Recent Advances and Future Directions in Causality, Prediction, and Specification Analysis

Recent Advances and Future Directions in Causality, Prediction, and Specification Analysis

Essays in Honor of Halbert L. White Jr

Xiaohong Chen · Norman R. Swanson
Editors

Recent Advances and Future Directions in Causality, Prediction, and Specification Analysis

Essays in Honor of Halbert L. White Jr

Springer

Editors
Xiaohong Chen
Yale University
New Haven, CT
USA

Norman R. Swanson
Hamilton Street 75
New Brunswick, NJ
USA

ISBN 978-1-4899-9971-9 ISBN 978-1-4614-1653-1 (eBook)
DOI 10.1007/978-1-4614-1653-1
Springer New York Heidelberg Dordrecht London

Printed on acid-free paper

Springer is part of Springer Science+Business Media (www.springer.com)

Editor's Introduction

With profound sadness, we are forced to note that Hal White passed away during the publication of this volume, at age 61. This Festschrift, thus, now honors both his academic prowess as well as his memory. During Hal's short stay on this earth, he touched so many lives in so many wonderful ways that it is impossible to enumerate all of them. All of those of us who know Hal have many stories to tell of how he has shaped our lives, both in academic and non-academic ways. Hal was always cheerful, intellectually curious, insightful, resourceful, considerate, tolerant, humble, hard-working, well spoken, efficient, engaging, encouraging and energizing. He truly loved and enjoyed everything he did, from teaching and researching, to working on government "think tank" projects and consulting projects of all types; and of course to playing his trumpets. His zest for life was extremely contagious. He gave of himself freely and in some sense with abandon, spearheading literally hundreds of path-breaking research projects in econometrics, financial economics, forecasting, labor economics, causality, law and economics, neural networks, and biostatistics. Hal was always optimistic and never complained about anything. He cared about doing things that would uplift others' spirits, too. He loved his family dearly, and treated all with a kindness not often seen. His work ethic was un-paralleled. Once, Norm was surprised to find, upon meeting Hal at 8am one morning to discuss research, that he had already, that day, written undergraduate and graduate lectures, worked on his new book, thought about and worked on research, and gone to the gym. He was one of the best undergraduate and graduate teachers we have ever known. He was the only undergraduate statistics/econometrics teacher we know of that was given a spontaneous standing ovation by more than 100 students at the end of a quarter's teaching introductory statistics. His exceptional graduate lectures resulted in so many of us pursuing careers in econometrics that we number in hundreds. Hal was extremely smart and knowledgeable, even brilliant, yet he never laughed at any naïve and sometimes stupid questions and comments from his students. He was always patient with his students. He believed in us and encouraged us even though some of us had no clue what we were doing or saying. Xiaohong still remembers vividly that, instead of trying to understand Hal's papers, she told him that his econometrics papers were boring and that some papers on bounded rationality in decision and game theories were much more interesting. To her surprise, Hal did not get angry but replied that he would be happy to supervise her even if she wanted to work on topics in microeconomics. Without Hal's guidance and encouragement, many of us would not have been enjoying our professional lives now.

Hal was not just a renaissance man, but so much more.

Dearly missed by all who have had the good fortune and pleasure to have known and interacted with him.

Xiaohong Chen and Norm Swanson—April 2012

This volume gathers together 20 original research papers which were presented at the conference in honor of the pre-eminent econometrician from the University of California, San Diego, Halbert L. White, organized on the occasion of his sixtieth birthday, and entitled *Causality, Prediction, and Specification Analysis: Recent Advances and Future Directions.* The conference was held at the Rady School of Management on the UCSD campus during May 6–7, 2011. The conference was attended by over 100 co-authors, colleagues, and students of White.

Some of Hal White's students that attended the conference.

There is little doubt that Hal White has been one of the most important researchers in econometric theory and in econometrics in general, over the last 35 years. There are many ways of measuring the role that he has played in the profession, and the impact that he has had on research. For example, *A Heteroskedasticity-Consistent Covariance Matrix Estimator and a Direct Test for Heteroskedasticity* (*Econometrica*, 1980), also often referred to as the "White Standard Error" paper, had 5738 citations on the Web of Science in one recent count, and is thus one of the most highly cited papers ever, both in econometrics and in the entire field of economics. Other seminal papers in econometrics have much lower citation numbers, which indicates the broad impact of White's work in economics in general.

According to one recent count, White had more than 130 full-length articles spanning all of the very top journals in economics, statistics, and finance. He has also written three seminal books in econometrics, and has edited more than 10 other volumes. His research has had a major impact not only in econometrics and in economics, but also in statistics, finance, and in computer and cognitive science; and in recent years his work has also had an impact even in medicine and the natural sciences. For example, his seminal paper on artificial neural networks (joint with Kurt Hornik and Max Stinchcombe) entitled *Multilayer Feedforward Networks are Universal Approximators* (Neural Networks, 1989) has 3862 Web of Science citations. He even has an article recently appearing in the Michigan Law Review. This multi-discliplinary diversity is indeed a characteristic unique to Hal.

In various discussions, Hal has recounted some details from his "early years".

I was born and raised in Kansas City, MO, where I attended Southwest High, graduating in 1968. There, I was salutatorian, having gotten edged out from the valedictorian spot by a few thousandths of a GPA point. If I had been smart enough not to take orchestra for credit, I could have been valedictorian, but since the valedictorian was smart enough to not do that (damned clarinet players!) I always figured she deserved it.

I applied to Harvard and Princeton for college and got rejected from Harvard. Later, when I was deciding whether to stay at Rochester or move, I ended up choosing the UCSD offer over that from Harvard, but not because of my undergrad admission experience. Like Groucho Marx, I apparently wouldn't want to belong to an organization that would admit someone like me (except in California).

Luckily, Princeton accepted me, and I was thrilled to go there, expecting to be a physics major. One problem: I couldn't understand physics to save my life. The only way I made it through physics to satisfy my science requirement was extensive tutoring by Vince Crawford, who was my hallmate (Dod Hall) freshman year. By second semester sophomore year, I had decided economics was much more interesting and doable, and I was fortunate in having great professors, among them Steven Goldfeld, Richard Quandt, Gregory Chow, Ray Fair, William Branson, George DeMenil, Orley Ashenfelter, Dan Hamermesh, and my senior thesis advisor, Alan Blinder. Alan was a new assistant professor then, fresh out of MIT.

At Princeton, I played my trumpet in the marching band, the orchestra (but not for credit), and the Triangle Club, plus a wide variety of student groups: a brass quintet, several big band jazz groups, and various soul/rhythm and blues bands, including The Nassau Brothers Soul Revue. This time I did manage to grab the valedictorian spot, although at Princeton, this is not determined by GPA, but by departmental nomination and election by the faculty.

Given the large number of my professors who came from MIT, that seemed to be the place to go next. So there I went in the Fall of 1972, along with Vince Crawford. My class at MIT has turned out to be quite distinguished, containing not only Vince, but also UCSD's Roger Gordon, who was my office mate in an office around the corner from Fisher Black and Robert Merton. Our office had no windows, but housed both of us (as well as Zvi Bodie), and gusts of sticky black soot would periodically blow out of the air vent. My illustrious classmates also include Peter Berck, Glenn Loury, Steven Sheffrin, Stephen Figlewski, Allan Drazen, Mario Draghi, Jeff Perloff, and Dennis Carlton. It was at MIT that I unknowingly established a later claim to fame by grading the homework of both Ben Bernanke and Paul Krugman as a TA for Jerry Hausman's econometrics classes. No surprise—they both did well. Frequently, I could use Bernanke's homework as an answer key!

Of course, the faculty at MIT while I was in grad school were stunning: Paul Samuelson, Robert Solow, Evsey Domar, Jagdish Bhagwati, Franco Modigliani, Charles Kindleberger, Frank Fisher, Peter Temin, Stan Fisher, Rudy Dornbusch, Hal Varian, Robert Hall, and very notably Rob Engle, a newly minted Ph.D. from Cornell, and a young Jerry Hausman, fresh out of Oxford.

I had somewhat of a hard time finding a thesis advisor to supervise my dissertation in labor economics, but eventually I knocked on the right door—Jerry's—and found the best advisor a young grad student could hope for. Jerry was always available and encouraging and provided ways forward whenever I hit what seemed to me to be a hopeless roadblock. My dissertation committee also included Lester Thurow (with whom I published my first Econometrica article, in international trade in 1976) and Bob Solow.

My job market experience in 1975–1976 was a harrowing one. I had 27 interviews, including the University of Chicago, where among my interviewers was Jim Heckman. The interview consisted of him demolishing my labor economics job market paper. I did end up with a good number of flybacks, including UCSD, but I did not get a UCSD offer (although Vince Crawford did, and took it!). Nor did I have any top 5 or 10 flybacks, and especially not Chicago! Only at the last minute, the night before I was just about to accept a very good but not great offer did I get a call from the University of Rochester offering me a flyout with a practically guaranteed offer. After consulting with Jerry, I decided to turn down my existing offer and bet my future on the Rochester possibility. In hindsight, I strongly suspect that Jerry was operating behind the scenes to generate that opportunity, making sure that his #2 thesis advisee (Roger Gordon was his first) was well treated in the market.

Rochester did come through with an offer, and an extremely attractive one at that—$16,000 for the academic year! Plus, I was thrilled to be going to a truly distinguished department, including, among others, Lionel McKenzie, Sherwin Rosen, Stanley Engerman, Robert Barro, Walter Oi, Eric Hanushek, Elhannon Helpman, and James Friedman. Econometrician G.S. Maddala had just left for Florida, but Charles Plosser and Bill Schwert were in the U of R Graduate School of Management just a few steps away, so I did have econometric colleagues handy. The thing was, at that time, I was a primarily a labor economist and only secondarily an econometrician. So there were some semesters that I taught macro and urban economics instead of econometrics. (Not that I knew macro or urban—these were just what was left over after the more senior faculty had chosen their courses!) I did accidentally learn a valuable lesson, though, in teaching those classes: make the first lecture about using the method of Lagrange multipliers to do constrained optimization. Not only is almost everything in economics a special case of this, but it causes half of those enrolled to drop the class immediately.

My transition from labor economist to econometrician took place in the first few years at U of R. One factor was that all of my labor economics articles based on my thesis chapters got rejected from all of the field journals. Another was that I learned measure theory from Bartle's superb book,

Measure and Integration, in a small study group consisting of game theorist Jim Friedman, general equilibrium theorist Larry Benveniste, and myself. Each week we met and worked through a chapter of Bartle's book and presented solutions to the exercises. From this, I finally began to understand asymptotic distribution theory.

At the same time, I was deeply concerned by the prevalence of misspecification in econometric models and the fact that not much was known at a general level about the consequences of misspecification. Especially puzzling was the then common wisdom that OLS applied to a misspecified model gave you a Taylor-series approximation to whatever the true relation was. This made no sense to me, so I wrote a paper called *Using Least Squares to Approximate Unknown Regression Functions*. Amazingly to me, this was accepted by the International Economic Review for publication. Since, thanks to measure theory, I now seemed to know what I was doing, and since I had finally succeeded in getting an article published, I then began to think that maybe econometrics was a better place for me than labor economics or international trade. (As an interesting aside, the IER paper now has nearly 300 citations, according to Google Scholar, but there are still lots of people who think least squares gives you a Taylor approximation!)

This paper then led to my famous Econometrica paper on heteroskedasticity, where my final conversion to an econometrician was effected by a referee who said that he would recommend publication, provided that the included labor economics example was removed. Finally, I got it! Econometrics was my way forward.

An especially outstanding feature of the U of R was the wonderful group of graduate students it attracted. Eventually, I did get to teach the graduate econometrics classes. Two of my now distinguished students there were Gary Gorton and Glenn MacDonald. And one of the most important relationships of my life began when Charley Bates showed up in my office one day with his little Lhasa Apso dog, Li Po, to see about studying econometrics. Charley had just finished an undergrad degree at UCSD with a double major in math and economics. Charley ended up taking my econometrics classes, and, after an interesting oddyssey, eventually became my thesis advisee. As it turned out, that was just the beginning of a lifelong friendship and collaboration with Charley that has had an extremely positive impact on both my professional and personal life. Among other things, we co-founded our economics consulting firm Bates White, LLC, together with a small group of econ Ph.D.s that Charley had hand-picked. The firm will soon celebrate its twelfth anniversary, and it now employs over 150 highly talented people, many of whom have direct or indirect connections to UCSD. I am especially gratified that the firm is now well known for setting new quality standards in the economic and econometric analysis of legal disputes.

Another transition began in those early days at the U of R, and that was my transformation from an East Coast type with a Midwestern background to a California type. That transition began with a phone call in early May of 1977 from Rob Engle, who was by then at UCSD with Clive Granger. Rob's call came just one day after Rochester had received three FEET of snow (in May!) in a still famous blizzard. He inquired if I might be interested in being a visiting assistant professor at UCSD. I had to think about that for a while—perhaps ten seconds. As it turned out, I was not able to visit the next academic year, but it did work out that I was able to visit UCSD in Winter and Spring quarters of 1979. So it was that in December of 1978 I flew out of Rochester during a blizzard and arrived in 75° San Diego sunshine to begin a visiting appointment at UCSD.

Hal in the early days

One of the things Hal first did upon arriving at UCSD was to write his book *Asymptotic Theory for Econometricians* (1984). This was path breaking. Hal realized that in order to develop econometric theory, and also in order to be a competent user, not limited by the availability of ready-to-use procedures, one should be able to understand and combine all of the relevant tools from probability theory and mathematical statistics. He was the first to develop and make accessible to econometricians the necessary tools for deriving the properties of estimators and constructing tests under a full menu of realistic settings. Hal was the first to teach us about the interplay between properties of the data (e.g., how much dependence there is in the series and how many moments are finite) and theoretical features of the model postulated by the researcher, as dictated by econometric theory. Whether an estimator has a well defined probability limit depends on the statistical properties of the data, but the meaning and economic interpretation of that probability limit depends on the theoretical model. One of the fundamental insights Hal emphasized is that all models are an approximation to reality, and are thus generally incorrect. Nevertheless, we can learn important things, even from an approximation of reality. Furthering this idea, a complete and rigorous treatment of estimation and inference with misspecified (i.e., generally incorrect models), is given in his book entitled *Estimation, Inference and Specification Analysis* (1994). There is little doubt that modern econometric theory was pioneered by Hal. Moreover, Hal's contributions have been fundamental not only to the field of theoretical econometrics, but also to the field of empirical economics. In particular, thanks to Hal's work, standard econometric tools, such as hypotheses testing and inference in general, are now utilized correctly, in a variety of realistic contexts.

It is impossible to list all of his contributions. Hence, we confine our attention to five particular standouts.

White Standard Errors

Empirical work often requires one to test the null hypothesis that a parameter, say that associated with conveying the returns to an extra year of schooling, is zero or is instead strictly positive. Standard computer packages have always provided a ready-to-use solution to this problem. However, the classical solution is correct only under a particular assumption, known as conditional homoskedasticity. This assumption states that the variance of the error in a given model, conditional on the explanatory variables, is constant. This is a very restrictive assumption, often violated in practice. In fact, often the variance of the error depends on the individual covariates, in an unknown manner. However, if conditional homoskedasticity fails to hold, the inference that we draw based on the classical solution is incorrect, and may lead to the wrong conclusion (e.g., we might conclude than an extra year of schooling has no effect on wages, when instead it does). This is because the variance/standard error estimator used by standard packages is only consistent for the "true" variance/standard error under conditional homoskedasticity. Hal, in *A Heteroskedasticity-Consistent Covariance Matrix Estimator and a Direct Test for Heteroskedasticity* (*Econometrica*, 1980), developed an estimator of the covariance which is robust to the presence of conditional heteroskedasticity of unknown form. This estimator is now routinely available in all computer packages, and is called "White Standard Errors". It is now common practice to report both "classical" and "White" standard errors.

White Standard Errors, although crucial to applied econometric analysis, still require that the error of the model is not autocorrelated (i.e. the error does not depend on its past). This is typically the case when we have cross-sectional observations, for example (e.g., we have data on a group of individuals at a given point in time, rather than data that are measured over time, such as the consumer price index). If we do have data measured over time, called time-series data, then the error is not autocorrelated only if the model is "dynamically correctly specified". For dynamic correct specification, we mean that both the functional form of the model and the dynamics specified for the model (e.g. the number of lags or past values) are correct. However, in practice, dynamic misspecification is more the rule than the exception. In articles co-authored with Ian Domowitz (*Journal of Econometrics*, 1982 and *Econometrica*, 1984) and as elaborated in his book *Asymptotic Theory for Econometricians* (1984), Hal proposed a variance estimator that is robust to both heteroskedasticity and autocorrelation of unknown form, and which is now known as a HAC (heteroskedasticity and autocorrelation robust) estimator. Whitney Newey and Ken West, in a famous *Econometrica* paper published in 1987, refined White's estimator to ensure positive definiteness, which is crucial for empirical application, yielding the famous so-called Newey-West estimator. Of course, all of this work was predicated in large part on the initial 1980 *Econometrica* paper and Hal's seminal work with Domowitz.

Maximum Likelihood Estimation of Misspecified Models

Another key contribution due to Hal is *Maximum Likelihood Estimation of Misspecified Models* (*Econometrica*, 1982). This paper is also among the most cited ever, with 1389 citations on the Web of Science. The idea underlying Maximum Likelihood Estimation (MLE) is that the estimators we compute are those maximizing the probability of observing the sample of data that we actually observe. If we correctly specify the conditional density of the data, then ML estimators are the "best estimators"—they are consistent, asymptotically efficient, and invariant to reparameterization. However, we almost never know the correct conditional density. For example, sometimes we are able to correctly specify only the conditional mean and maybe the conditional variance; and sometimes we are not even able to correctly specify the conditional mean. In the end, as Hal emphasized, models are just approximations of reality and so they are generally incorrect. But, what happens if we estimate misspecified models using Maximum Likelihood? Hal shows that the MLE generally converges to the parameter values minimizing the Kullback-Leibler Information Criterion (KLIC). Namely, MLE always converges to the parameters minimizing the "surprise" that we get when we believe that our data are generated by a given model, but instead we learn that they are generated by a different one. Further, if we misspecify the conditional distribution, but we still correctly specify the conditional mean, then the ML estimator, under very mild conditions, converges to the same value, as in the case of "full" correct specification. Nevertheless, the asymptotic variance is different, and this should be taken into account when performing hypothesis testing. This observation led to the celebrated Dynamic Fisher Information Matrix test due to Hal. The main practical implication of his work on MLE with misspecified models, is that one can simply estimate models via Gaussian Maximum Likelihood (i.e. one can proceed as if the errors are conditionally normal, even if they are not). This has had tremendous impact on applied work. Estimation with Gaussian likelihood is very simple to implement, and it's incredibly useful to know that it can deliver valid inference even if conditional normality does not hold.

This work also played a part in inspiring the subsequent literature on the estimation of conditional autoregressive models (ARCH and GARCH models). In this context, one postulates a model for the conditional mean and the conditional variance, even though the conditional density of the error is generally unknown, and typically has fatter tails than those associated with a normal random variable. However, Gaussian ML generally gives consistent parameter estimates and allows for correct inference as a consequence of Hal's theory. Hal's 1982 paper was also the starting point for a literature based on the use of the KLIC for model specification and testing (see e.g. the recent applications of the KLIC to measuring serial dependence by Yongmiao Hong and Hal White in *Econometrica* in 2005 and to forecast evaluation by Rafaella Giacomini and Hal White in *Econometrica* in 2006.

Neural Network and Consistent Specification Tests

Neural network models were introduced by cognitive scientists, in an attempt to build computers that could learn from experience instead of having to be programmed. Such models are characterized by input variables (sensory information) that "pass through" one (or more) hidden processing layers, yielding an "output" (a classification, prediction, or action) In a series of seminal papers, some joint with Ron Gallant or with Kurt Hornik and Max Stinchcombe, Hal has shown that such models have a "universal approximation" property, in the sense that they are able to approximate any generic function, as well as its derivatives, up to an arbitrary level of accuracy, given mild conditions. Although not as well known to economists, one of Hal's key papers on this subject, entitled *Multilayer Feedforward Networks are Universal Approximators* (Neural Networks, 1989) has received 3862 citations on the Web of Science, as mentioned above.

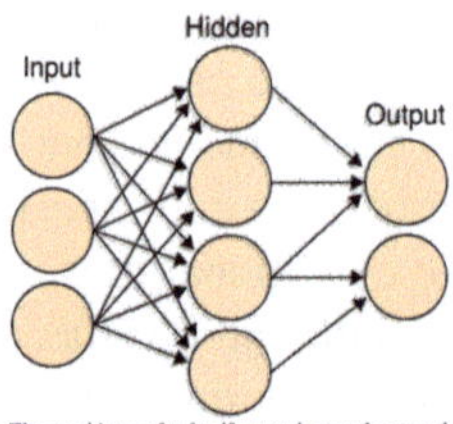

The workings of a feedforward neural network

The flexibility of a neural network model is ensured by its dependence on a number of parameters, which have to be estimated. Hal developed novel techniques for estimating neural network models and derived their statistical properties in a number of papers, including *Some Asymptotic Results for Learning in Single Hidden Layer Feedforward Network Models* (*Journal of the American Statistical Association*, 1989). These fundamental contributions to neural network theory have had a big impact in the cognitive sciences, medicine, engineering, and psychology. But what impact have they had in the field of econometrics? For one thing, artificial neural networks now have their own JEL number, C45. Further, neural networks play a major role in the crucially important literature on testing for the correct functional form of a model. Suppose that we want to test whether a linear model is correctly specified for the conditional mean. In this case, we want to have a test that is able to detect all possible departures from linearity, including small ones. A test that is able to detect any generic deviation from the null hypothesis is said to be "consistent". If the linear model is correctly specified, then the error is uncorrelated with any arbitrary function of the regressors. How can we approximate any arbitrary function of the regressors? With a neural network, of course, as they are capable of approximating any generic function. A very nice example of the use of neural network in testing for the correct functional form of a model is Hal's paper with T.H. Lee and Granger entitled *Testing for Neglected Nonlinearity in Time-Series Models: A Comparison of Neural Network Methods and Standard Tests* (*Journal of Econometrics*, 1993).

Nowadays, a new branch of economics, labeled neuro-economics, is rapidly gaining momentum. The objective is to study the link between the functioning of the brain and economic behavior. For example, which part of the brain controls our behavior when playing the stock market? Which characteristics of the brain make an individual a "better" player in the stock market? There is little doubt that in the near future, neural network theory will play a major role in the formalization and in the development of neuro-economics.

Reality Check and Data Snooping

A Reality Check for Data Snooping (*Econometrica*, 2000), is one of the most (if not the most) influential papers in the study of financial econometrics as well as in forecasting, over the last few years. Begin with a "benchmark" model, typically the most popular model, or the easiest to estimate, and consider a (potentially long) list of competing models. Assume that we want to test whether there exists at least one competitor that truly outperforms the benchmark. Hal starts from the observation that if we use the same dataset to sequentially test each model versus the benchmark, then eventually we're sure to find one or more models that beat it. This is because of the well known "data-mining" or "data-snooping" problem associated with sequentially comparing many models using classical statistical testing approaches. That is, we will eventually find a model that, simply due to luck, appears to be superior to the benchmark. Hal provides a novel solution to this problem. By jointly considering all competing models, his reality check procedure ensures that the probability of rejecting the null when it is false (i.e., the probability of a false discovery), is smaller than a prespecified level, say 5 %.

Evaluation of asset trading rules has been one of the most challenging issues in empirical finance. An investor can choose from a very long list of trading strategies. Say that she wants to pick the strategy giving the highest return. However, because of the data-snooping problem, she may simply pick a strategy that by luck appears to be successful, but it is truly not. Hal's Reality Check provides a formal way of choosing among trading strategies, controlling for the probability of picking "winners" just because of luck. This idea is clearly illustrated in his paper with Ryan Sullivan and Allan Timmermann, entitled, *Data Snooping, Technical Trading Rule Performance, and the Bootstrap* (*Journal of Finance*, 1999).

Causality and Structural Modeling

In recent years, Hal's interest has also focused on the issue of measuring causal effects, in very general settings. This is one of the most challenging problems in econometrics and statistics. Suppose that we want to evaluate the effect of an increase of police per capita on the crime rate. However, the crime rate may also increase in areas because of urban decay, which may be impossible to properly measure, and police per capita may be (positively or negatively) correlated with urban decay. Disentangling such cause/effect relationships is a problem that has been addressed numerous times over the last 100 years, and the problem remains vexing and complicated. Exactly how can we carry out valid statistical analysis of the sort needed? The difficulty is that we need to measure the effect of a cause or treatment that is "endogenous" – that is, the cause of interest (police per capita) is correlated with unobservable drivers (urban decay) of the response (the crime rate). The two most common solutions to this problem are the use of instrumental variables, i.e., the use of variables that are correlated with the observable cause but independent of the confounding, unobservable cause—i.e. the "error". The second approach consists of finding control variables, such that the endogenous cause, conditional on the control variables, is independent of the unobservable causes. There is growing consensus that the latter approach is preferable. However, it is often difficult to find adequate control variables. In this case, one has to rely on the instrumental variable approach. Still, there is a problem, as this approach works only for separable models, in which the error enters in an additive manner, that is, the unobservable causes do not interact with the observable causes.

In one of his recent important works in this area with Karim Chalak and Susanne Schennach, entitled *Estimating Average Marginal Effects in Nonseparable Structural Systems* (2011), Hal studies the case of nonseparable models, in which the effects of unobserved causes cannot be separated from those of the observable endogenous causes. They consider a different route to evaluate the marginal effect of an endogenous cause on the response variable, via use of the ratio of the marginal effect of the instrument on the response variables and the marginal effect of the instrument on the endogenous cause. In particular, they provide sufficient conditions on the structure of the model for the validity of the approach, and they develop a novel estimator. There is little doubt that this work will have a large impact on empirical microeconomics, as it considers very general and realistic settings. In another recent work with Stefan Hoderlein, entitled *Nonparametric Identification in Nonseparable Panel Data Models with Generalized Fixed Effects* (2011), Hal is also considering identification of marginal effects in nonseparable panel data models with non-additive fixed effects. This is a daunting challenge, and their results are bound to open new frontiers in both the nonparametric identification and the nonlinear panel data literatures.

In other recent work with UCSD Ph.D. Xun Lu, (*Granger Causality and Dynamic Structural Systems*, 2010) Hal shows that Granger causality is not devoid of true causal content. Instead, as Hal shows, it is equivalent to true structural causality under well defined conditions.

Hal and Teresa at the Xiamen Conference on Specification Testing in 30 Years

Turning our attention to the papers published in this volume, it is worth stressing that they comprise 20 original research papers. All of the papers investigate econometric questions in the broad areas of specification analysis, causality, and prediction. In the first paper, entitled: *Improving GDP Measurement: A Forecast Combination Perspective* by Boragan Aruoba, University of Maryland, Francis X. Diebold, University of Pennsylvania, Jeremy Nalewaik, Federal Reserve Board, Frank Schorfheide, University of Pennsylvania, and Dongho Song, University of Pennsylvania, the authors examine a forecast combination approach to "predict" GDP growth for the U.S., using both income side and expenditure side versions of GDP, and uncover interesting features of their new measure. In the second paper, entitled *Identification without Exogeneity under Equiconfounding in Linear Recursive Structural Systems* by Karim Chalak, Boston College, the author provides alternative identification results on structural coefficients in linear recursive systems of structural equations without requiring that observable variables are exogenous or conditionally exogenous. He provides conditions under which equiconfounding supports either full identification or partial identification.. In the third paper, entitled *Optimizing Robust Conditional Moment Tests: An Estimating Function Approach* by Yi-Ting Chen, Academia Sinica and Chung-Ming Kuan, National Taiwan University, survey robust conditional moment (RCM) tests under partial model specification, discuss a generalized RCM type test, and introduce methods for improving local asymptotic power of suboptimal RCM tests. In the fourth paper, entitled *Asymptotic Properties of Penalized M Estimators with Time Series Observations* by Xiaohong Chen, Yale University and Zhipeng Liao, University of California, Los Angeles, the authors establish convergence rates for penalized M estimators with weakly dependent data. They then derive root-n asymptotic normality results for plug-in penalized M estimators of regular functionals, and discuss consistent long-run covariance estimation. Turning our attention again to forecasting, in the fifth paper, entitled *A Survey of Recent*

Advances in Forecast Accuracy Comparison Testing with an Extension to Stochastic Dominance by Valentina Corradi, Warwick University and Norman R. Swanson, Rutgers University, the authors survey recent advances in predictive accuracy testing, with focus on distributional and density forecasting. They then introduce a new model selection type forecast accuracy test based on the use of standard principles of stochastic dominance. The sixth paper is entitled *New Directions in Information Matrix Testing: Eigenspectrum Tests* by Richard M. Golden, University of Texas at Dallas, Steven S. Henley, Martingale Research Corporation and Loma Linda University, Halbert White, University of California, San Diego, and T. Michael Kashner, Loma Linda University. In this paper, the information matrix test of White (1982) is extended by considering various nonlinear functions of the Hessian covariance matrices commonly used when carrying out such model specification tests. The paper entitled *Bayesian Estimation and Model Selection of GARCH Models with Additive Jumps* by Christian Haefke, Institute for Advanced Studies and Leopold Sogner, Institute for Advanced Studies is the seventh paper in this volume. In this paper, novel Bayesian simulation methods are used to carry out parameter estimation and model selection in a class of GARCH models with additive jumps. In the eighth paper, entitled *Hal White: Time at MIT and Early Days of Research* by Jerry Hausman, M.I.T., the author briefly discusses Hal White's early experiences at MIT, where he carried out his graduate work. Hausman then undertakes an interesting examination, via Monte Carlo simulation, of a variety of different estimators of White heteroskedasticity consistent standard errors, including one based on a Rothenberg second-order Edgeworth approximation. Turning now to the paper entitled *Open-model Forecast-error Taxonomies* by David F. Hendry, University of Oxford and Grayham E. Mizon, University of Southhampton, we are treated to a paper wherein "forecast-error taxonomies" are developed when there are unmodeled variables, and forecast failure to shifting intercept issues is discussed. The tenth paper in the volume is entitled *Heavy-Tail and Plug-In Robust Consistent Conditional Moment Tests of Functional Form* by Jonathan B. Hill, University of North Carolina. In this paper, the author considers consistent specification test of a parametric conditional mean function for heavy-tailed time series models, in which the dependent variable has only finite conditional first moment while all the higher moments could be infinite. The author derives chi-squared weak limit of his test statistics and provides a Monte Carlo study.. In the eleventh paper, entitled *Nonparametric Identification in Dynamic Nonseparable Panel Data Models* by Stefan Hoderlein, Boston College, and Halbert White, University of California, San Diego, the authors tackle the issue of nonparametric identification of covariate-conditioned and average partial effects in dynamic nonseparable panel data models. They show that the panel structure can be used to find control functions that in turn can be used for identification. The paper entitled *Consistent Model Selection Over Rolling Windows*, which is the twelfth paper in the volume, and which is written by Atsushi Inoue, North Carolina State University, Barabara Rossi, Duke University, and Lu Jin, North Carolina State University, analyzes the asymptotic properties of a test statistc based on the use of simulated out-of-sample predictive mean square errors when carrying out model selection amongst nested models using rolling data estimation windows. In particular, the authors discuss instances under which test consistency obtains, hence validating the use of the statistic in empirical contexts. Next, we have the paper entitled *Estimating Misspecified Moment Inequality Models* by Hiroaki Kaido, Boston University and Halbert White, University of California, San Diego. In this interesting paper, partially identified structures defined by a finite number of moment inequalities are examined, in the context on functional misspecification, a pseudo-true identified set whose elements can be interpreted as the least-squares projections of the moment functions that are observationally equivalent to the true moment function is found, and a set estimator for the pseudo-true identified set is proposed. The fourteenth paper in the volume is entitled *Model Adequacy Checks for Discrete Choice Dynamic Models* by Igor Kheifets, New Economic School and Carlos Velasco, Universidad Carlos III de Madrid. In this paper, the authors propose a consistent specification test for possibly nonstationary dynamic discrete choice models. They apply an extension of the probability integral transformation of data, and convert the null hypothesis of correct specification of conditional distribution of the original model into test of uniform marginal with no series dependence of the transformed data. This paper is followed by the piece entitled *On Long-Run Covariance Matrix Estimation with the Truncated Flat Kernel* by Chang-Ching Lin, Academia Sinica and Shinichi Sakata, University of Southern California, the authors propose simple modifications to truncated flat kernel estimators of long-run covariance matrices which enforce positive definiteness and have good small sample properties. The following paper, which is the sixteenth in the volume, and which is entitled *Predictability and Specification in Models of Exchange Rate Determination,* is authored by Esfandiar Maasoumi, Emory University and Levent Bulut, Emory University. In this paper, metric entropy tests are used to examine a variety of parametric models of exchange rate determination, and it is found that random walk models, both with and without drift, almost always dominate models based on various conditioning information sets. The seventeenth paper in the volume is entitled *Thirty Years of Heteroskedasticity-Robust Inference* by James G. MacKinnon, Queen's University. In this paper, the author discusses the revolutionary idea of White (1980) on inference that is robust to heteroskedasticity of unknown form. He also presents the recent developments to improve the finite sample properties of White's original standard error estimators. The eighteenth paper in the volume, entitled *Smooth Constrained Frontier Analysis,* is authored by Christopher F. Parmeter, McMaster University and Jeffrey S. Racine, McMaster University. In this paper, the authors propose a class of smooth constrained nonparametric and semiparametric estimators of production functions that are continuously differentiable and are consistent with the optimization axioms of production. Turning now to the second last paper in this volume, entitled *NoVaS Transformations: Flexible Inference for Volatility Forecasting* by Dimitris Politis, University of California, San Diego and Dimitrios D. Thomakos, University of Peloponesse, the authors present some new findings on the NoVas (''normalizing and variance stabilizing'') transformation approach to volatility prediction. They conduct detailed simulation studies about the relative forecasting performance of NoVaS with that of a benchmark GARCH(1,1) model.. Finally, we have an interesting paper entitled *Causal Efficacy and the Curse of Dimensionality* by Maxwell B. Stinchcombe, University of Texas, Austin and David M. Drukker, STATACorp Statistical Software. This paper gives a new geometric representation of various nonparametric conditional mean regression estimators, including the sieve least squares estimators (Fourier, wavelet, splines, artificial neural networks), the kernels and other locally weighted regressions. The authors establish that for any estimator having their new geometric representation, the nonparametric rate of convergence does not suffer the well-known curse of dimensionality, at least asymptotically.

Hal White's Key Publications

Books

1. H. White: *Asymptotic Theory for Econometricians*. New York: Academic Press (1984), revised edition (2001).
2. A.R. Gallant and H. White: *A Unified Theory of Estimation and Inference for Nonlinear Dynamic Models*. Oxford: Basil Blackwell (1988).
3. H. White: *Estimation, Inference, and Specification Analysis*. New York: Cambridge University Press (1994).

Edited Volumes

1. H. White: "Model Specification: Annals," *Journal of Econometrics*, 20 (1982).
2. H. White: "Non-Nested Models: Annals," *Journal of Econometrics*, 21 (1983).
3. W.A. Barnett, E. Berndt, and H. White: *Dynamic Econometric Modeling*. New York: Cambridge University Press (1988).
4. H. White: *Artificial Neural Networks: Approximation and Learning Theory*. Oxford: Basil Blackwell (1992).
5. Sejnowski, T. J. and H. White (eds): Nilsson, N., *Mathematical Foundations of Learning Machines*, 2nd Edition, San Mateo, CA: Morgan Kaufmann Publishers (1990).
6. H. White: *Advances in Econometric Theory: The Selected Works of Halbert White*. Cheltenham: Edward Elgar (1998).
7. A.-P. Refenes and H. White: "Neural Networks and Financial Economics," *International Journal of Forecasting*, 17 (1998).
8. R. Engle and H. White: *Cointegration, Causality, and Forecasting: A Festschrift in Honour of Clive W. J. Granger*. Oxford: Oxford University Press (1999).

9. Y.S. Abu-Mostafa, A.F. Atiya, M. Magdon-Ismail, and H. White: "Neural Networks in Financial Engineering," *IEEE Transactions on Neural Networks* 12 (2001).
10. H. White: New Perspectives in Econometric Theory: *The Selected Works of Halbert White, Volume 2*. Cheltenham: Edward Elgar, 2004.

Articles

1. H. White and A.P. Thirlwall: "U.S. Merchandise Imports and Dispersion of Demand," *Applied Economics*, 6, 275–292 (1974).
2. L. Thurow and H. White: "Optimum Trade Restrictions and Their Consequences," *Econometrica*, 44, 777–786 (1976).
3. L. Olson, H. White, and H. M. Shefrin: "Optimal Investment in Schooling When Incomes Are Risky," *Journal of Political Economy*, 87, 522–539 (1979).
4. H. White: "Using Least Squares to Approximate Unknown Regression Functions," *International Economic Review*, 21, 149–170 (1980).
5. G. MacDonald and H. White: "Some Large Sample Tests for Nonnormality in the Linear Regression Model," *Journal of the American Statistical Association*, 75, 16–27 (1980).
6. H. White: "Nonlinear Regression on Cross-Section Data," *Econometrica*, 48, 721–746 (1980).
7. H. White: "A Heteroskedasticity-Consistent Covariance Matrix Estimator and a Direct Test for Heteroskedasticity," *Econometrica*, 48, 817–838 (1980).
8. H. White: "Consequences and Detection of Misspecified Nonlinear Regression Models," *Journal of the American Statistical Association*, 76, 419–433 (1981).
9. H. White and L. Olson: "Conditional Distribution of Earnings, Wages and Hours for Blacks and Whites," *Journal of Econometrics*, 17, 263–285 (1981).
10. H. White: "Maximum Likelihood Estimation of Misspecified Models," *Econometrica*, 50, 1–25 (1982); Corrigendum, *Econometrica*, 51, 513 (1983).
11. H. White: "Instrumental Variables Regression with Independent Observations," *Econometrica*, 50, 483–500 (1982).
12. C. Plosser, W. Schwert and H. White: "Differencing As A Test of Specification," *International Economic Review*, 23, 535–552 (1982).
13. H. White: "Regularity Conditions for Cox's Test of Non-nested Hypotheses," *Journal of Econometrics*, 19, 301–318 (1982).
14. I. Domowitz and H. White: "Misspecified Models with Dependent Observations," *Journal of Econometrics*, 20, 35–50, (1982).
15. R. Davidson, J. MacKinnon and H. White: "Tests for Model Specification in the Presence of Alternative Hypotheses: Some Further Results," *Journal of Econometrics*, 21, 53–70 (1983).
16. H. White and I. Domowitz: "Nonlinear Regression with Dependent Observations," *Econometrica*, 52, 143–162 (1984).

17. H. White: "Maximum Likelihood Estimation of Misspecified Dynamic Models," in T.K. Dijkstra, ed., *Misspecification Analysis*. New York: Springer-Verlag, 1–19 (1984).
18. C. Bates and H. White: "A Unified Theory of Consistent Estimation for Parametric Models," *Econometric Theory*, 1, 151–178 (1985).
19. J. MacKinnon and H. White: "Some Heteroskedasticity Consistent Covariance Matrix Estimators with Improved Finite Sample Properties," *Journal of Econometrics*, 29, 305–325 (1985).
20. H. White: "Instrumental Variables Analogs of Generalized Least Squares Estimators," *Advances in Statistical Analysis and Statistical Computing*, 1, 173–227 (1986).
21. H. White: "Specification Testing in Dynamic Models," in Truman Bewley, ed., *Advances in Econometrics*. New York: Cambridge University Press (1987). Also appears in French as "Test de Specification dans les Modeles Dynamiques," *Annales de l'INSEE*, 59/60, 125–181 (1985).
22. C. Bates and H. White: "Efficient Instrumental Variables Estimation of Systems of Implicit Heterogeneous Nonlinear Dynamic Equations with Nonspherical Errors," in W.A. Barnett, E. Berndt, H. White, eds., *Dynamic Econometric Modelling*. New York: Cambridge University Press, 3–26 (1988).
23. J.M. Wooldridge and H. White: "Some Invariance Principles and Central Limit Theorems for Dependent Heterogeneous Processes," *Econometric Theory*, 4, 210–230 (1988).
24. A.R. Gallant and H. White: "There Exists a Neural Network That Does Not Make Avoidable Mistakes," *Proceedings of the Second Annual IEEE Conference on Neural Networks*, I:657–664 (1988).
25. H. White: "Economic Prediction Using Neural Networks: The Case of IBM Daily Stock Returns," *Proceedings of the Second Annual IEEE Conference on Neural Networks*, II:451–458. (1988).
26. H. White: "The Encompassing Principle for Non-Nested Dynamic Model Specification," *American Statistical Association/Proceedings of the Business and Economics Statistics Section*, 101–109 (1988).
27. C.W.J. Granger, H. White and M. Kamstra: "Interval Forecasting: An Analysis Based Upon ARCH-Quantile Estimators," *Journal of Econometrics*, 40, 87–96 (1989).
28. K. Hornik, M. Stinchcombe and H. White: "Multilayer Feedforward Networks are Universal Approximators," *Neural Networks*, 2, 359–366 (1989).
29. M. Stinchcombe and H. White: "Universal Approximation Using Feedforward Networks with Non-Sigmoid Hidden Layer Activation Functions," *Proceedings of the International Joint Conference on Neural Networks*, I: 612–617 (1989).
30. C.W.J. Granger, C.-M. Kuan, M. Mattson and H. White: "Trends in Unit Energy Consumption: The Performance of End-Use Models," *Energy*, 14, 943–960 (1989).

31. H. White: "A Consistent Model Selection Procedure Based on m-Testing," in C.W.J. Granger, ed., *Modelling Economic Series: Readings in Econometric Methodology*. Oxford: Oxford University Press, 369–403 (1989).
32. H. White: "Some Asymptotic Results for Learning in Single Hidden Layer Feedforward Network Models," *Journal of the American Statistical Association*, 84, 1003–1013 (1989).
33. H. White: "Learning in Artificial Neural Networks: A Statistical Perspective," *Neural Computation*, 1, 425–464 (1989).
34. K. Hornik, M. Stinchcombe and H. White: "Universal Approximation of an Unknown Mapping and Its Derivatives Using Multilayer Feedforward Networks," *Neural Networks*, 3, 551–560 (1990).
35. H. White: "Connectionist Nonparametric Regression: Multilayer Feedforward Networks Can Learn Arbitrary Mappings," *Neural Networks*, 3, 535–549 (1990).
36. M. Stinchcombe and H. White: "Approximating and Learning Unknown Mappings Using Multilayer Feedforward Networks with Bounded Weights," in *Proceedings of the International Joint Conference on Neural Networks*, III: 7–16 (1990).
37. H. White and J.M.Wooldridge: "Some Results for Sieve Estimation with Dependent Observations," in W. Barnett, J. Powell and G. Tauchen, eds., *Nonparametric and Semi-Parametric Methods in Econometrics and Statistics*. New York: Cambridge University Press, 459–493 (1991).
38. H. White and M. Stinchcombe: "Adaptive Efficient Weighted Least Squares with Dependent Observations," in W. Stahel and S. Weisberg (eds.) *Directions in Robust Statistics and Diagnostics*, IMA Volumes in Mathematics and Its Applications. New York: Springer-Verlag, 337–364 (1991).
39. H. White: "Nonparametric Estimation of Conditional Quantiles Using Neural Networks," in *Proceedings of the Symposium on the Interface*. New York: Springer-Verlag, 190–199 (1992).
40. M. Stinchcombe and H. White: "Some Measurability Results for Extrema of Random Functions over Random Sets," *Review of Economic Studies*, 495–514, (1992).
41. A.R. Gallant and H. White: "On Learning the Derivatives of an Unknown Mapping with Multilayer Feedforward Networks," *Neural Networks*, 5, 129–138 (1992).
42. C.-S. James Chu and H. White: "A Direct Test for Changing Trends," *Journal of Business and Economic Statistics*, 10, 289–299 (1992).
43. M. Stinchcombe and H. White: "Using Feedforward Networks to Distinguish Multivariate Populations," *Proceedings of the International Joint Conference on Neural Networks*, (1992).
44. T.-H. Lee, H. White and C.W.J. Granger: "Testing for Neglected Nonlinearity in Time-Series Models: A Comparison of Neural Network Methods and Standard Tests," *Journal of Econometrics*, 56, 269–290 (1993).

45. M. Plutowski and H. White: "Selecting Exemplars for Training Feedforward Networks From Clean Data," *IEEE Transactions on Neural Networks*, 4, 305–318 (1993).
46. C. Bates and H. White: "Determination of Estimators with Minimum Asymptotic Covariance Matrices," *Econometric Theory*, 9, 633–648 (1993).
47. C.-M. Kuan and H. White: "Artificial Neural Networks: An Econometric Perspective," *Econometric Reviews*, 13, 1–92 (1994).
48. M. Goldbaum, P. Sample, H. White and R. Weinreb: "Interpretation of Automated Perimetry for Glaucoma by Neural Networks," *Investigative Ophthalmology and Visual Science*, 35, 3362–3373 (1994).
49. C.-M. Kuan, K. Hornik and H. White: "A Convergence Result for Learning in Recurrent Neural Networks," *Neural Computation*, 6, 420–440 (1994).
50. C.-M. Kuan and H. White: "Adaptive Learning with Nonlinear Dynamics Driven by Dependent Processes," *Econometrica*, 62, 1087–1114 (1994).
51. K. Hornik, M. Stinchcombe, H. White and P. Auer: "Degree of Approximation Results for Feedforward Networks Approximating Unknown Mappings and Their Derivatives," *Neural Computation*, 6, 1262–1274 (1994).
52. H. White: "Parametric Statistical Estimation Using Artificial Neural Networks: A Condensed Discussion," in V. Cherkassky ed., *From Statistics to Neural Networks: Theory and Pattern Recognition Applications*. NATO-ASI Series F. New York: Springer-Verlag, 127–146 (1994).
53. C.W.J. Granger, M.L. King and H. White: "Comments on Testing Economic Theories and the Use of Model Selection Criteria," *Journal of Econometrics*, 67, 173–188 (1995).
54. S. Sakata and H. White: "An Alternative Definition of Finite Sample Breakdown Point with Applications to Regression Model Estimators," *Journal of the American Statistical Association*, 90, 1099–1106 (1995).
55. J. Yukich, M. Stinchcombe and H. White: "Sup-Norm Approximation Bounds for Networks through Probabilistic Methods," *IEEE Transactions on Information Theory*, 41, 1021–1027 (1995).
56. W. Baxt and H. White: "Bootstrapping Confidence Intervals for Clinical Input Variable Effects in a Network Trained to Identify the Presence of Acute Myocardial Infarction," *Neural Computation*, 7, 624–638 (1995).
57. N. Swanson and H. White: "A Model Selection Approach to Assessing the Information in the Term Structure Using Linear Models and Artificial Neural Networks," *Journal of Business and Economic Statistics*, 13, 265–276 (1995).
58. Y.-M. Hong and H. White: "Consistent Specification Testing Via Nonparametric Series Regression," *Econometrica*, 63, 1133–1159 (1995).
59. V. Corradi and H. White: "Regularized Neural Networks: Some Convergence Rate Results," *Neural Computation*, 7, 1201–1220 (1995).
60. H. White: "Parametric Statistical Estimation Using Artificial Neural Networks," in P. Smolensky, M.C. Mozer and D.E. Rumelhart, eds., *Mathematical Perspectives on Neural Networks*. Hilldale, NJ: L. Erlbaum Associates, 719–775 (1996).

61. C.-Y. Sin and H. White: "Information Criteria for Selecting Possibly Misspecified Parametric Models," *Journal of Econometrics*, 71, 207–225 (1996). Published in Spanish as "Criterios de Informacion para Seleccionar Modelos Parametricos Posiblemente Mal Especificados," in A. Escribano and J. Gonzalo eds., *Especificacion y Evaluacion de Modelos Econometricos*, vol. II, pp. 195–232 (1994).
62. M. Plutowski, G. Cottrell, and H. White: "Experience with Selecting Exemplars From Clean Data," *Neural Networks*, 9, 273–294 (1996).
63. X. Chen and H. White: "Laws of Large Numbers for Hilbert Space-Valued Mixingales with Applications," *Econometric Theory*, 12, 284–304 (1996).
64. C.-S. Chu, M. Stinchcombe, and H. White: "Monitoring Structural Change," *Econometrica*, 64, 1045–1066 (1996).
65. N. Swanson and H. White: "A Model Selection Approach to Real-Time Macroeconomic Forecasting Using Linear Models and Artificial Neural Networks," *Review of Economics and Statistics*, 79, 540–550 (1997).
66. N. Swanson and H. White: "Forecasting Economic Time Series Using Adaptive Versus Nonadapative and Linear Versus Nonlinear Econometric Models," *International Journal of Forecasting*, 13, 439–461 (1997).
67. S. Sakata and H. White: "High Breakdown Point Conditional Dispersion Estimation with Application to S&P 500 Daily Returns Volatility," *Econometrica*, 66, 529–568 (1998).
68. X. Chen and H. White: "Central Limit and Functional Central Limit Theorems for Hilbert Space-Valued Dependent Processes," *Econometric Theory*, 14, 260–284 (1998).
69. M. Stinchcombe and H. White: "Consistent Specification Testing with Nuisance Parameters Present Only Under the Alternative," *Econometric Theory*, 14, 295–324 (1998).
70. X. Chen and H. White: "Nonparametric Adaptive Learning with Feedback," *Journal of Economic Theory*, 82, 190–222 (1998).
71. X. Chen and H. White: "Improved Rates and Asymptotic Normality for Nonparametric Neural Network Estimators," *IEEE Transactions on Information Theory*, 45, 682–691 (1999).
72. V. Corradi and H. White: "Specification Tests for the Variance of a Diffusion," *Journal of Time Series Analysis*, 20, 253–270 (1999).
73. 73. R. Sullivan, A. Timmermann, and H. White: "Data Snooping, Technical Trading Rule Performance, and the Bootstrap," *Journal of Finance*, 54, 1647–1692 (1999).
74. 74. D. Ormoneit and H. White: "An Efficient Algorithm to Compute Maximum Entropy Densities," *Econometric Reviews*, 18, 127–141 (1999).
75. H. White and Y.-M. Hong: "M-Testing Using Finite and Infinite Dimensional Parameter Estimators," in R. Engle and H. White, eds., *Cointegration, Causality, and Forecasting: A Festschrift in Honor of Clive W.J. Granger*. Oxford: Oxford University Press, 326–345 (1999).

76. V. Corradi, N. Swanson, and H. White: "Testing for Stationarity-Ergodicity and for Comovement between Nonlinear Discrete Time Markov Processes," *Journal of Econometrics*, 96, 39–73. (2000).
77. H. White: "A Reality Check for Data Snooping," *Econometrica*, 68, 1097–1127 (2000).
78. S. Sakata and H. White: "S - Estimation of Nonlinear Regression Models With Dependent and Heterogenous Observations," *Journal of Econometrics*, 103, 5–72 (2001).
79. T.H. Kim and H. White: "James-Stein Type Estimators in Large Samples With Application to the Least Absolute Deviations Estimator," *Journal of the American Statistical Association*, 96, 697–705 (2001).
80. H. White and J. Racine: "Statistical Inference, the Bootstrap, and Neural Network Modeling with Application to Foreign Exchange Rates," *IEEE Transactions on Neural Networks*, 12, 1–19 (2001).
81. R. Sullivan, A. Timmermann, and H. White: "Dangers of Data Mining: The Case of Calendar Effects in Stock Returns," *Journal of Econometrics*, 105, 249–286 (2001).
82. S. Bagley, H. White, and B. Golomb: "Logistic Regression in the Medical Literature: Standards for Use and Reporting with Particular Attention to One Medical Domain," *Journal of Clinical Epidemiology*, 54, 979–985 (2001).
83. X. Chen and H. White: "Asymptotic Properties of Some Projection-Based Robbins-Monro Procedures in a Hilbert Space," *Studies in Nonlinear Dynamics and Econometrics*, 6, 1–53 (2002).
84. S. Gonçalves and H. White: "The Bootstrap of the Mean for Dependent Heterogenous Arrays," *Econometric Theory*, 18, 1367–1384 (2002).
85. T.H. Kim and H. White: "Estimation, Inference, and Specification Testing for Possibly Misspecified Quantile Regression," in T. Fomby and R.C. Hill, eds., *Maximum Likelihood Estimation of Misspecified Models: Twenty Years Later*. New York: Elsevier, 107–132 (2003).
86. R. Sullivan, A. Timmermann, and H. White: "Forecast Evaluation with Shared Data Sets," *International Journal of Forecasting*, 19, 217–228 (2003).
87. T. Perez-Amaral, G. Gallo, and H. White: "A Flexible Tool for Model Building: The Relevant Transformation of the Inputs Network Approach (RETINA)," *Oxford Bulletin of Economics and Statistics*, 65, 821–838 (2003).
88. Golomb, B., M. Criqui, H. White, and J. Dimsdale: "Conceptual Foundations of the UCSD Statin Study: A Randomized Controlled Trial Assessing the Impact of Statins on Cognition, Behavior, and Biochemistry," *Archives of Internal Medicine*, 164, 153–162 (2004).
89. J.M. Wooldridge and H. White: "Central Limit Theorems for Dependent Heterogeneous Processes with Trending Moments," in H. White, ed., *New Perspectives in Econometric Theory*. Cheltenham: Edward Elgar, 464–481 (2004).
90. Golomb, B., M. Criqui, H. White, and J. Dimsdale: "The UCSD Statin Study: A Randomized Controlled Trial Assessing the Impact of Statins on Selected Noncardiac Outcomes," *Controlled Clinical Trials*, 25, 178–202 (2004).

91. S. Gonçalves and H. White: "Maximum Likelihood and the Bootstrap for Nonlinear Dynamic Models," *Journal of Econometrics*, 119, 199–219 (2004).
92. T.-H. Kim and H. White: "On More Robust Estimation of Skewness and Kurtosis," *Finance Research Letters*, 1, 56–73 (2004).
93. D. Politis and H. White: "Automatic Block-Length Selection for the Dependent Bootstrap," *Econometric Reviews*," 23, 53–70 (2004).
94. P. Bertail, C. Haefke, D. Politis, and H. White: "Subsampling the Distribution of Diverging Statistics with Applications to Finance," *Journal of Econometrics*, 120, 295–326 (2004).
95. Y.-M. Hong and H. White: "Asymptotic Distribution Theory for An Entropy-Based Measure of Serial Dependence," *Econometrica*, 73, 837–902 (2005).
96. T.-H. Kim, D. Stone, and H. White: "Asymptotic and Bayesian Confidence Intervals for Sharpe Style Weights," *Journal of Financial Econometrics* 3, 315–343 (2005).
97. T. Perez-Amaral, G.M. Gallo, and H.L. White: "A Comparison of Complementary Automatic Modeling Methods: RETINA and PcGets." *Econometric Theory*, 21, 262–277 (2005).
98. S. Gonçalves and H. White: "Bootstrap Standard Error Estimation for Linear Regressions," *Journal of the American Statistical Association*, 100, 970–979 (2005).
99. H. White: "Approximate Nonlinear Forecasting Methods," in G. Elliott, C.W.J. Granger, and A. Timmermann, eds., *Handbook of Economic Forecasting*. New York: Elsevier, pp. 460–512 (2006).
100. H. White: "Time Series Estimation of the Effects of Natural Experiments," *Journal of Econometrics*, 135, 527–566 (2006).
101. R. Kosowski, A. Timmermann, H. White, and R. Wermers: "Can Mutual Fund 'Stars' Really Pick Stocks? New Evidence from a Bootstrap Analysis," *Journal of Finance*, 61, 2551–2596 (2006).
102. R. Giacomini and H. White: "Tests of Conditional Predictive Ability," *Econometrica*, 74, 1545–1578 (2006).
103. L. Su and H. White: "A Consistent Characteristic-Function-Based Test for Conditional Dependence," *Journal of Econometrics*, 141, 807–837 (2007).
104. J.-S. Cho and H. White: "Testing for Regime Switching," *Econometrica*, 75, 1671–1720 (2007).
105. H. Karimabadi, T. Sipes, H. White, M. Marinucci, A. Dmitriev, J. Chao, J. Driscoll, and N. Balac: "Data Mining in Space Physics: The Mine Tool Algorithm," *Journal of Geophysical Research*, 112, A11215 (2007).
106. R. Giacomini, A. Gottschling, C. Haefke, and H. White: "Mixtures of t-Distributions for Finance and Forecasting," *Journal of Econometrics*, 144, 175–192 (2008).
107. B. Golomb, J. Dimsdale, H. White, J. Ritchie, and M. Criqui: "Reductions in Blood Pressure with Statins," *Archives of Internal Medicine*, 168, 721–727 (2008).
108. L. Su and H. White: "A Nonparametric Hellinger Metric Test for Conditional Independence," *Econometric Theory*, 24, 829–864 (2008).

109. H. White and P. Kennedy: "Retrospective Estimation of Causal Effects Through Time," in J. Castle and N. Shephard (eds.) *The Methodology and Practice of Econometrics: A Festschrift in Honour of David F. Hendry*. Oxford: Oxford University Press, pp. 59–87 (2009).
110. H. Kaido and H. White: "Inference on Risk Neutral Measures for Incomplete Markets," *Journal of Financial Econometrics*, 7, 1–48 (2009).
111. H. White and K. Chalak: "Settable Systems: An Extension of Pearl's Causal Model with Optimization, Equilibrium, and Learning," *Journal of Machine Learning Research* 10, 1759–1799 (2009).
112. H. White, T.-H. Kim, and S. Manganelli: "Modeling Autoregressive Conditional Skewness and Kurtosis with Multi-Quantile CAViaR," in T. Bollerslev, J. Russell, and M. Watson (eds.) *Volatility and Time Series Econometrics: Essays in Honor of Robert F. Engle*. Oxford: Oxford University Press, pp. 231–256 (2010).
113. H. White and X. Lu, "Granger Causality and Dynamic Structural Systems," *Journal of Financial Econometrics*, 8, 193–243 (2010).
114. T.-H. Kim and H. White: "Bootstrapping the Shrinkage Least Absolute Deviations Estimator," *European Journal of Pure and Applied Mathematics*, 3, 371–381 (2010).
115. R. Lieli and H. White: "The Construction of Empirical Credit Scoring Models Based on Maximization Principles," *Journal of Econometrics* 157, 110–119 (2010).
116. T.M. Kashner, S. Henley, R. Golden, J. Byrne, S. Keitz, G. Cannon, B. Chang, G. Holland, D. Aron, E. Muchmore, A. Wicker, and H. White, "Studying the Effects of ACGME Duty Hours Limits on Resident Satisfaction: Results the from VA Learners' Perceptions Survey," *Academic Medicine*, 85, 1130 –1139 (2010).
117. A. Kane, T.-H. Kim, and H. White: "Forecast Precision and Portfolio Performance," *Journal of Financial Econometrics* 8, 265–304 (2010).
118. J.-S. Cho and H. White: "Testing for Unobserved Heterogeneity in Exponential and Weibull Duration Models," *Journal of Econometrics* 157, 458–480 (2010).
119. L. Su and H. White: "Testing Structural Change in Partially Linear Models," *Econometric Theory* 26, 1761–1806 (2010).
120. H. White and C.W.J. Granger: "Consideration of Trends in Time Series," *Journal of Time Series Econometrics* 3(1), Article 2 (2011).
121. K. Chalak and H. White: "An Extended Class of Instrumental Variables for the Estimation of Causal Effects," *Canadian Journal of Economics* 44, 1–51 (2011).
122. J.-S. Cho and H. White: "Generalized Runs Tests for the IID Hypothesis," *Journal of Econometrics*, 162, 326–344 (2011).
123. J.-S. Cho, I. Ishida, and H. White, "Revisiting Tests of Neglected Nonlinearity Using Artificial Neural Networks," *Neural Computation*, 33, 1133–1186 (2011).

124. J.S. Cho, T.U. Cheong, and H. White, "Experience with the Weighted Bootstrap in Testing for Unobserved Heterogeneity in Exponential and Weibull Duration Models," *Journal of Economic Theory and Econometrics*, 22, 60–91 (2011).
125. H. White, K. Chalak, and X. Lu, "Linking Granger Causality and the Pearl Causal Model with Settable Systems," *Journal of Machine Learning Research: Workshop and Conference Proceedings*, 12, 1–29 (2011).
126. J.-S. Cho and H. White, "Testing Correct Model Specification Using Extreme Learning Machines," *Neurocomputing*, 74, 2552–2565 (2011).
127. W. Kovacic, R. Marshall, L. Marx, and H. White, "Plus Factors and Agreement in Antitrust Law," *Michigan Law Review*, 110, 393–436 (2011).
128. H. White and J.S. Cho, "Higher-Order Approximations for Testing Neglected Nonlinearity," *Neural Computation*, 24, 273–287 (2012).
129. R. Golden, S. Henley, H. White, and T.M. Kashner, "New Directions in Information Matrix Testing: Eigenspectrum Tests," in X. Chen and N. Swanson (eds.) *Causality, Prediction, and Specification Analysis: Essays in Honor of Halbert White*. Berlin: Springer-Verlag (forthcoming).
130. H. Kaido and H. White, "Estimating Misspecified Moment Inequality Models," in X. Chen and N. Swanson (eds.) *Causality, Prediction, and Specification Analysis: Essays in Honor of Halbert White*. Berlin: Springer-Verlag (forthcoming).
131. S. Hoderlein and H. White, "Nonparametric Identification in Dynamic Nonseparable Panel Data Models," in X. Chen and N. Swanson (eds.) *Causality, Prediction, and Specification Analysis: Essays in Honor of Halbert White*. Berlin: Springer-Verlag (forthcoming).
132. S. Schennach, K. Chalak, and H. White: "Local Indirect Least Squares and Average Marginal Effects in Nonseparable Structural Systems," *Journal of Econometrics* (forthcoming).
133. H. White and K. Chalak: "Identification and Identification Failure for Treatment Effects using Structural Systems," *Econometric Reviews* (forthcoming).
134. K. Chalak and H. White, "Causality, Conditional Independence, and Graphical Separation in Settable Systems," *Neural Computation* (forthcoming).
135. L. Su and H. White, "Conditional Independence Specification Testing for Dependent Processes with Local Polynomial Quantile Regression," *Advances in Econometrics*, 29 (forthcoming).
136. A. Kane, T.-H. Kim, and H. White: "Active Portfolio Management: The Power of the Treynor-Black Model," in C. Kyrtsou and C. Vorlow (eds.) *Progress in Financial Markets Research*. New York: Nova Publishers (forthcoming).
137. L. Su, S. Hoderlein, and H. White: "Testing Monotonicity in Unobservables with Panel Data," submitted *Journal of Econometrics* (forthcoming).
138. H. White and X. Lu, "Robustness Checks and Robustness Tests in Applied Economics," *Journal of Econometric* (forthcoming).

Contents

Improving U.S. GDP Measurement: A Forecast Combination Perspective

S. Borağan Aruoba, Francis X. Diebold, Jeremy Nalewaik, Frank Schorfheide and Dongho Song

> *"A growing number of economists say that the government should shift its approach to measuring growth. The current system emphasizes data on spending, but the bureau also collects data on income. In theory the two should match perfectly—a penny spent is a penny earned by someone else. But estimates of the two measures can diverge widely, particularly in the short term..."*
>
> [Binyamin Appelbaum, New York Times, August 16, 2011]

Abstract Two often-divergent U.S. GDP estimates are available, a widely-used expenditure-side version GDP_E, and a much less widely-used income-side version GDP_I. We propose and explore a "forecast combination" approach to combining them. We then put the theory to work, producing a superior combined estimate of GDP growth for the U.S., GDP_C. We compare GDP_C to GDP_E and GDP_I, with particular attention to behavior over the business cycle. We discuss several variations and extensions.

S. Borağan Aruoba (✉)
University of Maryland, College Park, MD, USA
e-mail: aruoba@econ.umd.edu

F. X. Diebold · F. Schorfheide · D. Song
University of Pennsylvania, Philadelphia, PA, USA
e-mail: fdiebold@sas.upenn.edu

F. Schorfheide
e-mail: schorf@ssc.upenn.edu

D. Song
e-mail: donghos@sas.upenn.edu

J. Nalewaik
Federal Reserve Board, Washington, DC, USA
e-mail: jeremy.j.nalewaik@frb.gov

X. Chen and N. R. Swanson (eds.), *Recent Advances and Future Directions in Causality, Prediction, and Specification Analysis*, DOI: 10.1007/978-1-4614-1653-1_1,

1 Introduction

GDP growth is surely the most fundamental and important concept in empirical/applied macroeconomics and business cycle monitoring, yet significant uncertainty still surrounds its estimation. Two often-divergent estimates exist for the U.S., a widely-used expenditure-side version, GDP_E, and a much less widely-used income-side version, GDP_I. Nalewaik (2010) makes clear that, at the very least, GDP_I deserves serious attention and may even have properties in certain respects superior to those of GDP_E. That is, if forced to choose between GDP_E and GDP_I, a surprisingly strong case exists for GDP_I.

But of course one is *not* forced to choose between GDP_E and GDP_I, and a combined estimate that pools information in the two indicators GDP_E and GDP_I may improve on both. In this chapter, we propose and explore a method for constructing such a combined estimate, and we compare our new GDP_C ("combined") series to GDP_E and GDP_I over many decades, with particular attention to behavior over the business cycle, emphasizing comparative behavior during turning points.

Our work is motivated by, and builds on, five key literatures. First, and most pleasing to us, our work is very much related to Hal White's in its focus on dynamic modeling while acknowledging misspecification throughout.

Second, we obviously build on the literature examining GDP_I and its properties, notably Fixler and Nalewaik (2009) and Nalewaik (2010). GDP_I turns out to have intriguingly good properties, suggesting that it might be usefully combined with GDP_E.

Third, our work is related to the literature distinguishing between "forecast error" and "measurement error" data revisions, as for example in Mankiw et al. (1984), Mankiw and Shapiro (1986), Faust et al. (2005), and Aruoba (2008). In this chapter we work largely in the forecast error tradition.

Fourth, and related, we work in the tradition of the forecast combination literature begun by Bates and Granger (1969), viewing GDP_E and GDP_I as forecasts of GDP [actually a mix of "backcasts" and "nowcasts" in the parlance of Aruoba and Diebold (2010)]. We combine those forecasts by forming optimally weighted averages.[1]

Finally, we build on the literature on "balancing" the national income accounts, which extends back almost as far as national income accounting itself, as for example in Stone et al. (1942), who use a quadratic loss criterion to propose weighting different GDP estimates by the inverse of their squared "margins of error." Stone refined those ideas in his subsequent national income accounting work, and Byron (1978) and Weale (1985) formalized and refined Stone's approach. Indeed a number of papers by Weale and coauthors use subjective evaluations of the quality of different U.K. GDP estimates to produce combined estimates; see Barker et al. (1984), Weale

[1] For surveys of the forecast combination literature, see Diebold and Lopez (1996) and Timmermann (2006).

(1988), Solomou and Weale (1991), and Solomou and Weale (1993).[2] For example, Barker et al. (1984) and Weale (1988) incorporate data quality assessments from the U.K. Central Statistical Office. Weale also disaggregate some of their GDP estimates to incorporate information regarding differential quality of underlying source data. In that tradition, Beaulieu and Bartelsman (2004) use input–output tables to disaggregate GDP_E and GDP_I, using what they call "tuning" parameters to balance the accounts. We take a similar approach here, weighting competing GDP estimates in ways that reflect our assessment of their quality, but we employ more of a top-down, macro perspective.

We proceed as follows. In Sect. 2 we consider GDP combination under quadratic loss. This involves taking a stand on the values of certain unobservable parameters (or at least reasonable ranges for those parameters), but we argue that a "quasi-Bayesian" calibration procedure based on informed judgment is feasible, credible, and robust. In Sect. 3 we consider GDP combination under minimax loss. Interestingly, as we show, it does not require calibration. In Sect. 4 we apply our methods to provide improved GDP estimates for the U.S. In Sect. 5 we sketch several extensions, and we conclude in Sect. 6.

2 Combination Under Quadratic Loss

Optimal forecast combination typically requires knowledge (or, in practice, estimates) of forecast error properties such as variances and covariances. In the present context, we have two "forecasts," of true GDP, namely GDP_E and GDP_I, but true GDP is never observed, even after the fact. Hence we never see the "forecast errors," which complicates matters significantly but not hopelessly. In particular, in this section we work under quadratic loss and show that a quasi-Bayesian calibration based on informed judgment is feasible and credible, and simultaneously, that the efficacy of GDP combination is robust to the precise weights used.

2.1 Basic Results and Calibration

First assume that the errors in GDP_E and GDP_I growth are uncorrelated. Consider the convex combination[3]

$$\text{GDP}_C = \lambda \text{GDP}_E + (1 - \lambda)\, \text{GDP}_I,$$

---

[2] Weale also consider serial correlation and time-varying volatility in GDP measurement errors, as well as time-varying correlation between expenditure- and income-side GDP measurement errors.

[3] Throughout this chapter, the variables GDP, GDP_E, and GDP_I that appear in the equations refer to growth rates.

where $\lambda \in [0, 1]$.[4] Then the associated errors follow the same weighting,

$$e_C = \lambda e_E + (1 - \lambda)e_I,$$

where $e_C = \text{GDP}-\text{GDP}_C$, $e_E = \text{GDP}-\text{GDP}_E$ and $e_I = \text{GDP}-\text{GDP}_I$. Assume that both GDP_E and GDP_I are unbiased for GDP, in which case GDP_C is also unbiased, because the combining weights sum to unity.

Given the unbiasedness assumption, the minimum-MSE combining weights are just the minimum-variance weights. Immediately, using the assumed zero correlation between the errors,

$$\sigma_C^2 = \lambda^2\sigma_E^2 + (1 - \lambda)^2\sigma_I^2, \tag{1}$$

where $\sigma_C^2 = \text{var}(e_C)$, $\sigma_E^2 = \text{var}(e_E)$ and $\sigma_I^2 = \text{var}(e_I)$. Minimization with respect to λ yields the optimal combining weight,

$$\lambda^* = \frac{\sigma_I^2}{\sigma_I^2 + \sigma_E^2} = \frac{1}{1 + \phi^2}, \tag{2}$$

where $\phi = \sigma_E/\sigma_I$.

It is interesting and important to note that in the present context of zero correlation between the errors,

$$\text{var}(e_E) + \text{var}(e_I) = \text{var}(\text{GDP}_E - \text{GDP}_I). \tag{3}$$

The standard deviation of GDP_E minus GDP_I can be trivially estimated. Thus, an expression of a view about ϕ is in fact implicitly an expression of a view about not only the ratio of $\text{var}(e_E)$ and $\text{var}(e_I)$, but about their actual values. We will use this fact (and its generalization in the case of correlated errors) in several places in what follows.

Based on our judgment regarding U.S. GDP_E and GDP_I data, which we will subsequently discuss in detail in Sect. 2.2, we believe that a reasonable range for ϕ is $\phi \in [0.75, 1.45]$, with midpoint 1.10.[5] One could think of this as a quasi-Bayesian statement that prior beliefs regarding ϕ are centered at 1.10, with a 90 % prior credible interval of [0.75, 1.45]. In Fig. 1 we graph λ^* as a function of ϕ, for $\phi \in [0.75, 1.45]$. λ^* is of course decreasing in ϕ, but interestingly, it is only mildly sensitive to ϕ. Indeed, for our range of ϕ values, the optimal combining weight remains close to 0.5, varying from roughly 0.65 to 0.30. At the midpoint $\phi = 1.10$, we have $\lambda^* = 0.45$.

---

[4] Strictly speaking, we need not even impose $\lambda \in [0, 1]$, but $\lambda \notin [0, 1]$ would be highly nonstandard for two valuable and sophisticated GDP estimates such as GDP_E and GDP_I. Moreover, as we shall see subsequently, multiple perspectives suggest that for our application the interesting range of λ is well in the interior of the unit interval.

[5] Invoking Eq. (3), we see that the midpoint 1.10 corresponds to $\sigma_I = 1.30$ and $\sigma_E = 1.43$, given our estimate of $std(\text{GDP}_E - \text{GDP}_I) = 1.93\,\%$ using data 1947Q2-2009Q3.

Fig. 1 λ^* versus ϕ. λ^* constructed assuming uncorrelated errors. The *horizontal line* for visual reference is at $\lambda^* = 0.5$. See text for details

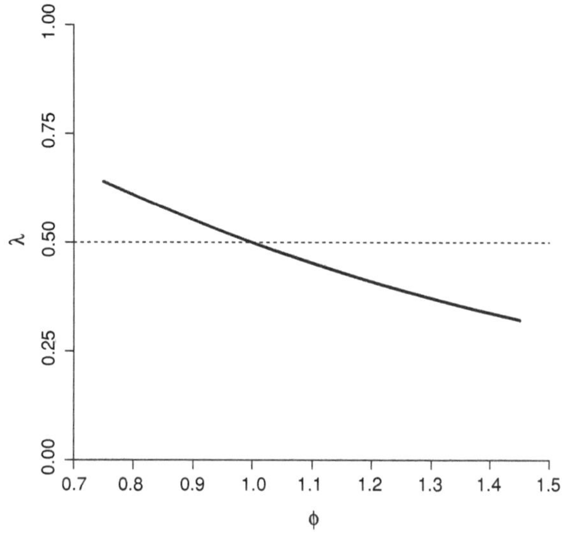

It is instructive to compare the error variance of combined GDP, σ_C^2, to σ_E^2 for a range of λ values (including $\lambda = \lambda^*$, $\lambda = 0$, and $\lambda = 1$).[6] From (1) we have:

$$\frac{\sigma_C^2}{\sigma_E^2} = \lambda^2 + \frac{(1-\lambda)^2}{\phi^2}.$$

In Fig. 2 we graph σ_C^2/σ_E^2 for $\lambda \in [0, 1]$ with $\phi = 1.1$. Obviously the maximum variance reduction is obtained using $\lambda^* = 0.45$, but even for nonoptimal λ, such as simple equal-weight combination ($\lambda = 0.5$), we achieve substantial variance reduction relative to using GDP_E alone. Indeed, a key result is that *for all* λ (except those very close to 1, of course) we achieve substantial variance reduction.

Now consider the more general and empirically-relevant case of correlated errors. Under the same conditions as earlier,

$$\sigma_c^2 = \lambda^2 \sigma_E^2 + (1-\lambda)^2 \sigma_I^2 + 2\lambda(1-\lambda)\sigma_{EI}, \tag{4}$$

so

[6] We choose to examine σ_C^2 relative to σ_E^2, rather than to σ_I^2, because GDP_E is the "standard" GDP estimate used in practice almost universally. A graph of σ_C^2/σ_I^2 would be qualitatively identical, but the drop below 1.0 would be less extreme.

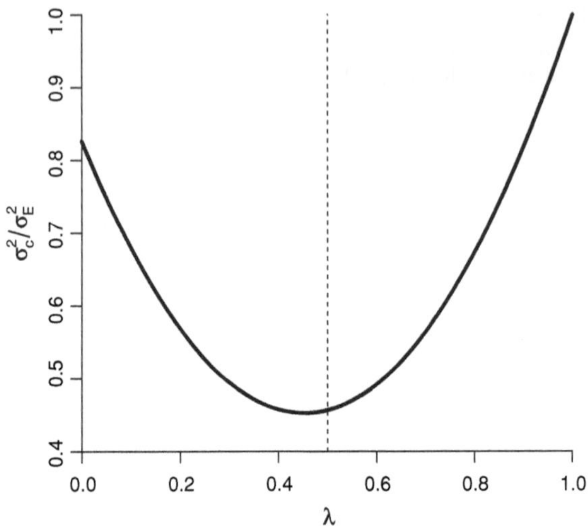

Fig. 2 σ_C^2/σ_E^2 for $\lambda \in [0, 1]$. We assume $\phi = 1.1$ and uncorrelated errors. See text for details

$$\lambda^* = \frac{\sigma_I^2 - \sigma_{EI}}{\sigma_I^2 + \sigma_E^2 - 2\sigma_{EI}} = \frac{1 - \phi\rho}{1 + \phi^2 - 2\phi\rho},$$

where $\sigma_{EI} = \text{cov}(e_E, e_I)$ and $\rho = \text{corr}(e_E, e_I)$.

It is noteworthy that—in parallel to the uncorrelated-error case in which beliefs about ϕ map one-for-one into beliefs about σ_E and σ_I— beliefs about ϕ and ρ now similarly map one-for-one into beliefs about σ_E and σ_I. Our definitions of σ_E^2 and σ_I^2 imply that

$$\sigma_j^2 = \text{var}[\text{GDP}_j] - 2\text{cov}[\text{GDP}_j, \text{GDP}] + \text{var}[\text{GDP}], \quad j \in \{E, I\}. \tag{5}$$

Moreover, the covariance between the GDP_E and GDP_I errors can be expressed as

$$\sigma_{EI} = \text{cov}[\text{GDP}_E, \text{GDP}_I] - \text{cov}[\text{GDP}_E, \text{GDP}] - \text{cov}[\text{GDP}_I, \text{GDP}] + \text{var}[\text{GDP}]. \tag{6}$$

Solving (5) for $\text{cov}[\text{GDP}_j, \text{GDP}]$ and inserting the resulting expressions for $j \in \{E, I\}$ into (6) yields

$$\sigma_{EI} = \text{cov}[\text{GDP}_I, \text{GDP}_E] - \frac{1}{2}\left(var[\text{GDP}_I] + \text{var}[\text{GDP}_E] - \sigma_I^2 - \sigma_E^2\right). \tag{7}$$

Finally, let $\sigma_{EI} = \rho\sigma_E\sigma_I$ and $\sigma_E^2 = \phi^2\sigma_I^2$. Then we can solve (7) for σ_I^2:

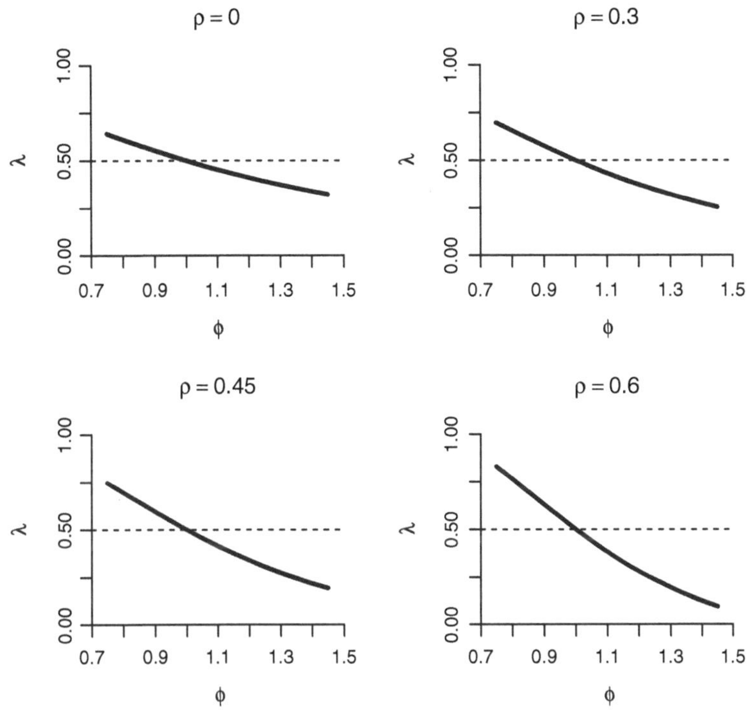

Fig. 3 λ^* versus ϕ for various ρ values. The *horizontal line* for visual reference is at $\lambda^* = 0.5$. See text for details

$$\sigma_I^2 = \frac{cov[\text{GDP}_I, \text{GDP}_E] - \frac{1}{2}\left(\text{var}[\text{GDP}_I] + \text{var}[\text{GDP}_E]\right)}{\rho\phi - \frac{1}{2}(1+\phi^2)} = \frac{N}{D}. \tag{8}$$

For given values of ϕ and ρ we can immediately evaluate the denominator D in (8), and using data-based estimates of $cov[\text{GDP}_I, \text{GDP}_E]$, $\text{var}[\text{GDP}_I]$, and $\text{var}[\text{GDP}_E]$ we can evaluate the numerator N.

Based on our judgment regarding U.S. GDP_E and GDP_I data (and again, we will discuss that judgment in detail in Sect. 2.2), we believe that a reasonable range for ρ is $\rho \in [0.30, 0.60]$, with midpoint 0.45. One could think of this as a quasi-Bayesian statement that prior beliefs regarding ρ are centered at 0.45, with a 90 % prior credible interval of [0.30, 0.60].[7]

---

[7] Again using GDP_E and GDP_I data 1947Q2-2009Q3, we obtain for the numerator $N = -1.87$ in Eq. (7) above. And using the benchmark values of $\phi = 1.1$ and $\rho = 0.45$, we obtain for the denominator $D = -0.61$. This implies $\sigma_I = 1.75$ and $\sigma_E = 1.92$. For comparison, the standard deviation of GDP_E and GDP_I growth rates is about 4.2. Hence our benchmark calibration implies that the error in measuring true GDP by the reported GDP_E and GDP_I growth rates is potentially quite large.

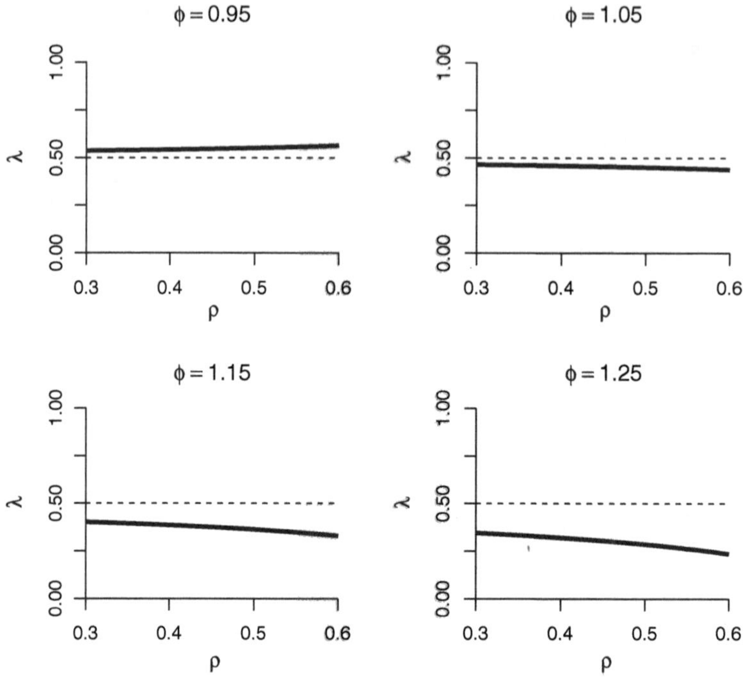

Fig. 4 λ^* versus ρ for various ϕ values. The *horizontal line* for visual reference is at $\lambda^* = 0.5$. See text for details

In Fig. 3 we show λ^* as a function of ϕ for $\rho = 0, 0.3, 0.45$, and 0.6; in Fig. 4 we show λ^* as a function of ρ for $\phi = 0.95, 1.05, 1.15$, and 1.25; and in Fig. 5 we show λ^* as a bivariate function of ϕ and ρ. For $\phi = 1$ the optimal weight is 0.5 for all ρ, but for $\phi \neq 1$ the optimal weight differs from 0.5 and is more sensitive to ϕ as ρ grows. The crucial observation remains, however, that under a wide range of conditions it is optimal to put significant weight on both GDP_E and GDP_I, with the optimal weights not differing radically from equality. Moreover, for all ϕ values greater than one, so that less weight is optimally placed on GDP_E under a zero-correlation assumption, allowance for positive correlation further decreases the optimal weight placed on GDP_E. For a benchmark calibration of $\phi = 1.1$ and $\rho = 0.45$, $\lambda^* \approx 0.41$.

Let us again compare σ_C^2 to σ_E^2 for a range of λ values (including $\lambda = \lambda^*$, $\lambda = 0$, and $\lambda = 1$). From (4) we have:

$$\frac{\sigma_C^2}{\sigma_E^2} = \lambda^2 + \frac{(1-\lambda)^2}{\phi^2} + 2\lambda(1-\lambda)\frac{\rho}{\phi}.$$

In Fig. 6 we graph σ_C^2/σ_E^2 for $\lambda \in [0, 1]$ with $\phi = 1.1$ and $\rho = 0.45$. Obviously the maximum variance reduction is obtained using $\lambda^* = 0.41$, but even for nonoptimal λ,

Fig. 5 λ^* versus ρ and ϕ. See text for details

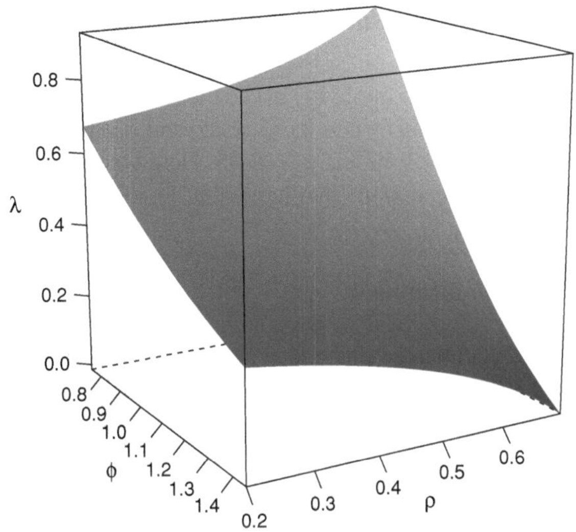

Fig. 6 σ_C^2/σ_E^2 for $\lambda \in [0, 1]$. We assume $\phi = 1.1$ and $\rho = 0.45$. See text for details

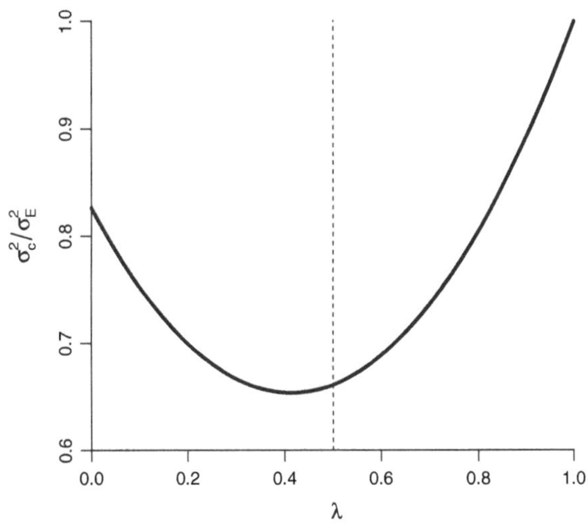

such as simple equal-weight combination ($\lambda = 0.5$), we achieve substantial variance reduction relative to using GDP_E alone.

2.2 On the Rationale for our Calibration

We have thus far implicitly asked the reader to defer to our judgment regarding calibration, focusing on $\phi \in [0.75, 1.45]$ and $\rho \in [0.30, 0.60]$ with benchmark midpoint values of $\phi = 1.10$ and $\rho = 0.45$. Here we explain the experience, reasoning, and research that supports that judgment.

2.2.1 Calibrating ϕ

The key prior view embedded in our choice of $\phi \in [0.75, 1.45]$, with midpoint 1.10, is that GDP_I is likely a somewhat more accurate estimate than GDP_E. This accords with the results of Nalewaik (2010), who examines the relative accuracy of the GDP_E and GDP_I in several ways, with results favorable to GDP_I, suggesting $\phi > 1$.

Let us elaborate. The first source of information on likely values of ϕ is from detailed examination of the source data underlying GDP_E and GDP_I. The largest component of GDP_I, wage, and salary income, is computed using quarterly data from tax records that are essentially universe counts, contaminated by neither sampling nor nonsampling errors. Two other very important components of GDP_I, corporate profits, and proprietors' income, are also computed using annual data from tax records.[8] Underreporting and nonreporting of income on tax forms (especially by proprietors) is an issue with these data, but the statistical agencies make adjustments for misreporting, and in any event the same misreporting issues plague GDP_E as well as GDP_I, as we discuss below.

In contrast to GDP_I, very little of the quarterly or annual data used to compute GDP_E is based on universe counts.[9] Rather, most of the quarterly GDP_E source data are from business surveys where response is voluntary. Nonresponse rates can be high, potentially introducing important sample-selection effects that may, moreover, vary with the state of the business cycle. Many annual GDP_E source data are from business surveys with mandatory response, but some businesses still do not respond to the surveys, and surely the auditing of these nonrespondents is less rigorous than the auditing of tax nonfilers. In addition, even the annual surveys do not attempt to collect data on some types of small businesses, particularly nonemployer businesses (i.e., businesses with no employees). The statistical agencies attempt to correct some of these omissions by incorporating data from tax records (making underreporting and nonreporting of income on tax forms an issue for GDP_E as well as GDP_I), but it is not entirely clear whether they adequately plug all the holes in the survey data.

---

[8] The tax authorities do not release the universe counts for corporate profits and proprietors' income; rather, they release results from a random sample of tax returns. But the sample they employ is enormous, so the variance of the sampling error is tiny for the top-line estimates. Moreover, the tax authorities obviously know the universe count, so it seems unlikely that they would release tabulations that are very different from the universe counts.

[9] Motor vehicle sales are a notable exception.

Although these problems plague most categories of GDP_E, some categories appear more severely plagued. In particular, over most of history, government statistical agencies have collected annual source data on less than half of personal consumption expenditures (PCE) for services, a very large category comprising between a quarter and a half of the nominal value of GDP_E over our sample. At the quarterly frequency, statistical agencies have collected even less source data on services PCE.[10] For this reason, statistical agencies have been forced to cobble together less-reliable data from numerous nongovernmental sources to estimate services PCE.

A second source of information on the relative reliability of GDP_E and GDP_I is the correlation of the two measures with other variables that should be correlated with output growth, as examined in Nalewaik (2010). Nalewaik (2010) is careful to pick variables that are not used in the construction of either GDP_E or GDP_I, to avoid spurious correlation resulting from correlated measurement errors.[11] The results are uniformly favorable to GDP_I and suggest that it is a more accurate measure of output growth than GDP_E. In particular, from the mid-1980s to the mid-2000s, the period of maximum divergence between GDP_E and GDP_I, Nalewaik (2010) finds that GDP_I growth has higher correlation with lagged stock price changes, the lagged slope of the yield curve, the lagged spread between high-yield corporate bonds and Treasury bonds, short and long differences of the unemployment rate (both contemporaneously and at leads and lags), a measure of employment growth computed from the same household survey, the manufacturing ISM PMI (Institute for Supply Management, Purchasing Managers Index), the nonmanufacturing ISM PMI, and dummies for NBER recessions. In addition, lags of GDP_I growth also predict GDP_E growth (and GDP_I growth) better than lags of GDP_E growth itself.

It is worth noting that, as regards our benchmark midpoint calibration of $\phi = 1.10$, we have deviated only slightly from an "ignorance prior" midpoint of 1.00. Hence our choice of midpoint reflects a conservative interpretation of the evidence discussed above. Similarly, regarding the width of the credible interval as opposed to its midpoint, we considered employing intervals such as $\phi \in [0.95, 1.25]$, for which $\phi > 1$ over most of the mass of the interval. The evidence discussed above, if interpreted aggressively, might justify such a tight interval in favor of GDP_I, but again we opted for a more conservative approach with $\phi < 1$ over more than a third of the mass of the interval.

2.2.2 Calibrating ρ

The key prior view embedded in our choice of $\rho \in [0.30, 0.60]$, with midpoint 0.45, is that the errors in GDP_E and GDP_I are likely positively correlated, with a

[10] This has begun to change recently, as the Census Bureau has expanded its surveys, but ϕ is meant to represent the average relative reliability over the sample we employ, so these facts are highly relevant.

[11] For example, the survey of households used to compute the unemployment rate is used in the construction of neither GDP_E nor GDP_I, so use of variables from that survey is fine.

moderately but not extremely large correlation value. This again accords with the results in Nalewaik (2010), who shows that 26 % of the nominal value of GDP_E and GDP_I is identical. Any measurement errors in that 26 % will be perfectly correlated across the two estimates. Furthermore, GDP_E and GDP_I are both likely to miss fluctuations in output occurring in the underground or "gray" economy, transactions that do not appear on tax forms or government surveys. In addition, the same price deflator is used to convert GDP_E and GDP_I from nominal to real values, so any measurement errors in that price deflator will be perfectly correlated across the two estimates.

These considerations suggest the lower bound for ρ should be well above zero, as reflected in our chosen interval. However, the evidence favoring an upper bound well below one is also quite strong, as also reflected in our chosen interval. First, and most obviously, the standard deviation of the difference between GDP_E and GDP_I is 1.9 %, far from the 0.0 % that would be the case if $\rho = 1.0$. Second, as discussed in the previous section, the source data used to construct GDP_E is quite different from the source data used to construct GDP_I, implying the measurement errors are likely to be far from perfectly correlated.

Of course, ρ could still be quite high if GDP_E and GDP_I were contaminated with enormous common measurement errors, as well as smaller, uncorrelated measurement errors. But if that were the case, GDP_E and GDP_I would fail to be correlated with other cyclically-sensitive variables, such as the unemployment rate, as they both are. The R^2 values from regressions of the output growth measures on the change in the unemployment rate are each around 0.50 over our sample, suggesting that at least half of the variance of GDP_E and GDP_I is true variation in output growth, rather than measurement error. The standard deviation of the residual from these regressions is 2.81 % using GDP_I and 2.95 % using GDP_E. For comparison, taking our benchmark value $\phi = 1.1$ and our upper bound $\rho = 0.6$ produces $\sigma_I = 2.05$ and $\sigma_E = 2.25$. Increasing ρ to 0.7 produces $\sigma_I = 2.36$ and $\sigma_E = 2.60$, approaching the residual standard error from our regression. This seems like an unreasonably high amount of measurement error, since the explained variation from such a simple regression is probably not measurement error, and indeed some of the unexplained variation from the regression is probably also not measurement error. Hence the upper bound of 0.6 for ρ seems about right.

3 Combination Under Minimax Loss

Here we take a more conservative perspective on forecast combination, solving a different but potentially important optimization problem. We utilize the minimax framework of Wald (1950), which is the main decision-theoretic approach for imposing conservatism and therefore of intrinsic interest. We solve a game between a benevolent scholar (the Econometrician) and a malevolent opponent (Nature). In that game the Econometrician chooses the combining weights, and Nature selects the stochastic properties of the forecast errors. The minimax solution yields the combining weights that deliver the smallest chance of the worst outcome for the Econometrician. Under the minimax approach knowledge or calibration of objects like ϕ and ρ is unnecessary, enabling us to dispense with judgment, for better or worse.

We obtain the minimax weights by solving for the Nash equilibrium in a two-player zero-sum game. Nature chooses the properties of the forecast errors and the Econometrician chooses the combining weights λ. For expositional purposes, we begin with the case of uncorrelated errors, constraining Nature to choose $\rho = 0$. To impose some constraints on the magnitude of forecast errors that Nature can choose, it is useful to re-parameterize the vector $(\sigma_I, \sigma_E)'$ in terms of polar coordinates; that is, we let $\sigma_I = \psi \cos\varphi$ and $\sigma_E = \psi \sin\varphi$. We restrict ψ to the interval $[0, \bar{\psi}]$ and let $\varphi \in [0, \pi/2]$. Because $\cos^2\varphi + \sin^2\varphi = 1$, the sum of the forecast error variances associated with GDP_E and GDP_I is constrained to be less than or equal to $\bar{\psi}^2$. The error associated with the combined forecast is given by

$$\sigma_C^2(\psi, \varphi, \lambda) = \psi^2 \left[\lambda^2 \sin^2\varphi + (1-\lambda)^2 \cos^2\varphi\right], \tag{9}$$

so that the minimax problem is

$$\max_{\psi \in [0, \bar{\psi}],\, \varphi \in [0, \pi/2]} \; \min_{\lambda \in [0,1]} \; \sigma_C^2(\psi, \varphi, \lambda), \tag{10}$$

The best response of the Econometrician was derived in (2) and can be expressed in terms of polar coordinates as $\lambda^* = \cos^2\varphi$. In turn, Nature's problem simplifies to

$$\max_{\psi \in [0, \bar{\psi}],\, \varphi \in [0, \pi/2]} \; \psi^2 (1 - \sin^2\varphi) \sin^2\varphi,$$

which leads to the solution

$$\varphi^* = \text{arc}\,\sin\sqrt{1/2}, \quad \psi^* = \bar{\psi}, \quad \lambda^* = 1/2. \tag{11}$$

Nature's optimal choice implies a unit forecast error variance ratio, $\phi = \sigma_E/\sigma_I = 1$, and hence that the optimal combining weight is 1/2. If, instead, Nature set $\varphi = 0$ or $\varphi = \pi/2$, that is $\phi = 0$ or $\phi = \infty$, then either GDP_E or GDP_I is perfect and the Econometrician could choose $\lambda = 0$ or $\lambda = 1$ to achieve a perfect forecast leading to a suboptimal outcome for Nature.

Now we consider the case in which Nature can choose a nonzero correlation between the forecast errors of GDP_E and GDP_I. The loss of the combined forecast can be expressed as

$$\sigma_C^2(\psi, \rho, \varphi, \lambda) = \psi^2 \left[\lambda^2 \sin^2\varphi + (1-\lambda)^2 \cos^2\varphi + 2\lambda(1-\lambda)\rho \sin\varphi \cos\varphi\right]. \tag{12}$$

It is apparent from (12) that as long as λ lies in the unit interval the most devious choice of ρ is $\rho^* = 1$. We will now verify that conditional on $\rho^* = 1$ the solution in

(11) remains a Nash equilibrium. Suppose that the Econometrician chooses equal weights, $\lambda^* = 1/2$. In this case

$$\sigma_C^2(\psi, \rho^*, \varphi, \lambda^*) = \psi^2 \left[\frac{1}{4} + \frac{1}{2} \sin \varphi \cos \varphi \right].$$

We can deduce immediately that $\psi^* = \bar{\psi}$. Moreover, first-order conditions for the maximization with respect to φ imply that $\cos^2 \varphi^* = \sin^2 \varphi^*$ which in turn leads to $\varphi^* = \text{arc} \sin \sqrt{1/2}$. Conditional on Nature choosing ρ^*, ψ^*, and φ^*, the Econometrician has no incentive to deviate from the equal-weights combination $\lambda^* = 1/2$, because

$$\sigma_C^2(\psi^*, \rho^*, \varphi^*, \lambda) = \frac{\bar{\psi}}{2} \left[\lambda^2 + (1-\lambda)^2 + 2\lambda(1-\lambda) \right] = \frac{\bar{\psi}}{2}.$$

In sum, the minimax analysis provides a rational for combining GDP_E and GDP_I with equal weights of $\lambda = 1/2$.

To the best of our knowledge, this section's demonstration of the optimality of equal forecast combination weights under minimax loss is original and novel. There does of course exist some related literature, but ultimately our approach and results are very different. For example, a branch of the machine-learning literature (e.g., Vovk 1998; Sancetta 2007) considers games between a malevolent Nature and a benevolent "Learner." The learner sequentially chooses weights to combine expert forecasts, and Nature chooses realized outcomes to maximize the Learner's forecast error relative to the best expert forecast. The Learner wins the game if his forecast loss is only slightly worse than the loss attained by the best expert in the pool, even under Nature's least favorable choice of outcomes. This game is quite different and much more complicated than ours, requiring different equilibrium concepts with different resultant combining weights.

4 Empirics

We have shown that combining using a quasi-Bayesian calibration under quadratic loss produces λ close to but less than 0.5, given our prior means for ϕ and ρ. Moreover, we showed that combining with λ near 0.5 is likely better—often much better—than simply using GDP_E or GDP_I alone, for wide ranges of ϕ and ρ. We also showed that combining under minimax loss always implies an optimal λ of exactly 0.5.

Here we put the theory to work for the U.S., providing arguably-superior combined estimates of GDP growth. We focus on quasi-Bayesian calibration under quadratic loss. Because the resulting combining weights are near 0.50, however, one could also view our combinations as approximately minimax. The point is that a variety of perspectives lead to combinations with weights near 0.50, and they suggest that

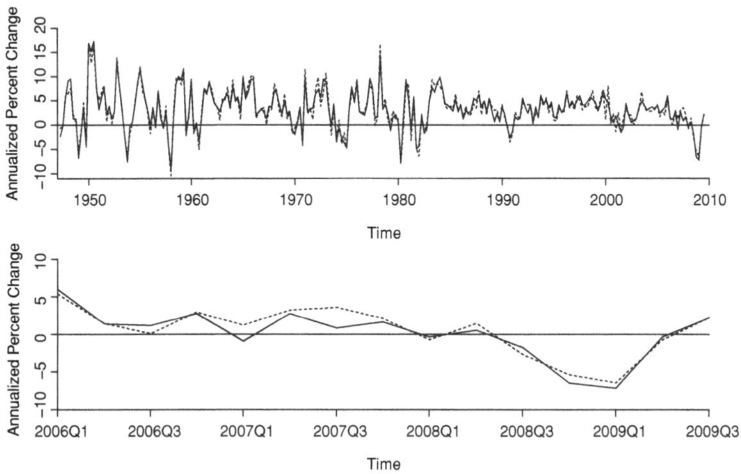

Fig. 7 U.S. GDP_C and GDP_E growth rates. GDP_C constructed assuming $\phi = 1.1$ and $\rho = 0.45$. GDP_C is *solid* and GDP_E is *dashed*. In the *top panel* we show a long sample, 1947Q2–2009Q3. In the *bottom panel*, we show a recent sample, 2006Q1–2009Q3. See text for details

such combinations are likely superior to using either of GDP_E or GDP_I alone, so that empirical examination of GDP_C is of maximal interest.

4.1 A Combined U.S. GDP Series

In the top panel of Fig. 7 we plot GDP_C constructed using $\lambda = 0.41$, which is optimal for our benchmark calibration of $\phi = 1.1$ and $\rho = 0.45$, together with the "conventional" GDP_E. The two appear to move closely together, and indeed they do, at least at the low frequencies emphasized by the long time-series plot. Hence for low-frequency analyses, such as studies of long-term economic growth, use of GDP_E, GDP_I or GDP_C is not likely to make a major difference.

At higher frequencies, however, important divergences can occur. In the bottom panel of Fig. 7, for example, we emphasize business cycle frequencies by focusing on a short sample 2006–2010, which contains the severe U.S. recession of 2007–2009. There are two important points to notice. First, the bottom panel of Fig. 7 makes clear that growth-rate assessments on particular dates can differ in important ways depending on whether GDP_C or GDP_E is used. For example, GDP_E is strongly positive for 2007Q3, whereas GDP_C for that quarter is close to zero, as GDP_I was strongly negative. Second, the bottom panel of Fig. 7 also makes clear that differing assessments can persist over several quarters, as for example during the financial crisis episode of 2007Q1–2007Q3, when GDP_E growth was consistently larger than GDP_C growth. One might naturally conjecture that such persistent and cumulative data distortions might similarly distort inferences, based on those data, about whether and when the U.S. economy was in recession. We now consider recession dating in some detail.

4.2 U.S. Recession and Volatility Regime Probabilities

Thus far we have assessed how combining produces changes in measured GDP. Now we assess whether and how it changes a certain important *transformation* of GDP, namely measured probabilities of recession regimes or high-volatility regimes based on measured GDP. We proceed by fitting a regime-switching model in the tradition of Hamilton (1989), generalized to allow for switching in both means and variances, as in Kim and Nelson (1999a),

$$\begin{aligned}(\text{GDP}_t - \mu_{s_{\mu t}}) &= \beta(\text{GDP}_{t-1} - \mu_{s_{\mu t-1}}) + \sigma_{s_{\sigma t}}\varepsilon_t \\ \varepsilon_t &\sim iidN(0,1) \\ s_{\mu t} &\sim \text{Markov}(P_\mu), \quad s_{\sigma t} \sim \text{Markov}(P_\sigma).\end{aligned} \tag{13}$$

Then, conditional on observed data, we infer the sequences of recession probabilities [$(P(s_{\mu t} = L)$, where L ("low") denotes the recession regime] and high-volatility regime probabilities [$(P(s_{\sigma_t} = H)$, where H ("high") denotes the high-volatility regime]. We perform this exercise using both GDP_E and GDP_C, and we compare the results.

We implement Bayesian estimation and state extraction using data 1947Q2-2009Q3.[12] In Fig. 8 we show posterior median smoothed recession probabilities. We show those calculated using GDP_C as solid lines with 90 % posterior intervals, we show those calculated using GDP_E as dashed lines, and we also show shaded NBER recession episodes to help provide context. Similarly, in Fig. 9 we show posterior median smoothed volatility regime probabilities.

Numerous interesting substantive results emerge. For example, posterior median smoothed recession regime probabilities calculated using GDP_C tend to be greater than those calculated using GDP_E, sometimes significantly so, as for example during the financial crisis of 2007. Indeed, using GDP_C one might date the start of the recent recession significantly earlier than did the NBER. As regards volatilities, posterior median smoothed high-volatility regime probabilities calculated by either GDP_E or GDP_C tend to show the post-1984 "great moderation" effect asserted by McConnell and Perez-Quiros (2000) and Stock and Watson (2002). Interestingly, however, those calculated using GDP_E also show the "higher recession volatility" effect in recent decades documented by Bloom et al. (2009) (using GDP_E data), whereas those calculated using GDP_C do not.

[12] We provide a detailed description in Appendix.

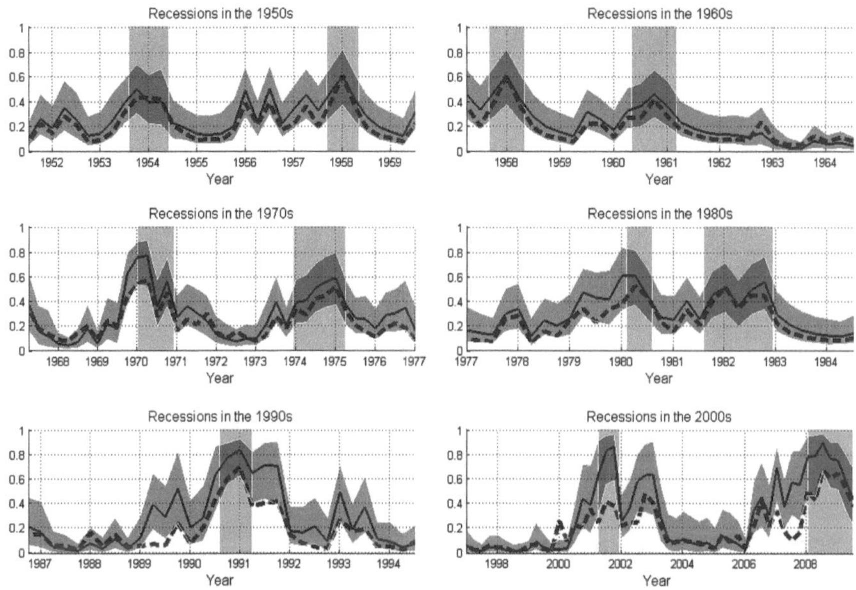

Fig. 8 Inferred U.S. Recession Regime Probabilities, calculated using GDP_C versus GDP_E. *Solid lines* are posterior median smoothed recession regime probabilities calculated using GDP_C, which we show with 90 % posterior intervals. *Dashed lines* are posterior median smoothed recession regime probabilities calculated using GDP_E. The sample period is 1947Q2-2009Q3. *Dark shaded bars* denote NBER recessions. See text and appendix for details

For our present purposes, however, none of those substantive results are of first-order importance, as the present chapter is not about business cycle dating, low-frequency versus high-frequency volatility regime dating, or revisionist history, *per se*. Indeed, thorough explorations of each would require separate and lengthy papers. Rather, our point here is simply that one's assessment and characterization of macroeconomic behavior can, and often does, depend significantly on use of GDP_C versus GDP_E. That is, choice of GDP_C versus GDP_E can *matter* for important tasks, whether based on direct observation of measured GDP, or on transformations of measured GDP such as extracted regime chronologies.

5 Extensions

Before concluding, we offer sketches of what we see as two important avenues for future research. The first involves real-time analysis and nonconstant combining weights, and the second involves combining from a measurement error as opposed to efficient forecast error perspective.

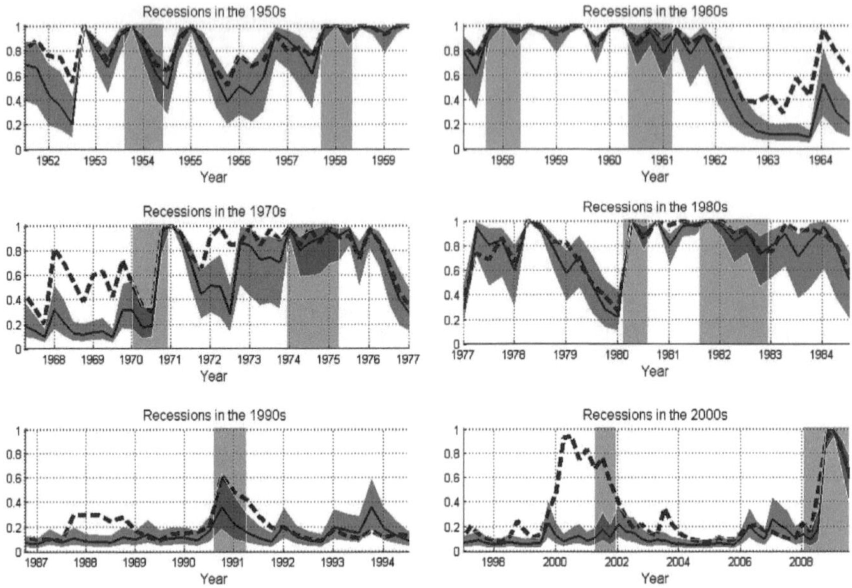

Fig. 9 Inferred U.S. high-volatility regime probabilities, calculated using GDP_C versus GDP_E. *Solid lines* are posterior median smoothed high-volatility regime probabilities calculated using GDP_C, which we show with 90 % posterior intervals. Dashed lines are posterior median smoothed high-volatility regime probabilities calculated using GDP_E. The sample period is 1947Q2-2009Q3. *Dark shaded bars* denote NBER recessions. See text and appendices for details.

5.1 Vintage Data, Time-Varying Combining Weights, and Real-Time Analysis

It is important to note that everything that we have done in this chapter has a retrospective, or "off-line," character. We work with a single vintage of GDP_E and GDP_I data and combine them, estimating objects of interest (combining weights, regime probabilities, etc.) for any period t using *all* data $t = 1, \ldots, T$. In all of our analyses, moreover, we have used time-invariant combining weights. Those two characteristics of our work thus far are not unrelated, and one may want to relax them eventually, allowing for time-varying weights, and ultimately, a truly real-time-analysis.

One may want to consider time-varying combining weights for several reasons. One reason is of near-universal and hence great interest, at least under quadratic loss. For any given vintage of data, error variances and covariances may naturally change, as we pass backward from preliminary data for the recent past, all the way through to "final revised" data for the more distant past.[13] More precisely, let t index time measured in quarters, and consider moving backward from "the present" quarter $t = T$.

[13] This is the so-called "apples and oranges" problem. To the best of our knowledge, the usage in our context traces to Kishor and Koenig (2011).

At instant $v \in T$ (with apologies for the slightly abusive notation), we have vintage-v data. Consider moving backward, constructing combined GDP estimates $GDP^{v}_{C,T-k}$, $k = 1, \ldots \infty$. For small k, the optimal calibrations might be quite far from benchmark values. As k grows, however, ρ and ϕ should approach benchmark values as the final revision is approached. The obvious question is how quickly and with what pattern should an optimal calibration move toward benchmark values as $k \rightarrow \infty$. We can offer a few speculative observations.

First consider ρ. GDP_I, and GDP_E share a considerable amount of source data in their early releases, before common source data are swapped out of GDP_I (e.g., when tax returns eventually become available and can be used). Indeed Fixler and Nalewaik (2009) show that the correlation between the earlier estimates of GDP_I and GDP_E growth is higher than the correlation between the later estimates. Hence ρ is likely higher for dates near the present (small k). This suggests calibrations with ρ dropping monotonically toward the benchmark value of 0.45 as k grows.

Now consider ϕ. How ϕ should deviate from its benchmark calibration value of 1.1 is less clear. On the one hand, early releases of GDP_I are missing some of their most informative source data (tax returns), which suggests a lower-than-benchmark ϕ for small k. On the other hand, early releases of GDP_E growth appear to be noisier than the early releases of GDP_I growth (see below), which suggests a higher-than-benchmark ϕ for small k. All told, we feel that a reasonable small-k calibration of ϕ is less than 1.1 but still above 1.

Note that our conjectured small-k effects work in different directions. Other things equal, bigger ρ pushes the optimal combining weight downward, away from 0.5, and smaller ϕ pushes the optimal combining weight upward, toward 0.5. In any particular data set the effects could conceivably offset more-or-less exactly, so that combination using constant weights for all dates would be fully optimal, but there is of course no guarantee.

Several approaches are possible to implement the time-varying weights sketched in the preceding paragraphs. One is a quasi-Bayesian calibration, elaborating on the approach we have taken in this chapter. However, such an approach would be more difficult in the more challenging environment of time-varying parameters. Another is to construct a real-time data set, one that records a snapshot of the data available at each point in time, such as the one maintained by the Federal Reserve Bank of Philadelphia. The key is to recognize that each quarter we get not simply one new observation on GDP_E and GDP_I, but rather an entire new vintage of data, all the elements of which could (in principle) change. One might be able to use the different data vintages, and related objects like revision histories, to infer properties of "forecast errors" of relevance for construction of optimal combining weights across various k.

One could go even further in principle, progressing to a truly real-time analysis, which is of intrinsic interest quite apart from addressing the issue of time-varying combining weights in the above "apples and oranges" environments. Tracking vintages, modeling the associated dynamics of revisions, and putting it all together to produce superior combined forecasts remains an outstanding challenge.[14] We look forward to its solution in future work, potentially in the state-space framework that we describe next.

5.2 A Model of Measurement Error

In parallel work in progress (Aruoba et al. 2011), we pursue a complementary approach based on a state-space model of measurement error. The basic model is

$$\begin{bmatrix} \mathrm{GDP}_{E,t} \\ \mathrm{GDP}_{I,t} \end{bmatrix} = \begin{bmatrix} 1 \\ 1 \end{bmatrix} \mathrm{GDP}_t + \begin{bmatrix} \varepsilon_{Et} \\ \varepsilon_{It} \end{bmatrix}$$

$$\mathrm{GDP_t} = \beta_0 + \beta_1 \mathrm{GDP_{t-1}} + \eta_\mathrm{t}, \tag{14}$$

where $\varepsilon_t = (\varepsilon_{Et}, \varepsilon_{It})' \sim WN(\underline{0}, \Sigma_\varepsilon)$, $\eta_t \sim WN(0, \sigma_\eta^2)$, and ε_t and η_t are uncorrelated at all leads and lags. In this model, both GDP_E and GDP_I are noisy measures of the latent true GDP process, which evolves dynamically. The expectation of true GDP conditional upon observed measurements may be extracted using optimal filtering techniques such as the Kalman filter.

The basic state-space model can be extended in various directions, for example to incorporate richer dynamics, and to account for data revisions and missing advance and preliminary releases of GDP_I.[15] Perhaps most important, the measurement errors ε may be allowed to be correlated with GDP, or more precisely, correlated with GDP innovations, η_t. Fixler and Nalewaik (2009) and Nalewaik (2010) document cyclicality in the "statistical discrepancy" ($\mathrm{GDP}_E - \mathrm{GDP}_I$), which implies failure of the assumption that ε_t and η_t are uncorrelated at all leads and lags. Of particular concern is contemporaneous correlation between η_t and ε_t. The standard Kalman filter cannot handle this, but appropriate modifications are available.

6 Conclusions

GDP growth is a central concept in macroeconomics and business cycle monitoring, so its accurate measurement is crucial. Unfortunately, however, the two available expenditure-side and income-side U.S. GDP estimates often diverge. In this chapter, we proposed a technology for optimally combining the competing GDP estimates,

---

[14] Nalewaik (2011) makes some progress toward real-time analysis in a Markov-switching environment.

[15] The first official estimate of GDP_I is released a month or two after the first official estimate of GDP_E, so for vintage v the available GDP_E^v data might be $\{\mathrm{GDP}_{E,t}^v\}_{t=1}^{T-1}$, whereas the available GDP_I^v vintage might be $\{GDP_{I,t}^v\}_{t=1}^{T-2}$. Note that for any vintage v, the available GDP_I data differ by at most one quarter from the available GDP_E data.

we examined several variations on the basic theme, and we constructed and examined combined estimates for the U.S.

Our results strongly suggest the desirability of separate and careful calculation of both GDP_E and GDP_I, followed by combination, which may lead to different and more accurate insights than those obtained by simply using expenditure-side or estimates alone. This prescription differs fundamentally from U.S. practice, where both are calculated but the income-side estimate is routinely ignored.

Our call for a combined U.S. GDP measure is hardly radical, particularly given current best-practice "balancing" procedures used at various non-U.S. statistical agencies to harmonize GDP estimates from different sources. We discussed U.K. GDP balancing at some length in the introduction, and some other countries also use various similar balancing procedures.[16] All such procedures recognize the potential inaccuracies of source data and have a similar effect to our forecast combination approach: the final GDP number lies between the alternative estimates.

Other countries use other approaches to combination. Indeed Australia uses an approach reminiscent of the one that we advocate in this chapter, albeit not on the grounds of our formal analysis.[17] In addition to GDP_E and GDP_I, the Australian Bureau of Statistics produces a production-side estimate, GDP_P, defined as total gross value added plus taxes and less subsidies, and its headline GDP number is the simple average of the three GDP estimates. We look forward to the U.S. producing a similarly-combined headline GDP estimate, potentially using the methods introduced in this chapter.

Acknowledgments We dedicate this chapter to Hal White, on whose broad shoulders we stand, on the occasion of his sixtieth birthday. For helpful comments we thank the editors and referees, as well as John Geweke, Greg Mankiw, Matt Shapiro, Chris Sims, and Justin Wolfers. For research support we thank the National Science Foundation and the Real-Time Data Research Center at the Federal Reserve Bank of Philadelphia. For research assistance we thank Ross Kelley and Matthew Klein.

Appendix: Estimation of U.S. Recession Probabilities

Here we provide details of Bayesian analysis of our regime-switching model.

A.1 Baseline Model

We work with a simple model with Markov regime-switching in mean and variance:

[16] Germany's procedures, for example, are described in Statistisches Bundesamt (2009).

[17] See http://www.abs.gov.au, under Australian National Accounts, Explanatory Notes for Australia.

$$\begin{aligned}(\text{GDP}_t - \mu_{s_{\mu t}}) &= \beta(\text{GDP}_{t-1} - \mu_{s_{\mu t-1}}) + \sigma_{s_{\sigma t}}\varepsilon_t \\ \varepsilon_t &\sim iidN(0,1)\end{aligned} \tag{A.1}$$

$$s_{\mu t} \sim \text{Markov}(P_\mu), \quad s_{\sigma t} \sim \text{Markov}(P_\sigma), \tag{A.2}$$

where P_μ and P_σ denote transition matrices for high and low mean and variance regimes,

$$P_\mu = \begin{bmatrix} p_{\mu H} & 1 - p_{\mu H} \\ 1 - p_{\mu L} & p_{\mu L} \end{bmatrix}$$

$$P_\sigma = \begin{bmatrix} p_{\sigma H} & 1 - p_{\sigma H} \\ 1 - p_{\sigma L} & p_{\sigma L} \end{bmatrix}.$$

Overall, then, there are four regimes:

$$\begin{aligned} S_t &= 1 \text{if } s_{\mu t} = H,\ s_{\sigma t} = H \\ S_t &= 2 \text{if } s_{\mu t} = H,\ s_{\sigma t} = L \\ S_t &= 3 \text{if } s_{\mu t} = L,\ s_{\sigma t} = H \\ S_t &= 4 \text{if } s_{\mu t} = L,\ s_{\sigma t} = L. \end{aligned} \tag{A.3}$$

For $t = 0$ the hidden Markov states are governed by the ergodic distribution associated with P_μ and P_σ.

A.2 Bayesian Inference

Priors. Bayesian inference combines a prior distribution with a likelihood function to obtain a posterior distribution of the model parameters and states. We summarize our benchmark priors in Table A.1. We employ a normal prior for μ_L, a gamma prior for $\mu_H - \mu_L$, inverted gamma priors for σ_H and σ_L, beta priors for the transition probabilities, and finally, a normal prior for β. Our prior ensures that $\mu_H \geq \mu_L$ and thereby deals with the "label switching" identification problem.

For μ_L, the average growth rate in the low-growth state, we use a prior distribution that is centered at 0, with standard deviation 0.70 %. Note that a priori we do not restrict the average growth rate to be negative. We also allow for (mildly) positive values. We choose the prior for $\mu_H - \mu_L$ such that the mean difference between the average growth rates in the two regimes is 2.00 %, with standard deviation 1.00 %. Our priors for the transition probabilities p_μ and p_σ are symmetric and imply a mean regime duration between three and 14 quarters. Finally, our choice for the prior of the autoregressive parameter β is normal with zero mean and unit variance, allowing a priori for both stable and unstable dynamics of output growth rates.

Table A.1 Prior choices and posterior distributions

	Prior Choice	GDP_E Median	5 %	95 %	GDP_C Median	5 %	95 %
$\mu_H - \mu_L$	Gamma(2, 1)	–	–	–	–	–	–
μ_H	–	3.50	[3.03	4.12]	3.76	[2.97	4.28]
μ_L	Normal(0, 0.5)	1.25	[0.34	2.29]	0.82	[0.17	1.64]
σ_H	InvGamma(2, 2)	4.82	[4.35	5.43]	4.64	[4.21	5.13]
σ_L	InvGamma(1, 2)	1.92	[1.55	2.34]	1.71	[1.74	2.05]
β	Normal(0, 1)	0.31	[0.17	0.45]	0.37	[0.27	0.53]
p_{μ_H}	Beta(25, 5)	0.91	[0.82	0.96]	0.92	[0.85	0.96]
p_{μ_L}	Beta(25, 5)	0.79	[0.64	0.87]	0.80	[0.67	0.88]
p_{σ_H}	Beta(25, 5)	0.91	[0.83	0.96]	0.91	[0.83	0.96]
p_{σ_L}	Beta(25, 5)	0.89	[0.81	0.95]	0.91	[0.85	0.95]

Implementation of Posterior Inference. Posterior inference is implemented with a Metropolis-within-Gibbs sampler, building on work by Carter and Kohn (1994) and Kim and Nelson (1999b). We denote the sequence of observations by $GDP_{1:T}$. Moreover, let $S_{1:T}$ be the sequence of hidden states, and let

$$\theta = (\mu_H, \mu_L, \sigma_H, \sigma_L, \beta)', \quad \text{and} \quad \phi = (p_{\mu_H}, p_{\mu_L}, p_{\sigma_L}, p_{\sigma_H})'.$$

Our Metropolis-within-Gibbs algorithm involves sampling iteratively from three conditional posterior distributions. To initialize the sampler we start from (θ^0, ϕ^0).
Algorithm: Metropolis-within-Gibbs Sampler
For $i = 1, \ldots, N$:

1. Draw $S_{1:T}^{i+1}$ conditional on θ^i, ϕ^i, $GDP_{1:T}$. This step is implemented using the multi-move simulation smoother described in Sect. 9.1.1 of Kim and Nelson (1999b).
2. Draw ϕ^{i+1} conditional on θ^i, $S_{1:T}^{i+1}$, $GDP_{1:T}$. If the dependence of the distribution of the initial state S_1 on ϕ is ignored, then it can be shown that the conditional posterior of ϕ is of the Beta form (see Sect. 9.1.2 of Kim and Nelson 1999b). We use the resulting Beta distribution as a proposal distribution in a Metropolis–Hastings step.
3. Draw θ^{i+1}, conditional on ϕ^{i+1}, $S_{1:T}^{i+1}$, $GDP_{1:T}$. Since our prior distribution is nonconjugate, we are using a random-walk Metropolis step to generate a draw from the conditional posterior of θ. The proposal distribution is $N(\theta^i, c\Omega)$.

We obtain the covariance matrix Ω of the proposal distribution in Step 3 as follows. Following Schorfheide (2005) we maximize the posterior density,

$$p(\theta, \phi | GDP_{1:T}) \propto p(GDP_{1:T} | \theta, \phi) p(\theta, \phi),$$

to obtain the posterior mode $(\tilde{\theta}, \tilde{\phi})$. We then construct the negative inverse of the Hessian at the mode and let Ω be the submatrix that corresponds to the parameter subvector θ. We choose the scaling factor c to obtain an acceptance rate of approximately 40 %. We initialize our algorithm choosing (θ^0, ϕ^0) in the neighborhood of $(\tilde{\theta}, \tilde{\phi})$ and use it to generate $N = 100,000$ draws from the posterior distribution.[18]

Posterior Estimates. Table A.1 also contains percentiles of posterior parameter distributions. The posterior estimates for the volatility parameters and the transition probabilities are similar across GDP_E and GDP_C. However, the posterior estimate for μ_L is higher using GDP_E than using GDP_C, while the opposite is true for β. Moreover, the differential between high and low mean regimes is bigger in the case of GDP_C, all of which can influence the time-series plot of the recession probabilities.

The Markov-switching means capture low-frequency shifts while the autoregressive coefficient captures high-frequency dynamics. Thus, the presence of the autoregressive term may complicate our analysis, because we are trying to decompose the GDP measurement discrepancy into both low- and highfrequency components. As a robustness check, we remove the autoregressive term in (A.1) and estimate an *iid* model specification. Although the posterior estimates for μ_L change, the remaining parameters are essentially identical to Table A.1. The smoothed recession probabilities remain nearly identical to Fig. 8.

References

Aruoba, B. (2008), "Data Revisions are not Well-Behaved", Journal of Money, Credit and Banking, 40, 319–340.

Aruoba, S.B. and F.X. Diebold (2010), "Real-Time Macroeconomic Monitoring: Real Activity, Inflation, and Interactions", American Economic Review, 100, 20–24.

Aruoba, S.B., F.X. Diebold, J. Nalewaik, F. Schorfheide, and D. Song (2011), "Improving GDP Measurement: A Measurement Error Perspective", Manuscript in progress, University of Maryland, University of Pennsylvania and Federal Reserve Board.

Barker, T., F. van der Ploeg, and M. Weale (1984), "A Balanced System of National Accounts for the United Kingdom", Review of Income and Wealth, 461–485.

Bates, J.M. and C.W.J. Granger (1969), "The Combination of Forecasts", Operations Research Quarterly, 20, 451–468.

Beaulieu, J. and E.J. Bartelsman (2004), "Integrating Expenditure and Income Data: What To Do With the Statistical Discrepancy?" FEDS Working Paper 2004, 39.

Bloom, N., M. Floetotto, and N. Jaimovich (2009), "Really Uncertain Business Cycles", Manuscript, Stanford University.

Byron, R. (1978), "The Estimation of Large Social Accounts Matrices", Journal of the Royal Statistical Society Series A, 141, Part 3, 359–367.

Carter, C.K. and R. Kohn (1994), "On Gibbs Sampling for State Space Models", Biometrika, 81, 541–553.

Diebold, F.X. and J.A. Lopez (1996), "Forecast Evaluation and Combination", In G.S. Maddala and C.R. Rao (eds.) Handbook of Statistics (Statistical Methods in Finance), North- Holland, 241–268.

[18] We performed several tests confirming that our choice of N yields an accurate posterior approximation.

Faust, J., J.H. Rogers, and J.H. Wright (2005), "News and Noise in G-7 GDP Announcements", Journal of Money, Credit and Banking, 37, 403–417.
Fixler, D.J. and J.J. Nalewaik (2009), "News, Noise, and Estimates of the "True" Unobserved State of the Economy", Manuscript, Bureau of Labor Statistics and Federal Reserve Board.
Hamilton, J.D. (1989), "A New Approach to the Economic Analysis of Nonstationary Time Series and the Business Cycle", Econometrica, 57, 357–384.
Kim, C.-J. and C.R. Nelson (1999a), "Has the U.S. Economy Become More Stable? A Bayesian Approach Based on a Markov-Switching Model of the Business Cycle", Review of Economics and Statistics, 81, 608–616.
Kim, C.-J. and C.R. Nelson (1999b), State Space Models with Regime Switching, MIT Press.
Kishor, N.K. and E.F. Koenig (2011), "VAR Estimation and Forecasting When Data Are Subject to Revision", Journal of Business and Economic Statistics, in press.
Mankiw, N.G., D.E. Runkle, and M.D. Shapiro (1984), "Are Preliminary Announcements of the Money Stock Rational Forecasts?" Journal of Monetary Economics, 14, 15–27.
Mankiw, N.G. and M.D. Shapiro (1986), "News or Noise: An Analysis of GNP Revisions", Survey of Current Business, May, 20–25.
McConnell, M. and G. Perez-Quiros (2000), "Output Fluctuations in the United States: What Has Changed Since the Early 1980s?" American Economic Review, 90, 1464–1476.
Nalewaik, J.J. (2010), "The Income- and Expenditure-Side Estimates of U.S. Output Growth", Brookings Papers on Economic Activity, 1, 71–127 (with discussion).
Nalewaik, J.J. (2011), "Estimating Probabilities of Recession in Real Time Using GDP and GDI", Journal of Money, Credit and Banking, in press.
Sancetta, A. (2007), "Online Forecast Combinations of Distributions: Worst Case Bounds", Journal of Econometrics, 141, 621–651.
Schorfheide, F. (2005), "Learning and Monetary Policy Shifts", Review of Economic Dynamics, 8, 392–419.
Solomou, S. and M. Weale (1991), "Balanced Estimates of U.K. GDP 1870–1913", Explorations in Economic History, 28, 54–63.
Solomou, S. and M. Weale (1993), "Balanced Estimates of National Accounts When Measurement Errors Are Autocorrelated: The U.K., 1920–1938", Journal of the Royal Statistical Society Series A, 156 Part 1, 89–105.
Statistisches Bundesamt, Wiesbaden (2009), "National Accounts: Gross Domestic Product in Germany in Accordance with ESA 1995 - Methods and Sources", Subject Matter Series, 18.
Stock, J.H. and M.W. Watson (2002), "Has the Business Cycle Changed and Why?" In M. Gertler and K. Rogoff (eds.), NBER Macroeconomics Annual, Cambridge, Mass.: MIT Press, 159–218.
Stone, R., D.G. Champernowne, and J.E. Meade (1942), "The Precision of National Income Estimates", Review of Economic Studies, 9, 111–125.
Timmermann, A. (2006), "Forecast Combinations", In G. Elliot, C.W.J. Granger and A. Timmermann (eds.), Handbook of Economic Forecasting, North-Holland, 136–196.
Vovk, V. (1998), "A Game of Prediction with Expert Advice", Journal of Computer and System Sciences, 56, 153–173.
Wald, A. (1950), Statistical Decision Functions, John Wiley, New York.
Weale, M. (1985), "Testing Linear Hypotheses on National Accounts Data", Review of Economics and Statistics, 90, 685–689.
Weale, M. (1988), "The Reconciliation of Values, Volumes, and Prices in the National Accounts", Journal of the Royal Statistical Society Series A, 151 Part 1, 211–221.

Identification Without Exogeneity Under Equiconfounding in Linear Recursive Structural Systems

Karim Chalak

Abstract This chapter obtains identification of structural coefficients in linear recursive systems of structural equations without requiring that observable variables are exogenous or conditionally exogenous. In particular, standard instrumental variables and control variables need not be available in these systems. Instead, we demonstrate that the availability of one or two variables that are equally affected by the unobserved confounder as is the response of interest, along with exclusion restrictions, permits the identification of all the system's structural coefficients. We provide conditions under which *equiconfounding* supports either full identification of structural coefficients or partial identification in a set consisting of two points.

Keywords Causality · Confounding · Covariance Restrictions · Identification · Structural systems

1 Introduction

This chapter obtains identification of structural coefficients in fully endogenous linear recursive systems of structural equations. In particular, standard exogenous instruments and control variables may be absent in these systems.[1] Instead, identification obtains under *equiconfounding* that is to say in the presence of (one or two) observable variables that are equally directly affected by the unobserved confounder as is the response. Examples of equiconfounding include cases in which the unobserved confounder directly affects the response and one or two observables by an equal

K. Chalak (✉)
Department of Economics, Boston College, 140 Commonwealth Ave.,
Chestnut Hill, MA 02467, USA
e-mail: chalak@bc.edu

[1] Standard instruments are uncorrelated with the unobserved confounder whereas conditioning on control variables renders the causes of interest uncorrelated with the confounder.

X. Chen and N. R. Swanson (eds.), *Recent Advances and Future Directions in Causality, Prediction, and Specification Analysis*, DOI: 10.1007/978-1-4614-1653-1_2,

proportion (proportional confounding) or an equal standard deviation shift. We show that the availability of one or two variables that are equally (e.g., proportionally) confounded in relation to the response of interest, along with exclusion restrictions, permits the identification of all the system's structural coefficients. We provide conditions under which we obtain either full identification of structural coefficients or partial identification in a set consisting of two points.

The results of this chapter echo a key insight in Halbert White's work regarding the importance of specifying causal relations governing the unobservables for the identification and estimation of causal effects (e.g., White and Chalak 2010, 2011; Chalak and White 2011; White and Lu 2011a,b; Hoderlein et al. 2011). A single chapter can do little justice addressing Hal's prolific and groundbreaking contributions to asymptotic theory, specification analysis, neural networks, time series analysis, and causal inference, to list a few areas, across several disciplines including economics, statistics, finance, and computer and cognitive sciences. Instead, here, we focus on one insight of Hal's recent work and build on it to introduce the notion of equiconfounding and demonstrate how it supports identification in structural systems.

To illustrate this chapter's results, consider the classic structural equation for the return to education (e.g., Mincer 1974; Griliches 1977)

$$Y = \beta_o X + \alpha_u U + \alpha_y U_y, \tag{1}$$

where Y denotes the logarithm of hourly wage, X determinants of wage with observed realizations, and U and U_y determinants of wage whose realizations are not observed by the econometrician. Elements of X may include years of education, experience, and tenure. Interest attaches to the causal effect of X on Y, assumed to be the constant β_o. Here, U denotes an index of unobserved personal characteristics that may determine wage and be correlated with X, such as cognitive and noncognitive skills, and U_y denote other unobserved determinants assumed to be uncorrelated with X and U. Endogeneity arises because of the correlation between X and $\alpha_u U$, leading to bias in the coefficient of a linear regression of Y on X. The method of instrumental variables (IV) permits identification of the structural coefficients under the assumption that a "valid" (i.e. uncorrelated with $\alpha_u U + \alpha_y U_y$) and "relevant" (i.e. $E(XZ')$ is full raw rank) vector Z excluded from Eq. (1) and whose dimension is at least as large as that of X is available (e.g., Wooldridge 2002, pp. 83–84). Alternatively, the presence of key covariates may ensure "conditional exogeneity" or "unconfoundedness" supporting identification (see e.g., White and Chalak 2011 and the citations therein). We do not assume the availability of standard instruments or control variables here, so these routes for identification are foreclosed.

Nevertheless, as we show, a variety of shape restrictions[2] on confounding can secure identification of β_o. To illustrate, begin by considering the simplest such

[2] Shape restrictions have been employed in a variety of different contexts. For example, Matzkin (1992) employs shape restrictions to secure identification in nonparametric binary threshold crossing models with exogeneity.

possibility in which data on a proxy for $\alpha_u U$, such as IQ score, is available. Let Z denote the logarithm of IQ and assume that the predictive proxy Z for U does not directly cause Y, and that Z and Y are equiconfounded. In particular, suppose that Z is structurally generated by

$$Z = \alpha_u U + \alpha_z U_z,$$

with U_z as a source of variation uncorrelated with other unobservables. Then, under this proportional confounding, a one unit increase in U leads to an approximate $100\alpha_u\%$ increase in wage and IQ ceteris paribus. It is straightforward to see that, by substitution, β_o is identified from a regression of $Y - Z$ on X. Note, however, that Z is not a valid instrument here ($E(Z\alpha_u U) \neq 0$) since Z is driven by U.

The above simple structure excludes IQ from the equation for Y to ensure that β_o is identified. Suppose instead that $X = (X_1, X_2, X_3')'$ and that the two variables X_1 and X_2 are structurally generated as follows

$$X_1 = \alpha_u U + \alpha_{x_1} U_{x_1} \quad \text{and} \quad X_2 = \alpha_u U + \alpha_{x_2} U_{x_2},$$

with U_{x_1} and U_{x_2} sources of variation, each uncorrelated with other unobservables. We maintain that the other elements of X are generally endogenous but we restrict X_1 and X_2 to be *equiconfounded joint causes* of Y. For example, X_1 may denote the logarithm of another test score, such as the Knowledge of World of Work (KWW) score (see e.g., Blackburn and Neumark 1992), and we relabel $\log(IQ)$ to X_2. Here, wage, KWW, and IQ are proportionally confounded by U. Substituting for $\alpha_u U = X_1 - \alpha_{x_1} U_{x_1}$ in (1) gives

$$Y - X_1 = \beta_o X - \alpha_{x_1} U_{x_1} + \alpha_y U_y,$$

and thus a regression of $Y - X_1$ on X does not identify β_o since X_1 is correlated with $\alpha_{x_1} U_{x_1}$. Further, although X_2 and X_3 are exogenous in this equation, they are not excluded from it and thus they cannot serve as instruments for X_1. Nevertheless, we demonstrate that in this case β_o is fully (over) identified.

In the previous example, two joint causes and a response that are equiconfounded secure identification. Similarly, one *cause* and two *joint responses* that are *equiconfounded* can ensure that β_o is identified. For example, let Y_1 and Y_2 denote two responses of interest (e.g., two measures of the logarithm of wage, one reported by the employer and another by the employee). In particular, suppose that

$$Y_1 = \beta_{1o} X + \alpha_u U + \alpha_{y_1} U_{y_1} \quad \text{and} \quad Y_2 = \beta_{2o} X + \alpha_u U + \alpha_{y_2} U_{y_2}.$$

Note that β_{1o} and β_{2o} need not be equal. As before, we maintain that an element X_1 (e.g., $\log(IQ)$) of X is structurally generated by

$$X_1 = \alpha_u U + \alpha_{x_1} U_{x_1},$$

with the remaining elements of X generally endogenous. We demonstrate that here $(\beta'_{1o}, \beta'_{2o})'$ is partially identified in a set consisting of two points.

Various other exclusion restrictions can secure identification of structural coefficients in the presence of equiconfounding. Consider the classic triangular structure:

$$Y = \beta_o X + \alpha_u U + \alpha_y U_y,$$
$$X = \gamma_o Z + \eta_u U + \alpha_x U_x.$$

As before, U_y and U_x denote exogenous sources of variation. The method of IV identifies β_o provided that the excluded vector Z is valid $(E(\alpha_u U Z') = 0)$ and relevant $(E(XZ')$ full raw rank) and thus has dimension at least as large as that of X. Suppose instead that Y, Z, and an element X_1 of X are equiconfounded by U:

$$X_1 = \gamma_{1o} Z + \alpha_u U + \alpha_{x_1} U_{x_1} \quad \text{and} \quad Z = \alpha_u U + \alpha_z U_z,$$

where U_{x_1} and U_z are each uncorrelated with other unobservables. The remaining elements of X are generally endogenous. For example, a researcher may wish to allow IQ to be a structural determinant of the subsequently administered KWW test, in order to capture learning effects, and to exclude IQ from the equation for Y if this test's information is unavailable to employers. Then Z denotes $\log(IQ)$ and X_1 denotes $\log(KWW)$. In this structure we refer to Z and X_1 as *equiconfounded pre-cause* and *intermediate-cause*, respectively. We demonstrate that $(\beta'_o, \gamma'_o)'$ is either fully identified or partially identified in a set consisting of two points. Importantly, in contrast to the method of IV, here Z is a *scalar endogenous* variable.

This chapter is organized as follows. Section 2 introduces notation. Formal identification results, including for the examples above, are discussed in Sects. 3 to 6. Often we present the identification results as adjustments to standard regression coefficients thereby revealing the regression bias arising due to endogeneity. Section 7 contains a discussion and Sect. 8 concludes. All mathematical proofs as well as constructive arguments for identification are gathered in the appendix.

2 Notation

Throughout, we let the random $k \times 1$ vector X and $p \times 1$ vector Y denote the observed direct causes and responses of interest, respectively.[3] If there are observed variables excluded from the equation for Y, we denote these by the $\ell \times 1$ vector Z. We observe independent and identically distributed realizations $\{Z_i, X_i, Y_i\}_{i=1}^n$ for

[3] This chapter considers linear recursive structural systems. Recursiveness rules out "simultaneity" permitting distinguishing the vectors of primary interest X and Y as the observed direct causes and responses, respectively. In particular, elements of Y are assumed to not cause elements of X. While mutual causality is absent here, endogeneity arises due to the confounder U jointly driving the causes X and responses Y.

Z, X, and Y and stack these into the $n \times \ell$, $n \times k$, and $n \times p$ matrices $\mathbf{Z}$, $\mathbf{X}$, and $\mathbf{Y}$, respectively. The matrices (or vectors) of structural coefficients γ_o and β_o denote finite causal effects determined by theory as encoded in a linear structural system of equations. The scalar index U denotes an unobserved confounder of X, Z, and Y and the vectors U_z, U_x, and U_y of positive dimensions denote unobserved causes of elements of Z, X and Y, respectively. Without loss of generality, we normalize the expectations of U, U_z, U_x, and U_y to zero. The structural coefficients matrices α_z, α_x and α_y denote the effects of elements of U_z, U_x and U_y on elements of Z, X and Y, respectively. Equiconfounding restricts the effect of the confounder U on Y and certain elements of X and Z to be equal; we denote this restricted effect by α_u and we denote unrestricted effects of U on elements of X by ϕ_u.

We employ the following notation for regression coefficients and residuals. Let Y, X, and Z be generic random vectors. We denote the coefficient and residual from a regression of Y on X by

$$\pi_{y.x} \equiv E(YX')E(XX')^{-1} \quad \text{and} \quad \epsilon_{y.x} \equiv Y - \pi_{y.x}X.$$

Similarly, we denote the coefficient associated with X from a regression of Y on X and Z by

$$\pi_{y.x|z} \equiv E(\epsilon_{y.z}\epsilon'_{x.z})E(\epsilon_{x.z}\epsilon'_{x.z})^{-1}.$$

This representation obtains from the Frisch-Waugh-Lovell theorem (Frisch and Waugh 1993; Lovell 1963; see e.g., Baltagi 1999, p. 159). Noting that

$$\begin{aligned} E(\epsilon_{y.z}\epsilon'_{x.z}) &= E(Y\epsilon'_{x.z}) - E(YZ')E(ZZ')^{-1}E(Z\epsilon'_{x.z}) = E(Y\epsilon'_{x.z}) \\ &= E(YX') - E(YZ')E(ZZ')^{-1}E(ZX') = E(\epsilon_{y.z}X'), \end{aligned}$$

we can rewrite $\pi_{y.x|z}$ as

$$\pi_{y.x|z} = E(Y\epsilon'_{x.z})E(X\epsilon'_{x.z})^{-1} = E(\epsilon_{y.z}X')E(\epsilon_{x.z}X')^{-1}.$$

Last, we denote sample regression coefficients by $\hat{\pi}_{y.x} \equiv (\mathbf{X}'\mathbf{X})^{-1}\mathbf{X}'\mathbf{Y}$ and residuals by $\hat{\epsilon}_{y.x,i} \equiv Y_i - \hat{\pi}_{y.x}X_i$, which we stack into the $n \times p$ vector $\hat{\epsilon}_{y.x}$. Similarly, we let $\hat{\pi}_{y.x|z} \equiv (\hat{\epsilon}'_{x.z}\mathbf{X})^{-1}\hat{\epsilon}'_{x.z}\mathbf{Y}$.

Throughout, we illustrate a structural system using a directed acyclic graph as in Chalak and White (2011). A graph $G_{\mathcal{S}}$ associated with a structural system $\mathcal{S}$ consists of a set of vertices (nodes) $\{V_g\}$, one for each variable in $\mathcal{S}$, and a set of arrows $\{a_{gh}\}$, corresponding to ordered pairs of distinct vertices. An arrow a_{gh} denotes that V_g is a potential direct cause for V_h, i.e., it appears directly in the structural equation for V_h with a corresponding possibly nonzero coefficient. We use solid nodes for observables and dashed nodes for unobservables. For convenience, we sometimes use vector nodes to represent vectors generated by structural system $\mathcal{S}$. In this case, an arrow from vector node Z to vector node X indicates that at least one element of Z is a direct cause of at least one element of X. We use solid nodes for observable vectors and dashed nodes for vectors with at least one unobservable element. For simplicity, we omit nodes for the exogenous vectors U_z, U_x, and U_y. Lastly, we use dashed arrows emanating from U to Y, X_1, Z , and possibly X_2 to denote equiconfounding.

3 Equiconfounded Predictive Proxy and Response

The simplest possibility arises when the response Y and a scalar predictive proxy Z for the unobserved confounder U are equiconfounded. The predictive proxy Z is excluded from the equation for Y. In particular, consider the structural system of equations $\mathcal{S}_1$ with causal graph G_1:

(1) $Z \stackrel{s}{=} \alpha_u U + \alpha_z U_z,$

(2) $X_1 \stackrel{s}{=} \phi_u U + \alpha_x U_x$

(3) $Y \stackrel{s}{=} \beta_o X + \alpha_u U + \alpha_y U_y$
with $U, U_z, U_x,$ and U_y
pairwise uncorrelated
and with $X = (X_1', 1)'$.

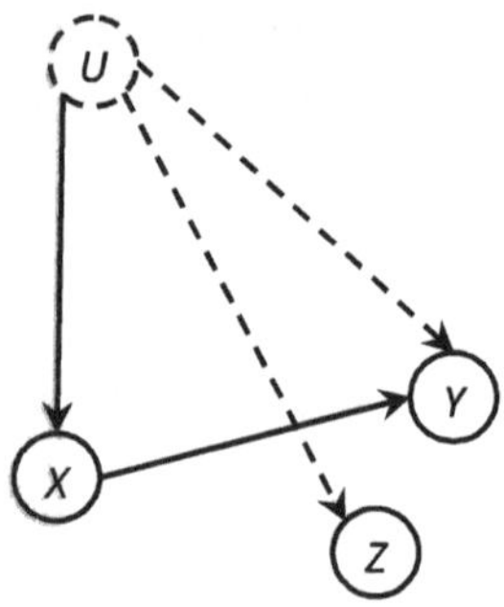

Graph 1 (G_1)
Equiconfounded Predictive Proxy
and Response

Similar to Chalak and White (2011), we use the "$\stackrel{s}{=}$" notation instead of "=" to emphasize structural equations. We let $\ell = p = 1$ in $\mathcal{S}_1$ as this suffices for identification. Here and in what follows, we let the last element of X be degenerate at 1. The next result shows that the structural vector β_o is point identified. This is obtained straightforwardly by substituting $\alpha_u U$ with $Z - \alpha_z U_z$ in the equation for Y.

Theorem 3.1 *Consider structural system $\mathcal{S}_1$ with $k > 0$, $\ell = p = 1$, and expected values of U, U_z, U_x, U_y normalized to zero. Suppose that $E(U^2)$ and $E(U_x U_x')$ exist and are finite. Then (i) $E(XX')$, $E(ZX')$, and $E(YX')$ exist and are finite. Suppose further that $E(XX')$ is nonsingular. Then (ii) β_o is fully identified as*

$$\beta_o = \pi_{y-z.x}.$$

Under standard conditions (e.g., White 2001) the estimator $\hat{\pi}_{y-z.x} \equiv (\mathbf{X}'\mathbf{X})^{-1}\mathbf{X}'(\mathbf{Y} - \mathbf{Z})$ is a consistent and asymptotically normal estimator for β_o. A heteroskedasticity robust estimator (White 1980) for the asymptotic covariance matrix for $\hat{\pi}_{y-z.x}$ is given by $(\mathbf{X}'\mathbf{X})^{-1}(\sum_{i=1}^{n} \hat{\epsilon}^2_{y-z.x,i} X_i X_i')(\mathbf{X}'\mathbf{X})^{-1}$.

4 Equiconfounded Joint Causes and Response

Identification in $\mathcal{S}_1$ requires the predictive proxy Z to be excluded from the equation for Y. However, β_o is also identified if two causes X_1 and X_2 and the response Y are equiconfounded. In particular, consider structural system $\mathcal{S}_2$ with causal graph G_2:

(1a) $X_1 \overset{s}{=} \alpha_u U + \alpha_{x_1} U_{x_1}$,

(1b) $X_2 \overset{s}{=} \alpha_u U + \alpha_{x_2} U_{x_2}$

(1c) $X_{31} \overset{s}{=} \phi_u U + \alpha_{x_3} U_{x_3}$

(2) $Y \overset{s}{=} \beta_o X + \alpha_u U + \alpha_y U_y$

with $U, U_{x_1}, U_{x_2}, U_{x_3},$ and U_y pairwise uncorrelated and $X = (X_1', X_2', X_{31}', 1)' = (X_1', X_2', X_3')'$.

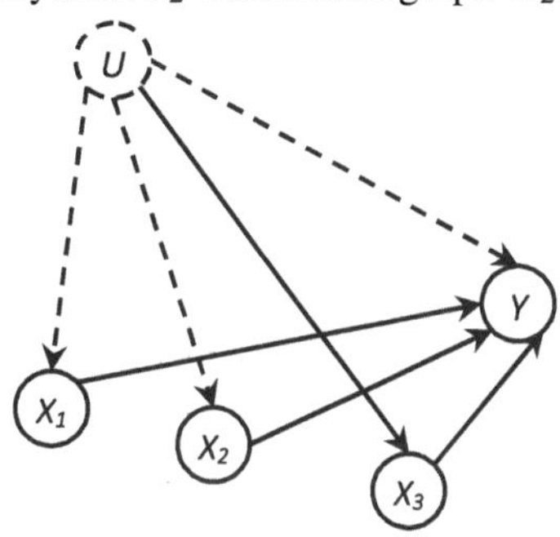

Graph 2 (G_2)
Equiconfounded Joint Causes and Response

We can rewrite $1(a, b, c)$ as

$$(1) \quad (X_1', X_2', X_{31}')' \overset{s}{=} \eta_u U + \alpha_x U_x,$$

with $\eta_u = (\alpha_u', \alpha_u', \phi_u')'$, $U_x = (U_{x_1}', U_{x_2}', U_{x_3}')'$, and α_x a block diagonal matrix with $\alpha_{x_1}, \alpha_{x_2}$, and α_{x_3} at the diagonal entries and zeros at the off-diagonal entries. Here, we let X_1 and X_2 be scalars, $k_1 = k_2 = 1$, as this suffices for identification. The next theorem shows that the structural vector β_o is point identified.

Theorem 4.1 *Consider structural system $\mathcal{S}_2$ with $\dim(X_3) \equiv k_3 \geq 0$, and $k_1 = k_2 = p = 1$, and expected values of U, U_z, U_x, U_y normalized to zero. Suppose that $E(U^2)$ and $E(U_x U_x')$ exist and are finite. Then (i) $E(XX')$ and $E(YX')$ exist and are finite. Suppose further that $E(XX')$ is nonsingular. Then (ii) the vector β_o is fully (over-)identified by:*

$$\begin{aligned}\beta_o = \beta_{JC}^* &\equiv \pi_{y.x} - [E(X_2X_1'), E(X_2X_1'), E(X_1X_3')]E(XX')^{-1} \\ = \beta_{JC}^\dagger &\equiv \pi_{y.x} - [E(X_2X_1'), E(X_2X_1'), E(X_2X_3')]E(XX')^{-1}.\end{aligned}$$

The above result obtains by noting that the moment $E(YX')$ identifies β_o when $E(XX')$ is nonsingular provided that $\alpha_u E(UX')$ is identified. But this holds since, $E(X_1X_3') = E(X_2X_3') = (\mathrm{Cov}(\phi_u U, \alpha_u U)', 0)$ and $E(X_1X_2) = \mathrm{Var}(\alpha_u U)$. The expressions for β_{JC}^* and $\beta_{JC}^\dagger$ emphasize the bias $\pi_{y.x} - \beta_{JC}^*$ (or $\pi_{y.x} - \beta_{JC}^\dagger$) in a regression of Y on X arising due to endogeneity. The plug-in estimators $\hat{\beta}_{JC}^*$ and $\hat{\beta}_{JC}^\dagger$ for β_{JC}^* and $\beta_{JC}^\dagger$, respectively:

$$\hat{\beta}^*_{JC} \equiv \hat{\pi}_{y.x} - \sum_{i=1}^{n}[X_{2i}X'_{1i}, X_{2i}X'_{1i}, X_{1i}X'_{31i}, 0](\mathbf{X}'\mathbf{X})^{-1}, \text{ and}$$

$$\hat{\beta}^*_{JC} \equiv \hat{\pi}_{y.x} - \sum_{i=1}^{n}[X_{2i}X'_{1i}, X_{2i}X'_{1i}, X_{2i}X'_{31i}, 0](\mathbf{X}'\mathbf{X})^{-1},$$

are consistent estimators under conditions sufficient to invoke the laws of large numbers.

A testable restriction of structure $\mathcal{S}_2$ is that $\text{Cov}(X_1, X_3) = \text{Cov}(X_2, X_3) = (\alpha_u E(U^2)\phi'_u, 0)$. Thus, $\mathcal{S}_2$ can be falsified by rejecting this null. In particular, one can reject the equiconfounding restrictions in equations $1(a, b, c)$ if $E(X_1 X'_3) \neq E(X_2 X'_3)$. For this, one can employ a standard F-statistic for the overall significance of the regression of $\mathbf{X}_1 - \mathbf{X}_2$ on $\mathbf{X}_3$.

5 Equiconfounded Cause and Joint Responses

The availability of a single cause and two responses that are equiconfounded also ensures the identification of causal coefficients. Specifically, consider structural system $\mathcal{S}_3$ given by:

$(1a)\ X_1 \overset{s}{=} \alpha_u U + \alpha_{x_1} U_{x_1}$

$(1b)\ X_{21} \overset{s}{=} \phi_u U + \alpha_{x_2} U_{x_2}$

$(2a)\ Y_1 \overset{s}{=} \beta_{1o} X + \alpha_u U + \alpha_{y_1} U_{y_1}$

$(2b)\ Y_2 \overset{s}{=} \beta_{2o} X + \alpha_u U + \alpha_{y_2} U_{y_2}$

with $U, U_{x_1}, U_{x_2}, U_{y_1},$ and U_{y_2} pairwise uncorrelated and

$X = (X'_1, X'_{21}, 1)' = (X'_1, X'_2)'$.

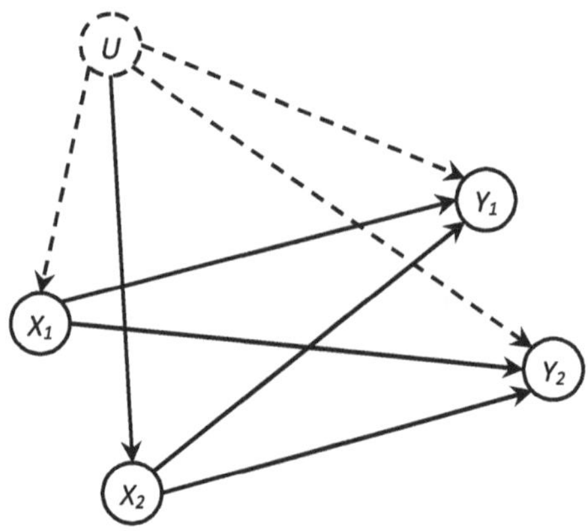

Graph 3 (G3)
Equiconfounded Cause and Joint Responses

Letting $Y = (Y'_1, Y'_2)'$, $\beta_o = (\beta'_{1o}, \beta'_{2o})'$, $U_x = (U'_{x_1}, U'_{x_2})'$, and $U_y = (U'_{y_1}, U'_{y_2})'$, and letting α_x be a block diagonal matrix with diagonal entries α_{x_1} and α_{x_2} and zero off-diagonal entries, and similarly for α_y, we can write $1(a, b)$ and $2(a, b)$ more compactly as

$$(1)\ (X'_1, X'_{21})' \overset{s}{=} \eta_u U + \alpha_x U_x$$

$$(2)\ Y \overset{s}{=} \beta_o X + \alpha_u \iota_p U + \alpha_y U_y,$$

with ι_p a $p \times 1$ vector with each element equal to 1 and $\eta_u = (\alpha_u', \phi_u')'$. Here it suffices for identification that $\dim(X_1) \equiv k_1 = 1$ and $p = 2$. The next theorem demonstrates that the structural matrix β_o is partially identified in a set consisting of two points.

Theorem 5.1 *Consider structural system* $\mathcal{S}_3$ *with* $\dim(X_2) \equiv k_2 \geq 0$, $k_1 = 1$, $p = 2$, *and expected values of* U, U_z, U_x, *and* U_y *normalized to zero. Suppose that* $E(U^2)$ *and* $E(U_x U_x')$ *exist and are finite, then (i)* $E(XX')$ *and* (YX') *exist and are finite. Suppose further that* $E(X_1 X_1')$ *and* $E(X_2 X_2')$ *are nonsingular then (ii.a)* $P_{x_1} \equiv E(\epsilon_{x_1.x_2}\epsilon_{x_1.x_2}')$ *and* $P_{x_2} \equiv E(\epsilon_{x_2.x_1}\epsilon_{x_2.x_1}')$ *exist and are finite. If also* P_{x_1} *and* P_{x_2} *are nonsingular then (ii.b)* $E(XX')$ *is nonsingular,* $\pi_{y.x}$ *and* $E(\epsilon_{y_1.x} Y_2')$ *exist and are finite, and (ii.c)*

$$\Delta_{JR} = \left[2P_{x_1}^{-1}E(X_1X_1') - 1\right]^2 - 4P_{x_1}^{-1}\left[E(X_1X_2')P_{x_2}^{-1}E(X_2X_1') + E(\epsilon_{y_1.x}Y_2')\right],$$

exists, is finite, and is nonnegative.

(iii) β_o *is partially identified in a set consisting of two points. In particular, (iii.a) if*

$$\begin{aligned}&\mathrm{Var}(\alpha_{x_1}U_{x_1}) + \mathrm{Cov}(\phi_u U, \alpha_u U)' \\ &\quad [\mathrm{Var}(\phi_u U) + \mathrm{Var}(\alpha_{x_2}U_{x_2})]^{-1}\mathrm{Cov}(\phi_u U, \alpha_u U) - \mathrm{Var}(\alpha_u U) < 0,\end{aligned}$$

then

$$\begin{aligned}0 \leq \sigma_{JR}^{\dagger} &\equiv E(X_1X_1') + \frac{1}{2}P_{x_1}(-1 - \sqrt{\Delta_{JR}}) < \alpha_u^2 E(U^2), \text{ and} \\ \sigma_{JR}^{*} &\equiv E(X_1X_1') + \frac{1}{2}P_{x_1}(-1 + \sqrt{\Delta_{JR}}) = \alpha_u^2 E(U^2),\end{aligned}$$

and thus

$$\beta_o = \beta_{JR}^{*} \equiv \pi_{y.x} - \iota_p[\sigma_{JR}^{*}, E(X_1X_2')]E(XX')^{-1}.$$

(iii.b) If instead the expression in (iii) is nonnegative then

$$\sigma_{JR}^{\dagger} = \alpha_u^2 E(U^2) \text{ and } 0 \leq \alpha_u^2 E(U^2) \leq \sigma_{JR}^{*},$$

and thus

$$\beta_o = \beta_{JR}^{\dagger} \equiv \pi_{y.x} - \iota_p[\sigma_{JR}^{\dagger}, E(X_1X_2')]E(XX')^{-1}.$$

Observe here that, unlike for the case of equiconfounded joint causes, β_o is not point identified but is partially identified in a set consisting of two points. Also, observe that $\beta_{1o} - \beta_{2o}$ is identified from a regression of $Y_1 - Y_2$ on X. However, $\beta_{1,JR}^{*} - \beta_{2,JR}^{*} = \beta_{1,JR}^{\dagger} - \beta_{2,JR}^{\dagger}$ and thus this does not help in fully identifying β_o. Similar to $\mathcal{S}_2$, with $E(XX')$ nonsingular, the moment $E(YX')$ identifies

β_o provided $\text{Cov}(\phi_u U, \alpha_u U)$ and $\text{Var}(\alpha_u U)$ are identified. While $E(X_{21} X_1) = \text{Cov}(\phi_u U, \alpha_u U)$, identification of $\text{Var}(\alpha_u U)$ is more involved here than in $\mathcal{S}_2$. Appendix B.1 presents a constructive argument showing that the moment $E(Y_1 Y_2)$ delivers a quadratic equation in $\text{Var}(\alpha_u U)$ with two positive roots, $\sigma^{\dagger}_{JR}$ and σ^{*}_{JR}.

Under suitable conditions sufficient to invoke the law of large numbers, the following plug-in estimators are consistent for Δ_{JR}, σ^{*}_{JR}, $\sigma^{\dagger}_{JR}$, β^{*}_{JR}, and $\beta^{\dagger}_{JR}$ respectively. To express these, let $\hat{P}_{x_1} = \frac{1}{n}\hat{\epsilon}'_{x_1.x_2}\mathbf{X}_1$ and $\hat{P}_{x_2} \equiv \frac{1}{n}\hat{\epsilon}'_{x_2.x_1}\mathbf{X}_2$. Then

$$\hat{\Delta}_{JR} \equiv \left[2\hat{P}_{x_1}^{-1}\,\frac{1}{n}\mathbf{X}_1'\mathbf{X}_1 - 1\right]^2 - 4\hat{P}_{x_1}^{-1}\left[\frac{1}{n}\mathbf{X}_1'\mathbf{X}_2\,\hat{P}_{x_2}^{-1}\,\frac{1}{n}\mathbf{X}_2'\mathbf{X}_1 + \frac{1}{n}\hat{\epsilon}'_{y_1.x}\mathbf{Y}_2\right],$$

$$\hat{\sigma}^{*}_{JR} \equiv \frac{1}{n}\mathbf{X}_1'\mathbf{X}_1 + \frac{1}{2}\hat{P}_{x_1}\left(-1 + \sqrt{\hat{\Delta}_{JR}}\right) \quad \text{and}$$

$$\hat{\sigma}^{\dagger}_{JR} \equiv \frac{1}{n}\mathbf{X}_1'\mathbf{X}_1 + \frac{1}{2}\hat{P}_{x_1}\left(-1 - \sqrt{\hat{\Delta}_{JR}}\right),$$

$$\hat{\beta}^{*}_{JR} \equiv \hat{\pi}_{y.x} - \iota_p\left[\hat{\sigma}^{*}_{JR}, \frac{1}{n}\mathbf{X}_1'\mathbf{X}_2\right]\left(\frac{1}{n}\mathbf{X}'\mathbf{X}\right)^{-1}, \quad \text{and}$$

$$\hat{\beta}^{\dagger}_{JR} \equiv \hat{\pi}_{y.x} - \iota_p\left[\hat{\sigma}^{\dagger}_{JR}, \frac{1}{n}\mathbf{X}_1'\mathbf{X}_2\right]\left(\frac{1}{n}\mathbf{X}'\mathbf{X}\right)^{-1}.$$

Thus, under suitable statistical assumptions, $\hat{\beta}^{*}_{JR}$ and $\hat{\beta}^{\dagger}_{JR}$ converge to β^{*}_{JR} and $\beta^{\dagger}_{JR}$, respectively; under the structural assumptions of $\mathcal{S}_3$, either β^{*}_{JR} or $\beta^{\dagger}_{JR}$ identifies the structural coefficient vector β_o.

6 Equiconfounding in Triangular Structures

Next, we consider the classic triangular structure discussed in the Introduction and show that if one excluded variable Z_1, one element X_1 of the direct causes X, and the response Y are equally confounded by U then all the system's structural coefficients are identified. Consider structural system $\mathcal{S}_4$ with causal graph G_4:

(1) $Z_1 \overset{s}{=} \alpha_u U + \alpha_z U_z$

(2a) $X_1 \overset{s}{=} \gamma_{1o} Z + \alpha_u U + \alpha_{x_1} U_{x_1}$

(2b) $X_{21} \overset{s}{=} \gamma_{2o} Z + \phi_u U + \alpha_{x_2} U_{x_2}$

(3) $Y \overset{s}{=} \beta_o X + \alpha_u U + \alpha_y U_y$,
with U_z, U, U_{x_1}, U_{x_2}, and U_y
pairwise uncorrelated,
and with $Z = (Z_1', 1')' = (Z_1', Z_2')'$,
and $X = (X_1', X_{21}', 1) = (X_1', X_2')'$.

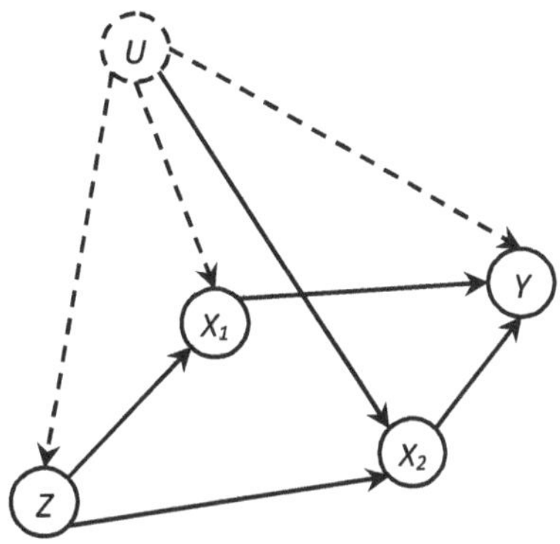

Graph 4 (G_4)
Equiconfounded Pre-Cause,
Intermediate-Cause, and Response

To rewrite 2(a, b) more compactly, let $\gamma_o = (\gamma_{1o}', \gamma_{2o}')'$ and $\eta_u = (\alpha_u', \phi_u')'$, and write $U_x' = (U_{x_1}', U_{x_2}')'$, with α_{x_1} and α_{x_2} the diagonals entries of the block diagonal matrix α_x with zero off-diagonal entries. Then

$$(2) \quad (X_1', X_{21}')' \overset{s}{=} \gamma_o Z + \eta_u U + \alpha_x U_x.$$

We sometimes refer to Z_1 as a *pre-cause* variable as it is excluded from the equation for Y and to X_1 as an *intermediate cause* as it mediates the effect of Z_1 on Y. As discussed in the Introduction, necessary conditions for the method of IV to identify β_o are that $E(Z(\alpha_u U + \alpha_y U_y)) = 0$ and that $E(XZ')$ is full raw rank. Both of these conditions can fail in $\mathcal{S}_4$, since $E(Z(\alpha_u U))$ is generally nonzero and only one excluded variable suffices for identification here so that $\dim(Z_1) \equiv \ell_1 = \dim(X_1) \equiv k_1 = p = 1$ and thus $\dim(Z) \equiv \ell \leq \dim(X) \equiv k$. Nevertheless, the next theorem demonstrates that the structural vectors γ_o and β_o are jointly either point identified or partially identified in a set consisting of two points.

Theorem 6.1 *Consider structural system $\mathcal{S}_4$ with $\dim(X_2) = k_2 \geq 0$, $\ell_1 = k_1 = p = 1$, and expected values of U, U_z, U_x, U_y normalized to zero. Suppose that $E(U^2)$, $E(U_z U_z')$, and $E(U_x U_x')$ exist and are finite. Then (i) $E(ZZ')$, $E(XZ')$, $E(XX')$, $E(YX')$, and $E(YZ')$ exist and are finite. (ii) Suppose further that $P_{z_1} \equiv E(\epsilon_{z_1.z_2} Z_1') = E(Z_1 Z_1')$, and thus $E(ZZ')$, and $E(XX')$ are nonsingular. Then (ii.a) $\pi_{x.z}, \pi_{z.x}$, $E(\epsilon_{x_1.z} X_2')$, and $E(\epsilon_{y.x} Z_1')$ exist and are finite and (ii.b)*

$$\Delta_{PC} = [-\pi_{x.z_1|z_2}' \, \pi_{z_1.x}' - \pi_{z_1.x_1|x_2}' + 1]^2 \\ + 4P_{z_1}^{-1} \, \pi_{z_1.x_1|x_2}' [E(\epsilon_{y.x} Z_1') + E(\epsilon_{x_1.z} X_2') \, \pi_{z_1.x_2|x_1}']$$

exists, is finite, and nonnegative.

(iii) β_o is either point identified or partially identified in a set consisting of two points. In particular, (iii.a) if

$$\pi'_{x.z_1|z_2}\pi'_{z_1.x} + \pi'_{z_1.x_1|x_2} - 1 - 2P_{z_1}^{-1}\pi'_{z_1.x_1|x_2}\alpha_u^2 E(U^2) < 0, \tag{2}$$

then

$$\sigma^{\dagger}_{PC} \equiv \frac{\pi'_{x.z_1|z_2}\,\pi'_{z_1.x} + \pi'_{z_1.x_1|x_2} - 1 - \sqrt{\Delta_{PC}}}{2P_{z_1}^{-1}\pi'_{z_1.x_1|x_2}} < \alpha_u^2 E(U^2) \quad \textit{and}$$

$$\sigma^{*}_{PC} \equiv \frac{\pi'_{x.z_1|z_2}\pi'_{z_1.x} + \pi'_{z_1.x_1|x_2} - 1 + \sqrt{\Delta_{PC}}}{2P_{z_1}^{-1}\,\pi'_{z_1.x_1|x_2}} = \alpha_u^2 E(U^2),$$

and we have

$$\begin{aligned}
\gamma_{1o} &= \gamma^{*}_{1,PC} \equiv \pi_{x_1.z} - [\sigma^{*}_{PC}, 0]E(ZZ')^{-1}, \\
\gamma_{2o} &= \gamma^{*}_{2,PC} \equiv \pi_{x_{21}.z} - [E(X_{21}\epsilon'_{x_1.z})[1 - \sigma^{*}_{PC}P_{z_1}^{-1}]^{-1}, 0]E(ZZ')^{-1}, \quad \textit{and} \\
\beta_o &= \beta^{*}_{PC} \equiv \pi_{y.x} - [\sigma^{*}_{PC}(\pi'_{x_1.z_1|z_2} - \sigma^{*}_{PC}\, P_{z_1}^{-1} + 1), E(\epsilon_{x_1.z}X'_2) \\
&\quad + \sigma^{*}_{PC}\pi'_{x_2.z_1|z_2}]E(XX')^{-1}.
\end{aligned}$$

(iii.b) If instead the expression in (2) *is nonnegative then* $\sigma^{\dagger}_{PC} = \alpha_u^2 E(U^2)$ *and* $\sigma^{*}_{PC} \geq \alpha_u^2 E(U^2)$*, and*

$$\begin{aligned}
\gamma_{1o} &= \gamma^{\dagger}_{1,PC} \equiv \pi_{x_1.z} - [\sigma^{\dagger}_{PC}, 0]E(ZZ')^{-1}, \\
\gamma_{2o} &= \gamma^{\dagger}_{2,PC} \equiv \pi_{x_{21}.z} - [\,E(X_{21}\epsilon'_{x_1.z})[1 - \sigma^{\dagger}_{PC}P_{z_1}^{-1}]^{-1}, 0]E(ZZ')^{-1}, \quad \textit{and} \\
\beta_o &= \beta^{\dagger}_{PC} \equiv \pi_{y.x} - [\sigma^{\dagger}_{PC}(\pi'_{x_1.z_1|z_2} - \sigma^{\dagger}_{PC}P_{z_1}^{-1} + 1), E(\epsilon_{x_1.z}X'_2) \\
&\quad + \sigma^{\dagger}_{PC}\pi'_{x_2.z_1|z_2}]E(XX')^{-1}.
\end{aligned}$$

Similar to $\mathcal{S}_3$, the moment $E(YX')$ identifies β_o provided $\alpha_u E(UX')$ is identified, which involves identifying $\text{Var}(\alpha_u U)$. Appendix B.2 provides a constructive argument showing that the moment $E(YZ')$ delivers a quadratic equation in $\text{Var}(\alpha_u U)$ which admits the two roots $\sigma^{\dagger}_{PC}$ and σ^{*}_{PC}. Note that it is possible to give primitive conditions in terms of system coefficients and covariances among unobservables for (2) to hold, similar to the condition given for the case of equiconfounded cause and joint responses. We forego this here but we note that, unlike for the case of equiconfounded cause and joint responses, if (2) holds, it is possible for $\sigma^{\dagger}_{PC}$ to be negative, leading to $\alpha_u^2 E(U^2)$, and thus (γ_o, β_o), to be point identified.

The following plug in estimators are consistent estimators under conditions suitable for the law of large numbers. First, we let $\hat{P}_{z_1} = \frac{1}{n}\hat{\epsilon}'_{z_1.z_2}\mathbf{Z}_1$, then

$$\hat{\Delta}_{PC} = [-\hat{\pi}'_{x.z_1|z_2}\hat{\pi}'_{z_1.x} - \hat{\pi}'_{z_1.x_1|x_2} + 1]^2$$
$$+ 4\hat{P}_{z_1}^{-1}\hat{\pi}'_{z_1.x_1|x_2}\left[\frac{1}{n}\hat{\epsilon}'_{y.x}\mathbf{Z}_1 + \left(\frac{1}{n}\hat{\epsilon}'_{x_1.z}\mathbf{X}_2\right)\hat{\pi}'_{z_1.x_2|x_1}\right],$$
$$\hat{\sigma}^*_{PC} \equiv (2\hat{P}_{z_1}^{-1}\hat{\pi}'_{z_1.x_1|x_2})^{-1}\left[\hat{\pi}'_{x.z_1|z_2}\hat{\pi}'_{z_1.x} + \hat{\pi}'_{z_1.x_1|x_2} - 1 + \sqrt{\hat{\Delta}_{PC}}\right],$$
$$\hat{\sigma}^\dagger_{PC} \equiv (2\hat{P}_{z_1}^{-1}\hat{\pi}'_{z_1.x_1|x_2})^{-1}\left[\hat{\pi}'_{x.z_1|z_2}\hat{\pi}'_{z_1.x} + \hat{\pi}'_{z_1.x_1|x_2} - 1 - \sqrt{\hat{\Delta}_{PC}}\right],$$
$$\hat{\gamma}^*_{1,PC} \equiv \hat{\pi}_{x_1.z} - [\hat{\sigma}^*_{PC}, 0]\left(\frac{1}{n}\mathbf{Z}'\mathbf{Z}\right)^{-1} \quad \text{and}$$
$$\hat{\gamma}^\dagger_{1,PC} \equiv \hat{\pi}_{x_1.z} - [\hat{\sigma}^\dagger_{PC}, 0]\left(\frac{1}{n}\mathbf{Z}'\mathbf{Z}\right)^{-1},$$
$$\hat{\gamma}^*_{2,PC} \equiv \hat{\pi}_{x_{21}.z} - \left[\left(\frac{1}{n}\mathbf{X}'_{21}\hat{\epsilon}_{x_1.z}\right)[1 - \hat{\sigma}^*_{PC}\hat{P}_{z_1}^{-1}]^{-1}, 0\right]\left(\frac{1}{n}\mathbf{Z}'\mathbf{Z}\right)^{-1},$$
$$\hat{\gamma}^\dagger_{2,PC} \equiv \hat{\pi}_{x_{21}.z} - \left[\left(\frac{1}{n}\mathbf{X}'_{21}\hat{\epsilon}_{x_1.z}\right)[1 - \hat{\sigma}^\dagger_{PC}\hat{P}_{z_1}^{-1}]^{-1}, 0\right]\left(\frac{1}{n}\mathbf{Z}'\mathbf{Z}\right)^{-1},$$
$$\hat{\beta}^*_{PC} \equiv \hat{\pi}_{y.x} - [\hat{\sigma}^*_{PC}\,(\hat{\pi}'_{x_1.z_1|z_2} - \hat{\sigma}^*_{PC}\hat{P}_{z_1}^{-1} + 1), \frac{1}{n}\hat{\epsilon}'_{x_1.z}\mathbf{X}_2$$
$$+ \hat{\sigma}^*_{PC}\hat{\pi}'_{x_2.z_1|z_2}]\left(\frac{1}{n}\mathbf{X}'\mathbf{X}\right)^{-1}, \text{ and}$$
$$\hat{\beta}^\dagger_{PC} \equiv \hat{\pi}_{y.x} - [\hat{\sigma}^\dagger_{PC}(\hat{\pi}'_{x_1.z_1|z_2}x - \hat{\sigma}^\dagger_{PC}\hat{P}_{z_1}^{-1} + 1), \frac{1}{n}\hat{\epsilon}'_{x_1.z}\mathbf{X}_2$$
$$+ \hat{\sigma}^\dagger_{PC}\hat{\pi}'_{x_2.z_1|z_2}]\left(\frac{1}{n}\mathbf{X}'\mathbf{X}\right)^{-1}.$$

7 Discussion

Structures $\mathcal{S}_1$, $\mathcal{S}_2$, $\mathcal{S}_3$, and $\mathcal{S}_4$ do not exhaust the possibilities for identification under equiconfounding. An example of another linear triangular structure with equiconfounding is one involving equiconfounded cause, response, and a *post-response* variable. For example, assuming that KWW score (a potential cause), hourly wage (a response), and the number of hours worked (a post response directly affected by hourly wage but not by the KWW score) are proportionally confounded, with other determinants of wage generally endogenous, may permit identification of this system's structural coefficients.

Roughly speaking, equiconfounding reduces the number of unknowns thereby permitting identification. In contrast, the method of IV supplies additional moments useful for identification. In general, equiconfounding leads to covariance restrictions (see e.g., Chamberlain 1977; Hausman and Taylor 1983) that, along with exclusion restrictions, permit identification. For example, in $\mathcal{S}_4$, the absence of a direct causal effect among X_1 and elements of X_2 and excluding Z_1 from the equation for Y permits identifying $\text{Cov}(\phi_u U, \alpha_u U)$ and $\text{Var}(\alpha_u U)$ given that Z_1, X_1, and Y are equiconfounded. This then permits identifying $\mathcal{S}_4$'s coefficients. Similar arguments apply to $\mathcal{S}_1$, $\mathcal{S}_2$, and $\mathcal{S}_3$. This is conveniently depicted in the causal graphs by (1) a missing arrow between two nodes, one of which is linked to U by a dashed arrow and the other by a solid arrow (e.g., X_1 and X_2 in $\mathcal{S}_4$) and (2) a missing arrow between two nodes that are both linked to U by a dashed arrow (e.g., Z and Y in $\mathcal{S}_4$). Recent papers which make use of alternative assumptions that lead to covariance restrictions useful for identification include Lewbel (2010); Altonji et al. (2011) and Galvao et al. (2012).

As discussed in Sect. 4, the availability of multiple equiconfounded variables can overidentify structural coefficients, leading to tests for equiconfounding. Further, equiconfounding can be used to conduct tests for hypotheses of interest. For example, one could test for endogeneity under equiconfounding without requiring valid exogenous instruments. To illustrate, consider the triangular structure discussed in structure $\mathcal{S}_4$ of Sect. 6 then Theorem 6.1 gives that under equiconfounding β_o is either fully identified or partially identified in $\{\beta^*_{PC}, \beta^\dagger_{PC}\}$. Theorem 6.1 allows for the possibility $\text{Var}(\alpha_u U) = 0$ of zero confounding or exogeneity. Further, if X is exogenous then clearly the regression coefficient $\pi_{y.x}$ also identifies β_o. This over identification provides the foundation for testing the exogeneity of X without requiring the availability of exogenous instruments with dimension at least as large as that of X. Instead, it suffices that a scalar Z_1 and one element X_1 of X are equally (un)affected by U as is Y. For example, in estimating an Engle curve for a particular commodity, total income Z_1 is often used as an instrument for total expenditures X_1 which may be measured with error. Nevertheless, as Lewbel (2010, Sect. 4) notes, "it is possible for reported consumption and income to have common sources of measurement errors" which could invalidate income as an instrument. One possibility for testing the absence of common sources of measurement error is to assume that the consumption Y of the commodity of interest, total expenditures X_1, and income Z_1 are misreported by an equal proportion. In the absence of common sources of measurement error, $\text{Var}(\alpha_u U) = 0$ and one of the equiconfounding estimands should coincide with the regression coefficient $\pi_{y.x}$, providing the foundation for such a test. A statistic for this test can be based on the difference between the regression estimator $\hat{\pi}_{y.x}$ and the equiconfounding estimators $\hat{\beta}^*_{PC}$ and $\hat{\beta}^\dagger_{PC}$ for β_o or alternatively on the estimators $\hat{\sigma}^*_{PC}$ and $\hat{\sigma}^\dagger_{PC}$ for $\text{Var}(\alpha_u U)$. Such a test statistic must account for $\text{Var}(\alpha_u U)$ being possibly partially identified in $\{\sigma^*_{PC}, \sigma^\dagger_{PC}\}$. We do not study formal properties of such tests here but we note the possibility of a test statistic based on $\min\{\hat{\sigma}^*_{PC}, \hat{\sigma}^\dagger_{PC}\}$. A similar test for exogeneity can be constructed in other structures, e.g., $\mathcal{S}_3$.

A key message of this chapter is that, when exogeneity and conditional exogeneity are not plausible, one can proceed to identify structural coefficients and test hypotheses in linear recursive structures by relying on a parsimonious alternative assumption that restricts the shape of confounding, namely equiconfounding. Here, we begin to study identification via restricting the shape of confounding by focusing on equiconfounding in linear structures but there are several potential extensions of interest. One possibility is to maintain the equiconfounding assumption and relax the constant effect structure, e.g., by allowing for random coefficients across individuals. Another possibility is to maintain the constant effect linear assumption and study bounding the structural coefficients under shape restrictions on confounding weaker than equiconfounding. Relaxing the restriction on the shape of confounding could potentially increase the plausibility of this restriction albeit while possibly leading to wider identification sets.

8 Conclusion

This chapter obtains identification of structural coefficients in linear systems of structural equations with endogenous variables under the assumption of equiconfounding. In particular, standard instrumental variables and control variables need not be available in these systems. Instead, we demonstrate an alternative way in which sufficiently specifying the causal relations among unobservables, as Hal White recommends (e.g., Chalak and White 2011; White and Chalak 2010, 2011; White and Lu 2011a,b; Hoderlein et al. 2011), can support identification of causal effects. In particular, we introduce the notion of *equiconfounding*, where one or two observables are equally affected by the unobserved confounder as is the response, and show that, along with exclusion restrictions, equiconfounding permits the identification of all the system's structural coefficients. We distinguish among several cases by the structural role of the equiconfounded variables. We study the cases of equiconfounded (1) predictive proxy and response, (2) joint causes and response, (3) cause and joint responses, and (4) and pre-cause, intermediate-cause, and response. We provide conditions under which we obtain either full identification of structural coefficients or partial identification in a set consisting of two points.

As discussed in Sect. 7, several extensions of this work are of potential interest including characterizing identification under equiconfounding in linear structural systems, developing the asymptotic distributions and properties for the plug-in estimators suggested here, extending the analysis to structures with heterogenous effects, relaxing the restriction on the shape of confounding, developing tests for equiconfounding and for endogeneity, as well as employing these results in empirical applications. We leave pursuing these extensions to future work.

Acknowledgments The author thanks participants of the Boston College Research in Econometrics Workshop and the Boston University/Boston College Green Line Econometrics Conference as well as Susanto Basu, McKinley Blackburn, Xiaohong Chen, Peter Gotschalk, Hiroaki Kaido, Arthur Lewbel, David Neumark, Jeffrey Wooldridge, an anonymous referee, and especially Halbert White for helpful discussions and suggestions. I also thank Lucrezio Figurelli and Michael Smith for their research assistance and Tao Yang for his help in the preparation of this manuscript. Any errors are solely the author's responsibility.

Appendix A: Mathematical Proofs

Proof of Theorem 3.1 (i) Given that the structural coefficients of S_1 are finite and that $E(U^2)$ and $E(U_x U_x')$ exist and are finite, the following moments exist and are finite:

$$E(XX') = \begin{bmatrix} \phi_u E(U^2)\phi_u' + \alpha_x E(U_x U_x')\alpha_x, & 0 \\ 0, & 1 \end{bmatrix}$$
$$E(ZX') = \alpha_u E(UX') = [\alpha_u E(U^2)\phi_u', 0]$$
$$E(YX') = \beta_o E(XX') + \alpha_u E(UX') = \beta_o E(XX') + [\alpha_u E(U^2)\phi_u', \quad 0].$$

(ii) Substituting for $\alpha_u U$ in (3) with its expression from (1), $\alpha_u U = Z - \alpha_z U_z$, gives

$$Y - Z = \beta_o X - \alpha_z U_z + \alpha_y U_y, \text{ and thus } E[(Y - Z)X'] = \beta_o E(XX').$$

It follows from the nonsingularity of $E(XX')$ that β_o is point identified as

$$\beta_o = \pi_{y-z.x} \equiv E[(Y - Z)X']E(XX')^{-1}.\square$$

Proof of Theorem 4.1 (i) Given that the structural coefficients of $\mathcal{S}_2$ are finite and that $E(U^2)$ and $E(U_x U_x')$ exist and are finite, we have that

$$E(XX') = \begin{bmatrix} \eta_u E(U^2)\eta_u' + \alpha_x E(U_x U_x')\alpha_x', & 0 \\ 0, & 1 \end{bmatrix}, \quad \text{and}$$
$$E(YX') = \beta_o E(XX') + [\alpha_u E(UX_1'), \ \alpha_u E(UX_2'), \ \alpha_u E(UX_{31}'), \ \alpha_u E(U)]$$
$$= \beta_o E(XX') + [\alpha_u^2 E(U^2), \ \alpha_u^2 E(U^2), \ \alpha_u E(U^2)\phi_u', \ 0]$$

exist and are finite. (ii) Further, $\alpha_u^2 E(U^2)$ is identified by $\alpha_u^2 E(U^2) = E(X_2 X_1')$ and $\phi_u E(U^2)\alpha_u$ is overidentified by $\phi_u E(U^2)\alpha_u = E(X_{31}X_1') = E(X_{31}X_2')$. Given that $E(XX')$ is nonsingular, it follows that β_o is fully (over)identified by

$$\beta_o = \beta_{JC}^* \equiv \pi_{y.x} - [E(X_2 X_1'), \ E(X_2 X_1'), \ E(X_1 X_3')]E(XX')^{-1}$$
$$= \beta_{JC}^\dagger \equiv \pi_{y.x} - [E(X_2 X_1'), \ E(X_2 X_1'), \ E(X_2 X_3')]E(XX')^{-1}.\square$$

Proof of Theorem 5.1 (i) Given that the structural coefficients of $\mathcal{S}_3$ and $E(U^2)$ and $E(U_x U_x')$ exist and are finite we have

$$E(XX') = \begin{bmatrix} \eta_u E(U^2)\eta_u' + \alpha_x E(U_x U_x')\alpha_x', & 0 \\ 0, & 1 \end{bmatrix}, \quad \text{and}$$
$$E(YX') = \beta_o E(XX') + \alpha_u \iota_p [E(UX_1'), \ E(UX_2')]$$

$$= \beta_o E(XX') + \iota_p[\alpha_u^2 E(U^2), [\alpha_u E(U^2)\phi_u', 0]]$$

exists and are finite.

$(ii.a)$ Given that $E(X_1X_1')$ and $E(X_2X_2')$ are nonsingular, we have

$$P_{x_1} \equiv E(\epsilon_{x_1.x_2}\epsilon_{x_1.x_2}') = E(\epsilon_{x_1.x_2}X_1') = E(X_1X_1') - \pi_{x_1.x_2}E(X_2X_1') \quad \text{and}$$
$$P_{x_2} \equiv E(\epsilon_{x_2.x_1}\epsilon_{x_2.x_1}') = E(\epsilon_{x_2.x_1}X_2') = E(X_2X_2') - \pi_{x_2.x_1}E(X_1X_2')$$

exist and are finite. $(ii.b)$ If also P_{x_1} and P_{x_2} are nonsingular, then $E(XX')^{-1}$ exists, is finite, and is given by (e.g., Baltagi 1999, p. 185):

$$E(XX')^{-1} = \begin{bmatrix} E(X_1X_1'), & E(X_1X_2') \\ E(X_2X_1'), & E(X_2X_2') \end{bmatrix}^{-1} = \begin{bmatrix} P_{x_1}^{-1}, & -\pi_{x_2.x_1}' P_{x_2}^{-1} \\ -\pi_{x_1.x_2}' P_{x_1}^{-1}, & P_{x_2}^{-1} \end{bmatrix},$$

with $P_{x_1}^{-1}\pi_{x_1.x_2} = \pi_{x_2.x_1}' P_{x_2}^{-1}$. It follows that $\pi_{y.x}$ exists and is finite. To show that

$$E(\epsilon_{y_1.x}Y_2') = E(Y_1Y_2') - E(Y_1X')E(XX')^{-1}E(XY_2')$$

exists and is finite, note that

$$\begin{aligned} E(YY') &= E[(\beta_o X + \alpha_u \iota_p U + \alpha_y U_y)(\beta_o X + \alpha_u \iota_p U + \alpha_y U_y)'] \\ &= \beta_o E(XX')\beta_o' + \beta_o E(XU)\iota_p'\alpha_u' + \alpha_u \iota_p E(UX')\beta_o' \\ &\quad + \iota_p \iota_p' \alpha_u^2 E(U^2) + \alpha_y E(U_y U_y')\alpha_y'. \end{aligned}$$

Substituting for the diagonal term $E(Y_1Y_2')$ in the above expression for $E(\epsilon_{y_1.x}Y_2')$ then gives

$$\begin{aligned} E(\epsilon_{y_1.x}Y_2') &= \beta_{1o}E(XX')\beta_{2o}' + \beta_{1o}\alpha_u E(XU) + \alpha_u E(UX')\beta_{2o}' \\ &\quad + \alpha_u^2 E(U^2) - E(Y_1X')E(XX')^{-1}E(XY_2'), \end{aligned}$$

and thus $E(\epsilon_{y_1.x}Y_2')$ exists and is finite given that $\alpha_u E(UX') = [\alpha_u^2 E(U^2), [\alpha_u E(U^2)\phi_u', 0]]$.

$(ii.c)$ Next, we have that

$$\Delta_{JR} = [2P_{x_1}^{-1}E(X_1X_1') - 1]^2 - 4P_{x_1}^{-1}[E(X_1X_2')P_{x_2}^{-1}E(X_2X_1') + E(\epsilon_{y_1.x}Y_2')],$$

exists and is finite as it is a function of finite moments and coefficients. We now show that Δ_{JR} is nonnegative. Given the nonsingularity of $E(XX')$, substituting for

$$\beta_o = [E(YX') - \alpha_u \iota_p E(UX')]E(XX')^{-1},$$

in the expression for $E(YY')$ gives

$$\begin{aligned}E(YY') &= [E(YX') - \alpha_u \iota_p E(UX')]E(XX')^{-1}E(XX')E(XX')^{-1}[E(XY') \\ &\quad - E(XU')\iota_p'\alpha_u'] + [E(YX') - \alpha_u \iota_p E(UX')]E(XX')^{-1}E(XU)\iota_p'\alpha_u' \\ &\quad + \alpha_u \iota_p E(UX')E(XX')^{-1}[E(XY') - E(XU)\iota_p'\alpha_u'] \\ &\quad + \iota_p \iota_p' \alpha_u^2 E(U^2) + \alpha_y E(U_y U_y')\alpha_y' \\ &= E(YX')E(XX')^{-1}E(XY') - \alpha_u \iota_p E(UX')E(XX')^{-1}E(XU')\iota_p'\alpha_u' \\ &\quad + \iota_p \iota_p' \alpha_u^2 E(U^2) + \alpha_y E(U_y U_y')\alpha_y'.\end{aligned}$$

The off-diagonal term then gives

$$\begin{aligned}E(\epsilon_{y_1.x} Y_2') &= E(Y_1 Y_2') - E(Y_1 X')E(XX')^{-1}E(XY_2') \\ &= \alpha_u^2 E(U^2) - \alpha_u E(UX')E(XX')^{-1}E(XU')\alpha_u'\end{aligned}$$

Substituting for $\alpha_u E(UX') = [\alpha_u^2 E(U^2), [\alpha_u E(U^2)\phi_u', 0]] = [\alpha_u^2 E(U^2), E(X_1 X_2')]$ gives

$$\begin{aligned}&\alpha_u E(UX')E(XX')^{-1}E(XU)\alpha_u' \\ &\quad = [\alpha_u^2 E(U^2), E(X_1 X_2')]\begin{bmatrix} P_{x_1}^{-1}, & -\pi_{x_2.x_1}' P_{x_2}^{-1} \\ -\pi_{x_1.x_2}' P_{x_1}^{-1}, & P_{x_2}^{-1}\end{bmatrix}[\alpha_u^2 E(U^2), E(X_1 X_2')]' \\ &\quad = \alpha_u^4 E(U^2)^2 P_{x_1}^{-1} - E(X_1 X_2')\pi_{x_1.x_2}' P_{x_1}^{-1}\alpha_u^2 E(U^2) \\ &\qquad - \alpha_u^2 E(U^2)\pi_{x_2.x_1}' P_{x_2}^{-1}E(X_2 X_1') + E(X_1 X_2')P_{x_2}^{-1}E(X_2 X_1').\end{aligned}$$

Thus, we expand the term $E(X_1 X_2')P_{x_2}^{-1}E(X_2 X_1') + E(\epsilon_{y_1.x} Y_2')$ in Δ_{JR} as:

$$\begin{aligned}&E(X_1 X_2')P_{x_2}^{-1}E(X_2 X_1') + E(\epsilon_{y_1.x} Y_2') \\ &\quad = E(X_1 X_2')P_{x_2}^{-1}E(X_2 X_1') + \alpha_u^2 E(U^2) - \alpha_u^4 E(U^2)^2 P_{x_1}^{-1} \\ &\qquad + E(X_1 X_2')\pi_{x_1.x_2}' P_{x_1}^{-1}\alpha_u^2 E(U^2) + \alpha_u^2 E(U^2)\pi_{x_2.x_1}' P_{x_2}^{-1}E(X_2 X_1') \\ &\qquad - E(X_1 X_2')P_{x_2}^{-1}E(X_2 X_1') \\ &\quad = -\alpha_u^4 E(U^2)^2 P_{x_1}^{-1} + \alpha_u^2 E(U^2)[2P_{x_1}^{-1}\pi_{x_1.x_2}E(X_2 X_1') + 1] \\ &\quad = -\alpha_u^4 E(U^2)^2 P_{x_1}^{-1} + \alpha_u^2 E(U^2)[2P_{x_1}^{-1}[E(X_1 X_1') - P_{x_1}] + 1] \\ &\quad = -\alpha_u^4 E(U^2)^2 P_{x_1}^{-1} + \alpha_u^2 E(U^2)[2P_{x_1}^{-1}E(X_1 X_1') - 1]\end{aligned}$$

where we use $P_{x_1}^{-1}\pi_{x_1.x_2} = \pi_{x_2.x_1}' P_{x_2}^{-1}$ and $P_{x_1} = E(X_1 X_1') - \pi_{x_1.x_2}E(X_2 X_1')$. Then

$$\begin{aligned}\Delta_{JR} &\equiv [2P_{x_1}^{-1}E(X_1 X_1') - 1]^2 - 4P_{x_1}^{-1}[E(X_1 X_2')P_{x_2}^{-1}E(X_2 X_1') + E(\epsilon_{y_1.x} Y_2')] \\ &= [2P_{x_1}^{-1}E(X_1 X_1') - 1]^2 + 4\alpha_u^4 E(U^2)^2 P_{x_1}^{-2} \\ &\quad - 4P_{x_1}^{-1}\alpha_u^2 E(U^2)[2P_{x_1}^{-1}E(X_1 X_1') - 1]\end{aligned}$$

$$= \{[2P_{x_1}^{-1}E(X_1X_1') - 1] - 2P_{x_1}^{-1}\alpha_u^2 E(U^2)\}^2 \geq 0.$$

(iii) We begin by showing that

$$\begin{aligned}&\mathrm{Var}(\alpha_{x_1}U_{x_1}) + \mathrm{Cov}(\phi_u U, \alpha_u U)' \\ &\quad \times [\mathrm{Var}(\phi_u U) + \mathrm{Var}(\alpha_{x_2}U_{x_2})]^{-1}\mathrm{Cov}(\phi_u U, \alpha_u U) - \mathrm{Var}(\alpha_u U)\end{aligned} \tag{A.1}$$

has the same sign as the expression $2P_{x_1}^{-1}E(X_1X_1') - 1 - 2P_{x_1}^{-1}\alpha_u^2 E(U^2)$ from Δ_{JR}. First, clearly, (A.1) can be negative, zero, or positive (e.g., set $\dim(X_{21}) = 1$, $\mathrm{Var}(\alpha_{x_1}U_{x_1}) = 1$, and $\mathrm{Var}(\alpha_{x_2}U_{x_2}) = \mathrm{Var}(\phi_u U) = \frac{1}{2}$. Then (A.1) reduces to $1 - \frac{1}{2}\mathrm{Var}(\alpha_u U)$ with sign depending on $\mathrm{Var}(\alpha_u U)$). Next, multiplying this expression by $P_{x_1} \equiv E(\epsilon_{x_1.x_2}\epsilon_{x_1.x_2}')$ preserves its sign and we obtain

$$\begin{aligned}&2E(X_1X_1') - P_{x_1} - 2\alpha_u^2 E(U^2) \\ &= 2E(X_1X_1') - [E(X_1X_1') - E(X_1X_2')E(X_2X_2')^{-1}E(X_2X_1')] - 2\alpha_u^2 E(U^2) \\ &= E(X_1X_1') + E(X_1X_2')E(X_2X_2')^{-1}E(X_2X_1') - 2\alpha_u^2 E(U^2).\end{aligned}$$

But we have

$$\begin{aligned}E(X_1X_1') &= \alpha_u^2 E(U^2) + \alpha_{x_1}E(U_{x_1}U_{x_1}')\alpha_{x_1}' \text{ and} \\ E(X_2X_2') &= \begin{bmatrix}\phi_u E(UU')\phi_u' + \alpha_{x_2}E(U_{x_2}U_{x_2}')\alpha_{x_2}', & 0 \\ 0, & 1\end{bmatrix}.\end{aligned}$$

Then using $[\alpha_u E(U^2)\phi_u', 0] = E(X_1X_2')$ gives

$$\begin{aligned}&E(X_1X_1') + E(X_1X_2')E(X_2X_2')^{-1}E(X_2X_1') - 2\alpha_u^2 E(U^2) \\ &\quad = \alpha_u^2 E(U^2) + \alpha_{x_1}E(U_{x_1}U_{x_1}')\alpha_{x_1}' + [\alpha_u E(U^2)\phi_u', 0] \\ &\qquad \times \begin{bmatrix}\phi_u E(UU')\phi_u' + \alpha_{x_2}E(U_{x_2}U_{x_2}')\alpha_{x_2}', & 0 \\ 0, & 1\end{bmatrix}^{-1} \begin{bmatrix}\phi_u E(U^2)\alpha_u \\ 0\end{bmatrix} - 2\alpha_u^2 E(U^2) \\ &\quad = \mathrm{Var}(\alpha_{x_1}U_{x_1}) + \mathrm{Cov}(\phi_u U, \alpha_u U)'[\mathrm{Var}(\phi_u U) + \mathrm{Var}(\alpha_{x_2}U_{x_2})]^{-1} \\ &\qquad \times \mathrm{Cov}(\phi_u U, \alpha_u U) - \mathrm{Var}(\alpha_u U).\end{aligned}$$

$(iii.a)$ Now, recall from $(ii.c)$ that

$$\Delta_{JR} = \{[2P_{x_1}^{-1}E(X_1X_1') - 1] - 2P_{x_1}^{-1}\alpha_u^2 E(U^2)\}^2.$$

Suppose that (3) is negative, then

$$\sqrt{\Delta_{JR}} = \left|2P_{x_1}^{-1}E(X_1X_1') - 1 - 2P_{x_1}^{-1}\alpha_u^2 E(U^2)\right|$$
$$= -2P_{x_1}^{-1}E(X_1X_1') + 1 + 2P_{x_1}^{-1}\alpha_u^2 E(U^2),$$

and we have

$$\begin{aligned}\sigma_{JR}^{\dagger} &\equiv E(X_1X_1') + \frac{1}{2}P_{x_1}(-1 - \sqrt{\Delta_{JR}})\\ &= 2E(X_1X_1') - P_{x_1} - \alpha_u^2 E(U^2)\\ &= \mathrm{Var}(\alpha_{x_1}U_{x_1}) + \mathrm{Cov}(\phi_u U, \alpha_u U)'[\mathrm{Var}(\phi_u U) + \mathrm{Var}(\alpha_{x_2}U_{x_2})]^{-1}\\ &\quad \times \mathrm{Cov}(\phi_u U, \alpha_u U)\\ &\quad < \alpha_u^2 E(U^2) \text{ (and } \geq 0),\end{aligned}$$

and

$$\sigma_{JR}^{*} \equiv E(X_1X_1') + \frac{1}{2}P_{x_1}(-1 + \sqrt{\Delta_{JR}}) = \alpha_u^2 E(U^2).$$

$(iii.b)$ Suppose instead that (A.1) is nonnegative then

$$\sqrt{\Delta_{JR}} = \left|2P_{x_1}^{-1}E(X_1X_1') - 1 - 2P_{x_1}^{-1}\alpha_u^2 E(U^2)\right|$$
$$= 2P_{x_1}^{-1}E(X_1X_1') - 1 - 2P_{x_1}^{-1}\alpha_u^2 E(U^2),$$

and we have

$$\sigma_{JR}^{\dagger} = \alpha_u^2 E(U^2),$$

and

$$\begin{aligned}\sigma_{JR}^{*} &= \mathrm{Var}(\alpha_{x_1}U_{x_1}) + \mathrm{Cov}(\phi_u U, \alpha_u U)'[\mathrm{Var}(\phi_u U)\\ &\qquad + \mathrm{Var}(\alpha_{x_2}U_{x_2})]^{-1}\mathrm{Cov}(\phi_u U, \alpha_u U)\\ &\geq \alpha_u^2 E(U^2) \geq 0.\end{aligned}$$

Thus, $\alpha_u^2 E(U^2)$ is partially identified in the set $\{\sigma_{JR}^{\dagger}, \sigma_{JR}^{*}\}$. It follows from the moment

$$E(YX') = \beta_o E(XX') + \iota_p[\alpha_u^2 E(U^2), E(X_1X_2')],$$

and the nonsingularity of $E(XX')$ that β_o is partially identified in the set $\{\beta_{JR}^{*}, \beta_{JR}^{\dagger}\}$. □

Proof of Theorem 6.1 (*i*) We have that

$$E(ZZ') = \begin{bmatrix} \alpha_u^2 E(U^2), & 0 \\ 0, & 1 \end{bmatrix},$$

$$E(XZ') = E\begin{pmatrix} [X_1', X_{21}']'Z' \\ Z' \end{pmatrix} = \begin{bmatrix} \gamma_o E(ZZ') + \begin{bmatrix} \eta_u E(U^2)\alpha_u' & 0 \end{bmatrix} \\ [0, \quad 1] \end{bmatrix},$$

$$E(XX') = \begin{bmatrix} \gamma_o E(ZX') + \eta_u E(UX') + \alpha_x E(U_x X'), & E(X) \\ E(X'), & 1 \end{bmatrix}$$
$$= \begin{bmatrix} \gamma_o E(ZX') + [[\eta_u E(U^2)\alpha_u', 0]\gamma_o' \\ \quad + \eta_u E(U^2)\eta_u', 0] + \begin{bmatrix} \alpha_x E(U_x U_x)'\alpha_x', & 0 \end{bmatrix}, & \begin{bmatrix} 0', & 1' \end{bmatrix}' \\ \begin{bmatrix} 0, & 1 \end{bmatrix}, & 1 \end{bmatrix},$$

$$E(YX') = \beta_o E(XX') + \alpha_u E(UX') = \beta_o E(XX')$$
$$+ [[\alpha_u^2 E(U^2), 0]\gamma_{1o}' + \alpha_u^2 E(U^2), [[\alpha_u^2 E(U^2), 0]\gamma_{2o}' + \alpha_u E(U^2)\phi_u', 0]],$$
$$E(YZ') = \beta_o E(XZ') + [\alpha_u^2 E(U^2), 0],$$

Thus, these moments exist and are finite since they are functions of existing finite coefficients and moments.

(*ii.a*) Given that $P_{z_1} \equiv E(\epsilon_{z_1.z_2} Z_1') = E(Z_1 Z_1')$ is nonsingular and $Z_2 = 1$, we have that

$$E(ZZ')^{-1} = \begin{bmatrix} P_{z_1}^{-1}, & -\pi_{z_2.z_1}' P_{z_2}^{-1} \\ -\pi_{z_1.z_2}' P_{z_1}^{-1}, & P_{z_2}^{-1} \end{bmatrix} = \begin{bmatrix} E(Z_1 Z_1')^{-1} & 0 \\ 0 & 1 \end{bmatrix}$$

is nonsingular and thus $\pi_{x.z}$ and $E(\epsilon_{x_1.z} X_2') = E(X_1 X_2') - \pi_{x_1.z} E(ZX_2')$ exist and are finite. With $E(XX')$ also nonsingular, $\pi_{z.x}$ exists and is finite. Also,

$$\begin{aligned} E(\epsilon_{y.x} Z_1') &= E(Y\epsilon_{z_1.x}') \\ &= \beta_o E(X\epsilon_{z_1.x}') + \alpha_u E(U\epsilon_{z_1.x}') + \alpha_y E(U_y \epsilon_{z_1.x}') \\ &= \alpha_u E(U\epsilon_{z_1.x}'). \end{aligned}$$

Using $E(X_1 X_2') = \gamma_{1o} E(ZX_2') + \alpha_u E(UX_2')$ then gives

$$\begin{aligned} E(\epsilon_{y.x} Z_1') &= \alpha_u E(U\epsilon_{z_1.x}') = \alpha_u E(UZ_1') - \alpha_u E(UX')E(XX')^{-1}E(XZ_1') \\ &= \alpha_u^2 E(U^2) - [[\alpha_u^2 E(U^2), 0]\gamma_{1o}' \\ &\quad + \alpha_u^2 E(U^2), E(X_1 X_2') - \gamma_{1o} E(ZX_2')]\pi_{z_1.x}' \end{aligned}$$

exists and is finite.

$(ii.b)$ We have that Δ_{PC} exists and is finite as it is a function of finite coefficients and moments. Next, we verify that $\Delta_{PC} \geq 0$. We begin by expanding the term $E(\epsilon_{y.x} Z_1')$ in Δ_{PC}. For this, we substitute for γ_{1o} with

$$\gamma_{1o} = \pi_{x_1.z} - [\alpha_u^2 E(U^2),\ 0]E(ZZ')^{-1},$$

in $-\alpha_u E(UX')\pi_{z.x}'$ which gives

$$\begin{aligned}
&- \alpha_u E(UX')\pi_{z.x}' \\
&= -[[\alpha_u^2 E(U^2),\quad 0]\gamma_{1o}' + \alpha_u^2 E(U^2),\quad E(X_1 X_2') - \gamma_{1o} E(ZX_2')]\pi_{z.x}' \\
&= -[\alpha_u^2 E(U^2),\quad 0]\pi_{x_1.z}'\pi_{z.x_1|x_2}' + [\alpha_u^2 E(U^2),\quad 0]E(ZZ')^{-1}[\alpha_u^2 E(U^2),\quad 0]'\pi_{z.x_1|x_2}' \\
&\quad - \alpha_u^2 E(U^2)\pi_{z.x_1|x_2}' - E(\epsilon_{x_1.z} X_2')\pi_{z.x_2|x_1}' - [\alpha_u^2 E(U^2),\quad 0]\pi_{x_2.z}'\pi_{z.x_2|x_1}' \\
&= -\alpha_u^2 E(U^2)\pi_{x_1.z_1|z_2}'\pi_{z.x_1|x_2}' + \alpha_u^4 E(U^2)^2 P_{z_1}^{-1}\pi_{z.x_1|x_2}' - \alpha_u^2 E(U^2)\pi_{z.x_1|x_2}' \\
&\quad - E(\epsilon_{x_1.z} X_2')\pi_{z.x_2|x_1}' - \alpha_u^2 E(U^2)\pi_{x_2.z_1|z_2}'\pi_{z.x_2|x_1}',
\end{aligned}$$

where we make use of $[\alpha_u^2 E(U^2),\ 0]E(ZZ')^{-1}[\alpha_u^2 E(U^2),\ 0]' = \alpha_u^4 E(U^2)^2 P_{z_1}^{-1}$. Thus,

$$\begin{aligned}
E(\epsilon_{y.x} Z_1') &= \alpha_u^2 E(U^2) - \alpha_u E(UX')\pi_{z_1.x}' \\
&= \alpha_u^2 E(U^2) - \alpha_u^2 E(U^2)\pi_{x_1.z_1|z_2}'\pi_{z_1.x_1|x_2}' + \alpha_u^4 E(U^2)^2 P_{z_1}^{-1}\pi_{z_1.x_1|x_2}' \\
&\quad - \alpha_u^2 E(U^2)\pi_{z_1.x_1|x_2}' - E(\epsilon_{x_1.z} X_2')\pi_{z_1.x_2|x_1}' - \alpha_u^2 E(U^2)\pi_{x_2.z_1|z_2}'\pi_{z_1.x_2|x_1}' \\
&= \alpha_u^2 E(U^2) - \alpha_u^2 E(U^2)\pi_{x.z_1|z_2}'\pi_{z_1.x}' + \alpha_u^4 E(U^2)^2 P_{z_1}^{-1}\pi_{z_1.x_1|x_2}' \\
&\quad - \alpha_u^2 E(U^2)\pi_{z_1.x_1|x_2}' - E(\epsilon_{x_1.z} X_2')\pi_{z_1.x_2|x_1}'.
\end{aligned}$$

Then

$$\begin{aligned}
\Delta_{PC} &\equiv [-\pi_{x.z_1|z_2}'\ \pi_{z_1.x}' - \pi_{z_1.x_1|x_2}' + 1]^2 + 4P_{z_1}^{-1}\ \pi_{z_1.x_1|x_2}'[E(\epsilon_{y.x} Z_1') \\
&\quad + E(\epsilon_{x_1.z} X_2')\ \pi_{z_1.x_2|x_1}'] \\
&= [-\pi_{x.z_1|z_2}'\pi_{z_1.x}' - \pi_{z_1.x_1|x_2}' + 1]^2 \\
&\quad + 4P_{z_1}^{-1}\pi_{z_1.x_1|x_2}'[\alpha_u^2 E(U^2) - \alpha_u^2 E(U^2)\pi_{x.z_1|z_2}'\pi_{z_1.x}' \\
&\quad + \alpha_u^4 E(U^2)^2 P_{z_1}^{-1}\pi_{z_1.x_1|x_2}' - \alpha_u^2 E(U^2)\pi_{z_1.x_1|x_2}' \\
&\quad - E(\epsilon_{x_1.z} X_2')\pi_{z_1.x_2|x_1}' + E(\epsilon_{x_1.z} X_2')\pi_{z_1.x_2|x_1}'] \\
&= \{[\pi_{x.z_1|z_2}'\pi_{z_1.x}' + \pi_{z_1.x_1|x_2}' - 1] - 2P_{z_1}^{-1}\pi_{z_1.x_1|x_2}'\alpha_u^2 E(U^2)\}^2 \geq 0.
\end{aligned}$$

(iii) Suppose that

$$\pi_{x.z_1|z_2}'\pi_{z_1.x}' + \pi_{z_1.x_1|x_2}' - 1 - 2P_{z_1}^{-1}\pi_{z_1.x_1|x_2}'\alpha_u^2 E(U^2) < 0.$$

Then

$$\sqrt{\Delta_{PC}} = \left|\pi'_{x.z_1|z_2}\pi'_{z_1.x} + \pi'_{z_1.x_1|x_2} - 1 - 2P_{z_1}^{-1}\pi'_{z_1.x_1|x_2}\alpha_u^2 E(U^2)\right|$$
$$= -\pi'_{x.z_1|z_2}\pi'_{z_1.x} - \pi'_{z_1.x_1|x_2} + 1 + 2P_{z_1}^{-1}\pi'_{z_1.x_1|x_2}\alpha_u^2 E(U^2),$$

and thus

$$\sigma^{\dagger}_{PC} \equiv \frac{\pi'_{x.z_1|z_2}\pi'_{z_1.x} + \pi'_{z_1.x_1|x_2} - 1 - \sqrt{\Delta_{PC}}}{2P_{z_1}^{-1}\pi'_{z_1.x_1|x_2}}$$
$$= \frac{\pi'_{x.z}\pi'_{z.x} + \pi'_{z.x_1|x_2} - 1 - P_{z_1}^{-1}\pi'_{z_1.x_1|x_2}\alpha_u^2 E(U^2)}{P_{z_1}^{-1}\pi'_{z_1.x_1|x_2}}$$
$$< \frac{P_{z_1}^{-1}\pi'_{z_1.x_1|x_2}\alpha_u^2 E(U^2)}{P_{z_1}^{-1}\pi'_{z_1.x_1|x_2}} = \alpha_u^2 E(U^2),$$

and

$$\sigma^{*}_{PC} \equiv \frac{\pi'_{x.z_1|z_2}\pi'_{z_1.x} + \pi'_{z_1.x_1|x_2} - 1 + \sqrt{\Delta_{PC}}}{2P_{z_1}^{-1}\pi'_{z_1.x_1|x_2}} = \alpha_u^2 E(U^2).$$

Now, with $E(ZZ')$ nonsingular, we have

$$E(X_1 Z') = \gamma_{1o}E(ZZ') + [\alpha_u^2 E(U^2),\, 0], \text{ or}$$
$$\gamma_{1o} = \pi_{x_1.z} - [\sigma^{*}_{PC},\, 0]E(ZZ')^{-1}.$$

Further, with $E(XX')$ nonsingular, we have

$$E(YX') = \beta_o E(XX') + \alpha_u E(UX'), \text{ or}$$
$$\beta_o = \{E(YX') - [[\alpha_u^2 E(U^2), 0]\gamma'_{1o}$$
$$+ \alpha_u^2 E(U^2), E(X_1 X_2') - \gamma_{1o}E(ZX_2')]\}E(XX')^{-1}.$$

Substituting for γ_{1o} gives

$$\left[\alpha_u^2 E(U^2),\, 0\right]\gamma'_{1o} + \alpha_u^2 E(U^2)$$
$$= \left[\alpha_u^2 E(U^2),\, 0\right]\pi'_{x_1.z} - \left[\alpha_u^2 E(U^2),\, 0\right]E(ZZ')^{-1}\left[\alpha_u^2 E(U^2),\, 0\right]' + \alpha_u^2 E(U^2)$$
$$= \left[\alpha_u^2 E(U^2),\, 0\right]\pi'_{x_1.z} - \alpha_u^4 E(U^2)^2\, P_{z_1}^{-1} + \alpha_u^2 E(U^2)$$
$$= \alpha_u^2 E(U^2)\,(\pi'_{x_1.z_1|z_2} - \alpha_u^2 E(U^2)\, P_{z_1}^{-1} + 1),$$

and

$$\begin{aligned}
&E(X_1X_2') - \gamma_{1o}E(ZX_2') \\
&\quad = E(X_1X_2') - [\pi_{x_1.z} - [\alpha_u^2 E(U^2),\, 0]E(ZZ')^{-1}]E(ZX_2') \\
&\quad = E(\epsilon_{x_1.z}X_2') + [\alpha_u^2 E(U^2),\, 0]\pi'_{x_2.z} = E(\epsilon_{x_1.z}X_2') + \alpha_u^2 E(U^2)\, \pi'_{x_2.z_1|z_2},
\end{aligned}$$

so that

$$\begin{aligned}
\beta_o = \pi_{y.x} - [&\sigma^*_{PC}\, (\pi'_{x_1.z_1|z_2} - \sigma^*_{PC}\, P_{z_1}^{-1} + 1),\, E(\epsilon_{x_1.z}X_2') \\
&+ \sigma^*_{PC}\, \pi'_{x_2.z_1|z_2}]E(XX')^{-1}.
\end{aligned}$$

Also, we have

$$\begin{aligned}
E(X_1X_{21}') &= \gamma_{1o}E(ZX_{21}') + \alpha_u E(UX_{21}') \\
&= \gamma_{1o}E(ZX_{21}') + \alpha_u E(UZ')\gamma_{2o}' + \alpha_u E(U^2)\phi_u' \\
&= \gamma_{1o}E(ZX_{21}') + [\alpha_u^2 E(U^2),\, 0]\gamma_{2o}' + \alpha_u E(U^2)\phi_u' \text{ and} \\
E(X_{21}Z') &= \gamma_{2o}E(ZZ') + [\phi_u E(U^2)\alpha_u',\, 0].
\end{aligned}$$

Substituting for

$$\gamma_{2o} = \pi_{x_{21}.z} - [\phi_u E(U^2)\alpha_u',\, 0]E(ZZ')^{-1}$$

in the expression for $E(X_1X_{21}')$ gives

$$\begin{aligned}
E(X_1X_{21}') &= \gamma_{1o}E(ZX_{21}') + [\alpha_u^2 E(U^2),\, 0]\pi'_{x_{21}.z} \\
&\quad - [\alpha_u^2 E(U^2),\, 0]E(ZZ')^{-1}[\phi_u E(U^2)\alpha_u',\, 0]' + \alpha_u E(U^2)\phi_u' \\
&= \gamma_{1o}E(ZX_{21}') + [\alpha_u^2 E(U^2),\, 0]\pi'_{x_{21}.z} \\
&\quad - \alpha_u^2 E(U^2)P_{z_1}^{-1}\alpha_u E(U^2)\phi_u' + \alpha_u E(U^2)\phi_u'.
\end{aligned}$$

Further substituting for γ_{1o} with $[E(X_1Z') - [\alpha_u^2 E(U^2),\, 0]]E(ZZ')^{-1}$ gives

$$\begin{aligned}
&E(X_1X_{21}') - [E(X_1Z') - [\alpha_u^2 E(U^2),\, 0]]E(ZZ')^{-1}E(ZX_{21}') - [\alpha_u^2 E(U^2),\, 0]\pi'_{x_{21}.z} \\
&\quad = -\alpha_u^2 E(U^2)P_{z_1}^{-1}\alpha_u E(U^2)\phi_u' + \alpha_u E(U^2)\phi_u',
\end{aligned}$$

or

$$E(X_1\epsilon'_{x_{21}.z}) = -\alpha_u^2 E(U^2)P_{z_1}^{-1}\alpha_u E(U^2)\phi_u' + \alpha_u E(U^2)\phi_u'.$$

Substituting for

$$\phi_u E(U^2)\alpha_u' = E(X_{21}\epsilon'_{x_1.z})[1 - \alpha_u^2 E(U^2)P_{z_1}^{-1}]^{-1}$$

in the expression for γ_{2o} gives

$$\gamma_{2o} = \pi_{x_{21}.z} - [\,\phi_u E(U^2)\alpha_u',\, 0\,]E(ZZ')^{-1}$$
$$= \pi_{x_{21}.z} - [\,E(X_{21}\epsilon_{x_1.z}')[1 - \sigma_{PC}^* P_{z_1}^{-1}]^{-1},\, 0\,]E(ZZ')^{-1}.$$

$(iii.b)$ Suppose instead that

$$\pi_{x.z_1|z_2}'\pi_{z_1.x}' + \pi_{z_1.x_1|x_2}' - 1 - 2P_{z_1}^{-1}\pi_{z_1.x_1|x_2}'\alpha_u^2 E(U^2) \geq 0.$$

Then

$$\sqrt{\Delta_{PC}} = \left|\pi_{x.z_1|z_2}'\pi_{z_1.x}' + \pi_{z_1.x_1|x_2}' - 1 - 2P_{z_1}^{-1}\pi_{z_1.x_1|x_2}'\alpha_u^2 E(U^2)\right|$$
$$= \pi_{x.z_1|z_2}'\pi_{z_1.x}' + \pi_{z_1.x_1|x_2}' - 1 - 2P_{z_1}^{-1}\pi_{z_1.x_1|x_2}'\alpha_u^2 E(U^2),$$

and thus

$$\sigma_{PC}^{\dagger} = \alpha_u^2 E(U^2),$$

and

$$\sigma_{PC}^* = \frac{\pi_{x.z_1|z_2}'\pi_{z_1.x}' + \pi_{z_1.x_1|x_2}' - 1 - P_{z_1}^{-1}\pi_{z_1.x_1|x_2}'\alpha_u^2 E(U^2)}{P_{z_1}^{-1}\pi_{z_1.x_1|x_2}'}$$
$$\geq \frac{P_{z_1}^{-1}\pi_{z_1.x_1|x_2}'\alpha_u^2 E(U^2)}{P_{z_1}^{-1}\pi_{z_1.x_1|x_2}'} = \alpha_u^2 E(U^2).$$

It follows that

$$\gamma_{1o} = \gamma_1^{\dagger} \equiv \pi_{x_1.z} - [\sigma_{PC}^{\dagger},\, 0]E(ZZ')^{-1},$$
$$\gamma_{2o} = \gamma_2^{\dagger} \equiv \pi_{x_2.z} - [\,E(X_{21}\epsilon_{x_1.z}')[1 - \sigma_{PC}^{\dagger}\, P_{z_1}^{-1}]^{-1},\, 0\,]E(ZZ')^{-1}, \text{ and}$$
$$\beta_o = \beta^{\dagger} \equiv \pi_{y.x} - [\sigma_{PC}^{\dagger}\,(\pi_{x_1.z_1|z_2}' - \sigma_{PC}^{\dagger}\, P_{z_1}^{-1} + 1),\, E(\epsilon_{x_1.z}X_2')$$
$$+ \sigma_{PC}^{\dagger}\, \pi_{x_2.z_1|z_2}']E(XX')^{-1}.\square$$

Appendix B: Constructive Identification

B.1 Equiconfounded Cause and Joint Responses: Constructive Identification

We present an argument to constructively demonstrate how the expression for Δ_{JR} and the identification of $\alpha_u^2 E(U^2)$, and thus β_o, in the proof of Theorem 5.1 obtain. Recall that in $\mathcal{S}_3$

$$E(YX') = \beta_o E(XX') + \iota_p[\alpha_u^2 E(U^2), [\alpha_u E(U^2)\phi_u', 0]].$$

We have that $\alpha_u E(U^2)\phi_u' = E(X_1 X_2')$. It remains to identify $\alpha_u^2 E(U^2)$. For this, recall that the proof of Theorem 5.1 gives

$$E(YY') = E(YX')E(XX')^{-1}E(XY') - \alpha_u \iota_p E(UX')E(XX')^{-1}\alpha_u E(XU)\iota_p' \\ + \iota_p \iota_p' \alpha_u^2 E(U^2) + \alpha_y E(U_y U_y')\alpha_y',$$

which we rewrite as

$$\iota_p \iota_p' \alpha_u^2 E(U^2) - \alpha_u \iota_p E(UX')E(XX')^{-1}E(XU)\iota_p' \alpha_u' \\ - E(\epsilon_{y.x} Y') + \alpha_y E(U_y U_y')\alpha_y' = 0. \qquad \text{(B.1)}$$

From the proof of Theorem 5.1, we also have

$$\alpha_u E(UX')E(XX')^{-1}E(XU)\alpha_u' \\ = \alpha_u^4 E(U^2)^2 P_{x_1}^{-1} - E(X_1 X_2')\pi_{x_1.x_2}' P_{x_1}^{-1} \alpha_u^2 E(U^2) \\ - \alpha_u^2 E(U^2)\pi_{x_2.x_1}' P_{x_2}^{-1} E(X_2 X_1') + E(X_1 X_2') P_{x_2}^{-1} E(X_2 X_1').$$

Thus, collecting the off-diagonal terms in Eq. (B.1) gives:

$$\alpha_u^2 E(U^2) - \alpha_u^4 E(U^2)^2 P_{x_1}^{-1} + E(X_1 X_2')\pi_{x_1.x_2}' P_{x_1}^{-1} \alpha_u^2 E(U^2) \\ + \alpha_u^2 E(U^2)\pi_{x_2.x_1}' P_{x_2}^{-1} E(X_2 X_1') - E(X_1 X_2') P_{x_2}^{-1} E(X_2 X_1') - E(\epsilon_{y_1.x} Y_2') = 0.$$

This is a quadratic equation in $\alpha_u^2 E(U^2)$ of the form

$$a\alpha_u^4 E(U^2)^2 + b\alpha_u^2 E(U^2) + c = 0,$$

with

$$a = P_{x_1}^{-1}, \\ b = -[1 + E(X_1 X_2')\pi_{x_1.x_2}' P_{x_1}^{-1} + \pi_{x_2.x_1}' P_{x_2}^{-1} E(X_2 X_1')] \\ = -[1 + E(X_1 X_2')\pi_{x_1.x_2}' P_{x_1}^{-1} + P_{x_1}^{-1}\pi_{x_1.x_2} E(X_2 X_1')] \\ = -[1 + 2P_{x_1}^{-1}\pi_{x_1.x_2} E(X_2 X_1')] \\ = -[1 + 2P_{x_1}^{-1}[E(X_1 X_1') - P_{x_1}]] = -[2P_{x_1}^{-1} E(X_1 X_1') - 1], \text{ and} \\ c = E(X_1 X_2') P_{x_2}^{-1} E(X_2 X_1') + E(\epsilon_{y_1.x} Y_2'),$$

where we make use of $P_{x_1}^{-1}\pi_{x_1.x_2} = \pi_{x_2.x_1}' P_{x_2}^{-1}$ and $P_{x_1} = E(X_1 X_1') - \pi_{x_1.x_2} E(X_2 X_1')$. The discriminant of this quadratic equation gives the expression for $\Delta_{JR} = b^2 - 4ac$. Theorem 5.1 (*ii.c*) gives that $\Delta_{JR} \geq 0$ and (*iii*) gives the two roots $\sigma^{\dagger}_{PC}$ and σ^{*}_{PC} of this quadratic equation

$$\frac{-b \pm \sqrt{\Delta_{JR}}}{2a} = \frac{1}{2} P_{x_1} \left\{ 2P_{x_1}^{-1} E(X_1 X_1') - 1 \pm \sqrt{\Delta_{JR}} \right\}$$
$$= E(X_1 X_1') + \frac{1}{2} P_{x_1} \left(-1 \pm \sqrt{\Delta_{JR}} \right),$$

and shows that these are nonnegative. One of these roots identifies $\alpha_u^2 E(U^2)$, depending on the sign of

$$\mathrm{Var}(\alpha_{x_1}' U_{x_1}) + \mathrm{Cov}(\phi_u U, \alpha_u U)' [\mathrm{Var}(\phi_u U)$$
$$+ \mathrm{Var}(\alpha_{x_2} U_{x_2})]^{-1} \mathrm{Cov}(\phi_u U, \alpha_u U) - \mathrm{Var}(\alpha_u U).$$

β_o is then identified from the moment $E(YX') = \beta_o E(XX') + \iota_p[\alpha_u^2 E(U^2), E(X_1 X_2')]$.

B.2 Equiconfounding in Triangular Structures: Constructive Identification

We present an argument to constructively demonstrate how the expression for Δ_{PC} and the identification of $\alpha_u^2 E(U^2)$ in the proof of Theorem 6.1 obtain. From the proof of Theorem 6.1, we have that

$$\beta_o = \{E(YX') - \alpha_u E(UX')\} E(XX')^{-1} = \pi_{y.x} - \alpha_u E(UX') E(XX')^{-1}.$$

Substituting for β_o in the expression for $E(YZ')$ gives

$$E(YZ') = \beta_o E(XZ') + [\alpha_u^2 E(U^2),\, 0],$$
$$= \pi_{y.x} E(XZ') - \alpha_u E(UX') E(XX')^{-1} E(XZ') + [\alpha_u^2 E(U^2),\, 0], \quad \text{or}$$
$$- E(\epsilon_{y.x} Z') - \alpha_u E(UX') \pi_{z.x}' + [\alpha_u^2 E(U^2),\, 0] = 0.$$

From the proof of Theorem 6.1, we have

$$- \alpha_u E(UX') \pi_{z.x}'$$
$$= -\alpha_u^2 E(U^2) \pi_{x_1.z_1|z_2}' \pi_{z.x_1|x_2}' + \alpha_u^4 E(U^2)^2 P_{z_1}^{-1} \pi_{z.x_1|x_2}' - \alpha_u^2 E(U^2) \pi_{z.x_1|x_2}'$$
$$- E(\epsilon_{x_1.z} X_2') \pi_{z.x_2|x_1}' - \alpha_u^2 E(U^2) \pi_{x_2.z_1|z_2}' \pi_{z.x_2|x_1}'.$$

Substituting for $-\alpha_u E(UX') \pi_{z.x}'$ in the above equality then gives

$$- E(\epsilon_{y.x}Z') - \alpha_u^2 E(U^2)\pi'_{x_1.z_1|z_2}\pi'_{z.x_1|x_2} + \alpha_u^4 E(U^2)^2 P_{z_1}^{-1}\pi'_{z.x_1|x_2}$$
$$- \alpha_u^2 E(U^2)\pi'_{z.x_1|x_2} - E(\epsilon_{x_1.z}X_2')\pi'_{z.x_2|x_1} - \alpha_u^2 E(U^2)\pi'_{x_2.z_1|z_2}\pi'_{z.x_2|x_1}$$
$$+ [\alpha_u^2 E(U^2), 0] = 0.$$

Collecting the first elements of this vector equality gives

$$- E(\epsilon_{y.x}Z_1') - \alpha_u^2 E(U^2)\pi'_{x_1.z_1|z_2}\pi'_{z_1.x_1|x_2} + \alpha_u^4 E(U^2)^2 P_{z_1}^{-1}\pi'_{z_1.x_1|x_2}$$
$$- \alpha_u^2 E(U^2)\pi'_{z_1.x_1|x_2} - E(\epsilon_{x_1.z}X_2')\pi'_{z_1.x_2|x_1} - \alpha_u^2 E(U^2)\pi'_{x_2.z_1|z_2}\pi'_{z_1.x_2|x_1}$$
$$+ \alpha_u^2 E(U^2) = 0.$$

This is a quadratic equation in $\alpha_u^2 E(U^2)$ of the from

$$a\alpha_u^4 E(U^2)^2 + b\alpha_u^2 E(U^2) + c = 0,$$

with

$$a = P_{z_1}^{-1}\pi'_{z_1.x_1|x_2},$$
$$b = -\pi'_{x.z_1|z_2}\pi'_{z_1.x} - \pi'_{z_1.x_1|x_2} + 1, \text{ and}$$
$$c = -E(\epsilon_{y.x}Z_1') - E(\epsilon_{x_1.z}X_2')\pi'_{z_1.x_2|x_1}.$$

The discriminant of this equation gives the expression for $\Delta_{PC} = b^2 - 4ac$ in Theorem 6.1 where it is shown that $\Delta_{PC} \geq 0$ and that the solutions to this quadratic equation are $\sigma^\dagger_{PC}$ and σ^*_{PC}:

$$\frac{-b \pm \sqrt{\Delta_{PC}}}{2a} = \frac{\pi'_{x.z_1|z_2}\pi'_{z_1.x} + \pi'_{z_1.x_1|x_2} - 1 \pm \sqrt{\Delta_{PC}}}{2P_{z_1}^{-1}\pi'_{z_1.x_1|x_2}}.$$

This then enables the identification of (β_o, γ_o) as shown in the proof of Theorem 6.1.

References

Altonji, J., T. Conley, T. Elder, and C. Taber (2011), "Methods for Using Selection on Observed Variables to Address Selection on Unobserved Variables", Yale University Department of Economics Working Paper.

Baltagi, B. (1999). Econometrics, 2nd Edition. Springer-Verlag, Berlin.

Blackburn, M. and D. Neumark (1992), "Unobserved Ability, Efficiency Wages, and Interindustry Wage Differentials", The Quarterly Journal of Economics, 107, 1421–1436.

Chalak, K. and H. White (2011), "An Extended Class of Instrumental Variables for the Estimation of Causal Effects", Canadian Journal of Economics, 44, 1–51.

Chamberlain, G. (1977), "Education, Income, and Ability Revisited", Journal of Econometrics, 241–257.

Frisch, R. and F. Waugh (1933), "Partial Regressions as Compared with Individual Trends", Econometrica, 1, 939–953.

Galvao, A., G. Montes-Rojasz, and S. Song (2012), "Endogeneity Bias Modeling Using Observables", University of Wisconsin-Milwaukee Department of Economics Working Paper.

Griliches, Z. (1977), "Estimating the Returns to Schooling: Some Econometric Problems", Econometrica, 45, 1–22.

Hausman, J. and W. Taylor (1983), "Identification in Linear Simultaneous Equations Models with Covariance Restrictions: An Instrumental Variables Interpretation", Econometrica, 51, 1527–1550.

Hoderlein, H., L. Su, and H. White (2011), "Specification Testing for Nonparametric Structural Models with Monotonicity in Unobservables", UCSD Department of Economics Working Paper.

Lewbel, A. (2010), "Using Heteroskedasticity to Identify and Estimate Mismeasured and Endogenous Regressor Models", Journal of Business and Economic Statistics, forthcoming.

Lovell, M., (1963), "Seasonal adjustment of economic time series," Journal of the American Statistical Association, 993–1010.

Matzkin, R. L. (1992), "Nonparametric and Distribution-Free Estimation of the Binary Threshold Crossing and the Binary Choice Models", Econometrica, 60, 239–270.

Mincer, J., (1974). Schooling, Experience, and Earning. New York: National Bureau of Economic Research.

White, H. (1980), "A Heteroskedasticity-Consistent Covariance Matrix Estimator and a Direct Test for Heteroskedasticity", Econometrica, 48, 817–838.

White, H. (2001). Asymptotic Theory for Econometricians. New York: Academic Press.

White, H. and K. Chalak (2010), "Testing a Conditional Form of Exogeneity", Economics Letters, 109, 88–90.

White and Chalak (2011), "Identification and Identification Failure for Treatment Effects using Structural Systems", Econometric Reviews, forthcoming.

White H. and X. Lu (2011a), "Causal Diagrams for Treatment Effect Estimation with Application to Efficient Covariate Selection", Review of Economics and Statistics, 93, 1453–1459.

White H. and X. Lu (2011b), "Robustness Checks and Robustness Tests in Applied Economics", UCSD Department of Economics Working Paper.

Wooldridge, J. M. (2002). Econometric Analysis of Cross Section and Panel Data. Cambridge: MIT Press.

Optimizing Robust Conditional Moment Tests: An Estimating Function Approach

Yi-Ting Chen and Chung-Ming Kuan

Abstract Robust conditional moment (RCM) tests for partial specifications are derived without a full specification assumption. Yet, researchers usually claim the optimality of these RCM tests by reinterpreting them as score tests under certain full specifications. This argument is in fact incompatible with the rationale of RCM tests. In this study, we consider a generalized RCM test based on the estimating function (EF) approach and explore a semi-parametric optimality criterion that does not require full specifications. Specifically, we derive the upper bound of the noncentrality parameter of the generalized RCM test and propose a method to optimize RCM tests so as to achieve this upper bound. The optimized RCM test is associated with the optimal EF method, and it is useful for improving the asymptotic local power of existing RCM tests. The proposed method thus permits researchers to pursue optimality without sacrificing robustness in estimating and testing partial specifications. We illustrate our method using various partial specifications and demonstrate the improved power property of the optimized tests by simulations.

Keywords Conditional mean-and-variance · Conditional quantile · Optimal estimating function · Quasi-maximum likelihood method · Robust conditional moment test · Semi-parametric optimality

1 Introduction

The correct specification of an econometric model can often be represented as a set of conditional moment (CM) restrictions and tested by checking the implied (finite-dimensional) unconditional moment restrictions. In the context of fully

Y.-T. Chen
Institute of Economics, Academia Sinica, Taipei, Taiwan

C.-M. Kuan (✉)
Department of Finance, National Taiwan University, Taipei, Taiwan
e-mail: ckuan@ntu.edu.tw

X. Chen and N. R. Swanson (eds.), *Recent Advances and Future Directions in Causality, Prediction, and Specification Analysis*, DOI: 10.1007/978-1-4614-1653-1_3,

specified conditional distribution models, Newey (1985) and Tauchen (1985) introduce a class of maximum-likelihood (ML)-based CM tests for static models; these tests are extended to dynamic models by White (1987). Such tests can be interpreted as Rao's score tests (Lagrange multiplier tests) for some parameter restrictions of conditional distribution models; see, e.g., White (1984, 1994), Chesher and Smith (1997), and Bera and Bilias (2001). An ML-based CM test is thus parametrically optimal against certain local alternatives *if* the conditional distribution is specified correctly.

Instead of specifying a complete model for conditional distribution, it is also common to postulate a partial specification, such as conditional mean, conditional mean-and-variance, or conditional quantile models. In this context, the ML-based CM tests need not be asymptotically valid because the underlying assumption of conditional distribution is likely to be misspecified. This motivates researchers to derive robust CM (RCM) tests without full specifications. For example, Wooldridge (1990a) propose a generalized RCM test based on "generalized residuals." This generalized test is also the omitted variable test of Davidson and MacKinnon (1990, 1993, 2000) for conditional-mean models and is readily applied to other partial specifications. RCM tests may also be obtained by replacing the ML method with certain quasi-ML (QML) methods, e.g., Wooldridge (1991), Berkes et al. (2003), Wong and Ling (2005), and Chen (2008).

Unlike test robustness, the optimality issue of RCM tests does not receive sufficient attention in the literature. Researchers usually reinterpret RCM tests as some ML-based CM tests (or score tests) and claim their parametric optimality. For example, the RCM tests for conditional mean (and variance) specifications are also the Gaussian ML-based CM tests under the conditional normality assumption and hence are as optimal as the latter when the full normality specification is correct. It is therefore said that the robustness of RCM tests "is obtained without sacrificing asymptotic efficiency" (Wooldridge 1990a). This optimality argument is, however, incompatible with the rationale of RCM tests. While parametric optimality requires full specifications being correctly specified, RCM tests are robust because they are constructed without full specifications. This suggests that the optimality of RCM tests should be studied under a different criterion.

The aim of this chapter is to explore "semi-parametric" optimality for RCM tests. We base our generalized RCM test on the estimating function (EF) approach, where the EF involves a generalized residual vector and a set of instrument variables. This generalized test encompasses many QML-based RCM tests for various partial specifications and is asymptotically equivalent to the test of Wooldridge (1990a). By exploring the noncentrality parameter of this generalized test, we observe that the parametric optimality of this test is crucially dependent on a generalized conditional homoskedasticity and standardization (GCHS) restriction, which requires the conditional covariance matrix of the generalized residual vector to be an identity matrix. Given this restriction, a generalized test can be understood as a score test if the associated EF is the same as the true score function. This motivates us to standardize the generalized residual vector using the matrix square root of its conditional covariance matrix for ensuring the GCHS restriction.

This standardization leads us to a particular version of the generalized RCM test. This test is parametrically optimal if its EF is the same as the true score function, whether or not the original GCHS restriction is satisfied. More importantly, it is semi-parametrically optimal in the sense that it achieves the upper bound of the non-centrality parameter of the generalized test without assuming a full specification. The associated EF is also Godambe (1960)-Durbin (1960)-optimal, in the sense that it attains the lower bound of the asymptotic covariance matrix of a generalized estimator for partial specifications; see, e.g., Godambe and Kale (1991), Vinod (1997), Mittelhammer et al. (2000), Bera et al. (2006) and the references therein for more discussions on the optimal EF. By combining the optimal EF method with this optimized test, we have an alternative approach to estimating and testing partial specifications in a semi-parametrically optimal way.

This approach has a simple generalized least square (GLS) interpretation in the linear regression context and depends on the conditional covariance matrix of the generalized residual vector. Since this matrix is typically unknown and needs to be estimated or approximated in applications, this approach would be semi-parametrically optimal if the conditional covariance matrix is consistently estimated; otherwise, this approach is suboptimal but remains robust. Thus, this approach permits us to *pursue asymptotic efficiency without sacrificing robustness* in estimating and testing partial specifications. To illustrate its usefulness, we consider the conditional mean, conditional mean-and-variance, and conditional quantile specifications. The GCHS restriction in these examples implies different higher order CM restrictions. Many existing RCM tests are likely to be suboptimal because they do not take into account these restrictions. The proposed method is therefore useful for improving the asymptotic local power of these suboptimal tests. We also demonstrate the proposed method in this respect using two Monte Carlo experiments.

The remainder of this chapter is organized as follows. In Sect. 2, we consider a generalized RCM test built on the EF approach. In Sect. 3, we provide examples of this generalized test in the conditional mean, mean-and-variance, and quantile contexts. In Sect. 4, we derive the upper bound of the noncentrality parameter, propose the optimized test, and link this test to the optimal EF method. We illustrate the applicability of the optimized test in Sect. 5, based on the examples in Sect. 3. Section 6 reports the simulation results. We conclude the chapter in Sect. 7. The Appendix summarizes some mathematical derivations.

2 A Generalized RCM Test

Let y_t be a finite-dimensional vector of dependent variable(s) with the time or cross-sectional index t, and $\mathcal{X}_t$ be the information set available in explaining y_t. Suppose that we are interested in testing a partial specification of $y_t|\mathcal{X}_t$ that has an $r \times 1$ vector of generalized residuals $\upsilon_t(\theta) := \upsilon_t(y_t, x_t; \theta)$ for some finite $r \geq \dim(y_t)$, in which x_t denotes a vector of $\mathcal{X}_t$-measurable explanatory variables, θ is a $p \times 1$ parameter vector in the compact set $\Theta \subset \mathbb{R}^p$. This partial specification is correctly specified if, and only if, the martingale difference condition,

$$H_o : \mathbb{E}[v_t(\theta_o)|\mathcal{X}_t] = 0, \tag{1}$$

is satisfied for some $\theta_o \in \Theta$. As in Wooldridge (1990a), we apply the concept of generalized residual to unify various partial specifications; see also Cox and Snell (1968), Gouriéroux et al. (1987), and Cameron and Trivedi (1998, Chap. 5). In certain applications, we may also be interested in testing

$$H_o' : \text{(1) and } v_t(\theta_o) \text{ is independent of } \mathcal{X}_t. \tag{2}$$

The following discussion focuses on H_o, but the results also hold for H_o' because the former is weaker than the latter.

Let $z_t(\theta)$ be a $q \times r$ matrix of $\mathcal{X}_t$-measurable misspecification indicators which may depend on the parameter vector θ, and $C_t(\theta)$ be an $r \times r$ $\mathcal{X}_t$-measurable weighting matrix that has a symmetric and positive-definite matrix square root $C_t(\theta)^{1/2}$ such that $C_t(\theta) = C_t(\theta)^{1/2}C_t(\theta)^{1/2}$. Denote the standardized vectors $v_t^s(\theta) := C_t(\theta)^{1/2}v_t(\theta)$ and $z_t^s(\theta) := z_t(\theta)C_t(\theta)^{1/2}$. Under H_o, the $q \times 1$ testing function $z_t^s(\theta)v_t^s(\theta)$ must satisfy the martingale difference condition:

$$\mathbb{E}[z_t^s(\theta_o)v_t^s(\theta_o)|\mathcal{X}_t] = z_t^s(\theta_o)\mathbb{E}[v_t^s(\theta_o)|\mathcal{X}_t] = 0, \tag{3}$$

which implies the unconditional moment restriction:

$$\mathbb{E}[z_t^s(\theta_o)v_t^s(\theta_o)] = 0. \tag{4}$$

Let T be the sample size, and $\{\theta_T\}$ be a sequence of parameters in Θ such that $\lim_{T\to\infty}\theta_T = \theta_o$. A testing of H_o that checks the validity of (4) is expected to be powerful against:

$$H_{1T} : \mathbb{E}[v_t(\theta_T)|\mathcal{X}_t] = z_t(\theta_T)^\top \delta T^{-1/2}, \tag{5}$$

with δ a $q \times 1$ non-zero vector, because $\mathbb{E}[z_t^s(\theta_T)v_t^s(\theta_T)|\mathcal{X}_t] = z_t^s(\theta_T)z_t^s(\theta_T)^\top \delta T^{-1/2}$ under H_{1T}. This implies that $\mathbb{E}[z_t^s(\theta_T)v_t^s(\theta_T)] = \mathbb{E}[z_t^s(\theta_T)z_t^s(\theta_T)^\top]\delta T^{-1/2}$ is a $q \times 1$ non-zero vector provided that $\mathbb{E}[z_t^s(\theta_T)z_t^s(\theta_T)^\top]$ is positive definite.

To check the validity of (4), we need to first estimate θ_o using the information implied by H_o. Let $\pi_t(\theta)$ be a $p \times r$ matrix of $\mathcal{X}_t$-measurable variables, and suppose that the row vectors of $\pi_t(\theta)$ and $z_t(\theta)$ are linearly independent of each other. In addition to (4), H_o also implies

$$\mathbb{E}[\pi_t(\theta_o)v_t(\theta_o)] = 0. \tag{6}$$

Using this information, we may estimate θ_o by the EF estimator $\bar{\theta}_T$, which solves the estimating equation:

$$\frac{1}{T}\sum_{t=1}^{T} g_t(\theta) = 0, \tag{7}$$

for some $g_t(\theta)$ from a class of linearly unbiased EFs:

$$\mathcal{G} := \{g_t(\theta)|g_t(\theta) = \pi_t(\theta)v_t(\theta)\}. \tag{8}$$

In this class of EFs, $g(\theta)$ and hence $\bar{\theta}_T$ are determined by the choice of $\pi_t(\theta)$; see, e.g., Bera and Bilias (2002) for a survey. Clearly, $\bar{\theta}_T$ can also be interpreted as a (just-identified) generalized-method-of-moments (GMM) estimator for θ_o.

Given the $p \times r$ matrix $w_t(\theta_o) := \left(\nabla_{\theta^\top}\mathbb{E}[v_t(\theta_o)|\mathcal{X}_t]\right)^\top$ which is evaluated under H_o, we denote $w_t(\theta)$ by using θ in place of the role of θ_o in $w_t(\theta_o)$. We also define $\hat{\theta}_T$ as the solution to (7) with the choice of $\pi_t(\theta) = -w_t(\theta)C_t(\theta)$. Put differently, $\hat{\theta}_T$ is a particular $\bar{\theta}_T$ with the EF:

$$g_t(\theta) = -w_t(\theta)C_t(\theta)v_t(\theta) = -w_t^s(\theta)v_t^s(\theta), \tag{9}$$

where $w_t^s(\theta) := w_t(\theta)C_t(\theta)^{1/2}$. Given this estimator, we can estimate $\mathbb{E}[z_t^s(\theta_o) v_t^s(\theta_o)]$ using the empirical moment $T^{-1}\sum_{t=1}^T z_t^s(\hat{\theta}_T)v_t^s(\hat{\theta}_T)$, and check (4) by evaluating the significance of this statistic. As will be discussed in Sect. 3, the estimator $\hat{\theta}_T$ encompasses the QML estimators (QMLEs) for some important partial specifications, and this EF approach is useful for unifying a number of existing tests proposed in different contexts.

Let $\Omega(\theta) := \mathbb{E}[\left(z_{wt}^s(\theta)v_t^s(\theta)\right)\left(z_{wt}^s(\theta)v_t^s(\theta)\right)^\top]$ be the $q \times q$ covariance matrix with

$$z_{wt}^s(\theta) := z_t^s(\theta) - \mathbb{E}[z_t^s(\theta)w_t^s(\theta)^\top]\mathbb{E}[w_t^s(\theta)w_t^s(\theta)^\top]^{-1}w_t^s(\theta). \tag{10}$$

The sample counterpart of $\Omega(\theta)$ is

$$\bar{\Omega}_T(\theta) := \frac{1}{T}\sum_{t=1}^{T}\left(\hat{z}_{w_t}^s(\theta)v_t^s(\theta)\right)\left(\hat{z}_{w_t}^s(\theta)v_t^s(\theta)\right)^\top,$$

with

$$\hat{z}_{w_t}^s(\theta) := z_t^s(\theta) - \left[\sum_{t=1}^{T} z_t^s(\theta)w_t^s(\theta)^\top\right]\left[\sum_{t=1}^{T} w_t^s(\theta)w_t^s(\theta)^\top\right]^{-1} w_t^s(\theta). \tag{11}$$

It is standard to derive the asymptotic distribution of $T^{-1/2}\sum_{t=1}^T z_t^s(\hat{\theta}_T)v_t^s(\hat{\theta}_T)$ under H_{1T}. This derivation involves a set of intermediate results that are presented as the "high-level" assumptions:

[A.1] The estimator $\bar{\theta}_T$ is consistent for θ_o and has the asymptotic linear representation:

$$\sqrt{T}(\bar{\theta}_T - \theta_o) = -\mathbb{E}[\pi_t(\theta_o)w_t(\theta_o)^\top]^{-1}\frac{1}{\sqrt{T}}\sum_{t=1}^{T}\pi_t(\theta_o)v_t(\theta_o) + o_{\mathbb{P}}(1). \quad (12)$$

[A.2] The statistic $T^{-1/2}\sum_{t=1}^{T} z_t^s(\bar{\theta}_T)v_t^s(\bar{\theta}_T)$ has the asymptotic expansion:

$$\frac{1}{\sqrt{T}}\sum_{t=1}^{T} z_t^s(\bar{\theta}_T)v_t^s(\bar{\theta}_T) = \frac{1}{\sqrt{T}}\sum_{t=1}^{T} z_t^s(\theta_o)v_t^s(\theta_o)$$
$$+ \mathbb{E}[z_t^s(\theta_o)w_t^s(\theta_o)^\top]\sqrt{T}(\bar{\theta}_T - \theta_o) + o_{\mathbb{P}}(1). \quad (13)$$

[A.3] The sequence $\{z_{w_t}^s(\theta_o)z_t^s(\theta_o)^\top\}$ is stationary and ergodic and $\{z_{w_t}^s(\theta_o)\big(v_t^s(\theta_o) - z_t^s(\theta_o)^\top\delta T^{-1/2}\big)\}$ obeys a central limit theorem (CLT).

[A.4] The statistic $\bar{\Omega}_T(\theta)$ is positive definite uniformly in T and θ and is uniformly consistent for $\Omega(\theta)$ over a neighborhood of θ_o.

These assumptions are quite standard for the first-order asymptotic analysis. Based on the GMM interpretation of $\bar{\theta}_T$, the consistency of $\bar{\theta}_T$ in [A.1] can be established using the conventional GMM theory, e.g., Hall (2005, Theorem 3.1). It is also common to obtain the asymptotic expansion in (12) when $\pi_t(\theta)v_t(\theta)$ is a smooth function of θ; see, e.g., Newey and McFadden (1994, Sect. 3). Similarly, the asymptotic expansion (13) in [A.2] can be obtained when $z_t^s(\theta)v_t^s(\theta)$ is a smooth function of θ, e.g., Wooldridge (1990a, pp. 40–42). In the Appendix, we provide a detailed discussion about [A.1] and [A.2] and their underlying conditions. Note that the asymptotic expansions in (12) and (13) may also hold when $\pi_t(\theta)v_t(\theta)$ and $z_t^s(\theta)v_t^s(\theta)$ are based on indicator functions of θ; see Phillips (1991), Andrews (1994, Sect. 3.2), and Newey and McFadden (1994, Sect. 7) for more discussions.

In [A.3], the stationarity and ergodicity of $\{z_{w_t}^s(\theta_o)z_t^s(\theta_o)^\top\}$ allow us to write $T^{-1}\sum_{t=1}^{T} z_{w_t}^s(\theta_o)z_t^s(\theta_o)^\top = \mathbb{E}[z_{w_t}^s(\theta_o)z_t^s(\theta_o)^\top]+o_{\mathbb{P}}(1)$ by the ergodic theorem when the elements of $z_{w_t}^s(\theta_o)z_t^s(\theta_o)^\top$ have finite absolute moments. Meanwhile, the CLT of $\{z_{w_t}^s(\theta_o)\big(v_t^s(\theta_o) - z_t^s(\theta_o)^\top\delta T^{-1/2}\big)\}$ is mainly due to the martingale difference property $\mathbb{E}[z_{w_t}^s(\theta_o)\big(v_t^s(\theta_o) - z_t^s(\theta_o)^\top\delta T^{-1/2}\big)|\mathcal{X}_t] = 0$ under H_{1T}; see White (White (1994), Theorem A.3.4) for a CLT for a double array of martingale difference and the associated technical conditions. This CLT requires that $\Omega(\theta_o)$ exists and has finite elements. This implicitly assumes that the matrix $\mathbb{E}[w_t^s(\theta_o)w_t^s(\theta_o)^\top]$ must be positive definite. In [A.4], the positive-definiteness condition is standard in defining a chi-square test statistic. This condition also requires that $\sum_{t=1}^{T} w_t^s(\theta)w_t^s(\theta)^\top$ is uniformly positive definite. In addition, the uniform consistency of $\bar{\Omega}_T(\theta)$ for $\Omega(\theta)$ holds when $\{w_t^s(\theta)w_t^s(\theta)^\top\}$, $\{z_t^s(\theta)w_t^s(\theta)^\top\}$, and $\{(z_{w_t}^s(\theta)v_t^s(\theta))(z_{w_t}^s(\theta)v_t^s(\theta))^\top\}$ are stationary and ergodic for each $\theta \in \Theta$ and obey a uniform law of larger numbers (ULLN); see, e.g., White (1994, Theorem A.2.2).

Given $\bar{\theta}_T = \hat{\theta}_T$, we can use (12), with the choice of $\pi_t(\theta) = -w_t(\theta)C_t(\theta)$, and (13) to show that

$$\frac{1}{\sqrt{T}}\sum_{t=1}^{T} z_t^s(\hat{\theta}_T)v_t^s(\hat{\theta}_T) = \frac{1}{\sqrt{T}}\sum_{t=1}^{T} z_{w_t}^s(\theta_o)v_t^s(\theta_o) + o_p(1)$$
$$= \frac{1}{\sqrt{T}}\sum_{t=1}^{T} z_{w_t}^s(\theta_o)\left(v_t^s(\theta_o) - z_t^s(\theta_o)^\top \delta T^{-1/2}\right)$$
$$+\left[\frac{1}{T}\sum_{t=1}^{T} z_{w_t}^s(\theta_o)z_t^s(\theta_o)^\top\right]\delta + o_p(1). \tag{14}$$

By [A.3] and the fact that $\mathbb{E}[z_{w_t}^s(\theta_o)w_t^s(\theta_o)^\top] = 0$, we then have under H_{1T} that

$$\frac{1}{\sqrt{T}}\sum_{t=1}^{T} z_t^s(\hat{\theta}_T)v_t^s(\hat{\theta}_T) \xrightarrow{\text{d}} N\left(\mathbb{E}[z_{w_t}^s(\theta_o)z_{w_t}^s(\theta_o)^\top]\delta,\, \Omega(\theta_o)\right). \tag{15}$$

Denote the $r \times r$ conditional covariance matrices:

$$\Sigma_t(\theta_o) := \mathbb{E}[v_t(\theta_o)v_t(\theta_o)^\top|\mathcal{X}_t] \tag{16}$$

and

$$\Sigma_t^s(\theta_o) := \mathbb{E}[v_t^s(\theta_o)v_t^s(\theta_o)^\top|\mathcal{X}_t] = C_t(\theta_o)^{1/2}\Sigma_t(\theta_o)C_t(\theta_o)^{1/2}. \tag{17}$$

We now define the generalized RCM test as

$$M_T = \left[\sum_{t=1}^{T} z_t^s(\hat{\theta}_T)v_t^s(\hat{\theta}_T)\right]^\top \left[\sum_{t=1}^{T}(\hat{z}_{w_t}^s(\hat{\theta}_T)v_t^s(\hat{\theta}_T))(\hat{z}_{w_t}^s(\hat{\theta}_T)v_t^s(\hat{\theta}_T))^\top\right]^{-1}$$
$$\times\left[\sum_{t=1}^{T} z_t^s(\hat{\theta}_T)v_t^s(\hat{\theta}_T)\right], \tag{18}$$

which will be referred to as the M test. In the light of (15), we can estimate $\Omega(\theta_o)$ by $\bar{\Omega}_T(\hat{\theta}_T)$ and obtain the following result.

Proposition 1 *Given [A.1]–[A.4],*

$$M_T \xrightarrow{\text{d}} \begin{cases} \chi^2(q), & \text{under } H_o, \\ \chi^2(q;\,\nu), & \text{under } H_{1T}, \end{cases}$$

with the noncentrality parameter:

$$\nu := \delta^\top\left(\mathbb{E}[z_{w_t}^s(\theta_o)z_{w_t}^s(\theta_o)^\top]\mathbb{E}[z_{w_t}^s(\theta_o)\Sigma_t^s(\theta_o)z_{w_t}^s(\theta_o)]^{-1}\mathbb{E}[z_{w_t}^s(\theta_o)z_{w_t}^s(\theta_o)^\top]\right)\delta. \tag{19}$$

The M test defines a class of RCM tests that, with suitable $v_t^s(\theta)$'s (and $z_t^s(\theta)$'s), are readily applied to check various partial specifications. The M test is robust to the unknown conditional distribution of $y_t|\mathcal{X}_t$ because the martingale difference property of the moment function $z_t^s(\theta)v_t^s(\theta)$ and the EF in (9) under H_o, as well as the consistency of $\bar{\Omega}_T(\hat{\theta}_T)$ for $\Omega(\theta_o)$, does not require a full specification. It is worth emphasizing that the asymptotic local power of the M test increases in the noncentrality parameter υ, which depends on the choice of $C_t(\theta)$. We will explore this issue again in Sect. 4.

In some applications, we need to extend $z_t(\theta)$ to admit a nuisance parameter vector ς and will write $z_t(\theta, \varsigma)$; see Sects. 4.1 and 6 for examples. Let $\bar{\varsigma}_T$ be a $T^{1/2}$-consistent estimator for some ς_o in the parameter space of ς. As discussed in Wooldridge (1990a), the asymptotic validity of an RCM test is not affected if we replace $z_t(\bar{\theta}_T)$ with $z_t(\bar{\theta}_T, \bar{\varsigma}_T)$, because the estimation effect generated by $\bar{\varsigma}_T$ is asymptotically negligible. For the same reason, we can use $z_t(\hat{\theta}_T, \bar{\varsigma}_T)$ in place of the role of $z_t(\hat{\theta}_T)$ in the M test without affecting its asymptotic validity.

The M test is asymptotically equivalent to Wooldridge (1990a) test:

$$W_T := \left[\sum_{t=1}^{T} \hat{z}_{w_t}^s(\bar{\theta}_T)v_t^s(\bar{\theta}_T)\right]^\top \left[\sum_{t=1}^{T} (\hat{z}_{w_t}^s(\bar{\theta}_T)v_t^s(\bar{\theta}_T))(\hat{z}_{w_t}^s(\bar{\theta}_T)v_t^s(\bar{\theta}_T))^\top\right]^{-1} \times \left[\sum_{t=1}^{T} \hat{z}_{w_t}^s(\bar{\theta}_T)v_t^s(\bar{\theta}_T)\right], \tag{20}$$

which can be computed as TR^2, where R^2 is the uncentered coefficient of determination from the artificial regression of 1 on $\hat{z}_{w_t}^s(\bar{\theta}_T)v_t^s(\bar{\theta}_T)$; see also Davidson and MacKinnon (1985) for a conditional mean example. Compared with the M test, W_T uses $\hat{z}_{w_t}^s(\bar{\theta}_T)$ in place of the role of $z_t^s(\bar{\theta}_T)$ in (13). This replacement is in spirit similar to the transformation in the $C(\alpha)$ test of Neyman (1959). While the $C(\alpha)$ test is designed for a full specification, W_T is for partial specifications; see Bera and Bilias (2001) for more discussion about the $C(\alpha)$ test. Note that by the restriction: $\mathbb{E}[z_{w_t}^s(\theta_o)w_t^s(\theta_o)^\top] = 0$, the estimation effect in (13) can be eliminated so that

$$\frac{1}{\sqrt{T}}\sum_{t=1}^{T} \hat{z}_{w_t}^s(\bar{\theta}_T)v_t^s(\bar{\theta}_T) = \frac{1}{\sqrt{T}}\sum_{t=1}^{T} z_{w_t}^s(\theta_o)v_t^s(\theta_o) + o_p(1). \tag{21}$$

Observe that the right-hand side of (21) is the same as the right-hand side of the first equality of (14). It follows that W_T is asymptotically equivalent to M_T; clearly, W_T would be the same as M_T when $\bar{\theta}_T = \hat{\theta}_T$. Moreover, W_T can be presented as a (conditional-heteroskedasticity-)robust Wald test statistic for checking the parameter restriction $\gamma = 0_{q\times 1}$ of the artificial regression:

$$v_t^s(\bar{\theta}_T) = w_t^s(\bar{\theta}_T)^\top\beta + z_t^s(\bar{\theta}_T)^\top\gamma + \text{error term}, \tag{22}$$

with β a $p \times 1$ parameter vector. Thus, we can also interpret W_T (or M_T) as an omitted variable test; see Davidson and MacKinnon (1990, 1993, 2000), Basawa (1991), MacKinnon (1992), Cameron and Trivedi (1998, 2005), and Godfrey and Orme (2001, Sects. 3.2 and 3.3).

Although the M test defines a wide class of RCM tests, it does not encompass nonparametric tests, score tests, and model selection tests. While the M test is based on a finite-dimensional moment restriction of H_o (or H_o'), the nonparametric test is for an infinite-dimensional moment restriction of the same hypothesis; see, e.g., Bierens (1982, 1994). An advantage of the nonparametric test over the M test is the consistency of testing H_o against all possible misspecifications in large samples. Nonetheless, the M test can be made powerful against specific misspecification by choosing a suitable $z_t(\theta)$; this advantage is especially important for refining a misspecified model. Compared with the M test, the score test also checks a finite-dimensional moment restriction, but it is developed from a conditional distribution assumption. The score test would be parametrically optimal or efficient (to be discussed in Sect. 4.1) if this assumption is true. However, the score test need not be optimal for partial specifications. The robustness to the unknown conditional distribution is an important advantage of the M test relative to the score test. The model selection test could also be based on a finite-dimensional moment restriction, but it focuses on the relative performance of models and does not deal with model correctness; see, e.g., Vuong (1989). Thus, the model selection test and the M test have different usages in empirical applications.

3 Examples: RCM Tests

In this section, we discuss a number of existing CM tests with $\dim(y_t) = 1$, provide the practical forms of $v_t(\theta)$, $w_t(\theta)$, $z_t(\theta)$, and $C_t(\theta)$ in the conditional mean, mean-and-variance, and quantile contexts, and demonstrate the general applicability of the M test in generating RCM tests.

3.1 Conditional-Mean Context

In the conditional-mean context, the partial specification of interest is the regression:

$$y_t = \mu_t(\theta) + u_t, \tag{23}$$

where $\mu_t(\theta)$ is a $\mathcal{X}_t$-measurable conditional mean specification for $y_t|\mathcal{X}_t$ and a smooth function of θ, and $u_t = u_t(\theta)$ denotes the error term. This model is correctly specified for $\mathbb{E}[y_t|\mathcal{X}_t]$ under H_o with $v_t(\theta) = u_t(\theta)$. This $v_t(\theta)$ implies that $w_t(\theta) = -\nabla_\theta \mu_t(\theta)$.

In the literature, there exist a variety of CM tests that check model (23) in different power directions by examining condition (4) with $v_t(\theta) = u_t(\theta), C_t(\theta) = 1$, and various $z_t(\theta)$'s. Examples include the tests of Breusch (1978), Godfrey (1978), and Dezhbakhsh (1990) that choose $z_t(\theta) = (u_{t-1}(\theta), \ldots, u_{t-m}(\theta))^\top$ for testing a linear regression against the remaining serial correlation. Similar to Ramsey (1969) regression specification error test (RESET), the tests of Keenan (1985), Tsay (1986), Luukkonen et al. (1988), Lee et al. (1993), and Eitrheim and Teräsvirta (1996) check model (23) against the remaining nonlinearity by choosing some nonlinear $z_t(\theta)$'s. The non-nested tests of Davidson and MacKinnon (1981) and Fisher and McAleer (1981) check model (23) against a competing model by setting $z_t(\theta, \varsigma)$ according to the difference between the non-nested specifications, where θ and ς are respectively, the parameter vectors of the model being tested and the alternative model. These existing tests are often presented as score tests under the conditional normality assumption: $u_t(\theta_o)|\mathcal{X}_t \sim N(0, \sigma_u^2)$, with $\sigma_u^2 := \mathbb{E}[u_t(\theta_o)^2]$.

By applying the M test in (18) to $v_t(\theta) = u_t(\theta)$, $w_t(\theta) = -\nabla_\theta \mu_t(\theta)$, $C_t(\theta) = 1$, and the aforementioned $z_t(\theta)$'s, we can easily make these existing tests free of the conditional normality assumption or the conditional homoskedasticity assumption: $\sigma_{u_t}^2 = \sigma_u^2$, where $\sigma_{u_t}^2 := \mathbb{E}[u_t(\theta_o)^2|\mathcal{X}_t]$. In this case, $\hat{\theta}_T$ is the least square (LS) estimator for θ_o because the EF in (9) is

$$g_t(\theta) = \nabla_\theta \mu_t(\theta) u_t(\theta).$$

The resulting RCM tests are asymptotically equivalent to the robust conditional mean tests in Wooldridge (1990b) that are obtained by Wooldridge (1990a) approach.

3.2 Conditional Mean-and-Variance Context

In the conditional mean-and-variance context, the partial specification is a location-scale model:

$$y_t = \mu_t(\theta) + h_t(\theta)^{1/2}\varepsilon_t, \tag{24}$$

where $h_t(\theta)$ is a $\mathcal{X}_t$-measurable conditional variance specification for $y_t|\mathcal{X}_t$ and a smooth function of θ, and $\varepsilon_t = \varepsilon_t(\theta)$ represents the standardized error with zero mean and unit variance. This model extends (23) by specifying the regression error as $u_t = h_t(\theta)^{1/2}\varepsilon_t$, and it is correctly specified for $\mathbb{E}[y_t|\mathcal{X}_t]$ and $\operatorname{var}[y_t|\mathcal{X}_t]$ under H_o with $v_t(\theta) = (\varepsilon_t(\theta), \varepsilon_t(\theta)^2 - 1)^\top$. It is also easy to see that $w_t(\theta) = -\left(\nabla_\theta \mu_t(\theta) h_t(\theta)^{-1/2}, \nabla_\theta h_t(\theta) h_t(\theta)^{-1}\right)^\top$.

Given the specification $\mu_t(\theta)$, there exist numerous CM tests that check the conditional variance specification of model (24) by examining condition (4) with $v_t(\theta) = \varepsilon_t(\theta)^2 - 1$, $C_t(\theta) = 1$, and various $z_t(\theta)$'s. Examples include the conditional heteroskedasticity tests of Breusch and Pagan (1979), White (1980), Engle (1982b), and McLeod and Li (1983) for the conditional-homoskedasticity model: $h_t(\theta_o) = \sigma_u^2$. In the generalized autoregressive conditional heteroskedasticity (GARCH) literature, examples also include the modified McLeod-Li test proposed by Li and Mak (1994) that chooses $z_t(\theta) = (\varepsilon_{t-1}(\theta)^2 - 1, \ldots, \varepsilon_{t-m}(\theta)^2 - 1)^\top$ for checking a GARCH-type $h_t(\theta)$ against remaining volatility clustering, the news impact curve test of Engle and

Ng (1993) that checks a GARCH-type $h_t(\theta)$ against remaining volatility asymmetry by setting $z_t(\theta) = I(\varepsilon_{t-1}(\theta) < 0)$, with the indicator function $I(\varepsilon_{t-1}(\theta) < 0) = 1$ if $\varepsilon_{t-1}(\theta) < 0$ and otherwise zero, and the tests of Lundbergh and Teräsvirta (2002). Similar to the tests in Sect. 3.1, these tests are often presented as score tests by adding the conditional normality assumption: $\varepsilon_t(\theta_o)|\mathcal{X}_t \sim N(0, 1)$ to model (24).

We can also remove the conditional normality assumption and estimate θ_o using the Gaussian QML method. This method shares the same log-likelihood function $T^{-1}\sum_{t=1}^{T} \ln f_t(\theta)$ as the Gaussian ML method, with the conditional normal probability density function (PDF):

$$f_t(\theta) = \frac{1}{\sqrt{2\pi} h_t(\theta)^{1/2}} \exp\left(-\frac{1}{2h_t(\theta)}(y_t - \mu_t(\theta))^2\right). \tag{25}$$

However, the asymptotic properties of the Gaussian QMLE are established without the conditional normality assumption; see, e.g., Bollerslev and Wooldridge (1992). In the GARCH literature, a number of RCM tests have been proposed for testing the independence hypothesis H_o' by using this QML method. Specifically, Berkes et al. (2003) used this QML method to robustify the Li-Mak test for H_o' in the presence of conditional non-normality. Wong and Ling (2005) derived an omnibus test for H_o' against the remaining serial correlation and volatility clustering based on $v_t(\theta) = (\varepsilon_t(\theta), \varepsilon_t(\theta)^2 - 1)^\top$. See also Chen (2008) for further extensions.

Let I_r be the $r \times r$ identity matrix. Note that we can rewrite the $v_t(\theta)$ for model (24) as:

$$v_t(\theta) = \left(\varepsilon_t(\theta), \frac{1}{\sqrt{2}}(\varepsilon_t(\theta)^2 - 1)\right)^\top \tag{26}$$

without distorting H_o. By applying the M test to this $v_t(\theta)$,

$$w_t(\theta) = -\left(\frac{\nabla_\theta \mu_t(\theta)}{h_t(\theta)^{1/2}}, \frac{\nabla_\theta h_t(\theta)}{\sqrt{2} h_t(\theta)}\right)^\top, \tag{27}$$

$C_t(\theta) = I_2$, and various $z_t(\theta)$'s, we can easily generate different RCM tests. The associated $\hat{\theta}_T$ is the Gaussian QMLE for θ_o because the EF in (9) is

$$g_t(\theta) = \frac{\nabla_\theta \mu_t(\theta)}{h_t(\theta)^{1/2}} \varepsilon_t(\theta) + \frac{\nabla_\theta h_t(\theta)}{2h_t(\theta)} \left(\varepsilon_t(\theta)^2 - 1\right), \tag{28}$$

so that the estimating equation with (28) is the same as the first-order condition of the Gaussian QML method. This particular M test extends the applicability of the aforementioned Gaussian QML-based tests for H_o. Wooldridge (1990a, Examples 3.2), considered a W_T-based conditional variance test with $v_t(\theta) = u_t(\theta)^2 - h_t(\theta)$ and $C_t(\theta)^{1/2} = h_t(\theta)^{-1}$, which is asymptotically equivalent to this M test, with $z_t(\theta)$ replaced by $(0_{q\times 1}, z_t(\theta))$. Lundbergh and Teräsvirta (2002) applied Wooldridge (1990a) approach to make their Gaussian ML-based score tests robust to conditional non-normality. These robust tests can also be linked to this particular M test.

3.3 Conditional Quantile Context

In the conditional quantile context, the partial specification is the quantile regression:

$$y_t = m_{\tau,t}(\theta) + u_t, \tag{29}$$

where $m_{\tau,t}(\theta)$ is a $\mathcal{X}_t$-measurable specification for the τ-th conditional quantile of $y_t|\mathcal{X}_t$ and a smooth function of θ, and $u_t(\theta)$ denotes the error term. This model is correctly specified under H_o with $v_t(\theta) = I(u_t(\theta) < 0) - \tau$. Let $p(\cdot|\mathcal{X}_t)$ be the conditional PDF of $u_t(\theta_o)|\mathcal{X}_t$. Under H_o, this $v_t(\theta)$ implies that $\mathbb{E}[v_t(\theta)|\mathcal{X}_t] = \int_{-\infty}^{m_{\tau,t}(\theta)} p(y - m_{\tau,t}(\theta_o)|\mathcal{X}_t)\mathrm{d}y - \tau$ and hence $w_t(\theta_o) = p(0|\mathcal{X}_t)\nabla_\theta m_{\tau,t}(\theta_o)$.

Given the tick function $\rho_\tau(u) := u(\tau - I(u < 0))$, $u \in \mathbb{R}$, θ_o can be estimated by minimizing

$$\frac{1}{T}\sum_{t=1}^{T} \rho_\tau(y_t - m_{\tau,t}(\theta));$$

see Koenker and Bassett (1978). The resulting estimator for θ_o is also the asymmetric Laplace QMLE and encompassed by the tick-exponential QMLE of Komunjer (2005). In addition, this estimator satisfies the asymptotic first-order condition:

$$\frac{1}{T}\sum_{t=1}^{T} \nabla_\theta m_{\tau,t}(\theta)\left(I(u_t(\theta) < 0) - \tau\right) = o_p(1), \tag{30}$$

and has asymptotic normality with the asymptotic covariance matrix:

$$\begin{aligned} V_\tau(\theta_o) := {}& \tau(1-\tau)\mathbb{E}[p(0|\mathcal{X}_t)\nabla_\theta m_{\tau,t}(\theta_o)\nabla_\theta m_{\tau,t}(\theta_o)^\top]^{-1} \\ & \times \mathbb{E}[\nabla_\theta m_{\tau,t}(\theta_o)\nabla_\theta m_{\tau,t}(\theta_o)^\top]\mathbb{E}[p(0|\mathcal{X}_t)\nabla_\theta m_{\tau,t}(\theta_o)\nabla_\theta m_{\tau,t}(\theta_o)^\top]^{-1}; \end{aligned} \tag{31}$$

see, e.g., Engle and Manganelli (2004, Theorem 2) and Koenker (2005, p. 124).

By applying the M test to $v_t(\theta) = I(u_t(\theta) < 0) - \tau$, $w_t(\theta) = p(0|\mathcal{X}_t)\nabla_\theta m_{\tau,t}(\theta)$, $C_t(\theta) = p(0|\mathcal{X}_t)^{-1}$, and various z_t's and by estimating $p(0|\mathcal{X}_t)$, we can generate different RCM tests. The associated $\hat{\theta}_T$ is based on the EF:

$$g_t(\theta) = -\nabla_\theta m_{\tau,t}(\theta)\left(I(u_t(\theta) < 0) - \tau\right), \tag{32}$$

which can be seen by introducing these $v_t(\theta)$, $w_t(\theta)$, and $C_t(\theta)$ into (9). This $\hat{\theta}_T$ is asymptotically equivalent to the asymmetric Laplace QMLE for θ_o. To see this point, note that since $\{\pi_t(\theta_o)v_t(\theta_o)\}$ is a martingale difference sequence under H_o, we may use (12) and a martingale difference CLT to show the result:

$$\sqrt{T}(\bar{\theta}_T - \theta_o) \xrightarrow{\mathrm{d}} N(0, V(\theta_o)), \tag{33}$$

in which the asymptotic covariance matrix $V(\theta_o)$ is of the "sandwich" form:

$$V(\theta_o) := \mathbb{E}[\pi_t(\theta_o)w_t(\theta_o)^\top]^{-1}\mathbb{E}[(\pi_t(\theta_o)v_t(\theta_o))\,(\pi_t(\theta_o)v_t(\theta_o))^\top]\mathbb{E}[w_t(\theta_o)\pi_t(\theta_o)^\top]^{-1},$$
$$= \mathbb{E}[\pi_t(\theta_o)w_t(\theta_o)^\top]^{-1}\mathbb{E}[\pi_t(\theta_o)\Sigma_t(\theta_o)\pi_t(\theta_o)^\top]\mathbb{E}[w_t(\theta_o)\pi_t(\theta_o)^\top]^{-1}, \qquad (34)$$

where the last equality is due to the law of iterated expectations. This result holds for general $\bar{\theta}_T$. By plugging $\pi_t(\theta) = -w_t(\theta)C_t(\theta)$ and $w_t(\theta)$ and $C_t(\theta)$ above into (34) and using the fact that $\Sigma_t(\theta_o) = \tau(1-\tau)$, we have $V(\theta_o) = V_\tau(\theta_o)$. This verifies that $\hat{\theta}_T$ is asymptotically equivalent to the asymmetric Laplace QMLE for θ_o.

The M test here is closely related to the dynamic quantile test of Engle and Manganelli (2004, Theorem 4) that checks condition (4) with $v_t(\theta) = I(u_t(\theta) < 0) - \tau$ and $C_t(\theta) = 1$. These two tests coincide when $p(0|\mathcal{X}_t)$ is a constant for all t's.

4 Optimization

4.1 Parametric Optimality

Let $f_t(\cdot|\mathcal{X}_t;\theta,\gamma)$ be a postulated conditional PDF of $y_t|\mathcal{X}_t$ with the score functions: $\ell_{\theta t}(\theta) := \nabla_\theta \ln f_t(y_t|\mathcal{X}_t;\theta,\gamma)$ and $\ell_{\gamma t}(\theta) := \nabla_\gamma \ln f_t(y_t|\mathcal{X}_t;\theta,\gamma)$. Suppose that H_o corresponds to the parameter restriction $\gamma = 0_{q\times 1}$ and H_{1T} corresponds to $\gamma = \delta T^{-1/2}$. Also let $\hat{\theta}_{\mathrm{ML}}$ be the MLE for θ_o under H_o. It is well known that the score test,

$$S_T := \left[\sum_{t=1}^{T}\ell_{\gamma t}(\hat{\theta}_{\mathrm{ML}})\right]^\top \left(\left[\sum_{t=1}^{T}\ell_{\gamma t}(\hat{\theta}_{\mathrm{ML}})\ell_{\gamma t}(\hat{\theta}_{\mathrm{ML}})^\top\right] - \left[\sum_{t=1}^{T}\ell_{\gamma t}(\hat{\theta}_{\mathrm{ML}})\ell_{\theta t}(\hat{\theta}_{\mathrm{ML}})^\top\right]\right.$$
$$\left.\times\left[\sum_{t=1}^{T}\ell_{\theta t}(\hat{\theta}_{\mathrm{ML}})\ell_{\theta t}(\hat{\theta}_{\mathrm{ML}})^\top\right]^{-1}\left[\sum_{t=1}^{T}\ell_{\theta t}(\hat{\theta}_{\mathrm{ML}})\ell_{\gamma t}(\hat{\theta}_{\mathrm{ML}})^\top\right]\right)^{-1}\left[\sum_{t=1}^{T}\ell_{\gamma t}(\hat{\theta}_{\mathrm{ML}})\right], \qquad (35)$$

is asymptotically most powerful for checking H_o against H_{1T}, if $f_t(y_t|\mathcal{X}_t;\theta,\gamma)$ is the true conditional PDF of $y_t|\mathcal{X}_t$; see also Newey (1985) for its optimal CM test interpretation. In this full specification context, S_T has the asymptotic distribution:

$$S_T \xrightarrow{\mathrm{d}} \begin{cases} \chi^2(q), & \text{under } H_o, \\ \chi^2(q;\nu^\dagger), & \text{under } H_{1T}, \end{cases}$$

with the noncentrality parameter:

$$\nu^{\dagger} := \delta^{\top}\Big(\mathbb{E}[\ell_{\gamma t}(\theta_o)\ell_{\gamma t}(\theta_o)^{\top}] \\ - \mathbb{E}[\ell_{\gamma t}(\theta_o)\ell_{\theta t}(\theta_o)^{\top}]\mathbb{E}[\ell_{\theta t}(\theta_o)\ell_{\theta t}(\theta_o)^{\top}]^{-1}\mathbb{E}[\ell_{\theta t}(\theta_o)\ell_{\gamma t}(\theta_o)^{\top}]\Big)\delta; \quad (36)$$

see, e.g., Eq. (51) of Engle (1982a) and Eq. (8.11) of Basawa (1991).

Under the conditional distribution assumption: $\ell_{\theta t}(\theta) = -w_t^s(\theta)v_t^s(\theta)$ and $\ell_{\gamma t}(\theta) = -z_t^s(\theta)v_t^s(\theta)$, we can write that $\hat{\theta}_T = \hat{\theta}_{\mathrm{ML}}$ and express the M test statistic in (18) as:

$$M_T = \left[\sum_{t=1}^{T}\ell_{\gamma t}(\hat{\theta}_{\mathrm{ML}})\right]^{\top}\left[\sum_{t=1}^{T}(\hat{z}^s_{w_t}(\hat{\theta}_{\mathrm{ML}})v_t^s(\hat{\theta}_{\mathrm{ML}}))(\hat{z}^s_{w_t}(\hat{\theta}_{\mathrm{ML}})v_t^s(\hat{\theta}_{\mathrm{ML}}))^{\top}\right]^{-1} \\ \times\left[\sum_{t=1}^{T}\ell_{\gamma t}(\hat{\theta}_{\mathrm{ML}})\right], \quad (37)$$

in which

$$\hat{z}^s_{w_t}(\theta)v_t^s(\theta) = -\left(\ell_{\gamma t}(\theta) - \left[\sum_{t=1}^{T}z_t^s(\theta)w_t^s(\theta)^{\top}\right]\left[\sum_{t=1}^{T}w_t^s(\theta)w_t^s(\theta)^{\top}\right]^{-1}\ell_{\theta t}(\theta)\right)$$

by (11). In general, this statistic needs not be asymptotically equivalent to the score test statistic (35). It is readily seen that, given

$$\Sigma_t^s(\theta_o) = I_r, \quad (38)$$

we can write $\mathbb{E}[z_t^s(\theta_o)w_t^s(\theta_o)^{\top}] = \mathbb{E}[\ell_{\gamma t}(\theta_o)\ell_{\theta t}(\theta_o)^{\top}]$ and $\mathbb{E}[w_t^s(\theta_o)w_t^s(\theta_o)^{\top}] = \mathbb{E}[\ell_{\theta t}(\theta_o)\ell_{\theta t}(\theta_o)^{\top}]$ by the law of iterated expectations. The restriction (38) will be referred to as the GCHS restriction, because it extends the conditional homoskedasticity and standardization restriction: $\mathbb{E}[v_t^2(\theta_o)|\mathcal{X}_t] = \mathbb{E}[v_t(\theta_o)^2]$ and $\mathbb{E}[v_t(\theta_o)^2] = 1$ from the special case $C_t(\theta) = 1$ to a general $C_t(\theta)$. The GCHS restriction yields asymptotic equivalence between (35) and (37) and also permits simplification of (19):

$$\nu = \delta^{\top}(\mathbb{E}[z^s_{w_t}(\theta_o)z^s_{w_t}(\theta_o)^{\top}])\delta, \\ = \delta^{\top}\Big(\mathbb{E}[z_t^s(\theta_o)z_t^s(\theta_o)^{\top}] \\ - \mathbb{E}[z_t^s(\theta_o)w_t^s(\theta_o)^{\top}]\mathbb{E}[w_t^s(\theta_o)w_t^s(\theta_o)^{\top}]^{-1}\mathbb{E}[w_t^s(\theta_o)z_t^s(\theta_o)^{\top}]\Big)\delta. \quad (39)$$

This ν is the same as $\nu^{\dagger}$ under the conditional distribution assumption. Thus, under the conditional distribution assumption and the GCHS restriction, the M test has the score test interpretation and hence is "parametrically optimal" for checking H_o against H_{1T}.

It is interesting to note that when $\ell_{\theta t}(\theta) = -w_t^s(\theta)v_t^s(\theta)$, we have $\mathbb{E}[\nabla_{\theta^\top}\ell_{\theta t}(\theta_o)] = -\mathbb{E}[w_t^s(\theta_o)w_t^s(\theta_o)^\top]$ under H_o. Recall that under the GCHS restriction, $\mathbb{E}[w_t^s(\theta_o) w_t^s(\theta_o)^\top] = \mathbb{E}[\ell_{\theta t}(\theta_o)\ell_{\theta t}(\theta_o)^\top]$. Thus, the GCHS restriction is analogous to the information matrix equality on the conditional distribution assumption: $\mathbb{E}[\nabla_{\theta^\top}\ell_{\theta t}(\theta_o)] + \mathbb{E}[\ell_{\theta t}(\theta_o)\ell_{\theta t}(\theta_o)^\top] = 0$.

4.2 Semi-Parametric Optimality

It is clear that the GCHS restriction would not be automatically satisfied for $v_t^s(\theta)$ with a general weighting matrix $C_t(\theta)$. However, by choosing $C_t(\theta) = \Sigma_t(\theta_o)^{-1}$, $v_t^s(\theta)$ becomes the standardized version of the generalized residual vector:

$$v_t^*(\theta) := \Sigma_t(\theta_o)^{-1/2}v_t(\theta),$$

where $\Sigma_t(\theta_o)^{1/2}$ is a symmetric and positive-definite matrix square root of $\Sigma_t(\theta_o)$. It follows from the definition of $\Sigma_t^s(\theta_o)$ in (17), the GCHS restriction holds:

$$\mathbb{E}[v_t^*(\theta_o)v_t^*(\theta_o)^\top|\mathcal{X}_t] = \Sigma_t(\theta_o)^{-1/2}\Sigma_t(\theta_o)\Sigma_t(\theta_o)^{-1/2} = I_r. \tag{40}$$

In view of the discussion in Sect. 4.1, it is natural to consider $C_t(\theta) = \Sigma_t(\theta_o)^{-1}$ in exploring the optimality of the M test.

Given $C_t(\theta) = \Sigma_t(\theta_o)^{-1}$, we write

$$w_t^*(\theta) := w_t(\theta)\Sigma_t(\theta_o)^{-1/2}, \quad z_t^*(\theta) := z_t(\theta)\Sigma_t(\theta_o)^{-1/2}, \tag{41}$$

and

$$z_{wt}^*(\theta) := z_t^*(\theta) - \mathbb{E}[z_t^*(\theta)w_t^*(\theta)^\top]\mathbb{E}[w_t^*(\theta)w_t^*(\theta)^\top]^{-1}w_t^*(\theta). \tag{42}$$

Then by (40), we obtain a particular ν:

$$\nu^* = \delta^\top\Big(\mathbb{E}[z_t^*(\theta_o)z_t^*(\theta_o)^\top] - \mathbb{E}[z_t^*(\theta_o)w_t^*(\theta_o)^\top]\mathbb{E}[w_t^*(\theta_o)w_t^*(\theta_o)^\top]^{-1}\mathbb{E}[w_t^*(\theta_o)z_t^*(\theta_o)^\top]\Big)\delta. \tag{43}$$

The proposition below is a key result of this study, and its proof is given in the Appendix.

Proposition 2 $\nu \leq \nu^*$ *for all possible* $C_t(\theta)$*'s.*

This result shows that ν^* is the upper bound of the noncentrality parameters within a class of M tests that have the same $v_t(\theta)$ and $z_t(\theta)$ but different $C_t(\theta)$'s. As the

M test is asymptotically equivalent to Wooldridge (1990a) test, the noncentrality parameter v and Proposition 2 also apply to W_T which allows a general $\bar{\theta}_T$. Let M_T^* be a particular M_T with $C_t(\theta) = \Sigma_t(\theta_o)^{-1}$ and $\hat{\theta}_T^*$ a particular $\hat{\theta}_T$ that solves the estimating equation: $T^{-1}\sum_{t=1}^{T} g_t^*(\theta) = 0$, with

$$g_t^*(\theta) = -w_t(\theta)\Sigma_t(\theta_o)^{-1}v_t(\theta). \tag{44}$$

By Proposition 1, M_T^* has the asymptotic distribution:

$$M_T^* \xrightarrow{\text{d}} \begin{cases} \chi^2(q), & \text{under } H_o, \\ \chi^2(q; \nu^*), & \text{under} H_{1T}, \end{cases} \tag{45}$$

with the noncentrality parameter ν^*. It is then clear from Proposition 2 that the M^* test is the optimized M test because its noncentrality parameter is ν^*.

By applying (40) and the law of iterated expectations to (43), we can see that $\nu^* = \nu^\dagger$ under the conditional distribution assumption: $\ell_{\theta t}(\theta) = -w_t^*(\theta)v_t^*(\theta)$ and $\ell_{\gamma t}(\theta) = -z_t^*(\theta)v_t^*(\theta)$. In this case, the M^* test has the score test interpretation for checking H_o against H_{1T}, and the estimator $\hat{\theta}_T^*$ is the same as the MLE for θ_o. Unlike the case in Sect. 4.1, this parametric optimality holds without the original GCHS restriction (38). Moreover, the M^* test is semi-parametrically optimal because it achieves the upper bound of ν without requiring any conditional distribution assumption.

Since $\hat{\theta}_T^*$ is a particular $\bar{\theta}_T$ with the choice of $\pi_t(\theta) = -w_t(\theta)\Sigma_t(\theta_o)^{-1}$, we can follow (33) to write

$$\sqrt{T}(\hat{\theta}_T^* - \theta_o) \xrightarrow{\text{d}} N(0, V^*(\theta_o)), \tag{46}$$

where the covariance matrix

$$V^*(\theta_o) := \mathbb{E}[w_t(\theta_o)\Sigma_t(\theta_o)^{-1}w_t(\theta_o)^\top]^{-1}, \tag{47}$$

is obtained from the $V(\theta_o)$ in (34) with this choice of $\pi_t(\theta)$. The following result holds without full specification; see Newey (1993, p. 423) for a proof.

Proposition 3 *$V(\theta_o) - V^*(\theta_o)$ is positive semidefinite for possible $\pi_t(\theta)$'s.*

This result means that the $g_t^*(\theta)$ in (44) is the optimal EF of $\mathcal{G}$, and $\hat{\theta}_T^*$ is the asymptotically most efficient version of $\bar{\theta}_T$. The optimal EF was first introduced by Godambe (1960) and Durbin (1960) for simple regressions and extended by Godambe (1985) and Godambe and Thompson (1989) to multiple linear regressions; see also Bera et al. (2006) for a recent survey. In the GMM literature, $\pi_t(\theta) = -w_t(\theta)\Sigma_t(\theta_o)^{-1}$ is known as the optimal instrument variable; see Chamberlain (1987) and Newey (1990, 1993). Also, the optimal EF has an information-matrix-equality-like interpretation under H_o, i.e.,

$$\mathbb{E}[\nabla_{\theta^\top} g_t^*(\theta_o)] + \mathbb{E}[g_t^*(\theta_o)g_t^*(\theta_o)^\top] = 0,$$

whether or not $g_t^*(\theta)$ is the same as the true score function. As discussed by Heyde (1997, p. 13), $g_t^*(\theta)$ is closer to the true score function (with respect to θ) than any other members of $\mathcal{G}$. As such, $g_t^*(\theta)$ may also be understood as the best "quasi-score" function for a partial specification.

It should be emphasized that, unlike the parametric optimality of the score test (the MLE), the semiparametric optimality of the M^* test (the estimator $\hat{\theta}_T^*$) is obtained without a full specification. Compared to the noncentrality parameter $\nu^\dagger$ for full specifications, the noncentrality parameter ν^* is the upper bound of υ for partial specifications. Similarly, compared to the Cramér-Rao lower bound for full specifications, the covariance matrix V_o^* is the lower bound of ν_o for partial specifications. This semiparametric optimality is thus compatible with the robustness to the unknown conditional distribution. This is particularly important for estimating and testing partial specifications.

This approach indeed has a very simple GLS interpretation in the linear regression context. To see this point, consider the linear regression $y_t = x_t^\top \theta + u_t$, such that $v_t(\theta) = u_t(\theta)$, $w_t(\theta) = -x_t$, $\Sigma_t(\theta) = \sigma_{ut}^2$. Recall that $\sigma_{\mathrm{ut}}^2 := \mathbb{E}[u_t(\theta_o)^2|\mathcal{X}_t]$. Thus, the optimal EF in (44) becomes $g_t^*(\theta) = x_t u_t(\theta)/\sigma_{\mathrm{ut}}^2$, and the estimator $\hat{\theta}_T^*$ reduces to the GLS estimator: $\hat{\theta}_T^* = \left[\sum_{t=1}^T x_t x_t^\top/\sigma_{ut}^2\right]^{-1}\left[\sum_{t=1}^T x_t y_t/\sigma_{ut}^2\right]$. Here, the M^* test is also a robust Wald test for checking the standardized regression of y_t/σ_{ut} on x_t/σ_{ut} against the artificial regression of y_t/σ_{ut} on x_t/σ_{ut} and z_t/σ_{ut}; see Engle (1982a, p. 790) for a "GLS-based Lagrange multiplier test" interpretation. This example provides an intuition underlying Propositions 2 and 3.

4.3 Computational Aspect

The optimized estimator and test, $\hat{\theta}_T^*$ and M_T^*, are both based on the unknown conditional covariance matrix $\Sigma_t(\theta_o)$. To compute the optimized estimator and test, we need to estimate or approximate $\Sigma_t(\theta_o)$ by a $r \times r$ matrix, denoted as $K_t(\hat{\theta}_T)$. Let $\dot{\theta}_T$ and $\dot{M}_T$ be, respectively, the feasible estimator and test that are obtained using $K_t(\hat{\theta}_T)$. Specifically, $\dot{\theta}_T$ is a particular $\bar{\theta}_T$ with the choice of $\pi_t(\theta) = -w_t(\theta)K_t(\hat{\theta}_T)^{-1}$, and $\dot{M}_T$ is a particular M_T with the choice of $C_t(\theta) = K_t(\theta)^{-1}$ and evaluated at $\theta = \dot{\theta}_T$. Since $\hat{\theta}_T$ is $T^{1/2}$-consistent for θ_o, $\dot{\theta}_T$ and $\dot{M}_T$ are, respectively, asymptotically equivalent to their $K_t(\theta_o)$-based counterparts. This means that $\dot{\theta}_T$ has the asymptotic null distribution (33) with $\pi_t(\theta) = -w_t(\theta)K_t(\theta)^{-1}$, and $\dot{M}_T$ has the asymptotic distribution in Proposition 1 with $C_t(\theta) = K_t(\theta)^{-1}$. In the case where $K_t(\theta_o) = \Sigma_t(\theta_o)$ (or in testing H_o', as will be explained shortly), the feasible statistics: $\dot{\theta}_T$ and $\dot{M}_T$ are, respectively, asymptotically equivalent to the infeasible statistics: $\hat{\theta}_T^*$ and M_T^*, and hence are of the semiparametric optimality. In other cases, the feasible statistics are not ensured to be optimal, but they remain robust to the unknown conditional distribution. Thus, we could pursue semiparametric optimality without sacrificing the robustness by choosing a proper $K_t(\hat{\theta}_T)$. The difficulty of this problem depends on the hypothesis being tested.

In testing the independence hypothesis H_o', it is natural to choose

$$K_t(\hat{\theta}_T) = \frac{1}{T}\sum_{t=1}^{T} v_t(\hat{\theta}_T)v_t(\hat{\theta}_T)^\top \tag{48}$$

for all the t's because $\Sigma_t(\theta_o)$ becomes $\mathbb{E}[v_t(\theta_o)v_t(\theta_o)^\top]$ under H_o' and the estimator in (48) is consistent for this matrix. In this case, we can easily implement the optimal-EF-based approach using the feasible statistics $\dot{\theta}_T$ and $\dot{M}_T$ with the choice of (48).

In testing H_o, it is challenging to choose a proper $K_t(\hat{\theta}_T)$. One possibility is to set $K_t(\hat{\theta}_T)$ as a nonparametric estimator for $\Sigma_t\theta_o$; see Newey (1993, Sects. 4 and 5). However, such an estimator may not be easy for practitioners. An alternative strategy is to choose $K_t(\hat{\theta}_T)$ as an estimated conditional covariance model, based on $\hat{\theta}_T$, for unknown $\Sigma_t(\theta_o)$. For instance, we may specify a conditional variance model for $K_t(\theta)$ in testing conditional mean or specify a conditional skewness-kurtosis model for $K_t(\theta)$ in testing conditional mean-and-variance. A sensible specification of $K_t(\theta)$ may be obtained by exploring the dynamic characteristics of the sequence $\{v_t(\hat{\theta}_T)v_t(\hat{\theta}_T)^\top\}$. This strategy does not ensure the semiparametric optimality of $\dot{\theta}_T$ and $\dot{M}_T$ because the postulated model $K_t(\theta)$ is likely to be misspecified for $\Sigma_t(\theta_o)$. Nonetheless, it is sensible because it reflects the fact that the semiparametric optimality of a "lower-order" CM estimation and testing method is obtained at the cost of exploiting the "higher-order" information contained in $\Sigma_t(\theta_o)$. Intuitively, the resulting $\dot{\theta}_T$ and $\dot{M}_T$ would be closer to the infeasible $\hat{\theta}_T^*$ and $\hat{M}_T^*$ if $K_t(\theta_o)$ provides a better approximation to $\Sigma_t(\theta_o)$.

In the case where the estimator $\dot{\theta}_T$ needs to be computed numerically (as in the GARCH example of Sect. 6), we may replace $\dot{\theta}_T$ in the proposed approach with the two-step estimator:

$$\ddot{\theta}_T := \hat{\theta}_T - \left[\sum_{t=1}^{T} w_t(\hat{\theta}_T)K_t(\hat{\theta}_T)^{-1}w_t(\hat{\theta}_T)^\top\right]^{-1}\left[\sum_{t=1}^{T} w_t(\hat{\theta}_T)K_t(\hat{\theta}_T)^{-1}v_t(\hat{\theta}_T)\right],$$

for computational simplicity. By definition, we have

$$\begin{aligned}\sqrt{T}(\ddot{\theta}_T - \dot{\theta}_T) &= \sqrt{T}(\hat{\theta}_T - \dot{\theta}_T) - \left[\frac{1}{T}\sum_{t=1}^{T} w_t(\hat{\theta}_T)K_t(\hat{\theta}_T)^{-1}w_t(\hat{\theta}_T)^\top\right]^{-1} \\ &\quad\times\left[\frac{1}{\sqrt{T}}\sum_{t=1}^{T} w_t(\hat{\theta}_T)K_t(\hat{\theta}_T)^{-1}v_t(\hat{\theta}_T)\right].\end{aligned} \tag{49}$$

Using the mean-value expansion and the $T^{1/2}$-consistency of $\hat{\theta}_T$ and $\dot{\theta}_T$, we obtain the asymptotic expansion:

$$\frac{1}{\sqrt{T}}\sum_{t=1}^{T} w_t(\dot{\theta}_T)K_t(\hat{\theta}_T)^{-1}v_t(\dot{\theta}_T) = \frac{1}{\sqrt{T}}\sum_{t=1}^{T} w_t(\hat{\theta}_T)K_t(\hat{\theta}_T)^{-1}v_t(\hat{\theta}_T)$$
$$-\left[\frac{1}{T}\sum_{t=1}^{T} w_t(\hat{\theta}_T)K_t(\hat{\theta}_T)^{-1}w_t(\hat{\theta}_T)^{\top}\right]$$
$$\sqrt{T}(\hat{\theta}_T - \dot{\theta}_T) + o_p(1). \tag{50}$$

Plugging (50) into (49) and using the estimating equation: $T^{-1}\sum_{t=1}^{T} w_t(\dot{\theta}_T)$ $K_t(\hat{\theta}_T)^{-1}v_t(\dot{\theta}_T) = 0$, we have $T^{1/2}(\ddot{\theta}_T - \dot{\theta}_T) = o_p(1)$. This shows the asymptotic validity of replacing $\dot{\theta}_T$ with $\ddot{\theta}_T$. Similarly, we can also replace $\dot{M}_T$ with $\ddot{M}_T$, where the latter is defined using $\ddot{\theta}_T$.

5 Examples: Optimized Tests

It is easy to observe from (18) that the test statistics: M_T and M_T^* are equivalent when $r = 1$, $C_t(\theta)$ is a constant, and the conditional homoskedasticity restriction holds:

$$\mathbb{E}[v_t(\theta_o)^2|\mathcal{X}_t] = \mathbb{E}[v_t(\theta_o)^2]. \tag{51}$$

Thus, the M test is semiparametrically optimal in this special case. In more general cases, the M test is not necessarily the same as the M^* test. We may apply the latter to refine the former; this is demonstrated below using the examples in Sect. 3.

5.1 Conditional-Mean Context

In Sect. 3.1, we considered a class of LS-based M tests for the conditional mean regression in (23) that are established for the case where $v_t(\theta) = u_t(\theta)$ (hence $r = 1$) and $C_t(\theta) = 1$. These particular M tests would be semi-parametrically optimal if the conditional homoskedasticity restriction: $\sigma_{ut}^2 = \sigma_u^2$ is satisfied. Since this restriction is implied by H_o', these tests are semiparametrically optimal in testing H_o'. However, they are not ensured to have this optimality in testing H_o because the conditional homoskedasticity restriction could be misspecified under H_o. In many applications, conditional heteroskedasticity is not exceptional. For instance, a Bernoulli-dependent variable with the conditional mean specification $\mu_t(\theta)$ is conditionally heteroskedastic with the conditional variance: $\sigma_{ut}^2 = \mu_t(\theta_o)(1 - \mu_t(\theta_o))$ under H_o; see also Cameron and Trivedi (1998, p. 347) for an example of the count data model. Conditional heteroskedasticity is also a well-known, stylized fact in financial time series.

In the presence of conditional heteroskedasticity, we may further improve the asymptotic local powers of the LS-based M tests by applying the M^* test to the same $z_t(\theta)$'s. By the same token, the asymptotic efficiency of the LS method can also be improved using the optimal EF method. In the example of binary choice models, the proposed optimization can be easily implemented by estimating θ_o using $\hat{\theta}_T$ because $\Sigma_t(\theta_o)$ has a closed form $\sigma_{ut}^2 = \mu_t(\theta_o)(1 - \mu_t(\theta_o))$. For financial time series, the functional form of $\Sigma_t(\theta)$ is unknown and can be approximated using a certain $K_t(\theta)$, as discussed in Sect. 4.3. For instance, we may compute $K_t(\hat{\theta}_T)$ as an estimated GARCH-type model. Such an approximation does not ensure semiparametric optimality but may be useful for improving the original LS-based M tests. This is because the original M tests are based on $C_t(\theta) = 1$, which amounts to approximating conditional heteroskedasticity using a constant. Yet, a GARCH-type $K_t(\hat{\theta}_T)$ ought to be a more sensible approximation to $\Sigma_t(\theta_o)$; our simulation in Sect. 6 provides evidence for this argument.

5.2 Conditional Mean-and-Variance Context

In Sect. 3.2, we discussed a class of Gaussian-QML-based M tests for the conditional mean-and-variance model in (24), where $v_t(\theta)$ follows (26) (hence $r = 2$) and $C_t(\theta) = I_2$. In this scenario, the M test would not be the same as the M^* test for both H_o and H_o', unless the condition $\Sigma_t(\theta_o) = I_2$ is satisfied. To ensure the GCHS restriction in (38) with $r = 2$, denote the conditional skewness $s_t(\theta) := \mathbb{E}[\varepsilon_t(\theta)^3|\mathcal{X}_t]$ and the conditional kurtosis $k_t(\theta) := \mathbb{E}[\varepsilon_t(\theta)^4|\mathcal{X}_t]$. To assess the validity of this condition, we can use (26) to write

$$\Sigma_t(\theta) = \begin{bmatrix} \mathbb{E}[\varepsilon_t(\theta)^2|\mathcal{X}_t] & \frac{1}{\sqrt{2}}\left(\mathbb{E}[\varepsilon_t(\theta)^3|\mathcal{X}_t] - \mathbb{E}[\varepsilon_t(\theta)|\mathcal{X}_t]\right) \\ \frac{1}{\sqrt{2}}\left(\mathbb{E}[\varepsilon_t(\theta)^3|\mathcal{X}_t] - \mathbb{E}[\varepsilon_t(\theta)|\mathcal{X}_t]\right) & \frac{1}{2}\left(\mathbb{E}[\varepsilon_t(\theta)^4|\mathcal{X}_t] - 2\mathbb{E}[\varepsilon_t(\theta)^2|\mathcal{X}_t] + 1\right) \end{bmatrix},$$

and simplify $\Sigma_t(\theta_o)$ as:

$$\Sigma_t(\theta_o) = \begin{bmatrix} 1 & \frac{1}{\sqrt{2}} s_t(\theta_o) \\ \frac{1}{\sqrt{2}} s_t(\theta_o) & \frac{1}{2}\left(k_t(\theta_o) - 1\right) \end{bmatrix} \tag{52}$$

under H_o with the $v_t(\theta)$ in (26). Clearly, the condition $\Sigma_t(\theta_o) = I_2$ amounts to imposing the conditional skewness and kurtosis restrictions: $s_t(\theta_o) = 0$ and $k_t(\theta_o) = 3$, which are satisfied under conditional normality: $\varepsilon_t(\theta_o)|\mathcal{X}_t \sim N(0, 1)$. This is consistent with the fact that the Gaussian QML-based M tests become the Gaussian ML-based tests and hence are parametrically optimal.

However, the conditional skewness and kurtosis restrictions are unlikely to be satisfied under conditional non-normality. This problem is empirically relevant in financial time series analysis. For example, the standardized errors of GARCH-type models for financial returns are usually found to be leptokurtic and/or asymmetric; see, e.g., Bollerslev (1987), Engle and González-Rivera (1991), and Park and Bera (2009), among others. In this scenario, the Gaussian QML method and the associated M tests may not be semiparametrically optimal. Li and Turtle (2000) suggested replacing the Gaussian QML method with the optimal EF method for estimating GARCH-type models. We may also improve the asymptotic local powers of the Gaussian QML-based M tests by applying the M^* test to the associated $v_t(\theta)$ and $z_t(\theta)$'s, i.e., by replacing the weighting matrix $C_t(\theta) = I_2$ with $C_t(\theta) = \Sigma_t(\theta_o)^{-1}$ for these particular M tests.

To see the relationship between the optimal EF method and the Gaussian QML method in this context, note that we can use (26), (27), and (52) to write the optimal EF in (44) as:

$$g_t^*(\theta) = \frac{1}{k_t(\theta_o) - 1 - s_t(\theta_o)^2}\left[\frac{\nabla_\theta \mu_t(\theta)}{h_t(\theta)^{1/2}}, \frac{\nabla_\theta h_t(\theta)}{\sqrt{2}h_t(\theta)}\right]\begin{bmatrix} k_t(\theta_o) - 1 & -\sqrt{2}s_t(\theta_o) \\ -\sqrt{2}s_t(\theta_o) & 2 \end{bmatrix}\begin{bmatrix} \varepsilon_t(\theta) \\ \frac{\varepsilon_t(\theta)^2 - 1}{\sqrt{2}} \end{bmatrix}$$

$$= \frac{\left((k_t(\theta_o) - 1)\frac{\nabla_\theta \mu_t(\theta)}{h_t(\theta)^{1/2}} - s_t(\theta_o)\frac{\nabla_\theta h_t(\theta)}{\sqrt{2}h_t(\theta)}\right)\varepsilon_t(\theta) - \left(s_t(\theta_o)\frac{\nabla_\theta \mu_t(\theta)}{h_t(\theta)^{1/2}} - \frac{\nabla_\theta h_t(\theta)}{\sqrt{2}h_t(\theta)}\right)(\varepsilon_t(\theta)^2 - 1)}{k_t(\theta_o) - 1 - s_t(\theta_o)^2}; \tag{53}$$

see also Li and Turtle (2000, Eq. 14) for the ARCH case of this optimal EF. Clearly, the optimal EF in (53) includes the Gaussian score function (28) as a special case where $s_t(\theta_o) = 0$ and $k_t(\theta_o) = 3$. Meanwhile, it is easy to see that the moment function $z_t^*(\theta)v_t^*(\theta) = z_t(\theta)\Sigma_t(\theta_o)^{-1}v_t(\theta)$ also reduces to the original testing function $z_t(\theta)v_t(\theta)$ in this case. Thus, the optimal EF method can be viewed as a generalization of the Gaussian QML method. Under conditional non-normality, this generalization improves the semiparametric optimality of the Gaussian QML method, because it combines the conditional mean-and-variance estimation and testing problems with the higher CM information $s_t(\theta_o)$ and $k_t(\theta_o)$.

Practical applications of this optimal approach involve the estimation or approximation of $s_t(\theta_o)$ and $k_t(\theta_o)$. As discussed in Sect. 4.3, the implementation of this approach would be semiparametrically optimal if the higher order CMs, $s_t(\theta_o)$ and $k_t(\theta_o)$, are consistently estimated; otherwise, this approach would be suboptimal but it remains robust. In testing H_o', it is easy to consistently estimate $s_t(\theta_o)$ and $k_t(\theta_o)$ using the sample skewness $T^{-1}\sum_{t=1}^T \varepsilon_t(\hat{\theta}_T)^3$ and the sample kurtosis $T^{-1}\sum_{t=1}^T \varepsilon_t(\hat{\theta}_T)^4$ autoedited1, respectively. In testing H_o, we may approximate $s_t(\theta_o)$ and $k_t(\theta_o)$ using a conditional skewness-kurtosis specification, such as that implied by the autoregressive conditional density model of Hansen (1994), Rockinger and Jondeau (2002), or Komunjer (2007). Unlike the case of score test, the higher order CM model discussed here is considered only for approximating the unknown $s_t(\theta_o)$ and $k_t(\theta_o)$, and the $\dot{M}$ test remains asymptotically valid even if this model is misspecified.

5.3 Conditional Quantile Context

In Sect. 3.3, we demonstrated that the M test is also applicable to the quantile regression in (29) when $v_t(\theta) = I(u_t(\theta) < 0) - \tau$ and $C_t(\theta) = p(0|\mathcal{X}_t)^{-1}$. In this example, we have $r = 1$, $\Sigma_t(\theta_o) = \tau(1 - \tau)$, but a non-constant $C_t(\theta)$ in general. (Note that the condition: $r = 1$ would not be satisfied when $v_t(\theta)$ is multidimensional, such as model (29) with various τ's.) Thus, the M test is not guaranteed to be the same as the M^* test.

In the conditional quantile context, the optimal EF in (44) is

$$g_t(\theta) = -\frac{1}{\tau(1-\tau)} p(0|\mathcal{X}_t) \nabla_\theta m_{\tau,t}(\theta) \left(I(u_t(\theta) < 0) - \tau \right), \tag{54}$$

which encompasses Godambe (2001) optimal EF for the conditional median model. By comparing (54) with Komunjer (2005, Eq. 8), we may also interpret this optimal EF as a particular tick-exponential score function. The resulting $\hat{\theta}_T^*$ has the asymptotic covariance matrix:

$$V^*(\theta_o) = \tau(1-\tau)\mathbb{E}[p(0|\mathcal{X}_t)^2 \nabla_\theta m_{\tau,t}(\theta_o) \nabla_\theta m_{\tau,t}(\theta_o)^\top]^{-1}, \tag{55}$$

which is obtained by plugging the associated $w_t(\theta)$ and $\Sigma_t(\theta)$ into (47). This estimator is asymptotically equivalent to the weighted estimator that minimizes the weighted objective function: $T^{-1}\sum_{t=1}^{T} p(0|\mathcal{X}_t)\rho_\tau(y_t - m_{\tau,t}(\theta))$; see, e.g., Koenker (2005, Theorem 5.1) for the latter. It is asymptotically more efficient than the asymmetric Laplace QMLE in Sect. 3.3. Given this $\hat{\theta}_T^*$, we can also apply the M^* test to the conditional quantile context by setting $C_t(\theta) = \Sigma_t(\theta_o)^{-1} = 1/(\tau(1-\tau))$ and using the associated $v_t(\theta)$ and $w_t(\theta)$. Interestingly, since the M and M^* tests both involve the conditional PDF $p(\cdot|\mathcal{X}_t)$, their computational cost in estimating this component are the same. This is different from the conditional mean(-and-variance) example where the M^* test typically has higher computational cost than the M test in applications.

6 Simulation

In this section, we conduct two Monte Carlo experiments to assess the finite-sample performance of the M test (with $C_t(\theta) = I_r$), the M^* test (with $C_t = \Sigma_t(\theta_o)^{-1}$), and the $\dot{M}$ (or $\ddot{M}$) test.

In the first experiment, we apply the M, M^*, and $\dot{M}$ tests to check H_o for the location model: $y_t = \theta + u_t$. The data generating processes (DGPs) are in the form of (24): $y_t = \mu_t + h_t^{1/2}\varepsilon_t$, with $\varepsilon_t|\mathcal{X}_t \sim N(0,1)$ and the following (μ_t, h_t)'s:

- AR-CHOMO (conditional homoskedasticity): $\mu_t = \theta_o + \gamma_1 y_{t-1}$ and $h_t = 1$;
- AR-EGARCH1: the AR μ_t and $h_t = \exp(\kappa_0 + \kappa_1 \ln h_{t-1} + \kappa_2\varepsilon_{t-1} + \kappa_3|\varepsilon_{t-1}|)$;
- AR-EGARCH2: the AR μ_t and $h_t = \exp(\kappa_0 + 2\kappa_1 \ln h_{t-1} + \kappa_2\varepsilon_{t-1} + \kappa_3|\varepsilon_{t-1}|)$;
- TAR (threshold AR)-CHOMO: $\mu_t = \theta_o + (\gamma_1 I(y_{t-1} \geq \gamma_3) + \gamma_2 I(y_{t-1} < \gamma_3))$ y_{t-1} and $h_t = 1$;
- TAR-EGARCH1: the TAR μ_t and the EGARCH1 h_t;
- TAR-EGARCH2: the TAR μ_t and the EGARCH2 h_t.

The parameters are set to be $\theta_o = 0$, $\gamma_1 = \delta T^{-1/2}$, with $\delta = 0, 1, 3, 5$, $\gamma_2 = -\gamma_1$, $\gamma_3 = 0$, $\kappa_0 = 0.1$, $\kappa_1 = 0.9$, $\kappa_2 = -0.15$, and $\kappa_3 = 0.05$. The strength of serial correlation (nonlinearity) of the AR (TAR) processes increases in δ, and the EGARCH2 process implies a stronger volatility asymmetry than the EGARCH1 process. The parameter $\gamma_1 = \delta T^{-1/2}$ controls the local powers of these tests. In particular, H_o holds under these DGPs when $\delta = 0$.

In this experiment, we have $v_t(\theta) = u_t(\theta) = y_t - \theta$, $w_t(\theta) = -1$, and $C_t(\theta) = 1$. Correspondingly, we estimate θ_o by the sample average $\hat{\theta}_T = T^{-1}\sum_{t=1}^{T} y_t$, and compute the test statistic M_T in (18) accordingly. The optimal EF estimator $\hat{\theta}_T^*$ and the optimized test statistic M_T^* are computed by setting $\Sigma_t(\theta_o)$ as the true h_t. Let $\hat{h}_t$ be the Gaussian QML-based fitted value of the GARCH(1,1) model for the residuals $\{u_t(\hat{\theta}_T)\}$. By approximating $\Sigma_t(\theta_o)$ using $K_t(\hat{\theta}_T) = \hat{h}_t$, we base the feasible test statistic $\dot{M}_T$ on this $K_t(\hat{\theta}_T)$ and the estimator $\dot{\theta}_T = \left[\sum_{t=1}^{T} 1/\hat{h}_t\right]^{-1}\left[\sum_{t=1}^{T} y_t/\hat{h}_t\right]$. This GARCH approximation is misspecified under the EGARCH1 and EGARCH2 processes because it ignores the volatility asymmetry, and the misspecification under EGARCH1 is milder than that under EGARCH2. This design reflects the fact that $K_t(\theta)$ could be misspecified for $\Sigma_t(\theta)$ in practical applications. In performing the tests, we consider two sets of $z_t(\theta, \varsigma)$'s: (i) $z_{k,lt} = u_{t-k}(\theta)$, with $k = 1, 2, 3$, and $z_{lt} = (z_{1,lt}^{\top}, z_{2,lt}^{\top}, z_{3,lt}^{\top})^{\top}$ for testing H_o against serial correlations and (ii) $z_{k,nt} = u_{t-1}(\theta)^k - \mathbb{E}[u_{t-1}(\theta)^k]$, with $k = 2, 3, 4$, and $z_{nt} = (z_{2,nt}^{\top}, z_{3,nt}^{\top}, z_{4,nt}^{\top})^{\top}$ for testing H_o against nonlinearity. Note that $z_{k,\mathrm{nt}}$ is centered and hence involves the nuisance parameter $\varsigma_o = \mathbb{E}[u_{t-1}(\theta_o)^k]$. We estimate ς_o using the statistic $\bar{\varsigma}_T = (T-1)^{-1}\sum_{t=2}^{T} u_{t-1}(\hat{\theta}_T)^k$ in th simulation. As explained in Sect. 2, this does not change the asymptotic validity of our tests.

In the second experiment, we apply the M, M^*, and $\ddot{M}$ tests to checking H_o' for the model:

$$y_t = \theta_0 + \varepsilon_t h_t^{1/2} \quad \text{and} \quad h_t = \theta_1 + \theta_2 h_{t-1} + \theta_3 u_{t-1}^2. \tag{56}$$

The DGPs are also in the form of (24) but with various ε_t's or (μ_t, h_t)'s:

- AR-GARCH-N: the AR μ_t, $h_t = \theta_1 + \theta_2 h_{t-1} + \theta_3 u_{t-1}^2$, and $\varepsilon_t|\mathcal{X}_t \sim N(0, 1)$;
- AR-GARCH-L1: the AR μ_t, the GARCH h_t, and $\varepsilon_t|\mathcal{X}_t \sim$ standardized log-normal distribution with the asymmetry parameter $\eta = 0.3$; specifically, $\varepsilon_t = (\exp(\eta\epsilon_t) - \omega^{1/2})/(\omega(\omega-1))^{1/2}$, $\omega := \exp(\eta^2)$, $\epsilon_t|\mathcal{X}_t \sim N(0, 1)$,
- AR-GARCH-L2: the AR μ_t, the GARCH h_t, and $\varepsilon_t|\mathcal{X}_t \sim$ standardized log-normal distribution with the asymmetry parameter $\eta = 0.6$;
- TAR-GARCH-N: the TAR μ_t, the GARCH h_t, and $\varepsilon_t|\mathcal{X}_t \sim N(0, 1)$;
- TAR-GARCH-L1: the TAR μ_t, the GARCH h_t, and $\varepsilon_t|\mathcal{X}_t \sim$ standardized log-normal distribution with the asymmetry parameter $\eta = 0.3$;
- TAR-GARCH-L2: the TAR μ_t, the GARCH h_t, and $\varepsilon_t|\mathcal{X}_t \sim$ standardized log-normal distribution with the asymmetry parameter $\eta = 0.6$.

We set $\theta_1 = 0.1$, $\theta_2 = 0.9$, and $\theta_3 = 0.05$. Other parameters are the same as those in the first experiment. The L2 process implies a stronger distributional asymmetry than the L1 process. In these DGPs, H_o' holds when $\delta = 0$, and the asymptotic local powers of the tests increase in δ.

In this experiment, we have $\theta = (\theta_0, \theta_1, \theta_2, \theta_3)^\top$, the $v_t(\theta)$ in (26) with the $\varepsilon_t(\theta)$ given by model (56), and $C_t = I_2$. We estimate the true parameter vector θ_o of (56) by the Gaussian QMLE $\hat{\theta}_T$ and compute the test statistic M_T accordingly. The estimator $\hat{\theta}_T^*$ and the test statistic M_T^* are computed using the H_o'-implied value of $\Sigma_t(\theta_o)$:

$$\Sigma_t(\theta_o) = \begin{bmatrix} 1 & \frac{1}{\sqrt{2}}\mathbb{E}[\varepsilon_t(\theta_o)^3] \\ \frac{1}{\sqrt{2}}\mathbb{E}[\varepsilon_t(\theta_o)^3] & \frac{1}{2}(\mathbb{E}[\varepsilon_t(\theta_o)^4] - 1) \end{bmatrix}, \tag{57}$$

that holds for all t's. Note that the standardized log-normal distribution implies $\mathbb{E}[\varepsilon_t(\theta_o)^3] = (\omega + 2)\sqrt{\omega - 1}$ and $\mathbb{E}[\varepsilon_t(\theta_o)^4] = \omega^4 + 2\omega^3 + 3\omega^2 - 3$; see, e.g., Johnson et al. (1994, p. 212). In testing H_o', we can consistently estimate $\Sigma_t(\theta_o)$ using $K_t(\hat{\theta}_T) = T^{-1}\sum_{t=1}^T v_t(\hat{\theta}_T)v_t(\hat{\theta}_T)^\top$, as mentioned in Sect. 4.3. The estimator $\ddot{\theta}_T$ and the test statistic $\ddot{M}_T$ are computed using this $K_t(\hat{\theta}_T)$, and they are, respectively, asymptotically equivalent to $\hat{\theta}_T^*$ and $\hat{M}_T^*$. In performing the tests, the $z_t(\theta, \varsigma)$'s being considered include (i) $z_{k,lt} = (\varepsilon_{t-k}(\theta), 0)$, with $k = 1, 2, 3$, and $z_{nt} = (z_{1,lt}^\top, z_{2,lt}^\top, z_{3,lt}^\top)^\top$ for testing H_o' against serial correlations and (ii) $z_{k,nt} = (\varepsilon_{t-1}(\theta)^k - \mathbb{E}[\varepsilon_{t-1}(\theta)^k], 0)$, with $k = 2, 3, 4$, and $z_{nt} = (z_{2,nt}^\top, z_{3,nt}^\top, z_{4,nt}^\top)^\top$ for testing H_o' against nonlinearity. To perform the tests with $z_{k,nt}$, we estimate the nuisance parameter $\varsigma_o = \mathbb{E}[\varepsilon_{t-1}(\theta_o)^k]$ using $\bar{\varsigma}_T = T^{-1}\sum_{t=2}^T \varepsilon_{t-1}(\hat{\theta}_T)^k$.

For each DGP, we generate $T + 100$ observations, and use the last T observations for estimation and testing. Given the nominal size 5 %, the sample sizes $T = 500$, 1,000, and the number of replications 1,000, we show the empirical rejection frequencies of the M, M^*, and $\dot{M}$ tests for the first experiment in Table 1 and their counterparts for the second experiment in Table 2. The main results of these two tables are summarized as follows.

First, the M test and the M^* test have the same empirical sizes and powers under the AR-CHOMO and TAR-CHOMO (AR-GARCH-N and TAR-GARCH-N) processes in the first (second) experiment. This is because these two tests are identical under conditional homoskedasticity (conditional normality), as discussed in Sect. 4.1 (Sect. 4.2). Table 1 (Table 2) also shows that the performance of the $\dot{M}$ test (the $\ddot{M}$ test) is very similar to that of the M test and the M^* test in these cases. This reflects the fact that the GARCH approximation encompasses the conditionally homoskedastic errors (the estimator $T^{-1}\sum_{t=1}^T v_t(\hat{\theta}_T)v_t(\hat{\theta}_T)^\top$ is consistent for (57)), so that these tests are asymptotically equivalent and share the same optimality property.

Second, the M tests with various $z_t(\theta, \varsigma)$'s have proper empirical sizes close to the 5 % nominal level in most cases. This shows that these tests are robust to the unknown conditional distribution in checking H_o and H_o'. The tests with $z_{4,nt}$ and $z_{\rm nt}$ are somewhat undersized for certain DGPs; this exceptional case is likely due to the fact that these nonlinear $z_t(\theta, \varsigma)$'s are highly sensitive to outliers. These two tables also show that the M tests with various $z_t(\theta, \varsigma)$'s have different power directions. In particular, the M test with $z_{1,lt}$ (or z_{lt}) and the test with $z_{2,nt}$ (or z_{nt}) are, respectively, powerful against the AR processes and the TAR processes. This is consistent with the power directions that these two $z_t(\theta, \varsigma)$'s are designed to have. In addition, the empirical powers of the M test at $T = 500$ are close to their counterparts

Table 1 Empirical rejection frequencies in the first experiment

DGP	Test	δ	$T = 500$								$T = 1{,}000$							
			$z_{1,lt}$	$z_{2,lt}$	$z_{3,lt}$	z_{lt}	$z_{2,nt}$	$z_{3,nt}$	$z_{4,nt}$	z_{nt}	$z_{1,lt}$	$z_{2,lt}$	$z_{3,lt}$	z_{lt}	$z_{2,nt}$	$z_{3,nt}$	$z_{4,nt}$	z_{nt}
		0	**6.2**	**5.2**	**4.2**	**6.0**	**5.3**	**3.7**	**3.5**	**4.4**	**5.1**	**4.7**	**4.8**	**4.8**	**5.6**	**4.6**	**5.2**	**4.1**
	M/M^*	1	21.3	11.9	10.0	17.0	9.3	14.9	7.2	11.2	21.6	9.8	9.5	16.3	11.4	16.5	10.0	11.8
		3	84.7	18.3	14.0	73.1	11.7	68.4	9.5	48.6	87.0	14.9	15.4	74.4	15.4	70.0	14.6	51.7
AR-CHOMO		5	100.0	35.1	19.6	100.0	14.9	99.4	12.0	96.4	100.0	26.0	19.8	99.7	19.3	99.2	18.0	96.8
		0	**6.0**	**5.2**	**4.6**	**6.0**	**5.2**	**3.8**	**3.7**	**4.4**	**5.2**	**4.7**	**4.8**	**4.7**	**5.5**	**4.7**	**5.3**	**4.4**
	$\dot{M}$	1	20.7	11.5	10.3	16.8	9.4	15.2	7.4	11.4	21.5	9.8	9.4	16.2	11.4	16.9	9.9	12.1
		3	84.5	17.7	14.5	72.2	12.1	69.9	9.9	51.4	87.4	14.8	15.1	74.8	16.0	71.6	14.5	54.1
		5	100.0	31.6	19.1	100.0	15.1	99.7	13.1	97.7	100.0	24.7	19.5	99.7	19.8	99.3	17.9	97.6
		0	**5.3**	**3.9**	**5.5**	**4.4**	**5.7**	**4.8**	**3.9**	**2.6**	**4.8**	**6.4**	**4.7**	**4.2**	**4.0**	**5.3**	**2.6**	**3.8**
	M	1	19.5	9.1	10.2	14.5	8.9	15.7	7.1	8.3	19.9	10.8	8.2	13.6	9.2	13.6	6.5	10.4
		3	81.7	14.7	15.4	64.4	14.3	52.0	11.5	37.0	83.0	15.4	13.7	68.2	13.8	51.7	9.9	39.6
		5	99.7	27.7	20.2	99.1	17.4	90.8	14.0	86.2	99.9	24.9	18.9	98.8	19.7	89.8	14.9	87.5
		0	**5.6**	**4.9**	**5.5**	**4.9**	**3.8**	**4.8**	**4.2**	**3.0**	**6.0**	**7.1**	**4.3**	**4.6**	**5.0**	**4.7**	**3.5**	**4.1**
AR-EGARCH1	M^*	1	20.3	9.4	9.7	15.5	7.4	16.5	7.3	9.1	22.9	11.6	8.5	15.8	10.1	17.1	8.4	11.8
		3	86.5	14.8	13.8	70.0	15.8	64.0	12.6	44.6	86.7	15.7	14.0	76.0	17.0	66.2	13.4	48.2
		5	99.9	28.4	18.1	99.9	25.6	98.1	17.1	92.7	99.9	25.3	18.9	99.7	28.3	97.7	19.4	93.6
		0	**6.2**	**4.1**	**5.1**	**4.9**	**5.1**	**5.2**	**4.1**	**3.1**	**4.8**	**6.3**	**4.5**	**4.1**	**4.4**	**5.1**	**2.8**	**3.4**
	$\dot{M}$	1	21.8	9.4	9.5	15.2	8.7	17.3	7.2	9.9	19.9	10.4	7.8	14.2	9.4	16.2	7.1	12.3
		3	83.6	13.8	14.3	66.2	14.0	62.6	12.1	46.6	86.0	14.5	12.8	71.8	13.5	63.0	11.3	51.6
		5	100.0	24.2	18.7	99.6	16.1	97.2	14.5	93.3	99.9	23.0	18.4	99.3	18.8	96.7	16.0	94.6
		0	**4.8**	**5.4**	**5.5**	**4.8**	**4.2**	**3.0**	**3.2**	**2.8**	**4.1**	**4.8**	**6.3**	**4.6**	**4.5**	**3.3**	**2.7**	**2.6**
	M	1	15.8	9.7	9.5	11.1	9.0	8.4	6.8	5.9	15.0	10.2	10.6	12.6	8.9	9.5	6.5	7.1
		3	67.4	16.5	14.2	51.6	13.2	30.1	9.9	24.6	67.1	14.8	14.0	49.4	12.7	29.4	9.1	23.7
		5	98.7	27.5	18.9	94.9	17.8	66.0	12.8	67.3	98.8	21.6	19.6	94.4	17.2	62.5	12.4	62.6
		0	**4.6**	**7.3**	**5.6**	**5.8**	**5.3**	**3.8**	**3.3**	**3.5**	**4.6**	**4.8**	**5.7**	**5.5**	**5.1**	**3.1**	**3.8**	**2.9**

(continued)

Table 1 (continued)

DGP	Test	δ	$T = 500$								$T = 1{,}000$							
			$z_{1,lt}$	$z_{2,lt}$	$z_{3,lt}$	z_{lt}	$z_{2,nt}$	$z_{3,nt}$	$z_{4,nt}$	z_{nt}	$z_{1,lt}$	$z_{2,lt}$	$z_{3,lt}$	z_{lt}	$z_{2,nt}$	$z_{3,nt}$	$z_{4,nt}$	z_{nt}
AR-EGARCH2	M^*	1	21.1	11.4	10.4	17.8	11.5	12.6	7.8	9.8	21.5	9.2	10.3	17.2	10.9	13.7	8.6	9.6
		3	87.9	16.5	15.3	73.9	26.9	59.3	16.2	42.6	88.4	14.3	14.2	74.9	25.2	57.3	15.0	42.0
		5	100.0	29.5	19.7	99.8	52.9	95.7	25.8	90.3	100.0	23.3	19.6	99.9	51.4	95.9	25.7	90.3
		0	**4.0**	**5.8**	**5.4**	**4.8**	**5.6**	**3.5**	**3.3**	**3.2**	**5.4**	**4.0**	**6.9**	**6.6**	**4.8**	**4.2**	**4.3**	**3.4**
	$\dot{M}$	1	16.7	10.7	10.3	13.4	10.7	11.8	8.1	8.5	19.0	9.0	11.7	15.6	10.1	13.4	8.6	10.2
		3	75.1	16.6	15.4	60.5	14.0	49.1	11.3	41.0	78.4	13.8	16.0	63.0	14.2	49.7	12.2	43.9
		5	99.7	28.7	18.7	98.1	18.7	92.3	15.1	92.4	99.9	20.7	20.3	98.6	18.1	91.9	16.9	91.3
		0	**5.1**	**3.8**	**5.3**	**4.0**	**3.7**	**4.3**	**2.8**	**3.9**	**5.6**	**3.9**	**4.7**	**5.0**	**4.4**	**4.9**	**4.1**	**4.1**
	M/M^*	1	8.8	9.6	9.7	8.7	10.4	8.4	7.9	8.3	10.5	9.2	10.7	10.5	13.3	10.4	9.6	10.5
		3	13.3	14.9	14.3	14.2	47.3	11.7	30.4	32.1	15.3	14.2	15.1	15.7	48.9	14.5	29.8	33.7
TAR-CHOMO		5	23.0	19.9	19.4	22.7	88.9	17.1	68.6	76.3	21.9	18.2	19.8	20.9	88.5	19.4	68.6	76.4
		0	**5.1**	**3.8**	**5.1**	**3.9**	**3.6**	**4.5**	**3.1**	**3.9**	**5.4**	**4.0**	**4.7**	**5.1**	**4.3**	**5.1**	**4.1**	**4.0**
	$\dot{M}$	1	8.9	9.3	9.4	8.8	10.6	8.8	8.4	8.3	10.3	9.3	10.7	10.5	13.3	10.7	9.9	10.4
		3	13.8	14.5	14.0	14.5	48.2	12.2	32.0	32.5	14.9	14.1	15.1	15.8	49.5	15.2	31.6	33.7
		5	23.5	19.6	19.1	23.5	89.7	17.6	72.4	76.1	21.6	18.0	19.8	20.9	89.0	20.5	71.1	76.3
		0	**4.2**	**6.0**	**4.3**	**4.8**	**5.1**	**4.5**	**2.9**	**4.3**	**4.1**	**5.1**	**5.1**	**4.5**	**5.6**	**4.3**	**5.1**	**4.2**
	M	1	7.8	10.7	10.3	9.4	13.8	8.9	8.4	9.4	10.0	10.5	9.5	9.3	15.4	9.2	10.1	10.5
		3	10.8	16.4	16.2	14.6	43.2	12.8	24.6	29.7	14.1	15.2	14.9	14.6	45.1	12.4	26.8	33.1
		5	18.6	21.3	21.1	22.6	84.1	16.4	56.9	74.0	19.3	20.5	19.3	20.8	83.3	15.6	54.6	76.6
		0	**5.0**	**5.5**	**4.5**	**4.5**	**4.7**	**5.1**	**3.1**	**5.1**	**5.0**	**4.6**	**4.3**	**4.2**	**6.1**	**5.1**	**4.9**	**4.9**
TAR-EGARCH1	M^*	1	9.2	10.6	10.6	9.2	13.9	9.5	9.5	10.7	10.5	9.3	9.2	9.3	15.0	10.2	11.1	12.1
		3	17.9	15.8	15.2	16.3	49.8	16.0	29.5	33.8	17.5	15.0	14.7	17.2	52.9	15.1	32.4	37.5
		5	37.0	20.6	20.5	30.9	91.5	27.0	66.7	80.0	32.7	20.2	19.6	28.8	93.2	25.9	67.1	82.8
		0	**5.3**	**5.9**	**4.8**	**4.2**	**5.0**	**4.7**	**3.7**	**4.7**	**4.0**	**5.9**	**4.9**	**4.3**	**5.8**	**4.8**	**4.9**	**4.7**
	$\dot{M}$	1	9.5	11.0	10.6	8.7	13.9	9.3	10.6	9.7	9.7	11.5	9.5	9.1	16.0	10.4	11.2	11.4
		3	13.7	16.7	15.9	13.9	46.8	13.6	31.0	31.1	14.1	16.2	15.8	14.6	50.3	13.8	32.7	34.6
		5	23.4	21.3	20.2	22.0	89.2	17.7	67.9	76.8	19.2	21.4	20.7	20.9	89.4	17.8	66.7	80.2

(continued)

Table 1 (continued)

DGP	Test	δ	$T = 500$								$T = 1{,}000$							
			$z_{1,\mathrm{lt}}$	$z_{2,\mathrm{lt}}$	$z_{3,\mathrm{lt}}$	z_{lt}	$z_{2,\mathrm{nt}}$	$z_{3,\mathrm{nt}}$	$z_{4,\mathrm{nt}}$	z_{nt}	$z_{1,\mathrm{lt}}$	$z_{2,\mathrm{lt}}$	$z_{3,\mathrm{lt}}$	z_{lt}	$z_{2,\mathrm{nt}}$	$z_{3,\mathrm{nt}}$	$z_{4,\mathrm{nt}}$	z_{nt}
		0	**4.5**	**5.2**	**4.9**	**4.3**	**3.9**	**3.5**	**2.3**	**3.5**	**4.9**	**4.8**	**5.2**	**5.0**	**3.6**	**3.8**	**2.4**	**3.8**
	M	1	8.9	11.8	10.2	8.5	11.2	6.5	7.1	8.1	9.6	9.7	9.6	9.2	10.4	7.3	7.0	8.6
		3	12.9	17.0	16.5	13.8	33.9	10.2	16.7	27.1	13.5	15.6	14.7	13.6	34.5	9.7	18.1	29.5
		5	19.4	22.4	21.4	19.4	75.9	13.3	41.9	69.9	18.3	22.2	21.2	20.4	71.1	12.5	40.8	69.0
		0	**5.6**	**5.2**	**4.7**	**5.3**	**3.8**	**3.9**	**2.7**	**4.3**	**6.1**	**5.4**	**6.4**	**6.8**	**5.0**	**5.0**	**3.0**	**4.4**
TAR-EGARCH2	M^*	1	12.1	10.1	9.1	10.4	13.9	8.3	8.6	10.3	11.9	10.4	11.2	11.2	15.5	10.3	8.8	10.5
		3	27.0	13.5	14.6	20.9	57.1	18.7	28.3	39.2	25.9	16.2	17.1	21.7	58.2	22.9	27.0	42.6
		5	64.4	18.3	19.9	47.9	94.8	41.7	62.4	84.8	56.1	22.1	23.2	46.0	96.2	45.1	62.7	88.9
		0	**5.0**	**5.5**	**5.0**	**4.8**	**4.5**	**3.5**	**2.8**	**3.8**	**5.4**	**3.9**	**5.6**	**5.7**	**4.8**	**4.5**	**3.3**	**4.9**
	$\dot{M}$	1	9.7	12.5	9.0	8.6	13.9	7.0	9.3	9.0	10.4	8.5	9.9	9.4	12.6	9.1	9.6	11.2
		3	14.3	16.0	15.3	13.9	44.9	10.3	25.5	34.7	14.8	13.5	14.6	14.9	47.3	12.9	28.5	39.0
		5	**23.5**	20.1	19.8	21.4	87.7	14.7	64.1	81.9	21.9	20.1	21.0	22.0	86.4	15.7	61.0	83.4

Note The entries are empirical rejection frequencies in percentage. The empirical sizes are in boldface

Table 2 Empirical rejection frequencies in the second experiment

DGP	Test	δ	$T = 500$								$T = 1{,}000$							
			$z_{1,\mathrm{lt}}$	$z_{2,\mathrm{lt}}$	$z_{3,\mathrm{lt}}$	z_{lt}	$z_{2,\mathrm{nt}}$	$z_{3,\mathrm{nt}}$	$z_{4,\mathrm{nt}}$	z_{nt}	$z_{1,\mathrm{lt}}$	$z_{2,\mathrm{lt}}$	$z_{3,\mathrm{lt}}$	z_{lt}	$z_{2,\mathrm{nt}}$	$z_{3,\mathrm{nt}}$	$z_{4,\mathrm{nt}}$	z_{nt}
		0	**5.7**	**5.5**	**6.0**	**5.5**	**5.1**	**5.5**	**4.4**	**4.7**	**5.5**	**6.4**	**6.5**	**6.2**	**5.3**	**4.5**	**4.5**	**5.3**
	M/M^*	1	19.9	11.9	11.7	16.2	8.7	14.8	8.0	10.1	18.9	11.0	10.0	15.8	9.4	13.9	7.3	10.6
		3	83.3	18.0	16.1	67.0	12.8	62.8	12.3	45.2	84.0	15.9	15.2	71.1	13.4	62.8	10.8	47.8
AR-GARCH-N		5	99.9	30.5	20.4	99.6	16.0	97.6	15.9	93.8	100.0	23.9	20.1	99.9	17.0	97.6	14.1	93.4
		0	**6.3**	**5.5**	**5.7**	**5.7**	**5.4**	**5.0**	**4.6**	**4.8**	**5.8**	**6.7**	**6.4**	**6.1**	**5.3**	**4.7**	**4.9**	**5.8**
	$\ddot{M}$	1	20.4	11.9	11.1	16.2	9.3	14.8	8.5	10.3	18.7	11.4	9.6	15.4	9.5	14.6	7.4	11.4
		3	83.3	18.0	15.6	67.2	13.8	62.1	12.5	45.0	84.0	16.5	14.8	70.7	13.4	63.3	11.0	48.3
		5	99.9	30.3	19.9	99.5	17.1	97.6	16.6	94.0	100.0	24.3	19.2	99.9	16.9	97.8	14.7	93.2
		0	**5.4**	**5.5**	**5.7**	**5.8**	**5.5**	**4.0**	**2.9**	**4.4**	**5.5**	**6.4**	**6.7**	**5.6**	**5.3**	**4.3**	**3.6**	**4.8**
	M	1	18.2	10.7	11.5	15.4	8.7	9.2	4.3	11.0	18.4	10.9	10.5	14.9	9.1	10.0	6.3	10.7
		3	83.8	16.5	16.1	67.1	22.2	44.9	14.5	48.6	83.8	16.2	15.3	68.0	25.1	44.6	16.4	51.5
		5	99.9	29.3	20.6	99.7	52.2	94.5	42.7	95.5	99.8	24.4	20.3	99.6	60.7	90.1	44.3	95.3
		0	**5.7**	**4.6**	**5.1**	**5.2**	**4.7**	**3.5**	**2.9**	**4.4**	**4.3**	**5.9**	**6.3**	**6.0**	**4.6**	**4.1**	**3.7**	**4.3**
AR-GARCH-L1	M^*	1	21.7	10.5	10.1	17.1	11.6	12.1	7.8	13.3	20.6	10.7	10.0	16.5	10.9	14.2	8.6	10.0
		3	90.4	16.8	13.9	78.2	35.1	61.4	27.3	61.8	92.0	16.2	14.5	80.1	37.5	61.8	30.4	64.4
		5	99.9	30.8	19.2	99.6	68.9	96.8	66.7	98.4	99.9	25.4	19.2	99.8	73.7	96.2	65.1	98.8
		0	**5.5**	**4.8**	**5.5**	**5.1**	**4.3**	**3.3**	**3.2**	**4.2**	**4.5**	**5.9**	**6.3**	**5.8**	**4.5**	**4.2**	**3.3**	**4.3**
	$\ddot{M}$	1	21.7	10.7	10.7	17.1	11.5	12.4	7.8	12.6	20.5	10.8	10.1	16.0	10.9	13.8	8.2	10.2
		3	90.3	17.1	14.6	78.3	35.1	62.0	27.7	60.6	92.2	16.4	14.4	80.0	37.0	61.2	29.9	64.6
		5	99.9	30.9	19.4	99.6	68.0	96.4	65.6	98.4	99.9	25.6	19.2	99.9	72.9	95.6	65.2	98.7
		0	**6.2**	**5.4**	**5.7**	**5.3**	**5.7**	**4.2**	**2.1**	**4.7**	**5.8**	**4.3**	**5.2**	**5.1**	**5.6**	**5.1**	**4.2**	**4.9**
	M	1	16.6	10.0	10.6	12.7	8.0	5.8	3.0	10.8	18.6	8.8	9.9	14.9	9.4	8.2	6.6	9.1
		3	82.3	14.9	15.8	64.1	31.2	29.7	12.4	42.6	81.2	13.7	15.7	63.0	32.0	26.0	13.2	38.6
		5	99.9	25.6	20.8	99.2	82.4	81.5	44.8	91.5	99.9	20.9	20.4	99.5	81.5	73.1	39.5	91.0
		0	**5.5**	**5.6**	**5.8**	**5.2**	**4.6**	**2.5**	**2.0**	**4.0**	**6.1**	**4.2**	**5.5**	**5.4**	**6.0**	**4.6**	**3.2**	**4.3**

(continued)

Table 2 (continued)

DGP	Test	δ	$T = 500$								$T = 1{,}000$							
			$z_{1,\mathrm{lt}}$	$z_{2,\mathrm{lt}}$	$z_{3,\mathrm{lt}}$	z_{lt}	$z_{2,\mathrm{nt}}$	$z_{3,\mathrm{nt}}$	$z_{4,\mathrm{nt}}$	z_{nt}	$z_{1,\mathrm{lt}}$	$z_{2,\mathrm{lt}}$	$z_{3,\mathrm{lt}}$	z_{lt}	$z_{2,\mathrm{nt}}$	$z_{3,\mathrm{nt}}$	$z_{4,\mathrm{nt}}$	z_{nt}
AR-GARCH-L2	M^*	1	21.6	10.5	10.1	16.6	11.4	6.5	4.6	12.0	27.1	8.0	9.6	18.1	13.4	9.7	5.6	11.4
		3	85.6	15.6	16.5	76.9	51.3	40.4	22.2	61.2	91.0	11.9	15.1	81.4	51.5	37.8	19.0	58.8
		5	97.8	29.2	21.4	96.5	87.6	78.5	54.2	93.8	99.1	18.0	19.8	98.7	90.3	78.7	51.3	94.7
		0	**4.8**	**4.1**	**5.2**	**4.8**	**4.6**	**2.4**	**2.2**	**4.1**	**5.5**	**5.0**	**5.9**	**5.1**	**5.2**	**4.0**	**2.5**	**4.3**
	$\ddot{M}$	1	22.1	9.8	10.1	16.4	12.3	8.0	5.6	13.2	27.5	8.7	11.0	19.0	13.4	10.1	5.6	12.0
		3	84.7	15.5	15.8	76.1	52.9	42.3	24.4	64.2	90.7	12.2	16.5	81.2	52.5	40.3	21.9	60.0
		5	97.4	28.5	20.8	95.9	84.7	77.0	54.1	93.5	99.2	17.7	21.3	98.3	88.5	78.3	53.1	94.8
		0	**5.7**	**5.5**	**6.0**	**5.5**	**5.1**	**5.5**	**4.4**	**4.7**	**6.9**	**5.6**	**5.3**	**5.8**	**4.0**	**5.9**	**3.7**	**3.9**
	M/M^*	1	11.3	11.2	11.1	11.8	11.7	10.6	9.2	10.2	12.9	11.2	11.1	12.2	12.0	11.7	9.8	9.4
		3	15.9	16.1	14.7	15.8	42.2	14.8	28.0	31.8	17.0	15.7	15.4	16.0	42.6	15.1	26.8	31.4
TAR-GARCH-N		5	24.6	20.6	18.6	21.9	86.0	20.2	65.4	75.6	23.0	21.7	19.5	21.8	85.6	19.5	61.2	72.9
		0	**6.3**	**5.5**	**5.7**	**5.7**	**5.4**	**5.0**	**4.6**	**4.8**	**7.1**	**5.6**	**5.3**	**5.7**	**4.1**	**6.0**	**3.7**	**4.1**
	$\ddot{M}$	1	11.8	11.5	11.4	12.1	11.9	10.1	9.9	10.7	13.3	10.9	11.3	12.0	12.1	11.8	10.0	9.6
		3	16.6	16.4	15.1	16.2	42.1	13.9	28.7	32.7	17.4	15.4	15.5	15.9	42.7	15.2	27.3	30.8
		5	25.4	21.2	19.1	22.3	85.1	20.0	65.4	75.6	23.1	21.3	19.7	21.5	85.4	19.8	61.1	73.3
		0	**5.4**	**5.5**	**5.7**	**5.8**	**5.5**	**4.0**	**2.9**	**4.4**	**5.5**	**6.4**	**6.7**	**5.6**	**5.3**	**4.3**	**3.6**	**4.8**
	M	1	10.4	10.9	11.4	11.8	9.7	7.4	4.2	8.8	11.7	11.1	10.4	10.2	9.4	7.8	6.5	8.4
		3	20.5	15.5	15.5	18.3	37.9	16.1	13.7	25.8	19.4	15.4	15.4	16.2	35.9	16.3	14.5	25.8
		5	45.9	20.3	19.4	33.7	86.4	42.1	42.1	71.5	41.0	20.9	20.0	30.6	83.1	43.1	40.8	71.4
		0	**5.7**	**4.6**	**5.1**	**5.2**	**4.7**	**3.5**	**2.9**	**4.4**	**4.3**	**5.9**	**6.3**	**6.0**	**4.6**	**4.1**	**3.7**	**4.3**
TAR-GARCH-L1	M^*	1	10.9	10.8	9.8	10.6	12.9	7.3	7.1	12.5	10.5	10.4	10.0	10.7	12.7	9.4	7.8	9.1
		3	22.2	15.9	13.3	17.4	50.9	22.2	23.7	39.9	19.5	15.2	14.8	17.3	51.0	27.3	25.9	38.5
		5	49.6	19.9	17.7	36.2	89.7	55.8	58.2	84.8	45.6	20.5	18.9	35.8	91.1	58.3	57.4	87.1
		0	**5.5**	**4.8**	**5.5**	**5.1**	**4.3**	**3.3**	**3.2**	**4.2**	**4.5**	**5.9**	**6.3**	**5.8**	**4.5**	**4.2**	**3.3**	**4.3**
	$\ddot{M}$	1	10.8	11.2	10.4	10.6	12.6	7.4	7.3	12.2	10.6	10.2	10.0	10.4	12.2	9.3	7.3	9.2
		3	21.8	16.2	13.7	17.3	49.8	21.9	23.0	38.9	19.5	14.7	14.7	16.9	50.1	26.7	25.4	38.2
		5	49.0	20.5	18.3	35.8	89.2	54.7	57.1	84.7	45.7	19.7	18.8	35.5	90.4	57.7	57.1	86.4
		0	**6.2**	**5.4**	**5.7**	**5.3**	**5.7**	**4.2**	**2.1**	**4.7**	**6.6**	**6.2**	**7.0**	**6.9**	**5.1**	**4.5**	**3.5**	**4.5**

(continued)

Table 2 (continued)

DGP	Test	δ	$T = 500$								$T = 1{,}000$							
			$z_{1,\mathrm{lt}}$	$z_{2,\mathrm{lt}}$	$z_{3,\mathrm{lt}}$	z_{lt}	$z_{2,\mathrm{nt}}$	$z_{3,\mathrm{nt}}$	$z_{4,\mathrm{nt}}$	z_{nt}	$z_{1,\mathrm{lt}}$	$z_{2,\mathrm{lt}}$	$z_{3,\mathrm{lt}}$	z_{lt}	$z_{2,\mathrm{nt}}$	$z_{3,\mathrm{nt}}$	$z_{4,\mathrm{nt}}$	z_{nt}
	M	1	10.8	9.9	10.3	10.0	8.1	5.6	3.3	8.1	11.8	11.1	12.4	12.1	9.8	7.8	6.2	8.0
		3	25.6	13.7	15.4	20.0	26.9	14.6	8.7	18.3	27.4	17.3	16.6	23.2	31.2	16.5	10.9	21.2
		5	62.2	18.3	20.3	46.5	79.4	49.0	30.0	59.6	62.7	21.4	20.6	46.5	79.4	45.3	27.7	66.4
		0	**5.5**	**5.6**	**5.8**	**5.2**	**4.6**	**2.5**	**2.0**	**4.0**	**5.3**	**5.1**	**5.0**	**5.7**	**4.6**	**3.9**	**2.8**	**5.1**
TAR-GARCH-L2	M^*	1	10.9	11.0	9.7	11.0	9.2	4.5	4.1	10.0	11.8	9.2	10.0	11.2	9.6	7.5	5.9	11.1
		3	32.9	16.5	14.6	24.4	43.1	20.9	15.8	38.2	32.4	15.3	14.7	26.9	39.8	23.2	14.7	40.3
		5	72.3	22.6	20.0	59.3	82.0	55.0	40.2	79.2	74.6	19.9	19.5	63.6	84.6	57.9	36.9	86.3
		0	**4.8**	**4.1**	**5.2**	**4.8**	**4.6**	**2.4**	**2.2**	**4.1**	**5.5**	**4.9**	**5.1**	**5.9**	**4.8**	**3.5**	**2.5**	**5.1**
	$\ddot{M}$	1	10.4	10.1	9.6	11.0	10.4	5.3	4.8	10.4	11.4	9.5	9.9	11.0	11.0	7.6	5.4	11.0
		3	31.4	15.9	14.6	24.7	44.2	23.0	16.9	40.9	30.9	14.8	14.3	26.9	41.9	22.8	14.8	38.9
		5	67.2	22.5	20.0	57.2	79.0	55.9	40.3	79.6	72.7	21.0	19.8	62.1	83.8	56.8	37.3	85.1

Note The entries are empirical rejection frequencies in percentage. The empirical sizes are in boldface

at $T = 1{,}000$. This is consistent with the parameter setting $\gamma_1 = \delta T^{-1/2}$ that we design to simulate the "local" powers of the M test. Importantly, the aforementioned size and power properties also hold for the M^* test and the $\dot{M}$ test (or the $\ddot{M}$ test). Thus, these tests are of the same robustness and power directions, and it is essential to discriminate between them by comparing their relative power performance.

Third, and more importantly, the relative power performance of these tests is consistent with our theoretical results. Specifically, Table 1 shows that the optimized M^* test and its approximation, the feasible $\dot{M}$ test, tend to outperform, or at least have very similar performance to, the (suboptimal) M test in the presence of conditional heteroskedasticity. Meanwhile, the $\dot{M}$ test provides a reasonable approximation to the M^* test in view of their power performance. To make these points clear, we simulate and plot the empirical power curves of the M, M^*, and $\dot{M}$ tests, under various AR (TAR) processes with $z_{1,lt}$ ($z_{2,nt}$), $T = 500$, and $\delta = 0, 0.5, 1, \ldots, 5$ in Fig. 1. We focus on this $z_t(\theta, \varsigma)$ because the testing powers of these tests under the AR (TAR) processes are mainly contributed by using this $z_t(\theta, \varsigma)$; see Table 1. Thus, we may evaluate our theoretical results in a more direct way by focusing on this $z_t(\theta, \varsigma)$.

This figure shows that these tests are indistinguishable under conditional homoskedasticity. By contrast, the M^* test and the $\dot{M}$ test outperform the M test under conditional heteroskedasticity. As implied by Proposition 2, the M^* test yields the upper bound of the power curve of the M test. A mild exception appears in Fig. 1f, in which the $\dot{M}$ test is marginally more powerful than the M^* test when $\delta \leq 1$. This might be due to sampling variation. In general, the power curve of the $\dot{M}$ test is between those of the M^* test and the M test. This suggests that the $\dot{M}$ test is useful for improving the local powers of the M test, even though it is not based on the true $\Sigma_t(\theta_o)$. This improvement is likely due to the fact that, despite the conditional homoskedasticity approximation ($C_t(\theta) = 1$) implicitly used by the M test and the GARCH approximation explicitly used by the $\dot{M}$ test are both misspecified for the EGARCH processes, the latter obviously provides a better approximation than the former.

From Table 1 and Fig. 1, we also observe that the "significance" of the power advantage of the M^* and $\dot{M}$ tests over the M test is data-dependent. Given $T = 500$ and $\delta = 3$ ($\delta = 5$), the M, M^*, and $\dot{M}$ tests with $z_{1,lt}$ ($z_{2,nt}$) have respective powers: 81.7 %, 86.5 %, and 83.6 % (43.2 %, 49.8 %, and 46.8 %) under AR-EGARCH1 (TAR-EGARCH1). These powers are not substantially different. In comparison, given the same T and δ, these tests have respective powers: 67.4 %, 87.9 %, and 75.1 % (33.9 %, 57.1 %, and 44.9 %) under AR-EGARCH2 (TAR-EGARCH2). The M^* and $\dot{M}$ tests outperform the M test in both cases, but it is particularly important to replace the suboptimal M test by the $\dot{M}$ test when conditional heteroskedasticity becomes stronger.

The second experiment also supports the validity of our theoretical results in finite samples. Table 2 shows that the M^* and $\ddot{M}$ tests tend to generate higher powers than, or at least very similar powers to, the M test under conditional asymmetry. For instance, the M, M^*, and $\ddot{M}$ tests with z_{lt} (z_{nt}) are, respectively, of the powers: 67.1 %, 78.2 %, and 78.3 % (25.8 %, 39.9 %, and 38.9 %) under AR-GARCH-L1

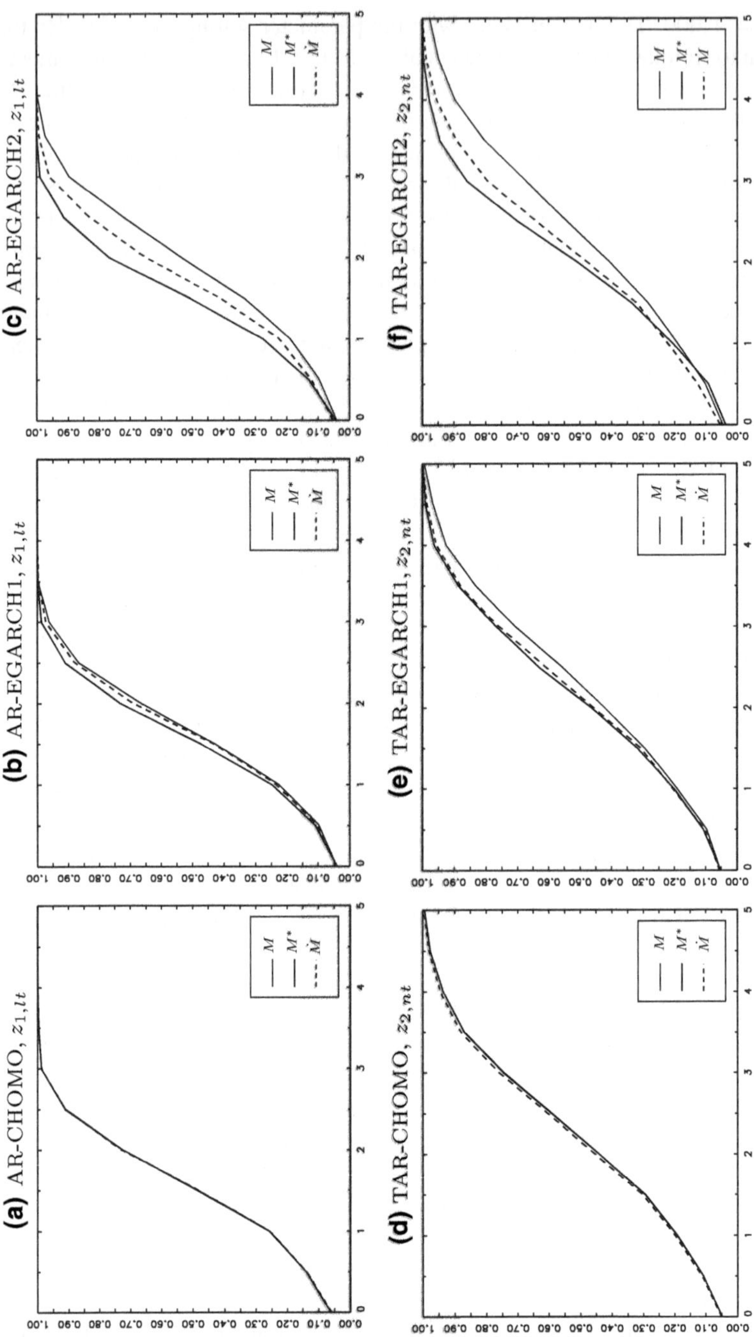

Fig. 1 Power curves of the M, M^*, and $\dot{M}$ tests. **a** AR-CHOMO, $z_{1,lt}$ **b** AR-EGARCH1, $z_{1,lt}$ **c** AR-EGARCH2, $z_{1,lt}$ **d** TAR-CHOMO, $z_{2,nt}$ **e** TAR-EGARCH1, $z_{2,nt}$ **f** TAR-EGARCH2, $z_{2,nt}$

(TAR-GARCH-L1) when $T = 500$ and $\delta = 3$. Similar to the first experiment, this also shows the power advantage of the M^* test and the $\ddot{M}$ test over the suboptimal M test. Note that the M^* test and the $\ddot{M}$ test have very similar empirical rejection frequencies in all cases for the second experiment. This reflects the fact that the feasible $\ddot{M}$ test is based on a consistent estimator for Σ_{ot} and hence is asymptotically equivalent to the infeasible M^* test. In this scenario, it is very easy to implement the optimized test.

From these two experiments, we see that the M^* and $\dot{M}$ (or $\ddot{M}$) tests are potentially useful for improving the local powers of the M test without sacrificing their size performance, that is, without sacrificing their robustness to the unknown conditional distribution.

7 Conclusions

This chapter is concerned with the optimality of RCM tests. We argue that the conventional score test interpretation is incompatible with the rationale of RCM tests. Instead, we explore a different type of test optimality by considering a generalized RCM test based on the EF approach and deriving the upper bound of its noncentrality parameter without a conditional distribution assumption. We then propose to optimize the generalized RCM test and show that the resulting test achieves this upper bound and is thus semiparametrically optimal. The optimized test is readily applicable to various partial specifications, such as the conditional mean, mean-and-variance, and quantile models. Thus, the proposed optimization method is useful for improving the power property of many existing RCM tests.

The implementation of the optimized test requires estimation (approximation) of the conditional covariance matrix of the generalized residual vector. The form of this matrix depends on the partial specifications being tested. When the covariance matrix can be consistently estimated, the optimized test constructed from this estimate is semiparametrically optimal. When the covariance matrix is difficult to estimate, it may be approximated using a sensible model. The power performance of the resulting test would be better if the postulated model provides a more accurate approximation to the covariance matrix. Even when the model is misspecified, the optimized test remains robust. Therefore, the approach proposed in this study allows us to pursue optimality of RCM tests without sacrificing their robustness to unknown conditional distributions. This makes the optimized test a practically useful tool.

Acknowledgments The authors are indebted to the co-editor, Norman Swanson, and an anonymous referee for their valuable comments and suggestions that led to a substantially improved version of this chapter. They also gratefully thank Cheng Hsiao, Biing-Shen Kuo, and Michael McAleer for helpful discussions. Yi-Tin Chen thanks the National Science Council of Taiwan (NSC 96-2415-H-001-016) for the research support.

Appendix

A.1 Assumptions: [A.1]–[A.2]

Because the derivation of the asymptotic results in [A.1] and [A.2] are known in the literature, the following discussions are provided only for completeness. For ease of exposition, the discussions are focused on the case where $\pi_t(\theta)v_t(\theta)$ and $z_t^s(\theta)v_t^s(\theta)$ are smooth functions of θ.

Recall that (i) Θ is a compact set. Let $Q_T(\theta)$ and $Q_o(\theta)$ be, respectively, the inner products of $T^{-1}\sum_{t=1}^{T}\pi_t(\theta)v_t(\theta)$ and $\mathbb{E}[\pi_t(\theta)v_t(\theta)]$. Given the following conditions for EF: (ii) $\{\pi_t(\theta)v_t(\theta)\}$ is stationary and ergodic for each $\theta \in \Theta$, (iii) $\mathbb{E}[\pi_t(\theta)v_t(\theta)]$ exists and is finite for each $\theta \in \Theta$, and is continuous on Θ, and (iv) $\mathbb{E}[\sup_{\theta\in\Theta}\|\pi_t(\theta)v_t(\theta)\|] < 0$, we may have the uniform convergence: $\sup_{\theta\in\Theta}|Q_T(\theta) - Q_o(\theta)| \xrightarrow{\text{p}} 0$; see, e.g., Hall (2005, Lemma 3.1). The consistency of $\bar{\theta}_T$ for θ_o, stated in [A.1], may follow this result and (v) the identifiable uniqueness condition: (6) only holds for a unique $\theta_o \in \Theta$; see, e.g., Hall (2005, Theorem 3.1).

If the EF is smooth in the sense that (vi) $\pi_t(\theta)v_t(\Theta)$ is continuously differentiable on Θ, then we can take the mean-value expansion of the estimating equation: $T^{-1}\sum_{t=1}^{T}\pi_t(\bar{\theta}_T)v_t(\bar{\theta}_T) = 0$ to write that

$$\frac{1}{\sqrt{T}}\sum_{t=1}^{T}\pi_t(\theta_o)v_t(\theta_o) + \frac{1}{T}\sum_{t=1}^{T}\nabla_{\theta^\top}\left(\pi_t(\tilde{\theta}_T)v_t(\tilde{\theta}_T)\right)\sqrt{T}(\bar{\theta}_T - \theta_o) = 0 \quad \text{(A.1)}$$

for some $\tilde{\theta}_T \in \Theta$ such that $\|\tilde{\theta}_T - \theta_o\| \leq \|\bar{\theta}_T - \theta_o\|$. Given the consistency of $\bar{\theta}_T$ for θ_o, the expansion in (A.1), and the conditions: (vii) $\{\nabla_{\theta^\top}(\pi_t(\theta)v_t(\theta))\}$ obeys a ULLN, (viii) $\mathbb{E}[\nabla_{\theta^\top}(\pi_t(\theta)v_t(\theta))]$ is continuous on Θ, and (ix) $\mathbb{E}[\nabla_{\theta^\top}(\pi_t(\theta_o)v_t(\theta_o))]$ is positive definite, it is easy to show that

$$\sqrt{T}(\bar{\theta}_T - \theta_o) = -\mathbb{E}[\nabla_{\theta^\top}(\pi_t(\theta_o)v_t(\theta_o))]^{-1}\frac{1}{\sqrt{T}}\sum_{t=1}^{T}\pi_t(\theta_o)v_t(\theta_o) + o_p(1); \quad \text{(A.2)}$$

see, e.g., Newey and McFadden (1994, Sect. 3). Following Magnus and Neudecker (1988, p. 30, Eq. 5), we can write that $\mathbb{E}[\pi_t(\theta)v_t(\theta)] = \mathbb{E}[(v_t(\theta)^\top \otimes I_p)\text{vec}(\pi_t(\theta))]$. Accordingly, we have

$$\begin{aligned}\mathbb{E}[\nabla_{\theta^\top}(\pi_t(\theta_o)v_t(\theta_o))] &= \mathbb{E}[\pi_t(\theta_o)\nabla_{\theta^\top}v_t(\theta_o)] + \mathbb{E}[(v_t(\theta_o)^\top \otimes I_p)\nabla_{\theta^\top}\text{vec}(\pi_t(\theta_o))] \\ &= \mathbb{E}[\pi_t(\theta_o)\mathbb{E}[\nabla_{\theta^\top}v_t(\theta_o)|\mathcal{X}_t]] \\ &\quad + \mathbb{E}[(\mathbb{E}[v_t(\theta_o)|\mathcal{X}_t]^\top \otimes I_p)\nabla_{\theta^\top}\text{vec}(\pi_t(\theta_o))], \qquad \text{(A.3)}\end{aligned}$$

where the second equality is due to the law of iterated expectations. Condition (vi) may allow us to write that $w_t(\theta_o) = \mathbb{E}[\nabla_\theta^\top v_t(\theta_o)|\mathcal{X}_t]$. Recall that $\mathbb{E}[v_t(\theta_o)|\mathcal{X}_t] = 0$ holds under H_o. Given condition (x): $\mathbb{E}[(z_t(\theta)\otimes I_p)\nabla_\theta^\top\text{vec}(\pi_t(\theta))]$ exists and is finite for each $\theta \in \Theta$, and is continuous on Θ, this restriction also holds under H_{1T} as $T \to \infty$ because

$$\mathbb{E}[(\mathbb{E}[v_t(\theta_T)|\mathcal{X}_t]^\top \otimes I_p)\nabla_\theta^\top \operatorname{vec}(\pi_t(\theta_T))] = T^{-1/2}\delta^\top \mathbb{E}[(z_t(\theta_T) \otimes I_p)\nabla_{\theta^\top} \operatorname{vec}(\pi_t(\theta_T))] \tag{A.4}$$
$$= o(1)$$

and $\theta_T \to \theta_o$ as $T \to \infty$. The asymptotic linear representation in (12) is obtained from (A.2) and these results. This shows that conditions (i)–(x) serve as a set of sufficient conditions underlying [A.1].

If the moment function $z_t^s(\theta)v_t^s(\theta)$ is smooth in the sense that (xi) $z_t^s(\theta)v_t^s(\theta)$ is continuously differentiable on Θ, then we can also take the mean-value expansion of the estimated moment: $T^{-1}\sum_{t=1}^T z_t^s(\bar{\theta}_T)v_t^s(\bar{\theta}_T)$. Given the consistency of $\bar{\theta}_T$ for θ_o, this expansion, and the conditions: (xii) $\{\nabla_{\theta^\top}(z_t^s(\theta)v_t^s(\theta))\}$ is stationary and ergodic, and obeys a ULLN and (xiii) $\mathbb{E}[\nabla_{\theta^\top}(z_t^s(\theta)v_t^s(\theta))]$ is continuous on Θ, it is also easy to show that

$$\frac{1}{\sqrt{T}}\sum_{t=1}^T z_t^s(\bar{\theta}_T)v_t^s(\bar{\theta}_T) = \frac{1}{\sqrt{T}}\sum_{t=1}^T z_t^s(\theta_o)v_t^s(\theta_o) \tag{A.5}$$
$$+ \mathbb{E}[\nabla_{\theta^\top}(z_t^s(\theta_o)v_t^s(\theta_o))]\sqrt{T}(\bar{\theta}_T - \theta_o) + o_p(1).$$

Similar to (A.3) and (A.4), given condition (xiii), we can show that, under H_o,

$$\mathbb{E}[\nabla_{\theta^\top}(z_t^s(\theta_o)v_t^s(\theta_o))] = \mathbb{E}[z_t^s(\theta_o)w_t^s(\theta_o))^\top].$$

Given condition (xiv): $\mathbb{E}[(z_t^s(\theta) \otimes I_p)\nabla_{\theta^\top}\operatorname{vec}(z_t^s(\theta))]$ exists and is finite for each $\theta \in \Theta$, and is continuous on Θ this restriction also holds under H_{1T} as $T \to \infty$. The asymptotic expansion in [A.2] is due to (A.5) and these results, and conditions: (i)–(v) and (xi)–(xiv) are a set of sufficient conditions underlying this assumption.

A.2 Proof of Proposition 2

The matrices considered in this proof are all evaluated at $\theta = \theta_o$. For notational brevity, we denote $C_t := C_t(\theta_o)$, $\Sigma_t := \Sigma_t(\theta_o)$, $\Sigma_t^s := \Sigma_t^s(\theta_o)$, $w_t^s := w_t^s(\theta_o)$, $w_t^* := w_t^*(\theta_o)$, $z_t^s := z_t^s(\theta_o)$, $z_t^* := z_t^*(\theta_o)$, $z_{wt}^s := z_{wt}^s(\theta_o)$, and $z_{wt}^* := z_{wt}^*(\theta_o)$ in the proof. Recall that $C_t^{1/2}$ and $\Sigma_t^{1/2}$ are symmetric and $\Sigma_t^{s1/2} := \Sigma_t^{1/2}C_t^{1/2}$. Therefore, we can write $\Sigma_t^s = (\Sigma_t^{s1/2})^\top\Sigma_t^{s1/2}$. By denoting $\xi_{1t} := z_{wt}^s\Sigma_t^{s-1/2}$ and $\xi_{2t} := z_{wt}^s(\Sigma_t^{s1/2})^\top$, we can rewrite (19) as

$$v = \delta^\top\left(\mathbb{E}[\xi_{1t}\xi_{2t}^\top]\mathbb{E}[\xi_{2t}\xi_{2t}^\top]^{-1}\mathbb{E}[\xi_{2t}\xi_{1t}^\top]\right)\delta. \tag{A.6}$$

By the definition of z^s_{wt}, w^*_t, and z^*_t, we can reexpress ξ_{1t} as:

$$\begin{aligned}\xi_{1t} &= (z^s_t - \mathbb{E}[z^s_t w^{s\top}_t]\mathbb{E}[w^s_t w^{s\top}_t]^{-1} w^s_t)\Sigma^{s-1/2}_t,\\ &= (z_t - \mathbb{E}[z^s_t w^{s\top}_t]\mathbb{E}[w^s_t w^{s\top}_t]^{-1} w_t)C^{1/2}_t \Sigma^{s-1/2}_t,\\ &= (z^*_t - \mathbb{E}[z^s_t w^{s\top}_t]\mathbb{E}[w^s_t w^{s\top}_t]^{-1} w^*_t)(\Sigma^{1/2}_t C^{1/2}_t \Sigma^{s-1/2}_t).\end{aligned}$$

Since

$$\Sigma^{1/2}_t C^{1/2}_t \Sigma^{s-1/2}_t = \Sigma^{1/2}_t C^{1/2}_t (\Sigma^{1/2}_t C^{1/2}_t)^{-1} = I_r,$$

we can simplify the above expression of ξ_{1t} as

$$\begin{aligned}\xi_{1t} &= z^*_t - \mathbb{E}[z^s_t w^{s\top}_t]\mathbb{E}[w^s_t w^{s\top}_t]^{-1} w^*_t\\ &= z^*_{\mathrm{wt}} + (\mathbb{E}[z^*_t w^{*\top}_t]\mathbb{E}[w^*_t w^{*\top}_t]^{-1} - \mathbb{E}[z^s_t w^{s\top}_t]\mathbb{E}[w^s_t w^{s\top}_t]^{-1}) w^*_t\end{aligned}$$

and show that

$$\mathbb{E}[\xi_{1t}\xi^\top_{2t}] = \mathbb{E}[z^*_{wt}\xi^\top_{2t}] + (\mathbb{E}[z^*_t w^{*\top}_t]\mathbb{E}[w^*_t w^{*\top}_t]^{-1} - \mathbb{E}[z^s_t w^{s\top}_t]\mathbb{E}[w^s_t w^{s\top}_t]^{-1})\mathbb{E}[w^*_t \xi^\top_{2t}].$$

Using the fact that

$$\begin{aligned}\mathbb{E}[w^*_t \xi^\top_{2t}] &= \mathbb{E}[w_t \Sigma^{-1/2}_t \Sigma^{s1/2}_t z^{s\top}_{wt}] = \mathbb{E}[w_t C^{1/2}_t z^{s\top}_{wt}]\\ &= \mathbb{E}[w^s_t z^{s\top}_{wt}] = (\mathbb{E}[z^s_{wt} w^{s\top}_t])^\top = 0,\end{aligned}$$

we obtain an important result: $\mathbb{E}[\xi_{1t}\xi^\top_{2t}] = \mathbb{E}[z^*_{wt}\xi^\top_{2t}]$. By this relationship, we can present (A.6) as

$$\nu = \delta^\top \left(\mathbb{E}[z^*_{wt}\xi^\top_{2t}]\mathbb{E}[\xi_{2t}\xi^\top_{2t}]^{-1}\mathbb{E}[\xi_{2t} z^{*\top}_{wt}]\right)\delta.$$

According to (43), we can write that $\upsilon^* = \delta^\top \mathbb{E}[z^*_{wt} z^{*\top}_{wt}]\delta$. Consequently, we have

$$\begin{aligned}\nu^* - \nu &= \delta^\top \left(\mathbb{E}[z^*_{wt} z^{*\top}_{wt}] - \mathbb{E}[z^*_{wt}\xi^\top_{2t}]\mathbb{E}[\xi_{2t}\xi^\top_{2t}]^{-1}\mathbb{E}[\xi_{2t} z^{*\top}_{wt}]\right)\delta\\ &= \delta^\top \mathbb{E}[\zeta_t \zeta^\top_t]\delta,\end{aligned}$$

in which $\zeta_t := z^*_{wt} - \mathbb{E}[z^*_{wt}\xi^\top_{2t}]\mathbb{E}[\xi_{2t}\xi^\top_{2t}]^{-1}\xi_{2t}$. Proposition 2 is proved because the matrix $\mathbb{E}[\zeta_t \zeta^\top_t]$ is positive semi-definite. □

References

Andrews, D. W. K. (1994). Empirical process methods in econometrics. In: R. F. Engle and D. L. McFadden (Eds.), Handbook of Econometrics, Volume 4, Amsterdam: Elsevier.

Basawa, I. V. (1991). Generalized score tests for composite hypotheses, In: V. P. Godambe (Ed), Estimating Functions, Oxford: Oxford University Press.

Bera, A. K. and Y. Bilias (2001). Rao's score, Neyman's $C(\alpha)$ and Silvey's LM tests: An essay on historical developments and some new results, Journal of Statistical Planning and Inference, 97, 9–44.
Bera, A. K. and Y. Bilias (2002). The MM, ME, ML, EL, EF and GMM approaches to estimation: A synthesis, Journal of Econometrics, 107, 51–86.
Bera, A. K., Y. Bilias, and P. Simlai (2006). Estimating functions and equations: An essay on historical developments with applications to econometrics, In: T. C. Mills, and K. Patterson (Eds), Palgrave Handbook of Econometrics, Volume 1, 427–476, London: Palgrave Macmillan.
Berkes, I., L. Horváth, and P. Kokoszka (2003). Asymptotics for GARCH squared residual correlations, Econometric Theory, 19, 515–540.
Bierens, H. J. (1982). Consistent model specification tests, Journal of Econometrics, 20, 105–134.
Bierens, H. J. (1994). Topics in Advanced Econometrics: Estimation, Testing, and Specification of Cross-section and Time Series Models, New York: Cambridge University Press.
Bollerslev, T. (1987). A conditionally heteroskedastic time series model for speculative prices and rates of return, Review of Economics and Statistics, 69, 542–547.
Bollerslev, T. and J. M. Wooldridge (1992). Quasi-maximum likelihood estimation and inference in dynamic models with time-varying covariances, Econometric Reviews, 11, 143–172.
Breusch, T. (1978). Testing for autocorrelation in dynamic linear models, Australian Economic Papers, 17, 334–355.
Breusch, T. and A. Pagan (1979). A simple test for heteroscedasticity and random coefficient variation, Econometrica, 47, 1287–1294.
Cameron, A. C. and P. K. Trivedi (1998). Regression Analysis of Count Data, New York: Cambridge University Press.
Cameron, A. C. and P. K. Trivedi (2005). Microeconometrics: Methods and Applications, New York: Cambridge University Press.
Chamberlain, G. (1987). Asymptotic efficiency in estimation with conditional moment restrictions, Journal of Econometrics, 34, 305–334.
Chen, Y.-T. (2008). A unified approach to standardized-residuals-based correlation tests for GARCH-type models, Journal of Applied Econometrics, 23, 111–133.
Chesher, A. and R. Smith (1997). Likelihood ratio specification tests, Econometrica, 65, 627–646.
Cox, D., and E. Snell (1968). A general definition of residuals, Journal of the Royal Statistical Society, B30, 248–V265.
Davidson, R. and J. G. MacKinnon (1981). Several tests for model specification in the presence of alternative hypotheses, Econometrica, 49, 781–793.
Davidson, R. and J. G. MacKinnon (1985). Heteroskedasticity-robust tests in regression directions. Annales de l' INSEE 59/60, 183–V218.
Davidson, R. and J. G. MacKinnon (1990). Specification tests based on artificial regressions, Journal of the American Statistical Association, 85, 220–227.
Davidson, R. and J. G. MacKinnon (1993). Estimation and Inference in Econometrics, New York: Oxford University Press.
Davidson, R. and J. G. MacKinnon (2000). Artificial regressions, In B. H. Baltagi (Ed), A Companion to Theoretical Econometrics, Oxford: Blackwell Publishing.
Dezhbakhsh, H. (1990). The inappropriate use of serial correlation tests in dynamic linear models, Review of Economics and Statistics, 72, 126–132.
Durbin, J. (1960). Estimation of parameters in time-series regression models, Journal of the Royal Statistical Society, B22, 139–153.
Eitrheim, Ø. and T. Teräsvirta (1996), Testing the adequacy of smooth transition autoregressive models, Journal of Econometrics, 74, 59–75.
Engle, R. F. (1982a), Wald, likelihood ratio, and Lagrange multiplier tests in econometrics, In Z. Griliches (Ed), Handbook of Econometrics, Volume 2, Amsterdam: Elsevier.
Engle, R. F. (1982b), Autoregressive conditional heteroscedasticity with estimates of the variance of United Kingdom inflation, Econometrica, 50, 987–1007.

Engle, R. F. and G. González-Rivera (1991). Semiparametric ARCH models, Journal of Business and Economic Statistics, 9, 345–359.
Engle, R. F. and V. K. Ng (1993). Measuring and testing the impact of news on volatility, Journal of Finance, 48, 1749–1778.
Engle, R. F. and S. Manganelli (2004). CAViaR: Conditional autoregressive value at risk by regression quantiles, Journal of Business and Economic Statistics, 22, 367–381.
Fisher, G. R. and M. McAleer (1981). Alternative procedures and associated tests of significance for non-nested hypotheses, Journal of Econometrics, 16, 103–119.
Godambe, V. P. (1960). An optimum property of regular maximum likelihood estimation, Annals of Mathematical Statistics, 31, 1208–1211.
Godambe, V. P. (1985). The foundations of finite sample estimation in stochastic processes, Biometrika, 72, 419–428.
Godambe, V. P. (2001). Estimation of median: Quasi-likelihood and optimum estimating functions, Discussion Paper 2001–2004, Department of Statistics and Actuarial Sciences, University of Waterloo.
Godambe, V. P. and M. E. Thompson (1989). An extension of quasi-likelihood estimation, Journal of Statistical Planning and Inference, 22, 137–152.
Godambe, V. P. and B. K. Kale (1991). Estimating functions: An overview, In: V. P. Godambe (Ed), Estimating Functions, Oxford: Oxford University Press.
Godfrey, L. G. (1978). Testing against general autoregressive and moving average error models when the regressors include lagged dependent variables, Econometrica, 46, 1293–1301.
Godfrey, L. G. and C.D. Orme (2001). On improving the robustness and reliability of Rao's score test, Journal of Statistical Planning and Inference, 97, 153–176.
Gouriéroux, C., A. Monfort, E. Renault, and A. Trognon (1987). Generalised residuals, Journal of Econometrics, 34, 5–32.
Hall, A. R. (2005). Generalized Method of Moments, Oxford: Oxford University Press.
Hansen, B. E. (1994). Autoregressive conditional density estimation, International Economic Review, 35, 705–730.
Heyde, C. (1997). Quasi-Likelihood and Its Application: A General Approach to Optimal Parameter Estimation, New York: Springer.
Johnson, N. L., S. Kotz, N. Balakrishnan (1994). Continuous Univariate Distribution, Volume 1, New York:Wiley.
Keenan, D. M. (1985). A Tukey non-additivity-type test for time series nonlinearity, Biometrika, 72, 39–44.
Koenker, R. (2005). Quantile Regression, New York: Cambridge University Press.
Koenker, R. and G. Bassett (1978). Regression quantiles, Econometrica, 46, 33–50.
Komunjer, I. (2005). Quasi-maximum likelihood estimation for conditional quantiles, Journal of Econometrics, 128, 137–164.
Komunjer, I. (2007). Asymmetric power distribution: Theory and applications to risk measurement, Journal of Applied Econometrics, 22, 891–921.
Lee, T.-H., H. White, and C. W. J. Granger (1993). Testing for neglected nonlinearity in time series models: A comparison of neural network methods and alternative tests, Journal of Econometrics, 56, 269–290.
Li, W. K. and T. K. Mak (1994). On the squared residual autocorrelations in nonlinear time series with conditional heteroskedasticity, Journal of Time Series Analysis, 15, 627–636.
Li, D. X. and H. J. Turtle (2000). Semiparametric ARCH models: An estimating function approach, Journal of Business and Economic Statistics, 18, 174–186.
Lundbergh S. and T. Teräsvirta (2002). Evaluating GARCH models, Journal of Econometrics, 110, 417–435.
Luukkonen, R., P. Saikkonen and T. Teräsvirta (1988), Testing linearity against smooth transition autoregressive models, Biometrika, 75, 491–499.
MacKinnon, J. G. (1992). Model specification tests and artificial regressions, Journal of Economic Literature, 30, 102–146.

Magnus, J. R. and H. Neudecker (1988). Matrix Differential Calculus with Applications in Statistics and Econometrics, New York: Wiley.
Mittelhammer, R., Judge, G., and Miller, D. (2000). Econometric Foundations. New York: Cambridge University Press.
McLeod, A. I. and W. K. Li (1983). Diagnostic checking ARMA time series models using squared-residual autocorrelations, Journal of Time Series Analysis, 4, 269–273.
Newey, W. K. (1985). Maximum likelihood specification testing and conditional moment tests, Econometrica, 53, 1047–1070.
Newey, W. K. (1990). Semiparametric efficiency bounds, Journal of Applied Econometrics, 5, 99–135.
Newey, W. K. (1993). Efficient estimation of models with conditional moment restrictions, In G. S. Maddala, C. R. Rao, and H. D. Vinod (Eds), Handbook of Statistics, Volume 11, Amsterdam: Elsevier.
Newey, W. K. and J.L. Powell (1990). Efficient estimation of linear and type I censored regression models under conditional quantile restrictions, Econometric Theory, 6, 295–317.
Newey, W. K. and D. L. McFadden (1994). Large sample estimation and hypothesis testing. In: R. F. Engle and D. L. McFadden (Eds), Handbook of Econometrics, Volume 4, Amsterdam: Elsevier.
Neyman, J. (1959). Optimal asymptotic tests of composite statistical hypothesis, In U. Grenander (Ed), Probability and Statistics: the Harald Cramér Volume, 213–234, Uppsala: Almqvist and Wiksell.
Park, S. Y. and A. K. Bera (2009). Maximum entropy autoregressive conditional heteroskedasticity model, Journal of Econometrics, 150, 219–230.
Phillips, P. C. B. (1991). A shortcut to LAD estimator asymptotics, Econometric Theory, 7, 450–463.
Ramsey, J. B. (1969). Tests for specification errors in classical linear least squares regression analysis, Journal of the Royal Statistical Society, B31, 350–371.
Rockinger, M. and E. Jondeau (2002). Entropy densities with an application to autoregressive conditional skewness and kurtosis, Journal of Econometrics, 106, 119–142.
Tauchen, G. (1985). Diagnostic testing and evaluation of maximum likelihood models, Journal of Econometrics, 30, 415–443.
Tsay, R. S. (1986). Nonlinearity tests for time series, Biometrika, 73, 461–466.
Vinod, H. D. (1997). Using Godambe-Durbin estimating functions in econometrics, Lecture Notes-Monograph Series, Vol. 32, Selected Proceedings of the Symposium on Estimating Functions, 215–237.
Vuong, Q. H. (1989). Likelihood ratio tests for model selection and non-nested hypotheses, Econometrica, 57, 307–333.
White, H. (1980). A heteroskedasticity-consistent covariance matrix estimator and a direct test for heteroskedasticity, Econometrica, 48, 817–838.
White, H. (1984). Comment on "Tests of specification in econometrics", Econometric Reviews, 3, 261–267.
White, H. (1987). Specification testing in dynamic models, In: T. Bewley (Ed.), Advances in Econometrics-Fifth World Congress, Volume I, 1–58, New York: Cambridge University Press.
White, H. (1994). Estimation, Inference and Specification Analysis. Cambridge University Press, New York.
Wong, H. and S. Ling (2005). Mixed portmanteau tests for time-series models, Journal of Time Series Analysis, 26, 569–579.
Wooldridge, J. M. (1990a). A unified approach to robust, regression-based specification tests, Econometric Theory, 6, 17–43.
Wooldridge, J. M. (1990b). An encompassing approach to conditional mean tests with applications to testing nonnested hypotheses, Journal of Econometrics, 45, 331–350.
Wooldridge, J. M. (1991). Specification testing and quasi-Maximum-Likelihood estimation, Journal of Econometrics, 48, 29–55.

Asymptotic Properties of Penalized M Estimators with Time Series Observations

Xiaohong Chen and Zhipeng Liao

Abstract The method of penalization is a general smoothing principle to solve infinite-dimensional estimation problems. In this chapter, we study asymptotic properties of penalized M estimators with weakly dependent data. We first establish the convergence rate for any penalized M estimators of unknown functions with stationary beta mixing observations. While the existing theories on the convergence rates with i.i.d. data require that the random criteria have exponential thin tails, we allow for unbounded random criteria with finite polynomial moments. When specializing to regression and density estimation of time series models, our rates coincide with Stone (*The Annals of Statistics*, 10: 1040–1053, 1982) optimal rates for i.i.d. data. We then derive root-n asymptotic normality for any plug-in penalized M estimators of regular functionals, and provide consistent estimates of their long-run variances.

Keywords Penalized M estimation · Weakly dependent data · Convergence rate · Asymptotic normality · HAC estimation

1 Introduction

Many estimators can be obtained by maximizing an empirical criterion of a sample average form, $L_n(\alpha) \equiv n^{-1}\sum_{t=1}^{n}\ell(\alpha, Z_t)$ over a parameter space $\mathcal{A}$ (e.g., log-likelihood, least squares, least absolute deviation). They are referred to as

X. Chen (✉)
Department of Economics, Yale University, 30 Hillhouse,
Box 208281, New Haven, CT 06520, USA
e-mail: xiaohong.chen@yale.edu

Z. Liao
Department of Economics, UC Los Angeles, 8379 Bunche Hall,
Mail Stop: 147703, Los Angeles, CA 90095, USA
e-mail: zhipeng.liao@econ.ucla.edu

X. Chen and N. R. Swanson (eds.), *Recent Advances and Future Directions in Causality, Prediction, and Specification Analysis*, DOI: 10.1007/978-1-4614-1653-1_4,

maximum-likelihood-like (M) estimators by Huber (1981), Gallant and White (1988), and Newey and McFadden (1994), among others.

When the parameter space $\mathcal{A}$ is a compact subset of a finite-dimensional Euclidean space, exact M estimates are easy to compute and their asymptotic properties are well established for both independent and dependent observations. For example, if $L_n(\alpha)$ is smooth in α almost surely and $\mathcal{A}$ has non-empty interior containing a pseudo-true parameter of interest $\alpha_0 = \arg\max_{\alpha \in \mathcal{A}} E[L_n(\alpha)]$, the asymptotic normality of the M estimator $\widehat{\alpha}_n$ can be obtained by Taylor expansion of the corresponding estimating equations (or the score equation $\nabla L_n(\widehat{\alpha}_n) = 0$, when $L_n(\alpha)$ is the sample average log-likelihood, or sample moment conditions) around α_0.

When $\mathcal{A}$ is an infinite-dimensional, non-compact function space, the *exact* M estimates for a general criterion $L_n(\alpha)$ may either not be defined or may have poor asymptotic properties such as the inconsistency or slow rate of convergence, see, e.g., Grenander (1981) for many such examples. Some *approximate* M estimation methods such as *sieve* method and *penalization* (or *regularization*) method can outperform the exact M estimation procedure in infinite-dimensional setting. The sieve M estimates maximize $L_n(\alpha)$ over a sequence of (smaller and typically compact) approximating parameter spaces $\mathcal{A}_n$, instead of the original infinite-dimensional parameter space $\mathcal{A}$; see e.g., Grenander (1981), White and Wooldridge (1991) and Chen (2007). The penalized (or regularized) M estimates (Tikhonov 1963) maximize $\tilde{L}_n(\alpha)$ (a penalized or regularized version of $L_n(\alpha)$) over the whole parameter space $\mathcal{A}$. Both these methods can provide consistent estimates that may have better asymptotic and finite sample properties than those of exact M estimates. Both methods are very flexible by combining different criterion functions with different sieves (for the sieve method) and different penalties (for the penalization method). For example, both could easily implement constraints such as monotonicity and convexity; and both could handle ill-posed inverse problems; see, e.g., Chen (2007, 2011), Chen and Pouzo (2012) and the references therein for details.

The asymptotic properties of general sieve M estimates have been relatively well developed. For example, for sieve M estimation with i.i.d. observations, Shen and Wong (1994), Birge and Massart (1994), Van de Geer (2000) derived the convergence rates; Shen (1997) established the $\sqrt{n}$ asymptotic normality of plug-in estimates of regular functions (i.e., functionals that could be estimated at a root-n rate); Chen and Liao (2008) derived the asymptotic normality for plug-in estimates of irregular functionals (i.e., functionals that could be at best estimated at a slower than root-n rate) and provided simple consistent variance estimates. For sieve M estimation with weakly dependent data, Chen and Shen (1998) obtained the non-parametric convergence rates and the $\sqrt{n}$-asymptotic normality for plug-in estimates of regular functionals; Chen et al. (2011) derived the asymptotic normality and proposed autocorrelation robust inference procedures for plug-in estimates of possibly irregular functionals.

There are some published work on the asymptotic properties of general penalized M estimators for i.i.d. data. Earlier theories developed by Wahba (1990), Gu (2002) and others are confined to the reproducing kernel Hilbert space framework, and relied on explicit solutions that can be exactly expressed as splines (i.e., smoothing splines).[1] The search for a spline representation for the exact solution often requires various boundary conditions on the space of functions, which are hard to justify in most economics applications. When the data are i.i.d. and when the centered random criterion function has an exponential thin tail, Shen (1997, 1998) and Van de Geer (2000) obtained the rate of convergence and the $\sqrt{n}$-asymptotic normality for general penalized M estimators that may not have a closed form solution expressed as splines.

In this chapter, we give up the search for the exact spline representation, but use the penalization to make the effective parameter space relatively compact. Thus, it is very flexible with the choice of parameter spaces as well as the choice of the penalization. We can use infinitely many terms of spline, Fourier series, wavelet, and many other basis expansions to implement the estimation with or without economics constraints. We study the rate of convergence (in a general pseudometric) and the asymptotic normality of penalized M estimates with weakly dependent data. Our sufficient conditions for asymptotic properties are more or less the same as those for sieve M estimates in Chen and Shen (1998) for time series data. Instead of imposing the strong exponential thin tail condition (as assumed in the existing penalization literature for i.i.d. data), we allow for polynomial tail of the centered random criterion function, which is important for economic time series applications. When specializing to time series regression and density estimation, our rates coincide with Stone's (1982) optimal rates for i.i.d. data. We then derive the root-n asymptotic normality for any plug-in penalized M estimators of regular functionals, and provide consistent estimates of their long-run variances (LRVs). We point out that this chapter is an updated and improved version of Chen (1997), which is an old unpublished working paper that established the rates of convergence of penalized M estimators and the root-n asymptotic normality of plug-in penalized M estimators of regular functionals for time series data. But Chen (1997) derived the rate result under the strong exponential thin tail condition and did not provide any consistent LRV estimators.

The rest of the chapter is organized as follows. Section 2 defines the general penalized M estimates and provides two illustrative examples. Section 3 establishes the rates of convergence for penalized M estimates with stationary weakly dependent observations. Section 4 develops the root-n asymptotic normality for plug-in penalized M estimates of regular functionals, and Sect. 5 provides consistent estimates of their LRVs. Section 6 briefly concludes. The Appendix contains all the technical proofs.

2 Definitions and Examples

Throughout the chapter, we let $\{Z_t\}_{t=1}^{n}$ be a weakly dependent sequence with $Z_t \in \mathcal{Z} \subset \mathcal{R}^{d_z}$ for each t, $(1 \le d_z < \infty)$, with marginal density $P_{0,t}(z)$ that is related to α_0, the pseudo-true parameter of interest. Let $d(\cdot, \cdot)$ be a general pseudometric on an

[1] Corradi and White (1995) applied this approach to establish convergence rate for Tikhonov-regularized neural networks.

infinite-dimensional parameter space $\mathcal{A}$ and $L_n(\alpha) \equiv n^{-1}\sum_{t=1}^{n}\ell(\alpha, Z_t)$ be an empirical criterion. We assume that the pseudo-true parameter $\alpha_0 \in \mathcal{A}$ satisfies:

$$E\left[L_n(\alpha_0)\right] \geq \sup_{\alpha\in\mathcal{A}} E\left[L_n(\alpha)\right].$$

Let $K(\alpha_0, \alpha) \equiv n^{-1}\sum_{t=1}^{n} E\left[\ell(\alpha_0, Z_t) - \ell(\alpha, Z_t)\right]$. Notice that $K(\alpha_0, \alpha)$ is the Kullback–Leibler information number based on n observations if the criterion is a log-likelihood.

One way to overcome the difficulties of optimizing over an infinite dimensional non-compact parameter space is to include a penalty describing the plausibility of each parameter value to the empirical criterion to be optimized. The penalty effectively forces the optimization to be carried out within compact subsets depending on sample size. More specifically, we denote

$$\tilde{L}_n(\alpha) \equiv L_n(\alpha) - \lambda_n J(\alpha),$$

where $J(\alpha)$ is a non-negative penalty function and λ_n is the tuning parameter. An *approximate penalized M estimate*, denoted by $\widehat{\alpha}_n$, is defined as an approximate maximizer of $\tilde{L}_n(\alpha)$ over $\mathcal{A}$, i.e.,

$$\tilde{L}_n(\widehat{\alpha}_n) \geq \sup_{\alpha\in\mathcal{A}} \tilde{L}_n(\alpha) - a_n, \tag{1}$$

where $a_n = o_p(1)$. The above procedure is called the method of penalization (see e.g., Tikhonov 1963 and Wahba 1990). Let $\rho(\cdot) : \mathcal{A} \to \mathcal{R}$ be a known functional. Sometimes $\rho(\alpha_0)$ is also the parameter of interest. The *plug-in penalized M estimate* for $\rho(\alpha)$ is simply $\rho(\widehat{\alpha}_n)$.

In this chapter, we study asymptotic properties of penalized M estimates with time series data. Let $\mathcal{I}_{-\infty}^{t}$ and $\mathcal{I}_{t+j}^{\infty}$ be $\sigma -$ fields generated, respectively, by $(Z_{-\infty}, \cdots, Z_t)$ and $(Z_{t+j}, \cdots, Z_\infty)$. Define

$$\phi(j) \equiv \sup_t \sup\{|P(B|A) - P(B)| : A \in \mathcal{I}_{-\infty}^{t}, P(A) > 0, B \in \mathcal{I}_{t+j}^{\infty}\}.$$

$$\beta(j) \equiv \sup_t E \sup\{|P(B|\mathcal{I}_{-\infty}^{t}) - P(B)| : B \in \mathcal{I}_{t+j}^{\infty}\}.$$

The process $\{Z_t\}_{t=-\infty}^{\infty}$ is called *uniform mixing* if $\phi(j) \to 0$ as $j \to \infty$; is *β-mixing or absolutely regular* if $\beta(j) \to 0$ as $j \to \infty$. The well-known relation is: $\beta(j) \leq \phi(j)$. There exist random sequences which are β-mixing but not uniform mixing; see Bradley (1986), Doukhan (1994) and White (2004) for details. Many nonlinear Markov processes have been shown to satisfy stationary β-mixing with exponential decay rates (i.e., $\beta(j) \leq \beta_0 \exp(-cj)$ for some $\beta_0, c > 0$); see, e.g., Chen (2011) for a long list of many econometrics time series models that are beta mixing.

Example 2.1 (Semiparametric additive AR(p) mean regression): suppose that the time series data $\{Y_t\}_{t=1}^n$ is generated according to

$$Y_t = \sum_{i=1}^{p_1} Y_{t-i}\theta_{0,i} + \sum_{i=p_1+1}^{p} h_{0,i-p_1}(Y_{t-i}) + e_t,\ E[e_t|Y_{t-i}, 1 \le i \le p] = 0.$$

The parameters of interest are $\theta \equiv (\theta_1, \cdots, \theta_{p_1})' \in \Theta$ and $h(\cdot) = (h_1(\cdot), \cdots, h_{p-p_1}(\cdot)) \in \mathcal{H}$, where $\Theta = (-1, 1)^{p_1}$, and $\mathcal{H} = \mathcal{H}_1 \times \cdots \times \mathcal{H}_{p-p_1}, \mathcal{H}_l = W^{m_{l,1}, m_{l,2}}([0, 1])$ is a Sobolev space with degree of smoothness $m_{l,1}$ measured by $L_{m_{l,2}}$(leb) norm (see, Adams 1975). Let $\alpha_0 = (\theta_0, h_0) \in \mathcal{A} = \Theta \times \mathcal{H}$.

Denote $X_{1,t} \equiv (Y_{t-1}, \cdots, Y_{t-p_1})'$ and $\eta_0(X_{2,t}) = \sum_{l=p_1+1}^{p} h_{0,l-p_1}(Y_{t-l})$. Let $L_n(\alpha) = n^{-1}\sum_{t=1}^n \ell(\alpha, Z_t)$, $\ell(\alpha, Z_t) = -\frac{1}{2}\left[Y_t - X_{1,t}'\theta - \eta(X_{2,t})\right]^2$. Let $\tilde{L}_n(\alpha) = L_n(\alpha) - \sum_{l=1}^{p-p_1} \lambda_{n,l} J_l(\alpha)$, where $J_l(\alpha) = \left[\int_0^1 |\nabla^{m_{l,1}} h_l(x)|^{m_{l,2}}\, dx\right]^{1/m_{l,2}}$ with $m_{l,1} > 1$ and $m_{l,2} \ge 1$. Then $\widehat{\alpha}_n = (\widehat{\theta}, \widehat{h}) \in \mathcal{A}$ that solves $\tilde{L}_n(\widehat{\alpha}_n) \ge \sup_{\alpha \in \mathcal{A}} \tilde{L}_n(\alpha) - o_p(1)$ becomes the penalized Least Squares estimator of α_0. To implement this, we can use wavelet to represent any functions in $\mathcal{H}$. The theory of this chapter can be applied to derive the convergence rate of $\widehat{h}$, the root-n asymptotic normality of $\widehat{\theta}$, and a consistent estimate of its asymptotic variance.

Example 2.2 (Non-parametric ARX(p,q) quantile regression): suppose $\{Y_t\}_{t=1}^n$ is generated according to:

$$\begin{aligned} Y_t &= h_0(Y_{t-1}, \cdots, Y_{t-p_1}, X_t, \cdots, X_{t-p_2+1}) + e_t \\ \text{with } &: E\left[\tau - I\{e_t \le 0\} | Y_{t-1}, \cdots, Y_{t-p_1}, X_t, \cdots, X_{t-p_2+1}\right] = 0. \end{aligned} \quad (2)$$

The function $h_0 : \mathcal{R}^{p_1} \times \mathcal{R}^{d_x p_2} \to \mathcal{R}$ is the parameter of interest, where $p_1, p_2, d_x \ge 1$ are fixed and known integers. $\{Y_t\}$ is stationary β-mixing under certain conditions on h_0, $\{X_t\}$ and $\{e_t\}$. Let $d \equiv p_1 + d_x p_2$. Suppose $h_0 \in \mathcal{H} = W^{m,p}([b_1, b_2]^d)$ (Sobolev space).

Previously Koenker et al. (1994) estimated a nonparametric quantile regression with i.i.d. data via the penalized smoothing spline technique. Chen and White (1999) estimated this time series quantile model via neural network sieve M estimation. Let $Z_t = (Y_t, W_t)$ and $W_t = (Y_{t-1}, \cdots, Y_{t-p_1}, X_t, \cdots, X_{t-p_2+1})$. Let $\tilde{L}_n(h) = n^{-1}\sum_{t=1}^n \ell(h, Z_t) - \lambda_n J(h)$, where $\ell(h, z) = [1(y < h(w)) - \tau](y - h(w))$ and $J(h) = \left[\int |h^{([m])}(w)|^p dw\right]^{1/p}$ with $m \ge 1$, $\min(p, 2) \times m > d$. Then $\widehat{h} \in \mathcal{H}$ that solves $\tilde{L}_n(\widehat{h}_n) \ge \sup_{h \in \mathcal{H}} \tilde{L}_n(h) - o_p(1)$ becomes the penalized quantile regression estimator of h_0. To implement this, we can use Fourier series, spline, or wavelet to represent any functions in $\mathcal{H}$. The theory of this chapter can be applied to derive the convergence rate of $\widehat{h}_n$, and the root-n asymptotic normality of plug-in penalized estimate $\rho(\widehat{h}_n)$ of any regular functionals $\rho(h_0)$.

3 Convergence Rate of the Penalized M Estimate

For simplicity we let the parameter space $(\mathcal{A}, d)$ be a Banach space, and $J(\alpha)$ be a semi-norm type of smoothness penalty such that $\lambda_n J(\alpha) \asymp J(\lambda_n \alpha) \geq 0$. In this section, we establish the convergence rate (in $d(\cdot, \cdot)$) of the approximate penalized M estimate with dependent data. We first provide a set of sufficient conditions.

Condition 3.1 (Dependence) *$\{Z_t\}_{t=1}^n$ is a strictly stationary process that is either uniform mixing with $\phi(j) \leq \phi_0 j^{-\varpi}$ for some $\phi_0 > 0$, $\varpi > 2$, or β-mixing with $\beta(j) \leq \beta_0 j^{-\varpi}$ for some $\beta_0 > 0$, $\varpi > 2$.*

Condition 3.2 (Identification) *There exist finite constants $c_0 > 0$, $\gamma_1 > 0$ such that for all small $\delta > 0$,*

$$\inf_{\{d(\alpha_0,\alpha)\geq\delta,\alpha\in\mathcal{A}\}} K(\alpha_0, \alpha) \geq c_0 \delta^{2\gamma_1}. \tag{3}$$

In the following, for any finite positive constants δ_1 and $\delta_2 \geq 1$, we denote

$$A_{\delta_1,\delta_2} \equiv \{\alpha \in \mathcal{A} : \delta_1/2 \leq d(\alpha_0, \alpha) \leq \delta_1, J(\alpha) \leq \delta_2\}$$
$$\text{and } \mathcal{F}_{\delta_1,\delta_2} \equiv \{\ell(\alpha, Z) - \ell(\alpha_0, Z) : \alpha \in A_{\delta_1,\delta_2}\}.$$

Condition 3.3 (Variance) *There exist finite constants $c_1 > 0$ and $\gamma_2 \in [0, 1)$ such that for all finite $\delta_1 > 0$ and $\delta_2 \geq 1$,*

$$\sup_{\alpha\in A_{\delta_1,\delta_2}} n^{-1} Var\left[\sum_{t=1}^{n} (\ell(\alpha, Z_t) - \ell(\alpha_0, Z_t))\right] \leq c_1 \delta_1^{2\gamma_1} [1 + (\delta_1^{2\gamma_1} + \delta_2)^{\gamma_2}].$$

Condition 3.4 (Tails behavior) *There exist finite constants $c_2 > 0$, $\gamma_3 \in (0, 2\gamma_1)$, $\gamma_4 \in [0, 1)$ and a random variable $U(Z)$ such that for all finite $\delta_1 > 0$ and $\delta_2 \geq 1$,*

$$\sup_{\alpha\in A_{\delta_1,\delta_2}} |\ell(\alpha, Z) - \ell(\alpha_0, Z)| \leq c_2 U(Z_t) \delta_1^{\gamma_3} \delta_2^{\gamma_4}$$

with $E[\{U(Z)\}^{\gamma_5}] < \infty$ for some $\gamma_5 > 2$.

Let $\mathcal{G} = \{g(\alpha, Z) : \alpha \in \mathcal{A}\}$ be a class of measurable functions mapping $\mathcal{A} \times \mathcal{Z}$ to $\mathcal{R}$ such that $E[g(\alpha, Z)]^2$ is finite for all $\alpha \in \mathcal{A}$. Let $\|\cdot\|_2$ be the L_2-norm on $\mathcal{G}$, i.e., for any $g(\alpha_1, z), g(\alpha_2, z) \in \mathcal{G}$,

$$||g(\alpha_1, Z) - g(\alpha_2, Z)||_2 = \left[E\,|g(\alpha_1, Z) - g(\alpha_2, Z)|^2\right]^{1/2}.$$

Let $\mathcal{L}_2$ be the completion of $\mathcal{G}$ under $\|\cdot\|_2$. We use the *bracketing average L_2 metric entropy* to measure the size of $\mathcal{G}$ (see, e.g., Pollard 1984), that is, for any given $\epsilon > 0$, suppose there exists $S(\epsilon, N) = \{g_1^l, g_1^u, \cdots, g_N^l, g_N^u\} \subset \mathcal{L}_2$ such that $\max_{1\leq j\leq N} \|g_j^u - g_j^l\|_2 \leq \epsilon$ and for any $g \in \mathcal{G}$, there exists a $j \in \{1, \cdots, N\}$ with

$g_j^l \leq g \leq g_j^u$ almost surely, then $H_{[]}(\epsilon, \mathcal{G}) = \log(\min\{N : S(\epsilon, N)\})$ is the bracketing L_2 metric entropy of the space $\mathcal{G}$, i.e., the logarithm of the minimal cardinality of ϵ-covering of the space $\mathcal{G}$ in the L_2 metric with bracketing.

Let $J(\alpha_0) < \infty$, $J_0 \equiv \max(J(\alpha_0), 1)$ and $\mathcal{F}_{\delta_1,\delta_2} \equiv \{\ell(\alpha, Z) - \ell(\alpha_0, Z) : \alpha \in A_{\delta_1,\delta_2}\}$.

Condition 3.5 (Size of the space) *There exists some* $\varepsilon_n \in (0, 1)$ *such that* $\lambda_n J_0 \leq c_3 \varepsilon_n^{2\gamma_1}$ *and*

$$\varepsilon_n = \inf \left\{ \varepsilon > 0 : \sup_{\{\delta_1 \geq 1, \delta_2 \geq 1\}} \frac{\int_{b\lambda_n(\delta_1^{2\gamma_1}+\delta_2)}^{a\varepsilon^{\gamma_1}(\delta_1^{2\gamma_1}+\delta_2)^{(1+\gamma_2)/2}} H_{[]}^{1/2}(w, \mathcal{F}_{\delta_1,\delta_2}) dw}{\lambda_n(\delta_1^{2\gamma_1} + \delta_2)} \leq c_4 n^{\frac{1}{2}} \right\}$$

for some constants $a, b, c_3, c_4 > 0$.

Condition 3.1 assumes that the data is mixing and imposes the decay rate on the weak dependence. Condition 3.2 is the identifiable uniqueness condition. Similar condition is used in White and Wooldridge (1991) to show the consistency of the sieve M estimates. In most applications, we can choose $d(\alpha_0, \alpha) = K^{1/2}(\alpha_0, \alpha)$ and $\gamma_1 = 1$ and then Condition 3.2 becomes the case considered in Shen (1998) for i.i.d. data. Condition 3.3 generalizes Assumption B in Shen (1998) for i.i.d. data to time series setting. Condition 3.4 relaxes the strong exponential thin tail Assumption C in Shen (1998) in order to allow for a wide range of semi-nonparametric time series applications. It is similar to the polynomial tail condition A.4 imposed in Chen and Shen (1998) for sieve M estimation of time series models. Condition 3.5 is similar to Assumption D in Shen (1998), which measures the complexity of the cell spaces $\mathcal{F}_{\delta_1,\delta_2}$.

In the following we let $P^*(\cdot)$ denote the outer measure (see, Pollard 1984).

Theorem 3.6 *Suppose that Conditions 3.1–3.5 hold. Then there exist finite constants* $d_1, d_2, d_3 > 0$ *such that for all large* $x \geq 1$ *and for all integer n,*

$$P^*\left(\sup_{\{d(\alpha_0,\alpha) \geq x\varepsilon_n, \alpha \in \mathcal{A}\}} \left[\widetilde{L}_n(\alpha) - \widetilde{L}_n(\alpha_0)\right] \geq -(x\varepsilon_n)^{2\gamma_1}/2 \right) \leq \eta_n(x), \text{ with}$$

$$\eta_n(x) \equiv \frac{d_1}{\exp(cx^{2\gamma_1(1-\gamma_2)} n \lambda_n^2 \varepsilon_n^{-2\gamma_1})} + \frac{d_2}{(x^{(2\gamma_1-\gamma_3)}\lambda_n)^{1+\varpi} n^{\varpi}} + \frac{d_3 \varepsilon_n^{\gamma_3\gamma_5}}{(x^{(2\gamma_1-\gamma_3)}\lambda_n)^{\gamma_5} n^{\gamma_5/2}}. \quad (4)$$

Hence for the penalized M estimate defined in (1) with $a_n = o(\varepsilon_n^{2\gamma_1})$, *we have for all* $x \geq 1$,

$$P\left(d(\alpha_0, \widehat{\alpha}_n) \geq x\varepsilon_n\right) \leq \eta_n(x).$$

We next show that the penalized M estimate falls into the set $\{\alpha \in \mathcal{A} : J(\alpha) \leq [1 + o(1)]J(\alpha_0)\}$ with probability approaching 1.

Theorem 3.7 *Let conditions in Theorem 3.6 hold. For any* $0 < \delta < 1/4$, *if* $(1 - \delta)(x\varepsilon_n)^{2\gamma_1} \leq \lambda_n$, *then:* $\Pr[J(\widehat{\alpha}_n) \geq (1 + 4\delta)J_0] \leq \eta_n(x)$.

Theorem 3.7 indicates that the penalized M estimation is effectively equivalent to the infeasible constrained M estimation over the subspace $\{\alpha \in \mathcal{A} : J(\alpha) \leq cJ(\alpha_0)\}$ where c is some large but finite positive constant.

Applying Theorems 3.6 and 3.7, we immediately obtain the following Corollary.

Corollary 3.8 *Let conditions of Theorem 3.6 hold with* $\gamma_1 = 1$. *If*

$$\min\left\{n\lambda_n^2\varepsilon_n^{-2}, n\lambda_n^2\varepsilon_n^{-2\gamma_3}, n^{\varpi}\lambda_n^{1+\varpi}\right\} \geq c > 0 \quad as\ n \to \infty,$$

then: (1) $d(\alpha_0, \widehat{\alpha}_n) = O_p(\delta_n)$ *with* $\delta_n = \max(\varepsilon_n, \lambda_n^{1/2})$; *(2)* $J(\widehat{\alpha}_n) \leq (1 + o_p(1))J_0$.

Remark 3.9 Corollary 3.8 implies that the convergence rate of the penalized M estimator depends on the local entropy ε_n of the parameter space and the tuning parameter λ_n. The optimal convergence rate is achieved by setting $\lambda_n \asymp \varepsilon_n^2$, and the optimal rate is $\delta_n \asymp \varepsilon_n$. This result is very similar to Theorem 1 in Chen and Shen (1998) for the convergence rate of sieve M estimator with dependent data. When $d(\alpha_0, \alpha) = K^{1/2}(\alpha_0, \alpha)$ (hence $\gamma_1 = 1$), and the data $\{Z_t\}$ is *i.i.d.*, our Corollary 3.8 becomes Corollary 2 in Shen (1998), except that we replace his strong exponential thin tail Assumption C by the weaker polynomial tail Condition 3.4.

4 Asymptotic Normality of Plug-In Penalized M Estimates

Since $\widehat{\alpha}_n$ is an approximate penalized M estimate over an infinite-dimensional function space, $\widehat{\alpha}_n$ may not be a solution to $\nabla L_n(\alpha) = 0$, and hence we could not follow the typical approach of Taylor expansion to derive the asymptotic normality of $\rho(\widehat{\alpha}_n) - \rho(\alpha_0)$.

Given the global convergence rate results in the previous section, to establish the asymptotic normality of $\rho(\widehat{\alpha}_n) - \rho(\alpha_0)$, it suffices to have "good" (to be more precise below) linear approximations to $L_n(\alpha) - L_n(\alpha_0)$ and $\rho(\alpha) - \rho(\alpha_0)$ within some shrinking neighborhood of α_0.

Let $(\mathcal{A}, d)$ be a subspace of a certain normed linear space $\mathcal{L}$ equipped with an inner product-induced norm $\|\cdot\|$ such that $\|\alpha - \alpha_0\| \leq cd(\alpha_0, \alpha)$ for some constant $c > 0$ and that $\|\alpha - \alpha_0\| \asymp K^{1/2}(\alpha_0, \alpha)$ within a small d-neighborhood of α_0. We assume that there exists some local approximation of $\ell(\alpha, Z)$, i.e.,

$$\ell(\alpha, Z) \simeq \ell(\alpha_0, Z) + \Delta(\alpha_0, Z)[\alpha - \alpha_0] + r(\alpha_0, Z)[\alpha - \alpha_0, \alpha - \alpha_0]/2, \quad (5)$$

for all α in a shrinking neighborhood of α_0, where $\Delta(\alpha_0, Z)[v]$ and $r(\alpha_0, Z)[v_1, v_2]$ are the (possibly smoothed) first and second pathwise derivatives of $\ell(\alpha, Z)$ w.r.t. α in the direction v and (v_1, v_2), respectively. Suppose the functional of interest $\rho(\cdot)$ has the following local linear approximation such that

$$|\rho(\alpha) - \rho(\alpha_0) - \rho'_{\alpha_0}[\alpha - \alpha_0]| \leq O(\|\alpha - \alpha_0\|^{\omega}) \text{ as } \|\alpha - \alpha_0\| \to 0, \quad (6)$$

where ω is a positive number, $\rho'_{\alpha_0}[\alpha - \alpha_0]$ is linear in $(\alpha - \alpha_0)$. We say that $\rho(\cdot)$ is a regular functional if the following condition holds

$$\|\rho'_{\alpha_0}\| \equiv \sup_{\{\alpha \in \mathcal{A}: \|\alpha - \alpha_0\| > 0\}} \frac{|\rho'_{\alpha_0}[\alpha - \alpha_0]|}{\|\alpha - \alpha_0\|} < \infty.$$

Let $\mathcal{V}$ be the Hilbert space generated by $\mathcal{A} - \{\alpha_0\}$ under the norm $\|\cdot\|$, with $\langle\cdot,\cdot\rangle$ denoting the corresponding inner product. By the Riesz representation theorem, there exists $v^* \in \mathcal{V}$ such that

$$\rho'_{\alpha_0}[v] = \langle v, v^* \rangle \quad \text{for all } v \in \mathcal{V},$$

and that $\|v^*\| = \|\rho'_{\alpha_0}\|$.

To derive the asymptotic normality for $n^{1/2}[\rho(\widehat{\alpha}_n) - \rho(\alpha_0)]$, we will approximate $\rho(\widehat{\alpha}_n) - \rho(\alpha_0)$ locally by a bounded linear functional $\langle \widehat{\alpha}_n - \alpha_0, v^* \rangle$. The latter can also be approximated by $n^{-1} \sum_{t=1}^{n} \Delta(\alpha_0, Z_t)[v^*]$, which is the local linear approximation to the random criterion difference of $L_n(\widehat{\alpha}_n) - L_n(\widehat{\alpha}_n \pm \varepsilon_n v^*)$, provided that $\alpha \pm \varepsilon_n v^* \in \mathcal{A}$ is a local alternative value of any α in a shrinking neighborhood of α_0, with $\varepsilon_n = o(n^{-1/2})$.

Essentially, the penalty $J(\alpha)$, which controls the global properties of the estimates, plays no role in the local approximation of the criterion difference within a neighborhood of α_0. However, to control the local behavior of the linear approximation of the criterion function with penalty, certain assumptions on $J(\alpha)$ and λ_n are needed.

Let δ_n be the convergence rate of the approximate penalized M estimate under the norm $\|\cdot\|$, i.e., $||\widehat{\alpha}_n - \alpha_0|| = O_p(\delta_n)$. Let C be a finite positive constant such that $C \geq \max\{J(\alpha_0), J(v^*)\} > 0$. Denote

$$\mathcal{N}_n \equiv \{\alpha \in \mathcal{A} : ||\alpha - \alpha_0|| \leq \delta_n \log\log n,\ J(\alpha) \leq C\}$$

as a shrinking neighborhood of α_0. Then $\widehat{\alpha}_n \in \mathcal{N}_n$ with probability approaching one (wpa1). Let $\mu_n[f(\alpha, Z)] = n^{-1} \sum_{t=1}^{n} \{f(\alpha, Z_t) - E[f(\alpha, Z_t)]\}$ be the empirical process indexed by α. Denote $u^* = \pm v^*$ and $\varepsilon_n = o(n^{-1/2})$. We now formulate the set of regularity conditions.

Condition 4.1 (Stochastic equicontinuity)

$$\sup_{\alpha\in\mathcal{N}_n} \mu_n(\ell(\alpha, Z) - \Delta(\alpha_0, Z)[\alpha - \alpha_0] - \{\ell(\alpha + \varepsilon_n u^*, Z) - \Delta(\alpha_0, Z)[\alpha + \varepsilon_n u^* - \alpha_0]\}) = O_p(\varepsilon_n^2)$$

Condition 4.2 (Expected value of criterion difference)

$$\sup_{\alpha\in\mathcal{N}_n} \left| E[\ell(\alpha, Z) - \ell(\alpha + \varepsilon_n u^*, Z)] - \frac{\|\alpha + \varepsilon_n u^* - \alpha_0\|^2 - \|\alpha - \alpha_0\|^2}{2} \right| = O(\varepsilon_n^2).$$

Condition 4.3 (Penalty) *There is a finite constant* $c > 0$ *such that*

$$J(\alpha_1 + \alpha_2) \le c \times [J(\alpha_1) + J(\alpha_2)] \textit{ for any } \alpha_1, \alpha_2 \in \mathcal{N}_n;$$

In addition $\lambda_n J(\varepsilon_n u^*) = O(\varepsilon_n^2)$.

Condition 4.4 (Gradient) $\sup_{\alpha\in\mathcal{N}_n} \mu_n \{\Delta(\alpha_0, Z)[\alpha - \alpha_0]\} = O_p(\varepsilon_n)$.

Condition 4.5 (CLT) $n^{1/2}\mu_n \{\Delta(\alpha_0, Z)[v^*]\} \to_d \mathcal{N}(0, \sigma_{v^*}^2)$ *with*

$$\sigma_{v^*}^2 \equiv \lim_{n\to\infty} n^{-1} Var\left(\sum_{t=1}^{n} \Delta(\alpha_0, Z_t)[v^*]\right) \in (0, \infty).$$

Condition 4.1 specifies linear approximation of the empirical criterion by its derivative within a small neighborhood of α_0. Condition 4.2 characterizes the local quadratic behavior of the expected value of the criterion difference. When $\mathcal{A}$ is an infinite-dimensional space, $\widehat{\alpha}_n$ is often on the boundary of $\mathcal{A}$, where interior points of $\mathcal{A}$ with respect to $\|\cdot\|$ may not exist. The corresponding score function specified by the directional derivative evaluated at $\widehat{\alpha}_n$ may not be close to zero when $\mathcal{A}$ is very large. Conditions 4.3 and 4.4 are generalization of the usual assumption that α_0 is an interior point of $\mathcal{A}$. Condition 4.5 only requires a traditional finite-dimensional CLT, which is weaker than the need of CLTs in an infinite-dimensional Hilbert space [see, e.g., Chen and White (1998)]. Condition 4.5 is satisfied by many weakly dependent data structures. For example, suppose that $\{Z_t\}_{t=1}^{\infty}$ is strictly stationary strong mixing with mixing coefficients $\alpha(i)$ satisfying $\sum_{i=1}^{\infty}[\alpha(i)]^{(q-2)/q} < \infty$ and that $\Delta(\alpha_0, Z)[v^*]$ has finite qth moments ($q > 2$). Then Condition 4.5 is satisfied with

$$\sigma_{v^*}^2 = Var(\Delta(\alpha_0, Z)[v^*]) + 2\sum_{j=2}^{\infty} Cov(\Delta(\alpha_0, Z_1)[v^*], \Delta(\alpha_0, Z_j)[v^*]).$$

Theorem 4.6 *Suppose that Conditions 4.1–4.5 hold and* $\rho(\cdot)$ *satisfies (6) with* $\|\widehat{\alpha}_n - \alpha_0\|^{\omega} = o_P(n^{-1/2})$. *Then for the plug-in penalized M estimate* $\rho(\widehat{\alpha}_n)$, *we have:*

$$\sqrt{n}\,[\rho(\widehat{\alpha}_n) - \rho(\alpha_0)] \to_d \mathcal{N}(0, \sigma_{v^*}^2).$$

This asymptotic normality result is very similar to that in Chen and Shen (1998) and Chen (2007, Theorem 4.3) for plug-in sieve M estimates. In particular, both estimators share the same asymptotic variance $\sigma_{v^*}^2$ for weakly dependent data. This confirms the well-known result by Newey (1994) for i.i.d. data that the asymptotic variances of $\sqrt{n}$-consistent semiparametric two-step estimators do not depend on the choice of first step nonparametric estimators.

5 Consistent Estimation of the Long-Run Variance

In this section, we provide a consistent estimator for the LRV $\sigma_{v^*}^2$ of the plug-in penalized M estimate $\rho(\widehat{\alpha}_n)$ of a regular functional $\rho(\alpha_0)$. Using the expression in (5), we define the norm $\|\cdot\|$ as $\|v\|^2 = -E\{r(Z, \alpha_0)[v, v]\}$. Let $\mathcal{V}$ be the Hilbert space generated by $\mathcal{A} - \alpha_0$ under the norm $\|\cdot\|$ with the corresponding inner product $\langle\cdot,\cdot\rangle$. Let $\mathcal{V}_n$ be a k_n−dimensional Hilbert space under the norm $\|\cdot\|$ that becomes dense in $\mathcal{V}$ as $k_n \to \infty$. We compute a sieve Riesz representor $v_n^* \in \mathcal{V}_n$ as

$$\rho'_{\alpha_0}[v_n^*] = \|v_n^*\|^2 \equiv \sup_{v\in\mathcal{V}_n, v\neq 0} \frac{\left|\rho'_{\alpha_0}[v]\right|^2}{\|v\|^2} < \infty.$$

Then by the property of Hilbert space we have: $\|v_n^*\|^2 \nearrow \|v^*\|^2$ and $\|v_n^* - v^*\| \to 0$ as $k_n \to \infty$.

We can define an empirical seminorm as $\|v\|_n^2 = \frac{-1}{n}\sum_{t=1}^{n} r(Z, \widehat{\alpha}_n)[v, v]$ for all $v \in \mathcal{V}$. Using the empirical seminorm $\|\cdot\|_n$ we can define an empirical Riesz representor $\widehat{v}_n^*$ as

$$\rho'_{\widehat{\alpha}_n}[\widehat{v}_n^*] = \|\widehat{v}_n^*\|_n^2 \equiv \sup_{v\in\mathcal{V}_n, v\neq 0} \frac{|\rho'_{\widehat{\alpha}_n}[v]|^2}{\|v\|_n^2} < \infty, \tag{7}$$

Using the penalized M estimate $\widehat{\alpha}_n$ and the empirical Riesz representor $\widehat{v}_n^*$, we introduce an estimator of $\sigma_{v^*}^2$ as

$$\widehat{\sigma}_n^2 \equiv \sum_{t=-n+1}^{n-1} \mathcal{K}\left(\frac{t}{m_n}\right) \Gamma_{n,t}(\widehat{\alpha}_n)\left[\widehat{v}_n^*, \widehat{v}_n^*\right], \tag{8}$$

where

$$\Gamma_{n,t}(\widehat{\alpha}_n)\left[\widehat{v}_n^*, \widehat{v}_n^*\right] = \begin{cases} \frac{1}{n}\sum_{k=t+1}^{n} \Delta(\widehat{\alpha}_n, Z_k)[\widehat{v}_n^*]\Delta(\widehat{\alpha}_n, Z_{k-t})[\widehat{v}_n^*] & \text{for } t \geq 0 \\ \frac{1}{n}\sum_{k=-t+1}^{n} \Delta(\widehat{\alpha}_n, Z_k)[\widehat{v}_n^*]\Delta(\widehat{\alpha}_n, Z_{k+t})[\widehat{v}_n^*] & \text{for } t < 0 \end{cases},$$

$\mathcal{K}(\cdot)$ is some kernel density function and m_n denotes its bandwidth. This estimator is an extension of Newey and West (1987) or Andrews' (1991) estimator for parametric time series models to the penalized M estimation of semi-nonparametric time series models.

We next present sufficient conditions for the consistency of $\widehat{\sigma}_n^2$.

Condition 5.1 *Let $\mathcal{W}_n = \{v \in \mathcal{V}_n : ||v|| = 1\}$ and $\delta_{v^*,n} = o(1)$ be some positive sequence.*

$$\textit{(i)} \quad \sup_{\alpha\in\mathcal{N}_n, v\in\mathcal{W}_n} \mu_n\{r(Z,\alpha)[v_1, v_2]\} = O_p(\delta_{v^*,n});$$

$$\textit{(ii)} \quad \sup_{\alpha\in\mathcal{N}_n, v\in\mathcal{W}_n} |E\{r(Z,\alpha)[v_1, v_2] - r(Z,\alpha_0)[v_1, v_2]\}| = O\left(\delta_{v^*,n}\right);$$

(iii) $\sup_{\alpha\in\mathcal{N}_n, v\in\mathcal{W}_n} \left|\rho'_\alpha[v] - \rho'_{\alpha_0}[v]\right| = O(\delta_{v^*,n})$; *(iv)* $\|v_n^* - v^*\| = O(\pi_n)$.

Under Condition 5.1(i)–(iii), we can invoke Lemma 5.1 of Chen et al. (2011) to deduce that $\|\widehat{v}_n^* - v_n^*\| = O_p(\delta_{v^*,n})$. By definitions of the Riesz representors $v^* \in \mathcal{V}$ and $v_n^* \in \mathcal{V}_n$ we have $\rho'_{\alpha_0}[v] = \langle v, v_n^*\rangle = \langle v, v^*\rangle$ for any $v \in \mathcal{V}_n$. Hence we can deduce that $v^* - v_n^*$ is orthogonal to $\mathcal{V}_n$. This and Condition 5.1(iv) imply that

$$\|\widehat{v}_n^* - v^*\|^2 = \|\widehat{v}_n^* - v_n^*\|^2 + \|v_n^* - v^*\|^2 = O_p(\delta_{v^*,n}^2 + \pi_n^2). \tag{9}$$

Denote $\delta_n^* = \max\{\delta_{v^*,n}, \pi_n\}$, then it is clear that under Condition 5.1, $\widehat{v}_n^*$ is a consistent estimate of v^* w.r.t. the norm $\|\cdot\|$ at the convergence rate δ_n^*.

Condition 5.2 *(i) There are $r \in (2, 4]$ and $p > r$ such that $\sum_{j=0}^{\infty} \beta(j)^{2(1/r-1/p)} < \infty$ and $\|\Delta(\alpha_0, Z)[v^*]\|_p < \infty$; (ii) there is a finite constant $c > 0$ such that for all $v \in \{\mathcal{V}_n : ||v - v^*|| \leq \delta_n^* \log\log n\}$, we have $E\left(|\Delta(\alpha_0, Z)[v - v^*]|^2\right) \leq c\|v - v^*\|^2$; (iii) there is a finite constant $c' > 0$ such that for all $\alpha \in \mathcal{N}_n$, we have $E\left[\sup_{v\in\mathcal{W}_n} |\Delta(Z,\alpha)[v] - \Delta(Z,\alpha_0)[v]|^2\right] \leq c'\|\alpha - \alpha_0\|^2$; (iv) $m_n(\delta_n \vee \delta_n^*) = o(1)$ and $n^{-1+2/r}m_n^2 = o(1)$; (v) $\mathcal{K}(\cdot)$ is symmetric, continuous at zero and satisfies $\mathcal{K}(0) = 1$, $\sup_x |\mathcal{K}(x)| \leq 1$, $\int_{\mathbb{R}} |\mathcal{K}(x)|dx < \infty$ and $\int_{\mathbb{R}} |x|\phi(x)dx < \infty$ where $\phi(x)$ is a nonincreasing function such that $|\mathcal{K}(x)| \leq \phi(x)$ for almost all $x \in \mathbb{R}$.*

Theorem 5.3 *Suppose that Conditions 5.1 and 5.2 hold and that $\widehat{\alpha}_n \in \mathcal{N}_n$ with probability approaching one. Then:*

$$\widehat{\sigma}_n^2 \to_p \sigma_{v^*}^2. \tag{10}$$

Using the results of Theorems 4.6 and 5.3, we can apply the Slutsky theorem to deduce that

$$\frac{\sqrt{n}\,[\rho(\widehat{\alpha}_n) - \rho(\alpha_0)]}{\widehat{\sigma}_n} = \frac{\sqrt{n}\,[\rho(\widehat{\alpha}_n) - \rho(\alpha_0)]}{\sigma_{v^*}} \frac{\sigma_{v^*}}{\widehat{\sigma}_n} \to_d \mathcal{N}(0, 1). \tag{11}$$

It is clear that confidence intervals (CIs) of $\rho(\alpha_0)$ can be constructed using the above Gaussian approximation.

6 Conclusion

In this chapter and for semi-nonparametric time series models with stationary beta-mixing observations, we provide a general theory on the convergence rate of penalized M estimates and root-n asymptotic normality of plug-in penalized M estimates of regular functionals. We establish these results under conditions similar to those for sieve M estimates in Chen and Shen (1998) for time series data. Instead of imposing the strong exponential thin tail condition as assumed in the existing theories on penalized M estimation with i.i.d. data, we allow for polynomial tail of the centered random criterion function, which is very important for time series applications. We also present simple consistent estimates of LRVs of the penalized M estimates of regular functionals, which can be used to construct confidence intervals or Wald-based tests.

We are working on various extensions. First, we plan to establish the asymptotic normality of the plug-in penalized M estimates of irregular (i.e., slower than root-n estimable) functionals. Second, we could entertain semi-nonparametric time series models with other types of temporal dependence properties, such as near epoch dependent functions of mixing processes considered in White and Wooldridge (1991).

Acknowledgments We thank co-editor Norm Swanson for his patience, encouragement, and useful comments. Chen acknowledges financial support from the National Science Foundation under Award Number SES0838161.

Appendix

The following Lemma is a useful exponential inequality for uniform mixing processes, which is similar to Lemma 1 in Chen and Shen (1998, Appendix) for beta-mixing processes.

Lemma A.1 *Let $\{Y_t\}$ be either m-dependent or uniform mixing. Suppose*

$$\sigma^2 \geq \sup_{f\in\mathcal{F}} n^{-1} Var\left[\sum\nolimits_{t=1}^{n} f(Z_t)\right] \text{ and } T \geq \sup_{f\in\mathcal{F}} \|f(Z)\|_{\sup}$$

and in addition, for any $0 < \xi < 1$,

$$M \leq \xi\sigma^2/4,$$

and

$$\int_{\xi M/32}^{\sigma T^{1/2}} H^{1/2}(u, \mathcal{F})du \leq Mn^{1/2}\xi^{3/2}/2^{10}.$$

Then

$$\begin{aligned} &P\left(\sup_{f\in\mathcal{F}} n^{-1}\sum_{t=1}^{n}(f(Y_t) - Ef(Y_t)) \geq M\right) \\ &\leq 3c\exp\left(-(1-\xi)\frac{nM^2}{2\sigma^2(1+T\xi/12)}\right). \end{aligned}$$

Proof of Theorem 3.6 We prove this theorem for beta-mixing processes, while the proof for uniform-mixing case is the same except using Lemma A.1 instead of Lemma 1 in Chen and Shen (1998). Without loss of generality, we assume that $x > 1$, $\max\{\lambda_n, \varepsilon_n\} \leq 1$ and we use c to denote a generic positive finite constant. Let $\widetilde{\ell}(\alpha, Z) \equiv \ell(\alpha, Z) - \lambda_n J(\alpha)$. Denote

$$\begin{aligned} I &= P^*\left(\sup_{\{d(\alpha_0,\alpha)\geq x\varepsilon_n,\alpha\in\mathcal{A}\}} \left[\widetilde{L}_n(\alpha) - \widetilde{L}_n(\alpha_0)\right] \geq -(x\varepsilon_n)^{2\gamma_1}/2\right) \\ &= P^*\left(\sup_{\{d(\alpha_0,\alpha)\geq x\varepsilon_n,\alpha\in\mathcal{A}\}} \left\{\mu_n\left[\widetilde{\ell}(\alpha, Z) - \widetilde{\ell}(\alpha_0, Z)\right]\right.\right. \\ &\qquad \left.\left. + E\left(\widetilde{L}_n(\alpha) - \widetilde{L}_n(\alpha_0)\right)\right\} \geq -(x\varepsilon_n)^{2\gamma_1}/2\right). \end{aligned}$$

Since

$$\begin{aligned} \mu_n\left[\widetilde{\ell}(\alpha, Z) - \widetilde{\ell}(\alpha_0, Z)\right] &= \mu_n\left[\ell(\alpha, Z) - \ell(\alpha_0, Z)\right], \\ E\left(\widetilde{L}_n(\alpha) - \widetilde{L}_n(\alpha_0)\right) &= -\left[K(\alpha_0, \alpha) + \lambda_n(J(\alpha) - J(\alpha_0))\right], \end{aligned}$$

we have:

$$\begin{aligned} I = P^*\Bigg(&\sup_{\{d(\alpha_0,\alpha)\geq x\varepsilon_n,\alpha\in\mathcal{A}\}} \mu_n\left[\ell(\alpha, Z) - \ell(\alpha_0, Z)\right] \\ &\geq \inf_{\{d(\alpha_0,\alpha)\geq x\varepsilon_n,\alpha\in\mathcal{A}\}} \left[K(\alpha_0, \alpha) + \lambda_n(J(\alpha) - J(\alpha_0))\right] - (x\varepsilon_n)^{2\gamma_1}/2\Bigg). \end{aligned}$$

For any $i, j \in N^+$, define

$$A_{i,j} = \left\{\alpha \in \mathcal{A} : 2^{i-1} x\varepsilon_n \leq d(\alpha_0, \alpha) < 2^i x\varepsilon_n \text{ and } 2^{j-1} J_0 \leq J(\alpha) < 2^j J_0\right\},$$
$$A_{i,0} = \left\{\alpha \in \mathcal{A} : 2^{i-1} x\varepsilon_n \leq d(\alpha_0, \alpha) < 2^i x\varepsilon_n \text{ and } J(\alpha) < J_0\right\},$$

then it is clear that

$$\bigcup_{j\geq 0} A_{i,j} = \left\{2^{i-1} x\varepsilon_n \leq d(\alpha_0, \alpha) < 2^i x\varepsilon_n, \alpha \in \mathcal{A}\right\},$$
$$\bigcup_{i\geq 1, j\geq 0} A_{i,j} = \{d(\alpha_0, \alpha) \geq x\varepsilon_n, \alpha \in \mathcal{A}\} \tag{A.1}$$

and A_{i_1,j_1} and A_{i_2,j_2} are disjoint for any $i_1 \neq i_2$ or $j_1 \neq j_2$. By Condition 3.2 (with $c_0 = 1$ for notational simplicity), we have

$$\inf_{A_{i,j}} [K(\alpha_0, \alpha) + \lambda_n(J(\alpha) - J(\alpha_0))] \geq (2^{i-1} x\varepsilon_n)^{2\gamma_1} + \lambda_n(2^{j-1} - 1)J(\alpha_0)$$
$$\text{and } \inf_{A_{i,0}} [K(\alpha_0, \alpha) + \lambda_n(J(\alpha) - J(\alpha_0))] \geq (2^{i-1} x\varepsilon_n)^{2\gamma_1} - \lambda_n J(\alpha_0), \tag{A.2}$$

Hence

$$\sup_{A_{i,j}} \left[\widetilde{L}_n(\alpha) - \widetilde{L}_n(\alpha_0)\right] \leq \sup_{A_{i,j}} \mu_n [\ell(\alpha, Z) - \ell(\alpha_0, Z)] - \left[(2^{i-1} x\varepsilon_n)^{2\gamma_1} + \lambda_n(2^{j-1} - 1)J(\alpha_0)\right] \tag{A.3}$$

for $j \geq 1$, and

$$\sup_{A_{i,0}} \left[\widetilde{L}_n(\alpha) - \widetilde{L}_n(\alpha_0)\right] \leq \sup_{A_{i,0}} \mu_n [\ell(\alpha, Z) - \ell(\alpha_0, Z)] - \left[(2^{i-1} x\varepsilon_n)^{2\gamma_1} - \lambda_n J(\alpha_0)\right]. \tag{A.4}$$

Since $x \geq 1$, $J_0\lambda_n \leq c_3(x\varepsilon_n)^{2\gamma_1}$, $\max\{\lambda_n, \varepsilon_n\} \leq 1$, using the results in (A.1), (A.2), (A.3) and (A.4), we can deduce that

$$I \leq \underbrace{\sum_{i,j=1}^{\infty} P^*\left(\sup_{A_{i,j}} \mu_n [\ell(\alpha, Z) - \ell(\alpha_0, Z)] \geq M_{i,j}\right)}_{I_1} + \underbrace{\sum_{i=1}^{\infty} P^*\left(\sup_{A_{i,0}} \mu_n [\ell(\alpha, Z) - \ell(\alpha_0, Z)] \geq M_i\right)}_{I_2}, \tag{A.5}$$

where $M_{i,j} \equiv \frac{\lambda_n}{2}\left[(2^{i-1}x)^{2\gamma_1} + (2^{j-1}-1)J(\alpha_0)\right]$ and $M_i \equiv c(2^{i-1}x\varepsilon_n)^{2\gamma_1}$. We now bound the term I_1 by modifying the proof of Theorem 3 in Chen and Shen (1998, Appendix). Let $B_{n,i,j}$ be some truncation sequence such that $B_{n,i,j} \to \infty$, $B_{n,i,j}\varepsilon_n^{\gamma_3} \to 0$ and $a_{n1,i,j}B_{n,i,j}^2\varepsilon_n^{2\gamma_3} \to 0$ as $n \to \infty$ for any fixed i and j, where $a_{n1,i,j}$ is defined later. Then we have

$$\begin{aligned} I_1 &\le \sum_{i,j=1}^{\infty} P^*\left(\sup_{A_{i,j}} \mu_n\left\{[\ell(\alpha,Z)-\ell(\alpha_0,Z)]I(U \le B_{n,i,j})\right\} \ge M_{i,j}\right) \\ &\quad + \sum_{i,j=1}^{\infty} P^*\left(\sup_{A_{i,j}} \mu_n\left\{[\ell(\alpha,Z)-\ell(\alpha_0,Z)]I(U > B_{n,i,j})\right\} \ge M_{i,j}\right) \\ &= \sum_{i,j=1}^{\infty} I_{11,i,j} + \sum_{i,j=1}^{\infty} I_{12,i,j} = I_{11} + I_{12}. \end{aligned} \tag{A.6}$$

We use Lemma 1 in Chen and Shen (1998) (on beta mixing) to bound $I_{11,i,j}$ for any fixed i and j. By Condition 3.3, we have

$$\begin{aligned} &\sup_{A_{i,j}} n^{-1}\mathrm{Var}\left[\sum_{t=1}^{n}(\ell(\alpha,Z_t)-\ell(\alpha_0,Z_t))\right] \\ &\quad \le v_{i,j}^2 \equiv c_1(2^i x\varepsilon_n)^{2\gamma_1}\left[1+((2^i x)^{2\gamma_1}+2^j J_0)^{\gamma_2}\right]. \end{aligned}$$

Under Condition 3.4 we have

$$\sup_{A_{i,j}} \left\|[\ell(\alpha,Z)-\ell(\alpha_0,Z)]I(U \le B_{n,i,j})\right\|_{\sup} \le B_{n,i,j}(2^i x\varepsilon_n)^{\gamma_3}(2^j J_0)^{\gamma_4}.$$

Denote $T_{i,j} \equiv \min\{B_{n,i,j}(2^i x\varepsilon_n)^{\gamma_3}(2^j J_0)^{\gamma_4}, 8/c_1\}$ and $\sigma_{i,j}^2 = v_{i,j}^2 T_{i,j}$. We can define $a_{n1,i,j} = [nM_{i,j}/(14T_{i,j})]$ and $a_{n2,i,j} = [n/(2a_{n1,i,j})] = [7T_{i,j}/M_{i,j}]$, then it is easy to see that $a_{n1,i,j} \to \infty$ and $a_{n2,i,j} \to \infty$ as $n \to \infty$, and $a_{n2,i,j} \ge 6T_{i,j}/M_{i,j}$. As $J_0\lambda_n \le c_4(x\varepsilon_n)^{2\gamma_1}$, we can deduce that $M_{i,j} \equiv \frac{\lambda_n}{2}\left[(2^{i-1}x)^{2\gamma_1} + (2^{j-1}-1)J(\alpha_0)\right] \le \xi\sigma_{i,j}^2/4$ for some $\xi \in (0,1)$. By the definition of ε_n and Condition 3.5 we have

$$\frac{\int_{bM_{i,j}}^{\sigma_{i,j}\sqrt{T_{i,j}}} H_{[]}^{\frac{1}{2}}(u,\mathcal{F}_{i,j})du}{M_{i,j}} \le c\frac{\int_{b\lambda_n(\delta_1^{2\gamma_1}+\delta_2)}^{a\varepsilon_n^{\gamma_1}(\delta_1^{2\gamma_1}+\delta_2)^{(1+\gamma_2)/2}} H_{[]}^{\frac{1}{2}}(u,\mathcal{F}_{i,j})du}{\lambda_n(\delta_1^{2\gamma_1}+\delta_2)} \le cn^{\frac{1}{2}}$$

where $\delta_1 = 2^i x$, $\delta_2 = 2^j J_0$ and $\mathcal{F}_{i,j} \equiv \{\ell(\alpha,Z)-\ell(\alpha_0,Z) : \alpha \in A_{i,j}\}$. Now we can invoke Lemma 1 in Chen and Shen (1998) to deduce that

$$
\begin{aligned}
I_{11,i,j} &= P^*\left(\sup_{A_{i,j}} \mu_n\left\{[\ell(\alpha)-\ell(\alpha_0)]\, I(U \le B_{n,i,j})\right\} \ge M_{i,j}\right) \\
&\le 6\exp\left\{-c\frac{nM_{i,j}^2}{\sigma_{i,j}^2\left[1+a_{n1,i,j}T_{i,j}\right]}\right\} + 2(a_{n2,i,j}-1)\beta(a_{n1,i,j}) \\
&\le 6\exp\left\{-\frac{cn\lambda_n^2\left[(2^i x)^{2\gamma_1}+2^j J(\alpha_0)\right]^{1-\gamma_2}}{\varepsilon_n^{2\gamma_1}}\right\} + 4\beta_0 n^{-\varpi}\left(T_{i,j}/M_{i,j}\right)^{1+\varpi}.
\end{aligned} \tag{A.7}
$$

Using virtually the same arguments as in the proof of Theorem 3 in Chen and Shen (1998, Appendix), we obtain

$$
\begin{aligned}
I_{11} &\le 6\sum_{i,j=1}^{\infty} \exp\left\{-cn\lambda_n^2\varepsilon_n^{-2\gamma_1}\left[(2^i x)^{2\gamma_1}+2^j J(\alpha_0)\right]^{1-\gamma_2}\right\} \\
&\quad + 4\beta_0 n^{-\varpi}\lambda_n^{-(1+\varpi)} x^{(\gamma_3-2\gamma_1)(1+\varpi)}\varepsilon_n^{\gamma_3(1+\varpi)} B_{n,i,j}^{1+\varpi} \\
&\quad \times \sum_{i,j=1}^{\infty}\left[\frac{(2^i)^{\gamma_3}(2^j J_0)^{\gamma_4}}{(2^i)^{2\gamma_1}+2^j J(\alpha_0)}\right]^{1+\varpi} \\
&\le d_1\exp\left\{-cx^{2\gamma_1(1-\gamma_2)} n\lambda_n^2\varepsilon_n^{-2\gamma_1}\right\} + d_2 x^{(\gamma_3-2\gamma_1)(1+\varpi)} n^{-\varpi}\lambda_n^{-(1+\varpi)}.
\end{aligned} \tag{A.8}
$$

To bound $\sum_{i,j=1}^{\infty} I_{12,i,j}$, following the proof of Theorem 3 in Chen and Shen (1998), we can show that, with $M_{i,j} \equiv \frac{\lambda_n}{2}\left[(2^{i-1}x)^{2\gamma_1} + (2^{j-1}-1)J(\alpha_0)\right]$,

$$
\begin{aligned}
I_{12} &\le \sum_{i,j=1}^{\infty} P^*\left(\frac{2}{n}\sum_{t=1}^{n}\sup_{A_{i,j}}|\ell(\alpha,Z)-\ell(\alpha_0,Z)|\, I(U > B_{n,i,j}) \ge M_{i,j}\right) \\
&\le \sum_{i,j=1}^{\infty} P^*\left(\sum_{t=1}^{n} U_t I(U_t > B_{n,i,j}) \ge \frac{cnM_{i,j}}{(2^i x\varepsilon_n)^{\gamma_3}(2^j J_0)^{\gamma_4}}\right) \\
&\le \sum_{i,j=1}^{\infty} P^*\left(n\mu_n\left[U_t I(U_t > B_{n,i,j})\right] \ge c'\frac{n\lambda_n}{\varepsilon_n^{\gamma_3}}\frac{\left[(2^{i-1}x)^{2\gamma_1}+(2^{j-1}-1)J(\alpha_0)\right]}{(2^i x)^{\gamma_3}(2^j J_0)^{\gamma_4}}\right) \\
&\le c\sum_{i,j=1}^{\infty} E\left[\left|n\mu_n\left[U_t I(U_t > B_{n,i,j})\right]\right|^{\gamma_5}\left|n\lambda_n\varepsilon_n^{-\gamma_3}\frac{\left[(2^i x)^{2\gamma_1}+2^j J_0\right]}{(2^i x)^{\gamma_3}(2^j J_0)^{\gamma_4}}\right|^{-\gamma_5}\right] \\
&\le cn^{\gamma_5/2}2^{\gamma_5/2}\left(\varepsilon_n^{\gamma_3}n^{-1}\lambda_n^{-1}\right)^{\gamma_5}\sum_{i,j=1}^{\infty}\left|\frac{(2^i x)^{\gamma_3}(2^j J_0)^{\gamma_4}}{\left[(2^i x)^{2\gamma_1}+2^j J(\alpha_0)\right]}\right|^{\gamma_5} \\
&\le cx^{(\gamma_3-2\gamma_1)\gamma_5}\left(n^{-\frac{1}{2}}\lambda_n^{-1}\varepsilon_n^{\gamma_3}\right)^{\gamma_5}.
\end{aligned} \tag{A.9}
$$

From the results in (A.8, A.9), we can deduce that

$$I_1 \leq \frac{d_1}{\exp(cx^{2\gamma_1(1-\gamma_2)}n\lambda_n^2\varepsilon_n^{-2\gamma_1})} + \frac{d_2}{x^{(2\gamma_1-\gamma_3)(1+\varpi)}n^{\varpi}\lambda_n^{1+\varpi}}$$
$$+ \frac{d_3\varepsilon_n^{\gamma_3\gamma_5}}{x^{(2\gamma_1-\gamma_3)\gamma_5}n^{\gamma_5/2}\lambda_n^{\gamma_5}} \equiv \eta_n(x).$$

I_2 can be bounded by the same bound using virtually the same arguments. Hence, we can deduce that $I \leq \eta_n(x)$. Finally, by definition of $\widehat{\alpha}_n$, we have for all $x \geq 1$ and with $a_n = o(\varepsilon_n^{2\gamma_1})$,

$$P\left(d(\alpha_0, \widehat{\alpha}_n) \geq x\varepsilon_n\right) \leq P^*\left(\sup_{\{d(\alpha_0,\alpha)\geq x\varepsilon_n, \alpha\in\mathcal{A}\}} \left[\widetilde{L}_n(\alpha) - \widetilde{L}_n(\alpha_0)\right] \geq -a_n\right)$$
$$\leq P^*\left(\sup_{\{d(\alpha_0,\alpha)\geq x\varepsilon_n, \alpha\in\mathcal{A}\}} \left[\widetilde{L}_n(\alpha) - \widetilde{L}_n(\alpha_0)\right] \geq -\frac{(x\varepsilon_n)^{2\gamma_1}}{2}\right)$$
$$\leq \eta_n(x).$$

Proof of Theorem 3.7 For any $x \geq 1$ and $j \in N$, define

$$A_j = \left\{\alpha \in \mathcal{A} : d(\alpha_0, \alpha) < x\varepsilon_n \text{ and } 2^{j-1}J_0 \leq J(\alpha) < 2^j J_0\right\},$$
$$A_0 = \{\alpha \in \mathcal{A} : d(\alpha_0, \alpha) < x\varepsilon_n \text{ and } J(\alpha) < J_0\}.$$

First note that

$$\Pr\left[J(\widehat{\alpha}_n) \geq \frac{\left[\lambda_n + \delta(x\varepsilon_n)^{2\gamma_1}\right] J(\alpha_0)}{\lambda_n - \delta(x\varepsilon_n)^{2\gamma_1}}\right]$$
$$\leq \Pr\left\{\lambda_n\left[J(\widehat{\alpha}_n) - J(\alpha_0)\right] \geq \delta(x\varepsilon_n)^{2\gamma_1}\left[J(\widehat{\alpha}_n) + J(\alpha_0)\right]\right\}. \quad \text{(A.10)}$$

By definition of $\widehat{\alpha}_n$, we have:

$$\mu_n\left[\ell(\widehat{\alpha}_n) - \ell(\alpha_0)\right] \geq \lambda_n\left[J(\widehat{\alpha}_n) - J(\alpha_0)\right] + K(\alpha_0, \widehat{\alpha}_n) - a_n,$$

which and (A.10) imply that

$$\Pr\left[J(\widehat{\alpha}_n) \geq \frac{\left[\lambda_n + \delta(x\varepsilon_n)^{2\gamma_1}\right] J(\alpha_0)}{\lambda_n - \delta(x\varepsilon_n)^{2\gamma_1}}\right] \leq I_3 + \Pr\left\{d(\alpha_0, \widehat{\alpha}_n) \geq x\varepsilon_n\right\},$$

where

$$I_3 = \Pr\Bigg[\mu_n[\ell(\widehat{\alpha}_n) - \ell(\alpha_0)] \geq \delta(x\varepsilon_n)^{2\gamma_1}[J(\widehat{\alpha}_n) + J(\alpha_0)] + K(\alpha_0, \widehat{\alpha}_n)$$
$$- a_n,\ d(\alpha_0, \widehat{\alpha}_n) \leq x\varepsilon_n\Bigg].$$

By Condition 3.2,

$$\inf_{\alpha \in A_j}\Big[K(\alpha_0, \alpha) + \delta(x\varepsilon_n)^{2\gamma_1}(J(\alpha) + J(\alpha_0))\Big] \geq M_j$$

where $M_j = 2^j \delta(x\varepsilon_n)^{2\gamma_1} J_0$, hence we get

$$I_3 \leq \sum_{j=1}^{\infty} \Pr\left\{\sup_{A_j} \mu_n\left[[\ell(\alpha) - \ell(\alpha_0)]\, I(U \leq B_{j,n})\right] \geq M_j\right\}$$
$$+ \sum_{j=1}^{\infty} \Pr\left\{\sup_{A_j} \mu_n\left[[\ell(\alpha) - \ell(\alpha_0)]\, I(U > B_{j,n})\right] \geq M_j\right\}.$$

Using the same arguments as in the proof of Theorem 3.6, we can show that $I_3 \leq \eta_n(x)$. By Theorem 3.6, we also have: $\Pr\{d(\alpha_0, \widehat{\alpha}_n) \geq x\varepsilon_n\} \leq \eta_n(x)$. Based on the above results, we can deduce that

$$\Pr\left[J(\widehat{\alpha}_n) \geq \frac{\lambda_n + \delta(x\varepsilon_n)^{2\gamma_1}}{\lambda_n - \delta(x\varepsilon_n)^{2\gamma_1}} J(\alpha_0)\right] \leq \eta_n(x). \tag{A.11}$$

Under $0 < \delta < 1/4$ and $(1 - \delta)(x\varepsilon_n)^{2\gamma_1} \leq \lambda_n$,

$$\frac{\lambda_n + \delta(x\varepsilon_n)^{2\gamma_1}}{\lambda_n - \delta(x\varepsilon_n)^{2\gamma_1}} = 1 + \frac{2\delta}{\lambda_n/(x\varepsilon_n)^{2\gamma_1} - \delta} \leq 1 + \frac{2}{1 - 2\delta}\delta < 1 + 4\delta. \tag{A.12}$$

The claimed result now follows from (A.11) and (A.12). □

Proof of Theorem 4.6 In the following we denote $R[\alpha - \alpha_0, z] \equiv \ell(\alpha, z) - \ell(\alpha_0, z) - \Delta(\alpha_0, z)[\alpha - \alpha_0]$ and $\alpha^*(\alpha, \varepsilon_n) = \alpha + \varepsilon_n u^* \in \mathcal{A}$ with $u^* = \pm v^*$ and $\varepsilon_n = o(n^{-1/2})$. By the definition of the penalized extremum estimator, we have

$$
\begin{aligned}
- O_p(\varepsilon_n^2) &\le n^{-1}\sum_{t=1}^{n}\left[\ell(\widehat{\alpha}_n, Z_t) - \ell(\alpha^*(\widehat{\alpha}_n, \varepsilon_n), Z_t)\right] - \lambda_n\left[J(\widehat{\alpha}_n) - J(\alpha^*(\widehat{\alpha}_n, \varepsilon_n))\right] \\
&= E[\ell(\widehat{\alpha}_n, Z_t) - \ell(\alpha^*(\widehat{\alpha}_n, \varepsilon_n), Z_t)] + \mu_n\left(\Delta(\alpha_0, Z)[\widehat{\alpha}_n - \alpha^*(\widehat{\alpha}_n, \varepsilon_n)]\right) \\
&\quad + \mu_n\left(R[\widehat{\alpha}_n - \alpha_0, Z] - R[\alpha^*(\widehat{\alpha}_n, \varepsilon_n) - \alpha_0, Z]\right) \\
&\quad + \lambda_n\left[J(\widehat{\alpha}_n + \varepsilon_n u^*) - J(\widehat{\alpha}_n)\right] \\
&\le \varepsilon_n\left[\langle \widehat{\alpha}_n - \alpha_0, u^*\rangle - \mu_n\left(\Delta(\alpha_0, Z)[u^*]\right)\right] + O_p(\varepsilon_n^2) + \lambda_n J(\varepsilon_n u^*) \\
&= \varepsilon_n\left[\langle \widehat{\alpha}_n - \alpha_0, u^*\rangle - \mu_n\left(\Delta(\alpha_0, Z)[u^*]\right)\right] + O_p(\varepsilon_n^2) \qquad \text{(A.13)}
\end{aligned}
$$

where the last equality is by Condition 4.1–4.4. By the definition of u^*, the inequality in (A.13) implies that

$$
\left|\langle \widehat{\alpha}_n - \alpha_0, v^*\rangle - \mu_n\left(\Delta(\alpha_0, Z)[v^*]\right)\right| = O_p(\varepsilon_n). \qquad \text{(A.14)}
$$

On the other hand, using (6) and the assumption on the convergence rate, we can deduce that

$$
\sqrt{n}\left[\rho(\widehat{\alpha}_n) - \rho(\alpha_0)\right] = \sqrt{n}\rho'_{\alpha_0}[\widehat{\alpha}_n - \alpha_0] + o_P(1) = \sqrt{n}\langle \widehat{\alpha}_n - \alpha_0, v^*\rangle + o_P(1). \qquad \text{(A.15)}
$$

The claimed result in Theorem 4.6 now follows from (A.14), (A.15) and the Condition 4.5. □

Proof of Theorem 5.3 This Theorem is proved by following similar arguments in Chen et al. (2011) for sieve semiparametric two-step GMM estimators with dependent data. See their paper for more details. Denote

$$
\widetilde{\sigma}_{v^*}^2 \equiv \sum_{t=-n+1}^{n-1} \mathcal{K}\left(\frac{t}{m_n}\right)\Gamma_{n,t}(\alpha_0)\left[v^*, v^*\right],
$$

then by the triangle inequality, we have

$$
\left|\widehat{\sigma}_n^2 - \sigma_{v^*}^2\right| \le \left|\widehat{\sigma}_n^2 - \widetilde{\sigma}_{v^*}^2\right| + \left|\widetilde{\sigma}_{v^*}^2 - E\left[\widetilde{\sigma}_{v^*}^2\right]\right| + \left|E\left[\widetilde{\sigma}_{v^*}^2\right] - \sigma_{v^*}^2\right|. \qquad \text{(A.16)}
$$

First note that by the triangle inequality

$$
\begin{aligned}
&\left|E\left[\widetilde{\sigma}_{v^*}^2\right] - \sigma_{v^*}^2\right| \\
&\le \frac{1}{n}\sum_{t=0}^{n-1}\left|\mathcal{K}\left(\frac{t}{m_n}\right) - 1\right|\sum_{k=t+1}^{n}\left|E\left\{\Delta(\alpha_0, Z_k)[v^*]\Delta(\alpha_0, Z_{k-t})[v^*]\right\}\right| \\
&\quad + \frac{1}{n}\sum_{t=-n+1}^{-1}\left|\mathcal{K}\left(\frac{t}{m_n}\right) - 1\right|\sum_{k=-t+1}^{n}\left|E\left\{\Delta(\alpha_0, Z_k)[v^*]\Delta(\alpha_0, Z_{k+t})[v^*]\right\}\right|,
\end{aligned}
$$

where

$$\left|E\left\{\Delta(\alpha_0, Z_k)[v^*]\Delta(\alpha_0, Z_{k-t})[v^*]\right\}\right| \leq 6\beta_i^{2\left(\frac{1}{2}-\frac{1}{p}\right)} \left\|\Delta(\alpha_0, Z_k)[v^*]\right\|_p^2 \leq c\beta_i^{2\left(\frac{1}{r}-\frac{1}{p}\right)}$$

for the beta mixing process. Thus we can deduce that

$$\left|E\left[\widetilde{\sigma}_{v^*}^2\right] - \sigma_{v^*}^2\right| \leq 2c\sum_{i=0}^{n-1}\left|\mathcal{K}\left(\frac{i}{m_n}\right) - 1\right|\beta_i^{2\left(\frac{1}{r}-\frac{1}{p}\right)} \to 0 \tag{A.17}$$

where the last result is by Condition 5.2(i) and the dominated convergence theorem.

For the second term at the right-hand side of inequality (A.16), note that by Minkowski's inequality

$$\begin{aligned}\left\|\widetilde{\sigma}_{v^*}^2 - E\left[\widetilde{\sigma}_{v^*}^2\right]\right\|_{r/2} &\leq \sum_{t=-n+1}^{n-1}\left|\mathcal{K}\left(\frac{t}{m_n}\right)\right|\left\|\Gamma_{n,t}(\alpha_0)\left[v^*, v^*\right]\right.\\ &\qquad \left. - E\left[\Gamma_{n,t}(\alpha_0)\left[v^*, v^*\right]\right]\right\|_{r/2}\\ &\leq cm_n^2 n^{-1+\frac{2}{r}}\sum_{t=-n+1}^{n-1}\left|\mathcal{K}\left(\frac{t}{m_n}\right)\right|\frac{1}{m_n} = o(1),\end{aligned} \tag{A.18}$$

where the second inequality follows from Lemma 2 in Hansen (1992) and the proof of Theorem 2 in Jong (2000), and the last equality is by Condition 5.2(iv)(v): $m_n^2 n^{-1+\frac{2}{r}} = o(1)$ and $\sum_{t=-n+1}^{n-1}\left|\mathcal{K}\left(\frac{t}{m_n}\right)\right|\frac{1}{m_n} \leq \int_R |\mathcal{K}(x)|\,dx < \infty$. Now, the result in (A.18) implies that

$$\left|\widetilde{\sigma}_{v^*}^2 - E\left[\widetilde{\sigma}_{v^*}^2\right]\right| = o_p(1) \tag{A.19}$$

We next deal with the first term at the right-hand side of inequality (A.16). First by the triangle inequality, we have

$$\begin{aligned}\left|\widehat{\sigma}_n^2 - \widetilde{\sigma}_{v^*}^2\right| &\leq \sum_{t=-n+1}^{n-1}\left|\mathcal{K}\left(\frac{t}{m_n}\right)\right|\left|\Gamma_{n,t}(\widehat{\alpha}_n)\left[\widehat{v}_n^*, \widehat{v}_n^*\right] - \Gamma_{n,t}(\alpha_0)\left[\widehat{v}_n^*, \widehat{v}_n^*\right]\right|\\ &\quad + \sum_{t=-n+1}^{n-1}\left|\mathcal{K}\left(\frac{t}{m_n}\right)\right|\left|\Gamma_{n,t}(\alpha_0)\left[\widehat{v}_n^*, \widehat{v}_n^*\right] - \Gamma_{n,t}(\alpha_0)\left[v^*, \widehat{v}_n^*\right]\right|\\ &\quad + \sum_{t=-n+1}^{n-1}\left|\mathcal{K}\left(\frac{t}{m_n}\right)\right|\left|\Gamma_{n,t}(\alpha_0)\left[v^*, \widehat{v}_n^*\right] - \Gamma_{n,t}(\alpha_0)\left[v^*, v^*\right]\right|\\ &\equiv I_{1,n} + I_{2,n} + I_{3,n}.\end{aligned} \tag{A.20}$$

For $I_{3,n}$, note that

$$\begin{aligned}
&E\left|\Gamma_{n,t}(\alpha_0)\left[v^*,\widehat{v}_n^*\right]-\Gamma_{n,t}(\alpha_0)\left[v^*,v^*\right]\right| \\
&\leq \frac{1}{n}\sum_{k=t+1}^{n} E\left|\Delta(\alpha_0,Z_{k-t})[v^*]\Delta(\alpha_0,Z_k)[\widehat{v}_n^*-v^*]\right| \\
&\leq \frac{n-i}{n}\left\|\Delta(\alpha_0,Z_{k-t})[v^*]\right\|_2\left\|\Delta(\alpha_0,Z_k)[\widehat{v}_n^*-v^*]\right\|_2, \qquad \text{(A.21)}
\end{aligned}$$

where the last inequality is by the Hölder inequality. Now using (A.21), the convergence rate of $\widehat{v}_n^*$ and Condition 5.2 (ii), we have

$$||I_{3,n}|\,|_1 \leq c m_n \delta_n^* \sum_{i=-n+1}^{n-1}\left|\mathcal{K}\left(\frac{i}{m_n}\right)\right| m_n^{-1} \leq c m_n \delta_n^* \int_R |\mathcal{K}(x)|\,dx = o(1). \qquad \text{(A.22)}$$

Using similar arguments, we can show that

$$||I_{2,n}|\,|_1 \leq c m_n \delta_n^* \sum_{i=-n+1}^{n-1}\left|\mathcal{K}\left(\frac{i}{m_n}\right)\right| m_n^{-1} \leq c m_n \delta_n^* \int_R |\mathcal{K}(x)|\,dx = o(1). \qquad \text{(A.23)}$$

Finally, we bound $I_{1,n}$. Since

$$\Gamma_{n,t}(\alpha)\left[\widehat{v}_n^*,\widehat{v}_n^*\right] = \begin{cases} \frac{1}{n}\sum\limits_{k=t+1}^{n} \Delta(\alpha,Z_k)[\widehat{v}_n^*]\Delta(\alpha,Z_{k-t})[\widehat{v}_n^*] & \text{for } t \geq 0 \\ \frac{1}{n}\sum\limits_{k=-t+1}^{n} \Delta(\alpha,Z_k)[\widehat{v}_n^*]\Delta(\alpha,Z_{k+t})[\widehat{v}_n^*] & \text{for } t < 0 \end{cases},$$

we have that for $t \geq 0$,

$$\begin{aligned}
&\left|\Gamma_{n,t}(\widehat{\alpha}_n)\left[\widehat{v}_n^*,\widehat{v}_n^*\right]-\Gamma_{n,t}(\alpha_0)\left[\widehat{v}_n^*,\widehat{v}_n^*\right]\right| \\
&\leq \frac{1}{n}\sum_{k=t+1}^{n}\left|\Delta(\widehat{\alpha}_n,Z_k)[\widehat{v}_n^*]\Delta(\widehat{\alpha}_n,Z_{k-t})[\widehat{v}_n^*]-\Delta(\alpha_0,Z_k)[\widehat{v}_n^*]\Delta(\alpha_0,Z_{k-t})[\widehat{v}_n^*]\right|
\end{aligned}$$

By the triangle inequality, Cauchy–Schwarz inequality and Minkowski inequality, we have uniformly in $t \geq 0$,

$$\begin{aligned}
&\left|\Gamma_{n,t}(\widehat{\alpha}_n)\left[\widehat{v}_n^*, \widehat{v}_n^*\right] - \Gamma_{n,t}(\alpha_0)\left[\widehat{v}_n^*, \widehat{v}_n^*\right]\right| \\
&\leq \frac{1}{n}\sum_{k=1}^{n}\left|\Delta(\widehat{\alpha}_n, Z_k)[\widehat{v}_n^*] - \Delta(\alpha_0, Z_k)[\widehat{v}_n^*]\right|^2 \\
&\quad +2\sqrt{\frac{1}{n}\sum_{k=1}^{n}\left|\Delta(\widehat{\alpha}_n, Z_k)[\widehat{v}_n^*] - \Delta(\alpha_0, Z_k)[\widehat{v}_n^*]\right|^2}\sqrt{\frac{1}{n}\sum_{k=1}^{n}\left|\Delta(\alpha_0, Z_k)[\widehat{v}_n^* - v^*]\right|^2} \\
&\quad +2\sqrt{\frac{1}{n}\sum_{k=1}^{n}\left|\Delta(\widehat{\alpha}_n, Z_k)[\widehat{v}_n^*] - \Delta(\alpha_0, Z_k)[\widehat{v}_n^*]\right|^2}\sqrt{\frac{1}{n}\sum_{k=1}^{n}\left|\Delta(\alpha_0, Z_k)[v^*]\right|^2} \\
&= O_p(\delta_n^2) + O_p(\delta_n \times \delta_n^*) + O_p(\delta_n)
\end{aligned}$$

where the last equality is due to Condition 5.2 (i)–(iii) and the Markov inequality. Similarly we get the same probability bound uniformly in $t < 0$. Hence,

$$\sup_t \left|\Gamma_{n,t}(\widehat{\alpha}_n)\left[\widehat{v}_n^*, \widehat{v}_n^*\right] - \Gamma_{n,t}(\alpha_0)\left[\widehat{v}_n^*, \widehat{v}_n^*\right]\right| = O_p(\delta_n). \tag{A.24}$$

Using (A.24), we get

$$I_{1,n} \leq m_n O_p(\delta_n) \sum_{i=-n+1}^{n-1}\left|\mathcal{K}\left(\frac{i}{m_n}\right)\right|\frac{1}{m_n} \leq m_n O_p(\delta_n)\int_R |\mathcal{K}(x)|\,dx = o_p(1). \tag{A.25}$$

From (A.20), (A.22), (A.23) and (A.25), we can deduce that $\left|\widehat{\sigma}_n^2 - \widetilde{\sigma}_{v^*}^2\right| = o_p(1)$, which together with the results in (A.17) and (A.19), gives the claimed result.

References

Adams, R. A. (1975): *Sobolev Spaces*. Academic Press, New York.

Andrews, D. W. K. (1991): "Heteroskedasticity and Autocorrelation Consistent Covariance Matrix Estimation", *Econometrica*, 59, 817–854.

Birge, L., and P. Massart (1998) "Minimum Contrast Estimators on Sieves: Exponential Bounds and Rates of Convergence", *Bernoulli*, 329–375.

Bradley, R. (1986) "Basic Properties of Strong Mixing Conditions", In E. Eberlein and M.S. Taqqu (Eds.), Dependence in Probability and Statistics.

Chen, X. (1997) "Rate and normality of penalized extremum estimates with tiem series observations", University of Chicago, *unpublished manuscript*.

Chen, X. (2007) "Large Sample Sieve Estimation of Semi-Nonparametric Models", In: James J. Heckman and Edward E. Leamer, Editor(s), Handbook of Econometrics, Elsevier, 2007, Volume 6B, Pages 5549–5632.

Chen, X. (2011): "Penalized Sieve Estimation and Inference of Semi-nonparametric Dynamic Models: A Selective Review". Cowles Foundation Discussion Paper 1804. Yale University.

Chen, X., and Z. Liao (2008) "On Limiting Distributions of Sieve M-estimators of Irregular Functionals", Yale and UCLA, *unpublished manuscript*.

Chen, X. and D. Pouzo (2012) "Estimation of Nonparametric Conditional Moment Models with Possibly Nonsmooth Generalized Residuals," *Econometrica* 80, 277–321.

Chen, X., and X. Shen (1998) "Sieve Extremum Estimates for Weakly Dependent Data", *Econometrica*, 66, 289–314.

Chen, X., and White, H. (1998) "Central Limit and Functional Central Limit Theorems for Hilbert-valued Dependent Heterogeneous Arrays with Applications", *Econometric Theory*, 14(2), 260–284.

Chen, X., and White, H. (1999) "Improved Rates and Asymptotic Normality for Nonparametric Neural Network Estimators", *IEEE Tran. Information Theory* 45, 682–691.

Chen, X., J. Hahn and Z. Liao (2011) "Sieve Semiparametric Two-Step GMM Estimation with Weakly Dependent Data", Yale and UCLA, *unpublished manuscript.*

Chen, X., Z. Liao and Y. Sun (2011) "Sieve Inference for Weakly Dependent Data", Yale, UCLA and UCSD, *unpublished manuscript.*

Corradi, V. and H. White (1995) "Regularized Neural Networks: Some Convergence Rate Results," *Neural Computation* 7, 1201–1220.

de Jong, R. (2000) "A Strong Consistency Proof for Heteroskedasticity and Autocorrelation Consistent Covariance Matrix Estimators", *Econometric Theory*, 16(2), 262–268.

Doukhan, P. (1994) *Mixing: Properties and Examples*, Lecture Notes in Statistics, Vol. 85. Springer, Berlin.

Gallant, A.R. and H. White (1988) *A Unified Theory of Estimation and Inference for Nonlinear Dynamic Models*. Oxford: Basil Blackwell.

Grenander, U. (1981) *Abstract Inference*, Wiley Series, New York.

Gu, C. (2002) Smoothing Spline ANOVA Models, Springer-Verlag, New York.

Hansen, B.E. (1992) "Consistent Covariance Matrix Estimation for Dependent Heterogeneous Processes", *Econometrica*, 60, 967–972.

Huber, P.J. (1981) *Robust Statistics*, Wiley Series, New York.

Koenker, R., P. Ng and S. Portnoy (1994) "Quantile Smoothing Splines", *Biometrika*, 81, 673–680.

Newey, W.K. (1994) "The Asymptotic Variance of Semiparametric Estimators", *Econometrica* 62, 1349–1382.

Newey, W.K. and D. F. McFadden (1994) "Large sample estimation and hypothesis testing", in R.F. Engle III and D.F. McFadden (eds.), *The Handbook of Econometrics*, vol. 4. North-Holland, Amsterdam.

Newey, W. K. and K. D. West (1987): "A Simple, Positive Semidefinite, Heteroskedasticity and Autocorrelation Consistent Covariance Matrix". *Econometrica* 55, 703–708.

Pollard, D. (1984) *Convergence of Statistical Processes*. Springer-Verlag, New York.

Shen, X. (1997) "On Methods of Sieves and Penalization", *The Annals of Statistics*, 25, 2555–2591.

Shen, X. (1998) "On the Method of Penalization", *Statistica Sinica*, 8, 337–357.

Shen, X. and W. Wong (1994) "Convergence Rate of Sieve Estimates", *The Annals of Statistics*, 22, 580–615.

Stone, C.J. (1982) "Optimal Global Rates of Convergence for Nonparametric Regression", *The Annals of Statistics*, 10, 1040–1053.

Van de Geer, S. (2000) *Empirical Processes in M Estimation*, Cambridge University Press.

Wahba, G. (1990) *Spline Models for Observational Data*, CBMS-NSF Regional Conference Series, Philadelphia.

White, H. (2004): *Asymptotic Theory for Econometricians*, Academic Press.

White, H., and J. Wooldridge (1991). "Some Results on Sieve Estimation with Dependent Observations". In: Barnett, W.A., Powell, J., Tauchen, G. (Eds.), Non-parametric and Semi-parametric Methods in Econometrics and Statistics. Cambridge University Press, Cambridge, pp. 459–493.

Tikhonov, T.N. (1963) "Solution of Incorrectly Formulated Problems and the Regularization Method", Soviet Math Dokl, 4, pp. 1035–1038. English translation of, Dokl Akad Nauk SSSR 151, 1963, 501–504.

A Survey of Recent Advances in Forecast Accuracy Comparison Testing, with an Extension to Stochastic Dominance

Valentina Corradi and Norman R. Swanson

Abstract In recent years, an impressive body of research on predictive accuracy testing and model comparison has been published in the econometrics discipline. Key contributions to this literature include the paper by Diebold and Mariano (J Bus Econ Stat 13:253–263, 1995) which sets the groundwork for much of the subsequent work in the area, West (Econometrica 64:1067–1084, 1996) who considers a variant of the DM test that allows for parameter estimation error in certain contexts, and White (Econometrica 68:1097–1126, 2000) who develops testing methodology suitable for comparing many models. In this chapter, we begin by reviewing various key testing results in the extant literature, both under vanishing and non-vanishing parameter estimation error, with focus on the construction of valid bootstrap critical values in the case of non-vanishing parameter estimation error, under recursive estimation schemes, drawing on Corradi and Swanson (Int Econ Rev 48:67–109, 2007a). We then review recent extensions to the evaluation of multiple confidence intervals and predictive densities, for both the case of a known conditional distribution Corradi and Swanson (J Econ 135:187–228, 2006a; Handbook of economic forecasting Elsevier, Amsterdam, pp 197–284) and of an unknown conditional distribution. Finally, we introduce a novel approach in which forecast combinations are evaluated via the examination of the quantiles of the expected loss distribution. More precisely, we compare models looking at cumulative distribution functions (CDFs) of prediction errors, for a given loss function, via the principle of stochastic dominance, and we choose the model whose CDF is stochastically dominated, over some given range of interest.

V. Corradi (✉)
Department of Economics, University of Warwick,
Coventry CV4 7AL, UK
e-mail: v.corradi@warwick.ac.uk

N. R. Swanson
Department of Economics, Rutgers University, 75 Hamilton Street,
New Brunswick NJ 08901, USA
e-mail: nswanson@econ.rutgers.edu

X. Chen and N. R. Swanson (eds.), *Recent Advances and Future Directions in Causality, Prediction, and Specification Analysis*, DOI: 10.1007/978-1-4614-1653-1_5,

Keywords Block bootstrap · Recursive estimation scheme · Reality check · Parameter estimation error · Stochastic dominance

1 Introduction

One of the key contributions permeating the econometric research of Halbert White is the development of statistical tools for specification, estimation, and inference with possibly misspecified models. His main message is that, even though models are merely (crude) approximations to reality, important things can be learned from carrying out inference and generally analyzing "wrong" models. Certainly, the notion of misspecification is absolutely crucial in the context of out-of-sample prediction. After all, if one is carrying out a predictive accuracy assessment in order to "choose" between two competing models, then, at the very least, one of the models is probably misspecified.

In this chapter, we begin by assuming that we are given multiple predictions, arising from multiple different models. Our objective is either to select the model(s) producing the more accurate predictions, for a given loss function, or alternatively, to eliminate the models giving the least accurate predictions. Furthermore, in many such situations, we can choose a benchmark or reference model. This can be a model suggested by economic theory, can be the winner of past competitions, or can simply be a model commonly used by practitioners. The key challenge in this case is to assess whether there exists a competing model that outperforms the benchmark. However, if we sequentially compare the reference model with each of its competitors, we may run into problems. In fact, as the number of competitors increases, the probability of picking an alternative model just by "luck", and not because of its intrinsic merit, increases and eventually will reach one. This is the well-known problem of data mining or data snooping.

The starting point for our discussion is Diebold and Mariano (1995), who develop the "workhorse" of predictive accuracy tests. Two models are compared by assessing their relative predictive losses, given a particular loss function. Assuming that parameter estimation error vanishes asymptotically and that the models are nonnested ensures that the DM test is asymptotically normally distributed, regardless of whether or not the loss function is differentiable.[1] West (1996) allows for non-vanishing parameter estimation error in the DM test, although at the cost of assuming differentiability. In White (2000), a sequence of DM tests are constructed, and the supremum thereof (called the reality check) is used to test whether a given "benchmark" model is at least as accurate as all competitors. The null hypothesis is thus that no competing model can produce a more accurate prediction than the benchmark model, for a given loss function. The key contribution of White (2000) is that he recognizes the importance of sequential test bias when comparing many (rather than two, say) models, and he develops the asymptotic theory allowing for the valid construc-

[1] For a discussion of nested models in the current context, see Clark and McCracken (2001); Corradi and Swanson (2006b).

tion of critical values for his reality check, using, for example, block bootstrap and related bootstrap techniques. In related work, Corradi and Swanson (2006a,2006b and 2007a,2007b) extend the reality check version of the DM test to the evaluation of confidence intervals and predictive densities (rather than focussing on the evaluation of point predictive loss measures). They additionally develop bootstrap techniques for addressing parameter estimation error, and allow for the evaluation of conditional distributions of both known and unknown functional form. By discussing all of the above papers, we undertake to construct a path describing developments in the predictive accuracy testing literature.

Of note is that if any of the above tests fail to reject the null hypothesis that no competitor outperforms the benchmark model, the obvious consequence is to base prediction only on the benchmark model. The tests, thus, are of a "model selection" variety. This is somewhat in contrast with the alternative approach of using forecast combination (see Elliott and Timmermann 2004) to construct "optimal" predictions. In light of this observation, we conclude this chapter by proposing a new stochastic dominance type test that combines features of DM and reality check tests with forecast combination. In particular, we suggest a model selection method for selecting among alternative combination forecasts constructed from panel of forecasters. More broadly, we close by arguing that the notions of stochastic dominance discussed in this context may have a variety of uses in the predictive accuracy testing literature.

Before turning to our discussion of the above tests, it is worth making two comments that further underscore the sense in which the results of the above papers build on one another. In particular, recall that the prediction errors used to construct DM-type tests arise in at least two ways. First, there are situations in which we have series of prediction errors, although we do not know the models used to generate the underlying predictions. For example, this situation arises when we have forecasts from different agents, or professional forecasters. Alternatively, we may have a sequence of Sharpe ratios or returns from different trading rules, as in the financial applications of Sullivan et al. (1999, 2001). Second, there are situations in which we are interested in comparing estimated models. For example, we may want to decide whether to predict tomorrow's inflation rate using an autoregressive model, a threshold model, or a Markov switching model. The parameters of these models are generally estimated. If the number of observations used to estimate the model is larger than the number of observations used for forecast evaluation, or if the same loss function is used for in-sample estimation and out-of-sample prediction (e.g., estimation by ordinary least squares (OLS) and a quadratic loss function), then the contribution of estimated parameters can be ignored. Otherwise, it has to be taken into account. Corradi and Swanson (2006a, 2007a) develop bootstrap procedures which properly capture the contribution of parameter estimation error in the case of rolling or recursive estimation schemes, respectively.

Additionally, and as mentioned above, DM- and reality check-type tests compare point forecasts (and forecast errors) from two or multiple models, respectively. For example, we may want to pick the model producing the most accurate point predictions of the inflation rate. However, there are situations in which we are instead interested in finding the model producing the most accurate interval predictions (e.g.

that inflation will be within a given interval). Predictive interval accuracy is particularly important in the management of financial risk in the insurance and banking industries, where confidence intervals or entire conditional distributions are often examined. Evaluation of Value at Risk and Expected Shortfall are two main examples (see Duffie and Pan (1997) for further discussion). Corradi and Swanson (2005, 2006a,b, 2007b) extend the DM and reality check tests to the case of intervals and conditional distributions, using both simulated and historical data.

The rest of the chapter is organized as follows. In Sect. 2 we discuss the DM and reality check tests, and outline how to construct valid bootstrap p-values in the case of non-vanishing parameter estimation error, with both recursive and rolling estimation schemes. In Sect. 3 we extend the DM and reality check tests to the evaluation of multiple confidence intervals and predictive densities. Finally, in Sect. 4 we outline a new technique that draws together concepts of forecast combination with multiple model evaluation. Namely, we introduce a stochastic dominance-type approach in which forecast combinations are evaluated via the examination of the quantiles of the expected loss distribution. More precisely, we compare models by prediction error CDFs, for given loss functions, via the principle of stochastic dominance, and we choose the model whose CDF is stochastically dominated, over some given range of interest.

2 DM and Reality Check Tests

2.1 The Case of Vanishing Estimation Error

We begin by outlining the DM (1995) and White (2000) tests, when parameter estimation error is asymptotically negligible. Consider a collection of $K+1$ models, where model 0 is treated as the benchmark or reference model and models $k = 1, \ldots, K$ compose the set of competing models. For the DM test, $K = 1$. For the reality check, $K > 1$. The h-step ahead forecast error associated with model k, is $u_{i,t+h} = y_{t+h} - \phi_k(Z^t, \theta_k^\dagger)$. As $\theta_k^\dagger$ is unknown, we do not observe the prediction error $u_{k,t+h}$, but we only observe $\widehat{u}_{k,t+h} = y_{t+h} - \phi_k(Z^t, \widehat{\theta}_{k,t})$, where $\widehat{\theta}_{k,t}$ is an estimator of $\theta_k^\dagger$ based on observations available at time t.

The common practice in out-of-sample prediction is to split the total sample of T observations into two subsamples of length R and P, with $R + P = T$. One uses the first R observations to estimate a candidate model, and construct the first h-step ahead prediction error. Then, one uses $R+1$ observations to re-estimate the model and compute the second h-step ahead prediction error, and so on, until one has a sequence of $(P - h + 1)$ h-step ahead prediction errors.[2] If we use this recursive

[2] Here, we use a recursive estimation scheme, where data up to time $t \geq R$ are used in estimation. West and McCracken (1998) also consider a rolling estimation scheme, in which a rolling windows of R observations is used for estimation.

estimation scheme, at each step the estimated parameters are given by

$$\widehat{\theta}_{k,t} = \arg\max_{\theta_k} \left\{ \frac{1}{t} \sum_{j=1}^{t} q_{k,j}\left(X_{k,t}, \theta_k\right) \right\} \text{ for } t \geq R, \tag{1}$$

where $q_{k,j}$ can be thought of as the quasi-likelihood function associated with model k.[3] Under stationarity, $\theta_k^{\dagger} = \arg\max_{\theta_i} E(q_{k,j}\left(X_{k,t}, \theta_k\right)$.

Hereafter, for notational simplicity, we consider only the case of $h = 1$.

For a given loss function, g, the DM test evaluates the following hypotheses[4]:

$$H_0 : E\left(g(u_{0,t+1}) - g(u_{1,t+1})\right) = 0$$

versus

$$H_A : E\left(g(u_{0,t+1}) - g(u_{1,t+1})\right) \neq 0.$$

If $R \to \infty$ at a faster rate than $P \to \infty$, as $T \to \infty$, then, assuming that models "0" and "1" are nonnested, the limiting distribution of

$$\widehat{DM}_P = \frac{1}{\sqrt{P}} \sum_{t=R}^{T-1} \left(g(\widehat{u}_{0,t+1}) - g(\widehat{u}_{1,t+1})\right) / \widehat{\sigma}_S$$

is $N(0, 1)$, when scaled appropriately by $\widehat{\sigma}_S$, a heteroscedasticity and autocorrelation consistent (HAC) estimation of the variance of $\frac{1}{\sqrt{P}} \sum_{t=R}^{T-1} g(\widehat{u}_{0,t+1}) - g(\widehat{u}_{1,t+1})$. Evidently, $\widehat{DM}_P$ is the HAC t-statistic associated with the intercept in a regression of the loss differential series, $g(\widehat{u}_{0,t+1}) - g(\widehat{u}_{1,t+1})$, on a constant. For a discussion of the limit distribution of this test statistic when the two forecasting models are nested, see Clark and McCracken (2001). Note also that g need not be differentiable, unless one wishes to adjust the limit distribution for the effect of parameter estimation error in cases where $P/R \to \pi$, as $P, R, T- > \infty$, $0 < \pi < \infty$, as in West (1996). Moreover, even if $P/R \to \pi$, as $P, R, T- > \infty$, $0 < \pi < \infty$, parameter estimation error is asymptotic negligible whenever we use the same loss function for in-sample estimation and out-of-sample prediction (see below for further discussion).

Now, for a given loss function, g, the reality check evaluates the following hypotheses:

---

[3] If we instead use a rolling estimation scheme, then

$$\widetilde{\theta}_{k,t} = \arg\max_{\theta_k} \left\{ \frac{1}{R} \sum_{j=t-R+1}^{t} q_{k,j}\left(X_{k,t}, \theta_k\right) \right\} \quad R \leq t \leq T.$$

[4] See Christoffersen and Diebold (1996, 1997) and Elliott and Timmermann (2004, 2005) for a detailed discussion of loss functions used in predictive evaluation.

$$H_0 : \max_{k=1,\ldots,K} E\left(g(u_{0,t+1}) - g(u_{k,t+1})\right) \leq 0$$

versus

$$H_A : \max_{k=1,\ldots,K} E\left(g(u_{0,t+1}) - g(u_{k,t+1})\right) > 0.$$

The null hypothesis is that no competing model outperforms the benchmark (i.e., model "0"), for a given loss function, while the alternative is that at least one competitor outperforms the benchmark. By jointly considering all competing models, the reality check controls the family-wise error rate (FWER), and circumvents so-called "data snooping" problems. In fact, the test is designed to ensure that the probability of rejecting the null when it is false is smaller than or equal to a fixed nominal level, α. The reality check statistic is given by:

$$\widehat{S}_P = \max_{k=1,\ldots,K} \widehat{S}_P(0,k), \tag{2}$$

where

$$\widehat{S}_P(0,k) = \frac{1}{\sqrt{P}} \sum_{t=R}^{T-1} \left(g(\widehat{u}_{0,t+1}) - g(\widehat{u}_{k,t+1})\right), \quad k = 1, \ldots, K.$$

Letting $S_P(0,k) = \frac{1}{\sqrt{P}} \sum_{t=R}^{T-1} \left(g(u_{0,t+1}) - g(u_{k,t+1})\right)$, it is immediate to see that,

$$\begin{aligned}\widehat{S}_P(0,k) - S_P(0,k) &= \mathrm{E}\left(\nabla_{\theta_0} g(u_{0,t+1})\right) \frac{1}{\sqrt{P}} \sum_{t=R+1}^{T} \left(\widehat{\theta}_{0,t} - \theta_0^{\dagger}\right) \\ &\quad - \mathrm{E}\left(\nabla_{\theta_k} g(u_{k,t+1})\right) \frac{1}{\sqrt{P}} \sum_{t=R+\tau}^{T} \left(\widehat{\theta}_{k,t} - \theta_k^{\dagger}\right) + o_P(1). \end{aligned} \tag{3}$$

Now, if $g = q_k$, then by the first-order conditions, $\mathrm{E}\left(\nabla_{\theta_k} g(u_{k,t+1})\right) = 0$. Thus, if we use the same loss function for estimation and prediction (e.g., we estimate the model by OLS and use a quadratic loss function), then parameter estimation error is asymptotically negligible. Furthermore, if $P/R \to 0$, as $P, R, T- > \infty$ (i.e., the sample used for estimation grows at a faster rate than the sample used for forecast evaluation), then parameter estimation is again asymptotically negligible. Otherwise, it has to be taken into account.

Proposition 2.2 in White (2000) establishes that

$$\max_{k=1,\ldots,K} \frac{1}{\sqrt{P}} \sum_{t=R}^{T-1} \left(\left(g(\widehat{u}_{0,t+1}) - g(\widehat{u}_{k,t+1})\right) - \mu_k\right) \xrightarrow{d} \max_{k=1,\ldots,K} Z_k,$$

where $\mu_k = \mathrm{E}\left(g(\widehat{u}_{0,t+1}) - g(\widehat{u}_{k,t+1})\right)$, $Z = (Z_1, \ldots, Z_k)^\top$ is distributed as $\mathrm{N}(0, V)$ and V has typical element

$$v_{j,k} = \lim_{P\to\infty} \mathrm{Cov}\left(\frac{1}{\sqrt{P}} \sum_{t=R+\tau}^{T} \left(g(\widehat{u}_{0,t+1}) - g(\widehat{u}_{j,t+1})\right), \right.$$
$$\left. \frac{1}{\sqrt{P}} \sum_{t=R+\tau}^{T} \left(g(\widehat{u}_{0,t+1}) - g(\widehat{u}_{k,t+1})\right)\right). \quad (4)$$

Because the maximum of a Gaussian process is not a Gaussian process, the construction of p-values for the limiting distribution above is not straightforward. White proposes two alternatives: (i) a simulation-based approach and (ii) a bootstrap-based approach. The first approach starts from a consistent estimator of V, say $\widehat{V}$. Then, for each simulation $s = 1, \ldots, S$, we construct

$$\widehat{d}_P^{(s)} = \begin{pmatrix} \widehat{d}_{1,P}^{(s)} \\ \vdots \\ \widehat{d}_{K,P}^{(s)} \end{pmatrix} = \begin{pmatrix} \widehat{v}_{1,1} & \cdots & \widehat{v}_{1,K} \\ \vdots & \ddots & \vdots \\ \widehat{v}_{K,1} & \cdots & \widehat{v}_{K,K} \end{pmatrix}^{1/2} \begin{pmatrix} \eta_1^{(s)} \\ \vdots \\ \eta_K^{(s)} \end{pmatrix},$$

where $\left(\eta_1^{(s)}, \ldots, \eta_K^{(s)}\right)^\top$ is drawn from a $\mathrm{N}(0, \mathbf{I}_K)$. Next, we compute $\max_{k=1,\ldots,K} \left|\widehat{d}_P^{(s)}\right|$, and the $(1-\alpha)$-percentile of its empirical distribution. This simulation- based approach requires the estimation of V. Note that we can use an estimator of V which captures the contribution of parameter estimation error, along the lines of West (1996) and West and McCracken (1998). However, if K is large, and forecasting errors exhibit a high degree of time dependence, estimators of the long-run variance become imprecise and ill-conditioned, making inference unreliable, especially in small samples. This problem can be overcome using bootstrap critical values.

White (2000) outlines the construction of bootstrap critical values when the contribution of parameter estimation error to the asymptotic covariance matrix is asymptotically negligible. In this case, we resample blocks of $g(\widehat{u}_{0,t+1}) - g(\widehat{u}_{k,t+1})$ and, for each bootstrap replication $b = 1, \ldots, B$, calculate

$$\widehat{S}_P^{*(b)}(0,k) = \frac{1}{\sqrt{P}} \sum_{t=R+\tau}^{T} \left(g^*(\widehat{u}_{0,t+1}) - g^*(\widehat{u}_{k,t+1})\right)$$
$$- \left(g(\widehat{u}_{0,t+1}) - g(\widehat{u}_{k,t+1})\right).$$

Then, we compute the bootstrap statistic as $\max_{k=1,\ldots,K} \left|\widehat{S}_P^{*(b)}(0,k) - \widehat{S}_P(0,k)\right|$ and the $(1-\alpha)$-percentile of the empirical distribution of B statistics is used for inference. Evidently, the same approach discussed above can be used for the DM test, although such is clearly not needed, given the earlier results discussed, in cases where parameter estimation error vanishes asymptotically.

Before turning to the issue of constructing DM and reality check p-values in the case of non-vanishing parameter estimation error, it is worthwhile to review some other recent developments in the reality check literature.[5]

2.1.1 Controlling for Irrelevant Models

From the statistic in (2), it is immediate to see that any model which is strictly dominated by the benchmark does not contribute to the limiting distribution, simply because it does not contribute to the maximum. On the other hand, all models contribute to the limiting distribution of either the simulated or the bootstrap statistic. Thus, by introducing irrelevant models, the overall p-value increases. In fact, for a given level α, the probability of rejecting the null when it is false is α when all models are as good as the benchmark (i.e. when $E\left(g(u_{0,t+1}) - g(u_{k,t+1})\right) = 0$ for $k = 1, \ldots, K$), otherwise the probability of rejecting the null is smaller than α, and decreases as the number of irrelevant models increases. While the reality check is able to control the family-wise error rate, and so avoids the issue of data snooping, it may thus be rather conservative.

For this reason, attempts have been made to modify the reality check in such a way as to control for both the family-wise error rate and the inclusion of irrelevant models. Hansen (2005) suggests a variant of the reality check, called the Superior Predictive Ability (SPA) test, which is less sensitive to the inclusion of poor models and thus less conservative. The SPA statistic is given by

$$T_P = \max\left\{0, \max_{k=1,\ldots,K} \frac{\frac{1}{\sqrt{P}}\sum_{t=R+\tau}^{T}\widehat{d}_{k,t}}{\sqrt{\widehat{v}_{k,k}}}\right\},$$

where $\widehat{d}_{k,t} = \left(g(\widehat{u}_{0,t+1}) - g(\widehat{u}_{k,t+1})\right)$ and $\widehat{v}_{k,k}$ is defined as in (4). The bootstrap counterpart to T_P at replication b, $T_P^{*(b)}$ is given by

$$T_P^{*(b)} = \max\left\{0, \max_{k=1,\ldots,K}\left\{\frac{\frac{1}{\sqrt{P}}\sum_{t=R+\tau}^{T}\left(\widehat{d}_{k,t}^{*(b)} - \widehat{d}_{k,t}1_{\left\{\widehat{m}_{k,P} > -\widehat{v}_{k,k}\sqrt{2\ln\ln P/P}\right\}}\right)}{\sqrt{\widehat{v}_{k,k}}}\right\}\right\}.$$

Here, p-values for the SPA statistic are given by $1/B\sum_{b=1}^{B}1_{\left\{T_P^{*(b)} > T_P\right\}}$. The logic underlying the construction of the SPA p-values is the following. When a model is too slack, and so it does not contribute to T_P, the corresponding bootstrap moment condition is not recentered, and so the bootstrap statistic is also not affected by the

---

[5] In the sequel, for ease of notation, the version of the DM test that we discuss will be $\widehat{S}_P(0, k)$, with $k = 1$.

irrelevant model. The fact that very poor models do not contribute to the bootstrap p-values makes the SPA p-values less conservative than the reality check p-values. Nevertheless, it cannot be established that the SPA test is uniformly more powerful than the reality check test. Corradi and Distaso (2011), using the generalized moment selection approach of Andrews and Soares (2010), derive a general class of superior predictive accuracy tests, that control for FWER and for the contribution of irrelevant models. They show that Hansen's SPA belongs to this class. Additionally, Romano and Wolf (2005) suggest a multiple step extension of the reality check which ensures tighter control of irrelevant models. A review of alternative ways of controlling for the overall error rate is provided in Corradi and Distaso (2011), and references contained therein.

2.1.2 Conditional Predictive Ability

In the Diebold-Mariano framework, as well as in the reality check framework, model k and model 0 are considered equally good, in terms of a given loss function, g, if $\mathrm{E}\big(g\left(u_{t,0}\right) - g\left(u_{t,k}\right)\big) = 0$. This is a statement about forecasting models. In fact, the null hypothesis is evaluated at the "pseudo-true" value for the parameters. Giacomini and White (2006) propose a novel approach in which model k and model 0 are considered equally good if $\mathrm{E}\big(g\left(\widehat{u}_{t,0}\right) - g\left(\widehat{u}_{t,k}\right) | \mathcal{G}_t\big) = 0$, where $\mathcal{G}_t$ is an information set, containing (part of) the history available up to time t. The two key differences between unconditional and conditional predictive accuracy tests are: (i) model comparison is based on estimated parameters in the GW approach, rather than on their probability limits, and (ii) models in the GW approach are evaluated according to the expected loss conditional on a given information set $\mathcal{G}_t$, rather than unconditionally. The above is a statement about forecasting methods rather than forecasting models. The notion is that not only the model, but also the way it is estimated matters. Needless to say, if a large number of observations is used for estimation, the estimated parameters get close to their probability limits. For this reason, GW suggest using relatively short observation windows, whose length is fixed and does increase with the sample size. In this way, estimated parameters can be treated as strong mixing random variables.

Recall also that the $\widehat{DM}_P$ is the HAC t-statistic associated with the intercept in a regression of the loss differential series, $g(\widehat{u}_{0,t+1}) - g(\widehat{u}_{1,t+1})$, on a constant. Evidently, DM and subsequent tests are easily made conditional by including other conditioning variables in the regression.

2.2 Bootstrap Critical Values for Recursive Estimation Schemes

Whenever $g \neq q_k$, for at least some k, and $P/R \to \pi \neq 0$, then parameter estimation error contributes to the variance of the limiting distribution of the DM and reality check tests. One reason for using a different loss function for estimation and prediction occurs when, for example, we use OLS for estimation, but then we want to use an asymmetric loss function which penalizes positive and negative errors in a different manner, when comparing predictive accuracy (see Zellner 1986; Christoffersen and Diebold 1997). More specifically, when parameter estimation error does not vanish, we need to take into account the contribution of $\frac{1}{\sqrt{P}}\sum_{t=R+\tau}^{T}\left(\widehat{\theta}_{k,t}-\theta_k^{\dagger}\right)$ to the asymptotic variance in (4). Hence, we need a bootstrap procedure which is valid for recursive m-estimators, in the sense that its use suffices to mimic the limiting distribution of $\frac{1}{\sqrt{P}}\sum_{t=R}^{T-1}\left(\widehat{\theta}_{k,t}-\theta_k^{\dagger}\right)$.

One approach to the above issue of parameter estimation error is to use the block bootstrap for recursive m-estimators for constructing critical values. In this context, it is important to note that earlier observations are used more frequently than temporally subsequent observations, when forming test statistics. On the other hand, in the standard block bootstrap, all blocks from the original sample have the same probability of being selected, regardless of the dates of the observations in the blocks. Thus, the bootstrap estimator which is constructed as a direct analog of $\widehat{\theta}_t$ is characterized by a location bias that can be either positive or negative, depending on the sample that we observe. In order to circumvent this problem, Corradi and Swanson (2007a) suggest a recentering of the bootstrap score which ensures that the new bootstrap estimator, which is no longer the direct analog of $\widehat{\theta}_{k,t}$, is asymptotically unbiased. It should be noted that the idea of recentering is not new in the bootstrap literature for the case of full sample estimation. In fact, recentering is necessary, even for first-order validity, in the case of overidentified generalized method of moments (GMM) estimators (see e.g. Hall and Horowitz 1996; Andrews 2002; Inoue and Shintani 2006). This is due to the fact that, in the overidentified case, the bootstrap moment conditions are not equal to zero, even if the population moment conditions are. However, in the context of $m-$estimators using the full sample, recentering is needed only for higher order asymptotics, but not for first-order validity, in the sense that the bias term is of smaller order than $T^{-1/2}$ (see e.g. Andrews 2002; Goncalves and White 2004). In the case of recursive $m-$estimators, on the other hand, the bias term is instead of the order $T^{-1/2}$, so that it does contribute to the limiting distribution. This points to a need for recentering when using recursive estimation schemes.

To keep notation simple, suppose that we want to predict, y_t using one of its past lags, and one lag of vector of additional variables, X_t, and let $Z_t=(y_t,X_t)$. Using the overlapping block resampling scheme of Kunsch (1989), at each replication, we draw b blocks (with replacement) of length l from the sample $W_t=(y_t,Z_{t-1})$, where $bl=T-1$. Let $W_t^*=(y_t^*,Z_{t-1}^*)$ denote the resampled observations. As a bootstrap counterpart to $\widehat{\theta}_{k,t}$, Corradi and Swanson (2007a) suggest constructing $\widehat{\theta}_{k,t}^*$, defined as follows:

$$\widehat{\theta}^*_{k,t} = \arg\min_{\theta_k} \frac{1}{t}\sum_{j=1}^{t}\left(q_k(y^*_j, Z^*_{j-1}, \theta_k) - \theta'_k\left(\frac{1}{T}\sum_{h=1}^{T-1}\nabla_{\theta_k} q_k(y_h, Z_{h-1}, \widehat{\theta}_{k,t})\right)\right), \tag{5}$$

where $R \leq t \leq T-1$, $k = 0, 1, \ldots, K$.

Note that $\widehat{\theta}^*_{k,t}$ is not the direct analog of $\widehat{\theta}_{k,t}$ in (1). Heuristically, the additional recentering term in (5) has the role of offsetting the bias that arises due to the fact in the that earlier observations have the same chance of being drawn as temporally subsequent observations. Theorem 1 in Corradi and Swanson (2007a) establishes that the limiting distribution of $\frac{1}{\sqrt{P}}\sum_{t=R}^{T-1}\left(\widehat{\theta}^*_{k,t} - \widehat{\theta}_{k,t}\right)$ is the same as that of $\frac{1}{\sqrt{P}}\sum_{t=R}^{T-1}\left(\widehat{\theta}_{k,t} - \theta^\dagger_k\right)$, conditional on the sample, and for all samples except a set with probability measure approaching zero. We can easily see how this result allows for the construction of valid bootstrap critical values for the reality check. Let $\widehat{u}_{k,t+1} = y_{t+1} - \phi_k\left(Z_t, \widehat{\theta}_{k,t}\right)$ and $\widehat{u}^*_{k,t+1} = y^*_{t+1} - \phi_k\left(Z^*_t, \widehat{\theta}^*_{k,t}\right)$, so that the reality check statistic $\widehat{S}_P$ is defined as in (2). The bootstrap counterpart of $\widehat{S}_P$ is given by

$$\widehat{S}^*_P = \max_{k=1,\ldots,K} S^*_P(0,k),$$

where

$$\widehat{S}^*_P(0,k) = \frac{1}{\sqrt{P}}\sum_{t=R}^{T-1}\Bigg[\left(g(y^*_{t+1} - \phi_0(Z^*_t, \widehat{\theta}^*_{0,t})) - g(y^*_{t+1} - \phi_k(Z^*_t, \widehat{\theta}^*_{k,t}))\right) - \left\{\frac{1}{T}\sum_{j=1}^{T}\left(g(y_{j+1} - \phi_0(Z_j, \widehat{\theta}_{0,t})) - g(y_{j+1} - \phi_k(Z_j, \widehat{\theta}_{k,t}))\right)\right\}\Bigg]. \tag{6}$$

It is important to notice that the bootstrap statistic in (6) is different from the "usual" bootstrap statistic, which is defined as the difference between the statistic computed over the sample observations and over the bootstrap observations. In fact, in $\widehat{S}^*_P(0,k)$, the bootstrap (resampled) component is constructed only over the last P observations, while the sample component is constructed over all T observations. The percentiles of the empirical distribution of $\widehat{S}^*_P$ can be used to construct valid bootstrap critical values for $\widehat{S}_P$, in the case of non-vanishing parameter estimation error. Their first-order validity is established in Proposition 2 in Corradi and Swanson (2007a). Valid bootstrap critical values for the rolling estimation case are outlined in Corradi and Swanson (2006a).

3 Extending the DM and Reality Check Tests to Forecast Interval Evaluation

3.1 The Case of Known Distribution Function

Thus far, we have discussed pointwise predictive accuracy testing (i.e. wherein models are evaluated on the basis of selecting the most accurate pointwise forecasts of a given variable). However, there are several instances in which merely having a "good" model for the conditional mean and/or variance may not be adequate for the task at hand. For example, financial risk management involves tracking the entire distribution of a portfolio, or measuring certain distributional aspects, such as value at risk (see e.g. Duffie and Pan 1997). In such cases, models of conditional mean and/or variance may not be satisfactory. A very small subset of important contributions that go beyond the examination of models of conditional mean and/or variance include papers which: assess the correctness of conditional interval predictions (see e.g. Christoffersen 1998); assess volatility predictability by comparing unconditional and conditional interval forecasts (see e.g. Christoffersen and Diebold 2000); and assess conditional quantiles (see e.g. Giacomini and Komunjer 2005). A thorough review of the literature on predictive interval and predictive density evaluation is given in Corradi and Swanson (2006b).

Corradi and Swanson (2006a) extend the DM and reality check tests to predictive density evaluation, and outline a procedure for assessing the relative out-of-sample predictive accuracy of multiple misspecified conditional distribution models that can be used with rolling and recursive estimation schemes. The objective is to compare these models in terms of their closeness to the true conditional distribution, $F_0(u|Z^t, \theta_0) = \Pr(y_{t+1} \leq u|Z^t)$.[6] In the spirit of White (2000), we choose a particular conditional distribution model as the "benchmark" and test the null hypothesis that no competing model can provide a more accurate approximation of the "true" conditional distribution, against the alternative that at least one competitor outperforms the benchmark model. Following Corradi and Swanson (2005), accuracy is measured using a distributional analog of mean square error. More precisely, the squared (approximation) error associated with model k, $k = 1, \ldots, K$, is measured in terms of the average over U of $E\left(\left(F_k(u|Z^t, \theta_k^\dagger) - F_0(u|Z^t, \theta_0)\right)^2\right)$, where $u \in U$, and U is a possibly unbounded set on the real line. Additionally, integration over u in the formation of the actual test statistic is governed by $\phi(u) \geq 0$, where $\int_U \phi(u) = 1$. Thus, one can control not only the range of u, but also the weights attached to different values of u, so that more weight can be attached to important tail events, for example. We also consider tests based on an analogous conditional confidence interval version of the above measure. Namely,

[6] With a slight abuse of notation, in this section the subscript 0 denotes the "true" conditional distribution model, rather than the benchmark model; and the subscript 1 thus now denotes the benchmark model.

$E\left(\left(\left(F_k(\overline{u}|Z^t,\theta_k^\dagger) - F_k(\underline{u}|Z^t,\theta_k^\dagger)\right) - (F_0(\overline{u}|Z^t,\theta_0) - F_0(\underline{u}|Z^t,\theta_0))\right)^2\right)$, where $\underline{u}$ and $\overline{u}$ are "lower" and "upper" bounds on the confidence interval to be evaluated. For notational simplicity, in the sequel we focus on conditional forecast interval comparison, and set $\underline{u} = -\infty$ and $\overline{u} = u$. For example, we say that model 1 is more accurate than model 2, if

$$E\left(\left(F_1(u|Z^t,\theta_1^\dagger) - F_0(u|Z^t,\theta_0)\right)^2 - \left(F_2(u|Z^t,\theta_2^\dagger) - F_0(u|Z^t,\theta_0)\right)^2\right) < 0.$$

This measure defines a norm and it implies a standard goodness of fit measure.

Another measure of distributional accuracy available in the literature is the Kullback-Leibler Information Criterion, KLIC (see e.g. White 1982; Vuong 1989; Fernandez-Villaverde and Rubio-Ramirez 2004; Amisano and Giacomini 2007; Kitamura 2004). According to the KLIC approach, we should choose Model 1 over Model 2 if

$$E\left(\log f_1\left(y_{t+1}|Z^t,\theta_1^\dagger\right) - \log f_2\left(y_{t+1}|Z^t,\theta_2^\dagger\right)\right) > 0.$$

The KLIC is a sensible measure of accuracy, as it chooses the model which on average gives higher probability to events which have actually occurred. The drawback is that the KLIC approach cannot be easily generalized to compare conditional intervals.

The hypotheses of interest are formulated as:

$$H_0 : \max_{k=2,\ldots,K}\left(\mu_1^2(u) - \mu_k^2(u)\right) \leq 0$$

versus

$$H_A : \max_{k=2,\ldots,K}\left(\mu_1^2(u) - \mu_k^2(u)\right) > 0,$$

where $\mu_k^2(u) = E\left(\left(1\{y_{t+1} \leq u\} - F_k(u|Z^t,\theta_k^\dagger)\right)^2\right)$, $k = 1,\ldots,K$. Note that for any given u, $E(1\{y_{t+1} \leq u\}|Z^t) = \Pr(y_{t+1} \leq u|Z^t) = F_0(u|Z^t,\theta_0)$. Thus, $1\{y_{t+1} \leq u\} - F_k(u|Z^t,\theta_i^\dagger)$ can be interpreted as an "error" term associated with computation of the conditional expectation under F_k.

The statistic is:

$$Z_P = \max_{k=2,\ldots,K} Z_{P,u,\tau}(1,k), \tag{7}$$

with

$$Z_{P,u}(1,k) = \frac{1}{\sqrt{P}} \sum_{t=R}^{T-1} \Big(\left(1\{y_{t+1} \leq u\} - F_1(u|Z^t, \widehat{\theta}_{1,t})\right)^2 - \left(1\{y_{t+1} \leq u\} - F_k(u|Z^t, \widehat{\theta}_{k,t})\right)^2 \Big),$$

where, as usual, $R + P = T$, and $\widehat{\theta}_{k,t}$ can be either a recursive or a rolling estimator. The limiting distribution of (7) is established in Proposition 1(a) in Corradi and Swanson (2006a), who also suggest how to construct valid bootstrap critical values, for both the recursive and the rolling estimation cases.

3.2 The Case of Unknown Distribution Function

There are cases in which the distribution function is not known in closed form. This problem typically arises when the variable we want to predict is generated by highly nonlinear dynamic models. Very important examples are Dynamic Stochastic General Equilibrium (DSGE) Models, which generally cannot be solved in closed form (see Bierens (2007), for a discussion of different ways of approximating DSGEs). Since the seminal papers by Kydland and Prescott (1982), Long and Plosser (1983) and King et al. (1988a,b), there has been substantial attention given to the problem of reconciling the dynamic properties of data simulated from DSGE models, and in particular from real business cycle (RBC) models, with the historical record. A partial list of advances in this area includes: (i) the examination of how RBC-simulated data reproduce the covariance and autocorrelation functions of actual time series (see e.g., Watson 1993); (ii) the comparison of DSGE and historical spectral densities (see e.g. Diebold et al. 1998); (iii) the evaluation of the difference between the second order time series properties of vector autoregression (VAR) predictions and out-of-sample predictions from DSGE models (see e.g. Schmitt-Grohe 2000); (iv) the construction of Bayesian odds ratios for comparing DSGE models with unrestricted VAR models (see e.g. Gomes and Schorfheide 2002; Fernandez-Villaverde and Rubio-Ramirez 2004); (v) the comparison of historical and simulated data impulse response functions (see e.g. Cogley and Nason 1995); (vi) the formulation of "Reality" bounds for measuring how close the density of an DSGE model is to the density associated with an unrestricted VAR model (see e.g. Bierens and Swanson 2000); and (vii) loss function based evaluation of DSGE models (see e.g. Schorfheide 2000).

The papers cited above evaluate the ability of a given DSGE model to reproduce a particular characteristic of the data. Corradi and Swanson (2007b) use a DM (reality check) approach to evaluate DSGEs in terms of their ability to match (with historical data) the joint distribution of the variables of interest, and provide an empirical application in terms of the comparison of several variants of the stochastic growth model of Christiano (1988). As the distribution function is not known in closed form, we replace it with its simulated counterpart.

To keep notation simple, as above, we consider the case of confidence intervals, setting $\underline{u} = -\infty$, and $u = \infty$. Hereafter, F represents the joint distribution of a variable of interest, say Y_t (e.g. output growth and hours worked). The hypotheses are:

$$H_0 : \max_{k=2,\ldots,K} \left(\left(F_0(u;\theta_0) - F_1(u;\theta_1^\dagger) \right)^2 - \left(F_0(u;\theta_0) - F_k(u;\theta_k^\dagger) \right)^2 \right) \leq 0$$

$$H_A : \max_{k=2,\ldots,K} \left(\left(F_0(u;\theta_0) - F_1(u;\theta_1^\dagger) \right)^2 - \left(F_0(u;\theta_0) - F_k(u;\theta_k^\dagger) \right)^2 \right) > 0.$$

Thus, under H_0, no model can provide a better approximation of the joint CDF than model 1. In order to test H_0 versus H_A, the relevant test statistic is $\sqrt{T} Z_{T,S}$, where

$$Z_{T,S} = \max_{k=2,\ldots,K} \sqrt{T} Z_{k,T,S}(u), \tag{8}$$

$$\begin{aligned} Z_{k,T,S}(u) = &\frac{1}{T}\sum_{t=1}^{T}\left(1\{Y_t \leq u\} - \frac{1}{S}\sum_{n=1}^{S} 1\{Y_{1,n}(\widehat{\theta}_{1,T}) \leq u\}\right)^2 \\ &-\frac{1}{T}\sum_{t=1}^{T}\left(1\{Y_t \leq u\} - \frac{1}{S}\sum_{n=1}^{S} 1\{Y_{k,n}(\widehat{\theta}_{k,T}) \leq u\}\right)^2, \end{aligned}$$

and $Y_{k,n}(\widehat{\theta}_{k,T})$ represents simulated counterparts of Y_t (i.e., the variables simulated under model k at simulation n, using the estimated parameters $\widehat{\theta}_{k,T}$). Heuristically, if S grows sufficiently fast with respect to T, then $\frac{1}{S}\sum_{n=1}^{S} 1\{Y_{k,n}(\widehat{\theta}_{k,T}) \leq u\}$ can be treated as the "true" distribution of the data simulated under model k. Broadly speaking, we are comparing different DSGE models, on the basis of their ability to match a given simulated joint CDF with that of the historical data. As we are comparing joint CDFs, the statistic in (8) provides an in-sample test.

When constructing the bootstrap counterpart of $Z_{k,T,S}$, we need to distinguish between the case in which $T/S \to 0$ and that in which $T/S \to \delta \neq 0$. Whenever $T/S \to 0$, simulation error is asymptotically negligible, and thus there is no need to resample the simulated observations. In this case, the bootstrap statistic is given by $\max_{k=2,\ldots,K} \sqrt{T} Z^*_{k,T,S}(u)$, where

$$\begin{aligned} &Z^*_{k,T,S}(u) \\ &= \frac{1}{T}\sum_{t=1}^{T}\left(\left(1\{Y_t^* \leq u\} - \frac{1}{S}\sum_{n=1}^{S} 1\{Y_{1,n}(\widehat{\theta}^*_{1,T}) \leq u\}\right)^2\right. \end{aligned}$$

$$-\left(1\{Y_t \leq u\} - \frac{1}{S}\sum_{n=1}^{S} 1\{Y_{1,n}(\widehat{\theta}_{1,T}) \leq u\}\right)^2\Bigg)$$

$$-\frac{1}{T}\sum_{t=1}^{T}\Bigg(\left(1\{Y_t^* \leq u\} - \frac{1}{S}\sum_{n=1}^{S} 1\{Y_{k,n}(\widehat{\theta}_{k,T}^*) \leq u\}\right)^2$$

$$-\left(1\{Y_t \leq u\} - \frac{1}{S}\sum_{n=1}^{S} 1\{Y_{k,n}(\widehat{\theta}_{k,T}) \leq u\}\right)^2\Bigg). \quad (9)$$

On the other hand, whenever $T/S \to \delta \neq 0$, then simulation error contributes to the limiting distribution. In this case, one has to additionally resample the simulated observations, and thus $Y_{1,n}(\widehat{\theta}_{1,T}^*)$ and $Y_{k,n}(\widehat{\theta}_{k,T}^*)$ in (9) should be replaced by $Y_{1,n}^*(\widehat{\theta}_{1,T}^*)$ and $Y_{k,n}^*(\widehat{\theta}_{k,T}^*)$. In both cases, the validity of bootstrap critical values is been established in Proposition 2 of Corradi and Swanson (2007b).

4 Stochastic Dominance: Predictive Evaluation Based on Distribution of Loss

In this section, we discuss a predictive accuracy testing approach based on distributional loss, as in the previous sections. However, rather than focusing on DM- and reality check-type approaches, we incorporate notions of stochastic dominance in our analysis. Namely, we introduce a criterion that is designed to include cases of generic predictive accuracy testing, forecast model selection, and forecast combination. The criterion is constructed via evaluation of error loss distributions using basic principles of stochastic dominance, wherein one examines whether or not one CDF lies "above" another, for example. In our discussion, we are concerned only with the evaluation of alternative panels or combinations of forecasts, such as are available when analyzing the Survey of Professional Forecasters (SPF) dataset available on the webpages of the Federal Reserve Bank of Philadelphia. Moreover, we consider first-order stochastic dominance. Evidently, the ideas presented here can be adapted to many varieties of predictive accuracy testing, and extension to second and higher order stochastic dominance will also play an important role in such applications. These and related issues are left to future research, and our example below is meant as a starting point in this sort of analysis.

4.1 Motivation

Central Banks and financial institutions have regular access to panels of forecasts for key macroeconomic variables that are made by professional forecasters. A leading example is the SPF. Using this dataset, much focus has centered on how to combine predictions (see e.g. Capistran and Timmermann 2009) and how to assess forecast rationality (see e.g. Elliott et al. 2008). With regard to forecast combination, Capistran and Timmermann (2009), as well as Elliott and Timmermann (2004, 2005), estimate combination weights by minimizing a given loss function, ensuring that the weights converge to those minimizing expected loss. Wallis (2005) proposes combining forecasts using a finite mixture distribution, and Smith and Wallis (2009) suggest the use of simple averages. With regard to rationality assessment, Elliott et al. (2008) test whether forecasters taking part in the SPF are rational for some parameterization of a flexible loss function. This is clearly an important approach when testing for rationality. However, in many instances, users already have a given loss function in mind, and only assess the accuracy of available forecasts under this loss function. Here, we take the loss function as given, and discuss predictive combination and accuracy assessment of datasets such as the SPF. However, this is done via analysis of cumulative loss distributions rather than synthetic measures of loss accuracy such as mean square error and mean absolute error.

More specifically, the objective is to introduce an alternative criterion for predictive evaluation which measures accuracy via examination of the quantiles of the expected loss distribution. The criterion is based on comparing empirical CDFs of predictive error loss, using the principle of stochastic dominance. The heuristic argument underpinning our approach is that the preferred model is one for which the error loss CDF is stochastically dominated by the error loss CDF of every competing model, at all evaluation points. In this sense, a model that has smaller quantiles at all regions of the loss distribution is selected, rather than a model that minimizes a single criterion, such as the mean square error. If a model is not strictly dominated, then our approach allows us to pinpoint the region of the loss distribution for which one model is preferred to another.

As alluded to above, applications for which the criterion is designed include: generic predictive accuracy testing; forecast model selection; and forecast combination. For example, in the context of the SPF, a panel of N_t forecasts for a given variable are made by professionals at each point in time, t. Both the number of individuals taking part in the survey, as well as the specific individuals generally change, from period to period. In this context, the criterion can be applied as follows. Assume that objective is to select and combine forecasts from the SPF. A set of rules, including for example, the simple mean or median across all forecasters, and quantile-based weighted combinations across forecasts are defined. Then, the loss function of the forecast errors implied by the rules are evaluated using tests based on the stochastic dominance criterion.

4.2 Setup

In each period t, we have a panel of N_t forecasts. The objective is to choose among k possible combinations of the available forecasts, under a given loss function, $g(\cdot)$.

In order to allow for frequent possible entry and exit into the panel, the combinations are simple rules, which are applied each period, regardless of the composition of the panels. Examples are: (i) simple average, (ii) simple average over a given range, such as the 25th-75th percentiles, or (iii) assigning different weights to different interquantile groups from the panel, such as a weight of 0.75 for the average over the 25th–75th percentile and 0.125 for the average over the first and last quartiles.

Define $e_{i,t} = y_t - y^f_{t,h,i}$, $i = 1, \ldots, k$, to be the forecast error associated with the $h-$step ahead prediction constructed using combination i. Let $g_{i,t} = g\left(e_{i,t}\right)$, where $g\left(\cdot\right)$ is a generic loss function. Also, let $F_{g,i}(x)$ be the empirical distribution of $g\left(e_{i,t}\right)$ evaluated at x, and let $\widehat{F}_{g,i,T}(x)$ be its sample analog, i.e.,

$$\widehat{F}_{g,i,T}(x) = \frac{1}{T}\sum_{t=1}^{T} 1\left\{g\left(e_{i,t}\right) \leq x\right\}.$$

The hypotheses of interest are:

$$H_0 : \max_{i>1} \inf_{x\in X} \left(F_{g,1}(x) - F_{g,i}(x)\right) \geq 0$$

versus

$$H_A : \max_{i>1} \inf_{x\in X} \left(F_{g,1}(x) - F_{g,i}(x)\right) < 0.$$

For the sake of simplicity suppose that $k = 2$. If $F_{g,1}(x) - F_{g,2}(x) \geq 0$ for all x, then the CDF associated with rule 1 always lies above the CDF associated with rule 2. Then, heuristically, $g\left(e_{1,t}\right)$ is (first order) stochastically dominated by $g\left(e_{2,t}\right)$ and rule 1 is the preferred combination. This is because all of the quantiles of $g\left(e_{1,t}\right)$ are smaller than the corresponding quantiles of $g\left(e_{2,t}\right)$. More formally, for a given x, suppose that

$$F_{g,1}(x) = \theta_1 \quad \text{and} \quad F_{g,2}(x) = \theta_2,$$

then we choose rule 1 if $\theta_1 > \theta_2$. This is because x is the θ_1-quantile under $F_{g,1}$ and the θ_2-quantile under $F_{g,2}$ and, as $\theta_1 > \theta_2$, the θ_2- quantile under $F_{g,1}$ is smaller than under $F_{g,2}$. Thus, for all evaluation points smaller than x, $g\left(e_{1,t}\right)$ has more probability mass associated with smaller values than $g\left(e_{2,t}\right)$ does.

It follows that if we fail to reject the null, rule 1 is selected. On the other hand, rejection of the null does not imply that rule 1 should be discarded. Instead, further analysis is required in order to select a rule. First, one needs to discriminate between the cases for which the various CDFs do not cross, and those for which they do cross. This is accomplished by proceeding sequentially as follows. For all $i \neq j$ $i, j = 1, \ldots, k$, sequentially test

$$H_0^{i,j} : \sup_{x\in X} \left(F_{g,i}(x) - F_{g,j}(x)\right) \leq 0 \tag{10}$$

versus its negation. Eliminate rule i, if $H_0^{i,j}$ is not rejected. Otherwise, retain rule i. There are two possible outcomes.

I: If there is a rule which is stochastically dominated by all other rules, we eventually discard all the "dominating" rules and remain with only the dominated one. This is always the case when no CDFs cross, and also clearly occurs in cases when various CDFs cross, as long as the dominated CDF cross no other CDF.

II: Otherwise, we remain with a subset of rules, all of which have crossing CDFs, and all of which are stochastically dominated by the eliminated rules.

Note that the logic underlying the outlined sequential procedure is reminiscent of the idea underlying the Model Confidence Set approach of Hansen et al. (2011), in which the worst models are eliminated in a sequential manner, and one remains with a set of models that are roughly equally good, according to the given evaluation criterion.

In the case where there are crossings, further investigation is needed. In particular, in this case, some rules are clearly dominant over certain ranges of loss, and are dominated over others. At this point, one might choose to plot the relevant CDFs, and examine their crossing points. Then, one has to make a choice. For example, one can choose a rule which is dominant over small values of x and is dominated over large values of x. This is the case in which one is concerned about making larger losses than would be incurred, where the other rule used, in a region where losses are large; while not being concerned with the fact that they are making larger losses, relative to those that would be incurred, where the other rule used, when losses are relatively small. Needless to say, one can also use a model averaging approach over the various survivor rules.

4.3 Statistic

In order to test H_0 versus H_A construct the following statistic:

$$L_{g,T} = -\max_{i>1} \inf_{x \in X} \sqrt{T}\left(\widehat{F}_{g,1,T}(x) - \widehat{F}_{g,i,T}(x)\right),$$

where $\widehat{F}_{g,j,T}(x)$, $j \geq 1$ is defined above; and where the negative sign in front of the statistic ensures that the statistic does not diverge to minus infinity under the null hypothesis. On the other hand, in order to test H_0^{ij}, we instead suggest the following statistic,

$$L_{g,T}^{i,j} = -\sup_{x \in X} \sqrt{T}\left(\widehat{F}_{g,i,T}(x) - \widehat{F}_{g,j,T}(x)\right).$$

In the context of testing for stochastic dominance, Linton et al. (2005) construct critical values via subsampling. Here we instead use the "m out of n" bootstrap.[7] Proceed to construct critical values as follows:

(i) We have T observations. Set $\Upsilon < T$.
(ii) Draw b blocks of length l, where $bl = \Upsilon$. One block consists, simultaneously, of draws on the actual data as well as the rule- based combination forecasts. Thus, if there are two rules, say, and the block length is 5, then a "block" consists of a 3×1 vector of length 5. This yields one bootstrap sample, which is used to construct a bootstrap statistic,

$$L_{g,\Upsilon}^{*} = -\max_{i>1} \inf_{x \in X} \sqrt{\Upsilon}\left(\widehat{F}_{g,1,\Upsilon}^{*}(x) - \widehat{F}_{g,i,\Upsilon}^{*}(x)\right)$$

where

$$\widehat{F}_{g,i,\Upsilon}^{*}(x) = \frac{1}{\Upsilon}\sum_{t=1}^{\Upsilon} 1\left\{g^{*}\left(e_{i,t}\right) \leq x\right\}$$

$$g^{*}\left(e_{i,t}\right) = g\left(y_{t}^{*} - y_{t,h,i}^{*f}\right)$$

(iii) Construct B bootstrap statistics and then compute their empirical distribution. The sample statistic is then compared against the percentile of this empirical distribution.

5 Concluding Remarks

In this chapter, we have reviewed the extant literature on Diebold and Mariano (1995) type predictive accuracy testing. We discuss pairwise and multiple model comparison (i.e., DM and reality check type predictive accuracy tests) using differentiable pointwise prediction accuracy measures such as mean square forecast error, as well as using non-differentiable loss functions. We also discuss valid inference under both asymptotically negligible and non-negligible parameter estimation error. Extensions to pairwise and multiple model comparison using predictive densities, distributions, intervals, and conditional distributions are then outlined, with emphasis on inference using these more complicated varieties of DM and reality check-type tests. Finally, extension and generalization of all of these testing approaches using notions of stochastic dominance are introduced, and future research directions, including the use of second and higher order stochastic dominance are outlined.

Acknowledgments This chapter has been prepared for the Festschrift in honor of Halbert L. White in the event of the conference celebrating his sixtieth birthday, entitled "Causality, Prediction, and

[7] The basic difference between subsampling and "m out of n" bootstrap is that in the latter case we resample overlapping blocks.

Specification Analysis: Recent Advances and Future Directions", and held at the University of California, San Diego on May 6–7, 2011. Swanson thanks the Rutgers University Research Council for financial support.

References

Amisano, G. and R. Giacomini, 2007, Comparing Density Forecasts via Weighted Likelihood Ratio Tests. Journal of Business and Economic Statistics 25, 177–190.

Andrews, D.W.K., 2002, Higher-Order Improvements of a Computationally Attractive $k-$step Bootstrap for Extremum Estimators, Econometrica 70, 119–162.

Andrews, D.W.K. and G. Soares, 2010, Inference for Parameters Defined by Moment Inequalities Using Generalized Moment Selection, Econometrica 78, 119–158.

Bierens, H.J., 2007, Econometric Analysis of Linearized Singular Dynamic Stochastic General Equilibrium Models, Journal of Econometrics, 136, 595–627.

Bierens, H.J., and N.R. Swanson, 2000, The Econometric Consequences of the Ceteris Paribus Condition in Theoretical Economics, Journal of Econometrics, 95, 223–253.

Capistran, C. and A. Timmermann, 2009, Disagreement and Biases in Inflation Expectations, Journal of Money, Credit and Banking 41, 365–396.

Chang, Y.S., J.F. Gomes, and F. Schorfheide, 2002, Learning-by-Doing as a Propagation Mechanism, American Economic Review 92, 1498–1520.

Christiano, L.J., 1988, Why Does Inventory Investment Fluctuate So Much, Journal of Monetary Economics 21, 247–280.

Christoffersen, P., 1998, Evaluating Interval Forecasts, International Economic Review 39, 841–862.

Christoffersen, P. and F.X. Diebold, 1996, Further Results on Forecasting and Model Selection under Asymmetric Loss, Journal of Applied Econometrics, 11, 561–572.

Christoffersen, P. and F.X. Diebold, 1997, Optimal Prediction Under Asymmetric Loss, Econometric Theory 13, 808–817.

Christoffersen, P. and F.X. Diebold, 2000, How Relevant is Volatility Forecasting for Financial Risk Management?, Review of Economics and Statistics 82, 12–22.

Clark, T.E. and M.W. McCracken, (2001), Tests of Equal Forecast Accuracy and Encompassing for Nested Models, Journal of Econometrics 105, 85–110.

Cogley, T., and J.M. Nason, 1995, Output Dynamics for Real Business Cycles Models, American Economic Review 85, 492–511.

Corradi, V. and W. Distaso, 2011, Multiple Forecast Evaluation, Oxford Handbook of Economic Forecasting, eds. D.F. Hendry and M.P. Clements, Oxford University Press, Oxford.

Corradi, V. and N.R. Swanson, 2005, A test for comparing multiple misspecified conditional intervals. Econometric Theory 21, 991–1016.

Corradi, V. and N.R. Swanson, 2006a, Predictive density and conditional confidence interval accuracy tests. Journal of Econometrics 135, 187–228.

Corradi, V. and N.R. Swanson, 2006b, Predictive density evaluation, in: C.W.J. Granger, G. Elliot and A. Timmermann, (Eds.), Handbook of economic forecasting Elsevier, Amsterdam, pp. 197–284.

Corradi, V. and N.R. Swanson, 2007a, Nonparametric bootstrap procedures for predictive inference based on recursive estimation schemes. International Economic Review 48, 67–109.

Corradi, V. and N.R. Swanson, 2007b, Evaluation of dynamic stochastic general equilibrium models based on distributional comparison of simulated and historical data. Journal of Econometrics 136, 699–723.

Diebold, F.X. and R.S. Mariano, 1995, Comparing predictive accuracy. Journal of Business and Economic Statistics 13, 253–263.

Diebold, F.X., L.E. Ohanian, and J. Berkowitz, 1998, Dynamic Equilibrium Economies: A Framework for Comparing Models and Data, Review of Economic Studies 65, 433–451.
Duffie, D. and J. Pan, 1997, An Overview of Value at Risk, Journal of Derivatives 4, 7–49.
Elliott, G. and A. Timmermann, 2004, Optimal Forecast Combinations Under General Loss Functions and Forecast Error Distributions, Journal of Econometrics 122, 47–79.
Elliott, G. and A. Timmermann, 2005, Optimal Forecast Combination Under Regime Switching, International Economic Review 46, 1081–1102.
Elliott, G., Komunjer I., and A. Timmermann, 2008, Biases in Macroeconomic Forecasts: Irrationality or Asymmetric Loss? 2008, Journal of the European Economic Association, 6, 122–157.
Fernandez-Villaverde, J. and J.F. Rubio-Ramirez, 2004, Comparing Dynamic Equilibrium Models to Data, Journal of Econometrics 123, 153–180.
Giacomini, R. and I. Komunjer, 2005, Evaluation and Combination of Conditional Quantile Forecasts, Journal of Business and Economic Statistics 23, 416–431.
Giacomini, R., and H. White, 2006, Conditional Tests for Predictive Ability, Econometrica 74, 1545–1578.
Goncalves, S., and H. White, 2004, Maximum Likelihood and the Bootstrap for Nonlinear Dynamic Models, Journal of Econometrics, 119, 199–219.
Hall, P., and J.L. Horowitz, 1996, Bootstrap Critical Values for Tests Based on Generalized Method of Moments Estimators. Econometrica 64, 891–916.
Hansen, P. R., 2005, A Test for Superior Predictive Ability, Journal of Business and Economic Statistics 23, 365–380.
Hansen, P.R., A. Lunde and J.M. Nason, 2011, The Model Confidence Set, Econometrica, 79, 453–497.
Inoue, A., and M. Shintani, 2006, Bootstrapping GMM Estimators for Time Series, Journal of Econometrics 133, 531–555.
King, R.G., C.I. Plosser, and S.T. Rebelo, 1988a, Production, Growth and Business Cycles 1: The Basic Neoclassical Model, Journal of Monetary Economics 21, 195–232.
King, R.G., C.I. Plosser, and S.T. Rebelo, 1988b, Production, Growth and Business Cycles 2: New Directions, Journal of Monetary Economics 21, 309–341.
Kitamura, Y., 2004, Econometric Comparisons of Conditional Models, Working Paper, Yale University.
Kunsch H.R., 1989, The Jackknife and the Bootstrap for General Stationary Observations. Annals of Statistics 17, 1217–1241.
Kydland, F.E., and E.C. Prescott, 1982, Time to Build and Aggregate Fluctuations, Econometrica 50, 1345–1370.
Linton, O., E. Maasoumi and Y.J. Whang, 2005, Consistent Testing for Stochastic Dominance Under General Sampling Schemes, Review of Economic Studies 72, 735–765.
Long, J.B. and C.I. Plosser, 1983, Real Business Cycles, Journal of Political Economy 91, 39–69.
Romano, J.P. and M. Wolf, 2005, Stepwise Multiple Testing as Formalized Data Snooping, Econometrica 73, 1237–1282.
Schorfheide, F., 2000, Loss Function Based Evaluation of DSGE Models, Journal of Applied Econometrics 15, 645–670.
Schmitt-Grohe, S., 2000, Endogenous Business Cycles and the Dynamics of Output, Hours and Consumption, American Economic Review 90, 1136–1159.
Smith, J. and K.F. Wallis, 2009, A Simple Explanation of the Forecast Combination Puzzle, Oxford Bullettin of Economics and Statistics 71, 331–355.
Sullivan R., A. Timmermann, and H. White, 1999, Data-Snooping, Technical Trading Rule Performance, and the Bootstrap, Journal of Finance 54, 1647–1691.
Sullivan, R., A. Timmermann, and H. White, 2001, Dangers of Data-Driven Inference: The Case of Calendar Effects in Stock Returns, Journal of Econometrics 105, 249–286.
Vuong, Q., 1989, Likelihood Ratio Tests for Model Selection and Non-Nested Hypotheses, Econometrica 57, 307–333.

Wallis, K.F., 2005, Combining Interval and Density Forecast: A Modest Proposal, Oxford Bullettin of Economics and Statistics 67, 983–994.
Watson, M.W., 1993, Measure of Fit for Calibrated Models, Journal of Political Economy 101, 1011–1041.
West, K.F., 1996, Asymptotic Inference About Predictive Ability, Econometrica 64, 1067–1084.
West, K.F., and M.W. McCracken, 1998, Regression Based Tests for Predictive Ability, International Economic Review 39, 817–840.
White, H., 1982, Maximum Likelihood Estimation of Misspecified Models, Econometrica 50, 1–25.
White, H., 2000, A reality check for Data Snooping, Econometrica 68, 1097–1126.
Zellner, A., 1986, Bayesian Estimation and Prediction Using Asymmetric Loss Function, Journal of the American Statistical Association 81, 446–451.

New Directions in Information Matrix Testing: Eigenspectrum Tests

Richard M. Golden, Steven S. Henley, Halbert White and T. Michael Kashner

Abstract Model specification tests are essential tools for evaluating the appropriateness of probability models for estimation and inference. White (*Econometrica*, 50: 1–25, 1982) proposed that model misspecification could be detected by testing the null hypothesis that the Fisher information matrix (IM) Equality holds by comparing

R. M. Golden (✉)
Cognitive Science and Engineering,
School of Behavioral and Brain Sciences,
University of Texas at Dallas,
GR4.1 800 W. Campbell Rd.,
Richardson, TX 75080-3021, USA
e-mail: golden@utdallas.edu

S. S. Henley
Martingale Research Corporation,
101 E. Park Blvd., Suite 600,
Plano, TX 75074, USA
e-mail: stevenh@martingale-research.com

S. S. Henley and T. Michael Kashner
Department of Medicine, Loma Linda University School of Medicine,
Loma Linda, CA 92357, USA

H. White
Department of Economics,
University of California San Diego,
La Jolla, CA 92093-0508, USA
e-mail: hwhite@ucsd.edu

T. Michael Kashner
Department of Psychiatry, University of Texas Southwestern Medical Center,
Dallas, TX 75390, USA
e-mail: Michael.kashner@va.gov

T. Michael Kashner
Office of Academic Affiliations,
Department of Veterans Affairs,
Washington, D.C. 20420, USA

X. Chen and N. R. Swanson (eds.), *Recent Advances and Future Directions in Causality, Prediction, and Specification Analysis*, DOI: 10.1007/978-1-4614-1653-1_6,

linear functions of the Hessian to outer product gradient (OPG) inverse covariance matrix estimators. Unfortunately, a number of researchers have reported difficulties in obtaining reliable inferences using White's (*Econometrica*, 50: 1–25, 1982) original information matrix test (IMT). In this chapter, we extend White (*Econometrica*, 50: 1–25, 1982) to present a new generalized information matrix test (GIMT) theory and develop a new Adjusted Classical GIMT and five new Eigenspectrum GIMTs that compare nonlinear functions of the Hessian and OPG covariance matrix estimators. We then evaluate the level and power of these new GIMTs using simulation studies on realistic epidemiological data and find that they exhibit appealing performance on sample sizes typically encountered in practice. Our results suggest that these new GIMTs are important tools for detecting and assessing model misspecification, and thus will have broad applications for model-based decision making in the social, behavioral, engineering, financial, medical, and public health sciences.

Keywords Eigenspectrum · Goodness-of-fit · Information matrix test · Logistic regression · Specification analysis

1 Introduction

A correctly specified probability model has the property that it contains the probability distribution that generates the observed data. Model specification tests examine the null hypothesis that a researcher's probability model is correctly specified. If the researcher's model of the observed data is not correct (i.e., misspecified), then the interpretation of parameter estimates and the validity of inferences obtained from the resulting probability model may be suspect. Thus, to avoid misleading inferences, the effects of model specification must be considered. For example, in the social and medical sciences (e.g., Kashner et al. 2010), the incompleteness of behavioral and medical theories mandates the need for principled specification analysis methods that use empirical observations to assess quality of a particular theory. This situation, all too common in statistical modeling, provides considerable impetus for the development of improved model specification tests.

1.1 Model Misspecification

When viewed from a practical perspective, the problem of model misspecification is essentially unavoidable. Although ideally a correctly specified model is always preferable, in many fields of science such as econometrics, medicine, and psychology some degree of model misspecification is inevitable. Indeed, all probability models are abstractions of reality, so the issue of model misspecification is fundamentally an empirical issue that is dependent upon how the model will be developed and applied in practice (e.g., Fisher 1922; White 1980, 1981, 1982, 1994; Begg and Lagakos 1990; Cox 1990; Lehmann 1990).

A variety of methods have been developed for the purpose of the assessment of model misspecification. For example, graphical residual diagnostics are useful for identifying the presence of model misspecification for the class of generalized linear models (e.g., Davison and Tsai 1992) and the larger class of exponential family nonlinear models (e.g., Wei 1998, Chap. 6). However, these methods require more subjective interpretations because results are expressed as measures of fit rather than as hypothesis tests. Moreover, specification tests such as chi-square goodness-of-fit tests (e.g., Hosmer et al. 1991, 1997) are not applicable in a straightforward manner when the observations contain continuous random variables. Link specification tests (Collett 2003; Hilbe 2009) are applicable for testing the assumption of linearity in the link function (e.g., logit), but are not designed to detect other types of model misspecification. Further, the applicability of these methods to more complex probability models such as hierarchical (e.g., Agresti 2002; Raudenbush and Bryk 2002), mixed (e.g., Verbeke and Lesaffre 1997), and latent variable (e.g., Gallini 1983; Arminger and Sobel 1990) models may not always be obvious.

1.2 Specification Analysis for Logistic Regression

Logistic regression modeling (Christensen 1997; Hosmer and Lemeshow 2000; Harrell 2001; Agresti 2002; Collett 2003; Hilbe 2009) is an important and widely used analysis tool in various fields; however, the number of available options for the assessment of model misspecification is relatively limited (see Sarkar and Midi 2010 for a review). Typically, the detection of model misspecification in logistic regression models is based upon direct comparison of the observed conditional frequencies of the response variable with predicted conditional probabilities (Hosmer et al. 1997). Unfortunately, the observed conditional frequencies of the response variable can only be compared with predicted conditional probabilities for a particular pattern of predictor variable values in a given data record. In practice, patterns of predictor variable values may rarely be repeated for more complex models involving either multiple categorical predictor variables or continuous-valued predictor variables. Because the number of distinct predictor patterns often increases as the number of records (i.e., sample size) increases, such applications of classical "fixed-cell asymptotic" results are problematic (e.g., Osius and Rojek 1992). To address this problem, "grouping" methods have been proposed that require artificially grouping similar, yet distinct predictor patterns (Bertolini et al. 2000; Archer and Lemeshow 2006).

A variety of test statistics that explicitly compare predicted probabilities with observed frequencies using grouping methods have been proposed, and include chi-square test methods (e.g., Hosmer and Lemeshow 1980; Tsiatis 1980; Hosmer et al. 1988, 1997; Copas 1989; Qin and Zhang 1997; Zhang 1999; Archer and Lemeshow 2006; Deng et al. 2009), sum-squared comparison methods (Copas 1989; Kuss 2002), and the closely related likelihood ratio test deviance-based comparison methods (e.g., Hosmer and Lemeshow 2000, pp. 145–146; Kuss 2002). Without employing such grouping methods, the resulting test statistics associated with direct comparison of observed conditional frequencies and predicted conditional probabilities will have excessive degrees of freedom and thus poor power. However, when such grouping methods are applied, they may actually have the unintended consequence of redefining the probability model whose integrity is being evaluated (Hosmer et al. 1997).

One solution to dealing with the "grouping" problem is to introduce appropriate regularity conditions intended to characterize the asymptotic behavior of the test statistics while allowing the number of distinct predictor patterns to increase with the sample size (e.g., Osius and Rojek 1992). Another important solution to the "grouping" problem is to embed the probability model whose specification is being scrutinized within a larger probability model and then compare the predicted probabilities of both models (e.g., Stukel 1988). Other approaches have explored improved approximations to Pearson's goodness-of-fit statistic (McCullagh 1985; Farrington 1996). Yet, despite these approaches, the variety of methods available for assessing the presence of model misspecification is surprisingly limited, and these limitations are particularly striking in the context of logistic regression modeling (e.g., Sarkar and Midi 2010).

1.3 Information Matrix Test

White (1982; also see 1987, 1994) proposed a particular model specification test called the *information matrix test* (IMT). Unlike chi-square goodness-of-fit tests and graphical diagnostics, IMTs are based upon the theoretical expectation that the Hessian inverse covariance matrix estimator (derived from the Hessian of the log-likelihood function) and the outer product gradient (OPG) inverse covariance matrix estimator (derived from the first derivatives of the log-likelihood function) are asymptotically equivalent whenever the researcher's probability model is correctly specified. We define a *full IMT* as a statistical test that tests the null hypothesis of asymptotic equivalence of the Hessian and OPG asymptotic covariance matrix estimators.

An important virtue of the IMT method is that it is applicable in a straightforward manner to a broad class of probability models. This includes not only linear and nonlinear regression models, but also even more complex models such as: limited dependent variables models (e.g., Maddala 1999; Greene 2003), exponential family nonlinear models (e.g., Wei 1998), generalized linear models (e.g., McCullagh and Nelder 1989), generalized additive models (e.g., Hastie and Tibshirani 1986, 1990), hierarchical models (e.g., Agresti 2002; Raudenbush and Bryk 2002), mixed models (e.g., Verbeke and Lesaffre 1997), latent variable models (e.g., Gallini 1983; Arminger and Sobel 1990), conditional random fields (e.g., Winkler 1991), and time series models (e.g., Hamilton 1994; White 1994; Box et al. 2008; Tsay 2010). However, despite the broad applicability of the IMT, the majority of the research in the development and evaluation of IMTs has focused on linear regression (Hall 1987; Taylor 1987; Davidson and MacKinnon 1992, 1998), logistic regression (Aparicio and Villanua 2001; Zhang 2001), probit (Davidson and MacKinnon 1992, 1998; Stomberg and White 2000; Dhaene and Hoorelbeke 2004), and Tobit (Horowitz 1994, 2003) modeling.

1.4 Empirical Performance of the Information Matrix Test

Although theoretically attractive, the IMT has not been widely used to detect model misspecification. In particular, some researchers have found the full IMT (White 1982) both analytically and computationally burdensome because its derivation and computation require third derivatives of the log-likelihood. To address this problem, Chesher (1983) and Lancaster (1984) demonstrated how the calculation of the third derivatives of the log-likelihood function could be avoided for the full IMT by showing that when the OPG and Hessian inverse covariance matrix estimators are asymptotically equivalent, the third derivatives of the log-likelihood may be expressed in terms of the first and second derivatives of the log-likelihood. This particular version of the White (1982) full IMT is commonly referred to as the *OPG IMT*. Unfortunately, OPG full IMTs were subsequently found to exhibit poor performance in various simulation studies for logistic regression (Aparicio and Villanua 2001) and linear regression (Taylor 1987; Davidson and MacKinnon 1992; Dhaene and Hoorelbeke 2004). This prompted some researchers (Davidson and MacKinnon 1992, 1998; Stomberg and White 2000; Dhaene and Hoorelbeke 2004) to re-evaluate the original formulation by White (1982), which involves explicit analytical computation of the third derivatives of the log-likelihood function.

In a series of simulation studies, researchers (e.g., Orme 1990; Stomberg and White 2000) have demonstrated that both the original White (1982) formulation and the OPG-IMT method exhibit relatively erratic performance and require excessively large sample sizes to ensure that the test statistic behaves properly. This led a number of researchers (e.g., Davidson and MacKinnon 1992; Stomberg and White 2000; Aparicio and Villanua 2001; Dhaene and Hoorelbeke 2004) to suggest that the erratic behavior of the full IMT for linear regression is due to excessive test statistic variance, since the degrees of freedom of the full IMT increase as a quadratic function of the number of free parameters of the probability model.

Further, researchers (Taylor 1987; Orme 1990; Horowitz 1994, 2003) have provided empirical evidence that the poor level performance of the OPG IMT is due to failure to incorporate the third derivatives of the log-likelihood functions as originally recommended by White (1982). Stomberg and White (2000) have shown demonstrable improvements using a bootstrapped version of the full IMT, but this method requires substantial computational resources.

1.5 Nondirectional and Directional Tests

A "nondirectional IMT" examines the null hypothesis that the Hessian and OPG covariance matrix estimators are asymptotically equivalent. White's (1982) Classical Full IMT is an example of a nondirectional information matrix test. If the null hypothesis of a nondirectional information test is false, it directly follows from Fisher's Information Matrix Equality that the probability model is misspecified.

A "directional IMT" compares functions of the OPG and Hessian covariance matrix estimators for the purpose of identifying specific types of model misspecification, rather than implementing a full covariance matrix estimator comparison. Two potential advantages of directional tests are: (1) gaining important insights regarding how to improve the quality of a misspecified model by identifying specific aspects of a model that appear to be correctly or incorrectly specified, and (2) better level performance and greater statistical power in the detection of model misspecification. White (1982) explicitly emphasized that improved specification testing performance and specific specification tests could be obtained through the use of directional information matrix tests. Nonetheless, as previously described, the majority of research has focused upon the full IMT rather than on particular directional versions of the full IMT as recommended by White (1982).

Directional tests also may, in some cases, provide improved statistical power if such tests are appropriately designed. However, despite the advantages of directional specification testing, little theoretical or empirical research has been conducted to more thoroughly explore directional IMTs as viable alternatives to White's (1982) nondirectional Classical Full IMT. Such insights may also be helpful for suggesting specific modifications to a researcher's model to improve its quality. Although, nondirectional tests are useful for overall assessments of model misspecification, but directional tests provide insights into which properties of a model are sensitive to the effects of model misspecification.

Prior research on directional versions of the full IMT has focused upon the detection of skewness, kurtosis, and heteroskedasticity in linear regression models, with a few notable exceptions (i.e., Henley et al. 2001, 2004; Alonso et al. 2008). For example, Bera and Lee (1993; also see Hall 1987; Chesher and Spady 1991) have shown how to derive directional information matrix tests for linear regression models using White's (1982) theoretical framework. These directional information matrix tests were shown to be mathematically equivalent (see White 1982; Hall 1987; Chesher and Spady 1991; Bera and Lee 1993 for relevant reviews) to commonly used statistical tests for checking for the presence of autoregressive conditional heteroskedasticity as well as checking for normality in the residual errors.

1.6 Logistic Regression Modeling IMTs

The IMT method is particularly attractive in the context of logistic regression modeling because it does not require the use of grouping mechanisms, and the degrees of freedom are solely dependent upon the number of free parameters in the model rather than the degree to which the predictor patterns in the data set are replicated. However, the application of IMTs to the problem of the detection of misspecification in categorical regression (Agresti 2002) and, in particular, logistic regression modeling (Hosmer and Lemeshow 2000; Hilbe 2009) is less common (but see Orme 1988; Aparicio and Villanua 2001; Zhang 2001; Kuss 2002), despite the major role that logistic regression plays in applied statistical analysis (Christensen 1997; Hosmer and Lemeshow 2000; Harrell 2001; Agresti 2002; Collett 2003; Hilbe 2009).

1.7 Generalized Information Matrix Test Theory

In this chapter, we introduce the essential ideas of our Generalized Information Matrix Test (GIMT) theory (Henley et al. 2001, 2004, 2008). GIMT theory includes the IMTs previously discussed in the literature, as well as a larger class of directional and nondirectional IMTs. We apply GIMT theory to develop six specific new GIMTs. We begin with a new version of the original $k(k+1)/2$ degrees of freedom White (1982) Classical Full IMT, called the "Adjusted Classical GIMT", which is applicable to a k parameter model. In addition, we explore information matrix testing by introducing and empirically evaluating five new Information Matrix Tests based upon comparing specific nonlinear functions of the eigenspectra of the Hessian and OPG covariance matrices (rather than their inverses) developed by Henley et al. (2001, 2004, 2008). The first of these directional tests is the k-degree of freedom "Log Eigenspectrum GIMT" based on the null hypothesis that the k eigenvalues of the Hessian and OPG covariance matrices are the same. The one-degree of freedom "Log Determinant GIMT" tests the null hypothesis that the products of the eigenvalues of the Hessian and OPG covariance matrices are identical. Log Determinant GIMTs are exceptionally sensitive to small differences in the eigenstructures. The "Log Trace GIMT" is a one-degree of freedom GIMT that tests the null hypothesis that the sums of the eigenvalues of the Hessian and OPG covariance matrices are identical. Log Trace GIMTs focus on differences in the major principal components of the Hessian and OPG covariance matrices. The fourth eigenspectrum test is the two-degree of freedom "Generalized Variance GIMT" that tests the composite null hypothesis that the Log Determinant and Log Trace GIMTs' null hypotheses hold. In particular, the Generalized Variance GIMT exploits the complementary features of the Log Trace and Log Determinant GIMTs, since the Log Determinant GIMT is sensitive to small differences in the entire eigenspectrum of the Hessian and OPG covariance matrices, while the Log Trace GIMT tends to focus on the larger eigenvalues. Finally, if the Hessian and OPG covariance matrices are identical, then the Hessian covariance matrix multiplied by the inverse of the OPG covariance matrix will be the identity matrix. This observation suggests a fifth type of GIMT called the "Log Generalized Akaike Information Criterion (GAIC) GIMT" for examining the average relative deviation between the eigenspectra of the Hessian and OPG covariance matrices. The Log GAIC GIMT, like the Log Determinant and Log Trace

GIMTs, is also a one-degree of freedom test sensitive to small differences in the eigenstructures of the Hessian and OPG covariance matrices.

We then provide a series of simulation studies to investigate the level and power properties of the new Eigenspectrum GIMTs and the Adjusted Classical GIMT. Our simulation studies are intended to achieve three specific objectives. First, we evaluate the reliability of the large sample approximations for estimating Type I error probabilities (level) for the Adjusted Classical GIMT and our five new Eigenspectrum GIMTs. Second, we evaluate the level-power performance of the new Eigenspectrum GIMTs relative to the Adjusted Classical GIMT. Finally, we evaluate the applicability of the new GIMTs to detect model misspecification in representative, realistic epidemiological data.

2 Theory

2.1 Information Matrix Equality

In what follows, we do not give formal results. For the most part, the necessary theory can already be found in White (1982, 1994). We use the following notation. Let the d-dimensional real column vectors $\mathbf{x}_1, \ldots, \mathbf{x}_n$ be realizations of the *i.i.d.* random variables $\mathbf{X}_1, \ldots, \mathbf{X}_n$ having support $\mathcal{R}^d$. Let the parameter space $\boldsymbol{\Theta} \subseteq \mathcal{R}^k$ be a compact set with non-empty interior. Let $f : \mathcal{X} \times \boldsymbol{\Theta} \rightarrow [0, \infty)$ be defined such that $f(\cdot\,; \boldsymbol{\theta})$ is a Radon-Nikodým density for each $\boldsymbol{\theta} \in \boldsymbol{\Theta}$. Let $f(\mathbf{x}_i; \boldsymbol{\theta})$ denote the likelihood of an observation $\boldsymbol{x}_i$ for parameter vector $\boldsymbol{\theta}$. Let $\bar{\mathbf{B}}_n = n^{-1} \sum_{i=1}^{n} \mathbf{B}_i$ where $\mathbf{B}_i = \mathbf{g}_i \mathbf{g}_i^T$ and $\mathbf{g}_i \equiv -\nabla_{\boldsymbol{\theta}} \log f(\mathbf{X}_i; \cdot)$. Let $\bar{\mathbf{A}}_n = n^{-1} \sum_{i=1}^{n} \mathbf{A}_i$ where $\mathbf{A}_i \equiv -\nabla_{\boldsymbol{\theta}}^2 \log f(\mathbf{X}_i; \cdot)$. Let $\mathbf{A}$ and $\mathbf{B}$ denote the respective expected values of $\bar{\mathbf{A}}_n$ and $\bar{\mathbf{B}}_n$ (when they exist). Suppose the *maximum likelihood estimator* $\hat{\boldsymbol{\theta}}_n$, which maximizes the *likelihood function* $\prod_{i=1}^{n} f(\mathbf{X}_i; \boldsymbol{\theta})$, converges almost surely to $\boldsymbol{\theta}^* \in \text{int}\,\Theta$. Let $\mathbf{A}^* \equiv \mathbf{A}(\boldsymbol{\theta}^*)$ and $\mathbf{B}^* \equiv \mathbf{B}(\boldsymbol{\theta}^*)$. Let $\hat{\mathbf{A}}_n \equiv \bar{\mathbf{A}}_n(\hat{\boldsymbol{\theta}}_n)$ and $\hat{\mathbf{B}}_n \equiv \bar{\mathbf{B}}_n(\hat{\boldsymbol{\theta}}_n)$. We say the model is *correctly specified* if there exists $\boldsymbol{\theta}_0$ such that $f(\cdot; \boldsymbol{\theta}_0)$ is the true density of $\mathbf{X}_i$. In this case, it holds under general conditions that $\boldsymbol{\theta}^* = \boldsymbol{\theta}_0$. The GIMT is based upon the critical observation that under correct specification, the Fisher Information Matrix equality holds, that is, $\mathbf{A}^* = \mathbf{B}^*$ (e.g., White 1982, 1994). This hypothesis may be tested by comparing $\hat{\mathbf{A}}_n$ and $\hat{\mathbf{B}}_n$. Rejecting the null hypothesis that $\mathbf{A}^* = \mathbf{B}^*$, thus indicates the presence of model misspecification. In this situation, the *classic Hessian covariance matrix estimator* $\hat{\mathbf{A}}_n^{-1}$ and *classic OPG covariance matrix* estimator $\hat{\mathbf{B}}_n^{-1}$ for $\sqrt{n}\left(\hat{\boldsymbol{\theta}}_n - \boldsymbol{\theta}^*\right)$ are inconsistent and the *robust estimator* $\hat{\mathbf{C}}_n \equiv \hat{\mathbf{A}}_n^{-1} \hat{\mathbf{B}}_n \hat{\mathbf{A}}_n^{-1}$ (e.g., Huber 1967; White 1982, 1994; Golden 1996) is consistent and should be used instead.

2.2 The Null Hypothesis for a Generalized IMT

Let $\Upsilon^{k\times k} \subseteq \mathcal{R}^{k\times k}$ be a compact set that contains $\mathbf{A}^*$ and $\mathbf{B}^*$ in its interior. Let $\mathbf{s}: \Upsilon^{k\times k} \times \Upsilon^{k\times k} \rightarrow \mathcal{R}^r$ be continuously differentiable in both of its matrix arguments where r is a positive integer less than or equal to $k(k+1)/2$. The function $\mathbf{s}$ is called a *Generalized Information Matrix Test (GIMT) Hypothesis Function* when it satisfies the condition that: For every $\mathbf{A}, \mathbf{B} \in \Upsilon^{k\times k}$, if $\mathbf{A} = \mathbf{B}$, then $\mathbf{s}(\mathbf{A}, \mathbf{B}) = \mathbf{0}_r$. Throughout this chapter, we assume that the GIMT Hypothesis function $\mathbf{s}: \Upsilon^{k\times k} \times \Upsilon^{k\times k} \rightarrow \mathcal{R}^r$ is a continuously differentiable function of both its arguments and that $\frac{d\mathbf{s}(\mathbf{A}(\boldsymbol{\theta}),\mathbf{B}(\boldsymbol{\theta}))}{d\boldsymbol{\theta}}$ evaluated at $\boldsymbol{\theta}^*$ has full row rank r. It will also be convenient to let $\mathbf{s}^* \equiv \mathbf{s}(\mathbf{A}^*, \mathbf{B}^*)$.

A GIMT is defined as a test statistic $\hat{\mathbf{s}}_n \equiv \mathbf{s}\left(\hat{\mathbf{A}}_n, \hat{\mathbf{B}}_n\right)$ that tests the null hypothesis:

$$H_0 : \mathbf{s}^* = \mathbf{0}_r.$$

We distinguish between "nondirectional" and "directional" GIMT hypothesis functions. A GIMT hypothesis function $\mathbf{s}$ is called *nondirectional* when $\mathbf{s}$ has the property that: For every $\mathbf{A}, \mathbf{B} \in \Upsilon^{k\times k}$, $\mathbf{A} = \mathbf{B}$, *if and only if* $\mathbf{s}(\mathbf{A}, \mathbf{B}) = \mathbf{0}_r$. Otherwise, the GIMT hypothesis function $\mathbf{s}$ is called *directional*.

2.3 Asymptotic Behavior of the Generalized IMT Statistic

We now define the *Generalized Information Matrix Test (GIMT)* statistic:

$$\hat{\mathcal{W}}_n \equiv n\left(\hat{\mathbf{s}}_n\right)^T \hat{\sum}_{n,\mathbf{s}}^{-1}\left(\hat{\mathbf{s}}_n\right). \tag{1}$$

where the estimator $\hat{\sum}_{n,\mathbf{s}}^{-1}$ is an estimator of the asymptotic covariance matrix of $n^{1/2}\hat{\mathbf{s}}_n$, $\sum_{\mathbf{s}}^{-1}(\boldsymbol{\theta}^*)$.

Under standard regularity conditions, $\hat{\mathcal{W}}_n$ has a chi-squared distribution with r degrees of freedom when the null hypothesis $H_0 : \mathbf{s}^* = \mathbf{0}_r$ holds. Let $\hat{\mathbf{g}}_i \equiv \mathbf{g}_i\left(\hat{\boldsymbol{\theta}}_n\right)$, $\mathbf{d}_i \equiv \begin{bmatrix} \mathbf{vec}(\mathbf{A}_i(\boldsymbol{\theta})) \\ \mathbf{vec}(\mathbf{B}_i(\boldsymbol{\theta})) \end{bmatrix}$, and $\nabla\bar{\mathbf{d}}_n(\boldsymbol{\theta}) \equiv n^{-1}\sum_{i=1}^n \nabla\mathbf{d}_i(\boldsymbol{\theta})$. The covariance matrix estimator $\hat{\sum}_{n,\mathbf{s}}$ is given by:

$$\hat{\sum}_{n,\mathbf{s}} \equiv \left[\frac{\partial\mathbf{s}}{\partial\mathbf{A}}\left(\hat{\mathbf{A}}_n\right)\frac{\partial\mathbf{s}}{\partial\mathbf{B}}\left(\hat{\mathbf{B}}_n\right)\right]^T \hat{\mathbf{Q}}_n \left[\frac{\partial\mathbf{s}}{\partial\mathbf{A}}\left(\hat{\mathbf{A}}_n\right)\frac{\partial\mathbf{s}}{\partial\mathbf{B}}\left(\hat{\mathbf{B}}_n\right)\right]$$

where $\hat{\mathbf{Q}}_n$ is computed from $\mathbf{d}_i$, $\hat{\mathbf{A}}_n$, $\nabla\bar{\mathbf{d}}_n$, $\mathbf{g}_i$ and $\hat{\boldsymbol{\theta}}_n$ following the approach of White (1982).

When the r-dimensional matrix $\sum_{\mathbf{s}}(\boldsymbol{\theta}^*)$ is singular and has rank g where $0 < g < r$, it is often possible to replace the original GIMT hypothesis function $\mathbf{s} : \Upsilon^{k \times k} \times \Upsilon^{k \times k} \to \mathcal{R}^r$ with an *alternative "adjusted" GIMT hypothesis function* $\tilde{\mathbf{s}} : \Upsilon^{k \times k} \times \Upsilon^{k \times k} \to \mathcal{R}^g$ that tests a similar null hypothesis yet has the property that the resulting asymptotic covariance matrix of $n^{1/2}\tilde{\mathbf{s}}_n$ is nonsingular. Let the *adjusted hypothesis projection matrix* $\mathbf{T}$ be a rectangular matrix with g rows and r columns with full row rank. Then, a decision indicating the "adjusted" null hypothesis $\tilde{H}_0 : \mathbf{Ts}^* = \mathbf{0}_g$ should be rejected also implies that the original null hypothesis $\mathrm{H}_0 : \mathbf{s}^* = \mathbf{0}_r$ should be rejected as well. Note that the adjusted null hypothesis projects the original GIMT hypothesis function from the original r-dimensional space into a g-dimensional subspace. Let $\tilde{\mathbf{s}}_n \equiv \mathbf{T}\hat{\mathbf{s}}_n$. Let $\tilde{\sum}_{n,\mathbf{s}} \equiv \mathbf{T}\hat{\sum}_{n,\mathbf{s}}\mathbf{T}^T$. Then $\tilde{\mathcal{W}}_n \equiv n\,(\tilde{\mathbf{s}}_n)^T \tilde{\sum}_{n,\mathbf{s}}^{-1}(\tilde{\mathbf{s}}_n)$ is called an "adjusted" GIMT, having g degrees of freedom (rather than r degrees of freedom) and testing the null hypothesis: $H_0 : \mathbf{Ts}^* = \mathbf{0}_g$.

Finally, although calculation of $\nabla \mathbf{d}_i(\boldsymbol{\theta})$ requires using the derivative of $\mathbf{A}_i$, which requires third derivatives of the log-likelihood, one can use the Lancaster-Chesher formula for $\nabla \mathbf{d}_i(\boldsymbol{\theta})$, denoted $\ddot{\nabla}\mathbf{d}_i(\boldsymbol{\theta})$. This avoids third derivatives by expressing $\nabla \mathbf{d}_i(\boldsymbol{\theta})$ in terms of the first and second derivatives of the log-likelihood function when the null hypothesis that the model is correctly specified holds (Lancaster 1984; also see Chesher 1983).

Thus, this yields six distinct GIMT statistics that can be used to test a single null hypothesis specified by a given GIMT Hypothesis function. When the GIMT null hypothesis holds either $\hat{\mathbf{B}}_n^{-1}$ or $\hat{\mathbf{C}}_n$ may be used instead of $\hat{\mathbf{A}}_n^{-1}$ to calculate $\hat{\mathbf{Q}}_n$. Furthermore, the assumption that the GIMT null hypothesis holds permits the use of the Lancaster-Chesher formula $\ddot{\nabla}\mathbf{d}_i(\boldsymbol{\theta})$ to avoid explicitly computing the third derivatives of the log-likelihood function (i.e., $\nabla \mathbf{d}_i(\boldsymbol{\theta})$). A *Hessian-GIMT statistic* corresponds to the case denoted by $\left\{\left(\hat{\mathbf{A}}_n\right)^{-1}, \nabla \mathbf{d}_i(\boldsymbol{\theta})\right\}$ where $\left(\hat{\mathbf{A}}_n\right)^{-1}$ is estimated by the Hessian covariance matrix estimator. An *OPG-GIMT statistic* corresponds to the case denoted by $\left\{\left(\hat{\mathbf{B}}_n\right)^{-1}, \ddot{\nabla}\mathbf{d}_i(\boldsymbol{\theta})\right\}$ where $\left(\hat{\mathbf{B}}_n\right)^{-1}$ is estimated by the OPG covariance matrix estimator (Lancaster 1984; also see Chesher 1983) and $\nabla \mathbf{d}_i(\boldsymbol{\theta})$ is calculated using the Lancaster-Chesher formula $\ddot{\nabla}\mathbf{d}_i(\boldsymbol{\theta})$. To the best of our knowledge, the use of the remaining four GIMT statistics $\left(\text{i.e., } \left\{\left(\hat{\mathbf{A}}_n\right)^{-1}, \ddot{\nabla}\mathbf{d}_i(\boldsymbol{\theta})\right\}, \left\{\hat{\mathbf{C}}_n, \ddot{\nabla}\mathbf{d}_i(\boldsymbol{\theta})\right\}, \left\{\left(\hat{\mathbf{B}}_n\right)^{-1}, \nabla \mathbf{d}_i(\boldsymbol{\theta})\right\}, \left\{\hat{\mathbf{C}}_n, \nabla \mathbf{d}_i(\boldsymbol{\theta})\right\}\right)$ associated with a single specific GIMT Hypothesis function for estimating the GIMT covariance matrix have not been discussed in the literature. However, in preliminary studies not reported here (Henley et al. 2001, 2004) we have found that these new statistics exhibit promising size and power properties.

It can be shown that for all six distinct GIMT statistics, the asymptotic distribution of $\hat{\mathcal{W}}_n$ is chi-square with r degrees of freedom when $H_0 : \mathbf{s}(\mathbf{A}^*, \mathbf{B}^*) = \mathbf{0}_r$ holds, under appropriate further regularity conditions and with a few minor modifications to the analysis presented by White (1982; see Proof of Theorem 4.1). Further, it can be shown that $\hat{\mathcal{W}}_n \to \infty$ almost surely when $H_0 : \mathbf{s}(\mathbf{A}^*, \mathbf{B}^*) = \mathbf{0}_r$ is false. Thus,

$\hat{\mathcal{W}}_n$ (or similarly the adjusted version $\hat{\mathcal{W}}_n$) can be used as a test statistic for the purpose of detecting the presence of model misspecification.

2.4 Classical IMT Family

White (1982) describes a family of IMTs that can be represented by a GIMT Hypothesis Function $\mathbf{s}$ of the form $\mathbf{s}(\mathbf{A}, \mathbf{B}) = \mathbf{S}\,\mathbf{vech}\,(\mathbf{A} - \mathbf{B})$, where the *selection matrix* $\mathbf{S} \in \mathcal{R}^{r \times k(k+1)/2}$ is some user-specified constant rectangular matrix of row rank r. The *Classical Full IMT* that has been widely discussed in the literature corresponds to the case where the selection matrix is a $k(k+1)/2$-dimensional identity matrix. White (1982) proposed the Classical Full IMT null hypothesis $H_0 : \mathbf{A}^* = \mathbf{B}^*$ that can be represented by a nondirectional GIMT hypothesis function. White (1982) also proposed a family of IMTs that could be represented as a set of directional GIMT hypothesis functions of the form: $\mathbf{s}(\mathbf{A}, \mathbf{B}) \equiv \mathbf{S}\,\mathbf{vech}\,(\mathbf{A} - \mathbf{B})$ where $\mathbf{S} \in \mathcal{R}^{r \times k(k+1)/2}$ has row rank r. Thus, the GIMT hypothesis function introduced in this chapter is a nonlinear generalization of the original Information Matrix Test hypothesis function described by White (1982), which is limited to the representation of linear combinations of the elements of the $\mathbf{A}$ and $\mathbf{B}$ matrices. Note that White's (1982) IMT theory may be viewed as special case of the GIMT theory presented in this chapter.

2.4.1 Classical Full IMT

The Classical Full IMT as described in White (1982, 1994) corresponds to the case where the *Classical Full IMT Hypothesis Function* $\mathbf{s} : \Upsilon^{k \times k} \times \Upsilon^{k \times k} \rightarrow \mathcal{R}^r$ is defined such that for every $\mathbf{A}, \mathbf{B} \in \Upsilon^{k \times k}$:

$$\mathbf{s}(\mathbf{A}, \mathbf{B}) = \mathbf{vech}(\mathbf{A}) - \mathbf{vech}(\mathbf{B})$$

yielding the null hypothesis $H_0 : \mathbf{vech}\,(\mathbf{A}^*) = \mathbf{vech}\,(\mathbf{B}^*)$. The Classical Full IMT is a nondirectional GIMT, but suffers from the disadvantage of an excessive number of degrees of freedom, $k(k+1)/2$. Thus, the associated excessive variance may yield erratic test performance for typical values of k.

2.4.2 Adjusted Classical GIMT

In simulation studies, we found that the covariance matrix of the GIMT hypothesis function estimator for White's (1982) Classical IMT tended to be singular and so we always used the "adjusted version" of the Classical Full IMT (see the discussion in Sect. 2.3), called the Adjusted Classical GIMT. We emphasize that although the performance of the Adjusted Classical GIMT has not been systematically investigated in previous empirical studies, it is actually a particular member of the family of directional IMTs explicitly discussed in White's (1982) original paper. We also comment that the performance of the adjusted version of the Classical Full IMT depends upon the researcher's choice of the row dimension g of the adjusted hypothesis projection matrix. Theoretically, the appropriate choice of g is straightforward, but in practice, numerical definitions of the presence of excessive multicollinearity are required. To examine the presence of excessive multicollinearity we compute the ratio of the largest to the smallest eigenvalues as well as the magnitude of the largest and smallest eigenvalues of the GIMT statistic covariance matrix estimator. The performance of the Adjusted Classical GIMT in our simulation studies (and other simulation studies not reported here) tended to vary depending upon how stringently we defined a GIMT statistic covariance matrix estimator as singular or non-singular (Henley et al. 2001, 2004). Our results suggest that care in this regard is a previously unappreciated crucial element to obtaining good IMT statistic performance.

2.5 Eigenspectrum GIMT Family

The essential idea of the classical IMT family (White 1982) was to directly compare linear combinations of the elements of and $\mathbf{A}^*$ and $\mathbf{B}^*$. In this section, we propose a new approach that compares the eigenvalues of $(\mathbf{A}^*)^{-1}$ and $(\mathbf{B}^*)^{-1}$ to determine if the Fisher Information Matrix Equality holds for a probability model.

Assume $\mathbf{A}^*$ is real symmetric positive definite and that all eigenvalues of $\mathbf{A}^*$ are distinct. Let $\lambda_{j,\mathbf{A}^*}$ denote the jth eigenvalue associated with the jth unique orthonormal eigenvector $\mathbf{e}_{j,\mathbf{A}^*}$ of $\mathbf{A}^*$. Then there exists a neighborhood of $\mathbf{A}^*$, $\mathcal{N}_{\mathbf{A}^*} \subseteq \mathcal{R}^{k\times k}$, such that: $\mathbf{A}\boldsymbol{\varepsilon}_{j,\mathbf{A}^*}(\mathbf{A}) = \Lambda_{j,\mathbf{A}^*}(\mathbf{A})\,\boldsymbol{\varepsilon}_{j,\mathbf{A}^*}(\mathbf{A})$ for all $\mathbf{A} \in \mathcal{N}_{\mathbf{A}^*}$ where $\Lambda_{j,\mathbf{A}^*} : \mathcal{N}_{\mathbf{A}^*} \to \mathcal{R}$ is an infinitely differentiable function such that $\Lambda_{j,\mathbf{A}^*}(\mathbf{A}^*) = \lambda_{j,\mathbf{A}^*}$, and $\boldsymbol{\varepsilon}_{j,\mathbf{A}^*} : \mathcal{N}_{\mathbf{A}^*} \to \mathcal{R}^k$ is an infinitely differentiable function such that $\boldsymbol{\varepsilon}_{j,\mathbf{A}^*}(\mathbf{A}^*) = \mathbf{e}_{j,\mathbf{A}^*}$ (Magnus (1985) Theorem 1; also see Magnus and Neudecker (1999) p. 180). Furthermore, $\frac{d\Lambda_{j,\mathbf{A}^*}}{d\mathbf{A}}(\mathbf{A}^*) = \mathbf{e}_{j,\mathbf{A}^*}\left(\mathbf{e}_{j,\mathbf{A}^*}\right)^T$. Let $\boldsymbol{\Lambda}_{\mathbf{A}^*} : \mathcal{N}_{\mathbf{A}^*} \to \mathcal{R}^k$ be defined such that for all $\mathcal{N}_{\mathbf{A}^*} \subseteq \mathcal{R}^{k\times k} : \boldsymbol{\Lambda}_{\mathbf{A}^*} \equiv \left[\Lambda_{1,\mathbf{A}^*}, \ldots, \Lambda_{k,\mathbf{A}^*}\right]$. Similarly, when $\mathbf{B}^*$ is real symmetric positive definite with distinct eigenvalues, there exists a neighborhood of $\mathbf{B}^*$, $\mathcal{N}_{\mathbf{B}^*} \subseteq \mathcal{R}^{k\times k}$, such that: $\mathbf{B}\boldsymbol{\varepsilon}_{j,\mathbf{B}^*}(\mathbf{B}) = \Lambda_{j,\mathbf{B}^*}(\mathbf{B})\,\boldsymbol{\varepsilon}_{j,\mathbf{B}^*}(\mathbf{B})$ for all $\mathbf{B} \in \mathcal{N}_{\mathbf{B}^*}$.

Let $\boldsymbol{\psi} : (0,\infty)^k \times (0,\infty)^k \to \mathcal{R}^r$ be continuously differentiable in both of its arguments. An *Eigenspectrum IMT Family* is a collection of GIMT selection functions where each selection function $\mathbf{s} : \mathcal{N}_{\mathbf{A}^*} \times \mathcal{N}_{\mathbf{B}^*} \to \mathcal{R}^r$ has the property that: $\mathbf{s}(\mathbf{A},\mathbf{B}) = \boldsymbol{\psi}(\boldsymbol{\Lambda}_{\mathbf{A}^*}(\mathbf{A}), \boldsymbol{\Lambda}_{\mathbf{B}^*}(\mathbf{B}))$ for all $\mathbf{A} \in \mathcal{N}_{\mathbf{A}^*}$ and for all $\mathbf{B} \in \mathcal{N}_{\mathbf{B}^*}$.

2.5.1 Log Eigenspectrum GIMT

Let $\mathbf{log}\,\boldsymbol{\Lambda}_{\mathbf{A}^*}(\mathbf{A}) \equiv \left[\log\Lambda_{1,\mathbf{A}^*}(\mathbf{A}), \ldots, \log\Lambda_{q,\mathbf{A}^*}(\mathbf{A})\right]^T$. The *Log Eigenspectrum GIMT Hypothesis Function* is defined such that for all $\mathbf{A}, \mathbf{B} \in \Upsilon^{k\times k}$:

$$\mathbf{s}(\mathbf{A},\mathbf{B}) = \left[\log\left(\frac{\Lambda_{1,\mathbf{A}^*}\left(\mathbf{A}^{-1}\right)}{\Lambda_{1,\mathbf{B}^*}\left(\mathbf{B}^{-1}\right)}\right), \ldots, \log\left(\frac{\Lambda_{k,\mathbf{A}^*}\left(\mathbf{A}^{-1}\right)}{\Lambda_{k,\mathbf{B}^*}\left(\mathbf{B}^{-1}\right)}\right)\right]$$
$$= \mathbf{log}\,\boldsymbol{\Lambda}_{\mathbf{A}^*}\left(\mathbf{A}^{-1}\right) - \mathbf{log}\,\boldsymbol{\Lambda}_{\mathbf{B}^*}\left(\mathbf{B}^{-1}\right).$$

Thus, the null hypothesis of the log eigenspectrum GIMT is given by:

$$H_0 : \mathbf{s}\left(\mathbf{A}^*,\mathbf{B}^*\right) = \mathbf{log}\,\boldsymbol{\Lambda}_{\mathbf{A}^*}\left(\left(\mathbf{A}^*\right)^{-1}\right) - \mathbf{log}\,\boldsymbol{\Lambda}_{\mathbf{B}^*}\left(\left(\mathbf{B}^*\right)^{-1}\right) = \mathbf{0}_k.$$

The Log Eigenspectrum GIMT is a directional GIMT because cases exist where $\mathbf{A}^* \neq \mathbf{B}^*$, yet the eigenspectra of $\mathbf{A}^*$ and $\mathbf{B}^*$ are identical. For example,

$$\mathbf{A}^* \equiv (1)\begin{bmatrix}0.7025\\-0.7117\end{bmatrix}\begin{bmatrix}0.7025 & -0.7117\end{bmatrix}$$
$$+(2)\begin{bmatrix}-0.7117\\-0.7025\end{bmatrix}\begin{bmatrix}-0.7117 & -0.7025\end{bmatrix} = \begin{bmatrix}1.5065 & 0.5\\0.5 & 1.4935\end{bmatrix}$$

and

$$\mathbf{B}^* \equiv (1)\begin{bmatrix}-0.8206\\0.5715\end{bmatrix}\begin{bmatrix}-0.8206 & 0.5715\end{bmatrix}$$
$$+(2)\begin{bmatrix}0.5715\\0.8206\end{bmatrix}\begin{bmatrix}0.5715 & 0.8206\end{bmatrix} = \begin{bmatrix}1.3266 & 0.4690\\0.4690 & 1.6734\end{bmatrix}$$

both have the same eigenvalues (1 and 2), yet $\mathbf{A}^* \neq \mathbf{B}^*$. On the other hand, such situations are rarely expected to occur in practice, so the Log Eigenspectrum GIMT essentially exhibits the behavioral properties of a nondirectional GIMT.

Note that the number of degrees of freedom for the Log Eigenspectrum GIMT is equal to the number of free parameters k, which is a substantial reduction from the $k(k+1)/2$ degrees of freedom of the Classical Full IMT statistic. Thus, it is expected that the variance of the Log Eigenspectrum GIMT statistic will be less than that of the Classical Full IMT statistic for even moderately small k.

2.5.2 Log Determinant GIMT

The *Log Determinant GIMT Hypothesis Function* is defined such that for every $\mathbf{A},\mathbf{B} \in \Upsilon^{k\times k}$:

$$\mathbf{s}(\mathbf{A},\mathbf{B}) = \log\det\left(\mathbf{A}^{-1}\mathbf{B}\right).$$

Thus, the null hypothesis of the Log Determinant GIMT is given by:

$$H_0 : \mathbf{s}\left(\mathbf{A}^*, \mathbf{B}^*\right) = \log\det\left(\left(\mathbf{A}^*\right)^{-1}\mathbf{B}^*\right)$$
$$= \log\det\left(\left(\mathbf{A}^*\right)^{-1}\right) - \log\det\left(\left(\mathbf{B}^*\right)^{-1}\right) = 0.$$

The determinant of $(\mathbf{A}^*)^{-1}$ (i.e., the product of the eigenvalues of $(\mathbf{A}^*)^{-1}$) can be interpreted as a measure of the magnitude of the Hessian covariance matrix $(\mathbf{A}^*)^{-1}$ and is sometimes referred to as the "generalized variance" (Cramér 1946, Sect. 22.7; Serfling 1980, p. 139). Thus, the Log Determinant GIMT hypothesis function compares the generalized variance of the Hessian covariance matrix $(\mathbf{A}^*)^{-1}$ to the generalized variance of the OPG covariance matrix $(\mathbf{B}^*)^{-1}$. The Log Determinant GIMT is expected to have good statistical power for two reasons: (1) it is a *one degree of freedom GIMT* regardless of the complexity of the model or the complexity of the data, and (2) it is equally sensitive to changes in the largest eigenvalues as well as changes in the smallest eigenvalues.

2.5.3 Log Trace GIMT

The Log Trace GIMT is a one-degree of freedom test that compares the magnitude of the Hessian covariance matrix $(\mathbf{A}^*)^{-1}$ to the magnitude of the OPG covariance matrix $(\mathbf{B}^*)^{-1}$ by constructing the Log Trace GIMT hypothesis function. The *Log Trace GIMT hypothesis function* is defined such that for every $\mathbf{A}, \mathbf{B} \in \Upsilon^{k \times k}$:

$$\mathbf{s}\left(\mathbf{A}, \mathbf{B}\right) = \log tr\left(\mathbf{A}^{-1}\right) - \log tr\left(\mathbf{B}^{-1}\right).$$

The null hypothesis of the Log Trace GIMT is given by:

$$H_0 : \mathbf{s}\left(\mathbf{A}^*, \mathbf{B}^*\right) = \log tr\left(\left(\mathbf{A}^*\right)^{-1}\right) - \log tr\left(\left(\mathbf{B}^*\right)^{-1}\right) = 0.$$

Note that the Log Trace GIMT hypothesis function may be interpreted as comparing the log sum of the on-diagonal variances of the Hessian covariance matrix $(\mathbf{A}^*)^{-1}$ to that of the OPG covariance matrix $(\mathbf{B}^*)^{-1}$ or equivalently, comparing the log sum of the eigenvalues of $(\mathbf{A}^*)^{-1}$ with that of $(\mathbf{B}^*)^{-1}$.

The Log Trace GIMT compares the Hessian and OPG covariance matrix structures based upon the larger eigenvalues while tending to ignore the smaller eigenvalues. This is equivalent to comparing the sums of the largest on-diagonal variance elements of both covariance matrices. Thus, the Log Trace GIMT is more sensitive to changes in the larger eigenvalues of the covariance matrices and less sensitive to changes in the smaller eigenvalues (i.e., focuses upon the major principal components of the Hessian and OPG covariance matrices). It is thus expected to be a less sensitive GIMT than the Log Determinant GIMT (i.e., it may have reduced statistical power). Depending upon the situation, this latter property of the Log Trace GIMT may be more or less desirable.

2.5.4 Log Generalized Variance GIMT

The *Log Generalized Variance GIMT Hypothesis Function* is defined such that for every $\mathbf{A}, \mathbf{B} \in \Upsilon^{k \times k}$:

$$\mathbf{s}(\mathbf{A}, \mathbf{B}) = \begin{bmatrix} \log\det\left(\mathbf{A}^{-1}\right) - \log\det\left(\mathbf{B}^{-1}\right) \\ \log tr\left(\mathbf{A}^{-1}\right) - \log tr\left(\mathbf{B}^{-1}\right) \end{bmatrix}.$$

The null hypothesis of the Log Generalized Variance GIMT is given by:

$$H_0 : \mathbf{s}\left(\mathbf{A}^*, \mathbf{B}^*\right) = \begin{bmatrix} \log\det\left((\mathbf{A}^*)^{-1}\right) - \log\det\left((\mathbf{B}^*)^{-1}\right) \\ \log tr\left((\mathbf{A}^*)^{-1}\right) - \log tr\left((\mathbf{B}^*)^{-1}\right) \end{bmatrix} = \begin{bmatrix} 0 \\ 0 \end{bmatrix}.$$

The Log Generalized Variance GIMT is a two degree of freedom GIMT and combines the Log Determinant GIMT, which focuses on both major and minor principal components of the Hessian and OPG covariance matrices, with the Log Trace GIMT, which focuses only upon the major principal components of the Hessian and OPG covariance matrices.

2.5.5 Log GAIC GIMT

Takeuchi (1976; for relevant reviews see Konishi and Kitagawa 1996; Bozdogan 2000) showed that the GAIC defined by the formula:

$$GAIC \equiv -2\log\prod_{i=1}^{n} f\left(\mathbf{X}_i; \hat{\boldsymbol{\theta}}_n\right) + 2TRACE\left(\hat{\mathbf{A}}_n^{-1}\hat{\mathbf{B}}_n\right)$$

is an unbiased estimator of the expected value of $-2\log\prod_{i=1}^{n} f\left(\mathbf{X}_i; \hat{\boldsymbol{\theta}}_n\right)$ in the presence of model misspecification. When the model is correctly specified, then almost surely: $\hat{\mathbf{A}}_n^{-1}\hat{\mathbf{B}}_n \rightarrow \mathbf{I}_k$ where $\mathbf{I}_k$ is the k-dimensional identity matrix. Furthermore, since $2TRACE\left(\hat{\mathbf{A}}_n^{-1}\hat{\mathbf{B}}_n\right) \rightarrow 2k$, GAIC reduces to Akaike's (1973) Akaike Information Criterion (AIC) defined as:

$$AIC \equiv -2\log\prod_{i=1}^{n} f\left(\mathbf{X}_i; \hat{\boldsymbol{\theta}}_n\right) + 2k.$$

Let $\left(\boldsymbol{\Lambda}_{\mathbf{A}^*}(\mathbf{A})\right)^{-1} \equiv \left[\left(\Lambda_{1,\mathbf{A}^*}(\mathbf{A})\right)^{-1}, \ldots, \left(\Lambda_{k,\mathbf{A}^*}(\mathbf{A})\right)^{-1}\right]$ and let $\odot$ denote the Hadamard product (i.e., element-wise vector multiplication) operator. If a simultaneous diagonalization of $\mathbf{A}^*$ and $\mathbf{B}^*$ exists, $TRACE\left[(\mathbf{A}^*)^{-1}\mathbf{B}^*\right] = (\mathbf{1}_k)^T \left[\left(\boldsymbol{\Lambda}_{\mathbf{A}^*}(\mathbf{A}^*)\right)^{-1} \odot \boldsymbol{\Lambda}_{\mathbf{B}^*}(\mathbf{B}^*)\right]$. This observation suggests a new GIMT called the Log

GAIC IMT. The *Log GAIC GIMT Hypothesis Function* is defined such that for every $\mathbf{A}, \mathbf{B} \in \Upsilon^{k \times k}$:

$$\mathbf{s}(\mathbf{A}, \mathbf{B}) = \log\left(\frac{1}{k}\sum_{j=1}^{k}\left(\frac{\tilde{\lambda}_{j,\mathbf{B}^*}(\mathbf{B})}{\tilde{\lambda}_{j,\mathbf{A}^*}(\mathbf{A})}\right)\right)$$
$$= \log\left(\frac{1}{k} TRACE\left[\left(\tilde{\boldsymbol{\lambda}}_{\mathbf{A}^*}(\mathbf{A})\right)^{-1} \odot \tilde{\boldsymbol{\lambda}}_{\mathbf{B}^*}(\mathbf{B})\right]\right).$$

Thus, the null hypothesis of the Log GAIC IMT is given by:

$$H_0 : \mathbf{s}\left(\mathbf{A}^*, \mathbf{B}^*\right) = \log\left(\frac{1}{k} TRACE\left[\left(\tilde{\boldsymbol{\lambda}}_{\mathbf{A}^*}\left(\mathbf{A}^*\right)\right)^{-1} \odot \tilde{\boldsymbol{\lambda}}_{\mathbf{B}^*}\left(\mathbf{B}^*\right)\right]\right) = 0.$$

The Log GAIC GIMT is also a one-degree of freedom IMT, and is more similar to the Log Determinant GIMT than to the Log Trace GIMT because the Log GAIC GIMT is sensitive to all differences in the eigenspectra of $(\mathbf{A}^*)^{-1}$ and $(\mathbf{B}^*)^{-1}$. However, the Log GAIC GIMT differs from the Log Determinant GIMT because these changes are combined additively instead of multiplicatively.

3 Simulation Studies

In this section we describe and report findings from simulation studies designed to investigate the level and power properties of the five new Eigenspectrum GIMTs and the Adjusted Classical GIMT. Our studies here investigate the reliability of the large sample approximations for estimating Type I error probabilities (level) and evaluate the performance of the new Eigenspectrum GIMTs relative to the new Adjusted Classical GIMT. They also demonstrate the applicability of the new Eigenspectrum GIMTs to detect and assess model misspecification using a realistic epidemiological data analysis problem.

3.1 Epidemiological Data Sample

Our simulation studies were conducted using a random sample ($n = 16{,}189$) of deidentified patient discharges from the Department of Veterans Affairs (VA) Patient Treatment File between October 1, 1995 and September 30, 1996. The "deidentified Extraction Sample" of 16,189 patients included a single binary response variable (ALC) indicating the presence or absence of a primary or secondary discharge diagnosis of either: (i) alcohol dependence (IDC9#303), or (ii) alcohol abuse (ICD9#305.0), based on diagnostic codes from the International Classification of Diseases 9th

Edition (ICD9) (DHHS 1980). The simulation data contains only adults, with the ICD9 alcohol disorders occurring in approximately 20.3 % (3,283) of all patients, where in the sample 4 % are female, 25.1 % are divorced, and 4.2 % are minorities.

3.2 Logistic Regression Models

In this chapter, we investigate the performance of our new GIMTs with respect to binary logistic regression (logit) models (Christensen 1997; Hosmer and Lemeshow 2000; Harrell 2001; Agresti 2002; Collett 2003; Hilbe 2009) in which the probability that a binary response random variable R takes on the values of zero or one is functionally dependent upon $d-1$ predictor variable values denoted by the $d-1$-dimensional vector $\mathbf{u} \in \mathcal{R}^{d-1}$. Define a logistic regression model using

$$\log\left[\frac{p\left(R=1|\mathbf{u};\boldsymbol{\beta}\right)}{p\left(R=0|\mathbf{u};\boldsymbol{\beta}\right)}\right]=\boldsymbol{\beta}^T\begin{bmatrix}\mathbf{u}\\1\end{bmatrix}$$

where the last element of the k-dimensional parameter vector $\boldsymbol{\beta}$ corresponds to the intercept parameter. In order to relate this logistic regression model to the discussion in Sect. 2, let $R \equiv x_1$ and $\mathbf{u} \equiv [x_2, \ldots, x_d]$ so that $\mathbf{x} \equiv [R, \mathbf{u}] \in \mathcal{R}^d$ and let $\boldsymbol{\theta} \equiv \boldsymbol{\beta} \in \Theta \subseteq \mathcal{R}^k$ where $d = k$. Using this notation, we define

$$f\left(\mathbf{x};\boldsymbol{\theta}\right)\equiv\left[x_1 p\left(R=1|\mathbf{u};\boldsymbol{\beta}\right)+\left(1-x_1\right)p\left(R=0|\mathbf{u};\boldsymbol{\beta}\right)\right]p\left(x_2,\ldots,x_d\right)$$

where the joint predictor density $p(x_2, \ldots, x_d)$ is not functionally dependent upon $\boldsymbol{\beta} \in \mathcal{R}^d$. Because of this latter property, the GIMT formulas are not functionally dependent on $p(x_2, \ldots, x_d)$. Thus in the *i.i.d.* case the log-likelihood for a logistic regression model with sample size n is

$$L\left(\boldsymbol{\beta}\right)=\sum_{i=1}^{n}\left\{R_i\ln\left[p\left(R_i=1|\mathbf{u}_i;\boldsymbol{\beta}\right)\right]+\left(1-R_i\right)\ln\left[1-p\left(R_i=1|\mathbf{u}_i;\boldsymbol{\beta}\right)\right]\right\}$$

where

$$p\left(R=1|\mathbf{u};\boldsymbol{\beta}\right)=\left(1+\exp\left[-\left(\mathbf{u}^T\boldsymbol{\beta}\right)\right]\right)^{-1}.$$

3.2.1 Logistic Regression Model with Binary Predictors

We first fitted a logistic regression model to the $n = 16{,}189$ deidentified Extraction Sample using maximum likelihood estimation to predict the presence or absence of "alcohol-disorder" (ALC) from the binary predictors "female" (FEMALE), "married" (MARRIED), recoded categorical predictor ethnicity containing "black" (BLACK) and "white" (WHITE), and the recoded predictor "age" (AGE).

The ethnicity variable was recoded into a three category design variable (white, black, other) using reference cell coding (Hosmer and Lemeshow 2000) where "other" is the reference variable. Also, the numerical AGE predictor was trichotomized into a three category design variable by applying optimally estimated cut values $\gamma_1 = 55.4$ and $\gamma_2 = 68.2$ (Henley et al. 2000; Kashner et al. 2002, 2003, 2007, 2010) where the first binary design variable $\text{AGE}_1(\text{age} \leq 55.4)$ is the reference variable.

In addition to reporting our model fit results using a negative log-likelihood score, we report fitness results in terms of a GAIC, also known as the Takeuchi Information Criterion (TIC) (Takeuchi 1976; Konishi and Kitagawa 1996; Bozdogan 2000). GAIC is a misspecification robust extension of the Akaike Information criterion (AIC) (Akaike 1973; Burnham and Anderson 2002, pp. 65, 362–372). The resulting fitted logistic regression model had a negative log-likelihood of 6,718.2 (GAIC/2n = 0.415420, $p = 0.0000$) with estimated parameter values

$$\hat{\beta}_0 = -0.7397, \quad \hat{\beta}_1 = -1.3099, \quad \hat{\beta}_2 = -2.2946, \quad \hat{\beta}_3 = -1.4249,$$
$$\hat{\beta}_4 = -0.9784, \quad \hat{\beta}_5 = 1.0000, \quad \hat{\beta}_6 = 0.6822$$

respectively for the intercept, AGE_2 ($55.4 < \text{age} \leq 68.2$), AGE_3 ($68.2 < \text{age} \leq 85$), FEMALE, MARRIED, BLACK, and WHITE predictors. Wald tests computed using robust standard errors (e.g., Wald 1943; White 1982; Golden 1996) showed each estimated parameter value was significantly different from zero ($p < 0.001$). All six GIMTs applied to this model failed to reject the null hypothesis (Adjusted Classical, $p = 0.6113$; Log Eigenspectrum, $p = 0.3618$; Log Determinant, $p = 0.6138$; Log Trace, $p = 0.4063$; Log Generalized Variance, $p = 0.6890$; Log GAIC, $p = 0.6004$) indicating no evidence of model misspecification. Thus, simulated data samples generated from this fitted model were expected to be more representative of real world data.

3.2.2 Alternative Logistic Regression Model with Numerical and Binary Predictors

We also fitted a different (alternative) logistic regression model that replaced the trichotomized age predictor with the numerical predictor for "age" (AGE*) and added a "divorced" (DIVORCED*) binary variable so each model had seven free parameters. The model was otherwise identical to the first one. The resulting fitted logistic regression model had a negative log-likelihood of 6,743 (GAIC/2n = 0.416965, $p = 0.0000$) with estimated parameter values

$$\hat{\beta}_0 = 1.8448, \quad \hat{\beta}_1 = -0.0646, \quad \hat{\beta}_2 = -1.6057, \quad \hat{\beta}_3 = -0.7972,$$
$$\hat{\beta}_4 = 0.3353, \quad \hat{\beta}_5 = 1.0082, \quad \hat{\beta}_6 = 0.7065$$

respectively for the intercept, AGE*, FEMALE, MARRIED, DIVORCED*, BLACK, and WHITE predictors. Wald tests computed using robust standard errors (e.g., Wald 1943; White 1982; Golden 1996) again showed each estimated parameter value was significantly different from zero ($p < 0.001$). All six GIMTs applied to the alternative logit model rejected the null hypothesis (Adjusted Classical, $p = 0.0000$; Log Eigenspectrum, $p = 0.0000$; Log Determinant, $p = 0.0028$; Log Trace, $p = 0.0282$; Log Generalized Variance, $p = 0.0112$; Log GAIC, $p = 0.0026$) indicating the presence of model misspecification.

In practice, researchers may inadvertently use a misspecified model that nevertheless provides a good fit, as measured by log-likelihood or GAIC, to the observed data. We selected an alternative logistic regression model, which provided a fit (GAIC/$2n = 0.416965$, $p = 0.0000$) to the observed data that is comparable to the fit (GAIC/$2n = 0.415420$, $p = 0.0000$) of the original logit model described in Sect. 3.2.1. This difference in model fit was not statistically significant ($p = 0.1960$) using the Discrepancy Risk Model Selection Test (DRMST) (Vuong 1989; Golden 2000, 2003; Henley et al. 2000, 2003, 2008) for comparing nonnested and possibly misspecified models.

3.3 *Simulation Study*

3.3.1 GIMT Level and Power Estimation Procedures

The procedure for estimating the observed level of a GIMT is shown in Fig. 1. Four simulated data samples of n^* records ($n^* = 1{,}619$, $n^* = 4{,}047$, $n^* = 8{,}095$, and $n^* = 16{,}189$) were generated by sampling with replacement from the original representative sample (see Politis et al. 1999; Davison et al. 2003). This process was repeated m times for each of four sample sizes. The conditional probability for the binary ALC outcome variable was then computed and assigned the value one or zero, based on the minimum probability of decision error rule, for each record using predictor values and the estimated coefficients of the seven-parameter logistic regression model with binary predictors. Thus, all simulated data samples had predictor values with synthetic ALC outcome values that had been generated from the specified logistic regression model estimated on the original representative sample ($n = 16{,}189$). To calculate level estimation results, we then fit the logistic regression model to each of the m simulated data samples for the four sample sizes and computed 10,000 significance levels in the range of zero to one for all the GIMTs. The percentage of times that a GIMT incorrectly rejects the null hypothesis of correct specification as the "observed incorrect rejection rate" or "observed level" was calculated.

The procedure for estimating the observed power of a GIMT is shown in (Fig. 2). In this experiment we created an alternative logistic regression model by changing two of the six binary predictor variables in the logistic regression model from the level estimation procedure (Fig. 1). As previously described, the numerical AGE and binary DIVORCED predictor variables in the original representative data sample replaced the binary design variables AGE_2 and AGE_3. This predictor variable change introduced a relatively subtle, but realistic misspecification into the alterna-

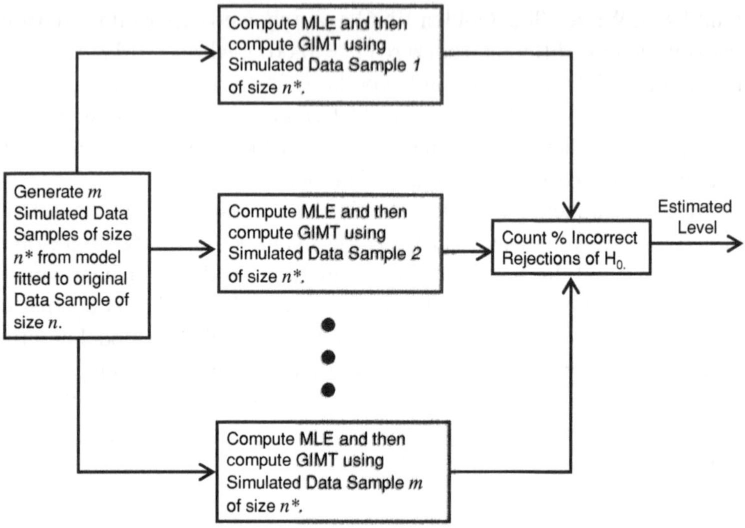

Fig. 1 Simulation procedure for estimation of level

tive model because the known (i.e., simulated) data generating process stems from the original logistic regression model containing only binary predictors. Further, the use of observationally equivalent original and alternative logit models (see discussion in Sect. 3.2.2) for the simulation design minimizes the confounding issue of model fit (GAIC) with specification, thus enabling the effects of model specification (goodness-of-fit) on GIMT performance to be more effectively studied. To calculate power estimation results, we then fit the alternative logistic regression model to each of the simulated data samples from the level analysis for the four sample sizes and computed 10,000 significance levels in the range of zero to one for all the GIMTs. The percentage of times that a GIMT correctly rejects the null hypothesis of correct specification as the "observed correct rejection rate" or "observed power" was calculated.

In our simulation studies, an MLE was defined as a set of parameter values such that the sup norm of the gradient of the negative log-likelihood evaluated at the MLE was less than 1e−8. Further, we avoided fitting models to degenerate simulated data by omitting samples with condition numbers greater than 4.5e+14 to insure numerical stability. The condition number is defined as the maximum eigenvalue divided by the minimum eigenvalue of the inverse of the Hessian covariance matrix estimator. Each simulation was run until $m = 100{,}000$ simulated data samples of size n^* was reached. The sample sizes n^* for the simulated data represented 10 %, 25 %, 50 %, and 100 % of the original 16,189 record data set. In all simulations, we utilized the Hessian-GIMT statistic as defined in Sect. 2.3.

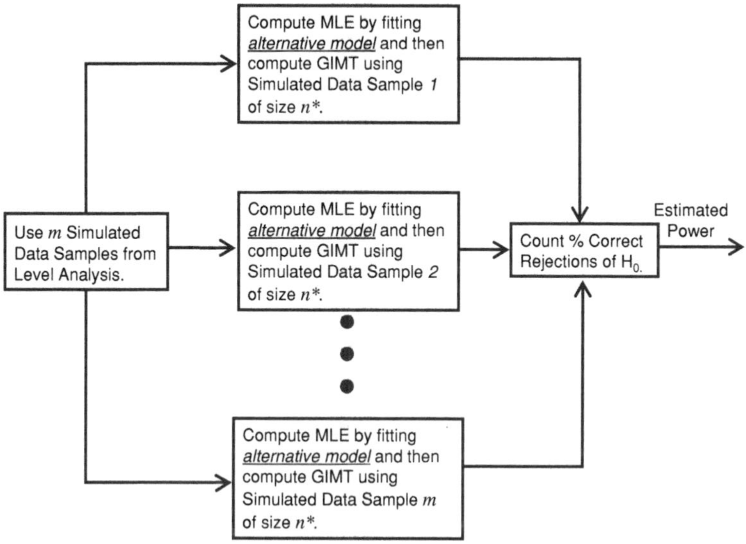

Fig. 2 Simulation procedure for estimation of power

3.3.2 Simulation Study Results

In this section we present level-discrepancy and level-power simulation results for the proposed GIMTs.

Level-Discrepancy Analyses

We first examined the performance for the six GIMTs using a *P*-value plot analysis (Davidson and MacKinnon 1998). This method plots the empirical level (observed rejection rate of the null hypothesis, i.e., Type I error) of a GIMT against its nominal level (specified rejection rate of the null hypothesis). To enable *P*-value plot comparisons, we also define a summary deviation measure for the *level-discrepancy* as the root mean square error (RMSE) between empirical and nominal levels over the specified range of interest (e.g., [0, 0.1] or [0, 1.0]). Thus, an ideal estimation of the Type I error rate corresponds to a level-discrepancy of zero (i.e., RMSE $= 0$). In our studies, the level-discrepancy for each GIMT was estimated on simulated data for each sample size.

The Adjusted Classical GIMT is a member of the family of Classical IMTs that includes White (1982) Full IMT. Figure 3 depicts the *P*-value plots with level-discrepancies for the Adjusted Classical GIMT on 100,000 simulated data samples for n ranging from 1,619 to 16,189 for level ranges on [0, 0.10]. These results show that the level-discrepancy deviation decreases from 0.0261 to 0.0091 RMSE as sample size increases, thus approaching an ideal estimation Type I error rate at larger sample sizes. Further, the exhibited Type I error rate convergence for the Adjusted Classical GIMT indicated level-discrepancy performance that was much better than the performance of the Classical Full IMT (not shown). We attribute this to the par-

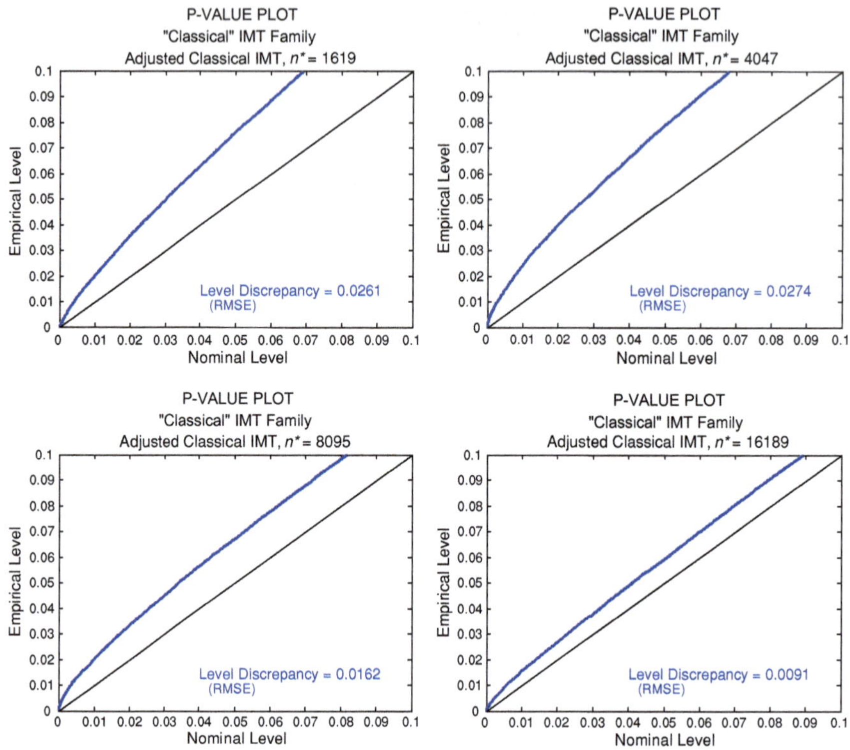

Fig. 3 *P*-value plots for the White's (1982) Adjusted Classical GIMT show empirical level [0, 0.1] versus nominal level [0, 0.1] by sample size. The displayed level-discrepancy is defined as the root mean square error (RMSE) between the empirical and nominal levels. Thus, an ideal estimation of the Type I error rate corresponds to a discrepancy between the empirical (simulated) and nominal levels of zero (i.e., RMSE $= 0$). The data points on the graphs are computed for 100,000 simulated data samples for $n^* = 1{,}619$, $n^* = 4{,}047$, $n^* = 8{,}095$ and $n^* = 16{,}189$

ticular care with which singularity or near-singularity of the test statistic covariance matrix is handled.

Next, we present the simulation results for the new Log Eigenspectrum GIMT. Figure 4 depicts the *P*-value plots with level-discrepancies for the Log Eigenspectrum GIMT on 100,000 simulated data samples for n ranging from 1,619 to 16,189, which again shows RMSE decreasing as sample size increases. Notably, the level-discrepancy (RMSE $= 0.0030$) for the Log Eigenspectrum GIMT at $n = 16{,}189$ is less than the level-discrepancy (RMSE $= 0.0091$) for the Adjusted Classical GIMT (Fig. 3).

The simulation results for the new Log GAIC GIMT, which is a directional GIMT, are also presented for comparison. Figure 5 shows the *P*-value plots with level-discrepancies for the Log GAIC GIMT on 100,000 simulated data samples for n ranging from 1,689 to 16,189. Again, the empirical and nominal levels of interest

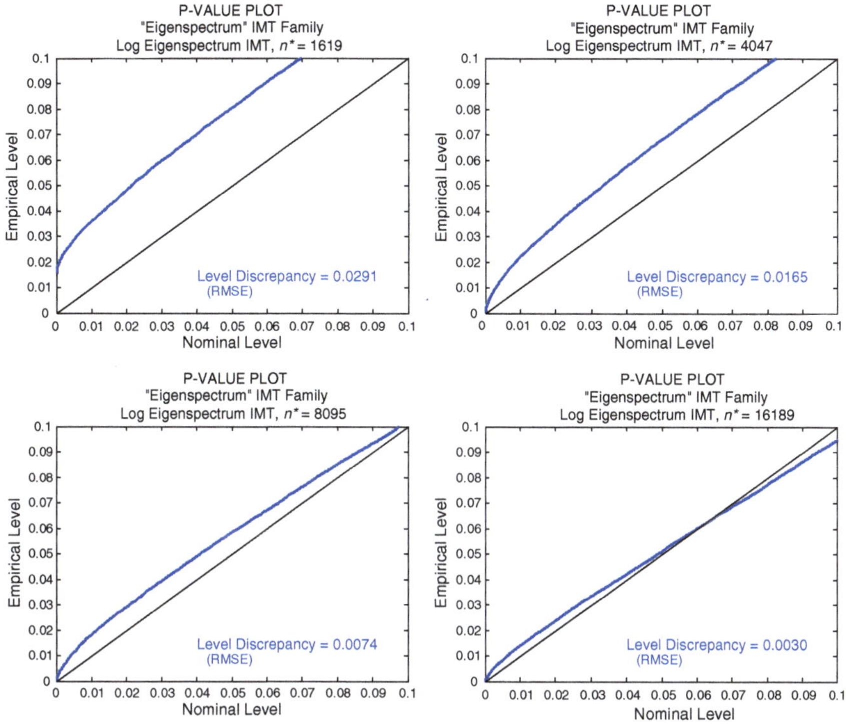

Fig. 4 *P*-value plots for the Log Eigenspectrum GIMT show empirical level [0, 0.1] versus nominal level [0, 0.1] by sample size. The level-discrepancy is defined as the deviation measured by root mean square error (RMSE) between the empirical and nominal levels. Thus, an ideal estimation of the Type I error rate corresponds to a discrepancy between the empirical (simulated) and nominal levels of zero (i.e., RMSE = 0). The data points on the graphs are computed for 100,000 simulated data samples for $n^* = 1{,}619$, $n^* = 4{,}047$, $n^* = 8{,}095$ and $n^* = 16{,}189$. The level-discrepancy (RMSE = 0.0030) at $n = 16{,}189$ for the Log Eigenspectrum GIMT with seven degrees of freedom is less than the level-discrepancy (RMSE = 0.0091) reported for the Adjusted Classical GIMT (Fig. 3), which has up to 28 degrees of freedom

range over [0, 0.10]. These simulation results show the level-discrepancy for the Log GAIC GIMT is converging to zero as sample size increases. The level-discrepancy (RMSE = 0.0045) at $n = 16{,}189$ for the directional Log GAIC GIMT is greater than the level-discrepancy (RMSE = 0.0030) reported for the Log Eigenspectrum GIMT (Fig. 4), but less than the level-discrepancy (RMSE = 0.0091) reported for the Adjusted Classical Full GIMT (Fig. 3). A similar pattern of results was observed using the *P*-value plot analyses for the remaining three new directional Eigenspectrum GIMTs. All observed rejection rates were very close to the nominal levels.

The level-discrepancy performance of all GIMTs is depicted in Fig. 6, which displays *P*-value plot results as a function of sample size. As shown, the new Eigenspectrum GIMTs exhibit excellent performance for large sample sizes. In addition, they exhibited better performance than the Adjusted Classical GIMT with

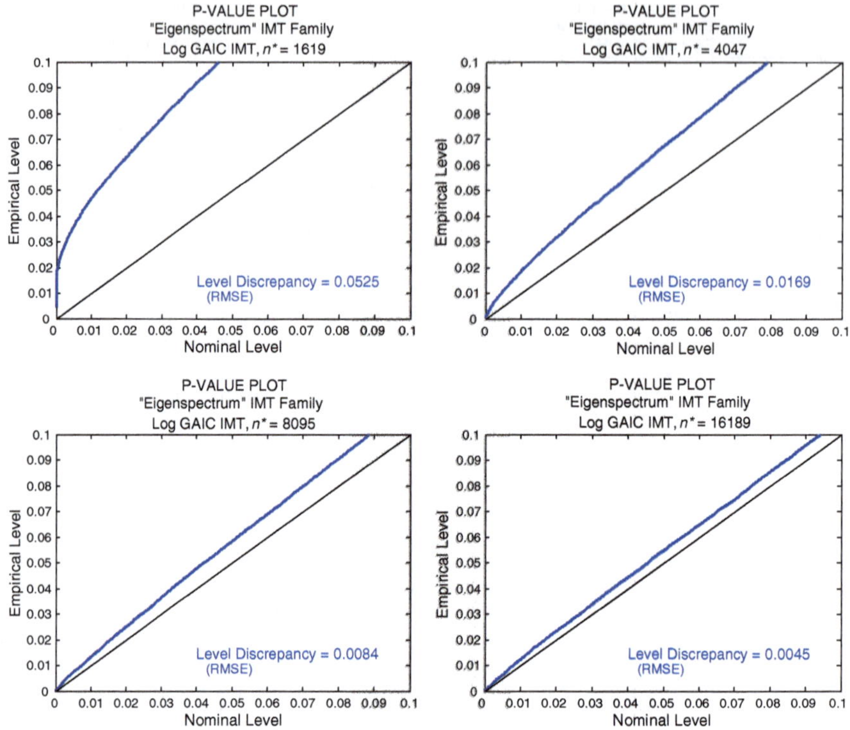

Fig. 5 *P*-value plots for the directional Log GAIC GIMT show empirical level [0, 0.1] versus nominal level [0, 0.1] by sample size. The level-discrepancy is defined as the deviation measured by root mean square error (RMSE) between the empirical and nominal levels. Thus, an ideal estimation of the Type I error rate corresponds to a discrepancy between the empirical (simulated) and nominal levels of zero (i.e., RMSE = 0). The data points on the graphs are computed for 100,000 simulated data samples for $n^* = 1{,}619$, $n^* = 4{,}047$, $n^* = 8{,}095$ and $n^* = 16{,}189$. The level-discrepancy (RMSE = 0.0045) at $n = 16{,}189$ for the directional Log GAIC GIMT with one-degree of freedom is larger than the level-discrepancies obtained for the Log Eigenspectrum GIMT (RMSE = 0.0030), though smaller than the Adjusted Classical GIMT (RMSE = 0.0091) shown respectively in Figs. 3 and 4

level-discrepancies approaching zero in all cases. The Log Eigenspectrum GIMT exhibited the best (i.e., smallest) level-discrepancy performance of all GIMTs at larger sample sizes.

The observed rejection rates (estimated Type I errors) for each of the six new GIMTs are reported in Table 1 for the nominal significance levels of 0.001, 0.005, 0.01, 0.025, 0.05, and 0.10 for the full sample size of $n = 16{,}189$. The simulated standard errors of the estimated Type I error rates are shown in parentheses. Note that these standard errors will converge to zero as $m \to \infty$ for a fixed sample size $n = 16{,}189$. Our findings show that the estimated Type I error rates for all six new GIMTs are, in general, very close to their specified error rates. The Log Eigenspectrum GIMT exhibited the smallest level-discrepancy of all GIMTs at the

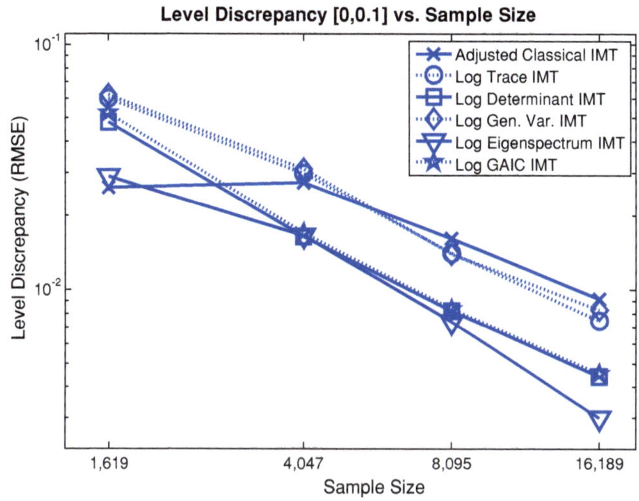

Fig. 6 Level-discrepancy performance by sample size for the six GIMTs in the simulation study. Each data point corresponds to 100,000 simulated data samples. The Adjusted Classical GIMT and all the Eigenspectrum GIMTs exhibit level-discrepancy convergence towards zero as sample size increases. The Log Eigenspectrum GIMT exhibited the smallest level-discrepancy of all GIMTs at the larger sample sizes

larger sample sizes. We also performed additional simulation studies (Henley et al. 2001, 2004), and found that the performance of the six new GIMTs was always better than White's (1982) Classical Full IMT.

Level-Power Analyses

Next, we perform a level-power analysis to examine all six GIMTs by generating a level-power curve (Davidson and MacKinnon 1998) for each GIMT. A level-power curve plots the power (i.e., 1-Type II error) of a statistical test as a function of the level (rejection rate or Type I error). Accordingly, we interpret a statistical test as a binary classifier that divides the decision space into two regions: *reject* or *fail to reject* (Wickens 2002; Pepe 2004, p. 152).

An important performance measure for the evaluation of binary classifiers is the Area Under the Response Operating Characteristic Curve (AUROC; also known as AUC) (Hanley and McNeil 1982; Bradley 1997; Wickens 2002; Pepe 2004; Fawcett 2006). In the context of a level-power analysis, this corresponds to the area under the level-power curve. A level-power AUROC equal to one corresponds to perfect classification (i.e. test) performance. Figure 7 shows the level-power curves for the Log Eigenspectrum GIMT for $m = 100{,}000$ simulated data samples with sample sizes of $n^* = 1{,}619$, $n^* = 4{,}047$, $n^* = 8{,}095$, and $n^* = 16{,}189$. The Log Eigenspectrum GIMT exhibited ideal level-power performance (AUROC $= 1.00$) at the two larger samples sizes (not shown).

Level-power curves for all sample sizes ($n^* = 1{,}619$, $n^* = 4{,}047$, $n^* = 8{,}095$, and $n^* = 16{,}189$) were also generated for the other GIMTs using 100,000 simulated

Table 1 Empirical level (observed Type I error rates) obtained in the simulation studies for pre-specified (nominal) significance levels: 0.001, 0.005, 0.01, 0.025, 0.05, and 0.10

Generalized IM test	Nominal level					
	$p = 0.001$	$p = 0.005$	$p = 0.01$	$p = 0.025$	$p = 0.05$	$p = 0.10$
Adjusted classical[a,b] (df ≤ 28)	0.0029 (0.0002)	0.0093 (0.0003)	0.0156 (0.0004)	0.0326 (0.0006)	0.0593 (0.0007)	0.1112 (0.0010)
Log eigenspectrum[b] (7 df)	0.0029 (0.0002)	0.0084 (0.0003)	0.0140 (0.0004)	0.0289 (0.0005)	0.0511 (0.0007)	0.0947 (0.0009)
Log determinant (1 df)	0.0013 (0.0001)	0.0061 (0.0002)	0.0120 (0.0003)	0.0282 (0.0005)	0.0548 (0.0007)	0.1063 (0.0010)
Log trace (1 df)	0.0017 (0.0001)	0.0072 (0.0003)	0.0134 (0.0004)	0.0306 (0.0005)	0.0576 (0.0007)	0.1101 (0.0010)
Log generalized variance (2 df)	0.0017 (0.0001)	0.0074 (0.0003)	0.0139 (0.0004)	0.0310 (0.0005)	0.0586 (0.0007)	0.1110 (0.0010)
Log GAIC (1 df)	0.0016 (0.0001)	0.0063 (0.0003)	0.0122 (0.0003)	0.0284 (0.0005)	0.0547 (0.0007)	0.1063 (0.0010)

Results are for the six GIMTs where the sample size $n^* = 16,189$ and the number of simulated data samples $m = 100,000$. Bootstrapped standard errors, reflecting simulation sampling error, are shown in parentheses. In general, empirical levels agreed with the prespecified nominal significance levels

[a]Adjusted to remove multicollinearity from the Classical Full IMT selection statistic covariance matrix

[b]Degrees of freedom (df) is a function of the number of free parameters

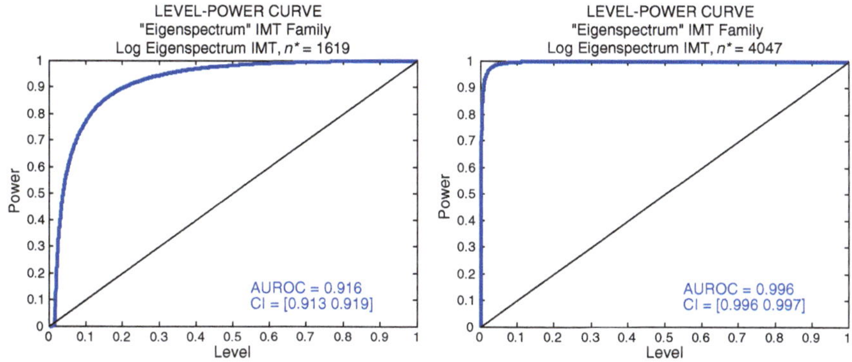

Fig. 7 Level-power curves for Log Eigenspectrum GIMT exhibit convergence to ideal GIMT decision performance as sample size increases using simulated epidemiological data. Each data point on the graphs represents 100,000 simulated data samples under the null and alternative hypotheses for the sample sizes $n^* = 1{,}619$ and $n^* = 4{,}047$ respectively. This two graph sequence depicts convergence to an ideal level-power curve (i.e., AUROC = 1.00). The level-power performance for the larger sample sizes $n^* = 8{,}095$ and $n^* = 16{,}189$ (not shown) achieved an ideal AUROC = 1.00

data samples per data point under the null and alternative hypotheses. Figure 8 depicts the level-power performance of all GIMTs as a function of sample size. As shown, the new Log Eigenspectrum GIMT and the Adjusted Classical GIMT have good power for both small and large sample sizes, although all of the GIMTs exhibit useful power for large sample sizes. A possible explanation for the increased power of the Log Eigenspectrum and the Adjusted Classical GIMTs is that these GIMTs test more comprehensive composite null hypotheses that result in increased opportunities to detect the presence of model misspecification.

4 Summary and Conclusions

In this chapter, we have introduced a general approach to the development of Generalized Information Matrix Tests that are intended to detect the presence of model misspecification. Such situations occur when the Hessian inverse covariance matrix $\mathbf{A}^*$ and the OPG inverse covariance matrix $\mathbf{B}^*$ are different. In particular, we introduced the new Generalized Information Matrix Test (GIMT) that tests $H_0 : \mathbf{s}(\mathbf{A}^*, \mathbf{B}^*) = \mathbf{0}_r$ and provided a Wald test version of the GIMT based on the asymptotic distribution of $n^{1/2}\hat{\mathbf{s}}_n \equiv n^{1/2}\mathbf{s}\left(\hat{\mathbf{A}}_n, \hat{\mathbf{B}}_n\right)$, along the lines of (White 1982, Theorem 4.2). For a given GIMT Selection Hypothesis Function, we also provided six distinct formulas for computing each GIMT test statistic and introduced the new concept of an "adjusted" GIMT statistic for dealing with issues of multicollinearity and demonstrated its utility by applying it to White's (1982) Classical Full IMT.

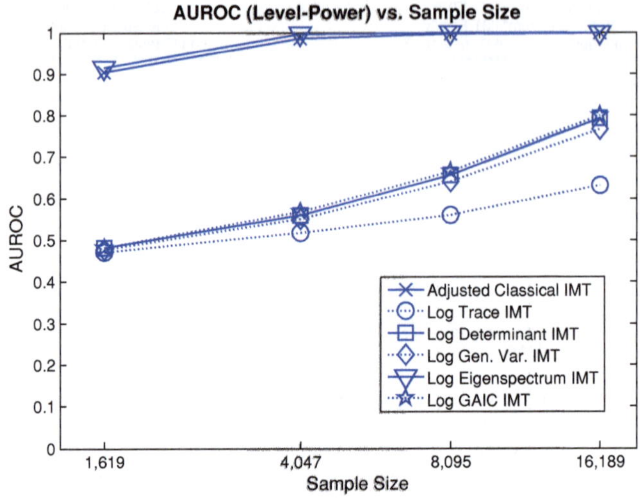

Fig. 8 AUROC (level-power) performance as a function of sample size for the six GIMTs in the simulation study. Each data point corresponds to 100,000 simulated data samples under the null and 100,000 simulated data samples under the alternative hypothesis. The Adjusted Classical and Log Eigenspectrum GIMTs converged at a faster rate to ideal level-power (i.e., AUROC = 1.00) as sample size increases, indicating more efficient level-power performance when compared to the other GIMTs

Further, we introduced the idea of constructing GIMTs by comparing nonlinear functions of the eigenspectra of the Hessian and OPG covariance matrices. Next, we developed five new GIMTs based upon the Eigenspectrum GIMT Family. These are the Log Eigenspectrum GIMT, Log Determinant GIMT, Log Trace GIMT, Generalized Variance GIMT, and Log GAIC GIMT. Analytic formulas for these five new Eigenspectrum GIMTs were derived and implemented in computer software.

We studied the performance of these five new Eigenspectrum GIMTs and an adjusted version of White's (1982) Classical Full IMT (i.e., Adjusted Classical GIMT) in a series of simulation experiments using a realistic 16,189 record data set typical of data encountered in epidemiological studies. By comparing a correctly specified model and a misspecified model with approximately equivalent fits to the observed data, our simulation studies focus specifically on the effects of model misspecification. Using *P*-value plots and level-power plots, we found that the Adjusted Classical GIMT and the five new Eigenspectrum GIMTs exhibited reliable performance, in the sense that their asymptotic behavior was correctly captured by the large sample statistical theory under the null. In particular, the empirically observed Type I error rates for all six new GIMTs were very close to their nominal error rates. Additionally, they also exhibited useful power. This is in stark contrast to the familiar poor performance of the unadjusted form of White (1982) Classical Full IMT (e.g., Davidson and MacKinnon 1992; Stomberg and White 2000; Aparicio and Villanua 2001).

For the larger sample sizes, the level-discrepancy performance (i.e., Type I error performance) of the high degree of freedom GIMT (i.e., Log Eigenspectrum) was better than those of all the low degree of freedom GIMTs (i.e., Log Determinant, Log Trace, Log Generalized Variance, Log GAIC), which in turn exceeded the performance of the high degree of freedom Adjusted Classical GIMT. However, the power performance (i.e., Type II error performance) of the Adjusted Classical and Log Eigenspectrum GIMTs was always superior to that of the low degree of freedom GIMTs over all sample sizes. We conjecture that the reduced variance of the low degree of freedom GIMTs decreased the efficiency of the large sample approximation when compared to the Log Eigenspectrum GIMT. We further conjecture that because the Eigenspectrum GIMTs have fewer degrees of freedom they were more robust to sampling error when compared to the Adjusted Classical GIMT, which adjusts its degrees of freedom to control for multicollinearity. The greater power of the larger degree of freedom GIMTs is most likely explained by noting that these GIMTs are simultaneously testing multiple hypotheses, thus providing additional opportunities to detect model misspecification.

We used our Adjusted Classical GIMT instead of White's (1982) Classical Full IMT because in additional simulation studies not reported here, the asymptotic covariance matrix for the Classical Full IMT was frequently observed to be singular and exhibited much worse performance in our investigations. However, in all cases, the level-discrepancy and the level-power performance of the new Adjusted Classical GIMT and the new Eigenspectrum GIMTs were superior to those of the Classical Full IMT. Moreover, the reliable performance of the Adjusted Classical GIMT as compared to the Classifical Full IMT is notable, and we emphasize that this GIMT is a special case of the original IMT theory proposed by White (1982).

In conclusion, the generalized IMT theory (Henley et al. 2001, 2004, 2008) presented here provides a novel framework for developing a wide range of model specification tests for a broad range of probability models. In particular, the new Eigenspectrum Family GIMTs have degrees of freedom less than or equal to k, in contrast to the Classical Full IMT (White 1982), which has $k(k+1)/2$ degrees of freedom for a k-parameter model. Further, our five new Eigenspectrum GIMTs and new Adjusted Classical GIMT for logistic regression models all have appealing level and power properties, as seen in a series of simulation experiments involving a realistic epidemiologic modeling problem. These six new GIMTs are therefore expected to provide useful new tools for detecting model misspecification across a broad class of probability models (Hastie and Tibshirani 1986; McCullagh and Nelder 1989; Wei 1998; Harrell 2001; Hastie et al. 2009), thus decreasing the chance that a misspecified model is inadvertently used to make inferences in practice. The reduction of incorrect statistical inferences, in turn, has fundamentally important consequences for making critical decisions in many areas, including the social, behavioral, and physical sciences, as well as engineering, financial, medical, and public health research (Kashner et al. 2002, 2003, 2007, 2010).

Acknowledgments This research was made possible by grants from the National Cancer Institute (NCI) (R44CA139607, PI: S.S. Henley) and the National Institute on Alcohol Abuse and Alcoholism

(NIAAA) (R43AA014302, PI: S.S. Henley; R43/44AA013351, PI: S.S. Henley; R44AA011607, PI: S.S. Henley) under the Small Business Innovation Research (SBIR) program. The authors wish to gratefully acknowledge this support. This chapter reflects the authors' views and not necessarily the opinions or views of the NCI or the NIAAA. The authors would also like to thank the anonymous referee for helpful comments and suggestions.

References

Agresti, A.: Categorical data analysis. New York: Wiley-Interscience, 2002.

Akaike, H.: "Information theory and an extension of the maximum likelihood principle", 1973.

Alonso, A., S. Litière, and G. Molenberghs: "A family of tests to detect misspecifications in the random-effects structure of generalized linear mixed models", Computational Statistics and Data Analysis, 52(2008), 4474–4486.

Aparicio, T., and I. Villanua: "The asymptotically efficient version of the information matrix test in binary choice models. A study of size and power", Journal of Applied Statistics, 28(2001), 167–182.

Archer, K. J., and S. Lemeshow: "Goodness-of-fit test for a logistic regression model fitted using survey sample data", The Stata Journal, 6(2006), 97–105.

Arminger, G., and M. E. Sobel: "Pseudo-maximum likelihood estimation of mean and covariance structures with missing data", Journal of the American Statistical Association, 85(1990), 195–203.

Begg, M. D., and S. Lagakos: "On the consequences of model misspecification in logistic regression", Environmental Health Perspectives, 87(1990), 69–75.

Bera, A. K., and S. Lee: "Information Matrix Test, Parameter Heterogeneity and ARCH: A Synthesis", The Review of Economic Studies, 60(1993), 229–240.

Bertolini, G., R. D'Amico, D. Nardi, A. Tinazzi, and G. Apolone: "One model, several results: the paradox of the Hosmer-Lemeshow goodness-of-fit test for the logistic regression model", Journal of Epidemiology and Biostatistics, 5(2000), 251–3.

Box, E. P., G. M. Jenkins, and G. C. Reinsel: Time Series Analysis: Forecasting and Control. New York: John Wiley & Sons, 2008.

Bozdogan, H.: "Akaike's Information Criterion and Recent Developments in Information Complexity", Journal of Mathematical Psychology, 44(2000), 62–91.

Bradley, A. P.: "The Use of the Area Under the ROC Curve in the Evaluation of Machine Learning Algorithms", Pattern Recognition, 30(1997), 1145–1159.

Burnham, K. P., and D. R. Anderson: Model selection and multimodel inference : a practical information-theoretic approach. New York: Springer, 2002.

Chesher, A.: "The information matrix test: Simplified calculation via a score test interpretation", Economics Letters, 13(1983), 45–48.

Chesher, A., and R. Spady: "Asymptotic Expansions of the Information Matrix Test Statistic", Econometrica, 59(1991), 787–815.

Christensen, R.: Log-Linear Models and Logistic Regression. Springer Texts in, Statistics, 1997.

Collett, D.: Modelling Binary Data. Chapman & Hall/CRC, 2003.

Copas, J.B.: "Unweighted sum of squares test for proportions", Applied Statistics, 38(1989), 71–80.

Cox, D.R.: "Role of models in statistical analysis", Statistical Science, 5(1990), 169–174.

Cramér, H.: Mathematical Methods of Statistics. Princeton: Princeton University Press, 1946.

Davidson, R., and J. G. MacKinnon: "A New Form of the Information Matrix Test", Econometrica, 60(1992), 145–157.

Davidson, R., and J. G. MacKinnon: "Graphical Methods for Investigating the Size and Power of Hypothesis Tests", The Manchester School, 66(1998), 1–26.

Davison, A. C., D. V. Hinkley, and G. A. Young: "Recent Developments in Bootstrap Methodology", Statistical Science, 18(2003), 141–157.
Davison, A. C., and C. L. Tsai: "Regression model diagnostics", International Statistical Review, 60(1992), 337–353.
Deng, X., S. Wan, and B. Zhang: "An improved goodness-of-test for logistic regression models based on case-control data by random partition", Communications in statistics: Simulations and computation, 38(2009), 233–243.
Dhaene, G., and D. Hoorelbeke: "The information matrix test with bootstrap-based covariance matrix estimation", Economics Letters, 82(2004), 341–347.
DHHS: "The International Classification of Diseases, 9th Revision, Clinical Modification (ICD-9-CM). DHHS Publication No. (PHS) 80–1280", Washington D.C.: Department of Health and Human Services, 1980.
Farrington, C.P.: "On assessing goodness of fit of generalized linear models to sparse data", Journal of the Royal Statistical Society, Series B, 58(1996), 349–360.
Fawcett, T.: "An introduction to ROC analysis", Pattern Recognition Letters, 27(2006), 861–874.
Fisher, R.A.: "On the mathematical foundations of theoretical statistics", Philosophical Transactions of the Royal Society of London, Series A, 222(1922), 309–368.
Gallini, J.: "Misspecifications that can result in path analysis structures", Applied Psychological Measurement, 7(1983), 125–137.
Golden, R.M.: Mathematical methods for neural network analysis and design. Cambridge, Mass.: MIT Press, 1996.
Golden, R. M.: "Statistical tests for comparing possibly misspecified and nonnested models", Journal of Mathematical Psychology, 44(2000), 153–170.
Golden, R.M.: "Discrepancy risk model selection test theory for comparing possibly misspecified or nonnested models", Psychometrika, 68(2003), 229–249.
Greene, W.: Econometric Analysis. New Jersey: Prentice-Hall, 2003.
Hall, A.: "The Information Matrix Test for the Linear Model", The Review of Economic Studies, 54(1987), 257–263.
Hamilton, J. D.: Time Series Analysis. Princeton, New Jersey: Princeton University Press, 1994.
Hanley, J. A., and B. J. McNeil: "The Meaning and Use of the Area under a Receiver Operating Characteristic (ROC) Curve", Radiology, 143(1982), 29–36.
Harrell, F. E.: Regression modeling strategies : with applications to linear models, logistic regression, and survival analysis. New York: Springer, 2001.
Hastie, T., R. Tibshirani, and J. Friedman: The Elements of Statistical Learning: Data Mining, Inference, and Prediction. Springer Series in, Statistics, 2009.
Hastie, T. J., and R. J. Tibshirani: "Generalized additive models", Statistical Science, 3(1986), 297–318.
Hastie, T. J., and R. J. Tibshirani: Generalized Additive Models. Chapman & Hall/CRC, 1990.
Henley, S. S., R. M. Golden, T. M. Kashner, and H. White: "Exploiting Hidden Structures in Epidemiological Data: Phase II Project", (R44AA011607) National Institute on Alcohol Abuse and Alcoholism, 2000. http://www.sbir.gov/sbirsearch/detail/223679
Henley, S. S., R. M. Golden, T. M. Kashner, H. White, and R. D. Katz: "Improving Validity Measures for Alcohol-Related Models: Phase I Project", (R43AA013351) National Institute on Alcohol Abuse and Alcoholism, 2001. http://www.sbir.gov/sbirsearch/detail/223681
Henley, S. S., R. M. Golden, T. M. Kashner, H. White, and R. D. Katz: "Robust Classification Methods for Categorical Regression: Phase I Project", (R43AA014302) National Institute on Alcohol Abuse and Alcoholism, 2003. http://www.sbir.gov/sbirsearch/detail/223689
Henley, S. S., R. M. Golden, T. M. Kashner, H. White, and D. Paik: "Robust Classification Methods for Categorical Regression: Phase II Project", (R44CA139607) National Cancer Institute, 2008. http://www.sbir.gov/sbirsearch/detail/223709
Henley, S. S., R. M. Golden, T. M. Kashner, H. White, L. Xuan, D. Paik, and R. D. Katz: "Improving Validity Measures in Alcohol-Related Models: Phase II Project", (R44AA013351) National Institute on Alcohol Abuse and Alcoholism, 2004. http://www.sbir.gov/sbirsearch/detail/223693

Hilbe, J. M.: Logistic Regression Models. New York: Chapman and Hall, 2009.
Horowitz, J.L.: "Bootstrap-based critical values for the information matrix test", Journal of Econometrics, 61(1994), 395–411.
Horowitz, J.L.: "The bootstrap in econometrics", Statistical Science, 18(2003), 211–218.
Hosmer, D. W., T. Hosmer, S. LeCessie, and S. Lemeshow: "A comparison of goodness-of-fit tests for the logistic regression model", Statistics in Medicine, 16(1997), 965–980.
Hosmer, D. W., and S. Lemeshow: "A goodness-of-fit test for the multiple logistic regression model", Communication in Statistics, A10(1980), 1043–1069.
Hosmer, D. W., and S. Lemeshow: Applied Logistic Regression. New York: John Wiley & Sons, 2000.
Hosmer, D. W., S. Lemeshow, and J. Klar: "Goodness-of-Fit Testing for Multiple Logistic Regression Analysis when the Estimated Probabilities are Small", Biometrical Journal, 30(1988), 1–14.
Hosmer, D. W., S. Taber, and S. Lemeshow: "The importance of assessing the fit of logistic regression models: a case study", American Journal of Public Health, 81(1991), 1630–1635.
Huber, P.: "The behavior of maximum likelihood estimates under non-standard conditions", University of California Press, 1967.
Kashner, T. M., T. J. Carmody, T. Suppes, A. J. Rush, M. L. Crismon, A. L. Miller, M. Toprac, and M. Trivedi: "Catching up on health outcomes: The Texas Medication Algorithm Project", Health Services Research, 38(2003), 311–331.
Kashner, T. M., S. S. Henley, R. M. Golden, J. M. Byrne, S. A. Keitz, G. W. Cannon, B. K. Chang, G. J. Holland, D. C. Aron, E. A. Muchmore, A. Wicker, and H. White: "Studying the Effects of ACGME Duty Hours Limits on Resident Satisfaction: Results From VA Learners' Perceptions Survey", Academic Medicine, 85(2010), 1130–1139.
Kashner, T. M., S. S. Henley, R. M. Golden, A. J. Rush, and R. B. Jarrett: "Assessing the preventive effects of cognitive therapy following relief of depression: A methodological innovation", Journal of Affective Disorders, 104(2007), 251–261.
Kashner, T. M., R. Rosenheck, A. B. Campinell, A. Suris, and C. W. T. S. Team: "Impact of work therapy on health status among homeless, substance-dependent veterans - A randomized controlled trial", Archives of General Psychiatry, 59(2002), 938–944.
Konishi, S., and G. Kitagawa: "Generalized information criteria in model selection", Biometrika, 83(1996), 875–890.
Kuss, O.: "Global goodness-of-fit tests in logistic regression with sparse data", Statistics in Medicine, 21(2002), 3789–3801.
Lancaster, T.: "The Covariance Matrix of the Information Matrix Test", Econometrica, 52(1984), 1051–1054.
Lehmann, E. L.: "Model specification: The views of Fisher and Neyman, and later developments", Statistical Science, 5(1990), 160–168.
Maddala, G. S.: Limited-dependent and Qualitative Variables in Econometrics. New York: Cambridge, 1999.
Magnus, J. R.: "On differentiating eigenvalues and eigenvectors", Econometric Theory, 1(1985), 179–191.
Magnus, J. R., and H. Neudecker: Matrix Differential Calculus with Applications in Statistics and Econometrics. New York: John Wiley & Sons, 1999.
McCullagh, P.: "On the asymptotic distribution of Pearson's statistic in linear exponential family models", International Statistical Review, 53(1985), 61–67.
McCullagh, P., and J. A. Nelder: Generalized linear models. New York: Chapman and Hall, 1989.
Orme, C.: "The Calculation of the Information Matrix Test for Binary Data Models", The Manchester School, 56(1988), 370–376.
Orme, C.: "The small-sample performance of the information-matrix test", Journal of Econometrics, 46(1990), 309–331.
Osius, G., and D. Rojek: "Normal goodness-of-fit tests for multinomial models with large degrees-of-freedom", Journal of the American Statistical Association, 87(1992), 1145–1152.

Pepe, M. S.: The Statistical Evaluation of Medical Tests for Classification and Prediction. Oxford: Oxford University Press, 2004.
Politis, D. N., J. P. Romano, and M. Wolf: Subsampling. New York: Springer, 1999.
Qin, J., and B. Zhang: "A goodness-of-fit test for logistic regression models based on case-control data", Biometrika, 84(1997), 609–618.
Raudenbush, S. W., and A. S. Bryk: Hierarchical Linear Models: Applications and Data Analysis Methods. Thousand Oaks, CA: Sage Publications, Inc., 2002.
Sarkar, S. K., and H. Midi: "Importance of assessing the model adequacy of binary logistic regression", Journal of Applied Sciences, 10(2010), 479–486.
Serfling, R. J.: Approximation theorems of mathematical statistics. New York: John Wiley & Sons, 1980.
Stomberg, C., and H. White: "Bootstrapping the Information Matrix Test", University of California, San Diego Department of Economics Discussion Paper, 2000.
Stukel, T.A.: "Generalized logistic models", Journal of the American Statistical Association, 83(1988), 426–431.
Takeuchi, K.: "Distribution of information statistics and a criterion of model fitting for adequacy of models", Mathematical Sciences, 153(1976), 12–18.
Taylor, L.W.: "The Size Bias of White's Information Matrix Test", Economics Letters, 24(1987), 63–67.
Tsay, R.S.: Analysis of Financial Time Series. New York: John Wiley & Sons, 2010.
Tsiatis, A.A.: "A Note on a goodness-of-fit test for the logistic regression model", Biometrika, 67(1980), 250–251.
Verbeke, G., and E. Lesaffre: "The effect of misspecifying the random-effects distribution in linear mixed models for longitudinal data", Computational Statistics and Data Analysis, 23(1997), 541–556.
Vuong, Q.H.: "Likelihood ratio tests for model selection and non-nested hypotheses", Econometrica, 57(1989).
Wald, A.: "Tests of Statistical Hypotheses Concerning Several Parameters When the Number of Observations is Large", Transactions of the American Mathematical Society, 54(1943), 426–482.
Wei, B.: Exponential Family Nonlinear Models. New York: Springer, 1998.
White, H.: "Using least squares to approximate unknown regression functions", International Economic Review, 21(1980), 149–170.
White, H.: "Consequences and detection of misspecified nonlinear regression models", Journal of the American Statistical Association, 76(1981), 419–433.
White, H.: "Maximum Likelihood Estimation of Misspecified Models", Econometrica, 50(1982), 1–25.
White, H.: "Specification Testing in Dynamic Models", Cambridge University Press, 1987.
White, H.: Estimation, inference, and specification analysis. Cambridge: Cambridge University Press, 1994.
Wickens, T.D.: Elementary Signal Detection Theory. New York: Oxford University Press, 2002.
Winkler, G.: Image Analysis, Random Fields, and Dynamic Monte Carlo Methods. New York: Springer-Verlag, 1991.
Zhang, B.: "A chi-squared goodness-of-fit test for logistic regression models based on case-control data", Biometrika, 86(1999), 531–539.
Zhang, B.: "An information matrix test for logistic regression models based on case-control data", Biometrika, 88(2001), 921–932.

Bayesian Analysis and Model Selection of GARCH Models with Additive Jumps

Christian Haefke and Leopold Sögner

Abstract This article investigates parameter estimation and model selection of GARCH models with additive jumps. Continuous noise is driven by Student-t innovations. Since the likelihood is not available in closed form, Bayesian simulation methods are applied to estimate the model parameters and perform model selection. Simulations suggest that the parameters of the jump process are difficult to estimate. Informative priors based on sample moments and tests on jumps are necessary to obtain reliable parameter estimates. In an application using S&P 500returns we estimate a 3 % jump intensity. In addition, our model allows us to infer the impact of a jump on future volatility. Our estimates show that the impact of jumps on the conditional volatility is large compared to the impact of continuous innovations.

Keywords GARCH · Additive jumps · Bayes factors · Model selection

1 Introduction

One of the recent challenges in modeling the volatility of asset returns is whether jumps are present in the time series and how—if there are any jumps—such drastic changes propagate forward into the asset's volatility. The literature on this topic (Sakata and White 1998; Harvey and Chakravarty 2008) suggests that jumps have no or only small impact on future volatility such that standard GARCH settings tend to overestimate the effect of jumps on volatility. The goal of this chapter is to estimate the effect of jumps on future volatility in a univariate GARCH specification.

C. Haefke (✉) · L. Sögner
Department of Economics and Finance, Institute for Advanced Studies,
Stumpergasse 56, 1060 Vienna, Austria
e-mail: Christian.haefke@ihs.ac.at

L. Sögner
e-mail: soegner@ihs.ac.at

X. Chen and N. R. Swanson (eds.), *Recent Advances and Future Directions in Causality, Prediction, and Specification Analysis*, DOI: 10.1007/978-1-4614-1653-1_7,

In addition, we perform Bayesian model selection to test whether a model with jumps is superior to a model without jumps.

Most models in the mathematical finance literature use Brownian motion to model asset returns. To account for drastic changes a jump component is included (see e.g. Duffie et al. 2000; Barndorff-Nielsen and Shephard 2001; Lamberton and Lapeyre 2008). Multivariate extensions with jumps in the return process and/or the underlying volatility process have been developed in recent years (see e.g. Aït-Sahalia et al. 2009; Barndorff-Nielsen and Stelzer 2009; Mayerhofer et al. 2010 etc.). Tests and evidence for jumps in financial time series, mostly constructed for high frequency data, have been provided e.g. in Barndorff-Nielsen and Shephard (2006), Andersen et al. (2007), Lee and Mykland (2008) and Corsi et al. (2008). With respect to GARCH models Grossi (2004) developed tools to detect jumps (which are outliers in this framework). Based on Engle (2002) and Engle and Gallo (2003), Hansen et al. (2010) proposed a GARCH setting which provides a nice mixture between the strengths of GARCH models and realized volatility estimates, where the realized volatility estimates enter into the conditional volatility term of a GARCH model. By this setting high degrees of persistence of GARCH conditional volatilities—already discussed in Andersen et al. (2003, 2007)—can be substituted for by a much smaller degree of serial correlation of the GARCH volatility term and a strong dependence on the realized volatility. The parameter estimates verify this claim.

Our setting approaches the modeling of jumps in a different way. Without working with high frequency data to estimate the realized volatility, a naïve estimate of the realized volatility is already given by the last squared return. The effect of this term is already included in usual GARCH settings. To overcome the potential problem of less persistence of the conditional GARCH volatility with respect to extreme events, we shall follow Boudt et al. (2011) and work with a setting with additive jumps (*bounded innovation propagation* GARCH). Other settings with jumps have been constructed in Duan et al. (2006, 2007).

For models with additive jumps estimation procedures taking care of outliers can be adapted. Usually, robust estimation is performed with a quasi maximum likelihood procedure where some down-weighting is applied to extreme events. Such estimators have been derived e.g. in Charles and Darn (2005), Muler and Yohai (2008) and Boudt and Croux (2010). Gran and Veiga (2010) use wavelet transforms to account for outliers. In contrast to these articles, our chapter explicitly specifies the distribution of jumps, performs an exact Bayesian analysis (alternatively the EM algorithm could be used in this setting), and—in contrast to robust estimation—allows us to study whether jumps impact future volatility differently than continuous innovations. Potentially, we can estimate the jump intensity, the distribution of the jump sizes and in addition, the posterior distribution of the latent jump process.

In this article, the continuous innovations follow an asymmetric t-distribution as applied in Mittnik and Paolella (2000) and Bauwens and Laurent (2005). The t-distribution is more flexible than the normal distribution to model tail behavior. Since financial returns are known for their fat tails, a model with t-distributions allows for parsimonious models with accurate fit in the tails, which is important for all kinds of risk management. To speed up computations we extend the results of Giacomini et al. (2008)—who provided closed form solutions for mixtures of cumulative distribution functions and quantiles for the Student t-distribution—to skew extensions of the t-distribution. Identification, however, is difficult to show for the general case, and we therefore restrict ourselves to mixtures of t-distributions with exogenously specified degrees of freedom. Yu and Daal (2005) claimed that an asymmetric t-model (of Hansen type) outperforms a jumps setting in the univariate case.

Parameter estimation is performed by means of Bayesian simulation techniques. Although the likelihood is not fully available in closed form, the likelihood conditional on the latent jump process will be given by an asymmetric t-distribution. This allows us to apply data augmentation (Tanner and Wong 1987) with the goal of simulating the joint posterior distribution of the model parameters and the latent processes.

We propose Bayesian model selection to test whether additive jumps play a significant role. Therefore, we are going to develop an algorithm to calculate Bayes factors (posterior odds-ratios) by means of importance sampling techniques (here we follow Frühwirth-Schnatter 2004, 2006). The latent jump process will be integrated out by means of particle filtering techniques recently developed in Shephard and Pitt (1999), Doucet and Johansen (2008) and Andrieu et al. (2010). The MCMC sampler successfully selects models for simulated data. When applied to S&P 500returns for the time span 11/2007–9/2009 the estimated number of jumps is between 9 and 16. Identified jumps differ from large innovations with respect to their persistence on future return volatility.

This chapter is organized as follows: Sect. 2 introduces and extends multivariate GARCH settings. Section 3 investigates parameter estimation in a Bayesian framework, while Sect. 4 describes Bayesian model selection. Then Sect. 5 applies our methodology to simulated and empirical data. Section 6 concludes.

2 A GARCH Setting with Additive Jumps

Consider a risky asset with one period—mean adjusted—net returns of r_n, $n = 1, \ldots, N$, that follow a GARCH process with additive jumps $J_n \in \mathrm{R}$:

$$\begin{aligned} r_n &= \sqrt{h_n} e_n + J_n \\ h_n &= A_0 + \sum_{j'=1}^{p} A_{j'}(r_{n-j'} - J_{n-j'})^2 + \sum_{j=1}^{q} B_j h_{n-j} + C J_{n-1}^2. \end{aligned} \qquad (1)$$

Let h_n describe the conditional volatility and e_n be a standardized iid noise term with absolutely continuous density. Fat tails for e_n will be modeled by means of t-distributed innovations. A_0 accounts for the level, $A_{j'}$ for the dependence of h_n on past realizations of $E_n = (r_n - J_n)^2 = h_n e_n^2$. Equation (1) implies that $E_n = r_n^2$ in the absence of jumps, which corresponds to the basic GARCH setting. While with a standard GARCH model (i.e. zero J and C), any $J_{n-1} \neq 0$ enters into h_n via r_{n-1}^2, the specification in (1) distinguishes between the impact of the "continuous" component e_n on asset volatility h_n and the impacts of jumps. The persistence of the volatility h_n is described by B_j while C captures the effect of jumps on h_n. To keep things simple—and in line with the later application where we restrict ourselves to $p = q = 1$—only J_{n-1} but no higher order lags are included in (1). The parameters are collected in the vector θ.

To allow for drastic changes in the yields, we include the jump component J_n by following Boudt et al. (2011) who introduced additive jumps in a GARCH setting. Their motivation for additive jumps was the observation of a short run impact of extreme returns on the future return. Our approach differs with respect to their model by including J_{n-1} in the conditional volatility function h_n. From a quantitative finance point of view, C measures how jumps propagate forward into volatility. If $C = 0$ then jumps have no memory. In addition since $A_{j'} \neq C$, different decays of different innovations in the volatility equation are allowed.

The econometric challenge is to estimate the model parameters θ. Note that, h_n depends on $E_0, E_1, \ldots, E_{n-1}$ and $J_0, J_1, \ldots, J_{n-1}$. Neither E_n nor J_n are observable which complicates the econometric analysis. Let us start a description of the *continuous noise* term e_n. Let ε_n follow an asymmetric t-distribution (see Mittnik and Paolella 2000; Bauwens and Laurent 2005) with density function $\pi_{\mathcal{T}}(\varepsilon_n|\nu, \zeta)$. As described in Appendix A this distribution has mean μ_e and variance $\sigma_e^2 > 0$ which depends on the degrees of freedom ν and the non-centrality parameter ζ. With $\zeta = 1$ we obtain a standard t-distribution with mean zero and variance $\nu/(\nu - 2)$; if $\zeta = 1$ we shall use the notation $\pi_{\mathcal{T}}(.|\nu)$. e_n is a standardized variable such that

$$e_n = \frac{\varepsilon_n - \mu_e}{\sigma_e}. \tag{2}$$

Appendix A provides more details on this distribution and extends the derivation of a closed form solution for the cumulative distribution function by Giacomini et al. (2008). Throughout the chapter, we assume that the fourth moment of e_n exists, which is guaranteed by the assumption $\nu > 4$. Summing up, the continuous noise part is described by the density

$$\pi(e_n|\theta) = \pi(e_n|\nu, \zeta, \mu_e, \sigma_e^2) = \sigma_e \pi_{\mathcal{T}}(\varepsilon_n|\nu, \zeta). \tag{3}$$

The *jumps* are constructed by means of

$$J_n = Y_n S_n. \tag{4}$$

The jump indicator Y_n equals one in the case of a jump in period n, otherwise it is zero. Following Duan et al. (2006, 2007) we use normal jump sizes. S_n is *iid* normal with mean zero and variance σ_J^2. For notational convenience define $r^N = (r_1, \ldots, r_n, \ldots, r_N)$, $Y^N = (Y_1, \ldots, Y_N)$, and $S^N = (S_1, \ldots, S_N)$.

Jump times and jump sizes are jointly independent. Each Y_n follows a Bernoulli distribution with probability $p_\lambda := 1 - \exp(-\lambda)$.[1] Hence $\pi(Y^N|\theta) = \prod_{n=1}^N p_\lambda^{\mathbf{1}_{\{Y_n=1\}}} (1-p_\lambda)^{\mathbf{1}_{\{Y_n=0\}}}$. S_n is normal with mean zero and variance σ_J^2. This yields

$$\pi(S_n|Y_n, \theta) = \mathbf{1}_{\{Y_n=1\}} \pi_{\mathcal{N}}(S_n|(0, \sigma_J^2)) + \mathbf{1}_{\{Y_n=0\}} \delta_{S_n=0}(S_n),$$
$$\pi(S^N|Y^N, \theta) = \prod_{n=1}^N \pi(S_n|Y_n, \theta) \tag{5}$$

$$\pi(Y^N|\theta) = \prod_{n=1}^N p_\lambda^{\mathbf{1}_{\{Y_n=1\}}} (1-p_\lambda)^{\mathbf{1}_{\{Y_n=0\}}} \text{and}$$
$$g(J^N|\theta) = \pi(S^N, Y^N|\theta) = \pi(S^N|Y^N, \theta)\pi(Y^N|\theta) \tag{6}$$

where $\pi_{\mathcal{N}}(.)$ stands for a standard normal density, $\delta_{S_n=0}(S_n)$ is the Dirac mass at $S_n = 0$, i.e., equal to one at $S_n = 0$ and zero elsewhere. The parameters θ consist of: ν, ζ (parameters of skewed-Student t-distributions), A_0, $A_{j'}$, B_j and C, with $j' = 1, \ldots, p$, $j = 1, \ldots, q$ (GARCH parameters) and the jump parameters λ and σ_J^2.

3 Parameter Estimation

For the model structure described in Sect. 2 Bayes' Theorem results in

$$\pi(r_n|r^{n-1}, \theta) \propto \pi(r_n|r^{n-1}, J^n, \theta) g(J^n|\theta)\pi(\theta). \tag{7}$$

Conditional on the current and past realizations of the jump process we derive

$$e_n = (h_n)^{-1/2}(r_n - J_n) \tag{8}$$

such that the *conditional density* of the returns is given by

$$\pi(r_n|r^{n-1}, J^n, \theta) = \frac{1}{|\det(h_n)^{1/2}|} \cdot \pi_e(e_n|\theta) = \frac{1}{|\sqrt{h_n}|} \cdot \sigma_e \pi_{\mathcal{T}}(\varepsilon_n|\nu, \zeta). \tag{9}$$

We get the joint density of returns and jumps by means of

[1] $\sum_{n=1}^N \mathbf{1}_{\{Y_n=1\}}$ follows binomial distribution with parameters N and $p_\lambda = 1 - \exp(\lambda)$.

$$\pi(r_n, J_n|r^{n-1}, J^{n-1}, \theta) = \pi(r_n, |r^{n-1}, J_n, J^{n-1}, \theta)g(J_n|\theta)$$
$$= \frac{1}{|\sqrt{h_n}|} \cdot \sigma_e \pi_{\mathcal{T}}(\varepsilon_n|\nu, \zeta)g(J_n|\theta)$$
$$\pi(r^N, J^N|r_0, J_0, e_0, h_0, \theta) = \Pi_{n=1}^N \pi(r_n, J_n|r^{n-1}, J^{n-1}, \theta). \quad (10)$$

Note that, if $C = 0$ then $\pi(r_n, |r^{n-1}, J^n, \theta)$ depends on J_n only, while for $C \neq 0$ this density depends of the whole history of J_n. That is to say we need the initial values $X_0 = (h_0, J_0, r_0)$ to reconstruct h_n. The distribution of the jumps J^n is given by densities already described by (5) and (6).

Posterior distribution. Although the density

$$\pi(r^N|\theta) = \int \left(\Pi_{n=1}^N \pi(r_n, S_n, Y_n|r^{n-1}, S^{n-1}, Y^{n-1}, X_0, \theta)\right) d\pi(S^n, Y^n, X_0) \quad (11)$$

is not available in closed from, the structure in (7) is sufficient to perform an exact Bayesian analysis. Given priors for the parameters θ and the initial values X_0, the joint posterior is given by Bayes' Theorem:

$$\pi(\theta, S^N, Y^N, X_0|r^N) \propto \pi(r^N|S^N, Y^N, X_0, \theta)\pi(S^N, Y^N|\theta)\pi(\theta, X_0)$$

where the jumps are parameterized by Y^N and S^N. The initial values X_0 are required to calculate h_1 (see (1)). If p or q are larger than one, then X_0 has to be adapted to the dimension required by the model. The set of augmented parameters consisting of θ, Y^N, S^N, and X_0 is collected in Ψ. Although not available in closed form, the log-likelihood $\ell(\theta; r^N)$ would be given by the log of Eq. (11) evaluated at the data r^N, while

$$\ell(\theta; r^N|S^N, Y^N) = \log \pi(r^N|S^N, Y^N, X_0, \theta) \quad (12)$$

will be called the *partial likelihood* in the following.

Prior distribution. To derive the joint posterior (12), we have to specify our prior $\pi(\theta, X_0)$. We assume that this prior factorizes into $\pi(\theta)\pi(Y_0, S_0|\theta)\pi(h_0)\pi(r_0)$. We put a Gamma prior ($\pi_{\mathcal{G}}(.|1, 1)$) on h_0, while for r_0 and S_0 we use a normal prior with mean zero and variance 1000. For Y_0 we use a Bernoulli distribution with probability $p_\lambda = 1 - \exp(-\lambda)$.

$\pi(\theta)$ is the prior for the parameters ν, ζ, λ, σ_J^2, A_0, $A_{j'}$, B_j and C, with $j' = 1, \ldots, p$ and $j = 1, \ldots, q$. ν is fixed at $\nu = 8$ and will not be estimated.[2] For the parameters λ and σ_J^2 informative priors based on sample moments and a priori running a Lee and Mykland (2008) jump test have been used. For more details see Appendix C. For λ we use a truncated normal prior $\pi_{\mathcal{TN}}(.|\lambda_0, \Lambda_0, \underline{\lambda}, \bar{\lambda})$. The left

[2] Sampling ν (with a truncated gamma distribution with truncation value 4, accounting for $\nu > 4$) resulted in a very poor performance of the sampler, the standard deviation of ν was high. This was observed in a model with and without jumps, respectively. Also maximum likelihood estimation in a model without jumps but with ν not fixed resulted in weak performance of the estimation procedure.

Table 1 Overview MCMC sampling

Step 1	sample $A_0, A_{j'}, B_j, C$	from $\pi(A_0, A_{j'}, B_j, C\|r^N, Y^N, S^N, X_0, \theta_{(-)})$
Step 2	sample λ, σ_J^2	from $\pi(\lambda, \sigma_J^2\|r^N, Y^N, S^N, X_0, \theta_{(-)})$
Step 3	sample ζ	from $\pi(\zeta\|r^N, Y^N, S^N, X_0, , \theta_{(-)})$
Step 4	sample Y^N, S^N	from $\pi(Y^N, S^N\|r^N, X_0, \theta)$
Step 5	sample X_0	from $\pi(X_0\|r^N, Y^N, S^N, \theta)$

MCMC Bayesian sampling of the augmented parameters Ψ is performed in five steps. $\theta_{(-)}$ always stands for the remaining parameters. After a burn-in phase, Steps 1–5 provide us with the samples Ψ^{v}, $\mathrm{v} = 1, \ldots, \mathrm{V}$, from the posterior

boundary, $\underline{\lambda}$ of this distribution is specified as one quarter of the jump probability obtained by the Lee and Mykland (2008) test. $\bar{\lambda}$ is set to 0.25, to prevent too frequent jumps.[3] Based on simulation evidence for our sample sizes we note that the Lee and Mykland (2008) test underestimates the number of jumps arising from our GARCH model approximately by a factor of two. Therefore, the location parameter λ_0 is set to two times the number of jumps inferred by the test, which turns out to give a relatively good proxy for the true jump intensity. The variance parameter Λ_0 is fixed at 0.1. Appendix C uses the output of the jump test to construct a truncated normal prior for σ_J^2 in a similar way.

To ensure non-negativity of A_0, $A_{j'}$, B_j, and C the support of these parameters has been truncated at zero. In addition, we constructed a prior based on the $\hat{\theta}^{MLO} = (\hat{A}_0^{MLO}, \hat{A}_{j'}^{MLO}, \hat{B}_j^{MLO}, \hat{C}^{MLO})^\top$ obtained in the starting phase of the sampler. Step 1 below describes how $\hat{\theta}^{\mathrm{ML}}$ is obtained. Based on this we use a truncated normal prior with mean parameter $\hat{A}_0^{MLO}$ and variance parameter c_{A0}^2; the support of A_0 is R^+. In the same way, $\pi(A_{j'}) = \pi_{\mathcal{TN}}(A_{j'}|\hat{A}_{j'}^{MLO}, c_{A1}^2)$, $\pi(B_j) = \pi_{\mathcal{TN}}(B_j|\hat{B}_j^{MLO}, c_{B1}^2)$ and $\pi(C) = \pi_{\mathcal{TN}}(C|\hat{C}^{MLO}, c_{C1}^2)$. We set c_{A0}^2, c_{A1}^2, c_{B1}^2 and c_{C1}^2 all equal to 0.1. We assume $|A_1^2\mathbb{E}(e_n^4) + B_1^2| < 1$ which implies weak stationarity for $p, q = 1$.[4] For more details see the derivation in Appendix B. In addition, we use the second to fourth sample moments of the returns to construct an informative prior for the parameters θ. For more details see Appendix C (Table 1).

MCMC Step 1: Sampling of the MGARCH parameters A_0, $A_{j'}$, B_j and C

We propose from the maximizer $\hat{\theta}^{\mathrm{ML}} = (\hat{A}_0^{\mathrm{ML}}, \hat{A}_{j'}^{\mathrm{ML}}, \hat{B}_j^{\mathrm{ML}}, \hat{C}^{\mathrm{ML}})^\top$ of the conditional likelihood (12). Then $A_0^{new} = \hat{A}_0^{\mathrm{ML}} + c_{A0}\varepsilon$ with $\varepsilon \sim \pi_{\mathcal{N}}(.|0, 1)$ or $\log A_0^{new} = \log \hat{A}_0^{\mathrm{ML}} + c_{A0}\varepsilon$, etc. Then c_{A0}, c_{A1}, c_{B1} and c_{C1} used here corre-

[3] This can be thought of an identification assumption to disentangle the innovation variance and the jump intensity.

[4] The innovation e_n was defined in Eq. (2) as the standardized innovation to our GARCH model.

spond to the parameters in the prior. The updates of A_0 and B_q are performed in one block, the remaining parameters are updated in separate Metropolis Hastings steps.

MCMC Step 2: Sampling of the jump intensity and size parameters λ, σ_J^2

For both parameters we apply log-random walk proposals. In addition, we use the fact that for $Y_n = 1$, the setting corresponds to a regression model with innovation given by S_n. Based on this we get $c_S = \sum_{n=1}^N \mathbf{1}_{\{Y_n=1\}}$ and $C_S = \sum_{n=1}^N \mathbf{1}_{\{Y_n=1\}} S_n^2$, where σ_J^2 is now proposed from an inverse gamma distribution with parameters c_s, C_S. This proposal is then used in a Metropolis–Hastings sampler. The Metropolis–Hastings step becomes necessary, since non-conjugate priors are used for this parameter.

For the jump probability $\frac{1}{N}\sum_{n=1}^N \mathbf{1}_{\{Y_n=1\}} = \frac{1}{N}\sum_{n=1}^N Y_n$ can be used. In a Bayesian context, we know that based on the model assumptions Y_n follows a binomial distribution with probability $p_\lambda = 1 - \exp(-\lambda)$, such that with a conjugate Beta prior with parameters α_0, β_0, the conditional posterior is given by $p_\lambda \sim \pi_{\mathcal{B}}(.|\alpha_0 + \sum_{n=1}^N \mathbf{1}_{\{Y_n=1\}}, \beta_0 + N - \sum_{n=1}^N \mathbf{1}_{\{Y_n=1\}})$ (see Robert 1994, p. 104); $\pi_{\mathcal{B}}(.|.)$ stands for a beta-distribution. This distribution can be used to propose λ as follows: sample p_λ from the above $\pi_{\mathcal{B}}(.|.)$ distribution. λ follows from $\lambda = -\log(1 - p_\lambda)$, while the proposal density $q(\lambda)$ is given by the product of a beta-density with the above parameters and factor $\frac{1}{1-p_\lambda}$ arising from the density transformation formula.

MCMC Step 3: Sampling of the parameter driving the asymmetric t-distribution ζ

For ζ a log proposal based on $\hat{\zeta}^{\mathrm{ML}}$ has been applied.

MCMC Step 4: Sampling of the latent jump indicators and jump sizes Y^N, S^N

Jumps are proposed from filtered estimates. To see how this works, first suppose that $Y_n = 1$ for all n. Then we get from (1):

$$\begin{aligned} r_n &= \sqrt{h_n} e_n + S_n \\ S_n &= 0 \cdot S_{n-1} + \zeta_n, \end{aligned} \tag{13}$$

where $\zeta_n \sim \mathcal{N}(0, \sigma_J^2)$, such that (13) corresponds to a model in state space form. Given the parameters θ and X_0, filtered estimates of S_n can be derived by means of the Kalman filter. E.g., from Frühwirth-Schnatter (2006) (p. 404) we get:

1. Propagation step—derive the predictive density $\pi(S_n|r^{n-1}, Y^n = 1)$:

$$S_n|r^{n-1} \sim \mathcal{N}(x_{n|n-1}, P_{n|n-1}) \text{ with } x_{n|n-1} = 0, \quad P_{n|n-1} = \sigma_J^2. \tag{14}$$

2. Prediction step—derive the forecast density $\pi(r_n|r^{n-1}, Y^n = 1)$:

$$y_n|y^{n-1} \sim \mathcal{N}(y_{n|n-1}, C_{n|n-1}) \text{ with } y_{n|n-1} = 0, \quad C_{n|n-1} = h_n + \sigma_J^2. \tag{15}$$

3. Correction step—derive the filter density $\pi(S_n|r^n, Y^n = 1)$:

$$S_n|r^n \sim \mathcal{N}(x_{n|n}, P_{n|n}) \text{ with } x_{n|n} = K_n y_n,$$
$$K_n = \frac{\sigma_J^2}{\sigma_J^2 + h_n}, \quad P_{n|n} = \sigma_J^2(1 - K_n). \tag{16}$$

Based on the filter we propose S_n from a normal distribution with mean $x_{n|n}$ and variance $P_{n|n}$. It is also worth noting that running the filter is not as simple as it looks, since J_{n-1}^2 enters into h_n. Therefore, we have to start with X_0 and run this filter from $n = 1, \ldots, N$. In each of these steps h_n has to be recalculated.

Now that we understand the choice of the parameters for the jump size, consider (1) as a regime switching state space model with a degenerated state at $Y_n = 0$. In other words, we consider a switching model with $S_n \sim \mathcal{N}(0, \sigma_J^2)$ in state $Y_n = 1$ with probability $p_\lambda = 1 - \exp(-\lambda)$, and a degenerated state with $Y_n, S_n = 0$ with probability $1 - p_\lambda = \exp(-\lambda)$ yielding $r_n = \sqrt{h_n} e_n + Y_n S_n$.

By means of Bayes' Theorem, we are able to calculate the conditional probabilities of the state indicators Y_n (see e.g. Frühwirth-Schnatter 2006, p. 324):

$$\begin{aligned}
&\pi(Y_n = 1|r^n, Y^{n-1}, S_n, S^{n-1}, \theta) \\
&= \frac{\pi(r_n|Y^n = 1, S_n, S^{n-1}, r^{n-1}, X_0, \theta)(1 - \exp(-\lambda))}{\pi(r_n|S_n, S^{n-1}, Y^{n-1}, r^{n-1}, X_0, \theta)} \\
&\pi(r_n|S_n, S^{n-1}, Y^{n-1}, r^{n-1}, X_0, \theta) \\
&= \pi(r_n|Y_n = 1, Y^{n-1}, S_n, S^{n-1}, r^{n-1}, X_0, \theta)(1 - \exp(-\lambda)) \\
&\quad + \pi(r_n|Y^n = 0, Y^{n-1}, S_n, S^{n-1}, r^{n-1}, X_0, \theta)\exp(-\lambda).
\end{aligned} \tag{17}$$

Therefore, the jump sizes S_n are proposed from a normal distribution with mean $x_{n|n}$ and variance $P_{n|n}$. For each $n = 1 \ldots N$ we propose Y_n from a Bernoulli trial with probability $\pi(Y_n = 1|r^n, Y^{n-1}, S_n, S^{n-1}, \theta)$. This results in the proposal density $q(Y_n, S_n)$, $n = 1, \ldots, N$. Equipped with samples from $q(Y_n, S_n)$, the jump flags and sizes are updated by means of the Metropolis Hastings algorithm. If only a block from $n_0 \geq 1$ to $n_1 \leq N$ should be updated we proceed in the same way. The filtering procedure works particularly well if p_λ is close to the true jump probability. In the applied part, we mix between full updates of (Y_n, S_n), $n = 1, \ldots, N$ and updates of smaller blocks of mean block size ten.

MCMC Step 5: Sampling of the initial values r_0, h_0, Y_0, S_0

X_0 is proposed by means of a normal random walk proposal. Note that, all of r_0, h_0 and Y_0, S_0 enter into h_1, and therefore propagate forward by the autoregressive structure of h_n.

MCMC: General considerations and pre-sampling phase

Before the sampler is started at sweep $\mathrm{v} = 1$, we alter between a maximization step of the partial likelihood given J^N and sampling J^N as described in `Step 4`; ν, ζ, λ are kept fixed here. For λ we used λ_0, $\nu = 8$ while ζ was fixed at one. This presampling phase corresponds to a basic EM update of the parameters (see e.g. McLachlan and Krishnan 1997). After a few steps, this procedure already approaches the true parameters given that λ is initially chosen rather close to the true jump intensity. Therefore, the Lee and Mykland (2008) test of jumps is necessary to obtain good starting values for the jump intensity. In the Bayesian estimation starting after this initial phase, λ is not kept fixed but rather sampled as one of the parameters of the MCMC sampler.

4 Model Selection

Consider a finite set of models $\mathcal{M}$, with elements $\mathcal{M}_l$ and the corresponding parameters and augmented parameters, θ_l and Ψ_l, respectively. The marginal likelihood $\pi(r^N|\mathcal{M}_l)$ follows from Bayes' Theorem:

$$\log \pi(r^N|\mathcal{M}_l) = \log \pi(r^N|\theta_l, \mathcal{M}_l) + \log \pi(\theta_l|\mathcal{M}_l) - \log \pi(\theta_l|r^N, \mathcal{M}_l). \quad (18)$$

The prior of the parameters described in Sect. 3 for any fixed $\mathcal{M}_l \in \mathcal{M}$ is denoted by $\pi(\theta_l|\mathcal{M}_l)$ and $\pi(\theta_l|r^N, \mathcal{M}_l)$ is the posterior density of model $\mathcal{M}_l$ where jumps and initial values have already been integrated out. While the non-normalized posterior (12) was sufficient to construct a Bayesian sampler, all terms in (18) have to be densities. Since the normalized $\pi(\theta_l|r^N, \mathcal{M}_l)$ is not available in closed form, a numerical estimate of the model likelihood $\pi(r^N|\mathcal{M}_l)$ has to be constructed. To this end, we derive a numerical approximation of the integral

$$\pi(r^N|\mathcal{M}_l) = \int \left[\prod_{n=1}^{N} \pi(r^n|r^{n-1}, J^N, X_0, \theta)\right] d\pi(J^N, X_0, \theta). \quad (19)$$

This will be done in two steps: First, we integrate out the jumps J^N and the initial values X_0 given a fixed latent parameter θ_l^{i}. This provides us with the likelihood $\pi(r^N|\theta_l^{\mathrm{i}}, \mathcal{M}_l)$ evaluated at θ_l^{i}. In a second step, we integrate over θ_l. In the following paragraphs we skip the model index l.

From Bayes' Theorem we get

$$\pi(r_n|r^{n-1}, \theta) \propto \pi(r_n|r^{n-1}, Y^n, S^n, X_0, \theta)\pi(Y^n, S^n|\theta)\pi(X_0|\theta). \quad (20)$$

To derive $\pi(r^N|\theta) = \prod_n \pi(r_n|r^{n-1}, \theta)$ the latent process J^N—parameterized by $X_n = (Y_n, S_n)$—and the initial values X_0 are integrated out by means of particle filtering. The recent literature on particle filtering e.g. Flury and Shephard (2009), Omori et al. (2007), Malik and Pitt (2009), Chib (1995), Pitt and Shephard (1999), Shephard and Pitt (1999), Doucet and Johansen (2008), Chib and Jeliazkov (2001) and Andrieu et al. (2010) provides tools to do this integration step. We denote the importance density by $q_\theta(X_n^{\mathrm{k}}|r^n)$ and will specify it later.[5]

We use a filter based on standard importance sampling. With θ fixed at θ^{i}, the joint distribution of r^N, X_0 and X^N is given by:

$$\begin{aligned}\pi_{\theta^{\mathrm{i}}}(r^N, X_0, X^N) &= \pi_{\theta^{\mathrm{i}}}(X_0)\pi(X^N)\cdot\prod_{n=1}^{N}\pi_{\theta^{\mathrm{i}}}(r_n|r^{n-1}, X^n)\\ &= \pi_{\theta^{\mathrm{i}}}(X_0)\pi_{\theta^{\mathrm{i}}}(Y^N, S^N)\cdot\prod_{n=1}^{N}\pi_{\theta^{\mathrm{i}}}(r_n|r^{n-1}, Y^n, S^n, X_0). \quad (21)\end{aligned}$$

The joint density of X^N follows from (5), and $\pi_{\theta^{\mathrm{i}}}(r_n|r^{n-1}, X_n)$ is defined in Eq. (7).[6] We sample the particles k, $\mathrm{k} = 1, \ldots, \mathrm{K}$, as follows:
Step P1. Create particles for the initial values X_0:

(a) Sample $X_0^{\mathrm{k}} = (h_0^{\mathrm{k}}, r_0^{\mathrm{k}}, Y_0^{\mathrm{k}}, S_0^{\mathrm{k}})$ from $q_{\theta^{\mathrm{i}}}(X_0)$.
(b) $\pi_{\theta^{\mathrm{i}}}(X_0)$ is a prior on the initial values.
(c) Compute the ratio:

$$w_0(X^{0,\mathrm{k}}) = \frac{\pi_{\theta^{\mathrm{i}}}(X_0^{\mathrm{k}})}{q_{\theta^{\mathrm{i}}}(X_0^{\mathrm{k}})}\,. \quad (22)$$

Step P2. Sample particles X_n^{k}: for $n = 1, \ldots, N$:

(a) Sample X_n^{k} from $q_{\theta^{\mathrm{i}}}(X_n)$.
(b) Compute the ratio

$$w_N(X^{N,\mathrm{k}}) = \frac{\pi_{\theta^{\mathrm{i}}}(X^{N,\mathrm{k}})}{q_{\theta^{\mathrm{i}}}(X^{N,\mathrm{k}})}\prod_{n=1}^{N}\pi_{\theta^{\mathrm{i}}}(r_n|r^{n-1}, X^{n,\mathrm{k}})\,. \quad (23)$$

Step P3. An estimate of the *marginal* likelihood $\pi_{\theta^{\mathrm{i}}}(r^N)$ is now derived as:

$$\hat{\pi}_{\theta^{\mathrm{i}}}(r^N) = \frac{1}{\mathrm{K}}\sum_{\mathrm{k}=1}^{\mathrm{K}} w_N(X^{N,\mathrm{k}})w_0(X^{0,\mathrm{k}}). \quad (24)$$

Importance Densities. We know from the literature (Shephard and Pitt 1999; Doucet and Johansen 2008) that the best way to sample is to use $q_{\theta^{\mathrm{i}}}(X_n) = \pi_{\theta^{\mathrm{i}}}(X_n|r^n, X_{n-1})$. However, for our setting the normalizing constant of the conditional posterior $X_n|r^n, X^{n-1}$ is not available. Based on the MCMC output Ψ^{v},

[5] We also implemented a sequential importance sampling scheme as e.g. used in Andrieu et al. (2010); however this algorithm was too demanding from a computational point of view.

[6] With MCMC we derived samples from $\pi(\theta, X^N|r^N) \propto \pi(y^N, X^N|\theta)\pi(\theta)$, where θ is a random variable.

$\mathrm{v} = 1, \ldots, \mathrm{V}$, we get an estimate of the jump probabilities $\hat{p}_{\lambda,n}$ by calculating the fractions Y_n^{v}/V. The sample means of S_n^{v}, $n = 1, \ldots, N$, result in $\hat{S}_n$, the estimates of sample variances are $\hat{s}_n^2$. Based on these estimates the particles Y_n^{k} are sampled from a Bernoulli distribution with a parameter $\breve{p}_{\lambda,n} := \max\{p_{\min}, \min\{p_{\max}, \hat{p}_{\lambda,n}\}\}$, for $n = 1, \ldots, N$ where $p_{\min} = 0.02$ and $p_{\max} = 0.98$. This results in $Y^{N,\mathrm{k}}$. For the jump sizes we sample S_n^{k} from a Student t-distribution with ten degrees of freedom; the level and variance are given by $\hat{S}_n$ and $\breve{s}_n^2 = \max\{0.01, \hat{s}_n^2\}$. We sample from a Student-t distribution to apply importance densities with sufficiently strong tails as required in Robert and Casella (1999) (p. 84) and the literature cited there. Similar to (5) we derive the proposal density $q_{\theta^{\mathrm{i}}}(Y^{N,\mathrm{k}}, S^{N,\mathrm{k}})$. The conditional distribution of $S^{N,\mathrm{k}}|Y^{N,\mathrm{k}}$ is given by $\prod_{n=1}^{N} \mathbf{1}_{\{Y_n^{\mathrm{k}}=1\}} \frac{1}{\sqrt{\breve{s}_n^2}} \pi_{\mathcal{T}}\left((S_n^{\mathrm{k}} - \hat{S}_n)/\sqrt{\breve{s}_n^2}|10\right) + \mathbf{1}_{\{Y_n^{\mathrm{k}}=0\}} \delta_{S_n^{\mathrm{k}}=0}$, where $\pi_{\mathcal{T}}(.|10)$ stands for a standard Student-t density with 10 degrees of freedom. The assumption of a Bernoulli distribution implies $q_\theta(Y_n^{\mathrm{k}})$ such that $q_\theta(Y^{N,\mathrm{k}}) = \prod_{n=1}^{N} q_\theta(Y_n^{\mathrm{k}}) = \prod_{n=1}^{N} \breve{p}_{\lambda,n}^{\mathbf{1}_{\{Y_n^{\mathrm{k}}=1\}}} (1 - \breve{p}_{\lambda,n})^{\mathbf{1}_{\{Y_n^{\mathrm{k}}=0\}}}$. This provides us with the proposal densities of $X^{N,\mathrm{k}}$. For $q_{\theta^{\mathrm{i}}}(X_0)$ we used the MCMC means and variances of this parameters and sample from t-distributions with the same level and scale parameter.

Model Likelihood. Last but not least, we calculate the model likelihood $\pi(r^N|M_l)$, by following some arguments in Malik and Pitt (2009). With the above particle filter we are already equipped with samples from $\pi(r^N|\theta_l^{\mathrm{i}}, M_l)$, which are $\pi_{\theta^{\mathrm{i}}}(r^N)$ for some fixed θ_l^{i}, $i = 1, \ldots, I$; l is the model index while i is a sample index. By means of importance sampling we sample an estimate of $\pi(r^N|M_l)$. $\pi(r^N|M_l) = \int \pi(r^N|\theta_l, \mathcal{M}_l) d\pi(\theta_l|\mathcal{M}_l)$, where $\pi(\theta_l|\mathcal{M}_l)$ is the prior in (18). By choosing an importance density $q(\theta|\mathcal{M}_l)$ we get the samples θ_l^{i}, $\mathrm{i} = 1, \ldots, \mathrm{I}$, and an estimate of the model likelihood

$$\hat{\pi}(r^N|\mathcal{M}_l) = \frac{1}{\mathrm{I}} \sum_{\mathrm{i}=1}^{\mathrm{I}} \frac{\pi(r^N|\theta_l^{\mathrm{i}}, \mathcal{M}_l)\pi(\theta_l^{\mathrm{i}}|\mathcal{M}_l)}{q(\theta_l^{\mathrm{i}}|\mathcal{M}_l)} . \tag{25}$$

Each $\pi(r^N|\theta_l^{\mathrm{i}}, \mathcal{M}_l)$ can now be estimated by Steps P1–P3.

5 Performance in Simulated and Empirical Data

5.1 Simulated Data

The objective of this exercise is to test the performance of the Bayesian sampler in a controlled environment similar to the data we are later going to use. Based on maximum likelihood estimates of a standard GARCH(1,1) model ($N = 500$ observations of S&P 500returns; November 2007–September 2009; parameter estimates in Table 2) we therefore pick the model parameters for the simulation to be $A_0 = 0.006$, $A_1 = 0.07$, $B_1 = 0.9$, and $\nu = 8$. In addition to these parameters we add a jump

Table 2 Maximum likelihood estimate for a GARCH(1,1)

ML estimates of S&P 500returns			
	MLE	SE	p-value
A_0	0.0064	0.0025	0.0102
A_1	0.0692	0.0096	<0.001
B_1	0.9284	0.0090	<0.001
ν	7.8708	1.1353	<0.001

Data are mean adjusted S&P 500returns from November 2007 to September 2009. $N = 500$ observations. MLE stands for the maximum likelihood estimate of the corresponding parameter, SE for the standard errors

component with an intensity $\lambda = 0.05$ and a jump size parameter of $\sigma_J^2 = 4$. The parameter C was set to 0.2 while $\zeta = 1$.

We use model (1) to generate series of $N = 500$ observations each. Table 3 presents typical output from the Bayesian sampler. The results presented in this table are descriptive statistics derived from the samples of the posterior Ψ^{v}, $\mathrm{v} = 1, \ldots, \mathrm{V}$, obtained by means of the Monte Carlo methods described in Sect. 3. IEF stands for the Chib (2001) inefficiency factor, which provides a measure of how many samples have to be generated by the Markov chain compared to a situation where we would be able to draw independent samples from the posterior. Although IEF is not low with our sampler, we observe that using the filter based updates of the jumps and proposals of the parameters based on a maximum likelihood routine results in fast convergence and stable sampling properties. The application of the filtered jump times and sizes and proposals based on maximizing the partial likelihood by far outperformed the other alternatives [e.g. a "regression based proposal" used in Kaufmann and Frühwirth-Schnatter (2002) or random walk proposals]. Although these two sampling steps are computationally demanding, they are very important to get reasonable parameter estimates—in addition convergence of the sampler is fast when using these tools.

To check the convergence properties of the sampler we checked/observed the following: With simulated data, we observed that our hybrid sampler starting with an EM type pre-sampling phase combined with the application of the Bayesian sampler as described in Sect. 3 quite rapidly arrives at samples concentrated around the true parameter values. In addition, we checked whether the sampler produces multimodal posteriors; however, this was not the case. Moreover, we compared the posterior distributions produced by the sampler when starting it with the same data with a different seed and different starting values. Here, the histograms from the posterior-samples are close to each other. In addition, we implemented the Gelman and Rubin (1992) test and its modified version in Brooks and Gelman (1998), the Geweke (1991) convergence diagnostic as well as the Geweke (1991) convergence diagnostic applied to the likelihood as proposed by Cowles and Carlin (1996). We observe that the Gelman and Rubin (1992) and Brooks and Gelman (1998) criterion based on comparing MCMC output of different chains is always passed. With the Geweke (1991) procedure we obtain reasonable results in most cases, however, as already pointed out by Cowles and Carlin (1996) the results of this test is sensitive

Table 3 Estimation results for simulated data with jumps

Data generated from model with jumps									
	true	mean	sd	min	max	Q(0.025)	median	Q(0.975)	IEF
Parameter estimates for model without jumps									
A_0	0.0060	0.0456	0.0265	0.0080	0.0981	0.0080	0.0470	0.0865	45.4807
A_1	0.0700	0.1505	0.0259	0.0959	0.2303	0.1198	0.1382	0.2132	101.1872
B_1	0.9000	0.8546	0.0266	0.7941	0.9019	0.7993	0.8539	0.9013	26.1383
C	0.2000	0.0000							Fixed
ν	8.0000	–							Fixed
ζ	1.0000	0.9892	0.0162	0.9495	1.0442	0.9554	0.9886	1.0218	2.4594
λ	0.0500	–							Fixed
σ_J^2	4.0000	–							Fixed
Parameter estimates for model with jumps									
A_0	0.0060	0.0155	0.0071	0.0055	0.0366	0.0055	0.0152	0.0249	111.2976
A_1	0.0700	0.1332	0.0149	0.0977	0.1647	0.0998	0.1324	0.1576	83.1306
B_1	0.9000	0.8399	0.0141	0.8057	0.8832	0.8226	0.8327	0.8763	179.1291
C	0.2000	0.1778	0.0403	0.0706	0.3304	0.1134	0.1768	0.2578	1.7911
ν	8.0000	–							Fixed
ζ	1.0000	1.0007	0.0152	0.9583	1.0472	0.9753	1.0018	1.0356	4.8794
λ	0.0500	0.0597	0.0054	0.0416	0.0658	0.0470	0.0596	0.0658	66.0968
σ_J^2	4.0000	3.6387	0.5911	2.4246	6.0296	2.6572	3.6085	5.0154	31.5103

$N = 500$ observations. The true parameter values are given in the column 'true'. 'mean' is the sample mean from the posterior, 'sd' the standard deviation, $Q(0.025)$, $Q(0.975)$ are quantiles. IEF is the Chib (2001) inefficiency factor

to the subsamples chosen to run this test. When the Geweke (1991) convergence test is applied to the log-likelihood, the test indicates good convergence properties.

Even with the strong priors on λ and σ_J^2, the estimated jump sizes exhibit some downward bias and still too many small jumps which are difficult to distinguish from large innovations e_n—especially if the innovations follow a Student-t distribution. The GARCH parameters A_0, A_1, B_1 and C are difficult to estimate. Especially the estimates of A_0 show a substantial degree of variation. Since A_0 accounts for the level of the conditional volatility, this high A_0 is compensated by a lower B_1 and a small jump intensity λ (see (B.6) in Appendix B).

We also simulated data without jumps and then again estimated parameters of a model with and without jumps. The parameter estimates are presented in Table 4. For both specifications the parameter ζ is estimated with high precision.

The second important insight—apart from the precision of the parameter estimates—that we would like to glean from the simulation is the reliability of the model selection step as described in Sect. 4. For each of our simulated time series we estimated a model with and without jumps[7] ($\mathcal{M}_{\text{jump}}$ and $\mathcal{M}_{\text{nojump}}$) and the marginal likelihood as described in Sect. 4. Then the estimation and model selection step is repeated with a different seed. In each step, we derive four estimates of the model likelihood and its standard deviation (SD). When comparing the model likelihoods

[7] Each of these estimation and model selection steps is done with the same seed.

Table 4 Estimation results for simulated data without jumps

Data generated from model without jumps	true	mean	sd	min	max	Q(0.025)	median	Q(0.975)	IEF
Parameter estimates for model without jumps									
A_0	0.0060	0.0202	0.0115	0.0049	0.0490	0.0049	0.0184	0.0412	105.9971
A_1	0.0700	0.0226	0.0178	0.0003	0.0984	0.0012	0.0235	0.0599	112.0275
B_1	0.9000	0.8832	0.0597	0.7455	0.9715	0.7496	0.8803	0.9715	110.0528
C	–	–							fixed
ν	8.0000	–							fixed
ζ	1.0000	1.0014	0.0136	0.9586	1.0456	0.9724	1.0011	1.0298	6.6382
λ	–	–							fixed
σ_J^2	–	–							fixed
Parameter estimates for model with jumps									
A_0	0.0060	0.0126	0.0071	0.0044	0.0499	0.0044	0.0096	0.0266	46.0598
A_1	0.0700	0.0346	0.0229	0.0026	0.1309	0.0064	0.0257	0.0851	99.8631
B_1	0.9000	0.9033	0.0497	0.7525	0.9549	0.8068	0.9246	0.9549	84.5283
C	–	0.0770	0.0551	0.0002	0.3332	0.0036	0.0681	0.2019	5.0042
ν	8.0000	–							fixed
ζ	1.0000	1.0004	0.0143	0.9645	1.0487	0.9719	1.0009	1.0266	5.2674
λ	–	0.0255	0.0066	0.0134	0.0351	0.0148	0.0250	0.0351	83.6257
σ_J^2	–	0.2029	0.0489	0.1552	0.4288	0.1560	0.1871	0.3451	36.6597

$N = 500$ observations, the data are generated from a model without jumps. The true parameter values are given in the second column. 'mean' is the sample mean from the posterior, sd the standard deviation, $Q(0.025)$, $Q(0.975)$ are quantiles. IEF is the Chib (2001) inefficiency factor

we observe that $\widehat{\log}\pi(r^N|\mathcal{M}_{\text{jump}}) > \widehat{\log}\pi(r^N|\mathcal{M}_{\text{nojump}})$ in all our simulation runs. In addition, we checked whether

$$\begin{aligned}\widehat{\log}\,\pi(r^N|\mathcal{M}_{\text{jump}}) - \alpha\widehat{\text{SD}}(\log\pi(r^N|\mathcal{M}_{\text{jump}}))\\ > \widehat{\log}\,\pi(r^N|\mathcal{M}_{\text{nojump}}) + \alpha\widehat{\text{SD}}(\log\pi(r^N|\mathcal{M}_{\text{nojump}}))\end{aligned} \tag{26}$$

for $\alpha = 1, 2, 3$. Inequality (26) was satisfied for all simulation runs with $\alpha = 1, 2$, and approximately 97.5 % of the simulation runs for $\alpha = 3$. That is to say, if the data was generated by a model with jumps, the marginal likelihood obtained by the sampler is a highly reliable tool to find the correct model.

If the true model is the model without jumps, the above inequality should not be satisfied, i.e., the marginal likelihood of the model without jumps should be higher, which was indeed the case *for all point estimates* of the marginal likelihood. To investigate the question whether the marginal likelihoods differ significantly, we once again look at (26) for $\alpha = -1, -2, -3$. With $\alpha = -1$, we observe that for approximately 70 % of the simulation runs inequality (26) does not hold; with $\alpha = -2$ and -3, these numbers decrease to 42 and 23 % respectively. So unlike the case with jumps, in the absence of jumps the distributions of marginal likelihoods overlap more for the two different specifications.

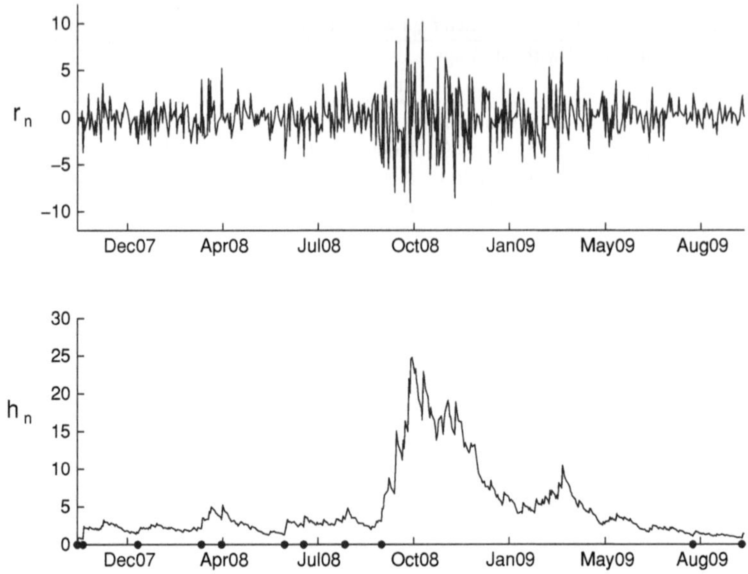

Fig. 1 S&P 500 returns and estimated volatility. *Top panel* S&P 500 returns form January 11, 2007 to September 30, 2009 measured in percentage terms. *Bottom panel* Estimated volatility process and jump dates (*dots*)

We summarize that the parameter estimation for A_0 and A_1 is rather imprecise in the simulation. Based on the marginal likelihood $\hat{\pi}(Y)$ and its standard deviation $\widehat{\text{SD}}(\pi(Y))$ the true model with jumps is clearly preferred to the model without jumps. When the artificial data is generated without jumps, the selection algorithm again always picks the correctly specified model.

5.2 Empirical Data

We applied the sampler to $N = 500$ daily S&P 500returns; the time span was November 2007 to September 2009. A maximum likelihood estimate with ζ fixed at one but with variable ν has already been presented in Table 2. Figures 1 and 2 provide a graphical illustration of our estimation results. Figure 1 shows the S&P 500 time series used to estimate the model parameters and the posterior estimates of h_n for the model with jumps. The posterior estimates of the jump times are denoted by dots. Interestingly, we infer jumps in the relatively calm periods of the time series. The more volatile last months of 2008 are driven by continuous innovations. To highlight these differences we focus on estimates of h_n for different sub-periods in Fig. 2 (upper panel with jumps, lower panel are estimates without jumps). E.g., at the first jump inferred in April 2008, the increase in h_n is smaller than in the estimates without jumps. In addition, we observe that especially in October and November 2008 h_n is much more volatile in the standard GARCH(1,1) model. Since the estimates of C are larger than zero, the jumps should not be considered as pure outliers. In addition, the impact of $\sqrt{h_n}e_n$ or J_n on future h_n is smaller in the model with jumps (parameter estimates of A_1 and C with jumps, smaller than A_1 without jumps in Table 5).

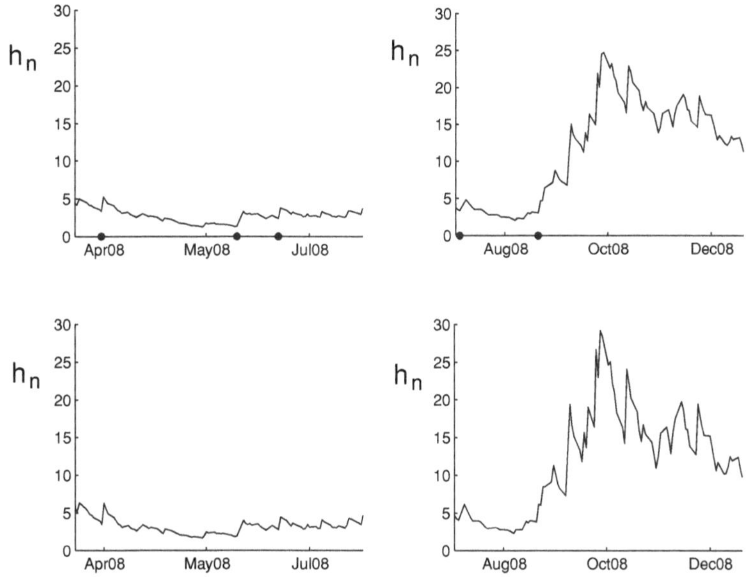

Fig. 2 Posterior estimates of of h_n, "zoom in" to modest period (*left* figures) and the beginning of the financial crises (*right* figures). *Top panel* Posterior estimates of a model with jumps, estimates of the jump dates marked by a dot. *Bottom panel* Posterior estimates of a model without jumps

The prior parameter $\lambda_0 = 0.022$ is obtained by the procedure described in Sect. 3 and data for the pre-estimation period 2000–2007. The estimated jump intensity based on the Lee and Mykland (2008) test for 2000–2007 data is slightly smaller than for the actual estimation sample 2007–2009, because the latter contains the financial crisis. However, as a robustness check we compared the posterior estimates for priors based on the pre-sample period 2000–2007 and priors based on 2007–2009 and found no important difference. The importance of the Lee and Mykland (2008) test is not to construct a "good" prior but to provide a reasonable initial value for the parameter λ which is important for step 4 of the MCMC sampler.

The Bayesian parameter estimates for a model with and without jumps are presented in Table 5. The upper part of this table shows the estimates for a model without jumps. Although the models considered are not exactly the same, compared to the maximum likelihood estimates (see Table 2) the Bayesian estimate of A_1 is larger while B_1 is smaller. More importantly, since the model likelihood is much larger with

Table 5 Estimation results for S&P 500returns

	mean	sd	min	max	Q(0.025)	median	Q(0.975)	IEF
Parameter estimates for model without jumps								
A_0	0.1792	0.0239	0.1328	0.2365	0.1328	0.1803	0.2365	51.6182
A_1	0.1136	0.0092	0.0996	0.1386	0.1018	0.1097	0.1380	137.5502
B_1	0.8549	0.0099	0.8307	0.8719	0.8307	0.8592	0.8719	112.6735
C	0.0000							fixed
ν	8.0000							fixed
ζ	0.9957	0.0112	0.9659	1.0233	0.9768	0.9958	1.0191	2.8678
$\widehat{\log\pi}(r^N \| \mathcal{M}_{\text{nojump}}) = -1236.4168$, $\widehat{\text{SD}}(\log \pi(r^N \| \mathcal{M}_{\text{nojump}})) = 6.1863$								
Parameter estimates for model with jumps								
A_0	0.0348	0.0087	0.0059	0.0631	0.0167	0.0356	0.0506	82.9480
A_1	0.0760	0.0060	0.0630	0.0922	0.0652	0.0753	0.0918	153.5819
B_1	0.9116	0.0067	0.8944	0.9264	0.8964	0.9115	0.9241	162.6749
C	0.1331	0.0426	0.0067	0.3211	0.0542	0.1307	0.2241	23.8281
ν	8.0000							fixed
ζ	0.9950	0.0116	0.9512	1.0403	0.9710	0.9952	1.0173	12.2026
λ_1	0.0302	0.0087	0.0099	0.0839	0.0162	0.0289	0.0515	61.5177
σ_J^2	7.9145	0.9969	5.1770	9.5260	5.8054	8.0274	9.4365	22.2376
$\widehat{\log\pi}(r^N \| \mathcal{M}_{\text{jump}}) = -1130.6176$, $\widehat{\text{SD}}(\log \pi(r^N \| \mathcal{M}_{\text{jump}})) = 10.8231$								

Time span from November 2007 to September 2009, $N = 500$. 'mean' is the sample mean from the posterior, sd the standard deviation, $Q(0.025)$, $Q(0.975)$ are quantiles. IEF is Chib (2001) inefficiency factor. $\widehat{\log\pi}(r^N|\mathcal{M}_.)$ is the point estimate of the log of the model likelihood, $\widehat{\text{SD}}(\log \pi(r^N|\mathcal{M}_.))$ is the estimated standard deviation. 10,000 MCMC steps, 1,000 burn in

jumps, the model selection tool clearly prefers a model with jumps. The estimated jump intensity is about 3 %, for the 500 periods considered we inferred 9–16 jumps.

Interestingly, the estimate of A_1 is substantially smaller than the estimate of C. Therefore, the persistence of non-jump innovations is much smaller than that of jump innovations. That is to say those drastic changes which have been inferred to be a jump have a higher impact on h_{n+j}, $j \geq 1$, than changes in $\sqrt{h_n}e_n$. While robust estimation techniques reduce the impact of extreme observations to improve parameter estimation, our estimates suggest that extreme observations picked up by J_n have a stronger impact on the volatility estimate than higher levels in $h_n e_n^2$ and allowing for them substantially improves the estimation.

6 Conclusions

This chapter developed tools for parameter estimation and model selection for a GARCH model with additive jumps. Lagged jumps significantly enter into the conditional volatility term. Simulation suggests, that the model selection algorithm is successful in distinguishing between models with and without jumps for samples of the same size as our actual data. The data clearly favor a model with additive jumps rather than a standard GARCH setting, even with Student-t distributed innovations.

Appendix A: The Skewed Student-t Distribution

In the following steps, we augment Giacomini et al. (2008) and calculate the cumulative distribution function for the univariate asymmetric Student-t distribution. First, we repeat some results concerning the distribution function for the univariate symmetric case. The density of a standard Student t-distribution with ν degrees of freedom is given by:

$$\pi_{\mathcal{T}}(x|\nu) = \frac{\Gamma\left(\frac{\nu+1}{2}\right)}{\sqrt{\nu\pi}\,\Gamma\left(\frac{\nu}{2}\right)}\left(1+\frac{x^2}{\nu}\right)^{-\frac{\nu+1}{2}}. \tag{A.1}$$

The random variable X has an expectation of zero and the variance $\frac{\nu}{\nu-2}$ if $\nu > 1$ and $\nu > 2$, respectively. Giacomini et al. (2008) derived the first and the second antiderivative for univariate t-distributed random variables by using the hypergeometric series

$$G_{12}(a,b,c,z) = \frac{\Gamma(c)}{\Gamma(a)\,\Gamma(b)}\sum_{k=0}^{\infty}\frac{\Gamma(a+k)\,\Gamma(b+k)}{\Gamma(c+k)}\frac{z^k}{k!}. \tag{A.2}$$

For $a, b, c, z \in \mathrm{C}$ and $|z| < 1$ this hypergeometric series converges, for non-negative integers $n = \nu/2 - 1$ the infinite sum stops after n terms. Then the first antiderivative $D^{-1}\pi_{\mathcal{T}}(x|\nu)$ provides us with the distribution function $F_{\mathcal{T}}(x|\nu)$:

$$F_{\mathcal{T}}(x|\nu) = \frac{1}{2} + \frac{x}{\kappa_\nu\sqrt{1+\frac{x^2}{\nu}}}\cdot G_{12}\left(\frac{1}{2}, 1-\frac{\nu}{2}, \frac{3}{2}, \frac{x^2}{x^2+\nu}\right) \tag{A.3}$$

where

$$\kappa_\nu = \frac{\sqrt{\nu\pi}\,\Gamma\left(\frac{\nu}{2}\right)}{\Gamma\left(\frac{\nu+1}{2}\right)}. \tag{A.4}$$

The second antiderivative of $\pi_{\mathcal{T}}(x|\nu)$ can be derived by means of

$$D^{-2}\pi_{\mathcal{T}}(x|\nu) = \frac{x}{2} + \frac{\nu\sqrt{1+\frac{x^2}{\nu}}}{(\nu-1)\kappa_\nu}\cdot G_{12}\left(-\frac{1}{2}, 1-\frac{\nu}{2}, \frac{1}{2}, \frac{x^2}{x^2+\nu}\right). \tag{A.5}$$

By the properties of (A.2), $G_{12}(.)$ terminates after $\nu/2 - 1$ terms.

Remark To derive (A.3) an incomplete beta integral has to be solved:

$$\int_0^x t^{\alpha-1}(1-t)^{\beta-1}\mathrm{d}t = \mathcal{B}(x,\alpha,\beta), \tag{A.6}$$

where $\mathcal{B}(x, \alpha, \beta)$ is the incomplete beta-function with parameters $\alpha, \beta > 0$. The regularized incomplete beta-function $\mathcal{B}_{\text{regularized}}(x, \alpha, \beta)$ is the fraction of $\mathcal{B}(x, \alpha, \beta)$ and $\mathcal{B}(\alpha, \beta)$, where $\mathcal{B}(\alpha, \beta)$ is the beta-function. For beta-functions we know that

$$1/\mathcal{B}(1/2, \nu/2) = \frac{\Gamma\left(\frac{\nu+1}{2}\right)}{\sqrt{\pi}\Gamma\left(\frac{\nu}{2}\right)}. \tag{A.7}$$

Therefore

$$\int_0^c \pi_{\mathcal{T}}(x|\nu)dx = \frac{1}{2}\frac{\mathcal{B}(c, 1/2, \nu/2)}{\mathcal{B}(1/2, \nu/2)} = \frac{\mathcal{B}_{\text{regularized}}(c, \alpha, \beta)}{2}. \tag{A.8}$$

By the definition and the properties of the hypergeometric function, the reader can verify that (A.3) and the calculation of the cumulative distribution function based on (A.8) have to agree.

Distribution Function—Asymmetric Case. Consider the scalar $\zeta > 0$. An asymmetric Student-t density can be derived by means of:

$$\pi_{\mathcal{T}}(x|\nu, \zeta) = 2\frac{\zeta}{1+\zeta^2}\frac{\Gamma\left(\frac{\nu+1}{2}\right)}{\Gamma\left(\frac{\nu}{2}\right)\sqrt{\pi\nu}} \times \left(\left(1 + \frac{x^2}{\zeta^2\nu}\right)^{-\frac{\nu+1}{2}} \mathbf{1}_{x\geq 0} + \left(1 + \frac{\zeta^2 x^2}{\nu}\right)^{-\frac{\nu+1}{2}} \mathbf{1}_{x<0}\right). \tag{A.9}$$

The construction of (A.9) follows from Fernandez and Steel (1998), Mittnik and Paolella (2000) and Bauwens and Laurent (2005). This construction allows us to get samples from this distribution as follows:

$$X = W|Z|\zeta - (1 - W)|Z|\zeta^{-1}, \tag{A.10}$$

where W is a Bernoulli random variable with probability $\zeta^2/(1 + \zeta^2)$; this is also the probability that $X \geq 0$. Z is standard t-distributed with mean zero and variance $\frac{\nu}{\nu-2}$. The moments of X are given by:

$$\mathbb{E}(X^r|\nu, \zeta) = \frac{\zeta^{r+1} + (-1)^r/\zeta^{r+1}}{\zeta + 1/\zeta} 2\mathbb{E}\left(Z^r|Z > 0, \zeta = 0\right). \tag{A.11}$$

In our application where the symmetric distribution is a Student-t distribution, we get $\mathbb{E}\left(X^r|X > 0, \zeta = 0\right)$ by means of Mittnik and Paolella (2000) or Paolella (2007) (p. 274). With $\nu > r$ we get

$$\mathbb{E}\left(X^r|X>0,\zeta=0\right)=\frac{\nu^{r/2}}{2\sqrt{\pi}}\frac{\Gamma(\frac{r+1}{2})\Gamma(\frac{\nu-r}{2})}{\Gamma(\frac{\nu}{2})}, \tag{A.12}$$

where $\Gamma(.)$ is the Euler-Gamma function. Equipped with (A.11) define $\mu_e = \mathbb{E}(X^1|\nu,\zeta)$ and $\sigma_e^2 = \mathbb{E}(X^2|\nu,\zeta) - \mu_e^2$. If the first and the second moments exist, we get the standardized random variable $\varepsilon = (X-\mu_e)/\sigma_e^{0.5}$.

Next we derive the cumulative distribution function: We abbreviate the factors of (A.9) as follows:

$$c_0 = 2\frac{\zeta}{1+\zeta^2},\quad c_1 = \frac{\Gamma\left(\frac{\nu+1}{2}\right)}{\Gamma\left(\frac{\nu}{2}\right)\sqrt{\pi\nu}}\ \text{and,}\ c_2 = \left(1+\frac{x^2(\zeta^I)^2}{\nu}\right)^{-\frac{\nu+1}{2}}.$$

where $\zeta^I = (\mathbf{1}_{x\geq 0}/\zeta + \mathbf{1}_{x<0}\zeta)$ and $I=-1$ if $x\geq 0$ and $I=1$ if $x<0$. To calculate the distribution function $P(X\leq x) := F_{\mathcal{T}}(x|\nu,\zeta)$, $x\in \mathrm{R}$, we have to solve the integral

$$F_{\mathcal{T}}(x|\nu,\zeta) = c_0c_1\int_{-\infty}^{x}\left(1+\frac{(z\zeta^I)^2}{\nu}\right)^{-\beta}\mathrm{d}z,\ \beta=\frac{\nu+1}{2}. \tag{A.13}$$

The transformation $y=\zeta^I z$ and the change of variable formula (such that $\mathrm{d}y = \zeta^I\mathrm{d}z$ and $\mathrm{d}z = \frac{1}{\zeta^I}\mathrm{d}y$) yield

$$F_{\mathcal{T}}(x|\nu,\zeta) = c_0c_1\int_{-\infty}^{y(x)}\frac{1}{\zeta^I}\left(1+\frac{y^2}{\nu}\right)^{-\beta}\mathrm{d}y. \tag{A.14}$$

$y(x)$ is the upper bound of the integral. $\frac{1}{\zeta^I}$ is constant on the sets $A_1=\{y|y\geq 0\}$ and $A_2=\{y|y<0\}$; i.e. we have $I=-1$ on A_1 while $I=1$ on A_2. The structure of the integrals remains the same, such that (A.14) becomes

$$\begin{aligned}F_{\mathcal{T}}(x|\nu,\zeta) =& \mathbf{1}_{x<0}c_0c_1\left(\frac{1}{\zeta}\int_0^{\infty}\left(1+\frac{y^2}{\nu}\right)^{-\beta}\mathrm{d}y - \frac{1}{\zeta}\int_0^{y(x)}\left(1+\frac{y^2}{\nu}\right)^{-\beta}\mathrm{d}y\right)\\ &+\mathbf{1}_{x\geq 0}c_0c_1\left(\frac{1}{\zeta}\int_0^{\infty}\left(1+\frac{y^2}{\nu}\right)^{-\beta}\mathrm{d}y + \zeta\int_0^{y(x)}\left(1+\frac{y^2}{\nu}\right)^{-\beta}\mathrm{d}y\right).\end{aligned} \tag{A.15}$$

Apply the following substitution:

$$\frac{\nu}{\nu + y^2} = 1 - t \text{ such that } t = 1 - \frac{\nu}{\nu - y^2} \text{ and } y = \sqrt{\frac{\nu t}{1-t}}. \tag{A.16}$$

For $y \in [0, \infty)$, $1 - t \in (0, 1)$ since $\nu > 0$. The first derivative is given by

$$\frac{\mathrm{d}y}{\mathrm{d}t} = \frac{1}{2}\sqrt{\frac{1-t}{\nu t}}\frac{\nu}{(1-t)^2} = \frac{1}{2}\nu^{0.5}t^{-0.5}(1-t)^{-1.5}. \tag{A.17}$$

Applying the substitution (A.16) in (A.15) and using (A.17) results in:

$$\begin{aligned} F_{\mathcal{T}}(x|\nu,\zeta) = {} & \mathbf{1}_{x<0}c_0c_1\nu^{0.5}\frac{1}{2}\left(\frac{1}{\zeta}\int_0^1 t^{-0.5}(1-t)^{\beta-1.5}\,\mathrm{d}t \right. \\ & \left. -\frac{1}{\zeta}\int_0^{b_u(y(x))} t^{-0.5}(1-t)^{\beta-1.5}\,\mathrm{d}t\right) \\ & + \mathbf{1}_{x\geq 0}c_0c_1\nu^{0.5}\frac{1}{2}\left(\frac{1}{\zeta}\int_0^1 t^{-0.5}(1-t)^{\beta-1.5}\,\mathrm{d}t \right. \\ & \left. +\frac{1}{\zeta}\zeta^2\int_0^{b_u(y(x))} t^{-0.5}(1-t)^{\beta-1.5}\,\mathrm{d}t\right). \end{aligned} \tag{A.18}$$

By (A.16) the lower bound of the integrals remain 0, the upper bound when integrating to z is $b_u(y(x)) = 1 - \frac{\nu}{\nu+y(x)^2}$ for the upper bound going to infinity this results in $b_u(\infty) = 1$. Therefore, the cumulative distribution function (A.18) is the sum of beta integrals. For the complete beta integral in (A.18) we directly apply (A.7) where $\int_0^1 t^{-0.5}(1-t)^{\beta-1.5}\,\mathrm{d}t = \mathcal{B}(1, \frac{1}{2}, \frac{\nu}{2}) = (1/c_1)(1/\nu^{0.5})$, while $\int_0^{b_u(y(x))} t^{-0.5}(1-t)^{\beta-1.5}\,\mathrm{d}t = \mathcal{B}(b_u(y(x)), \frac{1}{2}, \frac{\nu}{2})$ by (A.6). These facts, (A.7) and some algebra yield:

$$\begin{aligned} F_{\mathcal{T}}(x|\nu,\zeta) &= \mathbf{1}_{x<0}\frac{1}{1+\zeta^2}\left(1 - c_1\sqrt{\nu}\mathcal{B}\left(b_u(y(x)), \frac{1}{2}, \frac{\nu}{2}\right)\right) \\ &\quad + \mathbf{1}_{x\geq 0}\frac{1}{1+\zeta^2}\left(1 + \zeta^2 c_1\sqrt{\nu}\mathcal{B}\left(b_u(y(x)), \frac{1}{2}, \frac{\nu}{2}\right)\right) \\ &= \mathbf{1}_{x<0}\frac{1}{1+\zeta^2}\left(1 - \frac{\Gamma\left(\frac{\nu+1}{2}\right)}{\Gamma\left(\frac{\nu}{2}\right)\sqrt{\pi}}\mathcal{B}\left(b_u(y(x)), \frac{1}{2}, \frac{\nu}{2}\right)\right) \end{aligned}$$

$$+ \mathbf{1}_{x\geq 0}\frac{1}{1+\zeta^2}\left(1+\zeta^2\frac{\Gamma\left(\frac{\nu+1}{2}\right)}{\Gamma\left(\frac{\nu}{2}\right)\sqrt{\pi}}\mathcal{B}\left(b_u(y(x)),\frac{1}{2},\frac{\nu}{2}\right)\right)$$

$$= \mathbf{1}_{x<0}\frac{1}{1+\zeta^2}\left(1-\frac{\mathcal{B}(b_u(y(x)),\frac{1}{2},\frac{\nu}{2})}{\mathcal{B}(\frac{1}{2},\frac{\nu}{2})}\right)$$

$$+ \mathbf{1}_{x\geq 0}\frac{1}{1+\zeta^2}\left(1+\zeta^2\frac{\mathcal{B}(b_u(y(x)),\frac{1}{2},\frac{\nu}{2})}{\mathcal{B}(\frac{1}{2},\frac{\nu}{2})}\right). \quad \text{(A.19)}$$

Remark Note that we can easily check that (A.9) is a density. Since $\zeta + 1/\zeta = (1+\zeta^2)/\zeta$ we obtain

$$\int_{-\infty}^{\infty}\pi_{\mathcal{T}}(x|\nu,\zeta)\mathrm{d}x = \frac{c_0c_1\sqrt{\nu}}{2\zeta}\mathcal{B}\left(\frac{1}{2},\frac{\nu}{2}\right)+\frac{\zeta c_0c_1\sqrt{\nu}}{2}\mathcal{B}\left(\frac{1}{2},\frac{\nu}{2}\right)$$

$$= c_0c_1\frac{\sqrt{\nu}}{2}\left(1/\zeta+\zeta\right)\frac{1}{c_1\sqrt{\nu}} = 1.$$

Remark A further useful property is given by the fact that if Z is standard normal and $Y = \sqrt{U}/\nu$, where $U \sim \pi_{\chi^2}(.|\nu)$, then $X = Z/Y$ is standard t-distributed with ν degrees of freedom. If Z follows an asymmetric normal distribution based on Fernandez and Steel (1998), then $X = Z/Y$ follows the asymmetric t-distributed described by (A.9). To show this fact, it is sufficient to show that $\pi_{\mathcal{T}}(x/\zeta|\nu,1) = \int |y|\pi_{\mathcal{N}}(xy/\zeta)\pi(y)\mathrm{d}y$. $\pi(y) = \frac{2^{-\nu/2+1}\nu^{\nu/2}}{\Gamma(\nu/2)}y^{\nu-1}\exp(-(\nu y^2)/2)\mathbf{1}_{y\geq 0}$ follows from the χ^2 density and the transformation rule. $\pi_{\mathcal{N}}(.)$ and $\pi_{\chi^2}(.)$ are densities of the standard normal and a χ^2 distribution, respectively. This equality follows from straightforward integration. For the symmetric case this is presented in Paolella (2007) (p. 80).

Appendix B: Moments and Weak Stationarity

Conditions for strict stationarity for a GARCH setting without jumps have been derived in Francq and Zakoian (2005), Liu (2006) and Abramson and Cohen (2007). Here, we check whether our model with jumps is weakly stationary. A time series is called weakly stationary if the first and second moments exist and do not depend on the time index, in addition the autocovariances $\mathbb{C}\rtimes\gtrapprox(r_n, r_{n-s})$ are independent of n. Consider the model (1):

$$r_n = \sqrt{h_n}e_n + J_n \quad \text{(B.1)}$$

$$h_n = A_0 + \sum_{j'=1}^{p} A_{j'} E_{n-j'} + \sum_{j=1}^{q} B_j h_{n-j} + C J_{n-1}^2$$
$$= A_0 + A(L)E + B(L)h_n. \tag{B.2}$$

Since $\mathbb{E}(e_n) = \mathbb{E}(J_n) = 0$ we get $\mathbb{E}(r_n) = 0$. By the model assumptions we also know that $\mathbb{V}(e_n) = 1$. The k-th moment of e_n exists for $\nu > k$. $\mathbb{V}(J_n) = p_\lambda \sigma_J^2$ by the construction of the jump component J_n. J_n and $e_{n-j'}$ are independent for all $n, n-j$; $p_\lambda = 1 - \exp(-\lambda)$. With $E_n = (r_n - J_n)^2 = h_n e_n^2$ we get

$$h_n = A_0 + \sum_{j'=1}^{p} A_{j'} h_{n-1} e_{n-j'}^2 + \sum_{j=1}^{q} B_j h_{n-j} + C J_{n-1}^2. \tag{B.3}$$

By (B.3), h_n follows an $AR(\ell)$ process with random coefficients, such that

$$h_n = (A_0 + C J_{n-1}^2) + \sum_{j=1}^{\ell} (A_j e_{n-j}^2 + B_j) h_{n-j}, \tag{B.4}$$

$\ell = \max\{p, q\}$, where A_j or $B_j = 0$ for $j > p$ or $j > q$ respectively. Suppose the second moments of e_n and J_n exist.

Given $p = q = 1$, $\nu > 4$ and the assumptions from Sect. 2, Meyn and Tweedie (2009) (Theorem 16.5.1) imply that (h_n) is second order stationary if $|A_1^2 \mathbb{E}(e^4) + B_1^2| < 1$. For $p, q > 1$ this result can be adapted if necessary.[8] This yields

$$\mathbb{E}(h_n) = A_0 + \sum_{j'=1}^{p} A_{j'} \mathbb{E}(h_n) + \sum_{j=1}^{q} B_j \mathbb{E}(h_n) + C\mathbb{E}(J_{n-1}^2) \text{ such that}$$
$$\mathbb{E}(h_n) = \frac{1}{1 - \sum_{j'=1}^{p} A_{j'} + \sum_{j=1}^{q} B_j} \left(A_0 + C p_\lambda \sigma_J^2 \right). \tag{B.5}$$

Since $\mathbb{V}(X) = \mathbb{E}(\mathbb{V}(X|\mathcal{F})) + \mathbb{V}(\mathbb{E}(X|\mathcal{F}))$ (see e.g. Casella and Berger 2001) and $\mathbb{E}(r_n|h_n) = 0$ for any h_n, we get

$$\mathbb{V}(r_n) = \mathbb{E}(h_n) + p_\lambda \sigma_J^2. \tag{B.6}$$

For the autocovariance we also use the fact that $\mathbb{C}ov(r_n, r_{n-s}) = \mathbb{E}(\mathbb{C}ov(r_n, r_{n-s}|h_{n-s})) + \mathbb{C}ov(\mathbb{E}(r_n|h_{n-s}), \mathbb{E}(r_{n-s}|h_{n-s}))$. The second term is zero since

[8] This can be done by increasing the dimension of the process. While Meyn and Tweedie (2009) (Theorem 16.5.1) require a positive density with respect to the Lebesgue measure for the stochastic component, it should be noted that h_n lives on R_+. On this set there is always a density always positive. Following Meyn and Tweedie (2009) (Chap. 6) we observe that (h_n) is an aperiodic and irreducible T-chain as required in the proof of Theorem 16.5.1. Hence, Theorem 16.5.1 still holds with this slight modification of the process (h_n) living on non-negative reals.

$\mathbb{E}(r_{n-s}|h_{n-s}) = 0$ for arbitrary n and s, while $\mathbb{C}ov(X_n, X_{n-s}|h_{n-s}) = 0$ for any $s \neq 0$ since $e_n, e_{n-s}, J_n, J_{n-s}$ are jointly independent. This yields

$$\mathbb{C}ov(r_n, r_{n-s}) = 0 \quad \text{for all } s \neq 0. \tag{B.7}$$

In addition, we derive some higher order moments: by (A.11) from Appendix A the kth moment $M_{\varepsilon,k}$ of ε_n can be derived as long as $\nu > k$. Since $e_n = \frac{\varepsilon_n - \mu_e}{\sigma_e}$, where $\mu_e := M_{\varepsilon,1}$ and $\sigma_e^2 := M_{\varepsilon,2} - M_{\varepsilon,1}^2$, we get the moments of e_n by means of

$$M_{e,k} = \left(\frac{M_{\varepsilon,r} - \mu_e}{\sigma_e}\right)^r. \tag{B.8}$$

In the following, we shall approximate the skewness. To derive, it is necessary to calculate $\mathbb{E}(r_n^3)$; we already know that $\mathbb{E}(r_n) = 0$. Here, we get

$$\begin{aligned}
\mathbb{E}(r_n^3) &= \mathbb{E}((\sqrt{h_n}e_n + J_n)^3)\\
&= \mathbb{E}(h_n^{3/2}e_n^3) + 3\mathbb{E}(h_n e_n^2 J_n) + 3\mathbb{E}(\sqrt{h_n}e_n J_n^2) + \mathbb{E}(J_n^3)\\
&= \mathbb{E}(h_n^{3/2})\mathbb{E}(e_n^3).
\end{aligned} \tag{B.9}$$

The second on the third term become zero since h_n, e_n, J_n are independent and e_n and J_n have an expectation of zero. The expectation of J_n^3 is zero by the assumption of normal jump sizes. For the expected value of $\mathbb{E}(h_n^{3/2})$ we can perform a Taylor series approximation (see e.g. Paolella 2007, p. 86), such that

$$\mathbb{E}(h_n^{3/2}) \approx (\mathbb{E}(h_n))^{3/2} + \frac{3}{4}\frac{1}{\mathbb{E}(h_n)^2}. \tag{B.10}$$

By using only the constant term of this approximation we derive

$$\frac{\mathbb{E}(r_n^3)}{(\mathbb{E}(r_n^2))^{3/2}} = \frac{\mathbb{E}(h_n^{3/2})\mathbb{E}(e_n^3)}{(\mathbb{E}(h_n) + p_\lambda\sigma_J^2)^{3/2}} \approx \frac{\mathbb{E}(h_n)^{3/2}\mathbb{E}(e_n^3)}{(\mathbb{E}(h_n) + p_\lambda\sigma_J^2)^{3/2}}. \tag{B.11}$$

In a similar way we derive the kurtosis. Suppose $\nu > 4$, then

$$\begin{aligned}
\mathbb{E}(r_n^4) &= \mathbb{E}((\sqrt{h_n}e_n + J_n)^4)\\
&= \mathbb{E}(h_n^2 e_n^4) + 4\mathbb{E}(h_n^{3/2}e_n^3 J_n) + 6\mathbb{E}(h_n e_n^2 J_n^2) + 4\mathbb{E}(h_n^{1/2}e_n J_n^3) + \mathbb{E}(J_n^4)\\
&= \mathbb{E}(h_n^2)\mathbb{E}(e_n^4) + 4\cdot 0 + 6\mathbb{E}(h_n)p_\lambda\sigma_J^2 + 4\cdot 0 + p_\lambda 3\sigma_J^4.
\end{aligned} \tag{B.12}$$

The second and the fourth term in the second line are zero by the independence assumption and the fact that $\mathbb{E}(J_n) = \mathbb{E}(J_n^3) = 0$. The second term follows from the independence of J_n, e_n and h_n plus taking expectations. The last term follows from the independence of jump sizes and jump times and the properties of the normal distribution. $\mathbb{E}(e_n^4)$ follows from (A.11) and the discussion above. It remains to derive $\mathbb{E}(h_n^2)$. Thus,

$$
\begin{aligned}
\mathbb{E}(h_n^2) &= \mathbb{E}\left(\left(A_0 + \sum_{j'=1}^{p} A_{j'}E_{n-j'} + \sum_{j'=1}^{q} B_j h_{n-j} + CJ_{n-1}^2\right)^2\right) \\
&= \mathbb{E}\left(A_0^2 + 2A_0 \sum_{j'=1}^{p} A_{j'}E_{n-j'} + \left(\sum_{j'=1}^{p} A_{j'}E_{n-j'}\right)^2\right) \\
&+ 2\mathbb{E}\left(A_0 \sum_{j'=1}^{q} B_j h_{n-j} + A_0 C J_{n-1}^2 + \left(\sum_{j'=1}^{p} A_{j'}E_{n-j'}\right)\left(\sum_{j'=1}^{q} B_j h_{n-j}\right)\right. \\
&\left. + \left(\sum_{j'=1}^{q} B_j h_{n-j}\right) CJ_{n-1}^2\right) \\
&+ \mathbb{E}\left(\left(\sum_{j'=1}^{q} B_j h_{n-j}\right)^2 + 2\left(\sum_{j'=1}^{q} B_j h_{n-j}\right) CJ_{n-1}^2 + C^2 J_{n-1}^4\right) \\
&= A_0^2 + 2A_0 \sum_{j'=1}^{p} A_{j'}\mathbb{E}(E_n) + \mathbb{E}\left(\left(\sum_{j'=1}^{p} A_{j'}E_{n-j'}\right)^2\right) \\
&+ 2\left(A_0 \sum_{j'=1}^{q} B_j \mathbb{E}(h_n) + A_0 C p_\lambda \sigma_J^2 + \left(\sum_{j'=1}^{p} A_{j'}\mathbb{E}(E_n)\right)\left(\sum_{j'=1}^{q} B_j h_{n-j}\right)\right. \\
&\left. + \left(\sum_{j'=1}^{q} B_j \mathbb{E}(h_{n-j})\right) C\mathbb{E}(J_{n-1}^2)\right) \\
&+ \sum_{j'=1}^{q} B_j^2 \mathbb{E}(h_n^2) + 2\left(\sum_{j'=1}^{q} B_j \mathbb{E}(h_n)\right) C p_\lambda \sigma_J^2 + C^2 p_\lambda 3\sigma_J^4.
\end{aligned}
\tag{B.13}
$$

Note that $\mathbb{E}(h_n e_n^2) = \mathbb{E}(h_n)\mathbb{E}(e_n) = \mathbb{E}(h_n)$ and $\mathbb{E}(h_n^2 e_n^4) = \mathbb{E}(h_n^2)\mathbb{E}(e_n^4) = \mathbb{E}(h_n^2)M_{e,4}$. For $p, q \leq 1$ the above expression can be simplified. The kurtosis follows from the fraction $\frac{\mathbb{E}(r_n^4)}{(\mathbb{E}(r_n^2))^2}$ where the numerator follows from (B.12) while the denominator is given by (B.6).

Appendix C: Construction of an Informative Prior

To arrive at reliable parameter estimates, it was necessary to include some "additional" information in the data obtained by other statistical procedures. In the Bayesian sampler, this resulted in informative priors on λ and σ_J^2.

Tests on Jumps. Lee and Mykland (2008) developed a test on jumps for continuous time processes. This test is primary design for high frequency data. We apply this test to daily data. The test provides us with estimates of time point where the process r_n jumps, this estimates are abbreviated by Y_n^{LM}. Since $\mathbb{E}(\sqrt{h_n}e_n) = 0$ for our GARCH model we get an estimate of the jump size by means of $S_n^{\mathrm{LM}} = r_n$ with sample variance $\hat{\mathbb{V}}(S_n^{\mathrm{LM}})$

In the simulated data, we observe that for a sufficiently large σ_J^2, this test detects approximately 20–50 % of the jumps J_n. $\sum Y^{\mathrm{LM}}/N$, therefore underestimates the probability of a jump p_λ. Based on this observation we set the mean parameter used in the truncated normal prior to two times $p_\lambda^{\mathrm{LM}} = \sum Y^{\mathrm{LM}}/N$. In more details $\lambda_0 = -log(1 - \alpha p_\lambda^{\mathrm{LM}})$, with $\alpha = 2$. In addition, we observe that the test gets the large jumps, such that σ_J^2 should be smaller than the sample variance of the jumps heights inferred by this test. Thus, we calculated the variance of the jump size S_n^{LM} and constructed a truncated normal prior, such that the mean is half the variance of S_n^{LM}, the variance parameter is set to 2, the lower bound is the variance of the returns, while for the upper bound we used eight times $\hat{\mathbb{V}}(S_n^{\mathrm{LM}})$.

Moments of r_n. From (B.8) and Pascal's triangle we get

$$\mathbb{E}\left((e_n)^r|h_n\right) = \left(\frac{1}{\sigma_e}\right)^r \mathbb{E}\left((\varepsilon_n - \mu_e)^r\right) = \left(\frac{1}{\sigma_e}\right)^r \sum_{j=0}^{r} \binom{r}{j} \mathbb{E}\left(\varepsilon_n^{r-j}\right) \mu_e^j. \tag{C.1}$$

For the third moment we can use the proxy

$$\mathbb{E}(r_n^3) = \mathbb{E}(h_n^{3/2})\mathbb{E}(e_n^3) \approx \left((\mathbb{E}(h_n))^{3/2} + \frac{3}{4}\frac{1}{\mathbb{E}(h_n)^2}\right)\mathbb{E}(e_n^3), \tag{C.2}$$

where $\mathbb{E}(h_n)$ follows from (B.5). For the fourth moment (B.12) provides us with

$$\mathbb{E}(r_n^4) = \mathbb{E}(h_n^2)\mathbb{E}(e_n^4) + 6\mathbb{E}(h_n)p_\lambda\sigma_J^2 + p_\lambda 3\sigma_J^4\,. \tag{C.3}$$

With $p = q = 1$ the term $\mathbb{E}(h_n^2)$ becomes

$$\begin{aligned}\mathbb{E}(h_n^2) = {} & \frac{1}{1 - A_1^2\mathbb{E}(e_n^4) - B_1^2}\Big[A_0^2 + 2A_0A_1\mathbb{E}(h_n) \\ & + 2\left(A_0B_1\mathbb{E}(h_n) + A_0Cp_\lambda\sigma_J^2 + A_1B_1\mathbb{E}(h_n)^2 + B_1\mathbb{E}(h_n)Cp_\lambda\sigma_J^2\right)\Big] \\ & + \frac{1}{1 - A_1^2\mathbb{E}(e_n^4) - B_1^2}\left[2B_1\mathbb{E}(h_n)Cp_\lambda\sigma_J^2 + C^2p_\lambda 3\sigma_J^4\right].\end{aligned} \tag{C.4}$$

$\mathbb{E}(e_n^4)$ can be obtained by means of (C.1). By comparing the j-th moments based on these expressions to the sample moments $m_j(r^N)$ we get the scores $g_j(r^N, \theta) = \mathbb{E}_N(r_n^j) - m_j(r^N)$. By means of $d(r^N, \theta) = g_j(r^N, \theta)^\top \Omega g_j(r^N, \theta)$ we map these deviations to one real number. If the parameters perfectly match the empirical moments $d = 0$. Therefore, we also use the prior $d(r^N, \theta) \sim \pi_{\mathcal{N}}(d|0, \sigma_d^2)$, where $\sigma_d^2 = 100$ controls for the dispersion. The weight matrix Ω is diagonal with entries $(0, 1, 0.1, 0.0001)$. By this prior we put a joint prior on all model parameters. By our choice of Ω the impact of this prior on the parameters θ is neglectably small. This prior only puts low mass on those θ where the empirical moments and the model moments are very different.

References

Abramson, A. and Cohen, I. (2007). On the stationarity of markov switching garch processes. Econometric Theory, 23(3):485–500.

Aït-Sahalia, Y., Cacho-Diaz, J., and Hurd, T. R. (2009). Portfolio choice with a jumps: A closed form solution. Annals of Applied Probability, 19:556–584.

Andersen, T. G., Bollerslev, T., and Diebold, F. X. (2007). Roughing it up: Including jump components in the measurement, modeling and forecasting of return volatility. The Review of Economics and Statistics, 89(4):701–720.

Andersen, T. G., Bollerslev, T., Diebold, F. X., and Labys, P. (2003). Modeling and forecasting realized volatility. Econometrica, 71(2):579–625.

Andrieu, C., Doucet, A., and Holenstein, R. (2010). Particle Markov chain Monte Carlo methods. Journal of the Royal Statistical Society, 72(3):260–342.

Barndorff-Nielsen, O. and Shephard, N. (2001). Non-Gaussian Ornstein-Uhlenbeck-based models and some of their uses in financial economics. Journal of the Royal Statistical Society B, 63: 167-241.

Barndorff-Nielsen, O. and Shephard, N. (2006). Econometrics of testing jumps in financial economics using bipower variation. Journal of Financial Econometrics, 4(1):1–30.

Barndorff-Nielsen, O. E. and Stelzer, R. (2009). The multivariate supou stochastic volatility model. Working paper, Technische Universität München.

Bauwens, L. and Laurent, S. (2005). A new class of multivariate skew densities, with application to generalized autoregressive conditional heteroscedasticity models. Journal of Business and Economic Statistics, 23:346–354.

Boudt, K. and Croux, C. (2010). Robust m-estimation of multivariate garch models. Computational Statistics & Data Analysis, pages 2459–2469.

Boudt, K., Danielsson, J., and Laurent, S. (2011). Robust Forecasting of Dynamic Conditional Correlation GARCH Models. SSRN eLibrary.

Brooks, S. P. and Gelman, A. (1998). General methods for monitoring convergence of iterative simulations. Journal of Computational and Graphical Statistics, 7(4):434–455.

Casella, G. and Berger, R. (2001). Statistical Inference. Duxbury Resource Center, Boston, 2 edition.

Charles, A. and Darn, O. (2005). Outliers and garch models in financial data. Economics Letters, 86(3):347–352.

Chib, S. (1995). Marginal likelihood from the gibbs output. Journal of the American Statistical Association, 90(432):1313–1321.

Chib, S. (2001). Markov chain monte carlo methods: computation and inference. In Heckman, J. and Leamer, E., editors, Handbook of Econometrics, volume 5 of Handbook of Econometrics, chapter 57, pages 3569–3649. Elsevier.

Chib, S. and Jeliazkov, I. (2001). Marginal likelihood from the Metropolis-Hastings output. Journal of the American Statistical Association, 96:270–281.
Corsi, F., Pirino, D., and Renò, R. (2008). Threshold Bipower Variation and the Impact of Jumps on Volatility Forecasting. SSRN eLibrary.
Cowles, M. K. and Carlin, B. P. (1996). Markov chain monte carlo convergence diagnostics: A comparative review. Journal of the American Statistical Association, 91(434):883–904.
Doucet, A. and Johansen, A. M. (2008). A tutorial on particle filtering and smoothing: Fifteen years later. in Handbook of Nonlinear Filtering (eds. D. Crisan et B. Rozovsky), Oxford University Press, to appear.
Duan, J., Ritchken, P. H., and Sun, Z. (2006). Approximating Garch-Jump Models, Jump-Diffusion Processes, and Option Pricing. Mathematical Finance, 16(1):21–52.
Duan, J., Ritchken, P. H., and Sun, Z. (2007). Jump starting garch: Pricing options with jumps and returns and volatilities. Working paper, University of Toronto.
Duffie, D., Pan, J., and Singleton, K. (2000). Transform analysis and asset pricing for affine jump-diffusions. Econometrica, 68(6):1343–1376.
Engle, R. (2002). New frontiers for arch models. Journal of Applied Econometrics, 17(5):425–446.
Engle, R. F. and Gallo, G. M. (2003). A multiple indicators model for volatility using intra-daily data. Econometrics Working Papers Archive wp200307, Universita degli Studi di Firenze, Dipartimento di Statistica "G. Parenti".
Fernandez, C. and Steel, M. F. (1998). On bayesian modeling of fat tails and skewness. Journal of the American Statistical Association, 93(441):359–371.
Flury, T. and Shephard, N. (2009). Learning and filtering via simulation: smoothly jittered particle filters. Economics Series Working Papers 469, University of Oxford, Department of Economics.
Francq, C. and Zakoian, J.-M. (2005). L2 structures of standard and switching-regime garch models. Journal of the American Statistical Association, 115:1557–1582.
Frühwirth-Schnatter, S. (2004). Estimating marginal likelihoods for mixture and markov switching models using bridge sample techniques. The Econometrics Journal, 7:143–167.
Frühwirth-Schnatter, S. (2006). Finite Mixture and Markov Switching Models. Springer, New York.
Gelman, A. and Rubin, D. B. (1992). Statistical Science, 7(4):457–472.
Geweke, J. (1991). Evaluating the accuracy of sampling-based approaches to the calculation of posterior moments. Staff Report 148, Federal Reserve Bank of Minneapolis.
Giacomini, R., Gottschling, A., Haefke, C., and White, H. (2008). Mixtures of t-distributions for finance and forecasting. Journal of Econometrics, 144:175–192.
Gran, A. and Veiga, H. (2010). Outliers in garch models and the estimation of risk measures. Statistics and Econometrics Working Papers ws100502, Universidad Carlos III, Departamento de Estadstica y Econometra.
Grossi, L. (2004). Analyzing financial time series through robust estimators. Studies in Nonlinear Dynamics & Econometrics, 8(2).
Hansen, P. R., Zhuo, Z. H., and Shek, H. (2010). Realized garch: A joint model of returns and realized measures of volatility. SSRN eLibrary.
Harvey, A. and Chakravarty, T. (2008). Beta-t-(e)garch. Cambridge Working Papers in Economics 0840, Faculty of Economics, University of Cambridge.
Kaufmann, S. and Frühwirth-Schnatter, S. (2002). Bayesian analysis of switching arch-models. Journal of Time Series Analysis, 23:425–458.
Lamberton, D. and Lapeyre, B. (2008). Introduction to Stochastic Calculus Applied to Finance. Chapman & Hall, London, 2 edition.
Lee, S. S. and Mykland, P. A. (2008). Jumps in financial markets: A new nonparametric test and jump dynamics. Review of Financial Studies, 21(6):2535–2563.
Liu, J. (2006). Stationarity of a markov-switching garch model. Journal of Financial Econometrics, 4(4):573–593.
Malik, S. and Pitt, M. K. (2009). Modelling stochastic volatility with leverage and jumps: a simulated maximum likelihood approach via particle filtering. Working Paper. University of Warwick, Department of Economics, Coventry.

Mayerhofer, E., Pfaffel, O., and Stelzer, R. (2010). On strong solutions of matrix valued jump-diffusions. Preprint.

McLachlan, G. and Krishnan, T. (1997). The EM Algorithm and Extensions. Springer, New York.

Meyn, S. and Tweedie, R. L. (2009). Markov Chains and Stochastic Stability. Cambridge University Press (Cambridge Mathematical Library), New York, 2 edition.

Mittnik, S. and Paolella, M. S. (2000). Conditional density and value-at-risk prediction of asian currency exchange rates. Journal of Forecasting, 19(4):313–333.

Muler, N. and Yohai, V. J. (2008). Robust estimates for garch models. Journal of Statistical Planning and Inference, 138(10):2918–2940.

Omori, Y., Chib, S., Shephard, N., and Nakajima, J. (2007). Stochastic volatility with leverage: Fast and efficient likelihood inference. Journal of Econometrics, 140(2):425–449.

Paolella, M. (2007). Intermediate Probability-A Computational Approach. Wiley.

Pitt, M. K. and Shephard, N. (1999). Filtering via simulation: Auxiliary particle filters. Journal of the American Statistical Association, 94(446):590–599.

Robert, C. and Casella, G. (1999). Monte Carlo Statistical Methods. Springer, New York.

Robert, C. P. (1994). The Bayesian Choice. Springer, New York.

Sakata, S. and White, H. (1998). High breakdown point conditional dispersion estimation with application to s&p 500 daily returns volatility. Econometrica, 66(3):529–568.

Shephard, N. and Pitt, M. K. (1999). Filtering via simulation: auxiliary particle filters. Journal of the American Statistical Association, 94(446):590–599.

Tanner, M. A. and Wong, W. H. (1987). The calculation of posterior distributions by data augmentation. Journal of the American Statistical Association, 82:528–550.

Yu, J.-S. and Daal, E. (2005). A Comparison of Mixed GARCH-Jump Models with Skewed t-Distribution for Asset Returns. SSRN eLibrary.

Hal White: Time at MIT and Early Days of Research

Jerry Hausman

I am pleased to write a note in honor of Hal's sixtieth birthday. As memory is a tricky thing, I hope the following is accurate, but I can make no guarantees. Hal was among my first three Ph.D. students at MIT who are Roger Gordon, Hal White, and Paul Krugman. Since my first and only job has been at MIT, I found this supervision enjoyable and remarkably easy. However, using these three sample points to predict the future would have been grossly inaccurate, although mostly I have enjoyed the many MIT (and some Harvard) students I have supervised over the years.

Hal's thesis was in applied labor economics: "A Microeconomic Model of Wage Determination: Econometric Estimation and Application". His other supervisors were Bob Solow and Lester Thurow. While the thesis uses interesting econometric methods, the question may arise of why Hal did not write an econometric methodology thesis. My memory is as follows. In those days MIT students finished in four years. Then and now, MIT has much less fellowship money than Harvard and other universities which can guarantee a longer period. Nevertheless, MIT has far outdistanced other universities in the past 40 years in producing top graduate students. I told Hal that if by May of his third year he did not have an *Econometrica* level paper in process he should do an applied thesis so he could be sure to finish on time. Perhaps I was too young and inexperienced at the time to give better thesis advice. However, the initial conditions of his thesis being in an applied topic had no effect on his subsequent research which I now turn to.

Hal took three econometrics courses from me so, of course, I chose him as one of my teaching assistants (TA). He was the TA for all three courses so we talked about the topics in the courses a lot since my yellow note pages were just beginning to take shape at that time. Hal was a terrific TA, which the students appreciated given my teaching approach. He led the way for many subsequent TAs including Bernanke, Paul Ruud, Mark Machina, Whitney Newey, and Ken West over the next few years after Hal.

J. Hausman (✉)
MIT Department of Economics, Cambridge, MA, USA
e-mail: jhausman@mit.edu

X. Chen and N. R. Swanson (eds.), *Recent Advances and Future Directions in Causality, Prediction, and Specification Analysis*, DOI: 10.1007/978-1-4614-1653-1_8,

1 My Approach Before White Standard Errors

In the introductory econometrics course I discussed at length the problem of inference when the covariance matrix was not diagonal. How to estimate $(X'X)^{-1}(X'\Lambda X)(X'X)^{-1}$ where Λ is a diagonal matrix of unknown form? I pointed out that estimation of the middle matrix followed from the approach of the Berndt–Hall–Hall–Hausman (BHHH) algorithm: $D = \Sigma X_i \varepsilon_i \varepsilon_i' X_i'$ where D is an estimate of the middle matrix and (ε_i') is the least squares estimate of the residual. I missed the " White standard error" formula, but instead I took two alternative approaches. I taught that one could do FGLS (feasible GLS) using a specification for ε_i^2 using a general polynomial approach based on the X_is. I emphasized that the specification did not have to be "correct" since in large samples the estimates of the slope parameters would continue to be consistent and hopefully have reduced variance relative to the OLS estimates. However, in the absence of the correct specification for ε_i^2 the correct standard errors and t-tests were not available.

My other approach was to explore "how bad" things could be if one did OLS. Here I used " Watson's bound" (Watson 1967; Hannan 1970), to derive a formula in the single regressor setup.[1] The question at hand is how badly will OLS perform relative to GLS where the answer depends on both X and Λ. The efficiency measure is *EB* easy to compute:

$$EB(X, \Lambda) = \left(\sum_i \left(\frac{x_i^2}{\sigma_i^2}\right)\right)^{-1}.$$

Thus, the relationship of x_i and σ_i^2 is clear. Now for fixed X the approach is to maximize over Λ which is a straightforward characteristic value problem. Let us arrange the λ_is from smallest to largest, $0 \leq \lambda_1 \leq \cdots \leq \lambda_N$ where N is the sample size. Watson's bound, which is attainable, is

$$EB(X, \Lambda) \geq \frac{4\lambda_1^2\lambda_N^2}{2 + \left(\frac{\lambda_1^2}{\lambda_N^2}\right) + \left(\frac{\lambda_N^2}{\lambda_1^2}\right)}$$

where the estimates of σ_i^2 can replace the λ_i^2 in the efficiency bound formula. Calculating the bound for some illustrative values of the ratio of the largest to smallest variance yields:

Efficiency Bounds						
Ratio	1.2	1.5	2	5	10	100
Bound	0.992	0.960	0.889	0.556	0.331	0.039

[1] I also did analysis with multiple right-hand side variables but I will not discuss the results here since they are more complicated.

Thus, for cross-sectional data the loss in efficiency is typically not very large. Indeed, for typical *inid* cross-section Xs, a refined calculation demonstrates that the efficiency losses tend to be even smaller. However, as the number of right-hand side variables grows, the bound deteriorates. Thus, the efficiency loss in a given sample for fixed Xs could be calculated and a bound over all Xs was also available. However, unless we know the correct specification for the variances in the FGLS approach, we still did not have an estimate of the standard errors, since this period preceded the bootstrap approach.

Here, Hal solved the problem with his formula for "White standard errors", (White 1980). I first heard Hal's paper at the weekly joint Harvard–MIT Thursday econometrics seminar. I remember walking out of the seminar and saying to my close friend and co-author Zvi Griliches that Hal's paper would change the way we do econometrics. Zvi was less enthusiastic, perhaps since Hal had not been his student, but my prediction appears correct given the presence of Hal's formula in all econometric software packages and the large number of citations. Two further points. I talked with Hal when he was my TA about the "Hausman specification test" approach, and his comments were quite helpful. Second, the "Newey-West standard errors" for time series applications followed from two subsequent TAs for my econometrics courses. So I am pleased thinking that all applied econometrics computer output for regressions should have output arising from my TAs at MIT.

2 Finite Sample Approach

As Hal's thesis supervisor, I now propose a possible finite sample improvement to his approach. James MacKinnon (2011) in his paper in this volume has explored various bootstrap approaches to improve the finite sample performance of White standard error estimation. Since I am interested in inference, I will explore possible improvements in the behavior of the "t-test" using Hal's approach. However, if one is interested in the estimated standard errors, one can derive an estimate using division on the refined t-test divided by the OLS estimate of the parameter.

In large samples the asymptotic approximation assumes we know the true σ_i^2s. However, in finite samples we use estimates of these parameters. Guido Keurstiener and I explored this effect in inference from FGLS applied to difference-in-differences models in Hausman and Kuersteiner (2008). We found that taking account of the unknown variance estimates using Rothenberg (1988) second order Edgeworth expansion approach led to much more accurate sized tests. Also, we found that the second order expansion approach did better than the bootstrap in terms of power. Thus, I have applied a modification to the second order expansion to calculation of t-tests based on estimated White standard errors.[2] I have used the design framework

[2] This research is done jointly with Christopher Palmer, one of my current TAs. See Hausman and Palmer (2012).

from James MacKinnon's paper to see how his bootstrap approaches compare with the second-order refinement approach.

I consider the test statistic for linear combinations of the parameters and the null hypothesis $H_0 : c'\beta = c'\beta_0$. The associated t-statistic is

$$T = \frac{c'\hat{\beta} - c'\beta_0}{\sqrt{c'\hat{V}c}} \tag{1}$$

We first consider the size of various tests where the estimate of Σ in the middle matrix $X'\Sigma X$ takes various forms:[3]

1. HC0: White approach using the OLS residuals to estimate

$$\Sigma = \text{diag}\left\{\hat{u}_i^2\right\} \tag{2}$$

2. HC1: this approach adjusts for degrees of freedom and is the most commonly used form:

$$\Sigma = \frac{n}{n-k}\text{diag}\left\{\hat{u}_i^2\right\} \tag{3}$$

3. HC2: this approach adjusts for the "leverage" values h_i, where h is the diagonal of the projection matrix.

$$\Sigma = \text{diag}\left\{\frac{\hat{u}_i^2}{1-h_i}\right\} \tag{4}$$

where $h = \text{diag}\,(P_X)$ and $P_X = X(X'X)^{-1}X^1$ is the projection matrix of X.

4. HC3: this approach is an approximation to the jackknife covariance matrix HCJ, which I emit here because it is computationally more complicated and provides nearly identical results. HC3 is a slight modification of HC2:

$$\Sigma = \text{diag}\left\{\left(\frac{\hat{u}_i}{1-h_i}\right)^2\right\} \tag{5}$$

See MacKinnon (zou) for results containing HC4, which I omit because of its poor size performance in this design.

I compare these estimators to the Rothenberg second order Edgeworth approximation. This approach modifies the traditional two-sided critical values $Z_\alpha/2$ for a t-statistic of null hypothesis $\text{Ho}^2\ \text{C}'\beta = \text{C}'\beta_0$ with the equation:

$$t = \pm z_{\alpha/2}\left(1 - \frac{A}{2n}\right) \tag{6}$$

where n is the sample size and

[3] I use the same notation that MacKinnon uses in his paper in this volume.

$$
\begin{aligned}
A &= \frac{1}{4}(1 + z_{\alpha/2}^2)V_W - a(z_{\alpha/2}^2 - 1) - b \\
V_W &= \frac{2n}{3}\frac{\sum f_i^4 \hat{u}_i^4}{\left(\sum f_i^2 \hat{u}_i^2\right)^2} \\
a &= \frac{\sum f_i^2 g_i^2}{\sum f_i^2 \hat{u}_i^2} \\
b &= \frac{\sum f_i^2 Q_{ii}}{\sum f_i^2 \hat{u}_i^2} \\
f &= nX(X'X)^{-1}\mathrm{C} \\
g &= \frac{M\Sigma f}{\sqrt{f'\Sigma f/n}} \\
Q &= n(M\Sigma M - \Sigma) \\
M &= I - P_X
\end{aligned}
$$

and $\hat{u}_i$ are the fitted residuals.

However, the experience of applying this formula in Hausman and Palmer (2012) was that it has significant size distortions. Thus, I apply a non-parametric bootstrap to estimate β. For B bootstrap iterations, I resample (X, y) with replacement from the original data, forming a bootstrap sample (X^*, y^*). For each iteration j, I then calculate $\beta_j^* = (X^{*\prime}X^*)^{-1}X^{*\prime}y^*$, and take $\hat{V}$ to be

$$
\hat{V} = \frac{1}{B-1}\sum_{j=1}^{B}\left(\hat{\beta}_j^* - \bar{\hat{\beta}}^*\right)\left(\hat{\beta}_j^* - \bar{\hat{\beta}}^*\right)'. \tag{7}
$$

I use this estimated covariance matrix to calculate the test statistic in equation (1) and make interference by comparing it with the adjusted critical value obtained from equation (6), an approach. I refer to as the "second order bootstrap", or SOB, method.

To test our approach I use the same simulation design as MacKinnon (2011)

$$
\begin{aligned}
y_i &= \beta_1 + \sum_{k=2}^{5}\beta_k X_{ik} + u_i \\
u_i &= \sigma_i \varepsilon_i \\
\varepsilon_i &\sim \mathcal{N}(0, 1) \\
\sigma_i &= z(\gamma)\,(X_i\beta)^{\gamma} \\
X_{ik} &\sim LN(0, 1) \qquad \text{for} \quad k \geq 2 \\
\beta_k &= 1 \qquad \text{for} \quad k < 5 \\
\beta_5 &= 0
\end{aligned}
$$

where $\gamma = 0$ corresponds to homoskedasticity, and the degree of heteroskedasticity increases with γ, and $z(\gamma)$ is a scaling factor which ensures that the average variance of u_i is equal to 1.

I first consider the sizes of the various approaches. I test $H_0 : \beta_5 = 0$ with a size of $\alpha = 0.05$. In Graph 1 we see that HC0 rejects much too often as is well-recognized.

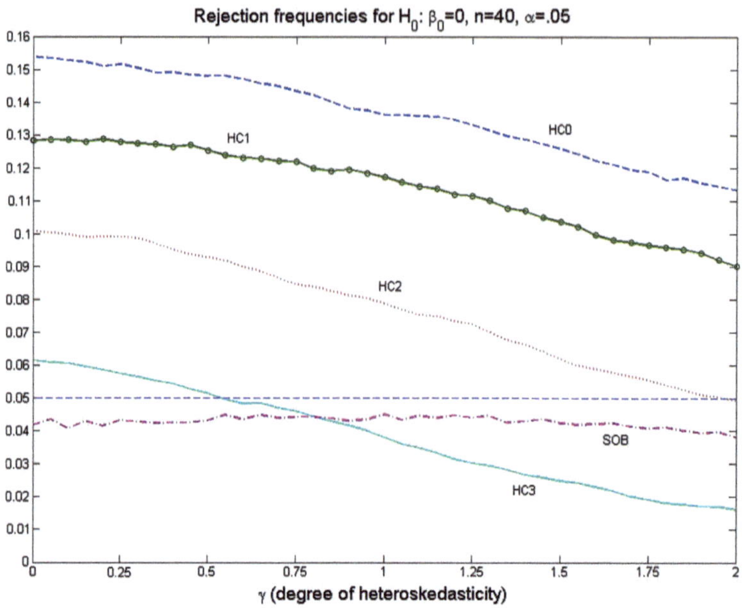

The alternatives HC1, HC2, and HC3 offer improvements, but all have significant size distortions. The "second order bootstrap" (SOB) approach has acceptable size performance, being the best of the alternatives considered.[4]

I now consider power performance and compare the SOB approach to a bootstrap approach to the White test. It is well recognized, e.g., (Hall 1992), the bootstrapped test statistic for a pivotal situation has the same order of approximation as the second-order approach. MacKinnon finds the wild bootstrap to perform the best using the following specification. The wild bootstrap involves forming B bootstrap samples using the data generating process

$$y_i^* = X_i\tilde{\beta} + f(\tilde{u}_i)v_i^*,$$

[4] I do not consider the bootstrap form of the White test since Hausman and Palmer (2012) find it has significant size distortions and will be inferior in terms of the higher order expansions to the bootstrap version of the test I consider below.

where $\tilde{u}_i$ are residuals from an estimate $\tilde{\beta}$ of β, $f(\cdot)$ is one of several candidate transformations of the estimated residuals, and v_i^* is a random variable with mean 0 and variance 1, such that $E\left(f(\tilde{u}_i)v_i^*\right) = 0$. For each bootstrap sample $\{X_i, y_i^*\}$, I estimate $\hat{\beta}_j^*$ where j indexes the bootstrap sample, $j = 1, \ldots, B$, and calculates the test statistic of interest, as in (1), using a particular heteroskedasticity-robust estimator of the variance of $\hat{\beta}$.

MacKinnon (2011) shows that using the wild bootstrap to estimate the distribution of test statistics based on $HC1$, using $v_i^* \in \{-1, 1\}$ with equal probability, restricted residuals (i.e. $\tilde{\beta}$ is estimated imposing the null hyptothesis), and a transformation of the residuals corresponding to $HC3$, $f(\tilde{u}_i) = \frac{\tilde{u}_i}{1-\tilde{h}_i}$ (where $\tilde{h}_i$ an element of the diagonal of the restricted projection matrix $P_{\tilde{X}}$) performs best in terms of size and power.

I now compare the second order-bootstrap (SOB) approach to the best bootstrap approach found by MacKinnon. In Graph 2, we see that the SOB approach has good size properties as does the wild bootstrap (WB), by construction.

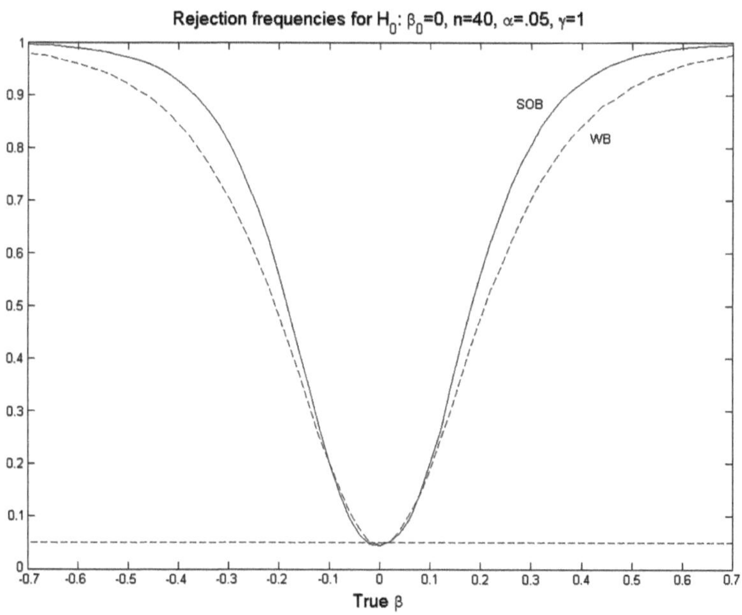

However, the SOB statistic has considerably greater power than the WB. In Graph 3 for the case of severe heteroskedasticity, we find a similar result.

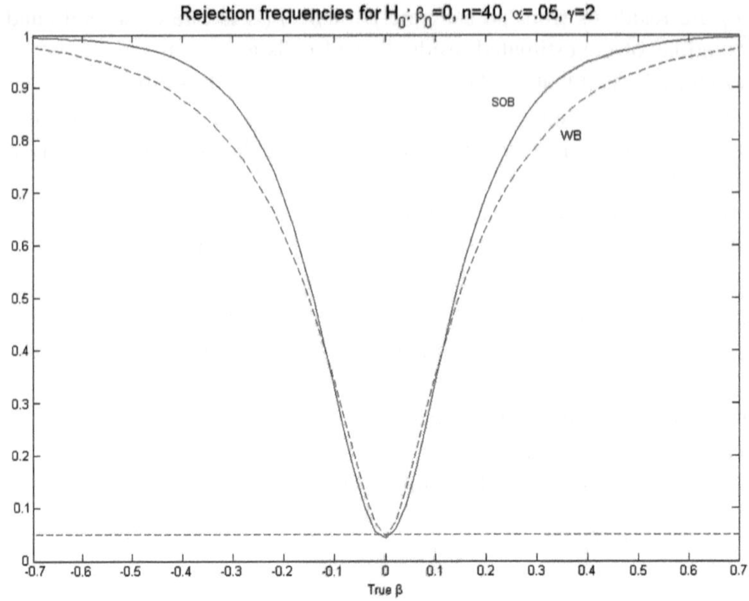

The size of both tests is quite accurate, but the power of the SOB approach exceeds the power of the WB by a considerable margin. Thus, I conclude that the second order bootstrap (SOB) approach appears to be better than alternative approaches to calculating the White test in finite samples.

The refinement to the t-tests arising from the second-order bootstrap approach is straightforward to program for econometric software. Thus, I recommend that econometric software providers include the refined SOB formula since it is typically (weakly) more accurate than the standard White formula.[5]

Hal has written many other important papers since his heteroscedasticity paper. I recommend to the reader the papers in this volume to see the breadth of Hal's research interests and contributions. I take great pride in Hal's accomplishments over the years and congratulate him and the conference organizers for celebrating Hal's sixtieth birthday.

Acknowledgments I thank Christopher Palmer for assisting in the preparation of this note.

[5] Similar refinements could be quite useful in the case of Newey-West and GMM estimated covariance matrices, where the number of unknown parameters estimates is significantly larger than in the heteroscedasticity situation.

References

Cribari-Neto, F. (2004). " Asymptotic inference under heteroskedasticity of unknown form", Computational Statistics and Data Analysis, 45, 215–233.
Davidson, R. and J. G. MacKinnon (1993). Estimation and Inference in Econometrics, New York, Oxford University Press.
Hall, P. (1992). The Bootstrap and Edgeworth Expansion, New York: Springer-Verlag.
Hannan, E.J. (1970). Multiple Time Series. New York: Wiley.
Hausman, J. and G. Kuersteiner (2008). " Difference in difference meets generalized least squares: higher order properties of hypotheses tests," Journal of Econometrics, 144, 371–391.
Hausman J. and C. Palmer (2012). " Heteroskedasticity Robust Inference in Finite Samples, Economics Letters, 116(2), 232–235.
MacKinnon, J.G. (2011). " Thirty years of heteroskedasticity-robust inference", Queen's Economics Department Working Paper No. 1268.
Rothenberg, T. J. (1988). " Approximate power functions for some robust tests of regression coefficients", Econometrica, 56, 997–1019.
Watson, G.S. (1967). " Linear least squares regression", Annals of Mathematical Statistics, 38, 1679–99.
White, H. (1980). " A heteroskedasticity-consistent covariance matrix estimator and a direct test for heteroskedasticity", Econometrica, 48, 817–838.

References

Open-Model Forecast-Error Taxonomies

David F. Hendry and Grayham E. Mizon

Abstract We develop forecast-error taxonomies when there are unmodeled variables, forecast 'off-line'. We establish three surprising results. Even when an open system is correctly specified in-sample with zero intercepts, despite known future values of strongly exogenous variables, changes in dynamics can induce forecast failure when they have nonzero means. The additional impact on forecast failure of incorrectly omitting such variables depends only on unanticipated shifts in their means. With no such shifts, there is no reduction in forecast failure from forecasting unmodeled variables relative to omitting them in 1-step or multi-step forecasts. Artificial data illustrations confirm these results.

Keywords Forecasting · Forecast-error taxonomies · Location shifts · Open models

1 Introduction

Our pleasure at contributing a chapter on forecasting to a volume in honor of Hal White, for whom forecasting was a salient research topic, has been completely dashed by Hal's tragic and premature death. Nevertheless, we should still celebrate a won-

---

Financial support from the Open Society Institute and the Oxford Martin School is gratefully acknowledged. We are indebted to Anindya Banerjee, Jennifer L. Castle, Mike Clements, Jurgen A. Doornik, Neil Ericsson, Katarina Juselius and John N.J. Muellbauer for helpful discussions about and comments on an earlier version.

D. F. Hendry (✉) · G. E. Mizon
Institute for New Economic Thinking at the Oxford Martin School,
University of Oxford, Oxford, UK
e-mail: david.hendry@nuffield.ox.ac.uk

G. E. Mizon
University of Southampton,Southampton, UK
e-mail: grayham.mizon@soton.ac.uk

X. Chen and N. R. Swanson (eds.), *Recent Advances and Future Directions in Causality, Prediction, and Specification Analysis*, DOI: 10.1007/978-1-4614-1653-1_9,

derful and generous individual who will be sorely, missed as well as the many major research findings that flowed from Hal's immensely creative mind.

There are a number of taxonomies of the sources of forecast errors in closed systems where every variable to be forecast is modeled: see for example, Clements and Hendry (1998), Clements and Hendry (2006) and Hendry and Hubrich (2011). Such taxonomies have clarified the problems facing forecasters when parameters change. Forecasting variables as part of systems that are subjected to unanticipated changes is difficult, as recent floods, tsunamis, and the financial crisis demonstrate. Systematic forecast errors and forecast failures are mainly due to location shifts, namely changes in the previous unconditional means of the variables being forecast, and changes in other parameters can be hard to detect, as shown in Hendry (2000) and illustrated by Hendry and Nielsen (2007).

In practice, many forecasting systems include unmodeled determinants, whose future values are determined 'off-line' by a separate process: examples include commodity prices, exchange rates, and outputs of trading partners. There are many reasons for not modeling some variables, namely those that are exceptionally difficult to forecast accurately, other variables that are policy instruments determined outside the system in use, and some weakly exogenous variables where conditioning on them incurs no loss of information for modeling: see Engle et al. (1983). Using a taxonomy of the consequences of including or excluding 'off-line' variables as inputs in forecasting models, we clarify the forecasting problems which could result. Even when the forecasting model is correctly specified in-sample having accurately estimated coefficients, with unmodeled variables that are strongly exogenous and *known* into the future, nevertheless changes in the dynamics of the system can induce forecast failure simply because the unmodeled variables have nonzero means.

At first sight such a claim seems counter-intuitive: if a variable y_t is determined by

$$y_t = \gamma y_{t-1} + \lambda z_t + \varepsilon_t$$

say, when $\varepsilon_t \sim \mathsf{IN}[0, \sigma_\varepsilon^2]$, and z_t is strongly exogenous, then for known λz_t:

$$(y_t - \lambda z_t) = \gamma y_{t-1} + \varepsilon_t \tag{1}$$

where the right-hand side has no intercept. Hence it might seem that (1) is in the class of models where change is hard to detect. However, if z_t has a nonzero mean, then so does y_t, and that alone makes the model susceptible to forecast failure after any parameters change, and as we show below, that result holds whether or not z_t is included in the model.

There are four distinct scenarios to consider for 1-step ahead forecasts, when facing parameter shifts in the data-generation process (DGP). First, where strongly exogenous variables with known future values are correctly included in the forecasting model and all parameters are known (or sufficiently precisely estimated that sampling variation is a second-order issue). Second, when the strongly exogenous variables are unknowingly and incorrectly omitted. Third, when the strongly exogenous variables need to be forecast, either within the system or 'off-line'. Finally, allowing for parameter-estimation uncertainty, model misspecification for the DGP and measurement errors at the forecast origin, a setting which in principle is applicable to all three previous cases but here is only considered for the third. An analogous four scenarios arise for multi-step forecasts, but as the key results seem little affected, we focus on the first four scenarios and briefly note extensions to forecasting more than one period ahead.

Section 2 investigates a correctly-specified $\mathsf{I}(0)$ open system to consider the sources of forecast failure that can result from changes in the parameters when the m unmodeled strongly exogenous variables, $\mathbf{z}_t$, have nonzero means. Section 2.1 investigates any additional impacts from unknowingly omitting the $\mathbf{z}_t$, and Sect. 2.2 compares 1-step forecasts one period later in both those settings. Section 3 develops 1-step taxonomies, first for excluding the $\mathbf{z}_t$, then in §3.1 when they are forecast 'off-line', also allowing for parameter-estimation uncertainty, measurement errors at the forecast origin, and mis-forecasting the $\mathbf{z}_t$. Section 4 provides an artificial data illustration of the analytical results. Section 5 considers multi-step forecasts when the exogenous process is known in the future, then §5.1, §5.2 and §5.3, respectively consider the impacts of omitting the unmodeled variables, forecasting them, then parameter estimation. Section 6 briefly notes the transformations needed to reduce an initially $\mathsf{I}(1)$ system to $\mathsf{I}(0)$. Section 7 concludes. The appendix compares forecasting in open and closed $\mathsf{I}(0)$ systems.

2 Forecasting in an Open I(0) System

Consider an open $\mathsf{I}(0)$ system conditional on a set of m strongly exogenous variables $\{\mathbf{z}_t\}$,[1] which are known into the future (lagged unmodeled variables can be stacked within $\mathbf{z}_t$) where the conditional DGP over $t = 1, \ldots T$ is:

$$\mathbf{y}_t = \tau + \Upsilon \mathbf{y}_{t-1} + \Gamma \mathbf{z}_t + \varepsilon_t \tag{2}$$

when $\varepsilon_t \sim \mathsf{IN}_n [\mathbf{0}, \Sigma]$ and $\mathsf{E}\left[\varepsilon_t | \mathbf{z}_1 \ldots \mathbf{z}_{T+H}\right] = \mathbf{0}$. A system which is $\mathsf{I}(1)$ and cointegrated is considered in §6. When all the variables are weakly stationary in-sample, so the eigenvalues of Υ lie within the unit circle, and we initially set all parameters to be constant, taking expectations in (2) when $\mathsf{E}[\mathbf{z}_t] = \rho$:

$$\mathsf{E}\left[\mathbf{y}_t\right] = \phi = \tau + \Upsilon\phi + \Gamma\mathsf{E}[\mathbf{z}_t] = \tau + \Upsilon\phi + \Gamma\rho,$$

so the in-sample equilibrium mean of $\mathbf{y}$ is:

$$\phi = (\mathbf{I}_n - \Upsilon)^{-1} (\tau + \Gamma\rho) \tag{3}$$

Consequently, we can re-write (2) as:

[1] Corresponding to $\Psi_{zy} = \mathbf{0}$ in the Appendix.

$$\mathbf{y}_t - \phi = \Upsilon (\mathbf{y}_{t-1} - \phi) + \Gamma (\mathbf{z}_t - \rho) + \varepsilon_t \tag{4}$$

Below, we use whichever parametrization (2) or (4) proves most convenient, although it must be remembered that how the means ϕ and ρ are connected in (3) depends on the invariants of the underlying behavior represented by agents' plans. For example, (3) only entails co-breaking between ϕ and ρ so long as the other parameters remain constant when ρ shifts: see Hendry and Massmann (2007), for an analysis of co-breaking. Concerning notation for forecast values, $\overline{\mathbf{y}}$ denotes a correctly specified model with known future $\mathbf{z}$; $\widetilde{\mathbf{y}}$ denotes when $\mathbf{z}$ is omitted from the model; and $\widehat{\mathbf{y}}$ is when the $\mathbf{z}$ are included in the model, but future values need to be forecast; and if needed, $\widehat{\widehat{\mathbf{y}}}$ for that last case when parameters are estimated. $\widehat{\mathbf{y}}_T$ denotes an estimated forecast-origin value.

We first consider a 1-step ahead forecast from time T for known $\mathbf{z}_{T+1}$ from a model that is correctly specified in-sample with known parameter values, denoted:

$$\overline{\mathbf{y}}_{T+1|T} = \tau + \Upsilon \mathbf{y}_T + \Gamma \mathbf{z}_{T+1} \tag{5}$$

However, the DGP in the next period in fact changes to:

$$\mathbf{y}_{T+1} = \tau^* + \Upsilon^* \mathbf{y}_T + \Gamma^* \mathbf{z}_{T+1} + \varepsilon_{T+1} \tag{6}$$

where all the parameters shift, including the dynamic feedback, and ρ shifts to $\mathsf{E}\left[\mathbf{z}_{T+1}\right] = \rho^*$. The resulting forecast error between (5) and (6) is $\overline{\varepsilon}_{T+1|T} = \mathbf{y}_{T+1} - \overline{\mathbf{y}}_{T+1|T}$ and hence:

$$\overline{\varepsilon}_{T+1|T} = \left(\tau^* - \tau\right) + \left(\Upsilon^* - \Upsilon\right) \mathbf{y}_T + \left(\Gamma^* - \Gamma\right) z_{T+1} + \varepsilon_{T+1} \tag{7}$$

so that:

$$\begin{aligned} \mathsf{E}\left[\overline{\varepsilon}_{T+1|T}\right] &= \left(\tau^* - \tau\right) + \left(\Upsilon^* - \Upsilon\right) \mathsf{E}\left[\mathbf{y}_T\right] + \left(\Gamma^* - \Gamma\right) \mathsf{E}\left[\mathbf{z}_{T+1}\right] \\ &= \left(\tau^* - \tau\right) + \left(\Upsilon^* - \Upsilon\right) \phi + \left(\Gamma^* - \Gamma\right) \rho^* \end{aligned} \tag{8}$$

Consequently, even if $\tau^* = \tau = \mathbf{0}$ so (7) has no intercept and $\Gamma^* = \Gamma$ and $\rho^* = \rho$, so (8) then does not depend directly on $\mathbf{z}_{T+1}$ which anyway has constant parameters, nevertheless forecast failure can occur for $\rho \neq \mathbf{0}$ when $\Upsilon^* \neq \Upsilon$ as then:

$$\mathsf{E}\left[\overline{\varepsilon}_{T+1|T}\right] = \left(\Upsilon^* - \Upsilon\right) (\mathbf{I}_n - \Upsilon)^{-1} \Gamma \rho \tag{9}$$

which reveals an equilibrium-mean shift occurs in $\{\mathbf{y}_t\}$.

This outcome may be clearer when (4) is written using (3) as:

$$\mathbf{y}_t = (\mathbf{I}_n - \Upsilon)^{-1} (\tau + \Gamma \rho) + \Upsilon (\mathbf{y}_{t-1} - \phi) + \Gamma (\mathbf{z}_t - \rho) + \varepsilon_t \tag{10}$$

so that even when $\tau = \mathbf{0}$, although $(\mathbf{y}_{t-1} - \phi)$, $\Gamma(\mathbf{z}_t - \rho)$ and ε_t all have expectations of zero, (10) entails an equilibrium mean of

$$(\mathbf{I}_n - \Upsilon)^{-1} \Gamma\rho \tag{11}$$

which is zero only if $\rho = \mathbf{0}$ when $\Gamma \neq \mathbf{0}$.

This is our first main result: despite correctly including unmodeled strongly exogenous variables $\mathbf{z}_t$ with known future values in a forecasting equation with no intercept and known parameters, a change in dynamics alone can induce forecast failure when the $\mathbf{z}_t$ have nonzero means.

More surprising still is that such failure is little different to that resulting either from modeling and forecasting $\mathbf{z}_t$ (see §3) possibly by a vector autoregression (VAR) say, or even excluding $\mathbf{z}_t$ entirely from the model, either deliberately or inadvertently, as we now show in §2.1.

2.1 Omitting the Exogenous Variables

If it is not known that $\mathbf{z}_t$ is relevant, so it is inadvertently omitted, the misspecified model of (4) is:

$$\mathbf{y}_t = \phi + \Upsilon_e (\mathbf{y}_{t-1} - \phi) + \mathbf{u}_t \tag{12}$$

where the subscript $_e$ in (12) denotes the finite-sample expected value following misspecification (i.e., $\mathsf{E}[\widetilde{\Upsilon}] = \Upsilon_e$). Then $\mathbf{u}_t = \Gamma_e(\mathbf{z}_t - \rho) + \varepsilon_t$ with $\mathsf{E}[\mathbf{u}_t] = \mathbf{0}$. Provided there have not been any equilibrium mean shifts in-sample, then $\phi_e = \phi$. The forecast using the expected parameter values (to abstract from sampling uncertainty) is:

$$\widetilde{\mathbf{y}}_{T+1|T} = \phi + \Upsilon_e (\mathbf{y}_T - \phi) \tag{13}$$

with $\widetilde{\mathbf{u}}_{T+1|T} = \mathbf{y}_{T+1} - \widetilde{\mathbf{y}}_{T+1|T}$ where (6) is reparametrized as:

$$\mathbf{y}_{T+1} = \phi^* + \Upsilon^* \left(\mathbf{y}_T - \phi^*\right) + \Gamma^* \left(\mathbf{z}_{T+1} - \rho^*\right) + \varepsilon_{T+1} \tag{14}$$

where $\phi^* = (\mathbf{I}_n - \Upsilon^*)^{-1} (\tau^* + \Gamma^*\rho^*)$. Then:

$$\begin{aligned}\widetilde{\mathbf{u}}_{T+1|T} &= \left(\phi^* - \phi\right) + \Upsilon^* \left(\mathbf{y}_T - \phi^*\right) - \Upsilon_e (\mathbf{y}_T - \phi) + \Gamma^* \left(\mathbf{z}_{T+1} - \rho^*\right) + \varepsilon_{T+1} \\ &= \left(\mathbf{I}_n - \Upsilon^*\right)\left(\phi^* - \phi\right) + \left(\Upsilon^* - \Upsilon_e\right)(\mathbf{y}_T - \phi) + \Gamma^* \left(\mathbf{z}_{T+1} - \rho^*\right) + \varepsilon_{T+1}\end{aligned} \tag{15}$$

with:

$$\mathsf{E}\left[\tilde{\mathbf{u}}_{T+1|T}\right] = \left(\mathbf{I}_n - \Upsilon^*\right)\left(\phi^* - \phi\right)$$
$$= \left(\tau^* - \tau\right) + \left(\Upsilon^* - \Upsilon\right)\phi + \left(\Gamma^* - \Gamma\right)\rho^* + \Gamma\left(\rho^* - \rho\right) \quad (16)$$

Thus, (8) and (16) only differ by $\Gamma\,(\rho^* - \rho)$, and hence are the same when $\rho^* = \rho$ despite the mis-specification. When also $\tau^* = \tau = \mathbf{0}$ and $\Gamma^* = \Gamma$, both are nonzero at the value in (9). However, the forecast-error variances will differ between (15) and (7), with the former being larger in general.

This is our second main result: the additional impact on forecast failure of incorrectly omitting strongly exogenous variables depends only on shifts in their means. Combining these first two results, as the comparison of and (8) (16) shows, when their means are constant at zero, then irrespective of whether or not these strongly exogenous variables are included in the forecasting system, they neither cause nor augment forecast failure.

2.2 1-Step Forecasts One Period Later

The analyses of forecasting one period after a break in Clements and Hendry (2011) show that results can be substantively altered because of the impacts of the breaks on later data. From (6):

$$\mathbf{y}_{T+2} = \tau^* + \Upsilon^*\mathbf{y}_{T+1} + \Gamma^* z_{T+2} + \varepsilon_{T+2} \quad (17)$$

so that as $\mathsf{E}\left[\mathbf{z}_{T+2}\right] = \rho^*$:

$$\mathsf{E}\left[\mathbf{y}_{T+2}\right] = \tau^* + \Upsilon^*\mathsf{E}\left[\mathbf{y}_{T+1}\right] + \Gamma^*\mathsf{E}\left[\mathbf{z}_{T+2}\right] = \left(\mathbf{I}_n - \left(\Upsilon^*\right)^2\right)\phi^* + \left(\Upsilon^*\right)^2\phi$$
$$= \phi^* - \left(\Upsilon^*\right)^2\left(\phi^* - \phi\right) \quad (18)$$

as $\phi^* = \left(\mathbf{I}_n - \Upsilon^*\right)^{-1}\left(\tau^* + \Gamma^*\rho^*\right)$ and $\mathsf{E}\left[\mathbf{y}_{T+1}\right] = \phi^* - \Upsilon^*\left(\phi^* - \phi\right)$. Forecasting from (5) updated one period, but still with in-sample known parameters, so:[2]

$$\overline{\mathbf{y}}_{T+2|T+1} = \tau + \Upsilon y_{T+1} + \Gamma\mathbf{z}_{T+2} \quad (19)$$

the resulting forecast error $\overline{\varepsilon}_{T+2|T+1} = \mathbf{y}_{T+2} - \overline{\mathbf{y}}_{T+2|T+1}$ is:

[2] Recursive or moving windows updating will drive the forecasting system toward the robust device considered in §2.3.

$$
\begin{aligned}
\overline{\varepsilon}_{T+2|T+1} = & \left(\mathbf{I}_n + \Upsilon^* - \Upsilon\right)\left(\mathbf{I}_n - \Upsilon^*\right)\left(\phi^* - \phi\right) && (Ia)\\
& + \left(\Upsilon^* - \Upsilon\right)\left(\mathbf{y}_{T+1} - \mathsf{E}\left[\mathbf{y}_{T+1}\right]\right) && (IIa)\\
& + \varepsilon_{T+2} && (IIIa)\\
& + \left(\Gamma^* - \Gamma\right)\left(\mathbf{z}_{T+2} - \rho^*\right) && (IVa)\\
& - \Gamma\left(\rho^* - \rho\right) && (Va)
\end{aligned}
\tag{20}
$$

with

$$
\mathsf{E}\left[\overline{\varepsilon}_{T+2|T+1}\right] = \left(\mathbf{I}_n + \Upsilon^* - \Upsilon\right)\left(\mathbf{I}_n - \Upsilon^*\right)\left(\phi^* - \phi\right) - \Gamma\left(\rho^* - \rho\right) \tag{21}
$$

Similarly, omitting the $\mathbf{z}_{T+2}$, so using:

$$
\widetilde{\mathbf{y}}_{T+2|T+1} = \phi + \Upsilon_e\left(\mathbf{y}_{T+1} - \phi\right) \tag{22}
$$

then as:

$$
\mathbf{y}_{T+2} = \phi^* - \left(\Upsilon^*\right)^2\left(\phi^* - \phi\right) + \Upsilon^*\left(\mathbf{y}_{T+1} - \mathsf{E}\left[\mathbf{y}_{T+1}\right]\right) + \Gamma^*\left(\mathbf{z}_{T+2} - \rho^*\right) + \varepsilon_{T+2} \tag{23}
$$

the forecast error $\widetilde{\varepsilon}_{T+2|T+1} = \mathbf{y}_{T+2} - \widetilde{\mathbf{y}}_{T+2|T+1}$ is:

$$
\begin{aligned}
\widetilde{\varepsilon}_{T+2|T+1} = & \left(\mathbf{I}_n + \Upsilon^* - \Upsilon_e\right)\left(\mathbf{I}_n - \Upsilon^*\right)\left(\phi^* - \phi\right) && (Ib)\\
& + \left(\Upsilon^* - \Upsilon_e\right)\left(\mathbf{y}_{T+1} - \mathsf{E}\left[\mathbf{y}_{T+1}\right]\right) && (IIb)\\
& + \varepsilon_{T+2} && (IIIb)\\
& + \Gamma^*\left(\mathbf{z}_{T+2} - \rho^*\right) && (IVb)
\end{aligned}
\tag{24}
$$

with:

$$
\mathsf{E}\left[\widetilde{\varepsilon}_{T+2|T+1}\right] = \left(\mathbf{I}_n + \Upsilon^* - \Upsilon_e\right)\left(\mathbf{I}_n - \Upsilon^*\right)\left(\phi^* - \phi\right) \tag{25}
$$

Consequently, unlike Clements and Hendry (2011), comparing (21) and (25) shows that there are no substantive changes compared to the baseline case here, and those two formulae are essentially the same when $\rho^* = \rho$.

2.3 Avoiding Systematic Forecast Failure

One implication of §2.2 is that until the forecasting model is changed, systematic forecast failure will persist. Out of the many possible methods for updating a model by intercept corrections, modeling the break, recursive or moving window re-estimation and differencing, we only note the last here: see Hendry (2006). In place of (22), consider simply using the first-difference forecast, $\Delta\widetilde{\mathbf{y}}_{T+2|T+1} = \mathbf{0}$:

$$\widetilde{\mathbf{y}}_{T+2|T+1} = \mathbf{y}_{T+1} = \phi^* + \Upsilon^* \left(\mathbf{y}_T - \phi^*\right) + \Gamma^* \left(\mathbf{z}_{T+1} - \rho^*\right) + \varepsilon_{T+1}$$

so that using (23), $\widetilde{\varepsilon}_{T+2|T+1} = \mathbf{y}_{T+2} - \widetilde{\mathbf{y}}_{T+2|T+1}$ is:

$$\begin{aligned}
\widetilde{\varepsilon}_{T+2|T+1} &= \phi^* - \left(\Upsilon^*\right)^2 \left(\phi^* - \phi\right) + \Upsilon^* \left(\mathbf{y}_{T+1} - \mathsf{E}\left[\mathbf{y}_{T+1}\right]\right) + \Gamma^* \left(\mathbf{z}_{T+2} - \rho^*\right) \\
&\quad + \varepsilon_{T+2} - \phi^* + \Upsilon^* \left(\phi^* - \phi\right) - \Upsilon^* \left(\mathbf{y}_T - \phi\right) - \Gamma^* \left(\mathbf{z}_{T+1} - \rho^*\right) - \varepsilon_{T+1} \\
&= \Upsilon^* \left(\mathbf{I}_n - \Upsilon^*\right) \left(\phi^* - \phi\right) + \Upsilon^* \left(\mathbf{y}_{T+1} - \mathsf{E}\left[\mathbf{y}_{T+1}\right]\right) \\
&\quad - \Upsilon^* \left(\mathbf{y}_T - \phi\right) + \Gamma^* \Delta \mathbf{z}_{T+2} + \Delta \varepsilon_{T+2}
\end{aligned}$$

so:

$$\mathsf{E}\left[\widetilde{\varepsilon}_{T+2|T+1}\right] = \Upsilon^* \left(\mathbf{I}_n - \Upsilon^*\right) \left(\phi^* - \phi\right) \tag{26}$$

which considerably dampens the forecast-error bias relative to (20) and (24) (e.g., for a univariate y_t, then $\Upsilon^* \left(1 - \Upsilon^*\right) \leq 0.25$).

3 1-Step Taxonomies

We now also allow for parameter estimation uncertainty, the misspecification of omitting **z**, and possible mismeasurement at the forecast origin, so the forecast-period DGP remains (14), whereas the forecasting model becomes:

$$\widetilde{\mathbf{y}}_{T+1|T} = \widetilde{\phi} + \widetilde{\Upsilon} \left(\widetilde{\mathbf{y}}_T - \widetilde{\phi}\right) \tag{27}$$

The forecast error, $\widetilde{\varepsilon}_{T+1|T} = \mathbf{y}_{T+1} - \widetilde{\mathbf{y}}_{T+1|T}$ can be decomposed into eleven empirically-relevant sources when $\phi_e \neq \phi$:

$$\begin{aligned}
\widetilde{\varepsilon}_{T+1|T} = & \left(\mathbf{I}_n - \Upsilon^*\right) \left(\phi^* - \phi\right) && \text{[1] equilibrium-mean shift} \\
& + \left(\Upsilon^* - \Upsilon\right) \left(\mathbf{y}_T - \phi\right) && \text{[2] dynamic shift} \\
& + \left(\mathbf{I}_n - \Upsilon_e\right) \left(\phi - \phi_e\right) && \text{[3] equilibrium-mean mis-specification} \\
& + \left(\Upsilon - \Upsilon_e\right) \left(\mathbf{y}_T - \phi\right) && \text{[4] dynamic mis-specification} \\
& + \left(\mathbf{I}_n - \Upsilon_e\right) \left(\phi_e - \widetilde{\phi}\right) && \text{[5] equilibrium-mean estimation} \\
& + \left(\Upsilon_e - \widetilde{\Upsilon}\right) \left(\mathbf{y}_T - \phi\right) && \text{[6] dynamic estimation} \\
& + \Upsilon_e \left(\mathbf{y}_T - \widetilde{\mathbf{y}}_T\right) && \text{[7] forecast origin mis-measurement} \\
& + \left(\widetilde{\Upsilon} - \Upsilon_e\right) \left(\widetilde{\phi} - \phi\right) && \text{[8] estimation covariance} \\
& + \left(\widetilde{\Upsilon} - \Upsilon_e\right) \left(\mathbf{y}_T - \widetilde{\mathbf{y}}_T\right) && \text{[9] measurement covariance} \\
& + \varepsilon_{T+1} && \text{[10] innovation error} \\
& + \Gamma^* \left(\mathbf{z}_{T+1} - \rho^*\right) && \text{[11] omitted variables}
\end{aligned} \tag{28}$$

As with earlier taxonomies, terms in (28) can be divided into those with nonzero expected values that lead to forecast biases, namely [1] and possibly [3] and [7] (noting that [8] is $\mathsf{O}_p(T^{-1})$), and those with zero means that only affect forecast error variances, namely all the other terms, noting that $\mathsf{E}[\mathbf{y}_T - \phi] = \mathsf{E}[\mathbf{z}_{T+1} - \rho^*] = \mathbf{0}$. Thus, despite estimating a misspecified system with omitted variables:

$$\mathsf{E}\left[\widetilde{\varepsilon}_{T+1|T}\right] \approx \left(\mathbf{I}_n - \Upsilon^*\right)\left(\phi^* - \phi\right) + \Upsilon_e\left(\phi - \mathsf{E}\left[\widetilde{\mathbf{y}}_T\right]\right)$$

which matches (16) when $\mathsf{E}\left[\widetilde{\mathbf{y}}_T\right] = \phi$.

This outcome could be compared directly with that from including the known $\mathbf{z}_t$ in estimation and forecasting by dropping line [10], stacking $\mathbf{x}_t' = \left(\mathbf{y}_t'\,\mathbf{z}_t'\right)$ and redefining parameters, estimates, and variables accordingly. Indeed, when $\Gamma^* = \Gamma = \mathbf{0}$, (28) becomes the forecast error taxonomy for a VAR.

3.1 Forecasting the Unmodeled Variables

However, the more interesting and realistic case is where $\mathbf{z}_{T+1}$ is known to be relevant and has to be forecast with its parameters estimated in (2), which we now consider via:

$$\widehat{\mathbf{y}}_{T+1|T} = \widehat{\phi} + \widehat{\Upsilon}\left(\widehat{\mathbf{y}}_T - \widehat{\phi}\right) + \widehat{\Gamma}\left(\widehat{\mathbf{z}}_{T+1} - \widehat{\rho}\right) \tag{29}$$

compared to (6). Although the following derivation is under the correct specification of (29), the results above show that misspecification does not create important additional problems, and for the dynamics, is already reflected in (28). Then, letting $\widehat{\varepsilon}_{T+1|T} = \mathbf{y}_{T+1} - \widehat{\mathbf{y}}_{T+1|T}$, all the terms from (28) remain other than [11] (still allowing for finite-sample biases in the dynamics, so $\Upsilon_e \neq \Upsilon$, but for simplicity taking $\mathsf{E}[\widehat{\rho}] = \rho$ and $\mathsf{E}[\widehat{\Gamma}] \approx \Gamma$) with the following 9 terms replacing the old [11].

$$\begin{array}{lll}
\widehat{\varepsilon}_{T+1|T} = & & \text{[1]–[10] in (28)} \\
& -\Gamma\left(\rho^* - \rho\right) & \text{[11] exogenous mean shift} \\
& +\left(\Gamma^* - \Gamma\right)\left(\mathbf{z}_{T+1} - \rho^*\right) & \text{[12] exogenous slope shift} \\
& +\Gamma\left(\widehat{\rho} - \rho\right) & \text{[13] exogenous-mean estimation} \\
& -\left(\widehat{\Gamma} - \Gamma\right)\left(\mathbf{z}_{T+1} - \rho^*\right) & \text{[14] exogenous slope estimation} \\
& +\Gamma\left(\mathbf{z}_{T+1} - \mathsf{E}\left[\widehat{\mathbf{z}}_{T+1}\right]\right) & \text{[15] exogenous mean mis-forecast} \\
& +\left(\widehat{\Gamma} - \Gamma\right)\left(\widehat{\rho} - \rho\right) & \text{[16] estimation covariance} \\
& -\left(\widehat{\Gamma} - \Gamma\right)\left(\rho^* - \rho\right) & \text{[17] exogenous mean shift covariance} \\
& +\Gamma\left(\mathsf{E}\left[\widehat{\mathbf{z}}_{T+1}\right] - \widehat{\mathbf{z}}_{T+1}\right) & \text{[18] exogenous mis-forecast.} \\
& +\left(\widehat{\Gamma} - \Gamma\right)\left(\mathbf{z}_{T+1} - \widehat{\mathbf{z}}_{T+1}\right) & \text{[19] exogenous mis-forecast covariance}
\end{array} \tag{30}$$

We focus on the terms in (30) with non-zero expectations, where $\mathsf{E}\left[\mathbf{z}_{T+1}\right] = \rho^*$, and for simplicity covariances are ignored as a smaller order of magnitude. Then combined with (28):

$$\begin{aligned}\mathsf{E}\left[\widehat{\varepsilon}_{T+1|T}\right] &\approx \left(\mathbf{I}_n - \Upsilon^*\right)\left(\phi^* - \phi\right) - \Gamma\left(\rho^* - \rho\right) + \Upsilon_e\left(\phi - \mathsf{E}\left[\widetilde{\mathbf{y}}_T\right]\right) \\ &\quad + \Gamma\left(\rho^* - \mathsf{E}\left[\widehat{\mathbf{z}}_{T+1}\right]\right) \\ &= \left(\tau^* - \tau\right) + \left(\Upsilon^* - \Upsilon\right)\phi + \left(\Gamma^* - \Gamma\right)\rho^* + \Upsilon_e\left(\phi - \mathsf{E}\left[\widetilde{\mathbf{y}}_T\right]\right) \\ &\quad + \Gamma\left(\rho^* - \mathsf{E}\left[\widehat{\mathbf{z}}_{T+1}\right]\right)\end{aligned}$$

from (16). As before, when $\tau^* = \tau = \mathbf{0}$ and $\Gamma^* = \Gamma$, with $\mathsf{E}\left[\widetilde{\mathbf{y}}_T\right] = \phi$:

$$\mathsf{E}\left[\widehat{\varepsilon}_{T+1|T}\right] \approx \left(\Upsilon^* - \Upsilon\right)\phi + \Gamma\left(\rho^* - \mathsf{E}\left[\widehat{\mathbf{z}}_{T+1}\right]\right)$$

compared to $\mathsf{E}\left[\widetilde{\mathbf{u}}_{T+1|T}\right] = \left(\Upsilon^* - \Upsilon\right)\phi + \Gamma\left(\rho^* - \rho\right)$, so:

$$\mathsf{E}\left[\widehat{\varepsilon}_{T+1|T}\right] - \mathsf{E}\left[\widetilde{\mathbf{u}}_{T+1|T}\right] \approx -\Gamma\left(\mathsf{E}\left[\widehat{\mathbf{z}}_{T+1}\right] - \rho\right) \tag{31}$$

This is our third main result: exogenous variable forecasts have to be closer to the new mean ρ^* than the old mean ρ to deliver a smaller forecast error bias than arises from omitting them.

When $\rho^* = \rho$, $\mathsf{E}\left[\widehat{\mathbf{z}}_{T+1}\right] = \rho$ is necessary for $\mathsf{E}\left[\widehat{\varepsilon}_{T+1|T}\right] = \mathsf{E}\left[\widetilde{\mathbf{u}}_{T+1|T}\right]$, and even then there will be variance effects both from parameter estimation and $\left(\mathsf{E}\left[\widehat{\mathbf{z}}_{T+1}\right] - \widehat{\mathbf{z}}_{T+1}\right)$. *This is our fourth main result*: when $\rho^* = \rho$, there is no reduction in forecast failure from accurately forecasting the exogenous variables relative to omitting them.

Our fifth main result is: this outcome does not depend on the strong exogeneity of the unmodeled variables, and holds even when they are only weakly exogenous.

Without strong assumptions about the dependencies between the many mean-zero terms in the taxonomy, it is not possible to derive explicit forecast error variances, but it is clear there are many contributions beyond the innovation error variance, some of which could well be $\mathsf{O}_p(1)$, such as mis-forecasting the unmodeled variables, and forecast-origin mismeasurement. Moreover, as forecast errors could arise from every possible (non-repetitive) selection from the 19 terms, namely $\sum_{k=1}^{19} 19!/\left(19-k\right)! \approx 3.3 \times 10^{17}$, delineating their source must be nearly impossible.

4 Artificial Data Illustration

We consider a bivariate system with one unmodeled (strongly exogenous) variable, with known future values, where the baseline parameter values are $\tau = \mathbf{0}$ and $\rho = 0$ when:

$$\Upsilon = \begin{pmatrix} 0.5 & 0 \\ 0 & 0.5 \end{pmatrix} \quad \Gamma = \begin{pmatrix} 1 \\ 1 \end{pmatrix} \tag{32}$$

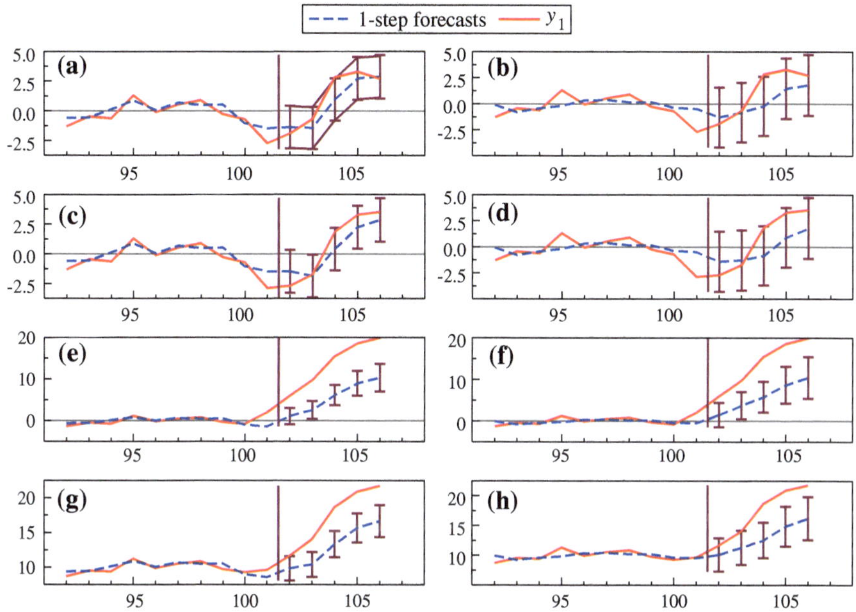

Fig. 1 Forecast failure for correct and misspecified models

with $\Sigma = \mathbf{I}_2$, $T = 100$, and $h = 1, \ldots, 5$ 1-step ahead forecasts after the break. The parameter shift investigated is:

$$\Upsilon^* = \begin{pmatrix} 0.75 & 0 \\ 0 & 0.5 \end{pmatrix} \tag{33}$$

first for the baseline, then when $\rho = 0$ but:

$$\tau = \begin{pmatrix} 5 \\ 0 \end{pmatrix} \tag{34}$$

and finally when $\tau = \mathbf{0}$ but $\rho = 5$.

The two equations are decoupled in this first experiment, whereas in the second:

$$\Upsilon = \begin{pmatrix} 0.5 & 0.5 \\ -0.3 & 0.5 \end{pmatrix} \tag{35}$$

again for the same scenarios.

The results of the first set are reported in Fig. 1.

Panel a records forecasts $\widehat{y}_{1,T+h|T+h-1}$ from a single draw of the initial process in (32) when parameters are estimated, shown with error bands of $\pm 2\widehat{\sigma}_{11}$, and when including parameter estimation uncertainty, shown with bars. There is a very small increase in forecast uncertainty from adding parameter variances, consistent with an $O_p(1/T)$ effect.

Panel b reports forecasts when z_t is omitted both in estimation and forecasting. Although the forecast intervals are wider, forecasts are similar and remain within their *ex ante* forecast intervals.

Panel c is for the correct specification but after the shift in (33), still with $\tau = \mathbf{0}$ and $\rho = 0$. Despite the break in the dynamics, forecasts remain within their *ex ante* forecast intervals, even though those are now incorrect. *Panel d* augments the problem by the incorrect omission of z_t, but hardly differs from *Panel b*.

Although we do not report the outcomes for a constant model and nonzero τ, they are well-behaved around the new data outcomes. The same cannot be said for the outcomes in *Panels e & f* for the nonzero value of τ in (34) after the break in Υ in (33): forecast failure is manifest, and almost unaffected by whether z_t is included or omitted.

Finally, for $\rho = 5$, *Panels g & h* show the forecasts for the same break when the model is correctly specified by including z_t, and incorrect by omitting it. Despite the known future values of z_t and the absence of forecast failure after the break when $\rho = 0$, failure is again manifest and similar to *Panels e & f*.

The second setting in (35) yielded similar results, even though throughout both sets of experiments, the second variable was correctly forecast. All these results are consistent with the implications of the taxonomy in (28).

5 *h*-Step Ahead Forecasts

We now consider the outcomes when an investigator needs to forecast h-steps ahead, $h > 1$. As the impacts of parameter-estimation uncertainty, mis-forecasting the unmodeled variables, and forecast-origin mismeasurement are similar to those derived above, we first derive the outcomes for known parameters to highlight the impacts of breaks when there are unmodeled variables. Thus, the in-sample system remains:

$$\mathbf{y}_t = \phi + \Upsilon\left(\mathbf{y}_{t-1} - \phi\right) + \Gamma\left(\mathbf{z}_t - \rho\right) + \epsilon_t$$

forecasting from $T + h - 1$ to $T + h$ by:

$$\mathbf{y}_{T+h|T+h-1} = \phi + \Upsilon\left(\mathbf{y}_{T+h-1|T+h-2} - \phi\right) + \Gamma\left(\mathbf{z}_{T+h} - \rho\right)$$

leading to the multi-step forecast:

$$\mathbf{y}_{T+h|T} = \phi + \sum_{i=0}^{h-1}\Upsilon^i\Gamma\left(\mathbf{z}_{T+h-i} - \rho\right) + \Upsilon^h\left(\mathbf{y}_T - \phi\right) \tag{36}$$

If the system remained constant, the outcome would be:

$$\mathbf{y}_{T+h} = \phi + \sum_{i=0}^{h-1} \left[\Upsilon^i \Gamma \left(\mathbf{z}_{T+h-i} - \rho \right) + \Upsilon^i \varepsilon_{T+h-i} \right] + \Upsilon^h \left(\mathbf{y}_T - \phi \right) \tag{37}$$

so a known future $\{\mathbf{z}_t\}$ enters the same way as the cumulative error process. Then $\sum_{i=0}^{h-1} \Upsilon^i \varepsilon_{T+h-i}$ would be the only source of forecast error when equation (36) was used. However, that will not remain the case once there are changes in parameters, misspecification of the model, or mis-estimation of Γ in (2), or unanticipated changes to ρ in the forecast period when the $\{\mathbf{z}_{T+h-i}\}$ are not known with certainty.

As before, we allow for structural change in the DGP, but to highlight the key problem, we first analyze a setting without estimation of, or misspecification in, the econometrician's model for the DGP in-sample, so the in-sample parameter values are known. Under changes in all parameters of (37), the actual future outcomes will be:

$$\mathbf{y}_{T+h} = \phi^* + \sum_{i=0}^{h-1} \left(\Upsilon^* \right)^i \left[\Gamma^* \left(\mathbf{z}_{T+h-i} - \rho^* \right) + \varepsilon_{T+h-i} \right] + \left(\Upsilon^* \right)^h \left(\mathbf{y}_T - \phi^* \right) \tag{38}$$

When (36) is used, the forecast error $\mathbf{v}_{T+h|T} = \mathbf{y}_{T+h} - \mathbf{y}_{T+h|T}$ becomes:

$$\begin{aligned}
\mathbf{v}_{T+h|T} = {} & \phi^* - \phi + \left(\Upsilon^* \right)^h \left(\mathbf{y}_T - \phi^* \right) - \Upsilon^h \left(\mathbf{y}_T - \phi \right) \\
& + \sum_{i=0}^{h-1} \left(\Upsilon^* \right)^i \Gamma^* \left(\mathbf{z}_{T+h-i} - \rho^* \right) - \sum_{i=0}^{h-1} \Upsilon^i \Gamma \left(\mathbf{z}_{T+h-i} - \rho \right) \\
& + \sum_{i=0}^{h-1} \left(\Upsilon^* \right)^i \varepsilon_{T+h-i}
\end{aligned}$$

Taking these rows one at a time, and using:

$$\sum_{i=0}^{h-1} \mathbf{A}^i = \left(\mathbf{I}_n - \mathbf{A}^h \right) \left(\mathbf{I}_n - \mathbf{A} \right)^{-1}$$

first:

$$\begin{aligned}
& \phi^* - \phi + \left(\Upsilon^* \right)^h \left(\mathbf{y}_T - \phi^* \right) - \Upsilon^h \left(\mathbf{y}_T - \phi \right) \\
& = \left(\mathbf{I}_n - \left(\Upsilon^* \right)^h \right) \left(\phi^* - \phi \right) + \left(\left(\Upsilon^* \right)^h - \Upsilon^h \right) \left(\mathbf{y}_T - \phi \right)
\end{aligned}$$

where the terms respectively represent equilibrium-mean and slope shifts. Next:

$$\sum_{i=0}^{h-1} (\Upsilon^*)^i \Gamma^* \left(\mathbf{z}_{T+h-i} - \rho^*\right) - \sum_{i=0}^{h-1} \Upsilon^i \Gamma \left(\mathbf{z}_{T+h-i} - \rho\right)$$
$$= \sum_{i=0}^{h-1} \left[(\Upsilon^*)^i \Gamma^* - \Upsilon^i \Gamma \right] \left(\mathbf{z}_{T+h-i} - \rho^*\right) - \sum_{i=0}^{h-1} \Upsilon^i \Gamma \left(\rho^* - \rho\right)$$

where the first component has mean zero and the second is part of the exogenous mean shift. Finally, combining:

$$\begin{aligned} \mathbf{v}_{T+h|T} = & \left(\mathbf{I}_n - (\Upsilon^*)^h\right)(\phi^* - \phi) && \text{[A] equilibrium-mean shift} \\ & + \left((\Upsilon^*)^h - \Upsilon^h\right)(\mathbf{y}_T - \phi) && \text{[B] dynamic shift} \\ & - \left(\mathbf{I}_n - \Upsilon^h\right)(\mathbf{I}_n - \Upsilon)^{-1} \Gamma \left(\rho^* - \rho\right) && \text{[C] exogenous mean shift} \end{aligned} \tag{39}$$
$$\begin{aligned} & + \sum_{i=0}^{h-1} \left[(\Upsilon^*)^i \Gamma^* - \Upsilon^i \Gamma \right] \left(\mathbf{z}_{T+h-i} - \rho^*\right) && \text{[D] exogenous slope shift} \\ & + \sum_{i=0}^{h-1} (\Upsilon^*)^i \varepsilon_{T+h-i} && \text{[E] innovation error} \end{aligned}$$

This outcome matches the earlier taxonomy specialized appropriately, namely [1], [2], [9], plus new [11], and [12]. As terms [A] and [C] have nonzero means, and the others have zero means:

$$\mathsf{E}\left[\mathbf{v}_{T+h}\right] = \left(\mathbf{I}_n - (\Upsilon^*)^h\right)(\phi^* - \phi) - \left(\mathbf{I}_n - \Upsilon^h\right)(\mathbf{I}_n - \Upsilon)^{-1} \Gamma \left(\rho^* - \rho\right) \tag{40}$$

Thus, even h-steps ahead, when $\rho^* = \rho$, forecast biases depend on $(\phi^* - \phi)$ which is nonzero whenever $\rho \neq \mathbf{0}$ despite $\tau^* = \tau = \mathbf{0}$.

This is our sixth main result: the first two results continue to hold for multi-step forecasts.

5.1 Omitting the Unmodeled Variables in h-Step Ahead Forecasts

The forecasting model in-sample is now (4) leading to the multi-step forecasts:

$$\widetilde{\mathbf{y}}_{T+h|T} = \phi + (\Upsilon_e)^h (\mathbf{y}_T - \phi) \tag{41}$$

When (41) is used, the forecast error $\widetilde{\mathbf{v}}_{T+h|T} = \mathbf{y}_{T+h} - \widetilde{\mathbf{y}}_{T+h|T}$ becomes:

$$\begin{aligned}
\widetilde{\mathbf{v}}_{T+h|T} &= \left(\phi^* - \phi\right) + \left(\Upsilon^*\right)^h \left(\mathbf{y}_T - \phi^*\right) - \left(\Upsilon_e\right)^h \left(\mathbf{y}_T - \phi\right) + \mathbf{v}_{T+h} \\
&= \left(\mathbf{I}_n - \left(\Upsilon^*\right)^h\right)\left(\phi^* - \phi\right) + \left(\left(\Upsilon^*\right)^h - \left(\Upsilon_e\right)^h\right)\left(\mathbf{y}_T - \phi\right) \\
&\quad + \sum_{i=0}^{h-1} \left(\Upsilon^*\right)^i \varepsilon_{T+h-i} + \sum_{i=0}^{h-1} \left(\Upsilon^*\right)^i \Gamma^* \left(\mathbf{z}_{T+h-i} - \rho^*\right)
\end{aligned} \tag{42}$$

matching the four terms in (15), where:

$$\mathbf{v}_{T+h} = \sum_{i=0}^{h-1} \left(\Upsilon^*\right)^i \left[\Gamma^* \left(\mathbf{z}_{T+h-i} - \rho^*\right) + \varepsilon_{T+h-i}\right]$$

with $\mathsf{E}\left[\mathbf{v}_{T+h}\right] = \mathbf{0}$, so that:

$$\mathsf{E}\left[\widetilde{\mathbf{v}}_{T+h|T}\right] = \left(\mathbf{I}_n - \left(\Upsilon^*\right)^h\right)\left(\phi^* - \phi\right) \tag{43}$$

This is our seventh main result: the previous conclusions about forecast failure based on the 1-step analyses are essentially unaltered: when $\rho^* = \rho$, (40) and (43) are equal, so forecast failure is only reduced by the inclusion of unmodeled variables when they have mean shifts.

5.2 Forecasting the Unmodeled Variables in h-Step Ahead Forecasts

Now:

$$\widehat{\mathbf{y}}_{T+h|T} = \phi + \sum_{i=0}^{h-1} \Upsilon^i \Gamma \left(\widehat{\mathbf{z}}_{T+h-i} - \rho\right) + \Upsilon^h \left(\mathbf{y}_T - \phi\right) \tag{44}$$

with the forecast error $\widehat{\mathbf{v}}_{T+h|T} = \mathbf{y}_{T+h} - \widehat{\mathbf{y}}_{T+h|T}$:

$$\widehat{\mathbf{v}}_{T+h|T} = (\phi^* - \phi) + (\Upsilon^*)^h (\mathbf{y}_T - \phi^*) - (\Upsilon_e)^h (\mathbf{y}_T - \phi) + \sum_{i=0}^{h-1} (\Upsilon^*)^i \varepsilon_{T+h-i}$$
$$+ \sum_{i=0}^{h-1} (\Upsilon^*)^i \Gamma^* (\mathbf{z}_{T+h-i} - \rho^*) - \sum_{i=0}^{h-1} \Upsilon^i \Gamma (\widehat{\mathbf{z}}_{T+h-i} - \rho)$$
$$= \left(\mathbf{I}_n - (\Upsilon^*)^h\right)(\phi^* - \phi) + \left((\Upsilon^*)^h - (\Upsilon_e)^h\right)(\mathbf{y}_T - \phi) + \sum_{i=0}^{h-1} (\Upsilon^*)^i \varepsilon_{T+h-i}$$
$$+ \sum_{i=0}^{h-1} \left((\Upsilon^*)^i \Gamma^* - \Upsilon^i \Gamma\right)(\mathbf{z}_{T+h-i} - \rho^*) - \sum_{i=0}^{h-1} \Upsilon^i \Gamma (\widehat{\mathbf{z}}_{T+h-i} - \mathbf{z}_{T+h-i})$$
$$- \sum_{i=0}^{h-1} \Upsilon^i \Gamma (\rho^* - \rho) \tag{45}$$

In the second block, the first three terms are identical to those in (42), and $\sum_{i=0}^{h-1} (\Upsilon^*)^i \Gamma^* (\mathbf{z}_{T+h-i} - \rho^*)$ has been replaced by terms relating to the shift in the dynamics (with mean zero), the forecast mistake, and the shift in the mean of the exogenous variables, as in (16).

5.3 Parameter Estimation in h-Step Ahead Forecasts

The estimated model forecasts are now:

$$\widehat{\widehat{\mathbf{y}}}_{T+h|T} = \widehat{\phi} + \sum_{i=0}^{h-1} \widehat{\Upsilon}^i \widehat{\Gamma} (\widehat{\mathbf{z}}_{T+h-i} - \widehat{\rho}) + \widehat{\Upsilon}^h (\widehat{\mathbf{y}}_T - \widehat{\phi}) \tag{46}$$

Thus, facing (38), the forecast error $\widehat{\widehat{\varepsilon}}_{T+h|T} = \mathbf{y}_{T+h} - \widehat{\widehat{\mathbf{y}}}_{T+h|T}$ is:

$$\widehat{\widehat{\varepsilon}}_{T+h|T} = \phi^* - \widehat{\phi} + (\Upsilon^*)^h (\mathbf{y}_T - \phi^*) - \widehat{\Upsilon}^h (\widehat{\mathbf{y}}_T - \widehat{\phi})$$
$$+ \sum_{i=0}^{h-1} (\Upsilon^*)^i \left[\Gamma^* (\mathbf{z}_{T+h-i} - \rho^*)\right] - \sum_{i=0}^{h-1} \widehat{\Upsilon}^i \widehat{\Gamma} (\widehat{\mathbf{z}}_{T+h-i} - \widehat{\rho})$$
$$+ \sum_{i=0}^{h-1} (\Upsilon^*)^i \varepsilon_{T+h-i}$$

which can be decomposed into the equivalent 19 terms as the earlier 1-step taxonomy in §3, analogous to the relation between (7) and (39). However, no new insights seem to be gained by doing so, and it is clear that the third result above still holds.

6 Transforming an I(1) System to I(0)

Consider an n-dimensional I(1) VAR with p lags and an innovation error $\eta_t \sim \mathsf{IN}_n\left[\mathbf{0}, \Omega_\eta\right]$ written as:

$$\mathbf{w}_t = \pi + \sum_{i=1}^{p} \Pi_i \mathbf{w}_{t-i} + \eta_t \tag{47}$$

where some of the np eigenvalues of the polynomial $\left|\mathbf{I}_n - \sum_{i=1}^{p} \Pi_i L^i\right|$ in L lie on, and the rest inside, the unit circle. Then $\Gamma = (\mathbf{I}_n - \sum_{i=1}^{p} \Pi_i)$ has reduced rank $0 < r < n$, and can be expressed as $\Gamma = \alpha\beta'$ where α and β are $n \times r$ with rank r: see e.g., Johansen (1995). Also $\pi = \gamma + \alpha\mu$, so when (e.g.) $p = 2$:

$$\Delta\mathbf{w}_t = \gamma + (\Pi_1 - \mathbf{I}_n)(\Delta\mathbf{w}_{t-1} - \gamma) - \alpha\left(\beta'\mathbf{w}_{t-2} - \mu\right) + \eta_t \tag{48}$$

with $\mathsf{E}\left[\beta'\mathbf{w}_t\right] = \mu$ and $\mathsf{E}\left[\Delta\mathbf{w}_t\right] = \gamma$ where both $\Delta\mathbf{w}_t$ and $\beta'\mathbf{w}_t$ are I(0) even though $\mathbf{w}_t$ is I(1). Then r of the $\mathbf{x}_t$ above are $\beta'\mathbf{w}_t$ and $n - r$ are $\alpha'_\perp\Delta\mathbf{w}_t$ where $\alpha_\perp$ is $n \times (n - r)$ with $\alpha'_\perp\alpha = \mathbf{0}$ and $(\alpha : \alpha_\perp)$ is non-singular.

Partitioning $\mathbf{w}_t$ into endogenous (modeled) variables $\mathbf{y}_t$ conditional on unmodeled $\mathbf{z}_t$ then produces an open system as analyzed in §7. Thus, our results hold in an open cointegrated system.

7 Conclusion

Even when a model is correctly specified in-sample, and the unmodeled variables, $\mathbf{z}_t$, are strongly exogenous with the correctly estimated coefficients, changes in the dynamics alone can induce forecast failure simply because the unmodeled variables have nonzero means. When the mean of $\mathbf{z}_t$ is constant, this forecast bias does not depend substantively on whether or not $\mathbf{z}_t$ is included in the forecasting model, but only on its nonzero mean. Including $\mathbf{z}_t$ in the forecasting model is beneficial when its mean shifts, but that advantage can be lost when future values $\mathbf{z}_{T+h}$ have to be forecast 'off-line'. These results are explicitly derived for 1-step ahead forecasts and known parameters, but continue to hold when extended to estimated models, to multi-step forecasting, and to a later forecast origin following a break.

Acknowledgments Financial support from the Open Society Foundation and the Oxford Martin School is gratefully acknowledged. We are indebted to Anindya Banerjee, Jennifer L. Castle, Mike Clements, Jurgen A. Doornik, Neil Ericsson, Katarina Juselius, and John N.J. Muellbauer for helpful discussions about and comments on an earlier version.

Appendix: Comparing Open with Closed I(0) Systems

Here, we relate the forecast error taxonomy of the open conditional I(0) system in (2) to that for a closed VAR(1). Let $\mathbf{x}_t' = (\mathbf{y}_t' \, \mathbf{z}_t')$, then the DGP over $t = 1, \ldots, T$ for $\mathbf{y}_t$ and $\mathbf{z}_t$ is now:

$$\mathbf{x}_t = \psi + \Psi \mathbf{x}_{t-1} + \mathbf{v}_t \tag{A.1}$$

when $\mathbf{v}_t' = \left(\mathbf{v}_{yt}', \mathbf{v}_{zt}'\right) \sim \mathsf{IN}_{n+m}\left[\mathbf{0}, \Omega\right]$ and $\Omega = \begin{pmatrix} \Omega_{yy} & \Omega_{yz} \\ \Omega_{zy} & \Omega_{zz} \end{pmatrix}$ with $\Omega_{zy} = \Omega_{yz}'$. When all the variables are weakly stationary in-sample, taking expectations in (A.1):

$$\mathsf{E}\left[\mathbf{x}_t\right] = \psi + \Psi \mathsf{E}\left[\mathbf{x}_{t-1}\right] = \psi + \Psi \mu = \mu,$$

so:

$$\mu = \left(\mathbf{I}_{n+m} - \Psi\right)^{-1} \psi = \begin{pmatrix} \mathsf{E}\left[\mathbf{y}_t\right] \\ \mathsf{E}\left[\mathbf{z}_t\right] \end{pmatrix} = \begin{pmatrix} \phi \\ \rho \end{pmatrix}. \tag{A.2}$$

Consequently, we can re-write (A.1) as:

$$\mathbf{x}_t - \mu = \Psi \left(\mathbf{x}_{t-1} - \mu\right) + \mathbf{v}_t \tag{A.3}$$

for $t = 1, 2, \ldots T$.

We first consider a 1-step ahead forecast from time T from a model that is correctly specified in-sample with known parameter values:

$$\overline{\mathbf{x}}_{T+1|T} = \psi + \Psi \mathbf{x}_T \tag{A.4}$$

but where the DGP in the next period has shifted to:

$$\mathbf{x}_{T+1} = \psi^* + \Psi^* \mathbf{x}_T + \mathbf{v}_{T+1} \tag{A.5}$$

with $\mathbf{v}_{T+1} \sim \mathsf{IN}_{n+m}\left[\mathbf{0}, \Omega\right]$. The resulting forecast error between (A.4) and (A.5) is $\overline{\mathbf{v}}_{T+1|T} = \mathbf{x}_{T+1} - \overline{\mathbf{x}}_{T+1|T}$ and hence:

$$\overline{\mathbf{v}}_{T+1|T} = \left(\psi^* - \psi\right) + \left(\Psi^* - \Psi\right) \mathbf{x}_T + \mathbf{v}_{T+1} \tag{A.6}$$

so that:[3]

[3] Note that although $\mathsf{E}\left[\mathbf{x}_t\right] = \psi + \Psi \mathsf{E}\left[\mathbf{x}_{t-1}\right] = \psi + \Psi\mu = \mu$ for $t = 1, 2, \ldots T$ when $t > T$ $\mathsf{E}\left[\mathbf{x}_{T+j}\right] = \sum_{i=0}^{j-1} (\Psi^*)^i \psi^* + (\Psi^*)^j \mu$ for $j \geqq 1$ which for an I(o) $\{\mathbf{x}_t\}$ process converges to $(\mathbf{I}_{n+m} - \Psi^*)^{-1} \psi^* = \mu^*$ as $j \to \infty$.

$$\mathsf{E}\left[\overline{\mathbf{v}}_{T+1|T}\right] = \left(\psi^* - \psi\right) + \left(\Psi^* - \Psi\right)\mathsf{E}\left[\mathbf{x}_T\right] = \left(\mu^* - \mu\right). \tag{A.7}$$

From (A.2), we can partition (A.7) as:

$$\begin{aligned}
\mathsf{E}\left[\overline{\mathbf{v}}_{T+1|T}\right] &= \begin{pmatrix} \phi^* - \phi \\ \rho^* - \rho \end{pmatrix} \\
&= \begin{pmatrix} \left(\psi_y^* - \psi_y\right) \\ \left(\psi_z^* - \psi_z\right) \end{pmatrix} + \begin{pmatrix} (\Psi_{yy}^* - \Psi_{yy}) & (\Psi_{yz}^* - \Psi_{yz}) \\ (\Psi_{zy}^* - \Psi_{zy}) & (\Psi_{zz}^* - \Psi_{zz}) \end{pmatrix} \begin{pmatrix} \phi \\ \rho \end{pmatrix} \\
&= \begin{pmatrix} \nabla\psi_y \\ \nabla\psi_z \end{pmatrix} + \begin{pmatrix} \nabla\Psi_{yy} & \nabla\Psi_{yz} \\ \nabla\Psi_{zy} & \nabla\Psi_{zz} \end{pmatrix} \begin{pmatrix} \phi \\ \rho \end{pmatrix}
\end{aligned}$$

where ∇ denotes a change in a parameter, with:

$$\begin{array}{lll}
\nabla\psi_y = \left(\psi_y^* - \psi_y\right) & \nabla\psi_z = \left(\psi_z^* - \psi_z\right) & \nabla\Psi_{yy} = (\Psi_{yy}^* - \Psi_{yy}) \\
\nabla\Psi_{yz} = (\Psi_{yz}^* - \Psi_{yz}) & \nabla\Psi_{zy} = (\Psi_{zy}^* - \Psi_{zy}) & \nabla\Psi_{zz} = (\Psi_{zz}^* - \Psi_{zz})
\end{array}$$

Partitioning $\mu = (\mathbf{I}_{n+m} - \Psi)^{-1}\,\psi$ yields:

$$\begin{aligned}
\begin{pmatrix} \phi \\ \rho \end{pmatrix} &= \begin{pmatrix} (\mathbf{I}_n - \Psi_{yy}) & -\Psi_{yz} \\ -\Psi_{zy} & (\mathbf{I}_m - \Psi_{zz}) \end{pmatrix}^{-1} \begin{pmatrix} \psi_y \\ \psi_z \end{pmatrix} \\
&= \begin{pmatrix} \mathbf{A}^{-1} & -\mathbf{A}^{-1}\Psi_{yz}(\mathbf{I}_m - \Psi_{zz})^{-1} \\ -(\mathbf{I}_m - \Psi_{zz})^{-1}\Psi_{zy}\mathbf{A}^{-1} & \mathbf{B} \end{pmatrix} \begin{pmatrix} \psi_y \\ \psi_z \end{pmatrix} \\
&= \begin{pmatrix} \mathbf{A}^{-1}\psi_y - \mathbf{A}^{-1}\Psi_{yz}(\mathbf{I}_m - \Psi_{zz})^{-1}\psi_z \\ \mathbf{B}\psi_z - (\mathbf{I}_m - \Psi_{zz})^{-1}\Psi_{zy}\mathbf{A}^{-1}\psi_y \end{pmatrix}
\end{aligned} \tag{A.8}$$

when $\mathbf{A} = [(\mathbf{I}_n - \Psi_{yy}) - \Psi_{yz}(\mathbf{I}_m - \Psi_{zz})^{-1}\Psi_{zy}]$ and $\mathbf{B} = (\mathbf{I}_m - \Psi_{zz})^{-1}[\mathbf{I}_m + \Psi_{zy}\mathbf{A}^{-1}\Psi_{yz}(\mathbf{I}_m - \Psi_{zz})^{-1}]$. Therefore (A.7) has the form:

$$\mathsf{E}\left[\overline{\mathbf{v}}_{T+1|T}\right] = \begin{pmatrix} \nabla\psi_y \\ \nabla\psi_z \end{pmatrix} + \begin{pmatrix} \nabla\Psi_{yy} & \nabla\Psi_{yz} \\ \nabla\Psi_{zy} & \nabla\Psi_{zz} \end{pmatrix} \begin{pmatrix} \mathbf{A}^{-1}\psi_y - \mathbf{A}^{-1}\Psi_{yz}(\mathbf{I}_m - \Psi_{zz})^{-1}\psi_z \\ \mathbf{B}\psi_z - (\mathbf{I}_m - \Psi_{zz})^{-1}\Psi_{zy}\mathbf{A}^{-1}\psi_y \end{pmatrix}$$

Hence, if the mean of the $\{\mathbf{z}_t\}$ process is constant ($\nabla\psi_z = \mathbf{0}$, $\nabla\Psi_{zy} = \mathbf{0}$, $\nabla\Psi_{zz} = \mathbf{0}$), and there is no intercept in the $\{\mathbf{y}_t\}$ process ($\psi_y^* = \psi_y = \mathbf{0}$), the mean of the forecast error becomes:

$$\mathsf{E}\left[\overline{\mathbf{v}}_{T+1|T}\right] = \begin{pmatrix} \left\{\nabla\Psi_{yz}\mathbf{B} - \nabla\Psi_{yy}\mathbf{A}^{-1}\Psi_{yz}(\mathbf{I}_m - \Psi_{zz})^{-1}\right\}\psi_z \\ \mathbf{0} \end{pmatrix}$$

so if there is a change in the dynamics of the $\{\mathbf{y}_t\}$ process and $\{\mathbf{z}_t\}$ has a nonzero mean, there will be forecast failure. Further, even if $\mathbf{z}_t$ is strongly exogenous for the parameters of the $\{\mathbf{y}_t\}$ process ($\Psi_{zy} = \mathbf{0}$), there will be forecast failure as:

$$\mathsf{E}\left[\overline{\mathbf{v}}_{T+1|T}\right] = \begin{pmatrix} \left\{\nabla\Psi_{yz} - \nabla\Psi_{yy}\mathbf{A}^{-1}\Psi_{yz}\right\}(\mathbf{I}_m - \Psi_{zz})^{-1}\psi_z \\ \mathbf{0} \end{pmatrix}$$

which will be nonzero provided $\psi_z \neq \mathbf{0}$ and there is a change in the dynamics of the $\{\mathbf{y}_t\}$ process, consistent with the closed system results in Clements and Hendry (1999).

These closed system results can be mapped to an open system using a conditional and marginal factorization of the joint distribution. From (A.1), the conditional distribution of $\mathbf{y}_t$ given $\mathbf{z}_t$ and the past is:

$$\begin{aligned} \mathbf{y}_t &= (\psi_y - \Xi\psi_z) + (\Psi_{yy} - \Xi\Psi_{zy})\,\mathbf{y}_{t-1} + \Xi\mathbf{z}_t + (\Psi_{yz} - \Xi\Psi_{zz})\,\mathbf{z}_{t-1} + (\mathbf{v}_{yt} + \Xi\mathbf{v}_{zt}) \\ &= \theta + \Theta y_{t-1} + \Xi\mathbf{z}_t + \Lambda z_{t-1} + \nu_t \end{aligned} \tag{A.9}$$

when $\Xi = \Omega_{yz}\Omega_{zz}^{-1}$. The initial VAR formulation induces one lag longer in $\mathbf{z}_t$ with:

$$\mathsf{E}\left[\mathbf{y}_t\right] = \theta + \Theta\mathsf{E}\left[\mathbf{y}_{t-1}\right] + \Xi\mathsf{E}\left[\mathbf{z}_t\right] + \Lambda\mathsf{E}\left[\mathbf{z}_{t-1}\right] = \theta + \Theta\phi + (\Xi + \Lambda)\,\rho = \phi$$

so that:

$$\phi = (\mathbf{I}_n - \Theta)^{-1}\left\{\theta + (\Xi + \Lambda)\,\rho\right\}$$

and:

$$(\mathbf{y}_t - \phi) = \Theta\,(\mathbf{y}_{t-1} - \phi) + \Xi\,(\mathbf{z}_t - \rho) + \Lambda\,(\mathbf{z}_{t-1} - \rho) + \nu_t.$$

The forecast error from predicting $\mathbf{y}_{T+1}$ by $\overline{\mathbf{y}}_{T+1|T} = \theta + \Theta\mathbf{y}_{t-1} + \Xi\mathbf{z}_{T+1} + \Lambda\mathbf{z}_T$ with known parameters and $\mathbf{z}_{T+1}$ and $\mathbf{z}_T$ is:

$$\overline{\nu}_{T+1} = \mathbf{y}_{T+1} - \overline{\mathbf{y}}_{T+1|T} = \nabla\theta + \nabla\Theta\mathbf{y}_{t-1} + \nabla\Xi\mathbf{z}_{T+1} + \nabla\Lambda\mathbf{z}_T + \nu_{T+1}$$

hence:

$$\begin{aligned} \mathsf{E}\left[\overline{\nu}_{T+1}\right] &= \nabla\theta + \nabla\Theta\phi + (\nabla\Xi + \nabla\Lambda)\,\rho \\ &= \nabla\theta + \nabla\Theta\,(\mathbf{I}_n - \Theta)^{-1}\left\{\theta + (\Xi + \Lambda)\,\rho\right\} + (\nabla\Xi + \nabla\Lambda)\,\rho \end{aligned}$$

with

$$\begin{aligned} \rho &= \mathbf{B}\psi_z - (\mathbf{I}_m - \Psi_{zz})^{-1}\Psi_{zy}\mathbf{A}^{-1}\psi_y \\ \nabla\theta &= (\nabla\psi_y - \nabla\Xi\psi_z - \Xi\nabla\psi_z) \\ \nabla\Theta &= (\nabla\Psi_{yy} - \nabla\Xi\Psi_{zy} - \Xi\nabla\Psi_{zy}) \\ \nabla\Lambda &= (\nabla\Psi_{yz} - \nabla\Xi\Psi_{zz} - \Xi\nabla\Psi_{zz}) \end{aligned}$$

If the $\{\mathbf{z}_t\}$ process is constant ($\nabla\psi_z = \mathbf{0}$, $\nabla\Psi_{zy} = \mathbf{0}$, $\nabla\Psi_{zz} = \mathbf{0}$) and there is no intercept in the $\{\mathbf{y}_t\}$ process ($\psi_y^* = \psi_y = \mathbf{0}$) then $\rho = \mathbf{B}\psi_z$ and the mean of the forecast error becomes:

$$\mathsf{E}\left[\overline{\nu}_{T+1}\right] = -[\nabla\Xi + (\nabla\Psi_{yy} - \nabla\Xi\Psi_{zy})\left(\mathbf{I}_n - \Psi_{yy} + \Xi\Psi_{zy}\right)^{-1}\Xi]\psi_z$$
$$+\left[(\nabla\Psi_{yy} - \nabla\Xi\Psi_{zy})\left(\mathbf{I}_n - \Psi_{yy} + \Xi\Psi_{zy}\right)^{-1}(\Xi + \Lambda) + (\nabla\Xi + \nabla\Lambda)\right]\mathbf{B}\psi_z$$

which, when $\mathbf{z}_t$ is strongly exogenous for the parameters of the $\{\mathbf{y}_t\}$ process ($\Psi_{zy} = \mathbf{0}$), simplifies to:

$$\mathsf{E}\left[\overline{\nu}_{T+1}\right] = -[\nabla\Xi + \nabla\Psi_{yy}\left(\mathbf{I}_n - \Psi_{yy}\right)^{-1}\Xi]\psi_z$$
$$+\left[\nabla\Psi_{yy}\left(\mathbf{I}_n - \Psi_{yy}\right)^{-1}(\Xi + \Lambda) + (\nabla\Xi + \nabla\Lambda)\right](\mathbf{I}_m - \Psi_{zz})^{-1}\psi_z$$

so again will be non-zero when $\psi_z \neq \mathbf{0}$ and there is a change in the dynamics of the $\{\mathbf{y}_t\}$ process (i.e., at least one of $\nabla\Psi_{yy}$, $\nabla\Xi$ and $\nabla\Lambda$ is non-zero). This result mirrors that in (8) noting that $\rho = (\mathbf{I}_m - \Psi_{zz})^{-1}\psi_z$ in this case.

An analogous result is obtained when we close the open conditional $\mathsf{I}(0)$ system in (2) by endogenizing $\mathbf{z}_t$ in:

$$\mathbf{y}_t = \tau + \Upsilon\mathbf{y}_{t-1} + \Gamma\mathbf{z}_t + \varepsilon_t \tag{A.10}$$
$$\mathbf{z}_t = \lambda + \Phi\mathbf{y}_{t-1} + \Pi\mathbf{z}_{t-1} + \eta_t \tag{A.11}$$

so that:

$$\mathsf{E}\left[\mathbf{z}_t\right] = \lambda + \Phi\mathsf{E}\left[\mathbf{y}_{t-1}\right] + \Pi\mathsf{E}\left[\mathbf{z}_{t-1}\right] = \lambda + \Phi\phi + \Pi\rho = \rho$$

or:

$$\lambda = (\mathbf{I}_m - \Pi)\,\rho - \Phi\phi$$

leading to:

$$(\mathbf{z}_t - \rho) = \Phi\left(\mathbf{y}_{t-1} - \phi\right) + \Pi\left(\mathbf{z}_{t-1} - \rho\right) + \eta_t$$

Then, as $\phi = (\mathbf{I}_n - \Upsilon)^{-1}(\tau + \Gamma\rho)$[4]:

$$\mathbf{y}_t - \phi = \Upsilon\left(\mathbf{y}_{t-1} - \phi\right) + \Gamma\left(\mathbf{z}_t - \rho\right) + \varepsilon_t$$
$$= (\Upsilon + \Gamma\Phi)\left(\mathbf{y}_{t-1} - \phi\right) + \Gamma\Pi\left(\mathbf{z}_{t-1} - \rho\right) + \left(\Gamma\eta_t + \varepsilon_t\right)$$

These results allow a general evaluation of the relative impacts of breaks when $\mathbf{z}_t$ is treated as 'external' or 'internal'.

[4] This is true whether or not $\mathbf{z}_t$ is strongly exogenous (i.e., $\Phi = \mathbf{0}$) for the parameters of $\mathbf{y}_t$ in the VAR.

References

Clements, M. P. and D. F. Hendry (1998). Forecasting Economic Time Series. Cambridge: Cambridge University Press.

Clements, M. P. and D. F. Hendry (1999). Forecasting Non-stationary Economic Time Series. Cambridge, Mass.: MIT Press.

Clements, M. P. and D. F. Hendry (2006). Forecasting with breaks. In G. Elliott, C. W. J. Granger, and A. Timmermann (Eds.), Handbook of Econometrics on Forecasting, pp. 605–657. Amsterdam: Elsevier.

Clements, M. P. and D. F. Hendry (2011). Forecasting from Mis-specified Models in the Presence of Unanticipated Location Shifts. In M. P. Clements and D. F. Hendry (Eds.), Oxford Handbook of Economic Forecasting, pp. 271–314. Oxford: Oxford University Press.

Engle, R. F., D. F. Hendry, and J.-F. Richard (1983). Exogeneity. Econometrica 51, 277–304.

Hendry, D. F. (2000). On detectable and non-detectable structural change. Structural Change and Economic Dynamics 11, 45–65.

Hendry, D. F. (2006). Robustifying forecasts from equilibrium-correction models. Journal of Econometrics 135, 399–426.

Hendry, D. F. and K. Hubrich (2011). Combining disaggregate forecasts or combining disaggregate information to forecast an aggregate. Journal of Business and Economic Statistics 29, 216–227.

Hendry, D. F. and M. Massmann (2007). Co-breaking: Recent advances and a synopsis of the literature. Journal of Business and Economic Statistics 25, 33–51.

Hendry, D. F. and B. Nielsen (2007). Econometric Modeling: A Likelihood Approach. Princeton: Princeton University Press.

Johansen, S. (1995). Likelihood-based Inference in Cointegrated Vector Autoregressive Models. Oxford: Oxford University Press.

Heavy-Tail and Plug-In Robust Consistent Conditional Moment Tests of Functional Form

Jonathan B. Hill

Abstract We present asymptotic power-one tests of regression model functional form for heavy-tailed time series. Under the null hypothesis of correct specification the model errors must have a finite mean, and otherwise only need to have a fractional moment. If the errors have an infinite variance then in principle any consistent plug-in is allowed, depending on the model, including those with non-Gaussian limits and/or a sub-$\sqrt{n}$-convergence rate. One test statistic exploits an orthogonalized test equation that promotes plug-in robustness irrespective of tails. We derive chi-squared weak limits of the statistics, we characterize an empirical process method for smoothing over a trimming parameter, and we study the finite sample properties of the test statistics.

1 Introduction

Consider a regression model

$$y_t = f(x_t, \beta) + \epsilon_t(\beta) \tag{1}$$

where $f : \mathbb{R}^p \times \mathcal{B} \to \mathbb{R}$ is a known response function for finite $p > 0$, continuous and differentiable in $\beta \in \mathcal{B}$ where $\mathcal{B}$ is a compact subset of $\mathbb{R}^q$, and the regressors $x_t \in \mathbb{R}^p$ may contain lags of y_t or other random variables. We are interested in testing whether $f(x_t, \beta)$ is a version of $E[y_t|x_t]$ for unique β^0, without imposing higher moments on y_t, while under misspecification we only require $E[\sup_{\beta\in\mathcal{B}} |\epsilon_t(\beta)|^\iota] < \infty$ and each $E[\sup_{\beta\in\mathcal{B}} |(\partial/\partial\beta_i) f(x_t, \beta)|^\iota] < \infty$ for some tiny $\iota > 0$. Heavy tails in macroeconomic, finance, insurance and telecommunication

The author thanks an anonymous referee and Co-Editor Xiaohong Chen for constructive remarks.

J. B. Hill
Department of Economics, University of North Carolina, Chapel Hill, NC, USA
e-mail: jbhill@email.unc.edu

X. Chen and N. R. Swanson (eds.), *Recent Advances and Future Directions in Causality, Prediction, and Specification Analysis*, DOI: 10.1007/978-1-4614-1653-1_10,

time series are now well-documented (Resnick 1987; Embrechts et al. 1997; Finkenstadt and Rootzen 2003; Gabaix 2008). Assume $E|y_t| < \infty$ to ensure $E[y_t|x_t]$ exists by the Radon–Nikodym theorem, and consider the hypotheses

$$H_0 : E\left[y_t|x_t\right] = f(x_t, \beta^0)\ a.s. \text{ for unique } \beta^0 \in \mathcal{B}, \quad \text{versus}$$
$$H_1 : \max_{\beta \in \mathcal{B}} P\left(E\left[y_t|x_t\right] = f(x_t, \beta)\right) < 1.$$

We develop consistent conditional moment (CM) test statistics for general alternatives that are both robust to heavy tails and to a plug-in for β^0. Our focus is Bierens' (1982, 1990) nuisance parameter indexed CM test for the sake of exposition, with neural network foundations in Gallant and White (1989), Hornik (1989, 1990), and White (1989a), and extensions to semi- and non-parametric models in Chen and Fan (1999). Let $\{y_t, x_t\}_{t=1}^n$ be the sample with size $n \geq 1$, let $\hat{\beta}_n$ be a consistent estimator of β^0, and define the residual $\epsilon_t(\hat{\beta}_n) := y_t - f(x_t, \hat{\beta}_n)$. The test statistic is

$$\hat{T}_n(\gamma) = \frac{1}{\hat{V}_n(\hat{\beta}_n, \gamma)} \left(\sum_{t=1}^{n} \epsilon_t(\hat{\beta}_n) F\left(\gamma' \psi_t\right) \right)^2$$
$$\text{where } F\left(\gamma'\psi_t\right) = \exp\left\{\gamma'\psi_t\right\} \text{ and } \psi_t := \psi(x_t), \tag{2}$$

where ψ is a bounded one-to-one Borel function from $\mathbb{R}^p$ to $\mathbb{R}^p$, $\hat{V}_n(\hat{\beta}_n, \gamma)$ estimates $E[(\sum_{t=1}^n \epsilon_t(\hat{\beta}_n)F(\gamma'\psi_t))^2]$, and $\gamma \in \mathbb{R}^p$ is a nuisance parameter.

If $E|\epsilon_t| < \infty$ and $E[\epsilon_t|x_t] \neq 0$ with positive probability then $E[\epsilon_t F(\gamma'\psi_t)] \neq 0$ for all γ on any compact $\Gamma \subset \mathbb{R}^p$ with positive Lebesgue measure, except possibly for γ in a countable subset $S \subset \Gamma$ (Bierens 1990, Lemma 1). This seminal result promotes a consistent test: if ϵ_t and $\sup_{\beta \in \mathcal{B}} |(\partial/\partial\beta_i) f(x_t, \beta)|$ have finite $4 + \iota$th-moments for tiny $\iota > 0$, and the NLLS estimator $\hat{\beta}_n = \beta^0 + O_p(1/n^{1/2})$ then $\hat{T}_n(\gamma) \xrightarrow{d} \chi^2(1)$ under H_0 and $\hat{T}_n(\gamma) \xrightarrow{p} \infty$ under H_1 for all $\gamma \in \Gamma/S$. Such moment and plug-in conditions are practically de rigueur (e.g. Hausman 1978; White 1981; Davidson et al. 1983; Newey 1985; White 1987; Bierens 1990; Jong 1996; Fan and Li 1996; Corradi and Swanson 2002; Hong and Lee 2005).

The property $E[\epsilon_t F(\gamma'\psi_t)] \neq 0$ under H_1 for all but countably many γ carries over to non-polynomial real analytic $F : \mathbb{R} \to \mathbb{R}$, including exponential and trigonometric classes (Lee et al. 1993; Bierens and Ploberger 1997; Stinchcombe and White 1998), and compound versions where S may be empty (Hill 2008a, 2008b), and has been discovered elsewhere in the literature on universal approximators (Hornik et al. 1989; 1990; Stinchcombe and White 1989; White 1989b; 1990). Stinchcombe and White (1998, Theorem 3.1) show boundedness of ψ ensures $\{F(\gamma'\psi(x_t)) : \gamma \in \Gamma\}$ is weakly dense on the space on which x_t lies, a property exploited to prove F is revealing.[1]

---

[1] We use the term "revealing" in the sense of "generically totally revealing" in Stinchcombe and White (Stinchcombe and White 1998, p. 299). A member h of a function space $\mathcal{H}$ reveals

The moment $E|\epsilon_t| < \infty$ is imposed to ensure $E[\epsilon_t|x_t]$ exists under *either* hypothesis, but if $f(x_t, \beta^0)$ is misspecified then there is no guarantee ϵ_t is integrable when $E[y_t^2] = \infty$ precisely because $f(x_t, \beta^0)$ need not be integrable. Suppose x_t is an integrable scalar with an infinite variance, and $f(x_t, \beta) = (x_t + \beta)^2$. Then $E|\epsilon_t(\beta)| = \infty$ for any $\beta \in \mathcal{B}$, hence $E[\epsilon_t(\beta)|x_t]$ is not well-defined for any β. Clearly we only need $E|y_t| < \infty$ to ensure $E[y_t|x_t]$ exists for a test of (1), while heavy tails can lead to empirical size distortions in a variety of test statistics (Lima 1997; Hill and Aguilar 2011).

In this chapter we apply a trimming indicator $\hat{I}_{n,t}(\beta) \in \{0, 1\}$ to $\epsilon_t(\beta)$ in order to robustify against heavy tails. Define the weighted and trimmed errors and test statistic

$$\hat{\mathcal{T}}_n(\gamma) = \frac{1}{\hat{S}_n^2(\hat{\beta}_n, \gamma)} \left(\sum_{t=1}^{n} \hat{m}_{n,t}^*(\hat{\beta}_n, \gamma) \right)^2 \quad \text{where } \hat{m}_{n,t}^*(\beta, \gamma) := \epsilon_t(\beta) \hat{I}_{n,t}(\beta) F\left(\gamma' \psi_t\right)$$

where $\hat{S}_n^2(\beta, \gamma)$ is a kernel estimator of $E[(\sum_{t=1}^n \hat{m}_{n,t}^*(\hat{\beta}_n, \gamma))^2]$ defined by

$$\hat{S}_n^2(\beta, \gamma) = \sum_{s,t=1}^{n} \omega\left((s-t)/b_n\right) \left\{\hat{m}_{n,s}^*(\beta, \gamma) - \hat{m}_n^*(\beta, \gamma)\right\} \left\{\hat{m}_{n,t}^*(\beta, \gamma) - \hat{m}_n^*(\beta, \gamma)\right\}$$

with $\hat{m}_n^*(\beta, \gamma) = 1/n \sum_{t=1}^n \hat{m}_{n,t}^*(\beta, \gamma)$, and $\omega(\cdot)$ is a kernel function with bandwidth $b_n \to \infty$ and $b_n/n \to 0$. By exploiting methods in the tail-trimming literature we construct $\hat{I}_{n,t}(\beta)$ in a way that ensures sufficient but *negligible trimming*: $\hat{I}_{n,t}(\beta) = 0$ for asymptotically infinitely many sample extremes of $\epsilon_t(\beta)$ representing a vanishing sample portion. This promotes both Gaussian asymptotics under H_0 *and* a consistent test.

Tail truncation by comparison is not valid when $E[\epsilon_t^2] = \infty$ because sample extremes of ϵ_t are replaced by a tail order statistic of ϵ_t that increases with n: too many large values are allowed for Gaussian asymptotics (Csörgo et al. 1986). On the other hand, trimming or truncating a *constant* sample portion of $\epsilon_t(\beta)$ leads to bias in general, unless ϵ_t is symmetrically distributed about zero under H_0 and symmetrically trimmed or truncated. In some cases, however, symmetry may be impossible as in a test of ARCH functional form (see Sect. 4.2).

We assume $F(u)$ is bounded on any compact subset of its support, covering exponential, logistic, and trigonometric weights, but not real analytic functions like $(1-u)^{-1}$ on $[-1, 1]$. Otherwise we must include $F\left(\gamma' \psi_t\right)$ in the trimming indicator $\hat{I}_{n,t}(\beta)$ which sharply complicates proving $\hat{\mathcal{T}}_n(\gamma)$ obtains an asymptotic power of

(Footnote 1 continued)
misspecification $E[y|x] \neq f$ when $E[(y-f)h] \neq 0$. A space $\mathcal{H}$ is generically totally revealing if all but a negligible number of $h \in \mathcal{H}$ have this property. In the index function case $h(x) = F(\gamma' \psi(x))$, where the weight h aligns with γ and the class $\mathcal{H}$ with Γ, this is equivalent to saying all $\gamma \in \Gamma/S$ where S has Lebesgue measure zero.

one on Γ/S. A HAC estimator $\hat{S}_n^2(\beta, \gamma)$ is required in general unless ϵ_t is iid under H_0: even if ϵ_t is a martingale difference $\hat{m}_{n,t}(\beta^0, \gamma)$ may not be due to trimming.

In lieu of the test statistic form a unique advantage exists in heavy-tailed cases since $1/n \sum_{t=1}^n \hat{m}_{n,t}^*(\beta^0, \gamma)$ is sub-$n^{1/2}$-convergent. Depending on the data generating process, a plug-in $\hat{\beta}_n$ may converge fast enough that it does not impact the limit distribution of $\hat{\mathcal{T}}_n(\gamma)$ under H_0, including estimators with a sub-$n^{1/2}$ rate and/or a non-Gaussian limit. Conversely, if $\hat{\beta}_n \xrightarrow{p} \beta^0$ at a sufficiently slow rate we either assume $\hat{\beta}_n$ is asymptotically linear, or in the spirit of Wooldridge (1990) exploit an orthogonal transformation of $\hat{m}_{n,t}^*(\beta, \gamma)$ that is robust to any $\hat{\beta}_n$ with a minimal convergence rate that may be below $n^{1/2}$ for heavy-tailed data. Orthogonal transformations have not been explored in the heavy-tail robust inference literature, and they do not require $n^{1/2}$-convergent or asymptotically normal $\hat{\beta}_n$ in heavy-tailed cases.

Model (1) covers Nonlinear ARX with random volatility errors of an unknown form, and Nonlinear strong and semi-strong ARCH. Note, however, that we do not test whether $E[y_t|z_{t-1}, z_{t-2}, ...] = f(x_t, \beta^0)$ $a.s.$, where $z_t = [y_t, x_{t+1}']'$ such that the error $\epsilon_t = y_t - f(x_t, \beta^0)$ is a martingale difference under H_0. This rules out testing whether a Nonlinear ARMAX or Nonlinear GARCH model is correctly specified. We can, however, easily extend our main results to allow such tests by mimicking de Jong's (1996, Theorem 2) extension of Bierens' (1990, Lemma 1) main result.

Consistent tests of functional form are widely varied with nonparametric, semiparametric, and bootstrap branches. A few contributions not cited above include White (1989a), Chan (1990), Eubank and Spiegelman (1990), Yatchew (1992), Hardle and Mammen (1993), Dette (1996), Zheng (1996), Fan and Li (1996, 2000), and Hill (2012). Inherently robust methods include distribution-free tests like indicator or sign-based tests (e.g. Brock et al. 1996), the m-out-of-n bootstrap with $m = o(n)$ applied to (2) (Arcones and Giné 1989; Lahiri 1995), and exact small sample tests based on sharp bounds (e.g. Dufour et al. 2006; Ibragimov and Muller 2010).

In Sect. 2 we construct $\hat{I}_{n,t}(\beta)$ and characterize allowed plug-ins. In Sect. 3 we discuss re-centering after trimming to remove small sample bias that may arise due to trimming. We then construct a p-value occupation time test that allows us to bypass choosing a particular number of extremes to trim and to commit only to a functional form for the sample fractile. Sect. 4 contains AR and ARCH examples where we present an array of valid plug-ins. In Sect. 5 we perform a Monte Carlo study and Sect. 6 contains concluding remarks.

We use the following notation conventions. Let $\Im_t := \sigma(y_\tau, x_{\tau+1} : \tau \leq 1)$, and let M and N be finite integers. $\lambda_{\min}(A)$ and $\lambda_{\max}(A)$ are the minimum and maximum eigenvalues of a square matrix $A \in \mathbb{R}^{M \times M}$. The L_p-norm of stochastic $A \in \mathbb{R}^{M \times N}$ is $||A||_p := (\sum_{i=1,j=1}^{M,N} E|A_{i,j}|^p)^{1/p}$, and the spectral norm of $A \in \mathbb{R}^{M \times N}$ is $||A|| = (\lambda_{\max}(A'A))^{1/2}$. For scalar z write $(z)_+ := \max\{0, z\}$, and let $[z]$ be the integer part of z. $K > 0$ is a finite constant and $\iota > 0$ is a tiny constant, the values of which may change from line-to-line; $L(n)$ is a slowly varying function where $L(n) \to \infty$ as $n \to \infty$, the rate of which may change from line-to-line.[2] If

$\{A_n(\gamma), B_n(\gamma)\}_{n\geq 1}$ are sequences of functions of γ and $\sup_{\gamma\in\Gamma}|A_n(\gamma)/B_n(\gamma)| \rightarrow 1$ we write $A_n(\gamma) \sim B_n(\gamma)$ *uniformly on* Γ, and if $\sup_{\gamma\in\Gamma}|A_n(\gamma)/B_n(\gamma)| \overset{p}{\rightarrow} 1$ we write $A_n(\gamma) \overset{p}{\sim} B_n(\gamma)$ *uniformly on* Γ. $\Longrightarrow$ denotes weak convergence on $\mathcal{C}[\Gamma]$, the space of continuous real functions on Γ. The indicator function is $I(a) = 1$ if a is true, and 0 otherwise. A random variable is *symmetric* if its distribution is symmetric about zero.

2 Tail-Weighted Conditional Moment Test

2.1 Tail-Trimmed Equations

Compactly denote the test equation, and the error evaluated at β^0:

$$m_t(\beta, \gamma) := \epsilon_t(\beta)F(\gamma'\psi_t) \text{ and } \epsilon_t = \epsilon_t(\beta^0).$$

By the mean-value-theorem the residuals $\epsilon_t(\hat{\beta}_n)$ reflect the plug-in $\hat{\beta}_n$, the regression error ϵ_t, and the response gradient written variously as

$$g_t(\beta) = \left[g_{i,t}(\beta)\right]_{i=1}^q = g(x_t, \beta) := \frac{\partial}{\partial\beta}f(x_t, \beta) \in \mathbb{R}^q.$$

We should therefore trim $\epsilon_t(\beta)$ by setting $\hat{I}_{n,t}(\beta) = 0$ when $\epsilon_t(\beta)$ *or* $g_{i,t}(\beta)$ is an extreme value. This idea is exploited for a class of heavy-tail robust M-estimators in Hill (2011b), and similar ideas are developed in Hill and Renault (2010) and Hill and Aguilar (2011).

In the following let $z_t(\beta) \in \{\epsilon_t(\beta), g_{i,t}\beta)\}$, define tail-specific observations

$$z_t^{(-)}(\beta) := z_t(\beta)I(z_t(\beta) < 0) \text{ and } z_t^{(+)}(\beta) := z_t(\beta)I(z_t(\beta) \geq 0),$$

and let $z_{(i)}^{(\cdot)}(\beta)$ be the ith sample order statistic of $z_t^{(\cdot)}(\beta)$: $z_{(1)}^{(-)}(\beta) \leq \cdots \leq z_{(n)}^{(-)}(\beta) \leq 0$ and $z_{(1)}^{(+)}(\beta) \geq \cdots \geq z_{(n)}^{(+)}(\beta) \geq 0$. Let $\{k_{j,\epsilon,n} : j = 1, 2\}$ and $\{k_{j,i,n} : j = 1, 2\}$ be sequences of positive integers taking values in $\{1, ..., n\}$, define trimming indicators

$$\hat{I}_{\epsilon,n,t}(\beta) := I\left(\epsilon_{(k_{1,\epsilon,n})}^{(-)}(\beta) \leq \epsilon_t(\beta) \leq \epsilon_{(k_{2,\epsilon,n})}^{(+)}(\beta)\right)$$
$$\hat{I}_{i,n,t}(\beta) := I\left(g_{i,(k_{1,i,n})}^{(-)}(\beta) \leq g_{i,t}(\beta) \leq g_{i,(k_{2,i,n})}^{(+)}(\beta)\right)$$
$$\hat{I}_{g,n,t}(\beta) := \prod_{i=1}^q \hat{I}_{i,n,t}(\beta)$$

[2] Slow variation implies $\lim_{n\rightarrow\infty} L(\lambda n)/L(n) = 1$ for any $\lambda > 0$ (e.g. a constant, or $(\ln(n))^a$ for finite $a > 0$: see Resnick 1987). In this chapter we always assume $L(n) \rightarrow \infty$.

$$\hat{I}_{n,t}(\beta) := \hat{I}_{\epsilon,n,t}(\beta) \times \hat{I}_{g,n,t}(\beta),$$

and trimmed test equations

$$\hat{m}^*_{n,t}(\beta, \gamma) := m_t(\beta, \gamma) \times \hat{I}_{n,t}(\beta) = \epsilon_t(\beta) \times \hat{I}_{n,t}(\beta) \times F(\gamma' \psi_t).$$

Thus $\hat{I}_{n,t}(\beta) = 0$ when any $\epsilon_t(\beta)$ or $g_{i,t}(\beta)$ is large. Together with some plug-in $\hat{\beta}_n$ and HAC estimator $\hat{S}^2_n(\hat{\beta}_n, \gamma)$ we obtain our test statistic $\hat{\mathcal{T}}_n(\gamma) = \hat{S}^{-2}_n(\hat{\beta}_n, \gamma)$ $(\sum_{t=1}^n \hat{m}^*_{n,t}(\hat{\beta}_n, \gamma))^2$.

We determine how many observations of $\epsilon_t(\beta)$ and $g_{i,t}(\beta)$ are extreme values by assuming $\{k_{j,\epsilon,n}\}$ and $\{k_{j,i,n}\}$ are *intermediate order sequences*. If $\{k_{j,z,n}\}$ denotes any one of them, then

$$1 \leq k_{1,z,n} + k_{2,z,n} < n, \quad k_{j,z,n} \rightarrow \infty \quad \text{and} \quad k_{j,z,n}/n \rightarrow 0.$$

The fractile $k_{j,z,n}$ represents the number of $m_t(\beta, \gamma)$ trimmed due to a large left- or right-tailed $\epsilon_t(\beta)$ or $g_{i,t}(\beta)$. Since we trim asymptotically infinitely many large values $k_{j,z,n} \rightarrow \infty$ we ensure Gaussian asymptotics, while trimming a vanishing sample portion $k_{j,z,n}/n \rightarrow 0$ promotes identification of H_0 and H_1.[3] The reader may consult Leadbetter et al. (1983, Chap. 2), Hahn et al. (1991) and Hill (2011a) for the use of intermediate order statistics in extreme value theory and robust estimation. See Sect. 3 for details on handling the fractiles $k_{j,z,n}$.

If any z_t is symmetric then symmetric trimming is used:

$$I\left(|z_t(\beta)| \leq z^{(a)}_{(k_{z,n})}(\beta)\right) \text{ where } z^{(a)}_t := |z_t|, \; k_{z,n} \rightarrow \infty \text{ and } k_{z,n}/n \rightarrow 0. \quad (3)$$

If a component takes on only one sign then one-sided trimming is appropriate, and if $z_t(\beta)$ has a finite variance then it can be dropped from $\hat{I}_{n,t}(\beta)$. In general tail thickness does not need to be known because our statistic has the same asymptotic properties for thin or thick tailed data, while unnecessary tail trimming is both irrelevant in theory, and does not appear to affect the test in small samples.

2.2 Plug-In Properties

The plug-in $\hat{\beta}_n$ needs to be consistent for a unique point $\beta^0 \in \mathcal{B}$.[4] In particular, we assume there exists a sequence of positive definite matrices $\{\tilde{V}_n\}$, where $\tilde{V}_n \in \mathbb{R}^{q \times q}$

---

[3] Consider if ϵ_t is iid and asymmetric under H_0, but symmetrically and non-negligibly trimmed with Tuesday, May 22, 2012 at 12:37 pm$k_{1,\epsilon,n} = k_{2,\epsilon,n} \sim \lambda n$ where $\lambda \in (0, 1)$. Then $\hat{\mathcal{T}}_n(\gamma) \xrightarrow{p} \infty$ under H_0 is easily verified. The test statistic reveals misspecification due entirely to trimming itself.

[4] Under the alternative β^0 is the unique probability limit of $\hat{\beta}_n$, a "quasi-true" point that optimizes a discrepancy function, for example, a likelihood function, method of moments criterion or the Kullback–Leibler Information Criterion. See White (1982) amongst many others.

and $\tilde{V}_{i,i,n} \to \infty$, and

$$\tilde{V}_n^{1/2}\left(\hat{\beta}_n - \beta^0\right) = O_p(1).$$

As we discuss below, in the presence of heavy tails $\hat{\beta}_n$ need not have $n^{1/2}$-convergent components, and depending on the model may have components with different rates $\tilde{V}_{i,i,n}^{1/2}$ below, at or above $n^{1/2}$.

Precisely how fast convergence $\hat{\beta}_n \xrightarrow{p} \beta^0$ is gauged by exploiting an asymptotic expansion of $\hat{S}_n^{-1}(\hat{\beta}_n, \gamma)\sum_{t=1}^n \hat{m}_{n,t}^*(\hat{\beta}_n, \gamma)$ around β^0. We therefore require the non-random quantile sequences in which the order statistics $\epsilon_{(k_{j,\epsilon,n})}^{(\cdot)}(\beta)$ and $g_{i,(k_{j,i,n})}^{(\cdot)}(\beta)$ approach asymptotically. The sequences are positive functions $\{l_{z,n}(\beta), u_{z,n}(\beta)\}$ denoting the lower $k_{1,z,n}/n$th and upper $k_{2,z,n}/n$th quantiles of $z_t(\beta)$ in the sense

$$P\left(z_t(\beta) < -l_{z,n}(\beta)\right) = \frac{k_{1,z,n}}{n} \quad \text{and} \quad P\left(z_t(\beta) > u_{z,n}(\beta)\right) = \frac{k_{2,z,n}}{n}. \qquad (4)$$

Distribution smoothness for $\epsilon_t(\beta)$ and $g_{i,t}(\beta)$ ensures $\{l_{z,n}(\beta), u_{z,n}(\beta)\}$ exist for all β and any chosen fractile policy $\{k_{1,z,n}, k_{2,z,n}\}$. See Appendix A for all assumptions. By construction $\{z_{(k_{1,z,n})}^{(-)}(\beta), z_{(k_{2,z,n})}^{(+)}(\beta)\}$ estimate $\{-l_{z,n}(\beta), u_{z,n}(\beta)\}$ and are uniformly consistent, e.g. $\sup_{\beta\in\mathcal{B}} |z_{(k_{2,z,n})}^{(+)}(\beta)/u_{z,n}(\beta) - 1| = O_p(1/k_{1,z,n}^{1/2})$. See Hill (2011b, Lemma C.2).

Now construct indicators and a trimmed test equation used solely for asymptotics: in general write $I_{z,n,t}(\beta) := I(-l_{z,n}(\beta) \le z_t(\beta) \le u_{z,n}(\beta))$, and define

$$I_{n,t}(\beta) := I_{\epsilon,n,t}(\beta) \times \prod_{i=1}^{q} I_{i,n,t}(\beta) = I_{\epsilon,n,t}(\beta) \times I_{g,n,t}(\beta) \text{ and}$$
$$m_{n,t}^*(\beta, \gamma) := m_t(\beta, \gamma) \times I_{n,t}(\beta).$$

We also require covariance, Jacobian, and scale matrices:

$$S_n^2(\beta, \gamma) := E\left(\sum_{t=1}^n \{m_{n,t}^*(\beta, \gamma) - E[m_{n,t}^*(\beta, \gamma)]\}\right)^2 \text{ and}$$
$$J_n(\beta, \gamma) := \frac{\partial}{\partial\beta} E\left[m_{n,t}^*(\beta, \gamma)\right] \in \mathbb{R}^{q\times 1}$$
$$V_n(\beta, \gamma) := n^2 S_n^{-2}(\beta, \gamma) \times J_n(\beta, \gamma)' J_n(\beta, \gamma) \in \mathbb{R}.$$

Now drop β^0 throughout, e.g. $g_t = g_t(\beta^0)$, $m_{n,t}^*(\gamma) = m_{n,t}^*(\beta^0, \gamma)$ and $S_n^2(\gamma) = S_n^2(\beta^0, \gamma)$. We may work with $m_{n,t}^*(\gamma)$ for asymptotic theory purposes since

$$\sup_{\gamma\in\Gamma}\left|\frac{1}{S_n(\gamma)}\sum_{t=1}^n \left\{\hat{m}_{n,t}^*(\gamma) - m_{n,t}^*(\gamma)\right\}\right| = o_p(1),$$

while trimming negligibility and response function smoothness ensure the following expansion:

$$\frac{1}{\hat{S}_n(\hat{\beta}_n,\gamma)}\sum_{t=1}^{n}\hat{m}^*_{n,t}(\hat{\beta}_n,\gamma) \overset{p}{\sim} \frac{1}{S_n(\gamma)}\sum_{t=1}^{n} m^*_{n,t}(\gamma) + V_n^{1/2}(\gamma)\left(\hat{\beta}_n - \beta^0\right). \quad (5)$$

See Lemmas B.2 and B.3 in Appendix A. Thus $\hat{\mathcal{T}}_n(\gamma)$ tests H_0 if $\hat{\beta}_n \overset{p}{\to} \beta^0$ fast enough in the sense $\sup_{\gamma\in\Gamma}||V_n(\gamma)\tilde{V}_n^{-1}|| = O(1)$. In the following we detail three plug-in cases denoted P1, P2, and P3.

Case P1 (fast (non)linear plug-ins). In this case $\sup_{\gamma\in\Gamma}||V_n(\gamma)\tilde{V}_n^{-1}|| \to 0$ hence $\hat{\beta}_n$ does not impact $\hat{\mathcal{T}}_n(\gamma)$ asymptotically, which is evidently only possible if ϵ_t and/or $g_{i,t}$ are heavy tailed. If $\{\epsilon_t, g_t\}$ are sufficiently thin tailed then under regularity conditions minimum distance estimators $\hat{\beta}_n$ are $n^{1/2}$-convergent while $V_n(\gamma)/n \to V(\gamma) = S^{-2}(\gamma)J(\gamma)'J(\gamma)$ is finite for each $\gamma \in \Gamma$.[5] In the presence of heavy tails, however, a unique advantage exists since $\sup_{\gamma\in\Gamma}||V_n^{1/2}(\gamma)|| = o(n^{1/2})$ may hold allowing many plug-ins to satisfy $\sup_{\gamma\in\Gamma}||V_n(\gamma)\tilde{V}_n^{-1}|| \to 0$. See Sect. 4 for examples.

Case P2 (slow linear plug-ins). If $\tilde{V}_n$ is proportional to $V_n(\gamma)$ then $\hat{\beta}_n$ impacts $\hat{\mathcal{T}}_n(\gamma)$ asymptotically. This is the case predominantly encountered in the literature since $\tilde{V}_n/n \to \tilde{V}$ and $V_n(\gamma)/n \to V(\gamma)$ for sufficiently thin tailed $\{\epsilon_t, g_t\}$. At least two solutions exist. First, under the present case $\hat{\beta}_n$ is assumed to be asymptotically linear and normal, covering many minimum discrepancy estimators when $\{\epsilon_t, g_t\}$ are sufficiently thin tailed, or heavy tail robust linear estimators like Quasi-maximum tail-trimmed likelihood (QMTTL) (Hill 2011b). Linearity rules out quantile estimators like LAD and its variants, including Log-LAD for GARCH models with heavy tailed errors (Peng and Yao 2003) and least absolute weighted deviations (LWAD) for heavytailed autoregressions (Ling 2005).

Case P3 ((non)linear plug-ins for orthogonal equations). If $\tilde{V}_n$ is proportional to $V_n(\gamma)$ then our second solution is to exploit (Wooldridge's 1990) orthogonal transformation for a new test statistic, ensuring plug-in robustness, and allowing nonlinear plug-ins. Other projection techniques are also evidently valid (e.g. Bai 2003).

Define a projection operator $\hat{\mathcal{P}}_{n,t}(\gamma)$ and filtered equations $\hat{m}^{\perp}_{n,t}(\beta,\gamma)$:

$$\hat{\mathcal{P}}_{n,t}(\gamma) = 1 - g_t'(\hat{\beta}_n)\hat{I}_{n,t}(\hat{\beta}_n)\left(\frac{1}{n}\sum_{t=1}^{n} g_t(\hat{\beta}_n)g_t'(\hat{\beta}_n)F(\gamma'\psi_t)\hat{I}_{n,t}(\hat{\beta}_n)\right)^{-1}$$

$$\times\frac{1}{n}\sum_{t=1}^{n} g_t(\hat{\beta}_n)F(\gamma'\psi_t)\hat{I}_{n,t}(\hat{\beta}_n)\hat{m}^{\perp}_{n,t}(\beta,\gamma) = \hat{m}^*_{n,t}(\beta,\gamma)\times\hat{\mathcal{P}}_{n,t}(\gamma).$$

[5] The rate of convergence for some minimum discrepancy estimators may be below $n^{1/2}$, even for thin tailed data, in contexts involving weak identification, kernel smoothing, and in-fill asymptotics. We implicitly ignored such cases here.

The test statistic is now

$$\hat{\mathcal{T}}_n^{\perp}(\gamma) = \frac{1}{\hat{S}_n^{\perp 2}(\hat{\beta}_n, \gamma)} \left(\sum_{t=1}^{n} \hat{m}_{n,t}^{\perp}(\hat{\beta}_n, \gamma) \right)^2 ,$$

where $\hat{S}_n^{\perp 2}(\beta, \gamma)$ is identically $\hat{S}_n^2(\beta, \gamma)$ computed with $\hat{m}_{n,t}^{\perp}(\beta, \gamma)$.

The asymptotic impact of $\hat{\beta}_n$ is again gauged by using the non-random thresholds $\{l_{z,n}, u_{z,n}\}$ to construct orthogonal equations and their variance and Jacobian:

$$\mathcal{P}_{n,t}(\gamma) := 1 - g_t' I_{n,t} \left(E\left[g_t g_t' F(\gamma'\psi_t) I_{n,t} \right] \right)^{-1} \times E\left[g_t F(\gamma'\psi_t) I_{n,t} \right] \text{ and}$$

$$m_{n,t}^{\perp}(\beta, \gamma) = m_{n,t}^{*}(\beta, \gamma) \times \mathcal{P}_{n,t}(\gamma)$$

$$S_n^{\perp 2}(\beta, \gamma) := E\left(\sum_{t=1}^{n} \left\{ m_{n,t}^{\perp}(\beta, \gamma) - E[m_{n,t}^{\perp}(\beta, \gamma)] \right\} \right)^2 \text{ and}$$

$$J_n^{\perp}(\beta, \gamma) := \frac{\partial}{\partial \beta} E\left[m_{n,t}^{\perp}(\beta, \gamma) \right] \in \mathbb{R}^{q \times 1}$$

$$V_n^{\perp}(\beta, \gamma) := n^2 S_n^{\perp -2}(\beta, \gamma) \times J_n^{\perp}(\beta, \gamma)' J_n^{\perp}(\beta, \gamma) \in \mathbb{R}.$$

Notice $\mathcal{P}_{n,t}(\gamma)$ is $\sigma(x_t)$-measurable, and uniformly L_1-bounded by Lyapunov's inequality and boundedness of $F(u)$, thus by dominated convergence $E[m_{n,t}^{\perp}(\gamma)] \to 0$ under H_0. By imitating expansion (5) and arguments in Wooldridge (1990), it can easily be shown if $V_n^{\perp}(\gamma)^{1/2}(\hat{\beta}_n - \beta^0) = O_p(1)$ then $\hat{S}_n^{\perp -1}(\hat{\beta}_n, \gamma) \sum_{t=1}^{n} \hat{m}_{n,t}^{\perp}(\hat{\beta}_n, \gamma) \overset{p}{\sim} S_n^{\perp -1}(\gamma) \sum_{t=1}^{n} m_{n,t}^{\perp}(\gamma)$. In general the new statistic $\hat{\mathcal{T}}_n^{\perp}(\gamma)$ is robust to $\hat{\beta}_n$, allowing nonlinear estimators, as long as

$$\tilde{V}_n^{1/2}\left(\hat{\beta}_n - \beta^0\right) = O_p(1) \text{ and } \lim \sup_{n \to \infty} \sup_{\gamma \in \Gamma} \left\| V_n^{\perp}(\gamma) \tilde{V}_n^{-1} \right\| < \infty. \tag{6}$$

2.3 Main Results

Appendix A contains all assumptions concerning the fractiles and non-degeneracy of trimmed moments (F1–F2); identification of the null (I1); the kernel and bandwidth for the HAC estimator (K1); the plug-in (P1–P3); moments and memory of regression components (R1–R4); and the test weight (W1). We state the main results for both $\hat{\mathcal{T}}_n(\gamma)$ and $\hat{\mathcal{T}}_n^{\perp}(\gamma)$, but for the sake of brevity limit discussions to $\hat{\mathcal{T}}_n(\gamma)$. Throughout Γ is a compact subset of $\mathbb{R}^p$ with positive Lebesgue measure.

Our first result shows tail-trimming does not impact the ability of $F(\gamma'\psi_t)$ to reveal misspecification.

Lemma 2.1 *Let $\mu_{n,t}(\gamma)$ denote either $m^*_{n,t}(\gamma)$ or $m^{\perp}_{n,t}(\gamma)$. Under the null $E[\mu_{n,t}(\gamma)] \to 0$. Further, if test weight property W1 and the alternative H_1 hold then $\liminf_{n\to\infty} |E[\mu_{n,t}(\gamma)]| > 0$ for all $\gamma \in \Gamma$ except possibly on a set $S \subset \Gamma$ with Lebesgue measure zero.*

Remark 1 Under H_1 it is possible in small samples for $E[m^*_{n,t}(\gamma)] = 0$ due to excessive trimming, and $|E[m^*_{n,t}(\gamma)]| \to \infty$ due to heavy tails. The test weight $F(u)$ therefore is still revealing under tail-trimming for sufficiently large n.

Next, the test statistics converge to chi-squared processes under H_0 and are consistent. Plug in cases are discussed in Sect. 2.2

Theorem 2.2 *Let F1–F2, I1, K1, R1–R4, and W1 hold.*

i. *Under H_0 and plug-in cases P1 or P2 there exists a Gaussian process $\{z(\gamma) : \gamma \in \Gamma\}$ on $C[\Gamma]$ with zero mean, unit variance, and covariance function $E[z(\gamma_1)z(\gamma_2)]$ such that $\{\hat{\mathcal{T}}_n(\gamma) : \gamma \in \Gamma\} \Longrightarrow \{z(\gamma)^2 : \gamma \in \Gamma\}$.*
ii. *UnderH_1 and P1 or P2, $\hat{\mathcal{T}}_n(\gamma) \xrightarrow{p} \infty \forall \gamma \in \Gamma/S$where S has Lebesgue measure zero.*
iii. *Under plug-in case P3 $\hat{\mathcal{T}}_n^{\perp}(\gamma)$ satisfies (i) and (ii).*

Remark 1 The literature offers a variety of ways to handle the nuisance parameter γ. Popular choices include randomly selecting $\gamma^* \in \Gamma$ (e.g. Lee et al. 1993), or computing a continuous test functional $h(\hat{\mathcal{T}}_n(\gamma))$ like the supremum $\sup_{\gamma\in\Gamma} \hat{\mathcal{T}}_n(\gamma)$ and average $\int_\Gamma \hat{\mathcal{T}}_n(\gamma)\mu(d\gamma)$, where $\mu(\gamma)$ is a continuous measure (Davies 1977; Bierens 1990). In the latter case $h(\hat{\mathcal{T}}_n(\gamma)) \xrightarrow{d} h(z(\gamma)^2) =: h_0$ under H_0 by the mapping theorem.

Hansen's 1996 bootstrapped p-value for non-standard h_0 exploits an iid Gaussian simulator. The method therefore applies only if ϵ_t is a martingale difference under H_0 and the trimmed error $\epsilon_t I_{\epsilon,n,t}$ becomes a martingale difference *sufficiently fast* in the sense $(n/E[m^{*2}_{n,t}(\gamma)])^{1/2} E[\epsilon_t I_{\epsilon,n,t}|\Im_{t-1}] \to 0$. It therefore suffices for ϵ_t to be iid and symmetric under H_0 and symmetrically trimmed since then $E[\epsilon_t I_{\epsilon,n,t}|\Im_{t-1}] = E[\epsilon_t I_{\epsilon,n,t}] = 0$, or if ϵ_t is asymmetric and $E[\epsilon_t] = 0$ under either hypothesis then ϵ_t can be symmetrically trimmed with re-centering as in Sect. 3, below. See Hill (2011c, Sect. C.1), the supplemental appendix to this chapter, for details on Hansen's p-value under tail-trimming.

Remark 2 As long as $S_n^2(\gamma) = E[m^*_{n,t}(\gamma)m^*_{n,t}(\gamma)'] \times (1 + o(1))$ then a HAC estimator is not required, including when $\epsilon_t I_{\epsilon,n,t}$ becomes a martingale difference sufficiently fast under H_0 as above. If we do not use a plug-in robust equation then an estimator $\hat{S}_n^2(\hat{\beta}_n, \gamma)$ must control for sampling error associated with $\hat{\beta}_n$. For example, if $\hat{\beta}_n$ is the NLLS estimator then (e.g. Bierens 1990, Eq. (14))

$$\hat{S}_n^2(\hat{\beta}_n, \gamma) = \sum_{t=1}^{n} \epsilon_t^2(\hat{\beta}_n)\hat{I}_{n,t}(\hat{\beta}_n) \times \left\{F(\gamma'\psi_t) - \hat{b}_n'\hat{A}_n^{-1}\hat{g}^*_{n,t}(\hat{\beta}_n)\right\}^2 \tag{7}$$

where $\hat{g}^*_{n,t}(\beta) := g_t(\beta)\hat{I}_{g,n,t}(\beta)$, $\hat{b}_n := 1/n\sum_{t=1}^n \hat{g}^*_{n,t}(\hat{\beta}_n)F(\gamma'\psi_t)$ and $\hat{A}_n := 1/n\sum_{t=1}^n \hat{g}^*_{n,t}(\beta)\hat{g}^*_{n,t}(\beta)'$. However, if $S_n^{\perp 2}(\gamma) \sim E[m^{\perp}_{n,t}(\gamma)m^{\perp}_{n,t}(\gamma)']$ then by orthogonality we need only use

$$\hat{S}_n^{\perp 2}(\hat{\beta}_n, \gamma) = \sum_{t=1}^n \hat{m}^{\perp}_{n,t}(\hat{\beta}_n, \gamma)\hat{m}^{\perp}_{n,t}(\hat{\beta}_n, \gamma)'. \tag{8}$$

3 Fractile Choice

We must choose how much to trim $k_{j,z,n}$ for each variable $z_t \in \{\epsilon_t, g_{i,t}\}$ and any given n. We first present a case when symmetric trimming with re-centering is valid even when ϵ_t is asymmetric under H_0. We then discuss an empirical process method that smooths over a class of fractiles.

Symmetric Trimming with Re-Centering. If $E[\epsilon_t] = 0$ even under the alternative, and ϵ_t is independent of x_t under H_0, then we may symmetrically trim for simplicity and re-center to eradicate bias that arises due to trimming, and still achieve a consistent test statistic. The test equation is

$$\hat{m}^*_{n,t}(\beta, \gamma) = \left(\epsilon_t(\beta)\hat{I}_{n,t}(\beta) - \frac{1}{n}\sum_{t=1}^n \epsilon_t(\beta)\hat{I}_{n,t}(\beta)\right) \times F(\gamma'\psi_t) \tag{9}$$

where $\hat{I}_{n,t}(\beta) = \hat{I}_{\epsilon,n,t}(\beta)\prod_{i=1}^q \hat{I}_{i,n,t}(\beta)$ as before, with symmetric trimming indicators $\hat{I}_{\epsilon,n,t}(\beta) := I(|\epsilon_t(\beta)| \leq \epsilon^{(a)}_{(k_{\epsilon,n})}(\beta))$, and $\hat{I}_{i,n,t}(\beta) := I(|g_{i,t}(\beta)| \leq g^{(a)}_{i,(k_{i,n})}(\beta))$. By independence $m^*_{n,t}(\beta, \gamma) = \left(\epsilon_t(\beta)I_{n,t}(\beta) - E[\epsilon_t(\beta)I_{n,t}(\beta)]\right) \times F(\gamma'\psi_t)$ satisfies $E[m^*_{n,t}(\gamma)] = 0$ under H_0 for any $\{k_{\epsilon,n}, k_{i,n}\}$, hence identification I1 is trivially satisfied. Under H_1 the weight $F(u)$ is revealing by Lemma 2.1 since $E[\epsilon_t] = 0$, $F(u)$ is bounded, and trimming is negligible: $\liminf_{n\to\infty} |E[m^*_{n,t}(\gamma)]| = \liminf_{n\to\infty} |E[\epsilon_t I_{n,t} F(\gamma'\psi_t)]| > 0\, \forall\gamma \in \Gamma/S$. A test of linear AR where the errors may be governed by a nonlinear GARCH process, or a test of linear ARCH, provide natural platforms for re-centering. See Sect. 4 for ARCH.

The moment condition $E[\epsilon_t] = 0$ under either hypothesis rules out some response functions depending on the tails of $\{y_t, x_t\}$. See Sect.1 for an example.

P–Value Occupation Time. Assume symmetric trimming to reduce notation and define the error moment supremum $\kappa_\epsilon := \arg\sup\{\alpha > 0 : E|\epsilon_t|^\alpha < \infty\}$. Under H_0 any intermediate order sequences $\{k_{\epsilon,n}, k_{i,n}\}$ are valid, but in order for our test to work under H_1 when ϵ_t may be exceptionally heavy tailed $\kappa_\epsilon < 1$, we must impose $k_{\epsilon,n}/n^{2(1-\kappa_\epsilon)/(2-\kappa_\epsilon)} \to \infty$ to ensure sufficient trimming for test consistency (see Assumption F1.b in Appendix A). Thus $k_{\epsilon,n} \sim n/L(n)$ is valid for any slowly varying $L(n) \to \infty$. Consider $k_{\epsilon,n} = k_{i,n} \sim \lambda n/\ln(n)$ where λ is taken from a compact set $\Lambda := [\underline{\lambda}, 1]$ for tiny $\underline{\lambda} > 0$, although any slowly varying $L(n) \to \infty$

may replace $\ln(n)$. The point $\lambda = 0$ is ruled out because the untrimmed $\hat{\mathcal{T}}_n(0)$ is asymptotically non-chi-squared under H_0 when $E[\epsilon_t^2] = \infty$.

We must now commit to some λ. Other than an arbitrary choice, Hill and Aguilar (2011) smooth over a space of feasible $\lambda's$ by computing p-value occupation time. We construct the occupation time below, and prove its validity for $\hat{\mathcal{T}}_n(\gamma)$ and $\hat{\mathcal{T}}_n^{\perp}(\gamma)$ in Appendix B. The following easily extends to $k_{\epsilon,n} \neq k_{i,n}$, asymmetric trimming, and functionals $h(\hat{\mathcal{T}}_n(\gamma))$ on Γ.

Write $\hat{\mathcal{T}}_n(\gamma, \lambda)$ and $\hat{\mathcal{T}}_n^{\perp}(\gamma, \lambda)$ to reveal dependence on λ, let $p_n(\gamma, \lambda)$ denote the asymptotic p-value $1 - F_\chi(\hat{\mathcal{T}}_n(\gamma, \lambda))$ where F_χ is the $\chi^2(1)$ distribution, and define the α-level occupation time

$$\tau_n(\gamma, \alpha) := \frac{1}{1 - \underline{\lambda}} \int_{\underline{\lambda}}^{1} I\left(p_n(\gamma, \lambda) < \alpha\right) d\lambda \in [0, 1], \quad \text{where } \alpha \in (0, 1).$$

Thus $\tau_n(\gamma, \alpha)$ is the proportion of $\lambda's$ satisfying $p_n(\gamma, \lambda) < \alpha$ hence rejection of H_0 at level α. Similarly, define the occupation time $\tau_n^{\perp}(\gamma, \alpha)$ for $\hat{\mathcal{T}}_n^{\perp}(\gamma, \lambda)$.

Theorem 3.1 *Let F1–F2, I1, K1, P1 or P2, R1–R4, and W1 hold. Let $\{u(\lambda) : \lambda \in \Lambda\}$ be a stochastic process that may be different in different places: in each case it has a version that has uniformly continuous sample paths, and $u(\lambda)$ is uniformly distributed on* $[0, 1]$. *Under the null $\tau_n(\gamma, \alpha) \stackrel{d}{\to} (1 - \underline{\lambda})^{-1} \int_{\underline{\lambda}}^1 I(u(\lambda) < \alpha)d\lambda$ and $\tau_n^{\perp}(\gamma, \alpha) \stackrel{d}{\to} (1 - \underline{\lambda})^{-1} \int_{\underline{\lambda}}^1 I(u(\lambda) < \alpha)d\lambda$, and under the alternative $\tau_n(\gamma, \alpha) \stackrel{p}{\to} 1$ and $\tau_n^{\perp}(\gamma, \alpha) \stackrel{p}{\to} 1 \, \forall \gamma \in \Gamma$ except possibly on subsets with measure zero.*

Remark 1 Since $u(\lambda)$ is a uniform random variable it follows $\lim_{n\to\infty} P(\tau_n(\gamma, \alpha) > \alpha | H_0) < \alpha$. A p-value occupation test therefore rejects H_0 at level α if $\tau_n(\gamma, \alpha) > \alpha$. In practice a discretized version is computed, for example

$$\hat{\tau}_n(\gamma, \alpha) := \frac{1}{n_{\underline{\lambda}}} \sum_{i=1}^{n} I\left(p_n(\gamma, i/n) < \alpha\right) \times I\left(i/n \geq \underline{\lambda}\right) \tag{10}$$

where $n_{\underline{\lambda}} := \sum_{i=1}^n I(i/n \geq \underline{\lambda})$ is the number of discretized points in $[\underline{\lambda}, 1]$.

Remark 2 In Sect. 4 we show $\hat{\beta}_n$ has a larger impact on $\hat{\mathcal{T}}_n(\gamma, \lambda)$ in small samples when the error has an infinite variance $\kappa_\epsilon < 2$, each $g_{i,t}$ has a finite mean $\kappa_i > 1$, and the number of trimmed errors $k_{\epsilon,n}$ is large (see Remark 3 of Lemma 4.1). This translates to the possibility of plug-in sensitivity of $\tau_n(\gamma, \alpha)$ in small samples. We show in our Monte Carlo study of Sect. 5 that when $\kappa_\epsilon < 2$ and $\kappa_i > 1$ the occupation time $\tau_n(\gamma, \alpha)$ results in size distortions that are eradicated when the plug-in robust $\hat{\tau}_n^{\perp}(\gamma, \alpha)$ is used.

In Fig. 1, we plot sample paths $\{p_n(\gamma, \lambda), p_n^{\perp}(\gamma, \lambda) : \lambda \in [0.01, 1.0]\}$ based on two samples $\{y_t\}_{t=1}^n$ of size $n = 200$: one sample is drawn from an AR(1) process

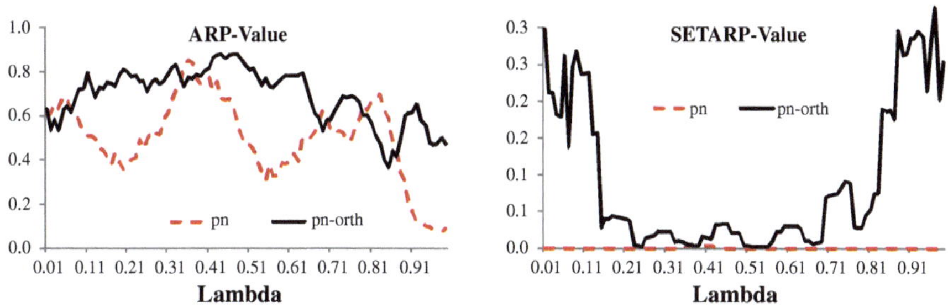

Fig. 1 P-value functions $p_n(\lambda)$ and $p_n^{\perp}(\lambda)$. *Note* pn $= p_n(\lambda)$, and pn-orth $= p_n^{\perp}(\lambda)$

and the other from a Threshold AR(1) process, each with iid Pareto errors ϵ_t and tail index 1.5. See Sect. 5 for simulation details. We estimate an AR(5) model by OLS, compute $\hat{\mathcal{T}}_n(\gamma, \lambda)$ and $\hat{\mathcal{T}}_n^{\perp}(\gamma, \lambda)$ with weight $F(\gamma'\psi(x_t)) = \exp\{\gamma'\psi(x_t)\}$, $\psi(x_t) = [1, \arctan(\tilde{x}_t^*)']'$ where $\tilde{x}_t^*$ is centered $\tilde{x}_t = [y_{t-1}, ..., y_{t-5}]'$, and γ is uniformly randomize on $[.1, 2]^6$. In this case at the 5 % level $\hat{\tau}_n, \hat{\tau}_n^{\perp} = 0, 0$ for the AR sample hence we fail to reject H_0, and $\hat{\tau}_n, \hat{\tau}_n^{\perp} = 0.59, 1.0$ for the SETAR sample hence we reject H_0.

Notice in the AR case $p_n(\gamma, \lambda)$ is smallest for large $\lambda \geq 0.9$, and $p_n(\gamma, \lambda) < p_n^{\perp}(\gamma, \lambda)$ for most $\lambda : p_n(\gamma, \lambda)$ is more likely to lead to a rejection than the plug-in robust $p_n^{\perp}(\gamma, \lambda)$ and for large λ. Although we only use one AR sample here, in Sect. 5 we show plug-in sensitivity does indeed lead to over-rejection of H_0.

4 Plug-In Choice and Verification of the Assumptions

We first characterize $V_n(\gamma)$ to show how fast $\hat{\beta}_n$ in $\hat{\mathcal{T}}_n(\gamma)$ must be in view of expansion (5). Synonymous derivations carry over to portray $V_n^{\perp}(\gamma)$. We then verify the assumptions for AR and ARCH models and several plug-in estimators. Define moment suprema $\kappa_\epsilon := \arg\sup\{\alpha > 0 : E|\epsilon_t|^\alpha < \infty\}$ and $\kappa_i := \arg\sup\{\alpha > 0 : E|g_{i,t}|^\alpha < \infty\}$.

Lemma 4.1 *Let F1–F2, I1, R1–R4 and W1 hold. If* $\kappa_i \leq 1$ *then assume* $P(|g_{i,t}| > g) = d_i g^{\kappa_i}(1 + o(1))$ *for some* $d_i > 0$. *Let* $L(n) \to \infty$ *be slowly varying, and let* $\{\mathfrak{L}_n\}$ *be a sequence of positive constants:* $\liminf_{n\to\infty} \mathfrak{L}_n \geq 1$ *and* $\mathfrak{L}_n = O(\ln(n))$, *and if* ϵ_t *is finite dependent then* $\mathfrak{L}_n = K$. *In the following* $L(n)$ *and* $\mathfrak{L}_n$ *may be different in different places.*

i. Let $\min\{\kappa_i\} > 1$. *If* $\kappa_\epsilon > 2$ *then* $V_n(\gamma) = O(n)$ *; if* $\kappa_\epsilon = 2$ *then* $V_n(\gamma) \sim n/L(n)$*; and if* $\kappa_\epsilon < 2$ *then* $V_n(\gamma) \sim Kn(k_{\epsilon,n}/n)^{2/\kappa_\epsilon - 1}/\mathfrak{L}_n$.
ii. Let some $\kappa_i < 1$. *If* $\kappa_\epsilon > 2$ *then* $V_n(\gamma) \sim Kn \max_{i:\kappa_i<1}\{(n/k_{i,n})^{2/\kappa_i - 2}\}$*; if* $\kappa_\epsilon = 2$ *then* $V_n(\gamma) \sim Kn \max_{i:\kappa_i<1}\{(n/k_{i,n})^{2/\kappa_i-2}\}/L(n)$*; and if* $\kappa_\epsilon < 2$ *then* $V_n(\gamma) \sim Kn \max_{i:\kappa_i<1}\{(n/k_{i,n})^{2/\kappa_i-2}\} \times (k_{\epsilon,n}/n)^{2/\kappa_\epsilon-1}/\mathfrak{L}_n$.

iii. *If* $\min\{\kappa_i\} = 1$ *then replace* $\max_{i:\kappa_i<1}\{(n/k_{i,n})^{2/\kappa_i-2}\}$ *in (b) with* $L(n)$.

Remark 1 The term $\mathfrak{L}_n$ arises due to β-mixing *and* heavy tails: clearly $S_n^2(\gamma) \sim KnE[m_{n,t}^2]$ if ϵ_t is finite dependent or has a finite variance, but otherwise we can only show $S_n^2(\gamma) \sim nE[m_{n,t}^2] \times O(\ln(n))$, cf. Hill (2011b, Lemma B.2)

Remark 2 If $E[\epsilon_t^2] = \infty$ then $V_n(\gamma) = o(n)$ as long as all $\kappa_i > 1$, hence $\hat{\beta}_n$ may be sub-$n^{1/2}$-convergent. This arises, for example, in integrable AR models or ARCH models with square integrable errors as we verify below.

Remark 3 If $\kappa_\epsilon < 2$ and each $\kappa_i > 1$ then $V_n(\gamma) \sim Kn(k_{\epsilon,n}/n)^{2/\kappa_\epsilon - 1}/\mathfrak{L}_n$. Combine this with expansion (5) to deduce a higher error trimming rate $k_{\epsilon,n} \to \infty$ *amplifies* the impact of $\hat{\beta}_n$ on the test statistic $\hat{\mathcal{T}}_n(\gamma)$ in small samples, even when fast plug-in Assumption P1 holds. This suggests the plug-in robust statistic $\hat{\mathcal{T}}_n^{\perp}(\gamma)$ should be used when $k_{\epsilon,n}$ is chosen to be large relative to n. This is supported by experiments in Sect. 5 where the p-value occupation which smooths over small and large $k_{\epsilon,n}$ performs substantially better when $\hat{\mathcal{T}}_n^{\perp}(\gamma)$ is used.

4.1 Linear AR

Consider a stationary AR(p) $y_t = \beta^{0\prime} x_t + \epsilon_t$ where $x_t = [y_{t-1}, ..., y_{t-p}]'$, ϵ_t is iid and $E[\epsilon_t] = 0$. Assume ϵ_t has an absolutely continuous symmetric distribution with a uniformly bounded density $\sup_{c\in\mathbb{R}}(\partial/\partial c)P(\epsilon_t \leq c) < \infty$, and Paretian tail:

$$P(|\epsilon_t| > \epsilon) = d\epsilon^{-\kappa}(1 + o(1)), \quad d > 0, \quad \kappa > 1. \tag{11}$$

Since y_t is symmetric with a power law tail and the same index κ (Brockwell and Cline 1985), and $g_{i,t} = y_{t-i}$, we use symmetric trimming (3) with common fractiles $k_{\epsilon,n} = k_{y,n}$ denoted k_n. Let $\hat{\beta}_n$ be computed by OLS, LAD, LWAD by Ling (2005), least tail-trimmed squares (LTTS) by Hill (2011b), or generalized method of tail-trimmed moments (GMTTM) by Hill and Renault (2010) with estimating equations $[\epsilon_t(\beta)y_{t-i}]_{i=1}^r$ for some $r \geq p$.[6]

Lemma 4.2 *Assumptions F2, I1, and R1–R4 hold. If* $\kappa < 2$ *then* $V_n(\gamma) \sim Kn(k_n/n)^{2/\kappa-1}$ *and if then* $V_n(\gamma) \sim Kn/L(n)$ *uniformly on* Γ. *Therefore each* $\hat{\beta}_n$ *satisfies P1 and P3 if* $E[\epsilon_t^2] = \infty$ *and P3 if* $E[\epsilon_t^2] < \infty$*; and if* $E[\epsilon_t^2] < \infty$ *then only OLS, LTTS, and GMTTM satisfy P2.*

Remark 1 The F1 fractile properties are controlled by the analyst. Each plug-in is super-$n^{1/2}$-convergent when $E[\epsilon_t^2] = \infty$, and OLS and LAD have non-Gaussian limits when $E[\epsilon_t^2] = \infty$ (Davis et al. 1992; Ling 2005; Hill and Renault 2010; Hill

[6] Other over-identifying restrictions can easily be included, but the GMTTM rate may differ from what we cite in the proof of Lemma 4.2 if they are not lags of y_t. See Hill and Renault (2010).

2011b) while $V_n^{1/2}(\gamma) = o(n^{1/2})$ by Lemma 4.1. Hence each $\hat{\beta}_n$ satisfies fast plug-in P1. However, if ϵ_t has a finite variance then $V_n(\gamma) \sim Kn$ and each $\hat{\beta}_n$ has rate $n^{1/2}$, ruling out LAD and LWAD for the non-orthogonalized $\hat{\mathcal{T}}_n(\gamma)$ since P2 requires estimator linearity.

4.2 *Linear ARCH*

Now consider a strong-ARCH(p) $y_t = h_t u_t$ where $u_t \overset{iid}{\sim} (0, 1)$ and $h_t^2 = \omega^0 + \sum_{i=1}^p \alpha_i^0 y_{t-i}^2 = \beta^{0\prime} x_t$, $\omega^0 > 0$, and $\alpha_i^0 \geq 0$. Assume at least one $\alpha_i^0 > 0$ for brevity, let $\sum_{i=1}^p \alpha_i^0 < 1$, and assume the distribution of u_t is non-degenerate, symmetric, absolutely continuous, and bounded $\sup_{c \geq 0}(\partial/\partial c)P(u_t \leq c) < \infty$. Let κ_u be the moment supremum arg $\sup\{\alpha > 0 : E|u_t|^\alpha < \infty\}$. If $\kappa_u \in (2, 4]$ then assume u_t has tail (11) with index κ_u.

A test of omitted ARCH nonlinearity can be framed in terms of errors $u_t^2 - 1$ or $y_t^2 - \beta^{0\prime} x_t = (u_t^2 - 1)h_t^2$. Since the former only requires u_t^2 and not y_t^2 to be integrable, consider $\epsilon_t(\beta) := u_t^2(\beta) - 1 := y_t^2/(\beta' x_t) - 1$. In this case $(\partial/\partial\beta)\epsilon_t(\beta)|_{\beta^0} = -u_t^2 x_t / h_t^2$ has tails that depend solely on the iid error u_t since we impose ARCH effects $\alpha_i^0 > 0$: $||x_t/h_t^2|| \leq K a.s.$ We therefore do not need to use information from x_t for trimming. The error $\epsilon_t = u_t^2 - 1$ may be asymmetric but we can symmetrically trim with re-centering as in Sect. 3. The trimmed equation with re-centering assuming ARCH effects is $\hat{m}_{n,t}^*(\beta, \gamma) = \{\epsilon_t \hat{I}_{\epsilon,n,t}(\beta) - 1/n \sum_{t=1}^n \epsilon_t \hat{I}_{\epsilon,n,t}(\beta)\} \times F(\gamma' \psi_t)$ where $\hat{I}_{\epsilon,n,t}(\beta) := I(|\epsilon_t(\beta)| \leq \epsilon_{(k_{\epsilon,n})}^{(a)}(\beta))$.

In the following we consider plug-ins $\hat{\beta}_n$ computed by QML, Log-LAD by Peng and Yao (2003), QMTTL by Hill (2011b), or GMTTM with QML-type equations $\{u_t^2(\beta) - 1\} z_t(\beta)$ where $z_t(\beta) = [(\beta' x_{t-i})^{-1} x_{t-i}]_{i=0}^r$ for some $r \geq 0$ (Hill and Renault 2010).

Lemma 4.3 *Assumptions F2, I1, and R1–R4 hold. Further a. GMTTM and QMTTL satisfy P1 if* $\kappa_u \in (2, 4]$, *P2 if* $\kappa_u > 4$, *and P3 in general; b. QML satisfies P2 and P3 if* $\kappa_u \geq 4$, *but does not satisfy P1–P3 when* $\kappa_u \in (2, 4)$; *c. Log-LAD satisfies P1 if* $E[u_t^4] = \infty$, *it does not satisfy P2 if* $\kappa_u > 4$, *and it satisfies P3 in general.*

Remark 1 QML is too slow when the ARCH error has an infinite fourth moment $\kappa_u \in (2, 4)$. This arises due both to feedback with the error u_t, and to the F1.b lower bound on the error trimming rate $k_{j,\epsilon,n}/n^{2(1-\kappa_\epsilon)/(2-\kappa_\epsilon)} \to \infty$ which ensures test consistency when $E|\epsilon_t| = \infty$: the former implies $||\tilde{V}_n|| = Kn^{1-2/\kappa_u} = o(n^{1/2})$ (Hall and Yao 2003), while the latter guarantees $\inf_{\gamma \in \Gamma} ||V_n(\gamma)||/n^{1-2/\kappa_u} \to \infty$. Each remaining estimator has a Gaussian limit since $\kappa_u > 2$. Log-LAD is not linear so orthogonalization is required when $E[u_t^4] < \infty$.

5 Simulation Study

We now present a small-scale simulation study where we test for omitted nonlinearity in three models: linear AR(2) $y_t = 0.8y_{t-1} - 0.4y_{t-2} + \epsilon_t$, Self-Exciting Threshold AR(1) [SETAR] $y_t = 0.8y_{t-1}I(y_{t-1} < 0) - 0.4y_{t-1}I(y_{t-1} \geq 0) + \epsilon_t$, and Bilinear [BILIN] $y_t = 0.9y_{t-1}\epsilon_{t-1} + \epsilon_t$. We generate 10,000 samples of size $n \in \{200, 800, 5000\}$ by using a starting value $y_1 = \epsilon_1$, generating $2n$ observations of y_t, and retaining the last n. The errors $\{\epsilon_t\}$ are either iid $N(0, 1)$; symmetric Pareto $P(\epsilon_t \leq -c) = P(\epsilon_t \geq c) = 0.5(1 + c)^{-\kappa_\epsilon}$ with index $\kappa_\epsilon = 1.5$; or IGARCH(1,1) $\epsilon_t = h_t u_t$ where $h_t^2 = 0.3 + .4u_{t-1}^2 + 0.6h_{t-1}^2$ and $u_t \overset{iid}{\sim} N(0, 1)$, with starting value $h_1^2 = 0.3$. The errors ϵ_t therefore have possible moment suprema $\kappa_\epsilon \in \{1.5, 2, \infty\}$. Each process is stationary geometrically ergodic and therefore geometrically β-mixing (Pham and Tran 1985; An and Huang 1996; Meitz and Saikkonen 2008). We estimate an AR(5) model $y_t = \sum_{i=1}^{5} \beta_i^0 y_{t-i} + \epsilon_t$ by OLS for each series, although LTTS and LWAD render essentially identical results.

5.1 Tail-Trimmed CM Test

Write $x_t := [y_{t-1}, ..., y_{t-p}]'$. Recall from Sect. 3 $k_{j,\epsilon,n} \sim n/L(n)$ for slowly varying $L(n) \to \infty$ promotes test consistency when $E|\epsilon_t| = \infty$ under the alternative. Considering ϵ_t and y_{t-i} have the same moment supremum κ_ϵ and are symmetric under H_0, we simply use symmetric trimming with $k_n = [\lambda n/\ln(n)]$ for each ϵ_t and y_{t-i}. We re-center by using $\hat{m}_{n,t}^*(\beta, \gamma)$ defined in (9), and compute the orthogonal equations $\hat{m}_{n,t}^{\perp}(\beta, \gamma)$ with the re-centered $\hat{m}_{n,t}^*(\beta, \gamma)$ and operator $\hat{\mathcal{P}}_{n,t}(\gamma) = 1 - x_t'\hat{I}_{n,t}(\hat{\beta}_n) \times (\sum_{t=1}^{n} x_t x_t' F(\gamma'\psi_t)\hat{I}_{n,t}(\hat{\beta}_n))^{-1} \times \sum_{t=1}^{n} x_t F(\gamma'\psi_t)\hat{I}_{n,t}(\hat{\beta}_n)$. We use an exponential weight $F(\gamma'\psi(x_t)) = \exp\{\gamma'\psi(x_t)\}$ and argument $\psi(x_t) = [1, \arctan(x_t^*)']' \in \mathbb{R}^6$ with $x_{i,t}^* = x_{i,t} - 1/n \sum_{t=1}^{n} x_{i,t}$ (cf. Bierens 1990, Sect. 5), and then compute $\hat{\mathcal{T}}_n(\gamma)$ and $\hat{\mathcal{T}}_n^{\perp}(\gamma)$. We use scale estimators (7) and (8) with $g_t = x_t$ for the sake of comparison with our choice of additional test statistics discussed below. We randomly draw γ from a uniform distribution on $\Gamma = [0.1, 2]^6$ for each sample generated, and fix $\lambda = 0.025$ or compute p-value occupation times $\hat{\tau}_n(\gamma, \alpha)$ and $\hat{\tau}_n^{\perp}(\gamma, \alpha)$ on $[0.01, 1.0]$ a la (10) for nominal levels $\alpha \in \{0.01, 0.05, 0.10\}$. Notice $\lambda = 0.025$ implies very few observations are trimmed, e.g. at most 1.5 % of a sample of size 800.[7]

[7] If $n = 800$ then $k_n = [0.025 \times 800/\ln(800)] = 2$ for each $\{\epsilon_t, y_{t-1}, ..., y_{t-5}\}$. Hence at most $2 \times 6 = 12$ observations are trimmed, which is 1.5 % of 800.

5.2 Tests of Functional Form

The remaining tests are based on *untrimmed* versions of $\hat{\mathcal{T}}_n(\gamma)$ and $\hat{\mathcal{T}}_n^{\perp}(\gamma)$ where critical values are obtained from a $\chi^2(1)$ distribution; Hong and White's 1995 nonparametric test, Ramsey's 1969 regression error specification test (RESET), Li's 1983 test, and a test proposed by Tsay (1986). Hong and White's 1995 statistic is $\hat{M}_n = (2\ln n)^{-1/2}(s_n^{-2}\sum_{t=1}^n \hat{\epsilon}_t \hat{v}_{n,t} - \ln n)$ with components $s_n^2 := 1/n\sum_{t=1}^n \hat{\epsilon}_t^2$ and $\hat{v}_{n,t} := \hat{f}_t - \hat{\beta}_n' x_t$, and nonparametric estimator $\hat{f}_t = \sum_{i=1}^{[\ln(n)]} \phi_i \exp\{\gamma_i' x_t\}$ of $E[y_t|x_t]$, cf. Gallant (1981) and Bierens (Bierens 1990, Corollary 1). The parameters γ_i are for each sample uniformly randomly selected from Γ, and ϕ is estimated by least squares.[8] If certain regularity conditions hold, including independence of ϵ_t and $E[\epsilon_t^4] < \infty$, then $\hat{M}_n \overset{d}{\to} N(0,1)$ under H_0, while $\hat{M}_n \to \infty$ in probability under H_1, hence a one-sided test is performed. The RESET test is an F-test on the auxiliary regression $\hat{\epsilon}_t = \phi_0' x_t + \sum_{i=2}^{k_1}\sum_{j=2}^{k_2} \phi_{i,j} x_{t-j}^i + u_t$ where we use $k_1 = k_2 = 3$; the McLeod-Li statistic is $\sum_{t=1}^n (\hat{\epsilon}_t^2 - s_n^2)(\hat{\epsilon}_{t-h}^2 - s_n^2)/\sum_{t=1}^n (\hat{\epsilon}_t^2 - s_n^2)^2$ with lags $h = 3$; and Tsay's test is based on first regressing $vech[x_t x_t'] = \xi' x_t + u_t$, and then computing $F_n := \sum_{t=1}^n (\hat{\epsilon}_t \hat{u}_t)[\sum_{t=1}^n \hat{u}_t \hat{u}_t']^{-1} \sum_{t=1}^n (\hat{\epsilon}_t \hat{u}_t')$: $F_n \overset{d}{\to} \chi^2(p(p+1)/2)$ under H_0 as long as $E[\epsilon_t^4] < \infty$.

5.3 Simulation Results

See Tables 1, 2, 3 for test results, where empirical power is adjusted for size distortions. We only present results for $n \in \{200, 800\}$: see the supplemental appendix Hill (2011c, Sect. C.4) for $n = 5{,}000$.

Write $\hat{\mathcal{T}}_n$-Fix or $\hat{\mathcal{T}}_n$-OT for tests based on fixed $\lambda = 0.025$ or occupation time. The results strongly suggest orthogonalization is required if we use occupation time because $\hat{\mathcal{T}}_n$-OT exhibits large size distortions, while $\hat{\mathcal{T}}_n^{\perp}$-OT has fairly sharp size and good power. This follows from the dual impact of sampling error associated with $\hat{\beta}_n$ and the loss of information associated with trimming. Our simulations show this applies in general, irrespective of heavy tails, while Remark 3 of Lemma 4.1 shows when $\kappa_\epsilon = \kappa_i \in (1,2)$ then a *large amount of trimming* k_n *amplifies sensitivity* of $\hat{\mathcal{T}}_n$ to $\hat{\beta}_n$ in small samples. Orthogonalization *should* play a stronger role when λ is large, hence $\hat{\mathcal{T}}_n^{\perp}$-OT *should* dominate $\hat{\mathcal{T}}_n$-OT, at least when the variance is infinite.

In heavy-tailed cases $\hat{\mathcal{T}}_n$-Fix and $\hat{\mathcal{T}}_n^{\perp}$-OT in general exhibit the highest power, although all tests exhibit low power when the errors are IGARCH and $n \in \{200, 800\}$. It should be noted the Hong-White, RESET, McLeod-Li, and Tsay tests are all designed under the assumption ϵ_t is independent under H_0 and $E[\epsilon_t^4] < \infty$, hence IGARCH errors are invalid due both to feedback and heavy tails. If ϵ_t is iid Gaussian

---

[8] See Hong and White (1995, Theorem 3.2) for defense of a slowly varying series length $\ln(n)$.

Table 1 Empirical size (linear AR)

n	iid ϵ_t ($\kappa = 1.5$)[a]		GARCH ϵ_t ($\kappa = 2$)		iid ϵ_t ($\kappa = \infty$)	
	200	800	200	800	200	800
	1 %, 5 %, 10 %	1 %, 5 %, 10 %	1 %, 5 %, 10 %	1 %, 5 %, 10 %	1 %, 5 %, 10 %	1 %, 5 %, 10 %
TT-Orth-Fix[b,c]	0.00, 0.01, 0.04[d]	0.00, 0.02, 0.06	0.00, 0.01, 0.05	0.00, 0.03, 0.09	0.00, 0.02, 0.05	0.00, 0.03, 0.07
TT-Fix	0.00, 0.02, 0.07	0.01, 0.04, 0.08	0.00, 0.01, 0.04	0.00, 0.02, 0.05	0.00, 0.02, 0.06	0.00, 0.02, 0.04
TT-Orth-OT	0.01, 0.04, 0.06	0.02, 0.06, 0.12	0.01, 0.03, 0.04	0.01, 0.02, 0.04	0.01, 0.03, 0.09	0.02, 0.07, 0.12
TT-OT	0.23, 0.41, 0.52	0.31, 0.46, 0.54	0.04, 0.17, 0.27	0.15, 0.31, 0.40	0.04, 0.12, 0.20	0.06, 0.14, 0.23
CM-Orth[e]	0.00, 0.01, 0.05	0.00, 0.03, 0.07	0.00, 0.04, 0.11	0.00, 0.04, 0.10	0.00, 0.04, 0.09	0.00, 0.03, 0.09
CM	0.00, 0.01, 0.04	0.01, 0.02, 0.08	0.00, 0.00, 0.02	0.00, 0.01, 0.03	0.00, 0.01, 0.03	0.00, 0.02, 0.04
HW[f]	0.17, 0.22, 0.25	0.21, 0.24, 0.27	0.06, 0.15, 0.24	0.80, 0.87, 0.89	0.00, 0.02, 0.05	0.02, 0.05, 0.07
RESET[g]	0.00, 0.00, 0.02	0.00, 0.01, 0.02	0.00, 0.03, 0.09	0.01, 0.05, 0.11	0.00, 0.03, 0.08	0.01, 0.05, 0.10
McLeod-Li[g]	0.02, 0.03, 0.03	0.01, 0.02, 0.02	0.58, 0.70, 0.78	1.0, 1.0, 1.0	0.01, 0.04, 0.07	0.02, 0.05, 0.09
Tsay[g]	0.98, 0.99, 1.0	1.0, 1.0, 1.0	0.37, 0.47, 0.51	0.72, 0.77, 0.80	0.01, 0.05, 0.10	0.01, 0.05, 0.10

[a] Moment supremum of the test error ϵ_t: $\kappa = \sup\{\alpha : E|\epsilon_t|^{\alpha} < \infty\}$ [b] *TT* tail-trimmed CM test with randomized nuisance parameter γ. *Fix* fixed trimming parameter λ [c] *Orth* orthogonal equation transformation. *OT* occupation time test over set of λ [d] Rejection frequencies at 1, 5, and 10 % nominal levels [e] Untrimmed randomized and sup-CM tests [f] Hong and White's (1995) nonparametric test [g] Ramsey's RESET test with 3 lags; McLeod and Li's test with 3 lags; Tsay's F-test

Table 2 Empirical power[a] (self-exciting threshold AR)

	iid ϵ_t ($\kappa = 1.5$)		GARCH ϵ_t ($\kappa = 2$)		iid ϵ_t ($\kappa = \infty$)	
n	200	800	200	800	200	800
	1 %, 5 %, 10 %	1 %, 5 %, 10 %	1 %, 5 %, 10 %	1 %, 5 %, 10 %	1 %, 5 %, 10 %	1 %, 5 %, 10 %
TT-Orth-Fix	0.02, 0.12, 0.22	.08, 0.26, 0.38	0.01, 0.06, 0.11	0.01, 0.05, 0.11	0.02, 0.05, 0.11	0.02, 0.08, 0.15
TT-Fix	0.12, 0.18, 0.24	0.21, 0.32, 0.39	0.01, 0.05, 0.11	0.03, 0.12, 0.23	0.02, 0.07, 0.12	0.09, 0.27, 0.43
TT-Orth-OT	0.19, 0.35, 0.46	0.65, 0.83, 0.93	0.08, 0.17, 0.25	0.12, 0.24, 0.39	0.06, 0.13, 0.24	0.16, 0.28, 0.42
TT-OT	0.28, 0.30, 0.32	0.38, 0.35, 0.37	0.11, 0.13, 0.21	0.24, 0.25, 0.39	0.04, 0.13, 0.22	0.39, 0.52, 0.57
CM-Orth	0.05, 0.21, 0.33	0.11, 0.27, 0.42	0.02, 0.07, 0.13	0.01, 0.05, 0.09	0.01, 0.04, 0.08	0.02, 0.06, 0.10
CM	0.04, 0.11, 0.18	0.12, 0.23, 0.29	0.01, 0.05, 0.10	0.02, 0.12, 0.24	0.01, 0.07, 0.14	0.08, 0.30, 0.44
HW	0.06, 0.10, 0.16	0.17, 0.15, 0.30	0.04, 0.05, 0.09	0.04, 0.07, 0.12	0.02, 0.06, 0.11	0.16, 0.29, 0.40
RESET	0.03, 0.14, 0.28	0.08, 0.28, 0.45	0.02, 0.12, 0.24	0.15, 0.38, 0.53	0.20, 0.54, 0.73	1.0, 1.0, 1.0
McLeod-Li	0.29, 0.45, 0.55	0.71, 0.76, 0.83	0.00, 0.00, 0.07	0.01, 0.05, 0.10	0.07, 0.19,.27	0.51, 0.69, 0.79
Tsay	0.02, 0.02, 0.02	0.00, 0.00, 0.00	0.13, 0.17, 0.19	0.15, 0.17, 0.21	0.45, 0.65, 0.70	1.0, 1.0, 1.0

[a] The rejection frequencies are adjusted for size distortions based on Table 1

Table 3 Empirical power[a] (bilinear AR)

	iid ϵ_t ($\kappa = 1.5$)		GARCH ϵ_t ($\kappa = 2$)		iid ϵ_t ($\kappa = \infty$)	
n	200	800	200	800	200	800
	1 %, 5 %, 10 %	1 %, 5 %, 10 %	1 %,5 %, 10 %	1 %, 5 %, 10 %	1 %, 5 %, 10 %	1 %, 5 %, 10 %
TT-Orth-Fix	0.04, 0.16, 0.26	0.22, 0.39, 0.49	0.01, 0.07, 0.11	0.02, 0.08, 0.14	0.01, 0.05, 0.09	0.01, 0.05, 0.11
TT-Fix	0.04, 0.13, 0.21	0.13, 0.31, 0.42	0.02, 0.09, 0.17	0.02, 0.09, 0.18	0.01, 0.04, 0.07	0.01, 0.04, 0.10
TT-Orth-OT	0.08, 0.14, 0.18	0.36, 0.38, 0.37	0.02, 0.05, 0.10	0.04, 0.06, 0.09	0.01, 0.05, 0.05	0.00, 0.01, 0.02
TT-OT	0.57, 0.61, 0.61	0.68, 0.58, 0.60	0.27, 0.30, 0.36	0.57, 0.52, 0.55	0.01, 0.07, 0.13	0.06, 0.12, 0.16
CM-Orth	0.03, 0.14, 0.24	0.21, 0.40, 0.51	0.02, 0.11, 0.21	0.03, 0.13, 0.26	.01, 0.04, 0.11	0.01, 0.05, 0.11
CM	0.02, 0.08, 0.16	0.08, 0.30, 0.41	0.01, 0.05, 0.10	0.01, 0.05, 0.11	.01, 0.04, 0.09	0.01, 0.04, 0.09
HW	0.00, 0.00, 0.00	0.00, 0.00, 0.00	0.02, 0.07, 0.07	0.00, 0.00, 0.00	0.24, 0.38, 0.47	0.87, 0.92, 0.97
RESET	0.02, 0.07, 0.14	0.01, 0.06, 0.14	0.03, 0.07, 0.11	0.01, 0.05, 0.09	0.02, 0.06, 0.12	0.03, 0.17, 0.28
McLeod-Li	0.19, 0.26, 0.33	0.35, 0.43, 0.51	0.00, 0.02, 0.04	0.00, 0.00, 0.00	0.86, 0.93, 0.98	0.99, 1.0, 1.0
Tsay	0.03, 0.06, 0.10	0.01, 0.05, 0.10	0.36, 0.36, 0.37	0.20, 0.20, 0.23	.76, 0.84, 0.88	0.91, 0.95, 0.96

[a] The rejection frequencies are adjusted for size distortions based on Table 1

then trimming does not affect the power of the CM statistic, although Hong-White, McLeod-Li, and Tsay tests exhibit higher power.

The untrimmed CM statistics tend to under-reject H_0 and obtain lower power when the error variance is infinite. RESET and McLeod-Li statistics under-reject when $\kappa_\epsilon < 2$, while RESET performs fairly well for an AR model with IGARCH error, contrary to asymptotic theory. The McLeod-Li statistic radically over-rejects H_0 for AR-IGARCH, merely verifying the statistic was designed for iid normal errors under H_0. Tsay's F-statistic radically over-rejects for iid and GARCH errors with infinite variance: empirical power *and* size are above 0.60. In these cases heavy tails and/or conditional heteroscedasticity simply appear as nonlinearity (cf. Lima 1997; Hong and Lee 2005; Hill and Aguilar 2011). Hong and White's (1995) nonparametric test exhibits large, and sometimes massive, size distortions when variance is infinite, even for iid errors.

6 Conclusion

We develop tail-trimmed versions of Bierens' (1982, 1990), and Lee et al. (1993) tests of functional form for heavy-tailed time series. The test statistics are robust to heavy tails since trimming ensures standard distribution limits, while negligible trimming ensures the revealing nature of the test weight is not diminished. We may use plug-ins that are sub-$n^{1/2}$-convergent or do not have a Gaussian limit when tails are heavy, depending on the model and error-regressor feedback, and Wooldridge's (1990) orthogonal projection promotes robustness to an even larger set of plug-ins.

A p-value occupation time test allows the analyst to by-pass the need to choose a trimming portion by smoothing over a class of fractiles. A large amount of trimming, however, may have an adverse impact on the test in small samples due to the loss of information coupled with sampling error due to the plug-in. This implies the p-value occupation time may be sensitive to the plug-in in small samples, but when computed with the plug-in robust orthogonal test equation delivers a sharp test in controlled experiments.

Future work may seek to include other trimming techniques like smooth weighting; adaptive methods for selecting the fractiles; and extensions to other classes of tests like Hong and White (1995) nonparametric test for iid data, and Hong and Lee (2005) spectral test which accommodates conditional heteroscedasticity of unknown form.

Acknowledgments The author thanks an anonymous referee and Co-Editor Xiaohong Chen for constructive remarks.

Appendix A: Assumptions[9]

Write thresholds and fractiles compactly $c_{z,n}(\cdot) = \max\{l_{z,n}(\cdot), u_{z,n}(\cdot)\}$ and $k_{j,n} = \max\left\{k_{j,\epsilon,n}, k_{j,1,n}, ..., k_{j,q,n}\right\}$, define $\sigma_n^2(\beta,\gamma) := E\left[m_{n,t}^{*2}(\beta,\gamma)\right]$ and

$$J_t(\beta,\gamma) := -g_t(\beta) F\left(\gamma'\psi_t\right), \; J_{n,t}^*(\beta,\gamma) := J_t(\beta,\gamma) I_{n,t}(\beta),$$

$$\hat{J}_{n,t}^*(\beta,\gamma) = J_t(\beta)\hat{I}_{n,t}(\beta) J_n^*(\beta,\gamma) := \frac{1}{n}\sum_{t=1}^{n} J_{n,t}^*(\beta,\gamma),$$

$$\hat{J}_n^*(\beta,\gamma) := \frac{1}{n}\sum_{t=1}^{n} \hat{J}_{n,t}^*(\beta,\gamma).$$

Drop β^0, define $\Im_t = \sigma(x_{\tau+1}, y_\tau : \tau \leq t)$, and let Γ be any compact subset of $\mathbb{R}^p$ with positive Lebesgue measure. Six sets of assumptions are employed. First, the test weight is revealing.

W1 (weight). *a.* $F : \mathbb{R} \rightarrow \mathbb{R}$ *is Borel measurable, analytic, and nonpolynomial on some open interval* $R_0 \subseteq \mathbb{R}$ *containing* 0. *b.* $\sup_{u\in U}|F(u)| \leq K$ *and* $\inf_{u\in U}|F(u)| > 0$ *on any compact subset* $U \subset S_F$, *with* S_F *the support of* F.

Remark 1 The W1.b upper bound allows us to exclude $F(\gamma'\psi_t)$ from the trimming indicators which greatly simplifies proving test consistency under trimming, and is mild since it applies to repeatedly cited weights (exponential, logistic, sine, cosine). The lower bound in W1.b helps to establish a required stochastic equicontinuity condition for weak convergence when ϵ_t may be heavy tailed, and is easily guaranteed by centering $F(\gamma'\psi_t)$ if necessary.

Second, the plug-in $\hat{\beta}_n$ is consistent. Let $\tilde{m}_{n,t}$ be $\Im_t$-measurable mappings from $\mathcal{B} \subset \mathcal{R}^q$ to $\mathcal{R}^r$, $r \geq q$, and $\{\tilde{V}_n\}$ a sequence of non-random matrices $\tilde{V}_n \in \mathbb{R}^{q\times q}$ where $\tilde{V}_{i,i,n} \rightarrow \infty$. Stack equations $\mathcal{M}_{n,t}^*(\beta,\gamma) := [m_{n,t}^*(\beta,\gamma), \tilde{m}_{n,t}'(\beta)]' \in \mathcal{R}^{r+1}$, and define the covariances $\tilde{S}_n(\beta) := \sum_{s,t=1}^n E[\{\tilde{m}_{n,s}(\beta) - E[\tilde{m}_{n,s}(\beta)]\} \times \{\tilde{m}_{n,t}(\beta) - E[\tilde{m}_{n,t}(\beta)]\}']$ and $\mathfrak{S}_n^*(\beta,\gamma) := \sum_{s,t=1}^n E[\{\mathcal{M}_{n,s}^*(\beta,\gamma) - E[\mathcal{M}_{n,s}^*(\beta,\gamma)]\} \times \{\mathcal{M}_{n,t}^*(\beta,\gamma) - E[\mathcal{M}_{n,t}^*(\beta,\gamma)]\}']$, hence $[\mathfrak{S}_{i,j,n}^*(\beta,\gamma)]_{i=2,j=2}^{r+1,r+1} = \tilde{S}_n(\beta)$. We abuse notation since $\mathfrak{S}_n^*(\beta,\gamma)$ may not exist for some or any β. Let *f.d.d.* denote *finite dimensional distributions*.

P1 (*fast (non)linear plug-ins*). $\tilde{V}_n^{1/2}(\hat{\beta}_n - \beta^0) = O_p(1)$ *and* $\sup_{\gamma\in\Gamma}||V_n(\gamma)\tilde{V}_n^{-1}|| \rightarrow 0$.

P2 (*slow linear plug-ins*). $\mathfrak{S}_n^*(\gamma)$ *exists for each n, specifically* $\sup_{\gamma\in\Gamma}||\mathfrak{S}_n^*(\gamma)|| < \infty$ *and* $\liminf_{n\rightarrow\infty}\inf_{\gamma\in\Gamma}\lambda_{\min}(\mathfrak{S}_n^*(\gamma)) > 0$. *Further:*

[9] We ignore for notational economy measurability issues that arise when taking a supremum over an index set. Assume all functions in this chapter satisfy Pollard (1984) permissibility criteria, the measure space that governs all random variables is complete, and therefore all majorants are measurable. Probability statements are therefore with respect to outer probability, and expectations over majorants are outer expectations. Cf. Dudley (1978) and Stinchcombe and White (1992).

a. $\tilde{V}_n^{1/2}(\hat{\beta}_n - \beta^0) = O_p(1)$ *and* $\tilde{V}_n \sim \mathcal{K}(\gamma)V_n(\gamma)$, *where* $\mathcal{K} : \Gamma \to \mathbb{R}^{q\times q}$ *and* $\inf_{\gamma\in\Gamma} \lambda_{\min}(\mathcal{K}(\gamma)) > 0$.
b. $\tilde{V}_n^{1/2}(\hat{\beta}_n - \beta^0) = \tilde{A}_n \sum_{t=1}^{n}\{\tilde{m}_{n,t} \ -E[\tilde{m}_{n,t}]\}\times\ (1 + o_p(1)) +\ o_p(1)$ *where nonstochastic* $\tilde{A}_n \in \mathbb{R}^{q\times r}$ *has full column rank and* $\tilde{A}_n\tilde{S}_n^{-1}\tilde{A}_n' \to I_q$.
c. *The f.d.d. of* $\mathfrak{S}_n^*(\gamma)^{-1/2}\{\mathcal{M}_{n,t}^*(\gamma) - E[\mathcal{M}_{n,t}^*(\gamma)]\}$ *belong to the same domain of attraction as the f.d.d. of* $S_n^{-1}(\gamma)\{m_{n,t}^*(\gamma) \ -E[m_{n,t}^*(\gamma)]$.

P3 (*orthogonal equations and (non)linear plug-ins*). $\tilde{V}_n^{1/2}(\hat{\beta}_n - \beta^0) = O_p(1)$ *and* $\limsup_{n\to\infty}\sup_{\gamma\in\Gamma}||V_n^{\perp}(\gamma)\tilde{V}_n^{-1}|| < \infty$.

Remark 2 $\hat{\beta}_n$ effects the limit distribution of $\hat{\mathcal{T}}_n(\gamma)$ under P2 hence we assume $\hat{\beta}_n$ is linear. P3 is invoked for orthogonalized equations $\hat{m}_{n,t}^{\perp}(\beta, \gamma)$.

Third, identification under trimming.
I1 (*identification by* $m_{n,t}^*(\gamma)$). *Under the null* $\sup_{\gamma\in\Gamma}|nS_n^{-1}(\gamma)E[m_{n,t}^*(\gamma)]| \to 0$.

Remark 3 If $m_t(\gamma)$ is asymmetric there is no guarantee $E[m_{n,t}^*(\gamma)] = 0$, although $E[m_{n,t}^*(\gamma)] \to 0$ under H_0 by trimming negligibility and dominated convergence. The fractiles $\{k_{j,\epsilon,n}, k_{j,i,n}\}$ must therefore promote I1 for asymptotic normality in view of expansion (5) and mean centering. Since $\sup_{\gamma\in\Gamma}\{S_n(\gamma)/n\} = o(1)$ by Lemma B.1, below, I1 implies identification of H_0 *sufficiently fast*. The property is superfluous if $E[\epsilon_t] = 0$ under either hypothesis, ϵ_t is independent of x_t under H_0, and re-centering is used since then $E[m_{n,t}^*(\gamma)] = 0$ under H_0 (see Sect. 3).

Fourth, the DGP and properties of regression model components.

R1 (response). $f(\cdot, \beta)$ is for each $\beta \in \mathcal{B}$ a Borel measurable function, continuous, and differentiable on $\mathcal{B}$ with Borel measurable gradient $g_t(\beta) = g(x_t, \beta) := (\partial/\partial\beta)f(x_t, \beta)$.
R2 (moments). $E|y_t| < \infty$, and $E(\sup_{\beta\in\mathcal{B}}|f(x_t, \beta)|^{\iota}) < \infty$ and $E(\sup_{\beta\in\mathcal{B}}|(\partial/\partial\beta_i)f(x_t, \beta)|^{\iota}) < \infty$ for each i and some tiny $\iota > 0$.
R3 (*distribution*).

a. *The finite dimensional distributions of* $\{y_t, x_t\}$ *are strictly stationary, non-degenerate, and absolutely continuous. The density function of* $\epsilon_t(\beta)$ *is uniformly bounded* $\sup_{\beta\in\mathcal{B}}\sup_{a\in\mathbb{R}}\{(\partial/\partial a)P(\epsilon_t(\beta) \le a)\} < \infty$.
b. *Define* $\kappa_\epsilon(\beta) := \text{argsup}_{\alpha>0}\{E|\epsilon_t(\beta)|^\alpha < \infty\} \in (0, \infty]$, *write* $\kappa_\epsilon = \kappa_\epsilon(\beta^0)$, *and let* $\mathcal{B}_{2,\epsilon}$ *denote the set of* β *such that the error variance is infinite* $\kappa_\epsilon(\beta) \le 2$. *If* $\kappa_\epsilon(\beta) \le 2$ *then* $P(|\epsilon_t(\beta)| > c) = d(\beta)\epsilon^{-\kappa_\epsilon(\beta)}(1 + o(1))$ *where* $\inf_{\beta\in\mathcal{B}_{2,\epsilon}} d(\beta) > 0$ *and* $\inf_{\beta\in\mathcal{B}_{2,\epsilon}}\kappa_\epsilon(\beta) > 0$, *and* $o(1)$ *is not a function of* β, *hence* $\lim_{c\to\infty}\sup_{\beta\in\mathcal{B}_{2,\epsilon}}|d(\beta)^{-1}\epsilon^{\kappa_\epsilon(\beta)}P(|\epsilon_t(\beta)| > c) - 1| = 0$.

R4 (*mixing*). $\{y_t, x_t\}$ *are geometrically* β*-mixing:* $\sup_{\mathcal{A}\subset\Im_{t+l}^{+\infty}} E|P(\mathcal{A}|\Im_{-\infty}^{t}) - P(\mathcal{A})| = o(\rho^l)$ *for* $\rho \in (0, 1)$.

Remark 1 Response function smoothness R1 coupled with distribution continuity and boundedness R3.a imply $\sum_{t=1}^{n} \hat{m}_{n,t}^{*}(\hat{\beta}_n, \gamma)$ can be asymptotically expanded around β^0, cf. Hill (2011b, Appendices B and C). Power-law tail decay R3.b is mild since it includes weakly dependent processes that satisfy a central limit theorem (Leadbetter et al. 1983), and simplifies characterizing tail-trimmed variances in heavy-tailed cases by Karamata's Theorem.

Remark 2 The mixing property characterizes nonlinear AR with nonlinear random volatility errors (Pham and Tran 1985; An and Huang 1996; Meitz and Saikkonen 2008).

Fifth, we restrict the fractiles and impose nondegeneracy under trimming. Recall $k_{j,n} = \max\{k_{j,\epsilon,n}, k_{j,1,n}, ..., k_{j,q,n}\}$, the R3.b moment supremum $\kappa_\epsilon > 0$, and $\sigma_n^2(\beta, \gamma) = E[m_{n,t}^{*2}(\beta, \gamma)]$.

F1 (fractiles).

a. $k_{j,\epsilon,n}/\ln(n) \to \infty$;
b. *If* $\kappa_\epsilon \in (0, 1)$ *then* $k_{j,\epsilon,n}/n^{2(1-\kappa_\epsilon)/(2-\kappa_\epsilon)} \to \infty$.

F2 (nondegenerate trimmed variance). $\liminf_{n\to\infty} \inf_{\beta\in\mathcal{B},\gamma\in\Gamma}\{S_n^2(\beta, \gamma)/n\} > 0$ *and* $\sup_{\beta\in\mathcal{B},\gamma\in\Gamma}\{n\sigma_n^2(\beta, \gamma)/S_n^2(\beta, \gamma)\} = O(1)$.

Remark 1 F1.a sets a mild lower bound on $k_{\epsilon,n}$ that is useful for bounding trimmed variances $\sigma_n^2(\beta, \gamma)$ and $S_n^2(\beta, \gamma)$. F1.b sets a harsh lower bound on $k_{\epsilon,n}$ if, under misspecification, ϵ_t is not integrable: as $\kappa_\epsilon \searrow 0$ we must trim more $k_{\epsilon,n} \nearrow n$ in order to prove a LLN for $m_{n,t}^{*}(\gamma)$ which is used to prove $\hat{\mathcal{T}}_n(\gamma)$ is consistent. Any $k_{\epsilon,n} \sim n/L(n)$ for slowly varying $L(n) \to \infty$ satisfies F1.

Remark 2 Distribution nondegeneracy under R3.a coupled with trimming negligibility ensure trimmed moments are not degenerate for sufficiently large n, for example $\liminf_{n\to\infty} \inf_{\beta\in\mathcal{B},\gamma\in\Gamma} \sigma_n^2(\beta, \gamma) > 0$. The long-run variance $S_n^2(\beta, \gamma)$, however, can in principle be degenerate due to negative dependence, hence F2 is imposed. F2 is standard in the literature on dependent CLT's and exploited here for a CLT for $m_{n,t}^{*}(\beta, \gamma)$, cf. Dehling et al. (1986) .

Finally, the kernel $\omega(\cdot)$ and bandwidth b_n.

K1 (kernel and bandwidth). $\omega(\cdot)$ is integrable, and a member of the class $\omega : \mathbb{R} \to [-1, 1]|\omega(0) = 1, \omega(x) = \omega(-x)\forall x \in \mathbb{R}, \int_{-\infty}^{\infty} |\omega(x)|dx < \infty, \int_{-\infty}^{\infty} |\vartheta(\xi)|d\xi < \infty$, $\omega(\cdot)$ is continuous at 0 and all but a finite number of points }, where $\vartheta(\xi) := (2\pi)^{-1} \int_{-\infty}^{\infty} \omega(x)e^{i\xi x}dx < \infty$. Further $\sum_{s,t=1}^{n} |\omega((s-t)/b_n)| = o(n^2)$, $\max_{1\leq s\leq n} | \sum_{t=1}^{n} \omega((s-t)/b_n)| = o(n)$ and $b_n = o(n)$.

Remark 1 Assumption K1 includes Bartlett, Parzen, Quadratic Spectral, Tukey-Hanning, and other kernels. See Jong and Davidson (2000) and their references.

Appendix B: Proofs of Main Results

We require several preliminary results proved in the supplemental appendix Hill (2011c, Sect. C.3). Throughout the terms $o_p(1)$, $O_p(1)$, $o(1)$ and $O(1)$, do not depend on β, γ, and t. We only state results that concern $\hat{m}^*_{n,t}(\beta,\gamma)$, and $m^*_{n,t}(\beta,\gamma)$, since companion results extend to $\hat{m}^{\perp}_{n,t}(\beta,\gamma)$, and $m^{\perp}_{n,t}(\beta,\gamma)$. Let F1–F2, K1, R1–R4, and W1.b hold. Recall $\sigma^2_n(\beta,\gamma) = E[m^{*2}_{n,t}(\beta,\gamma)]$.

Lemma B.1 (variance bounds)

a. $\sigma^2_n(\beta,\gamma) = o\left(n \max\left\{1, (E[m^*_{n,t}(\beta,\gamma)])^2\right\}\right)$, $\sup_{\gamma\in\Gamma}\left\{\frac{\sigma^2_n(\gamma)}{\max\left\{1, (E[m^*_{n,t}(\gamma)])^2\right\}}\right\} = o(n/\ln(n))$;

b. $S^2_n(\gamma) = \mathfrak{L}_n n \sigma^2_n(\gamma) = o(n^2)$ *for some sequence* $\{\mathfrak{L}_n\}$ *that satisfies* $\liminf_{n\to\infty} \mathfrak{L}_n > 0$, $\mathfrak{L}_n = K$ *if* ϵ_t *is finite dependent or* $E[\epsilon^2_t] < \infty$, *and otherwise* $\mathfrak{L}_n \leq K \ln(n/\min_{j\in\{1,2\}}\{k_{j,\epsilon,n}\}) \leq K \ln(n)$.

Lemma B.2 (variance bounds)

a. $\sup_{\gamma\in\Gamma} |S^{-1}_n(\gamma)\sum_{t=1}^n \{\hat{m}^*_{n,t}(\gamma) - m^*_{n,t}(\gamma)\}| = o_p(1)$.

b. Define $\hat{\mu}^*_{n,t}(\beta,\gamma) := \hat{m}^*_{n,t}(\beta,\gamma) - \hat{m}^*_n(\beta,\gamma)$ *and* $\mu^*_{n,t}(\beta,\gamma) := m^*_{n,t}(\beta,\gamma) - m^*_n(\beta,\gamma)$. *If additionally P1 or P2 holds* $\sup_{\gamma\in\Gamma} |S^{-2}_n(\gamma)\sum_{s,t=1}^n \omega((s-t)/b_n) \{\hat{\mu}^*_{n,s}(\hat{\beta}_n,\gamma)\hat{\mu}^*_{n,t}(\hat{\beta}_n,\gamma) - \mu^*_{n,s}(\gamma)\mu^*_{n,t}(\gamma)\}| = o_p(1)$.

Lemma B.3 (variance bounds) *Let* $\beta, \tilde{\beta} \in \mathcal{B}$. *For some sequence* $\{\beta_{n,*}\}$ *in* $\mathcal{B}$ *satisfying* $||\beta_{n,*} - \tilde{\beta}|| \leq ||\beta - \tilde{\beta}||$, *and for some tiny* $\iota > 0$ *and arbitrarily large finite* $\delta > 0$ *we have* $\sup_{\gamma\in\Gamma} |\hat{m}^*_n(\beta,\gamma) - \hat{m}^*_n(\tilde{\beta},\gamma) - \hat{J}^*_n(\beta_{n,*},\gamma)'(\beta - \tilde{\beta})| = n^{-\delta} \times ||\beta - \tilde{\beta}||^{1/\iota} \times o_p(1)$.

Lemma B.4 (Jacobian) *Under P1 or P2* $\sup_{\gamma\in\Gamma} ||J^*_n(\hat{\beta}_n,\gamma) - J_n(\gamma)(1+o_p(1))|| = o_p(1)$.

Lemma B.5 (HAC) *Under P1 or P2* $\sup_{\gamma\in\Gamma} |\hat{S}^2_n(\hat{\beta}_n,\gamma)/S^2_n(\gamma) - 1| \xrightarrow{p} 0$.

Lemma B.6 (ULLN) *Let* $\inf_{n\geq N} |E[m^*_{n,t}(\gamma)]| > 0$ *for some* $N \in \mathbb{N}$ *and all* $\gamma \in \Gamma/S$ *where S has measure zero. Then* $\sup_{\gamma\in\Gamma/S}\{1/n\sum_{t=1}^n m^*_{n,t}(\gamma)/E[m^*_{n,t}(\gamma)]\} \xrightarrow{p} 1$.

Lemma B.7 (UCLT) $\{S^{-1}_n(\gamma)\sum_{t=1}^n (m^*_{n,t}(\gamma) - E[m^*_{n,t}(\gamma)]) : \gamma \in \Gamma\} \Longrightarrow \{z(\gamma) : \gamma \in \Gamma\}$, *a scalar* $(0,1)$*-Gaussian process on* $\mathcal{C}[\Gamma]$ *with covariance function* $E[z(\gamma_1)z(\gamma_2)]$ *and a.s. bounded sample paths. If P2 also holds then* $\{\mathfrak{S}^{-1/2}_n(\gamma)\sum_{t=1}^n \{\mathcal{M}^*_{n,t}(\gamma) - E[\mathcal{M}^*_{n,t}(\gamma)] : \gamma \in \Gamma\} \Longrightarrow \{\mathcal{Z}(\gamma) : \gamma \in \Gamma\}$ *an* $r+1$ *dimensional Gaussian process on* $\mathcal{C}[\Gamma]$ *with zero mean, covariance* I_{r+1}, *and covariance function* $E[\mathcal{Z}(\gamma_1)\mathcal{Z}(\gamma_2)']$.

Proof of Lemma 2.1 We only prove the claims for $m^*_{n,t}(\beta,\gamma)$. In view of the $\sigma(x_t)$ -measurability of $\mathcal{P}_{n,t}(\gamma)$ and $\sup_{\gamma\in\Gamma} E|\mathcal{P}_{n,t}(\gamma)| < \infty$ the proof extends to $m^{\perp}_{n,t}(\beta,\gamma)$ with few modifications. Under H_0 the claim follows from trimming negligibility and Lebesgue's dominated convergence: $E[m^*_{n,t}(\gamma)] \to E[m_t(\gamma)] = 0$.

Under the alternative there are two cases: $E|\epsilon_t| < \infty$, or $E|\epsilon_t| = \infty$ such that $E[\epsilon_t|x_t]$ may not exist.
Case 1 ($E|\epsilon_t| < \infty$). Property W1, compactness of Γ, and boundedness of ψ imply $F(\gamma'\psi_t)$ is uniformly bounded and revealing: $E[\epsilon_t F(\gamma'\psi_t)] \neq 0$ for all $\gamma \in \Gamma/S$ where S has Lebesgue measure zero. Now invoke boundedness of $F(\gamma'\psi_t)$ with Lebesgue's dominated convergence theorem and negligibility of trimming to deduce $|E[\epsilon_t(1 - I_{n,t}(\beta^0))F(\gamma'\psi_t)]| \to 0$, hence $E[\epsilon_t I_{n,t}(\beta^0)F(\gamma'\psi_t)] = E\left[\epsilon_t F(\gamma'\psi_t)\right] + o(1) \neq 0$ for all $\gamma \in \Gamma/S$ and all $n \geq N$ for sufficiently large N.
Case 2 ($E|\epsilon_t| = \infty$). Under H_1 since $I_{n,t}(\beta) \to 1\, a.s.$ and $E|\epsilon_t| = \infty$, by the definition of conditional expectations there exists sufficiently large N such that $\min_{n\geq N} |E[\epsilon_t I_{n,t}(\beta^0)|x_t]| > 0$ with positive probability $\forall n \geq N$. The claim therefore follows by Theorem 1 of Bierens and Ploberger (1997) and Theorem 2.3 of Stinchcombe and White (1998): $\liminf_{n\to\infty} |E[\epsilon_t I_{n,t}(\beta^0)F(\gamma'\psi_t)]| > 0$ for all $\gamma \in \Gamma/S$. $\mathcal{QED}$.

Proof of Theorem 2.2 Define $M^*_{n,t}(\beta,\gamma) := m^*_{n,t}(\beta,\gamma) - E[m^*_{n,t}(\beta,\gamma)]$ and $\hat{M}^*_{n,t}(\beta,\gamma) := \hat{m}^*_{n,t}(\beta,\gamma) - E[\hat{m}^*_{n,t}(\beta,\gamma)]$. We first state some required properties. Under plug–in properties P1 or P2 $\hat{\beta}_n - \beta^0 = o_p(1)$. Identification I1 imposes under H_0

$$\sup_{\gamma\in\Gamma} \left| S_n^{-1}(\gamma) E[m^*_{n,t}(\gamma)] \right| = o(1/n), \tag{B.1}$$

which implies the following long-run variance relation uniformly on Γ:

$$E\left(\sum_{t=1}^{n} M^*_{n,t}(\gamma)\right)^2 = S_n^2(\gamma) - n^2\left(E\left[m^*_{n,t}(\beta,\gamma)\right]\right)^2 = S_n^2(\gamma)\left(1 + o\left(1\right)\right). \tag{B.2}$$

Uniform expansion Lemma B.3, coupled with Jacobian consistency Lemma B.4 and $\hat{\beta}_n \xrightarrow{p} \beta^0$ imply for any arbitrarily large finite $\delta > 0$,

$$\sup_{\gamma\in\Gamma} \left| \frac{1}{n} \sum_{t=1}^{n} \left\{ \hat{m}^*_{n,t}(\hat{\beta}_n,\gamma) - \hat{m}^*_{n,t}(\gamma) \right\} - J_n(\gamma)' \left(\hat{\beta}_n - \beta^0\right) \left(1 + o_p(1)\right) \right| = o_p\left(n^{-\delta}\right). \tag{B.3}$$

Finally, by uniform approximation Lemma B.2.a

$$\sup_{\gamma\in\Gamma} \left| \frac{1}{S_n(\gamma)} \sum_{t=1}^{n} \left\{ \hat{m}^*_{n,t}(\gamma) - m^*_{n,t}(\gamma) \right\} \right| = o_p(1), \tag{B.4}$$

and by Lemma B.5 we have uniform HAC consistency:

$$\sup_{\gamma \in \Gamma} \left| \hat{S}_n^2(\hat{\beta}_n, \gamma)/S_n^2(\gamma) - 1 \right| = o_p(1). \tag{B.5}$$

Claim i ($\hat{T}_n(\gamma)$: Null H_0). Under fast plug-in case P1 we assume $\sup_{\gamma \in \Gamma} ||V_n(\gamma) \tilde{V}_n^{-1}|| \to 0$, hence

$$\sup_{\gamma \in \Gamma} \left| n S_n^{-1}(\gamma) J_n(\gamma)' \left(\hat{\beta}_n - \beta^0 \right) \right| = o_p(1). \tag{B.6}$$

Since $\delta > 0$ in (B.3) may be arbitrarily large, $\liminf_{n \to \infty} \inf_{\gamma \in \Gamma} S_n(\gamma) > 0$ by nondegeneracy F2, and Eqs. (B.1)–(B.6) are uniform properties, it follows uniformly on Γ

$$\hat{T}_n(\gamma) \overset{p}{\sim} \left(\frac{1}{S_n(\gamma)} \sum_{t=1}^{n} M_{n,t}^*(\gamma) + \frac{n J_n(\gamma)'}{S_n(\gamma)} \left(\hat{\beta}_n - \beta^0 \right) + o_p\left(\frac{n}{S_n(\gamma)} n^{-\delta} \right) \right)^2$$
$$= \left(\frac{1}{S_n(\gamma)} \sum_{t=1}^{n} M_{n,t}^*(\gamma) + o_p(1) \right)^2 = \mathcal{M}_n^2(\gamma), \tag{B.7}$$

say. Now apply variance relation (B.2), UCLT Lemma B.7 and the mapping theorem to conclude $E[\mathcal{M}_n^2(\gamma)] \to 1$ and $\{\hat{T}_n(\gamma) : \gamma \in \Gamma\} \Longrightarrow \{z^2(\gamma) : \gamma \in \Gamma\}$, where $z(\gamma)$ is (0, 1)-Gaussian process on $\mathcal{C}[\Gamma]$ with covariance function $E[z(\gamma_1)z(\gamma_2)]$.

Under slow plug-in case P2 a similar argument applies in lieu of plug-in linearity and UCLT Lemma B.7. Since the steps follow conventional arguments we relegate the proof to Hill (Hill 2011c, Sect. C.2).

Claim ii ($\hat{T}_n(\gamma)$: Alternative H_1). Lemma 2.1 ensures $\inf_{n \geq N} \left| E[m_{n,t}^*(\gamma)] \right| > 0$ for some $N \in \mathbb{N}$ and all $\gamma \in \Gamma/S$ where $S \subset \Gamma$ has Lebesgue measure zero. Choose any $\gamma \in \Gamma/S$, assume $n \geq N$ and write

$$\hat{T}_n(\gamma) = \left(\frac{1}{\hat{S}_n(\hat{\beta}_n, \gamma)} \sum_{t=1}^{n} \hat{m}_{n,t}^*(\hat{\beta}_n, \gamma) \right)^2$$
$$= \frac{n^2 \left(E\left[m_{n,t}^*(\gamma) \right] \right)^2}{\hat{S}_n^2(\hat{\beta}_n, \gamma)} \left(\frac{\left| 1/n \sum_{t=1}^{n} \hat{m}_{n,t}^*(\hat{\beta}_n, \gamma) \right|}{\left| E\left[m_{n,t}^*(\gamma) \right] \right|} \right)^2.$$

In lieu of (B.5) and the Lemma B.1.a,b variance property $n|E[m_{n,t}^*(\gamma)]|/S_n(\gamma) \to \infty$, the proof is complete if we show $\mathcal{M}_n(\hat{\beta}_n, \gamma) := |1/n \sum_{t=1}^{n} \hat{m}_{n,t}^*(\hat{\beta}_n, \gamma)|/|E[m_{n,t}^*(\gamma)]| \xrightarrow{p} 1$.

By (B.3), (B.4) and the triangle inequality $\mathcal{M}_n(\hat{\beta}_n, \gamma)$ is bounded by

$$\frac{1}{\left|E\left[m_{n,t}^{*}(\gamma)\right]\right|}\left|\frac{1}{n}\sum_{t=1}^{n}m_{n,t}^{*}(\gamma)\right|+\frac{1}{\left|E\left[m_{n,t}^{*}(\gamma)\right]\right|}$$
$$\left|J_n(\gamma)'\left(\hat{\beta}_n-\beta^0\right)(1+o_p(1))\right|+o_p\left(\frac{S_n(\gamma)}{n\left|E\left[m_{n,t}^{*}(\gamma)\right]\right|}\right),$$

where $\sup_{\gamma\in\Gamma/S}\{1/n\sum_{t=1}^{n}m_{n,t}^{*}(\gamma)/E[m_{n,t}^{*}(\gamma)]\}\stackrel{p}{\to}1$ by Lemma B.6. Further, combine fast or slow plug-in P1 or P2, the construction of $V_n(\gamma)$ and variance relation Lemma B.1.a,b to obtain

$$\frac{\left|J_n(\gamma)'\left(\hat{\beta}_n-\beta^0\right)(1+o_p(1))\right|}{\left|E\left[m_{n,t}^{*}(\gamma)\right]\right|}\leq\frac{S_n(\gamma)}{n\left|E\left[m_{n,t}^{*}(\gamma)\right]\right|}nJ_n(\gamma)'S_n^{-1}(\gamma)$$
$$V_n^{-1/2}(\gamma)\sim K\frac{S_n(\gamma)}{n\left|E\left[m_{n,t}^{*}(\gamma)\right]\right|}=o(1).$$

Therefore $\mathcal{M}_n(\hat{\beta}_n,\gamma)\stackrel{p}{\to}1$.
Claim iii ($\hat{T}_n^{\perp}(\gamma)$). The argument simply mimics claims (i) and (ii) since under plug-in case P3 it follows $\hat{S}_n^{\perp}(\hat{\beta}_n,\gamma)^{-1}\sum_{t=1}^{n}\hat{m}_{n,t}^{\perp}(\hat{\beta}_n,\gamma)\stackrel{p}{\sim}S_n^{\perp}(\gamma)^{-1}\sum_{t=1}^{n}m_{n,t}^{\perp}(\gamma)$ by construction of the orthogonal equations (Wooldridge 1990), and straightforward generalizations of the supporting lemmas. $\mathcal{QED}$.

The remaining proofs exploit the fact that for each $z_t\in\{\epsilon_t,g_{i,t}\}$ the product $z_tF\left(\gamma'\psi_t\right)$ has the same tail decay rate as z_t: by weight boundedness W1.b $P(|z_t\sup_{u\in\mathbb{R}}F(u)|>c)\geq P(|z_tF_t(\gamma)|>c)\geq P(|z_t\inf_{u\in\mathbb{R}}F(u)|>c)$. Further, use $I_{n,t}=I_{\epsilon,n,t}I_{g,n,t}$, dominated convergence and each $I_{z,n,t}\stackrel{a.s.}{\to}1$ to deduce $E[|z_tF(\gamma'\psi_t)|^rI_{n,t}]=E[|z_tF(\gamma'\psi_t)|^rI_{z,n,t}]\times(1+o(1))$ for any $r>0$. Hence higher moments of $z_tF(\gamma'\psi_t)I_{n,t}$ and $z_tI_{z,n,t}$ are equivalent up to a constant scale.

Proof of Theorem 3.1 The claim under H_1 follows from Theorem 2.2. We prove $\tau_n(\alpha)\stackrel{d}{\to}(1-\underline{\lambda})^{-1}\int_{\underline{\lambda}}^{1}I(u(\lambda)<\alpha)d\lambda$ under H_0 for plug-in case P1 since the remaining cases follow similarly. Drop γ and write $\hat{m}_{n,t}^{*}(\hat{\beta}_n,\lambda)$ and $\hat{S}_n^2(\hat{\beta}_n,\lambda)$ to express dependence on $\lambda\in\Lambda:=[\underline{\lambda},1]$. Define $\hat{Z}_n(\lambda):=\hat{S}_n^{-1}(\hat{\beta}_n,\lambda)\sum_{t=1}^{n}\hat{m}_{n,t}^{*}(\hat{\beta}_n,\lambda)$. We exploit weak convergence on a Polish space[10]: we write $\{\hat{Z}_n(\lambda):\lambda\in\Lambda\}\Longrightarrow^{*}\{z(\lambda):\lambda\in\Lambda\}$ on $l_\infty(\Lambda)$, where $\{z(\lambda):\lambda\in\Lambda\}$ is a Gaussian process with a version that has uniformly bounded and uniformly continuous sample paths with respect to $||\cdot||_2$, if $\hat{Z}_n(\lambda)$ converges in *f.d.d.* and tightness applies: $\lim_{\delta\to0}\limsup_{n\to\infty}P(\sup_{||\lambda-\tilde{\lambda}||\leq\delta}|\hat{Z}_n(\lambda)-\hat{Z}_n(\tilde{\lambda})|>\varepsilon)=0\forall\varepsilon>0$.

We need only prove $\{\hat{Z}_n(\lambda):\lambda\in\Lambda\}\Longrightarrow^{*}\{z(\lambda):\lambda\in\Lambda\}$ since the claim follows from multiple applications of the mapping theorem. Convergence in *f.d.d.*

---

[10] See Hoffmann-Jørgensen (1991), cf. Dudley (1978).

follows from $\sup_{\lambda\in\Lambda}|\hat{S}_n^{-1}(\hat{\beta}_n,\lambda)\sum_{t=1}^n \hat{m}_{n,t}^*(\hat{\beta}_n,\lambda) - S_n^{-1}(\lambda)\sum_{t=1}^n m_{n,t}^*(\lambda)| \xrightarrow{p} 0$ by (B.3)–(B.5) under plug-in case P1, and the proof of UCLT Lemma B.7.

Consider tightness and notice by (B.3)–(B.6) and plug-in case P1

$$\sup_{\lambda\in\Lambda}\left|\hat{\mathcal{Z}}_n(\lambda) - \mathcal{Z}_n(\lambda)\right| \xrightarrow{p} 0 \text{ where } \mathcal{Z}_n(\lambda) := \sum_{t=1}^n \frac{1}{S_n(\lambda)} m_t I_{n,t}(\lambda) = \sum_{t=1}^n \mathcal{Z}_{n,t}(\lambda),$$

hence we need only to consider $\mathcal{Z}_n(\lambda)$ for tightness. By Lemma B.1.b and $\inf\{\Lambda\} > 0$ it is easy to verify $\inf_{\lambda\in\Lambda} S_n^2(\lambda) = n\sigma_n^2$ for some sequence $\{\sigma_n^2\}$ that satisfies $\liminf_{n\to\infty}\sigma_n^2 > 0$. Therefore

$$\begin{aligned}\left|\sum_{t=1}^n\left\{\mathcal{Z}_{n,t}(\lambda) - \mathcal{Z}_{n,t}(\tilde{\lambda})\right\}\right| &\leq \left|\frac{1}{n^{1/2}\sigma_n}\sum_{t=1}^n m_t\left\{I_{n,t}(\lambda) - I_{n,t}(\tilde{\lambda})\right\}\right| \\ &\quad + \left|\frac{S_n(\lambda)}{S_n(\tilde{\lambda})} - 1\right| \times \left|\frac{1}{S_n(\lambda)}\sum_{t=1}^n m_t I_{n,t}(\lambda)\right| = \mathcal{A}_{1,n}(\lambda,\tilde{\lambda}) \\ &\quad + \mathcal{A}_{2,n}(\lambda,\tilde{\lambda}).\end{aligned}$$

By subadditivity it suffices to prove each $\lim_{\delta\to 0}\limsup_{n\to\infty} P(\sup_{||\lambda-\tilde{\lambda}||\leq\delta}\mathcal{A}_{i,n}(\lambda,\tilde{\lambda}) > \varepsilon) = 0 \forall\varepsilon > 0$.

Consider $\mathcal{A}_{1,n}(\lambda,\tilde{\lambda})$ and note $I_{n,t}(\lambda)$ can be approximated by a sequence of continuous, differentiable functions. Let $\{\mathcal{N}_n\}$ be a sequence of positive numbers to be chosen below, and define a smoothed version of $I_{n,t}(\lambda)$,

$$\begin{aligned}\mathfrak{I}_{\mathcal{N}_n,n,t}(\lambda) &:= \int_0^1 I_{n,t}(\varpi)\mathrm{S}\left(\mathcal{N}_n(\varpi - \lambda)\right)d\varpi \\ &= \int_{\lambda-1/\mathcal{N}_n}^{\lambda+1/\mathcal{N}_n} I_{n,t}(\varpi)\left\{\frac{e^{-1/(1-\mathcal{N}_n^2(\varpi-\lambda)^2)}}{\int_{-1}^1 e^{-1/(1-w^2)}dw} \times \frac{\mathcal{N}_n}{e^{\varpi^2/\mathcal{N}_n^2}}\right\}d\varpi,\end{aligned}$$

where $\mathrm{S}(u)$ is a so-called "smudge" function used to blot out $I_{n,t}(\varpi)$ when ϖ is outside the interval $(\lambda - 1/\mathcal{N}_n, \lambda + 1/\mathcal{N}_n)$. The term $\{\cdot\}$ after the second equality defines $\mathrm{S}(u)$ on $[-1, 1]$. The random variable $\mathfrak{I}_{\mathcal{N}_n,n,t}(\lambda)$ is $\Im_t$ -measurable, uniformly bounded, continuous, and differentiable for each $\mathcal{N}_n$, and since $k_n(\lambda) \geq k_n(\tilde{\lambda})$ for $\lambda \geq \tilde{\lambda}$ then $\mathfrak{I}_{\mathcal{N}_n,n,t}(\lambda) \leq \mathfrak{I}_{\mathcal{N}_n,n,t}(\tilde{\lambda}) a.s.$ Cf. Phillips (1995).

Observe $\mathcal{A}_{1,n}(\lambda,\tilde{\lambda}) = \mathcal{B}_{1,\mathcal{N}_n,n}(\lambda,\tilde{\lambda}) + \mathcal{B}_{2,\mathcal{N}_n,n}(\lambda) + \mathcal{B}_{2,\mathcal{N}_n,n}(\tilde{\lambda})$ where

$$\mathcal{B}_{1,\mathcal{N}_n,n}(\lambda,\tilde{\lambda}) = \sum_{t=1}^{n} \frac{m_t \left\{\mathfrak{I}_{\mathcal{N}_n,n,t}(\lambda) - \mathfrak{I}_{\mathcal{N}_n,n,t}(\tilde{\lambda})\right\}}{n^{1/2}\sigma_n},$$

$$\mathcal{B}_{2,\mathcal{N}_n,n}(\lambda) = \sum_{t=1}^{n} \frac{m_t \left\{I_{n,t}(\lambda) - \mathfrak{I}_{\mathcal{N}_n,n,t}(\lambda)\right\}}{n^{1/2}\sigma_n}.$$

Consider $\mathcal{B}_{1,\mathcal{N}_n,n}(\lambda,\tilde{\lambda})$, define $\mathcal{D}_{\mathcal{N}_n,n,t}(\lambda) := (\partial/\partial\lambda)\mathfrak{I}_{\mathcal{N}_n,n,t}(\lambda)$, and let $\{b_n(\lambda,\iota)\}$ for infinitesimal $\iota > 0$ be any sequence of positive numbers that satisfies $P(|m_t| > b_n(\lambda,\iota)) \to \lambda - \iota \in (0,1)$, hence $\lim_{n\to\infty}\sup_{\lambda\in\Lambda} b_n(\lambda,\iota) < \infty$. By the mean-value-theorem $\mathfrak{I}_{\mathcal{N}_n,n,t}(\lambda) - \mathfrak{I}_{\mathcal{N}_n,n,t}(\tilde{\lambda}) = \mathcal{D}_{\mathcal{N}_n,n,t}(\lambda_*)(\lambda - \tilde{\lambda})$ for some $\lambda_* \in \Lambda$, $|\lambda - \lambda_*| \leq |\lambda - \tilde{\lambda}|$. But since $\sup_{\lambda\in\Lambda}|I_{n,t}(\lambda) - 1| \overset{a.s.}{\to} 0$ it must be the case that $\sup_{\lambda\in\Lambda}|\mathcal{D}_{\mathcal{N}_{nn},n,t}(\lambda)| \to 0 a.s.$ as $n \to \infty$ for any $\mathcal{N}_n \to \infty$. Therefore, for N sufficiently large, all $n \geq N$, any $p > 0$ and some $\{b_n(\lambda,\iota)\}$ we have $\sup_{\lambda\in\Lambda} E|m_t\mathcal{D}_{\mathcal{N}_n,n,t}(\lambda)|^p \leq K\sup_{\lambda\in\Lambda} E|m_t I(|m_t| \leq b_n(\lambda,\iota))|^p \leq K\sup_{\lambda\in\Lambda} b_n^p(\lambda,\iota)$ which is bounded on $\mathbb{N}$. This implies $m_t\mathcal{D}_{\mathcal{N}_n,n,t}(\lambda)$ is L_p-bounded for any $p > 2$ uniformly on $\Lambda \times \mathbb{N}$, and geometrically β-mixing under R4. In view of $\liminf_{n\to\infty}\sigma_n^2 > 0$ we may therefore apply Lemma 3 in Doukhan et al. (1995) to obtain $\sup_{\lambda\in\Lambda}|n^{-1/2}\sigma_n^{-1}\sum_{t=1}^n m_t\mathcal{D}_{\mathcal{N}_n,n,t}(\lambda)| = O_p(1)$. This suffices to deduce $\lim_{\delta\to 0}\limsup_{n\to\infty} P(\sup_{||\lambda-\tilde{\lambda}||\leq\delta}|\mathcal{B}_{1,\mathcal{N}_n,n}(\lambda,\tilde{\lambda})| > \varepsilon)$ is bounded by

$$\lim_{\delta\to 0}\limsup_{n\to\infty} P\left(K\sup_{\lambda\in\Lambda}\left|\frac{1}{n^{1/2}\sigma_n}\sum_{t=1}^{n} m_t\mathcal{D}_{\mathcal{N}_n,n,t}(\lambda)\right| \times \delta > \varepsilon\right) = 0.$$

Further, since the rate $\mathcal{N}_n \to \infty$ is arbitrary, we can always let $\mathcal{N}_n \to \infty$ so fast that $\limsup_{n\to\infty} P(\sup_{\lambda\in\Lambda}|\mathcal{B}_{2,\mathcal{N}_n,n}(\lambda)| > \varepsilon) = 0$, cf. Phillips (1995). By subadditivity this proves $\lim_{\delta\to 0}\limsup_{n\to\infty} P(\sup_{||\lambda-\tilde{\lambda}||\leq\delta}\mathcal{A}_{1,n}(\lambda,\tilde{\lambda}) > \varepsilon) = 0 \forall\varepsilon > 0$.

Now consider $\mathcal{A}_{2,n}(\lambda,\tilde{\lambda})$. By UCLT Lemma B.7 $\sup_{\lambda\in\Lambda}|S_n^{-1}(\lambda)\sum_{t=1}^n m_t I_{n,t}(\lambda)| = O_p(1)$ for any compact subset Λ of $(0,1]$. The proof is therefore complete if we show $|S_n(\lambda)/S_n(\tilde{\lambda}) - 1| \leq K|\lambda - \tilde{\lambda}|^{1/2}$. By Lemma B.1.b $S_n^2(\lambda) = \mathfrak{L}_n(\lambda) n E[m_t^2 I_{n,t}(\lambda)]$. Compactness of $\Lambda \subset (0,1]$ ensures $\liminf_{n\to\infty}\inf_{\lambda\in\Lambda}\mathfrak{L}_n(\lambda) > 0$ and $\sup_{\lambda\in\Lambda}\mathfrak{L}_n(\lambda) = O(\ln(n))$, and by distribution continuity $E[m_t^2 I_{n,t}(\lambda)]$ is differentiable, hence $|S_n(\lambda)/S_n(\tilde{\lambda}) - 1| \leq K(\sup_{\lambda\in\Lambda}\{|G_n(\lambda)|\}/E[m_t^2 I_{n,t}(\lambda)])^{1/2} \times |\lambda - \tilde{\lambda}|^{1/2} =: \mathcal{E}_n|\lambda - \tilde{\lambda}|^{1/2}$ where $G_n(\lambda) := (\partial/\partial\lambda) E[m_t^2 I_{n,t}(\lambda)]$. Since $k_n \sim \lambda n/\ln(n)$ it is easy to verify $\limsup_{n\to\infty}\sup_{\lambda\in\Lambda}\mathcal{E}_n < \infty$: if $E[m_t^2] < \infty$ then the bound is trivial, and if $E[m_t^2] = \infty$ then use $c_{\epsilon,n} = K(n/k_n)^{1/\kappa} = K(\ln(n))^{1/\kappa}\lambda^{-1/\kappa}$ and Karamata's Theorem (Resnick 1987, Theorem 0.6). $\mathcal{QED}$.

Proof of Lemma 4.1 By Lemma B.7 in Hill (2011b) $J_n(\gamma) = -E[g_t F_t(\gamma) I_{n,t}] \times (1 + o(1))$ hence it suffices to bound $(E[g_{i,t} F_t(\gamma) I_{n,t}])^2/S_n^2(\gamma)$. The claim follows from Lemma B.1.b, and the following implication of Karamata's theorem (e.g. Resnick 1987, Theorem 0.6): if any random variable w_t has tail $P(|w_t| > w) = dw^{-\kappa}(1 + o(1))$, and $w_{n,t}^* := w_t I(|w_t| \leq c_{w,n})$, $P(|w_t| > c_{w,n}) = k_{w,n}/n = o(1)$

and $k_{w,n} \rightarrow \infty$, then $E|w^*_{n,t}|^p$ is slowly varying if $p = \kappa$, and $E|w^*_{n,t}|^p \sim Kc^p_{w,n}(k_{w,n}/n) = K(n/k_{w,n})^{p/\kappa-1}$ if $p > \kappa$. $\mathcal{QED}$.

Proof of Lemma 4.2 First some preliminaries. Integrability of ϵ_t is assured by $\kappa > 1$, and y_t has tail (11) with the same tail index κ (Brockwell and Cline 1985). Stationarity ensures $\epsilon_t(\beta) = \sum_{i=0}^{\infty} \psi_i(\beta)\epsilon_{t-i}$, where $\sup_{\beta \in \mathcal{B}} |\psi_i(\beta)| \leq K\rho^i$ for $\rho \in (0, 1)$, $\psi_0(\beta^0) = 1$ and $\psi_i(\beta^0) = 0 \forall i \geq 1$. Since ϵ_t is iid with tail (11) it is easy to show $\epsilon_t(\beta)$ satisfies uniform power law property R3.b by exploiting convolution tail properties developed in Embrechts and Goldie (1980). Use (4) and (11) to deduce $c_{\epsilon,n} = K(n/k_n)^{1/\kappa}$.

F2 follows from the stationary AR data generating process and distribution continuity. I1 holds since $E[m^*_{n,t}(\gamma)] = 0$ by independence, symmetry, and symmetric trimming. R1 and R2 hold by construction; (11) and the stated error properties ensure R3; see Pham and Tran (1985) for R4.

Now P1–P3. OLS and LAD are $n^{1/\kappa}$-convergent if $\kappa \in (1, 2]$ (Davis et al. 1992); LTTS and GMTTM are $n^{1/\kappa}/L(n)$ -convergent if $\kappa \in (1, 2]$ (Hill and Renault 2010; Hill 2011b)[11]; and LWAD is $n^{1/2}$-convergent in all cases (Ling 2005). It remains to characterize $V_n(\gamma)$. Each claim follows by application of Lemma 4.1. If $\kappa > 2$ then $V_n(\gamma) \sim Kn$, so OLS, LTTS and GMTTM satisfy P2 [LAD and LWAD are not linear: see Davis et al. (1992)]. If $\kappa \in (1, 2)$ then $V_n(\gamma) \sim Kn\,(k_n/n)^{2/\kappa-1} = o(n)$, while each $\hat{\beta}_n$ satisfies $\tilde{V}^{1/2}_{i,i,n}/n^{1/2} \rightarrow \infty$, hence P1 applies for any intermediate order $\{k_n\}$. The case $\kappa = 2$ is similar.

Finally, Lemma 4.1 can be shown to apply to $V^{\perp}_n(\gamma)$ by exploiting the fact that $\epsilon_t g_{i,t} = \epsilon_t y_{t-i}$ have the same tail index as ϵ_t (Embrechts and Goldie 1980). The above arguments therefore extend to $m^{\perp}_{n,t}(\beta, \gamma)$ under P3. $\mathcal{QED}$.

Proof of Lemma 4.3 The ARCH process $\{y_t\}$ is stationary geometrically β-mixing (Carrasco and Chen 2002). In lieu of re-centering after trimming and error independence, all conditions except P1–P3 hold by the arguments used to prove Lemma 4.2.

Consider P1–P3. Note $\epsilon_t = u_t^2 - 1$ is iid, it has tail index $\kappa_u/2 \in (1, 2]$ if $E[u_t^4] = \infty$, and $(\partial/\partial\beta)\epsilon_t(\beta)|_{\beta^0} = -u_t^2 x_t/h_t^2$ is integrable. Further $S^2_n(\gamma) = nE[m^{*2}_{n,t}(\gamma)]$ by independence and re-centering. Thus $V_n(\gamma) \sim Kn$ if $E[u_t^4] < \infty$, and otherwise apply Lemma 4.1 to deduce $V_n(\gamma) \sim Kn\,(k_n/n)^{4/\kappa_u-1}$ if $\kappa_u < 4$, and $V_n(\gamma) \sim n/L(n)$ if $\kappa_u = 4$.

GMTTM with QML-type equations and QMTTL have a scale $||\tilde{V}_n|| \sim n/L(n)$ if $E[u_t^4] = \infty$, hence P1, otherwise $||\tilde{V}_n|| \sim Kn$ hence P2 (Hill and Renault 2010; Hill 2011b). Log-LAD is $n^{1/2}$-convergent if $E[u_t^2] < \infty$, hence P1 if $\kappa_u \leq 4$, and if $\kappa_u > 4$ then it does not satisfy P2 since it is not linear. QML is $n^{1/2}$-convergent

[11] LTTS and GMTTM require trimming fractiles for estimation: GMTTM requires fractiles $\tilde{k}_{i,n}$ for each estimating equation $\tilde{m}_{i,n,t}$, and LTTS requires fractiles $\tilde{k}_{\epsilon,n}$ and $\tilde{k}_{y,n}$ for ϵ_t and y_{t-i}. The given rates of convergence apply if for GMTTM $\tilde{k}_{i,n} \sim \lambda \ln(n)$ (Hill and Renault 2010), and for LTTS $\tilde{k}_{\epsilon,n} \sim \lambda n/\ln(n)$ and $\tilde{k}_{y,n} \sim \lambda \ln(n)$ (Hill 2011b), where $\lambda > 0$ is chosen by the analyst and may be different in different places.

if $E[u_t^4] < \infty$ hence P2, and if $E[u_t^4] = \infty$ then the rate is $n^{1-2/\kappa_u}/L(n)$ when $\kappa_u \in (2, 4]$ (Hall and Yao 2003, Theorem 2.1). But if $\kappa_u < 4$ then $n(k_n/n)^{4/\kappa_u - 1} = k_n^{4/\kappa_u - 1} n^{2-4/\kappa_u} > n^{2-4/\kappa_u}/L(n)$ for any slowly varying $L(n) \to \infty$ and intermediate order $\{k_n\}$ hence QML does not satisfy P1 or P2. Synonymous arguments extend to $m_{n,t}^{\perp}(\gamma)$ under P3 by exploiting Lemma 4.1. $\mathcal{QED}$.

References

An H.Z., Huang F.C. (1996) The Geometrical Ergodicity of Nonlinear Autoregressive Models, Stat. Sin. 6, 943–956.

Arcones M., Giné E. (1989) The Bootstrap of the Mean with Arbitrary Bootstrap Sample Size, Ann.I H. P. 25, 457–481.

Bai J. (2003) Testing Parametric Conditional Distributions of Dynamic Models, Rev. Econ. Stat. 85, 531–549.

Bierens H.J. (1982) Consistent Model Specification Tests, J. Econometric 20, 105–13.

Bierens H.J. (1990) A Consistent Conditional Moment Test of Functional Form, Econometrica 58, 1443–1458.

Bierens H.J., Ploberger W. (1997) Asymptotic Theory of Integrated Conditional Moment Tests, Econometrica 65, 1129–1151.

Brock W.A., Dechert W.D., Scheinkman J.A., LeBaron B. (1996) A Test for Independence Based on the Correlation Dimension, Econometric Rev. 15, 197–235.

Brockwell P.J., Cline D.B.H. (1985) Linear Prediction of ARMA Processes with Infinite Variance, Stoch. Proc. Appl. 19, 281–296.

Carrasco M., Chen X. (2002) Mixing and Moment Properties of Various GARCH and Stochastic Volatility Models, Econometric Theory 18, 17–39.

Chan K.S. (1990) Testing for Threshold Autoregression, Ann. Stat. 18, 1886–1894.

Chen X. and Fan Y. (1999) Consistent Hypothesis Testing in Semiparametric and Nonparametric Models for Econometric Time Series, J. Econometrics 91, 373–401.

Corradi V., Swanson N.R. (2002) A Consistent Test for Nonlinear Out-of-Sample Predictive Accuracy, J. Econometrics 110, 353–381.

Csörgo S., Horváth L., Mason D. (1986) What Portion of the Sample Makes a Partial Sum Asymptotically Stable or Normal? Prob. Theory Rel. Fields 72, 1–16.

Davidson R., MacKinnon J., White H. (1983) Tests for Model Specification in the Presence of Alternative Hypotheses: Some Further Results, J. Econometrics 21, 53–70.

Davies R.B. (1977) Hypothesis Testing when a Nuisance Parameter is Present Only under the Alternative, Biometrika 64, 247–254.

Davis R.A., Knight K., Liu J. (1992) M-Estimation for Autoregressions with Infinite Variance, Stoch. Proc. Appl. 40, 145–180.

de Jong R.M. (1996) The Bierens Test under Data Dependence, J. Econometrics 72, 1–32.

de Jong R.M., Davidson J. (2000) Consistency of Kernel Estimators of Heteroscedastic and Autocorrelated Covariance Matrices, Econometrica 68, 407–423.

de Lima P.J.F. (1997) On the Robustness of Nonlinearity Tests to Moment Condition Failure, J. Econometrics 76, 251–280.

Dehling, H., M. Denker, W. Phillip (1986) Central Limit Theorems for Mixing Sequences of Random Variables under Minimal Conditions, Ann. Prob. 14, 1359–1370.

Dette H. (1999) A Consistent Test for the Functional Form of a Regression Based on a Difference of Variance Estimators, Ann. Stat.27, 1012–1040.

Dufour J.M., Farhat A., Hallin M. (2006) Distribution-Free Bounds for Serial Correlation Coefficients in Heteroscedastic Symmetric Time Series, J. Econometrics 130, 123–142.

Doukhan P., Massart, P., Rio E. (1995) Invariance Principles for Absolutely Regular Empirical Processes, Ann. I. H. P. 31, 393–427.

Dudley R. M. (1978) Central Limit Theorem for Empirical Processes. Ann. Prob. 6, 899–929.
Embrechts P., Goldie C.M. (1980) On Closure and Factorization Properties of Subexponential Distributions, J. Aus. Math. Soc. A, 29, 243–256.
Embrechts P., Klüppelberg C., Mikosch T. (1997) Modelling Extremal Events for Insurance and Finance. Springer-Verlag: Frankfurt.
Eubank R., Spiegelman S. (1990) Testing the Goodness of Fit of a Linear Model via Nonparametric Regression Techniques, J. Amer. Stat. Assoc. 85, 387–392.
Fan Y., Li Q. (1996) Consistent Model Specification Tests: Omitted Variables and Semiparametric Functional Forms, Econometrica 64, 865–890.
Fan Y., Li Q. (2000) Consistent Model Specification Tests: Kernel-Based Tests Versus Bierens' ICM Tests, Econometric Theory 16, 1016–1041.
Finkenstadt B., Rootzén H. (2003) Extreme Values in Finance, Telecommunications and the Environment. Chapman and Hall: New York. Parameter Space, Econometric Theory 26, 965–993.
Gabaix, X. (2008) Power Laws, in The New Palgrave Dictionary of Economics, 2nd Edition, S. N. Durlauf and L. E. Blume (eds.), MacMillan.
Gallant A.R. (1981) Unbiased Determination of Production Technologies. J. Econometrics, 20, 285–323.
Gallant A.R., White H. (1989) There Exists a Neural Network That Does Not Make Avoidable Mistakes, Proceedings of the Second Annual IEEE Conference on Neural Net., I:657–664.
Hall P., Yao Q. (2003) Inference in ARCH and GARCH Models with Heavy-Tailed Errors, Econometrica 71, 285–317.
Hahn M.G., Weiner D.C., Mason D.M. (1991) Sums, Trimmed Sums and Extremes, Birkhäuser: Berlin.
Hansen B.E. (1996). Inference When a Nuisance Parameter Is Not Identified Under the Null Hypothesis, Econometrica 64, 413–430.
Härdle W., Mammen E. (1993) Comparing Nonparametric Versus Parametric Regression Fits, Ann. Stat. 21, 1926–1947.
Hausman J.A. (1978) Specification Testing in Econometrics, Econometrica 46, 1251–1271.
Hill J.B. (2008a) Consistent and Non-Degenerate Model Specification Tests Against Smooth Transition and Neural Network Alternatives, Ann. D'Econ. Statist. 90, 145–179.
Hill J.B. (2008b) Consistent GMM Residuals-Based Tests of Functional Form, Econometric Rev.: forthcoming.
Hill J.B. (2011a) Tail and Non-Tail Memory with Applications to Extreme Value and Robust Statistics, Econometric Theory 27, 844–884.
Hill J.B. (2011b) Robust M-Estimation for Heavy Tailed Nonlinear AR-GARCH, Working Paper, University of North Carolina - Chapel Hill.
Hill J.B. (2011c) Supplemental Appendix for Heavy-Tail and Plug-In Robust Consistent Conditional Moments Tests of Functional Form, www.unc.edu/jbhill/ap_cm_trim.pdf.
Hill J.B. (2012) Stochastically Weighted Average Conditional Moment Tests of Functional Form: Stud. Nonlin. Dyn. Econometrics 16: forthcoming.
Hill, J.B., Aguilar M. (2011) Moment Condition Tests for Heavy Tailed Time Series, J. Econometrics: Annals Issue on Extreme Value Theory: forthcoming.
Hill J.B., Renault E. (2010) Generalized Method of Moments with Tail Trimming, submitted; Dept. of Economics, University of North Carolina - Chapel Hill.
Hoffmann-Jørgensen J. (1991) Convergence of Stochastic Processes on Polish Spaces, Various Publication Series Vol. 39, Matematisk Institute, Aarhus University.
Hong Y., White H. (1995) Consistent Specification Testing Via Nonparametric Series Regression, Econometrica 63, 1133–1159.
Hong Y., Lee Y-J. (2005) Generalized Spectral Tests for Conditional Mean Models in Time Series with Conditional Heteroscedasticity of Unknown Form, Rev. Econ. Stud. 72, 499–541.
Hornik K., Stinchcombe M., White H. (1989) Multilayer Feedforward Networks are Universal Approximators, Neural Net. 2, 359–366.

Hornik K., Stinchcombe M., White H. (1990) Universal Approximation of an Unknown Mapping and Its Derivatives Using Multilayer Feedforward Networks, Neural Net., 3, 551–560.

Ibragimov R., Müller U.K. (2010) t-Statistic based Correlation and Heterogeneity Robust Inference, J. Bus. Econ. Stat. 28, 453–468.

Lahiri S.N. (1995) On the Asymptotic Beahiour of the Moving Block Bootstrap for Normalized Sums of Heavy-Tailed Random Variables, Ann. Stat. 23, 1331–1349.

Leadbetter M.R., Lindgren G., Rootzén H. (1983) Extremes and Related Properties of Random Sequences and Processes. Springer-Verlag: New York.

Lee T., White H., Granger C.W.J. (1993) Testing for Neglected Nonlinearity in Time-Series Models: A Comparison of Neural Network Methods and Alternative Tests, J. Econometrics 56, 269–290.

Ling S. (2005) Self-Weighted LAD Estimation for Infinite Variance Autoregressive Models, J. R. Stat. Soc. B 67, 381–393.

McLeod A.I., Li W.K. (1983) Diagnostic Checking ARMA Time Series Models Using Squared Residual Autocorrelations, J. Time Ser. Anal. 4, 269–273.

Meitz M., Saikkonen P. (2008) Stability of Nonlinear AR-GARCH Models, J. Time Ser. Anal. 29, 453–475.

Newey W.K. (1985) Maximum Likelihood Specification Testing and Conditional Moment Tests, Econometrica 53, 1047–1070.

Peng L., Yao Q. (2003) Least Absolute Deviation Estimation for ARCH and GARCH Models, Biometrika 90, 967–975.

Pham T., Tran L. (1985) Some Mixing Properties of Time Series Models. Stoch. Proc. Appl. 19, 297–303.

Pollard D. (1984) Convergence of Stochastic Processes. Springer-Verlang New York.

Ramsey J.B. (1969) Tests for Specification Errors in Classical Linear Least-Squares Regression, J. R. Stat. Soc. B 31, 350–371.

Resnick S.I. (1987) Extreme Values, Regular Variation and Point Processes. Springer-Verlag: New York.

Stinchcombe M., White H. (1989) Universal Approximation Using Feedforward Networks with Non-Sigmoid Hidden Layer Activation Functions, Proceedings of the International Joint Conference on Neural Net., I, 612–617.

Stinchcombe M.B., White H. (1992) Some Measurability Results for Extrema of Random Functions Over Random Sets, Rev. Economic Stud., 59, 495–514.

Stinchcombe M.B., White H. (1998) Consistent Specification Testing with Nuisance Parameters Present Only Under the Alternative, Econometric Theory 14, 295–325.

Tsay R. (1986) Nonlinearity Tests for Time Series, Biometrika 73, 461–466.

White H. (1981) Consequences and Detection of Misspecified Nonlinear Regression Models, J. Amer. Stat. Assoc. 76, 419–433.

White H. (1982) Maximum Likelihood Estimation of Misspecified Models, Econometrica 50, 1–25.

White H. (1987) Specification Testing in Dynamic Models, in Truman Bewley, ed., Advances in Econometrics. Cambridge University Press: New York.

White H. (1989a) A Consistent Model Selection Procedure Based on m-Testing, in C.W.J. Granger, ed., Modelling Economic Series: Readings in Econometric Methodology, p. 369–403. Oxford University Press: Oxford.

White H. (1989b) Some Asymptotic Results for Learning in Single Hidden Layer Feedforward Network Models, J. Amer. Stat. Assoc., 84, 1003–1013.

White H. (1990) Connectionist Nonparametric Regression: Multilayer Feedforward Networks Can Learn Arbitrary Mappings, Neural Net., 3, 535–549.

Wooldridge J.M. (1990) A Unified Approach to Robust, Regression-Based Specification Tests, Econometric Theory 6, 17–43.

Yatchew A.J. (1992) Nonparametric Regression Tests Based on Least Squares, Econometric Theory 8, 435–451.

Zheng J.X. (1996) A Consistent Test of Functional Form via Nonparametric Estimation Techniques, J. Econometrics 75, 263–289.

Nonparametric Identification in Dynamic Nonseparable Panel Data Models

Stefan Hoderlein and Halbert White

Abstract We consider the identification of covariate-conditioned and average partial effects in dynamic nonseparable panel data structures. We demonstrate that a control function approach is sufficient to identify the effects of interest, and we show how the panel structure may be helpful in finding control functions. We also provide new results for the nonparametric binary dependent variable case with a lagged dependent variable.

Keywords Nonseparable Models · Identification · Dynamic · Panel data · Semiparametric · Binary choice

1 Introduction

We consider nonparametric identification of covariate-conditioned and average partial effects of causes of interest ("effects of interest") in panel structures. Identification is nonparametric in that the structural relations generating the data are not assumed to have a parametric representation, nor do we assume that this structure is separable between observables and unobservables or that it possesses any monotonicity properties on the right-hand-side variables. We permit the observable causes of interest to be endogenous, as they need not be independent of the unobservables. Compared to previous work, a key innovation is that we allow for lagged dependent variables, and we analyze both the effect of the lagged dependent variable as well as the effect

S. Hoderlein (✉)
Department of Economics, Boston College, 140 Commonwealth Ave,
Chestnut Hill, MA 02467, USA
e-mail: stefan_hoderlein@yahoo.com

H. White
Department of Economics, University of California San Diego,
9500 Gilman Drive, La Jolla, CA 92093-0508, USA
e-mail: hwhite@weber.ucsd.edu

X. Chen and N. R. Swanson (eds.), *Recent Advances and Future Directions in Causality, Prediction, and Specification Analysis*, DOI: 10.1007/978-1-4614-1653-1_11,

of other explanatory variables in structural systems with lagged dependent variables. We consider both continuous and binary lagged dependent variables.

For the same structure but without lagged dependent variables (the "static case"), Hoderlein and White (2011, henceforth HW) establish nonparametric identification of covariate-conditioned and average partial effects of endogenous causes for the subpopulation of "stayers" (i.e., the subpopulation for which the explanatory variables stay unchanged between two time periods), without imposing independence between the persistent unobservables and the causes of interest. A similar result is obtained in Graham and Powell (2010, henceforth GP) for the subpopulation of "movers" (the complement population to the stayers), if the structure is known to be linear in the explanatory variables. Finally, Chernozhukov, Fernandez-Val, Hahn, and Newey (2009) obtain results for average discrete variation in causes of interest for the subpopulation of stayers, without imposing independence.

Both the HW and the GP approaches restrict the dependence of the regressors on the past in a way that rules out lagged dependent variables. In contrast, Altonji and Matzkin (2005) and Bester and Hansen (2008) restrict the dependence in a way that may allow for lagged dependent variables. We follow a similar strategy here, as it does not appear that effects in the general dynamic case can be point identified otherwise. To make the main ideas clear, we first lay out this strategy in the static case, followed by an analysis of the dynamic case. An important feature of our contribution here is our focus on the content of the identifying assumptions, especially for the dynamic case.

Although our main focus is on providing new identification results, we also consider their implications for estimation. We recommend local linear regression, with explicit allowance for the case of mixed continuous-discrete regressors, as in Li and Racine (2004). Interestingly, the asymptotic theory relevant to our estimators has not yet been fully settled; development is ongoing. As the challenges of this theory are significant, its further development lies beyond the scope of this chapter. Thus, we focus on describing our proposed estimators, discussing their known properties, suggesting useful directions for the further development of the asymptotic theory, and examining estimator finite-sample properties via simulation experiments.

The structure of the chapter is as follows: In the second section, we set out the main structural assumptions and briefly describe the effects of interest. In Sect. 3, we present our main identification results. We start with the static case and then discuss in more detail the dynamic case. Section 4 discusses estimation. Section 5 contains a summary and concluding remarks.

2 The Data Generating Process and Effects of Interest

In this section we specify the structure generating the data and describe the effects of interest. We begin by specifying a dynamic triangular structural system that generates the data. We write $\mathbb{N}^+ := \{1, 2, \ldots\}$ and $\mathbb{N} := \{0\} \cup \mathbb{N}^+$. We also write $\bar{\mathbb{N}}^+ := \mathbb{N}^+ \cup \{\infty\}$ and $\bar{\mathbb{N}} := \{0\} \cup \bar{\mathbb{N}}^+$.

Assumption A.1 (a)(i) Let $(\Omega, \mathcal{F}, P)$ be a complete probability space. Let $k_y \in \mathbb{N}^+$, let Y_0 be a $k_y \times 1$ random vector on $(\Omega, \mathcal{F}, P)$, and let the random $k_y \times 1$ vectors Y_t be determined by a dynamic triangular structural system as

$$Y_t = \phi(Y_{t-1}, X_t, S_t, U_t; A, B), \quad t = 1, 2, \ldots,$$

where ϕ is an unknown measurable $k_y \times 1$ function; X_t, S_t, and U_t are vectors of time-varying random variables on $(\Omega, \mathcal{F}, P)$ of dimensions $k_x \in \mathbb{N}^+$, $k_s \in \mathbb{N}$, and $k_u \in \bar{\mathbb{N}}^+$; and A and B are vectors of time-invariant random variables on $(\Omega, \mathcal{F}, P)$ of dimensions $k_a \in \bar{\mathbb{N}}^+$ and $k_b \in \mathbb{N}$.

Suppose also that W_t and C are random vectors on $(\Omega, \mathcal{F}, P)$ of dimensions $k_w \in \mathbb{N}$ and $k_c \in \mathbb{N}$, time-varying and time-invariant, respectively. (ii) The triangular structure is such that neither Y_t, Y_{t-1}, nor X_t structurally determines W_t; Y_{t-1} does not structurally determine X_t, S_t, or U_t; and X_t does not structurally determine S_t or U_t.

(b) Realizations of U_t and A are not observed. Realizations of all other random variables are observed.

We observe a panel of data generated according to Assumption A.1, e.g.,

$$Y_{i,t} = \phi(Y_{i,t-1}, X_{i,t}, S_{i,t}, U_{i,t}; A_i, B_i), \quad t = 1, 2, \ldots; \quad i = 1, 2, \ldots.$$

We assume the data are identically distributed across i and accordingly drop the i subscript.

We are interested only in the effects of X_t on Y_t or of Y_{t-1} on Y_t (the dynamics). A finite number of lags is readily accommodated; for simplicity, we specify only a single lag of Y_t. Given these interests, we also write

$$\phi_t(Y_{t-1}) = \phi(Y_{t-1}, X_t, S_t, U_t; A, B) \quad \text{or} \quad \phi_t(X_t) = \phi(Y_{t-1}, X_t, S_t, U_t; A, B),$$

suppressing all but the causes of interest. Interest attaches to the marginal effects

$$D_y\phi_t(Y_{t-1}) \quad \text{and} \quad D_x\phi_t(X_t),$$

where $D_y = \partial/\partial y_{-1}$ and $D_x = \partial/\partial x$ and denote the derivatives with respect to the first and second arguments of ϕ, respectively. The triangularity restrictions imposed in $A.2(a.ii)$ ensure that these are the full effects of the variables of interest; there are no indirect effects here. Because ϕ is unknown and U_t and A are unobservable, these effects cannot be directly measured. Instead, we consider identifying the conditionally expected effects

$$\mathbb{E}[D_y\phi_t(Y_{t-1})|\mathcal{G}_t] \quad \text{and} \quad \mathbb{E}[D_x\phi_t(X_t)|\mathcal{H}_t],$$

where $\mathcal{G}_t$ and $\mathcal{H}_t$ denote suitable conditioning information sets. As the notation suggests, different conditioning information may be involved in identifying the effects of Y_{t-1} and X_t. The random variables W_t and C will be used in generating $\mathcal{G}_t$ and $\mathcal{H}_t$.

Observe that covariate-conditioned effects of this sort are more informative about the underlying effects, $D_y\phi_t(Y_{t-1})$ or $D_x\phi_t(X_t)$, than are unconditional averages or partial means, as conditional expectations give mean-squared-error optimal predictions and thus necessarily have smaller prediction variance for effects of interest than unconditional averages or partial means.

3 Identification of Average Marginal Effects

3.1 The Static Case

For clarity and to ease the notational burden, we begin with an analysis of the static case, $\phi_t(X_t) := \phi(X_t, S_t, U_t; A, B)$. A direct way to identify effects in this case makes use of the conditional expectation

$$\mathbb{E}[Y_t|X_t = x, Q_t = q] = \mathbb{E}[\phi_t(X_t) \mid X_t = x, Q_t = q], \tag{1}$$

where Q_t represents observable "covariates," both time-varying and time-invariant. For example, time-varying components of Q_t include S_t, as well as observed drivers of X_t, such as lagged X_t's, together with W_t's acting as proxies for U_t and for unobserved drivers of X_t. The time-invariant components of Q_t are B and C. C may include observable proxies for A; observable attributes explaining X_t; and observable proxies for unobservable attributes explaining X_t. For concreteness, let $Q_t = (S_t, X_{t-1}, W_t, B, C)$ for the moment. We further discuss Q_t below.

The conditional expectation on the left of Eq. (1) exists whenever $\mathbb{E}(Y) < \infty$; it has no necessary structural meaning. Under Assumption A.1 $(a.i)$, however, the structurally meaningful representation on the left of Eq. (1) holds. It is helpful to also provide an integral representation of this object. For this, we suppress the dependence of ϕ on S_t and B, and write

$$\mathbb{E}[\phi_t(X_t) \mid X_t = x, Q_t = q] = \int \phi(x, u; a)\, \mathrm{d}F(u, a \mid x, q).$$

Here, $\mathrm{d}F(u, a \mid x, q)$ defines the conditional density of (U_t, A) given $(X_t = x, Q_t = q)$. This distribution may depend on t, but we suppress this dependence here and in what follows for notational simplicity. We also let the argument list implicitly specify the relevant random variables. This integral representation holds, provided that the associated conditional distribution is regular (e.g., Dudley (2002), Chap. 10.2). In what follows, we assume implicitly that any referenced conditional distribution is regular.

As interest attaches to the marginal effect of X_t, we take the derivative of $\mathbb{E}[Y_t \mid X_t = x, Q_t = q]$ with respect to x. This gives

$$D_x \mathbb{E}[Y_t | X_t = x, Q_t = q] \\ = \int D_x \phi(x, u; a) \, \mathrm{d}F(u, a \mid x, q) + \int \phi(x, u; a) D_x \, \mathrm{d}F(u, a \mid x, q).$$

The representation holds with differentiability for ϕ and $\mathrm{d}F(u, a \mid x, q)$ and regularity permitting the interchange of derivative and integral. This includes an assumption that the domain of integration does not depend on x. Under mild conditions, $D_x \mathrm{d}F = D_x \ln \mathrm{d}F \, \mathrm{d}F$; letting

$$\delta_t := D_x \ln \mathrm{d}F(U_t, A \mid X_t, Q_t),$$

be the exogeneity score of White and Chalak (2011), we can write

$$D_x \mathbb{E}[Y_t \mid X_t = x, Q_t = q] \\ = \mathbb{E}[D_x \phi_t(X_t) \mid X_t = x, Q_t = q] + \mathbb{E}[\phi_t(X_t) \delta_t \mid X_t = x, Q_t = q].$$

The first term on the right is a main item of interest: it is an average marginal effect of the sort discussed above. The second term on the right is an "endogeneity" bias. Whenever this is nonzero, it interferes with using $D_x \mathbb{E}[Y_t \mid X_t = x, Q_t = q]$ to measure the effect of interest. See White and Chalak (2011) and White and Lu (2011) for further discussion.

We thus seek conditions that make this bias vanish. A standard condition for this is the assumption that (U_t, A) is independent of X_t given Q_t. Following Dawid (1979), we write this

$$(U_t, A) \perp X_t \mid Q_t. \tag{2}$$

This type of "control function" assumption has been used in related contexts by Altonji and Matzkin (2005), Imbens and Newey (2009), and Hoderlein (2011), to name just a few. White and Chalak (2011) refer to this as a "conditional exogeneity" assumption, given its similarity to the assumption of strict exogeneity (here, $(U_t, A) \perp X_t$). When $(U_t, A) \perp X_t$ fails, we have the case commonly referred to as "fixed effects" (Wooldridge, 2002). Condition (2) allows fixed effects ($(U_t, A) \not\perp X_t$), while still delivering identification of effects of interest.

To see how, observe that (2) ensures that for all (u, a, x, q), we have

$$\mathrm{d}F(u, a \mid x, q) = \mathrm{d}F(u, a \mid q),$$

so that δ_t is identically zero. This guarantees that the effect bias vanishes, so that

$$D_x \mathbb{E}[Y_t | X_t = x, Q_t = q] \\ = \mathbb{E}[D_x \phi_t(X_t) \mid X_t = x, Q_t = q] = \mathbb{E}[D_x \phi_t(x) \mid Q_t = q].$$

The first equality holds because the effect bias vanishes. The second equality follows as a further consequence of conditional independence.

Thus, under Assumption A.1(a), conditional exogeneity, and sufficient differentiability and regularity, $D_x\mathbb{E}[Y_t \mid X_t = x, Q_t = q]$ has a clear structural interpretation as an average marginal effect. In this case, we say that $D_x\mathbb{E}[Y_t \mid X_t = x, Q_t = q]$ is "identified" (cf. Hurwicz, 1950). Under Assumption A.1(b), all variables entering the conditional expectation on the right are observable, so this effect measure can be straightforwardly estimated from available data.

Before stating a formal result, we offer further insight into the content of the conditional exogeneity assumption. To develop this, it is useful to split Q_t explicitly into its time-varying and time-invariant components, say $Q_t := (\xi_t, B, C)$, and to write the conditional exogeneity restriction $(U_t, A) \perp X_t \mid \xi_t, B, C$ equivalently as

$$U_t \perp X_t \mid \xi_t, A, B, C \tag{3}$$

$$A \perp X_t \mid \xi_t, B, C. \tag{4}$$

This representation permits us to appreciate the differing roles of (B, C) and ξ_t.

The role of ξ_t is foremost in (3). The more closely related are ξ_t and U_t, the less useful X_t is as a predictor of U_t (given ξ_t, etc.) and therefore the more plausible is (3). Viewed in this way, it is useful to have ξ_t include proxies for U_t. Specifically, ξ_t should include variables W_t driven by U_t. Components of S_t may also act as proxies for U_t. Symmetrically, the more closely related are ξ_t and X_t, the less useful U_t is as a predictor of X_t (given ξ_t, etc.) and therefore the more plausible is (3). Accordingly, one might choose ξ_t to include drivers of X_t, such as S_t, X_{t-1}, and W_t, or to include proxies for unobserved drivers of X_t. Nevertheless, as White and Lu (2011) show, including drivers of X_t in ξ_t leads to less precise effect estimates; in the limit, predicting X_t too well leads to the analog of extreme multicollinearity.

The role of (B, C) is foremost in (4), where it acts as a proxy for A. Here, the more closely related are (B, C) and A, the less useful X_t is as a predictor of A (given (B, C), etc.) and therefore the more plausible is (4). Similarly, the more closely related are ξ_t and X_t, the less useful A is as a predictor of X_t, and the more plausible is (4). Again, however, efficiency considerations suggest that it is preferable to include proxies for A and avoid including variables correlated with X_t. These considerations motivate our specification that $Q_t = (S_t, X_{t-1}, W_t, B, C)$ above.

Finally, observe that if one's goal is to estimate $\mathbb{E}[D_x\phi_t(X_t) \mid X_t = x, Q_t = q]$ for arbitrary ϕ, x, and q, then Eq. (2) is necessary, as otherwise the effect bias is nonzero for some (generally most) values of x and/or q. Fortunately, the latitude in choosing Q_t (afforded by the latitude in the choice of W_t and C) provides flexibility in plausibly ensuring conditional exogeneity.

As White and Kennedy (2009) discuss, suitable covariates can contain further lags of X_{t-1} and lags (or even leads) of S_t and W_t. We let $X_{t-\tau_x}^{t-1} := (X_{t-\tau_x}, \ldots, X_{t-1})$ denote a lag history of X_t, and we let $S_{t-\tau_{s,1}}^{t+\tau_{s,2}} := (S_{t-\tau_{s,1}}, \ldots, S_{t+\tau_{s,2}})$ and $W_{t-\tau_{w,1}}^{t+\tau_{w,2}} := (S_{t-\tau_{w,1}}, \ldots, S_{t+\tau_{w,2}})$ denoted lead and lag histories of S_t and W_t. We adopt the convention that when $\tau_x = 0$, $X_{t-\tau_x}^{t-1}$ is empty. Formally, $\sigma(\mathcal{X})$ denotes the $\sigma-$field (information set) generated by the random vector $\mathcal{X}$; we impose

Assumption A.2 Let τ_x, $\tau_{s,1}$, $\tau_{s,2}$, $\tau_{w,1}$, and $\tau_{w,2}$ belong to $\mathbb{N}$, and let $k_q \in \mathbb{N}^+$. The observable $k_q \times 1$ random vector Q_t is measurable$-\sigma(X_{t-\tau_x}^{t-1}, S_{t-\tau_{s,1}}^{t+\tau_{s,2}}, W_{t-\tau_{w,1}}^{t+\tau_{w,2}}, B, C)$, and (S_t, B) is measurable $-\sigma(Q_t)$.

Assumption A.2 potentially extends the observability of the covariates Q_t to periods before $t = 1$. We understand implicitly that these observations are generated by the structure of A.1 for whatever time periods are required. The requirement that (S_t, B) is measurable$-\sigma(Q_t)$ ensures that Q_t essentially includes (S_t, B).

To proceed, we impose the validity of the interchange of integral and derivative used above. White and Chalak (2011) give detailed primitive conditions for this. For simplicity and conciseness here, we just impose the needed high-level assumption.

Assumption A.3 The distribution of $(U_t, A) \mid (X_t, Q_t)$ and the structural function ϕ are such that for all admissible (x, q), we have

$$\begin{aligned} D_x \int \phi(x, s, u; a, b)\, \mathrm{d}F(u, a \mid x, q) \\ = \int D_x\phi(x, s, u; a, b)\, \mathrm{d}F(u, a \mid x, q) \\ + \int \phi(x, s, u; a, b) D_x \ln\, \mathrm{d}F(u, a \mid x, q)\, \mathrm{d}F(u, a \mid x, q). \end{aligned}$$

Next, we impose conditional exogeneity.

Assumption A.4 $(U_t, A) \perp X_t \mid Q_t$.

To state our first formal result, we let supp$(\cdot)$ denote the support of the indicated random variable, that is, the smallest closed set containing that random variable with probability one. We also let supp$(\cdot \mid \cdot)$ denote the support of the first indicated random variable, given the specified value for the second. The identification result for the static case is

Proposition 3.1 *Given A.1–A.4 with* $Y_t = \phi(X_t, S_t, U_t; A, B)$, *for all* $q \in supp(Q_t)$ *and* $x \in supp(X_t \mid Q_t = q)$,

$$\begin{aligned} D_x\mathbb{E}[Y_t|X_t = x, Q_t = q] &= \mathbb{E}[D_x\phi_t(X_t) \mid X_t = x, Q_t = q] \\ &= \mathbb{E}[D_x\phi_t(x) \mid Q_t = q], t = 1, 2, \ldots . \end{aligned}$$

Averaged versions of these effect measures are also recoverable. Specifically, when the conclusions of Proposition 3.1 hold, then one can recover average marginal effects of the form

$$\mathbb{E}_F[D_x\phi_t(X_t)] := \int \mathbb{E}[D_x\phi_t(x) \mid Q_t = q]\, \mathrm{d}F(x, q),$$

where $\mathrm{d}F$ is some density of interest specified by the researcher. Specifically, we have

$$\mathbb{E}_F[D_x\phi_t(X_t)] = \int D_x\mathbb{E}\left[Y_t \mid X_t = x, Q_t = q\right] \, \mathrm{d}F(x, q).$$

3.2 The Dynamic Case

Now suppose data are generated according to the fully dynamic version of Assumption A.1(a),

$$Y_t = \phi(Y_{t-1}, X_t, S_t, U_t; A, B). \tag{5}$$

We consider two different effects. First, we consider the effect of X_t on Y_t. Then we consider dynamic effects, that is, the effect of Y_{t-1} on Y_t.

3.2.1 The Effect of X_t

Given the results above, extending the static case to include Y_{t-1} is now easy. We therefore keep our discussion here to a minimum. With $\phi_t(X_t) := \phi(Y_{t-1}, X_t, S_t, U_t; A, B)$, A.1 gives

$$\mathbb{E}[Y_t \mid Y_{t-1} = y, X_t = x, Q_t = q] = \mathbb{E}[\phi_t(X_t) \mid Y_{t-1} = y, X_t = x, Q_t = q].$$

The content of Q_t is still governed by A.2. The analog of A.3 is simply

Assumption A.3′ The distribution of $(U_t, A) \mid (Y_{t-1}, X_t, Q_t)$ and the structural function ϕ are such that for all admissible (y, x, q), we have

$$\begin{aligned} D_x &\int \phi(y, x, s, u; a, b)\mathrm{d}F(u, a \mid y, x, q) \\ &= \int D_x\phi(y, x, s, u; a, b)\mathrm{d}F(u, a \mid y, x, q) \\ &\quad + \int \phi(y, x, s, u; a, b)D_x \ln \mathrm{d}F(u, a \mid y, x, q)\,\mathrm{d}F(u, a \mid y, x, q). \end{aligned}$$

The conditional exogeneity assumption becomes

Assumption A.4′ $(U_t, A) \perp X_t \mid Y_{t-1}, Q_t$.

The dynamic version of Proposition 3.1 is

Proposition 3.2 *Given A.1, A.2, A.3′, and A.4′, for all* $(y, q) \in$ *supp* (Y_{t-1}, Q_t) *and* $x \in$ *supp* $(X_t \mid Y_{t-1} = y, Q_t = q)$,

$$\begin{aligned} &D_x \mathbb{E}[Y_t | Y_{t-1} = y, X_t = x, Q_t = q] \\ &\quad = \mathbb{E}[D_x \phi_t(X_t) \mid Y_{t-1} = y, X_t = x, Q_t = q] \\ &\quad = \mathbb{E}[D_x \phi_t(x) \mid Y_{t-1} = y, Q_t = q], \quad t = 1, 2 \ldots . \end{aligned} \tag{6}$$

Using the obvious notation, an analogous argument applied to

$$\lambda_t(Y_{t-2}, X_t, X_{t-1}) := \phi_t(\phi_t(Y_{t-2}, X_{t-1}), X_t)$$

under the assumption[1] that for all t,

$$(U_t, U_{t-1}, A) \perp X_t \mid Y_{t-2}, X_{t-1}, Q_t$$

yields

$$\begin{aligned} &D_x \mathbb{E}[Y_t \mid Y_{t-2} = y, X_t = x, X_{t-1} = x_{-1}, Q_t = q] \\ &\qquad = \mathbb{E}[D_x \phi_t(Y_{t-1}, x) \mid Y_{t-2} = y, X_{t-1} = x_{-1}, Q_t = q]. \end{aligned} \tag{7}$$

Generally, the average marginal effects measured by Eqs. (6) and (7) will differ. Nevertheless, in special cases, these may coincide; examples are when ϕ is suitably separable or partially linear. Comparing estimators of the conditional expectations on the left in Eqs. (19) and (7) may therefore support tests of these properties.

3.2.2 The Effect of Y_{t-1}

We emphasize that the results so far identify only average marginal effects of X_t. They do not identify any dynamic impacts associated with $D_y \phi$. Nevertheless, under suitable conditions we can recover certain dynamic effects. Because X_t is no longer a cause of interest, we absorb it into S_t, and drop explicit reference to X_t. Thus, we write $Y_t = \phi_t(Y_{t-1}) := \phi(Y_{t-1}, S_t, U_t; A, B)$.

Now consider

$$\mathbb{E}[Y_t | Y_{t-1} = y, Q_t^* = q^*] = \mathbb{E}[\phi_t(Y_{t-1}) \mid Y_{t-1} = y, Q_t^* = q^*]. \tag{8}$$

We write Q_t^* instead of Q_t to make it clear that different covariates may be relevant here than when considering the effects of X_t. Similar to Q_t, Q_t^* represents both observable time-varying covariates and observable time-invariant covariates. Q_t^* obeys an analog of A.2:

---

[1] The elements of Q_t may need to be augmented with elements of Q_{t-1} here. We leave the notation unchanged for simplicity.

Assumption A.2′ Let $\tau_y, \tau_{s,1}, \tau_{s,2}, \tau_{w,1}$, and $\tau_{w,2}$ belong to $\mathbb{N}$, and let $k_{q^*} \in \mathbb{N}^+$. The observable $k_{q^*} \times 1$ random vector Q_t^* is measurable $-\sigma(Y_{t-\tau_y}^{t-2}, S_{t-\tau_{s,1}}^{t+\tau_{s,2}}, W_{t-\tau_{w,1}}^{t+\tau_{w,2}}, B, C)$, and (S_t, B) is measurable $-\sigma(Q_t^*)$.

We further discuss the content of Q_t^* below.

Suppressing the dependence of ϕ on S_t and B, we have the integral representation

$$\mathbb{E}[\phi_t(Y_{t-1}) \mid Y_{t-1} = y, Q_t^* = q^*] = \int \phi(y, u; a)\, \mathrm{d}F(u, a \mid y, q^*).$$

Taking the derivative of $\mathbb{E}[Y_t \mid Y_{t-1} = y, Q_t^* = q^*]$ with respect to y gives

$$\begin{aligned} D_y\mathbb{E}[Y_t|Y_{t-1} = y, Q_t^* = q^*] &= \int D_y\phi(y, u; a)\, \mathrm{d}F(u, a \mid y, q^*) \\ &\quad + \int \phi(y, a; u) D_y \mathrm{d}F(u, a \mid y, q^*) \\ &= \mathbb{E}[D_y\phi_t(Y_{t-1}) \mid Y_{t-1} = y, Q_t^* = q^*] \\ &\quad + \mathbb{E}[\phi_t(Y_{t-1})\delta_t^* \mid Y_{t-1} = y, Q_t^* = q^*], \end{aligned}$$

where

$$\delta_t^* := D_y \ln \mathrm{d}F(U_t, A \mid Y_{t-1}, Q_t^*),$$

following an argument precisely parallel to that for the static case.

From this, we see that we can recover a useful measure of the effect of Y_{t-1} on Y_t, provided that the effect bias δ_t^* vanishes. An analog of A.4′ will ensure this. The analog of A.3′ is

Assumption A.3″ The distribution of $(U_t, A) \mid (Y_{t-1}, Q_t^*)$ and the structural function ϕ are such that for all admissible (y, q^*), we have

$$\begin{aligned} &D_y \int \phi(y, s, u; a, b)\, \mathrm{d}F(u, a \mid y, q^*) \\ &= \int D_y\phi(y, s, u; a, b)\, \mathrm{d}F(u, a \mid y, q^*) \\ &+ \int \phi(y, s, u; a, b) D_y \ln\, \mathrm{d}F(u, a \mid y, q^*)\, \mathrm{d}F(u, a \mid y, q^*). \end{aligned}$$

Assumption A.4″ $(U_t, A) \perp Y_{t-1} \mid Q_t^*$.

Making the time-varying and time invariant components of Q_t^* explicit, as say $Q_t^* := (\xi_t^*, B, C)$, this condition is equivalent to

$$U_t \perp Y_{t-1} \mid \xi_t^*, A, B, C \tag{9}$$

$$A \perp Y_{t-1} \mid \xi_t^*, B, C. \tag{10}$$

To investigate the plausibility of A.4$''$, we separately consider (9) and (10). As we see, this provides insight into appropriate choices for ξ_t^*.

First, consider the plausibility of (9). For simplicity and concreteness, let $\xi_t^* = (S_t, S_{t-1}, S_{t-2}, Y_{t-2}, Y_{t-3})$, and for now let B and C have dimension zero, so that $Y_t = \phi(Y_{t-1}, S_t, U_t; A)$. Suppose further that

$$U_t \perp U_{t-1} \mid \xi_t^*, A, \tag{11}$$

which is plausible when $\{U_t\}$ is viewed as a sequence of innovations. This corresponds to (and extends) the strict exogeneity assumption usually made in this literature.

By Dawid (1979, lemmas 4.1 and 4.2(i)), this implies that for any function f we have

$$U_t \perp f(U_{t-1}, \xi_t^*, A) \mid \xi_t^*, A.$$

Now $Y_{t-1} = \phi(Y_{t-2}, S_{t-1}, U_{t-1}; A)$; taking $f(U_{t-1}, \xi_t^*, A) = \phi(Y_{t-2}, S_{t-1}, U_{t-1}; A)$ gives

$$U_t \perp Y_{t-1} \mid \xi_t^*, A,$$

as desired. Note that we did not use the S_{t-2} or Y_{t-3} components of ξ_t^*; we use these next. We also did not use the S_t component of ξ_t^*, but we carry this along to ensure A.2$'$.

Now consider $A \perp Y_{t-1} \mid \xi_t^*$. For this, suppose that ϕ depends invertibly on an index of A :

$$\phi(Y_{t-2}, S_{t-1}, U_{t-1}; A) = \phi_0(Y_{t-2}, S_{t-1}, U_{t-1}; \phi_1(A)). \tag{12}$$

This includes the separable case, $\phi(Y_{t-2}, S_{t-1}, U_{t-1}; A) = \phi_0(Y_{t-2}, S_{t-1}, U_{t-1}) + \phi_1(A)$, popular in the literature. Then

$$\phi_1(A) = \phi_0^{-1}(Y_{t-2}, S_{t-1}, U_{t-1}; Y_{t-1}).$$

If we also assume

$$A \perp U_{t-1}, U_{t-2} \mid S_t, S_{t-1}, S_{t-2}, Y_{t-2}, Y_{t-3}, \tag{13}$$

we have by Dawid (1979, lemmas 4.1 and 4.2(i)) that

$$A \perp \phi_0(Y_{t-2}, S_{t-1}, U_{t-1}; \phi_0^{-1}(Y_{t-3}, S_{t-2}, U_{t-2}; Y_{t-2})) \mid \xi_t^*,$$

that is, as desired,

$$A \perp Y_{t-1} \mid \xi_t^*.$$

Here, we use each component of ξ_t^* except S_t.

More generally, ϕ may depend on multiple indexes of A. This dependence need not create difficulties for identification, as the panel structure of the data can be exploited to ensure the needed conditional exogeneity, provided ϕ is sufficiently well behaved. Specifically, suppose that ϕ depends on T indexes of A such that

$$\phi(Y_{t-1}, S_t, U_t; A) = \phi_0(Y_{t-1}, S_t, U_t; \phi_1(A), \ldots, \phi_T(A)). \tag{14}$$

Write the T equations for $t = 1, \ldots, T$ as

$$Y^T = \phi_{0,T}(Y_0^{T-1}, S^T, U^T; \phi^T(A)),$$

where $Y^T := (Y_1, \ldots, Y_T)$ (and similarly for S^T, U^T, and ϕ^T) and $Y_0^{T-1} := (Y_0, \ldots, Y_{T-1})$.

Now suppose that this system of T equations in the T unknowns $\phi^T(A)$ has a unique solution, the natural extension of the invertibility imposed in the single index case:

$$\phi^T(A) = \phi_{0,T}^{-1}(Y_0^{T-1}, S^T, U^T; Y^T).$$

To ensure that, as desired, $A \perp Y_{T-1} \mid \xi_T^*$, i.e.,

$$A \perp \phi_0(Y_{T-2}, S_{T-1}, U_{T-1}; \phi_{0,T-2}^{-1}(Y_{-2}^{T-3}, S_{-1}^{T-2}, U_{-1}^{T-2}; Y_{-1}^{T-2})) \mid \xi_T^*,$$

it suffices to assume

$$A \perp U_{-1}^{T-1} \mid S_{-1}^{T-1}, Y_{-2}^{T-2}. \tag{15}$$

From this, we see that the appropriate choice for ξ_T^* is

$$\xi_T^* = S_{-1}^{T-1}, Y_{-2}^{T-2}.$$

If the first observation available is for $t = 0$, this implies that $t = T + 2$ is the first observation to have available all the data required for estimation.

So far, we have not taken advantage of the availability of observable time-invariant covariates B and C. These can help ensure (10) for general contexts in which ϕ does not have the index structure just discussed. Specifically, suppose there exists an unobservable random variable ε such that for an (unknown) measurable function α,

$$A = \alpha(B, C, \varepsilon), \tag{16}$$

where

$$\varepsilon \perp Y_{t-1} \mid \xi_t^*, B, C, \tag{17}$$

with, for example, $\xi_t^* = (S_t, S_{t-1}, Y_{t-2})$. Then Dawid (1979, 4.1 and 4.2(i)) ensures that, as desired, (10) holds:

$$A \perp Y_{t-1} \mid \xi_t^*, B, C.$$

We also require (9), $U_t \perp Y_{t-1} \mid \xi_t^*, A, B, C$. Given $A = \alpha(B, C, \varepsilon)$ and (17), a straightforward derivation shows that it suffices that

$$U_t \perp U_{t-1} \mid \xi_t^*, B, C, \varepsilon. \tag{18}$$

Given the latitude in choosing C, this provides another means[2] of plausibly ensuring A.3$''$.

The identification of dynamic effects now follows:

Proposition 3.3 *Given A.1, A.2$'$, A.3$''$, and A.4$''$, for all* $(y, q^*) \in$ *supp* (Y_{t-1}, Q_t),

$$\begin{aligned} D_y\mathbb{E}[Y_t|Y_{t-1} = y, Q_t^* = q^*] &= \mathbb{E}[D_y\phi_t(Y_{t-1}) \mid Y_{t-1} = y, Q_t^* = q^*] \\ &= \mathbb{E}[D_y\phi_t(y) \mid Q_t^* = q^*], \quad t = 1, 2, \ldots. \end{aligned} \tag{19}$$

3.3 Binary Choice Structures

Now consider the case of a binary dependent variable, Y_t, and continuous X_t, with potential dependence between (Y_{t-1}, X_t) and (U_t, A). As mentioned in the introduction, this case can be treated with arguments similar to those above, but not exactly in the same fashion.

3.3.1 Effects of X_t

To obtain identification results for the effects of X_t, we suitably modify our previous assumptions. In particular, we specify the structure of interest as follows, absorbing B into S_t.

Assumption A.1$'$ Assumption A.1 holds with

$$\phi(Y_{t-1}, X_t, S_t, U_t; A) = \mathbb{I}\{\phi_0(Y_{t-1}, X_t, S_t; A) + U_t > 0\},$$

where ϕ_0 is an unknown measurable function and U_t is a random scalar.

---

[2] With the structure imposed here, one can define $\tilde{\phi}$, say, such that $\tilde{\phi}(Y_{t-1}, X_t, U_t, B, C, \varepsilon) := \phi(Y_{t-1}, X_t, U_t, \alpha(B, C, \varepsilon), B)$. In the $\tilde{\phi}$ representation, ε plays the role previously played in the ϕ representation by A, and (B, C) now plays the role previously played by B alone. It is thus natural that the conditions to be satisfied with respect to ε are entirely parallel to those previously required with respect to A. We maintain our original representation in terms of ϕ, because we wish to maintain variable interpretations and analysis for the non-invertible dynamic case as parallel as possible to the other cases, and the assumption that $A = \alpha(B, C, \varepsilon)$ with suitably behaved ε need not play an explicit role elsewhere. Moreover, explicitly introducing this relation here provides insight into the roles of B and C generally.

Assumption A.1′ formally specifies a data generating process where a latent variable determined by a separable structure determines a binary outcome. This reduces to the textbook binary choice fixed-effects case if $\phi_0(Y_{t-1}, X_t, S_t; A) = Y_{t-1}\delta_o + X_t'\beta_o + S_t'\gamma_o + \alpha(A)$ for some unknown vectors δ_o, β_o, and γ_o and some unknown function α. Here, however, the effect of X_t may depend on its own level and may also vary across the population as a function of both the persistent unobservable A (e.g., think of A as preferences) and the observable S_t. For simplicity, we restrict U_t to enter in an additively separable fashion. In view of previous results, this is not necessary, but to provide concrete results, we refrain from the greatest possible generality. Instead, we specify a structure that immediately nests the textbook case where $Y_t = \mathbb{I}\left\{Y_{t-1}\delta_o + X_t'\beta_o + S_t'\gamma_o + U_t + A > 0\right\}$, with $(\delta_o, \beta_o, \gamma_o)$ nonrandom and A a scalar. We also provide results covering this important special case below. Our more general case is nevertheless useful, as it nests random coefficient structures (e.g., $Y_t = \mathbb{I}\left\{Y_{t-1}\delta(A) + X_t'\beta(A) + S_t'\gamma(A) + U_t + \alpha(A) > 0\right\}$), allowing us to treat applications in, e.g., consumer demand or empirical industrial organizations, where individual consumers have heterogeneous responses, or in other fields where heterogeneity in individual responses is crucial.

Parallel to our approach in the previous sections, consider

$$\begin{aligned}\beta^*(y, x, q) :&= D_x \mathbb{E}[Y_t \mid Y_{t-1} = y, X_t = x, Q_t = q] \\ &= D_x \int \mathbb{P}\left[Y_t = 1 | Y_{t-1} = y, X_t = x, Q_t = q, A = a\right] \mathrm{d}F(a \mid y, x, q).\end{aligned}$$

We also consider the average partial derivative

$$\beta_\tau^* := \mathbb{E}\left[\beta^*(Y_{t-1}, X_t, Q_t)\tau(Y_{t-1}, X_t, Q_t)\right],$$

where τ is a user-supplied measurable weighting or trimming function. Both $\beta^*(y, x, q)$ and β_τ^* involve only the joint distribution of observable random variables and can therefore be recovered from the available data.

Parallel to A.3′, we ensure the validity of the interchange of derivative and integral with

Assumption A.3‴ The distribution of $(U_t, A) \mid (Y_{t-1}, X_t, Q_t)$ and the structural function ϕ are such that for all admissible (y, x, q), we have

$$\begin{aligned}&D_x \int \mathbb{P}\left[Y_t = 1 | Y_{t-1} = y, X_t = x, Q_t = q, A = a\right] \mathrm{d}F(a \mid y, x, q) \\ &= \int D_x \mathbb{P}\left[Y_t = 1 | Y_{t-1} = y, X_t = x, Q_t = q, A = a\right] \mathrm{d}F(a \mid y, x, q) \\ &\quad + \int \mathbb{P}\left[Y_t = 1 | Y_{t-1} = y, X_t = x, Q_t = q, A = a\right] D_x \\ &\quad \times \ln \mathrm{d}F(a \mid y, x, q)\, \mathrm{d}F(a \mid y, x, q).\end{aligned}$$

Here, A.4′ continues to apply. We also add convenient properties for ϕ_0 and U_t.

Assumption A.5 (i) For each admissible (y, s, a), $\phi_0(y, \cdot, s; a)$ is differentiable on $supp(X_t)$; (ii) For each admissible (a, y, q), $U_t \mid (A = a, Y_{t-1} = y, Q_t = q)$ has a continuous distribution with conditional density $f(\cdot \mid a, y, q)$.

We obtain the following identification result for the case of binary Y_t.

Proposition 3.4 *Suppose A.1′, A.2, A.3‴, A.4′, and A.5 hold. (i) Then for all* $(y, q) \in$ *supp* (Y_{t-1}, Q_t), $x \in$ *supp* $(X_t \mid Y_{t-1} = y, Q_t = q)$, *and* $t = 1, 2, \ldots,$

$$\begin{aligned}\beta^*(y, x, q) &= \mathbb{E}[D_x \mathbb{P}\left[Y_t = 1 | Y_{t-1}, X_t, Q_t, A\right] \mid Y_{t-1} = y, X_t = x, Q_t = q] \\ &= -\mathbb{E}(D_x \phi_0(Y_{t-1}, x, S_t; A) \\ &\quad \times f(-\phi_o(Y_{t-1}, x, S_t; A) \mid A, Y_{t-1}, Q_t) \mid Y_{t-1} = y, Q_t = q).\end{aligned}$$

(ii) If $\phi_0(y, x, s, a) = x'\beta_o + \tilde{\phi}_0(y, s, a)$, *where* β_o *is an unknown real vector and* $\tilde{\phi}_0$ *is an unknown measurable function, then for all* $(y, q) \in$ *supp* (Y_{t-1}, Q_t) *and* $x \in$ *supp* $(X_t \mid Y_{t-1} = y, Q_t = q)$,

$$\begin{aligned}&\beta^*(y, x, q) = \beta_o \, \bar{\psi}(y, x, q) \quad where \\ &\bar{\psi}(y, x, q) := -\mathbb{E}(f(-\phi_0(Y_{t-1}, x, S_t; A) \mid A, Y_{t-1}, Q_t) \mid Y_{t-1} = y, Q_t = q).\end{aligned}$$

Consequently,

$$\beta_\tau^* \propto \beta_o.$$

3.3.2 Effects of Y_{t-1}

Because Y_{t-1} is binary, we are interested in discrete effects, and not marginal effects. The situation is closely parallel to the classical treatment effects framework, where interest attaches to the effects of a binary treatment, such as the average effect of treatment on the treated or the average affect of treatment.

Here, we relax Assumption A.1′ to remove the separability in U_t. We now absorb both X_t and B into S_t.

Assumption A.1″ Assumption A.1 holds with

$$\phi(Y_{t-1}, S_t, U_t; A) = \mathbb{I}\{\phi_1(Y_{t-1}, S_t, U_t; A) > 0\},$$

where ϕ_1 is an unknown measurable function.

To define the effects of interest, we first define the potential responses associated with our data generating process. The potential responses for $y = 0, 1$ are

$$Y_{y,t} := \mathbb{I}\{\phi_1(y, S_t, U_t; A) > 0\}.$$

The analog of the covariate-conditioned effect of treatment on the treated is then

$$\gamma_1(q^*) := \mathbb{E}[Y_{1,t} - Y_{0,t} \mid Y_{t-1} = 1, Q_t^* = q^*].$$

The analog of the average effect of treatment on the treated is

$$\bar{\gamma}_1 := \mathbb{E}[Y_{1,t} - Y_{0,t} \mid Y_{t-1} = 1] = \mathbb{E}(\mathbb{E}[Y_{1,t} - Y_{0,t} \mid Y_{t-1} = 1, Q_t^*] \mid Y_{t-1} = 1).$$

Analogous effects can be defined for the effect of treatment on the untreated or the average effect of treatment, but, as the analysis is similar, we leave this aside for brevity.

To identify the desired effects, we observe that for all $y, y' \in \{0, 1\}$ we have

$$\begin{aligned}
\mathbb{E}\Big[Y_t | Y_{t-1} &= y, Q_t^* = q^*\Big] \\
&= \int \mathbb{I}\{\phi_1(y, s, u; a) > 0\}\, \mathrm{d}F(u, a \mid y, q^*) \quad (\text{by} A.1'') \\
&= \int \mathbb{I}\{\phi_1(y, s, u; a) > 0\}\, \mathrm{d}F(u, a \mid q^*) \quad (\text{by} A.4'') \\
&= \int \mathbb{I}\{\phi_1(y, s, u; a) > 0\}\, \mathrm{d}F(u, a \mid y', q^*) \quad (\text{by} A.4'') \\
&= \int [\int \mathbb{I}\{\phi_1(y, s, u; a) > 0\}\, \mathrm{d}F(u \mid y', q^*, a)]\, \mathrm{d}F(a \mid y', q^*) \\
&= \int \mathbb{E}[Y_{y,t} \mid Y_{t-1} = y', Q_t^* = q^*, A = a]\, \mathrm{d}F(a \mid y', q^*).
\end{aligned}$$

It follows that

$$\begin{aligned}
\mathbb{E}\Big[Y_{1,t} &- Y_{0,t} \mid Y_{t-1} = 1, Q_t^* = q^*\Big] \\
&= \int \mathbb{E}[Y_{1,t} - Y_{0,t} \mid Y_{t-1} = 1, Q_t^* = q^*, A = a] \mathrm{d}F(a \mid 1, q^*) \\
&= \int \mathbb{E}[Y_{1,t} \mid Y_{t-1} = 1, Q_t^* = q^*, A = a]\, \mathrm{d}F(a \mid 1, q^*) \\
&\quad - \int \mathbb{E}[Y_{0,t} \mid Y_{t-1} = 1, Q_t^* = q^*, A = a]\, \mathrm{d}F(a \mid 1, q^*) \\
&= \mathbb{E}[Y_t \mid Y_{t-1} = 1, Q_t^* = q^*] - \mathbb{E}[Y_t \mid Y_{t-1} = 0, Q_t^* = q^*].
\end{aligned}$$

Formally, we have

Proposition 3.5 *Suppose A.1″, A.2′, and A.4″ hold. (i) Then for all* $q^* \in$ *supp* (Q_t^*)

$$\gamma_1(q^*) = \mathbb{E}[Y_t \mid Y_{t-1} = 1, Q_t^* = q^*] - \mathbb{E}[Y_t \mid Y_{t-1} = 0, Q_t^* = q^*].$$

(ii) We also have

$$\bar{\gamma}_1 = \mathbb{E}[Y_t \mid Y_{t-1} = 1] - \mathbb{E}(\mathbb{E}[Y_t \mid Y_{t-1} = 0, Q_t^*] \mid Y_{t-1} = 1).$$

4 Estimation

Although our main goal is to obtain the new identification results of Sect. 3, the implications of these results for estimation deserve careful consideration. The identified effects can be represented either in terms of conditional expectations (Proposition 3.5(i)), derivatives of conditional expectations (Proposition 3.1–3.4(i)), or partial means (averages) of conditional expectations or their derivatives (Proposition 3.5(ii) and 3.4(ii)). To estimate these effects, we thus seek a convenient estimator of conditional expectation that also reliably estimates the conditional expectation derivatives and lends itself to averaging. We propose using local linear regression (e.g., Cleveland 1979), as it readily meets these criteria.

Significantly, the presence of both continuous and discrete regressors is essential for realistic application of Propositions 3.1–3.3 and necessary for application of Propositions 3.4 and 3.5. The traditional analysis of local linear regression (e.g., Fan (1992), Ruppert and Wand (1994), Fan and Gijbels (1996), and Masry (1997)) assumes continuous regressors. The available asymptotic theory for local linear regression in the mixed continuous-discrete case rests on foundational work by Li and Racine (2004). Nevertheless, the theory required for our proposed estimators is not yet available. Development of this theory is actively under way, but the challenges it presents place further development here well beyond our present scope. Accordingly, our goals for this section are restricted to describing our proposed estimators, discussing their known or expected properties, and suggesting useful directions for their further development.

4.1 Estimating Covariate-Conditioned Effects

We assume that for each period t we have data on a panel of $n = n_t$ individuals. For simplicity, we assume that observations are independent and identically distributed (IID) and that any missing observations are missing at random. Consistent with our nonparametric approach, we propose estimating separate relationships for each time period. This is the nonparametric analog of the parametric practice of including time dummies for each period.

The local linear regression estimator solves the weighted least squares problem

$$\hat{\theta}_{n,t}(w) = \arg\min_{\theta \in \Theta} \sum_{i=1}^{n} [Y_{i,t} - g(W_{i,t}^c, \theta)]^2 K_{\hat{h}}(W_{i,t} - w).$$

Depending on the application, $W_{i,t}$ may be $(X_{i,t}, Q_{i,t})$ (Proposition 3.1), $(Y_{i,t-1}, X_{i,t}, Q_{i,t})$ (Proposition 3.2 and 3.4), or $(Y_{i,t-1}, Q^*_{i,t})$ (Proposition 3.3 and 3.5). $W^c_{i,t}$ denotes the continuously distributed elements of $W_{i,t}$. The term $g(W^c_{i,t}, \theta) = \alpha + W^{c\prime}_{i,t}\beta$ represents the local linear regression, with parameters $\theta := (\alpha, \beta')'$. For Propositions 3.4 and 3.5, we have a binary lagged dependent variable, $Y_{i,t-1}$, so $W_{i,t}$ necessarily contains one or more discretely distributed components, denoted $W^d_{i,t}$. Whenever derivatives of the conditional expectation are of interest, the associated variables (i.e., $X_{i,t}$ and $Y_{i,t-1}$) are elements of $W^c_{i,t}$. Other regressors may belong to either $W^c_{i,t}$ or $W^d_{i,t}$.

When all elements of $W_{i,t} := (W_{i,t,\ell}, \ell = 1, \ldots, q)$ are continuous, $K_{\hat{h}}$ is a product kernel:

$$K_{\hat{h}}(W_{i,t} - w) = \prod_{\ell=1}^{q} \hat{h}_\ell^{-1} k(\frac{W_{i,t,\ell} - w_\ell}{\hat{h}_\ell}),$$

where $w := (w_1, \ldots, w_q)'$ defines the regressor values of interest; k is a univariate kernel; and $\hat{h}_\ell$ is a variable-specific bandwidth, either given a priori or data determined. Li and Racine (2004) recommend choosing $\hat{h}_\ell$ by cross-validation or by using the corrected AIC method of Hurvich, Simonoff and Tsai (1998).

When $W_{i,t}$ contains discrete regressors, Li and Racine (2004) distinguish between discrete variables having a natural ordering (e.g., income categories), denoted $\tilde{W}^d_{i,t}$, and those that do not (e.g., ethnicity), denoted $\bar{W}^d_{i,t}$, so that $W^d_{i,t} := (\tilde{W}^{d\prime}_{i,t}, \bar{W}^{d\prime}_{i,t})'$. In this case the kernel is

$$K_{\hat{h}}(W_{i,t} - w) = \prod_{\ell=1}^{q} \hat{h}_\ell^{-1} k(\frac{W^c_{i,t,\ell} - w^c_\ell}{\hat{h}_\ell}) \times \prod_{\ell=1}^{r_1} \hat{\lambda}_\ell^{|\tilde{W}^d_{i,t,\ell} - \tilde{w}^d_\ell|} \times \prod_{\ell=r_1+1}^{r} \hat{\lambda}_\ell^{\mathbb{I}\{\bar{W}^d_{i,t,\ell} \neq \bar{w}^d_\ell\}},$$

where $\hat{\lambda}_\ell \in [0, 1]$ is a variable-specific weighting parameter, either given a priori or data determined (e.g., using the corrected AIC). See Li and Racine (2004) and Li, Racine, and Wooldridge (2009) for further background and details. A computer implementation of these procedures is available in the R library package *np*.

When we are interested in covariate-conditioned average marginal effects, i.e., for all cases except that of Proposition 3.5, we use $\hat{\beta}_{n,t}(w)$ as our estimator. When we are interested in the conditional expectation, as in Proposition 3.5(i), we use $\hat{\alpha}_{n,t}(w)$.

Determining the properties of $\hat{\theta}_{n,t}(w)$ is an active area of research. So far, only the properties of $\hat{\alpha}_{n,t}(w)$ in the mixed continuous-discrete case with data-determined $\hat{h}$ and $\hat{\lambda}$ have been fully settled (Li and Racine 2004, Theorem 3.2). Study of the properties of $\hat{\beta}_{n,t}(w)$ in the mixed continuous-discrete case with data-determined $\hat{h}$ and $\hat{\lambda}$ is underway, but so far results for this case are not available. In fact, results are not yet available even for $\hat{\beta}_{n,t}(w)$ in the mixed continuous-discrete case with $\hat{h}$ and $\hat{\lambda}$ given a priori (rather than being data determined). Nevertheless, based on results so far available, we may expect that $\hat{\beta}_{n,t}(w)$ will be asymptotically normal, with a rate identical to that known for $\hat{\alpha}_{n,t}(w)$.

On the other hand, results for given $\hat{h} = h_n$ when all regressors are continuous, as may hold for Propositions 3.1–3.3, are immediately available from Li and Racine (2007, Theorem 2.7). As the currently available asymptotic normality results of Li and Racine (2007, Theorem 2.7) and Li and Racine (2004, Theorem 3.2) apply to the estimators recommended here directly and without any modification in this case, we conserve space by not restating those results. See also Hoderlein and White (2011).

We hope that the identification results of the previous section will act as motivation and encouragement for the development of asymptotic distribution results for $\hat{\beta}_{n,t}(w)$ in the general case. We further suggest that it would be of interest to have results describing the joint distribution of $\hat{\beta}_{n,t}(w)$, $t = 1, \ldots, T$, for fixed finite T. Such results could be used to test whether effects are stable across time. Moreover, when effects are plausibly stable over time (either a priori or empirically) such results would enable construction of a more efficient estimator of the effects of interest as a suitably weighted average of the estimators for individual time periods.

4.2 Estimating Partial Means

To estimate the average partial derivative

$$\beta_\tau^* := \mathbb{E}\left[\beta^*(Y_{t-1}, X_t, Q_t)\tau(Y_{t-1}, X_t, Q_t)\right],$$

one can form

$$\hat{\beta}_{\tau,n,t} := n^{-1}\sum_{i=1}^{n} \hat{\beta}_{n,t}(Y_{i,t-1}, X_{i,t}, Q_{i,t})\ \tau(Y_{i,t-1}, X_{i,t}, Q_{i,t}).$$

This quantity is a partial mean, so once a suitable asymptotic representation is available for $\hat{\beta}_{n,t}(w)$, Theorem 4.1 of Newey (1994) can be applied to give conditions ensuring the asymptotic normality of $\hat{\beta}_{\tau,n,t}$. The analysis for this is expected to closely parallel that of Hoderlein and White (2011, Theorem 5).

For the binary lagged dependent variable case, we avoid problems associated with the tails of Q_t^* by considering a trimmed version of $\bar{\gamma}_1$ analogous to β_τ^*, namely

$$\gamma_{1,\tau}^* := \mathbb{E}\left[\gamma_1(Q_t^*)\ \tau_1(Q_t^*) \mid Y_{t-1} = 1\right],$$

where τ_1 is a trimming function that downweights observations in the tails of Q_t^*. A straightforward estimator of $\gamma_{1,\tau}^*$ follows by averaging $\hat{\alpha}_{n,t}(Y_{i,t-1}, Q_{i,t}^*)$ over the sample where $Y_{i,t-1} = 1$:

$$\hat{\gamma}_{1,\tau,n,t} := n_1^{-1} \sum_{\{i:Y_{i,t-1}=1\}} \hat{\alpha}_{n,t}(1, Q_{i,t}^*)\tau_1(Q_{i,t}^*),$$

where n_1 is the number of observations in period t with $Y_{i,t-1} = 1$.

Alternatively, one can form an estimator using the propensity score, parallel to Li, Racine, and Wooldridge (2009). Following their approach, we can write

$$Y_t = Y_{0,t} + \gamma(Q_t^*)Y_{t-1} + \varepsilon_t,$$

where $\varepsilon_t := Y_t - E(Y_t \mid Y_{t-1}, Q_t^*)$ and $\gamma(Q_t^*) := \mathbb{E}[Y_{1,t} - Y_{0,t} \mid Y_{t-1}, Q_t^*] = \mathbb{E}[Y_{1,t} - Y_{0,t} \mid Q_t^*]$. It follows that

$$\bar{\gamma}_1 = \mathbb{E}(\mathbb{E}[Y_{1,t} - Y_{0,t} \mid Y_{t-1} = 1, Q_t^*] \mid Y_{t-1} = 1) = \mathbb{E}(\gamma(Q_t^*) \mid Y_{t-1} = 1).$$

We also have $\gamma(Q_t^*) = cov(Y_t, Y_{t-1} \mid Q_t^*)/var(Y_{t-1} \mid Q_t^*)$. Letting $p(Q_t^*) := \mathbb{P}[Y_{t-1} = 1 \mid Q_t^*]$ represent the propensity score relevant here, we have

$$\begin{aligned}\bar{\gamma}_1 &= \mathbb{E}\left(\frac{Y_t(Y_{t-1} - p(Q_t^*))}{var(Y_{t-1} \mid Q_t^*)} \mid Y_{t-1} = 1\right) = \mathbb{E}\left(\frac{Y_t(1 - p(Q_t^*))}{var(Y_{t-1} \mid Q_t^*)} \mid Y_{t-1} = 1\right)\\ &= \mathbb{E}\left(\frac{Y_t(1 - p(Q_t^*))}{p(Q_t^*)(1 - p(Q_t^*))} \mid Y_{t-1} = 1\right) = \mathbb{E}\left(\frac{Y_t}{p(Q_t^*)} \mid Y_{t-1} = 1\right),\end{aligned}$$

where we use the fact that $var(Y_{t-1} \mid Q_t^*) = p(Q_t^*)(1 - p(Q_t^*))$, since Y_{t-1} is binary.

Li, Racine, and Wooldridge (2009) propose a local linear estimator of $p(Q_t^*)$ for the mixed continuous-discrete case, say $\hat{p}_{n,t}(Q_t^*)$. Using this, we can construct an estimator of $\gamma_{1,\tau}^*$ as

$$\tilde{\gamma}_{1,\tau,n,t} := n_1^{-1} \sum_{\{i: Y_{i,t-1}=1\}} \frac{Y_{i,t}}{\hat{p}_{n,t}(Q_{i,t}^*)} \tau_1(Q_{i,t}^*).$$

From this, it is clear that the trimming should remove values of $\hat{p}_{n,t}(Q_{i,t}^*)$ close to zero.

Developing the formal asymptotic distribution theory for $\hat{\gamma}_{1,\tau,n,t}$ and $\tilde{\gamma}_{1,\tau,n,t}$ is beyond our scope here. But see Li, Racine, and Wooldridge (2009) for further details and a complete asymptotic theory for a nonparametric propensity score-based estimator of the average effect of treatment in the mixed continuous-discrete case.

5 Summary and Concluding Remarks

This chapter provides an approach to identifying effects of interest in nonseparable panel data models when the relationship of interest depends structurally on the lagged dependent variable. This case is important, as it falls outside the scope of the approaches of Graham and Powell (2010) and Hoderlein and White (2011).

Our approach relies on the use of control functions (covariates) to ensure the independence between the causes of interest (Y_{t-1} or X_t) and the transitory and persistent unobservables, U_t and A, conditional on appropriate controls, which may contain both time-varying and time-invariant components. The time-varying components may include both leads and lags relative to time t. We further show how suitable control variable candidates can arise from the panel data structure. Finally, we show how this method extends to cover the identification of effects in dynamic panel data binary choice models with endogenous causes and state dependence.

As we discuss, convenient estimators for the effects identified here can be constructed using local linear regression for the mixed continuous-discrete regressor case. Theory for these estimators applicable to the present context is still under development. The results given here should serve as motivation and encouragement for this effort. We also suggest useful directions for the further development of this theory.

Mathematical Appendix

The proofs of Propositions 3.1–3.3 and 3.5 are as given in the text.

Proof of Proposition 3.4 (i) Given A.1′, A.2, and A.3‴, we have

$$\begin{aligned}\beta^*(y,x,q) &= D_x \int \mathbb{P}\left[Y_t = 1 | Y_{t-1} = y, X_t = x, Q_t = q, A = a\right] \mathrm{d}F(a \mid y,x,q)\\ &= \int D_x\mathbb{P}\left[Y_t = 1 | Y_{t-1} = y, X_t = x, Q_t = q, A = a\right] \mathrm{d}F(a \mid y,x,q)\\ &\quad + \int \mathbb{P}\left[Y_t = 1 | Y_{t-1} = y, X_t = x, Q_t = q, A = a\right] D_x\\ &\quad \times \ln \mathrm{d}F(a \mid y,x,q)\, \mathrm{d}F(a \mid y,x,q).\end{aligned}$$

Given A.4′, this becomes

$$\beta^*(y,x,q) = \int D_x\mathbb{P}\left[Y_t = 1 | Y_{t-1} = y, X_t = x, Q_t = q, A = a\right] \mathrm{d}F(a \mid y,q).$$

Now

$$\begin{aligned}D_x\mathbb{P}[Y_t &= 1 | Y_{t-1} = y, X_t = x, Q_t = q, A = a]\\ &= D_x \int \mathbb{I}\{\phi_0(y,x,s;a) + u > 0\}\, \mathrm{d}F(u \mid a,y,x,q) \quad \text{(by A.1}'\text{)}\\ &= D_x \int \mathbb{I}\{\phi_0(y,x,s;a) + u > 0\}\, \mathrm{d}F(u \mid a,y,q) \quad \text{(by A.4}'\text{)}\\ &= D_x F(-\phi_0(y,x,s;a) \mid a,y,q)\end{aligned}$$

$$= -D_x\phi_0(y,x,s;a)\, f(-\phi_0(y,x,s;a) \mid a,y,q). \quad \text{(by A.5)}$$

Thus,

$$\begin{aligned}\beta^*(y,x,q) &= \int -D_x\phi_0(y,x,s;a)\, f(-\phi_0(y,x,s;a) \mid a,y,q)\,\mathrm{d}F(a \mid y,q)\\ &= -\mathbb{E}(D_x\phi_0(Y_{t-1},x,S_t;A)\\ &\quad \times f(\phi_0(Y_{t-1},x,S_t;A) \mid A, Y_{t-1}, Q_t) \mid Y_{t-1}=y, Q_t=q).\end{aligned}$$

(ii) The proof is immediate and is omitted.

References

Altonji, J., and R. Matzkin (2005): "Cross Section and Panel Data Estimators for Nonseparable Models with Endogenous Regressors", Econometrica, 73, 1053–1103.

Arellano, M. (2003): "Discrete Choice with Panel Data", Investigaciones Economicas, 27, 423–458.

Arellano, M. and R. Carrasco (2003): "Binary Choice Panel Data Models with Predetermined Variables", Journal of Econometrics, 115, 125–157.

Bester, A. and C. Hansen (2008),"Identification of Marginal Effects in a Nonparametric Correlated Random Effects Model", Journal of Business and Economic Statistics, forthcoming.

Chamberlain, G. (1982), "Multivariate Regression Models for Panel Data", Journal of Econometrics, 18(1), 5–46.

Chamberlain, G. (1984): "Panel Data", in Z. Griliches and M.D. Intriligator (eds.), Handbook of Econometrics, Vol. 2. New York: North Holland.

Chamberlain, G. (1992): "Binary Response Models for Panel Data: Identification and Information", Harvard University Working Paper.

Chernozhukov, V., I. Fernandez-Val, J. Hahn, and W. Newey (2009): "Identification and Estimation of Marginal Effects in Nonlinear Panel Models", MIT Working Paper.

Cleveland, W.S. (1979): "Robust Locally Weighted Regression and Smoothing Scatterplots", Journal of the American Statistical Association, 74, 829–836.

Dawid, A.P. (1979): "Conditional Independence in Statistical Theory", Journal of the Royal Statistical Society Series B, 41, 1–31.

Dudley, R.M. (2002). Real analysis and probability. Cambridge: Cambridge University Press.

Evdokimov, K. (2009): "Identification and Estimation of a Nonparametric Panel Data Model with Unobserved Heterogeneity", Yale University, Working paper.

Fan, J. (1992): "Design-adaptive Nonparametric Regression", Journal of the American Statistical Association, 87, 998–1004.

Fan J., and I. Gijbels (1996). Local Polynomial Modelling and its Applications. London: Chapman and Hall.

Fan, J. and Q. Yao (1998): "Efficient Estimation of Conditional Variance Functions in Stochastic Regression", Biometrika, 85, 645–660.

Graham, B., and J. Powell (2010): "Identification and Estimation of 'Irregular' Correlated Random Coefficient Models", NBER Working Paper 14469.

Hausman, J., B. Hall, and Z. Griliches (1984): "Econometric Models for Count Data with an Application to the Patents-R&D Relationship", Econometrica, 52, 909–938.

Heckman, J. and T. MaCurdy, (1980), "A Life-Cycle Model of Female Labour Supply", Review of Economic Studies, 47, pp. 47–74.

Heckman, J. J. Smith, and N. Clements (1997): "Making The Most Out of Programme Evaluations and Social Experiments: Accounting for Heterogeneity in Programme Impacts", Review of Economic Studies, 64, 487–535.

Heckman, J. and E. Vytlacil (2007): "Econometric Evaluation of Social Programs", in: Handbook of Econometrics, Vol. 6b, Heckman, J. and E. Leamer (eds.), North Holland.

Hoderlein, S. (2005): "Nonparametric Demand Systems, Instrumental Variables and a Heterogeneous Population", Brown University Working Paper.

Hoderlein, S. (2011): "How Many Consumers are Rational?", Journal of Econometrics, forthcoming.

Hoderlein, S., and E. Mammen (2007): "Identification of Marginal Effects in Nonseparable Models without Monotonicity", Econometrica, 75, 1513–1519.

Hoderlein, S., and Y. Sasaki (2011): "On the Role of Time in Nonseparable Panel Data Models", Boston College Working Paper.

Hoderlein, S. and H. White (2011): "Nonparametric Identification in Nonseparable Panel Data Models with Generalized Fixed Effects", Boston College Working Paper.

Honore, B. and E. Kyriazidou (2000): "Panel Data Discrete Choice Models with Lagged Dependent Variables", Econometrica, 68, 839–874.

Hurvich, C.M., Simonoff J.S. and C.-L. Tsai (1998): "Smoothing Parameter Selection in Nonparametric Regression Using an Improved Akaike Information Criterion", Vol. 60, part 2, pp. 271–293.

Imbens, G. and W. Newey (2009): "Identification and Estimation of Triangular Simultaneous Equations Models Without Additivity", Econometrica, 77, 1481–1512.

Li, Q. and J. Racine (2004): "Cross-Validated Local Linear Nonparametric Regression", Statistica Sinica, 14, 485–512.

Li, Q. and J. Racine (2007): Nonparametric Econometrics: Theory and Practice. Princeton: Princeton University Press.

Li, Q., Racine, J. and J. Wooldridge (2009). "Efficient Estimation of Average Treatment Effects with Mixed Categorical and Continuous Data", Journal of Business & Economic Statistics, American Statistical Association, vol. 27(2), 206–223.

Newey, W. (1994): "Kernel Estimation of Partial Means and a General Variance Estimator", Econometric Theory, 10, 233–253.

Schennach, S., H. White, and K. Chalak (2011): "Local Indirect Least Squares and Average Marginal Effects in Nonseparable Structural Systems", UCSD Working Paper.

White, H. and K. Chalak (2011): "Identification and Identification Failure for Treatment Effects using Structural Models", UCSD Working Paper.

White, H. and P. Kennedy (2009):"Retrospective Estimation of Causal Effects Through Time", in J. Castle and N. Shephard (eds.) The Methodology and Practice of Econometrics: A Festschrift in Honour of David F. Hendry. Oxford: Oxford University Press, pp. 59–87.

White, H. and X. Lu (2011): "Efficient Estimation of Treatment Effects and Underlying Structure", UCSD Working Paper.

Wooldridge, J. (2002): Econometrics of Cross Section and Panel Data. Cambridge, MA: MIT Press.

Wooldridge, J. (2005): "Fixed-Effects and Related Estimators for Correlated Random-Coefficient and Treatment-Effect Panel Data Models", The Review of Economics and Statistics, 87, 385–390.

Consistent Model Selection: Over Rolling Windows

Atsushi Inoue, Barbara Rossi and Lu Jin

Abstract In this chapter we analyze asymptotic properties of the simulated out-of -sample predictive mean squared error (PMSE) criterion based on a rolling window when selecting among nested forecasting models. When the window size is a fixed fraction of the sample size, Inoue and Kilian (J Econ 130: 273–306, 2006) show that the PMSE criterion is inconsistent. We consider alternative schemes under which the rolling PMSE criterion is consistent. When the window size diverges slower than the sample size at a suitable rate, we show that the rolling PMSE criterion selects the correct model with probability approaching one when parameters are constant or when they are time varying. We provide Monte Carlo evidence and illustrate the usefulness of the proposed methods in forecasting inflation.

1 Introduction

It is a common practice to compare models by out-of-sample predictive mean squared error (PMSE). For example, Meese and Rogoff (1983a,b) and Swanson and White (1997) compare models according to their PMSE calculated in rolling windows. Another common practice is to use a consistent information criterion such as the

A. Inoue (✉)
Department of Agricultural and Resource Economics, North Carolina State University, Campus Box 8109, Raleigh, NC 27695-8109, USA
e-mail: atsushi@unity.ncsu.edu

B. Rossi
ICREA-UPF, Barcelona GSE and CR, calle Ramon Trias Fargas 25-27, Barcelona 08005, SPAIN
e-mail: barbara.rossi@upf.edu

L. Jin
Department of Economics, North Carolina State University, Campus Box 8110, Raleigh, NC 27695-8110, USA
e-mail: ljin@unity.ncsu.edu

X. Chen and N. R. Swanson (eds.), *Recent Advances and Future Directions in Causality, Prediction, and Specification Analysis*, DOI: 10.1007/978-1-4614-1653-1_12,

Schwarz Information Criterion (SIC), used for example in Swanson and White (1997). Information criteria and the out-of-sample PMSE criteria deal with the issue of overfitting inherent in the in-sample PMSE criterion. Information criteria penalizes overparameterized models via penalty terms and are easy to compute. The out-of-sample PMSE criteria simulate out-of-sample forecasts and are very intuitive.[1]

In a recent chapter, Inoue and Kilian (2006) show that the recursive and rolling PMSE criteria are inconsistent and recommend that consistent in-sample information criteria, such as the SIC, be used in model selection. They also show that even when there is structural change these out-of-sample PMSE criteria are not necessarily consistent. Their results are based on the assumption that the window size is proportional to the sample size.

In this chapter we consider an alternative framework in which the window size goes to infinity at a slower rate than the sample size. Under this assumption we show that the rolling-window PMSE criterion is consistent for selecting nesting linear forecasting models. When the nesting model is the truth, the criterion selects the nesting model with probability approaching one because the parameters and thus the PMSE are consistently estimated as the window size diverges. When the nested model is generating the data, the quadratic term in the quadratic expansion of the loss difference becomes dominant when the window size is small. Because the quadratic form is always positive, the criterion will select the nested model with probability approaching one. When the window size is large, however, the linear term and the quadratic term are of the same order and the sign cannot be determined. By letting the window size diverge slowly, the rolling PMSE criterion is consistent under a variety of environments, when parameters are constant or when they are time varying.

When the window size diverges at a slower rate than the sample size, the rolling regression estimator can be viewed as a nonparametric estimator (Giraitis et al. 2011) and time-varying parameters are consistently estimated. We show that our rolling-window PMSE criterion remains consistent even when parameters are time varying. When the window size is large, that is, when it is assumed to go to infinity at the same rate as the total sample size, the criterion is not consistent because the rolling regression estimator is oversmoothed. In the time-varying parameter case, the conventional information criterion is not consistent in general.

This chapter is related to, and different from, the works by West (1996); Clark and McCracken (2001); Giacomini and White (2006); Giacomini and Rossi (2010), and Rossi and Inoue (2011) in several ways. West (1996) and Clark and McCracken (2001) focus on comparing models' relative to forecasting performance when the window size is a fixed fraction of the total sample size,whereas Giacomini and

[1] The out-of-sample PMSE criteria are based on simulated out-of-sample predictions where parameters are estimated from a subsample to predict an observation outside the subsample. When subsamples always start with the first observation and use consecutive observations whose number is increasing, we call the simulated quadratic loss the recursive PMSE criterion. When subsamples are based on the same number of observations and are moving, we call the simulated quadratic loss the rolling PMSE criterion and the number of observations in the subsamples is the window size. See Inoue and Kilian (2006) for more technical definitions of these criteria.

White (2006) focus on the case where the window size is constant; this chapter focuses instead on the case where the window size goes to infinity but at a slower rate than the total sample size. Giacomini and Rossi (2010) argue that, in the presence of instabilities, traditional tests of predictive ability may be invalid, since they focus on the forecasting performance of the models on average over the out-of-sample portion of the data. To avoid the problem, they propose to compare models' relative predictive ability in the presence of instabilities by using a rolling window approach over the out-of-sample portion of the data. The latter helps them to follow the relative performance of the models as it evolves over time. In this chapter we focus on consistent model selection procedures, instead, rather than testing; furthermore, our focus is not to compare models' predictive performance over time, rather to select the best forecasting model asymptotically. Rossi and Inoue (2011) focus on the problem of performing inference on predictive ability that is robust to the choice of the window size. In this chapter, instead, we take as given the choice of the window size and our objective is not to perform tests; we focus instead on understanding whether it is possible to consistently select the true model depending on the size of the window relative to the total sample size.

The rest of this chapter is organized as follows: In Sect. 2 we establish the consistency of the rolling PMSE criterion under the standard stationary environment as well as under the time-varying parameter environment. In Sect. 3 we investigate the finite-sample properties of the rolling-window PMSE criterion. Section 4 demonstrates the usefulness of our criteria in forecasting inflation. Section 5 concludes.

2 Asymptotic Theory

Consider two nesting linear forecasting models, models 1 and 2, to generate h-steps ahead direct forecasts (where h is finite):

$$\text{Model 1}: y_{t+h} = \alpha^{*\prime} x_t + u_{t+h}, \tag{1}$$

$$\text{Model 2}: y_{t+h} = \beta' z_t + v_{t+h} \quad = \quad \alpha' x_t + \gamma' w_t + v_{t+h}, \tag{2}$$

where $\dim(\alpha) = k$ and $\dim(\beta) = l$. The first terms on the right-hand sides of Eqs. (1) and (2), $\alpha^{*\prime} x_t$ and $\beta' z_t$ are the population linear projections of y_{t+h} on x_t and z_t, respectively. Thus, z_t is uncorrelated with v_{t+h}, $\alpha^* = [E(x_t x_t')]^{-1} E(x_t y_{t+h})$ and $\beta = [E(z_t z_t')]^{-1} E(z_t y_{t+h})$.

Define the population quadratic loss of each model by

$$\sigma_1^2 = \lim_{T\to\infty} \tfrac{1}{T-h} \sum_{t=1}^{T-h} E[(y_{t+h} - \alpha' x_t)^2] = \lim_{T\to\infty} \tfrac{1}{T-h} \sum_{t=1}^{T-h} E(u_{t+h}^2),$$

$$\sigma_2^2 = \lim_{T\to\infty} \tfrac{1}{T-h} \sum_{t=1}^{T-h} E[(y_{t+h} - \beta' z_t)^2] = \lim_{T\to\infty} \tfrac{1}{T-h} \sum_{t=1}^{T-h} E(v_{t+h}^2).$$

Our goal is to select the model with smallest quadratic loss.

Let the window size used for parameter estimation be denoted by W for some $W > h$. Define the rolling ordinary least squares (OLS) estimators as follows, for $t = W + 1, ..., T$:

$$\hat{\alpha}_{t,W} = \left(\sum_{s=t-W}^{t-h} x_s x_s' \right)^{-1} \sum_{s=t-W}^{t-h} x_s y_{s+h}, \tag{3}$$

$$\hat{\beta}_{t,W} = \left(\sum_{s=t-W}^{t-h} z_s z_s' \right)^{-1} \sum_{s=t-W}^{t-h} z_s y_{s+h}, \tag{4}$$

and the associated rolling PMSEs by:

$$\hat{\sigma}^2_{1,W} = \frac{1}{T-h-W} \sum_{t=W+1}^{T-h} \hat{u}^2_{t+h}, \tag{5}$$

$$\hat{\sigma}^2_{2,W} = \frac{1}{T-h-W} \sum_{t=W+1}^{T-h} \hat{v}^2_{t+h}, \tag{6}$$

where $\hat{u}_{t+h} = y_{t+h} - \hat{\alpha}'_{t,W} x_t$, $\hat{v}_{t+h} = y_{t+h} - \hat{\beta}'_{t,W} z_t$. We say that the rolling PMSE criterion is consistent if

- $\hat{\sigma}^2_{1,W} < \hat{\sigma}^2_{2,W}$ with probability approaching one if $\sigma_1^2 = \sigma_2^2$; and
- $\hat{\sigma}^2_{1,W} > \hat{\sigma}^2_{2,W}$ with probability approaching one if $\sigma_1^2 > \sigma_2^2$.

Under what conditions on the window size is the rolling PMSE criterion consistent? The existing results are not positive. When the window size is *large relative to the sample size* (i.e., $\exists\lambda \in (0, 1)$ s.t. $W = \lambda T + o(T)$), Inoue and Kilian (2005) show that the criterion is not consistent. Specifically, when $\sigma_1^2 = \sigma_2^2$, they show that the criterion selects model 2 with a positive probability resulting in the overparameterized model. We will discuss this result in more detail in the next section, where we will compare it with the theoretical results proposed in this chapter.

When the window size is *very small* (i.e., W is a fixed constant), it is straightforward to show that the criterion may not be consistent. For example, compare the zero-forecast model ($x_t = \emptyset$) and the constant-forecast model ($w_t = 1$) with $W = h = 1$. Suppose that $y_{t+1} = c + u_{t+1}$, where $u_t \sim iid(c, \sigma^2)$. Note that $\sigma_1^2 = c^2 + \sigma^2$ and $\sigma_2^2 = \sigma^2$. Since

$$\hat{\sigma}^2_{1,1} = \tfrac{1}{T-1} \sum_{t=1}^{T-1} y^2_{t+1} \xrightarrow{p} c^2 + \sigma^2,$$
$$\hat{\sigma}^2_{2,1} = \tfrac{1}{T-1} \sum_{t=1}^{T-1} (y_{t+1} - y_t)^2 \xrightarrow{p} 2\sigma^2,$$

however, $\hat{\sigma}_{1,1}^2 < \hat{\sigma}_{2,1}^2$ with probability approaching one whenever $c^2 < \sigma^2$. This is because parameter estimation uncertainty never vanishes even asymptotically, when the window size is fixed.

The goal of the next section is to show that the criterion is consistent if the window size is small, but not too small, relative to the sample size in the following sense: $W \to \infty$ and $W/T \to 0$ as $T \to \infty$. Following Clark and McCracken (2000), we use the following notation: Let $q_{2,t} = z_t z_t'$, $q_{1,t} = x_t x_t'$, $B_i = [E(q_{it})]^{-1}$, $B_i(t) = \left[\frac{1}{W_h}\sum_{s=t-W}^{t-h} q_{i,s}\right]^{-1}$, $H_1(t) = \frac{1}{W_h}\sum_{s=t-W}^{t-h} x_s(y_{s+h} - \alpha^{*\prime}x_s)$, $H_2(t) = \frac{1}{W_h}\sum_{s=t-W}^{t-h} z_s v_{s+h}$, where i is either 1 or 2 and $W_h = W - h + 1$.

2.1 Consistency of the Rolling-Window PMSE Criterion When Parameters are Constant

First, consider the case where the parameters are constant.

Assumption 1 As $T \to \infty$, $T^{1/2}/W = O(1)$ and $W/T \to 0$.

Assumption 2 (a) $\{[x_t' \; z_t' \; y_{t+h}]'\}$ is covariance stationary and has finite 10 moments with $E(z_t z_t')$ positive definite and $B_2(t)$ positive definite for all t almost surely.
(b) $W^{1/2}(B_i(t) - B_i)$ and $W^{1/2}H_i(t)$ have finite fourth moments uniformly in t for $i = 1, 2$.
(c) $E(v_{t+h}|\mathcal{F}_t) = 0$ with probability one for $1, 2, \ldots$, where $\mathcal{F}_t$ is the σ field generated by $\{(y_{s+h}, z_s)\}_{s=1}^{t-h}$.
(d) $E[H_1'(t)B_1(x_t x_t' - E(x_t x_t'))B_1 H_1(t)] = o(W^{-1})$ and $E[H_2'(t)B_2(z_t z_t' - E(z_t z_t'))B_2 H_2(t)] = o(W^{-1})$ uniformly in t.
(e)

$$\operatorname{Cov}\left[\operatorname{vech}\left(\sum_{t=W+1}^{T-h} H_i'(t)(B_i(t) - B_i)q_{i,t}(B_i(t) - B_i)H_i(t)\right)\right]$$
$$= O\left(\sum_{t=W+1}^{T-h} \operatorname{Cov}\left[\operatorname{vech}\left(H_i'(t)(B_i(t) - B_i)q_{i,t}(B_i(t) - B_i)H_i(t)\right)\right]\right),$$

$$\operatorname{Cov}\left[\operatorname{vec}\left(\sum_{t=W+1}^{T-h} H_i'(t)B_i q_{i,t}(B_i(t) - B_i)H_i(t)\right)\right]$$
$$= O\left(\sum_{t=W+1}^{T-h} \operatorname{Cov}\left[\operatorname{vec}\left(H_i'(t)B_i q_{i,t}(B_i(t) - B_i)H_i(t)\right)\right]\right),$$

$$\text{Cov}\left[\text{vech}\left(\sum_{t=W+1}^{T-h} H_i'(t)B_i q_{i,t} B_i H_i(t)\right)\right]$$
$$= O\left(\sum_{t=W+1}^{T-h} \text{Cov}\left[\text{vech}\left(H_i'(t)B_i q_{i,t} B_i H_i\right)\right]\right),$$

for $i = 1, 2$.

Remark When the window size is assumed to be proportional to the sample size, $W = [rT]$ for $r \in [0, 1]$, the functional central limit theorem (FCLT) is often used to find the asymptotic properties of the recursive and rolling regression estimators (e.g., Clark and McCracken 2001). For example, if $h = 1$,

$$\sqrt{T}(\hat{\beta}_{t,W} - \beta) = \left(\frac{1}{T}\sum_{s=t-W}^{t-1} z_s z_s'\right)^{-1} \frac{1}{\sqrt{T}} \sum_{s=t-W}^{t-1} z_s v_{s+1}$$

and if $\text{vech}(z_t z_t')$ and $z_t v_{t+1}$ satisfy the FCLT, we obtain

$$\sqrt{T}(\hat{\beta}_{[rT]} - \beta) \Rightarrow \frac{\sigma}{r}[E(z_t z_t')]^{-1/2} B_l(r)$$

where $B_l(r)$ is the l-dimensional standard Brownian motion, provided $[z_t' \; v_{t+1}]'$ is covariance stationary. Thus, we have $\hat{\beta}_{t,W} - \beta = O_p(T^{-1/2})$ uniformly in t. When the window size diverges slower than the sample size it is tempting to use the same analogy and claims $\hat{\beta}_{t,W} - \beta = O_p(W^{-1/2})$ uniformly in t. This result does not follow from the FCLT, however, even though $\hat{\beta}_{t,W} - \beta = O_p(W^{-1/2})$ pointwise in t. To see why, let $z_t = 1$. Then

$$\hat{\beta}_{t,W} - \beta = \frac{1}{W}\sum_{s=1}^{t-1} v_{s+1} - \frac{1}{W}\sum_{s=1}^{t-W-1} v_{s+1}$$
$$= \frac{\sqrt{T}}{W}\frac{1}{\sqrt{T}}\sum_{s=1}^{t-1} v_{s+1} - \frac{\sqrt{T}}{W}\frac{1}{\sqrt{T}}\sum_{s=1}^{t-W-1} v_{s+1}$$
$$= o_p\left(\frac{\sqrt{T}}{W}\right)$$

uniformly in t, where the last equality follows from $\frac{1}{\sqrt{T}}\sum_{s=1}^{t-1} v_{s+1} - \frac{1}{\sqrt{T}}\sum_{s=1}^{t-W-1} v_{s+1} = o_p(1)$ by the FCLT and $W = o(T)$. Thus, the FCLT alone does not imply $\hat{\beta}_{t,W} - \beta = O_p(W^{-1/2})$ uniformly in t in general. This is why we need some high-level assumption, such as Assumptions 2(b)(d)(e).

Assumption 1 requires that W diverges slower than T. This assumption makes the convergence rates of terms in the expansion of the PMSE differential uneven which helps to establish the consistency of this criterion when the nested model is generating the data. Assumption 2(c) requires that the nesting model is (dynamically) correctly specified. Assumption 2(d) is trivially satisfied if z_t is strictly exogenous and allows for weak correlations between z_t and v_s. Assumption 2(e) is a high-level assumption and imposes that the variance of the sum is in the same order of the sum of variances. In other words, the summands are only weakly serially correlated so that their autocovariances decay fast enough. This assumption is somewhat related to the concept of essential stationarity of Wooldridge (1994, pp. 2643–2644). Assumptions somewhat similar to this condition are used in the central limit theorem for stationary and ergodic processes (e.g., Theorem 5.6 of Hall and Heyde 1980, p. 148) and the central limit theorem for near epoch-dependent processes (e.g., Theorem 5.3 of Gallant and White 1988, p. 76; Assumption C1 of Wooldridge and White 1988).

Theorem 1 *Under Assumptions 1 and 2, the rolling-window PMSE criterion is consistent.*

To compare our consistency result and the inconsistency result of Inoue and Kilian (2006), consider two simple competing models, $y_{t+h} = u_{t+h}$ (model 1) and $y_{t+h} = c + v_{t+h}$ (model 2) where v_{t+h} is i.i.d. with mean zero and variance σ_2^2 and $h = 1$. The difference of the out-of-sample PMSE can be written as

$$\hat{\sigma}_{2,W}^2 - \hat{\sigma}_{1,W}^2 = -\frac{2}{T-W-1}\sum_{t=W+1}^{T-1}(\hat{c}_t - c)v_{t+1} + \frac{1}{T-W-1}\sum_{t=W+1}^{T-1}(\hat{c}_t - c)^2$$

where $\hat{c}_t = (1/W)\sum_{s=t-W}^{t-1} y_{s+1}$. Assume that $c = 0$ in population.

When $W = [\lambda T]$ for some $\lambda \in (0,1)$, it follows from Lemmas A6 and A7 of Clark and McCracken (2000) that

$$T\left(\hat{\sigma}_{2,W}^2 - \hat{\sigma}_{1,W}^2\right) \xrightarrow{d} -\frac{2}{\lambda(1-\lambda)}\sigma_2^2\int_\lambda^1 (B(r) - B(r-\lambda))\mathrm{d}B(r)$$
$$+\frac{1}{\lambda^2(1-\lambda)}\sigma_2^2\int_\lambda^1 (B(r) - B(r-\lambda))'(B(r) - B(r-\lambda))\mathrm{d}r$$

where $B(\cdot)$ is the standard Brownian motion. Because the probability that the right-hand side is negative is nonzero, the criterion is inconsistent when $c = 0$. This is the inconsistency result in Inoue and Kilian (2006).

When $W = o(T^{1/(1+2\varepsilon)})$ for some $\varepsilon \in (0, 1/2)$, the case considered in this chapter, we have:

$$
\begin{aligned}
W(\hat{\sigma}_{2,W}^2 - \hat{\sigma}_{1,W}^2) &= -\frac{2W^{\frac{1}{2}+\varepsilon}}{T-W-1}\sum_{t=W+1}^{T-1}\left(\frac{1}{W^{\frac{1}{2}+\varepsilon}}\sum_{s=t-W}^{t-1} v_{s+1}\right)v_{t+1} \\
&\quad + \frac{1}{T-W-1}\sum_{t=W+1}^{T-1}\left(\frac{1}{W^{\frac{1}{2}}}\sum_{s=t-W}^{t-1} v_{s+1}\right)^2 \\
&= \frac{1}{T-W-1}\sum_{t=W+1}^{T-1}\left(\frac{1}{W^{\frac{1}{2}}}\sum_{s=t-W}^{t-1} v_{s+1}\right)^2 + o_p(1)
\end{aligned}
$$

Because the right-hand side remains positive even asymptotically, the criterion will choose model 1 with probability approaching one. The key for the consistency result is that the last quadratic term in the expansion dominates the middle cross-term when the window size is small.

Lastly, it should be noted that our consistency result does not imply that the resulting forecast based on a slowly diverging window size is optimal. When parameters are constant, one would expect that the optimal forecast for the $T+1$st observation should be based on all T observations, not on the last W observations. Assumption 1 is merely a device to obtain the consistency of the rolling PMSE criterion.

2.2 *Consistency of the Rolling-Window PMSE Criterion When Parameters are Time Varying*

Sometimes it is claimed that out-of-sample PMSE comparisons are used to protect practitioners from parameter instability. As Inoue and Kilian (2006) show this is not always the case. In this section we show that the rolling PMSE criterion with small window sizes delivers consistent model selection even when parameters are time varying.

Suppose that the slope coefficients are time varying in the sense that

$$
y_{T,t+h} = \beta\left(\frac{t}{T}\right)' z_{T,t} + v_{T,t+h} \tag{7}
$$

where $\beta(r) = [\alpha(r)' \ \gamma(r)']'$ for $r \in [0,1]$. When the slope coefficients are time varying, the second moments are also time varying. Let

$$
\begin{aligned}
\begin{bmatrix} \Gamma_{zz}\left(\frac{t}{T}\right) & \Gamma_{zy}\left(\frac{t}{T}\right) \\ \Gamma_{yz}\left(\frac{t}{T}\right) & \Gamma_{yy}\left(\frac{t}{T}\right) \end{bmatrix} &= \begin{bmatrix} \Gamma_{xx}\left(\frac{t}{T}\right) & \Gamma_{xw}\left(\frac{t}{T}\right) & \Gamma_{xy}\left(\frac{t}{T}\right) \\ \Gamma_{wx}\left(\frac{t}{T}\right) & \Gamma_{ww}\left(\frac{t}{T}\right) & \Gamma_{wy}\left(\frac{t}{T}\right) \\ \Gamma_{yx}\left(\frac{t}{T}\right) & \Gamma_{yw}\left(\frac{t}{T}\right) & \Gamma_{yy}\left(\frac{t}{T}\right) \end{bmatrix} \\
&= \begin{bmatrix} E[x_{T,t}x_{T,t}'] & E[x_{T,t}w_{T,t}'] & E[x_{T,t}y_{T,t}] \\ E[w_{T,t}x_{T,t}'] & E[w_{T,t}w_{T,t}'] & E[w_{T,t}y_{T,t}] \\ E[y_{T,t}x_{T,t}'] & E[y_{T,t}w_{T,t}'] & E[y_{T,t}^2] \end{bmatrix},
\end{aligned}
$$

for $t = 1, 2, ..., T$ and $T = 1, 2, ...$ Let $\bar{B}_1\left(\frac{t}{T}\right) = [E(x_{T,t}x'_{T,t})]^{-1}$ and $\bar{B}_2\left(\frac{t}{T}\right) = [E(z_{T,t}z'_{T,t})]^{-1}$. Then $\beta(\cdot) = [\Gamma_{zz}(\cdot)]^{-1}\Gamma_{zy}(\cdot)$. We compare

$$y_{T,t+h} = \alpha\left(\frac{t}{T}\right)' x_{T,t} + u_{T,t+h} \tag{8}$$

and (7), where (7) simplifies to (8) if $\gamma(u) = 0$ for all $u \in [0, 1]$.

Assumption 3 As $T \to \infty$, $T^{1/2}/W = O(1)$ and $W = o(T^{2/3})$.

Assumption 4 (a)

$$\xi_t = \text{vech}\left\{\begin{bmatrix} z_{T,t}z'_{T,t} & z_{T,t}y_{T,t+h} \\ y_{T,t+h}z'_{T,t} & y^2_{T,t+h}\end{bmatrix} - \begin{bmatrix}\Gamma_{zz}\left(\frac{t}{T}\right) & \Gamma_{zy}\left(\frac{t}{T}\right) \\ \Gamma_{yz}\left(\frac{t}{T}\right) & \Gamma_{yy}\left(\frac{t}{T}\right)\end{bmatrix}\right\} \tag{9}$$

has finite fifth moments with $B_2(t)$ positive definite for all t almost surely.

(b) $W^{1/2}\left(B_i(t) - \bar{B}_i\left(\frac{t}{T}\right)\right)$ and $W^{1/2}H_i(t)$ have finite fourth moments uniformly in t for $i = 1, 2$.

(c) $E(v_{T,t+h}|\mathcal{F}_{Tt}) = 0$ with probability one for 1, 2, ..., where $\mathcal{F}_{Tt}$ is the σ field generated by $\{(y_{T,s+h}, z_{Ts})\}_{s=1}^{t-h}$.

(d) $E[H'_i(t)\bar{B}_i\left(\frac{t}{T}\right)(q_{i,T,t} - E(q_{i,T,t}))\bar{B}_i\left(\frac{t}{T}\right)H_i(t)] = o(W^{-1})$ uniformly in t for $i = 1, 2$, where $q_{1,T,t} = x_{T,t}x_{T,t}$ and $q_{2,T,t} = z_{T,t}z'_{T,t}$.

(e)

$$\text{Cov}\left[\text{vech}\left(\sum_{t=W+1}^{T-h} H'_i(t)\left(B_i(t) - \bar{B}_i\left(\frac{t}{T}\right)\right)q_{i,T,t}\left(B_i(t) - \bar{B}_i\left(\frac{t}{T}\right)\right)H_i(t)\right)\right]$$
$$= O\left(\sum_{t=W+1}^{T-h}\text{Cov}\left[\text{vech}\left(H'_i(t)\left(B_i(t) - \bar{B}_i\left(\frac{t}{T}\right)q_{i,T,t}\left(B_i(t) - \bar{B}_i\left(\frac{t}{T}\right)\right)H_i(t)\right)\right]\right),$$

$$\text{Cov}\left[\text{vec}\left(\sum_{t=W+1}^{T-h} H'_i(t)\bar{B}_i\left(\frac{t}{T}\right)q_{i,T,t}\left(B_i(t) - \bar{B}_i\left(\frac{t}{T}\right)\right)H_i(t)\right)\right]$$
$$= O\left(\sum_{t=W+1}^{T-h}\text{Cov}\left[\text{vec}\left(H'_i(t)\bar{B}_i\left(\frac{t}{T}\right)q_{i,T,t}\left(B_i(t) - \bar{B}_i\left(\frac{t}{T}\right)\right)H_i(t)\right)\right]\right),$$
$$\text{Cov}\left[\text{vech}\left(\sum_{t=W+1}^{T-h} H'_i(t)\bar{B}_i\left(\frac{t}{T}\right)q_{i,T,t}\bar{B}_i\left(\frac{t}{T}\right)H_i(t)\right)\right]$$
$$= O\left(\sum_{t=W+1}^{T-h}\text{Cov}\left[\text{vech}\left(H'_i(t)\bar{B}_i\left(\frac{t}{T}\right)q_{i,T,t}\bar{B}_i\left(\frac{t}{T}\right)H_i\right)\right]\right),$$

where $i = 1, 2$.

(f) $\Gamma_{zz}(u)$ is positive definite for all $u \in [0, 1]$, and $\alpha(.) \equiv \Gamma_{xx}(\cdot)^{-1}\Gamma_{xy}(\cdot)$ and $\beta(.) \equiv \Gamma_{zz}(\cdot)^{-1}\Gamma_{zy}(\cdot)$ satisfy a Lipschitz condition of order 1.

Remark Assumption 3 is more restrictive than Assumption 1 to keep the bias of the rolling regression estimator from interfering the consistency of the rolling PMSE estimator. Assumptions 4(a)(b) requires that ξ_t behaves like a stationary process with enough many moments. Assumptions 4(b)–(e) are analogs of Assumptions 2(b)–(e). Assumption 4(f) requires that the second moments change very smoothly.

Theorem 2 *Suppose Assumptions 3 and 4 hold. Then the rolling-window PMSE criterion is consistent.*

Remark The above consistency result is intuitive once it is recognized that the rolling regression estimator is a nonparametric regression estimator of parameters with a truncated kernel. For example, Cai (2007) establish the consistency and asymptotic normality of nonparametric estimators of time-varying parameters, and Giraitis et al. (2011) prove the consistency and asymptotic normality of nonparametric estimators for stochastic time-varying coefficient AR(1) models.

In general, the conventional information criteria, such as SIC, are not consistent when parameters are time varying. To show why that is the case consider comparing two competing models $y_{t+h} = u_{t+h}$ and $y_{t+h} = c + v_{t+h}$ for $h = 1$ when the data are generated from:

$$y_t = \frac{t}{T} - \frac{1}{2} + \varepsilon_t \tag{10}$$

where ε_t is i.i.d. with mean zero and variance σ^2. Then the population in-sample PMSE of the zero forecast model is

$$\lim_{T\to\infty} E\left(\frac{1}{T-1}\sum_{t=1}^{T-1} y_{t+1}^2\right) = \sigma^2 + \int_0^1 \left(r - \frac{1}{2}\right)^2 dr = \sigma^2 + \frac{1}{12}$$

The population in-sample PMSE of the forecast model that estimates the constant in rolling windows is also

$$\lim_{T\to\infty} \min_c E\left(\frac{1}{T-1}\sum_{t=1}^{T-1} (y_{t+1} - c)^2\right) = \min_c \left(\sigma^2 + \int_0^1 (r-c)^2 dr\right) = \sigma^2 + \frac{1}{12}$$

Thus, the SIC would select the zero forecast model while the true DGP is a time-varying constant forecast model. Our criterion, by re-estimating the constant in rolling windows, is robust to time variation in the parameters and will select the second model with probability approaching unity asymptotically.

3 Monte Carlo Evidence

In this section we investigate the finite-sample performance of the rolling-window PMSE criterion in two Monte Carlo experiments. In the first experiment, we use the data generating process (DGP) of Clark and McCracken (2005) as it is similar to the empirical application that we will consider in the next section. In the second experiment, we use a simple DGP in which the dependent and independent variables both follow first-order autoregressive processes, and consider both constant parameter and time-varying parameter cases.

3.1 Simulation 1: DGP2 in Clark and McCracken (2005)

The second DGP of Clark and McCracken (2005) is based on estimates based on quarterly 1957:1–2004:3 data of inflation (Y) and the rate of capacity utilization in manufacturing (x). We consider restricted and unrestricted forecasting models as follows:

$$\text{Model 1}: \ \Delta Y_{t+1} = \alpha_0 + \alpha_1 \Delta Y_t + \alpha_2 \Delta Y_{t-1} + u_{1,t+1} \tag{11}$$

$$\begin{aligned}\text{Model 2}: \ \Delta Y_{t+1} = {} & \alpha_0 + \alpha_1 \Delta Y_t + \alpha_2 \Delta Y_{t-1} + \gamma_1 x_{t-1} + \gamma_2 x_{t-2} + \gamma_3 x_{t-3} \\ & + \gamma_4 x_{t-4} + u_{2,t+1}\end{aligned} \tag{12}$$

When the restricted model (11) is true, the DGP is parameterized using Eq. (7) in Clark and McCracken (2005):

$$\Delta Y_t = -0.316\Delta Y_{t-1} - 0.214\Delta Y_{t-2} + u_{y,t}, \tag{13}$$

$$\begin{aligned}x_t = {} & -0.193\Delta Y_{t-1} - 0.242\Delta Y_{t-2} - 0.240\Delta Y_{t-3} - 0.119\Delta Y_{t-4} \\ & + 1.427x_{t-1} - 0.595x_{t-2} + 0.294x_{t-3} - 0.174x_{t-4} + u_{x,t},\end{aligned} \tag{14}$$

where

$$\begin{bmatrix} u_{y,t} \\ u_{x,t} \end{bmatrix} \overset{iid}{\sim} N\left(\begin{bmatrix} 0 \\ 0 \end{bmatrix}, \begin{bmatrix} 1.792 & 0.244 \\ 0.244 & 1.463 \end{bmatrix}\right). \tag{15}$$

When the unrestricted model (12) is the truth, the DGP is parameterized using Eq. (9) in Clark and McCracken (2005).

$$\begin{aligned}\Delta Y_t = {} & -0.419\Delta Y_{t-1} - 0.258\Delta Y_{t-2} \\ & + 0.331x_{t-1} - 0.423x_{t-2} + 0.309x_{t-3} - 0.139x_{t-4} + u_{y,t},\end{aligned} \tag{16}$$

where x_t is defined as in Eq. (14) and

Table 1 Selection probabilities of the SIC

T	The restricted model is true	The unrestricted model is true
100	0.9901	0.6640
250	0.9977	0.9847
500	0.9997	1
1000	0.9997	1

Table 2 Selection probabilities of the PMSE criterion when the window size is a fixed fraction of the total sample size

π	T	The restricted model is true	The unrestricted model is true
0.2	100	0.9955	0.2326
	250	0.9914	0.9113
	500	0.9907	0.9997
	1000	0.9916	1
0.5	100	0.7459	0.8101
	250	0.7353	0.9845
	500	0.7383	0.9995
	1000	0.7427	1
0.8	100	0.3385	0.8476
	250	0.3682	0.9411
	500	0.3735	0.9841
	1000	0.3719	0.9985

$$\begin{bmatrix} u_{y,t} \\ u_{x,t} \end{bmatrix} \overset{iid}{\sim} N\left(\begin{bmatrix} 0 \\ 0 \end{bmatrix}, \begin{bmatrix} 1.517 & 0.244 \\ 0.244 & 1.463 \end{bmatrix}\right), \tag{17}$$

In both (15) and (17), the initial values of ΔY_t and x_t are generated with draws from the unconditional normal distribution. We compare the performance of the SIC and the rolling window PMSE criteria; the latter is implemented with a window size that is either (i) fixed relative to the sample size; (ii) proportional to the sample size; or (iii) diverging slower than the sample size. The number of Monte Carlo replications is set to 10,000. Tables 1, 2, 3, 4 report the empirical probabilities of selecting the correct model. If the procedure is correct, the corresponding probabilities in the tables should be unity.

Tables 1, 2 and 3 report the results for the SIC, the PMSE criterion with W proportional to T, and the PMSE criterion with fixed W, respectively. As expected, the SIC selects the correct model with probability approaching one as the sample size increases. The second last column of Table 2 shows that, when the window size is set to a fraction of the total sample size, $W = [\pi T]$, the PMSE criterion tends to overparameterize the model when π is not very small. When the window size is fixed to a small number ($W = 10$), the PMSE criterion tends to underparameterize the model. The results for $W = [0.2T]$, $W = 50$, and $W = 90$ seem to contradict our claim that these specifications of the window size should yield inconsistent

Table 3 Selection probabilities of the PMSE criterion when the window size is constant

W	T	The restricted model is true.	The unrestricted model is true.
10	100	1	0.0008
	250	1	0
	500	1	0
	1000	1	0
50	100	0.7459	0.8101
	250	0.9914	0.9113
	500	1	0.9729
	1000	1	0.9972
90	100	0.1937	0.8612
	250	0.8959	0.9840
	500	0.9954	0.9990
	1000	1	1

Table 4 Selection probabilities of the PMSE criterion when the window size is slowly diverging

W	T	The restricted model is true	The unrestricted model is true
$T^{1/3}$	100	N/A	N/A
	250	1	0
	500	1	0
	1000	1	0
$T^{1/2}$	100	1	0.0008
	250	1	0.0016
	500	1	0.0532
	1000	1	0.5512
$T^{3/4}$	100	0.9500	0.5947
	250	0.9749	0.9619
	500	0.9883	0.9998
	1000	0.9953	1

model selection; however, for reasonably large sample sizes, these specifications are observationally equivalent to the small window size specification we propose. Table 4 shows the results when the window size is small but diverging, $W = o(T)$. The results for $W = T^{3/4}$ support our consistency results. Although the window size $W = T^{1/3}$ and $W = T^{1/2}$ does not satisfy our sufficient condition (Assumption 1), the resulting criterion chooses the restricted model with probability approaching one when it is true. However, the PMSE criterion with $W = T^{1/3}$ fails to choose the unrestricted model when it is the truth.[2]

Overall, our results suggest that a window size that is a fixed fraction of the total sample size does not appear to give consistent results when Model 1 is the true data generating process. On the other hand, a constant window size $W = 10$ is not

[2] When $T = 100$, $W = T^{1/3}$ is too small to compute a rolling estimator.

consistent when Model 2 is true. The divergent window size, in general, consistently selects the correct model, asymptotically. When $W = T^{1/3}$, the consistency is not obvious due to the small window size, but unreported results show that the frequency of consistency will eventually converge to 1 when the total sample size becomes infinitely large.

The SIC does select the correct model asymptotically, and it appears to do so with an even higher probability that the PMSE criterion with a slowly diverging window size. However, as we will show in the next set of Monte Carlo simulations, the SIC will not select the correct model in the presence of time variation.

3.2 Simulation 2:Autoregressive DGP With/Without a Time-Varying Parameter

Next we consider two forecasting models

$$\text{Model 1: } y_t = \alpha y_{t-1} + u_{1,t}$$
$$\text{Model 2: } y_t = \alpha y_{t-1} + \gamma x_t + u_{2,t}$$

where the data are generated by

$$x_t = 0.5x_{t-1} + u_{x,t},$$
$$y_t = 0.5y_{t-1} + \gamma x_t + u_{y,t},$$

$u_{x,t} \sim iid\ N(0,1)$ and $u_{y,t} \sim iid\ N(0,1)$ are independent of each other. We consider four cases: $\gamma = 0$; $\gamma = 0.25$; $\gamma = 0.5$ and $\gamma = t/T - 0.5$. When $\gamma = 0$ Model 1 is true. Under the cases where $\gamma = 0.5$ or 0.25, Model 2 is true. Even when $\gamma_{T,t} = t/T - 0.5$, Model 2 should be selected since the true data generating process does include a constant, although the constant is time varying. The number of Monte Carlo replications is set to 10,000.

Tables 5, 6, 7, and 8 report the empirical probabilities of selecting the right model for the SIC and the rolling-window PMSE criterion with $W = [\pi T]$, W being a constant, and $W = o(T)$, respectively, when γ is time invariant. As before, the SIC is consistent and the PMSE criterion tends to either overparameterize or underparameterize the model when W is a large fraction of T or when W is a small constant. The results when W is a small fraction of T ($\pi = 0.2$) or when W is 50 or 90 show that the PMSE criterion selects the correct model. This may be due to finite samples in which these window sizes are consistent with slowing diverging ones. The results in Table 8 show that the PMSE criterion selects the correct forecasting model with probability approaching one as the sample size increases when $W \to \infty$ and $T^{1/2}/W = O(1)$ as T grows.

The aforementioned results indicate that while the PMSE criterion with a slowly diverging window size is consistent the SIC tends to perform better. One advantage of the PMSE criterion over the SIC is that the PMSE criterion is robust to parameter

Table 5 Selection probabilities of the SIC

T	$\gamma = 0$	$\gamma = 0.25$	$\gamma = 0.5$
100	0.9645	0.7548	0.9989
250	0.9815	0.9826	1
500	0.9881	1	1
1000	0.9926	1	1

Table 6 Selection probabilities of the PMSE criterion when the window size is a fixed fraction of the sample

π	T	$\gamma = 0$	$\gamma = 0.25$	$\gamma = 0.5$
0.2	100	0.9364	0.5497	0.9795
	250	0.9411	0.9360	1
	500	0.9414	0.9981	1
	1000	0.9422	1	1
0.5	100	0.8075	0.7433	0.9759
	250	0.8100	0.9368	0.9998
	500	0.8089	0.9914	1
	1000	0.8182	0.9998	1
0.8	100	0.6724	0.6944	0.8784
	250	0.6787	0.8338	0.9753
	500	0.6882	0.9205	0.9971
	1000	0.6963	0.9800	0.9999

Table 7 Selection probabilities of the PMSE criterion when the window size is constant

W	T	$\gamma = 0$	$\gamma = 0.25$	$\gamma = 0.5$
10	100	0.9859	0.2170	0.8569
	250	0.9998	0.1118	0.9591
	500	1	0.0449	0.9945
	1000	1	0.0054	0.9996
50	100	0.8075	0.7433	0.9759
	250	0.9411	0.9360	1
	500	0.9856	0.9909	1
	1000	0.9982	1	1
90	100	0.6145	0.6421	0.7845
	250	0.8688	0.9568	1
	500	0.9479	0.9980	1
	1000	0.9885	1	1

instabilities. Table 9 reports the selection probabilities of the SIC and PMSE criterion when $\gamma_{T,t} = t/T - 0.5$. $\gamma_{T,t}$ is modeled so that the in-sample PMSE of Model 2 equals that of Model 1 while the out-of-sample PMSE of Model 2 is smaller than that

Table 8 Selection probabilities of the PMSE criterion when the window size is slowly diverging

W	T	$\gamma = 0$	$\gamma = 0.25$	$\gamma = 0.5$
$T^{1/3}$	100	0.9983	0.0092	0.0970
	250	0.9999	0.0040	0.4060
	500	1	0.0008	0.7201
	1000	1	0.0016	0.9959
$T^{1/2}$	100	0.9859	0.2170	0.8569
	250	0.9982	0.4115	0.9987
	500	0.9997	0.7848	1
	1000	1	0.9901	1
$T^{3/4}$	100	0.8909	0.6889	0.9858
	250	0.9213	0.9506	1
	500	0.9361	0.9980	1
	1000	0.9551	1	1

Table 9 Selection probabilities when a parameter is time varying

T	SIC	$W = T^{\frac{1}{3}}$	$W = T^{\frac{1}{2}}$	$W = T^{\frac{2}{3}}$
100	0.0489	0.0063	0.1943	0.4904
250	0.0313	0.0026	0.4567	0.8703
500	0.0215	0.0005	0.8664	0.9953
1000	0.0139	0.0015	0.9982	1.0000

of Model 1. Table 9 shows that the PMSE criterion selects Model 2 with empirical probability approaching one while the SIC selects Model 1.[3]

To summarize, the Monte Carlo results are consistent with our asymptotic theory and the PMSE criterion with a slowly diverging window size chooses the correct forecasting model with probability approaching one, no matter whether the parameters are time varying or not. On the other hand, although the SIC is consistent when the parameter is constant over time, it is inconsistent when the parameter is time varying.

4 Empirical Application

We consider forecasting quarterly inflation h -periods into the future. Let the regression model be:

$$y_{t+h}^{h} = \gamma_0 + \gamma_1 (L) x_t + \gamma_2 (L) y_t + u_{t+h}^{h}, t = 1, \ldots, T \tag{18}$$

[3] Technically, the window size $W = T^{2/3}$ does not satisfy our sufficient condition but yields good results.

where the dependent variable is $y_{t+h}^{h} = (400/h)\ln(P_{t+h}/P_t) - 400\ln(P_t/P_{t-1})$ where P_t is the price level (CPI) at time t, h is the forecast horizon and equals four, so that the forecasts involve annual percent growth rates of inflation. $\gamma_1(L) = \sum_{j=0}^{p}\gamma_{1j}L^j$ and $\gamma_2(L) = \sum_{j=0}^{q}\gamma_{2j}L^j$, where L is the lag operator. Following Stock and Watson (2003), we consider several explanatory variables, x_t, one at a time. The explanatory variable, x_t, is either an interest rate or a measure of real output, unemployment, price, money, or earnings. The data are transformed to eliminate stochastic or deterministic trends and to quarterly frequencies. For a detailed description of the variables that we consider, see Table 10. We utilize quarterly, finally revised data available in January 2011. The earliest starting point of the sample that we consider is January 1959, although both M3 and the exchange rate series have a later starting date due to data availability constraints. Overall, this implies that the total sample size is about 240 observations. In the out-of-sample forecasting exercise, we estimate the number of lags (p and q) recursively by BIC; the estimation scheme is rolling with a window size of 40 observations. The benchmark model is an autoregressive model:

$$y_{t+h}^{h} = \gamma_0 + \gamma_2(L)\,y_t + u_{t+h}^{h},\ t = 1, ..., T. \tag{19}$$

Results are reported in Fig. 1. The figure reports the ratio of the MSFE of the model, Eq. (18), relative to the MSFE of the autoregressive benchmark model, Eq. (19). According to the Monte Carlo simulations in the previous section, the most successful window sizes are between $T^{1/2}$ and $T^{2/3}$, which, given the available sample of data, implies between 16 and 39 observations.

Panel A reports results for predictors (x_t) that include real output measures. It is well known that such measures should be good predictors of inflation according to the Phillips curve. Several studies have documented the empirical success of Phillips curve models, see for example Stock et al. (1999a,b) and 2003, although the empirical results in Marcellino et al. (2003) suggests that the ability of such measures to forecast inflation in Europe is more limited than in the United States. The figure shows that capacity utilization, employment, and unemployment measures are very useful predictors for inflation. In fact, when the window size is less than about 80, the MSFE of the model is always smaller than that of the autoregressive benchmark, sometimes even substantially. Note that for larger window sizes the PMSE criterion would however suggest that the AR benchmark forecasts better than the economic model.

Earnings, instead, is not a successful predictor: in window sizes in the range between $T^{1/2}$ and $T^{2/3}$, it is significantly worse, and occasionally better, although only for larger window sizes. However, recall from the discussion in Sect. 2 that when the window size is large relative to the total sample size, Inoue and Kilian (2005) have shown that the PMSE criterion tends to select overparameterized models. When the window sizes are between $T^{1/2}$ and $T^{2/3}$, the previous sections showed that the PMSE criterion tends to select the correct model. This suggests that earnings are particularly unreliable for forecasting inflation.

Table 10 Series description

Label	Name	Period		Description	Source
Asset Prices					
rovnght@us	FEDFUNDS	1959 M1	2010 M9	Int rate: Fed funds (effective)	F
rtbill@us	TB3MS	1959 M1	2010 M9	Int rate: 3-month treasury bill, Sec Mkt rate	F
rbnds@us	GS1	1959 M1	2010 M9	Int rate: US treasury constant maturity, 1-Yr	F
rbndm@us	GS5	1959 M1	2010 M9	Int rate: US treasury constant maturity, 5-Yr	F
rbndl@us	GS10	1959 M1	2010 M9	Int rate: US treasury constant maturity, 10-Yr	F
stockp@us	SP500	1959 Q1	2010 Q3	US share prices: S&P 500	F
exrate@us	111..NELZF...	1960 M1	2010 M9	NEER from ULC	I
Activity					
rgdp@us	GDPC96	1959 Q1	2010 Q3	Real GDP	F
ip@us	INDPRO	1959 M1	2010 M9	Industrial Prod. index, (sa)	F
capu@us	CAPUB04	1959 M1	2010 M9	Capacity utilization rate: manufacturing (sa)	F
emp@us	CE16OV	1959 M1	2010 M9	Civilian employment: thou. persons	F
unemp@us	UNRATE	1959 M1	2010 M9	Civilian Unemp rate (sa)	F
Money					
mon0@us	AMBSL	1959 M1	2010 M9	Monetary base: St. Louis Adj. (sa)	F
mon1@us	M1SL	1959 M1	2010 M9	Money: M1 (sa)	F
mon2@us	M2SL	1959 M1	2010 M9	Money: M2 (sa)	F
mon3@us	M3SL	1959 M1	2006 M2	Money: M3 (sa)	F
Wages and Prices					
ppi@us	PPIACO	1959 M1	2010 M9	Producer price index	F
earn@us	AHEMAN	1959 M1	2010 M9	Hourly earnings: Manufact. (nsa)	F

Notes Sources are abbreviated as follows: *D*, datastream; *F*, federal reserve economic data; *I*, IMF international financial statistics; *O*, OECD main economic indicators; *G*, global insight

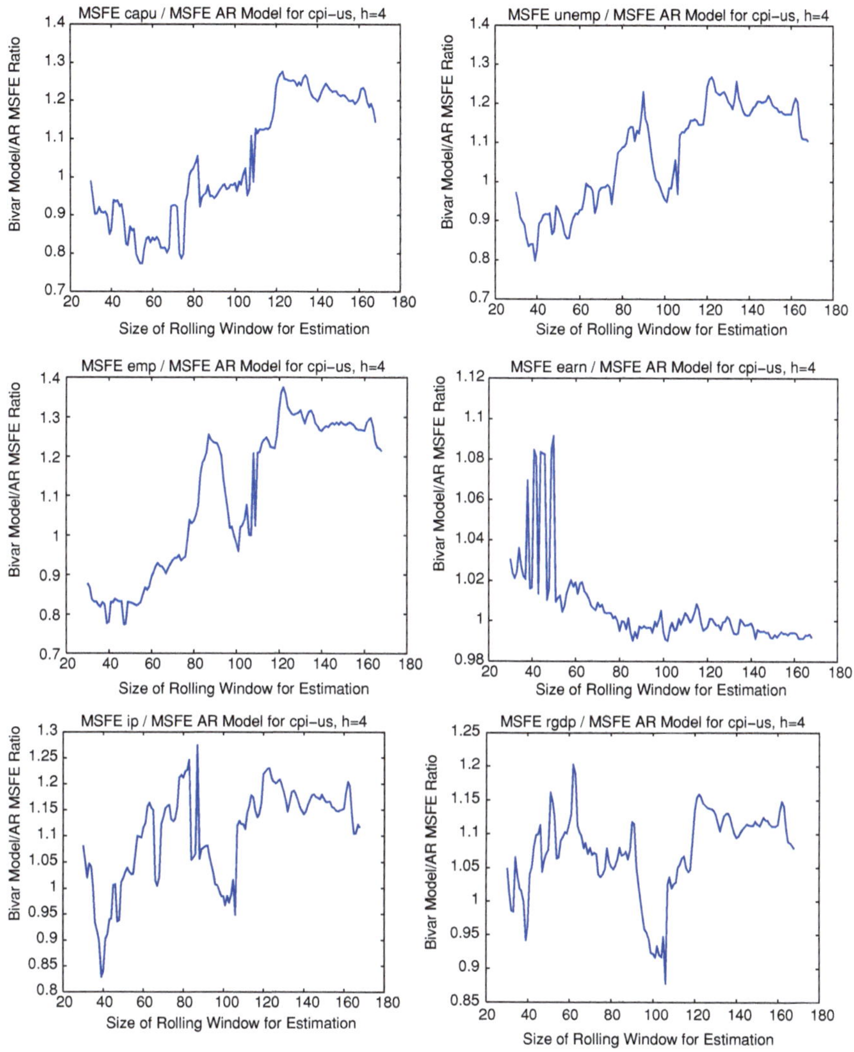

Fig. 1 QLR break test

The performance of industrial production and real GDP predictors, instead, is less clear: the ratio can be either above or below unity depending on the window size. Even for window sizes in the range between $T^{1/2}$ and $T^{2/3}$, the ratio can be either above or below unity. These results suggest instabilities in the forecasting performance of these predictors, and are consistent with the results in Rossi and Sekhposyan (2010), although the latter were interested in testing equal predictive ability rather than consistently selecting the correct model, as we do here. Rossi and Sekhposyan (2010) empirical evidence documented that the economic predictors have forecasting

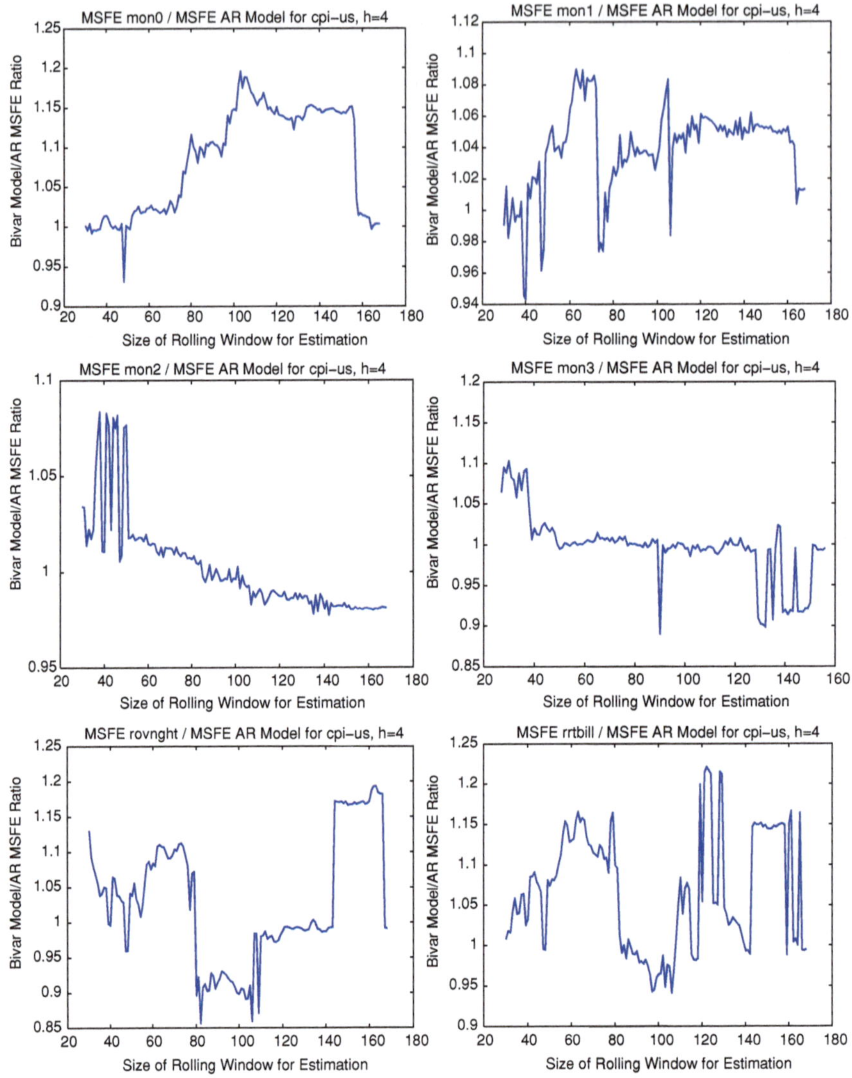

Fig. 1 continued

ability in the early part of their sample, but the predictive ability disappears in the later part of their sample. The reversals in predictive ability happened, according to their tests, around the time of the Great Moderation, which the literature dates back to 1983–1984 (see McConnell and Perez-Quiros 2000), similar to the results in D'Agostino et al. (2006).

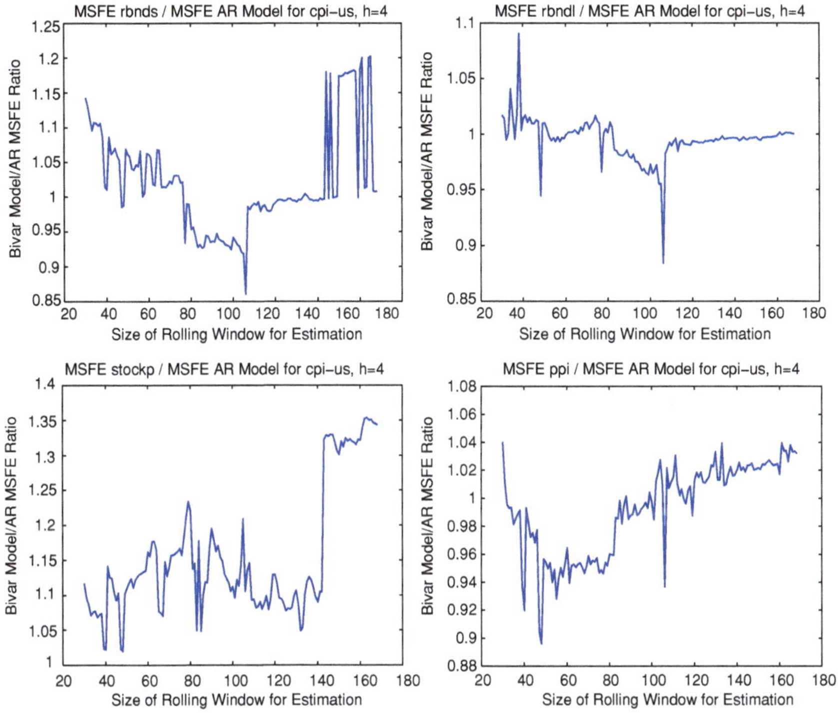

Fig. 1 continued

Panel B focuses on monetary measures. M1, M2, and M3 never have predictive ability except for some selected window sizes, again pointing to the presence of instabilities.

Panel C focuses on interest rates. The results are quite interesting. They show that interest rates (such as 1-year or 10-year bonds) appear to be very good predictors of inflation for medium window sizes, below 120–140 observations. Again, however, for very large window sizes the PMSE criterion would select the smaller model. Short-term interest rates tend to be useful predictors only when the window size is large, but again the ratio is below unity for some selected window sizes and above unity for others. Again, we conjecture that instabilities are important, as discussed in Rossi and Sekhposyan (2010).

Panel D focuses on other monetary variables. Stock prices are never useful for predicting inflation. Interestingly, the producer price index is a good predictor for inflation: the figure shows that for the relevant window sizes, the ratio of the MSFE of the model relative to that of the benchmark is always lower than unity, and it becomes higher than unity only for large window sizes.

Overall, our empirical results suggest that traditional Phillips curve predictors such as capacity utilization and unemployment are useful in forecasting inflation, as well as the producer price index. The empirical results for the other macroeconomic

Table 11 QLR break test P-values

Indicator	P-value
A. Real output measures	
Capacity utilization	0.00
Unemployment	0.00
Employment	0.00
Earnings	0.00
Industrial production	0.05
Real GDP	0.00
B. Money measures	
M0	0.00
M1	0.00
M2	0.00
M3	0.00
C. Interest rates	
Fed funds	0.00
Real 3-mo. Treasury bill	0.00
1-Year bond	0.04
10-Year bond	0.04
D. Other nominal measures	
Stock prices	0.03
Producer price index	0.00

Notes The table reports results for Andrews (1993) QLR test for structural breaks implemented with a HAC covariance estimator with a bandwidth equal to (1/5)T

predictors are not clearcut, and might signal the importance of instabilities in the data. In order to provide more information on the instability in the forecasting regressions we consider, we report joint tests for structural breaks in the parameters of Eq. (18) using Andrews (1993) test for structural breaks. Table 11 reports the p-values of the test, which confirm that instabilities are extremely important.

5 Concluding Remarks

There is a known break, forecasters tend to use post-break observations when they make forecasts. In other words, they base their forecasts on a "truncated window" instead of the full sample. This chapter shows that this type of ideas can deliver the consistency of the rolling PMSE criterion not only when parameters are time varying but also when they are constant over time.

In this chapter we focus on the rolling scheme. Inoue and Kilian (2006) show that the PMSE criterion based on the recursive scheme is inconsistent if the number of initial observations is large, i.e., a fixed fraction of the sample size, while Wei (1992) proves that it is consistent if the number of initial observations is very small, i.e., a fixed constant. One might be able to extend Wei (1992) result to the case in which the number of initial observations diverges at a rate slower than the sample size. However, such a model selection criterion might not be robust to parameter instability.

It should be noted that our consistency results are based on correctly specified nested models. Although information criteria are not robust to parameter instabilities, they are robust to misspecification and nonnestedness (Sin and White 1996). We leave PMSE criterion-based model comparison of misspecified or non-nested models for future research.

The main object of forecasters is often to minimize PMSE rather than identify the true model. We are currently developing a data-dependent method for choosing the window size to achieve this goal in a separate chapter

Appendix

A.1 Lemmas

Next, we present a lemma similar to Lemma A2 of Clark and McCracken (2000).

Lemma 1 *Suppose that Assumptions 1 and 2 hold and that* $\gamma = 0$. *Then:*

(a) $\frac{1}{T-h-W}\sum_{t=W+1}^{T-h} u_{t+h}x_t B_1(t)H_1(t) = o_p\left(\frac{1}{W}\right)$.

(b) $\frac{1}{T-h-W}\sum_{t=W+1}^{T-h} v_{t+h}z_t B_2(t)H_2(t) = o_p\left(\frac{1}{W}\right)$.

(c) $\frac{1}{T-h-W}\sum_{t=W+1}^{T-h} H_1'(t)B_1(t)x_t x_t' B_1(t)H_1(t) = \frac{1}{T-h-W}\sum_{t=W+h}^{T-1} H_1'(t)B_1 H_1(t) + o_p\left(\frac{1}{W}\right)$.

(d) $\frac{1}{T-h-W}\sum_{t=W+1}^{T-h} H_2'(t)B_2(t)z_t z_t' B_2(t)H_2(t) = \frac{1}{T-h-W}\sum_{t=W+1}^{T-h} H_2'(t)B_2 H_2(t) + o_p\left(\frac{1}{W}\right)$.

Proof of Lemma 1: The proofs for (a) and (c) are very similar to those for (b) and (d), respectively. For brevity, we only provide the proofs of (b) and (d). The results for (a) and (c) can be easily derived by replacing z_t and β by x_t and α, respectively.

Note that

$$\frac{1}{T-h-W}\sum_{t=W+1}^{T-h} v_{t+h}z_t B_2(t)H_2(t) = \frac{1}{T-h-W}\sum_{t=W+1}^{T-h} v_{t+h}z_t B_2 H_2(t) + \frac{1}{T-h-W}\sum_{t=W+1}^{T-h} v_{t+h}z_t (B_2(t) - B_2)H_2(t)$$

By Assumption 2(b) and Hölder's inequality, the second moments of the summands on the right-hand side are of order $O(W^{-1})$ and $O(W^{-2})$, respectively. Thus, it follows from Assumption 2(c) that the variance of the left-hand side is of order

$O(T^{-1}W^{-1})$. By the Chebyshev inequality and Assumption 1, the left-hand side is $o_p(W^{-1})$.

The proof of (d) is composed of two stages. In the first stage, we show that $B_2(t)$ in the equation can be approximated by its expectation B_2, which is

$$\frac{1}{T-h-W}\sum_{t=W+1}^{T-h} H_2'(t)B_2(t)z_t z_t' B_2(t)H_2(t)$$
$$= \frac{1}{T-h-W}\sum_{t=W+1}^{T-h} H_2'(t)B_2 z_t z_t' B_2 H_2(t) + o_p\left(\frac{1}{W}\right) \tag{A.1}$$

Since the left-hand side of Eq. (A.1) contains four terms,

$$\frac{1}{T-h-W}\sum_{t=W+1}^{T-h} H_2'(t)B_2(t)z_t z_t' B_2(t)H_2(t)$$
$$= \frac{1}{T-h-W}\sum_{t=W+1}^{T-h} H_2'(t)B_2 z_t z_t' B_2 H_2(t)$$
$$+ \frac{1}{T-h-W}\sum_{t=W+1}^{T-h} H_2'(t)(B_2(t)-B_2)z_t z_t'(B_2(t)-B_2)H_2(t)$$
$$+ \frac{1}{T-h-W}\sum_{t=W+1}^{T-h} H_2'(t)B_2 z_t z_t'(B_2(t)-B_2)H_2(t)$$
$$+ \frac{1}{T-h-W}\sum_{t=W+1}^{T-h} H_2'(t)(B_2(t)-B_2)z_t z_t' B_2 H_2(t), \tag{A.2}$$

which include the first term in the right-hand side of Eq. (A.1).

By Assumption 2(b) and Hölder's inequality, the second moments of the summands in the last three terms are of order $O(W^{-4})$, $O(W^{-3})$, and $O(W^{-3})$, respectively. Thus, their first moments are at most $O(W^{-3}) = o(W^{-1})$. By using these and Assumption 2(e), the second moments of the last three terms are thus of the order $O(T^{-1}W^{-4})$, $O(T^{-1}W^{-3})$ and $O(T^{-1}W^{-1})$, respectively. By the Chebyshev inequality and Assumption 1, these last three terms are of the order $o_p(W^{-1})$, proving (A.1).

The second stage of the proof of (d) is to show that we can further approximate $z_t z_t'$ in the first term in the right-hand side of Eq. (A.2) by its expectation $E(z_t z_t')$. Adding and subtracting $E(z_t z_t')$, we obtain

$$\frac{1}{T-h-W}\sum_{t=W+1}^{T-h} H_2'(t)B_2 z_t z_t' B_2 H_2(t)$$

$$= \frac{1}{T-h-W}\sum_{t=W+1}^{T-h} H_2'(t)B_2E(z_tz_t')B_2H_2(t)$$
$$+ \frac{1}{T-h-W}\sum_{t=W+1}^{T-h} H_2'(t)B_2(z_tz_t' - E(z_tz_t'))B_2H_2(t) \tag{A.3}$$

The mean of the second term is $o_p(W^{-1})$ by Assumption 2(d). The second moments of the summand in the second term is $O(W^{-2})$ by Assumption 2(b). Using these and Assumption 2(e), the second moment of the second term is of the order $o(W^{-2})$. By the Chebyshev inequality, (A.3) is $o_p(W^{-1})$.

Lemma 2 *Suppose that Assumptions 3 and 4 hold and that* $\gamma(\cdot) = 0$.

(a) $\frac{1}{T-h-W}\sum_{t=W+1}^{T-h} u_{T,t+h}x_{T,t}B_1(t)H_1(t) = o_p\left(\frac{1}{W}\right)$.
(b) $\frac{1}{T-h-W}\sum_{t=W+1}^{T-h} v_{T,t+h}z_{T,t}B_2(t)H_2(t) = o_p\left(\frac{1}{W}\right)$.
(c) $\frac{1}{T-h-W}\sum_{t=W+1}^{T-h} H_1'(t)B_1(t)x_{T,t}x_{T,t}'B_1(t)H_1(t)$
$= \frac{1}{T-h-W}\sum_{t=W+1}^{T-h} H_1'(t)\bar{B}_1\left(\frac{t}{T}\right)H_1(t) + o_p\left(\frac{1}{W}\right)$.
(d) $\frac{1}{T-h-W}\sum_{t=W+1}^{T-h} H_2'(t)B_2(t)z_{T,t}z_{T,t}'B_2(t)H_2(t)$
$= \frac{1}{T-h-W}\sum_{t=W+1}^{T-h} H_2'(t)\bar{B}_2\left(\frac{t}{T}\right)H_2(t) + o_p\left(\frac{1}{W}\right)$.

Proof of Lemma 2 Under Assumptions 3 and 4 the proof of Lemma 2 takes exactly the same steps as the proof of Lemma 1 except that B_i, u_t, and v_t are replaced by $\bar{B}_i\left(\frac{t}{T}\right)$, $u_{T,t}$, and $v_{T,t}$, respectively. This is because Lemma 2 is written in terms of $u_{T,t}$ and $v_{T,t}$ rather than in terms of $\hat{\alpha}_{t,W} - \alpha\left(\frac{t}{T}\right)$ and $\hat{\beta}_{t,W} - \beta\left(\frac{t}{T}\right)$ which we deal with in the proof of Theorem 2.

A.2 Proofs of Theorems

Proof of Theorem 1 Note that the PMSEs $\hat{\sigma}_{1,W}^2$ and $\hat{\sigma}_{2,W}^2$ can be expanded as

$$\hat{\sigma}_{1,W}^2 = \frac{1}{T-h-W}\sum_{t=W+1}^{T-h}\left(y_{t+h} - \widehat{\alpha}_t'x_t\right)^2$$
$$= \frac{1}{T-h-W}\sum_{t=W+1}^{T-h}\left(y_{t+h} - \alpha^{*\prime}x_t - \left(\widehat{\alpha}_t'x_t - \alpha^{*\prime}x_t\right)\right)^2$$

$$= \frac{1}{T-h-W} \sum_{t=W+1}^{T-h} \left(y_{t+h} - \alpha^{*\prime} x_t \right)^2$$

$$- \frac{2}{T-h-W} \sum_{t=W+1}^{T-h} \left(y_{t+h} - \alpha^{*\prime} x_t \right) x_t' \left(\widehat{\alpha}_t - \alpha^* \right)$$

$$+ \frac{1}{T-h-W} \sum_{t=W+1}^{T-h} \left(\widehat{\alpha}_t' - \alpha^{*\prime} \right) x_t x_t' \left(\widehat{\alpha}_t - \alpha^* \right) \tag{A.4}$$

and

$$\hat{\sigma}_{2,W}^2 = \frac{1}{T-h-W} \sum_{t=W+1}^{T-h} \left(y_{t+h} - \widehat{\beta}_t' z_t \right)^2$$

$$= \frac{1}{T-h-W} \sum_{t=W+1}^{T-h} \left(y_{t+h} - \beta' z_t - \left(\widehat{\beta}_t' z_t - \beta' z_t \right) \right)^2$$

$$= \frac{1}{T-h-W} \sum_{t=W+1}^{T-h} \left(y_{t+h} - \beta' z_t \right)^2$$

$$- \frac{2}{T-h-W} \sum_{t=W+1}^{T-h} \left(y_{t+h} - \beta' z_t \right) z_t' \left(\widehat{\beta}_t - \beta \right)$$

$$+ \frac{1}{T-h-W} \sum_{t=W+1}^{T-h} \left(\widehat{\beta}_t' - \beta' \right) z_t z_t' \left(\widehat{\beta}_t - \beta \right), \tag{A.5}$$

respectively, where $\alpha^* = [E(x_t x_t')]^{-1} E(x_t y_{t+h})$. There are two cases: the case in which the data are generated from model 1, i.e., $\gamma = 0$ (case 1) and the case in which the data are generated from model 2, i.e., $\gamma \neq 0$ (case 2).

In case 1, the actual model is $y_{t+h} = \alpha' x_t + v_{t+h}$. The first component of $\hat{\sigma}_{2,W}^2$ in Eq. (A.5) is numerically identical to the first component of $\hat{\sigma}_{1,W}^2$ in Eq. (A.4) because $\gamma = 0$ and $\alpha - \alpha^* = 0$. Note that all the other components converge to zero faster since all parameters are consistently estimated. Under the case where Model 1 is true, the difference between the probability limit of $\hat{\sigma}_{1,W}^2$ and $\hat{\sigma}_{2,W}^2$ is zero, which does not identify which model is the true model. Only comparing the probability limits of $\hat{\sigma}_{1,W}^2$ and $\hat{\sigma}_{2,W}^2$ as T and W go to infinity and W diverges slowly than T is not sufficient for the model selection to indicate that $\lim_{T\to\infty,\, W\to\infty} P(\hat{\sigma}_{1,W}^2 < \hat{\sigma}_{2,W}^2) = 1$. However, if we can tell whether $\hat{\sigma}_{1,W}^2$ is always smaller than $\hat{\sigma}_{2,W}^2$ along the path of convergence of T and W toward infinity, the true model can still be identified. Since the models are nested $u_{t+h} = v_{t+h}$, it follows from (A.4) and (A.5) that

$$
\begin{aligned}
\hat{\sigma}^2_{2,W} - \hat{\sigma}^2_{1,W} &= \frac{2}{T-h-W} \sum_{t=W+1}^{T-h} \left[v_{t+h} z_t' (\widehat{\beta}_t - \beta) - v_{t+h} x_t' (\widehat{\alpha}_t - \alpha) \right] \\
&\quad + \frac{1}{T-h-W} \sum_{t=W+1}^{T-h} \big[(\widehat{\beta}_t' - \beta') z_t z_t' (\widehat{\beta}_t - \beta) \\
&\qquad - (\widehat{\alpha}_t' - \alpha') x_t x_t' (\widehat{\alpha}_t - \alpha) \big] \\
&= \frac{2}{T-h-W} \sum_{t=W+1}^{T-h} \left[v_{t+h} z_t' B_2(t) H_2(t) - v_{t+h} x_t' B_1(t) H_1(t) \right] \\
&\quad + \frac{1}{T-h-W} \sum_{t=W+1}^{T-h} \big[H_2(t)' B_2(t) z_t z_t' B_2(t) H_2(t) \\
&\qquad - H_1(t)' B_1(t) x_t x_t' B_1(t) H_1(t) \big] \\
&= \frac{1}{T-h-W} \sum_{t=W+1}^{T-h} \left[H_2(t)' B_2 H_2(t) - H_1(t)' B_1 H_1(t) \right] + o_p\left(\frac{1}{W}\right)
\end{aligned}
\tag{A.6}
$$

where the last equality follows from Lemma 1(a)–(d).

To get the sign of Eq. (A.6), we first define Q by

$$
Q = [E(z_t z_t')]^{\frac{1}{2}} \left\{ [E(z_t z_t')]^{-1} - \begin{bmatrix} [E(x_t x_t')]^{-1} & \mathbf{0}_{l \times (k-l)} \\ \mathbf{0}_{(k-l) \times l} & \mathbf{0}_{(k-l) \times (k-l)} \end{bmatrix} \right\} [E(z_t z_t')]^{\frac{1}{2}}
\tag{A.7}
$$

as in Lemma A.4 of Clark and McCracken (2000). Clark and McCracken (2000) show that the Q matrix is symmetric and idempotent. An idempotent matrix is positive semidefinite, which means for all $v \in \Re^k$, $v^T Q v \geq 0$. It implies that

$$
\begin{aligned}
&\left[\frac{1}{W_h^{\frac{1}{2}}} \sum_{s=t-W}^{t-h} z_s v_{s+h} \right]' [E(z_t z_t')]^{-1} \left[\frac{1}{W_h^{\frac{1}{2}}} \sum_{s=t-W}^{t-h} z_s v_{s+h} \right] \\
&- \left[\frac{1}{W_h^{\frac{1}{2}}} \sum_{s=t-W}^{t-h} x_s v_{s+h} \right]' [E(x_t x_t')]^{-1} \left[\frac{1}{W_h^{\frac{1}{2}}} \sum_{s=t-W}^{t-h} x_s v_{s+h} \right] \\
&= \left[\frac{1}{W_h^{\frac{1}{2}}} \sum_{s=t-W}^{t-h} z_s v_{s+h} \right]' \left\{ [E(z_t z_t')]^{-1} - \begin{bmatrix} [E(x_t x_t')]^{-1} & \mathbf{0}_{l \times (k-l)} \\ \mathbf{0}_{(k-l) \times l} & \mathbf{0}_{(k-l) \times (k-l)} \end{bmatrix} \right\} \\
&\quad \times \left[\frac{1}{W_h^{\frac{1}{2}}} \sum_{s=t-W}^{t-h} z_s v_{s+h} \right]
\end{aligned}
$$

$$= \left[\frac{1}{W_h^{\frac{1}{2}}} \sum_{s=t-W}^{t-h} z_s v_{s+h} \right]' [E(z_t z_t')]^{-\frac{1}{2}} \cdot Q \cdot [E(z_t z_t')]^{-\frac{1}{2}}$$

$$\times \left[\frac{1}{W_h^{\frac{1}{2}}} \sum_{s=t-W}^{t-h} z_s v_{s+h} \right] \geq 0 \qquad \text{(A.8)}$$

Note that the probability that $[E(z_t z_t')]^{-1/2} W_h^{-1/2} \sum_{s=t-W}^{t-h} z_s v_{s+h}$ lies in the null space of Q for infinitely many t approaches zero because the dimension of the null space is $l < k$. Thus, the average of (A.8) over t is positive with probability approaching one. Combining the results in Eqs. (A.6) and (A.8), we find that the sign of $W(\hat{\sigma}_{2,W}^2 - \hat{\sigma}_{1,W}^2)$ is always positive with probability approaching one. Therefore, when $\gamma = 0$, $\hat{\sigma}_{1,W}^2 < \hat{\sigma}_{2,W}^2$ with probability approaching one.

In case 2, that is, when Model 2 is the true model, we have $y_{t+h} = \beta' z_t + v_{t+h} = \alpha' x_t + \gamma' w_t + v_{t+h}$. By Assumptions 2(a)(b), the second and third terms on the right-hand sides of (A.4) and (A.5) are both $o_p(T^{1/2}/W)$ and $o_p(T/W^2)$, respectively. Thus, they are $o_p(1)$ by Assumption 1. The first term on the right-hand side of Eq. (A.5) converges to the variance of v_{t+h} as the sample size T goes to infinity:

$$\frac{1}{T-h-W} \sum_{t=W+1}^{T-h} \left(y_{t+h} - \beta' z_t\right)^2 = \frac{1}{T-h-W} \sum_{t=W+1}^{T-h} v_{t+h}^2 \xrightarrow{p} \sigma_2^2. \qquad \text{(A.9)}$$

Similarly, the first term on the right-hand side of Eq. (A.4) converges in probability to the variance of $u_{t+h} \equiv y_{t+h} - \alpha^{*\prime} x_t$:

$$\begin{aligned}
\hat{\sigma}_{1,W}^2 &= \frac{1}{T-h-W} \sum_{t=W+h}^{T-1} \left(y_{t+h} - \alpha^{*\prime} x_t\right)^2 + o_p(1) \\
&\xrightarrow{p} E\left[(y_{t+h} - \alpha^{*\prime} x_t)^2\right] \\
&= E\left[(\alpha' x_t + \gamma' w_t + v_{t+h} - \alpha^{*\prime} x_t)^2\right] \\
&= E\left[(v_{t+h} + (\alpha' - \alpha^{*\prime}) x_t + \gamma' w_t)^2\right] \\
&= \sigma_2^2 + \begin{bmatrix} \alpha - \alpha^* \\ \gamma \end{bmatrix}' \begin{bmatrix} E(x_t x_t') & E(x_t w_t') \\ E(w_t x_t') & E(w_t w_t') \end{bmatrix} \begin{bmatrix} \alpha - \alpha^* \\ \gamma \end{bmatrix} > \sigma_2^2. \qquad \text{(A.10)}
\end{aligned}$$

Therefore, when Model 2 is true, the PMSEs satisfy $P(\hat{\sigma}_{1,W}^2 > \hat{\sigma}_{2,W}^2) = 1$ as $T \to \infty$ and $W \to \infty$, where W diverges slower than T.

Proof of Theorem 2 Note that the PMSEs, $\hat{\sigma}_{1,W}^2$ and $\hat{\sigma}_{2,W}^2$ can be expanded as

$$\hat{\sigma}_{1,W}^{2} = \frac{1}{T-h-W}\sum_{t=W+1}^{T-h}\left(y_{T,t+h} - \alpha^{*}\left(\frac{t}{T}\right)' x_{T,t}\right)^{2}$$
$$- \frac{2}{T-h-W}\sum_{t=W+1}^{T-h}\left(y_{T,t+h} - \alpha^{*}\left(\frac{t}{T}\right)' x_{T,t}\right) x_{T,t}'\left(\widehat{\alpha}_t - \alpha^{*}\left(\frac{t}{T}\right)\right)$$
$$+ \frac{1}{T-h-W}\sum_{t=W+1}^{T-h}\left(\widehat{\alpha}_t' - \alpha^{*}\left(\frac{t}{T}\right)\right)' x_{T,t}x_{T,t}'\left(\widehat{\alpha}_t - \alpha^{*}\left(\frac{t}{T}\right)\right) \tag{A.11}$$

and

$$\hat{\sigma}_{2,W}^{2} = \frac{1}{T-h-W}\sum_{t=W+1}^{T-h}\left(y_{T,t+h} - \beta'\left(\frac{t}{T}\right) z_{T,t}\right)^{2}$$
$$- \left(\frac{2}{T-h-W}\right)\sum_{t=W+1}^{T-h}\left(y_{T,t+h} - \beta'\left(\frac{t}{T}\right) z_{T,t}\right) z_{T,t}'\left(\widehat{\beta}_t - \beta\left(\frac{t}{T}\right)\right)$$
$$+ \frac{1}{T-h-W}\sum_{t=W+1}^{T-h}\left(\widehat{\beta}_t' - \beta'\left(\frac{t}{T}\right)\right)' z_t z_t'\left(\widehat{\beta}_t - \beta\left(\frac{t}{T}\right)\right), \tag{A.12}$$

respectively. If we show that each of

$$\frac{1}{T-h-W}\sum_{t=W+1}^{T-h}\left(y_{T,t+h} - \alpha^{*}\left(\frac{t}{T}\right)' x_{T,t}\right) x_t'\left(\widehat{\alpha}_t - \alpha^{*}\left(\frac{t}{T}\right)\right)$$
$$- \frac{1}{T-h-W}\sum_{t=W+1}^{T-h} u_{T,t+h}x_{T,t}' B_1(t) H_1(t), \tag{A.13}$$

$$\frac{1}{T-h-W}\sum_{t=W+1}^{T-h}\left(\widehat{\alpha}_t' - \alpha^{*}\left(\frac{t}{T}\right)\right)' x_{T,t}x_{T,t}'\left(\widehat{\alpha}_t - \alpha^{*}\left(\frac{t}{T}\right)\right)$$
$$- \frac{1}{T-h-W}\sum_{t=W+1}^{T-h} H_1(t)' B_1(t) z_{T,t} z_{T,t}' B_2(t) H_2(t), \tag{A.14}$$

$$\frac{1}{T-h-W}\sum_{t=W+1}^{T-h}\left(y_{T,t+h} - \beta\left(\frac{t}{T}\right)' z_{T,t}\right) z_{T,t}'\left(\widehat{\beta}_t - \beta\left(\frac{t}{T}\right)\right)$$
$$- \frac{1}{T-h-W}\sum_{t=W+1}^{T-h} v_{T,t+h}z_{T,t}' B_2(t) H_2(t), \tag{A.15}$$

$$\frac{1}{T-h-W}\sum_{t=W+1}^{T-h}\left(\widehat{\beta_t'}-\beta\left(\frac{t}{T}\right)'\right)' z_{T,t}z_{T,t}'\left(\widehat{\beta_t}-\beta\left(\frac{t}{T}\right)\right)$$
$$-\frac{1}{T-h-W}\sum_{t=W+1}^{T-h} H_2(t)'B_2(t)z_{T,t}z_{T,t}'B_2(t)H_2(t), \tag{A.16}$$

are $o_p(1/W)$ when the data are generated from model 1 (case 1) and are $o_p(1)$ when the data are generated from model 2 (case 2), the proof of Theorem 2 takes exactly the same steps as the proof of Theorem 1. Thus, it remains to show that (A.13)–(A.16) are $o_p(W^{-1})$ in case 1 and $o_p(1)$ in case 2. Note that the bias of the rolling regression estimator can be written as:

$$\hat{\beta}_{W,t}-\beta\left(\frac{t}{T}\right) = B_2(t)\frac{1}{W_h}\sum_{s=t-W}^{t-h} z_s\left[v_{s+h}+z_s'\left(\beta\left(\frac{s}{T}\right)-\beta\left(\frac{t}{T}\right)\right)\right]$$
$$= B_2(t)H_2(t)+\frac{B_2(t)}{W_h}\sum_{s=t-W}^{t-h} z_sz_s'\left(\beta\left(\frac{s}{T}\right)-\beta\left(\frac{t}{T}\right)\right) \tag{A.17}$$

Thus, the difference (A.15) is

$$\frac{1}{T-h-W}\sum_{t=W+1}^{T-h} v_{T,t+h}z_{T,t}'B_2(t)\frac{1}{W_h}\sum_{s=t-W}^{t-h} z_sz_s'\left(\beta\left(\frac{s}{T}\right)-\beta\left(\frac{t}{T}\right)\right).$$
$$=\frac{1}{T-h-W}\sum_{t=W+1}^{T-h} v_{T,t+h}z_{T,t}'\bar{B}_2\left(\frac{t}{T}\right)\frac{1}{W_h}\sum_{s=t-W}^{t-h} z_sz_s'\left(\beta\left(\frac{s}{T}\right)-\beta\left(\frac{t}{T}\right)\right)$$
$$+\frac{1}{T-h-W}\sum_{t=W+1}^{T-h} v_{T,t+h}z_{T,t}'\left(B_2(t)-\bar{B}_2\left(\frac{t}{T}\right)\right)\frac{1}{W_h}$$
$$\times\sum_{s=t-W}^{t-h} z_sz_s'\left(\beta\left(\frac{s}{T}\right)-\beta\left(\frac{t}{T}\right)\right). \tag{A.18}$$

By Assumption 4(c), the summands have zero mean. By Hölder's inequality and Assumptions 4(b)(c)(e)(f), the second moments of the right-hand side terms are $O(W/T^2)$. By Chebyshev's inequality, (A.15) is $O_p(W^{1/2}/T)$ which is $o_p(1/W)$ by Assumption 3. It can be shown that (A.13) is also $o_p(1/W)$ in a similar fashion.

The difference (A.16) is the sum of the following three terms:

$$\frac{1}{T-h-W}\sum_{t=W+1}^{T-h} v_{T,t+h}z_{T,t}z_{T,t}'B_2(t)\frac{1}{W_h}\sum_{s=t-W}^{t-h} z_sz_s'\left(\beta\left(\frac{s}{T}\right)-\beta\left(\frac{t}{T}\right)\right), \tag{A.19}$$

$$\frac{1}{T-h-W}\sum_{t=W+1}^{T-h}\left(\beta\left(\frac{s}{T}\right)-\beta\left(\frac{t}{T}\right)\right)'\frac{1}{W_h}\sum_{s=t-W}^{t-h} z_s z_s' B_2(t) z_{T,t} z_{T,t}' v_{T,t+h}, \tag{A.20}$$

$$\frac{1}{T-h-W}\sum_{t=W+1}^{T-h}\left(\beta\left(\frac{s}{T}\right)-\beta\left(\frac{t}{T}\right)\right)'\frac{1}{W_h}\sum_{s=t-W}^{t-h} z_s z_s' B_2(t) z_{T,t}$$
$$\times z_{T,t}' B_2(t)\frac{1}{W_h}\sum_{s=t-W}^{t-h} z_s z_s'\left(\beta\left(\frac{s}{T}\right)-\beta\left(\frac{t}{T}\right)\right), \tag{A.21}$$

Using Chebyshev's inequality, Hölder's inequality, Assumptions 3 and 4(b)(c)(e)(f), it can be shown that (A.19), (A.20), and (A.21) are $O_p(W^{1/2}T^{-2})$, $O_p(W^{1/2}T^{-2})$ and $O_p(W^2T^{-2})$ all of which are $o_p(W^{-1})$. It can be shown that (A.14) is also $o_p(1/W)$ when $\gamma(\cdot) = 0$ in an analogous fashion.

The rest of the proof of Theorem 2 takes exactly the same steps as the proof of Theorem 1 except that α^*, β, B_i, u_t, v_t, x_t, y_t, z_t and Lemma 1 is replaced by $\alpha\left(\frac{t}{T}\right)$, $\beta\left(\frac{t}{T}\right)$, $\bar{B}_i\left(\frac{t}{T}\right)$, u_{Tt}, v_{Tt}, x_{Tt}, y_{Tt}, z_{Tt} and Lemma 2, respectively.

References

Andrews, D.W.K. (1993), "Tests for Parameter Instability and Structural Change with Unknown Change Point", Econometrica 61, 821–856.

D'Agostino, A., D. Giannone, and P. Surico (2006), "(Un)Predictability and Macroeconomic Stability" ECB Working Paper 605.

Cai, Z., (2007), "Trending Time-Varying Coefficient Time Series Models with Serially Correlated Errors", Journal of Econometrics, 136, 163–188.

Clark, T.E., and M.W. McCracken (2000), "Not-for-Publication Appendix to " Tests of Equal Forecast Accuracy and Encompassing for Nested Models, unpublished manuscript, Federal Reserve Bank of Kansas City and Louisiana State Unviersity.

Clark, T.E., and M.W. McCracken (2001) "Tests of Equal Forecast Accuracy and Encompassing for Nested Models", Journal of Econometrics, 105, 85–110.

Clark, T.E., and M.W. McCracken (2005), "Evaluating Direct Multistep Forecasts", Econometric Reviews, 24, 369–404.

Gallant, A.R., and H. White (1988), A Unified Theory of Estimation and Inference for Nonlinear Dynamic Models, Basil Blackwell: New York, NY.

Giacomini, R. and B. Rossi (2010), "Forecast Comparisons in Unstable Environments", Journal of Applied Econometrics 25(4), 595–620.

Giacomini, R. and H. White (2006), "Tests of Conditional Predictive Ability", Econometrica 74(6), 1545–1578.

Giraitis, L., G. Kapetanios and T. Yates (2011),"Inference on Stochastic Time-Varying Coefficient Models", unpublished manuscript, Queen Mary, University of London, and the Bank of England.

Hall, P., and C.C. Heyde (1980), Martingale Limit Theory and its Application, Academic Press: San Diego CA.

Inoue, A., and L. Kilian (2006), "On the Selection of Forecasting Models", Journal of Econometrics, 130, 273–306.

Marcellino, Massimiliano, James H. Stock and Mark W. Watson (2003), "Macroeconoinic Forecasting in the Euro Area: Country-Speci...c vs. Area-Wide Information", European Economic Review, 47(1), pages 1–18.
McConnell, M.M., and G. Perez-Quiros (2000), "Output Fluctuations in the United States: What Has Changed Since the Early 1980" American Economic Review, 90(5), 1464–1476.
Meese, R. and K.S. Rogoff (1983a), "Exchange Rate Models of the Seventies. Do They Fit Out of Sample?", The Journal of International Economics 14, 3–24.
Meese, R. and K.S. Rogoff (1983b), "The Out of Sample Failure of Empirical Exchange Rate Models", in Jacob Frankel (ed.), Exchange Rates and International Macroeconomics, Chicago: University of Chicago Press for NBER.
Rossi, B., and A. Inoue (2011), "Out-of-Sample Forecast Tests Robust to the Choice of Window Size", mimeo.
Rossi, B., and T. Sekhposyan (2010), "Have Models™ Forecasting Performance Changed Over Time, and When?", International Journal of Forecasting, 26(4).
Sin, C.-Y., and H. White (1996), "Information Criteria for Selecting Possibly Misspecified Parametric Models", Journal of Econometrics, 71, 207–225.
Stock, James H. and Mark W. Watson (1999a), "Business Cycle Fluctuations in U.S. Macroeconomic Time Series", in Handbook of Macroeconomics, Vol. 1, J.B. Taylor and M. Woodford, eds, Elsevier, 3–64.
Stock, James H. and Mark W. Watson (1999b), "Forecasting In ation", Journal of Monetary Economics, 44, 293–335.
Swanson, N.R., and H. White (1997), "A Model Selection Approach to Real-Time Macroeconomic Forecasting Using Linear Models and Artificial Neural Networks", Review of Economics and Statistics.
Wei, C.Z. (1992), "On Predictive Least Squares Principles", Annals of Statistics, 20, 1–42.
West, K.D. (1996), "Asymptotic Inference about Predictive Ability", Econometrica 64, 1067–1084.
Wooldridge, J.M., and H. White (1988), Some Invariance Principles and Central Limit Theorems for Dependent Heterogeneous Processes, Econometric Theory 4, 210–230.
Wooldridge, J.M. (1994), "Estimation and Inference for Dependent Processes", in the Handbook of Econometrics, Volume IV, Edited by R.F. Engle and D.L. McFadden, Chapter 45, pp. 2639–2738.

Estimating Misspecified Moment Inequality Models

Hiroaki Kaido and Halbert White

Abstract This chapter studies partially identified structures defined by a finite number of moment inequalities. When the moment function is misspecified, it becomes difficult to interpret the conventional identified set. Even more seriously, this can be an empty set. We define a pseudo-true identified set whose elements can be interpreted as the least-squares projections of the moment functions that are observationally equivalent to the true moment function. We then construct a set estimator for the pseudo-true identified set and establish its $O_p(n^{-1/2})$ rate of convergence.

1 Introduction

This chapter develops a new approach to estimating structures defined by moment inequalities. Moment inequalities often arise as optimality conditions in discrete choice problems or in structures where economic variables are subject to some type of censoring. Typically, parametric models are used to estimate such structures. For example, in their analysis of an entry game in the airline markets, Ciliberto and Tamer (2009) use a linear specification for airlines' profit functions and assume that unobserved heterogeneity in the profit functions can be captured by independent normal random variables. In asset pricing theory with short sales prohibited, Luttmer (1996) specifies the functional form of the pricing kernel as a power function of

H. Kaido (✉)
Department of Economics, Boston University, 270 Bay State Rd., Boston, MA 02215, USA
e-mail: hkaido@bu.edu

H. White
Department of Economics (0508), University of California, San Diego, 9500 Gilman Dr., La Jolla, CA 92093-0508, USA
e-mail: hwhite@ucsd.edu

X. Chen and N. R. Swanson (eds.), *Recent Advances and Future Directions in Causality, Prediction, and Specification Analysis*, DOI: 10.1007/978-1-4614-1653-1_13,

consumption growth, based on the assumption that the investor's utility function is additively separable and isoelastic.

Any conclusions drawn from such methods rely on the validity of the model specification. Although commonly used estimation and inference methods for moment inequality models are robust to potential lack of identification, typically they are not robust to misspecification. Compared to cases where the parameter of interest is point identified, much less is known about the consequences of misspecified moment inequalities. As we will discuss, these can be serious. In general, misspecification makes it hard to interpret the estimated set of parameter values; an even more serious possibility is that the identified set could be an empty set. If the identified set is empty, every nonempty estimator sequence is inconsistent. Furthermore, it is often hard to see if the estimator is converging to some object that can be given any meaningful interpretation. An exception is the estimation method developed by Ponomareva and Tamer (2010), which focuses on estimating a regression function with interval censored outcome variables.

This chapter develops a new estimation method that is robust to potential parametric misspecification in general moment inequality models. Our contributions are three-fold. First, we define a pseudo-true identified set that is nonempty under mild assumptions and that can be interpreted as the projection of the set of function-valued parameters identified by the moment inequalities. Second, we construct a set estimator using a two-stage estimation procedure, and we show that the estimator is consistent for the pseudo-true identified set in Hausdorff metric. Third, we give conditions under which the proposed estimator converges to the pseudo-true identified set at the $n^{-1/2}$-rate.

The first stage is a nonparametric estimator of the true moment function. Given this, why perform a parametric second-stage estimation? After all, the nonparametric first stage estimates the same object of interest, without the possibility of parametric misspecification. There are a variety of reasons a researcher may nevertheless prefer to implement the parametric second stage: first is the undeniably appealing interpretability of the parametric specification; second is the much more precise estimation and inference afforded by using a parametric specification; and third, the second term of the second-stage objective function may offer a potentially useful model specification diagnostic. Future research may permit deriving the asymptotic distribution of this term under the null of correct parametric specification to provide a formal test. The two-stage procedure proposed here delivers these benefits, while avoiding the more serious adverse consequences of potential misspecification.

The chapter is organized as follows. Section 2 describes the data generating process and gives examples that fall within the scope of this chapter. We also introduce our definition of the pseudo-true identified Sect. 3 defines our estimator and presents our main results. We conclude in Sect. 4. We collect all proofs into the appendix.

2 The Data Generating Process and the Model

Our first assumption describes the data generating process (DGP).

Assumption 2.1 Let $(\Omega, \mathfrak{F}, \mathbb{P}_0)$ be a complete probability space. Let $k, \ell \in \mathbb{N}$. Let $X : \Omega \to \mathbb{R}^k$ be a Borel measurable map, let $\mathcal{X} \subseteq \mathbb{R}^k$ be the support of X, and let P_0 be the probability measure induced by X on $\mathcal{X}$. Let $\rho_0 : \mathcal{X} \to \mathbb{R}^\ell$ be an unknown measurable function such that $E[\rho_0(X)]$ exists and

$$E[\rho_0(X)] \leq 0, \tag{1}$$

where the expectation is taken with respect to P_0.

In what follows, we call ρ_0 the *true moment function*. The moment inequalities (1) often arise as an optimality condition in game-theoretic models (Bajari et al. 2007; Ciliberto and Tamer 2009) or models that involve variables that are subject to some kind of censoring (Manski and Tamer 2002). In empirical studies of such models, it is common to specify a parametric model for ρ_0.

Assumption 2.2 Let $p \in \mathbb{N}$ and let Θ be a subset of $\mathbb{R}^p$ with nonempty interior. Let $m : \mathcal{X} \times \Theta \to \mathbb{R}^\ell$ be such that $m(\cdot, \theta)$ is measurable for each $\theta \in \Theta$ and $m(x, \cdot)$ is continuous on Θ, a.e. $- P_0$. For each $\theta \in \Theta$, $m(\cdot, \theta) \in L^2_\ell := \{f : \mathcal{X} \to \mathbb{R}^\ell : E[f(X)'f(X)] < \infty\}$.

Throughout, we call $m(\cdot, \cdot)$ the *parametric moment function*.

Definition 2.1 Let $m_\theta(\cdot) := m(\cdot, \theta)$. Define $\mathcal{M}_\Theta := \{m_\theta \in L^2_\ell : \theta \in \Theta\}$. $\mathcal{M}_\Theta$ is *correctly specified* $(-P_0)$ if there exists $\theta_0 \in \Theta$ such that

$$P_0[\rho_0(X) = m(X, \theta_0)] = 1.$$

Otherwise, the model is misspecified.

If the model is correctly specified, we may define the set of parameter values that can be identified by the inequalities in (1):

$$\Theta_I := \{\theta \in \Theta : E[m(X, \theta)] \leq 0\}.$$

We call Θ_I the *conventional identified set*. This set collects all parameter values that yield parametric moment functions that are observationally equivalent to ρ_0.

It becomes difficult to interpret Θ_I when the model is misspecified, as pointed out by Ponomareva and Tamer (2010) for a regression model with an interval-valued outcome variable. Suppose first that the model is misspecified but Θ_I is nonempty. The set is still a collection of parameter values that are observationally equivalent to each other, but since there is no θ in Θ_I that corresponds to the true moment function, further structure is required to unambiguously interpret Θ_I as a collection of "pseudo-true parameter(s)". Further, Θ_I may be empty, especially if $\mathcal{M}_\Theta$ is a small class of functions. This makes the interpretation of Θ_I even more difficult. In fact, interpretation is impossible, as there is nothing to interpret.

Often, the economics of a given problem impose further structure on the DGP. To specify this, we let $0 < L \leq \ell$, and for measurable $s : \mathcal{X} \to \mathbb{R}^L$, let $\|s\|_L := E[s(X)'s(X)]^{1/2}$. Let $L^2_L := \{s : \mathcal{X} \to \mathbb{R}^L, \|s\|_L < \infty\}$, and let $\mathcal{S} \subseteq L^2_L$.

Assumption 2.3 There exists $\varphi : \mathcal{X} \times \mathcal{S} \to \mathbb{R}^\ell$ such that for each $x \in \mathcal{X}$, $\varphi(x, \cdot)$ is continuous on $\mathcal{S}$ and for each $s \in \mathcal{S}$, $\varphi(\cdot, s)$ is measurable. Further, there exists $s_0 \in \mathcal{S}$ such that

$$\rho_0(x) = \varphi(x, s_0), \quad \forall x \in \mathcal{X}.$$

When $\rho_0 \in L^2_\ell$ and there is no further structure on ρ_0 available, we let $L = \ell$, $\mathcal{S} = L^2_\ell$, and take φ to be the evaluation functional $e : \mathcal{X} \times \mathcal{S} \to \mathbb{R}^\ell$:

$$\varphi(x, s) = e(x, s) \equiv s(x),$$

as then $\varphi(x, \rho_0) = e(x, \rho_0) \equiv \rho_0(x)$ and $s_0 = \rho_0$. In this case, it is not necessary to explicitly introduce φ. Often, however, further structure on the form of ρ_0 is available. Typically, this is reflected in s depending non-trivially only on a strict subvector of X, say X_1. In such cases, we may write $\mathcal{S} \subseteq L^2_{\mathcal{X}_1}$ for clarity. We give several examples below.

When Assumption 2.3 holds, we typically parametrize the unknown function s_0. For example, it is common to specify s_0 as a linear function of some of the components of x. As we will see in the examples, a common modeling assumption is

Assumption 2.4 There exists $r : \mathcal{X} \times \Theta \to \mathbb{R}^L$ such that with $r_\theta := r(\cdot, \theta)$,

$$m(x, \theta) = \varphi(x, r_\theta), \quad \forall (x, \theta) \in \mathcal{X} \times \Theta.$$

Thus, misspecification occurs when there is no θ_0 in Θ such that $s_0 = r_{\theta_0}$.

More generally, misspecification can occur because the researcher mistakenly imposes Assumption 2.3, in which case s_0 fails to exist and there is again no θ_0 in Θ such that $\rho_0(x) = \varphi(x, r_{\theta_0})$. As s_0 is an element of an infinite-dimensional space, we may refer to this as "nonparametric" misspecification. To proceed, we assume that, as is often plausible, the researcher is sufficiently able to specify the structure of interest that nonparametric misspecification is not an issue, either because correct φ restrictions are imposed or no φ restrictions are imposed. We thus focus on the case of parametric misspecification, where s_0 exists but there is no θ_0 in Θ such that $s_0 = r_{\theta_0}$.

2.1 Examples

In this section, we present several motivating examples and also give commonly used parametric specifications in these examples. For any vector x, we use $x^{(j)}$ to denote the jth component of the vector. Similarly, for a vector valued function $f(x)$, we use $f^{(j)}(x)$ to denote the jth component of $f(x)$.

Example 2.1 (Interval censored outcome) Let $Z : \Omega \to \mathbb{R}^{d_Z}$ be a regressor with support $\mathcal{Z}$. Let $Y : \Omega \to \mathbb{R}$ be an outcome variable that is generated as:

$$Y = s_0(Z) + \epsilon, \tag{2}$$

where $s_0 \in \mathcal{S} := L^2_{\mathcal{Z}}$, say, and ϵ satisfies $E[\epsilon|Z] = 0$. We let $\mathcal{Y}$ denote the support of Y. Suppose Y is unobservable, but there exist $(Y_L, Y_U)' : \Omega \to \mathcal{Y} \times \mathcal{Y}$ such that $Y_L \le Y \le Y_U$ almost surely. Then, $(Y_L, Y_U, Z)'$ satisfies the following inequalities almost surely:

$$E[Y_L|Z] - s_0(Z) \le 0 \tag{3}$$
$$s_0(Z) - E[Y_U|Z] \le 0. \tag{4}$$

Let $x = (y_L, y_U, z)' \in \mathcal{X} := \mathcal{Y} \times \mathcal{Y} \times \mathcal{Z}$. Given a collection $\{A_1, \ldots, A_K\}$ of Borel subsets of $\mathcal{Z}$, the inequalities in (3), (4) imply that the moment inequalities in (1) hold with

$$\rho_0(x) = \varphi(x, s_0) := \begin{bmatrix} y_L - s_0(z) \\ s_0(z) - y_U \end{bmatrix} \otimes 1_A(z), \tag{5}$$

where $1_A(z) := (1\{z \in A_1\}, \ldots, 1\{z \in A_K\})'$.[1] For each $x \in \mathcal{X}$ and $s \in \mathcal{S}$, the functional φ evaluates vertical distances of $r(z)$ from y_L and y_U and multiplies them by the indicator function evaluated at z. Additional information on ρ_0 available in this example is that the moment functions are based on the vertical distances.

A common specification for s_0 is $s_0(z) = r_{\theta_0}(z) = z'\theta_0$ for some $\theta_0 \in \Theta \subseteq \mathbb{R}^{d_Z}$. The parametric moment function is then given for each $x \in \mathcal{X}$ by $m(x, \theta) = \varphi(x, r_\theta)$. Therefore, this example satisfies Assumption 2.4.

Example 2.2 Tamer (2003) considers a simultaneous game of complete information. For each $j = 1, 2$, let $Z_j : \Omega \to \mathbb{R}^{d_Z}$ and $\epsilon_j : \Omega \to \mathbb{R}$ be firm j's characteristics that are observable to the firms. The econometrician observes the Z's but not the ϵ's. For each j, let $g_j : \mathcal{Z} \times \{0, 1\} \to \mathbb{R}$. These functions are known to the firms but not to the econometrician. Suppose that each firm's payoff is given by

$$\pi_j(Z_j, Y_j, Y_{-j}) = (\epsilon_j - g_j(Z_j, Y_{-j}))Y_j, \quad j = 1, 2,$$

[1] Here, we take the indicators (or instruments) $1_A(z)$ as given. The indicators $1_A(z)$ could be replaced by any finite vector of measurable non-negative functions of z. Andrews and Shi (2011) give examples of such functions.

where $Y_j \in \mathcal{Y} := \{0, 1\}$ is firm j's entry decision, and $Y_{-j} \in \mathcal{Y}$ is the other firm's entry decision. The econometrician observes these decisions. Given (z_1, z_2), the firms' payoffs can be summarized in Table 1.

Suppose the firms and the econometrician know that $g(z, 1) \geq g(z, 0)$ for any value of z. This means that, other things equal, the opponent's entry would reduce the firm's own profit. In this setting, there are several possible equilibrium outcomes depending on the realization of (ϵ_1, ϵ_2). If $\epsilon_1 > g_1(z_1, 1)$ and $\epsilon_2 > g_2(z_2, 1)$, then $(1, 1)$ is the unique Nash equilibrium (NE) outcome. Similarly, if $\epsilon_1 > g_1(z_1, 1)$ and $\epsilon_2 < g_2(z_2, 1)$, $(1, 0)$ is the unique NE outcome, and if $\epsilon_1 < g_1(z_1, 1)$ and $\epsilon_2 > g_2(z_2, 1)$, $(0, 1)$ is the unique NE outcome. Now, if $\epsilon_1 < g_1(z_1, 1)$ and $\epsilon_2 < g_2(z_2, 1)$, there are two Nash equilibria, and they give the outcomes $(1, 0)$ and $(0, 1)$. Let $F_j, j = 1, 2$ be the unknown CDFs of ϵ_1 and ϵ_2.[2] Without any assumptions on the equilibrium selection mechanism, the model predicts the following set of inequalities:

$$P(Y_1 = 1, Y_2 = 1|Z_1 = z_1, Z_2 = z_2) = (1 - F_1(g_1(z_1, 1)))(1 - F_2(g_2(z_2, 1))) \tag{6}$$

$$P(Y_1 = 1, Y_2 = 0|Z_1 = z_1, Z_2 = z_2) \geq (1 - F_1(g_1(z_1, 1)))F_2(g_2(z_2, 1)) \tag{7}$$

$$P(Y_1 = 1, Y_2 = 0|Z_1 = z_1, Z_2 = z_2) \leq F_2(g_2(z_2, 1)). \tag{8}$$

Let $x := (y_1, y_2, z_1, z_2)' \in \mathcal{X} := \mathcal{Y} \times \mathcal{Y} \times \mathcal{Z} \times \mathcal{Z}$. Let $s_0 \in \mathcal{S} := \{s \in L^2_{\mathcal{Z}\times\mathcal{Z}} : s(z_1, z_2) \in [0, 1]^2, \forall (z_1, z_2) \in \mathcal{Z} \times \mathcal{Z}\}$ be defined by

$$s_0^{(1)}(z_1, z_2) := F_1(g_1(z_1, 1))$$
$$s_0^{(2)}(z_1, z_2) := F_2(g_2(z_2, 1)).$$

Here, $s_0^{(j)}(z_1, z_2)$ is the conditional probability that firm j's profit upon entry is negative given z_1 and z_2. Given a collection $\{A_j, j = 1, \ldots, K\}$ of Borel subsets of $\mathcal{Z} \times \mathcal{Z}$, let $1_A(z) := (1\{(z_1, z_2) \in A_1\}, \ldots, 1\{(z_1, z_2) \in A_K\})'$. The inequalities (6)–(8) imply the moment inequalities in (1) hold with

$$\begin{aligned}\rho_0(x) &= \varphi(x, s_0)\\ &= \begin{pmatrix} 1\{y_1 = 1, y_2 = 1\} - (1 - s_0^{(1)}(z_1, z_2))(1 - s_0^{(2)}(z_1, z_2)) \\ (1 - s_0^{(1)}(z_1, z_2))(1 - s_0^{(2)}(z_1, z_2)) - 1\{y_1 = 1, y_2 = 1\} \\ (1 - s_0^{(1)}(z_1, z_2))s_0^{(2)}(z_1, z_2) - 1\{y_1 = 1, y_2 = 0\} \\ 1\{y_1 = 1, y_2 = 0\} - s_0^{(2)}(z_1, z_2) \end{pmatrix} \otimes 1_A(z).\end{aligned}$$

The additional information on ρ_0 is that it is based on the differences between some combinations of the conditional probabilities $s_0(z_1, z_2)$ and indicators for specific events.

[2] The players do not need to know the F's, but these are important to the econometrician.

Table 1 The entry game payoff matrix

$Y_1\backslash Y_2$	0	1
0	$(0, 0)$	$(0, \epsilon_2 - g_2(z_2, 0))$
1	$(\epsilon_1 - g_1(z_1, 0), 0)$	$(\epsilon_1 - g_1(z_1, 1), \epsilon_2 - g_2(z_2, 1))$

A common parametric specification for g_j is $g_j(z_j, y_{-j}) = z_j'\gamma_0 - y_{-j}\beta_{j,0}$ for some $\beta_{j,0} \in B \subseteq \mathbb{R}_+$ and $\gamma_0 \in \Gamma \subseteq \mathbb{R}^{dz}$. It is also common to assume that F_j, $j = 1, 2$ belong to a known parametric class $\{F(\cdot; \alpha), \alpha \in \mathcal{A}\}$ of distributions. Then the parametric moment function can be defined for each x by $m(x, \theta) := \varphi(x, r_\theta)$, where $\theta := (\alpha_1, \alpha_2, \beta_1, \beta_2, \gamma)'$ and

$$r_\theta^{(1)}(z_1, z_2) = F(z_1'\gamma - \beta_1; \alpha_1) \tag{9}$$

$$r_\theta^{(2)}(z_1, z_2) = F(z_2'\gamma - \beta_2; \alpha_2). \tag{10}$$

This example also satisfies Assumption 2.4.

Example 2.3 (Discrete choice) Suppose an agent chooses $Z \in \mathbb{R}^{dz}$ from a set $\mathcal{Z} := \{z_1, \ldots, z_K\}$ in order to maximize her expected payoff $E[s_0(Y, Z) \mid \mathcal{I}]$, where Y is a vector of observable random variables, $s_0 \in \mathcal{R} := L^2_{\mathcal{Y}\times\mathcal{Z}}$ is the payoff function, and $\mathcal{I}$ is the agent's information set. The optimality condition for the agent's choice is given by:

$$E[s_0(Y, z_j) - s_0(Y, Z) \mid \mathcal{I}] \leq 0, \quad j = 1, \ldots, K. \tag{11}$$

Let $x := (y, z)' \in \mathcal{X} := \mathcal{Y} \times \mathcal{Z}$. The optimality conditions in (11) imply that the unconditional moment inequalities in (1) hold with

$$\rho_0(x) = \varphi(x, s_0) = \begin{pmatrix} \begin{bmatrix} s_0(y, z_1) - s_0(y, z_1) \\ \vdots \\ s_0(y, z_K) - s_0(y, z_1) \end{bmatrix} \times 1\{z = z_1\} \\ \vdots \\ \begin{bmatrix} s_0(y, z_1) - s_0(y, z_K) \\ \vdots \\ s_0(y, z_K) - s_0(y, z_K) \end{bmatrix} \times 1\{z = z_K\} \end{pmatrix}.$$

For given y, the functional φ evaluates the profit differences between a given choice z (e.g., z_1) and every other possible choice. The additional information on ρ_0 is that it is based on the profit differences.

A common specification for s_0 is $s_0(y, z) = r_{\theta_0}(y, z) = \psi(y, z; \alpha_0) + z'\beta_0 + \epsilon_z$ for some known function ψ, unknown $(\alpha_0, \beta_0) \in \Theta \subset \mathbb{R}^{d_\alpha + d_\beta}$, and an unobservable choice-dependent error ϵ_z. For simplicity, we assume that ϵ_z satisfies $E[\epsilon_{z_i} - \epsilon_{z_j} \mid \mathcal{I}] = 0$ for any i, j; see Pakes et al (2006) and Pakes (2010) for detailed discussions.

The parametric moment function is then given for each $x \in \mathcal{X}$ by $m(x, \theta) = \varphi(x, r_\theta)$. This example satisfies Assumption 2.4.

Example 2.4 (Pricing kernel) Let $Z : \Omega \to \mathbb{R}^{d_Z}$ be the payoffs of d_Z securities that are traded at a price of $P \in \mathcal{P} \subseteq \mathbb{R}^{d_Z}$. If short sales are not allowed for any securities, then the feasible set of portfolio weights is restricted to $\mathbb{R}_+^{d_Z}$ and the standard Euler equation does not hold. Instead, the following Euler inequalities hold (see Luttmer 1996):

$$E[s_0(Y)Z - P] \leq 0,$$

where $Y : \Omega \to \mathcal{Y}$ is a state variable, e.g. consumption growth, and $s_0 \in \mathcal{S} := \{s \in L^2_{\mathcal{Y}} : s(y) \geq 0, \forall y \in \mathcal{Y}\}$ is the pricing kernel function. The moment inequalities thus hold with the true moment function:

$$\rho_0(x) = \varphi(x, s_0) = s_0(y)z - p,$$

where $x := (y, z, p)' \in \mathcal{Y} \times \mathcal{Z} \times \mathcal{P}$. This function evaluates the pricing kernel r at y and computes a vector of pricing errors. The additional information on ρ_0 is that it is based on the pricing errors.

A common specification for s_0 is $s_0(y) = r_{\theta_0}(y) = \beta_0 y^{-\gamma_0}$, where $\beta_0 \in B \subseteq [0, 1]$ is the investor's subjective discount factor and $\gamma_0 \in \Gamma \subseteq \mathbb{R}_+$ is the relative risk aversion coefficient. Let $\theta := (\beta, \gamma)'$. The parametric moment function is then given for each $x \in \mathcal{X}$ by $m(x, \theta) = \varphi(x, r_\theta)$, satisfying Assumption 2.4.

2.2 Projection

The inequality restrictions $E[\varphi(X, s_0)] \leq 0$ may not uniquely identify s_0. Define

$$\mathcal{S}_0 := \{s \in \mathcal{S} : E[\varphi(X, s)] \leq 0\}.$$

We define a pseudo-true identified set of parameters as a collection of projections of elements in $\mathcal{S}_0$. Let W be a given non-random finite $L \times L$ symmetric positive-definite matrix. For each $s \in \mathcal{S}$, define the norm $\|s\|_W := E[s(X)'Ws(X)]^{1/2}$. For each $s \in \mathcal{S}$ and $A \subseteq \mathcal{S}$, the projection map $\Pi_A : \mathcal{S} \to A$ is the map such that

$$\|s - \Pi_A s\|_W = \inf_{a \in A} \|s - a\|_W.$$

Let $\mathcal{R}_\Theta := \{r_\theta \in \mathcal{S} : \theta \in \Theta\}$. Given Assumption 2.4, we can define

$$\Theta_* := \{\theta \in \Theta : r_\theta = \Pi_{\mathcal{R}_\Theta} s, s \in \mathcal{S}_0\}.$$

When φ is the evaluation map e, Θ_* is simply $\Theta_* := \{\theta \in \Theta : m_\theta = \Pi_{\mathcal{M}_\Theta} s, s \in \mathcal{S}_0\}$.

Θ_* can be interpreted as the set of parameters that correspond to the elements m_θ in the $\mathcal{R}_\Theta$ -projection of $\mathcal{S}_0$. This set is nonempty (under some regularity conditions), and each element can be interpreted as a projection of s inducing a functional $\varphi(\cdot, s)$ that is observationally equivalent to ρ_0. In this sense, each element in Θ_* has an interpretation as a pseudo-true value. Thus, we call Θ_* the *pseudo-true identified set*. [White (1982) uses θ_* to denote the unique pseudo-true value in the fully identified case.]

We illustrate the relationship between Θ_I and Θ_* with an example. Consider Example 2.1. Let $\Theta \subseteq \mathbb{R}^{d_Z}$. The conventional identified set is given by

$$\Theta_I = \{\theta \in \Theta : E[(Y_L - Z'\theta)1\{Z \in A_j\}] \le 0, \\ \text{and } E[(Z'\theta - Y_U)1\{Z \in A_j\}] \le 0, \quad j = 1, \dots, K\}. \tag{12}$$

The pseudo-true identified set is given by

$$\Theta_* = \{\theta \in \Theta : \theta = E[ZZ']^{-1}E[Zs(Z)], s \in \mathcal{S}_0\}. \tag{13}$$

Let D be a $d_Z \times K$ matrix whose jth column is $E[Z\,1\{Z \in A_j\}]$. For this example, the following result holds:

Proposition 2. 1 *Let the conditions of Example 2.1 hold, and let Θ_* be given as in (13). Let Θ_I be given as in (12). Then $\Theta_I \subseteq \Theta_*$. Suppose further that $\mathcal{M}_\Theta$ is correctly specified, that $E[Y_U|Z] = E[Y_L|Z] = Z'\theta_0$ a.s, and that $d_Z \le rank(D)$. Then $\Theta_I = \Theta_* = \{\theta_0\}$.*

As this example shows, unless there is some information that helps restrict $\mathcal{S}_0$ very tightly, Θ_I is often a proper subset of Θ_*. This is because without such information, $\mathcal{S}_0$ is typically a much richer class of functions than $\mathcal{R}_\Theta$. Another important point to note is that, although Θ_* is well-defined generally, Θ_I can be empty quite easily. In particular, for any $x, x' \in \mathcal{X}$, let $x_\lambda := \lambda x + (1-\lambda)x', 0 \le \lambda \le 1$. Θ_I is empty if there exists (x, x') and $\lambda \in [0, 1]$ such that (i) $x_\lambda \in \mathcal{X}$ and $(E[Y_L|x_\lambda] - E[Y_U|x])/\|x_\lambda - x\| > (E[Y_U|x'] - E[Y_U|x])/\|x' - x\|$ or (ii) $x_\lambda \in \mathcal{X}$ and $(E[Y_U|x_\lambda] - E[Y_L|x])/\|x_\lambda - x\| < (E[Y_L|x'] - E[Y_L|x])/\|x' - x\|$.[3] Figure 1, which is similar to Fig. 1 in Ponomareva and Tamer (2010), illustrates an example that satisfies condition (i) for the one-dimensional case.

In this example, each element in Θ_* solves the following moment restrictions:

$$E[Z(Z'\theta - Y)] = E[Zu(X)], \tag{14}$$

with $u(x) = s(z) - y$ for some $s \in \mathcal{S}_0$. This can be viewed as a special case of *incomplete linear moment restrictions* studied in Bontemps, Magnac, and Maurin (2011)

[3] For this example, Θ_I is never empty as long as the number $(2K)$ of moment inequalities equals the number of parameters (ℓ).

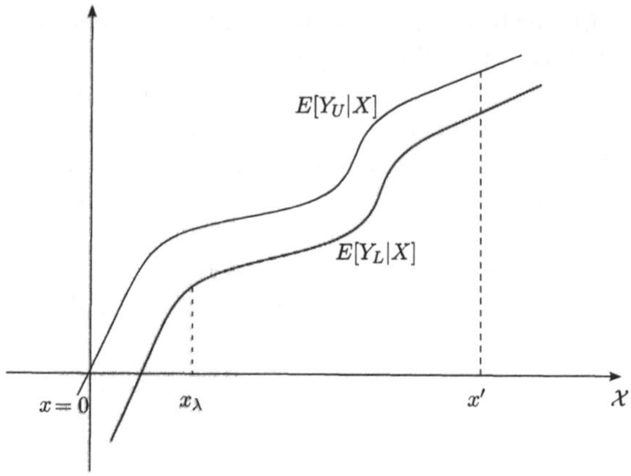

Fig. 1 An example with an empty conventional identified set

(BMM, henceforth).[4] BMM shows that the set of parameters that solves incomplete linear moment restrictions is necessarily convex and develops an inference method that exploits this property.

We note here that this connection to BMM's work only occurs when the parametric class is of the form: $\mathcal{R}_\Theta = \{r_\theta : r_\theta(z) = z'\theta,\ \theta \in \Theta\}$. The elements of Θ_*, however, do not generally solve incomplete linear moment restrictions when $\mathcal{R}_\Theta$ includes nonlinear functions of θ. Therefore, BMM's inference method is only applicable when r_θ is linear. Our estimation procedure is more flexible than theirs in the following two respects. First, one may allow projection to a more general class of parametric functions that includes nonlinear functions of θ. Second, as a consequence of the first point, we do not require Θ_* to be convex. We, however, pay a price for achieving this generality. We require s to satisfy suitable smoothness conditions, which are not required by BMM. We discuss these conditions in detail in the following section.

3 Estimation

3.1 Set Estimator

For W as above and each $(\theta, s) \in \Theta \times \mathcal{S}$, let the *population criterion function* be defined by

$$\begin{aligned} Q(\theta, s) = {} & E[(s(X_i) - r_\theta(X_i))' W (s(X_i) - r_\theta(X_i))] \\ & - \inf_{\vartheta \in \Theta} E[(s(X_i) - r_\vartheta(X_i))' W (s(X_i) - r_\vartheta(X_i))]. \end{aligned} \tag{15}$$

[4] We are indebted to an anonymous referee for pointing out a relationship between BMM's framework and ours. General incomplete linear moment restrictions are given by $E[V(Z'\theta - Y)] = E[Vu(V)]$, where V is a vector of random variables, and u is an unknown bounded function. See BMM for details.

Using the population criterion function, the "pseudo-true" identified set Θ_* can be equivalently written as

$$\Theta_* = \{\theta : Q(\theta, s) = 0, \quad s \in \mathcal{S}_0\}.$$

Given a sample $\{X_1, \ldots, X_n\}$ of observations, let the *sample criterion function* be defined for each $(\theta, s) \in \Theta \times \mathcal{S}$ by

$$Q_n(\theta, s) := \frac{1}{n}\sum_{i=1}^{n}(s(X_i) - r_\theta(X_i))'W(s(X_i) - r_\theta(X_i))$$
$$- \inf_{\vartheta \in \Theta} \frac{1}{n}\sum_{i=1}^{n}(s(X_i) - r_\vartheta(X_i))'W(s(X_i) - r_\vartheta(X_i)). \qquad (16)$$

Ideally, we would like to estimate Θ_* by $\tilde{\Theta}_n$, say, where $\tilde{\Theta}_n := \{\theta : Q_n(\theta, s) \leq c_n, s \in \mathcal{S}_0\}$. But $\mathcal{S}_0$ is unknown, so we must estimate it. Thus, we employ a two-stage procedure, similar to that studied in Kaido and White (2010). Section 3.3 discusses how to construct a first-stage estimator of $\mathcal{S}_0$. For now, we suppose that such an estimator exists. For this, let $\mathcal{F}(A)$ be the set of closed subsets of a set A. See Kaido and White (2010) for background, including discussion of Effros measurability.

Assumption 3.1 (First-stage estimator) For each n, let $\mathcal{S}_n \subseteq \mathcal{S}$. $\hat{\mathcal{S}}_n : \Omega \to \mathcal{F}(\mathcal{S}_n)$ is (Effros-) measurable.

Given a first-stage estimator, we define a set estimator for the pseudo-true identified set. Let $\{c_n\}$ be a sequence of non-negative constants. The set estimator for Θ_* is defined by

$$\hat{\Theta}_n := \{\theta \in \Theta : Q_n(\theta, s) \leq c_n, s \in \hat{\mathcal{S}}_n\}. \qquad (17)$$

We establish our consistency results using the Hausdorff metric. Let $||\cdot||$ denote the Euclidean norm, and for any closed subsets A and B of a finite-dimensional Euclidean space (e.g., containing θ), let

$$d_H(A, B) := \max\{\vec{d}_H(A, B), \vec{d}_H(B, A)\}, \quad \vec{d}_H(A, B) := \sup_{a \in A} \inf_{b \in B} \|a - b\|, \quad (18)$$

where d_H and $\vec{d}_H$ are the Hausdorff metric and directed Hausdorff distance respectively.

Before stating our assumptions, we introduce some additional notation. Let D_θ^α denote the differential operator $\partial^\alpha / \partial\theta_1^{\alpha_1} \cdots \partial\theta_p^{\alpha_p}$ with $|\alpha| := \sum_{j=1}^{p} \alpha_j$. Similarly, we let D_x^β denote the differential operator $\partial^\beta / \partial x_1^{\beta_1} \cdots \partial x_k^{\beta_k}$ with $|\beta| := \sum_{j=1}^{k} \beta_j$. For a function $f : \mathcal{X} \to \mathbb{R}$ and $\gamma > 0$, let $\underline{\gamma}$ be the smallest integer smaller than γ and define

$$\|f\|_\gamma := \max_{|\beta|\le\underline{\gamma}} \sup_{x\in\mathcal{X}} \left|D_x^\beta f(x)\right| + \max_{|\beta|=\underline{\gamma}} \sup_{x,y\in\mathcal{X}} \frac{\left|D_x^\beta f(x) - D_x^\beta f(x)\right|}{\|x - -y\|^{\gamma-\underline{\gamma}}}.$$

Let $\mathcal{C}_M^\gamma(\mathcal{X})$ be the set of all continuous functions $f : \mathcal{X} \to \mathbb{R}$ such that $\|f\|_\gamma \le M$. Let $\mathcal{C}_{M,L}^\gamma(\mathcal{X}) := \{f : \mathcal{X} \to \mathbb{R}^L : f^{(j)} \in \mathcal{C}_M^\gamma(\mathcal{X}), j = 1, \ldots, L\}$. Finally, for any $\eta > 0$, let $\mathcal{S}_0^\eta := \{s \in \mathcal{S} : \inf_{s'\in\mathcal{S}_0} \|s - s'\|_W < \eta\}$.

Our first assumption places conditions on the parameter spaces Θ and $\mathcal{S}$. We let $int(\Theta)$ denote the interior of Θ.

Assumption 3.2 (i) Θ is compact; (ii) $\mathcal{S}$ is a compact convex set with nonempty interior; (iii) there exists $\gamma > k/2$ such that $\mathcal{S} \subseteq \mathcal{C}_{M,L}^\gamma(\mathcal{X})$; (iv) $\mathcal{R}_\Theta$ is a convex subset of $\mathcal{S}$; (v) $\Theta_* \subseteq int(\Theta)$.

Assumption 3.2 (i) is standard in the literature of extremum estimation and also ensures the compactness of the pseudo-true identified set. Assumption 3.2 (iii) imposes a smoothness requirement on each component of $s \in \mathcal{S}$. Together with Assumption (ii), this implies that $\mathcal{S}$ is compact under the uniform norm, which will be also used for establishing the Hausdorff consistency of $\hat{\mathcal{S}}_n$ in the following section. For the Hausdorff consistency of $\hat{\Theta}_n$, the requirement $\gamma > k/2$ can be relaxed to $\gamma > 0$, and it also suffices that the smoothness requirement holds for functions in neighborhoods of $\mathcal{S}_0$. The stronger requirement given here, however, will be useful for deriving the rates of convergence of $\hat{\Theta}_n$ and $\hat{\mathcal{S}}_n$.

For ease of analysis, we assume below that the observations are from a sample of IID random vectors.

Assumption 3.3 The observations $\{X_i, i = 1, \ldots, n\}$ are independently and identically distributed.

The following two assumptions impose regularity conditions on r_θ.

Assumption 3.4 (i) $r(x, \cdot)$ is twice continuously differentiable on the interior of Θ a.e. $- P_0$, and for any j, x, and $|\alpha| \le 2$, there exists a measurable bounded function $C : \mathcal{X} \to \mathbb{R}$ such that $|D_\theta^\alpha r_\theta^{(j)}(x) - D_\theta^\alpha r_{\theta'}^{(j)}(x)| \le C(x)\|\theta - \theta'\|$; (ii) there exists a measurable bounded function $R : \mathcal{X} \to \mathbb{R}$ such that

$$\max_{\substack{j=1,\ldots,l\\|\alpha|\le2}} \sup_{\theta\in\Theta} \left|D_\theta^\alpha r_\theta^{(j)}(x)\right| \le R(x).$$

For each x, let $\nabla_\theta r_\theta(x)$ be a $L \times p$ matrix whose jth row is the gradient vector of $r_\theta^{(j)}$ with respect to θ. For each $x \in \mathcal{X}$ and $i, j \in \{1, \ldots, L\}$, let $\partial^2/\partial\theta_i\partial\theta_j r_\theta(x)$ be a $L \times 1$ vector whose kth component is given by $\partial^2/\partial\theta_i\partial\theta_j r_\theta^{(k)}(x)$. For each $\theta \in \Theta$, $s \in \mathcal{S}$, and $x \in \mathcal{X}$, let $H_W(\theta, s, x)$ be a $p \times p$ matrix whose (i, j)th component is given by

$$H_W^{(i,j)}(\theta, s, x) = 2\left(\frac{\partial^2}{\partial\theta_i\partial\theta_j} r_\theta(x)\right)' W(r_\theta(x) - s(x)). \tag{19}$$

Let $\eta > 0$. For each $s \in \mathcal{S}_0^\eta$ and $\epsilon > 0$, let $V^\epsilon(s)$ be the neighborhood of $\theta_*(s)$ defined by

$$V^\epsilon(s) := \{\theta \in \Theta : \|\theta - \theta_*(s)\| \leq \epsilon\}.$$

Let $\mathcal{N}_{\epsilon,\eta} := \{(\theta, s) : \theta \in V^\epsilon(s), s \in \mathcal{S}_0^\eta\}$ be the graph of the correspondence V^ϵ on $\mathcal{S}_0^\eta$.

Assumption 3.5 There exist $\bar{\epsilon} > 0$ and $\bar{\eta} > 0$ such that the Hessian matrix $\nabla_\theta^2 Q(\theta, s) := E[H_W(\theta, s, X_i) + 2\nabla_\theta r_\theta(X_i)' W \nabla_\theta r_\theta(X_i)]$ is positive definite uniformly over $\mathcal{N}_{\bar{\epsilon},\bar{\eta}}$.

Assumption 3.4 imposes a smoothness requirement on r_θ as a function of θ, enabling us to expand the first order condition for minimization, as is standard in the literature. Assumption 3.5 requires that Hessian of $Q(\theta, s)$ with respect to θ to be positive definite uniformly on a suitable neighborhood of $\Theta_* \times \mathcal{S}_0$. For the consistency of $\hat{\Theta}_n$, it suffices to assume that the Hessian is uniformly non-singular over $\mathcal{N}_{\bar{\epsilon},\bar{\eta}}$, but a stronger condition given here will be useful to ensure a quadratic approximation of the criterion function, which is crucial for the $\sqrt{n}$-consistency of $\hat{\Theta}_n$.

Further, we assume that $\hat{\mathcal{S}}_n$ is consistent for $\mathcal{S}_0$ in a suitable Hausdorff metric. Specifically, for subsets A, B of $\mathcal{S}$, let

$$d_{H,W}(A, B) := \max\left\{\sup_{a \in A} \inf_{b \in B} \|a - b\|_W, \sup_{b \in B} \inf_{a \in A} \|a - b\|_W\right\}.$$

Assumption 3.6 $d_{H,W}(\hat{\mathcal{S}}_n, \mathcal{S}_0) = o_p(1)$.

Theorem 3.1 is our first main result, which establishes the consistency of the set estimator defined in (17) with c_n set to 0. This result is established by extending the standard consistency proof for extremum estimators to the current setting. Note that, under Assumption 3.2 (iv), the projection $\theta_*(s) := \Pi_{\mathcal{R}_\Theta} s$ of each point $s \in \mathcal{S}$ to $\mathcal{R}_\Theta$ exists and is uniquely determined. In other words, for each $s \in \mathcal{S}$, $\theta_*(s)$ is point identified. By setting $c_n = 0$, the set estimator is then asymptotically equivalent to the collection of minimizers $\hat{\theta}_n(s) := \text{argmin}_{\theta' \in \Theta} Q_n(\theta, s)$ of the sample criterion function. The main challenge for establishing Hausdorff consistency is to show that $\hat{\theta}_n(s) - \theta_*(s)$ vanishes in probability over a sufficiently large neighborhood of $\mathcal{S}_0$. The proof of the theorem in the appendix formally establishes this and gives the desired result.

Theorem 3.1 *Suppose Assumptions 2.1–2.4 and 3.1–3.6 hold. Let $\hat{\Theta}_n$ be defined as in (17) with $c_n = 0$ for all n. Then $d_H(\hat{\Theta}_n, \Theta_*) = o_p(1)$.*

The result of Theorem 3.1 is similar to that of Theorem 3.2 in Chernozhukov et al. (2007), who establish the Hausdorff consistency of a level-set estimator with $c_n = 0$

when Q_n degenerates on a neighborhood of the identified set.[5] When Assumption 3.2 (iv) fails to hold, this estimator may not be consistent. We, however, conjecture that it would be possible to construct a Hausdorff consistent estimator of Θ_* even in such a setting by choosing a positive sequence $\{c_n\}$ of levels that tends to 0 as $n \to \infty$ and by exploiting the fact that $\hat{\mathcal{S}}_n$ converges to $\mathcal{S}_0$ in a suitable Hausdorff metric. In fact, Kaido and White (2010) establish the Hausdorff consistency of their two-stage set estimator using this argument, but in their analysis, the first-stage parameter (s in our setting) must be finite dimensional. Extending Theorem 3.1 to a more general one that allows non-convex parametric classes is definitely of interest, but to keep our tight focus here, we leave this as a future work.

3.2 The Rate of Convergence

Theorem 3.1 uses the fact that $d_H(\hat{\Theta}_n, \Theta_*)$ can be bounded by $d_{H,W}(\hat{\mathcal{S}}_n, \mathcal{S}_0)$. Although $\hat{\mathcal{S}}_n$ does not converge at a parametric rate generally, the convergence rate of $\hat{\Theta}_n$ can be improved when $\hat{\mathcal{S}}_n$ converges to $\mathcal{S}_0$ at a rate $o_p(n^{-1/4})$. This is analogous to the results obtained for the point identified case; see, for example, Newey (1994), Ai and Chen (2003), and Ichimura and Lee (2010).

Assumption 3.7 $d_{H,W}(\hat{\mathcal{S}}_n, \mathcal{S}_0) = o_p(n^{-1/4})$.

Theorem 3.2 *Suppose the conditions of Theorem 3.1 hold. Suppose in addition Assumption 3.7 holds. Let $\hat{\Theta}_n$ be defined as in (17) with $c_n = 0$ for all n. Then, $d_H(\hat{\Theta}_n, \Theta_*) = O_p(n^{-1/2})$.*

For this, setting c_n to 0 is crucial for achieving the $O_p(n^{-1/2})$ rate. We here note that Theorem 3.2 builds on Lemma A.2 in the appendix, which establishes the convergence rate (in directed Hausdorff distance) of $\hat{\Theta}_n$ in (17) with a possibly nonzero level c_n. This lemma does not require Assumption 3.2 (iv) but assumes the Hausdorff consistency of $\hat{\Theta}_n$ as a high-level condition. This is why Theorem 3.2 is stated for $\hat{\Theta}_n$ with $c_n = 0$. As previously discussed, however, if Theorem 3.1 is extended to allow non-convex parametric classes, this lemma can be used to characterize the estimator's convergence rate under a more general setting.

3.3 The First-Stage Estimator

This section discusses how to construct a first-stage set estimator. A challenge is that the object of interest $\mathcal{S}_0$ is a subset of an infinite-dimensional space. This requires us to use a nonparametric estimation technique for estimating $\mathcal{S}_0$. This type of estimation

[5] Their framework does not consider misspecification. Their object of interest is therefore the conventional identified set Θ_I. In our setting, the sample criterion function degenerates, i.e., $Q_n(\theta, s) = 0$, on a neighborhood of $\Theta_* \times \mathcal{S}_0$ under Assumption 3.2 (iv).

problem was recently analyzed in Santos (2011), who studies estimation of linear functionals of function-valued parameters in nonparametric instrumental variable problems. We rely on his results on consistency and the rate of convergence, which extend Chernozhukov et al. (2007) analysis to a nonparametric setting. Specifically, for each $s \in \mathcal{S}$, let

$$\mathcal{Q}_n(s) := \sum_{j=1}^{l} \Big(\frac{1}{n} \sum_{i=1}^{n} \varphi^{(j)}(X_i, s)\Big)_+^2. \tag{20}$$

This is a sample criterion function defined on $\mathcal{S}$. For instance, $\mathcal{Q}_n$ for Example 2.1 is given by

$$\mathcal{Q}_n(s) = \sum_{j=1}^{K} \Big(\frac{1}{n} \sum_{i=1}^{n} (Y_{L,i} - s(Z_i))1_{A_j}(Z_i)\Big)_+^2 + \sum_{j=1}^{K} \Big(\frac{1}{n} \sum_{i=1}^{n} (s(Z_i) - Y_{U,i})1_{A_j}(Z_i)\Big)_+^2.$$

Our first-stage set estimator is a level set of $\mathcal{Q}_n$ over a sieve $\mathcal{S}_n \subseteq \mathcal{S}$. Given a sequence of non-negative constants $\{a_n\}$ and $\{b_n\}$, define

$$\hat{\mathcal{S}}_n := \{s \in \mathcal{S}_n : \mathcal{Q}_n(s) \le b_n/a_n\}. \tag{21}$$

We add regularity conditions on φ, $\{\mathcal{S}_n\}$, and $\{(a_n, b_n)\}$ to ensure the Hausdorff consistency of $\hat{\mathcal{S}}_n$ and derive its convergence rate. The following two assumptions impose smoothness requirements on the map φ.

Assumption 3.8 For each j, there is a function $B_j : \mathcal{X} \to \mathbb{R}_+$ such that

$$|\varphi^{(j)}(x, s) - \varphi^{(j)}(x, s')| \le B_j(x)\rho(s, s'), \quad \forall s, s' \in \mathcal{S},$$

where $\rho(s, s') := \sup_{x \in \mathcal{S}} \max_{j=1,\dots,l} |s^{(j)}(x) - s'^{(j)}(x)|$.

For each $s \in \mathcal{S}$, let $\mathcal{I}(s) := \{j \in \{1, \dots, l\} : E[\varphi^{(j)}(X_i, s)] > 0\}$. $\mathcal{I}(s)$ is the set of indexes whose associated moments violate the inequality restrictions. For each j, let $\bar{\varphi}^{(j)} := E[\varphi^{(j)}(X_i, s)]$.

Assumption 3.9 (i) For each $s \in \mathcal{S}$ and j, $\bar{\varphi}^{(j)} : \mathcal{S} \to \mathbb{R}$ is continuously Fréchet differentiable with the Fréchet derivative $\dot{\varphi}_s^{(j)} : \mathcal{S} \to \mathbb{R}$, and for each $s \in \mathcal{S}$, the operator norm $\|\dot{\varphi}_s^{(j)}\|_{op}$ of $\dot{\varphi}_s^{(j)}$ is bounded away from 0 for some $j \in \{1, \dots, l\}$; (ii) for each $s \notin \mathcal{S}_0$, there exist $j \in \mathcal{I}(s)$ and $C_j > 0$ such that $E[\varphi^{(j)}(X_i, s)] \ge C_j \|s - s_0\|_W$ for some $s_0 \in \mathcal{S}_0$.

We also add regularity conditions on $\mathcal{S}_n$, which can be satisfied by commonly used sieves including polynomials, splines, wavelets, and certain artificial neural network sieves.

Assumption 3.10 (i) For each n, $\mathcal{S}_n \subseteq \mathcal{S}$, and both $\mathcal{S}_n$ and $\mathcal{S}$ are closed with respect to ρ; (ii) for every $s \in \mathcal{S}$, there is $\Pi_n s \in \mathcal{S}_n$ such that $\sup_{s \in \mathcal{S}} \|s - \Pi_n s\|_W = O(\delta_n)$ for some sequence $\{\delta_n\}$ of non-negative constants such that $\delta_n \to 0$.

Theorem 3.3 *Suppose Assumptions 2.1–2.3, 3.2 (i)–(iii), 3.3, 3.8, 3.9 (i), and 3.10 hold. Let* $a_n = O(\max\{n^{-1}, \delta_n^2\}^{-1})$ *and* $b_n \to \infty$ *with* $b_n = o(a_n)$. *Then*

$$d_{H,W}(\hat{\mathcal{S}}_n, \mathcal{S}_0) = o_p(1).$$

In addition, suppose that Assumption 3.9 (ii) holds. Then

$$d_{H,W}(\hat{\mathcal{S}}_n, \mathcal{S}_0) = O_p\big(\sqrt{b_n/a_n}\big).$$

Theorem 3.3 can be used to establish Assumptions 3.6 and 3.7, which are imposed in Theorems 3.1 and 3.2. These conditions are satisfied for Example 2.1 with a single regressor.

In what follows, for any two sequences of positive constants $\{c_n\}$, $\{d_n\}$, let $c_n \asymp d_n$ mean there exist constants $0 < C_1 < C_2 < \infty$ such that $C_1 \le |c_n/d_n| \le C_2$ for all n.

Corollary 3.1 *In Example 2.1, suppose that* $\mathcal{Z}$ *is a compact convex subset of the real line and* $r_\theta(z) = \theta^{(1)} + \theta^{(2)} z$, *where* $\theta \in \Theta \subseteq \mathbb{R}^2$. *Suppose that* Θ *is compact and convex. Suppose further that* $\{(Y_{L,i}, Y_{U,i}, Z_i)\}_{i=1,\ldots,n}$ *is a random sample from* P_0 *and that* $P_0(Z \in A_k) > 0$ *for all* k *and* $Var(Z) > 0$. *Let* $\mathcal{S} := \{s \in L^2_{\mathcal{Z},1} : \mathcal{Z} \to \mathbb{R} : \|s\|_\infty \le M, |s(z) - s(z')| \le M\|z - z'\|, \forall z, z' \in \mathcal{Z}\}$ *for some* $M > 0$. *Let* $\{r_q(\cdot)\}_{q=1}^{J_n}$ *be splines of order two with* J_n *knots on* $\mathcal{Z}$. *Define* $\mathcal{S}_n := \{s : s(z) = \sum_{q=1}^{J_n} \beta_q r_q(z)\}$ *with* $J_n \asymp n^{c_1}$, $c_1 > 1/3$. *Let* $\hat{\mathcal{S}}_n$ *be defined as in (21) with* $a_n \asymp n^{c_2}$, *where* $2/3 < c_2 < 1$ *and* $b_n \asymp \ln n$. *Then: (i)* $\hat{\mathcal{S}}_n$ *is (Effros-) measurable;*
(ii) $d_{H,W}(\hat{\mathcal{S}}_n, \mathcal{S}_0) = o_p(1)$; *(iii)* $d_{H,W}(\hat{\mathcal{S}}_n, \mathcal{S}_0) = o_p(n^{-1/4})$.

Given these results, we further show that the estimator of the pseudo-true identified set is consistent and converges at a $n^{-1/2}$-rate.

Corollary 3.2 *Suppose that the conditions of Corollary 3.1 hold. Let* Q *be defined as in (15) with* $W = 1$. *Let* Q_n *be defined as in (16) and* $\hat{\Theta}_n$ *be defined as in (17) with* $c_n = 0$ *and* $\hat{\mathcal{S}}_n$ *as in Corollary 3.1. Then* $d_H(\hat{\Theta}_n, \Theta_*) = O_p(n^{-1/2})$.

4 Concluding Remarks

Moment inequalities are widely used to estimate discrete choice problems and structures that involve censored variables. In many empirical applications, potentially misspecified parametric models are used to estimate such structures. This chapter studies a novel estimation procedure that is robust to misspecification of moment inequalities. To overcome the challenge that the conventional identified set may be empty under misspecification, we defined a pseudo-true identified set as the least squares projection of the set of functions at which the moment inequalities are satisfied. This set is nonempty under mild assumptions. We also proposed a two-stage set estimator for estimating the pseudo-true identified set. Our estimator first estimates the identified set of function-valued parameters by a level-set estimator over a suitable sieve. The pseudo-true identified set can then be estimated by projecting the first-stage estimator to a finite-dimensional parameter space. We give conditions, under which the estimator is consistent for the pseudo-true identified set in the Hausdorff metric and converges at a rate $O_p(n^{-1/2})$. Developing inference procedures based on the proposed estimator would be an interesting future work. Another interesting extension would be to study the optimal choice of the weighting matrix. In this chapter, we maintained the assumption that W is fixed and does not depend on (θ, s). Given the form of the criterion function, the most natural choice of W would be the inverse matrix of the variance covariance matrix of $s(X_i) - r_\theta(X_i)$. This matrix is generally unknown but can be consistently estimated by its sample analog: $\hat{W}_n(\theta, s) := (\frac{1}{n}\sum_{i=1}^n (s(X_i) - r_\theta(X_i))(s(X_i) - r_\theta(X_i))')^{-1}$. Defining a sample criterion function using $\hat{W}_n(\theta, s)$ as a weighting matrix would lead to a three-step procedure. Such a procedure may result in more efficient estimation of Θ_*.[6] Yet, another interesting direction would be to develop a specification test for the moment inequality models based on the current framework. This direction would extend the results of Guggenberger et al. (2008), which studies a testing procedure that tests the nonemptiness of the identified set.

A Mathematical Proofs

A.1 Notation

Throughout the appendix, let $\|\cdot\|$ denote the usual Euclidean norm. For each $s, s' \in \mathcal{S}$, let $\rho(s, s') := \sup_{x \in \mathcal{S}} \max_{j=1,\dots,l} |s^{(j)}(x) - s'^{(j)}(x)|$. For each $a \times b$ matrix A, let $\|A\|_{op} := \min\{c : \|Av\| \le c\|v\|, v \in \mathbb{R}^b\}$ be the operator norm. For any symmetric matrix A, let $\xi(A)$ denote the smallest eigenvalue of A.

For a given pseudometric space (T, ρ), let $N(\epsilon, T, \rho)$ be the *covering number*, i.e., the minimal number of ϵ-balls needed to cover T. For each measurable function $f : \mathcal{X} \to \mathbb{R}$ and $1 \le p < \infty$, let $\|f\|_{L^p} := E[|f(X)|^p]^{1/p}$ provided that the integral exists. Similarly, let $\|f\|_\infty := \inf\{c : P(|f(X)| > c) = 0\}$. For a given function space $\mathcal{G}$ equipped with a norm $\|\cdot\|_\mathcal{G}$ and $l, u \in \mathcal{G}$, let $[l, u] := \{f \in \mathcal{G} : l \le f \le u\}$. For each $f \in \mathcal{G}$, let $B_{\epsilon, f} := \{[l, u] : l \le f \le u, \|l - u\|_\mathcal{G} < \epsilon\}$ be the ϵ-bracket of f. The *bracketing number* $N_{[\,]}(\epsilon, \mathcal{G}, \|\cdot\|_\mathcal{G})$ is the minimum number of ϵ-brackets needed to cover $\mathcal{G}$. An *envelope function* G of a function

[6] We are indebted to an anonymous referee for this point.

class $\mathcal{G}$ is a measurable function such that $g(x) \leq G(x)$ for all $g \in \mathcal{G}$. For each $\delta > 0$, the *bracketing integral* of $\mathcal{G}$ with an envelope function G is defined as $J_{[]}(\delta, \mathcal{G}, \|\cdot\|_{\mathcal{G}}) := \int_0^\delta \sqrt{1 + \ln N_{[]}(\epsilon \|G\|_{\mathcal{G}}, \mathcal{G}, \|\cdot\|_{\mathcal{G}})} d\epsilon$.

A.2 Projection

Proof of Proposition 2.1 Note that under the conditions of Example 2.1, Assumption 2.3 holds. This ensures $\mathcal{S}_0$ is nonempty. By Eq. (13), Θ_* is nonempty. Furthermore, let $\theta \in \Theta_I$, and for each $z \in \mathcal{Z}$, let $r_\theta(z) := z'\theta$. Note that $r_\theta \in \mathcal{S}_0$. Thus, (13) holds with $s = r_\theta$, which ensures the first claim.

For the second claim, note that the condition $E[Y_U|Z] = E[Y_L|Z] = Z'\theta_0$ a.s implies that any $\theta \in \Theta_I$ must satisfy

$$E[Z1\{Z \in A_j\}]'(\theta_0 - \theta) = 0, \quad j = 1, 2, \ldots, K. \tag{A.1}$$

By the rank condition on D, the unique solution to (A.1) is $\theta_0 - \theta = 0$. Thus, $\{\theta_0\} = \Theta_I$. Since $\{\theta_0\} \subseteq \Theta_*$ by the first claim, it suffices to show that θ_0 is the unique element of Θ_*. For this, note that under our assumptions, $\mathcal{S}_0 = \{s_0\}$ with $s_0(z) = z'\theta_0$. Thus, $\Theta_* = \{\theta_0\}$. This completes the proof. □

A.3 Consistency of the Parametric Part

For each $s \in \mathcal{S}$, let $\theta_*(s) := \arg\min_{\theta \in \Theta} Q(\theta, s)$ and $\hat{\theta}_n(s) := \arg\min_{\theta \in \Theta} Q_n(\theta, s)$.

Lemma A.1 *Suppose that Assumptions 3.4 and 3.2 (iv) hold. Then, (i) for each $x \in \mathcal{X}$ and any $s, s' \in \mathcal{S}$, there exists a function $C_1 : \mathcal{X} \to \mathbb{R}_+$ such that*

$$\left\| r_{\theta_*(s)}(x) - r_{\theta_*(s')}(x) \right\| \leq C_1(x)\rho(s, s'); \tag{A.2}$$

(ii) For each $x \in \mathcal{X}$, $j = 1, \ldots, L$, and any $s, s' \in \mathcal{S}$, there exists a function $C_2 : \mathcal{X} \to \mathbb{R}_+$ such that

$$\left\| \nabla_\theta^{(j)} r_{\theta_*(s)}(x) - \nabla_\theta^{(j)} r_{\theta_*(s')}(x) \right\| \leq C_2(x)\rho(s, s'). \tag{A.3}$$

Proof of Lemma A.1 Assumption 3.4 ensures that

$$\left\| r_{\theta_*(s)}(x) - r_{\theta_*(s')}(x) \right\| \leq L^{1/2} C(x) \left\| \theta_*(s) - \theta_*(s') \right\|. \tag{A.4}$$

Assumption 3.2 (iv) ensures that for each $s \in L^2_{\mathcal{S},L}$, $\theta_*(s) = \Pi_{\mathcal{R}_\Theta} s$ is uniquely determined, where $\Pi_{\mathcal{R}_\Theta}$ is the projection mapping from the Hilbert space $L^2_{\mathcal{S},L}$ to the closed convex subset $\mathcal{R}_\Theta$. Furthermore, Lemma 6.54 (*d*) in Aliprantis and Border (2006) and the fact that ρ is stronger than $\|\cdot\|_W$ imply

$$\left\|\theta_*(s) - \theta_*(s')\right\| \le \left\|s - s'\right\|_W \le c\rho(s, s'), \tag{A.5}$$

for some $c > 0$. Combining (A.4) and (A.5) ensures (i). Similarly, Assumption 3.4 ensures that for each $x \in \mathcal{X}$

$$\left\|\nabla_\theta^{(j)} r_{\theta_*(s)}(x) - \nabla_\theta^{(j)} r_{\theta_*(s')}(x)\right\| \le J^{1/2} C(x) \left\|\theta_*(s) - \theta_*(s')\right\|. \tag{A.6}$$

Combining (A.5) and (A.6) ensures (ii). □

Proof of Theorem 3.1 Step 1: Let $s \in \mathcal{S}$ be given. For each $\theta \in \Theta$, let $Q_s(\theta) := Q(\theta, s)$ and $Q_{n,s}(\theta) := Q_n(\theta, s)$. By Assumption 3.2 (iv) and Theorem 6.53 in Aliprantis and Border (2006), Q_s is uniquely minimized at $\theta_*(s)$. By Assumption 3.2 (i), Θ is compact. By Assumption 3.2, $Q(\theta)$ is continuous. Furthermore, Assumption 3.4 ensures the applicability of the uniform law of large numbers. Thus, $\sup_{\theta\in\Theta} |Q_{n,s}(\theta) - Q_s(\theta)| = o_p(1)$. Hence, by Theorem 2.1 in Newey and McFadden (1994), $\hat\theta_n(s) - \theta_*(s) = o_p(1)$.

By Assumptions 3.2 (v), 3.4 (ii), and the fact that $\hat\theta_n(s)$ is consistent for $\theta_*(s)$, $\hat\theta_n(s)$ solves the first order condition:

$$\nabla_\theta Q_n(\theta, s) = \frac{1}{n}\sum_{i=1}^n \nabla_\theta r_\theta(X_i)' W(s(X_i) - r_\theta(X_i)) = 0, \tag{A.7}$$

with probability approaching one. Expanding this condition at $\theta_*(s)$ using the mean-value theorem applied to each element of $\nabla_\theta Q_n(\theta, s)$ yields

$$\nabla_\theta^2 Q_n(\bar\theta_n(s), s)(\hat\theta_n(s) - \theta_*(s)) = \frac{1}{n}\sum_{i=1}^n \nabla_\theta r_{\theta_*(s)}(X_i)' W(s(X_i) - r_{\theta_*(s)}(X_i)), \tag{A.8}$$

where $\bar\theta_n(s)$ lies on the line segment that connects $\hat\theta_n(s)$ and $\theta_*(s)$.[7] For each $s \in \mathcal{S}_0^{\bar\eta}$, let

$$\psi_s(x) := \nabla_\theta r_{\theta_*(s)}(x)' W(s(x) - r_{\theta_*(s)}(x)). \tag{A.9}$$

Below, we show that the function class $\Psi := \{f_s : f_s = \psi_s^{(j)}, s \in \mathcal{S}_0^{\bar\eta}, j = 1, 2, \ldots, J\}$ is a Glivenko–Cantelli class.

---

[7] Since the mean value theorem only applies element by element to the vector in (A.8), the mean value $\bar\theta_n$ differs across the elements. For notational simplicity, we use $\bar\theta_n$ in what follows, but the fact that they differ element to element should be understood implicitly. For the measurability of these mean values, see Jennrich (1969) for example.

By Assumption 3.4 (ii), Lemma A.1, the triangle inequality, and the Cauchy–Schwarz inequality, for any $s, s' \in \mathcal{S}$,

$$\begin{aligned}|\psi_s^{(j)}(x) - \psi_{s'}^{(j)}(x)| &\leq \left\|(\nabla_\theta^{(j)} r_{\theta_*(s)}(x) - \nabla_\theta^{(j)} r_{\theta_*(s')}(x))' W\right\| \\ &\quad \times \left\|s(x) - r_{\theta_*(s)}(x)\right\| + \left\|\nabla_\theta^{(j)} r_{\theta_*(s')}(x)' W\right\| \\ &\quad \times \left\|[s(x) - s'(x)] + [r_{\theta_*(s')}(x) - r_{\theta_*(s)}(x)]\right\| \\ &\leq (C_2(x)\|W\|_{op}(M + R(x)) + (1 + C_1(x))\|W\|_{op} R(x)) \\ &\qquad \times \sup_{x \in \mathcal{S}} \left\|s(x) - s'(x)\right\| \\ &\leq F(x)\rho(s, s'), \end{aligned} \tag{A.10}$$

where $F(x) := (C_2(x)\|W\|_{op}(M + R(x)) + (1 + C_1(x))\|W\|_{op} R(x)) \times \sqrt{L}$. For any $\epsilon > 0$, let $u := \epsilon/2\|F\|_{L^1}$. By, Theorem 2.7.11 in van der Vaart and Wellner (1996) and Assumption 3.2 (ii), we obtain

$$\begin{aligned} N_{[]}(\epsilon, \Psi, \|\cdot\|_{L^1}) &= N_{[]}(2u\|F\|_{L^1}, \Psi, \|\cdot\|_{L^1}) \\ &\leq N(u, \mathcal{S}_0^{\bar{\eta}}, \rho). \end{aligned} \tag{A.11}$$

For each $j = 1, \ldots, L$, let $\mathcal{S}_0^{\bar{\eta},(j)} := \{s^{(j)} : s \in \mathcal{S}_0^{\bar{\eta}}\}$. For each $j, g \in \mathcal{S}_0^{\bar{\eta},(j)}$, and $\epsilon > 0$, let $B_\epsilon^{(j)}(g) := \{f \in \mathcal{S}_0^{\bar{\eta},(j)} : \|f - g\|_\infty < \epsilon\}$. Similarly, for each $s \in \mathcal{S}_0^{\bar{\eta}}$, let $B_{u,\rho}(s) := \{f \in \mathcal{S}_0^{\bar{\eta},(j)} : \rho(f, s) < \epsilon\}$. As we will show below, $N_j := N(u, \mathcal{S}_0^{\bar{\eta},(j)}, \|\cdot\|_\infty)$ is finite for all j. Thus, for each j there exist $f_{1,j}, \ldots, f_{N_j,j} \in \mathcal{S}_0^{\bar{\eta},(j)}$ such that $\mathcal{S}_0^{\bar{\eta},(j)} \subseteq \bigcup_{l=1}^{N_j} B_u^{(j)}(f_{l,j})$. We can then obtain a grid of distinct points $f_1, \ldots, f_N \in \mathcal{S}_0^{\bar{\eta}}$ such that $f_i^{(j)} = f_{l,j}$ for some $1 \leq l \leq N_j$, where $N = \prod_{j=1}^L N_j$. Then, by the definition of ρ, $\mathcal{S}_0^{\bar{\eta}} \subseteq \bigcup_{i=1}^N B_{u,\rho}(f_i)$. Thus,

$$N\big(u, \mathcal{S}_0^{\bar{\eta}}, \rho\big) \leq \prod_{j=1}^L N\big(u, \mathcal{S}_0^{\bar{\eta},(j)}, \|\cdot\|_\infty\big) \leq N\big(u, \mathcal{C}_M^\gamma(\mathcal{X}), \|\cdot\|_\infty\big)^L < \infty, \tag{A.12}$$

where the last inequality follows from Assumption 3.2 (ii)–(iii) and Theorem 2.7.1 in van der Vaart and Wellner (1996). By Theorem 2.4.1 in van der Vaart and Wellner (1996), Ψ is a Glivenko–Cantelli class.

Note that, by Assumptions 3.2 (v) and 3.4, $\theta^*(s)$ solves the population analog of (A.7). Thus,

$$E[\nabla_\theta r_{\theta_*(s)}(X_i)' W(s(X_i) - r_{\theta_*(s)}(X_i))] = E[\psi_s(x)] = 0. \tag{A.13}$$

These results together with the strong law of large numbers whose applicability is ensured by Assumptions 3.3 and 3.4 (ii) imply

$$\sup_{s\in\mathcal{S}_0^{\bar{\eta}}}\left|\frac{1}{n}\sum_{i=1}^{n}\psi_s^{(j)}(X_i)\right| = o_p(1), \quad j = 1,\dots,J. \tag{A.14}$$

Step 2: In this step, we show that the Hessian $\nabla_\theta^2 Q_n(\theta, s)$ is invertible with probability approaching 1 uniformly over $\mathcal{N}_{\bar{\epsilon},\bar{\eta}}$. Let $\mathcal{H} := \{h_{\theta,s} : \mathcal{X} \to \mathbb{R} : h_{\theta,s}(x) = H_W^{(i,j)}(\theta, s, x) + 2\nabla_\theta r_\theta^{(i)}(x)'W\nabla_\theta r_\theta^{(j)}(x), 1 \le i, j \le p, \theta \in \Theta, s \in \mathcal{S}_0^{\bar{\eta}}\}$. Note that $h_{\theta,s}$ takes the form:

$$\begin{aligned} h_{\theta,s}(x) &= 2\sum_{k=1}^{L}\sum_{h=1}^{L}\frac{\partial^2 r_\theta^{(h)}(x)}{\partial\theta_i\partial\theta_j}W^{(h,k)}\big(s^{(k)}(x) - r_\theta^{(k)}(x)\big)\\ &\quad+\sum_{k=1}^{L}\sum_{h=1}^{L}\frac{\partial r_\theta^{(h)}(x)}{\partial\theta_i}W^{(h,k)}\frac{\partial r_\theta^{(k)}(x)}{\partial\theta_j}\end{aligned}$$

for some $1 \le i, j \le p, \theta \in \Theta$, and $s \in \mathcal{S}_0^{\bar{\eta}}$. Consider the function classes $\mathcal{F}_1 := \{D_\theta^\alpha r_\theta^{(k)} : \theta \in \Theta, |\alpha| \le 2, k = 1,\dots,L\}$ and $\mathcal{F}_2 := \{s^{(k)} : s \in \mathcal{S}_0^{\bar{\eta}}, k = 1,\dots,L\}$. Assumptions 3.2 (i), 3.4, and Theorem 2.7.11 in van der Vaart and Wellner (1996) ensure $N_{[]}(\epsilon, \mathcal{F}_1, \|\cdot\|_{L^2}) \le N(u, \Theta, \|\cdot\|) < \infty$ with $u := \epsilon/2\|C\|_{L^2}$. Assumption 3.2 (ii)–(iii) and Corollary 2.7.2 in van der Vaart and Wellner (1996) ensure $N_{[]}(\epsilon, \mathcal{F}_2, \|\cdot\|_{L^2}) \le N_{[]}(\epsilon, C_M^\gamma(\mathcal{X}), \|\cdot\|_{L^2}) < \infty$. Since $\mathcal{H}$ can be obtained by combining functions in $\mathcal{F}_1$ and $\mathcal{F}_2$ by additions and pointwise multiplications, Theorem 6 in Andrews (1994) implies $N_{[]}(\epsilon, \mathcal{H}, \|\cdot\|_{L^2}) < \infty$. This bracketing number is given in terms of the L^2-norm, but we can also obtain a bracketing number in terms of the L^1-norm. For this, let $h_1,\dots,h_p$ be the centers of $\|\cdot\|_{L^2}$-balls that cover $\mathcal{H}$. Then, the brackets $[h_i - \epsilon, h_i + \epsilon], i = 1,\dots,p$ cover $\mathcal{H}$, and each bracket has length at most 2ϵ in $\|\cdot\|_{L^1}$. Thus, $N_{[]}(\epsilon, \mathcal{H}, \|\cdot\|_{L^1}) < \infty$. By Theorem 2.7.1 in van der Vaart and Wellner (1996), $\mathcal{H}$ is a Glivenko–Cantelli class. Hence, uniformly over $\Theta \times \mathcal{S}_0^{\bar{\eta}}$,

$$\begin{aligned}\nabla_\theta^2 Q_n(\theta, s) &= \frac{1}{n}\sum_{i=1}^{n} H_W(\theta, s, X_i) + 2\nabla_\theta r_\theta(X_i)'W\nabla_\theta r_\theta(X_i)\\ &\xrightarrow{p} E[H_W(\theta, s, X_i) + 2\nabla_\theta r_\theta(X_i)'W\nabla_\theta r_\theta(X_i)]. \end{aligned}\tag{A.15}$$

Note that $d_{H,W}(\hat{\mathcal{S}}_n, \mathcal{S}_0) = o_p(1)$ by Assumption 3.6. Thus, $(\bar{\theta}_n(s), s) \in \mathcal{N}_{\bar{\epsilon},\bar{\eta}}$ with probability approaching one. By Assumption 3.5 and (A.15), there exists $\delta > 0$ such that $\nabla_\theta^2 Q_n(\bar{\theta}_n(s), s)$'s smallest eigenvalue is above δ uniformly over $\mathcal{N}_{\bar{\epsilon},\bar{\eta}}$. Thus, the Hessian $\nabla_\theta^2 Q_n(\bar{\theta}_n(s), s)$ in (A.8) is invertible with probability approaching 1.

Step 3: Steps 1–2 imply that, uniformly over $\mathcal{S}_0^{\bar{\eta}}$,

$$\begin{aligned}\|\theta_*(s) - \hat{\theta}_n(s')\| &= \|\theta_*(s) - \theta_*(s') + \theta_*(s') - \hat{\theta}_n(s')\| \\ &\le \|\theta_*(s) - \theta_*(s')\| + 2\delta^{-1} \sup_{s\in\mathcal{S}_0^{\bar{\eta}}} \left\| \frac{1}{n}\sum_{i=1}^{n} \psi_s(X_i) \right\| \\ &\le \|s - s'\|_W + o_p(1),\end{aligned} \tag{A.16}$$

where we used the fact that $\|\theta_*(s) - \theta_*(s')\| \le \|s - s'\|_W$ by Lemma 6.54 (*d*) in Aliprantis and Border (2006).

Step 4: Finally, note that by Step 3,

$$\begin{aligned}\vec{d}_H(\Theta_*, \hat{\Theta}_n) &= \sup_{\theta\in\Theta_*} \inf_{\theta'\in\hat{\Theta}_n} \|\theta - \theta'\| = \sup_{s\in\mathcal{S}_0} \inf_{s'\in\hat{\mathcal{S}}_n} \|\theta_*(s) - \hat{\theta}_n(s')\| \\ &\le \sup_{s\in\mathcal{S}_0} \inf_{s'\in\hat{\mathcal{S}}_n} \|s - s'\|_W + o_p(1)\end{aligned} \tag{A.17}$$

$$\begin{aligned}\vec{d}_H(\hat{\Theta}_n, \Theta_*) &= \sup_{\theta'\in\hat{\Theta}_n} \inf_{\theta\in\Theta_*} \|\theta - \theta'\| = \sup_{s'\in\hat{\mathcal{S}}_n} \inf_{s\in\mathcal{S}_0} \|\theta_*(s) - \hat{\theta}_n(s')\| \\ &\le \sup_{s'\in\hat{\mathcal{S}}_n} \inf_{s\in\mathcal{S}_0} \|s - s'\|_W + o_p(1).\end{aligned} \tag{A.18}$$

Equation (18) and Assumption 3.6 then ensure the desired result. □

A.4 Convergence Rate

The following lemma controls the rate at which $\hat{\Theta}_n$ covers Θ_*. Given a sequence $\{\eta_n\}$ such that $\eta_n \to 0$, we let $V^{\delta_{1n}}(s) := \{\theta' : \|\theta' - \theta(s)\| \le e_n, \quad e_n = O_p(\eta_n)\}$ and let $\mathcal{N}_{\eta_n,0} := \{(\theta, s) : \theta \in V^{\eta_n}(s), s \in \mathcal{S}_0\}$.

Lemma A.2 *Suppose Assumptions 2.1–2.3, 3.1–3.2, and 3.6 hold. Let $\{\delta_{1n}\}$ and $\{\epsilon_n\}$ be sequences of non-negative numbers converging to 0 as $n \to \infty$. Let $G : \Theta \times \mathcal{S} \to \mathbb{R}_+$ be a function such that G is jointly measurable and lower semicontinuous. For each n, let $G_n : \Omega \times \Theta \times \mathcal{S} \to \mathbb{R}$ be a function such that for each $\omega \in \Omega$, $G_n(\omega, \cdot, \cdot)$ is jointly measurable and lower semicontinuous, and for each $(\theta, s) \in \Theta \times \mathcal{S}$, $G_n(\cdot, \theta, s)$ is measurable. Let $\Theta_* := \{G(\theta, s) = 0, s \in \mathcal{S}_0\}$ and $\hat{\Theta}_n := \{\theta \in \Theta : G_n(\theta, s) \le \inf_{\theta\in\Theta} G_n(\theta, s) + c_n, s \in \hat{\mathcal{S}}_n\}$. Suppose that $d_H(\hat{\Theta}_n, \Theta_*) = O_p(\delta_{1n})$. Suppose further that there exists a positive constant κ and a neighborhood $V(s)$ of $\theta_*(s)$ such that*

$$G(\theta, s) \ge \kappa\|\theta - \theta_*(s)\|^2 \tag{A.19}$$

for all $\theta \in V(s)$, $s \in \mathcal{S}_0$. Suppose that uniformly over $\mathcal{N}_{\delta_{1n},0}$,

$$G_n(\theta, s) = G(\theta, s) + O_p(\|\theta - \theta_*(s)\|/\sqrt{n}) + o_p(\|\theta - \theta_*(s)\|^2) + O_p(\epsilon_n). \tag{A.20}$$

Then

$$\vec{d}_H(\Theta_*, \hat{\Theta}_n) = O_p(\max\{c_n^{1/2}, \epsilon_n^{1/2}, 1/\sqrt{n}\}).$$

Proof of Lemma A.2 The proof of this Lemma is similar to Theorem 1 in Sherman (1993). By (A.19), (A.20), and the Hausdorff consistency of $\hat{\Theta}_n$, it follows that, uniformly over $\mathcal{N}_{\delta_{1n},0}$,

$$c_n \geq \kappa\|\theta - \theta_*(s)\|^2 + O_p(\|\theta - \theta_*(s)\|/\sqrt{n}) + o_p(\|\theta - \theta_*(s)\|^2) + O_p(\epsilon_n), \quad \text{(A.21)}$$

with probability approaching 1. As in Theorem 1 in Sherman (1993), write $K_n\|\theta - \theta(s)\|$ for the $O_p(\|\theta - \theta_*(s)\|/\sqrt{n})$ term, where $K_n = O_p(1/\sqrt{n})$ and also note that $o_p(\|\theta - \theta_*(s)\|^2)$ is bounded from below by $-\frac{\kappa}{2}\|\theta - \theta^*(s)\|^2$ with probability approaching 1. Thus, we obtain

$$\frac{\kappa}{2}\|\theta - \theta_*(s)\|^2 + K_n\|\theta - \theta_*(s)\| \leq c_n + O_p(\epsilon_n). \quad \text{(A.22)}$$

Completing the square, we obtain

$$\frac{1}{2}\kappa(\|\theta - \theta_*(s)\| - K_n/\kappa)^2 \leq c_n + O_p(\epsilon_n) + \frac{1}{2}K_n^2/\kappa = c_n + O_p(\epsilon_n) + O_p(1/n). \quad \text{(A.23)}$$

Taking square roots gives

$$\begin{aligned} \|\theta - \theta_*(s)\| &\leq (2/\kappa)^{1/2}c_n^{1/2} + K_n/\kappa + O_p(\epsilon_n^{1/2}) + O_p(1/\sqrt{n}) && \text{(A.24)} \\ &= O_p(c_n^{1/2}) + O_p(\epsilon_n^{1/2}) + O_p(1/\sqrt{n}). && \text{(A.25)} \end{aligned}$$

Thus,

$$\begin{aligned} \vec{d}_H(\Theta_*, \hat{\Theta}_n) &= \sup_{s\in\mathcal{S}_0} \inf_{\theta\in\hat{\Theta}_n} \|\theta - \theta_*(s)\| && \text{(A.26)} \\ &\leq \sup_{s\in\mathcal{S}_0} \inf_{\theta\in V^{\delta_{1n}}(s)} \|\theta - \theta_*(s)\| \\ &\leq O_p(c_n^{1/2}) + O_p(\epsilon_n^{1/2}) + O_p(1/\sqrt{n}). && \text{(A.27)} \end{aligned}$$

This completes the proof. □

The following lemma controls the rate at which $\hat{\Theta}_n$ is contracted into a neighborhood of Θ_*. Given $s \in \mathcal{S}$ and a sequence $\{\delta_n\}$ such that $\delta_n \to 0$, let $U^{\delta_n}(s) := \{\theta \in \Theta : \|\theta - \theta_*(s)\| \geq \delta_n\}$.

Lemma A.3 *Suppose Assumptions 2.1–2.3, 3.1–3.2, and 3.6 hold. Let G_n be defined as in Lemma A.2. Suppose that there exist positive constants (k, κ_2) and a sequence $\{\delta_{1n}\}$ such that*

$$G_n(\theta, s) \geq \kappa_2\|\theta - \theta_*(s)\|^2 \quad \text{(A.28)}$$

with probability approaching 1 for all $\theta \in U^{\delta_n}(s)$ *with* $\delta_n := (k\delta_{1n}/\sqrt{n})^{1/2}$ *and* $s \in \mathcal{S}_0^{\bar{\eta}}$. *Then,*

$$\vec{d}_H(\hat{\Theta}_n, \Theta_*) = O_p(\delta_{1n}^{1/2}/n^{1/4}) + O_p(c_n^{1/2}).$$

Proof of Lemma A.3 Note first that $\hat{\mathcal{S}}_n$ is in $\mathcal{S}_0^{\bar{\eta}}$ with probability approaching 1 by Assumption 3.6. Let $\tilde{c}_n := \sqrt{n}c_n$ and $\bar{c}_n := \max\{\kappa_2 k\delta_{1n}, \tilde{c}_n\}$. Let $\epsilon_n := (\bar{c}_n/\kappa_2\sqrt{n})^{1/2}$. Then, uniformly over $\mathcal{S}_0^{\bar{\eta}}$,

$$\inf_{\Theta \cap U^{\epsilon_n}(s)} \sqrt{n}G_n(\theta, s) \geq \kappa_2\sqrt{n}\epsilon_n^2 \geq \bar{c}_n. \tag{A.29}$$

Since $\sqrt{n}G_n(\hat{\theta}_n(s), s) \leq \tilde{c}_n$ for all $s \in \hat{\mathcal{S}}_n$, the results above ensure

$$\begin{aligned}\vec{d}_H(\hat{\Theta}_n, \Theta_*) &= \sup_{s\in\hat{\mathcal{S}}_n} \inf_{\theta\in\Theta_*} \|\hat{\theta}_n(s) - \theta\| \\ &\leq \sup_{s\in\hat{\mathcal{S}}_n} \|\hat{\theta}_n(s) - \theta_*(s)\| \leq \epsilon_n = O_p(\delta_{1n}^{1/2}/n^{1/4}) + O_p(\tilde{c}_n^{1/2}/n^{1/4}).\end{aligned}$$

This ensures the claim of the Lemma. □

Proof of Theorem 3.2 We first show (A.19) holds with $G(\theta, s) = Q(\theta, s)$. For this, we use the second-order Taylor expansion of $Q(\theta, s)$. For $\theta \in V^{\delta_{1n}}(s)$, it holds by Assumptions 3.2 (v) and 3.4 that

$$\begin{aligned}Q(\theta, s) = {} & Q(\theta_*(s), s) + \nabla_\theta Q(\theta_*(s), s)'(\theta - \theta_*(s)) \\ & + \frac{1}{2}(\theta - \theta_*(s))'\nabla_\theta^2 Q(\bar{\theta}(s), s)(\theta - \theta_*(s)),\end{aligned} \tag{A.30}$$

where $\bar{\theta}(s)$ is on the line segment that connects θ and $\theta_*(s)$. By (15), $Q(\theta_*(s), s) = 0$, and by the first order condition of the optimality, $\nabla_\theta Q(\theta_*(s), s) = 0$. Thus, it follows that

$$Q(\theta, s) = \frac{1}{2}(\theta - \theta_*(s))'\nabla_\theta^2 Q(\bar{\theta}(s), s)(\theta - \theta_*(s)) \geq \kappa\|\theta - \theta_*(s)\|^2, \tag{A.31}$$

where $\kappa := \inf_{\theta\in\Theta, s\in\mathcal{S}_0} \xi(\nabla_\theta^2 Q(\theta, s))/2$, and $\kappa > 0$ by Assumption 3.5.

We next show that (A.20) holds for

$$\begin{aligned}G_n(\theta, s) = {} & \frac{1}{n}\sum_{i=1}^n (s(X_i) - r_\theta(X_i))'W(s(X_i) - r_\theta(X_i)) \\ & - \frac{1}{n}\sum_{i=1}^n (s(X_i) - r_{\theta_*(s)}(X_i))'W(s(X_i) - r_{\theta_*(s)}(X_i)).\end{aligned} \tag{A.32}$$

In what follows, let $\hat{E}_n$ denote the expectation with respect to the empirical distribution. Using the Taylor expansion of G_n and G with respect to θ at $\theta_*(s)$, we may write

$$G_n(\theta,s)-G(\theta,s)=S_{1,n}(\theta,s)+S_{2,n}(\theta,s), \tag{A.33}$$

where

$$\begin{aligned} S_{1n}(\theta,s) &:= -2(\theta-\theta_*(s))'(\hat{E}_n-E)[\nabla_\theta r_{\theta_*(s)}(x)'W(s(x)-r_{\theta_*}(x))] \\ &\quad +o_p(\|\theta-\theta_*(s)\|^2) &\text{(A.34)}\\ S_{2n}(\theta,s) &:= (\theta-\theta_*(s))'(\hat{E}_n-E)[\nabla_\theta r_{\theta_*(s)}(x)'W\nabla_\theta r_{\theta_*(s)}(x)](\theta-\theta_*(s)). &\text{(A.35)}\end{aligned}$$

Thus, for (A.20) to hold, it suffices to show that $S_{1n}(\theta,s)=O_p(\|\theta-\theta_*(s)\|/\sqrt{n})+o_p(\|\theta-\theta_*(s)\|^2)$ and $S_{2n}(\theta,s)=O_p(\epsilon_n)$ for some $\epsilon_n\to 0$. For S_{1n}, note that our assumptions suffice for the conditions of Lemma A.4. Thus, Φ is a P_0-Donsker class. This ensures $S_{1n}(\theta,s)=O_p(\|\theta-\theta_*(s)\|/\sqrt{n})+o_p(\|\theta-\theta_*(s)\|^2)$. We now consider S_{2n}. For each $s\in\mathcal{S}_0$ and $x\in\mathcal{X}$, let $\phi_s(x):=\nabla_\theta r_{\theta_*(s)}(x)'W\nabla_\theta r_{\theta_*(s)}(x)$. Note that

$$\begin{aligned} E\left[\sup_{(\theta,s)\in\mathcal{N}_{\delta_{1n},0}}|S_{2n}(\theta,s)|\right] &\le \delta_{1n}^2 n^{-1/2}E\left[\sup_{s\in\mathcal{S}_0}|\mathbb{G}_n\phi_s|\right]\\ &\le n^{-1/2}\delta_{1n}^2 C J_{[]}(1,\mathcal{S}_0,\|\cdot\|_{L^2})\left\|\sup_{s\in\mathcal{S}_0}|\phi_s|\right\|_{L^2}, &\text{(A.36)}\end{aligned}$$

where the last inequality follows from Lemma B.1 of Ichimura and Lee (2010). Now, Markov's inequality, Lemma A.4, and Assumption 3.4 (ii) ensure that $S_{2n}=O_p(\epsilon_n)$, where $\epsilon_n=n^{-1/2}\delta_{1n}^2$.

We further set $c_n=0$. Note that the estimator defined in (17) with $c_n=0$ equals the set estimator $\hat{\Theta}_n=\{\theta:G_n(\theta,s)\le\inf_{\theta\in\Theta}G_n(\theta,s)\}$. By Assumption 3.7 and Step 4 of the proof of Theorem 3.1, we may take $\delta_{1n}=O_p(n^{-1/4})$ as an initial rate. Lemma A.2 then implies that $\vec{d}_H(\Theta_*,\hat{\Theta}_n)=O_p(\epsilon_n^{1/2})$, where $\epsilon_n=O_p(n^{-1/2}\delta_{1n}^2)=O_p(n^{-1})$. Thus, $\vec{d}_H(\Theta_*,\hat{\Theta}_n)=O_p(n^{-1/2})$.

Now we consider $\vec{d}_H(\hat{\Theta}_n,\Theta_*)$. We show that (A.28) holds for G_n. For each θ and s, let $L_n(\theta,s):=\frac{1}{n}\sum_{i=1}^n(s(X_i)-r_\theta(X_i))'W(s(X_i)-r_\theta(X_i))$. Let $s\in\mathcal{S}_0^{\bar{\eta}}$ and $\theta\in U^{\delta_{1n}}(s)$. A second-order Taylor expansion of $G_n(\theta,s)=L_n(\theta,s)-L_n(\theta_*(s),s)$ with respect to θ at $\theta_*(s)$ gives

$$\begin{aligned} G_n(\theta,s) &= \nabla_\theta L_n(\theta_*(s),s)'(\theta-\theta_*(s))+\frac{1}{2}(\theta-\theta_*(s))'\nabla^2_\theta L_n(\bar{\theta}_n(s),s)(\theta-\theta_*(s))\\ &= o_p(1)+\frac{1}{2}(\theta-\theta_*(s))'\nabla^2_\theta L_n(\bar{\theta}_n(s),s)(\theta-\theta_*(s))\\ &\ge \kappa_2\|\theta-\theta_*(s)\|^2, &\text{(A.37)}\end{aligned}$$

with probability approaching 1 for some $\kappa_2 > 0$, where $\bar{\theta}_n(s)$ is a point on the line segment that connects θ and $\theta_*(s)$. The last inequality follows from Step 3 of the proof of Theorem 3.1 and Assumption 3.5.

Set $\tilde{c}_n = 0$. Then, Lemma A.3 implies $\vec{d}_H(\hat{\Theta}_n, \Theta_*) = O_p(\delta_{1n}^{1/2}/n^{1/4})$. Setting $\delta_{1n} = O_p(n^{-1/4})$ refines this rate to $O_p(n^{-3/8})$. Repeated applications of Lemma A.3 then implies $\vec{d}_H(\hat{\Theta}_n, \Theta_*) = O_p(n^{-1/2})$. As both of the directed Hausdorff distances converge to 0 at the stochastic order of $n^{-1/2}$, the claim of the theorem follows. □

Lemma A.4 *Suppose Assumptions 3.2 and 3.4 hold. Then Φ is a P_0-Donsker class.*

Proof of Lemma A.4 The proof of Theorem 3.1 shows that each $f_s \in \Phi$ is Lipschitz in s. For any $\epsilon > 0$, Assumption 3.2 (ii)–(iii), Theorems 2.7.11 and 2.7.2 in van der Vaart and Wellner (1996), and (A.12) imply

$$\ln N_{[]}(\epsilon\|F\|_{L^2}, \Psi, \|\cdot\|_{L^2}) \leq \ln N(\epsilon/2, \mathcal{S}_0^{\delta_2}, \rho)^L \leq C(1/\epsilon)^{k/\gamma}, \tag{A.38}$$

where C is a constant that depends only on k, γ, L, and $\mathrm{diam}(\mathcal{X})$. Thus, for any $\delta > 0$,

$$J_{[]}(\delta, \Phi, \|\cdot\|_{L^2}) \leq \int_0^\delta \sqrt{1 + C(1/\epsilon)^{k/\gamma}}\,d\epsilon < \infty. \tag{A.39}$$

Example 2.14.4 in van der Vaart and Wellner (1996) ensures that Ψ is P_0-Donsker. □

A.5 First Stage Estimation

In the following, we work with the following population criterion function. For each $s \in \mathcal{S}$, let $\mathcal{Q}$ be defined by

$$\mathcal{Q}(s) := \sum_{j=1}^{l} E[\varphi^{(j)}(X_i, s)]_+^2. \tag{A.40}$$

Lemma A.5 *Suppose that Assumption 3.9 (i) holds. Let the criterion function be given as in (A.40). Then, there exists a positive constant C_2 such that*

$$\mathcal{Q}(s) \leq \inf_{s_0 \in \mathcal{S}_0} C_2 \|s - s_0\|_W^2.$$

Proof of Lemma A.5 Let $s \in \mathcal{S}$ be arbitrary. For any $s_0 \in \mathcal{S}$, $E[\varphi^{(j)}(X, s_0)] \leq 0$ for $j = 1, \ldots, l$. Let V be an open set that contains s and s_0. Assumption 3.9 (i) and Theorem 1.7 in Lindenstrauss et al. (2007), it holds that

$$\mathcal{Q}(s) \le \sum_{j=1}^{l} \left(E[\varphi^{(j)}(X_i, s)] - E[\varphi^{(j)}(X_i, s_0)] \right)_+^2$$
$$\le \left(\sum_{j=1}^{l} \| \sup_{g \in \tilde{V}_j} \dot{\varphi}_g^{(j)} \|_{op}^2 \right) \|s - s_0\|_W^2, \tag{A.41}$$

where $\tilde{V}_j := \{g \in V : \dot{\varphi}_g^{(j)} \text{ exists}\}$. Let $C_2 := \sum_{j=1}^{l} \| \sup_{g \in \mathcal{S}} \dot{\varphi}_g^{(j)} \|_{op}^2$. It holds that $0 < C_2 < \infty$ by the hypothesis. We thus obtain

$$\mathcal{Q}(s) \le C_2 \|s - s_0\|_W^2 \tag{A.42}$$

for all $s_0 \in \mathcal{S}_0$. Note that $s_0 \mapsto \|s - s_0\|_W$ is continuous and $\mathcal{S}_0$ is compact by Assumption 3.2 (ii)–(iii) and Assumption 3.10 (i). Taking infimum over $\mathcal{S}_0$ then ensures the desired result. □

Lemma A.6 *Suppose Assumption 3.9 (ii) holds. Let the criterion function be given as in (A.40). Then there exists a positive constant C such that*

$$\mathcal{Q}(s) \ge \inf_{s_0 \in \mathcal{S}_0} C_3 \|s - s_0\|_W^2.$$

Proof of Lemma A.6 If $s \in \mathcal{S}_0$, the conclusion is immediate. Suppose that $s \notin \mathcal{S}_0$. By Assumption 3.9 (ii), there exists $s_0 \in \mathcal{S}_0$

$$\mathcal{Q}(s) = \sum_{j \in \mathcal{I}(s)} (E[\varphi^{(j)}(X_i, s)])^2 \ge C_j \|s - s_0\|_W^2. \tag{A.43}$$

Let $C_3 := C_j$. Thus, the claim of the lemma follows. □

In the following, let $\mathcal{G} := \{g : g(x) = \varphi_s^{(j)}(x), s \in \mathcal{S}, j = 1, \ldots, l\}$.

Lemma A.7 *Suppose Assumptions 3.2, 3.4 , and 3.8 hold. Then $\mathcal{G}$ is a P_0-Donsker class.*

Proof of Lemma A.7 By Assumption 3.8, $\varphi_s^{(j)}$ is Lipschitz in s. The rest of the proof is the same as that of Lemma A.4. □

Proof of Theorem 3.3 We establish the claims of the theorem by applying Theorem B.1 in Santos (2011). Note first that Assumption 3.2 (ii)–(iii) and Assumption 3.10 (i) ensure that $\mathcal{S}$ is compact. This ensures condition (i) of Theorem B.1 in Santos (2011). Condition (ii) of Theorem B.1 in Santos (2011) is ensured by Assumption 3.10. Lemma A.7 ensures that uniformly over Θ_n

$$\mathcal{Q}_n(s) = \mathcal{Q}(s) + O_p(n^{-1}). \tag{A.44}$$

Thus, condition (iii) of Theorem B.1 in Santos (2011) hold with $C_1 = 1$ and $c_{2n} = n^{-1}$. Lemma A.5 ensures that $\mathcal{Q}(s) \le \inf_{s_0 \in \mathcal{S}_0} C_2 \|s - s_0\|_W^2$ for some $C_2 > 0$. Thus, condition (iv) of Theorem B.1 in Santos (2011) hold with $\kappa_1 = 2$. Now, the first claim of Theorem B.1. in Santos (2011) establishes

$$d_{H,W}(\hat{\mathcal{S}}_n, \mathcal{S}_0) = o_p(1). \tag{A.45}$$

Furthermore, Lemma A.6 ensures $\mathcal{Q}(s) \ge \inf_{s_0 \in \mathcal{S}_0} C_3 \|s - s_0\|^2$ for some $C_3 > 0$. This ensures condition (v) of Theorem B.1 in Santos (2011) with $\kappa_2 = 2$. Now, the second claim of Theorem B.1. in Santos (2011) ensures

$$d_{H,W}(\hat{\mathcal{S}}_n, \mathcal{S}_0) = O_p(\max\{(b_n/a_n)^{1/2}, \delta_n\}). \tag{A.46}$$

Since $(b_n/a_n)^{1/2}/\delta_n \to \infty$, the claim of the theorem follows. □

Proof of Corollary 3.1 In what follows, we explicitly show $\mathcal{Q}_n$'s dependence on $\omega \in \Omega$. Let $\mathcal{Q}_n : \Omega \times \mathcal{S} \to \mathbb{R}$ be defined by $\mathcal{Q}_n(\omega, s) = \sum_{j=1}^{l} (\frac{1}{n} \sum_{i=1}^{n} \varphi(X_i(\omega), s))_+^2$. By Assumption 2.3, φ is continuous in s for every x and measurable for every s. Also note that X_i is measurable for every i. Thus, by Lemma 4.51 in Aliprantis and Border (2006), $\mathcal{Q}_n$ is jointly measurable in (ω, s) and lower semicontinuous in s for every ω. Note that $\mathcal{S}$ is compact by Assumptions 3.2 (ii)–(iii) and 3.10 (i), which implies $\mathcal{S}$ is locally compact. Since $\mathcal{S}$ is a metric space, it is a Hausdorff space. Thus, by Proposition 5.3.6 in Molchanov (2005), $\mathcal{Q}_n$ is a normal integrand defined on a locally compact Hausdorff space. Proposition 5.3.10 in Molchanov (2005) then ensures the first claim.

Now we show the second claim using Theorem 3.3 (i). Assumptions 2.1–2.3 hold with φ defined in (5). Assumption 3.2 holds by our hypothesis with $\gamma = 1$. Assumption 3.3 is also satisfied by the hypothesis. Note that for each j, $\varphi^{(j)}(x, s) = (y_L - s(z))1_{A_k}(z)$ or $\varphi^{(j)}(x, s) = (s(z) - y_U)1_{A_k}(z)$ for some $k \in \{1, \ldots, K\}$. Without loss of generality, let j be an index for which $\varphi^{(j)}(x, s) = (y_L - s(z))1_{A_k}(z)$ for some Borel set A_k. For any $s, s' \in \mathcal{S}$,

$$|\varphi^{(j)}(x, s) - \varphi^{(j)}(x, s')| = |(s'(z) - s(z))1_{A_k}(z)| \le \rho(s, s'). \tag{A.47}$$

It is straightforward to show the same result for other indexes. Thus, Assumption 3.8 is satisfied.

Now for j such that $\varphi^{(j)}(x, s) = (y_L - s(z))1_{A_k}(z)$, note that

$$|\bar{\varphi}^{(j)}(s + h) - \bar{\varphi}^{(j)}(s) - E[h(Z)(-1_{A_k}(Z))]| = 0. \tag{A.48}$$

Thus, the Fréchet derivative is given by $\dot{\varphi}_s^{(j)}(h) = E[h(Z)(-1_{A_k}(Z))]$. By Proposition 6.13 in Folland (1999), the norm of the operator is given by $\|\dot{\varphi}_s^{(j)}\|_{op} = E[| - 1_{A_k}(Z)|^2]^{1/2} = P_0(Z \in A_k) > 0$, which ensures the boundedness (continuity) of the operator. It is straightforward to show the same result for other indexes. Hence, Assumption 3.9 (i) is satisfied. By construction, Assumption 3.10 (i) is satisfied, and Assumption 3.10 (ii) holds with $\delta_n \asymp J_n^{-1}$ (See Chen 2007). These ensure the conditions of Theorem 3.3 (i). Thus, the second claim follows.

For the third claim, let $s \in \mathcal{S} \setminus \mathcal{S}_0$. Then, there exists j such that $E[\varphi^{(j)}(X_i, s)] > 0$. Without loss of generality, suppose that $E[\varphi^{(j)}(X_i, s)] = E[(Y_{L,i} - s(Z_i))1_{A_k}(Z_i)] \geq \delta > 0$. Let $s_0 \in \mathcal{S}_0$ be such that

$$E[(Y_{L,i} - s_0(Z_i))1_{A_k}(Z_i)] = 0. \tag{A.49}$$

Such s_0 always exists by the intermediate value theorem. Then, for j with which $\varphi^{(j)}(x, s) = (y_L - s(z))1_{A_k}(z)$, it follows that

$$\begin{aligned} E[\varphi^{(j)}(X_i, s)] &= E[(Y_{L,i} - s(Z_i))1_{A_k}(Z_i)] - E[(Y_{L,i} - s_0(Z_i))1_{A_k}(Z_i)] \\ &= E[(s_0(Z_i) - s(Z_i))1_{A_k}(Z_i)] > 0 \end{aligned} \tag{A.50}$$

Thus, we have

$$E[\varphi^{(j)}(X_i, s)] \geq C\|s_0 - s\|_W, \tag{A.51}$$

where $C := \inf_{q \in E} E[q(Z_i)1_{A_k}(Z_i)]$ and $E := \{q \in \mathcal{S} : \|q\|_W = 1, E[q(Z_i)1_{A_k}(Z_i)] > 0\}$. Since C is the minimum value of a linear function over a convex set, it is finite. Furthermore, by the construction of E, it holds that $C > 0$. Thus, Assumption 3.9 (ii) holds. Thus, by Theorem 3.3 (ii), the third claim follows. □

Proof of Corollary 3.2 We show the claim of the corollary using Theorem 3.2. Note that we have shown, in the proof of Corollary 3.1, that Assumptions 2.1–2.3, 3.2 (i)–(iii), and 3.3 hold. Thus, to apply Theorem 3.2, it remains to show Assumptions 2.4, 3.2 (iv), and 3.4–3.7.

Assumption 2.4 is satisfied by the parameterization $r_\theta(z) = \theta^{(1)} + \theta^{(2)}z$. For Assumption 3.2 (iv), note that $\mathcal{R}_\Theta$ is given by

$$\mathcal{R}_\Theta = \left\{r_\theta : r_\theta = \theta^{(1)} + \theta^{(2)}z, \quad \theta \in \Theta\right\}.$$

Since Θ is convex, for any $\lambda \in [0, 1]$, it holds that $\lambda r_\theta + (1 - \lambda)r_{\theta'} = r_{\lambda\theta+(1-\lambda)\theta'} \in \mathcal{R}_\Theta$. Thus, Assumption 3.2 (iv) is satisfied. For Assumption 3.4, note first that r_θ is twice continuously differentiable on the interior of Θ. Because r_θ is linear, $\max_{|\alpha|\leq 2} |D_\theta^\alpha r_\theta(z) - D_\theta^\alpha r_{\theta'}(z)| = (1 + z^2)^{1/2}\|\theta - \theta'\|$ by the Cauchy–Schwarz inequality. By the compactness of $\mathcal{Z}$, $C(z) := (1+z^2)^{1/2}$ is bounded. Thus, Assumption 3.4 (i) is satisfied. Similarly, $\max_{|\alpha|\leq 2} \sup_{\theta\in\Theta} |D_\theta^\alpha r_\theta| \leq \max\{1, |z|, C(1 + z^2)^{1/2}\} =: R(z)$, where $C := \sup_{\theta\in\Theta} \|\theta\|$. By the compactness of $\mathcal{Z}$ and Θ, R is bounded. Thus, Assumption 3.4 (ii) is satisfied. Note that the Hessian of $Q(\theta, s)$ with respect to θ is given by $2E[(1, z)(1, z)']$, which does not depend on θ nor s and is positive definite by the assumption that $Var(Z) > 0$. Thus, Assumption 3.5 is satisfied. Assumptions 3.6 and 3.7 are ensured by Corollary 3.1. Now the conditions of Theorem 3.2 are satisfied. Thus, the claim of the Corollary follows. □

References

Ai, C., and X. Chen (2003): "Efficient Estimation of Models with Conditional Moment Restrictions Containing Unknown Functions", Econometrica, 71(6), 1795–1843.

Aliprantis, C. D., and K. C. Border (2006): Infinite Dimensional Analysis-A Hitchhiker's Guide. Springer, Berlin.

Andrews, D. W. K. (1994): "Chapter 37: Empirical Process Methods in Econometrics", vol. 4 of Handbook of Econometrics, pp. 2247–2294. Elsevier, Amsterdam.

Andrews, D. W. K., and X. Shi (2011): "Inference for Parameters Defined by Conditional Moment Inequalities", Discussion Paper, Yale University.

Bajari, P., C. L. Benkard, and J. Levin (2007): "Estimating Dynamic Models of Imperfect Competition", Econometrica, 75(5), 1331–1370.

Bontemps, C., T. Magnac, and E. Maurin (2011): "Set Identified Linear Models", CeMMAP Working Paper.

Chen, X. (2007): "Large Sample Sieve Estimation of Semi-Nonparametric Models", Handbook of Econometrics, 6, 5549–5632.

Chernozhukov, V., H. Hong, and E. Tamer (2007): "Estimation and Confidence Regions for Parameter Sets in Econometric Models1", Econometrica, 75(5), 1243–1284.

Ciliberto, F., and E. Tamer (2009): "Market Structure and Multiple Equilibria in Airline Markets", Econometrica, 77(6), 1791–1828.

Folland, G. (1999): Real Analysis: Modern Techniques and Their Applications, vol. 40. Wiley-Interscience, New York.

Guggenberger, P., J. Hahn, and K. Kim (2008): "Specification Testing under Moment Inequalities", Economics Letters, 99(2), 375–378.

Ichimura, H., and S. Lee (2010): "Characterization of the Asymptotic Distribution of Semiparametric M-Estimators", Journal of Econometrics, 159(2), 252–266.

Jennrich, R. I. (1969): "Asymptotic Properties of Nonlinear Least Squares Estimators", Annals of Mathematical Statistics, 40(2), 633–643.

Kaido, H., and H. White (2010): "A Two-Stage Approach for Partially Identified Models", Discussion Paper, University of California San Diego.

Lindenstrauss, J., D. Preiss, and J. Tiser (2007): "Differentiability of Lipschitz Maps", in Banach Spaces and Their Applications in, Analysis, pp. 111–123.

Luttmer, E. G. J. (1996): "Asset Pricing in Economies with Frictions", Econometrica, 64(6), 1439–1467.

Manski, C. F., and E. Tamer (2002): "Inference on Regressions with Interval Data on a Regressor or Outcome", Econometrica, 70(2), 519–546.

Molchanov, I. S. (2005): Theory of Random Sets. Springer, Berlin.

Newey, W. (1994): "The Asymptotic Variance of Semipara metric Estimators," Econometrica, 62(6), 1349–1382.

Newey, W. K., and D. McFadden (1994): "Large Sample Estimation and Hypothesis Testing", Handbook of Econometrics, 4, 2111–2245.

Pakes, A. (2010): "Alternative Models for Moment Inequalities", Econometrica, 78(6), 1783–1822.

Pakes, A., J. Porter, K. Ho, and J. Ishii (2006): "Moment Inequalities and Their Application", Working Paper, Harvard University.

Ponomareva, M., and E. Tamer (2010): "Misspecification in Moment Inequality Models: Back to Moment Equalities?" Econometrics Journal, 10, 1–21.

Santos, A. (2011): "Instrumental Variables Methods for Recovering Continuous Linear Functionals", Journal of Econometrics, 161, 129–146.

Sherman, R. P. (1993): "The Limiting Distribution of the Maximum Rank Correlation Estimator", Econometrica, 61(1), 123–137.
Tamer, E. (2003): "Incomplete Simultaneous Discrete Response Model with Multiple Equilibria", The Review of Economic Studies, 70(1), 147–165.
van der Vaart, A. W., and J. A. Wellner (1996): Weak Convergence and Empirical Processes: with Applications to Statistics. Springer, New York.
White, H. (1982): "Maximum Likelihood Estimation of Misspecified Models", Econometrica, 50(1), 1–25.

Model Adequacy Checks for Discrete Choice Dynamic Models

Igor Kheifets and Carlos Velasco

Abstract This chapter proposes new parametric model adequacy tests for possibly nonlinear and nonstationary time series models with noncontinuous data distribution, which is often the case in applied work. In particular, we consider the correct specification of parametric conditional distributions in dynamic discrete choice models, not only of some particular conditional characteristics such as moments or symmetry. Knowing the true distribution is important in many circumstances, in particular to apply efficient maximum likelihood methods, obtain consistent estimates of partial effects, and appropriate predictions of the probability of future events. We propose a transformation of data which under the true conditional distribution leads to continuous uniform iid series. The uniformity and serial independence of the new series is then examined simultaneously. The transformation can be considered as an extension of the integral transform tool for noncontinuous data. We derive asymptotic properties of such tests taking into account the parameter estimation effect. Since transformed series are iid we do not require any mixing conditions and asymptotic results illustrate the double simultaneous checking nature of our test. The test statistics converges under the null with a parametric rate to the asymptotic distribution, which is case dependent, hence we justify a parametric bootstrap approximation. The test has power against local alternatives and is consistent. The performance of the new tests is compared with classical specification checks for discrete choice models.

Keywords Goodness of fit · Diagnostic test · Parametric conditional distribution · Discrete choice models · Parameter estimation effect · Bootstrap.

I. Kheifets (✉)
New Economic School, Nakhimovskii prospekt 47,
Moscow, Russian Federation
e-mail: ikheifets@nes.ru

C. Velasco
Department of Economics, Universidad Carlos III de Madrid,
calle Madrid 128 Getafe, Madrid, Spain
e-mail: carlos.velasco@uc3m.es

X. Chen and N. R. Swanson (eds.), *Recent Advances and Future Directions in Causality, Prediction, and Specification Analysis*, DOI: 10.1007/978-1-4614-1653-1_14,

1 Introduction

Dynamic choice models are important econometric tools in applied macroeconomics and finance. These are used to describe the monetary policy decisions of central banks (Hamilton and Jorda 2002; Basu and de Jong 2007), for recession forecasting (Kauppi and Saikkonen 2008; Startz 2008) and to model the behavior of agents in financial markets (Rydberg and Shephard 2003). In the simplest framework, a binary dynamic model explains the value of an indicator variable in period t, $Y_t \in \{0, 1\}$, in terms of an information set Ω_t available at this period. Then Y_t conditional on Ω_t is distributed as a Bernoulli variable with expectation $p_t = E(Y_t|\Omega_t) = \mathrm{P}(Y_t = 1|\Omega_t) = F(\pi_t)$ where $\pi_t = \pi(\Omega_t)$ summarizes the relevant information and F is a cumulative probability distribution function (cdf) monotone increasing.Typical specifications of the link function F are the standard normal cdf, Φ, and the logistic cdf.

We can describe the observed values of Y_t as $Y_t = 1\left\{Y_t^* > 0\right\}$ where Y_t^* is given by the latent variable model

$$Y_t^* = \pi_t + \varepsilon_t$$

and $\varepsilon_t \sim F = F_\varepsilon$ are iid observations with zero mean.

In a general specification π_t is a linear combination of a set of exogenous variables X_t observable in t, but not necessarily contemporaneous, plus lags of Y_t and π_t itself,

$$\pi_t = \alpha_0 + \alpha(L)\,\pi_t + \delta(L)\,Y_t + X_t'\beta,$$

where $\delta(L) = \delta_1 L + \cdots + \delta_q L^q$ and $\alpha(L) = \alpha_1 L + \cdots + \alpha_p L^p$. When $q = 0$, $p = 1$ and $F_\varepsilon = \Phi$ this leads to the dynamic probit model of Dueker (1997),

$$\pi_t = \pi_0 + \delta_1 Y_{t-1} + X_t'\beta,$$

and if the roots of $1 - \alpha(L)$ are out of the unit circle, π_t can be represented in terms of infinite lags of Y_t and X_t.

Many nonlinear extensions have been considered in the literature, such as interactions with lags of Y_t, to describe the state of the economy in the past,

$$\pi_t = \pi_0 + \delta_1 Y_{t-1} + X_t'\beta + (Y_{t-1}X_t)'\,\gamma$$

or with the sign of other variables in X_t, both stressing different reaction functions in several regimes defined in terms of exogenous variables at period t. Other specifications consider heteroskedasticity corrections, so that $\mathrm{Var}(\varepsilon_t) = \sigma^2(\Omega_t)$, for example a two regimes conditional variance, $\mathrm{Var}(\varepsilon_t) = \sigma^2(Y_{t-1})$.

In the general ordered discrete choice model, the dependent variable takes $J + 1$ values in a set $\mathcal{J}$, and the parametric distribution $\mathrm{P}(Y_t = j|\Omega_t)$ can be modeled using the unobserved latent continuous dependent variable Y_t^*. In the typical case where $Y_t = j$ if $\mu_{j-1} \le Y_t^* \le \mu_j$ for $j \in \mathcal{J}$, $\mathcal{J} = \{0, 1, 2, ..., J\}$ and $\varepsilon_t \sim F_\varepsilon$, with $\mu_{-1} = -\infty$ and $\mu_J = \infty$, we have that

$$\mathrm{P}(Y_t = j|\Omega_t) = F_\varepsilon(\mu_j - \pi_t) - F_\varepsilon(\mu_{j-1} - \pi_t)$$

with $\alpha_0 = 0$.

Forecasting is one of the main uses of discrete choice models. In that case for the calculation of predictions it might be necessary to resource to recursive methods when $\delta(L) \neq 0$. However, in almost all situations parameters are unknown, but conditional maximum likelihood (ML) estimation is straightforward given the binomial or discrete nature of data, with typically well-behaved likelihoods and asymptotic normal estimates if the model is properly specified. The existence, representation and probability properties of these models have been studied under general conditions by de Jong and Woutersen (2011), who also report the consistency and asymptotic normality of ML estimates when the parametric model is correct. However, if not, estimates will be inconsistent and predictions can be severely biased.

This leads to the need of diagnostic and goodness-of-fit techniques, which should account for the main features of these models, discrete nature, and dynamic evolution. The first property entails nonlinear modeling and renders invalid many methods specifically tailored for continuous distributions. Although the latent disturbance ε_t is continuous and with a well-specified distribution, it is unobservable. Simulation methods could be used to estimate the distribution of such innovations, but we follow an alternative route by "*continuing*" the discrete observations Y_t, so that they have a continuous and strictly increasing conditional distribution in $[-1, J]$ given Ω_t. This distribution inherits the dependence on a set of parameters and on a conditional information set and can serve as a main tool to evaluate the appropriateness of the hypothesized model.

Conditional distribution specification tests are often based on comparing parametric and nonparametric estimation as in Andrews (1997) conditional Kolmogorov test, or on the integral transform (see Bai 2003; Corradi and Swanson 2006). The former approach is developed for different data types, while the latter can be used only for data with continuous distribution. The integral transform does not require strong conditions on the data dependence structure, so it is very useful in testing dynamic models. However, applying the integral transform to noncontinuous data will not bring to uniform on [0, 1] series, and therefore this approach can not be applied directly to dynamic discrete choice models. To guarantee that adequacy tests based on the integral transform enjoy nice asymptotic properties we propose the following procedure: first, make data continuous by adding a continuous random noise and then apply the modified conditional distribution transformation to get uniform iid series.

The first step can be called the *continuous extension of a discrete variable* which has been employed in different situations. For example Ferguson (1967) uses some type of extension for simple hypothesis testing, Denuit and Lambert (2005) and Neslehova (2006) use it to apply a copulas technique for discrete and discontinuous variables. The second step is the probability integral transform (PIT) of the continued variables, which we will call *randomized PIT*. Resulting uniform iid series can be tested using Bai (2003) or Corradi and Swanson (2006) tests. However, in some cases these tests can not distinguish certain alternatives, so we also propose test based on comparing joint empirical distribution functions with the product of its theoretical uniform marginals by means of Cramer-von Mises or Kolmogorov-Smirnov (KS) type statistics, developed by Kheifets (2011) for continuous distributions.

In a general setup, we do not know the true parameters, while the integral transform using estimated parameters does not necessary provide iid uniform random variates. Hence, asymptotic properties and critical values of the tests with estimated parameters have to be addressed. The estimation effect changes the asymptotic distribution of the statistics and makes it *data dependent*. Andrews (1997) proves that parametric bootstrap provides correct critical values in this case using linear expansion of the estimation effect, which arises naturally under the ML method. The idea of orthogonal projecting the test statistics against the estimation effect due to Wooldridge (1990) has been used in parametric moment tests, see Bontemps and Meddahi (2005). The continuous version of the projection, often called Khmaladze (1981) transformation, was employed in the tests of Koul and Stute (1999) to specify the conditional mean, and of Bai and Ng (2001), Bai (2003), Delgado and Stute (2008) to specify the conditional distribution. These projection tests are not model invariant since they require to compute conditional mean and variance derivatives, and also projections may cause a loss in power. In this paper, we apply a bootstrap approach instead. In the case of ordered choice models an extensive Monte Carlo comparison of specification tests has been done by Mora and Moro-Egido (2007) in a static cross-section context. They study two types of tests based on moment conditions and on comparison of parametric and nonparametric estimates.

Despite that there is some work on nonstationary discrete data models, cf. Phillips and Park (2000), we stress stationary situations, but some ideas could be extended to a more general setup as far as the conditional model provides a full specification of the distribution of the dependent discrete variable.

The contributions of this paper are following: (1) a new specification test for dynamic discontinuous models is proposed, (2) we show that the test is invariant to the choice of distribution of the random noise added, (3) parameter estimation effect of the test is studied, (4) under standard conditions we show the asymptotic properties of such tests, and (5) since asymptotic distribution is case dependent, critical values can not be tabulated and we prove that a bootstrap distribution approximation is valid.

The rest of the paper is organized as follows. Section 2 introduces specification test statistics. Asymptotic properties and bootstrap justification provided in Sect. 3. Monte Carlo experiments are reported in Sect. 4. Section 5 concludes.

2 Test Statistics

In this section we introduce our goodness-of-fit statistics. Suppose that a sequence of observations $(Y_1, X_1), (Y_2, X_2), ..., (Y_T, X_T)$ is given. Let $\Omega_t = \{X_t, X_{t-1}, \ldots; Y_{t-1}, Y_{t-2}, \ldots\}$ be the information set at time t (not including Y_t).

We consider a family of conditional cdf's $F(y|\Omega_t, \theta)$, parameterized by $\theta \in \Theta$, where $\Theta \subseteq R^L$ is a finite dimensional parameter space. We could allow for non-stationarity by permitting the change in the functional form of the cdf of Y_t using subscript t in F_t. Our null hypothesis of correct specification is

H_0 : The conditional distribution of Y_t conditional on Ω_t is in the parametric family $F(y|\Omega_t, \theta)$ for some $\theta_0 \in \Theta$.

For example, for dynamic ordered discrete choice model the null hypothesis would mean that $\exists\theta_0 \in \Theta,\ \forall j = 0, \dots, J,\ \mathrm{P}(Y_t = j|\,\Omega_t) = p_j(\Omega_t, \theta_0)$, i.e. that all conditional probabilities are in a given parametric family.

For further analysis, we assume that the support of the conditional distributions $F(y|\Omega_t, \theta)$ is a finite set of nonnegative integers $\{0, \dots, J\}$ and $F(y|\Omega_t, \theta) = \sum_{j \le y} \mathrm{P}_F(j|\Omega_t, \theta)$, where P_F is the probability function at the discrete points.

The first step is to obtain a *continuous version* of Y. For any random variable $Z \sim F_z$ with support in [0, 1] and F_z continuous (but not necessary strictly increasing) define the *continued by* Z version of Y,

$$Y^\dagger = Y + Z - 1.$$

Then the distribution of the continued version of Y is

$$F^\dagger(y|\Omega_t) = \mathrm{P}\left(Y^\dagger \le y|\Omega_t\right) = F([y]|\Omega_t) + F_z(y - [y])\mathrm{P}([y] + 1|\Omega_t), \quad (1)$$

which is strictly increasing on $[-1, J]$. The typical choice for Z is the uniform in $[0, 1]$, so that

$$F^\dagger(y|\Omega_t) = F([y]|\Omega_t) + (y - [y])\mathrm{P}([y] + 1|\Omega_t). \quad (2)$$

The binary choice case renders $F^\dagger(y|\Omega_t) = (y - [y])(1 - p_t)$ for $y \in [-1, 0)$ and $F^\dagger(y|\Omega_t) = (1 - p_t) + (y - [y])p_t$ for $y \in [0, 1]$. Note, that $F^\dagger$ coincides with F in the domain of F. We state next an "invariance property": for our purpose, it does not matter how to continue Y and what distribution F_z of the noise Z to add. The unit support of Z is needed to get a simple expression for $F^\dagger$ in (1), otherwise the resulting distribution will be a convolution $F^\dagger(y|\Omega_t) = \sum_{j=0}^{J} F_z(y + 1 - j)\,\mathrm{P}(j|\Omega_t)$. Continuation idea has been used to deal with discrete distributions, for example, to work with copulas with discrete marginals as in Denuit and Lambert (2005).

The following proposition generalizes results about the PIT.

Proposition 1 *(a) Under H_0 random variables $U_t = F^\dagger(Y_t^\dagger|\Omega_t, \theta_0)$ are iid uniform; (b) Invariant property of randomized PIT: realizations of U_t are the same for any distribution F_z in* (1) *both under H_0 and under the alternative.*

Part (a) is a property of usual PIT with a continuous distribution $F^\dagger$. Part (b) that realizations of U_t are the same, means the following. Consider continuations of Y_t by arbitrary $Z \sim F_z$ and uniform $Z_u \sim F_U$. Fix realizations $\{y_t\}$, $\{z_t\}$ and $\{z_{ut}\}$ from respective distributions. If $z_{ut} = F_z(z_t)$, then

$$F^{\dagger F_z}(y_t + z_t - 1|\Omega_t, \theta_0) = F^{\dagger F_U}(y_t + z_{ut} - 1|\Omega_t, \theta_0),$$

where $F^{\dagger F_z}$ stresses dependence of $F^\dagger$ on F_z in (1), $F^{\dagger F_U}$ is as $F^\dagger$ in (2), continued by uniform, and Ω_t denotes here realized past. Therefore, although a continued variable $Y_t^\dagger$ and its distribution $F^\dagger$ depends on F_z, $F^\dagger(Y_t^\dagger|\Omega_t, \theta_0)$ is not and we can always use uniform variables Z for continuation without affecting any properties of tests based on U_t.

Now we can use the fact that under the null hypothesis $U_t = F^\dagger(Y_t^\dagger|\Omega_t, \theta_0)$, $t = 1, \ldots, T$, are uniform on [0,1] and iid random variables, so that $\mathrm{P}(U_{t-1} \leq r_1, U_{t-2} \leq r_2, \ldots, U_{t-p} \leq r_p) = r_1 r_2 \ldots r_p$, for $r = (r_1, \ldots, r_p) \in [0, 1]^p$. This motivates us to consider the following empirical processes

$$V_{pT}(r) = \frac{1}{\sqrt{T-(p+1)}} \sum_{t=p+1}^{T} \left[\prod_{j=1}^{p} I(U_{t-j} \leq r_j) - r_1 r_2 \ldots r_p \right].$$

If we do not know θ_0 either $\{(Y_t, X_t), t \leq 0\}$, we approximate U_t with $\hat{U}_t = F_t^\dagger(Y_t^\dagger|\tilde{\Omega}_t, \hat{\theta})$ where $\hat{\theta}$ is an estimator of θ_0 and the truncated information set is $\tilde{\Omega}_t = \{X_t, X_{t-1}, \ldots, X_1; Y_{t-1}, Y_{t-2}, \ldots, Y_1\}$ and write

$$\hat{V}_{pT}(r) = \frac{1}{\sqrt{T-(p+1)}} \sum_{t=p+1}^{T} \left[\prod_{j=1}^{p} I(\hat{U}_{t-j} \leq r_j) - r_1 r_2 \ldots r_p \right] \tag{3}$$

and

$$D_{pT} = \Gamma(\hat{V}_{pT}(r))$$

for any continuous functional $\Gamma(\cdot)$ from $\ell^\infty([0, 1]^p)$, the set of uniformly bounded real functions on $[0, 1]^p$, to R. In particular we use the Cramer-von Misses (CvM) and Kolmogorov Smirnov test statistics

$$D_{pT}^{\mathrm{CvM}} = \int_{[0,1]^p} \hat{V}_{pT}(r)^2 dr \quad \text{or} \quad D_{pT}^{\mathrm{KS}} = \max_{[0,1]^p} \left| \hat{V}_{pT}(r) \right|. \tag{4}$$

One further possibility is to test for j-lag pairwise independence, using the process

$$\hat{V}_{2T,j}(r) = \frac{1}{\sqrt{T-j}} \sum_{t=j+1}^{T} \left[I(\hat{U}_t \leq r_1) I(\hat{U}_{t-j} \leq r_2) - r_1 r_2 \right], \tag{5}$$

and corresponding test statistics $D_{2T,j}^{\mathrm{CvM}}$ and $D_{2T,j}^{\mathrm{KS}}$, say.

We can aggregate across p or j summing possibly with different weights $k(\cdot)$, obtaining generalized statistics

$$\mathrm{ADP}_T = \sum_{p=1}^{T-1} k(p) D_{pT}, \quad \text{or} \quad \mathrm{ADJ}_T = \sum_{j=1}^{T-1} k(j) D_{2T,j}. \tag{6}$$

For $p = 1$, D_{1T}^{KS} delivers a generalization of Kolmogorov test to discrete distributions. Usually, this test captures general deviations of marginal distribution but lacks power if only dynamics is misspecified. In particular, it does not have power against alternatives where U_t are uniform on [0,1] but not independent. For general p, V_{pT} delivers a generalization of Kheifets (2011) to discrete distributions. This test should capture both deviations of marginal distribution and deviations in dynamics.

A more direct approach is based in Box and Pierce (1970) type of statistics, we could consider

$$\mathrm{BPU}_m := T \sum_{j=1}^{m} \hat{\rho}_{T,U}\,(j)^2,$$

$m = 1, 2, \ldots,$ and $\hat{\rho}_{T,U}\,(j)$ are the sample correlation coefficients of the $U_t's$ at lag j. Noting that U_t should be uniform continuous iid random variables under the null of correctly specified model, but might be correlated under alternative hypothesis of wrong specification, BPU_m is a good basis to design goodness-of-fit tests. This idea is related to the tests of Hong (1998). Alternatively, we can check autocorrelations of Gaussian residuals $\Phi(U_t)$

$$\mathrm{BPN}_m := T \sum_{j=1}^{m} \hat{\rho}_{T,\Phi(U)}\,(j)^2,$$

and normality of $\Phi(U_t)$ with Jarque-Bera test (JB). In addition we can check autocorrelations of discrete innovations,

$$e_t = \frac{Y_t - E\,[Y_t|\Omega_t]}{(\mathrm{Var}\,[Y_t|\Omega_t])^{1/2}},$$

which are just the usual standardized probit residuals. We can define

$$\mathrm{BPD}_m := T \sum_{j=1}^{m} \hat{\rho}_{T,e}\,(j)^2$$

and other statistics based on autocorrelations of squares of different types of residuals. The asymptotic distribution of these statistics can be approximated by chi square distributions when the true parameters θ_0 are known. Unlike tests based on empirical process, these tests can not capture some alternatives, for example if misspecification involves only higher order moments.

Parameter estimation affects the asymptotic distribution of these statistics, as well as that of those tests based on the empirical distribution of the $U_t's$. There are different bootstrap and sampling techniques to approximate asymptotic distribution, see for example Shao and Dongsheng (1995), Politis et al. (1999). Since under H_0 we know the parametric conditional distribution, we apply parametric bootstrap to mimic the H_0 distribution. We introduce the algorithm now for statistics $\Gamma(\hat{V}_{2T})$.

1. Estimate model with initial data $(Y_t, X_t), t = 1, 2, \ldots, T$, get parameter estimator $\hat{\theta}$, get test statistic $\Gamma(\hat{V}_{2T})$.
2. Simulate Y_t^* with $F(\cdot|\Omega_t^*, \hat{\theta})$ recursively for $t = 1, 2, \ldots, T$, where the bootstrap information set is $\Omega_t^* = (X_t, X_{t-1}, \ldots, Y_{t-1}^*, Y_{t-2}^*, \ldots)$.
3. Estimate model with simulated data Y_t^*, get θ^*, get bootstrapped statistics $\Gamma(\hat{V}_{2T}^*)$.
4. Repeat 2–3 B times, compute the percentiles of the empirical distribution of the B boostrapped statistics.
5. Reject H_0 if $\Gamma(\hat{V}_{2T})$ is greater than the corresponding $(1 - \alpha)$th percentile.

We will prove that $\Gamma(\hat{V}_{2T}^*)$ has the same limiting distribution as $\Gamma(\hat{V}_{2T})$. Bootstrapping other statistics is similar.

3 Asymptotic Properties of Specification Tests

In this section, we derive asymptotic properties of the statistics based on V_{2T}. We start with the simple case when we know parameters, then study how the asymptotic distribution changes if we estimate parameters. We provide analyses under the null, under the local and fixed alternatives. We first state all necessarily assumptions and propositions, then discuss them.

Let $\|\cdot\|$ denote Euclidean norm for matrices, i.e. $\|A\| = \sqrt{\mathrm{tr}(A'A)}$ and for $\varepsilon > 0$, $B(a, \varepsilon)$ is an open ball in R^L with the center in the point a and the radius ε. In particular, for some $M > 0$ denote $B_T = B\left(\theta_0, MT^{-1/2}\right) = \{\theta : \|\theta - \theta_0\| \leq MT^{-1/2}\}$.

For any discrete distributions G and F, with probability functions P_G and P_F, and $r \in [0, 1]$ define

$$d(G, F, r) = G\left(F^{-1}(r)\right) - F\left(F^{-1}(r)\right) + \frac{r - F\left(F^{-1}(r)\right)}{\mathrm{P}_F\left(F^{-1}(r) + 1\right)}\left(\mathrm{P}_G\left(F^{-1}(r) + 1\right) - \mathrm{P}_F\left(F^{-1}(r) + 1\right)\right).$$

We have $d(F, F, r) = 0$, but $d(G, F, r)$ is not symmetric in G and F.

Assumption 1 Uniform boundedness away from zero: $\forall \varepsilon > 0$, $\exists \delta > 0$, such that $|F(0|\Omega_t, \theta)| > \varepsilon$ and $|F(j|\Omega_t, \theta) - F(j-1|\Omega_t, \theta)| > \varepsilon$ for $j = 1, \ldots, J$ uniformly in $\theta \in B(\theta_0, \delta)$.

Assumption 2 Smoothness with respect to parameters:

(2.1)

$$E \max_{t=1,\dots,T} \sup_{u \in B_T} \max_y |F(y|\Omega_t, u) - F(y|\Omega_t, \theta_0)| = O\left(T^{-1/2}\right).$$

(2.2) $\forall M \in (0, \infty)$, $\forall M_2 \in (0, \infty)$ and $\forall \delta > 0$

$$\max_y \frac{1}{\sqrt{T}} \sum_{t=1}^{T} \sup_{\substack{||u-v|| \le M_2 T^{-1/2-\delta} \\ u,v \in B_T}} |F(y|\Omega_t, u) - F(y|\Omega_t, v)| = o_p(1).$$

(2.3) $\forall M \in (0, \infty)$, there exists a uniformly continuous (vector) function $h(r)$ from $[0, 1]^2$ to R^L, such that

$$\sup_{v \in B_T} \sup_{r \in [0,1]^2} \left| \frac{1}{\sqrt{T}} \sum_{t=2}^{T} h_t(r, v) - h(r)' \sqrt{T} (\theta_0 - v) \right| = o_p(1),$$

where

$$\begin{aligned} h_t(r, v) &= d\left(F(\cdot|\Omega_{t-1}, \theta_0), F(\cdot|\Omega_{t-1}, v), r_2\right) r_1 \\ &\quad + d\left(F(\cdot|\Omega_t, \theta_0), F(\cdot|\Omega_t, v), r_1\right) I\left(F(Y_{t-1}|\Omega_{t-1}, \theta_0) \le r_2\right). \end{aligned}$$

Assumption 3 A Linear expansion of the estimator: when the sample is generated by the null $F_t(y|\Omega_t, \theta_0)$, the estimator $\hat{\theta}$ admits a linear expansion

$$\sqrt{T}(\hat{\theta} - \theta_0) = \frac{1}{\sqrt{T}} \sum_{t=1}^{T} \ell(Y_t, \Omega_t) + o_p(1), \tag{7}$$

with $E_{F_t}(\ell(Y_t, \Omega_t)|\Omega_t) = 0$ and $\frac{1}{T}\sum_{t=1}^{T} \ell(Y_t, \Omega_t)\ell(Y_t, \Omega_t)' \overset{p_{F_t}}{\to} \Psi$.

Dynamic probit/logit and general discrete choice models considered in Introduction can easily be adjusted to satisfy all these assumptions. Discrete support allows a simple analytical closed form of conditional distribution of continued variable by any continuous random variable on unit support as in (2). Assumption 1 in particular requires that $F(0|\Omega_t, \theta)$ and $F(j|\Omega_t, \theta) - F(j-1|\Omega_t, \theta)$ for $j = 1, \dots, J$ are bounded away from zero uniformly around θ_0. To study parameter estimation effect we need to assume some smoothness of the distribution with respect to the parameter in Assumption 2 and a linear expansion of the estimator in Assumption 3. Note, the smoothness of the distribution with respect to the parameter is preserved after continuation, therefore Assumption 2 is similar to continuous case in Kheifets (2011); local Lipschitz continuity or existence of uniformly bounded first derivative of the distribution w.r.t. parameter is sufficient. For bootstrap we will need to strengthen Assumption 3 (see Assumption 3B below), although both conditions are standard and satisfied for many estimators, for example for MLE. Note, that to establish the convergence of the process V_{2T} (with known θ_0) under the null (the following Proposition 2), we do not need these assumptions.

We now describe the asymptotic behavior of the process $V_{2T}(r)$ under H_0. Denote by "$\Rightarrow$" weak convergence of stochastic processes as random elements of the Skorokhod space $D\left([0,1]^2\right)$.

Proposition 2 *Under* H_0

$$V_{2T} \Rightarrow V_{2\infty},$$

where $V_{2\infty}(r)$ *is bi-parameter zero mean Gaussian process with covariance*

$$\mathrm{Cov}_{2\infty}(r,s) = (r_1 \wedge s_1)(r_2 \wedge s_2) + (r_1 \wedge s_2) r_2 s_1 + (r_2 \wedge s_1) r_1 s_2 - 3 r_1 r_2 s_1 s_2.$$

To take into account the estimation effect on the asymptotic distribution, we use a Taylor expansion to approximate $\hat{V}_{2T}(r)$ with $V_{2T}(r)$,

$$\hat{V}_{2T}(r) = V_{2T}(r) + \sqrt{T}\left(\hat{\theta} - \theta_0\right)' h(r) + o_p(1)$$

uniformly in r. To identify the limit of $\hat{V}_{2T}(r)$, we need to study limiting distribution of $\sqrt{T}(\hat{\theta} - \theta_0)$, using the expansion from Assumption 3. Define

$$C_T(r,s,\theta) = E\left(\begin{array}{c} V_{2T}(r) \\ \frac{1}{\sqrt{T}}\sum_{t=1}^{T} \ell\left(Y_t, \Omega_t\right) \end{array}\right)\left(\begin{array}{c} V_{2T}(s) \\ \frac{1}{\sqrt{T}}\sum_{t=1}^{T} \ell\left(Y_t, \Omega_t\right) \end{array}\right)'$$

and let $(V_{2\infty}(r), \psi'_\infty)'$ be a zero mean Gaussian process with covariance function $C(r,s,\theta_0) = \lim_{T\to\infty} C_T(r,s,\theta_0)$. Dependence on θ on right hand side (rhs) comes through U_t and $\ell\left(\cdot,\cdot\right)$.

Suppose the conditional distribution function $H(y|\Omega_t)$ is not in the parametric family $F(y|\Omega_t,\theta)$ but has the same support. For any $T_0 \in \{0,1,2,\ldots,\}$ and $T \geq T_0$ define conditional on Ω_t conditional df

$$G_T(y|\Omega_t,\theta) = \left(1 - \frac{\sqrt{T_0}}{\sqrt{T}}\right) F(y|\Omega_t,\theta) + \frac{\sqrt{T_0}}{\sqrt{T}} H(y|\Omega_t).$$

Now we define local alternatives:

H_{1T}: Conditional cdf of Y_t is equal to $G_T(y|\Omega_t,\theta_0)$ with $T_0 \neq 0$.

Conditional cdf $G_T(y|\Omega_t,\theta_0)$ allow us to study all three cases: H_0 if $T_0 = 0$, H_{1T} if $T = T_0, T_0+1, T_0+2, \ldots$ and $T_0 \neq 0$ and H_1 if we fix $T = T_0$. In the next proposition we provide the asymptotic distribution of our statistics under the null and under the local alternatives.

Proposition 3 *a) Suppose Assumptions 1–3 hold. Then under* H_0

$$\Gamma(\hat{V}_{2T}) \xrightarrow{d} \Gamma(\hat{V}_{2\infty}),$$

where $\hat{V}_{2\infty}(r) = V_{2\infty}(r) - h(r)'\psi_{\infty}$.

b) Suppose Assumptions 1–3 hold. Then under H_{1T}

$$\Gamma(\hat{V}_{2T}) \xrightarrow{d} \Gamma\left(\hat{V}_{2\infty} + \sqrt{T_0}k - \sqrt{T_0}\xi'h\right),$$

where

$$k(r) = \operatorname*{plim}_{T\to\infty} \frac{1}{T}\sum_{t=2}^{T} \{d\left(H\left(\cdot|\Omega_{t-1}\right), F\left(\cdot|\Omega_{t-1}, \theta_0\right), r_2\right) r_1$$
$$+ d\left(H\left(\cdot|\Omega_t\right), F\left(\cdot|\Omega_t, \theta_0\right), r_1\right) I\left(F\left(Y_{t-1}|\Omega_{t-1}, \theta_0\right) \le r_2\right)\},$$

and

$$\xi = \operatorname*{plim}_{T\to\infty} \frac{1}{T}\sum_{t=1}^{T} \ell\left(Y_t, \Omega_t\right). \tag{8}$$

Under G_T, the random variables $U_t = F^{\dagger}(Y_t^{\dagger}|\Omega_t, \theta_0)$ are not anymore iid, instead $U_t^* = G_T^{\dagger}(Y_t^{\dagger}|\Omega_t, \theta_0)$ are uniform iid. The first term in $k(r)$ controls for the lack of uniformity of U_t (and it is similar to Bai's (2003) $k(r)$), it is zero when U_t are uniform. The second term in $k(r)$ adds control for independence of U_t, cf. Kheifets (2011).

Under the alternative we may have also that (7) is not centered around zero, since $E_{G_T}\left(\ell\left(Y_t, \Omega_t\right)|\Omega_t\right) = \frac{\sqrt{T_0}}{\sqrt{T}} E_H\left(\ell\left(Y_t, \Omega_t\right)|\Omega_t\right)$, therefore ξ may be nonzero, which stands for information from estimation. This term does not appear in Bai (2003) method, since his method projects out the estimation effect.

For the case of the one parameter empirical process, we can provide the following corollary, which is similar to Bai (2003)'s single parameter results.

Corollary 1 *a) Suppose Assumptions 1–3 hold. Then under* H_0

$$\Gamma(\hat{V}_{1T}(\cdot)) \xrightarrow{d} \Gamma(\hat{V}_{2\infty}(\cdot, 1)),$$

where $\hat{V}_{1\infty}(\cdot) = V_{1\infty}(\cdot) - h(\cdot, 1)'\psi_{\infty}$ *and* $V_{1\infty}(\cdot) = V_{2\infty}(\cdot, 1)$.

b) Suppose Assumptions 1–3 hold. Then under H_{1T}

$$\Gamma(\hat{V}_{1T}(\cdot)) \xrightarrow{d} \Gamma(\hat{V}_{1\infty}(\cdot) + \sqrt{T_0}k_1(\cdot) - \sqrt{T_0}h(\cdot, 1)'\xi),$$

where for $r \in [0, 1]$

$$k_1(r) = \operatorname*{plim}_{T\to\infty} \frac{1}{T}\sum_{t=2}^{T} d\left(H\left(\cdot|\Omega_t\right), F\left(\cdot|\Omega_t, \theta_0\right), r\right).$$

Note then that tests based on $\hat{V}_{1T}$ are not consistent against alternatives for which $k_1 = 0$ and $h(\cdot, 1) = 0$ but $k \neq 0$ or $h(\cdot, 1) \neq 0$ on some set of positive measure.

We will justify our bootstrap procedure now, i.e., we prove that $\Gamma(\hat{V}^*_{2T})$ has the same limiting distribution as $\Gamma(\hat{V}_{2T})$. We say that the sample is distributed under $\{\theta_T : T \geq 1\}$ when there is a triangular array of random variables $\{Y_{Tt} : T \geq 1, t \leq T\}$ with (T, t) element generated by $F(\cdot|\Omega_{Tt}, \theta_T)$, where $\Omega_{Tt} = (X_{t-1}, X_{t-2}, \ldots, Y_{Tt-1}, Y_{Tt-2}, \ldots)$. Similar arguments can be applied to other statistics.

Assumption 3B For all nonrandom sequences $\{\theta_T : T \geq 1\}$ for which $\theta_T \to \theta_0$, we have

$$\sqrt{T}(\hat{\theta} - \theta_T) = \frac{1}{\sqrt{T}} \sum_{t=1}^{T} \ell\left(Y_{Tt}, \Omega_{Tt}\right) + o_p(1),$$

under $\{\theta_T : T \geq 1\}$, where $E\left[\ell\left(Y_{Tt}, \Omega_{Tt}\right)|\Omega_{Tt}\right] = 0$ and

$$\frac{1}{T} \sum_{t=1}^{T} \ell\left(Y_{Tt}, \Omega_{Tt}\right) \ell\left(Y_{Tt}, \Omega_{Tt}\right)' \xrightarrow{p} \Psi.$$

Note that the function $\ell\left(\cdot, \cdot\right)$ now depends on θ_T and is assumed to be the same as in Assumption 3. We require that estimators of close to θ_0 points have *the same* linear representation as the estimator of θ_0 itself.

Proposition 5 *Suppose Assumptions 1, 2, and 3B hold. Then for any nonrandom sequence* $\{\theta_T : T \geq 1\}$ *for which* $\theta_T \to \theta_0$, *under* $\{\theta_T : T \geq 1\}$,

$$\Gamma(\hat{V}_{2T}(r)) \xrightarrow{d} \Gamma(\hat{V}_{2\infty}(r)).$$

4 Monte Carlo Simulation

In this section, we investigate the finite sample properties of our bootstrap tests using Monte Carlo exercise. We use a simple dynamic Probit model with one exogenous regressor with autoregressive dynamics. We consider three specifications of dynamics

$$\begin{aligned}
\text{Static model}: \ \pi_t &= \pi_0 + \beta X_t, \\
\text{Dynamic model}: \ \pi_t &= \pi_0 + \delta_1 Y_{t-1} + \beta X_t, \\
\text{Dynamic model with interactions}: \ \pi_t &= \pi_0 + \delta_1 Y_{t-1} + \gamma_1 Y_{t-1} X_t + \beta X_t, \ \gamma_1 = -2\beta,
\end{aligned}$$

Table 1 Different scenarios for Monte Carlo experiments

	DGP	Null
1	probti static	probit static
2	probit dynamic	probit dynamic
3	probit interactions	probit interactions
4	logit static	probit static
5	chi2 static	probit static
6	logit dynamic	probit static
7	chi2 dynamic	probit static
8	logit interactions	probit dynamic
9	chi2 interactions	probit dynamic
10	logit interactions	probit static
11	chi2 interactions	probit static

where in all specifications X_t follows an AR(1) process,

$$X_t = \alpha_1 X_{t-1} + e_t, \quad e_t \sim IIN\,(0, 1)\,,$$

and we set $\pi_0 = 0, \beta = 1, \delta_1 = 0.8, \alpha_1 = 0.8.$

We try 11 different scenarios of data generating processes (DGP) and null hypotheses (see Table 1). In the first three, we study the size properties of static, dynamic, and dynamic with interactions probit models. Other scenarios check power when dynamics and/or marginals are misspecified. We take logit and $\left(\chi_1^2 - 1\right)/2^{1/2}$ as alternative distributions. We use sample sizes $T = 100$ (Table 2), 300 (Table 3) and 500 (Table 4) with 1,000 replications. To estimate the Bootstrap percentages of rejections we use a Warp bootstrap Monte Carlo (see Giacomini et al. 2007) for all considered test statistics. For tests based on "continued" residuals we consider one-parameter ($p = 1$) and two-parameter empirical processes ($p = 2$) with $j = 1$ and $j = 2$ lags and CvM and KS criterions. To make the results more readable, we denote them as $\text{CvM}_0 = D_{1T}^{\text{CvM}}$, $\text{CvM}_1 = D_{2T,1}^{\text{CvM}}$, $\text{CvM}_2 = D_{2T,2}^{\text{CvM}}$ and $\text{KS}_0 = D_{1T}^{\text{KS}}$, $\text{KS}_1 = D_{2T,1}^{\text{KS}}$, $\text{KS}_2 = D_{2T,2}^{\text{KS}}$. We consider Box-Pierce type tests for Gaussian and discrete residuals with $m = 1, 2, 25$. We also check normality of Gaussian residuals with a bootstrapped JB. The results of empirical process tests with further lags $j = 3, 4, 5$ and correlation tests on uniform residuals do not provide additional information and are omitted.

Now we discuss the performance of empirical process based tests in comparison with traditional correlation tests. For $T = 100$ almost all test statistics are slightly undersized (cases 1–3). The situation improves with larger T, and CvM statistics approach faster to nominal rates than KS. Overall, empirical size at $T = 500$ is very good. The situation with power is not unambiguous. No test can capture static logit alternative to the null hypothesis of static probit model even at $T = 500$ (case 4). On the other hand, when static χ^2 alternative to the null hypothesis of static probit is considered (case 5), there is some power at $T = 300$ which improves with $T = 500$ for all empirical process based tests. Since under the null and under the alternative

Table 2 Percentage of rejections of test statistics with $T = 100$

		CvM_0	CvM_1	CvM_2	KS_0	KS_1	KS_2	BPN_1	BPN_2	BPN_{25}	JB	BPD_1	BPD_2	BPD_{25}
1	10%	8.8	7.4	10.4	8.4	10.1	9.2	9.5	9.6	9.3	8.3	10.1	10.6	8.8
	5%	3.5	4.3	4.3	3.9	4.8	4.7	4.6	3.7	3.8	4.4	5.5	5.1	3.4
	1%	0.3	0.9	0.4	0.5	1.1	1.7	1.5	0.8	0.3	2.1	0.8	0.6	0.3
2	10%	7.9	8.3	8.7	7.0	9.6	9.2	9.0	10.6	7.0	11.2	9.5	10.7	12.8
	5%	3.0	3.6	4.0	2.8	4.9	4.5	6.0	4.0	2.1	5.9	4.0	4.4	6.1
	1%	0.0	0.4	0.1	0.8	1.2	1.0	0.9	1.3	0.3	1.5	0.4	1.1	0.7
3	10%	8.9	10.0	9.5	7.7	10.6	9.4	10.1	11.3	8.9	10.7	9.2	9.2	10.1
	5%	4.1	4.1	3.9	3.6	4.9	5.0	5.5	5.5	4.5	5.4	5.5	3.8	5.4
	1%	0.1	0.1	0.2	1.1	0.5	0.8	1.2	1.1	0.5	1.1	0.6	0.8	0.5
4	10%	8.1	9.0	7.6	8.4	8.9	9.9	7.2	8.8	7.5	9.9	9.0	9.2	9.0
	5%	3.9	4.6	3.5	3.6	4.1	3.7	3.5	4.1	3.6	3.0	5.1	4.6	4.1
	1%	0.5	0.4	0.3	0.6	0.6	0.6	1.2	0.7	0.6	0.5	1.0	1.9	0.7
5	10%	10.4	9.5	10.2	12.0	10.1	11.1	9.2	11.5	10.7	20.3	8.0	7.5	9.2
	5%	4.9	6.1	5.6	5.9	5.2	5.7	5.7	6.3	6.1	12.6	4.6	3.7	4.8
	1%	0.5	0.9	0.3	0.8	1.2	0.3	1.0	1.0	0.7	4.3	1.8	1.6	0.9
6	10%	9.5	11.0	7.6	9.2	9.8	9.3	19.1	15.4	11.7	11.0	43.0	35.3	16.8
	5%	4.6	4.9	3.5	3.5	5.2	4.6	10.7	9.0	6.6	4.7	29.4	20.5	9.4
	1%	0.4	0.5	0.8	0.5	1.4	0.9	2.9	2.3	0.8	0.9	11.0	5.7	2.9
7	10%	10.3	10.9	9.4	9.2	10.0	9.3	28.3	26.4	14.5	13.7	60.0	50.6	24.6
	5%	4.8	5.2	4.7	3.9	4.7	5.2	20.6	16.4	8.5	7.7	47.1	37.0	16.7
	1%	0.1	1.5	0.1	1.2	1.3	0.5	9.4	6.0	2.6	2.3	26.0	16.4	5.6
8	10%	9.7	9.2	13.7	9.9	10.1	13.0	14.0	26.6	16.2	9.9	46.2	57.4	30.1
	5%	4.0	3.7	7.8	3.6	5.5	7.8	6.5	18.8	10.1	3.8	36.9	45.1	18.6
	1%	0.8	0.8	2.5	0.8	1.1	1.3	0.6	6.4	2.3	0.3	17.1	27.6	5.0
9	10%	14.4	16.9	29.1	16.0	20.6	34.4	18.1	55.7	33.5	20.0	79.0	82.2	64.9
	5%	8.9	10.0	21.1	9.9	12.5	18.5	11.2	48.4	23.1	12.4	72.9	81.0	59.8
	1%	0.9	1.8	3.9	1.4	4.2	3.8	3.4	26.9	11.6	3.1	58.1	77.2	43.8
10	10%	8.6	14.7	18.1	7.6	15.5	13.0	28.0	42.0	21.3	9.2	50.1	79.8	43.6
	5%	2.8	8.5	9.5	3.8	7.6	6.6	17.5	29.0	12.9	3.9	35.7	69.8	30.4
	1%	0.6	1.4	2.1	0.4	1.3	0.5	5.3	12.4	4.4	0.3	22.4	45.6	10.7
11	10%	9.0	28.1	33.6	8.1	29.2	28.4	53.1	85.1	60.3	8.8	72.0	99.9	94.2
	5%	3.4	17.6	19.8	3.3	17.1	11.8	40.7	76.3	43.1	5.3	61.6	99.7	90.5
	1%	0.2	6.1	4.2	0.2	3.4	1.4	23.2	57.1	22.0	0.6	40.8	98.4	72.3

we have static models, correlation tests do not have power. Normality test (JB) is doing well only in the latter case. When there is a slight dynamic misspecification added to logit (case 6), CvM_1 and KS_1 improve, but when it is added to χ^2 our tests and JB doing worse (case 7). Correlation tests, on the contrary display power against these dynamic alternatives. When the alternative has dynamic interactions, and the null is a dynamic probit (cases 8 and 9), all tests (but JB for logit) are doing well, and even better if higher lags are taken into account. Finally, when dynamic interactions are taken versus static model (cases 10 and 11), power is very good, and increases when more lags are considered. Exceptions are "marginal tests" CvM_0, KS_0, and JB.

Table 3 Percentage of rejections of test statistics with $T = 300$

		CvM$_0$	CvM$_1$	CvM$_2$	KS$_0$	KS$_1$	KS$_2$	BPN$_1$	BPN$_2$	BPN$_{25}$	JB	BPD$_1$	BPD$_2$	BPD$_{25}$
1	10 %	8.3	9.2	9.2	9.1	9.0	10.4	8.0	8.3	8.6	8.0	8.3	8.2	10.2
	5 %	4.1	4.7	4.6	5.2	4.8	4.6	3.6	3.9	4.4	2.7	4.2	3.1	4.8
	1 %	0.7	1.0	0.6	0.8	0.6	0.4	0.6	0.7	1.1	0.6	0.6	0.6	1.0
2	10 %	9.3	8.9	10.2	9.3	9.8	11.6	7.6	10.0	9.7	9.6	9.0	6.9	7.4
	5 %	5.5	4.4	5.9	5.2	4.9	6.4	3.8	4.6	4.8	3.8	3.7	3.6	3.2
	1 %	1.0	1.1	0.9	1.4	1.1	0.9	0.5	0.7	1.4	0.7	0.5	0.2	0.6
3	10 %	8.5	12.3	8.7	8.7	12.2	9.9	8.1	9.9	10.1	9.0	10.1	9.4	13.5
	5 %	4.5	5.1	5.1	3.3	5.4	5.3	4.4	5.2	5.9	4.2	5.3	4.2	5.1
	1 %	1.1	1.0	1.5	1.2	0.6	0.9	0.9	1.0	1.3	0.5	0.6	1.2	1.5
4	10 %	9.9	10.2	9.2	9.5	10.8	9.8	8.6	9.3	10.0	11.2	8.5	9.6	8.5
	5 %	4.8	4.9	4.6	5.3	5.2	4.9	4.4	5.1	4.0	6.1	3.3	3.2	3.6
	1 %	0.9	1.1	0.6	0.9	1.3	1.1	0.5	0.5	1.0	0.7	0.8	0.5	0.9
5	10 %	16.5	15.1	14.9	15.8	14.9	14.4	11.8	11.2	8.7	41.4	6.0	7.2	9.0
	5 %	8.8	7.9	8.3	9.6	7.5	8.5	5.0	6.1	4.1	30.4	4.6	6.3	6.7
	1 %	1.6	2.0	1.8	1.8	2.2	1.4	0.9	1.4	1.0	9.6	3.0	3.1	2.9
6	10 %	8.8	15.4	11.3	9.0	13.7	10.1	38.3	29.9	16.0	9.6	79.1	69.0	29.2
	5 %	4.7	9.8	4.8	5.4	7.9	6.1	25.1	21.8	8.5	5.8	65.2	58.1	19.3
	1 %	0.5	2.0	0.3	0.6	1.5	1.5	11.8	5.8	1.5	0.7	43.7	36.6	6.8
7	10 %	11.8	12.2	14.4	12.3	8.8	13.2	42.5	35.1	15.6	24.5	55.6	47.1	24.0
	5 %	7.0	5.9	9.4	6.2	4.1	6.3	31.2	25.0	9.9	16.3	44.6	39.5	15.0
	1 %	1.1	1.3	1.9	1.2	1.2	2.0	15.3	9.2	2.6	3.3	35.3	20.2	5.8
8	10 %	12.5	18.3	44.9	13.0	17.2	44.0	19.5	67.0	30.0	12.6	91.4	96.5	72.0
	5 %	6.3	12.5	31.6	6.4	10.3	28.9	10.6	55.7	19.3	6.2	85.6	94.0	59.5
	1 %	1.0	2.6	9.8	0.9	2.7	8.5	2.7	31.3	7.4	1.4	71.4	87.7	37.3
9	10 %	32.9	42.5	81.0	29.5	46.9	88.8	34.3	92.0	71.3	24.8	99.0	99.7	98.8
	5 %	17.3	25.9	65.2	19.7	36.3	80.2	25.2	88.8	64.7	17.6	98.0	99.6	97.8
	1 %	3.0	7.8	36.3	3.9	14.3	56.4	12.3	77.1	42.1	4.0	94.5	99.1	95.6
10	10 %	8.7	33.1	44.9	9.7	28.3	33.7	51.9	83.2	49.4	9.3	81.7	99.6	84.6
	5 %	4.4	22.4	30.0	4.7	17.7	21.4	36.8	74.5	35.2	5.5	69.5	98.8	78.7
	1 %	1.1	9.0	11.1	0.8	6.8	5.2	18.2	54.0	17.0	1.2	37.9	97.1	48.1
11	10 %	8.6	46.2	76.7	9.1	46.7	76.9	63.8	99.5	89.7	11.0	81.5	100.0	100.0
	5 %	4.3	32.8	63.9	4.3	36.1	67.8	51.0	98.8	81.8	5.6	68.2	100.0	100.0
	1 %	0.4	11.7	37.3	0.4	18.4	42.8	31.7	94.9	63.9	0.9	39.4	100.0	99.3

To summarize, dynamic misspecification can be captured well by empirical process statistics and correlation tests. Misspecification in marginals, on the contrary, can not be distinguished at all by correlation tests but empirical process statistics, possibly multi-parameter, still work, although further research in improving power of these tests is needed.

To develop our omnibus type tests we introduce additional continuous noise. An important question is the effect of this noise on the power of the tests. Since correlation tests based on discrete residuals BPD$_j$ do not use additional noise, while correlation tests based on continuous residuals BPN$_j$ do, we can use the difference in

Table 4 Percentage of rejections of test statistics with $T = 500$

		CvM_0	CvM_1	CvM_2	KS_0	KS_1	KS_2	BPN_1	BPN_2	BPN_{25}	JB	BPD_1	BPD_2	BPD_{25}
1	10 %	10.2	8.1	9.2	9.8	8.6	8.0	11.9	11.7	11.1	11.3	10.1	8.6	9.8
	5 %	4.7	4.5	4.9	4.2	3.9	4.3	6.0	5.4	5.6	5.3	5.2	4.7	4.7
	1 %	0.5	1.0	0.7	0.7	0.6	1.0	0.6	0.8	0.8	1.2	1.1	0.4	1.1
2	10 %	9.1	8.0	8.3	10.2	8.6	10.7	11.6	11.5	8.4	9.2	8.6	9.9	10.6
	5 %	4.3	4.9	4.4	4.7	3.8	4.1	5.6	4.8	3.9	4.6	4.3	5.7	5.6
	1 %	0.7	0.8	0.8	0.5	0.2	0.6	0.6	1.4	0.5	0.5	1.4	0.8	0.8
3	10 %	9.1	8.9	9.9	9.2	8.6	8.5	10.0	11.6	10.7	11.0	10.7	10.2	10.0
	5 %	4.1	3.9	3.1	4.8	4.5	4.9	5.7	7.1	5.4	5.2	4.6	5.3	4.8
	1 %	0.7	1.1	1.0	1.0	0.4	0.4	1.1	1.0	1.9	1.5	1.5	2.0	1.6
4	10 %	10.7	8.9	10.9	10.7	10.8	8.8	11.5	9.2	10.2	7.8	10.0	10.4	12.3
	5 %	5.2	4.3	4.8	5.2	3.9	4.1	6.1	3.5	5.2	4.4	5.1	6.7	7.2
	1 %	0.4	0.8	1.0	0.7	0.6	0.4	0.7	1.1	0.7	0.7	1.4	1.3	1.9
5	10 %	17.1	16.8	17.0	20.0	19.4	17.8	11.8	12.1	8.5	53.2	7.9	8.0	14.0
	5 %	11.4	10.0	9.7	13.4	12.0	12.1	4.4	5.5	3.8	45.1	5.6	5.4	9.1
	1 %	3.6	3.7	3.2	4.5	4.9	3.3	1.3	1.7	0.7	23.6	3.4	3.7	5.3
6	10 %	8.7	17.1	9.8	10.2	15.5	8.9	46.1	36.2	17.6	9.3	88.7	81.2	42.0
	5 %	5.3	8.9	4.9	4.9	6.9	3.4	32.9	27.3	11.8	3.7	82.9	69.0	y29.5
	1 %	0.6	1.5	1.0	0.9	1.1	0.8	17.2	8.9	2.4	0.6	53.0	46.8	8.5
7	10 %	15.2	11.9	14.8	13.3	11.3	15.9	39.9	36.3	18.0	38.0	53.7	42.6	21.5
	5 %	8.1	5.6	10.8	7.5	4.8	8.0	28.5	28.0	10.6	27.9	41.0	34.4	16.5
	1 %	2.2	1.3	2.8	2.5	1.7	3.0	12.0	9.4	3.0	8.2	18.2	19.5	9.4
8	10 %	22.6	34.0	90.1	25.1	35.9	92.9	23.7	97.6	76.7	10.0	99.9	100.0	99.6
	5 %	12.6	23.3	83.8	14.7	25.9	86.5	16.7	95.9	65.1	5.0	99.7	100.0	99.2
	1 %	3.4	7.6	53.9	4.0	10.4	65.0	5.1	87.6	44.7	1.1	99.2	99.9	97.1
9	10 %	56.1	73.2	98.8	58.3	78.1	99.6	62.6	99.5	96.9	30.4	100.0	100.0	100.0
	5 %	39.9	59.9	97.0	41.9	69.9	98.8	51.2	99.3	95.4	20.5	100.0	100.0	100.0
	1 %	13.4	38.7	88.5	16.1	48.2	95.6	31.1	98.6	91.4	10.7	100.0	100.0	99.8
10	10 %	9.9	58.4	90.5	10.3	52.8	88.7	74.8	99.6	93.6	7.9	98.7	100.0	100.0
	5 %	5.2	43.1	82.2	5.0	38.2	79.8	65.2	99.3	89.4	4.5	95.9	100.0	100.0
	1 %	1.1	14.3	59.4	0.6	14.1	39.6	44.5	97.3	78.0	1.3	86.0	100.0	99.7
11	10 %	10.0	74.7	99.1	11.3	81.3	98.0	86.8	100.0	100.0	9.4	99.6	100.0	100.0
	5 %	3.6	62.5	96.7	4.8	71.3	95.6	78.9	100.0	99.9	4.6	98.6	100.0	100.0
	1 %	0.5	38.5	87.5	0.8	33.1	80.7	64.0	100.0	99.9	1.3	87.1	100.0	100.0

rejection rates between these sets of statistics under dynamic misspecification as an indirect measure of the effect of the introduced noise, though correlation tests are not consistent against static alternatives. From our Monte Carlo simulations we see that for all scenarios we consider, correlation tests based on discrete residuals perform better, indicating that some power losses may indeed be attributed to the introduced noise. To overcome this problem, we plan to develop tests for discrete models based on alternative transformations of the data without introducing additional noise, but still consistent against a wide range of nonparametric alternative hypotheses.

5 Conclusion

In this chapter, we have proposed new tests for checking goodness-of-fit of conditional distributions in nonlinear discrete time series models. Specification of the conditional distribution (but not only conditional moments) is important in many macroeconomics and financial applications. Due to the parameter estimation effect, the asymptotic distribution depends on the model and specific parameter values. We show that our parametric bootstrap provides a good approximation to asymptotic distributions and renders feasible and simple tests. Monte Carlo experiments have shown that tests based on empirical processes have power if misspecification comes from dynamics. If misspecification affects marginals alone, correlation tests are inconsistent, while tests based on empirical processes have some power. Comparing to the continuous case, we may conclude that there is a reduction of power due to the additional noise which distribution is known under the alternative too.

Acknowledgments We thank Juan Mora for useful comments. Financial support from the Fundación Ramón Areces and from the Spain Plan Nacional de I+D+I (SEJ2007-62908) is gratefully acknowledged.

Appendix

Proof of Proposition 1 Part (a) is a property of dynamic PIT with a continuous conditional distribution $F_t^{\dagger}$, the proof can be found in Bai (2003). Part (b) follows from the fact that (omitting dependence on t, Ω_t and θ)

$$\begin{aligned} F^{\dagger}(Y+Z-1) &= F([Y+Z-1]) + Z^U \mathrm{P}([Y+Z]) \\ &= F(Y-1) + Z^U \mathrm{P}(Y), \end{aligned}$$

where

$$Z^U = F_z(Y+Z-1-[Y+Z-1]) = F_z(Z)$$

is uniform for any $Z \sim F_z$ continuous and with $[0, 1]$ support, by the usual static PIT property. Therefore, although a continued variable $Y^{\dagger}$ and its distribution $F^{\dagger}$ depends on F_z, $F^{\dagger}(Y^{\dagger})$ does not.

□

Proof of Proposition 2 Assumption 1 in Kheifets (2011) is satisfied automatically after applying continuation defined in (2), therefore Proposition 1 of Kheifets (2011) holds.

□

Proof of Proposition 3 Follows from Kheifets (2011), we need only to check that Assumption 2 in Kheifets (2011) is satisfied.

Let $r = F^{\dagger}(y)$. Note that $[y] = F^{-1}(r)$ but $F([y]) = F\left(F^{-1}(r)\right)$ equals r only when $y = [y]$. The inverse of $F^{\dagger}$ is

$$y = \left(F^{\dagger}\right)^{-1}(r) = [y] + \frac{r - F([y])}{\mathrm{P}([y]+1)} = [y] + 1 + \frac{r - F([y]+1)}{\mathrm{P}([y]+1)}$$
$$= F^{-1}(r) + \frac{r - F\left(F^{-1}(r)\right)}{\mathrm{P}\left(F^{-1}(r)+1\right)}.$$

Note also that $(r - F([y]))/\mathrm{P}([y]+1) = y - [y] \in [0, 1]$. Take distribution G with the same support as F. We have different useful ways to write $d(G, F, r)$:

$$d(G, F, r) = \eta^{\dagger}(r) - r = G^{\dagger}\left(\left(F^{\dagger}\right)^{-1}(r)\right) - r = G^{\dagger}(y) - r$$
$$= G([y]) - F([y]) + (y - [y])(\mathrm{P}_G([y]+1) - \mathrm{P}_F([y]+1)) \quad \text{(A.1)}$$
$$= G([y]+1) - F([y]+1)$$
$$+ (y - [y] - 1)(\mathrm{P}_G([y]+1) - \mathrm{P}_F([y]+1)) \quad \text{(A.2)}$$
$$= G\left(F^{-1}(r)\right) - F\left(F^{-1}(r)\right)$$
$$+ \frac{r - F\left(F^{-1}(r)\right)}{\mathrm{P}_F\left(F^{-1}(r)+1\right)}\left(\mathrm{P}_G\left(F^{-1}(r)+1\right) - \mathrm{P}_F\left(F^{-1}(r)+1\right)\right). \quad \text{(A.3)}$$

Thus, noting that $\mathrm{P}(\cdot)$ is bounded away from zero, we have that Assumption 2 in this paper is sufficient for Assumption 2 in Kheifets (2011):

(K2.1)

$$E \sup_{t=1,\ldots,T} \sup_{u \in B_T} \sup_{r \in [0,1]} \left|\eta_t^{\dagger}(r, u, \theta_0) - r\right| = O\left(T^{-1/2}\right).$$

(K2.2) $\forall M \in (0, \infty)$, $\forall M_2 \in (0, \infty)$ and $\forall \delta > 0$

$$\sup_{r \in [0,1]} \frac{1}{\sqrt{T}} \sum_{t=1}^{T} \sup_{\substack{||u-v|| \le M_2 T^{-1/2-\delta} \\ u,v \in B_T}} \left|\eta_t^{\dagger}(r, u, \theta_0) - \eta_t^{\dagger}(r, v, \theta_0)\right| = o_p(1).$$

(K2.3) $\forall M \in (0, \infty)$, $\forall M_2 \in (0, \infty)$ and $\forall \delta > 0$

$$\sup_{|r-s| \le M_2 T^{-1/2-\delta}} \frac{1}{\sqrt{T}} \sum_{t=1}^{T} \sup_{u \in B_T} \left|\eta_t^{\dagger}(r, u, \theta_0) - \eta_t^{\dagger}(s, u, \theta_0)\right| = o_p(1).$$

(K2.4) $\forall M \in (0, \infty)$, there exists a uniformly continuous (vector) function $h(r)$ from $[0, 1]^2$ to R^L, such that

$$\sup_{u \in B_T} \sup_{r \in [0,1]^2} \left| \frac{1}{\sqrt{T}} \sum_{t=2}^{T} h_t - h(r)' \sqrt{T} (u - \theta_0) \right| = o_p(1).$$

where

$$h_t = \left(\eta_{t-1}^{\dagger}(r_2, u, \theta_0) - r_2\right) r_1 + \left(\eta_t^{\dagger}(r_1, u, \theta_0) - r_1\right) I\left(F_{t-1}^{\dagger}\left(Y_{t-1}^{\dagger}|u\right) \le r_2\right).$$

For Part (a), take $d(F(\cdot|\Omega_t, \theta_0), F(\cdot|\Omega_t, \hat{\theta}))$. Then (K2.1), (K2.2), (K2.4) follow from (2.1), (2.2) and (2.3) because of representation (A.3). If we compare (A.1) and (A.2) we see that $d(\cdot)$ is not only continuous in r, but piece-wise linear, so (K2.3) is satisfied automatically.

For Part (b), take $d(G_T(\cdot|\Omega_t, \theta_0), F(\cdot|\Omega_t, \hat{\theta}))$ and use the additivity of $d(\cdot)$ in the first arguments:

$$d(G_T(\cdot|\Omega_t, \theta_0), F(\cdot|\Omega_t, \hat{\theta})) = \left(1 - \frac{\sqrt{T_0}}{\sqrt{T}}\right) d(F(\cdot|\Omega_t, \theta_0), F(\cdot|\Omega_t, \hat{\theta})) + \frac{\sqrt{T_0}}{\sqrt{T}} d(H(\cdot|\Omega_t), F(\cdot|\Omega_t, \hat{\theta})).$$

□

Proof of Proposition 5 The proof is similar if we consider $d(F(\cdot|\Omega_t, \theta_T), F(\cdot|\Omega_t, \hat{\theta}_T))$ under $\{\theta_T : T \ge 1\}$.

□

References

Andrews, D.W.K. (1997). A conditional Kolmogorov test. Econometrica 65, 1097–1128.

Bai, J. (2003). Testing Parametric Conditional Distributions of Dynamic Models. Review of Economics and, Statistics 85, 531–549.

Bai, J. and S. Ng (2001). A consistent test for conditional symmetry in time series models. Journal of Econometrics 103, 225–258.

Basu, D. and R. de Jong (2007). Dynamic Multinomial Ordered Choice with an Application to the Estimation of Monetary Policy Rules. Studies in Nonlinear Dynamics and Econometrics 4, article 2.

Blum, J. R., Kiefer, J. and M. Rosenblatt (1961). Distribution free tests of independence based on sample distribution function. Annals of Matematical Statistics 32, 485–98.

Bontemps, C. and N. Meddahi (2005). Testing normality: a GMM approach. Journals of Econometrics 124, 149–186.

Box, G. and D. Pierce (1970). Distribution of residual autocorrelations in autorregressive integrated moving average time series models. Journal of the American Statistical Association 65, 1509–1527.

Corradi, V. and R. Swanson (2006). Bootstrap conditional distribution test in the presence of dynamic misspecification. Journal of Econometrics 133, 779–806.

de Jong, R.M. and T. Woutersen (2011). Dynamic time series binary choice. Econometric Theory 27, 673–702.

Delgado, M. (1996). Testing serial independence using the sample distribution function, Journal of Time Series Analysis 17, 271–285.

Delgado, M. and J. Mora (2000). A nonparametric test for serial independence of regression errors, Biometrika 87, 228–234.

Delgado, M. and W. Stute (2008). Distribution-free specification tests of conditional models. Journal of Econometrics 143, 37–55.

Denuit, M. and P. Lambert (2005). Constraints on concordance measures in bivariate discrete data. Journal of Multivariate Analysis 93, 40–57.

Dueker, M. (1997). Strengthening the case for the yield curve as a predictor of U.S. recessions. Review, Federal Reserve Bank of St. Louis, issue Mar, 41–51.

Ferguson, T.S. (1967). Mathematical Statistics: A Decision Theoretic Approach. Academic Press.

Giacomini, R., D.N. Politis, and H. White (2007). A Warp-Speed Method for Conducting Monte Carlo Experiments Involving Bootstrap Estimators. Mimeo.

Hamilton, J. and O. Jorda (2002). A model of the Federal Funds rate target. Journal of Political Economy 110, 1135–1167.

Hoeffding W. (1948). A nonparametric test of independence. Annals of Mathematical Statistics 26, 189–211.

Hong, Y. (1998). Testing for pairwise serial independence via the empirical distribution function. Journal Royal Statistical Society 60, 429–453.

Kauppi, H. and P. Saikkonen (2008). Predicting U.S. recessions with dynamic binary response models. Review of Economics and Statistics 90, 777–791.

Kheifets, I.L. (2011). Specification tests for nonlinear time series. Mimeo.

Khmaladze, E.V. (1981). Martingale approach in the theory of goodness-of-tests. Theory of Probability and its Applications 26, 240–257.

Koul, H.L. and W. Stute (1999). Nonparametric model checks for time series. Annals of Statistics 27, 204–236.

Mora, J. and A.I. Moro-Egido (2007). On specification testing of ordered discrete choice models. Journal of Econometrics 143, 191–205.

Neslehova, J. (2006). Dependence of Non Continuous Random Variables. Springer-Verlag.

Phillips, P.C.B. and J.Y. Park (2000). Nonstationary Binary Choice. Econometrica 68, 1249–1280.

Politis, D., J. Romano and M. Wolf (1999). Subsampling. New York: Springer-Verlag.

Rosenblatt, M. (1975) A quadratic measure of deviation of two-dimensional density estimates and a test of independence. Annals of Statistics 3, 1–14.

Rydberg, T.N. and N. Shephard (2003). Dynamics of trade-by-trade price movements: decomposition and models. Journal of Financial Econometrics 1, 2–25.

Shao, J. and T. Dongsheng (1995). The Jackknife and bootstrap. New York: Springer-Verlag.

Skaug, H.J. and D. Tjøstheim (1993). Nonparametric test of serial independence based on the empirical distribution function. Biometrika 80, 591–602.

Startz, R. (2008). Binomial Autoregressive Moving Average Models with an Application to U.S. Recessions. Journal of Business and Economic Statistics 26, 1–8.

Wooldridge, J.M. (1990). An encompassing approach to conditional mean tests with applications to testing nonnested hypotheses. Journal of Econometrics 45, 331–350.

On Long-Run Covariance Matrix Estimation with the Truncated Flat Kernel

Chang-Ching Lin and Shinichi Sataka

Abstract Despite its large sample efficiency, the truncated flat kernel (TF) estimator of long-run covariance matrices is seldom used, because it occasionally gives a non-positive semidefinite estimate and sometimes performs poorly in small samples, compared to other familiar kernel estimators. This paper proposes simple modifications to the TF estimator to enforce the positive definiteness without sacrificing the large sample efficiency and make the estimator more reliable in small samples through better utilization of the bias-variance trade-off. We study the large sample properties of the modified TF estimators and verify their improved small-sample performances by Monte Carlo simulations.

1 Introduction

The precision of an estimator is often assessed using its consistently estimated (asymptotic) covariance matrix or standard error. When using time series data, the asymptotic covariance matrix can be consistently estimated by a long-run covariance matrix. This paper is concerned with kernel estimation of long-run covariance matrices using the truncated flat kernel proposed by White and Domowitz (1984), which we call the truncated flat kernel (TF) estimator.

While the TF estimator is a natural method to estimate long-run covariance matrices in the presence of serial correlations in an unknown form, it has a drawback

C.-C. Lin
Institute of Economics, Academia Sinica,
Taiwan
e-mail: lincc@econ.sinica.edu.tw

S. Sataka (✉)
Department of Economics, University of Southern California,
Los Angles, CA, USA
e-mail: shinichi.sakata@gmail.com

X. Chen and N. R. Swanson (eds.), *Recent Advances and Future Directions in Causality, Prediction, and Specification Analysis*, DOI: 10.1007/978-1-4614-1653-1_15,

that it may deliver a non-positive semidefinite estimate. A conventional solution to overcome this difficulty is to suitably downweight the estimated autocovariances, as Newey and West's (1987) Bartlett kernel (BT) and Andrews' (1991) Quadratic Spectral kernel (QS) estimators do. As demonstrated in Gallant and White (1988), there are many kernels that guarantees positive semidefiniteness of long-run covariance matrices. Hansen (1992), de Jong and Davidson (2000), and Jansson (2003) show the general conditions sufficient for the kernel estimators to be consistent.

An interesting fact pointed out in the literature on spectral density estimation (e.g., Priestley (1981) and Hannan (1970)) is that the asymptotic bias is negligible relative to the asymptotic variance in TF estimation unless the growth rate of the bandwidth is very low. This means that, unlike the other familiar kernel estimators subject to the usual trade-off between the asymptotic bias and variance, use of a slowly growing bandwidth can make the variance converge fast in the TF estimation, still keeping the bias negligible. The TF estimator is thus asymptotically efficient relative to the other familiar kernel estimators in typical scenarios. The small-sample behavior of the TF estimator is, however, sometimes dissimilar to what the large-sample theory indicates. As shown in Andrews (1991), the TF estimator performs considerably better or worse than the other commonly used kernel estimators. This counterintuitive fact has not been investigated at our best knowledge.

The contribution of this paper is twofold. First, we propose a simple method to modify a non-positive semidefinite estimator to generate a positive semidefinite (p.s.d.) estimator. Unlike the other approach in the literature such as the one in Politis (2011) that replaces all negative eigenvalues in the eigenvalue decomposition of the non-p.s.d.estimate with zeros, our method never makes the mean square error (MSE) of the estimator larger than the original one.

Second, we reconcile the puzzling discrepancy between the asymptotic efficiency and finite sample performance of the TF estimator. Unlike the other familiar estimators that are continuously related to their bandwidths, a change in the bandwidth affects the TF (and ATF) estimate only when crossing an integer value. This feature severely limits the opportunity to balance the finite sample bias and variance of the TF (and ATF) estimator. To eliminate this restriction, we propose linearly interpolating the TF estimators at the nearest two integer bandwidths for each non-integer bandwidth. Though the kernel used in the extended TF (ETF) estimation is analogous to the flat-top kernel estimators of Politis and Romano (1996, 1999), the width of the sloped part of the kernel is always one in the ETF estimation, while it is proportional to the bandwidth in the flat-top kernel estimation. For this reason, the ETF estimator is more closely linked to the TF estimator than the latter. Our Monte Carlo simulations verify that the relationship between the ETF and QS estimators in small samples is in line with the large sample theory.

The rest of the paper is organized as follows. We introduce a simple method to generate a p.s.d. covariance matrix estimator from a non-p.s.d. estimator in Sect. 2 and discuss its computation and basic properties in Sects. 3 and 4, respectively. We then establish the asymptotic properties of the ATF estimator in Sect. 5 and propose the ETF estimator in Sect. 6. We also assess the finite sample performance of the proposed estimators relative to those of the QS and BT estimators by

Monte Carlo experiments in Sect. 7. Further, we discuss the behavior of our estimators with data-based bandwidths in Sect. 8 and examine the finite sample performance of the estimators with data-based bandwidths by Monte Carlo experiments in Sect. 9. The mathematical proofs of selected results are found in the Appendix, while the proofs of the other results are available from the authors upon request.

Throughout this paper, each vector is a column vector, and limits are taken along the sequence of sample sizes (denoted T) growing to infinity, unless otherwise indicated. For each metric space A, $\mathscr{B}(\mathsf{A})$ denotes the Borel σ-field on A. For the Euclidean spaces, write $\mathscr{B}^p \equiv \mathscr{B}(\mathbb{R}^p)$ for simplicity.

2 Estimators Adjusted for Positive Semidefiniteness

In this section, we propose a method to adjust a square-matrix-valued estimate to obtain an estimate with guaranteed positive semidefiniteness. As its usefulness is not limited to estimation of covariance matrices. we keep our analysis in this section general, though we make the following assumption for concreteness.

Assumption 1 Let $(\Omega, \mathscr{F}, P)$ be a probability space, and Θ a nonempty subset of $\mathbb{R}^p$ $(p \in \mathbb{N})$. The sequence $\{Z_t\}_{t\in\mathbb{Z}}$ consists of measurable functions from $(\Omega \times \Theta, \mathscr{F} \otimes \mathscr{B}(\Theta))$ to $(\mathbb{R}^v, \mathscr{B}^v)$ $(v \in \mathbb{N})$ such that for each $\theta \in \Theta$ and each $t \in \mathbb{Z}$, $\mathrm{E}[Z_t(\cdot,\theta)' Z_t(\cdot,\theta)] < \infty$. Also, for each $T \in \mathbb{N}$, $\hat{\theta}_T$ is a $p \times 1$ Θ-valued estimator of $\theta^* \in \Theta$. Further, $\{Z_t^* \equiv Z_t(\cdot, \theta^*)\}_{t\in\mathbb{Z}}$ is a zero-mean covariance stationary process.

The random function Z_t in Assumption 1 is the score vector for the tth observation in maximum likelihood estimation (MLE). In the generalized method-of-moment (GMM) estimation, Z_t is a vector consisting of moment functions. Suppose that $\{Z_t^*\}_{t\in\mathbb{N}}$ is not a martingale difference sequence, and its autocovariance function is not truncated at a known lag. Our goal is to accurately estimate $S_T \equiv \mathrm{var}[T^{-1/2}\sum_{t=1}^T Z_t^*] = \Gamma_T(0) + \sum_{\tau=1}^{T-1}(\Gamma_T(\tau) + \Gamma_T'(\tau))$, where $T \in \mathbb{N}$ is the sample size, and for each $\tau \in \{1, 2, \ldots, T-1\}$, $\Gamma_T(\tau) \equiv (T-\tau)/T \; \mathrm{cov}[Z_{\tau+1}^*, Z_1^*]$.

Let k be an even function from $\mathbb{R}$ to $\mathbb{R}$ that is continuous at the origin and discontinuous at most at a finite number of points. Suppose that θ^* is known. Then a kernel estimator of S_T using the kernel k and a bandwidth $m_T \in (0, \infty)$ is

$$\tilde{S}_T^k \equiv k(0)\,\tilde{\Gamma}_T(0) + \sum_{\tau=1}^{T-1} k\Big(\frac{\tau}{m_T}\Big)\big(\tilde{\Gamma}_T(\tau) + \tilde{\Gamma}_T'(\tau)\big), \quad T \in \mathbb{N}, \tag{1}$$

where $\tilde{\Gamma}_T(\tau) \equiv T^{-1}\sum_{t=\tau+1}^T Z_t^* Z_{t-\tau}^{*\prime}$, $(\tau \in \{1, 2, \ldots, T-1\}$, $T \in \mathbb{N})$. When θ^* is unknown, as is the case in typical applications, we need to replace the unknown θ^* with its estimator $\hat{\theta}_T$ to obtain a feasible estimator of S_T. Let $\hat{Z}_{T,t}$ denote the random vector obtained by replacing θ^* with $\hat{\theta}_T$ in Z_t^*. Also, set

$\hat{\Gamma}_T(\tau) \equiv T^{-1}\sum_{t=\tau+1}^{T} \hat{Z}_t\hat{Z}_{t-\tau}'$, ($\tau \in \{1, 2, \ldots, T-1\}$, $T \in \mathbb{N}$). Then the feasible estimator is

$$\hat{S}_T^k \equiv k(0)\hat{\Gamma}_T(0) + \sum_{\tau=1}^{T-1} k\Big(\frac{\tau}{m_T}\Big)\big(\hat{\Gamma}_T(\tau) + \hat{\Gamma}_T'(\tau)\big), \quad T \in \mathbb{N}.$$

While S_T is p.s.d., being a covariance matrix, $\tilde{S}_T^k$ and $\hat{S}_T^k$ may not be so, depending on the kernel k. A way to avoid a non-p.s.d. estimate is to use certain kernels such as BT or QS. Here, we instead propose pushing a non-p.s.d. estimate back to the space of symmetric p.s.d. matrices. This approach has an advantage that no limit is imposed on our choice of the kernel.

On $\mathbb{R}^{a_1 \times a_2}$, where $(a_1, a_2) \in \mathbb{N}^2$, define a real valued function $\|\cdot\|_W : \mathbb{R}^{a_1 \times a_2} \to \mathbb{R}$ by $\|A\|_W \equiv (\text{vec}(A)' \, W \, \text{vec}(A))^{1/2}$ ($A \in \mathbb{R}^{a_1 \times a_2}$), where W is a $(a_1a_2) \times (a_1a_2)$ symmetric p.s.d. matrix, and vec(A) is the column vector made by stacking the columns of A vertically from left to right. If W is the identity matrix, $\|\cdot\|_W$ becomes the Frobenius norm, denoted $\|\cdot\|$ for simplicity. Let P_v be the set of all $v \times v$, symmetric p.s.d. matrices.

Definition 1 Given an estimator $\hat{S}_T$ of S_T and a $v^2 \times v^2$ symmetric p.s.d. random matrix W_T for each $T \in \mathbb{N}$, the P_v-valued random matrix $\hat{S}_T^A$ satisfying that for each $T \in \mathbb{N}$, $\|\hat{S}_T - \hat{S}_T^A\|_{W_T} = \inf_{s \in \mathsf{P}_v} \|\hat{S}_T - s\|_{W_T}$, provided that it exists, is called *the estimator that adjusts $\hat{S}_T$ for positive semidefiniteness* or simply *the adjusted estimator (with weighting matrix W_T).*

Because P_v is a convex set, and $s \mapsto \|\hat{S}_T - s\|_{W_T}$ is a convex function, the minimization problem in the adjustment is a convex programming. It is easy to verify that the solution of the minimization problem exists for every possible realization. Given this fact, the existence of the adjusted estimator can be established by using Brown and Purves (1973, Corollary 1, pp. 904–905).

Theorem 2.1 *Suppose that Assumption 1 holds. Then for each estimator $\hat{S}_T$ of S_T and each symmetric p.s.d. random matrix W_T, the estimator that adjusts $\hat{S}_T$ for positive semidefiniteness with the weighting matrix W_T exists.*

3 Algorithm of Adjustment for Positive Definiteness

The minimization problem in the adjustment for positive definiteness has no closed-form solution. Despite that it is a convex programming problem with a smooth objective function, a challenge is that our choice set is P_v, the set of all symmetric p.s.d. matrices. Though Pinheiro and Bates (1996) list a few ways to parameterize P_v, the objective function becomes non-convex, once we employ such a parameterization. In addition the number of parameters in this approach is large. Thus, the gradient search combined with Pinheiro and Bates' (1996) parameterization is slow and unreliable in our problem. We below take a different approach.

Let $\mathbb{S}^v$ denote the space of all $v \times v$ *symmetric* matrices. Define a objective linear function ϕ from $\mathbb{R}^{(v(v+1)/2)}$ to $\mathbb{S}^v$ by

$$\phi(x) \equiv \begin{pmatrix} x_1 & x_2 & x_3 & \cdots & x_v \\ x_2 & x_{v+1} & x_{v+2} & \cdots & x_{2v-1} \\ x_3 & x_{v+2} & x_{2v} & \cdots & x_{3v-3} \\ \vdots & \vdots & \vdots & \cdots & \vdots \\ x_v & x_{2v-1} & x_{3v-3} & \cdots & x_{v(v+1)/2} \end{pmatrix}, \quad x \equiv \begin{pmatrix} x_1 \\ x_2 \\ \vdots \\ x_{v(v+1)/2} \end{pmatrix} \in \mathbb{R}^{(v(v+1)/2)}.$$

Let $\hat{S}_T$ be an estimator of S_T. If x^* is a solution of the problem:

$$\min_{x \in \mathbb{R}^{v(v+1)/2}} \|\hat{S}_T - \phi(x)\|_{W_T} \text{ subject to the constraint that } \phi(x) \text{ is p.s.d.,} \tag{2}$$

then $\phi(x^*)$ is $\hat{S}_T^A$, the estimator that adjusts $\hat{S}_T$ for positive definiteness.

Now, decompose W_T as $W_T = V_T V_T'$ by the Cholesky decomposition. Then we have that

$$\|\hat{S}_T - \phi(x)\|_{W_T} = (V_T'(\text{vec}(\hat{S}_T) - \text{vec}(\phi(x))))'(V_T'(\text{vec}(\hat{S}_T) - \text{vec}(\phi(x)))).$$

Note that for each $(v(v+1)/2) \times 1$ vector y and each $g \in \mathbb{R}$, it holds that $y'y \leq g$ if and only if

$$\begin{pmatrix} I_{v(v+1)/2} & y \\ y' & g \end{pmatrix} = \begin{pmatrix} I_{v(v+1)/2} & 0_{(v(v+1)/2)\times 1} \\ y' & 1 \end{pmatrix} \times \begin{pmatrix} I_{v(v+1)/2} & 0 \\ 0 & g - y'y \end{pmatrix} \begin{pmatrix} I_{v(v+1)/2} & 0_{(v(v+1)/2)\times 1} \\ y' & 1 \end{pmatrix}'$$

is p.s.d. It follows that for each $g \in \mathbb{R}$, it holds that $\|\hat{S}_T - \phi(x)\|_{W_T} \leq g$ if and only if

$$D(x, g) \equiv \begin{pmatrix} I_{v(v+1)/2} & V_T'(\text{vec}(\hat{S}_T) - \text{vec}(\phi(x))) \\ (V_T'(\text{vec}(\hat{S}_T) - \text{vec}(\phi(x))))' & g \end{pmatrix} \text{ is p.s.d.}$$

Thus, the problem (2) is equivalent to choice of $(x, g) \in \mathbb{R}^{v(v+1)/2} \times \mathbb{R}$ to minimize g subject to the constraint that

$$\begin{pmatrix} \phi(x) & 0_{v\times(v(v+1)/2+1)} \\ 0_{(v(v+1)/2+1)\times v} & D(x,g) \end{pmatrix} = \begin{pmatrix} 0 & 0_{v\times(v(v+1)/2)} & 0_{v\times 1} \\ 0_{(v(v+1)/2)\times v} & I_{v(v+1)/2} & V_T'\operatorname{vec}(\hat{S}_T) \\ 0_{1\times v} & (V_T'\operatorname{vec}(\hat{S}_T))' & 0 \end{pmatrix}$$
$$- \begin{pmatrix} -\phi(x) & 0_{v\times(v(v+1)/2)} & 0_{v\times 1} \\ 0_{(v(v+1)/2)\times v} & 0_{(v(v+1)/2)\times(v(v+1)/2)} & V_T'\operatorname{vec}(\phi(x)) \\ 0_{1\times v} & (V_T'\operatorname{vec}(\phi(x)))' & -g \end{pmatrix} \quad (3)$$

is p.s.d. In this problem, the objective function is a linear function of x and g. Also, on the right-hand side in (3), both terms are symmetric matrices, and the second term is linear in x and g. Thus, this problem is a (dual-form) semidefinite programming problem, which can be solved quickly and reliably using existing computation algorithms (see, e.g., Vandenberghe and Boyd (1996) for the semidefinite programming in general). In our Monte Carlo simulations, we use SeDuMi Sturm (1999) among them.

4 Properties of Adjustment for Positive Definiteness

Now, let $\hat{S}_T$ be an arbitrary estimator of S_T and W_T a symmetric p.s.d. $v^2 \times v^2$ random matrix ($T \in \mathbb{N}$). Then, whenever $\hat{S}_T \in \mathsf{P}_v$, it apparently holds that $\|\hat{S}_T^A - \hat{S}_T\|_{W_T} = 0$. Moreover:

Theorem 4.1 *Suppose that Assumption 1 holds. Then:*

(a) For every possible realization of the data and each $T \in \mathbb{N}$, it holds that $\|\hat{S}_T^A - S_T\|_{W_T} \leq \|\hat{S}_T - S_T\|_{W_T}$, where the equality holds if and only if $\|\hat{S}_T^A - \hat{S}_T\|_{W_T} = 0$.
(b) For each $T \in \mathbb{N}$, the adjusted estimator $\hat{S}_T^A$ uniquely minimizes the function $s \mapsto \|s - S_T\|_{W_T}$ over P_v whenever W_T is positive definite (p.d.).

Because Theorem 4.1(a) means that the adjustment moves the estimator toward S_T in terms of the norm $\|\cdot\|_{W_T}$ for sure, the performance of the adjusted estimator cannot be worse than the original estimator. Theorem 4.1(b) means that the adjusted estimator is unique with a probability approaching one as $T \to \infty$ in a typical application, in which the weighting matrix W_T is positive definite with a probability approaching one. The violation of the positive definiteness of W_T possibly arises, however, when a user desires to estimate a covariance matrix of a subvector of $T^{-1/2}\sum_{t=1}^{T} Z_t^*$ and puts zeros in the weighting matrix W_T to ignore the part of the covariance matrix irrelevant in the user's analysis. In such a situation, the adjusted estimator is equivalent to the procedure that first eliminates from $\hat{S}_T$ and W_T their rows and columns corresponding to the irrelevant elements in $T^{-1/2}\sum_{t=1}^{T} Z_t^*$ and then adjusts the resulting $\hat{S}_T$ using the resulting W_T (which should be p.d.). Thus, the adjusted estimator again has the uniqueness property in estimation the submatrix of S_T the user cares. The positive definiteness of W_T or its limit is imposed in some of the results presented later. The above discussion on Theorem 4.1(b) would apply to such results.

Here are a few implications of Theorem 4.1(a).

Corollary 4.2 *Under Assumption 1:*

(a) For each $T \in \mathbb{N}$, $\mathrm{E}\big[\|\hat{S}_T^A - S_T\|_{W_T}^2\big] \le \mathrm{E}\big[\|\hat{S}_T - S_T\|_{W_T}^2\big]$.

(b) If $\{\hat{S}_T\}_{T\in\mathbb{N}}$ *is consistent for* $\{S_T\}_{T\in\mathbb{N}}$ *(i.e.,* $\{\|\hat{S}_T - S_T\|\}_{T\in\mathbb{N}}$ *converges in probability-P to zero), and* $W_T = \mathrm{O}_P(1)$, *then* $\{\|\hat{S}_T^A - S_T\|_{W_T}\}_{T\in\mathbb{N}}$ *converges in probability-P to zero. If in addition* $\{W_T\}_{T\in\mathbb{N}}$ *converges in probability-P to a nonsingular matrix W, then* $\{\hat{S}_T^A\}_{T\in\mathbb{N}}$ *is consistent for* $\{S_T\}_{T\in\mathbb{N}}$.

(c) Let $\{b_T\}_{T\in\mathbb{N}}$ *be an arbitrary sequence of positive real numbers. If* $\{\hat{S}_T\}_{T\in\mathbb{N}}$ *is consistent for* $\{S_T\}_{T\in\mathbb{N}}$, *and* $\{S_T\}$ *is asymptotically uniformly p.d., then* $\|\hat{S}_T^A - \hat{S}_T\|_{W_T} = \mathrm{o}_P(b_T)$. *If in addition* W_T *converges in probability-P to a nonsingular matrix W, then* $\hat{S}_T^A - \hat{S}_T = \mathrm{o}_P(b_T)$.

Corollary 4.2 demonstrates that adjustment for positive definiteness never worsens the performance of an estimator. It improves the MSE of the estimator. If the estimator is consistent, so is the adjusted estimator. If $\{S_T\}_{T\in\mathbb{N}}$ is asymptotically uniformly p.d. as is typically expected, the difference between the original and adjusted estimators is asymptotically negligible in a very strict sense, as the difference converges to zero at an arbitrary fast rate.

In our asymptotic analysis of consistent estimators, we magnify the MSE of each of the estimators, because otherwise, the MSEs would converge to zero as $T \to \infty$ in a typical setup. Given an estimator $\hat{S}_T$ of S_T, a $v^2 \times v^2$ symmetric p.s.d. random matrix W_T, and a positive real constant a_T (magnification factor), write $\mathrm{MSE}(a_T, \hat{S}_T, W_T) \equiv a_T \mathrm{E}\big[\|\hat{S}_T - S_T\|_{W_T}^2\big]$. Using this scaled MSE, we now state asymptotic equivalence of the adjusted and original estimators.

Theorem 4.3 *Suppose that Assumption 1 holds. If for some sequence* $\{a_T \in (0,\infty)\}_{T\in\mathbb{N}}$, $\{a_T\|\hat{S}_T - S_T\|_{W_T}^2\}_{T\in\mathbb{N}}$ *is uniformly integrable, then* $\mathrm{MSE}(a_T, \hat{S}_T, W_T) - \mathrm{MSE}(a_T, \hat{S}_T^A, W_T) \to 0$.

In this theorem, the required uniform integrability of $\{a_T\|\hat{S}_T - S_T\|_{W_T}^2\}_{T\in\mathbb{N}}$ implies uniform integrability of $\{a_T\|\hat{S}_T^A - S_T\|_{W_T}^2\}_{T\in\mathbb{N}}$, so that both MSE $(a_T, \hat{S}_T, W_T)$ and $\mathrm{MSE}(a_T, \hat{S}_T^A, W_T)$ are finite under the conditions imposed in Theorem 4.3.

When the parameter θ^* is unknown, our analysis must take into account the effect of the parameter estimation on the long-run covariance estimators. In order for $\mathrm{MSE}(a_T, \hat{S}_T, W_T)$ to be finite, $\hat{Z}_{T,t}$ must have finite fourth moments. Nevertheless, the fourth moments of $\hat{Z}_{T,t}$ may be infinity due to the effect of the estimation of θ^*, even when the fourth moments of Z_t^* are finite. For this reason, Andrews (1991) uses the truncated MSE instead of the MSE defined above, and so do we.

The truncated MSE of an estimator $\hat{S}_T$ of S_T scaled by a_T and truncated at $h \in (0,\infty)$ is defined to be $\mathrm{MSE}_h(a_T, \hat{S}_T, W_T) \equiv \mathrm{E}[\min\{a_T\|\hat{S}_T - S_T\|_{W_T}^2, h\}]$.

The MSEs of multiple estimators truncated at a high value h allow us to compare the performance of the estimators, ignoring the far tails of the distributions of the estimators. In reflection of this feature, most of our results presented below focus on the limit of the truncated MSEs, letting the truncation point grow to infinity.

Because for each $h \in (0, \infty)$, the function $x \mapsto \min\{x, h\} : [0, \infty) \to \mathbb{R}$ is a nondecreasing function, the relationship between the adjusted and original estimators stated in Corollary 4.2(a) carries over even if we replace the MSEs with the truncated MSEs, i.e., $\text{MSE}_h(a_T, \hat{S}_T^A, W_T) \le \text{MSE}_h(a_T, \hat{S}_T, W_T)$.

A consistent estimator and its adjusted estimator are asymptotically only negligibly different. If $\{S_T\}_{T\in\mathbb{N}}$ is asymptotically uniformly p.d., as Corollary 4.2(c) states. The asymptotically negligible difference between the original and adjusted estimators is inherited by the truncated MSE, when a suitable scaling factor is used. That is:

Theorem 4.4 *Suppose that Assumption 1 holds. If* $\lim_{h\to\infty}\lim_{T\to\infty}\text{MSE}_h(a_T, \hat{S}_T, W_T)$ *exists and is finite,* $\{S_T\}_{T\in\mathbb{N}}$ *is asymptotically uniformly p.d., and* $a_T^{1/2}(\hat{S}_T - S_T) = O_P(1)$*, then*

$$\lim_{h\to\infty}\lim_{T\to\infty}\text{MSE}_h(a_T, \hat{S}_T^A, W_T) = \lim_{h\to\infty}\lim_{T\to\infty}\text{MSE}_h(a_T, \hat{S}_T, W_T).$$

5 Truncated Flat Kernel Estimator Adjusted for Positive Semidefiniteness

For each $\tau \in \mathbb{Z}$, write $\Gamma(\tau) \equiv \text{cov}[Z_0^*, Z_\tau^*]$. Also, for arbitrary a_1, a_2, a_3, a_4 in $\{1, \ldots, v\}$ and arbitrary t_1, t_2, t_3, t_4 in $\mathbb{Z}$, let $\kappa_{a_1,a_2,a_3,a_4}(t_1, t_2, t_3, t_4)$ denote the fourth-order cumulant of $(Z_{t_1,a_1}^*, Z_{t_2,a_2}^*, Z_{t_3,a_3}^*, Z_{t_4,a_4}^*)$. Andrews (1991, Proposition 1) shows the asymptotic bias and variance of each kernel estimator with known θ^*, imposing the following memory conditions on $\{Z_t^*\}_{t\in\mathbb{Z}}$.

Assumption 2 $\sum_{\tau=-\infty}^{\infty}\|\Gamma(\tau)\| < \infty$, and for each a, b, c, d in $\{1, 2, \ldots, v\}$,

$$\sum_{\tau_1=-\infty}^{\infty}\sum_{\tau_2=-\infty}^{\infty}\sum_{\tau_3=-\infty}^{\infty}|\kappa_{a,b,c,d}(0, \tau_1, \tau_2, \tau_3)| < \infty.$$

Andrews (1991, pp. 827 and 853) also demonstrates that a wide range of kernel estimators satisfy the uniform integrability condition imposed in Theorem 4.3 with a suitably chosen scaling factor, if:

Assumption 3 The process $\{Z_t^*\}_{t\in\mathbb{Z}}$ is an eighth-order stationary process with

$$\sum_{\tau_1=-\infty}^{\infty}\cdots\sum_{\tau_7=-\infty}^{\infty}\kappa_{a_1,\ldots,a_8}(0, \tau_1, \cdots, \tau_7) < \infty, \qquad (a_1, \ldots, a_8) \in \{1, \ldots, v\}^8,$$

where for arbitrary $t_1, \ldots, t_8$ in $\mathbb{Z}$, $\kappa_{a_1,\cdots,a_8}(t_1, \ldots, t_8)$ denotes the eighth-order cumulant of $(Z^*_{t_1,a_1}, \ldots, Z^*_{t_8,a_8})$.

Write $S^{(q)} \equiv (2\pi)^{-1} \sum_{\tau=-\infty}^{\infty} |\tau|^q \Gamma(\tau)$ for each $q \in [0, \infty)$. Then, under Assumption 2, the series $S \equiv S^{(0)}$ converges, and $\{S_T\}_{T\in\mathbb{N}}$ converges to S. In most applications, it is reasonable to assume:

Assumption 4 The matrix S is p.d.

Given Assumptions 1–4, we can assess the asymptotic MSEs of the TF estimator (without the estimated parameters) and its adjusted version by applying Andrews (1991, Proposition 1(c)) along with Corollary 4.2(a) and Theorem 4.3 of this paper. Let $\tilde{S}_T^{\text{TF}}(m_T)$ denote the TF estimator with bandwidth m_T, which is obtained by setting the TF kernel to k in (1), and $\tilde{S}_T^{\text{TF},A}(m_T)$ the estimator that adjusts $\hat{S}_T^{\text{TF}}(m_T)$ for positive semidefiniteness. Also, let $K_{v,v}$ denote the $v^2 \times v^2$ commutation matrix, i.e., $K_{v,v} \equiv \sum_{i=1}^{v} \sum_{j=1}^{v} e_i e_j' \otimes e_j e_i'$, where e_i is the ith elementary $v \times 1$ vector, and $\otimes$ is the Kronecker product operator.

Proposition 5.1 *Suppose that Assumptions 1 and 2 hold and that $\{m_T \in (0, T-1)\}_{T\in\mathbb{N}}$ satisfies that $m_T^{2q+1}/T \to \gamma \in (0, \infty)$ for some $q \in (0, \infty)$ for which the series $S^{(q)}$ converges. Also, let W be a $v^2 \times v^2$ symmetric p.s.d. matrix. Then we have:*

(a)

$$\lim_{T\to\infty} \text{MSE}\Big(\frac{T}{m_T}, \tilde{S}_T^{TF,A}(m_T), W\Big) \le \lim_{T\to\infty} \text{MSE}\Big(\frac{T}{m_T}, \tilde{S}_T^{TF}(m_T), W\Big)$$
$$= 8\pi^2 \text{tr}(W(I + K_{v,v})S \otimes S). \qquad (4)$$

(b) If in addition Assumptions 3 and 4 hold, (4) holds with equality.

Proposition 5.1 means that the convergence rates of both the ATF and TF estimators can be made as fast as $T^{-q/(2q+1)}$, provided that the bandwidth is suitably chosen, and $S^{(q)}$ converges. In particular, when $S^{(q)}$ converges for some $q > 2$, employing a bandwidth $m_T \sim T^{1/(2q+1)}$ (i.e., $m_T = O(T^{1/(2q+1)})$ and $T^{1/(2q+1)} = O(m_T)$) makes the TF estimators converge to S_T faster in terms of the MSE than the QS and BT estimator, whose convergence rates never exceed $T^{-1/3}$ and $T^{-2/5}$, respectively.

We next investigate the behavior of the adjusted and unadjusted TF estimators with θ^* estimated by $\hat{\theta}_T$. To do this, we add a few assumptions related to the effect of the parameter estimation on the long-run covariance matrix estimation.

Assumption 5 (a) $\hat{\theta}_T - \theta^* = O_p(T^{-1/2})$.

(b) There exists a uniformly L_2-bounded sequence of random variables $\{\eta_{1,t}\}_{t\in\mathbb{Z}}$ such that for each $t \in \mathbb{Z}$, $\|Z_t^*\| \le \eta_{1,t}$ and $\sup_{\theta\in\Theta} \|\partial/\partial\theta Z_t(\cdot, \theta)\| \le \eta_{1,t}$.

Assumption 6 (a) The sequence $\{\zeta_t \equiv (Z_t^{*\prime}, \text{vec}(\partial/\partial\theta' Z_t(\cdot,\theta^*) - \text{E}[\partial/\partial\theta' Z_t(\cdot,\theta^*)])')'\}_{t\in\mathbb{Z}}$ is a fourth-order stationary process such that Assumption 2 holds with Z_t replaced by ζ_t.

(b) There exists a uniformly L_2-bounded sequence of random variables $\{\eta_{2,t}\}_{t\in\mathbb{Z}}$ such that for each $t \in \mathbb{Z}$ $\sup_{\theta\in\Theta} \|\partial^2/\partial\theta\partial\theta' Z_{t,a}(\cdot,\theta)\| \le \eta_{2,t}, (a = 1,\ldots,v)$.

Assumption 5 requires that $\{\hat{\theta}_T\}_{T\in\mathbb{N}}$ is $\sqrt{T}$-consistent, as is typically the case in ML and GMM estimation. The Lipschitz type conditions imposed on the derivatives of the random function Z_t in Assumptions 5 and 6 are standard. The higher order stationarity and memory condition stated in Assumption 6(a) is natural given Assumptions 1–3. For simplicity, we hereafter focus on the case, in which the weighting matrix is convergent in probability.

Assumption 7 $\{W_T\}_{T\in\mathbb{N}}$ is a sequence of $v^2 \times v^2$ symmetric p.s.d. random matrices that converges in probability-P to a constant $v^2 \times v^2$ matrix W.

Under Assumptions 1 and 4, the difference between any estimator consistent for S and the estimator that adjusts it for positive definiteness converges in probability to zero at an arbitrarily fast rate (Corollary 4.2(c)). The ATF estimator therefore inherits the large sample properties of the TF kernel estimator.

Theorem 5.2 *Let $\{m_T\}_{T\in\mathbb{N}}$ be a sequence of positive real numbers growing to infinity.*

(a) If Assumptions 1, 2, 5, and 7 hold, and $m_T^2/T \to 0$, then $\|\hat{S}_T^{TF,A}(m_T) - S_T\|_{W_T} \to 0$ in probability-P. If in addition W is p.d., then $\{\hat{S}_T^{TF,A}(m_T)\}_{T\in\mathbb{N}}$ is consistent for $\{S_T\}_{T\in\mathbb{N}}$.

(b) If Assumptions 1 and 4–7 hold, and $m_T^{2q+1}/T \to \gamma \in (0,\infty)$ for some $q \in (0,\infty)$ for which $S^{(q)}$ converges, then $\|\hat{S}_T^{TF,A}(m_T) - S_T\|_{W_T} = \text{O}_P((m_T/T)^{-1/2})$ and $\|\hat{S}_T^{TF,A}(m_T) - \hat{S}_T^{TF}(m_T)\|_{W_T} = \text{o}_P((m_T/T)^{1/2})$.

(c) If, in addition to the conditions of part (b), W is p.d., then $\hat{S}_T^{TF,A}(m_T) - S_T = \text{O}_P((m_T/T)^{1/2})$ and $\hat{S}_T^{TF,A}(m_T) - \hat{S}_T^{TF}(m_T) = \text{o}_P((m_T/T)^{1/2})$.

(d) Under the conditions of part (b) plus Assumption 3,

$$\begin{aligned}
&\lim_{h\to\infty}\lim_{T\to\infty} \text{MSE}_h(T/m_T, \hat{S}_T^{TF,A}(m_T), W_T) \\
&= \lim_{h\to\infty}\lim_{T\to\infty} \text{MSE}_h(T/m_T, \hat{S}_T^{TF}(m_T), W_T) \\
&= \lim_{T\to\infty} \text{MSE}(T/m_T, \tilde{S}_T^{TF}(m_T), W)
\end{aligned}$$

As Theorem 5.2 shows, the presence of the estimated parameters has no effect on the asymptotic properties of ATF estimators, as is the case for the TF estimator. In particular, it enjoys the same large sample efficiency as the TF estimator does.

6 Extended Truncated Flat Kernel Estimator

In the TF estimation, all bandwidths between two adjacent nonnegative integers give the same estimator. Suppose that we have two adjacent integer bandwidths that result in good performances of the TF estimator. Given the familiar argument that the bandwidth should be chosen to balance the bias and variance of the estimator, one might desire to consider an estimator "between" the two estimators picked by the two integer bandwidths. A natural way to create a smooth transition path from an integer bandwidth to the next is to linearly interpolate the TF estimator between each pair of adjacent integer bandwidths. We call such estimators the extended TF (ETF) estimators. The ETF estimator based on $\hat{S}_T^{\text{TF}}$ with bandwidth $m \in [0, \infty)$ is defined to be

$$\begin{aligned}\hat{S}_T^{\text{ETF}}(m) &\equiv (\lfloor m \rfloor + 1 - m)\, \hat{S}_T^{\text{TF}}(m) + (m - \lfloor m \rfloor)\, \hat{S}_T^{\text{TF}}(m+1) \\ &= \hat{S}_T^{\text{TF}}(m) + (m - \lfloor m \rfloor)\, (\hat{\Gamma}_T(\lfloor m \rfloor + 1) + \hat{\Gamma}_T(\lfloor m \rfloor + 1)'), \quad T \in \mathbb{N},\end{aligned}$$

where $\lfloor \cdot \rfloor : \mathbb{R} \to \mathbb{R}$ is the floor function, which returns the greatest integer not exceeding the value of the argument, and we employ the rule that $\hat{S}^{\text{TF}}(0) = \hat{\Gamma}_T(0)$. The ETF estimator based on $\tilde{S}_T^{\text{TF}}$ is analogously defined. Each version of the ETF estimators coincides with the corresponding version of the TF estimator if the bandwidth m is an integer. In general, provided that the bandwidth m is less than $T - 1$, each version of the ETF estimator with a bandwidth m, compared to the corresponding version of the TF estimator with the same bandwidth, brings in the fraction $(m - \lfloor m \rfloor)$ of the autocovariance matrix estimator at lag $\lfloor m \rfloor + 1$.

We below investigate the large sample behavior of the ETF estimators. We first study the large sample properties of $\tilde{S}_T^{\text{ETF}}$, the ETF estimator with known θ^*. To do this, we examine the behavior of the last autocovariance matrix estimator fractionally incorporated in the ETF estimator.

Lemma 6.1 *Suppose that Assumptions 1 and 2 hold. Then:*

(a) $\sup_{\tau \in \{0,1,\ldots,T-1\}} \mathrm{E}[\, \|\tilde{\Gamma}_T(\tau) - \Gamma_T(\tau)\|^2\,] = O(T^{-1})$.
(b) Suppose that $\{m_T \in (0, T-1)\}_{T \in \mathbb{N}}$ *grows to* ∞. *If* $S^{(q)}$ *converges for some* $q \in (0, \infty)$, *then* $m_T^q\, \mathrm{E}[\tilde{\Gamma}_T(\lfloor m_T + 1 \rfloor)] \to 0$.
(c) Suppose that $\{m_T \in (0, T-1)\}_{T \in \mathbb{N}}$ *grows to* ∞. *If, in addition,* $m_T^{2q+1}/T \to \gamma \in (0, \infty)$ *for some* $q \in (0, \infty)$ *for which the series* $S^{(q)}$ *converges, then* $\mathrm{E}[\|\tilde{\Gamma}_T(\lfloor m_T + 1 \rfloor)\|^2] = o(m_T/T)$.

From Lemma 6.1(c), one might conjecture that the autocovariance estimator at the last lag is asymptotically negligible in the ETF estimation. It is indeed the case as the next proposition states.

Proposition 6.2 *Suppose that Assumptions 1, and 2 hold and* $\{m_T \in (0, T-1)\}_{T \in \mathbb{N}}$ *satisfies that* $m_T^{2q+1}/T \to \gamma \in (0, \infty)$ *for some* $q \in (0, \infty)$ *for which the series* $S^{(q)}$ *converges. Also, let* W *be a* $v^2 \times v^2$ *symmetric p.s.d. matrix. Then*

$$\lim_{T\to\infty} \text{MSE}(T/m_T,\ \tilde{S}_T^{ETF}(m_T),\ W) = \lim_{T\to\infty} \text{MSE}(T/m_T,\ \tilde{S}_T^{TF}(m_T),\ W).$$

Note that the ETF estimator may deliver a non-p.s.d. estimate, being a convex combination of the TF estimators that have the same problem. Thus, the estimator that adjusts it for positive semidefiniteness is useful. As is the case with the TF estimation, the adjustment improves the MSE of the ETF estimator in small samples (Corollary 4.2(a)). The next proposition states that the adjusted ETF (AETF) estimator performs at least as well as the ETF estimator in large samples.

Proposition 6.3 *Proposition 5.1 holds when* $\{\tilde{S}_T^{TF}\}_{T\in\mathbb{N}}$ *and* $\{\tilde{S}_T^{TF,A}\}_{T\in\mathbb{N}}$ *are replaced with* $\{\tilde{S}_T^{ETF}\}_{T\in\mathbb{N}}$ *and* $\{\tilde{S}_T^{ETF,A}\}_{T\in\mathbb{N}}$*, respectively.*

We now turn to $\hat{S}_T^{\text{ETF}}$, the ETF estimator in the presence of estimated parameters, $\hat{\theta}_T$. The next theorem demonstrates that $\hat{\theta}_T$ has no effect on the large sample properties on the ETF estimator, as is the case for the TF and ATF estimators.

Theorem 6.4 *Suppose that* $\{m_T \in (0, T-1)\}_{T\in\mathbb{N}}$ *grows to infinity.*

(a) If Assumptions 1, 2, and 5 hold, and $m_T^2/T \to 0$*, then* $\{\hat{S}_T^{ETF}(m_T)\}_{T\in\mathbb{N}}$ *is consistent for* $\{S_T\}_{T\in\mathbb{N}}$.

(b) If Assumptions 1, 5, and 6 hold, and $m_T^{2q+1}/T \to \gamma \in (0,\infty)$ *for some* $q \in (0,\infty)$ *for which* $S^{(q)}$ *converges, then* $\hat{S}_T^{ETF}(m_T) - S_T = O_P((m_T/T)^{1/2})$ *and* $\hat{S}_T^{ETF}(m_T) - \tilde{S}_T^{ETF}(m_T) = o_P((m_T/T)^{1/2})$.

(c) Under the conditions of part (b) plus Assumption 3,

$$\begin{aligned}
&\lim_{h\to\infty}\lim_{T\to\infty} \text{MSE}_h(T/m_T,\ \hat{S}_T^{ETF}(m_T),\ W_T)\\
&= \lim_{T\to\infty} \text{MSE}(T/m_T,\ \tilde{S}_T^{ETF}(m_T),\ W)\\
&= \lim_{T\to\infty} \text{MSE}(T/m_T,\ \tilde{S}_T^{TF}(m_T),\ W)
\end{aligned}$$

Also, it follows from Corollary 4.2, that the relationship between the ETF estimator and the AETF estimator is parallel to that between the TF estimator and the ATF estimator. Thus:

Theorem 6.5 *Theorem 5.2 holds when* $\{\hat{S}_T^{TF}\}_{T\in\mathbb{N}}$ *and* $\{\hat{S}_T^{TF,A}\}_{T\in\mathbb{N}}$ *are replaced with* $\{\hat{S}_T^{ETF}\}_{T\in\mathbb{N}}$ *and* $\{\hat{S}_T^{ETF,A}\}_{T\in\mathbb{N}}$*, respectively.*

In sum, the ETF and AETF estimators have the same large sample properties as TF and ATF estimators. In particular, the TF, ATF, ETF, and AETF estimators share the large sample efficiency.

7 Finite-Sample Performance of the ATF and AETF Estimators

In this section, we conduct Monte Carlo simulations to examine the small-sample performance of the proposed estimators in comparison with the familiar QS and BT estimators, borrowing the experiment setups from Andrews (1991). In each of the experiments, $\{(y_t, x_t')'\}_{t\in\mathbb{N}}$ is a stationary process, where y_t is a random variable, and x_t is a $v \times 1$ random vector. The coefficients θ^* in the population regression of y_t on x_t are parameters of interest. In this setup, we examine the MSE of each of the covariance matrix estimators and the size of the t-test of an exclusion restriction in the OLS regression, using each of the covariance matrix estimators. Thus, we have that $Z_t(\cdot, \theta^*) = x_t u_t$ $(t \in \mathbb{N})$, where $u_t = y_t - x_t'\theta^*$. The regressor vector x_t consists of a constant set equal to one and four random variables x_{t2}, x_{t3}, x_{t4}, and x_{t5}, i.e., $x_t = [1, x_{t2}, x_{t3}, x_{t4}, x_{t5}]'$. The regression coefficients θ^* are set equal to zeros.

The experiments are split into two groups: the AR(1)-HOMO and MA(1)-HOMO experiments. In the AR(1)-HOMO experiments, the sequence of disturbances $\{u_t\}_{t\in\mathbb{N}}$ is a univariate stationary Gaussian AR(1) process with mean zero and variance one. To generate the four nonconstant regressors, we first generate four independent sequences (that are also independent from the disturbance u_t) in the same way as we generate the disturbance sequence; then normalize them to obtain x_t such that $T^{-1}\sum_{t=1}^{T} x_t x_t' = I$. Because of this normalization, the estimated long-run covariance matrix is equal to the estimated asymptotic covariance matrix of the OLS estimator of θ^*. The data generating process in MA(1)-HOMO experiments are the same as the AR(1)-HOMO experiments, except that the disturbance term and the regressors (prior to the normalization) are Gaussian stationary MA(1) processes with mean zero and variance one. The number of Monte Carlo replications is 25,000 in each of the experiments. In each replication, $500 + T$ observations are generated and the last T observations are used.

We first compare the performance of the ATF estimator against that of the TF estimator to assess the effect of the adjustment for positive semidefiniteness on the performance. While Corollary 4.2 claims that the MSE of the ATF estimator never exceeds that of the TF estimator, Theorem 5.2(d) suggests that the efficiency gain from the adjustment is asymptotically negligible. We seek to check if the negligibility of the efficiency gain by the adjustment carries over in small samples.

We calculate the efficiency of the ATF estimator relative to that of TF estimator in the AR(1)-HOMO and MA(1)-HOMO experiments with sample size $T = 128$ and bandwidths $m \in \{1, 3, 5, 7\}$, where the efficiency of an estimator relative to another is the MSE of the latter divided by that of the former. We use the AR coefficients $\rho \in \{0, 0.3, 0.5, 0.7, 0.9, 0.95, -0.3, -0.5\}$ in the AR(1)-HOMO experiments and the MA coefficients $\vartheta \in \{0.1, 0.3, 0.5, 0.7, 0.99, -0.3, -0.7\}$ in the MA(1)-HOMO experiments. Following Andrews (1991, p. 836), we employ the weighting matrix

$$W_T = \left(\left(T^{-1}\sum_{t=1}^{T} x_t x_t'\right)^{-1} \otimes \left(T^{-1}\sum_{t=1}^{T} x_t x_t'\right)^{-1}\right) \tilde{W} \left(\left(T^{-1}\sum_{t=1}^{T} x_t x_t'\right)^{-1} \otimes \left(T^{-1}\sum_{t=1}^{T} x_t x_t'\right)^{-1}\right),$$

where $\tilde{W}$ is a $v^2 \times v^2$ diagonal matrix whose diagonal elements are set equal to

$$\text{vec}\begin{pmatrix} 0 & 0 & 0 & 0 & 0 \\ 0 & 2 & 1 & 1 & 1 \\ 0 & 1 & 2 & 1 & 1 \\ 0 & 1 & 1 & 2 & 1 \\ 0 & 1 & 1 & 1 & 2 \end{pmatrix}.$$

(We ignore the normalization of the regressors, i.e., $T^{-1}\sum_{t=1}^{T} x_t x_T' = I$, just for now, to explain the role of W_T.) With the weighting matrix W_T, the MSE of an estimator $\hat{S}_T$ of S_T is

$$\mathrm{E}\left[\left\| \left(T^{-1}\sum_{t=1}^{T} x_t x_t'\right)^{-1} \hat{S}_T \left(T^{-1}\sum_{t=1}^{T} x_t x_t'\right)^{-1} - \left(T^{-1}\sum_{t=1}^{T} x_t x_t'\right)^{-1} S_T \left(T^{-1}\sum_{t=1}^{T} x_t x_t'\right)^{-1}\right)' \right\|_{\tilde{W}}\right]$$

(note that the weighting matrix in the formula on the right-hand side of the above equality is $\tilde{W}$). Thus, the MSE measures the discrepancy between the estimated covariance matrix of the OLS estimator of θ^* using $\hat{S}_T$ and the estimated covariance matrix using S_T (the true covariance matrix unknown to us in practice), using the weighting matrix $\tilde{W}$. The zeros among the diagonal elements of $\tilde{W}$ let us focus on the covariance matrix of the slopes in the OLS estimator of θ^*. The weighting matrix $\tilde{W}$ puts equal weights on all elements in the upper (or lower) triangle of the covariance matrix of the slope estimators, taking into account that the estimated covariance matrix is symmetric.

Once we put the normalization of the regressors back into the picture, the MSE of $\hat{S}_T$ simply equals $\mathrm{E}\big[\|\hat{S}_T - S_T\|_{\tilde{W}}\big] = \mathrm{E}\big[\text{vec}(\hat{S}_T - S_T)'\tilde{W}\text{vec}(\hat{S}_T - S_T)\big]$. Nevertheless, it should be understood that the MSE still measures the discrepancy between the estimated covariance matrix of the OLS estimator of θ^* using $\hat{S}_T$ with the estimated covariance matrix using S_T, as discussed above.

Our simulation results on the efficiency of the ATF estimator relative to the TF estimator are so simple that we do not tabulate them. Our finding is that the efficiency of the ATF estimator relative to the TF estimator is 1.00 in the vast majority of our experiments, and it exceeds 1.01 in none of the experiments. This reflects the fact

Table 1 The Efficiency of the estimators relative to the QS estimator using fixed optimum bandwidths in Andrews (1991) experiments

AR(1)-HOMO

T	Estimator	ρ 0	0.3	0.5	0.7	0.9	0.95	-0.3	-0.5
64	BT	1.00	1.00	0.99	0.96	0.97	0.98	1.00	0.99
	ATF	1.00	1.00	0.91	1.05	1.03	1.02	1.00	0.89
	AETF	1.00	1.00	0.99	1.05	1.03	1.02	1.00	0.99
128	BT	1.00	1.00	0.97	0.94	0.95	0.96	1.00	0.97
	ATF	1.00	0.99	0.99	1.04	1.04	1.03	0.99	0.97
	AETF	1.00	1.00	1.02	1.06	1.04	1.03	1.00	1.02
256	BT	1.00	1.00	0.95	0.92	0.93	0.95	1.00	0.95
	ATF	1.00	0.91	1.08	1.09	1.06	1.05	0.90	1.08
	AETF	1.00	1.00	1.08	1.09	1.06	1.05	1.00	1.08

MA(1)-HOMO

T	Estimator	ϑ 0.1	0.3	0.5	0.7	0.9	0.99	-0.3	-0.7
64	BT	1.00	1.00	1.00	0.99	0.99	0.99	0.99	0.99
	ATF	1.00	1.00	0.99	0.94	0.91	0.91	0.99	0.94
	AETF	1.00	1.00	1.00	0.99	0.99	0.99	0.99	0.99
128	BT	1.00	1.00	0.99	0.99	0.99	0.99	1.00	0.99
	ATF	1.00	1.00	0.89	0.84	0.87	0.87	1.00	0.80
	AETF	1.00	1.00	0.99	1.00	1.00	1.00	1.00	0.99
256	BT	1.00	1.00	0.99	0.96	0.95	0.95	1.00	0.96
	ATF	1.00	0.95	0.84	0.93	0.96	0.96	0.95	0.91
	AETF	1.00	1.00	1.00	1.03	1.04	1.04	1.00	1.02

Note The efficiency of each estimator is the ratio of the MSE of the QS estimator to that of the estimator

that the probability that the TF estimator is not p.s.d. is close to zero in all of the experiments.

We next investigate the potential efficiency gain from using the estimators in the TF family instead of the QS, BT, ATF, and AETF estimators. In this comparison, we let each of the estimators use its fixed optimum bandwidth. We here mean by the fixed optimum bandwidth of a kernel estimator the nonstochastic bandwidth that minimizes the (finite sample) MSE of the estimator, which we numerically find by using the grid search method through the Monte Carlo experiments. Table 1 displays the efficiency of the BT, TF, ATF, ETF, and AETF estimators relative to the QS estimator with sample sizes 64, 128, and 256.

The relationship between the ATF and QS estimators is similar to that between the TF and QS estimators reported in Andrews (1991). The ATF estimator outperforms the QS estimator clearly in some cases, and the complete opposite happens in some other cases. On the other and, the AETF estimator never has a MSE larger than the ATF estimator and sometimes brings in substantial improvement over the ATF estimator, in particular, when the ATF estimator poorly performs relatively to the QS estimator. As a result, the MSE of the AETF estimator is smaller than or about the same as that of the QS estimator in all experiments. Not surprisingly, the fixed optimum bandwidth for the AETF estimator is close to the midpoint between a pair of adjacent integers when the AETF estimator outperforms the ATF estimator by a large margin.

The large sample theory indicates that the efficiency of the ATF and AETF estimators relative to the QS and BT estimators becomes higher as the sample size increases. Table 1 indeed confirms that the relative efficiency of the AETF increases, though gradually, as the sample size grows. On the other hand, the relative efficiency of the ATF estimator shows more complicated moves. That is, the relative efficiency of the ATF may decrease when the sample size increases. To understand why this happens, it is useful to view the ATF estimator as a restricted version of the AETF estimator that can only use an integer bandwidth in the AETF estimation. Suppose that the fixed optimum bandwidth for the AETF estimator is close to an integer with the initial sample size. Then the ATF and AETF estimators perform equally well with the initial sample size. When the sample size increases, however, the optimum bandwidth for the AETF may be close to the midpoint between a pair of adjacent integers. The restriction imposed on the ATF estimator now becomes a severe penalty. Thus, the efficiency of the ATF estimator relative to the QS estimator can decrease, while the relative efficiency of the AETF increases.

8 TF Estimation with Data-Based Bandwidth

The optimum bandwidth is unknown in practice. We need a way to choose a bandwidth based on data. For consistency of the TF, ATF, ETF, and AETF estimators with data-based bandwidths, a data-based bandwidth $\hat{m}_T$ only needs to satisfy the following assumption.

Assumption 8 The sequence $\{m_T \in (0, T-1)\}_{T\in\mathbb{N}}$ satisfies that $m_T \to \infty$ and $m_T^2/T \to 0$. Also, a sequence of random variables $\{\hat{m}_T\}_{T\in\mathbb{N}}$ satisfies that $|\log(\hat{m}_T/m_T)| = \mathrm{O}_P(1)$. Note that Assumption 8 imposes the same conditions on $\{m_T\}_{T\in\mathbb{N}}$ as the consistency results for the ATF, ETF, and AETF estimators in Theorems 5.2(a), 6.4(a), and 6.5(a).

To establish results on the rate of convergence and the asymptotic truncated MSE of the estimators, we impose stronger conditions on the bandwidth.

Assumption 9 The sequence $\{m_T \in (0, T-1)\}_{T\in\mathbb{N}}$ satisfies that $m_T \to \infty$ and $m_T^{2q+1}/T \to \gamma \in (0,\infty)$ for some $q \in (0,\infty)$ for which $S^{(q)}$ absolutely converges. Also, a sequence of random variables $\{\hat{m}_T\}_{T\in\mathbb{N}}$ satisfies that for some sequence $\{d_T \in (0,\infty)\}_{T\in\mathbb{N}}$ such that $d_T^{-1} m_T^{1/2} \to 0$, $d_T|\hat{m}_T - m_T|/m_T = \mathrm{O}_P(1)$.

The conditions imposed on $\{m_T\}$ in Assumption 9 are the same as those imposed in Theorems 5.2(b)–(d), 6.4(b), (c), and 6.5(b)–(d).

Remark In Andrews (1991) and Newey and West (1994), though they do not consider the TF estimator, the data-based bandwidth takes a form of $\hat{m}_T = \hat{c}_T T^r$ where r is some positive real number and $\hat{c}_T$ is an estimator of some constant $c \in (0, \infty)$. With such $\hat{m}_T$, the condition $|\log(\hat{m}_T/m_T)| = O_P(1)$ in Assumption 8 coincides with Assumption E of Andrews (1991), because $\log(\hat{m}_T/m_T) = \log(\hat{c}_T/c_T)$. Also, we have that $d_T|\hat{m}_T - m_T|/m_T = d_T(\hat{c}_T - c) = O_P(1)$ for a suitably chosen $d_T \in (0, \infty)$ under Assumption 9. In order for $d_T^{-1} m_T^{1/2}$ to converge to zero, q in Assumption 9 needs to be sufficiently large. If $d_t = T^{1/2}$, as is the case in the data-based bandwidth of Andrews (1991), it must hold that $q > 1/2$.

We are now ready to state results on the large sample behavior of the TF, ATF, ETF, and AETF estimators with data-based bandwidths.

Theorem 8.1 *(a) Suppose that Assumptions 1, 2, 5, and 8 hold. Then the estimators* $\{\hat{S}_T^{TF}(\hat{m}_T)\}_{T\in\mathbb{N}}$ *and* $\{\hat{S}_T^{ETF}(\hat{m}_T)\}_{T\in\mathbb{N}}$ *are consistent for* $\{S_T\}_{T\in\mathbb{N}}$*, and it holds that*

$$\|\hat{S}_T(\hat{m}_T)-S_T\|_{W_T} \to 0 \text{ in probability-}P, \quad \hat{S}_T \in \{\hat{S}_T^{TF},\ \hat{S}_T^{TF,A},\ \hat{S}_T^{ETF},\ \hat{S}_T^{ETF,A}\}. \tag{5}$$

If in addition W is p.d., then $\{\hat{S}_T^{TF,A}(\hat{m}_T)\}_{T\in\mathbb{N}}$ *and* $\{\hat{S}_T^{ETF,A}(\hat{m}_T)\}_{T\in\mathbb{N}}$ *are also consistent for* $\{S_T\}_{T\in\mathbb{N}}$.

(b) If Assumptions 1, 4–7, and 9 hold. Then we have:

$$\begin{aligned}(T/m_T)^{1/2}(\hat{S}_T^{TF}(\hat{m}_T) - \hat{S}_T^{TF}(m_T)) &= o_P(1),\\ (T/m_T)^{1/2}(\hat{S}_T^{TF}(\hat{m}_T) - S_T) &= O_P(1),\end{aligned} \tag{6}$$

$$\begin{aligned}(T/m_T)^{1/2}(\hat{S}_T^{ETF}(\hat{m}_T) - \hat{S}_T^{ETF}(m_T)) &= o_P(1),\\ (T/m_T)^{1/2}(\hat{S}_T^{ETF}(\hat{m}_T) - S_T) &= O_P(1),\end{aligned} \tag{7}$$

$$\begin{aligned}&(T/m_T)^{1/2}\|\hat{S}_T(\hat{m}_T) - S_T\|_{W_T} = O_P(1),\\ &\hat{S}_T \in \{\hat{S}_T^{TF},\ \hat{S}_T^{TF,A},\ \hat{S}_T^{ETF},\ \hat{S}_T^{ETF,A}\},\end{aligned} \tag{8}$$

$$\begin{aligned}&(T/m_T)^{1/2}\|\hat{S}_T(\hat{m}_T) - \hat{S}_T(m_T)\|_{W_T} = o_P(1),\\ &\hat{S}_T \in \{\hat{S}_T^{TF},\ \hat{S}_T^{TF,A},\ \hat{S}_T^{ETF},\ \hat{S}_T^{ETF,A}\}.\end{aligned} \tag{9}$$

(c) If, in addition to the conditions of part (b), W is p.d., then

$$\begin{aligned}(T/m_T)^{1/2}(\hat{S}_T^{TF,A}(\hat{m}_T) - \hat{S}_T^{TF,A}(m_T)) &= o_P(1),\\ (T/m_T)^{1/2}(\hat{S}_T^{TF,A}(\hat{m}_T) - S_T) &= O_P(1),\end{aligned} \tag{10}$$

$$\begin{aligned}(T/m_T)^{1/2}(\hat{S}_T^{ETF,A}(\hat{m}_T) - \hat{S}_T^{ETF,A}(m_T)) &= o_P(1),\\ (T/m_T)^{1/2}(\hat{S}_T^{ETF,A}(\hat{m}_T) - S_T) &= O_P(1).\end{aligned} \tag{11}$$

(d) *Under the conditions of part (b) plus Assumption 3, for each* $\hat{S}_T \in \{\hat{S}_T^{TF}, \hat{S}_T^{TF,A}, \hat{S}_T^{ETF}, \hat{S}_T^{ETF,A}\}$,

$$\begin{aligned}&\lim_{h\to\infty}\lim_{T\to\infty}\mathrm{MSE}_h(T/m_T, \hat{S}_T(\hat{m}_T), W_T)\\&\quad= \lim_{h\to\infty}\lim_{T\to\infty}\mathrm{MSE}_h(T/m_T, \hat{S}_T(m_T), W_T).\end{aligned}$$

The results presented in Theorem 8.1 indicate that the more slowly the bandwidth grows, the faster the MSE shrinks in the TF, ATF, ETF, and AETF estimation, provided that $\Gamma(\tau)$ converges to zero fast enough as $\tau \to \infty$. The complete flat shape of the TF kernel at the origin makes the convergence rate of the bias so fast that the bias is asymptotically negligible relative to the variance in the TF estimation, virtually regardless of the growth rate of the bandwidth. This means that given a sequence of bandwidths in TF estimation, we can always find another sequence of bandwidths with a slower growth rate that makes faster the convergence rate of the TF estimator. The rate results in Theorem 8.1 reflect this fact.

Andrews (1991) and Newey and West (1994) propose ways to choose bandwidths based on data in kernel estimation. Their approach is based on the trade-off between the asymptotic bias and asymptotic variance of typical kernel estimators: the more slowly the bandwidth grows, the more slowly the asymptotic bias shrinks and the faster the variance shrinks, loosely speaking. Their approach sets the growth rate of the bandwidth in such a way that the convergence rates of the squared bias and the variance are equated, so that the MSE of the estimator reaches the fastest possible convergence rate. It then chooses the proportional constant for the bandwidth by minimizing the suitably scaled asymptotic MSE.

The approach of Andrews (1991) and Newey and West (1994) is inapplicable in the TF estimation, given the absence of the trade-off between the asymptotic bias and asymptotic variance of the TF estimator. Nevertheless, it is possible to choose a bandwidth sequence that makes the TF estimator asymptotically more efficient than the QS estimator. Let m_T^{QS} and $\tilde{m}_T^{QS}$ denote the "oracle" and data-based bandwidths of Andrews (1991), respectively (for the precise mathematical formulas of m_T^{QS} and $\tilde{m}_T^{QS}$, see Eqs. (5.1), (6.1), and (6.8) in Andrews (1991)). If we set $\hat{m}_T = a\tilde{m}_T^{QS}$ for any $a \in (0, 1/2]$, then we have by Theorem 8.1(d) that

$$\begin{aligned}&\lim_{h\to\infty}\lim_{T\to\infty}\mathrm{MSE}_h(T/m_T^{QS}, \hat{S}_T^{\mathrm{TF}}(\hat{m}_T), W_T)\\&\quad= \lim_{h\to\infty}\lim_{T\to\infty} a\mathrm{MSE}_h(T/(am_T^{QS}), \hat{S}_T^{\mathrm{TF}}(\hat{m}_T), W_T)\\&\quad= 8a\pi^2\mathrm{tr}(W(I + K_{v,v})S \otimes S) \le 4\pi^2\mathrm{tr}(W(I + K_{v,v})S \otimes S).\end{aligned}$$

Because the right-hand side of this equality is equal to the asymptotic variance of the QS estimator with bandwidth $\tilde{m}_T^{QS}$, which is no greater than the asymptotic MSE of the QS estimator, the TF estimator with bandwidth $\hat{m}_T$ is asymptotically more efficient than the QS estimator with bandwidth $\tilde{m}_T^{QS}$. We can, of course, apply the same bandwidth $\hat{m}_T$ in the ATF and AETF estimation to attain the same asymptotic MSE.

A practical question is what value we should use for a. Though the asymptotic MSE of the TF estimator with the bandwidth $\hat{m}_T$ can be made arbitrarily small by setting a sufficiently small value to a, too small a value for a would result in a large magnitude of bias in the TF estimation in small samples, because there is a trade-off between the bias and the variance in finite samples. In our Monte Carlo simulations in the next section, we use $a = 1/2$ for the ATF estimator and $a = 1/3$ for the AETF estimator, though these choices are arguably ad hoc. We use a larger value for a in the ATF estimation than in the AETF estimation, because the ATF estimator effectively rounds down the data-based bandwidth $\hat{m}_T$, due to the equality $\hat{S}^{\text{ATF}}(\hat{m}_T) = \hat{S}^{\text{ATF}}(\lfloor \hat{m}_T \rfloor)$.

9 Finite-Sample Performance of the ATF and AETF Estimators with Data-Based Bandwidths

In this section, we conduct Monte Carlo experiments to examine the performances of the ATF and AETF estimators in comparison with the BT, QS, and Politis and Romano's (1996, 1999) flat-top kernel estimators using data-based bandwidths, borrowing the experiment designs from Newey and West (1987) and Politis (2011) in addition to the design of Andrews (1991) used earlier in Sect. 7. In what follows, PoID, PoPR, PoQS, and PoBT denote the flat-top kernel estimators with infinitely differential tail, Parzen's type tail, QS type tail, and Bartlett tail, respectively. The shape parameters of these flat-top kernel estimators are set to the values used in Politis (2011) (i.e., for PoID: $c = 0.05$, $b = 0.25$; for PoPR: $c = 0.75$; for PoQS: $c = 1$, $b = 4$; and for PoBT: $c = 0.5$).

Our experiments use the bandwidth selection methods that work stably in all of our experiments *without manual tuning or intervention*. Our choice of the data-based bandwidth for the QS and BT estimators are that of Andrews (1991). In the ATF and AETF estimation, we use the method described in Sect. 8. For the flat-top kernel estimators, we adjust the bandwidth for the ATF and AETF, replacing the formula for the asymptotic variance for the TF estimator with those of the flat-top kernel estimators (the bandwidths for the PoID, PoPR, PoQS, and PoBT are $0.6439\tilde{m}_T^{QS}$, $0.3269\tilde{m}_T^{QS}$, $0.2266\tilde{m}_T^{QS}$ and $0.5\tilde{m}_T^{QS}$). Though we in theory could use Newey and West's (1994) method instead of Andrews' (1991) method in the bandwidth selection, we have found that Newey and West's (1994) method is not suitable for our purpose, because the simulation results heavily depend on its tuning parameter. We have also found that the bandwidth selection method recommended by Politis (2011) sometimes results in terrible performance without some human intervention (which is impossible in Monte Carlo experiments).

Table 2 reports the efficiency of the estimators relative to the QS estimator in the AR(1)-HOMO and MA(1)-HOMO experiments. The relationship among the estimators are analogous to that in Table 1 of the experiments with fixed optimum bandwidths, though the randomness of the data-based bandwidth introduces extra variability in the results. The MSE of the AETF estimator is smaller than or at least comparable to that of the QS estimator in all of our experiments, while the efficiency of the ATF estimator relative to the QS estimator varies from an experiment to another. The efficiency of the PoID, PoPR, PoQS, and PoBT varies across different underlying data generating processes, and the flat-top kernel estimators do not uniformly outperform the other estimators.

We now turn to the experiments of Newey and West (1994) and Politis (2011). The first two experiments borrowed from Newey and West (1994), NW-A1 and NW-A2, feature a time-series regression model with AR processes for its regressors and disturbance, while the third experiment NW-B1 incorporates truncated memory and GARCH(1,1) effects. In Politis (2011) experiments, Po1 and Po2, $\{Z_t^*\}_{t\in\mathbb{N}}$ is a bivariate process that involves no unknown parameter θ^*. In Po1, the two components of $\{Z_t^*\}$ are independent from each other. The first component is an AR(1) process with coefficient 0.75, while the second component is an MA(1) process weighting the current and lagged innovations equally. In Po2, the first component is an MA(1) process with coefficient -1, and the second component is the sum of an AR(1) process with coefficient -0.75 and the first component at the seventh lag, so that its cross-autocovariance jumps up at lag 7.

Table 3 presents the efficiency of the estimators relative to the QS estimator in NW-A1, NW-A2, NW-B1, Po1, and Po2. In NW-A1, NW-A2, NW-B1, and Po1, the QS, AETF, and flat-top kernel estimators perform comparably. In Po2, however, the QS, BT, and Politis flat-top estimators clearly outperform the ATF and AETF estimators. This seems to reflect the unusual feature of Po2 that the cross autocovariance jumps at the seventh lag. The ATF and AETF estimators miss the jump completely unless their bandwidths are greater than six, while the other estimators more easily capture the jump at least partially thorough the sloped part of the kernel. This reveals a possible drawback of the ATF and AETF estimators, though we doubt typical economic applications involve such an exotic autocovariance structure.

In summary, the relationship between the AETF and QS estimators is consistent with what the large sample theory suggests, unlike the relationship between the ATF and QS estimators. Though the relationship between flat-top kernel estimators and the AETF estimator is somewhat unclear, they perform comparably in many cases.

10 Conclusion

In this paper, we modify the truncated flat kernel (TF) estimator of long-run covariance matrices proposed by White and Domowitz (1984) to propose estimators with guaranteed positive semidefiniteness and finite sample performance stably consistent with the large sample efficiency of the TF estimator. We analytically prove the "large sample equivalence" of the proposed estimators and the TF estimator and

Table 2 The efficiency of the estimators relative to the QS estimator using data-dependent bandwidths in Andrews (1991) experiments

AR(1)-HOMO

		ρ							
T	Estimator	0	0.3	0.5	0.7	0.9	0.95	-0.3	-0.5
64	BT	1.02	1.01	1.00	0.99	1.00	1.00	1.01	1.00
	ATF	1.03	1.01	1.01	1.01	1.00	1.00	1.01	1.02
	AETF	1.01	1.01	1.02	1.01	1.00	1.00	1.01	1.02
	PoID	1.03	1.00	0.97	0.99	1.00	1.00	0.99	0.98
	PoPR	1.03	1.00	0.97	0.99	1.00	1.00	0.99	0.97
	PoQS	1.03	1.00	0.97	0.99	1.00	1.00	0.99	0.97
	PoBT	1.03	1.00	0.97	0.99	1.00	1.00	0.99	0.97
128	BT	1.03	1.02	0.99	0.98	0.99	1.00	1.02	1.00
	ATF	1.03	1.00	1.03	1.02	1.01	1.00	1.00	1.03
	AETF	1.01	1.01	1.03	1.02	1.00	1.00	1.01	1.03
	PoID	1.06	1.00	0.98	0.99	1.00	1.00	1.00	0.99
	PoPR	1.07	1.00	0.98	0.99	1.00	1.00	1.00	0.98
	PoQS	1.07	1.00	0.98	0.99	1.00	1.00	1.00	0.98
	PoBT	1.07	1.00	0.98	0.99	1.00	1.00	1.00	0.98
256	BT	1.04	1.02	0.99	0.97	0.98	0.99	1.02	0.99
	ATF	1.04	0.99	1.03	1.03	1.01	1.01	0.99	1.03
	AETF	1.01	1.01	1.05	1.03	1.00	1.00	1.01	1.05
	PoID	1.08	0.99	0.99	1.00	1.00	1.00	0.99	1.00
	PoPR	1.09	0.98	1.00	0.99	1.00	1.00	0.98	1.01
	PoQS	1.09	0.98	1.00	0.99	1.00	1.00	0.98	1.01
	PoBT	1.09	0.99	0.99	0.99	1.00	1.00	0.99	1.00

MA(1)-HOMO

		ϑ							
T	Estimator	0.1	0.3	0.5	0.7	0.9	0.99	-0.3	-0.7
64	BT	1.02	1.01	1.00	0.99	0.99	0.99	1.01	1.00
	ATF	1.02	1.01	1.01	1.01	1.02	1.02	1.01	1.02
	AETF	1.01	1.01	1.01	1.02	1.02	1.02	1.01	1.02
	PoID	1.03	1.00	0.97	0.97	0.97	0.97	1.00	0.97
	PoPR	1.03	1.00	0.97	0.96	0.96	0.96	1.00	0.97
	PoQS	1.03	1.00	0.97	0.96	0.96	0.96	1.00	0.97
	PoBT	1.03	1.00	0.97	0.97	0.97	0.97	1.00	0.97
128	BT	1.03	1.02	1.00	1.00	0.99	0.99	1.02	1.00
	ATF	1.01	1.01	1.02	1.03	1.04	1.04	1.01	1.04
	AETF	1.01	1.01	1.02	1.03	1.04	1.04	1.01	1.04
	PoID	1.06	1.01	0.98	0.98	0.99	0.99	1.01	0.99
	PoPR	1.06	1.01	0.97	0.97	0.98	0.98	1.01	0.98
	PoQS	1.06	1.01	0.97	0.97	0.98	0.98	1.01	0.98
	PoBT	1.06	1.01	0.97	0.98	0.98	0.99	1.01	0.99

(continued)

Table 2 Continued

AR(1)-HOMO

T	Estimator	ρ 0	0.3	0.5	0.7	0.9	0.95	-0.3	-0.5
256	BT	1.04	1.02	1.00	0.99	0.99	0.99	1.02	0.99
	ATF	1.03	0.98	1.04	1.05	1.06	1.05	0.98	1.05
	AETF	1.01	1.01	1.03	1.06	1.07	1.07	1.01	1.06
	PoID	1.08	1.01	0.99	1.02	1.03	1.03	1.01	1.02
	PoPR	1.08	1.00	0.97	1.01	1.03	1.04	1.00	1.01
	PoQS	1.08	1.00	0.97	1.01	1.03	1.04	1.00	1.02
	PoBT	1.08	1.01	0.98	1.01	1.03	1.03	1.01	1.01

See the note of Table 1

Table 3 The efficiency of the estimators relative to the QS estimator using data-dependent bandwidths in Newey and West (1994) and Politis' (2011) experiments

	NW-A1	NW-A2	NW-B1	Po1	Po1	Po2	Po2
T	100	200	300	100	500	100	500
BT	0.97	1.00	0.84	1.13	1.07	1.15	1.10
ATF	0.97	0.95	0.98	0.98	0.99	0.94	0.83
AETF	0.99	0.98	1.01	1.01	1.00	0.95	0.88
PoID	0.99	1.01	1.02	1.06	1.01	1.37	1.20
PoPR	0.99	0.99	1.02	1.05	1.01	1.40	1.21
PoQS	0.99	0.99	1.02	1.05	1.01	1.40	1.21
PoBT	0.99	1.00	1.02	1.06	1.00	1.40	1.23

See the note of Table 1

demonstrate the improved performance of the proposed estimators over that of the TF estimator in Monte Carlo experiments.

Acknowledgments The authors are grateful for helpful comments and suggestions the anonymous referee gave to them. They also benefited from discussion with Lutz Kilian, Chung-Ming Kuan, Serena Ng, Dimitris Politis, and the participants of the 2008 Far Eastern Meeting of Econometric Society and the Conference in Honor of Halbert L. White, Jr.

Appendix A Mathematical Proofs

For each symmetric p.s.d. matrix A, $A^{1/2}$ denotes a p.s.d. symmetric matrix such that $A^{1/2}A^{1/2} = A$. Also, for each $(a, b) \in \mathbb{R}^2$, $a \vee b$, and $a \wedge b$ denote the smaller and larger between a and b, respectively. In some of the proofs given below, we will use the following lemma.

Lemma A.1 *Suppose that Assumption 1 holds. Let $\hat{S}_{1,T}$ and $\hat{S}_{2,T}$ be estimators of S_T, W_T a $v^2 \times v^2$ symmetric p.s.d. random matrix, and a_T a positive real number ($T \in \mathbb{N}$). If $a_T^{1/2}(\hat{S}_{1,T} - S_T) = \mathrm{O}_P(1)$, and $a_T^{1/2}\|\hat{S}_{1,T} - \hat{S}_{2,T}\|_{W_T} \to 0$*

in probability-P, then for each $h \in (0, \infty)$ *for which* $\text{MSE}_h(a_T, \hat{S}_{1,T}, W_T)$ *converges to a (finite) real number, it holds that* $\lim_{T\to\infty} \text{MSE}_h(a_T, \hat{S}_{2,T}, W_T) = \lim_{T\to\infty} \text{MSE}_h(a_T, \hat{S}_{1,T}, W_T)$.

Proof of Lemma A.1 The proof is available upon request. Q.E.D.

We omit the proofs of Theorem 2.1, Corollary 4.2, Proposition 5.1, Theorem 5.2, Propositions 6.2, 6.3, Lemma 6.1, Theorem 6.4, and Theorem 6.5, given the imposed space constraint. They are available from the authors upon request.

Proof of Theorem 4.1 To prove (a), fix $T \in \mathbb{N}$, and $\omega \in \Omega$ arbitrarily and suppose that $\hat{S}_T(\omega) \notin \mathsf{P}_v$. Write $\hat{s}^A \equiv \hat{S}_T^A(\omega)$ and $w \equiv \hat{W}_T(\omega)$, and let A, V, $\hat{x}$, and $\hat{x}^A$ be as in the proof of Theorem 2.1. Also, let $\bar{x} \equiv A'\text{vec}(S_T)$. Then the desired inequality is equivalent to $\|\hat{x} - \bar{x}\| \geq \|\hat{x}^A - \bar{x}\|$. Also, the equality of $\|\hat{s}^A - \hat{s}\|_w$ to zero is equivalent to the equality of $\|\hat{x} - \hat{x}^A\| = \inf_{x\in\mathsf{V}} \|\hat{x} - x\|$ to zero, which is further equivalent to that $\hat{x} \in \mathsf{V}$, because V is closed.

The inequality in question trivially holds with equality if $\hat{x} \in \mathsf{V}$, because it then holds that $\hat{x}^A = \hat{x}$. Now, suppose that $\hat{x} \notin \mathsf{V}$ and let B denote the Euclidean closed ball in $\mathbb{R}^{\text{rank}(A)}$ with radius $\|\hat{x}^A - \hat{x}\|$ centered at $\hat{x}$. It then clearly holds that $\mathsf{V} \cap \text{int}\,\mathsf{B} = \emptyset$. Also, V is convex, and B is convex with a nonempty interior, having a positive radius. By the Eidelheit Separation Theorem (Luenberger 1969, pp. 133–134,Theorem3), it follows that there exists a hyperplane H_1 separating V and B. Because $\hat{x}^A$ belongs to both V and B, H_1 contains $\hat{x}^A$, so that H_1 is the unique tangency plane of the Euclidean closed ball B at $\hat{x}^A$.

Now shift H_1 so that it contains $\bar{x}$ and call the resulting hyperplane H_2. Let $\check{x}$ be the projection of $\hat{x}$ onto H_2. Then $\hat{x}^A$ is on the line segment connecting $\hat{x}$ and $\check{x}$, and $\check{x} - \bar{x}$ is perpendicular to both $\hat{x} - \check{x}$ and $\hat{x}^A - \check{x}$. We thus have that

$$\|\hat{x} - \bar{x}\|^2 = \|\hat{x} - \check{x}\|^2 + \|\check{x} - \bar{x}\|^2 > \|\hat{x}^A - \check{x}\|^2 + \|\check{x} - \bar{x}\|^2 = \|\hat{x}^A - \bar{x}\|^2$$

The desired result therefore follows.

The claim of (b) immediately follows from the fact that if W_T is p.d., $\hat{S}_T^A$ is the minimizer of a function $s \mapsto \|\hat{S}_T - s\|_{W_T}$ that is strictly convex on the convex set P^v. Q.E.D.

Proof of Theorem 4.3 The sequence $\{a_T \|\hat{S}_T - S_T\|_{W_T}^2\}_{T\in\mathbb{N}}$ converges in probability-P to zero, because $P[\hat{S}_T - S_T = 0] \to 1$ by the consistency of $\{\hat{S}_T\}_{T\in\mathbb{N}}$ for $\{S_T\}_{T\in\mathbb{N}}$ and the asymptotic uniform positive definiteness of $\{S_T\}$. Because

$$\begin{aligned}
&\text{MSE}(a_T, \hat{S}_T, W_T) - \text{MSE}(a_T, \hat{S}_T^A, W_T) \\
&= \text{E}[a_T \|\hat{S}_T - S_T\|_{W_T}^2 - a_T \|\hat{S}_T^A - S_T\|_{W_T}^2], \qquad T \in \mathbb{N},
\end{aligned}$$

and $\{a_T \|\hat{S}_T - S_T\|_{W_T}^2 - a_T \|\hat{S}_T^A - S_T\|_{W_T}^2\}_{T\in\mathbb{N}}$ is uniformly integrable under the current assumption, it suffices to show that $\{a_T \|\hat{S}_T - S_T\|_{W_T}^2 - a_T \|\hat{S}_T^A - S_T\|_{W_T}^2\}$ converges to zero in probability-P. Let ϵ be an arbitrary positive real number.

Then

$$P\big[\big|\, a_T \,\|\hat{S}_T - S_T\|^2_{W_T} - a_T \,\|\hat{S}^A_T - S_T\|^2_{W_T} \,\big| > \epsilon\big]$$
$$\leq P\big[\big|\, a_T \,\|\hat{S}_T - S_T\|^2_{W_T} - a_T \,\|\hat{S}^A_T - S_T\|^2_{W_T} \,\big| \neq 0\big] \leq P[\hat{S}_T \notin \mathsf{P}] \to 0,$$

where the last inequality follows from the consistency of $\{\hat{S}_T\}_{T\in\mathbb{N}}$ for $\{S_T\}_{T\in\mathbb{N}}$ and the asymptotic uniform positive definiteness of $\{S_T\}$ by Theorem 4.1(a). The result therefore follows. Q.E.D.

Proof of Theorem 4.4 By Corollary 4.2(c), $a_T^{1/2}(\hat{S}^A_T - \hat{S}_T) \to 0$ in probability-P. Applying Lemma A.1, taking $\{\hat{S}_T\}_{T\in\mathbb{N}}$ for $\{\hat{S}_{1,T}\}_{T\in\mathbb{N}}$ and $\{\hat{S}^A_T\}_{T\in\mathbb{N}}$ for $\{\hat{S}_{2,T}\}_{T\in\mathbb{N}}$ respectively yields the desired result. Q.E.D.

Proof of Theorem 8.1 (a) Suppose that $\hat{S}^{\mathrm{TF}}_T(\hat{m}_T) - \hat{S}^{\mathrm{TF}}_T(m_T) \to 0$ in probability-P. Then $\{\hat{S}^{\mathrm{TF}}_T(\hat{m}_T)\}_{T\in\mathbb{N}}$ is consistent for $\{S_T\}_{T\in\mathbb{N}}$, because

$$\|\hat{S}^{\mathrm{TF}}_T(\hat{m}_T) - S_T\| \leq \|\hat{S}^{\mathrm{TF}}_T(\hat{m}_T) - \hat{S}^{\mathrm{TF}}_T(m_T)\| + \|\hat{S}^{\mathrm{TF}}_T(m_T) - S_T\|, \quad T \in \mathbb{N},$$

where the first term on the right-hand side converges to zero by hypothesis, and the second term converges in probability-P to zero by Andrews (1991, Theorem 1(a)). Also, $\{\hat{S}^{\mathrm{ETF}}_T(\hat{m}_T)\}_{T\in\mathbb{N}}$ is consistent for $\{S_T\}_{T\in\mathbb{N}}$ by Theorem 6.4(a). The convergences of (5) with $\hat{S}_T = \hat{S}^{\mathrm{TF}}_T$ and $\hat{S}_T = \hat{S}^{\mathrm{ETF}}_T$ respectively follow from the consistency of $\{\hat{S}^{\mathrm{TF}}_T(\hat{m}_T)\}_{T\in\mathbb{N}}$ and $\{\hat{S}^{\mathrm{ETF}}_T(\hat{m}_T)\}_{T\in\mathbb{N}}$ by the Slutsky Theorem. Then, applying Corollary 4.2(b) to $\{\hat{S}^{\mathrm{TF},A}_T(\hat{m}_T)\}_{T\in\mathbb{N}}$ and $\{\hat{S}^{\mathrm{ETF},A}_T(\hat{m}_T)\}_{T\in\mathbb{N}}$ establishes the rest of the claims in (a). Thus, it suffices to show that $\hat{S}^{\mathrm{TF}}_T(\hat{m}_T) - \hat{S}^{\mathrm{TF}}_T(m_T) \to 0$ in probability-P, i.e., for each $\epsilon \in (0, 1]$, $P[\|\hat{S}^{\mathrm{TF}}_T(\hat{m}_T) - \hat{S}^{\mathrm{TF}}_T(m_T)\| \geq \epsilon] < \epsilon$ for almost all $T \in \mathbb{N}$.

Pick $\epsilon \in (0, 1]$ arbitrarily. Then, by Assumption 8, there exists $\Delta_\epsilon \in (1, \infty)$ such that for each $T \in \mathbb{N}$, $P[\hat{m}_T \notin [(1/\Delta_\epsilon)m_T,\ \Delta_\epsilon m_T]] < \epsilon/2$. When $\hat{m}_T \in [(1/\Delta_\epsilon)m_T,\ \Delta_\epsilon m_T]$, we have that

$$\begin{aligned}
&\|\hat{S}^{\mathrm{TF}}_T(\hat{m}_T) - \hat{S}^{\mathrm{TF}}_T(m_T)\| \\
&\quad = \Bigg\| \sum_{\tau=\lfloor \hat{m}_T \wedge m_T \rfloor + 1}^{\lfloor \hat{m}_T \vee m_T \rfloor} \big(\hat{\Gamma}_T(\tau) + \hat{\Gamma}'_T(\tau)\big) \Bigg\| \\
&\quad \leq \Bigg\| \sum_{\tau=\lfloor \hat{m}_T \wedge m_T \rfloor + 1}^{\lfloor \hat{m}_T \vee m_T \rfloor} \big((\hat{\Gamma}_T(\tau) - \Gamma_T(\tau)) + (\hat{\Gamma}_T(\tau) - \Gamma_T(\tau))'\big) \Bigg\| \\
&\qquad + \Bigg\| \sum_{\tau=\lfloor \hat{m}_T \wedge m_T \rfloor + 1}^{\lfloor \hat{m}_T \vee m_T \rfloor} \big(\Gamma_T(\tau) + \Gamma(\tau)'\big) \Bigg\| \\
&\quad \leq 2A_{1,T} + 2A_{2,T}, \quad T \in \mathbb{N}, \quad \text{where}
\end{aligned} \tag{A.1}$$

$$A_{1,T} \equiv \sum_{\tau=\lfloor(1/\Delta_\epsilon)m_T\rfloor+1}^{\lfloor\Delta_\epsilon m_T\rfloor} \|\hat{\Gamma}_T(\tau) - \Gamma_T(\tau))\|,$$

$$A_{2,T} \equiv \sum_{\tau=\lfloor(1/\Delta_\epsilon)m_T\rfloor+1}^{\lfloor\Delta_\epsilon m_T\rfloor} \|\Gamma_T(\tau)\|, \quad T \in \mathbb{N}.$$

By using the Minkowski inequality and Lemma 6.1(a), we obtain that

$$\begin{aligned} \mathrm{E}[A_{1,T}^2]^{1/2} &\leq \sum_{\tau=\lfloor(1/\Delta_\epsilon)m_T\rfloor+1}^{\lfloor\Delta_\epsilon m_T\rfloor} \mathrm{E}[\|\hat{\Gamma}_T(\tau) - \Gamma_T(\tau))\|^2]^{1/2} \\ &= O(m_T/T^{1/2}) = o(1). \end{aligned}$$

By the Markov inequality, it follows that $A_{1,T} \to 0$ in probability-P. Also, the absolute convergence of $S^{(0)}$ implies that $A_{2,T} \leq \sum_{\tau=\lfloor(1/\Delta_\epsilon)m_T\rfloor+1}^{\lfloor\Delta_\epsilon m_T\rfloor} \|\Gamma(\tau)\| \leq \sum_{\tau=\lfloor(1/\Delta_\epsilon)m_T\rfloor+1}^{\infty} \|\Gamma(\tau)\| = o(1)$. Thus, $2A_{1,T} + A_{2,T} \to 0$ in probability-P. We now have that

$$\begin{aligned} P[\|\hat{S}_T^{\mathrm{TF}}(\hat{m}_T) - \hat{S}_T^{\mathrm{TF}}(m_T)\| \geq \epsilon] \leq P[\,&\hat{m}_T \notin [(1/\Delta_\epsilon)m_T,\ \Delta_\epsilon m_T]] \\ &+ P[2A_{1,T} + 2A_{2,T} \geq \epsilon], \quad T \in \mathbb{N}. \end{aligned}$$

The first term on the right-hand side of this equality is no greater than $\epsilon/2$ for each $T \in \mathbb{N}$, while the second term is smaller than $\epsilon/2$ for almost all $T \in \mathbb{N}$. The desired result therefore follows.

(b) Suppose that the first equality in (6) holds. Then the second equality also holds, because

$$\begin{aligned} \|(T/m_T)^{1/2}(\hat{S}_T^{\mathrm{TF}}(\hat{m}_T) - S_T)\| \leq\ &\|(T/m_T)^{1/2}(\hat{S}_T^{\mathrm{TF}}(\hat{m}_T) - \hat{S}_T^{\mathrm{TF}}(m_T))\| \\ &+ \|(T/m_T)^{1/2}(\hat{S}_T^{\mathrm{TF}}(m_T) - S_T)\|, \end{aligned}$$

$T \in \mathbb{N}$, where the first term on the right-hand side converges to zero by hypothesis, and the second term is $O_P(1)$ by Andrews (1991, Theorem 1(b)). Also, (7) can be easily derived from (6) by using the definition of the ETF estimator and the triangle inequality. Given (6)–(7), it is straightforward to establish (8) and (9) by using the definition of $\|\cdot\|_{W_T}$ and applying the basic rules about stochastic order of magnitudes in additions and multiplications. Thus, it suffices to show the first equality in (6) to prove the current claim.

The first equality in (6) is equivalent to that for each $\epsilon \in (0, 1]$,

$$P[(T/m_T)^{1/2}\|\hat{S}_T^{\mathrm{TF}}(\hat{m}_T) - \hat{S}_T^{\mathrm{TF}}(m_T)\| \geq \epsilon] < \epsilon \quad \text{for almost all } T \in \mathbb{N}. \quad (\mathrm{A.2})$$

Pick $\epsilon \in (0, 1]$ arbitrarily. Then, by Assumption 9, there exists $\Delta_\epsilon \in (0, \infty)$ such that for each $T \in \mathbb{N}$, $P[\hat{m}_T \notin [(1 - d_T^{-1}\Delta_\epsilon)m_T, (1 + d_T^{-1}\Delta_\epsilon)m_T]] < \epsilon/2$. Derivation analogous to (A.1) yields that when $\hat{m}_T \in [(1 - d_T^{-1}\Delta_\epsilon)m_T, (1 + d_T^{-1}\Delta_\epsilon)m_T]$,

$$\|(T/m_T)^{1/2}(\hat{S}_T^{\mathrm{TF}}(\hat{m}_T) - \hat{S}_T^{\mathrm{TF}}(m_T))\| \leq 2A_{3,T} + 2A_{4,T}, \quad T \in \mathbb{N}, \quad \text{where}$$

$$A_{3,T} \equiv (T/m_T)^{1/2} \sum_{\tau=\lfloor(1-d_T^{-1}\Delta_\epsilon)m_T\rfloor+1}^{\lfloor(1+d_T^{-1}\Delta_\epsilon)m_T\rfloor} \|\hat{\Gamma}_T(\tau) - \Gamma_T(\tau))\|,$$

$$A_{4,T} \equiv (T/m_T)^{1/2} \sum_{\tau=\lfloor(1-d_T^{-1}\Delta_\epsilon)m_T\rfloor+1}^{\lfloor(1+d_T^{-1}\Delta_\epsilon)m_T\rfloor} \|\Gamma_T(\tau)\|.$$

By using the Minkowski inequality and Lemma 6.1(a), we obtain that

$$\mathrm{E}[A_{3,T}^2]^{1/2} \leq (T/m_T)^{1/2} \sum_{\tau=\lfloor(1-d_T^{-1}\Delta_\epsilon)m_T\rfloor+1}^{\lfloor(1+d_T^{-1}\Delta_\epsilon)m_T\rfloor}$$

$$\mathrm{E}[\|\hat{\Gamma}_T(\tau) - \Gamma_T(\tau))\|^2]^{1/2} = O(d_T^{-1}m_T^{1/2}).$$

Because $d_T^{-1}m_T^{1/2} \to 0$ by Assumption 9, it follows that $\mathrm{E}[A_{3,T}^2]^{1/2} \to 0$. By the Markov inequality, $A_{3,T} \to 0$ in probability-P. Also, we have that

$$\begin{aligned}
A_{4,T} &\leq (T/m_T)^{1/2} \sum_{\tau=\lfloor(1-d_T^{-1}\Delta_\epsilon)m_T\rfloor+1}^{\lfloor(1+d_T^{-1}\Delta_\epsilon)m_T\rfloor} \|\Gamma_T(\tau)\| \\
&\leq (T/m_T)^{1/2} \sum_{\tau=\lfloor(1-d_T^{-1}\Delta_\epsilon)m_T\rfloor+1}^{\lfloor(1+d_T^{-1}\Delta_\epsilon)m_T\rfloor} \|\Gamma(\tau)\| \\
&\leq (T/m_T)^{1/2} \sum_{\tau=\lfloor(1-d_T^{-1}\Delta_\epsilon)m_T\rfloor+1}^{\infty} \|\Gamma(\tau)\| \\
&\leq (T/m_T)^{1/2} \sum_{\tau=\lfloor m_T/2\rfloor+1}^{\infty} \|\Gamma(\tau)\|,
\end{aligned}$$

where the last inequality holds for almost all $T \in \mathbb{N}$, as $1 - d_T^{-1}\Delta_\epsilon \geq 1/2$ for almost all $T \in \mathbb{N}$. Write $\gamma_T \equiv (m_T^{2q+1}/T)$ for each $T \in \mathbb{N}$. Then γ_T converges to Γ, and

$$\begin{aligned}(T/m_T)^{1/2} &= (T/m_T)^{1/2}\gamma_T^{1/2}\gamma_T^{-1/2} \\ &= \gamma_T^{-1/2} m_T^q = 2^q \gamma_T^{-1/2}(m_T/2)^q, \quad T \in \mathbb{N}.\end{aligned}$$

It follows that $A_{4,T} \leq 2^q \gamma_T^{-1/2} \sum_{\tau=\lfloor m_T/2 \rfloor+1}^{\infty} \tau^q \|\Gamma(\tau)\| = o(1)$, given the absolute convergence of $S^{(q)}$.

We now have that for each $T \in \mathbb{N}$,

$$\begin{aligned}&P\left[\left(\frac{T}{m_T}\right)^{1/2} \|\hat{S}_T^{\mathrm{TF}}(\hat{m}_T) - \hat{S}_T^{\mathrm{TF}}(m_T)\| \geq \epsilon\right] \\ &\quad \leq P\left[\hat{m}_T \notin \left[\left(1-\frac{\Delta_\epsilon}{d_T}\right)m_T, \left(1+\frac{\Delta_\epsilon}{d_T}\right)m_T\right]\right] + P[2A_{3,T} + 2A_{4,T} \geq \epsilon].\end{aligned}$$

Because the first term on the right-hand side of this equality is no greater than $\epsilon/2$ for each $T \in \mathbb{N}$, and the second term is smaller than $\epsilon/2$ for almost all $T \in \mathbb{N}$, (A.2) holds, and the desired result follows.

(c) The results follow from (8) and (9) setting $\hat{S}_T = \hat{S}_T^{\mathrm{TF},A}$ and $\hat{S}_T = \hat{S}_T^{\mathrm{ETF},A}$, respecitvely, by arguments analogous to the proof of Theorem 4.2(b).

(d) The result follows from the corresponding result (9) by Lemma A.1. Q.E.D.

References

Andrews, D. W. K., 1991. Heteroskedasticity and Autocorrelation Consistent Covariance Matrix Estimation, Econometrica, 59, 817–858.

Brown, L. D. and Purves, R., 1973. Measurable Selections of Extrema, The Annals of Statistics, 1, 902–912.

de Jong, R. M. and Davidson, J., 2000. Consistency of Kernel Estimators of Heteroscedastic and Autocorrelated Covariance Matrices, Econometrica, 68, 407–423.

Gallant, A. R. and White, H., 1988. A Unified Theory of Estimation and Inference for Nonlinear Dynamic Models. Basil Blackwell, New York.

Hannan, E. J., 1970. Multiple Time Series, A Wiley Publications in Applied Statistics. Wiley.

Hansen, B. E., 1992. Consistent Covariance Matrix Estimation for Dependent Heterogeneous Processes, Econometrica, 60, 967–972.

Jansson, M., 2003. Consistent Covariance Matrix Estimation for Linear Processes, Econometric Theory, 18, 1449–1459.

Luenberger, D. G., 1969. Optimization by Vector Space Methods, Series in Decision and Control. Wiley, New York, NY.

Newey, W. K. and West, K. D., 1987. A Simple Positive Semi-Definite, Heteroskedasticity and Autocorrelation Consistent Covariance Matrix, Econometrica, 55, 703–708.

Newey, W. K. and West, K. D., 1994. Automatic Lag Selection in Covariance Matrix Estimation, Review of Economic Studies, 61, 631–653.

Pinheiro, J. C. and Bates, D. M., 1996. Unconstrained Parametrizations for Variance-Covariance Matrices, Statistics and Computing, 6, 289–296.

Politis, D. N., 2011. Higher-Order Accurate, Positive Semidefinite Estimation of Large-Sample Covariance and Spectral Density Matrices, Econometric Theory, Available on CJO 2011 doi:10.1017/S0266466610000484.

Politis, D. N. and Romano, J. P., 1996. On Flat-Top Kernel Spectral Density Estimators for Homogeneous Random Fields, Journal of Statistical Planning and Inference, 51, 41–53.

Politis, D. N. and Romano, J. P., 1999. Multivariate Density Estimation with General Flat-Top Kernels of Infinite Order, Journal of Multivariate Analysis, 68, 1–25.

Priestley, M. B., 1981. Spectral Analysis and Time Series. Academic Press, New York.

Sturm, J. F., 1999. Using SeDuMi 1.02, a MATLAB toolbox for optimization over symmetric cones, Optimation Methods and Sotfware, 11, 625–653.

Vandenberghe, L. and Boyd, S., 1996. Semidefinite Programming, SIAM Review, 38, 49–95.

White, H. and Domowitz, I., 1984. Nonlinear Regression with Dependent Observations, Econometrica, 52, 143–161.

Predictability and Specification in Models of Exchange Rate Determination

Esfandiar Maasoumi and Levent Bulut

Abstract We examine a class of popular structural models of exchange rate determination and compare them to a random walk with and without drift. Given almost any set of conditioning variables, we find parametric specifications fail. Our findings are based on a broad entropy function of the whole distribution of variables and forecasts. We also find significant evidence of nonlinearity and/or "higher moment" influences which seriously questions the habit of forecast and model evaluation based on mean-variance criteria. Taylor rule factors may improve out of sample "forecasts" for some models and exchanges, but do not offer similar improvement for in-sample (historical) fit. We estimate models of exchange rate determination non-parametrically so as to avoid functional form issues. Taylor rule and some other variables are smoothed out, being statistically irrelevant in sample. The metric entropy tests suggest significant differences between the observed densities and their in- and out- of sample forecasts and fitted values. Much like the Diebold-Mariano approach, we are able to report statistical significance of the differences with our more general measures of forecast performance.

1 Introduction

Rational expectation hypothesis is at the core of the modern exchange rate determination models: assuming the "true" structural model of the economy is known,

E. Maasoumi (✉)
Arts and Sciences Distinguished Professor of Economics,
Emory University, Atlanta GA 30322, USA
e-mail: esfandiar.maasoumi@emory.edu

L. Bulut
Visiting Assistant Professor of Economics, Andrew Young School of Policy Studies,
Georgia State University, Atlanta GA 30303, USA
e-mail: bulut@gsu.edu

X. Chen and N. R. Swanson (eds.), *Recent Advances and Future Directions in Causality, Prediction, and Specification Analysis*, DOI: 10.1007/978-1-4614-1653-1_16,

forecasts are unbiased, uncorrelated, and efficient. In out of sample forecastabality of the *change* in spot rates, popular models seemingly fail to systematically beat a random walk based on *standard point forecast criteria*. In an influential chapter, Meese and Rogoff (1983) examined this "puzzle," and based on data from 1970s, they found that the random walk model performs as well as any estimated structural or various time series models. In other words, knowing the past, current and even one period ahead true values of exchange rate fundamentals, such as income, money supply growth rates, inflation rates, output gaps, and interest rates for two countries seemingly fails to produce better forecasts of the change in the nominal exchange rate, than simply using the current nominal exchange rate. This uncomfortable finding is known as the "Exchange rate disconnect puzzle" or the "Meese–Rogoff Puzzle."

Meese and Rogoff (1983) findings have been reexamined in the literature. One line of research reexamines different currency pairs, different time periods, real time versus revised macrodata, and different linear structural models to assess the evidence based on the first and second moments of the distribution of the forecast errors. In this line of research, until recently, different attempts had failed to show forecasting power in the short run. A few, for example, Mark (1995) and Engel et al. (2007), find better performing structural models only at horizons 2–4 years out! Cheung et al. (2005) applied a wide range of structural models and adopted different test statistics, yet failed to show that structural models consistently outperform the random walk model. Some researchers, instead of revised data, examined real-time data since it was the only available information at the time of decision making. Faust et al. (2003) found better performing structural models in out-of-sample by using fully revised data, yet they failed to outperform random walk model. Other studies extend the set of structural models by including further macro variables such as the Taylor-rule principles. Molodtsova and Papell (2009) test the out-of-sample predictive power of Taylor-rule based exchange rate models and find that those models significantly outperform the random walk model in the short horizon. Rogoff and Stavrakeva (2008), on the other hand, are critical of the findings in Molodtsova and Papell (2009); Gourinchas and Rey (2007), and Engel et al. (2007), arguing that they are not robust to alternative time windows and alternative tests. They notably speculate that this lack of robustness to alternative time windows may be due to potential nonlinearities and/or structural breaks. We agree, and would add inadequate conditioning sets and other mispecifications to the list of potential culprits. A very recent literature pioneered by Evans and Lyons (2002, 2005) incorporates the micro determinants of exchange rates (micro-structured models) into macro exchange rate models to form a "hybrid" model. In this approach, the order flows (the detail on the size, direction, and initiator of the transactions of exchange rates) are considered as signals of heterogeneous investor expectations and it is suggested that the order flows contain information on (and changing expectations of) exchange rate fundamentals that are more timely than the data releases. While there is some evidence of exchange rate predictability and forecastability of the "hybrid" model with the very high frequency data (where data on exchange rate fundamentals do not exist), at higher forecast horizons (one month or longer), the evidence based on the conventional point forecast accuracy criteria is mixed (see Berger et al. (2008) and Chinn and Moore (2011)).[1]

A second related line of research questions model specification and seeks alternative, mostly nonlinear/nonparametric, specifications to overcome the Meese and Rogoff (1983) findings. Diebold and Nason (1990) use univariate nonparametric time series methods to forecast the *conditional mean* of the spot exchange rates but fail to find better prediction performance over the random walk. Meese and Rose (1991) look for nonlinear relationship between the exchange rates and their fundamentals to minimize the potential misspecification in the linear models. They use nonparametric techniques and conclude that the poorer explanatory power of the structural models over random walk cannot be attributed to nonlinearities. This is suggestive of inadequate conditioning variables which we confirm in this chapter.

Finally, an emergent third strand in the literature questions the conventional point forecast accuracy criteria and offers some alternatives, such as the density forecast approach. In this approach, the model-based forecast distributions are compared with the true (data-driven) distribution of the actual change in exchange rate series. Were these densities to be fully characterized by second moments, as in the case of the linear/Gaussian processes, this approach would find the same results obtained with Diebold and Mariano (1995) and West (1996) type second moment tests. As for the evaluation of density forecasts, several different methods have been proposed. Diebold et al. (1998) propose to first estimate the forecast density of the model and transform it by the probability integral at each observed value over the forecast period. They suggest testing the implied i.i.d.'ness of these uniformly distributed transformed series. Clements and Smith (2000) test for the implied uniform distribution using the Kolmogorov-Smirnov statistic. In particular, Berkowitz (2001) proposes to transform Diebold et al. (1998) transformed statistics to a normal distribution to avoid the difficulties of testing for a uniform null. Although Berkowitz (2001) methodology helps understanding how well a model's predictive density approximates the predictive density of the data, it does not allow for model comparison. To solve that problem Corradi and Swanson (2006), in the spirit of Diebold and Mariano (1995), test for equal point forecast accuracy by proposing a testing strategy which tests the null of equal density forecast accuracy of two competing models. Along this line of research, and more encouragingly, Wang and Wu (2010) estimate the semiparametric interval distribution of change in exchange rates to compare their forecast interval range with random walk model. They find supporting evidence of better forecast performance of Taylor-rule based structural models over the random walk model.

The approach in this chapter encompasses the second and third strands of research highlighted above. We examine the same set of popular structural models of exchange rate determination, and compare them to a random walk with and without drift. Our criterion for assessment of closeness between distributions is a general entropy functional of such distributions. This reflects our critical view of mean squared type

[1] It might be interesting to evaluate the performance of the "hybrid" model by using the metric entropy criterion, but we leave that to future studies.

performance criteria as inadequate and/or inappropriate. Given almost any set of conditioning variables, we find parametric specifications fail by our criterion. We find significant evidence of nonlinearity and/or "higher moment" influences which seriously questions the habit of forecast and model evaluation based on mean-variance criteria. Conditioning variables, such as Taylor rule factors may improve out-of-sample "forecasts" for some models and exchanges, but do not offer uniform improvement for in-sample (historical) fit. Our findings benefit from nonparametric estimation. This is consistent with findings of nonlinear effects of fundamental and Taylor rule variables, as in this chapter, Wang and Wu (2010), and Rogoff and Stavrakeva (2008). Such findings suggest the "Meese-Rogoff puzzle" may be an artifact of the parametric specifications of the traditional models, as well as due to inordinate focus on the first two moments of the forecast distributions. The tightness of the distribution of the forecast errors reported by Wang and Wu (2010) may be accompanied by other differences in asymmetry, kurtosis, and higher order moments. This is important information in risk management. All of the potential additional effects can be picked up by broader "distribution metrics", such as "entropy" that go well beyond the variance for non-Gaussian/nonlinear processes.

The metric entropy criterion was suggested in Maasoumi and Racine (2002), and Granger et al. (2004). It is capable of contrasting whole distributions of (conditional) predictions of parametric and nonparametric models, as well as that of random walk. It serves equally well as a measure of in-sample and out-of-sample fit or model adequacy, and it can assess the (nonlinear) affinity between the actual series and their predictions obtained from various models. This same metric serves as a measure of generic "dependence" in time series, as demonstrated in Granger et al. (2004).

Our findings, being robust to functional form misspecification, forecast criteria limitations, and a large set of popular explanatory variables, indicate the parametric forms are misspecified, and no current theory provides uniformly good forecast of the distribution of the observed changes in exchange rates.

The nonparametric approach suggests Taylor rule and some other variables are smoothed out, being statistically irrelevant in sample. The metric entropy tests suggest significant difference between forecast and fitted densities, on the one hand, and densities of the corresponding observed series. We are able to report statistical significance of differences for our more general measures of forecast performance. A by-product of our work is a more complete characterization of the gains over traditional specifications obtained from nonparametric implementations and additional fundamental variables and Taylor rule effects.

1.1 Entropy Measure of Dependence for Forecast Performance

- **As a Measure of Association**

Diebold and Mariano (1995) employed a quadratic loss function and computed the squared prediction errors. They tested the null of equal predictive accuracy by estimating whether the population mean of the difference between loss differential functions of two contestant models is zero. Such testing strategy is focused on the first and second moments of functions of predictions errors, and not designed to capture differences in higher moments. Given a set of conditioning variables, conditional mean is known as the best predictor under mean squared error criterion. Here we adopt the nonparametric entropy measure of dependence, as suggested in Granger et al. (2004), to compare forecasting power of several different models. It has been documented that this metric entropy has good power in detecting dependence structure of various linear and nonlinear models. The measure is similar to the Kullback–Leibler information criteria, but unlike the latter, it satisfies the triangularity property of metrics, and is a normalized Bhattacharya-Matusita-Hellinger measure as follows:

$$S\rho_1 = \frac{1}{2}\int_{-\infty}^{\infty}\int_{-\infty}^{\infty}\left(f_1^{1/2} - f_2^{1/2}\right)^2 dadb, \tag{1}$$

where $f_1 = f(a,b)$ is a joint density and $f_2 = g(a)h(b)$ is the product of the marginal densities of the random variables a and b. Two random variables are independent if and only if $f_1 = f_2$ which implies $S\rho_1 = 0$. For continuous variables, the upper limit of the function is normalized to unity, but for discrete variables the upper limit depends on the underlying distributions (see Giannerini et al. (2011) for details). A statistically significant positive value of $S\rho_1$ implies existence of possibly nonlinear dependence/association. Theoretical properties of the cross validated, nonparametric estimation of $S\rho_1$ are examined in a number of chapter by Skaug and Tjøstheim (1996); Su and White (2008); Granger et al. (2004), and lately by Giannerini et al. (2011) under more demanding sample dependence assumptions for time series. Giannerini et al. (2011) consider both surrogate method and bootstrap resampling approaches. Bootstrap is adequate to the task at hand in this chapter, and is widely known to be a major improvement over the asymptotic approximate theory for these entropy measures.

In this chapter, we utilize this entropy-based measure of dependence for two traditionally distinct purposes: as an in-sample *goodness-of-fit* measurement, and as a test of predictive performance of alternative models. To measure the in-sample goodness-of-fit of a model i, we set $a = y_t$ and $b = \hat{y}_t^i$ $(t = 1, 2, ..., T)$, where y_t refers to observed change in nominal exchange rate, while $\hat{y}_t^i$ indicates the fitted value for y_t generated by model i. Based on existing empirical evidence, we assume that the change in nominal exchange rate is a stationary continuous random variable with a marginal density $g(y_t)$. An adequate model is expected to produce strong relationship between the actual and the fitted values of exchange rate change series. Therefore, *higher* values of $S\rho_1$ imply well-performing models with higher predictive ability, much as R^2 as a goodness of fit measure for linear models. This metric reduces to a monotonically increasing function of the correlation coefficient for linear Gaussian processes. Nothing is lost by employing this metric when correlation analysis may suffice!

Similarly, when measuring and testing *predictive performance* of model i, we set $a = y_t$ and $b = \hat{y}_t^i$ $(t = R+1, R+2, ..., T)$, where y_t refers to actual out-of-sample change in nominal exchange rate, whereas $\hat{y}_t^i$ indicates the non-recursive forecast of y_t generated by model i based on the estimates obtained from the training sample of size R.[2] The *higher* $S\rho_1$ the better the fit and forecast performance of a model.

- **As an Alternative Measure of Density**

We also use the same entropy measure to test the equality of densities for two univariate random variable a and b as suggested in Maasoumi and Racine (2002).We use the nonparametric kernel estimates of the following metric entropy statistics:

$$S\rho_2 = \frac{1}{2}\int \left(f_1^{1/2} - f_2^{1/2}\right)^2 da \tag{2}$$

but, now $f_1 = f(a)$ and $f_2 = f(b)$ are both marginal densities of the random variables a and b. As before, $a = y_t$ and $b = \hat{y}_t^i$ may indicate either the in-sample fitted values or the non-recursive forecast of y_t generated by model i. Specifically random variables y_t and $\hat{y}_t^i$ are identically distributed if and only if the marginal densities are equal. Under the null of equality, $S\rho_2 = 0$. Here the *lower* values of $S\rho_2$ indicate *better* predictive performance, or better fit.

In the following sections, we will first discuss the exchange rate forecasting methodology, then we will briefly summarize the data and the structural models considered in this chapter. Finally, we will discuss our estimation results and compare them with the traditional point forecast accuracy criterion.

2 Out-of-Sample Exchange Rate Forecasting

For each model, we construct the first 1 month ahead forecast with the first estimation window, then repeat the process by rolling the window one period ahead in the sample until all the observations are exhausted. Let s_t denote the natural logarithm of the nominal exchange rate at time t, and the change in the logged nominal exchange rate as $y_{t+1} = s_{t+1} - s_t$. If X_t is a vector of "fundamentals" at time t, a typical parametric model in our set may be represented as follows:

$$y_{t+1} = \alpha + \beta' X_t + \varepsilon_{t+1}. \tag{3}$$

In this regression equation (3), the change in the natural logarithm of exchange rates is determined by some fundamentals and unexpected shocks. Under rational expectations, the unobservable expectation of one period ahead exchange rate will be the conditional expectation implied by the structural model, assuming uncorrelated,

[2] The detailed information about the structural models and the out-of-sample forecasting methodology will be provided in the following section.

Table 1 Model description

	Model name	List of explanatory variables
Model 1:	Asymmetric taylor rule with no smoothing	$(y_{\text{gap}} - y^*_{\text{gap}})$, $(\pi - \pi^*)$, q and *a constant*
Model 2:	Symmetric taylor rule with no smoothing	$(y_{\text{gap}} - y^*_{\text{gap}})$, $(\pi - \pi^*)$, and *a constant*
Model 3:	Asymmetric taylor rule with smoothing	$(y_{\text{gap}} - y^*_{\text{gap}})$, $(\pi - \pi^*)$, q, i_{t-1}, i^*_{t-1}, and *a constant*
Model 4:	Symmetric taylor rule with smoothing	$(y_{\text{gap}} - y^*_{\text{gap}})$, $(\pi - \pi^*)$, i_{t-1}, i^*_{t-1} and *a constant*
Model 5:	Purchasing power parity model	q and *a constant*
Model 6:	Interest parity model	$(i - i*)$ and *a constant*
Model 7:	Monetary model	$(m - m^*) - (y - y^*) - s$
Model 8:	Driftless random walk	*none*
Model 9:	Random walk with a drift	*a constant*

Variable definitions	
y_{gap}	Quasi-real quadratic trending based measure of the output gap in US.
y^*_{gap}	Quasi-real quadratic trending based measure of the output gap in the foreign country.
π	Inflation rate in US.
π^*	Inflation rate in the foreign country.
p	Price level in US.
p^*	Price level in the foreign country.
q	Real exchange rate in the foreign country. It is calculated as: $q = p - p^* - s$.
i	Monthly nominal interest rate in U.S.
i_{t-1}	One-month lagged monthly interest rate in U.S.
i^*	Monthly nominal interest rate in the foreign country.
i^*_{t-1}	One-month lagged monthly interest rate in the foreign country.
m	Natural logarithm of the money supply in U.S.
m^*	Natural logarithm of the money supply in the foreign country.
y	Natural logarithm of the real GDP in U.S.
y^*	Natural logarithm of the real GDP in the foreign country.
s	Natural logarithm of the dollar price of foreign currency.
Δs	Percentage change in the Natural logarithm of the nominal spot exchange rate.

In outputgap measurement, we follow Molodtsova and Papell (2009) and calculate the potential output (quadratic trending output) by using the "quasi-real-time" data: we still use ex-post revised output data at time $t - 1$ (not the future observations) to calculate the potential output at time t, and for the following each year, we update the sample and calculate potential output at that year accordingly

and mean-zero error terms. In rolling regressions with a sample of size N, a sub-sample of size R is designated as the training or estimation sample to produce P forecasts where $N = R + P$. For example, the first R observations may be used to obtain estimates $\widehat{\alpha}$ and $\widehat{\beta}$; then the realized values of economic fundamentals at time $(t + 1)$ are employed to produce an out-of-sample forecast as follows:

Table 2 Kernel consistent model specification test results

Models	1	2	3	4	5	6	7
AUS	0.032**	0.452	0.068*	0.288	0.540	0.136	0.126
CAN	0.566	0.564	0.106	0.202	0.540	0.268	0.044**
DEN	0.362	0.544	0.030**	0.000***	0.536	0.002***	0.548
FRA	0.014**	0.008***	0.002***	0.012**	0.546	0.040**	0.008***
GER	0.810	0.456	0.048**	0.006***	0.596	0.002***	0.010**
ITL	0.074*	0.092*	0.000***	0.000***	0.582	0.020**	0.004***
JPN	0.000***	0.004***	0.000***	0.014**	0.556	0.004***	0.002***
NTH	0.556	0.118	0.002***	0.004***	0.552	0.000***	0.152
POR	0.032**	0.144	0.052*	0.294	0.546	0.526	0.032**
SWE	0.020**	0.022**	0.006***	0.000***	0.626	0.000***	0.046**
SWI	0.202	0.482	0.060*	0.058*	0.542	0.314	0.532
U.K.	0.000***	0.000***	0.022**	0.004***	0.592	0.066*	0.592

The table shows the test results for correct specification of parametric regression models as described in Hsiao et al. (2007). The numbers show the p-values at which we reject the null of correctly specified parametric model. The distribution of the test statistics is derived with 500 IID bootstrapped replications. ***, **, and * denote significance at 1%, 5%, and 10%, respectively

$$\hat{y}_{t+1} = \widehat{\alpha} + \widehat{\beta}' X_{t+1}. \tag{4}$$

The process is repeated by rolling the window by one period ahead: the first observation is dropped from the sample and $(R + 1)$th observation is added to the sample, leaving the sample size constant. This produces the new estimates of $\widehat{\alpha}$ and $\widehat{\beta}$. Eventually, P number of forecasts are produced for each model to be used for forecast comparison.

2.1 Data and the "Structural" Models

In the selection of countries, data coverage and model selection, we follow the predominant choices in the recent literature. The data is taken from Molodtsova and Papell (2009) who employed monthly data from March 1973 through December 1998 for Euro area countries (France, Germany, Italy, Netherlands, and Portugal), and through June 2006 for the remaining OECD countries (Australia, Canada, Denmark, Japan, Sweden, Switzerland, and the United Kingdom).[3] The US dollar is treated as the "home currency," and exchange rate is defined as the US Dollar price of one unit of foreign currency. An increase in the exchange rate indicates depreciation of the dollar.

The conditioning variables are total income $y_t(y_t^*)$, inflation rate $\Pi_t(\Pi_t^*)$, output gap $y_{\text{gap}}(y_{\text{gap}}^*)$, the real exchange rate $q_t(q_t^*)$, money supply $m_t(m_t^*)$, price level

[3] Meese and Rogoff (1983) also uses monthly data in their chapter, while some studies such as Engel and West (2005); Cheung et al. (2005), and Gourinchas and Rey (2007) use quarterly data.

Table 3 Cross-validated bandwidths in out-of-sample forecasts

		Cross-validated bandwidths in each rolling window			
		Bandwidths			
		Median	10th percentile	90th percentile	st. dev.
AUS	$\tilde{y}_t^{gap}$	35260.74	0.02	218779.24	0.04
	$\tilde{\Pi}_t$	1.59	0.80	5877020.38	2.54
	q_t	0.04	0.03	9925.49	0.11
	i_{t-1}	1.95	0.66	2508301.63	2.42
	i_{t-1}^*	0.88	0.44	4973632.00	2.74
CAN	$\tilde{y}_t^{gap}$	0.04	0.02	366035.50	0.03
	$\tilde{\Pi}_t$	4973061.80	1.21	26125346.44	1.36
	q_t	0.28	0.02	703888.32	0.08
	i_{t-1}	228159.48	0.54	17470521.79	2.28
	i_{t-1}^*	185809.19	1.36	310479024.80	2.58
DEN	$\tilde{y}_t^{gap}$	241385.39	0.11	1201050.51	0.06
	$\tilde{\Pi}_t$	0.91	0.45	8097023.70	1.53
	q_t	101566.07	0.08	1946581.91	0.15
	i_{t-1}	4.42	0.73	25549599.61	2.42
	i_{t-1}^*	4.71	1.62	101520853.43	2.88
FRA	$\tilde{y}_t^{gap}$	0.03	0.02	271520.01	0.04
	$\tilde{\Pi}_t$	228337.87	0.74	11918011.74	1.86
	q_t	215631.05	0.25	1050485.47	0.16
	i_{t-1}	2897456.10	1.12	46750812.45	2.84
	i_{t-1}^*	12.50	0.82	31944044.52	2.50
GER	$\tilde{y}_t^{gap}$	82145.73	0.03	410423.70	0.04
	$\tilde{\Pi}_t$	14.81	0.98	9947322.06	1.99
	q_t	64493.60	0.07	1434618.94	0.16
	i_{t-1}	2.55	0.83	11222742.85	2.84
	i_{t-1}^*	0.96	0.80	3867907.12	2.34
ITL	$\tilde{y}_t^{gap}$	39073.22	0.02	548697.67	0.04
	$\tilde{\Pi}_t$	890113.88	0.98	13898521.08	2.49
	q_t	0.26	0.03	926787.13	0.15
	i_{t-1}	2.79	1.07	17138191.42	2.84
	i_{t-1}^*	1.93	0.67	22555640.87	2.92
JPN	$\tilde{y}_t^{gap}$	0.03	0.02	148294.40	0.05
	$\tilde{\Pi}_t$	0.62	0.41	2.09	1.68
	q_t	23719.70	0.12	853226.44	0.15
	i_{t-1}	1.61	0.67	1295104.14	2.42
	i_{t-1}^*	1.01	0.64	1.76	1.81
NTH	$\tilde{y}_t^{gap}$	0.04	0.02	22294.20	0.04
	$\tilde{\Pi}_t$	1657121.24	2.41	12788187.32	2.06
	q_t	148929.61	0.24	1138899.70	0.16
	i_{t-1}	10.29	0.64	20898299.67	2.84
	i_{t-1}^*	2.48	1.06	7561953.49	2.32

(continued)

Table 3 (continued)

		Cross-validated bandwidths in each rolling window			
		Bandwidths			
		Median	10th percentile	90th percentile	st. dev.
POR	$\widetilde{y_t}^{gap}$	150939.94	0.07	632244.74	0.06
	$\widetilde{\Pi}_t$	1.97	1.49	3485564.84	3.46
	q_t	218204.39	0.23	1160393.73	0.15
	i_{t-1}	0.53	0.43	0.68	2.04
	i^*_{t-1}	8548160.95	29.25	63600482.45	3.50
SWE	$\widetilde{y_t}^{gap}$	0.04	0.02	120508.07	0.05
	$\widetilde{\Pi}_t$	348965.98	0.91	13828866.69	2.34
	q_t	37012.03	0.19	1427051.78	0.20
	i_{t-1}	6.13	0.85	12613983.53	3.18
	i^*_{t-1}	7.14	1.72	9869856.03	3.09
SWI	$\widetilde{y_t}^{gap}$	0.04	0.02	228780.81	0.04
	$\widetilde{\Pi}_t$	652660.54	0.40	18467288.02	1.55
	q_t	338518.86	0.17	1588662.72	0.15
	i_{t-1}	2.00	0.39	8179778.01	2.23
	i^*_{t-1}	3.95	0.70	22462155.95	2.00
UK	$\widetilde{y_t}^{gap}$	16759.44	0.02	297811.95	0.03
	$\widetilde{\Pi}_t$	2411331.57	1.61	13253603.52	1.76
	q_t	29224.76	0.07	818628.17	0.12
	i_{t-1}	2.22	0.67	9449292.76	2.42
	i^*_{t-1}	1.72	0.60	7189358.43	2.77

The table shows the summary statistics of the least squared cross-validated bandwidth selections for each explanatory variable of Model 3 (the largest model) in each rolling window. The last column shows the standard deviation of the regressor

$p(p^*)$, and short-term interest rates $i_t\,(i_t^*)$.[4] Nominal interest rates are defined in percentages, while all other variables are transformed by taking the natural logarithm multiplied by 100. In the original database the seasonally adjusted industrial production index is used as proxy for total income. Inflation rate is measured by the annual growth rate of monthly CPI index p_t. Output gap is measured (by using the quasi-real data) as the percentage deviation of industrial production from its quadratic trending level. Real exchange rate for the foreign country is calculated as $q_t = s_t + p_t^* - p_t$. As for the money supply, for the majority of countries with available data, M1 is used as a proxy for the quantity of money, and M2 for a few.

We estimate nine exchange rate models, Models 1–7 are the structural models extant in the literature, Model 8 is the driftless random walk model, and Model 9 is the random walk with drift. These models are not nested. An "encompassing model" is sometimes a convenient statistical construct, and may be stated as follows:

$$\Delta y_{t+1} = \alpha + \beta_1 \widetilde{y_t}^{gap} + \beta_2 \widetilde{\Pi}_t + \beta_3 q_t + \beta_4 i_{t-1} + \beta_5 i^*_{t-1} + \beta_6 \widetilde{i_t} + \beta_7 m_t^* + \varepsilon_{t+1}. \quad (5)$$

[4] Variables in parentheses denote the foreign country counterparts.

Table 4 P-values for the CW test under the null of driftless random walk

	Model 1		Model 2		Model 3		Model 4		Model 5		Model 6		Model 7		Model 9
	Lin	NP	Lin	NP	Lin	NP	Lin	NP	Lin	NP	Lin	NP	Lin	NP	Lin
AUS	−0.524	0.619	0.299	1.653	1.055	2.115	1.691	2.434	−0.801	0.082	1.551	1.992	0.199	−0.810	0.317
	0.700	0.268	0.383	0.050	0.146	0.018	0.046	0.008	0.788	0.467	0.061	0.024	0.421	0.791	0.376
CAN	2.006	−0.145	2.122	2.501	1.295	−0.964	1.657	1.431	−0.837	−2.233	1.886	1.306	1.898	1.364	0.393
	0.023	0.558	0.017	0.006	0.098	0.832	0.049	0.077	0.798	0.987	0.030	0.096	0.029	0.087	0.347
DEN	0.018	0.203	0.096	−0.515	0.119	0.489	0.589	1.185	−1.034	−0.992	−0.259	1.285	0.855	0.247	−0.920
	0.493	0.420	0.462	0.696	0.453	0.312	0.278	0.119	0.849	0.839	0.602	0.100	0.197	0.402	0.821
FRA	0.594	0.083	0.133	0.707	1.568	1.249	1.521	1.073	−0.315	−0.352	−1.194	−0.216	−0.067	2.005	−0.758
	0.277	0.467	0.447	0.240	0.059	0.107	0.065	0.142	0.624	0.638	0.883	0.585	0.527	0.023	0.775
GER	−0.317	1.281	0.222	2.147	0.168	2.650	1.210	3.370	−0.150	−0.196	0.659	0.281	−0.487	2.364	0.209
	0.624	0.101	0.412	0.017	0.433	0.004	0.114	0.000	0.560	0.578	0.255	0.389	0.687	0.010	0.417
ITL	2.568	1.580	1.714	1.487	2.773	1.883	2.741	2.288	−0.544	−0.817	0.354	0.862	−0.926	0.573	−0.433
	0.006	0.058	0.044	0.069	0.003	0.031	0.003	0.012	0.706	0.793	0.362	0.195	0.822	0.284	0.667
JPN	0.860	1.104	0.849	0.653	2.536	2.387	2.859	2.169	1.268	−0.437	2.537	2.762	0.967	1.677	1.346
	0.195	0.135	0.198	0.257	0.006	0.009	0.002	0.015	0.103	0.669	0.006	0.003	0.167	0.047	0.090
NTH	−0.915	1.002	−0.496	1.751	−0.101	1.801	0.460	2.383	−0.065	−0.051	0.947	2.816	−0.116	0.330	0.018
	0.819	0.159	0.690	0.041	0.540	0.037	0.323	0.009	0.526	0.520	0.172	0.003	0.546	0.371	0.493
POR	−0.622	−0.176	0.308	1.452	−1.319	0.966	0.389	1.631	−2.298	−2.119	0.609	0.679	0.200	−0.169	−1.298
	0.733	0.570	0.379	0.074	0.904	0.169	0.349	0.054	0.989	0.982	0.272	0.250	0.421	0.567	0.902
SWE	0.539	0.226	0.745	1.173	−0.981	0.256	−0.790	2.301	−0.561	−1.811	−1.116	0.644	0.284	0.607	−1.168
	0.295	0.411	0.228	0.121	0.836	0.399	0.785	0.011	0.712	0.964	0.867	0.260	0.388	0.272	0.878
SWI	−0.666	1.344	−0.053	1.910	0.992	2.125	1.342	2.579	−0.782	−1.066	1.996	3.143	0.893	2.475	0.382
	0.747	0.090	0.521	0.029	0.161	0.017	0.090	0.005	0.783	0.856	0.024	0.001	0.186	0.007	0.351
UK	0.885	1.171	0.751	1.031	0.490	2.109	0.370	0.610	−0.081	−0.148	0.403	0.819	−0.282	−0.453	−0.370
	0.188	0.121	0.227	0.152	0.312	0.018	0.356	0.271	0.532	0.559	0.344	0.207	0.611	0.674	0.644

The Table shows the Clark and West (CW) test results (p-values are in the second rows) for the OLS and NP out-of-sample forecasts for alternative exchange rate models under the null of driftless random walk. We use rolling regression method with a window of 120 observations. In the NP forecasts, we compute the least-squares cross-validated bandwidths for the local linear estimators. For each currency model pair, the first data shows the CW test statistics while the second data shows the p-values. CW assumes two models compared are nested, under the null the exchange rate follows a driftless RW. The limiting distribution of the CW under the null is standard normal

For any variable x, we denote by $\widetilde{x}$ the fundamental variable x in the home country (United States), minus the fundamental variable x^* in the foreign country (such that $\widetilde{x} = x - x^*$). $m_t^* = (m_t - m_t^*) - (y_t - y_t^*) - s_t$ refers to the predictor in the monetary model. Each parametric model may be viewed as a restricted form of the this artificial comprehensive form.

Table 1 in the appendix summarizes these models. Model 1 is the Taylor rule model examined in Wang and Wu (2010) as their benchmark. It is asymmetric with no smoothing. Models 2–4 are also Taylor rule models studied in Molodtsova and Papell (2009). Model 2 is the constrained (symmetric) Taylor rule that assumes PPP, Model 3 is the smoothing Taylor rule, and Model 4 is the constrained (symmetric) smoothing Taylor rule model where the lagged value of interest rate is included to control for the potential interest rate smoothing affect. Model 5 is the PPP model with a single variable q_t. Model 6 is the uncovered interest parity model, and Model 7 is the monetary model.[5]

2.2 Evaluating Point Forecasts

The literature does the out-of-sample forecast comparison by comparing the prediction error implied by the structural model with the one implied by the benchmark model; here in our chapter, we will use both the driftless random walk (Model 8) and random walk with drift (Model 9) for model comparison. 2-state markov-switching model is commonly used in the literature to control for long periods of appreciations and depreciations in nominal exchange rates. Instead, we follow a strategy which can be characterized as a P-period markov-switching model when the model produces P out-of-sample forecasts. In other words, we define the drift in each estimation window as the mean of the first differences of the actual exchange rates in the training sample.

Following the methodology of Diebold and Mariano (1995) and West (1996), we first evaluate the out-of-sample performance of the models based on the mean-squared prediction error (MSPE) comparison. In this approach, the quadratic loss functions for the structural model i and the benchmark model b are defined as follows:

$$L(y_t^i) = (y_t - \hat{y}_t^i)^2, \qquad L(y_t^b) = (y_t - \hat{y}_t^b)^2, \tag{6}$$

where y_t is the actual series and $\hat{y}_t^i$ and $\hat{y}_t^b$ are the forecasts obtained from the structural model i and the benchmark model b, respectively. The forecast accuracy

[5] See Molodtsova and Papell (2009) and Wang and Wu (2010) for the derivation of the models. A specification search approach to these models may be a worthy topic of research. The appropriate approach in that setting would be the data snooping techniques proposed by White (2000) in which no model may be correctly specified. This realism is an enduring aspect of techniques developed by Hal White. The object of inference in such settings would be the "pseudo parameters" which are afforded a compelling and clear definition based on entropy concepts such as the ones employed in this chapter.

Table 5 *P*-values for the CW test under the null of random walk with a drift

	Model 1		Model 2		Model 3		Model 4		Model 5		Model 6		Model 7		Model 8
	Lin	NP	Lin	NP	Lin	NP	Lin	NP	Lin	NP	Lin	NP	Lin	NP	Lin
AUS	−0.527	0.363	−0.014	1.394	1.225	2.078	1.684	2.446	−1.631	−0.133	1.480	2.039	−0.343	−0.900	1.404
	0.701	0.359	0.505	0.082	0.111	0.019	0.047	0.008	0.948	0.553	0.070	0.021	0.634	0.815	0.081
CAN	2.407	0.134	2.335	2.697	1.957	−0.932	1.939	1.453	−0.281	−1.737	2.353	1.545	1.812	1.282	1.804
	0.008	0.447	0.010	0.004	0.026	0.824	0.027	0.074	0.610	0.958	0.010	0.062	0.036	0.100	0.036
DEN	0.492	0.686	0.892	0.123	0.619	0.943	1.322	1.402	−0.521	−0.711	−0.278	2.324	1.290	0.517	2.518
	0.312	0.246	0.187	0.451	0.268	0.173	0.094	0.081	0.699	0.761	0.610	0.010	0.099	0.303	0.006
FRA	1.770	1.038	1.383	1.506	2.359	1.325	2.184	1.145	0.111	0.082	−0.934	0.550	0.420	2.138	2.304
	0.039	0.150	0.084	0.067	0.010	0.093	0.015	0.127	0.456	0.468	0.824	0.291	0.338	0.017	0.011
GER	0.259	1.217	0.349	2.221	0.281	2.876	1.095	3.393	0.543	0.628	0.338	0.215	0.324	2.356	1.178
	0.398	0.113	0.364	0.014	0.390	0.002	0.137	0.000	0.294	0.265	0.368	0.415	0.373	0.010	0.120
ITL	3.264	1.982	2.641	1.846	3.293	2.054	3.549	2.630	−0.370	−0.800	1.025	1.352	0.821	1.532	2.575
	0.001	0.024	0.004	0.033	0.001	0.021	0.000	0.005	0.644	0.788	0.153	0.089	0.207	0.064	0.005
JPN	−0.033	0.543	−0.388	−0.229	2.013	2.136	2.505	1.849	0.630	−0.739	1.880	2.437	0.201	1.042	0.709
	0.513	0.294	0.651	0.591	0.023	0.017	0.006	0.033	0.264	0.770	0.031	0.008	0.420	0.149	0.239
NTH	−0.236	1.164	−0.767	1.693	−0.281	1.656	−0.005	2.465	0.570	0.653	0.642	2.872	0.336	0.548	1.358
	0.593	0.123	0.778	0.046	0.611	0.050	0.502	0.007	0.285	0.257	0.261	0.002	0.369	0.292	0.088
POR	2.352	2.265	2.490	3.586	−1.103	0.701	−0.338	1.247	−0.526	−0.383	−0.287	−0.155	−0.133	−0.482	4.634
	0.010	0.012	0.007	0.000	0.863	0.243	0.632	0.108	0.700	0.649	0.613	0.561	0.553	0.684	0.000
SWE	1.486	0.637	1.489	1.271	−0.868	0.792	−0.522	2.685	−0.269	−1.355	−0.699	0.860	1.081	1.275	3.246
	0.069	0.262	0.069	0.102	0.807	0.215	0.699	0.004	0.606	0.912	0.758	0.195	0.140	0.102	0.001
SWI	−0.578	1.129	−0.426	1.818	0.758	1.916	0.857	2.516	0.004	−0.201	1.537	2.905	0.458	2.286	1.040
	0.718	0.130	0.665	0.035	0.225	0.028	0.196	0.006	0.498	0.580	0.063	0.002	0.324	0.012	0.150
UK	1.291	1.235	1.144	1.034	0.944	2.279	0.948	0.751	0.296	0.044	0.924	1.350	0.146	−0.236	1.391
	0.099	0.109	0.127	0.151	0.173	0.012	0.172	0.227	0.384	0.482	0.178	0.089	0.442	0.593	0.083

The Table shows the Clark and West (CW) test results for the OLS and NP out-of-sample forecasts for alternative exchange rate models under the null of random walk with a drift model (we allow drift to change in every forecast window). We use rolling regression method with a window of 120 observations. In the NP forecasts, we compute the least-squares cross-validated bandwidths for the local linear estimators. For each currency model pair, the first row shows the CW test statistics while the second row shows the p-values. The limiting distribution of the CW under the null is standard normal

Table 6 S-rho 1 ($S\rho_1$) Measure of goodness of fit: In-sample NP fits versus the actual series

Models	1	2	3	4	5	6	7
AUS	0.019	0.011	0.181	0.024	0.026	0.014	0.018
	0.000	0.016	0.000	0.000	0.000	0.006	0.094
CAN	0.021	0.007	0.034	0.014	0.011	0.011	0.010
	0.000	0.024	0.000	0.000	0.068	0.116	0.000
DEN	0.015	0.005	0.024	0.016	0.010	0.011	0.008
	0.000	0.546	0.000	0.000	0.264	0.000	0.572
FRA	0.016	0.018	0.034	0.016	0.009	0.012	0.017
	0.000	0.096	0.000	0.000	0.182	0.472	0.000
GER	0.019	0.018	0.042	0.018	0.016	0.012	0.019
	0.000	0.000	0.000	0.000	0.386	0.158	0.000
ITL	0.024	0.019	0.084	0.049	0.010	0.016	0.018
	0.000	0.000	0.000	0.000	0.006	0.280	0.000
JPN	0.010	0.007	0.034	0.018	0.011	0.021	0.047
	0.000	0.002	0.000	0.000	0.026	0.000	0.006
NTH	0.012	0.015	0.034	0.038	0.012	0.011	0.011
	0.140	0.000	0.000	0.000	0.070	0.000	0.448
POR	0.023	0.014	0.108	0.041	0.024	0.011	0.035
	0.000	0.000	0.000	0.000	0.268	0.174	0.752
SWE	0.015	0.013	0.021	0.042	0.010	0.007	0.000
	0.000	0.000	0.000	0.000	0.546	0.000	0.000
SWI	0.030	0.034	0.032	0.060	0.010	0.014	0.010
	0.000	0.000	0.000	0.000	0.052	0.000	0.520
UK	0.030	0.022	0.088	0.036	0.010	0.016	0.014
	0.000	0.000	0.000	0.000	0.002	0.000	0.124

The first row for each country gives the integral version of the nonparametric metric entropy $S\rho_1$ for testing pairwise nonlinear dependence between the densities of the actual series and the NP fits in-sample. The second row shows the p-values generated with 500 bootstrap replications. Under the null, actual series and the in-sample NP fits are independent, hence the integrated value of the dependence matrix $S\rho_1$ (Maasoumi and Racine 2002) takes the value of zero

testing is based on whether the population mean of the loss differential series d_t is zero where:

$$d_t = L(y_t^b) - L(y_t^i) = (y_t - \hat{y}_t^b)^2 - (y_t - \hat{y}_t^i)^2. \tag{7}$$

In Diebold and Mariano (1995) and West (1996), the null of equal predictive accuracy is:

$$H_0 : E[d_t] = E[L(y_t^b) - L(y_t^i)] = \text{MSPE}^b - \text{MSPE}^i = 0. \tag{8}$$

Clark and McCracken (2001) show that when comparing nested models, Diebold and Mariano (1995) test statistics will be non-normal and the use of standard critical values results in poorly sized tests. Accordingly, Clark and West (2006) propose a corrected Diebold-Mariano statistic which takes into account the fact that under the null, MSPE of the structural model and the benchmark model are not the same. If the null is true, estimation of the structural model produces a noisy estimate

Table 7 S-rho 1 ($S\rho_1$) Measure of predictability:
Out-of-sample NP forecasts versus the actual series

Models	1	2	3	4	5	6	7	9
AUS	0.011	0.005	0.008	0.005	0.015	0.020	0.010	0.016
	0.888	0.906	0.640	0.380	0.650	0.000	0.094	0.126
CAN	0.007	0.005	0.008	0.010	0.002	0.013	0.007	0.012
	0.342	0.164	0.036	0.390	0.258	0.030	0.014	0.174
DEN	0.008	0.006	0.005	0.003	0.008	0.006	0.004	0.011
	0.110	0.146	0.942	0.882	0.328	0.504	0.652	0.768
FRA	0.005	0.005	0.005	0.007	0.006	0.004	0.008	0.018
	0.654	0.632	0.022	0.460	0.704	0.916	0.134	0.344
GER	0.005	0.010	0.011	0.016	0.011	0.004	0.013	0.008
	0.342	0.048	0.088	0.012	0.978	0.312	0.006	0.852
ITL	0.010	0.006	0.009	0.010	0.011	0.014	0.008	0.012
	0.026	0.020	0.008	0.006	0.100	0.000	0.172	0.090
JPN	0.009	0.004	0.004	0.008	0.003	0.007	0.006	0.017
	0.162	0.892	0.274	0.230	0.172	0.024	0.314	0.166
NTH	0.005	0.006	0.006	0.006	0.009	0.007	0.004	0.007
	0.498	0.400	0.736	0.178	0.930	0.340	0.876	0.786
POR	0.007	0.007	0.010	0.007	0.021	0.027	0.014	0.023
	0.196	0.290	0.764	0.864	0.018	0.412	0.664	0.018
SWE	0.006	0.009	0.011	0.008	0.011	0.006	0.004	0.012
	0.138	0.010	0.034	0.016	0.102	0.006	0.910	0.262
SWI	0.008	0.009	0.008	0.003	0.006	0.011	0.012	0.014
	0.898	0.356	0.110	0.336	0.882	0.096	0.302	0.118
UK	0.004	0.006	0.006	0.010	0.009	0.014	0.002	0.015
	0.636	0.018	0.366	0.164	0.020	0.014	0.448	0.032

The first row for each country gives the integral version of the nonparametric metric entropy $S\rho_1$ for testing pairwise nonlinear dependence between the densities of the actual series and the NP out-of-sample forecasts. The second row shows the p-values generated with 500 bootstrap replications. Under the null, actual series and the out-of-sample NP forecasts are independent, hence the integrated value of the dependence matrix $S\rho_1$ (Maasoumi and Racine 2002) takes the value of zero

of the parameter, supposed to be zero in population, increasing the MSPE in the sample. They suggest an adjusted MSPE for the alternative model which is adjusted downwards to have equal MSPEs under the null. Accordingly, the loss differential function can be adjusted as follows:

$$d - \text{adj}_t = L(y_t^b) - L(y_t^i) - \text{adj} = (y_t - \hat{y}_t^b)^2 - (y_t - \hat{y}_t^i)^2 - (\hat{y}_t^b - \hat{y}_t^i)^2. \quad (9)$$

Clark and West (2006) test if the population mean of the adjusted series $d - adj_t$ is zero, based on the following statistic:

$$\text{CW} = \frac{\widetilde{d}}{(\widehat{\text{avar}}(\widetilde{d}))^{1/2}} = \frac{\text{MSPE}^b - \text{MSPE}^i_{\text{adj}}}{(\widehat{\text{avar}}(\text{MSPE}^b - \text{MSPE}^i_{\text{adj}}))^{1/2}}, \quad (10)$$

Table 8 S-rho 2 ($S\rho_2$): Metric Entropy Density Equality Test Results for the Fitted (in-sample) Values

Models	1	2	3	4	5	6	7
AUS	0.257*	0.549*	0.023*	0.188*	0.552*	0.453*	0.607*
CAN	0.273*	0.517*	0.182*	0.344*	0.635*	0.571*	0.668*
DEN	0.380*	0.703*	0.241*	0.360*	0.721*	0.551*	0.788*
FRA	0.325*	0.581*	0.177*	0.347*	0.685*	0.714*	0.458*
GER	0.336*	0.353*	0.144*	0.364*	0.671*	0.638*	0.433*
ITL	0.269*	0.273*	0.096*	0.169*	0.780*	0.712*	0.452*
JPN	0.380*	0.451*	0.144*	0.289*	0.712*	0.468*	0.541*
NTH	0.662*	0.397*	0.224*	0.268*	0.667*	0.451*	0.830*
POR	0.192*	0.291*	0.039*	0.185*	0.625*	0.584*	0.627*
SWE	0.408*	0.407*	0.246*	0.128*	0.659*	0.588*	0.632*
SWI	0.253*	0.243*	0.206*	0.138*	0.590*	0.534*	0.788*
UK	0.195*	0.299*	0.082*	0.218*	0.680*	0.533*	0.742*

The table shows the consistent univariate density difference metric entropy test statistics for the NP fitted values (in-sample) and the actual series. Under the null of equality of densities, * denote significance at 1 %. The null distribution is obtained with 500 bootstrap replications

where $\widetilde{d}$ refers to mean of $d - \text{adj}_t$, and $\text{MSPE}^i_{\text{adj}}$ refers to MSPE for the structural model adjusted for the bias. If the CW test statistics is significantly positive, one may conclude that the structural model outperforms the random walk model. Clark and West (2006) suggest standard normal critical values for inference in comparing these nested models.[6]

Note that, these procedures assume an encompassing form that correctly nests the competing models. Misspecifications of functional form and/or omitted variables are not accommodated. We find evidence for both types of misspecification. To see this, consider Table 2 in which the parametric models are subjected to the nonparametric specification test proposed by Hsiao et al. (2007). Note that for each model, this test takes the conditioning variables as given. But cross validation in NP estimation is indeed capable of identifying irrelevant variables (see Table 3 in the appendix on full sample smoothing of the largest model, Model 3, through least-square cross validated bandwidth selection).

As can be seen from Table 2 p-values, most parametric model-currency combinations are rejected. Only Model 5, with a single variable q, is generally parametrically (linearly) well-specified! Additional variables appear to have nonlinear effects, to various degrees, for different exchange rates. In relative terms, the Symmetric Taylor rule models with no smoothing (Model 2) do better in sample. Addition of linear interest rate smoothing variables (in Models 3 and 4) tends to be rejected.

A shed further light on the possibility of irrelevant explanatory variables, we examine more closely a nonparametric estimation of the largest model above, Model 3

[6] Rogoff and Stavrakeva (2008) argue that CW test statistics cannot be used to evaluate forecasting performance as it is not testing the null of equal predictive accuracy, hence they suggest to use bootstrapped critical values. There is less evidence in favor of Taylor-rule based models when CW test statistics with bootstrapped critical values are used.

(Asymmetric Taylor Rule with no smoothing), which contains the majority of explanatory variables in any of the 7 models. Smoothing with cross validation in kernel estimation is known to be able to smooth out irrelevant regressors; see Li and Racine 2007, Chap. 4. Table 3 in the appendix supports the following inferences: Taylor rule variables appear to be insignificant in the full sample, when all the conditioning variables are considered together! Output gap differences, inflation differences, and real exchange rates are smoothed out in at least 5 currencies for the full sample (not-shown in the appendix) and in at least half of the currencies for the rolling regressions. While irrelevant variables may not generally induce bias or inconsistency in estimation, they do increase uncertainty, be it through MSPEs (as observed in the CW tests), and as will be seen in our metric entropy examination of the whole forecast distribution. Combined with the parametric tests in Table 2, it would seem that many of these models suffer from parametric misspecifications, as well as inappropriate set of conditioning variables. In this setting one has to seriously question the propriety of the conditional mean forecasting paradigm based on the mean squared error assessments.

With above caveat in mind, in Table 4, we report the CW test statistics and p-values for each model and currency when the benchmark model is the driftless random walk. This is done to provide a benchmark for what can be learned from our broader distribution metrics. For 1-month ahead forecasts of exchange rates changes, the following observations are indicated:

(a) Neither OLS nor NP forecasts provide enough evidence in favor of the exchange rate models 1 (Asymmetric Taylor Rule with no smoothing) and 5 (PPP); (b) With NP out-of-sample forecasting, there is some evidence in favor of models for five currencies in Models 2 and 3, and for four currencies in Models 4 and 7 where OLS estimates did not do well; (c) For Model 3, only NP forecasts provide favorable evidence for five currencies (Australian Dollar, British Pound, Deutsche Mark, Dutch Guilder, and Swiss Franc), all of which exhibit specification problems (see Table 2). For Model 4, with NP forecasts, there is evidence in favor for four currencies, three of which involve specification issues. A similar pattern is present in the rest of the models except Models 1 and 2; (d) Out of 15 currency–model pairs where both OLS and NP forecasts produce favorable results, nine cases have parametric specification problems. This does not support the idea that NP estimation is a panacea for prediction from misspecified models. Out of 20 currency-model pairs where we have evidence in favor of some NP empirical exchange rate models, we reject the null of parametric specification in 12 cases. So, NP forecasts tend to produce better results in favor of the exchange rate models relative to a driftless random walk; (e) Only for the Japanese yen, we see evidence in favor of the random walk with drift against driftless random walk. This suggests a constant growth in that exchange series.

In Table 5 the CW test results are given with the null of a random walk with drift. In CW test of equal predictability of two nested models, under the null the series follows a martingale difference against the alternative that the series is linearly predictable. However, Clark and West (2006) argue that the same asymptotic distribution critical values can be applied even for nonlinear and Markov Switching models. Nikolsko-Rzhevskyy and Prodan (2011) also show that their simulation results imply properly

Table 9 S-rho 2 ($S\rho_2$): Metric entropy density equality test results for forecasted (out-of-sample) values

PANEL-A: Metric entropy density equality test Statistics (NP Forecasts vs. Actual series)

Models	1	2	3	4	5	6	7
AUS	0.063*	0.206*	0.025*	0.040*	0.507*	0.279*	0.200*
CAN	0.188*	0.284*	0.086*	0.143*	0.523*	0.338*	0.287*
DEN	0.166*	0.350*	0.080*	0.119*	0.448*	0.425*	0.218*
FRA	0.215*	0.270*	0.103*	0.115*	0.424*	0.335*	0.127*
GER	0.201*	0.220*	0.075*	0.071*	0.506*	0.241*	0.161*
ITL	0.195*	0.202*	0.090*	0.114*	0.477*	0.490*	0.235*
JPN	0.131*	0.151*	0.021*	0.027*	0.575*	0.193*	0.178*
NTH	0.223*	0.206*	0.113*	0.120*	0.483*	0.239*	0.310*
POR	0.163*	0.157*	0.083*	0.082*	0.405*	0.569*	0.257*
SWE	0.147*	0.173*	0.066*	0.078*	0.480*	0.289*	0.309*
SWI	0.057*	0.144*	0.023*	0.046*	0.518*	0.296*	0.193*
UK	0.168*	0.338*	0.078*	0.125*	0.489*	0.327*	0.277*

PANEL-B: Relative $S\rho_2$ against random walk with a drift null in out-of-sample forecasting

Models	1	2	3	4	5	6	7
AUS	0.097	0.318	0.039	0.062	0.784	0.431	0.308
CAN	0.302	0.457	0.138	0.230	0.841	0.543	0.461
DEN	0.278	0.586	0.134	0.199	0.750	0.712	0.364
FRA	0.394	0.495	0.189	0.211	0.777	0.614	0.233
GER	0.312	0.342	0.116	0.110	0.786	0.374	0.251
ITL	0.329	0.341	0.152	0.193	0.806	0.828	0.396
JPN	0.231	0.266	0.037	0.048	1.014	0.340	0.314
NTH	0.356	0.329	0.180	0.191	0.770	0.381	0.494
POR	0.331	0.319	0.169	0.167	0.823	1.157	0.523
SWE	0.236	0.277	0.106	0.125	0.769	0.463	0.495
SWI	0.087	0.219	0.035	0.070	0.788	0.451	0.294
UK	0.271	0.546	0.126	0.202	0.790	0.528	0.448

Panel-A shows the consistent univariate density difference metric entropy test statistics for the NP forecasted values (out-of-sample) and the actual series. Under the null of equality of densities ($S\rho_2 = 0$), * *denote significance at 1 %. The null distribution is obtained with 500 bootstrap replications. Panel-B shows, in out-of-sample forecasting, the ratio of the integrated value of the metric entropy measure of univariate density differences, Srho-2 ($S\rho_2$), for each model to the ($S\rho_2$) for the benchmark (random walk drift) model. Higher Srho-2 measures imply lower predictive powers. Therefore, a ratio less than 1 implies that structural model out-predicts the null (random walk with a drift) model*

sized CW test in the case of the nonlinear models. Therefore, we use the asymptotic normal critical values. We allow drift to change for every forecast window. In the NP forecasts, we compute the least-squares cross-validated bandwidths for the local linear estimators. For each currency model pair, the first entry shows the CW statistics while the one below it is the p-value. The first columns are parametric (OLS), the second columns are NP values. Our results show that random walk with drift model outperforms the driftless random walk model in 3 out of 12 currencies.

Table 10 S-rho 1 ($S\rho_1$) Measure of goodness of fit: In-sample OLS fits versus the actual series

Models	1	2	3	4	5	6	7
AUS	0.016	0.017	0.011	0.010	0.026	0.013	0.025
	0.000	0.020	0.002	0.008	0.000	0.002	0.016
CAN	0.008	0.007	0.008	0.009	0.011	0.011	0.019
	0.014	0.024	0.000	0.000	0.068	0.084	0.002
DEN	0.007	0.005	0.007	0.008	0.010	0.014	0.008
	0.102	0.546	0.000	0.000	0.264	0.008	0.572
FRA	0.010	0.011	0.013	0.018	0.009	0.015	0.010
	0.066	0.302	0.012	0.002	0.182	0.266	0.332
GER	0.008	0.008	0.007	0.010	0.016	0.010	0.014
	0.070	0.022	0.002	0.000	0.386	0.008	0.004
ITL	0.010	0.015	0.010	0.012	0.010	0.006	0.021
	0.002	0.014	0.002	0.046	0.006	0.334	0.000
JPN	0.009	0.010	0.014	0.010	0.011	0.018	0.012
	0.034	0.636	0.000	0.000	0.026	0.000	0.068
NTH	0.012	0.009	0.008	0.008	0.012	0.013	0.009
	0.142	0.132	0.050	0.090	0.070	0.000	0.660
POR	0.009	0.010	0.012	0.013	0.024	0.011	0.037
	0.002	0.004	0.058	0.206	0.268	0.174	0.366
SWE	0.010	0.006	0.004	0.004	0.010	0.004	0.014
	0.058	0.142	0.000	0.000	0.546	0.000	0.032
SWI	0.009	0.008	0.009	0.015	0.010	0.016	0.010
	0.062	0.364	0.014	0.000	0.052	0.034	0.520
UK	0.014	0.012	0.007	0.010	0.010	0.013	0.013
	0.006	0.008	0.002	0.000	0.002	0.000	0.120

The first row for each country gives the integral version of the nonparametric metric entropy $S\rho_1$ for testing pairwise nonlinear dependence between the densities of the actual series and the OLS fits in-sample. The second row shows the p-values generated with 500 bootstrap replications. Under the null, actual series and the in-sample OLS fits are independent, hence the integrated value of the dependence matrix $S\rho_1$ (Maasoumi and Racine 2002) takes the value of zero

According to the results in Table 5, when the null is a random walk with a drift, parametric, and NP forecasts reach the same conclusion (in favor of the empirical models) more than the case where the null is a driftless random walk. One noteworthy finding is that, similar to the results in Table 4, out of 21 currency-model pairs where we have evidence in favor of the NP models, we reject the null of parametric models in 16 cases. So, at times where we have a model specification problem, NP forecasts tend to produce better results in favor of exchange rate models against the null of random walk with drift.

3 Constructing and Evaluating Density Forecasts

In estimating $S\rho_1$, we use Guassian kernel density estimates of the marginal density functions for the actual series $g(y_t)$, the in-sample fitted values for each structural model $h(\hat{y}_t^i)(i = 1, 2, .., 7)$, and the bivariate density of the actual and fitted values

Table 11 S-rho 1 ($S\rho_1$) Measure of predictability: Out-of-sample OLS forecasts versus the actual series

Models	1	2	3	4	5	6	7	9
AUS	0.009	0.019	0.007	0.012	0.011	0.013	0.014	0.016
	0.256	0.800	0.262	0.098	0.336	0.016	0.014	0.126
CAN	0.011	0.012	0.009	0.009	0.008	0.014	0.011	0.012
	0.026	0.108	0.080	0.076	0.346	0.024	0.030	0.174
DEN	0.005	0.009	0.005	0.005	0.009	0.009	0.007	0.011
	0.696	0.476	0.126	0.062	0.446	0.446	0.072	0.768
FRA	0.005	0.011	0.008	0.010	0.015	0.015	0.007	0.018
	0.478	0.174	0.338	0.086	0.830	0.008	0.832	0.344
GER	0.006	0.008	0.007	0.007	0.012	0.011	0.008	0.008
	0.506	0.360	0.140	0.120	0.986	0.226	0.146	0.852
ITL	0.011	0.014	0.010	0.012	0.011	0.031	0.012	0.012
	0.030	0.070	0.000	0.000	0.024	0.000	0.106	0.090
JPN	0.007	0.010	0.010	0.011	0.011	0.012	0.011	0.017
	0.346	0.114	0.018	0.006	0.004	0.000	0.018	0.166
NTH	0.008	0.016	0.005	0.010	0.011	0.013	0.010	0.007
	0.258	0.534	0.434	0.222	0.970	0.006	0.230	0.786
POR	0.014	0.015	0.016	0.022	0.020	0.024	0.023	0.023
	0.100	0.012	0.264	0.350	0.008	0.278	0.428	0.018
SWE	0.011	0.007	0.008	0.009	0.015	0.003	0.013	0.012
	0.022	0.054	0.020	0.024	0.138	0.184	0.134	0.262
SWI	0.007	0.007	0.007	0.014	0.015	0.013	0.012	0.014
	0.848	0.920	0.080	0.106	0.802	0.120	0.750	0.118
UK	0.007	0.008	0.008	0.015	0.012	0.013	0.017	0.015
	0.150	0.362	0.030	0.150	0.000	0.002	0.010	0.032

The first row for each country gives the integral version of the nonparametric metric entropy $S\rho_1$ for testing pairwise nonlinear dependence between the densities of the actual series and the OLS out-of-sample forecasts. The second row shows the p-values generated with 500 bootstrap replications. Under the null, actual series, and the out-of-sample OLS forecasts are independent, hence the integrated value of the dependence matrix $S\rho_1$ Maasoumi and Racine 2002 takes the value of zero

$f(y_t, \hat{y}_t^i)$. Least-squares cross-validation is employed to select the optimal bandwidth. Results are shown in Table 6.[7] As stated earlier, this is a "goodness of fit" indicator of general dependence, comparable to "R^2" assessments of "association" in linear models. The higher the values of the $S\rho_1$ the better is the in-sample and out-of-sample performance of a model. The critical levels under the null were generated by bootstrap methods as described in the NP package in R (see Hayfield and Racine (2008)).

Only Models 3 and 4 perform consistently well across different currencies, and only Australian Dollar and Japanese Yen can be consistently predicted well by all models. We do find the fitted values are statistically significantly "related" with the actual series in more than half of the currencies. Specifically, Model 3, Constrained

[7] Metric entropy measurements are done in R by using the np package (Hayfield and Racine (2008))

Table 12 S-rho 2 ($S\rho_2$): Metric entropy density equality test results for the OLS fitted (in-sample) and forecasted (out-of-sample) values

PANEL-A: S-rho 2 ($S\rho_2$): Metric entropy density equality test Results for the OLS fitted (in-sample) values

Models	1	2	3	4	5	6	7
AUS	0.464*	0.547*	0.374*	0.377*	0.552*	0.570*	0.622*
CAN	0.507*	0.517*	0.420*	0.445*	0.635*	0.497*	0.560*
DEN	0.689*	0.703*	0.437*	0.464*	0.721*	0.602*	0.788*
FRA	0.479*	0.602*	0.441*	0.498*	0.685*	0.649*	0.960*
GER	0.579*	0.577*	0.420*	0.466*	0.671*	0.686*	0.665*
ITL	0.440*	0.559*	0.365*	0.510*	0.780*	0.718*	0.622*
JPN	0.563*	0.649*	0.341*	0.386*	0.712*	0.436*	0.706*
NTH	0.662*	0.786*	0.469*	0.569*	0.667*	0.546*	0.930*
POR	0.353*	0.375*	0.396*	0.483*	0.625*	0.584*	0.622*
SWE	0.652*	0.718*	0.399*	0.396*	0.659*	0.741*	0.853*
SWI	0.580*	0.674*	0.431*	0.506*	0.590*	0.527*	0.788*
UK	0.510*	0.553*	0.390*	0.443*	0.680*	0.537*	0.742*

PANEL-B: S-rho 2 ($S\rho_2$): Metric entropy density equality test Results for the OLS forecasted (out-of-sample) values

Models	1	2	3	4	5	6	7	9
AUS	0.320*	0.448*	0.230*	0.278*	0.550*	0.358*	0.487*	0.647*
CAN	0.355*	0.392*	0.314*	0.284*	0.553*	0.476*	0.391*	0.622*
DEN	0.339*	0.439*	0.305*	0.334*	0.484*	0.485*	0.338*	0.597*
FRA	0.335*	0.439*	0.328*	0.299*	0.441*	0.526*	0.450*	0.546*
GER	0.325*	0.426*	0.316*	0.293*	0.527*	0.399*	0.320*	0.644*
ITL	0.327*	0.306*	0.245*	0.272*	0.479*	0.426*	0.349*	0.592*
JPN	0.282*	0.276*	0.220*	0.168*	0.611*	0.339*	0.272*	0.567*
NTH	0.411*	0.454*	0.332*	0.305*	0.492*	0.331*	0.501*	0.627*
POR	0.339*	0.328*	0.438*	0.375*	0.397*	0.571*	0.500*	0.492*
SWE	0.334*	0.309*	0.279*	0.275*	0.496*	0.418*	0.421*	0.624*
SWI	0.364*	0.412*	0.268*	0.235*	0.544*	0.419*	0.332*	0.657*
UK	0.264*	0.376*	0.221*	0.275*	0.493*	0.370*	0.432*	0.619*

Panel-A shows the consistent univariate density difference metric entropy test statistics for the OLS fitted values (in-sample) and the actual series. Panel-B shows the consistent univariate density difference metric entropy test statistics for the OLS forecasted values (out-of-sample) and the actual series. Under the null of equality of densities ($S\rho_2 = 0$), * denote significance at 1 %. The null distribution is obtained with 500 bootstrap replications

(Asymmetric) smoothing Taylor-rule model, is the best performing as it produces significant relation with the actual series for all currencies, having the highest dependence in 8 out of 12 currencies.

To consider the performance of the random walk models with or without drift, we note that these models have unique values for $S\rho_1$. A driftless random walk (RW) model suggests $y_{t+1} = \varepsilon_{t+1}$, predicting a zero change. On the other hand, the RW model with drift, Model 9, is $y_{t+1} = c + \varepsilon_{t+1}$ where c is a constant. For each period, it will predict c as its forecast. The marginal density functions for RW models are thus degenerate. Accordingly, the bivariate density of the actual values and the forecasts from RW models will be the marginal density function for the actual series. Therefore $S\rho_1 = 0$ for RW models. Consequently, the rejection of the null hypothesis of "independence" with the entropy metric constitutes a rejection of the random walk hypothesis, supporting the inference that the models with statistically significant non-zero $S\rho_1$ perform better than the random walk model. And the findings indicate that, quite a few models for each currency do a better job than the random walk model in terms of our general in-sample goodness of fit criteria, especially so when the models are estimated nonparametrically.

Table 7 shows the out-of-sample predictive performance of alternative models. While there are a few model-currency pairs which suggest some predictability, these results indicate a generally poor in-and out-of-sample association between the actual series and the forecast values from these models. Very few of these values are significantly larger than zero. The fact that some of these distributions may have lower second moments, when suggested by the CW type tests, is not comforting, given significant evidence of higher order differences between the series and its forecasts.

In Table 7 where the higher moment effects are considered, we find that the performance of the structural models against the driftless random walk model improves significantly. We find that for those models where CW test has failed to show a better performance, metric entropy $S\rho_1$ values show that, out of 12 countries, structural models outperform the random walk model in three currencies for Models 2, 5, and 6, and in two currencies for Models 3, 4, and 7.

By including higher moment effects, our entropy-based nonparametric $S\rho_1$ statistic reveals that the RW with drift does even better against the linear models compared with the assessments based on the traditional second moment tests, see Table 7: for Italy, RW with drift has higher pairwise relation with the actual series than five out of six well-performing models. For Portugal, RW with drift produces higher pairwise relation with the actual series than the single well-performing structural model. Finally, for the UK, RW with drift has the highest pairwise relation with the observed series over the three well-performing models.

3.1 Density of Forecasts

Table 8 and Panel-A of Table 9 show the nonparametric estimation results of the metric $S\rho_2$ tests. Large values of this statistic provide evidence against the structural models. The results are rather emphatic with these consistent and powerful entropy tests. These models generally fail to produce forecasts close in distributions to observed series. There is good reason why they do not forecast well, "on average." Broadly speaking Taylor-rule based models produce smaller $S\rho_2$ values both in-and out-of-sample. We also calculate the $S\rho_2$ value for the RW with drift for out-of-sample forecasting. Therefore, we can calculate the relative $S\rho_2$ values for model comparison. As shown in Panel-B of Table 9, except for two currency/model pairs, the relative $S\rho_2$ value is less than 1, indicating that structural models produce

Table 13 Relative $S\rho_1$ and $S\rho_2$ values (against random walk with a drift null) in out-of-sample forecasting

PANEL-A: Relative $S\rho_1$ (against random walk with a drift null) in out-of-sample forecasting

	Model 1		Model 2		Model 3		Model 4		Model 5		Model 6		Model 7	
	Lin	NP	Lin	NP	Lin	NP	Lin	NP	Lin	NP	Lin	NP	Lin	NP
AUS	0.563	0.688	1.188	0.313	0.438	0.500	0.750	0.313	0.688	0.938	0.813	1.250	0.851	0.642
CAN	0.917	0.583	1.000	0.417	0.750	0.667	0.750	0.833	0.667	0.167	1.167	1.083	0.892	0.598
DEN	0.455	0.727	0.818	0.545	0.455	0.455	0.455	0.273	0.818	0.727	0.818	0.545	0.674	0.389
FRA	0.278	0.278	0.611	0.278	0.444	0.278	0.556	0.389	0.833	0.333	0.833	0.222	0.396	0.447
GER	0.750	0.625	1.000	1.250	0.875	1.375	0.875	2.000	1.500	1.375	1.375	0.500	0.985	1.651
ITL	0.917	0.833	1.167	0.500	0.833	0.750	1.000	0.833	0.917	0.917	2.583	1.167	0.997	0.626
JPN	0.412	0.529	0.588	0.235	0.588	0.235	0.647	0.471	0.647	0.176	0.706	0.412	0.668	0.345
NTH	1.143	0.714	2.286	0.857	0.714	0.857	1.429	0.857	1.571	1.286	1.857	1.000	1.435	0.590
POR	0.609	0.304	0.652	0.304	0.696	0.435	0.957	0.304	0.870	0.913	1.043	1.174	1.020	0.594
SWE	0.917	0.500	0.583	0.750	0.667	0.917	0.750	0.667	1.250	0.917	0.250	0.500	1.109	0.315
SWI	0.500	0.571	0.500	0.643	0.500	0.571	1.000	0.214	1.071	0.429	0.929	0.786	0.877	0.859
UK	0.467	0.267	0.533	0.400	0.533	0.400	1.000	0.667	0.800	0.600	0.867	0.933	1.161	0.128

(continued)

Table 13 (continued)

PANEL-B: Relative $S\rho_2$ (against random walk with a drift null) in out-of-sample forecasting	Model 1		Model 2		Model 3		Model 4		Model 5		Model 6		Model 7	
	Lin	NP	Lin	NP	Lin	NP	Lin	NP	Lin	NP	Lin	NP	Lin	NP
AUS	0.495	0.097	0.692	0.318	0.355	0.039	0.430	0.062	0.850	0.784	0.553	0.431	0.753	0.308
CAN	0.571	0.302	0.630	0.457	0.505	0.138	0.457	0.230	0.889	0.841	0.765	0.543	0.629	0.461
DEN	0.568	0.278	0.735	0.586	0.511	0.134	0.559	0.199	0.811	0.750	0.812	0.712	0.567	0.364
FRA	0.614	0.394	0.804	0.495	0.601	0.189	0.548	0.211	0.808	0.777	0.963	0.614	0.824	0.233
GER	0.505	0.312	0.661	0.342	0.491	0.116	0.455	0.110	0.818	0.786	0.620	0.374	0.497	0.251
ITL	0.552	0.329	0.517	0.341	0.414	0.152	0.459	0.193	0.809	0.806	0.720	0.828	0.590	0.396
JPN	0.497	0.231	0.487	0.266	0.388	0.037	0.296	0.048	1.078	1.014	0.598	0.340	0.480	0.314
NTH	0.656	0.356	0.724	0.329	0.530	0.180	0.486	0.191	0.785	0.770	0.528	0.381	0.800	0.494
POR	0.689	0.331	0.667	0.319	0.890	0.169	0.762	0.167	0.807	0.823	1.161	1.157	1.017	0.523
SWE	0.535	0.236	0.495	0.277	0.447	0.106	0.441	0.125	0.795	0.769	0.670	0.463	0.674	0.495
SWI	0.554	0.087	0.627	0.219	0.408	0.035	0.358	0.070	0.828	0.788	0.638	0.451	0.506	0.294
UK	0.426	0.271	0.607	0.546	0.357	0.126	0.444	0.202	0.796	0.790	0.598	0.528	0.698	0.448

Panel-A shows, in out-of-sample forecasting, the ratio of the integrated value of the dependence metric for each model (estimated in OLS and NP, respectively) to the S-rho for the random walk drift model. Higher Srho-1 values imply better forecast. Hence, a ratio higher than 1 implies that structural model out-predicts the null of random walk with a drift. Benchmark is Random walk with drift. Since S-rho is a metric, the relative Srho shows the relative performance of the structural models against random walk drift model. The numbers in bold indicate the well-performing structural models against the random walk with drift. Panel-B shows, in out-of-sample forecasting, the ratio of the integrated value of the metric entropy measure of univariate density differences, Srho-2 ($S\rho_2$), for each model to the ($S\rho_2$) for the benchmark (random walk drift) model. Higher Srho-2 measures imply lower predictive powers. Therefore, a ratio less than 1 implies that structural model out-predicts the null of random walk with a drift. The numbers in bold indicate the well-performing structural models against the random walk with drift densities of exchange rate forecasts out-of-sample that are closer than the densities implied by the RW with drift model (Tables 10, 11, 12, 13).

4 Conclusion

Whether structural models of exchange rate movements are predictive or not is not well suited to mean squared prediction error criteria, and the underlying series appear to have distributions with significant higher order moments characteristics. Conditioning variables such as have been proposed so far appear to have nonlinear effects, at best, which are more robustly examined with nonparametric estimation. Comparison with forecasts from random walk models is somewhat misleading, as this may indicate "good relative performance" for models that have very poor forecasting ability, as clearly demonstrated with our entropy distance metrics. Our measures are metric and allow a ranking of closeness of forecasts to realized values.

References

Berger, David W. and Chaboud, Alain P. and Chernenko, Sergey V. and Howorka, Edward and Jonathan H. Wright (2008). "Order Flow and Exchange Rate Dynamics in Electronic Brokerage System Data", Journal of International Economics, Elsevier, vol. 75(1), pages 93–109, May.

Berkowitz, Jeremy (2001). "Testing Density Forecasts with Applications to Risk Management", Journal of Business and Economic Statistics, 19, 465–474.

Cheung, Yin-Wong & Chinn, Menzie D. & Antonio G. Pascual (2005)."Empirical Exchange Rate Models of the Nineties: Are any Fit to Survive?" Journal of International Money and Finance, Elsevier, vol. 24(7), pages 1150–1175, November.

Chinn, Menzie D. & Michael J. Moore (2011)."Order Flow and the Monetary Model of Exchange Rates: Evidence from a Novel Data Set", Forthcoming in Journal of Money, Credit and Banking.

Clark, Todd E. & Michael W. McCracken (2001)."Tests of Equal Forecast Accuracy and Encompassing for Nested Models", Journal of Econometrics, Elsevier, vol. 105(1), pages 85–110, November.

Clark, Todd E. & Kenneth D. West (2006)."Using out-of-sample Mean Squared Prediction Errors to Test the Martingale Difference Hypothesis", Journal of Econometrics, Elsevier, vol. 135(1–2), pages 155–186.

Clements, Michael P. & Jeremy Smith (2000). "Evaluating the Forecast Densities of Linear and Non-Linear Models: Applications to Output Growth and Unemployment", Journal of Forecasting, 19, 255–276.

Corradi, Valentina & Norman R. Swanson (2006). "Predictive Density Evaluation", in: Handbook of Economic Forecasting, eds. Clive W.J. Granger, Graham Elliot and Allan Timmerman, Elsevier, Amsterdam, pp. 197–284.

Diebold, Francis X & Gunther, Todd A. & Anthony S. Tay (1998)."Evaluating Density Forecasts with Applications to Financial Risk Management", International Economic Review, vol. 39(4), pages 863–83, November.

Diebold, Francis X & Roberto S. Mariano (1995)."Comparing Predictive Accuracy", Journal of Business & Economic Statistics, American Statistical Association, vol. 13(3), pages 253–63, July.

Diebold, Francis X & James A. Nason (1990)."Nonparametric Exchange Rate Prediction?" Journal of International Economics, Elsevier, vol. 28(3–4), pages 315–332, May.

Engel, Charles & Mark, Nelson C. & Kenneth D. West (2007)."Exchange Rate Models are not as Bad as You Think", NBER Chapters, in: NBER Macroeconomics Annual 2007, Volume 22, pages 381–441 National Bureau of Economic Research, Inc.
Engel, Charles & Kenneth D. West (2005). "Exchange Rates and Fundamentals", Journal of Political Economy, vol. 113(3), pages 485–517, June.
Evans, M.D.D. & Richard K. Lyons (2002). "Order Flow and Exchange Rate Dynamics", Journal of Political Economy, vol. 110(1), 170–180.
Evans, M.D.D. & Richard K. Lyons (2005). "Meese and Rogoff Redux: Micro-Based Exchange Rate Forecasting", American Economic Review, vol. 95(2), pages 405–414, May.
Faust, Jon & Rogers, John H. & Jonathan H. Wright (2003)."Exchange Rate Forecasting: The Errors We've Really Made", Journal of International Economics, Elsevier, vol. 60(1), pages 35–59, May.
Giannnerini, Simone & Dagum, Estela B. & Esfandiar Maasoumi (2011)."A Powerful Entropy Test for Linearity Against Nonlinearity in Time Series", Working Paper Series.
Gourinchas, Pierre-Olivier & Helene Rey (2007)."International Financial Adjustment", Journal of Political Economy, vol. 115(4), pages 665–703.
Granger, Clive W. J. & Maasoumi, Esfandiar & Jeff Racine (2004)."A Dependence Metric For Possibly Nonlinear Processes", Journal of Time Series Analysis, 25, Issue 5, pp. 649–669.
Hayfield, Tristen & Jeffrey S. Racine (2008). "Nonparametric Econometrics: The np Package", Journal of Statistical Software, Volume 27 (5).
Hsiao, Cheng & Li, Qi & Jeffrey S. Racine (2007)."A Consistent Model Specification Test with Mixed Discrete and Continuous Data", Journal of Econometrics, Elsevier, vol. 140(2), pages 802–826, October.
Li, Qi & Jeffrey S. Racine (2007). Nonparametric Econometrics: Theory and Practice, Princeton University Press, ISBN: 0691121613, 768 Pages.
Maasoumi, Esfandiar & Jeff Racine (2002)."Entropy and Predictability of Stock Market Returns", Journal of Econometrics, Elsevier, vol. 107(1–2), pages 291–312, March.
Mark, Nelson C. (1995)."Exchange Rates and Fundamentals: Evidence on Long-Horizon Predictability", American Economic Review, American Economic Association, vol. 85(1), pages 201–18, March.
Meese, Richard A. & Kenneth Rogoff (1983)."Empirical Exchange Rate Models of the Seventies : Do They Fit out of Sample?" Journal of International Economics, Elsevier, vol. 14(1–2), pages 3–24, February.
Meese, Richard A & Andrew K. Rose (1991)."An Empirical Assessment of Non-linearities in Models of Exchange Rate Determination", Review of Economic Studies, Wiley Blackwell, vol. 58(3), pages 603–19, May.
Molodtsova, Tanya & David H. Papell (2009)."Out-of-sample Exchange Rate Predictability with Taylor Rule Fundamentals", Journal of International Economics, Elsevier, vol. 77(2), pages 167–180, April.
Nikolsko-Rzhevskyy, Alex & Ruxandra Prodan (2011)."Markov Switching and Exchange Rate Predictability", Forthcoming in International Journal of Forecasting.
Rogoff, Kenneth S. & Vania Stavrakeva (2008)."The Continuing Puzzle of Short Horizon Exchange Rate Forecasting", NBER Working Papers 14071, National Bureau of Economic Research, Inc.
Skaug, H. & Dag Tjøstheim (1996). "Testing for Serial Independence Using Measures of Distance Between Densities", in P. Robinson & M. Rosenblatt, eds, Athens Conference on Applied Probability and Time Series, Springer Lecture Notes in Statistics, Springer.
Su, Liangjun & Halbert White (2008). "Nonparametric Hellinger Metric Test for Conditional Independence", Econometric Theory, vol. 24, pages 829–864.
Wang, Jian & Jason J. Wu (2010)."The Taylor Rule and Forecast Intervals for Exchange Rates", Forthcoming in Journal of Money, Credit and Banking.
West, Kenneth D. (1996)."Asymptotic Inference about Predictive Ability", Econometrica, Econometric Society, vol. 64(5), pages 1067–84, September.
White, Halbert (2000). "A Reality Check for Data Snooping", Econometrica, Econometric Society, vol. 68(5), pages 1097–1126, September.

Thirty Years of Heteroskedasticity-Robust Inference

James G. MacKinnon

Abstract White (*Econometrica*, 48:817–838, 1980) marked the beginning of a new era for inference in econometrics. It introduced the revolutionary idea of inference that is robust to heteroskedasticity of unknown form, an idea that was very soon extended to other forms of robust inference and also led to many new estimation methods. This paper discusses the development of heteroskedasticity-robust inference since 1980. There have been two principal lines of investigation. One approach has been to modify White's original estimator to improve its finite-sample properties, and the other has been to use bootstrap methods. The relation between these two approaches, and some ways in which they may be combined, are discussed. Finally, a simulation experiment compares various methods and shows how far heteroskedasticity-robust inference has come in just over 30 years.

1 Introduction

White (1980), which appears to be the most cited paper in economics, ushered in a new era for inference in econometrics. The defining feature of this new era is that the distributional assumptions needed for asymptotically valid inference are no longer the same as the ones needed for fully efficient asymptotic inference. The latter still requires quite strong assumptions about disturbances, but the former generally requires much weaker assumptions. In particular, for many econometric models, valid inference is possible in the presence of heteroskedasticity of unknown form, and it

Research for this paper was supported, in part, by a grant from the Social Sciences and Humanities Research Council of Canada. I am grateful to Dimitris Politis, Patrik Guggenberger, and an anonymous referee for comments.

J. G. MacKinnon (✉)
Department of Economics, Queen's University, Kingston, ON K7L 3N6, Canada
e-mail: jgm@econ.queensu.ca

X. Chen and N. R. Swanson (eds.), *Recent Advances and Future Directions in Causality, Prediction, and Specification Analysis*, DOI: 10.1007/978-1-4614-1653-1_17,

is often possible as well in the presence of various types of unknown dependence, such as serial correlation and clustered disturbances.

The linear regression model dealt with in White (1980) can be written as

$$y_i = \boldsymbol{X}_i \boldsymbol{\beta} + u_i, \quad i = 1, \ldots, n, \tag{1}$$

where the $1 \times k$ vectors of regressors $\boldsymbol{X}_i$ may be fixed or random, the disturbances u_i are independent but, in general, not identically distributed, with unknown variances σ_i^2 that may depend on the $\boldsymbol{X}_i$, and certain regularity conditions must be imposed on the pairs $(\boldsymbol{X}_i, u_i)$. The paper proved a number of important asymptotic results, of which the key one is that

$$\hat{\boldsymbol{V}}_n \equiv \frac{1}{n} \sum_{i=1}^{n} \hat{u}_i^2 \boldsymbol{X}_i^\top \boldsymbol{X}_i \overset{\text{a.s.}}{\longrightarrow} \frac{1}{n} \sum_{i=1}^{n} \mathrm{E}(u_i^2 \boldsymbol{X}_i^\top \boldsymbol{X}_i), \tag{2}$$

where $\hat{u}_i \equiv y_i - \boldsymbol{X}_i \hat{\boldsymbol{\beta}}$ is the ith OLS residual.

In 1980, this was a startling result. The rightmost quantity in (2) is an average of n matrix expectations, and each of those expectations is unknown and impossible to estimate consistently. For many decades, despite a few precursors in the statistics literature such as Eicker (1963, 1967) and Hinkley (1977), econometricians believed that it is necessary to estimate each expectation separately in order to estimate an average of expectations consistently. The key contribution of White (1980) was to show that it is not necessary at all.

The result (2) makes it easy to obtain the asymptotic covariance matrix estimator

$$(\boldsymbol{X}^\top \boldsymbol{X}/n)^{-1} \hat{\boldsymbol{V}}_n (\boldsymbol{X}^\top \boldsymbol{X}/n)^{-1}, \tag{3}$$

and it is shown in White (1980) that (3) consistently estimates the asymptotic covariance matrix of $\sqrt{n}(\hat{\boldsymbol{\beta}} - \boldsymbol{\beta}_0)$. As the author remarks in a masterpiece of understatement, "This result fills a substantial gap in the econometrics literature, and should be useful in a wide variety of applications."

The finite-sample covariance matrix estimator that corresponds to (3) is

$$(\boldsymbol{X}^\top \boldsymbol{X})^{-1} \Big(\sum_{i=1}^{n} \hat{u}_i^2 \boldsymbol{X}_i^\top \boldsymbol{X}_i \Big) (\boldsymbol{X}^\top \boldsymbol{X})^{-1}, \tag{4}$$

in which the factors of n have been removed. This estimator, which later came to be known as HC0, was the first *heteroskedasticity-consistent covariance matrix estimator*, or *HCCME*, in econometrics. Estimators that look like (4) are generally referred to as *sandwich covariance matrix estimators*.

Although White (1980) uses the notation $\sum_{i=1}^{n} \hat{u}_i^2 \boldsymbol{X}_i^\top \boldsymbol{X}_i$ to denote the filling of the sandwich, most discussions of HCCMEs use the notation $\boldsymbol{X}^\top \hat{\boldsymbol{\Omega}} \boldsymbol{X}$ instead, where $\hat{\boldsymbol{\Omega}}$ is an $n \times n$ diagonal matrix with typical diagonal element $\hat{u}_i^2$. The latter notation is certainly more compact, and I will make use of it in the rest of the paper. However, the more compact notation has two disadvantages. It tends to obscure the fundamental result (2), and it can lead to very inefficient computer programs if they are written in a naive way, because it involves an $n \times n$ matrix.

The key result that averages of expectations can be estimated consistently even when individual ones cannot has had profound implications for econometric theory and practice. It did not take long for econometricians to realize that, if heteroskedasticity-robust inference is possible, then so must be inference that is robust to both heteroskedasticity and autocorrelation of unknown form. Key early papers on what has come to be known as *HAC estimation* include Hansen (1982), White and Domowitz (1984), Newey and West (1987, 1994), Andrews (1991), and Andrews and Monahan (1992). New estimation methods, notably the generalized method of moments (Hansen 1982) and its many variants and offshoots, which would not have been possible without HCCMEs and HAC estimators, were rapidly developed following the publication of White (1980). There were also many important theoretical developments, including White (1982), the key paper on misspecified models in econometrics.

This paper discusses the progress in heteroskedasticity-robust inference since White (1980). Section 2 deals with various methods of heteroskedasticity-consistent covariance matrix estimation. Section 3 deals with bootstrap methods both as an alternative to HCCMEs and as a way of obtaining more reliable inferences based on HCCMEs. Section 4 briefly discusses robust inference for data that are clustered as well as heteroskedastic. Section 5 presents simulation results on the finite-sample properties of some of the methods discussed in Sects. 2 and 3, and the paper concludes in Sect. 6.

2 Better HCCMEs

The HC0 estimator given in expression (4) is not the only finite-sample covariance matrix estimator that corresponds to the asymptotic estimator (3). The matrix (4) depends on squared OLS residuals. Since OLS residuals are on average too small, it seems very likely that (4) will underestimate the true covariance matrix when the sample size is not large. The easiest way to improve (4) is to multiply it by $n/(n-k)$, or, equivalently, to replace the OLS residuals by ones that have been multiplied by $\sqrt{n/(n-k)}$. This is analogous to dividing the sum of squared residuals by $n-k$ instead of by n when we estimate the error variance. This estimator was called HC1 in MacKinnon and White (1985).

MacKinnon and White (1985) also discussed two more interesting procedures. The first of these, which they called HC2 and was inspired by Horn et al. (1975), involves replacing the squared OLS residuals $\hat{u}_i^2$ in (4) by

$$\grave{u}_i^2 \equiv \hat{u}_i^2/(1-h_i),$$

where h_i is the ith diagonal element of the projection matrix $\boldsymbol{P_X} \equiv \boldsymbol{X}(\boldsymbol{X}^\top\boldsymbol{X})^{-1}\boldsymbol{X}^\top$, which is sometimes called the *hat matrix*. Because $\mathrm{E}(\hat{u}_i^2) = (1 - h_i)\sigma^2$ when the disturbances are homoskedastic with variance σ^2, it is easy to see that HC2 will be unbiased in that case. In contrast, for HC1 to be unbiased under homoskedasticity, the experimental design must be balanced, which requires that $h_i = k/n$ for all i, a very special case indeed.

The final procedure discussed in MacKinnon and White (1985) was based on the jackknife. In principal, the jackknife involves estimating the model n additional times, each time dropping one observation, and then using the variation among the delete-1 estimates that result to estimate the covariance matrix of the original estimate. For the model (1), this procedure was shown to yield the (finite-sample) estimator

$$\frac{n-1}{n}(\boldsymbol{X}^\top\boldsymbol{X})^{-1}\Big(\sum_{i=1}^{n} \acute{u}_i^2\boldsymbol{X}_i^\top\boldsymbol{X}_i - \frac{1}{n}\boldsymbol{X}^\top\acute{\boldsymbol{u}}\acute{\boldsymbol{u}}^\top\boldsymbol{X}\Big)(\boldsymbol{X}^\top\boldsymbol{X})^{-1}, \tag{5}$$

where the vector $\acute{\boldsymbol{u}}$ has the typical element

$$\acute{u}_i = \hat{u}_i/(1 - h_i).$$

Notice that, since $\grave{u}_i$ is unbiased when the disturbances are homoskedastic, $\acute{u}_i$ must actually be biased upwards in that case, since $\acute{u}_i = \grave{u}_i/(1 - h_i)^{1/2}$, and the denominator here is always less than one.

MacKinnon and White (1985) called the jackknife estimator (5) HC3, and that is how it is referred to in much of the literature. However, Davidson and MacKinnon (1993) observed that the first term inside the large parentheses in (5) will generally be much larger than the second, because the former is $O_p(n)$ and the latter $O_p(1)$. They therefore (perhaps somewhat cavalierly) redefined HC3 to be the covariance matrix estimator

$$(\boldsymbol{X}^\top\boldsymbol{X})^{-1}\Big(\sum_{i=1}^{n} \acute{u}_i^2\boldsymbol{X}_i^\top\boldsymbol{X}_i\Big)(\boldsymbol{X}^\top\boldsymbol{X})^{-1}, \tag{6}$$

which has exactly the same form as HC0, HC1 when the individual OLS residuals are rescaled, and HC2. The modern literature has generally followed this naming convention, and so I will refer to (6) as HC3 and to (5) as HCJ.

Another member of this series of estimators was proposed in Cribari-Neto (2004). The HC4 estimator uses

$$\ddot{u}_i^2 = \hat{u}_i^2/(1 - h_i)^{\delta_i}, \quad \delta_i = \min(4, nh_i/k),$$

instead of the $\hat{u}_i^2$ in (4). The idea is to inflate the ith residual more (less) when h_i is large (small) relative to the average of the h_i, which is k/n. Cribari-Neto and Lima (2009) provide simulation results which suggest that, for the set of models they study, the coverage of confidence intervals based on HCj for $j = 0, \ldots, 4$ always increases monotonically with j. However, HC4 actually overcovers in some cases, so it is not always better than HC3. Poirier (2010) provides an interpretation of HC2 through HC4 in terms of the Bayesian bootstrap. There is also an HC5 estimator, which is quite similar to HC4; see Cribari-Neto et al. (2007).

All of the HCj series of estimators simply modify the (squared) residuals in various ways, but a few papers have taken different approaches. Furno (1996) uses residuals based on robust regression instead of OLS residuals in order to minimize the impact of data points with high leverage. Qian and Wang (2001) and Cribari-Neto and Lima (2010) explicitly correct the biases of various HCCMEs in the HCj series. The formulae that result generally appear to be complicated and perhaps expensive to program when n is large. Both papers present evidence that bias-corrected HCCMEs do indeed reduce bias effectively. However, there appears to be no evidence that they perform particularly well in terms of either coverage for confidence intervals or rejection frequencies for tests. Since those are the things that matter in practice, and bias-corrected HCCMEs are more complicated to program than any of the HCj series, there does not seem to be a strong case for employing the former in applied work.

The relative performance of test statistics and confidence intervals based on different HCCMEs depends principally on the h_i, which determine the leverage of the various observations, and on the pattern of heteroskedasticity. There are valuable analytical results in Chesher and Jewitt (1987), Chesher (1989), and Chesher and Austin (1991). When the sample is balanced, with no points of high leverage, these papers find that HC1, HC2, and HCJ all tend to work quite well. But even a single point of high leverage, especially if the associated disturbance has a large variance, can greatly distort the distributions of test statistics based on some or all of these estimators. Thus, it may be useful to see whether the largest value of h_i is unusually large.

The papers just cited make it clear that HCJ is not always to be preferred to HC2, or even to HC1. In some cases, tests based on HCJ can underreject, and confidence intervals can overcover. The results for HCJ must surely apply to HC3 as well. Similar arguments probably apply with even more force to HC4, which inflates some of the residuals much more than HC3 does; see Sect. 5.

3 Bootstrap Methods

There are two widely used methods for bootstrapping regression models with independent but possibly heteroskedastic disturbances. Both methods can be used to estimate covariance matrices, but they do so in ways that are computationally inefficient and have no theoretical advantages over much simpler methods like HC2 and HC3. In most cases, this is not very useful. What is much more useful is to combine these bootstrap methods with statistics constructed using HCCMEs in order to obtain more reliable inferences than the latter can provide by themselves.

The oldest of the two methods is the *pairs bootstrap* (Freedman 1981), in which the investigator resamples from the entire data matrix. For a linear regression model, or any other model where the data matrix can be expressed as $[\boldsymbol{y}\ \boldsymbol{X}]$, each bootstrap sample $[\boldsymbol{y}^* \ \boldsymbol{X}^*]$ simply consists of n randomly chosen rows of the data matrix. We can write a typical bootstrap sample as

$$[\boldsymbol{y}^* \ \boldsymbol{X}^*] = \begin{bmatrix} y_{1^*} & \boldsymbol{X}_{1^*} \\ y_{2^*} & \boldsymbol{X}_{2^*} \\ \vdots & \vdots \\ y_{n^*} & \boldsymbol{X}_{n^*} \end{bmatrix},$$

where each of the indices 1^* through n^*, which are different for each bootstrap sample, takes the values 1 through n with probability $1/n$. Thus if, for example, $1^* = 27$ for a particular bootstrap sample, the first row of the data matrix for that sample will consist of the 27th row of the actual data matrix. Technically, the pairs bootstrap data are drawn from the empirical distribution function, or EDF, of the actual data. This is similar to bootstrap resampling for a single variable as originally proposed in Efron (1979, 1982).

Since the regressor matrix will be different for each of the bootstrap samples, the pairs bootstrap does not make sense if the regressors are thought of as fixed in repeated samples. Moreover, to the extent that the finite-sample properties of estimators or test statistics depend on a particular $\boldsymbol{X}$ matrix, the pairs bootstrap may not mimic these properties as well as we would hope because it does not condition on $\boldsymbol{X}$. The pairs bootstrap as just described does not impose any restrictions. However, a modified version for regression models that does allow one to impose restrictions on the bootstrap DGP was proposed in Flachaire (1999).

The original idea of bootstrapping was to estimate standard errors, or more generally the covariance matrices of estimates of parameter vectors, by using the variation among the estimates from the bootstrap samples. If $\hat{\boldsymbol{\beta}}_j^*$ denotes the estimate of $\boldsymbol{\beta}$ from the jth bootstrap sample and $\bar{\boldsymbol{\beta}}^*$ denotes the average of the $\hat{\boldsymbol{\beta}}_j^*$ over B bootstrap samples, the bootstrap estimate of the covariance matrix of $\hat{\boldsymbol{\beta}}$ is simply

$$\widehat{\mathrm{Var}}^*(\hat{\boldsymbol{\beta}}) = \frac{1}{B-1}\sum_{j=1}^{B}(\hat{\boldsymbol{\beta}}_j^* - \bar{\boldsymbol{\beta}}^*)(\hat{\boldsymbol{\beta}}_j^* - \bar{\boldsymbol{\beta}}^*)^{\top}. \tag{7}$$

Although bootstrap covariance matrix estimators like (7) can be useful in some cases (for example, complicated nonlinear models or nonlinear functions of the coefficient estimates in regression models), the matrix (7) is actually just another HCCME, and not one that has any particular merit in finite samples. In fact, Lancaster (2006) shows that the covariance matrix of a delta method approximation to the distribution of the $\hat{\boldsymbol{\beta}}_j^*$ is simply HC0. In practice, when B is large enough, the matrix (7) is probably somewhat better than HC0, but no better than HC2 or HC3.

The main advantage of the pairs bootstrap is that it can be used with a very wide variety of models. For regression models, however, what is generally acknowledged to be a better way to deal with heteroskedasticity is the *wild bootstrap*, which was proposed in Liu (1988) and further developed in Mammen (1993). For the model (1) with no restrictions, the wild bootstrap DGP is

$$y_i^* = \boldsymbol{X}_i\hat{\boldsymbol{\beta}} + f(\hat{u}_i)v_i^*, \tag{8}$$

where $f(\hat{u}_i)$ is a transformation of the ith residual $\hat{u}_i$, and v_i^* is a random variable with mean 0 and variance 1. A natural choice for the transformation $f(\cdot)$ is

$$f(\hat{u}_i) = \frac{\hat{u}_i}{(1-h_i)^{1/2}}. \tag{9}$$

Since this is the same transformation used by HC2, we will refer to it as w2. Using (9) ensures that the $f(\hat{u}_i)$ must have constant variance whenever the disturbances are homoskedastic. Alternatively, one could divide $\hat{u}_i$ by $1 - h_i$, which is the transformation that we will refer to as w3 because it is used by HC3. The fact that v_i^* has mean 0 ensures that $f(\hat{u}_i)v_i^*$ also has mean 0, even though $f(\hat{u}_i)$ may not.

Transformations very similar to w2 and w3 can also be useful in the context of bootstrap prediction with homoskedastic errors, where the bootstrap DGP resamples from the rescaled residuals. Stine (1985) suggested using what is essentially w2, and Politis (2010) has recently shown that using predictive (or jackknife) residuals, which effectively use w3, works better.

There are, in principle, many ways to specify the random variable v_i^*. The most popular is the two-point distribution

$$F_1: \quad v_i^* = \begin{cases} -(\sqrt{5}-1)/2 & \text{with probability } (\sqrt{5}+1)/(2\sqrt{5}), \\ (\sqrt{5}+1)/2 & \text{with probability } (\sqrt{5}-1)/(2\sqrt{5}). \end{cases}$$

This distribution was suggested in Mammen (1993). Its theoretical advantage is that the skewness of the bootstrap error terms is the same as the skewness of the residuals. A simpler two-point distribution, called the *Rademacher distribution*, is just

$$F_2: \quad v_i^* = \begin{cases} -1 & \text{with probability } \frac{1}{2}, \\ 1 & \text{with probability } \frac{1}{2}. \end{cases}$$

This distribution imposes symmetry on the bootstrap error terms, which it is good to do if they actually are symmetric.

In some respects, the error terms for the wild bootstrap DGP (8) do not resemble those of the model (1) at all. When a two-point distribution like F_1 or F_2 is used, the bootstrap error term can take on only two possible values for each observation. Nevertheless, the wild bootstrap mimics the essential features of the true DGP well enough for it to be useful in many cases.

For any bootstrap method,

$$\begin{aligned}\hat{\boldsymbol{\beta}}_j^* - \bar{\boldsymbol{\beta}}^* &= (\boldsymbol{X}^\top\boldsymbol{X})^{-1}\boldsymbol{X}^\top\boldsymbol{y}_j^* - \bar{\boldsymbol{\beta}}^* \\ &= (\boldsymbol{X}^\top\boldsymbol{X})^{-1}\boldsymbol{X}^\top(\boldsymbol{X}\hat{\boldsymbol{\beta}} + \boldsymbol{u}_j^*) - \bar{\boldsymbol{\beta}}^* \\ &= (\boldsymbol{X}^\top\boldsymbol{X})^{-1}\boldsymbol{X}^\top\boldsymbol{u}_j^* + (\hat{\boldsymbol{\beta}} - \bar{\boldsymbol{\beta}}^*),\end{aligned} \tag{10}$$

where $\boldsymbol{y}_j^*$ and $\boldsymbol{u}_j^*$ denote, respectively, the regressand and the vector of error terms for the jth bootstrap sample. If we use the wild bootstrap DGP (8), and the OLS estimator is unbiased, then the expectation of the bootstrap estimates $\hat{\boldsymbol{\beta}}_j^*$ will just be $\hat{\boldsymbol{\beta}}$, and so the last term in the last line of (10) should be zero on average.

The first term in the last line of (10) times itself transposed looks like a sandwich covariance matrix, but with $\boldsymbol{u}_j^*\boldsymbol{u}_j^{*\top}$ instead of a diagonal matrix:

$$(\boldsymbol{X}^\top\boldsymbol{X})^{-1}\boldsymbol{X}^\top\boldsymbol{u}_j^*\boldsymbol{u}_j^{*\top}\boldsymbol{X}(\boldsymbol{X}^\top\boldsymbol{X})^{-1}.$$

It is particularly easy to see what this implies when the bootstrap errors are generated by F_2. In that case, the diagonal elements of $\boldsymbol{u}_j^*\boldsymbol{u}_j^{*\top}$ are simply the squares of the $f(\hat{u}_i)$. The off-diagonal elements must have expectation zero, because, for each bootstrap sample, every off-diagonal element is a product of the same two transformed residuals multiplied either by $+1$ or -1, each with probability one-half. Thus, as B becomes large, we would expect the average of the $\boldsymbol{u}_j^*\boldsymbol{u}_j^{*\top}$ to converge to a diagonal matrix with the squares of the $f(\hat{u}_i)$ on the diagonal. It follows that, if the transformation $f(\cdot)$ is either w2 or w3, the bootstrap covariance matrix estimator (7) must converge to either HC2 or HC3 as $B \to \infty$.

So far, we have seen only that the pairs bootstrap and the wild bootstrap provide computationally expensive ways to approximate various HCCMEs. If that was all these bootstrap methods were good for, there would be no point using them, at least not in the context of making inferences about the coefficients of linear regression models. They might still be useful for calculating covariance matrices for nonlinear functions of those coefficients.

Where these methods, especially the wild bootstrap, come into their own is when they are used together with heteroskedasticity-robust test statistics in order to obtain more accurate P values or confidence intervals. There is a great deal of evidence that the wild bootstrap outperforms the pairs bootstrap in these contexts; see Horowitz (2001), MacKinnon (2002), Flachaire (2005), and Davidson and Flachaire (2008), among others. Therefore, only the wild bootstrap will be discussed.

Consider the heteroskedasticity-robust t statistic

$$\tau(\hat{\beta}_l - \beta_l^0) = \frac{\hat{\beta}_l - \beta_l^0}{\sqrt{\left[(\boldsymbol{X}^\top\boldsymbol{X})^{-1}\boldsymbol{X}^\top\hat{\boldsymbol{\Omega}}\boldsymbol{X}(\boldsymbol{X}^\top\boldsymbol{X})^{-1}\right]_{ll}}}, \tag{11}$$

in which the difference between $\hat{\beta}_l$, the OLS estimate of the lth element of $\boldsymbol{\beta}$ in (1) and its hypothesized value β_l^0 is divided by the square root of the lth diagonal element of any suitable HCCME, such as HC2, HC3, or HC4, depending on precisely how $\hat{\boldsymbol{\Omega}}$ is defined. This test statistic is asymptotically distributed as N(0, 1) under quite weak assumptions. But its finite-sample distribution may or may not be well approximated by the standard normal distribution. Because (11) is asymptotically pivotal, bootstrap methods should provide an asymptotic refinement, that is, more rapid convergence as the sample size increases.

To calculate a wild bootstrap P value for the test statistic (11), we first estimate the model (1) under the null hypothesis to obtain restricted estimates $\tilde{\boldsymbol{\beta}}$ and restricted residuals $\tilde{\boldsymbol{u}}$. We then generate B bootstrap samples, using the DGP

$$y_i^* = \boldsymbol{X}_i \tilde{\boldsymbol{\beta}} + f(\tilde{u}_i) v_i^*. \tag{12}$$

As in (8), there are several choices for the transformation $f(\cdot)$. We have already defined w2 in Eq. (9) and w3 just afterwards. Another possibility, which we will call w1, is just $\sqrt{(n/(n-k+1)}\,\tilde{u}_i$. The random variates v_i^* could be drawn from F_1, F_2, or possibly some other distribution with mean 0 and variance 1.

For each bootstrap sample, indexed as usual by j, we calculate $\tau_j^*(\beta_l)$, the bootstrap analog of the test statistic (11), which is

$$\tau_j^*(\hat{\beta}_{lj}^* - \beta_l^0) = \frac{\hat{\beta}_{lj}^* - \beta_l^0}{\sqrt{\left[(\boldsymbol{X}^\top\boldsymbol{X})^{-1}\boldsymbol{X}^\top\hat{\boldsymbol{\Omega}}_j^*\boldsymbol{X}(\boldsymbol{X}^\top\boldsymbol{X})^{-1}\right]_{ll}}}. \tag{13}$$

Here, $\hat{\beta}_{lj}^*$ is the OLS estimate for the jth bootstrap sample, and $\boldsymbol{X}^\top\hat{\boldsymbol{\Omega}}_j^*\boldsymbol{X}$ is computed in exactly the same way as $\boldsymbol{X}^\top\hat{\boldsymbol{\Omega}}\boldsymbol{X}$ in (11), except that it uses the residuals from the bootstrap regression.

Davidson and Flachaire (2008) have shown, on the basis of both theoretical analysis and simulation experiments, that wild bootstrap tests based on the Rademacher distribution F_2 can be expected to perform better, in finite samples, than ones based on the Mammen distribution F_1, even when the true disturbances are moderately skewed. Some of the results in Sect. 5 strongly support this conclusion.

Especially when one is calculating bootstrap P values for several tests, it is easier to use unrestricted rather than restricted estimates in the bootstrap DGP, because there is no need to estimate any of the restricted models. The bootstrap data are then generated using (8) instead of (12), and the bootstrap t statistics are calculated as $\tau_j^*(\hat{\beta}_{lj}^* - \hat{\beta}^l)$, which means replacing β_l^0 by $\hat{\beta}_l$ on both sides of Eq. (13). This ensures that the bootstrap test statistics are testing a hypothesis which is true for the bootstrap data.

When using studentized statistics like (11) and other statistics that are asymptotically pivotal, it is almost always better to use restricted estimates in the bootstrap DGP, because the DGP is estimated more efficiently when true restrictions are imposed; see Davidson and MacKinnon (1999). However, this is not true for statistics which are not asymptotically pivotal; see Paparoditis and Politis (2005). The advantage of using restricted estimates can be substantial in some cases, as will be seen in Sect. 5.

Once we have computed $\hat{\tau} = \tau(\hat{\beta}_l - \beta_l^0)$ and B instances of τ_j^*, which be either $\tau_j^*(\hat{\beta}_{lj}^* - \beta_l^0)$ or $\tau_j^*(\hat{\beta}_{lj}^* - \hat{\beta}_l)$, the bootstrap P value is simply

$$\hat{p}^*(\hat{\tau}) = 2\min\left(\frac{1}{B}\sum_{j=1}^{B}\mathrm{I}(\tau_j^* \leq \hat{\tau}), \frac{1}{B}\sum_{j=1}^{B}\mathrm{I}(\tau_j^* > \hat{\tau})\right). \tag{14}$$

This is an *equal-tail bootstrap P value*, so called because, for a test at level α, the rejection region is implicitly any value of $\hat{\tau}$ that is either less than the $\alpha/2$ quantile or greater than the $1-\alpha/2$ quantile of the empirical distribution of the τ_j^*. It is desirable to choose B such that $\alpha(B+1)/2$ is an integer; see Racine and MacKinnon (2007).

For t statistics, it is generally safest to use an equal-tail P value like (14) unless there is good reason to believe that the test statistic is symmetrically distributed around zero. For any test that rejects only when the test statistic is in the upper tail, such as a heteroskedasticity-robust F statistic or the absolute value of a heteroskedasticity-robust t statistic, we would instead compute the bootstrap P value as

$$\hat{p}^*(\hat{\tau}) = \frac{1}{B}\sum_{j=1}^{B}\mathrm{I}(\tau_j^* > \hat{\tau}). \tag{15}$$

In this case, it is desirable to choose B such that $\alpha(B+1)$ is an integer, which must of course be true whenever $\alpha(B+1)/2$ is an integer.

In many cases, we are interested in confidence intervals rather than tests. The most natural way to obtain a bootstrap confidence interval in this context is to use the *studentized bootstrap*, which is sometimes known as the *percentile-t method*. The bootstrap data are generated using the wild bootstrap DGP (8), which does not impose the null hypothesis. Each bootstrap sample is then used to compute a bootstrap test statistic $\tau_j^*(\hat{\beta}_{lj}^* - \hat{\beta}^l)$. These are sorted, and their $\alpha/2$ and $1-\alpha/2$ quantiles obtained, which is particularly easy to do if $\alpha(B+1)/2$ is an integer. If $q_{\alpha/2}^*$ and $q_{1-\alpha/2}^*$ denote these empirical quantiles, and $s(\hat{\beta}^l)$ denotes the (presumably heteroskedasticity-robust) standard error of $\hat{\beta}^l$, then the studentized bootstrap interval at level α is

$$\left[\hat{\beta}^l - s(\hat{\beta}^l)q_{1-\alpha/2}^*, \quad \hat{\beta}^l - s(\hat{\beta}^l)q_{\alpha/2}^*\right]. \tag{16}$$

As usual, the lower limit of this interval depends on the upper tail quantile of the bootstrap test statistics, and the upper limit depends on the lower tail quantile. Even if the true distribution of the τ_j^* happens to be symmetric around the origin, it is highly unlikely that the empirical distribution will be. Therefore, the interval (16) will almost never be symmetric.

Another way to find confidence intervals is explicitly to invert bootstrap P values. The confidence interval then consists of all points for which the bootstrap P value (14) is greater than α. Solving for such an interval can be a bit complicated, since the null hypotheses that correspond to each end of the interval must be imposed on the bootstrap DGP. However, this technique can be more reliable than the studentized bootstrap method; see Davidson and MacKinnon (2010, 2011).

The discussion so far may have incorrectly given the impression that the only reason to use the wild bootstrap is to reduce the size distortion of tests, or the coverage errors of confidence intervals, that are associated with HCCMEs which are not entirely reliable in finite samples. In cross-section regressions with samples of several hundred observations or more, those errors are often quite modest. But there may well be other sources of much larger size distortions or coverage errors that can also be reduced by using bootstrap methods. Although the primary reason for bootstrapping may not be heteroskedasticity of unknown form, it is often wise to use a technique like the wild bootstrap together with heteroskedasticity-robust covariance matrices.

An important example is two-stage least squares (or generalized IV) estimation with possibly heteroskedastic disturbances when the instruments are not strong. Davidson and MacKinnon (2010) proposed a wild bootstrap procedure for this case. When there are just two endogenous variables, the model is

$$\boldsymbol{y}_1 = \beta \boldsymbol{y}_2 + \boldsymbol{Z}\boldsymbol{\gamma} + \boldsymbol{u}_1 \tag{17}$$

$$\boldsymbol{y}_2 = \boldsymbol{W}\boldsymbol{\pi} + \boldsymbol{u}_2. \tag{18}$$

Equation (17) is a structural equation, and Eq. (18) is a reduced-form equation. The n-vectors $\boldsymbol{y}_1$ and $\boldsymbol{y}_2$ are vectors of observations on endogenous variables, $\boldsymbol{Z}$ is an $n \times k$ matrix of observations on exogenous variables, and $\boldsymbol{W}$ is an $n \times l$ matrix of exogenous instruments with the property that $\mathcal{S}(\boldsymbol{Z})$, the subspace spanned by the columns of $\boldsymbol{Z}$, lies in $\mathcal{S}(\boldsymbol{W})$, the subspace spanned by the columns of $\boldsymbol{W}$. Typical elements of $\boldsymbol{y}_1$ and $\boldsymbol{y}_2$ are denoted by y_{1i} and y_{2i} respectively, and typical rows of $\boldsymbol{Z}$ and $\boldsymbol{W}$ are denoted by $\boldsymbol{Z}_i$ and $\boldsymbol{W}_i$.

Davidson and MacKinnon (2010) discusses several wild bootstrap procedures for testing the hypothesis that $\beta = \beta_0$. The one that works best, which they call the *wild restricted efficient* (or *WRE*) bootstrap, uses the bootstrap DGP

$$y_{1i}^* = \beta_0 y_{2i}^* + \boldsymbol{Z}_i\tilde{\boldsymbol{\gamma}} + f_1(\tilde{u}_{1i})v_i^* \tag{19}$$

$$y_{2i}^* = \boldsymbol{W}_i\tilde{\boldsymbol{\pi}} + f_2(\tilde{u}_{2i})v_i^*, \tag{20}$$

where $\tilde{\boldsymbol{\gamma}}$ and the residuals $\tilde{u}_{1i}$ come from an OLS regression of $\boldsymbol{y}_1 - \beta_0\boldsymbol{y}_2$ on $\boldsymbol{Z}$, $\tilde{\boldsymbol{\pi}}$ comes from an OLS regression of $\boldsymbol{y}_2$ on $\boldsymbol{W}$ and $\tilde{\boldsymbol{u}}_1$, and $\tilde{\boldsymbol{u}}_2 \equiv \boldsymbol{y}_2 - \boldsymbol{W}\tilde{\boldsymbol{\pi}}$. The transformations $f_1(\cdot)$ and $f_2(\cdot)$ could be any of w1, w2, or w3.

This bootstrap DGP has three important features. First, the structural Eq. (19) uses restricted (OLS) estimates instead of unrestricted (2SLS) ones. This is very important for the finite-sample properties of the bootstrap tests. Note that, if 2SLS estimates were used, it would no longer make sense to transform the $\hat{u}_{1i}$, because 2SLS residuals are not necessarily too small. Second, the parameters of the reduced-form Eq. (20) are estimated efficiently, because the structural residuals are included as an additional regressor. This is also very important for finite-sample properties. Third, the same random variable v_i^* multiplies the transformed residuals for both equations. This ensures that the correlation between the structural and reduced-form residuals is retained by the structural and reduced-form bootstrap error terms.

Davidson and MacKinnon (2010) provides evidence that bootstrap tests of hypotheses about β based on the WRE bootstrap perform remarkably well whenever the sample size is not too small (400 seems to be sufficient) and the instruments are not very weak. What mostly causes asymptotic tests to perform poorly is simultaneity combined with weak instruments, and not heteroskedasticity. The main reason to use the WRE bootstrap is to compensate for the weak instruments.

Ideally, one should always use a heteroskedasticity-robust test statistic together with the wild bootstrap, or perhaps some other bootstrap method that is valid in the presence of heteroskedasticity. However, it is also asymptotically valid to use a nonrobust test statistic together with the wild bootstrap, or a robust test statistic together with a bootstrap method that does not take account of heteroskedasticity. The simulation evidence in Davidson and MacKinnon (2010) suggests that both of these approaches, while inferior to the ideal one, can work reasonably well.

4 Cluster-Robust Covariance Matrices

An important extension of heteroskedasticity-robust inference is cluster-robust inference. Consider the linear regression model

$$\boldsymbol{y} \equiv \begin{bmatrix} \boldsymbol{y}_1 \\ \boldsymbol{y}_2 \\ \vdots \\ \boldsymbol{y}_m \end{bmatrix} = \begin{bmatrix} \boldsymbol{X}_1 \\ \boldsymbol{X}_2 \\ \vdots \\ \boldsymbol{X}_m \end{bmatrix} \boldsymbol{\beta} + \begin{bmatrix} \boldsymbol{u}_1 \\ \boldsymbol{u}_2 \\ \vdots \\ \boldsymbol{u}_m \end{bmatrix} \equiv \boldsymbol{X}\boldsymbol{\beta} + \boldsymbol{u}.$$

Here, there are m clusters, indexed by j, the observations for which are stacked into the vector $\boldsymbol{y}$ and the matrix $\boldsymbol{X}$. Clusters might correspond to cities, counties, states, or countries in a cross-section of households or firms, or they might correspond to cross-sectional units in a panel dataset. The important thing is that there may be correlation among the disturbances within each cluster, but not across clusters.

If we know nothing about the pattern of variance and covariances within each cluster, then it makes sense to use a cluster-robust covariance matrix estimator. The simplest such estimator is

$$\widehat{\mathrm{Var}}(\hat{\boldsymbol{\beta}}) = (\boldsymbol{X}^\top\boldsymbol{X})^{-1}\Big(\sum_{j=1}^{m} \boldsymbol{X}_j^\top \hat{\boldsymbol{u}}_j \hat{\boldsymbol{u}}_j^\top \boldsymbol{X}_j\Big)(\boldsymbol{X}^\top\boldsymbol{X})^{-1}, \tag{21}$$

where $\hat{\boldsymbol{u}}_j$ is the vector of OLS residuals for the jth cluster. This has the familiar sandwich form of an HCCME, except that the filling in the sandwich is more complicated. It is robust to heteroskedasticity of unknown form as well as to within-cluster correlation. The estimator (21) was first proposed by Froot (1989), introduced into Stata by Rogers (1993), and extended to allow for serial correlation of unknown form, as in HAC estimation, by Driscoll and Kraay (1998). It is widely used in applied work.

Cameron et al. (2008) recently proposed a wild bootstrap method for clustered data. As in the usual wild bootstrap case, where the bootstrap disturbance for observation i depends on the residual $\hat{u}_i$, all the bootstrap disturbances for each cluster depend on the residuals for that cluster. The wild bootstrap DGP is

$$y_{ji}^* = \boldsymbol{X}_{ji}\hat{\boldsymbol{\beta}} + f(\hat{u}_{ji})v_j^*, \tag{22}$$

where j indexes clusters, i indexes observations within each cluster, and the v_j^* follow the Rademacher (F_2) distribution. The key feature of (22) is that there are only as many v_j^* as there are clusters. Thus, the bootstrap DGP preserves the variances and covariances of the residuals within each cluster. This method apparently works surprisingly well even when the number of clusters is quite small.

5 Simulation Evidence

Simulation experiments can be used to shed light on the finite-sample performance of various HCCMEs, either used directly for asymptotic tests or combined with various forms of the wild bootstrap. This section reports results from a number of experiments that collectively deal with a very large number of methods. Most of the experiments were deliberately designed to make these methods perform poorly.

Many papers that use simulation to study the properties of HCCMEs, beginning with MacKinnon and White (1985) and extending at least to Cribari-Neto and Lima (2010), have simply chosen a fixed or random $\boldsymbol{X}$ matrix for a small sample size—just 10 in the case of Davidson and Flachaire (2008)—and formed larger samples by repeating it as many times as necessary. When $\boldsymbol{X}$ matrices are generated in this way, there will only be as many distinct values of h_i as the number of observations in the original sample. Moreover, all of those values, and in particular the largest one, must be exactly proportional to $1/n$; see Chesher (1989). This ensures that inference based on heteroskedasticity-robust methods improves rapidly as n increases. Since very few real datasets involve $\boldsymbol{X}$ matrices for which all of the h_i are proportional to $1/n$, this sort of experiment almost certainly paints an excessively optimistic picture. Some evidence on this point is provided below.

In contrast, the model employed here, which is similar to one used for a much more limited set of experiments in MacKinnon (2002), is

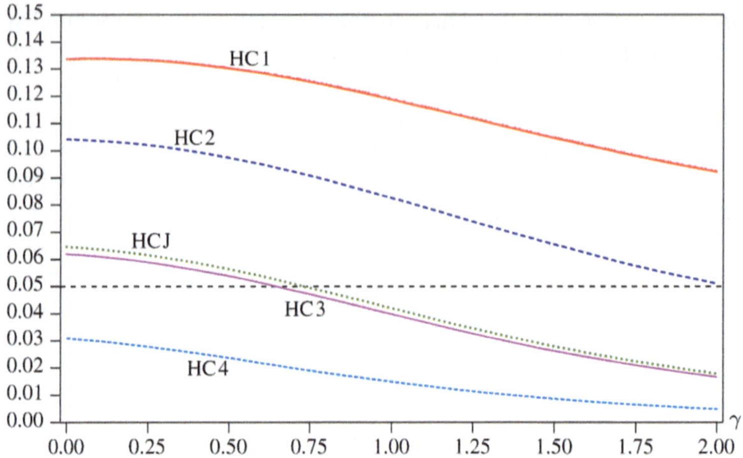

Fig. 1 Rejection frequencies for heteroskedasticity-robust t tests, $n = 40$

$$y_i = \beta_1 + \sum_{k=2}^{5} \beta_k X_{ik} + u_i, \quad u_i = \sigma_i \epsilon_i, \quad \epsilon_i \sim \mathrm{N}(0, 1), \tag{23}$$

where all regressors are drawn randomly from the standard lognormal distribution, $\beta_k = 1$ for $k \leq 4$, $\beta_5 = 0$, and

$$\sigma_i = z(\gamma)\big(\beta_1 + \sum_{k=2}^{5} \beta_k X_{ik}\big)^{\gamma}. \tag{24}$$

Here, $z(\gamma)$ is a scaling factor chosen to ensure that the average variance of u_i is equal to 1. Thus, changing the parameter γ changes how much heteroskedasticity there is but does not, on average, change the variance of the disturbances. In the experiments, $0 \leq \gamma \leq 2$. Note that $\gamma = 0$ implies homoskedasticity, and $\gamma >> 1$ implies rather extreme heteroskedasticity.

The DGP consisting of Eqs. (23) and (24) was deliberately chosen so as to make heteroskedasticity-robust inference difficult. Because the regressors are lognormal, many samples will contain a few observations on the X_{ik} that are quite extreme, and the most extreme observation in each sample will tend to become more so as the sample size increases. Therefore, the largest value of h_i will tend to be large and to decline very slowly as $n \to \infty$. In fact, the average value of $h_i^{\max}$ is nearly 0.80 when $n = 20$ and declines by a factor of only about 3.5 as the sample size increases to 1,280, with the rate of decline increasing somewhat as n becomes larger. It is likely that few real datasets have h_i which are as badly behaved as the ones in these experiments, so their results almost certainly paint an excessively pessimistic picture.

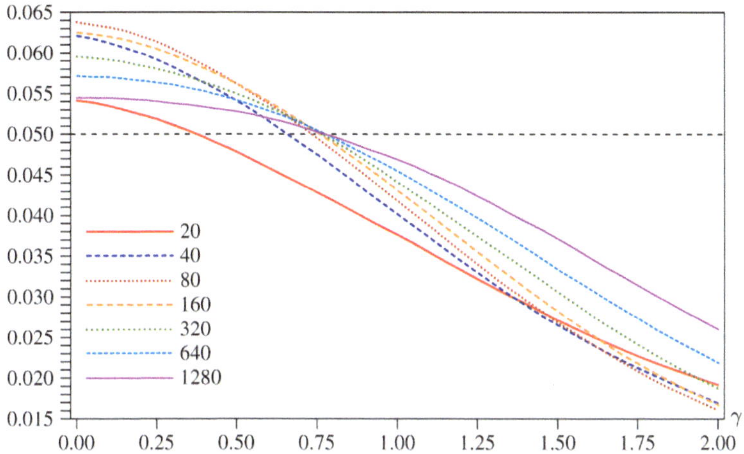

Fig. 2 Rejection frequencies for asymptotic HC3 t tests, various sample sizes

Figures 1 and 2 show the results of several sets of experiments for asymptotic tests of the hypothesis that $\beta_5 = 0$ based on test statistics like (11) and the standard normal distribution. The figures show rejection frequencies as functions of the parameter γ. They are based on 1,000,000 replications for each of 41 values of γ between 0.00 and 2.00 at intervals of 0.05.

Rejection frequencies for five different HCCMEs when $n = 40$ are shown in Fig. 1. As expected, tests based on HC1 always overreject quite severely. Perhaps somewhat unexpectedly, tests based on HC4 always underreject severely. This is presumably a consequence of the very large values of $h_i^{\max}$ in these experiments. Tests based on the other estimators sometimes overreject and sometimes underreject. In every case, rejection frequencies decline monotonically as γ increases. For any given value of γ, they also decline as j increases from 1 to 4 in HCj. It is reassuring to see that the results for HC3 and HCJ are extremely similar, as predicted by Davidson and MacKinnon (1993) when they introduced the former as an approximation to the latter and appropriated its original name.

Note that, as Davidson and Flachaire (2008) emphasized, restricting attention to tests at the 0.05 level is not inconsequential. All the tests are more prone to overreject at the 0.01 level and less prone to overreject at the .10 level than they are at the 0.05 level. In other words, the distributions of the test statistics have much thicker tails than does the standard normal distribution. Even HC4, which underrejects at the 0.05 level for every value of n and γ, always overrejects at the 0.01 level for some small values of γ.

Figure 2 focuses on HC3, which seems to perform best among the HCj estimators for $n = 40$. It shows results for seven values of n from 20 to 1,280. The surprising thing about this figure is how slowly the rejection frequency curves become flatter as the sample size increases. The curves actually become steeper as n increases from 20 to 40 and then to 80. The worst overrejection for $\gamma = 0$ and the worst underrejection

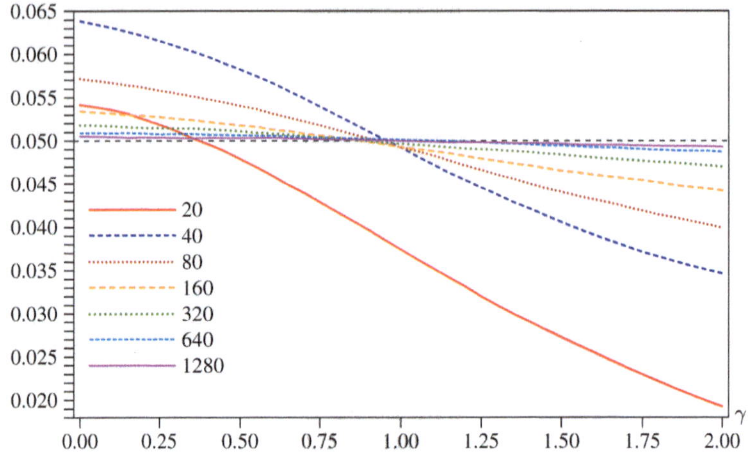

Fig. 3 Rejection frequencies for asymptotic HC3 t tests, 20 rows of $\boldsymbol{X}$ repeated

for $\gamma = 2$ both occur when $n = 80$. As n increases from 80 to 160, 320, 640, and finally 1280, the curves gradually become flatter, but they do so quite slowly. It seems likely that we would need extremely large samples for rejection frequencies to be very close to the nominal level of 0.05 for all values of γ. This is a consequence of the experimental design, which ensures that $h_i^{\max}$ decreases very slowly as n increases.

An alternative to generating the entire regressor matrix for each sample size is simply to generate the first 20 rows and then repeat them as many times as necessary to form larger samples with integer multiples of 20 observations. As noted earlier, $h_i^{\max}$ would then be proportional to $1/n$. Figure 3 contains the same results as Fig. 2, except that the matrix $\boldsymbol{X}$ is generated in this way. The performance of asymptotic tests based on HC3 now improves much faster as n increases. In particular, the rejection frequency curve changes dramatically between $n = 20$ and $n = 40$. It is evident that the way in which $\boldsymbol{X}$ is generated matters enormously.

The remaining figures deal with wild bootstrap tests. Experiments were performed for 12 variants of the wild bootstrap. There are three transformations of the residuals (denoted by w1, w2, or w3, because they are equivalent to HC1, HC2, or HC3), two types of residuals (restricted and unrestricted, denoted by r or u), and two ways of generating the v_j^* (F_1 or F_2, denoted by 1 or 2). The 12 variants are

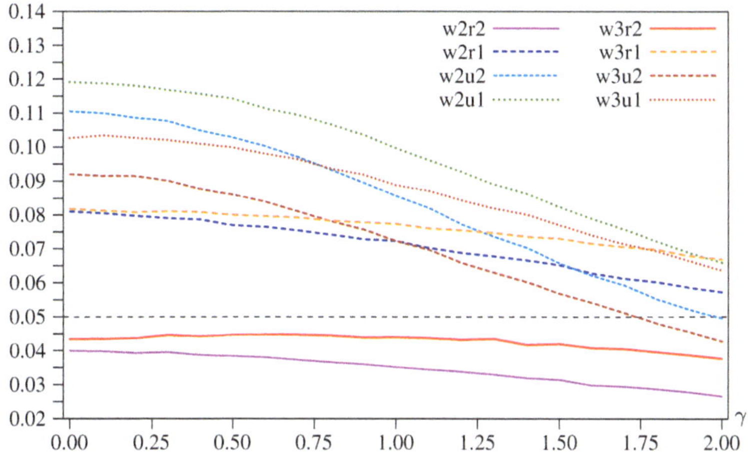

Fig. 4 Rejection frequencies for bootstrap HC3 t tests, $n = 40$

$$\text{w1r1 and w1r2: } u_i^* = \sqrt{n/(n-k+1)}\,\tilde{u}_i$$

$$\text{w1u1 and w1u2: } u_i^* = \sqrt{n/(n-k)}\,\hat{u}_i$$

$$\text{w2r1 and w2r2: } u_i^* = \frac{\tilde{u}_i}{(1-\tilde{h}_i)^{1/2}}$$

$$\text{w2u1 and w2u2: } u_i^* = \frac{\hat{u}_i}{(1-h_i)^{1/2}}$$

$$\text{w3r1 and w3r2: } u_i^* = \frac{\tilde{u}_i}{(1-\tilde{h}_i)}$$

$$\text{w3u1 and w3u2: } u_i^* = \frac{\hat{u}_i}{(1-h_i)}$$

In the expressions for w2r1, w2r2, w3r1, and w3r2, $\tilde{h}_i$ denotes the ith diagonal of the hat matrix for the restricted model.

The experimental results are based on 100,000 replications for each of 21 values of γ between 0.0 and 2.0 at intervals of 0.1, with $B = 399$. In practice, it would be better to use a larger number for B in order to obtain better power, but 399 is adequate in the context of a simulation experiment; see Davidson and MacKinnon (2000). There are five different HCCMEs and 12 different bootstrap DGPs. Thus, each experiment produces 60 sets of rejection frequencies. It would be impossible to present all of these graphically without using an excessively large number of figures.

Figures 4 and 5 present results for HC3 and HC1 respectively, combined with eight different bootstrap DGPs for $n = 40$. Results are shown only for w2 and w3, because the diagram would have been too cluttered if w1 had been included, and methods based on w1 usually performed less well than ones based on w2. HC3 was chosen because asymptotic tests based on it performed best, and HC1 was chosen

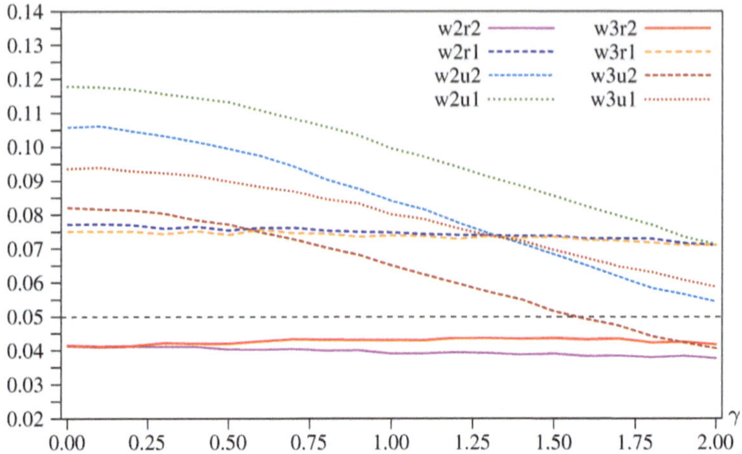

Fig. 5 Rejection frequencies for bootstrap HC1 t tests, $n = 40$

because asymptotic tests based on it performed worst. Note that the results for HC0 would have been identical to the ones for HC1, because the former is just a multiple of the latter. This implies that the position of $\hat{\tau}$ in the sorted list of $\hat{\tau}$ and the τ_j^* must be the same for HC0 and HC1, and hence the P value must be the same.

In Fig. 4, we see that only two of the wild bootstrap methods (w3r2 and w2r2) yield tests that never overreject. The size distortion for w3r2 is always less than for w2r2. The curve for w1r2, not shown, lies everywhere below the curve for w2r2. The other six wild bootstrap methods do not perform particularly well. They all overreject for all or most values of γ. For small values of γ, the four worst methods are the ones that use unrestricted residuals. But w2r1 and w3r1 also work surprisingly poorly.

Figure 5 shows results for the same eight wild bootstrap methods as Fig. 4, but this time the test statistic is based on HC1. The results are similar to those in Fig. 4, but they are noticeably better in several respects. Most importantly, w3r2 and, especially, w2r2 underreject less severely, and all of the tests that use unrestricted residuals overreject somewhat less severely.

The remaining figures focus on the effects of sample size. Figure 6 shows rejection frequencies for tests based on HC1 for six sample sizes, all using the w3r2 wild bootstrap. In striking contrast to the asymptotic results in Fig. 2, the improvement as n increases is quite rapid. Except for the largest values of γ, the rejection frequencies are very close to 0.05 for $n = 640$.

Figure 7 shows that using unrestricted residuals harms performance greatly for all sample sizes. Although there is much faster improvement with n than for the asymptotic tests in Fig. 2, overrejection for small values of γ is actually more severe for the smaller sample sizes. Both overrejection for small values of γ and underrejection for large ones remain quite noticeable even when $n = 640$.

Figure 8 is similar to Fig. 6, except that the matrix $\boldsymbol{X}$ consists of the first 20 rows repeated as many times as necessary. Results are presented only for $n = 40$, 60, 80,

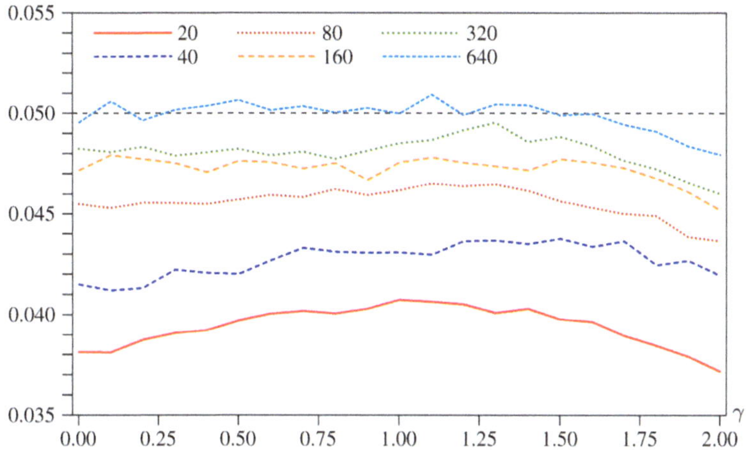

Fig. 6 Rejection frequencies for w3r2 bootstrap HC1 t tests

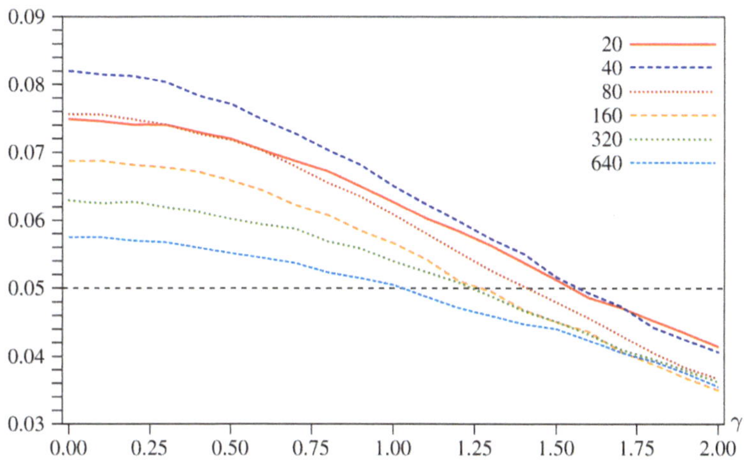

Fig. 7 Rejection frequencies for w3u2 bootstrap HC1 t tests

120, and 160. Results for $n = 20$ are omitted, because they may be found in Fig. 6, and including them would have required a greatly extended vertical axis. Results for sample sizes larger than 160 are omitted for obvious reasons. To reduce experimental error, these results are all based on 400,000 replications.

The performance of all the bootstrap tests in Fig. 8 is extremely good. Simply making the bottom half of the $\boldsymbol{X}$ matrix repeat the top half, as happens when $n = 40$, dramatically improves the rejection frequencies. Results would have been similar for tests based on HC2, HC3, HCJ, or HC4. It is now very difficult to choose among bootstrap tests that use different HCCMEs, as they all work extremely well.

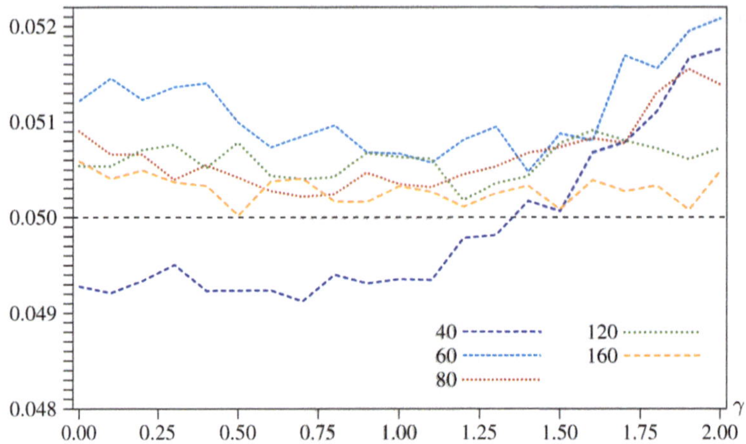

Fig. 8 Rejection frequencies for w3r2 bootstrap HC1 t tests, 20 rows of $\boldsymbol{X}$ repeated

Although Fig. 8 only shows results for the w3r2 variant of the wild bootstrap, other bootstrap methods also perform much better when the regressor matrix consists of the first 20 rows repeated than when the entire matrix is generated randomly. But there still seem to be clear benefits from using restricted residuals and the F_2 distribution, at least for smaller values of n.

Like most of the work in this area, the experiments described so far focus exclusively on the performance of tests under the null. However, test power can be just as important as test size. The remaining experiments therefore address two important questions about power. The first is whether the choice of HCCME matters, and the second is whether there is any advantage to using unrestricted rather than restricted residuals in the bootstrap DGP. These experiments use the w3 bootstrap and the F_2 distribution. The sample size is 40, there are 100,000 replications, and $B = 999$. The number of bootstrap samples is somewhat larger than in the previous experiments, because power loss is proportional to $1/B$; see Jöckel (1986).

Figure 9 shows power functions for wild bootstrap (w3r2) tests of the hypothesis that $\beta_5 = 0$ in Eq. 11 as a function of the actual value of β_5 when $\gamma = 1$. Experiments were performed for 71 values of β_5: $-0.70, -0.68, \ldots, 0.68, 0.70$. This figure has two striking features. First, the power functions are not symmetric. There is evidently greater power against negative values of β_5 than against positive ones. This occurs because of the pattern of heteroskedasticity in Eq. (24). For $\gamma > 0$, there is more heteroskedasticity when $\beta_5 > 0$ than when $\beta_5 < 0$. This causes the estimate of β_5 to be more variable as the true value of β_5 increases. When $\gamma = 0$, the power functions are symmetric.

The second striking feature of Fig. 9 is that power decreases monotonically from HC1 to HC2, HC3, and finally HC4. Thanks to the bootstrap, all the tests have essentially the same performance under the null. Thus, what we see in the figure is a real, and quite substantial, reduction in power as we move from HC1, which pays

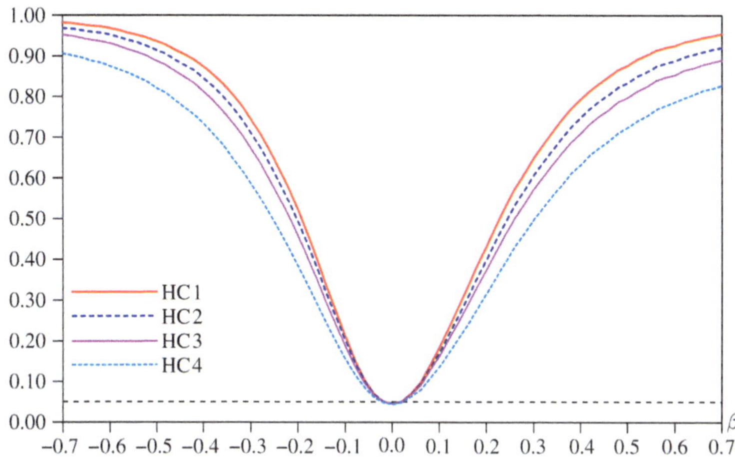

Fig. 9 Power of wild bootstrap (w3r2) heteroskedasticity-robust t tests, $\gamma = 1$, $n = 40$

no attention to the leverage of each observation, to robust covariance matrices that take greater and greater account thereof. At least in this case, there appears to be a real cost to using HCCMEs that compensate for leverage (they overcompensate, in the case of HC3 and HC4). It seems to be much better to correct for the deficiencies of HC1 by bootstrapping rather than by using a different HCCME.

Although there is still the same pattern for similar experiments in which the $\boldsymbol{X}$ matrix is generated by repeating the first 20 observations (results not shown), the loss of power is much less severe. Thus, it may well be that the power loss in Fig. 9 is just about as severe as one is likely to encounter.

It is widely believed that using unrestricted residuals in a bootstrap DGP yields greater power than using restricted residuals. The argument is that, when the null is false, restricted residuals will be larger than unrestricted ones, and so the bootstrap error terms will be too big if restricted residuals are used. Paparoditis and Politis (2005) show that there is indeed a loss of power from using restricted residuals whenever a test statistic is asymptotically nonpivotal. However, their theoretical analysis yields no such result for asymptotically pivotal statistics like the robust t statistic (11) studied here. Using restricted residuals does indeed cause the bootstrap estimates to be more variable, but it also causes the standard errors of those estimates to be larger. Thus, there is no presumption that bootstrap critical values based on the distribution of the bootstrap t statistics will be larger if one uses restricted residuals.

Figure 10 shows two power functions, one for the w3r2 bootstrap, which is identical to the corresponding one in Fig. 9, and one for the w3u2 bootstrap. Using unrestricted residuals causes the test to reject more frequently for most, but not all, values of β_5, including $\beta_5 = 0$. Ideally, one would like to adjust both tests to have precisely the correct size, but this is very difficult to do in a way that is unambiguously correct; see Davidson and MacKinnon (2006). If one could do so, it is not clear that the w3u2 bootstrap would ever have greater power than the w3r2 bootstrap, and it is clear that it would actually have less power for many positive values of β_5.

It can be dangerous to draw conclusions from simulation experiments, especially in a case like this where the details of the experimental design are evidently very important. Nevertheless, it seems to be possible to draw several qualified conclusions from these experiments. Many of these echo previous theoretical and simulation results that may be found in Chesher and Austin (1991), Davidson and Flachaire (2008), and other papers, but others appear to be new.

- The best HCCME for asymptotic inference may not be the best one for bootstrap inference.
- When regressor matrices of various sizes are created by repeating a small number of observations as many times as necessary, both asymptotic and bootstrap tests perform better than they do when there is no repetition and $h_i^{\max}$ decreases slowly as n increases.
- Rejection frequencies for bootstrap tests can improve much more rapidly as n increases than ones for asymptotic tests, even when $h_i^{\max}$ decreases very slowly as n increases.
- Although well-chosen bootstrap methods can work much better than purely asymptotic ones, not all bootstrap methods work particularly well when $h_i^{\max}$ decreases slowly as n increases.
- There can be a substantial gain from using restricted residuals in the wild bootstrap DGP, especially when $h_i^{\max}$ decreases slowly as n increases.
- There can be a substantial gain from using F_2 rather than F_1 to generate the bootstrap error terms, especially when $h_i^{\max}$ decreases slowly as n increases.
- The power of bootstrap tests based on different HCCMEs can differ substantially. The limited evidence presented here suggests that HC1 may yield the greatest power and HC4 the least.
- There is no theoretical basis for, and no evidence to support, the idea that using unrestricted residuals in the bootstrap DGP will yield a more powerful test than using restricted residuals when the test statistic is asymptotically pivotal.

All the experiments focused on testing rather than confidence intervals. However, studentized bootstrap confidence intervals like (16) simply involve inverting bootstrap t tests based on unrestricted residuals. Thus, the poor performance of tests that use unrestricted residuals in the bootstrap DGP when $h_i^{\max}$ decreases slowly suggests that studentized bootstrap confidence intervals may not be particularly reliable when the data have that feature. In such cases, it is likely that one can obtain bootstrap confidence intervals with much better coverage by inverting bootstrap P values based on restricted residuals; see Davidson and MacKinnon (2011).

The base case for these experiments, in which the regressors are randomly generated from the log-normal distribution, is probably unrealistic. In practice, the performance of heteroskedasticity-robust tests may rarely be as bad for moderate and large sample sizes as it is in these experiments. But the other case, in which the rows of the regressor matrix repeat themselves every 20 observations, is even more

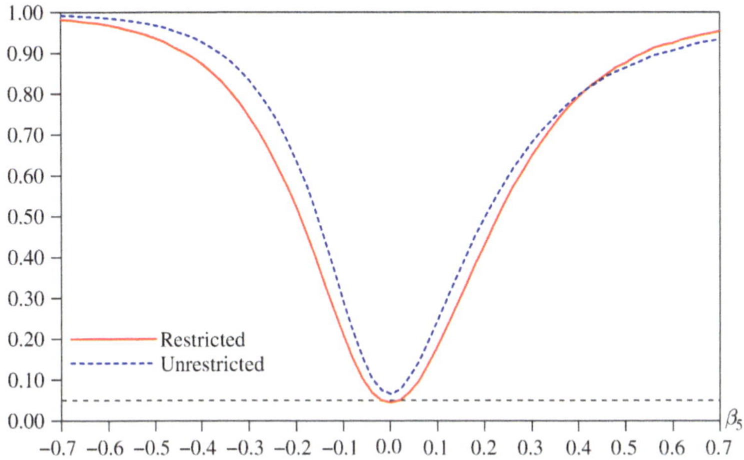

Fig. 10 Power of wild bootstrap HC1 t tests, $\gamma = 1$, $n = 40$

unrealistic. The many published simulation results that rely on this type of experimental design are almost certainly much too optimistic in their assessments of how well heteroskedasticity-robust tests and confidence intervals perform.

6 Conclusion

White (1980) showed econometricians how to make asymptotically valid inferences in the presence of heteroskedasticity of unknown form, and the impact of that paper on both econometric theory and empirical work has been enormous. Two strands of later research have investigated ways to make more accurate inferences in samples of moderate size. One strand has concentrated on finding improved covariance matrix estimators, and the other has focused on bootstrap methods. The wild bootstrap is currently the technique of choice. It has several variants, some of which are closely related to various HCCMEs. The wild bootstrap is not actually a substitute for a good covariance matrix estimator. Instead, it should be used in conjunction with one to provide more accurate tests and confidence intervals. This paper has discussed both strands of research and presented simulation results on the finite-sample performance of asymptotic and bootstrap tests.

Acknowledgments Research for this paper was supported, in part, by a grant from the Social Sciences and Humanities Research Council of Canada. I am grateful to Dimitris Politis, Patrik Guggenberger, and an anonymous referee for comments.

References

Andrews, D.W.K. (1991). "Heteroskedasticity and autocorrelation consistent covariance matrix estimation", Econometrica, 59:817–858.

Andrews, D.W.K., and J. C. Monahan (1992). "An improved heteroskedasticity and autocorrelation consistent covariance matrix estimator", Econometrica, 60, 953–966.

Cameron, A. C., J. B. Gelbach, and D. L. Miller (2008). "Bootstrap-based improvements for inference with clustered errors", Review of Economics and Statistics, 90, 414–427.

Chesher, A. (1989). "Hájek inequalities, measures of leverage and the size of heteroskedasticity robust tests", Journal of Econometrics, 57, 971–977.

Chesher, A., and G. Austin (1991). "The finite-sample distributions of heteroskedasticity robust Wald statistics", Journal of Econometrics, 47, 153–173.

Chesher, A., and I. Jewitt (1987). "The bias of a heteroskedasticity consistent covariance matrix estimator", Econometrica, 55, 1217–1222.

Cribari-Neto, F. (2004). "Asymptotic inference under heteroskedasticity of unknown form", Computational Statistics and Data Analysis, 45, 215–233.

Cribari-Neto, F., and M. G. A. Lima (2009). "Heteroskedasticity-consistent interval estimators", Journal of Statistical Computation and Simulation, 79, 787–803.

Cribari-Neto, F., and M. G. A. Lima (2010). "Sequences of bias-adjusted covariance matrix estimators under heteroskedasticity of unknown form", Annals of the Institute of Mathematical Statistics, 62, 1053–1082.

Cribari-Neto, F., T. C. Souza, and K. L. P. Vasconcellos (2007). "Inference under heteroskedasticity and leveraged data", Communications in Statistics: Theory and Methods, 36, 1977–1988 [see also Erratum (2008), 37, 3329–3330.].

Davidson, R., and E. Flachaire (2008). "The wild bootstrap, tamed at last", Journal of Econometrics, 146, 162–169.

Davidson, R. and J. G. MacKinnon (1993). Estimation and Inference in Econometrics, New York, Oxford University Press.

Davidson, R., and J. G. MacKinnon (1999). "The size distortion of bootstrap tests", Econometric Theory, 15, 361–376.

Davidson, R., and J. G. MacKinnon (2000). "Bootstrap tests: How many bootstraps?" Econometric Reviews, 19, 55–68.

Davidson, R., and J. G. MacKinnon (2006). "The power of bootstrap and asymptotic tests", Journal of Econometrics, 133, 421–441.

Davidson, R., and J. G. MacKinnon (2010). "Wild bootstrap tests for IV regression", Journal of Business and Economic Statistics, 28, 128–144.

Davidson, R., and J. G. MacKinnon (2011). "Confidence sets based on inverting Anderson-Rubin tests", Queen's University, QED Working Paper No. 1257.

Driscoll, J. C., and A. C. Kraay (1998). "Consistent covariance matrix estimation with spatially dependent panel data", Review of Economics and Statistics, 80, 549–560.

Efron, B. (1979). "Bootstrap methods: Another look at the jackknife", Annals of Statistics, 7, 1–26.

Efron, B. (1982). The Jackknife, the Bootstrap and Other Resampling Plans. Philadelphia, Society for Industrial and Applied Mathematics.

Eicker, F. (1963). "Asymptotic normality and consistency of the least squares estimators for families of linear regressions", Annals of Mathematical Statistics, 34, 447–456.

Eicker, F. (1967). "Limit theorems for regressions with unequal and dependent errors", in Fifth Berkeley Symposium on Mathematical Statistics and Probability, ed. L. M. Le Cam and J. Neyman, Berkeley, University of California Press, 1, 59–82.

Flachaire, E. (1999). "A better way to bootstrap pairs", Economics Letters, 64, 257–262.

Flachaire, E. (2005). "Bootstrapping heteroskedastic regression models: Wild bootstrap vs pairs bootstrap", Computational Statistics and Data Analysis, 49, 361–376.

Freedman, D. A. (1981). "Bootstrapping regression models", Annals of Statistics, 9, 1218–1228.

Froot, K. A. (1989). "Consistent covariance matrix estimation with cross-sectional dependence and heteroskedasticity in financial data", Journal of Financial and Quantitative Analysis, 24, 333–355.
Furno, M. (1996). "Small sample behavior of a robust heteroskedasticity consistent covariance matrix estimator", Journal of Statistical Computation and Simulation, 54, 115–128.
Hansen, L. P. (1982). "Large sample properties of generalized method of moments estimators", Econometrica, 50, 1029–1054.
Hinkley, D.V. (1977). "Jackknifing in unbalanced situations", Technometrics, 19, 285–292.
Horn, S. D., R. A. Horn, and D. B. Duncan (1975). "Estimating heteroskedastic variances in linear models", Journal of the American Statistical Association, 70, 380–385.
Horowitz, J. L. (2001). "The bootstrap", in Handbook of Econometrics, Vol. 5, ed. J. J. Heckman and E. E. Leamer. Amsterdam, North-Holland, 3159–3228.
Jöckel, K.-H. (1986). "Finite sample properties and asymptotic efficiency of Monte Carlo tests", Annals of Statistics, 14, 336–347.
Lancaster, T. (2006). "A note on bootstraps and robustness", Brown University Working Paper 2006–6.
Liu, R.Y. (1988). "Bootstrap procedures under some non-I.I.D. models", Annals of Statistics, 16, 1696–1708.
MacKinnon, J. G. (2002). "Bootstrap inference in econometrics", Canadian Journal of Economics, 35, 615–645.
MacKinnon, J. G., and H. White (1985). "Some heteroskedasticity consistent covariance matrix estimators with improved finite sample properties", Journal of Econometrics, 29, 305–325.
Mammen, E. (1993). "Bootstrap and wild bootstrap for high dimensional linear models", Annals of Statistics, 21, 255–285.
Newey, W.K., and K. D. West (1987). "A simple, positive semi-definite, heteroskedasticity and autocorrelation consistent covariance matrix", Econometrica, 55, 703–708.
Newey, W. K., and K. D. West (1994). "Automatic lag selection in covariance matrix estimation", Review of Economic Studies, 61,631–653.
Paparoditis, E., and D. N. Politis (2005). "Bootstrap hypothesis testing in regression models", Statistics and Probability Letters, 74, 356–365.
Poirier, D. J. (2010). "Bayesian interpretations of heteroskedastic consistent covariance estimators using the informed Bayesian bootstrap", Econometric Reviews, 30, 457–468.
Politis, D.N. (2010). "Model-free model-fitting and predictive distributions", Department of Economics, Univ. of California-San Diego.
Qian, L., and S. Wang (2001). "Bias-corrected heteroscedasticity robust covariance matrix (sandwich) estimators", Journal of Statistical Computation and Simulation, 70, 161–174.
Racine, J. S., and J. G. MacKinnon (2007). "Simulation-based tests that can use any number of simulations", Communications in Statistics: Simulation and Computation, 36, 357–365.
Rogers, W. H. (1993). "Regression standard errors in clustered samples", STATA Technical Bulletin, 13, 19–23.
Stine, R. A. (1985). "Bootstrap prediction intervals for regression", Journal of the American Statistical Association, 80, 1026–1031.
White, H. (1980). "A heteroskedasticity-consistent covariance matrix estimator and a direct test for heteroskedasticity", Econometrica, 48, 817–838.
White, H. (1982). "Maximum likelihood estimation of misspecified models", Econometrica, 50, 1–25.
White, H., and I. Domowitz (1984). "Nonlinear regression with dependent observations", Econometrica, 52, 143–161.

Smooth Constrained Frontier Analysis

Christopher F. Parmeter and Jeffrey S. Racine

Abstract Production frontiers (i.e., "production functions") specify the maximum output of firms, industries, or economies as a function of their inputs. A variety of innovative methods have been proposed for estimating both "deterministic" and "stochastic" frontiers. However, existing approaches are either parametric in nature, rely on nonsmooth nonparametric methods, or rely on nonparametric or semiparametric methods that ignore theoretical axioms of production theory, each of which can be problematic. In this chapter we propose a class of smooth constrained nonparametric and semiparametric frontier estimators that may be particularly appealing to practitioners who require smooth (i.e., continuously differentiable) estimates that, in addition, are consistent with theoretical axioms of production.

Keywords Efficiency · Concavity · Monotonicity · Constrained Kernel Estimator

We would like to thank but not implicate Subal Kumbhakar, Peter Schmidt, Paul Wilson and Jeff Wooldridge for their insightful comments and suggestions. All errors in this chapter are due to technical inefficiency and not noise. Racine would like to gratefully acknowledge support from Natural Sciences and Engineering Research Council of Canada (NSERC:www.nserc.ca), the Social Sciences and Humanities Research Council of Canada (SSHRC:www.sshrc.ca), and the Shared Hierarchical Academic Research Computing Network (SHARCNET:www.sharcnet.ca).

C. F. Parmeter (✉)
Department of Economics, University of Miami,
517-E Jenkins Building University of Miami Coral Gables,
FL 33124-6520, USA
e-mail: cparmeter@bus.miami.edu

J. S. Racine
Department of Economics, University of Miami,
Kenneth Taylor Hall, Rm 431,
1280 Main Street West HamiltonON L8S 4M4, Canada
e-mail: racinej@mcmaster.ca

X. Chen and N. R. Swanson (eds.), *Recent Advances and Future Directions in Causality, Prediction, and Specification Analysis*, DOI: 10.1007/978-1-4614-1653-1_18,

1 Overview

Estimating production relationships is a key component of both applied micro- and macroeconomic research. Modern analysis traces its roots to the pioneering empirical work of Cobb and Douglas (1928), Klein (1947) and Arrow et al. (1961). Though this work was notable for the application of statistical methodology to the estimation of a fundamental object in economics (the "production function"), the field continues to evolve in innovative and sometimes controversial ways; see Leibenstein (1966) for a case in point. The theory of production has matured considerably since its early days. The modern theoretical framework for production analysis stems from the path breaking work of Debreu (1951), Shephard (1953, 1970), and Diewert (1971), to name a few.

A continuing theme in applied production analysis is the specification of economic functionals of interest, specifically production, profit and cost functions. The appeal of deploying nonparametric methods in these settings is that "Approximation of these functions and their derivatives can aid in confirmation or refutation of particular theories of the firm..." (Hornik et al. 1990, p. 552). Here we embrace the full essence of these considerations and develop nonparametric estimators for both deterministic and stochastic frontiers which respect theoretical conditions on the derivatives.

We do not restrict *ex ante* which constraints should be imposed in a given setting as this is clearly application specific. Rather, we propose an approach that can easily handle numerous constraints simultaneously. As such, the methods proposed herein ought to be of general utility in keeping with Amsler et al. (2009, p. 22) who comment "Of course we can always estimate a regression consistently by purely nonparametric methods like kernels or nearest neighbors, but there ought to be advantages of imposing the restrictions that economic theory dictates." We demonstrate that indeed there are substantial advantages to imposing restrictions dictated by economic theory on nonparametric frontier methods, thus the constrained nonparametric kernel estimators we propose address one of the outstanding issues in applied frontier analysis.[1] The interpretation of the "advantages" that using constrained methods provides does not necessarily lie on the statistical side. Rather, while constrained nonparametric methods may fail to improve rates of convergence or are asymptotically equivalent to their unconstrained counterparts (when the constraints are "correct," i.e., consistent with the data generating process ("DGP")), the real benefits lie in the ability to implement estimators which respect economic theory for the data at hand and the ability to test economic restrictions.

In this chapter we propose three kernel-based frontier estimators that satisfy requisite axioms of production and are continuously differentiable. Two are deterministic frontier estimators while the third is a stochastic frontier estimator. All three of these methods incorporate general axioms of production by exploiting recent advances in constrained kernel estimation; see Hall and Huang (2001) and Du et al. (2010) for

[1] Amsler et al. (2009) continue, "We predict that in the foreseeable future the methodology will exist for routine application of the stochastic frontier model without a parametric specification of the frontier."

details. They therefore represent smooth nonparametric generalizations of Aigner and Chu (1968) goal programming approach, Winsten (1957) constrained ordinary least squares (COLS) method, and Aigner et al. (1977) stochastic frontier approach. The first deterministic frontier method envelopes the data directly and is termed "smooth goal programming" (SGP) and may be of interest to those currently using data envelopment analysis (DEA) approaches. The second deterministic frontier method "corrects" a smooth nonparametric conditional mean function and is termed "smooth corrected programming" (SCP), and may be of interest to those currently using corrected deterministic frontier methods. As such, the second approach can be thought of as the smooth counterpart of Kuosmanen and Johnson (2010). The third method is a constrained version of Fan et al. (1996) but where the resulting estimator is guaranteed to satisfy general production axioms and is termed "smooth stochastic frontier" (SSF), and this method may be of interest to those using flexible stochastic frontier methods. Additionally, we show how concavity can be imposed using simple linear constraints as opposed to more computationally demanding nonlinear constraints (O'Donnell and Coelli 2005; Henderson and Parmeter 2009), which constitutes an extension to constrained kernel methods not done elsewhere that may be of general interest.

The appeal of this chapter lies in its contribution to the applied econometric literature on empirical constrained nonparametric methods. A number of empirical chapters use constrained nonparametric methods to investigate a range of topics including Briesch et al. (2002), who estimate a constrained nonparametric model of consumer brand choice focusing on the utility of price and discounts, Yatchew and Härdle (2006), who deploy constrained methods to estimate the state price density (a key object of interest in option pricing theory), Haag et al. (2009), who impose the Slutsky symmetry conditions in a demand system (which they estimate using nonparametric kernel methods), and Blundell et al. (2012), who use methods similar to those contained herein to measure the price elasticity of gasoline demand imposing the Slutsky shape restriction, to name but a few.[2]

The outline of the rest of this chapter is as follows. Section 2 outlines the restricted nonparametric estimators upon which our proposed smooth constrained frontier estimators are based. Section 3 formally describes our approach and establishes the requisite theoretical properties. Section 4 provides several Monte Carlo simulations designed to examine the finite-sample performance of the methods while Sect. 5 provides an illustrative example. Section 6 provides concluding remarks.

[2] See the webpage for the conference "Shape Restrictions in Non- and Semiparametric Estimation of Econometric Models" hosted by Northwestern University's Center for Econometrics on November 5-6, 2010 (http://www.wcas.northwestern.edu/cfe/conferences.html).

2 Constrained Nonparametric Regression

The three frontier methods we outline below require as input a nonparametric model constrained to obey axioms of production theory. We adopt the approach of Du et al. (2010) and direct the reader to that article for theoretical underpinnings and further details. Below we provide a brief sketch of their approach for the interested reader.

In what follows we let $\{(x_i, y_i)\}_{i=1}^n$ denote sample pairs of inputs and outputs and x a point of support at which we evaluate the frontier. Our goal is to nonparametrically estimate the unknown production frontier $m(x)$ subject to constraints on $m^{(\mathbf{s})}(x)$ where $\mathbf{s}$ is a k-vector corresponding to the dimension of x. The elements of $\mathbf{s}$ represent the order of the partial derivative corresponding to each element of x. Thus $\mathbf{s} = (0, 0, \ldots, 0)$ represents the function itself, while $\mathbf{s} = (1, 0, \ldots, 0)$ represents $\partial m(x)/\partial x_1$. In general, for $\mathbf{s} = (s_1, s_2, \ldots, s_k)$ we have

$$m^{(\mathbf{s})}(x) = \frac{\partial^{s_1} m(x)}{\partial x_1^{s_1}}, \ldots, \frac{\partial^{s_k} m(x)}{\partial x_k^{s_k}}. \tag{1}$$

We consider the class of kernel regression smoothers that can be written as linear combinations of the output y_i, i.e.,

$$\hat{m}(x) = \sum_{i=1}^{n} n^{-1} A_i(x) y_i, \tag{2}$$

which is a very broad class. For instance, the local constant Nadaraya-Watson estimator uses

$$A_i(x) = \frac{n K_\gamma(x_i, x)}{\sum_{j=1}^{n} K_\gamma(X_j, x)}, \tag{3}$$

where $K_\gamma(\cdot)$ is a generalized product kernel that admits both continuous and categorical inputs, and γ is a vector of bandwidths; see Racine and Li (2004) for details. Though we restrict attention to the class of kernel regression smoothers, there is no barrier preventing the application of these methods to other nonparametric estimators such as artificial neural networks (White 1989).

In order to impose constraints on a nonparametric frontier, we shall require a nonparametric estimator that satisfies constraints of the form

$$l(x) \le \hat{m}^{(\mathbf{s})}(x) \le u(x) \tag{4}$$

for arbitrary $l(\cdot)$, $u(\cdot)$, and $\mathbf{s}$, where $l(\cdot)$ and $u(\cdot)$ represent (local) lower and upper bounds, respectively.

The constrained estimator is obtained by introducing an n-vector of weights, p, chosen so that the resulting estimator satisfies (4). We define the constrained estimator to be

$$\hat{m}(x|p) = \sum_{i=1}^{n} p_i A_i(x) y_i, \tag{5}$$

such that (4) is satisfied. Construction of (5) proceeds as follows. Let p_u be an n-vector with elements $1/n$ and let p be the vector of weights to be selected. In order to impose our constraints, we choose $p = \hat{p}$ to minimize the distance from p to the uniform weights p_u using the distance metric $D(p) = (p_u - p)'(p_u - p)$. The constrained estimator is then obtained by selecting those weights p that minimize $D(p)$ subject to constraints such as those given in (8), (9) and (10) below, which can be cast as a general nonlinear programming problem. For the constraints we need to impose (frontier behavior, monotonicity and concavity) we will have inequalities that are linear in p, which can be solved using standard quadratic programming methods and off-the-shelf software.[3] The appropriate bandwidth(s) for our unknown function can be estimated using any of the commonly available data-driven procedures and require estimation of the unrestricted function only. For notational simplicity we shall drop the "$|p$" notation with the understanding that the constrained estimator is that defined in (5) above.

Before proceeding to discuss constrained estimation of frontier functions, we note that the derivatives which the constraints are applied to depend on the estimator used. For example, consider the local linear estimator of $m(x)$ and its derivatives,

$$\hat{\delta}(x) = \min_{\delta(x)} (\mathcal{Y} - \mathcal{X}\delta(x))'\mathcal{K}(x)(\mathcal{Y} - \mathcal{X}\delta(x)),$$

where $\mathcal{Y}$ is an $n \times 1$ vector with ith component y_i, $\mathcal{X}$ is an $n \times (1+d)$ matrix with ith row $\left(1, (x_i - x)'\right)$, $\mathcal{K}(x)$ is the $n \times n$ diagonal matrix having ith diagonal element $K_\gamma(x_i, x)$, and γ is a vector of bandwidths. The vector $\delta(x)$ contains the conditional mean evaluated at x (first component) as well as the d first order derivatives of $m(x)$ (the 2 through $d+1$ components). The vector $\hat{\delta}(x)$ is a consistent estimator for $m(x)$ and its d first order derivatives (Li and Racine 2007, Theorem 2.7).

The derivative estimates arising directly from the local linear estimator (elements 2 through $d+1$ of $\hat{\delta}(x)$), will differ from the analytical derivatives, even though they are asymptotically equivalent under standard conditions required for consistency. Thus, if economic constraints are imposed on the direct derivatives, this may produce an estimated surface which is not consistent with the constraints. Fortunately this can be avoided by imposing the constraints on the analytical derivatives of the local polynomial estimator being used.

We now deploy the constrained estimator outlined above for smooth constrained nonparametric estimation of both deterministic and stochastic frontier models.

---

[3] For example, in the `R` language it is solved using the `quadprog` package, in GAUSS it is solved using the `qprog` command, and in MATLAB the `quadprog` command. Even when n is quite large the solution is computationally fast using any of these packages.

3 Smooth Constrained Nonparametric Frontier Estimation

The starting point for modeling production frontiers is

$$y_i = m(x_i) + \varepsilon_i, \quad i = 1, \ldots, n, \tag{6}$$

where y_i represents output, x_i a k-vector of inputs, $m(\cdot)$ the frontier (i.e., maximum output given x), and ε_i is either one-sided technical inefficiency (deterministic frontier) or a two-part composed error term (stochastic frontier) consisting of a one-sided term representing inefficiency (u_i) and a two-sided term representing statistical noise (v_i) such that $\varepsilon_i = v_i - u_i$.

We shall first consider constrained nonparametric extensions of two popular approaches used to estimate deterministic frontiers, and then proceed to estimate constrained semiparametric stochastic frontiers (SSFs). Naturally, the constraints will be those dictated by the axioms of production theory.

3.1 Constrained Nonparametric Deterministic Frontiers

The deterministic frontier approach models $\varepsilon_i = -u_i$ as a one-sided process, i.e., $\varepsilon_i \leq 0$. One could estimate the frontier directly using programming type methods such as DEA or, by specifying the functional form for $m(\cdot)$, could proceed indirectly via COLS,[4] which necessarily places joint restrictions on ε_i and $m(\cdot)$. We briefly outline COLS in a linear production function setting by way of illustration. Presume that the deterministic frontier model is

$$y_i = \alpha + x_i'\beta + \varepsilon_i, \quad i = 1, \ldots, n, \tag{7}$$

and that one estimates this model ignoring the error structure to obtain estimates $\hat{\alpha}$ and $\hat{\beta}$. Since $E[\varepsilon_i|x_i] \neq 0$, $\hat{\alpha}$ is a biased estimate of α. Moreover, the production function will not lie above all of the data which is inconsistent with the notion that $m(x_i) = \alpha + x_i'\beta$ is a frontier. To remedy this COLS corrects the estimated intercept to guarantee that the adjusted frontier function does indeed lie above the observed outputs. That is $\hat{\alpha}_c = \hat{\alpha} + \max_i \hat{\varepsilon}_i$ and the residuals are corrected in the opposite direction, $\hat{\varepsilon}_i^c = \hat{\varepsilon}_i - \max_i \hat{\varepsilon}_i$. Greene (1980) shows that this procedure will produce consistent estimates for α and ε_i^c *presuming the model is correctly specified and given that a set of regularity conditions hold.* However, in applied settings one may worry about misspecification, or one may test for correct parametric specification

[4] The idea of shifting an estimated production function stems from Winsten (1957) comment on Farrell (1957) description of an industry "envelope" isoquant, namely, that the estimated regression represents an average production function which could be shifted vertically to estimate the production frontier itself.

and reject one's model using, say, Hong and White (1995) test. In either case, models that are robust to misspecification would have obvious appeal.

In what follows we propose two alternate nonparametric deterministic frontier estimators, one that bounds the data and (unlike DEA) is smooth everywhere, requiring only one stage, and one that can be considered the smoothed version of the estimator proposed by Kuosmanen and Johnson (2010). Due to the fact that this setup will allow us to incorporate restrictions on the frontier and on its derivatives, imposing bounds, monotonicity and concavity is straightforward. Let our constrained estimator defined in (5) satisfy the following restrictions:

$$\sum_{i=1}^{n} p_i A_i(x_i) y_i - y_i \geq 0, \tag{8}$$

$$\sum_{i=1}^{n} p_i \left[\sum_{\mathbf{s} \in \mathbf{S}_1} A_i^{(\mathbf{s})}(x) \right] y_i \geq 0, \tag{9}$$

$$\sum_{i=1}^{n} p_i \left[\sum_{\mathbf{s} \in \mathbf{S}_2} A_i^{(\mathbf{s})}(x) \right] y_i \leq 0, \tag{10}$$

where $\mathbf{S}_1$ is

$$\left[(1, 0, \ldots, 0)\ (0, 1, \ldots, 0) \cdots (0, 0, \ldots, 1) \right]_k ,$$

while $\mathbf{S}_2$ is

$$\left[(2, 0, \ldots, 0)\ (0, 2, \ldots, 0) \cdots (0, 0, \ldots, 2) \right]_k .$$

These three conditions guarantee that the estimated frontier lies (weakly) above all observed output while respecting monotonicity and *necessary* conditions for concavity. This direct one-step estimator can be thought of as the smooth, nonparametric variant of Aigner and Chu (1968) parametric goal programming approach which we term $\hat{m}^{\mathrm{SGP}}(x_i)$ SGP.

Note that for $k = 1$ the above conditions are both necessary and sufficient for concavity, however, for $k \geq 2$ they may not be sufficient. To ensure that sufficiency is met we shall, in addition, impose additional linear conditions. While these additional conditions are known under a variety of names, they are commonly termed the Afriat conditions (or inequalities); see Kuosmanen (2008). Note that if, instead, one were to focus attention on the matrix of second derivatives this would involve nonlinear constraints which are more complicated, computationally speaking, than Afriat (1967) approach (the Afriat conditions are linear in the constraint weights).[5] Assuming that the unknown frontier is first order differentiable,[6] Afriat (1967) conditions state that a function is (globally) concave if and only if

---

[5] See Henderson and Parmeter (2009) for a detailed exposition on imposing concavity using the Hessian in this setting.

[6] Note that the class of nonparametric estimators considered herein also rely on this assumption.

$$m(\mathbf{z}) - m(\mathbf{x}) \leq \frac{\partial m}{\partial x_1}(\mathbf{x})(z_1 - x_1) + \cdots + \frac{\partial m}{\partial x_k}(\mathbf{x})(z_k - x_k), \quad \forall \mathbf{z}, \mathbf{x}. \tag{11}$$

In our framework these inequalities can be handled directly without resorting to nonlinear constrained optimization, though of course this does not reduce the number of overall inequalities that must be imposed (a total of $n \times (n-1) \times k$ inequalities for $k \geq 2$).[7]

Before proceeding, a few words on constraining production frontiers are in order. Though concavity[8] is sometimes warranted and imposed on estimated production functions (Chambers 1988), it may be viewed as a special case and practitioners frequently estimate models (e.g., the translog) which, by definition, cannot be concave without destroying their flexibility (Ryan and Wales 2000). The failure to verify whether concavity is satisfied using well-established tests (Hanoch and Rothschild 1972) is not uncommon; see the discussion in O'Donnell and Coelli (2005, p. 495) on the importance of imposing and checking theoretical constraints when estimating production relationships. Functional forms which can accommodate both long and short run behavior have been proposed in the literature, and by construction are not globally concave. By way of example, Duggal et al. (1999, p. 47) note that their production function has a form which "allows for an S-shaped production function which embodies not only the properties of a long-run production function but also those exhibited in the short run." We therefore wish to alert the reader to the fact that, though our method is capable of imposing concavity (in addition to a range of other constraints), in applied production settings it may be unwise to impose concavity on production functions without further investigation (Duggal et al. 2007). Of course, it is trivial to drop this restriction while maintaining (weak) monotonicity, and our method is quite general and can handle concavity which is theoretically needed in the context of cost (revenue) function estimation, concavity (convexity) in prices, and so forth.

Powerful and flexible nonsmooth conditional mean-based deterministic frontier methods that satisfy requisite constraints have been proposed (Kuosmanen and Johnson 2010; Kuosmanen and Kortelainen 2011). The following corrected method will produce a smooth counterpart to Kuosmanen and Johnson (2010). Thus, as an alternative to the SGP estimator proposed above, if one is willing to impose a set of regularity conditions on the inefficiency and base the frontier on a conditional mean, then a simple two step estimator can be constructed by estimating the mean production function in Eq. (5) subject to the constraints in (9) and (11) (Eq. (10) would suffice if $k = 1$). Having estimated the constrained conditional mean (which we shall call $\hat{g}(x_i)$ to distinguish it from the frontier estimator $\hat{m}(x_i)$) we can obtain residuals (i.e., $\hat{\varepsilon}_i = y_i - \hat{g}(x_i)$) and then use $\max_i \hat{\varepsilon}_i$ to correct our estimate. The following procedure will yield our SCP deterministic frontier estimator:

---

[7] The use of these conditions to impose concavity is not uncommon and is used by Matzkin (1991) in a utility theoretic context and also by Kuosmanen and Johnson (2010) in the nonsmooth production context.

[8] In some settings quasi-concavity is assumed instead of concavity, and our approach is applicable for both.

(i) First, estimate the conditional mean $\hat{g}(x_i)$ imposing the constraints in (9) and (11) (or (10)) and obtain the residuals, $\hat{\varepsilon}_i$.
(ii) Second, shift the estimated conditional mean so that it envelopes the data, i.e., construct

$$\hat{m}^{\mathrm{SCP}}(x_i) = \hat{g}(x_i) + \max_i \hat{\varepsilon}_i .$$

(iii) Finally, calculate estimates of producer inefficiency,

$$\hat{\varepsilon}_i^{\mathrm{SCP}} = \hat{m}^{\mathrm{SCP}}(x_i) - y_i = \hat{\varepsilon}_i - \max_i \hat{\varepsilon}_i .$$

We drop the lower bound constraint on $\hat{g}(x_i)$ since Kuosmanen and Johnson (2010, Theorem 4.2) show that the discriminatory power of C^2NLS is greater than that of a DEA estimator. The reason for this is as follows; input values in either the extreme lower or upper end of the support tend to reflect the frontier estimator downward, resulting in a biased estimate of a firm's efficiency level. The two-step procedure that corrects the entire frontier is not impacted to the same degree as the one step method since all observations are used in the smoothing. Below we show that this relationship holds between our SGP and SCP estimators.

3.2 Constrained Semiparametric Stochastic Frontiers

Unlike the fully nonparametric deterministic approach outlined above, the approach we now outline for stochastic frontiers is, strictly speaking, a semiparametric method as it relies on parametric structure for the composed error distribution. Smooth estimation of a stochastic frontier was proposed by Fan et al. (1996). They note that standard maximum likelihood methods are infeasible when one does not specify (i.e., parameterize) the production function. They further note that direct nonparametric estimation of the conditional mean would result in a biased estimate when one ignores the inefficiency term. Fan et al. (1996) solution is to correct this (downward) bias by retaining standard distributional assumptions from the SFA literature (e.g., normal noise, half-normal inefficiency) and estimating the corresponding distributional parameters via maximum likelihood on the nonparametric residuals from a standard kernel regression. Once these parameters are determined, the estimated conditional mean can be shifted (bias-corrected) by the estimated mean of the inefficiency distribution (mean correction factor). Under weak conditions Fan et al. (1996) show that the parameters of the composed error distribution can be estimated at the parametric $\sqrt{n}$ rate. Their simulations reveal that the semiparametric method produces estimates of the distributional parameters that are competitive with the same distributional parameter estimates produced from correctly specified production frontiers in the standard maximum likelihood framework. One drawback of their approach, however, is that they do not constrain the estimator so that it satisfies general axioms of production. As such, there is room for improvement.

A key distinction between the previous work of Fan et al. (1996) and that proposed here is that the proposed semiparametric estimator is guaranteed to satisfy the theoretical axioms of producer theory (production, cost, profit, etc.). This is especially important if one is interested in returns to scale or technical change. For example, returns to scale is defined as the sum of input elasticities (which are to be non-negative), and it is essential that these restrictions are satisfied at all data points. In an unconstrained semiparametric setting this is not guaranteed to be the case. Furthermore, empirical results may not be of much use for policy purposes if, for example, the scale measure is defined at the mean (which may not be indicative of any producer in the sample), or if production restrictions are violated for individual producers. These situations could arise in an unconstrained semiparametric framework which underscores the importance of deploying constrained nonparametric estimation in a production setting.

Our approach to estimating stochastic frontiers follows directly along the lines of Fan et al. (1996) thereby affording the researcher the same flexibility that the estimator of Fan et al. (1996) provides, but in addition we constrain the resulting stochastic frontier to satisfy general axioms of production as was done for the two deterministic approaches defined above. This is achieved by replacing the unknown conditional mean in Fan et al. (1996, (13), p. 462) with one based upon (5) defined above. No further changes are necessary, and all results of Fan et al. (1996) follow without modification.

Fan et al. (1996) assume that the noise follows a mean zero normal distributive law and that the technical inefficiency stems from a half-normal distributive law. Given these presumptions and given the constrained estimate (5) one would construct the smooth constrained stochastic semiparametric frontier model as follows:

(i) Compute the (constrained) smooth conditional expectation, $E[y_i|x_i]$, as described above and call this $\hat{g}(x_i)$. Let the residuals be denoted $\hat{\varepsilon}_i = y_i - \hat{g}(x_i)$.
(ii) Define the concentrated variance of the composed error term $\sigma^2(\lambda)$ as a function of $\lambda = \sigma_u/\sigma_v$, $\sigma^2 = \sigma_u^2 + \sigma_v^2$, as follows:

$$\hat{\sigma}^2(\lambda) = \frac{n^{-1}\sum_{i=1}^{n}\hat{\varepsilon}_i^2}{1 - \frac{2\lambda^2}{\pi(1+\lambda^2)}}. \tag{12}$$

(iii) Define the mean correction factor $\mu(\lambda)$ as a function of λ, i.e.,

$$\hat{\mu}(\lambda) = \frac{\sqrt{2}\hat{\sigma}\lambda}{\left\{\pi(1+\lambda^2)\right\}^{1/2}}. \tag{13}$$

(iv) Estimate λ by maximizing the concentrated log likelihood function consistent with the presumed distributional assumptions. In this setting we have

$$\hat{\lambda} = \max_{\lambda}\left(-n\ln\hat{\sigma}(\lambda) + \sum_{i=1}^{n}\ln(\Phi(-\tilde{\varepsilon}_i\lambda/\hat{\sigma}(\lambda)) - (2\hat{\sigma}^2(\lambda))^{-1}\sum_{i=1}^{n}\tilde{\varepsilon}_i^2\right), \quad (14)$$

where $\tilde{\varepsilon}_i = \hat{\varepsilon}_i - \hat{\mu}(\lambda)$ and $\Phi(\cdot)$ is the cumulative distribution function for a standard normal random variate.

(v) The constrained smooth stochastic production frontier $m(x_i)$ is consistently estimated by

$$\hat{m}^{\mathrm{SSF}}(x_i) = \hat{g}(x_i) + \hat{\mu}, \quad (15)$$

where $\hat{\mu} = \sqrt{2}\hat{\sigma}\hat{\lambda}/\left(\pi(1+\hat{\lambda}^2)\right)$ and where $\hat{\sigma} = \sqrt{\hat{\sigma}^2(\hat{\lambda})}$. See Fan et al. (1996) for further details.

Again, the sole difference between the approach of Fan et al. (1996) and $\hat{m}^{\mathrm{SSF}}(x_i)$ defined above is that, in addition to being a semiparametric smooth estimate, $\hat{m}^{\mathrm{SSF}}(x_i)$ will satisfy the axioms of production which it inherits from $\hat{g}(x_i)$ above. We show below that this difference is non-trivial.

3.3 Theoretical Properties

We now outline some elementary properties of the proposed estimators.

Theorem 3.1 *For independent and identically distributed inefficiency terms, $\varepsilon_1, \ldots, \varepsilon_n$, which are uncorrelated with the covariates X, if $f(\varepsilon_i) > 0$ at $\varepsilon_i = 0$, the SCP efficiency estimator is consistent. That is*

$$\operatorname*{plim}_{n\to\infty} \hat{\varepsilon}_i^{\mathrm{SCP}} = \varepsilon_i, \quad \forall i = 1, \ldots, n.$$

Proof of Theorem 3.1 Letting $\mu = E[\varepsilon_i]$, Du et al. (2010) (Theorem 2.2(i)) guarantees that $\hat{\varepsilon}_i$ (obtained from the first stage) is a consistent estimator for $\varepsilon_i - \mu\ \forall\, i$ since $E[\varepsilon_i - \mu] = 0$. The arguments in Greene (1980, pp. 32–34) show that $\operatorname*{plim}_{n\to\infty} \varepsilon_{(1)} = 0$, where $\varepsilon_{(1)}$ is the first order statistic of ε. This implies that $\operatorname*{plim}_{n\to\infty} \hat{\varepsilon}_{(1)} = \mu$. Therefore, $\operatorname*{plim}_{n\to\infty} \hat{\varepsilon}_i^{\mathrm{SCP}} = \operatorname*{plim}_{n\to\infty} \hat{\varepsilon}_i - \operatorname*{plim}_{n\to\infty} \max_j \hat{\varepsilon}_j = (\varepsilon_i - \mu) - \operatorname*{plim}_{n\to\infty} \hat{\varepsilon}_{(1)} = \varepsilon_i$. □

This result implies that our corrected procedure will produce consistent estimates of producer inefficiency when regularity conditions on the inefficiency distribution are met. Moreover, this result implies that our efficiency estimates are asymptotically unbiased as well, albeit only in an iid framework. Additionally, in a comment to Schmidt (1985), Yatchew (1985, Proposition 1) proves consistency of a nonparametric deterministic frontier assuming compact support of the vector of inputs and that the unknown function comes from a family of functions which are equicontinuous and bounded. Consistency is also obtained by replacing the equicontinuity assumption with an appropriate Lipschitz condition on the family of functions.

Theorem 3.2 *We have that a)* $\hat{\varepsilon}_i^{SCP} \leq \hat{\varepsilon}_i^{SGP} \leq 0\ \forall i$ *and b)* $\hat{\varepsilon}_i^{SCP} \leq \hat{\varepsilon}_i^{SSF}\ \forall i$.

Proof of Theorem 3.2 For (a), suppose not. Then for an arbitrary firm j, $\hat{\varepsilon}_j^{SCP} \geq \hat{\varepsilon}_j^{SGP}$. Since our nonparametric goal programming method envelopes the data and both the SGP and SCP frontiers are concave there must exist at least one firm such that $\hat{\varepsilon}_i^{SGP} = 0$ and $\hat{\varepsilon}_i^{SCP} \geq 0$. However, this implies that $\hat{\varepsilon}_i^{SCP} = \hat{\varepsilon}_i - \max_j \hat{\varepsilon}_j \geq 0$ which implies that $\hat{\varepsilon}_i \geq \max_j \hat{\varepsilon}_j$ which is a contradiction.

For (b) we see immediately that since $\hat{\varepsilon}_i^{SCP} = \hat{\varepsilon}_i - \max_j \hat{\varepsilon}_j$ and $\hat{\varepsilon}_i^{SSF} = \hat{\varepsilon}_i - \hat{\mu}(\lambda)$, $\hat{\varepsilon}_i^{SCP} \leq \hat{\varepsilon}_i^{SSF}$ since the estimator of the mean of the one-sided distribution cannot be larger than the largest composed error residual. Moreover, since both $\hat{m}^{SCP}(x)$ and $\hat{m}^{SSF}(x)$ employ identical first stage estimates, they differ only in the amount of their (upward) correction. □

Theorem 3.2 states that our two stage corrected deterministic estimator lies everywhere above our single stage goal programming approach. This result does not, however, provide insight into the efficiency (statistically speaking) of the estimates which we therefore investigate via Monte Carlo simulation in the next section. Additionally, because the SCP estimator (as well as COLS, MOLS and C^2NLS) is based upon a (shifted) conditional mean, there is no guarantee that the microeconomic features of interest (returns to scale (henceforth RTS), technical change, elasticities of substitution) are equivalent among methods. This can be seen immediately in Fig. 1.[9] Here we have generated data from a single input frontier with one-sided inefficiency and fit the model using both SGP and SCP. If we were to shift the average production frontier so that it encapsulated all of the data, it would severely distort estimates of inefficiency.

The second part of Theorem 3.2 states that our SSF estimator is everywhere below our SCP estimator, which is intuitive since the SSF estimator and the SCP estimator use identical first stage estimates. We cannot generalize a result between the SSF estimator and the SGP estimator without further assumptions on the error terms (composed or not). Even though both the SGP and SSF estimators have the same smoothness constraints imposed (monotonicity and concavity), the SGP constraint is imposed at the frontier while the SSF constraint is imposed at the mean thus the shape of the SGP and the SSF curves could well differ. Further, this implies that there could exist a crossing of the SGP and SSF frontiers which rules out a strict relationship between their inefficiency estimates.

The point here is that while these estimators may be consistent, the behavior of shifted average estimators may not be consistent with direct frontier estimators in finite-sample settings. Unfortunately, the fact that SGP and DEA bound the data leaves them susceptible to outliers.[10] Kuosmanen and Johnson (2010, pp. 17–18) note that "In contrast to DEA, however, all observations influence the shape of the C^2NLS

---

[9] For this figure, the input was generated $\mathcal{U}[0, 5]$, the frontier was given by $\sqrt{\text{input}/2}$, the inefficiency was half-normal with mean zero and standard deviation 0.15, and negative output values were set to zero.

[10] Timmer (1971) proposed an *ad hoc* upper bound to mitigate the effect of outliers in a goal programming setting. Alternative strategies for dealing with outliers in the DEA context include Cazals et al. (2002) who proposed a robust method for approximating the frontier for the free

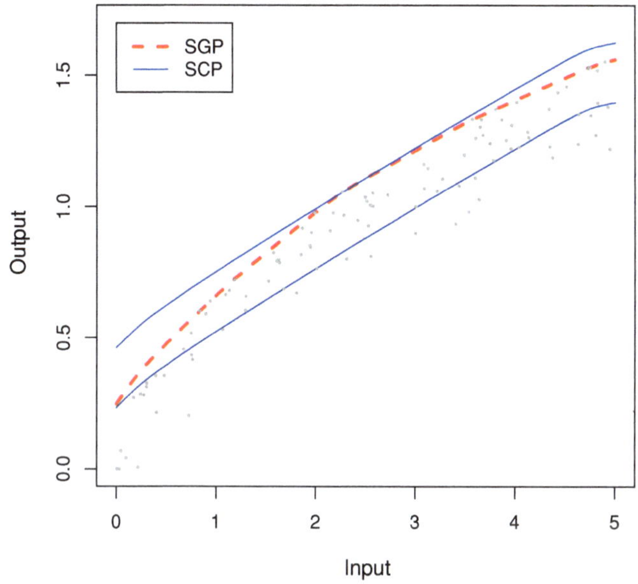

Fig. 1 Deterministic Frontier. Conditional mean-based (SCP) versus maximal (SGP) output Estimation. The top two lines represent frontier estimates, the bottom line the conditional mean

frontier. Thus, a single outlier located above the frontier does not distort the shape of the C^2NLS frontier as severely as in DEA. Further, C^2NLS utilizes the information that inefficient observations contain about the frontier." We note that SGP contains the same desirable features of C^2NLS, i.e., all observations influence the shape of the frontier (via local smoothing) but the presence of outliers can (and will) distort both the SGP and SCP estimators described here as well as the C^2NLS estimator. Again, these estimators are designed for estimation of deterministic frontiers and data with substantial noise should not be modelled using these methods. We do, however, wish to point out that kernel methods have recently been proposed that admit outliers and these approaches might be applicable in such instances; we direct the interested reader to Leung (2005) and the references therein.

Figure 2 presents the counterpart to Fig. 1 for a stochastic frontier. In Fig. 2 we compare the proposed smooth corrected semiparametric frontier (SSF) versus the smooth uncorrected semiparametric frontier ("U-SSF") of Fan et al. (1996). It is evident that imposing the requisite constraints of production theory can bring the semiparametric estimate in line with basic production axioms (one can observe neg-

---

(Footnote 10 continued)
disposal hull (FDH) estimator. This estimator is known as the "order-m frontier estimator" (as $m \to \infty$ this approaches the standard FDH estimator). For small values of m the order-m frontier does not bound the data and is not heavily influenced by outliers, while if one were to convexify the estimator it represents a robust (to outliers) DEA type estimator.

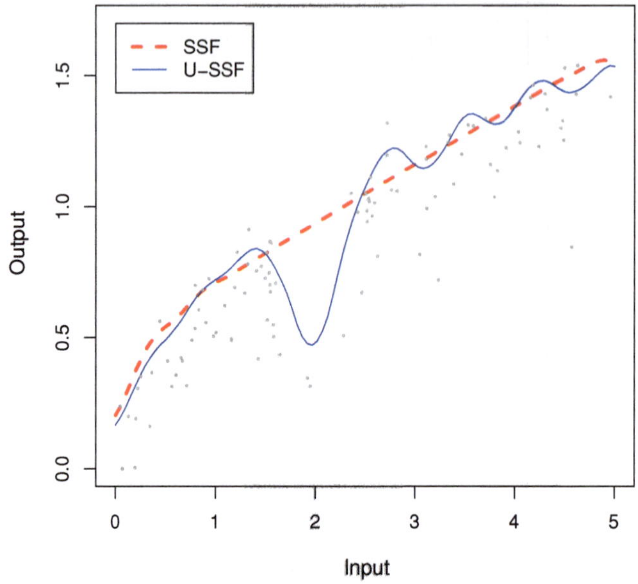

Fig. 2 Stochastic Frontier. Smooth corrected semiparametric frontier (SSF) versus the smooth uncorrected semiparametric frontier (U-SSF)

ative marginal productivity estimates present in the U-SSF estimator, for example, i.e., a negative slope of the U-SSF frontier for some firms).

4 Finite-Sample Behavior

In this section we undertake a series of Monte Carlo experiments designed to assess the finite-sample performance of the proposed approaches. The same underlying models are used for both the deterministic and stochastic frontier simulations though with differential treatment of ε. For simulations we make use of the `R` environment for statistical computing (R Development Core Team 2009) and the `R` packages `np` (Hayfield and Racine 2008), `DEA` (Diaz-Martinez and Fernandez-Menendez. 2008), `cobs` (Ng and Maechler 2009) and `quadprog` (Berwin A. Turlach 2007).

4.1 Deterministic Frontiers

First, we restrict our attention to the two deterministic frontier estimators considered above as well as COLS using a correctly specified parametric model ("COLS"), COLS using an incorrectly specified linear parametric model ("L-COLS"), COLS using an incorrectly specified quadratic parametric model ("Q-OLS"), the DEA approach ("DEA"), and where appropriate the SGP model that does not impose concavity but does impose monotonicity ("M-SGP"). We consider the following DGPs:

(i) $m(x) = 3 + 4 \times \ln(x) + 3 \times \sqrt{x}$,
(ii) $m(x) = 3 + \Phi(x - 3.5)$.

For each experiment we consider sample sizes of $n = 200, 400, 600, 800$ while x is distributed independently $\mathcal{U}[1, 10]$. Our one-sided error is generated as $|N(0, \sigma_\varepsilon^2)|$. For each scenario we conduct $M = 1{,}000$ Monte Carlo simulations. Note that DGP (i) is globally concave while DGP (ii) uses the `R` function `pnorm(·)`, the Standard Gaussian CDF which delivers a frontier having a sigmoidal shape consistent with parametric specifications outlined in Duggal et al. (1999, p. 47).

To assess the finite-sample performance of the deterministic frontier estimators, we consider the above DGPs and let σ_ε^2 equal 0.2, 0.4 and 0.8. We use the local linear[11] kernel estimator with bandwidths obtained via least squares cross-validation. For DGP (i) our monotonicity and concavity constraints are imposed on a grid of 100 equally spaced points while for DGP (ii) we impose monotonicity only. We report ratios of median mean square error (MSE) taken over all M Monte Carlo replications, with the numeraire being that for the SGP estimator. For each run MSE is calculated as the average squared difference between each estimators' fit and the true frontier values on the same set of grid points used to impose the constraints. Results for the deterministic frontier simulation are reported in Table 1.

4.2 Stochastic Frontiers

In order to assess the finite-sample performance of the SSF estimator we consider the same DGPS as above, but now add noise in addition to inefficiency. In our setting we use the same values of λ and σ^2 as Fan et al. (1996) did in their simulations.[12] Here we estimate the unrestricted nonparametric stochastic frontier as in Fan et al. (1996) ("U-SSF"), the proposed smooth constrained "SSF" as well as shifted parametric conditional mean models, both correctly and incorrectly specified ("COLS," "L-COLS" and "Q-COLS," respectively), and where appropriate the SSF model that does not impose concavity but does impose monotonicity ("M-SSF"). As with our previous simulations we consider sample sizes of $n = 200, 400, 600, 800$. Our one-sided error is generated as $|N(0, \sigma_u^2)|$ while our two-sided error, generated independently from u and x is $N(0, \sigma_v^2)$. For each scenario we conduct 1,000 Monte Carlo simulations and let $(\lambda, \sigma^2) = (1.66, 1.88)$, $(1.24, 1.63)$ and $(0.83, 1.35)$.[13]

---

[11] Results for the local constant estimator are qualitatively similar and are excluded for space considerations.

[12] These are also identical to the values employed by Aigner et al. (1977).

[13] This corresponds to $\sigma_u^2 = 1.379, 0.901, 0.536$ and $\sigma_v^2 = 0.500, 0.339, 0.294$, respectively.

Table 1 Deterministic Frontier Monte Carlo

			DGP (i), Deterministic Frontier			
	$m(x) = 3 + 4 \times \ln(x) + 3 \times \sqrt{x}$					
	SCP	COLS	L-COLS	Q-COLS	DEA	M-SGP
	$\sigma_u^2 = 0.2$					
200	1.01	0.147	250	36	0.833	1.48
400	1.68	0.181	603	91.9	0.879	1.44
600	2.62	0.245	1100	175	1.14	1.48
800	3.37	0.255	1590	263	1.27	1.45
	$\sigma_u^2 = 0.4$					
200	1.19	0.2	163	23	0.919	1.44
400	2.04	0.273	409	60.7	1.07	1.44
600	2.96	0.343	717	110	1.38	1.43
800	3.69	0.399	1040	162	1.54	1.41
	$\sigma_u^2 = 0.8$					
200	1.21	0.228	96	13.3	0.89	1.38
400	2.51	0.401	279	41.1	1.29	1.42
600	3.5	0.444	478	72.2	1.62	1.44
800	4.32	0.492	746	114	2.27	1.45
	DGP (ii), Deterministic Frontier					
	$m(x) = 3 + \text{pnorm}(x - 3.5)$					
		SCP	COLS	L-COLS	Q-COLS	
	$\sigma_u^2 = 0.2$					
	200	5.44	0.399	151	28.8	
	400	9.44	0.476	398	92.8	
	600	12.7	0.668	714	189	
	800	14.8	0.621	1030	300	
				$\sigma_u^2 = 0.4$		
	200	5.99	0.531	97.6	18.8	
	400	10.3	0.685	259	53.4	
	600	13.8	0.904	458	106	
	800	17.2	1.15	720	191	
				$\sigma_u^2 = 0.8$		
	200	6.05	0.593	56.4	11.8	
	400	11.1	0.889	164	35.9	
	600	13.7	1.04	274	62.3	
	800	18.1	1.27	427	100	

Ratio of median MSE for each estimator in the respective column heading relative to that for the SGP estimator. Numbers larger than 1 indicate superior MSE performance of the SGP method (results accurate to three significant digits)

As before, we use the local linear estimator with bandwidths obtained via least squares cross-validation. Our monotonicity and concavity constraints are imposed on a grid of 100 equally spaced points. We report the ratio between each estimator's MSE against that for the SSF estimator where the median is taken over all $M =$ 1,000 replications. For each run MSE is calculated as the average squared difference

Table 2 Stochastic Frontier Monte Carlo

			DGP (i), Stochastic Frontier $m(x) = 3 + 4 \times \ln(x) + 3 \times \sqrt{x}$		
	U-SSF	COLS	L-COLS	Q-COLS	M-SSF
			$\sigma_u^2 = 0.536, \sigma_v^2 = 0.294$		
200	1.51	0.525	30.9	3.22	1.12
400	1.42	0.513	50.6	4.88	1.13
600	1.33	0.585	58.2	5.5	1.1
800	1.37	0.606	75.9	7.02	1.12
			$\sigma_u^2 = 0.901, \sigma_v^2 = 0.339$		
200	1.33	0.582	18.1	2.29	1.09
400	1.34	0.609	28.5	3.26	1.13
600	1.32	0.673	34	3.79	1.1
800	1.24	0.705	36.2	3.99	1.07
			$\sigma_u^2 = 1.379, \sigma_v^2 = 0.500$		
200	1.35	0.544	12.3	1.76	1.12
400	1.32	0.617	19.2	2.53	1.1
600	1.25	0.714	20.1	2.66	1.07
800	1.18	0.743	22.9	2.95	1.06
			$\sigma_u^2 = 1.379, \sigma_v^2 = 0.500$ $m(x) = 3 + \text{pnorm}(x - 3.5)$		
	U-SSF	COLS	L-COLS	Q-COLS	
			$\sigma_u^2 = 0.536, \sigma_v^2 = 0.294$		
	200	1.25	0.527	1.95	0.919
	400	1.27	0.578	2.68	1.07
	600	1.24	0.615	3.27	1.14
	800	1.12	0.672	3.32	1.23
			$\sigma_u^2 = 0.901, \sigma_v^2 = 0.339$		
	200	1.23	0.596	1.53	0.888
	400	1.22	0.676	1.99	1.02
	600	1.17	0.718	2.23	1.08
	800	1.14	0.794	2.2	1.09
			$\sigma_u^2 = 1.379, \sigma_v^2 = 0.500$		
	200	1.19	0.683	1.3	0.937
	400	1.24	0.711	1.6	0.956
	600	1.18	0.755	1.75	1.02
	800	1.17	0.826	1.89	1.06

Ratio of median MSE for each estimator in the respective column heading relative to that for the SSF estimator. Numbers larger than 1 indicate superior MSE performance of the SSF approach (results accurate to three significant digits)

between each of the estimators and the true frontier values on the same set of grid points used to impose the constraints.[14] Results for the stochastic frontier simulation are reported in Table 2.

[14] Note that frontier behavior is evaluated at the sample realizations, not the grid points, and the DEA estimator is evaluated at the sample realizations for all constraints.

4.3 Discussion

First, consider results for the deterministic frontier case summarized in Table 1. Of the two direct nonparametric frontier estimators (SGP and DEA), the proposed SGP approach dominates except in quite small samples. Of the shifted methods (SCP, COLS, L-COLS, Q-COLS), the proposed SCP estimator improves dramatically over the misspecified linear and quadratic COLS estimators (L-COLS, Q-COLS) that are prevalent in applied settings. Furthermore, the nonparametric SGP estimator can even outperform a correctly specified parametric model as n increases which some may consider impossible (DGP ii), COLS). The key to interpreting these entries is to recognize that the proposed SGP estimator is a direct estimator of the frontier, while COLS and its ilk (including Kuosmanen and Johnson (2010)) involve shifting a conditional mean.[15] These entries simply highlight potential benefits of direct estimation of the frontier. Finally, imposing concavity where appropriate appears to improve on that imposing monotonicity only (M-SGP).

It is worth noting that the performance gains of SGP relative to DEA are to be expected given the theoretical results of Banker and Maindiratta (1988) which show that DEA delivers a lower bound on the family of production possibilities sets which rationalize the observed data. Given the concavity of the SGP estimator it cannot lie below the DEA estimator which may therefore result in improved estimates of the frontier.

Next, consider results for the stochastic frontier case summarized in Table 2. Recall that each of these methods involve shifting a conditional mean model, hence in this case the correctly specified parametric model cannot be beat. However, as n increases the proposed nonparametric method converges to the correctly specified parametric model for both DGPs considered (consider the COLS column as n increases). Furthermore, the proposed smooth SSF method outperforms the popular linear and quadratic specifications (except for small samples for DGP ii) for Q-OLS) with the relative performance improving as n increases. Finally, as expected, the restricted SSF estimator proposed here dominates the unrestricted nonparametric stochastic frontier ("U-SSF").

The simulation results comparing the performance of unrestricted and restricted nonparametric conditional mean models are also novel for the class of estimators proposed in Du et al. (2010). While Hall and Huang (2001) did quantify the gains from imposing monotonicity on a conditional mean, their simulations were limited to a single simulated example. Our work here shows that imposing conditions consistent with economic theory can have large impacts on the finite-sample performance of a nonparametric estimator, regardless of context.

[15] Though we do not include Kuosmanen and Johnson (2010) approach in our simulation, theirs is a "shifted" (indirect) method that relies on a nonparametric estimate of the conditional mean, thus its performance would be comparable to the SCP approach and it too would be dominated by the (direct) SGP approach.

5 Application

To illustrate how the proposed methods perform in applied settings we use the classic production data of U.S. electricity companies in 1970 studied by Christensen and Greene (1976).[16] The data consist of a single output, millions of kilowatt hours of electricity generated (y), and three inputs, labor (l), capital (c) and fuel (f). Overall, though this data set is small ($n = 123$), it provides us with a well known setting in which we can evaluate the proposed methods. The dimensionality of the data is consistent with a large number of applied production studies; Kumbhakar and Tsionas (2011) analyze electricity generation using the same three inputs to the production process.

Our production frontier is

$$y_i = m(l_i, c_i, f_i) + \varepsilon_i, \quad i = 1, \ldots, n, \tag{16}$$

which we estimate using a local constant estimator with cross-validated bandwidths. Our primary interest is in deviations from the frontier (inefficiency) and RTS. Since we are not using a logarithmic transformation, RTS is defined here as

$$\widehat{\text{RTS}}_i = \left(\frac{\partial \hat{m}(l_i, c_i, f_i)}{\partial l} \cdot l_i + \frac{\partial \hat{m}(l_i, c_i, f_i)}{\partial c} \cdot c_i + \frac{\partial \hat{m}(l_i, c_i, f_i)}{\partial f} \cdot f_i \right) \frac{1}{\hat{m}(l_i, c_i, f_i)}. \tag{17}$$

We use both of the frontier methods described above, SGP and SCP, as well as SSF to analyze RTS and inefficiency. We impose both monotonicity and concavity across the inputs and bandwidths are selected using least squares cross validation (Li and Racine 2004). We summarize the distribution of RTS and inefficiency for both methods by plotting their (smooth) CDFs, which are provided in Figs. 3 and 6, respectively.

Figure 3 displays the CDF of estimated RTS[17] using a standard unrestricted kernel estimator of the production function, a monotonically restricted (in all inputs) kernel estimator, the SCP estimator (which is equivalent to imposing monotonicity and concavity since the frontier is a neutral shift) and our SGP estimator (which also bounds the data). As noted above, the distribution of RTS differs considerably across the SGP and SCP methods. Also, it appears that imposing *both* monotonicity and concavity severely limits the RTS across all firms in the sample. This is consistent with the parametric cost function findings of Christensen and Greene (1976) who find mostly decreasing RTS and several firms with estimated diseconomies of scale.

Delving further into this issue, consider Figs. 4 and 5 which plot the unrestricted output against the restricted output, i.e., q_i versus $n\hat{p}_i \cdot q_i$, when imposing monotonicity only and both monotonicity and concavity, respectively. Deviations from the 45 degree line signify observations for which the constraint weights deviate from the

[16] This data is freely available in cost function form in the Ecdat library (Croissant 2006) in R (R Development Core Team 2009).

[17] We use Silverman's rule-of-thumb bandwidth for all smoothed distribution plots.

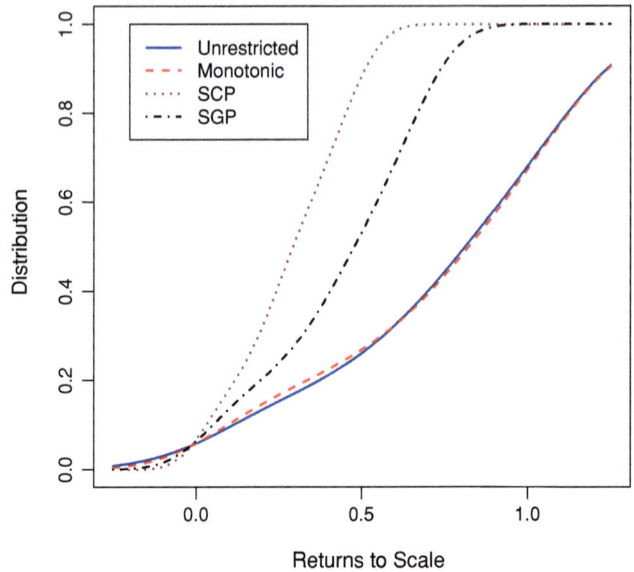

Fig. 3 Estimated distributions of RTS for four nonparametric production function/frontier estimators

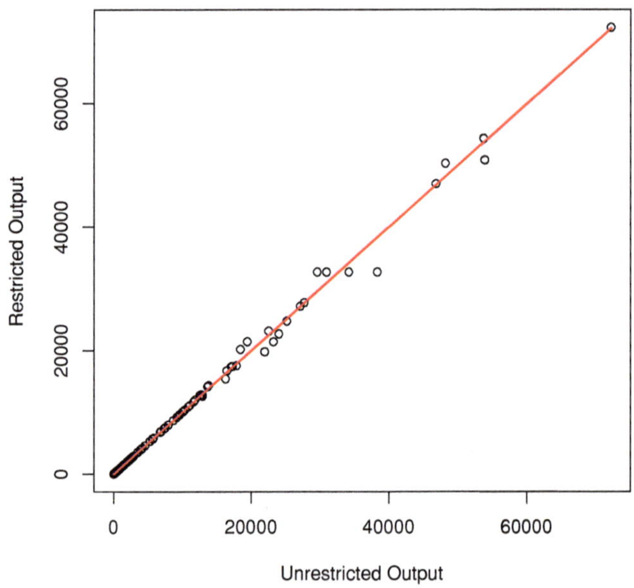

Fig. 4 Constraint weighted output ($n\hat{p}_i \cdot q_i$) against actual output (q_i) imposing monotonicity

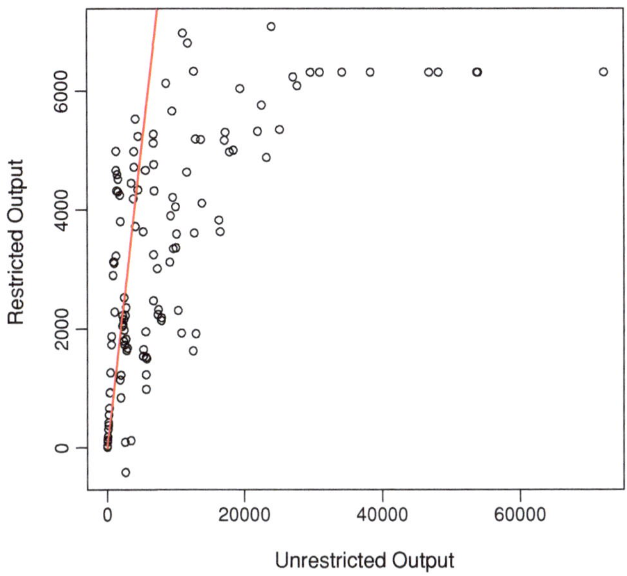

Fig. 5 Constraint weighted output ($n\hat{p}_i \cdot q_i$) against actual output (q_i) imposing monotonicity and concavity

uniform (unconstrained) weights. These plots are useful for understanding how much "movement" of the regressand is required in order to satisfy the constraints. We notice that for imposing monotonicity only, a majority of the points lie along the 45 degree line, while those that differ are still close, suggesting very little difference between $\hat{p}_i$ and p_u. However, Fig. 5 implies that almost every point received a constraint weight different from the uniform weights in order to impose both monotonicity and concavity. This is suggestive that imposing concavity on top of monotonicity is not only more restrictive, but also impacts the estimation of the surface everywhere, as opposed to being more of a localized issue which is the case when we impose monotonicity only.

We note that an apparent first order stochastic dominance relationship exists between the estimated RTS for the SGP and SCP estimators, while the unrestricted and monotonically restricted nonparametric production function produce nearly identical distributions of RTS. The imposition of concavity on our frontier produces a flatter estimate of the production frontier which is what produces the noticeably left shifted distributions of RTS relative to the estimators that do not impose concavity. It appears that almost all firms possess estimated RTS less than 0.5 when using the SCP estimator whereas roughly 60 % of firms have estimated RTS less than 0.5 when using the SGP estimator. This is in contrast to the approximately 20 % of firms who have RTS less than 0.5 using either a standard nonparametric conditional mean model or a monotonically constrained conditional mean model. This is to be expected as con-

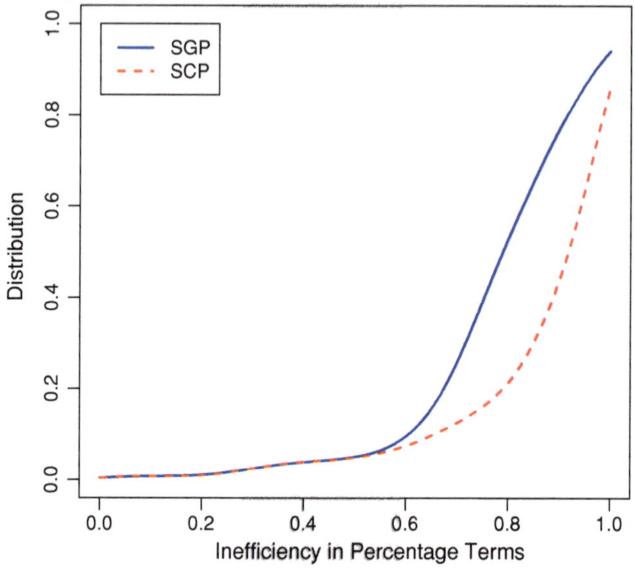

Fig. 6 Estimated distributions of estimates of inefficiency (% terms) for SGP and SCP

cave functions are more severely shaped constrained than monotonically restricted estimators.

The estimated CDFs of inefficiency measured in percentage terms, i.e., $(\hat{m}-y)/\hat{m}$, for our SGP and SCP estimation routines presented in Fig. 6 both tend to suggest that a majority of electricity plants are largely inefficient. Inefficiency estimates from the SCP estimator are stochastically dominated by those from the SGP estimator. What this apparent dominance relationship suggests, along with our results from the distribution of estimated RTS, is that the SGP and SCP estimators provide different estimates of the frontier, which we highlighted earlier as a fundamental difference between direct estimation of the frontier and estimation of a conditional mean that is shifted to allow it to mimic a frontier. This is particularly noteworthy as both RTS and efficiency are measures routinely used by policy makers, thus estimator choice matters. Furthermore, SFA and COLS/MOLS, being conditional-mean based, are liable to the same critique as all such shifted estimators. Moreover, this result is to be expected in light of Theorem 3.2.

What is missing from Fig. 6 is the distributions of inefficiency for our stochastic methods, SSF and U-SSF. But for this application we obtain residuals with the wrong skewness (positive instead of negative) implying that estimation of σ^2 and λ is trivial as in these cases it is widely known that $\hat{\lambda} = 0$ (Olson et al. 1980).

We tested our residuals for symmetry using the bootstrap test of Kuosmanen and Fosgerau (2009), who follow the time series procedure of Pérez-Alonso (2007). This test provides evidence against negative symmetry of the residuals. With 1,000 bootstrap replications, we obtain a bootstrap p-value of 0.795 with no constraints imposed, 0.790 with monotonicity imposed and 0.99 with both monotonicity and concavity imposed. In sum, the outcomes of this test lend further statistical credence to the finding of no inefficiency for the SSF and U-SSF estimators. Interestingly, Kuosmanen and Fosgerau (2009) use the same data deployed here and find contrasting results. The reason for the difference in findings is that Kuosmanen and Fosgerau take natural logarithms of all of their variables prior to estimation of the production function whereas we elect to keep all of our variables in level form given the use of a nonparametric model. It should also be noted that Kuosmanen and Fosgerau (2009) find several instances of the wrong skew using logarithms albeit when focusing attention on the cost function.

Simar and Wilson (2010) show that even with one million observations, the probability of observing a random draw of composed errors with the wrong skewness is almost 50 % when the variance ratio is set equal to 0.01. They also mention "... we know of no published chapters reporting an estimate of zero for the variance parameter of the one-sided component in a stochastic frontier model." (Simar and Wilson (2010, p. 10)). A common response to this issue is to either select a different sample or to re-specify one's model, neither of which is attempted here. In our case re-specification is of no value as we are using methods robust to misspecification. An alternative would be to resort to either local polynomial methods or ad hoc methods of bandwidth selection. However, this is not necessary. Simar and Wilson (2010) have proposed a simple bagging approach to handle samples that display the wrong skewness so that inference can still be conducted.

The finding of such high levels of inefficiency (in % terms) may seem troubling. However, our data stem from electricity generation plants in the 1970s, which was a heavily regulated industry (Christensen and Greene 1976 as discussed in). Also, given the limited nature of the data we cannot control for additional differences of firms which may be misconstrued as inefficiency, such as age of the firm or how the electricity is generated (coal or gas-fired). Further, as presented, these measures of inefficiency do not allow for statistical inference and it very well could be the case that many of these firms have inefficiency levels that do not differ significantly from 0. Beyond this, deterministic frontier methods usually have higher levels of inefficiency given that all unobservable features are characterized as inefficiency, whereas stochastic methods do not. This example was adopted primarily to showcase how the proposed methods can be used to impose economic constraints within the applied production arena.

6 Concluding Remarks

Frontier methods provide powerful tools for assessing technical inefficiency among a sample of firms. The results from a frontier study have played important roles in guiding policy and assessing which firms are performing well (or poorly) in a given industry. Flexible estimation methodologies that impose as little structure as possible are axiomatically desirable, however, one can run the risk of not imposing sufficient structure. In this chapter we propose a triad of methods for flexible frontier analysis that place minimal structure on the frontier while delivering a smooth continuously differentiable frontier that, in addition, satisfies requisite conditions dictated by basic axioms of production theory. We propose two deterministic frontier methods and one stochastic frontier method that each exploit recent developments in constrained kernel estimation techniques. Our two deterministic alternatives have close links to the earlier goal programming literature as well as to the recent work on corrected concave nonparametric least squares.

A simulation study reveals that the methods perform remarkably well relative to their peers, while an empirical example illustrates the ease with which these methods can be employed. Additionally, the empirical example highlights the differences that can arise between the use of a shifted average production estimate versus an estimator that attempts to estimate the frontier directly. We find that, in a cross section of electricity generating plants, decreasing RTS is indicative of the entire sample while a majority of firms are inefficient.

We hope that these approaches are of interest to practitioners who worry about parametric misspecification and who are looking for smooth flexible alternatives that are consistent with basic production axioms. We further hope that our discussion underscores the importance of sound specification analysis which incorporates imposing economic constraints in nonparametric settings, a point that Hal White has championed throughout his career.

References

Afriat, S. N. (1967), 'The construction of utility functions from expenditure data', International Economic Review 8, 67–77.

Aigner, D. and Chu, S. (1968), 'On estimating the industry production function', American Economic Review 58, 826–839.

Aigner, D. J., Lovell, C. A. K. and Schmidt, P. (1977), 'Formulation and estimation of stochastic frontier production functions', Journal of Econometrics 6(1), 21–37.

Amsler, C., Lee, Y. H. and Schmidt, P. (2009), 'A survey of stochastic frontier models and likely future developments', Seoul Journal of Economics 22, 5–27.

Arrow, K. J., Chenery, H. B., Minhas, B. S. and Solow, R. M. (1961), 'Capital-labor substitution and economic efficiency', Review of Economics and Statistics 63(3), 225–250.

Banker, R. D. and Maindiratta, A. (1988), 'Nonparametric analysis of technical and allocative efficiencies in production', Econometrica 56(6), 1315–1332.

Blundell, R., Horowitz, J. L. and Parey, M. (2012), 'Measuring the price responsiveness of gasoline', Quantitative Economics 3, 29–51.

Briesch, R. A., Chintagunta, P. K. and Matzkin, R. L. (2002), 'Semiparametric estimation of brand choice behavior', Journal of the American Statistical Association 97, 973–982.

Cazals, C., Florens, J. P. and Simar, L. (2002), 'Nonparametric frontier estimation: A robust approach', Journal of Econometrics 106, 1–25.

Chambers, R. (1988), Applied production analysis, Cambridge University Press, Cambridge.

Christensen, L. R. and Greene, W. H. (1976), 'Economies of scale in u.s. electric power generation', The Journal of Political Economy 84(1), 655–676.

Cobb, C. and Douglas, P. H. (1928), 'A theory of production', American Economic Review 18, 139–165.
Croissant, Y. (2006), Ecdat: Data sets for econometrics. R package version 0.1-5. http://www.r-project.org
Debreu, G. (1951), 'The coefficient of resource utilization', Econometrica 19(3), 273–292.
Diaz-Martinez, Z. and Fernandez-Menendez., J. (2008), DEA: Data Envelopment Analysis. R package version 0.1-2.
Diewert, W. E. (1971), 'An application of the Shepard duality theorem: A generalized Leontief production function', Journal of Political Economy 79(3), 481–507.
Du, P., Parmeter, C. F. and Racine, J. S. (2010), Constrained nonparametric kernel regression: Estimation and inference. Working Paper.
Duggal, V. G., Saltzman, C. and Klein, L. R. (1999), 'Infrastructure and productivity: a nonlinear approach', Journal of Econometrics 92, 47–74.
Duggal, V. G., Saltzman, C. and Klein, L. R. (2007), 'Infrastructure and productivity: An extension to private infrastructure and it productivity', Journal of Econometrics 140, 485–502.
Fan, Y., Li, Q. and Weersink, A. (1996), 'Semiparametric estimation of stochastic production frontier models', Journal of Business & Economic Statistics 14(4), 460–468.
Farrell, M. J. (1957), 'The measurement of productive efficiency', Journal of the Royal Statistical Society Series A, General 120(3), 253–281.
Greene, W. H. (1980), 'Maximum likelihood estimation of econometric frontier functions', Journal of Econometrics 13(1), 27–56.
Haag, B. R., Hoderlein, S. and Pendakur, K. (2009), 'Testing and imposing Slutsky symmetry in nonparametric demand systems', Journal of Econometrics 153(1), 33–50.
Hall, P. and Huang, H. (2001), 'Nonparametric kernel regression subject to monotonicity constraints', The Annals of Statistics 29(3), 624–647.
Hanoch, G. and Rothschild, M. (1972) 'Testing the assumptions of production theory: a nonparametric approach', Journal of Political Economy 80, 256–275.
Hayfield, T. and Racine, J. S. (2008), 'Nonparametric econometrics: The np package', Journal of Statistical Software 27(5). http://www.jstatsoft.org/v27/i05/
Henderson, D. J. and Parmeter, C. F. (2009), Imposing economic constraints in nonparametric regression: Survey, implementation and extension, in Q. Li and J. S. Racine, eds, 'Advances in Econometrics: Nonparametric Econometric Methods', Vol. 25, Emerald Group Publishing.
Hong, Y. and White, H. (1995), 'Consistent specification testing via nonparametric series regression', Econometrica 63(5), 1133–1159.
Hornik, K., Stinchcombe, M. and White, H. (1990), 'Universal approximations of an unknown mapping and its derivatives using multilayer feedforward networks', Neural Networks 3(5), 551–560.
Klein, L. R. (1947), The use of cross-section data in econometrics with application to the study of production of railroad services in the United States. Mimeo, National Bureau of Economic Research, New York.
Kumbhakar, S. C. and Tsionas, E. G. (2011), 'Stochastic error specification in primal and dual production systems', Journal of Applied Econometrics. 26(2), 270–297.
Kuosmanen, T. (2008), 'Representation theorem for convex nonparametric least squares', The Econometrics Journal 11, 308–325.
Kuosmanen, T. and Fosgerau, M. (2009), 'Neoclassical versus frontier production models? Testing for the skewness of regression residuals', Scandinavian Journal of Economics 111(2), 317–333.
Kuosmanen, T. and Johnson, A. (2010), 'Data envelopment analysis as nonparametric least squares regression', Operations Research 58(1), 149–160.
Kuosmanen, T. and Kortelainen, M. (2011), 'Stochastic non-smooth envelopment of data semi-parametric: Frontier estimation subject to shape constraints', Journal of Productivity Analysis. Forthcoming.
Leibenstein, H. (1966), 'Allocative efficiency vs. 'X-efficiency'', American Economic Review 56(3), 392–415.

Leung, D. (2005), 'Cross-validation in nonparametric regression with outliers', The Annals of Statistics 33, 2291–2310.

Li, Q. and Racine, J. S. (2004), 'Cross-validated local linear nonparametric regression', Statistica Sinica 14, 485–512.

Li, Q. and Racine, J. S. (2007), Nonparametric Econometrics: Theory and Practice, Princeton University Press.

Matzkin, R. L. (1991), 'Semiparametric estimation of monotone and concave utility functions for polychotomous choice models', Econometrica 59, 1315–1327.

Ng, P. T. and Maechler, M. (2009), cobs: COBS - Constrained B-splines (Sparse matrix based). R package version 1.2-0. http://wiki.r-project.org/rwiki/doku.php?id=packages:cran:cobs

O'Donnell, C. J. and Coelli, T. J. (2005), 'A Bayesian approach to imposing curvature on distance functions', Journal of Econometrics 126(2), 493–523.

Olson, J. A., Schmidt, P. and Waldman, D. A. (1980), 'A monte carlo study of estimators of stochastic frontier production functions', Journal of Econometrics 13, 67–82.

Turlach, B. A. (2007), quadprog: Functions to solve Quadratic Programming Problems. R package version 1.4-11. R port by A. Weingessel.

Pérez-Alonso, A. (2007), 'A bootstrap approach to test the conditional symmetry in time series models', Computational Statistics and Data Analysis 51, 3484–3504.

R Development Core Team (2009), R: A Language and Environment for Statistical Computing, R Foundation for Statistical Computing, Vienna, Austria. ISBN 3-900051-07-0. http://www.R-project.org

Racine, J. S. and Li, Q. (2004), 'Nonparametric estimation of regression functions with both categorical and continuous data', Journal of Econometrics 119(1), 99–130.

Ryan, D. L. and Wales, T. J. (2000), 'Imposing local concavity in the translog and generalized Leontief cost functions', Economics Letters 67, 253–260.

Schmidt, P. (1985), 'Frontier production functions', Econometric Reviews 4(2), 289–328.

Shephard, R. W. (1953), Cost and production functions, Princeton University Press.

Shephard, R. W. (1970), The theory of cost and production functions, Princeton University Press.

Simar, L. and Wilson, P. W. (2010), 'Estimation and inference in stochastic frontier models', Econometric Reviews 29, 62–98.

Timmer, C. P. (1971), 'Using a probabilistic frontier production function to measure technical efficiency', The Journal of Political Economy 79(4), 776–794.

White, H. (1989), 'Learning in artificial neural networks: A statistical perspective', Neural Computation 1(4), 425–464.

Winsten, C. B. (1957), 'Discussion on Mr. Farrell's paper', Journal of the Royal Statistical Society Series A, General 120(3), 282–284.

Yatchew, A. and Härdle, W. (2006), 'Nonparametric state price density estimation using constrained least squares and the bootstrap', Journal of Econometrics 133, 579–599.

Yatchew, A. J. (1985), 'Comment on 'Frontier production functions'', Econometric Reviews 4(2), 345–352.

NoVaS Transformations: Flexible Inference for Volatility Forecasting

Dimitris N. Politis and Dimitrios D. Thomakos

Abstract In this chapter we present several new findings on the NoVaS transformation approach for volatility forecasting introduced by Politis (Model-Free Volatility Prediction, UCSD Department of Economics Discussion Paper 2003–16; Recent advances and trends in nonparametric statistics, Elsevier, North Holland; J Financ Econ 5:358–389, 2007). In particular: (a) we present a new method for accurate volatility forecasting using NoVaS; (b) we introduce a "time-varying" version of NoVaS and show that the NoVaS methodology is applicable in situations where (global) stationarity for returns fails such as the cases of local stationarity and/or structural breaks and/or model uncertainty; (c) we conduct an extensive simulation study on the forecasting ability of the NoVaS approach under a variety of realistic data generating processes (DGP); and (d) we illustrate the forecasting ability of NoVaS on a number of real data sets and compare it to realized and range-based volatility measures. Our empirical results show that the NoVaS -based forecasts lead to a much 'tighter' distribution of the forecasting performance measure. Perhaps our

Earlier results from this research were presented in seminars in the Departments of Economics of the University of California at San Diego, University of Cyprus, and the University of Crete, as well as several conferences. We would like to thank Elena Andreou, conference and seminar participants for useful comments and suggestions. Many thanks are also due to an anonymous referee for a most constructive report, and to the Editors, Xiaohong Chen and Norman Swanson, for all their hard work in putting this volume together.

D. N. Politis (✉)
Department of Mathematics and Department of Economics,
University of California, San Diego, USA
e-mail: politis@math.ucsd.edu

D. D. Thomakos
Department of Economics,
University of Peloponnese, Tripolis, Greece
e-mail: thomakos@uop.gr

D. D. Thomakos
Rimini Center for Economic Analysis, Rimini, Italy

X. Chen and N. R. Swanson (eds.), *Recent Advances and Future Directions in Causality, Prediction, and Specification Analysis*, DOI: 10.1007/978-1-4614-1653-1_19,

most remarkable finding is the *robustness* of the NoVaS forecasts in the context of structural breaks and/or other nonstationarities of the underlying data. Also striking is that forecasts based on NoVaS invariably outperform those based on the benchmark *GARCH*(1,1) even when the true DGP *is* *GARCH*(1,1) when the sample size is moderately large, e.g., 350 daily observations.

Keywords ARCH · Forecasting · GARCH · Local stationarity · Robustness · Structural breaks · Volatility.

1 Introduction

Accurate forecasts of the volatility of financial returns is an important part of empirical financial research. In this chapter we present a number of new findings on the NoVaS transformation approach to volatility prediction. The NoVaS methodology was introduced by Politis (2003a,b, 2007) and further expanded in Politis and Thomakos (2008). The name of the method is an acronym for 'Normalizing and Variance Stabilizing' transformation. NoVaS is based on exploratory data analysis ideas, it is model-free, data-adaptive, and—as the chapter at hand hopes to demonstrate—especially relevant when making forecasts in the context of underlying data generating processes (DGPs) that exhibit nonstationarities (e.g. locally stationary time series, series with parameter breaks or regime switching, etc.). In general, NoVaS allows for a flexible approach to inference, and is also well suited for application to short time series.

The original development of the NoVaS approach was made in Politis (2003a,b, 2007) having as its 'spring board' the popular ARCH model with normal innovations. In these chapters, the main application was forecasting squared returns (as a proxy for forecasting volatility), and the evaluation of forecasting performance was addressed via the L_1-norm (instead of the usual MSE) since the case was made that financial returns might not have finite 4th moment.

In the chapter at hand we further investigate the performance of NoVaS in a pure forecasting context.[1] First, we present a method for *bona fide* volatility forecasting, extending the original NoVaS notion of forecasting squared returns. Second, we conduct a very comprehensive simulation study about the relative forecasting performance of NoVaS: we consider a wide variety of volatility models as data generating processes (DGPs), and we compare the forecasting performance of NoVaS with that of a benchmark *GARCH*(1,1) model. We introduce the notion of a "time-varying" NoVaS approach and show that it is especially relevant in these cases where the assumption of global stationarity fails. The results of our simulations show that NoVaS forecasts lead to a much 'tighter' distribution of the forecasting performance measure (mean absolute deviation of the forecast errors), when compared to the benchmark model, for all DGPs we consider. This finding is especially relevant in

[1] See also Politis and Thomakos (2008).

the context of volatility forecasting for risk management. We further illustrate the use of NoVaS for a number of real data sets and compare the forecasting performance of NoVaS-based volatility forecasts with realized and range-based volatility measures, which are frequently used in assessing the performance of volatility forecasts.

The literature on volatility modeling, forecasting, and the evaluation of volatility forecasts is very large and varied in the topics covered. Possibly related to the chapter at hand is the work by Hansen (2006) in which the problem of forming predictive intervals is addressed using a semiparametric, transformation-based approach. Hansen works with a set of (standardized) residuals from a parametric model, and then uses the empirical distribution function of these residuals to compute conditional quantiles that can be used in forming prediction intervals. The main similarity between Hansen's work and NoVaS is that both approaches use a transformation of the original data and the empirical distribution to make forecasts. The main difference, however, is that Hansen works in the context of a (possibly misspecified) model whereas NoVaS is totally model-free.

We can only selectively mention here some recent literature related to the forecasting problems we address: Mikosch and Starica (2004) for change in structure in volatility time series and GARCH modeling; Meddahi (2001) for an eigenfunction volatility modeling approach; Peng and Yao (2003) for robust LAD estimation of GARCH models; Poon and Granger (2003) for assessing the forecasting performance of various volatility models; Hansen Lunde and Nason (2003) on selecting volatility models; Andersen et al. (2004, 2005) on analytic evaluation of volatility forecasts and the use of realized volatilities in evaluating volatility forecasts; Ghysels and Forsberg (2007) on the use and predictive power of absolute returns; Francq and Zakoïan (2005), Lux and Morales-Arias (2010) and Choi et al. (2010) on switching regime GARCH models, structural breaks and long memory in volatility; Hillebrand (2005) on GARCH models with structural breaks; Hansen and Lunde (2005, 2006) for comparing forecasts of volatility models against the standard $GARCH(1,1)$ model and for consistent ranking of volatility models and the use of an appropriate series as the 'true' volatility; Ghysels et al. (2006) for predicting volatility by mixing data at different frequencies and Ghysels and Sohn (2009) for the type of power variation that predicts well volatility in the context of mixed data frequencies. Andersen et al. (2007) for modeling realized volatility when jump components are included; Chen et al. (2008) examine volatility forecasting in the context of threshold models coupled with volatility measurement based on intraday range. The whole line of work of Andersen, Bollerslev, Diebold, and their various co-authors on realized volatility and volatility forecasting is nicely summarized in their review article "Volatility and Correlation Forecasting", in the *Handbook of Economic Forecasting*, see Andersen et al. (2006). Bandi and Russell (2008) discuss the selection of optimal sampling frequency in realized volatility estimation and forecasting; Patton and Sheppard (2008) discuss the evaluation of volatility forecasts while Patton and Sheppard (2009) present results on optimal combinations of realized volatility estimators in the context of volatility forecasting. Fryzlewicz et al. (2006, 2008) and Dahlhaus and Subba-Rao (2006, 2007) all work in the context of local stationarity and a new class of ARCH processes with slowly varying parameters. Of course this list is by no means complete.

The rest of the chapter is organized as follows: in Sect. 2 we briefly review the general development of the NoVaS approach; in Sect. 3 we present the design of our simulation study and discuss the simulation results on forecasting performance; in Sect. 4 we present empirical applications of NoVaS using real-world data; finally, in Sect. 5 we offer some concluding remarks.

2 Review of the NoVaS Methodology

In this section we present a brief overview of the NoVaS transformation, the implied NoVaS distribution, the methods for distributional matching, and NoVaS forecasting. For a more comprehensive review of the NoVaS methodology see Politis and Thomakos (2008).

2.1 NoVaS Transformation and Implied Distribution

Let us consider a zero mean, strictly stationary time series $\{X_t\}_{t\in\mathbb{Z}}$ corresponding to the returns of a financial asset. We assume that the basic properties of X_t correspond to the 'stylized facts'[2] of financial returns:

1. X_t has a non-Gaussian, approximately symmetric distribution that exhibits excess kurtosis.
2. X_t has time-varying conditional variance (volatility), denoted by $h_t^2 \stackrel{\text{def}}{=} \mathsf{E}\left[X_t^2|\mathcal{F}_{t-1}\right]$ that exhibits strong dependence, where $\mathcal{F}_{t-1} \stackrel{\text{def}}{=} \sigma(X_{t-1}, X_{t-2}, \ldots)$.
3. X_t is dependent although it possibly exhibits low or no autocorrelation which suggests possible nonlinearity.

These well-established properties affect the way one models and forecasts financial returns and their volatility and form the starting point of the NoVaS methodology.

The first step in the NoVaS transformation is variance stabilization to address the time-varying conditional variance property of the returns. We construct an empirical measure of the *time-localized* variance of X_t based on the information set $\mathcal{F}_{t|t-p} \stackrel{\text{def}}{=} \{X_t, X_{t-1}, \ldots, X_{t-p}\}$

$$\gamma_t \stackrel{\text{def}}{=} G(\mathcal{F}_{t|t-p}; \alpha, \boldsymbol{a}), \gamma_t > 0\ \forall t \tag{1}$$

[2] Departures from the assumption of these 'stylized facts' have been discussed in Politis and Thomakos (2008); in this chapter, we are mostly concerned about departures/breaks in stationarity—see Sect. 2.4 in what follows.

where α is a scalar control parameter, $\boldsymbol{a} \stackrel{\text{def}}{=} (a_0, a_1, \ldots, a_p)^\top$ is a $(p+1) \times 1$ vector of control parameters and $G(\cdot; \alpha, \boldsymbol{a})$ is to be specified.[3] The function $G(\cdot; \alpha, \boldsymbol{a})$ can be expressed in a variety of ways, using a parametric or a semiparametric specification. To keep things simple we assume that $G(\cdot; \alpha, \boldsymbol{a})$ is additive and takes the following form:

$$\begin{aligned} G(\mathcal{F}_{t|t-p}; \alpha, \boldsymbol{a}) &\stackrel{\text{def}}{=} \alpha s_{t-1} + \sum_{j=0}^{p} a_j g(X_{t-j}) \\ s_{t-1} &= (t-1)^{-1} \sum_{j=1}^{t-1} g(X_j) \end{aligned} \tag{2}$$

with the implied restrictions (to maintain positivity for γ_t) that $\alpha \geq 0$, $a_i \geq 0$, $g(\cdot) > 0$ and $a_p \neq 0$ for identifiability. Although other choices are possible, the natural choices for $g(z)$ are $g(z) = z^2$ or $g(z) = |z|$. With these designations, our empirical measure of the time-localized variance becomes a combination of an unweighted, recursive estimator s_{t-1} of the unconditional variance of the returns $\sigma^2 = \mathsf{E}\left[X_1^2\right]$, or of the mean absolute deviation of the returns $\delta = \mathsf{E}|X_1|$, and a weighted average of the current[4] and the past p values of the squared or absolute returns.

Using $g(z) = z^2$ results in a measure that is reminiscent of an $ARCH(p)$ model which was employed in Politis (2003a,b, 2007). The use of absolute returns, i.e., $g(z) = |z|$ has also been advocated for volatility modeling; see e.g., Ghysels and Forsberg (2007) and the references therein. Robustness in the presence of outliers in an obvious advantage of absolute versus squared returns. In addition, note that the mean absolute deviation is *proportional* to the standard deviation for the symmetric distributions that will be of current interest.

The second step in the NoVaS transformation is to use γ_t in constructing a studentized version of the returns, akin to the standardized innovations in the context of a parametric (e.g. GARCH-type) model. Consider the series W_t defined as:

$$W_t \equiv W_t(\alpha, \boldsymbol{a}) \stackrel{\text{def}}{=} \frac{X_t}{\phi(\gamma_t)} \tag{3}$$

where $\phi(z)$ is the time-localized standard deviation that is defined relative to our choice of $g(z)$, for example $\phi(z) = \sqrt{z}$ if $g(z) = z^2$ or $\phi(z) = z$ if $g(z) = |z|$. The aim now is to choose the NoVaS parameters in such a way as to make W_t follow as closely as possible a chosen target distribution that is easier to work with. The natural choice for such a distribution is the normal—hence the 'normalization' in the NoVaS acronym; other choices (such as the uniform) are also possible in applications, although perhaps not as intuitive. Note that by solving for X_t in Eq. (3), and using the fact that γ_t depends on X_t, it follows that we have the *implied* model representation:

---

[3] See the discussion about the calibration of α and $\boldsymbol{a}$ in the next section.

[4] The necessity and advantages of including the current value is elaborated upon by Politis (2003a,b, 2004, 2007).

$$X_t = U_t A_{t-1} \tag{4}$$

where U_t is the series obtained from the transformed series W_t in (3) and is required for forecasting—see Politis and Thomakos (2008). The component A_{t-1} depends only on past square or absolute returns, similar to the ARCH component of a GARCH model.

Remark 1 Politis (2003b, 2004, 2007) makes the case that financial returns seem to have finite second moment but infinite 4th moments. In that case, the normal target does not seem to be compatible with the choice of absolute returns—and the same is true of the uniform target—as it seems that the case $g(z) = |z|$ might be better suited for data that do not have a finite second moment. Nevertheless, there is always the possibility of encountering such extremely heavy-tailed data, e.g., in emerging markets, for which the absolute returns might be helpful.[5] The setup of potentially infinite 4th moments has been considered by Hall and Yao (2003) and Berkes and Horvath (2004) among others, and has important implications on an issue crucial in forecasting, namely the choice of loss function for evaluating forecast performance. The most popular criterion for measuring forecasting performance is the mean-squared error (MSE) which, however, is inapplicable in forecasting squared returns (and volatility) when the 4th moment is infinite. In contrast, the mean absolute deviation (MAD) is as intuitive as the MSE but does not suffer from this deficiency, and can thus be used in evaluating the forecasts of either squared or absolute returns and volatility; this L_1 loss criterion will be our preferred choice in this chapter.[6]

2.2 NoVaS Distributional Matching

We next turn to the issue of optimal selection of the NoVaS parameters. The free parameters are p (the NoVaS order), and $(\alpha, \boldsymbol{a})$. The parameters α and $\boldsymbol{a}$ are constrained to be non-negative to ensure the same for the variance. In addition, motivated by unbiasedness considerations, Politis (2003a,b, 2007) suggested the convexity condition $\alpha + \sum_{j=0}^{p} a_j = 1$. Finally, thinking of the coefficients a_i as local smoothing weights, it is intuitive to assume $a_i \geq a_j$ for $i > j$. We now discuss in detail the case when $\alpha = 0$; see Remark 2 for the case of nonzero α. A suitable scheme that satisfies the above conditions is given by exponential weights in Politis (2003a,b, 2007):

$$a_j = \begin{Bmatrix} 1/\sum\limits_{j=0}^{p} \exp(-bj) & \text{for} \quad j = 0 \\ a_0 \exp(-bj) & \text{for} \quad j = 1, 2, \ldots, p \end{Bmatrix} \tag{5}$$

[5] This might well be the case of the EFG data set of Sect. 4 in what follows.

[6] See also the recent chapter by Hansen and Lunde (2006) about the relevance of MSE in evaluating volatility forecasts.

where b is the exponential rate. We require the calibration of two parameters: a_0 and b. In this connection, let $\boldsymbol{\theta} \stackrel{\text{def}}{=} (p, b) \mapsto (\alpha, \boldsymbol{a})$, and denote the studentized series as $W_t \equiv W_t(\boldsymbol{\theta})$ rather than $W_t \equiv W_t(\alpha, \boldsymbol{a})$. For any given value of the parameter vector $\boldsymbol{\theta}$ we need to evaluate the 'closeness' of the marginal distribution of W_t with the target distribution.

Many different objective functions could be used for this. Let us denote such an objective function by $D_n(\boldsymbol{\theta})$, that obeys $D_n(\boldsymbol{\theta}) \geq 0$ and consider the following algorithm given in Politis (2003a, 2007):

- Let p take a very high starting value, e.g., let $p_{\max} \approx n/4$.
- Let $\alpha = 0$ and consider a discrete grid of b values, say $B \stackrel{\text{def}}{=} (b_{(1)}, b_{(2)}, \ldots, b_{(M)})$, $M > 0$. Find the optimal value of b, say b^*, that minimizes $D_n(\boldsymbol{\theta})$ over $b \in B$, and compute the optimal parameter vector $\boldsymbol{a}^*$ using Eq. (5).
- Trim the value of p by removing (i.e., setting to zero) the a_j parameters that do not exceed a pre-specified threshold, and renormalize the remaining parameters so that their sum equals one.

The solution then takes the general form:

$$\boldsymbol{\theta}_n^* \stackrel{\text{def}}{=} \underset{\boldsymbol{\theta}}{\operatorname{argmin}}\, D_n(\boldsymbol{\theta}) \tag{6}$$

Such an optimization procedure will always have a solution in view of the intermediate value theorem and is discussed in the previous work on NoVaS.[7] In empirical applications with financial returns it is usually sufficient to consider kurtosis-matching and thus to have $D_n(\boldsymbol{\theta})$ to take the form:

$$\mathcal{D}_n(\boldsymbol{\theta}) \stackrel{\text{def}}{=} \left| \frac{\sum_{t=1}^{n} (W_t - \bar{W}_n)^4}{n s_n^4} - \kappa^* \right| \tag{7}$$

where $\bar{W}_n \stackrel{\text{def}}{=} (1/n) \sum_{t=1}^{n} W_t$ denotes the sample mean, $s_n^2 \stackrel{\text{def}}{=} (1/n) \sum_{t=1}^{n} (W_t - \bar{W}_n)^2$ denotes the sample variance of the $W_t(\boldsymbol{\theta})$ series, and κ^* denotes the theoretical kurtosis coefficient of the target distribution. For the normal distribution $\kappa^* = 3$.

Remark 2 The discussion so far was under the assumption that the parameter α, that controls the weight given to the recursive estimator of the unconditional variance, is zero. If desired one can select a non-zero value by doing a direct search over a discrete grid of possible values while obeying the summability condition $\alpha + \sum_{j=0}^{p} a_j = 1$.

[7] This part of the NoVaS application appears similar at the outset to the Minimum Distance Method (MDM) of Wolfowitz (1957). Nevertheless, their objectives are quite different since the latter is typically employed for parameter estimation and testing whereas in NoVaS there is little interest in parameters—the focus lying on effective forecasting.

For example, one can choose the value of α that optimizes out-of-sample predictive performance; see Politis (2003a,b, 2007) for more details.

2.3 NoVaS Forecasting

Once the NoVaS parameters are calibrated one can compute volatility forecasts. In fact, as Politis (2003a,b, 2007) has shown, one can compute forecasts for different functions of the returns, including higher powers (with absolute value or not). The choice of an appropriate forecasting loss function, both for producing and for evaluating the forecasts, is crucial for maximizing forecasting performance. As per our Remark 1, we focus on the L_1 loss function for producing the forecasts and the mean absolute deviation (MAD) of the forecast errors for assessing forecasting performance. After optimization of the NoVaS parameters we now have both the optimal transformed series $W_t^* = W_t(\boldsymbol{\theta}_n^*)$ but also the series U_t^*, the optimized version of the component of the *implied* model of Eq. (4). For a complete discussion of how one obtains NoVaS forecasts see Politis and Thomakos (2008). In this section we present new results on NoVaS volatility forecasting.

Consider first the case where forecasting is performed based on squared returns. In Politis and Thomakos (2008) it is explained in detail that we require two components to forecast squared returns: one component is the conditional median of U_{n+1}^{2*} series and the other is the (known at time n) component A_n^{2*}. The rest of the procedure depends on the dependence properties of the studentized series W_n^* and the target distribution. From our experience, what has invariably been observed with financial returns is that their corresponding W_n^* series appears—for all practical purposes—to be uncorrelated.[8] If the target distribution is the normal then—by the approximate normality of its *joint* distributions—the W_n^* series would be independent as well. The series U_n^* would inherit the W_n^*s independence by Eqs. (3) and (4), and therefore the best estimate of the conditional median of U_{n+1}^{2*} is the unconditional sample median. Based on the above discussion we are now able to obtain volatility forecasts $\widehat{h}_{n+1}^2$ in a variety of ways: (a) we can use the forecasts of squared (or absolute) returns; (b) we can use only the component of the conditional variance A_n^2 for $\phi(z) = \sqrt{z}$ or A_n for $\phi(z) = z$, akin to a GARCH approach; (c) we can combine (a) and (b) and use the forecast of the empirical measure $\widehat{\gamma}_{n+1}$.

The volatility forecast based on (a) above would be:

$$\widehat{h}_{n+1,1}^2 \equiv \widehat{X}_{n+1}^2 \stackrel{\text{def}}{=} \widehat{\mathsf{Med}}\left[U_n^{2*}\right] A_n^{2*}. \tag{8}$$

When using (b) the corresponding forecast would just be the power of the A_n^* component, something very similar to an $ARCH(\infty)$ forecast:

[8] This is an empirical finding; if, however, the W_n^* series is not independent then a slightly different procedure involving a (hopefully) linear predictor would be required—see Politis (2003a, 2007) and Politis and Thomakos (2008) for details.

$$\widehat{h}^2_{n+1,2} \stackrel{\text{def}}{=} A_n^{2*}. \tag{9}$$

However, the most relevant and appropriate volatility forecast in the NoVaS context should be based on (c), i.e., on a forecast of the estimate of the time-localized variance measure $\widehat{\gamma}_{n+1}$, which was originally used to initiate the NoVaS procedure in Eq. (1). What is important to note is that forecasting based on $\widehat{\gamma}_{n+1}$ is neither forecasting of squared returns nor forecasting based on past information alone. It is, in fact, a linear combination of the two, thus incorporating elements from essentially two approaches. Combining Eqs. (1–4), (8) and (9) it is straightforward to show that $\widehat{\gamma}_{n+1}$ can be expressed as:

$$\begin{aligned}\widehat{\gamma}_{n+1} \equiv \widehat{h}^2_{n+1,3} &\stackrel{\text{def}}{=} \left\{a_0^* \widehat{\mathsf{Med}}\left[U_n^{2*}\right] + 1\right\} A_n^{2*} \\ &= a_0^* \widehat{h}^2_{n+1,1} + \widehat{h}^2_{n+1,2}.\end{aligned} \tag{10}$$

Equation (10) is our new proposal for volatility forecasting using NoVaS. In his original work, Politis (2003a) used Eq. (8), and in effect conducted forecasting of the one-step-ahead squared returns via NoVaS. By contrast, Eq. (10) is a *bona fide* predictor of the one-step-ahead *volatility,* i.e., the conditional variance. For this reason, Eq. (10) will be the formula used in what follows, our simulations and real data examples.

Forecasts using absolute returns are constructed in a similar fashion, the only difference being that we will be forecasting *directly* standard deviations $\widehat{h}_{n+1}$ and not variances. It is straightforward to show that the forecast based on (c) would be given by:

$$\begin{aligned}\widehat{\gamma}_{n+1} \equiv \widehat{h}_{n+1,3} &\stackrel{\text{def}}{=} \left\{a_0^* \widehat{\mathsf{Med}}\left[|U_n^*|\right] + 1\right\} |A_n^*| \\ &= a_0^* \widehat{h}_{n+1,1} + \widehat{h}_{n+1,2}\end{aligned} \tag{11}$$

with $\widehat{h}_{n+1,1}$ and $\widehat{h}_{n+1,2}$ being identical expressions to Eqs. (8) and (9) which use the absolute value transformation.

2.4 Departures from the Assumption of Stationarity: Local Stationarity and Structural Breaks

Consider the case of a very long time series $\{X_1, \ldots, X_n\}$, e.g., a daily series of stock returns spanning a decade. It may be unrealistic to assume that the stochastic structure of the series has stayed invariant over such a long stretch of time. A more realistic model might assume a slowly changing stochastic structure, i.e., a locally stationary model as given by Dahlhaus (1997).

Recent research has tried to address this issue by fitting time-varying GARCH models to the data but those techniques have not found global acceptance yet, in part due to their extreme computational cost. Fryzlewicz et al. (2006, 2008) and Dahlhaus and Subba-Rao (2006, 2007) all work in the context of local stationarity for a new class of ARCH processes with slowly varying parameters.

Surprisingly, NoVaS is flexible enough to accommodate such smooth/slow changes in the stochastic structure. All that is required is a *time-varying* NoVaS fitting, i.e., selecting/calibrating the NoVaS parameters on the basis of a *rolling* window of data as opposed to using the entire available past. Interestingly, as will be apparent in our simulations, the time-varying NoVaS method works well even in the presence of *structural breaks* that would typically cause a breakdown of traditional methods unless explicitly taken into account. The reason for this robustness is the simplicity in the NoVaS estimate of local variance: it is just a linear combination of (present and) past squared returns. Even if the coefficients of the linear combination are not optimally selected (which may happen in the neighborhood of a break), the linear combination remains a reasonable estimate of local variance.

By contrast, the presence of structural breaks can throw off the (typically nonlinear) fitting of GARCH parameters. Therefore, a GARCH practitioner must always be on the lookout for structural breaks, essentially conducting a hypothesis test before each application. While there are several change point tests available in the literature, the risk of non-detection of a change point can be a concern. Fortunately, the NoVaS practitioner does not have to worry about structural breaks because of the aforementioned *robustness* of the NoVaS approach.

3 NoVaS Forecasting Performance: A Simulation Analysis

It is of obvious interest to compare the forecasting performance of NoVaS-based volatility forecasts with the standard benchmark model, the *GARCH*(1,1), under a variety of different underlying DGPs. Although there are numerous models for producing volatility forecasts, including direct modeling of realized volatility series, it is not clear which of these models should be used in any particular situation, and whether they can always offer substantial improvements over the GARCH benchmark. In the context of a simulation, we will be able to better see the relative performance of NoVaS -based volatility forecasts versus GARCH-based forecasts and, in addition, we will have available the true volatility measure for forecast evaluation. This latter point, the availability of an appropriate series of true volatility, is important since in practice we do not have such a series of true volatility. The proxies range from realized volatility—generally agreed to be one of the best (if not the best) such measure—, to range-based measures, and to squared returns. We use such proxies in the empirical examples of the next section.

3.1 Simulation Design

We consider a variety of models as possible DGPs.[9] Each model $j = 1, 2, \ldots, M(=7)$ is simulated over the index $i = 1, 2, \ldots, N(=500)$ with time indices $t = 1, 2, \ldots, T(=1250)$. The sample size T amounts to about 5 years of daily data. The parameter values for the models are chosen so as to reflect annualized volatilities between about 8 to 25 %, depending on the model being used. For each model we simulate a volatility series and the corresponding returns series based on the standard representation:

$$\begin{aligned} X_{t,ij} &\stackrel{\text{def}}{=} \mu_j + h_{t,ij} Z_{t,ij} \\ h^2_{t,ij} &\stackrel{\text{def}}{=} h_j(h^2_{t-1,ij}, X^2_{t-1,ij}, \boldsymbol{\theta}_{tj}) \end{aligned} \tag{12}$$

where $h_j(\cdot)$ changes depending on the model being simulated.

The seven models simulated are: a standard GARCH, a GARCH with discrete breaks (B-GARCH), a GARCH with slowly varying parameters (TV-GARCH), a Markov switching GARCH (MS-GARCH), a smooth transition GARCH (ST-GARCH), a GARCH with an added deterministic function (D-GARCH), and a stochastic volatility model (SV-GARCH). Note that the parameter vector $\boldsymbol{\theta}_t$ will be time-varying for the Markov switching model, the smooth transition model, the time-varying parameters model, and the discrete breaks model. For the simulation we set $Z_t \sim t_{(3)}$, standardized to have unit variance.[10]

We next present the volatility equations of the above models. For ease of notation we drop the i and j subscripts when presenting the models. The first model we simulate is a standard *GARCH*(1,1) with volatility equation given by:

$$h_t^2 = \omega + \alpha h_{t-1}^2 + \beta(X_{t-1} - \mu)^2 \tag{13}$$

The parameter values were set to $\alpha = 0.9$, $\beta = 0.07$ and $\omega = 1.2e{-}5$, corresponding to an annualized volatility of 10 %. The mean return was set to $\mu = 2e - 4$ (same for all models, except the MS-GARCH) and the volatility series was initialized with the unconditional variance.

The second model we simulate is a *GARCH*(1,1) with discrete changes (breaks) in the variance parameters. These breaks depend on changes in the annualized unconditional variance, ranging from about 8 % to about 22 % and we assume two equidistant changes per year for a total of $B = 10$ breaks. The model form is identical to the *GARCH*(1,1) above:

---

[9] In our design we do not just go for a limited number of DGPs but for a wide variety and we also generate a large number of observations, totalling over 4 million, across models and replications. Note that the main computational burden is the numerical (re)optimization of the *GARCH* model over 300 K times across all simulations—and that involves (re)optimization only every 20 observations!.

[10] We fix the degrees of freedom to their true value of 3 during estimation and forecasting, thus giving GARCH a relative advantage in estimation.

$$h_t^2 = \omega_b + \alpha_b h_{t-1}^2 + \beta_b (X_{t-1} - \mu)^2, \quad b = 1, 2, \ldots, B \tag{14}$$

The α_b parameters were drawn from a uniform distribution in the interval [0.8, 0.99] and the β_b parameters were computed as $\beta_b = 1 - \alpha_b - c$, for c either 0.015 or 0.02. The ω_b parameters were computed as $\omega_b = \sigma_b^2(1 - \alpha_b - \beta_b)/250$, where σ_b^2 is the annualized variance.

The third model we simulate is a *GARCH*(1,1) with slowly varying variance parameters, of a nature very similar to the time-varying ARCH models recently considered by Dahlhaus and Subba-Rao (2006, 2007). The model is given by:

$$h_t^2 = \omega(t) + \alpha(t) h_{t-1}^2 + \beta(t)(X_{t-1} - \mu)^2 \tag{15}$$

where the parameters satisfy the finite unconditional variance assumption $\alpha(t) + \beta(t) < 1$ for all t. The parameters functions $\alpha(t)$ and $\beta(t)$ are sums of sinusoidal functions of different frequencies ν_k of the form $c(t) = \sum_{k=1}^{K} \sin(2\pi \nu_k t)$, for $c(t) = \alpha(t)$ or $\beta(t)$. For $\alpha(t)$ we set $K = 4$ and $\nu_k = \{1/700, 1/500, 1/250, 1/125\}$ and for $\beta(t)$ we set $K = 2$ and $\nu_k = \{1/500, 1/250\}$. That is, we set the persistence parameter function $\alpha(t)$ to exhibit more variation than the parameter function $\beta(t)$ that controls the effect of squared returns.

The fourth model we simulate is a two-state Markov Switching $GARCH(1,1)$ model, after Francq and Zakoïan (2005). The form of the model is given by:

$$h_t^2 = \sum_{s=1}^{2} \mathbf{1}\{\mathsf{P}(S_t = s)\} \left[\omega_s + \alpha_s h_{t-1}^2 + \beta_s (X_{t-1} - \mu_s)^2\right] \tag{16}$$

In the first regime (high persistence and high volatility state) we set $\alpha_1 = 0.9$, $\beta_1 = 0.07$ and $\omega_1 = 2.4e-5$, corresponding to an annualized volatility of 20 %, and $\mu_1 = 2e-4$. In the second regime (low persistence and low volatility state) we set $\alpha_2 = 0.7$, $\beta_2 = 0.22$ and $\omega_2 = 1.2e-4$ corresponding to an annualized volatility of 10 %, and $\mu_2 = 0$. The transition probabilities for the first regime are $p_{11} = 0.9$ and $p_{12} = 0.1$ while for the second regime we try two alternative specifications $p_{21} = \{0.3, 0.1\}$ and $p_{22} = \{0.7, 0.9\}$.

The fifth model we simulate is a (logistic) smooth transition $GARCH(1,1)$; see Taylor (2004) and references therein for a discussion on the use of such models. The form the model takes is given by:

$$h_t^2 = \sum_{s=1}^{2} Q_s(X_{t-1}) \left[\omega_s + \alpha_s h_{t-1}^2 + \beta_s (X_{t-1} - \mu_s)^2\right] \tag{17}$$

where $Q_1(\cdot) + Q_2(\cdot) = 1$ and $Q_s = \left[1 + \exp(-\gamma_1 X_{t-1}^{\gamma_2})\right]^{-1}$ is the logistic transition function. The parameters α_s, β_s, ω_s and μ_s are set to the same values as in the previous MS-GARCH model. The parameters of the transition function are set to $\gamma_1 = 12.3$ and $\gamma_2 = 1$.

The sixth model we simulate is a $GARCH(1, 1)$ model with an added smooth deterministic function yielding a *locally stationary* model as a result. For the convenient case of a linear function we have that the volatility equation is the same as in the standard $GARCH(1, 1)$ model in Eq. (13) while the return equation takes the following form:

$$X_t = \mu + [a - b(t/T)]\, h_t Z_t \tag{18}$$

To ensure positivity of the resulting variance we require that $(a/b) > (t/T)$. Since $(t/T) \in (0, 1]$ we set $a = \alpha + \beta = 0.97$ and $b = (\beta/\alpha) \approx 0.078$ so that the positivity condition is satisfied for all t.

Finally, the last model we simulate is a stochastic volatility model with the volatility equation expressed in logarithmic terms and taking the form of an autoregression with normal innovations. The model now takes the form:

$$\log h_t^2 = \omega + \alpha \log h_{t-1}^2 + w_t, w_t \sim \mathcal{N}(0, \sigma_w^2) \tag{19}$$

and we set the parameter values to $\alpha = 0.95$, $\omega \approx -0.4$ and $\sigma_w = 0.2$.

For each simulation run i and for each model j we split the sample into two parts $T = T_0 + T_1$, where T_0 is the estimation sample and T_1 is the forecast sample. We consider two values for T_0, namely 250 or 900, which correspond respectively to about a year and three and a half years of daily data. We roll the estimation sample T_1 times and thus generate T_1 out-of-sample forecasts. In estimation the parameters are re-estimated (for GARCH) or updated (for NoVaS) every 20 observations (about one month for daily data). We always forecast the volatility of the corresponding return series we simulate (Eqs. (10) and (11)) and evaluate it with the known, one-step-ahead simulated volatility. NoVaS forecasts are produced for using a normal target distribution and both squared and absolute returns. The nomenclature used in the tables is as follows:

1. SQNT, NoVaS forecasts made using squared returns and normal target.
2. ABNT, NoVaS forecasts made using absolute returns and normal target.
3. GARCH, L_2-based GARCH forecasts.
4. M-GARCH, L_1-based GARCH forecasts.

The naïve forecast benchmark is the sample variance of the rolling estimation sample. Therefore, for each model j being simulated we produce a total of $F = 4$ forecasts; the forecasts are numbered $f = 0, 1, 2, \ldots, F$ with $f = 0$ denoting the naïve forecast. We then have to analyze T_1 forecast errors $e_{t,ijf} \stackrel{\text{def}}{=} h_{t+1,ij}^2 - \widehat{h}_{t+1,ijf}^2$. Using these forecast errors we compute the mean absolute deviation for each model; each forecast method and each simulation run as:

$$m_{ijf} = MAD_{ijf} \stackrel{\text{def}}{=} \frac{1}{T_1} \sum_{t=T_0+1}^{T} |e_{t,ijf}| \tag{20}$$

The values $\{m_{ijf}\}_{i=1,\dots,N;j=1,\dots,M;f=0,\dots,F}$ now become our data for meta-analysis. We compute various descriptive statistics about their distribution (across i, the independent simulation runs and for each f the different forecasting methods) like mean ($\bar{x}_f$ in the tables), std. deviation ($\widehat{\sigma}_f$ in the tables), min, the 10, 25, 50, 75, 90 % quantiles and max (Q_p in the tables, $p = 0, 0.1, 0.25, 0.5, 0.75, 0.9, 1$). For example, we have that:

$$\bar{x}_{jf} \stackrel{\text{def}}{=} \frac{1}{N}\sum_{i=1}^{N} m_{ijf} \tag{21}$$

We also compute the percentage of times that the relative (to the benchmark) MAD's of the NoVaS forecasts are better than the GARCH forecasts. Define $m_{ij,N} \stackrel{\text{def}}{=} m_{ijf}/m_{ij0}$, $f = 1, 2$ to be the ratio of the MAD of any of the NoVaS forecasts relative to the benchmark and $m_{ij,G} \stackrel{\text{def}}{=} m_{ijf}/m_{ij0}$, $f = 3, 4$ to be the ratio of the MAD of the two GARCH forecasts relative to the benchmark. That is, for each model j and forecasting method f we compute (dropping the j model subscript):

$$\widehat{P}_f \stackrel{\text{def}}{=} \frac{1}{N}\sum_{i=1}^{N} \mathbf{1}\left(m_{ij,N} \leq m_{ij,G}\right). \tag{22}$$

Then, we consider the total number of times that any NoVaS forecasting method had a smaller relative MAD compared to the relative MAD of the GARCH forecasts and compute also $\widehat{P} \stackrel{\text{def}}{=} \cup_f \widehat{P}_f$ as the union across. So $\widehat{P}_f$, for $f = 1, 2$ corresponds to the aforementioned methods NoVaS methods SQNT and ABNT, respectively, and $\widehat{P}$ corresponds to their union.

3.2 Discussion of Simulation Results

The simulation helps compare the NoVaS forecasts to the usual GARCH forecasts, i.e., L_2-based GARCH forecasts, and also to the M-GARCH forecasts, i.e., L_1-based GARCH forecasts, the latter being recommended by Politis (2003a, 2004, 2007). All simulation results, that is the statistics of the MAD's of Eq. (20) and the probabilities of Eq. (22), are compacted in three tables, Table 1 through Table 3. In Tables 1 and 2 we have the statistics for the MAD's (Table 1 has the case of 1000 forecasts (smaller estimation sample) while Table 2 has the case of 350 forecasts (larger estimation sample). Table 3 has the statistics on the probabilities.

The main result that emerges from looking at these tables is the very good and competitive performance of NoVaS forecasts, even when the the true DGP is GARCH (DGP1 in the tables).[11] While it would seem intuitive that GARCH forecasts would

[11] The phenomenon of poor performance of GARCH forecasting when the DGP is actually GARCH may seem puzzling and certainly deserves further study. Our experience based on the simulations

Table 1 Summary of simulation results across DGP and models, $T_1 = 1{,}000$

$\bar{x}_f$	DGP1	DGP2	DGP3	DGP4a	DGP4b	DGP5	DGP6	DGP7
Naive	0.24	0.43	0.31	0.36	0.48	0.32	0.16	0.26
SQNT	0.14	0.17	0.14	0.20	0.18	0.15	0.12	0.21
ABNT	0.21	0.28	0.15	0.30	0.26	0.24	0.18	0.23
GARCH	2.64	29.10	1.70	1.33	3.21	2.05	1.62	1.50
M-GARCH	1.56	16.15	1.02	0.88	1.91	1.25	0.98	0.95
$\widehat{\sigma}_f$	DGP1	DGP2	DGP3	DGP4a	DGP4b	DGP5	DGP6	DGP7
Naive	0.33	0.96	0.53	0.42	2.34	0.34	0.17	0.16
SQNT	0.08	0.47	0.23	0.12	0.15	0.07	0.04	0.13
ABNT	0.09	0.47	0.16	0.14	0.15	0.10	0.05	0.11
GARCH	13.43	385.48	14.11	3.04	23.07	10.15	9.01	8.74
M-GARCH	7.39	212.13	7.78	1.68	12.71	5.60	4.96	4.81
$Q_{0.10}$	DGP1	DGP2	DGP3	DGP4a	DGP4b	DGP5	DGP6	DGP7
Naive	0.09	0.13	0.12	0.15	0.13	0.12	0.08	0.17
SQNT	0.09	0.10	0.06	0.14	0.12	0.11	0.10	0.15
ABNT	0.16	0.17	0.09	0.23	0.19	0.19	0.15	0.18
GARCH	0.10	0.15	0.10	0.17	0.13	0.12	0.09	0.18
M-GARCH	0.16	0.18	0.11	0.24	0.19	0.18	0.14	0.22
$Q_{0.50}$	DGP1	DGP2	DGP3	DGP4a	DGP4b	DGP5	DGP6	DGP7
Naive	0.15	0.22	0.19	0.24	0.23	0.21	0.10	0.23
SQNT	0.11	0.12	0.09	0.17	0.15	0.13	0.10	0.19
ABNT	0.19	0.20	0.11	0.27	0.23	0.22	0.16	0.22
GARCH	0.34	0.50	0.20	0.41	0.31	0.26	0.21	0.33
M-GARCH	0.29	0.40	0.17	0.37	0.30	0.26	0.20	0.32
$Q_{0.90}$	DGP1	DGP2	DGP3	DGP4a	DGP4b	DGP5	DGP6	DGP7
Naive	0.45	0.71	0.51	0.61	0.62	0.62	0.28	0.32
SQNT	0.19	0.21	0.19	0.26	0.24	0.20	0.15	0.26
ABNT	0.28	0.36	0.20	0.37	0.33	0.32	0.22	0.28
GARCH	3.53	4.19	1.51	2.88	2.83	2.53	1.78	2.71
M-GARCH	2.04	2.51	0.91	1.79	1.69	1.53	1.13	1.62

Notes (1) DGP*i* denotes the *i*th data generating process as follows: *1* for GARCH, *2* for B-GARCH, *3* for TV-GARCH, *4a* and *4b* for MS-GARCH, *5* for ST-GARCH, *6* for D-GARCH, and *7* for SV-GARCH (2) Table entries give statistics of the MAD of the forecast errors over 500 replications and $T_1 = 1{,}000$ denotes the number of forecasts generated for computing MAD in each replication (3) $\bar{x}_f$ denotes the sample mean, $\widehat{\sigma}_f$ denotes the sample std. deviation, and Q_p denotes the pth sample quantile of the MAD distribution over 500 replications (4) Naïve denotes forecasts based on the rolling sample variance, SQNT (ABNT) denotes NoVaS forecasts based on a normal target distribution and squared (absolute) returns, GARCH and M-GARCH denote L_2 and L_1 based forecasts from a standard GARCH model

(Footnote 11 continued)
suggests that the culprit is the occasional instability of the numerical MLE used to fit the GARCH model (computations performed in R using an explicit log-likelihood function with R optimization routines). Although in most trials the GARCH fitted parameters were accurate, every so often the numerical MLE gave grossly inaccurate answers which, of course, affect the statistics of forecasting performance. This instability was less pronounced when the fitting was done based on a large sample

Table 2 Summary of simulation results across DGP and models, $T_1 = 350$

$\bar{x}_f$	DGP1	DGP2	DGP3	DGP4a	DGP4b	DGP5	DGP6	DGP7
Naive	0.26	0.39	0.31	0.37	0.47	0.31	0.13	0.26
SQNT	0.14	0.10	0.13	0.20	0.20	0.15	0.11	0.22
ABNT	0.21	0.22	0.15	0.32	0.27	0.25	0.17	0.24
GARCH	0.22	0.65	0.20	2.70	5.56	0.19	0.12	0.24
M-GARCH	0.24	0.47	0.20	1.65	3.21	0.24	0.15	0.27
$\widehat{\sigma}_f$	DGP1	DGP2	DGP3	DGP4a	DGP4b	DGP5	DGP6	DGP7
Naive	0.39	0.87	0.58	0.70	1.95	0.42	0.19	0.33
SQNT	0.13	0.09	0.30	0.16	0.30	0.12	0.05	0.36
ABNT	0.13	0.32	0.19	0.33	0.26	0.17	0.06	0.28
GARCH	0.75	4.99	0.37	42.77	84.17	0.31	0.22	0.98
M-GARCH	0.49	2.75	0.38	23.68	46.39	0.27	0.14	0.58
$Q_{0.10}$	DGP1	DGP2	DGP3	DGP4a	DGP4b	DGP5	DGP6	DGP7
Naive	0.07	0.12	0.13	0.11	0.11	0.10	0.04	0.16
SQNT	0.09	0.07	0.06	0.13	0.11	0.10	0.10	0.13
ABNT	0.15	0.12	0.09	0.21	0.18	0.17	0.14	0.16
GARCH	0.04	0.07	0.08	0.08	0.07	0.06	0.04	0.13
M-GARCH	0.09	0.09	0.10	0.14	0.12	0.12	0.08	0.16
$Q_{0.50}$	DGP1	DGP2	DGP3	DGP4a	DGP4b	DGP5	DGP6	DGP7
Naive	0.14	0.21	0.19	0.22	0.20	0.20	0.08	0.22
SQNT	0.11	0.08	0.08	0.16	0.14	0.12	0.10	0.19
ABNT	0.18	0.15	0.11	0.25	0.21	0.21	0.15	0.21
GARCH	0.10	0.13	0.12	0.15	0.13	0.12	0.07	0.18
M-GARCH	0.17	0.15	0.13	0.23	0.19	0.19	0.13	0.23
$Q_{0.90}$	DGP1	DGP2	DGP3	DGP4a	DGP4b	DGP5	DGP6	DGP7
Naive	0.48	0.56	0.49	0.64	0.67	0.56	0.24	0.34
SQNT	0.20	0.13	0.19	0.27	0.27	0.21	0.13	0.28
ABNT	0.29	0.28	0.20	0.40	0.37	0.30	0.20	0.30
GARCH	0.35	0.37	0.28	0.45	0.42	0.34	0.18	0.26
M-GARCH	0.33	0.34	0.29	0.47	0.46	0.34	0.20	0.34

Notes (1) DGPi denotes the ith data generating process as follows: *1* for GARCH, *2* for B-GARCH, *3* for TV-GARCH, *4a* and *4b* for MS-GARCH, *5* for ST-GARCH, *6* for D-GARCH, and *7* for SV-GARCH (2) Table entries give statistics of the MAD of the forecast errors over 500 replications and $T_1 = 1{,}000$ denotes the number of forecasts generated for computing MAD in each replication (3) $\bar{x}_f$ denotes the sample mean, $\widehat{\sigma}_f$ denotes the sample std. deviation and Q_p denotes the pth sample quantile of the MAD distribution over 500 replications (4) Naïve denotes forecasts based on the rolling sample variance, SQNT (ABNT) denotes NoVaS forecasts based on a normal target distribution and squared (absolute) returns, GARCH and M-GARCH denote L_2 and L_1 based forecasts from a standard GARCH model

have an advantage in this case we find that *any* of the NoVaS methods (SQNT, ABNT) is seen to outperform both GARCH and M-GARCH in *all* measured areas: mean

(Footnote 11 continued)
(case of 900). Surprisingly, a training sample as large as 250 (e.g. a year of daily data) was not enough to ward off the negative effects of this instability in fitting (and forecasting) based on the GARCH model.

Table 3 Summary of simulation results across DGP and models percentage of times that NoVaS forecasts are better than the benchmarks

DGP	Benchmark	$\widehat{P}_1$	$\widehat{P}_2$	$\widehat{P}$	$\widehat{P}_1$	$\widehat{P}_2$	$\widehat{P}$
DGP1	GARCH	0.93	0.66	0.93	0.43	0.13	0.43
	M-GARCH	1.00	0.74	1.00	0.86	0.35	0.86
DGP2	GARCH	0.98	0.76	0.98	0.86	0.35	0.86
	M-GARCH	0.99	0.87	0.99	0.96	0.42	0.96
DGP3	GARCH	0.98	0.85	1.00	0.89	0.52	0.98
	M-GARCH	0.99	0.98	1.00	0.96	0.91	0.99
DGP4a	GARCH	0.94	0.62	0.94	0.42	0.14	0.42
	M-GARCH	1.00	0.73	1.00	0.85	0.30	0.86
DGP4b	GARCH	0.90	0.60	0.90	0.45	0.18	0.46
	M-GARCH	1.00	0.75	1.00	0.87	0.36	0.89
DGP5	GARCH	0.91	0.55	0.91	0.47	0.14	0.47
	M-GARCH	1.00	0.67	1.00	0.91	0.31	0.92
DGP6	GARCH	0.76	0.55	0.76	0.24	0.09	0.24
	M-GARCH	1.00	0.61	1.00	0.77	0.19	0.77
DGP7	GARCH	0.90	0.70	0.91	0.36	0.17	0.40
	M-GARCH	0.97	0.99	1.00	0.84	0.73	0.91

Notes (1) DGP*i* denotes the *i*th data generating process as follows: *1* for GARCH, *2* for B-GARCH, *3* for TV-GARCH, *4a* and *4b* for MS-GARCH, *5* for ST-GARCH, *6* for D-GARCH, and *7* for SV-GARCH (2) Table entries give the proportion of times that the NoVaS MAD relative to the naïve benchmark was smaller than the GARCH MAD relative to the same benchmark, see Eq. (22) in the main text

of the MAD distribution ($\bar{x}_f$, mean error), tightness of MAD distribution ($\hat{\sigma}_f$ and the related quantiles), and finally the % of times NoVaS MAD was better. Actually, in this setting, the GARCH forecasts are vastly underperforming as compared to the Naive benchmark. The best NoVaS method here is the SQNT that achieves a mean error $\bar{x}_f$ almost half of that of the benchmark, and with a much tighter MAD distribution. Comparing Tables 1 and 2 sheds more light in this situation: it appears that a training sample of size 250 is just too small for GARCH to work well; with a training sample of size 900 the performance of GARCH is greatly improved, and GARCH manages to beat the benchmark in terms of mean error (but not variance). SQNT NoVaS however is *still* the best method in terms of mean error and variance; it beats M-GARCH in terms of the $\widehat{P}_1$ percentage, and narrowly underperforms as compared to GARCH in this criterion. All in all, SQNT NoVaS volatility forecasting appears to beat GARCH forecasts when the DGP *is* GARCH—a remarkable finding. Furthermore, GARCH apparently requires a very large training sample in order to work well; but with a sample spanning 3–4 years questions of non-stationarity may arise that will be addressed in what follows.

When the DGP is a GARCH with discrete breaks (B-GARCH, DGP2 in the tables) it is apparent here that ignoring possible structural breaks when fitting a GARCH model can be disastrous. The GARCH forecasts vastly underperform compared to the Naive benchmark with either small (Table 1) or big training sample (Table 2).

Interestingly, *both* NoVaS methods are better than the benchmark with SQNT seemingly the best again. The SQNT method is better than either GARCH method at least 86 % of the time. It should be stressed here that NoVaS does *not* attempt to estimate any breaks; it applies totally automatically, and is seemingly unperturbed by structural breaks. When we have a DGP of a GARCH with slowly varying parameters (TV-GARCH) the results are similar to the previous case except that the performance of GARCH is a little better as compared to the benchmark—but only when given a big training sample (compare Tables 1 and 2 for DGP3). However, still *both* NoVaS methods are better than either GARCH method. The best is again SQNT. Either of those beats either GARCH method at least 88 % of the time (Table 3). For the Markov switching GARCH (MS-GARCH) (DGPs 4a and 4b in the tables) the results are essentially the same as with DGP2: GARCH forecasts vastly underperform the Naive benchmark with either small or big training sample. Again, *all* NoVaS methods are better than the benchmark with SQNT being the best.

For the fifth DGP, the smooth transition GARCH (ST-GARCH) (DGP5 in the tables) the situation is more like the first one (where the DGP is plain GARCH); with a large enough training sample, GARCH forecasts are able to beat the benchmark, and be competitive with NoVaS. Still, however, SQNT NoVaS is best, not only because of smallest mean error but also in terms of tightness of MAD distribution. The results are also similar to the next DGP, GARCH with deterministic function (D-GARCH) (DGP6 in the tables), where given a large training sample, GARCH forecasts are able to beat the benchmark, and be competitive with NoVaS. Again, SQNT NoVaS is best, not only because of smallest mean error but also in terms of tightness of MAD distribution. Finally, for the last DGP, stochastic volatility model (SV-GARCH) (DGP7 in the tables) a similar behavior to the above two cases is found, but although (with a big training sample) GARCH does well in terms of mean error, note the large spread of the MAD distribution.

The results from the simulations can be summarized as follows:

- GARCH forecasts are extremely off-the-mark when the training sample is not large (of the order of 2–3 years of daily data). Note that large training sample sizes are prone to be problematic if the stochastic structure of the returns changes over time.
- Even given a large training sample, NoVaS forecasts are best; this holds *even when the true DGP is actually GARCH!*
- Ignoring possible breaks (B-GARCH), slowly varying parameters (TV-GARCH), or a Markov switching feature (MS-GARCH) when fitting a GARCH model can be disastrous in terms of forecasts. In contrast, NoVaS forecasts seem unperturbed by such gross nonstationarities.
- Ignoring the presence of a smooth transition GARCH (ST-GARCH), a GARCH with an added deterministic function (D-GARCH), or a stochastic volatility model (SV-GARCH) does not seem as crucial at least when the the implied nonstationarity features are small and/or slowly varying.

- Overall, it seems that SQNT NoVaS is the volatility forecasting method of choice since it is the best in all examples except TV-GARCH (in which case it is a close second to ABNT NoVaS).

4 Empirical Application

In this section we provide an empirical illustration of the application and potential of the NoVaS approach using four real data sets. In judging the forecasting performance for NoVaS we consider different measures of 'true' volatility, including realized and range-based volatility.

4.1 Data and Summary Statistics

Our first data set consists of monthly returns and associated realized volatility for the S&P500 index, with the sample extending from February 1970 to May 2007 for a total of $n = 448$ observations. The second data set consists of monthly returns and associated realized, range-based volatility for the stock of Microsoft (MSFT). The sample period is from April 1986 to August 2007 for a total of $n = 257$ observations. For both these data sets the associated realized volatility was constructed by summing daily squared returns (for the S&P500 data) or daily range-based volatility (for the MSFT data). Specifically, if we denote by $r_{t,i}$ the ith daily return for month t then the monthly realized volatility is defined as $\sigma_t^2 \stackrel{\text{def}}{=} \sum_{i=1}^{m} r_{t,i}^2$, where m is the number of days. For the calculation of the realized range-based volatility denote by $H_{t,i}$ and $L_{t,i}$ the daily high and low prices for the ith day of month t. The daily range-based volatility is defined as in Parkinson (1980) as $\sigma_{t,i}^2 \stackrel{\text{def}}{=} \left[\ln(H_{t,i}) - \ln(L_{t,i})\right]^2 / [4\ln(2)]$; then, the corresponding monthly realized measure would be defined as $\sigma_t^2 \stackrel{\text{def}}{=} \sum_{i=1}^{m} \sigma_{t,i}^2$. Our third data set consists of daily returns and realized volatility for the US dollar/Japanese Yen exchange rate for a sample period between 1997 and 2005 for a total of $n = 2236$ observations. The realized volatility measure was constructed as above using intraday returns. The final data set we examine is the stock of a major private bank in the Athens Stock Exchange, EFG Eurobank. The sample period is from 1999 to 2004 for a total of $n = 1403$ observations. For lack of intraday returns we use the daily range-based volatility estimator as defined before.

Descriptive statistics of the returns for all four of our data sets are given in Table 4. We are mainly interested in the kurtosis of the returns, as we will be using kurtosis-based matching in performing NoVaS. All series have unconditional means that are not statistically different from zero and no significant serial correlation, with the exception of the last series (EFG) that has a significant first order serial correlation estimate. Also, all four series have negative skewness which is, however, statistically insignificant except for the monthly S&P500 and MSFT series where it is significant

Table 4 Descriptive statistics for empirical series

Series	n	$\bar{x}$ (%)	$\widehat{\sigma}$ (%)	$\mathcal{S}$	$\mathcal{K}$	$\mathcal{N}$	$\widehat{r}(1)$
S&P500, monthly	448	1.01	4.35	−0.37	5.04	0.00	0.00
MSFT, monthly	257	0.00	1.53	−1.75	9.00	0.00	−0.10
USD/Yen, daily	2236	−0.00	0.72	−0.70	8.52	0.00	0.00
EFG, daily	1403	−0.07	2.11	−1.24	24.32	0.00	0.14

Notes (1) n denotes the number of observations, $\bar{x}$ denotes the sample mean, $\widehat{\sigma}$ denotes the sample standard deviation, $\mathcal{S}$ denotes the sample skewness, $\mathcal{K}$ denotes the sample kurtosis (2) $\mathcal{N}$ is the p-value of the Cramer-Von Misses test for normality of the underlying series (3) $\widehat{r}(1)$ denotes the estimate of the first order serial correlation coefficient

at the 5 % level. Finally, all series are characterized by heavy tails with kurtosis coefficients ranging from 5.04 (monthly S&P500) to 24.32 (EFG). The hypothesis of normality is strongly rejected for all series.

In Figs. 1, 2, 3, 4, 5, 6, 7, 8 we present graphs for the return series, the corresponding volatility and log volatility, the quantile–quantile (QQ) plot for the returns and four recursive moments. The computation of the recursive moments is useful for illustrating the potential unstable nature that may be characterizing the series. Figures 1 and 2 are for the monthly S&P500 returns, Figs. 3 and 4 are for monthly MSFT returns, Figs. 5 and 6 are for the daily USD/Yen returns and Figs. 7 and 8 are for the daily EFG returns. Of interest are the figures that plot the estimated recursive moments. In Fig. 2 we see that the mean and standard deviation of the monthly S&P500 returns are fairly stable while the skewness and kurtosis exhibit breaks. In fact, the kurtosis exhibits the tendency to rise in jolts/shocks and does not retreat to previous levels thereby indicating that there might not be an finite 4th moment for this series. Similar observations can be made for the other four series as far as recursive kurtosis goes. This is especially relevant about our argument that NoVaS can handle such possible global nonstationarities.

4.2 NoVaS Optimization and Forecasting Specifications

Our NoVaS in-sample analysis is performed for two possible combinations of target distribution and variance measures, i.e, squared and absolute returns using a normal target, as in the simulation analysis. We use the exponential NoVaS algorithm as discussed in Sect. 2, with $\alpha = 0.0$, a trimming threshold of 0.01 and $p_{\max} = n/4$. The objective function for optimization is kurtosis-matching, i.e., $D_n(\boldsymbol{\theta}) = |\mathcal{K}_n(\boldsymbol{\theta})|$, as in Eq. (7)—robustness to deviations from these baseline specification is also discussed below. The results of our in-sample analysis are given in Table 5. In the table we present the optimal values of the exponential constant b^*, the first coefficient a_0^*, the implied optimal lag length p^*, the value of the objective function $D_n(\boldsymbol{\theta}^*)$, and two measures of distributional fit. The first is the QQ correlation coefficient for the original series, QQ_X, and the second is the QQ correlation coefficient for the

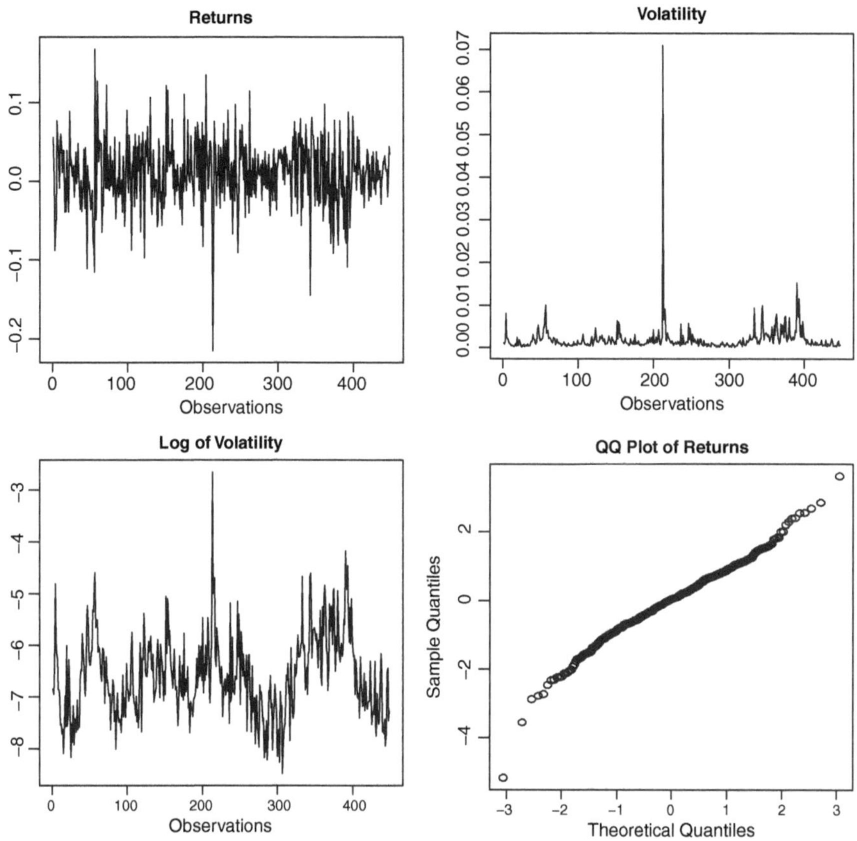

Fig. 1 Return, volatility, and QQ plots for the monthly S&P500 series

transformed series $W_t(\boldsymbol{\theta}^*)$ series, QQ_W. These last two measures are used to gage the 'quality' of the attempted distributional matching before and after the application of the NoVaS transformation.

Our NoVaS out-of-sample analysis is reported in Tables 6, 7, 8 and 9. All forecasts are based on a rolling sample whose length n_0 differs according to the series examined: for the monthly S&P500 series we use $n_0 = 300$ observations; for the monthly MSFT series we use $n_0 = 157$ observations; for EFG series we use $n_0 = 900$ observations; for the daily USD/Yen series we use $n_0 = 1250$ observations. The corresponding evaluation samples are $n_1 = \{148, 100, 986, 503\}$ for the four series respectively. Note that our examples cover a variety of different lengths, ranging from 157 observations for the MSFT series to 1250 observations for the USD/Yen series. All forecasts we make are 'honest' out-of-sample forecasts: they use only observations prior to the time period to be forecasted. The NoVaS parameters are reoptimized as the window rolls over the entire evaluation sample (every month for the monthly series and every 20 observations for the daily series). We forecast

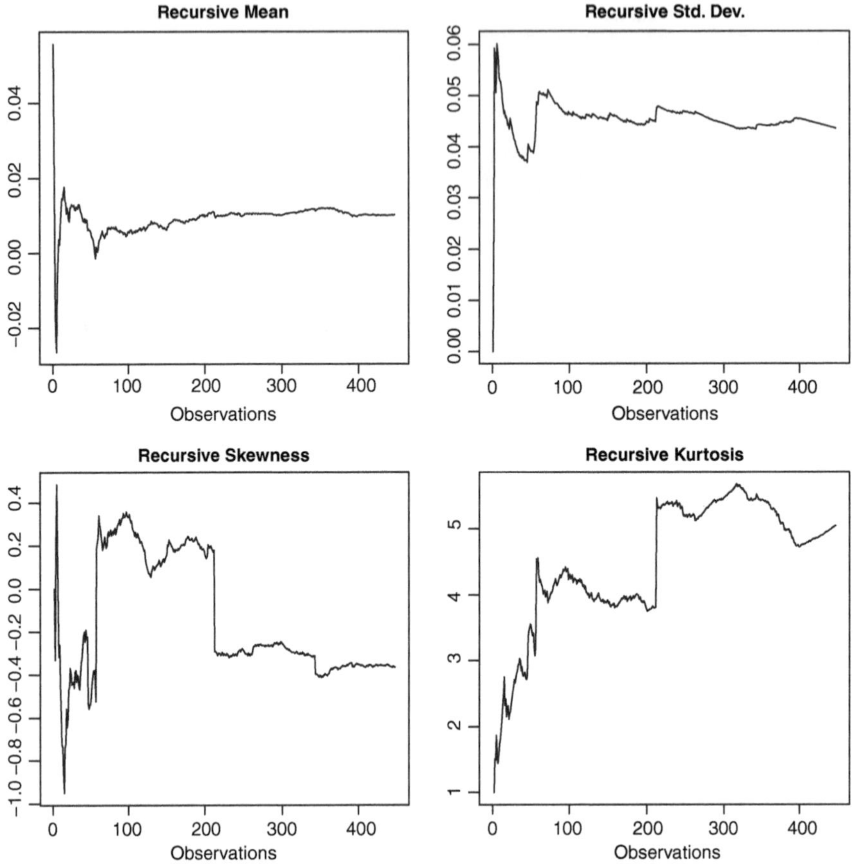

Fig. 2 Recursive moments for the monthly S&P500 series

volatility both by using absolute or squared returns (depending on the specification), as described in the section on NoVaS forecasting, and by using the empirical variance measure $\widehat{\gamma}_{n+1}$—see Eqs. (10) and (11).[12] To compare the performance of the NoVaS approach we estimate and forecast using a standard $GARCH(1, 1)$ model for each series, assuming a $t_{(\nu)}$ distribution with degrees of freedom estimated from the data. The parameters of the model are re-estimated as the window rolls over, as described above. As noted in Politis (2003a,b, 2007), the performance of GARCH forecasts is found to be improved under an L_1 rather than L_2 loss. We therefore report standard mean forecasts as well as median forecasts from the GARCH models. We always evaluate our forecasts using the 'true' volatility measures given in the previous section and report several measures of forecasting performance. This is important

[12] All NoVaS forecasts were made without applying an explicit predictor as all $W_t(\boldsymbol{\theta}^*)$ series were found to be uncorrelated.

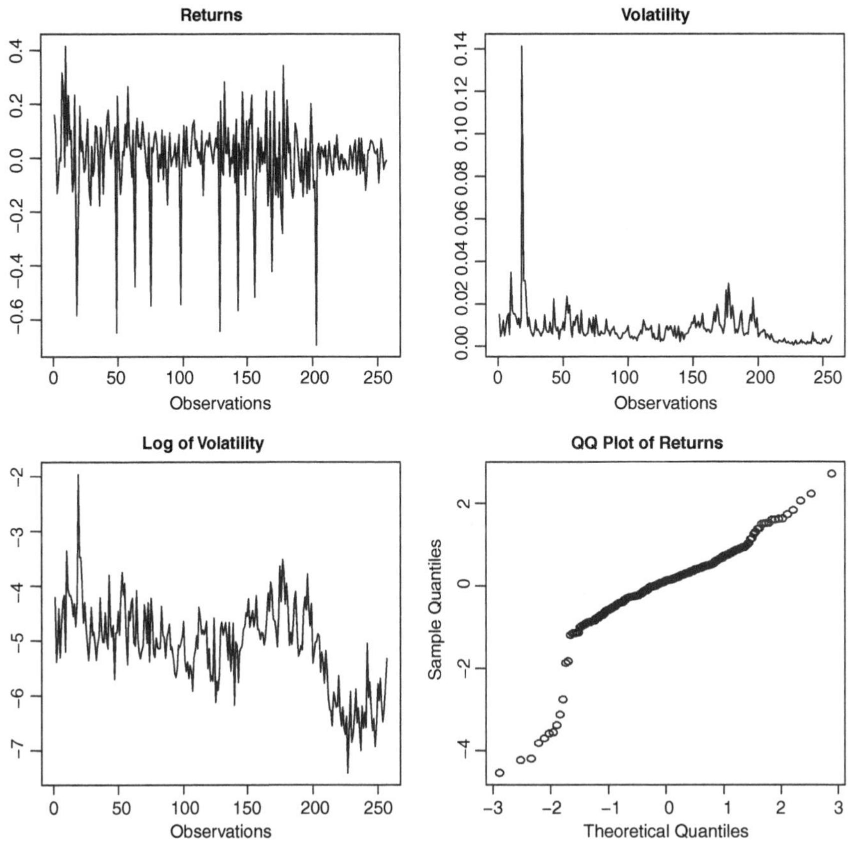

Fig. 3 Return, volatility, and QQ plots for the monthly MSFT series

as a single evaluation measure may not always provide an accurate description of the performance of competing models.

We first calculate the mean absolute deviation (MAD) and root mean-squared (RMSE) of the forecast errors $e_t \stackrel{\text{def}}{=} \sigma_t^2 - \widehat{\sigma}_t^2$, given by:

$$MAD(e) \stackrel{\text{def}}{=} \frac{1}{n_1} \sum_{t=n_0+1}^{n} |e_t|, \quad RMSE(e) \stackrel{\text{def}}{=} \sqrt{\frac{1}{n_1} \sum_{t=n_0+1}^{n} (e_t - \bar{e})^2} \tag{23}$$

where $\widehat{\sigma}_t^2$ denotes the forecast for any of the methods/models we use. As a Naive benchmark we use the (rolling) sample variance. We then calculate the Diebold and Mariano (1995) test for comparing forecasting models. We use the absolute value function in computing the relevant statistic and so we can formally compare the MAD rankings of the various models.

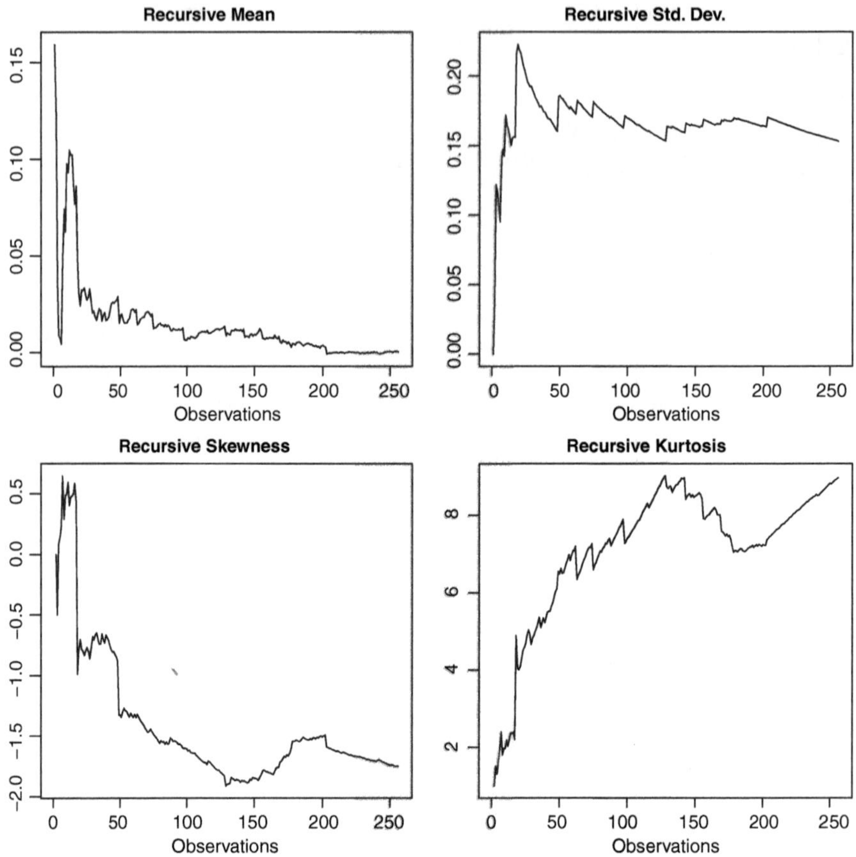

Fig. 4 Recursive moments for the monthly MSFT series

Finally, we calculate and report certain statistics based on the forecasting unbiasedness regression (also known as 'Mincer-Zarnowitz regression'). This regression can be expressed in several ways and we use the following representation:

$$e_t = a + b\widehat{\sigma}_t^2 + \zeta_t \tag{24}$$

where ζ_t is the regression error. Under the hypothesis of forecast unbiasedness we expect to have $\mathsf{E}\left[e_t|\mathcal{F}_{t-1}\right] = 0$ and therefore we expect $a = b = 0$ (and $\mathsf{E}\left[\zeta_t|\mathcal{F}_{t-1}\right] = 0$ as well.) Furthermore, the R^2 from the above regression is an indication as to how much of the forecast error variability can still be explained by the forecast. For any two competing forecasting models A and B we say that model A is superior to model B if $R_A^2 < R_B^2$, i.e., if we can make no further improvements in our forecast.

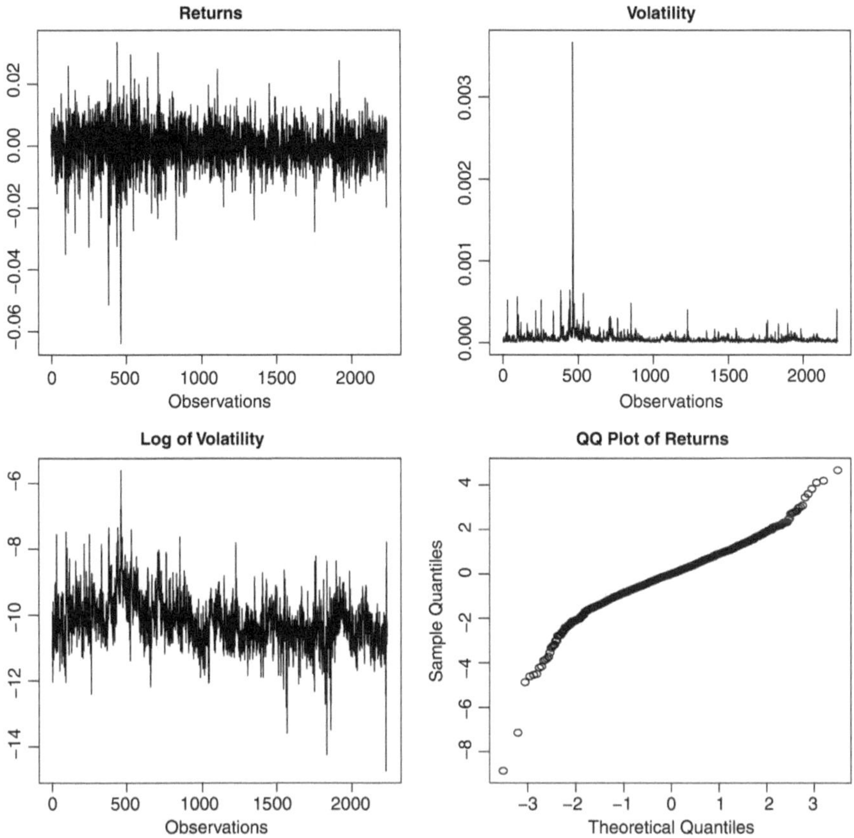

Fig. 5 Return, volatility, and QQ plots for the daily USD/Yen series

Our forecasting results are summarized in Tables 6 and 7 for the MAD and RMSE rankings and in Tables 8 and 9 for the Diebold-Mariano test and forecasting unbiasedness regressions. Similar results were obtained when using a recursive sample and are available on request.

4.3 Discussion of Results

We begin our discussion with the in-sample results and, in particular, the degree of normalization achieved by NoVaS. Looking at the value of the objective function in Table 5 we see that it is zero to three decimals for practically all cases. Therefore, NoVaS is very successful in reducing the excess kurtosis in the original return series. In addition, the quantile–quantile correlation coefficient is very high (in excess of 0.99 in all cases examined, frequently being practically one). One should compare the two QQ measures of *before and after* the NoVaS transformation to see the difference

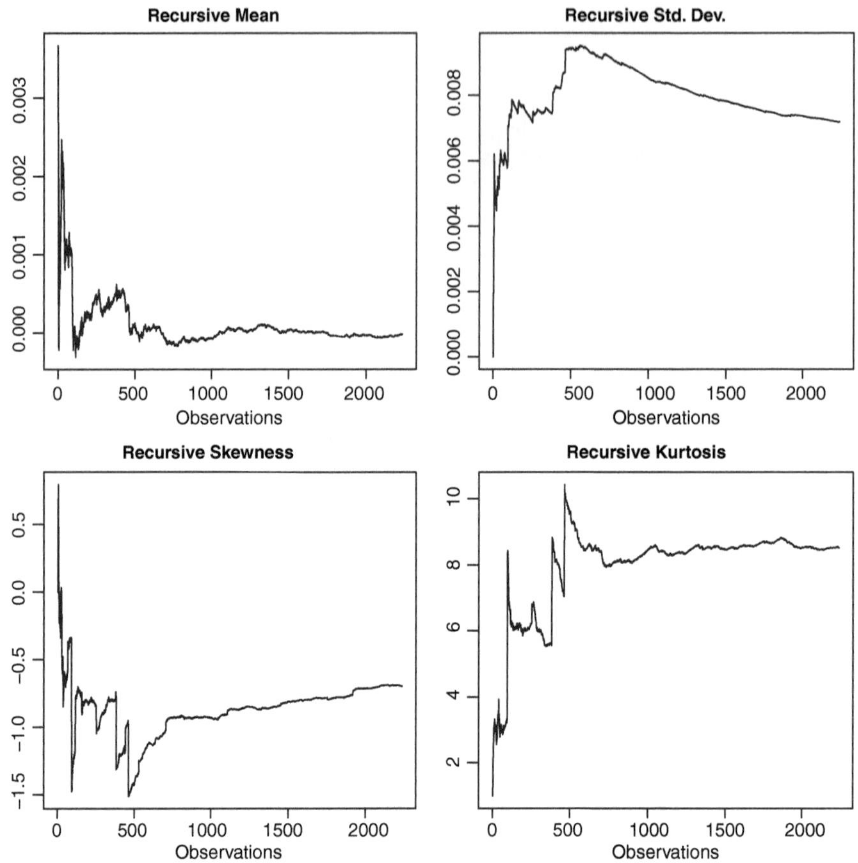

Fig. 6 Recursive moments for the daily USD/Yen series

that the transformation has on the data. The case of the EFG series is particularly worth mentioning as that series has the highest kurtosis: we can see from the table that we get a QQ correlation coefficient in excess of 0.998; this is a very clear indication that the desired distributional matching has been achieved for all practical purposes. A visual confirmation of the differences in the distribution of returns before and after NoVaS transformations is given in Figs. 9, 10, 11 and 12. In these figures we have QQ plots for all the series and four combinations of return distributions, including the uniform for visual comparison. It is apparent from these figures that normalization has been achieved in all cases examined. Finally, a second noticeable in-sample result is the optimal lag length chosen by the different NoVaS specifications. In particular, we see from Table 16 that the optimal lag length is greater when using squared returns than when using absolute returns. As expected, longer lag lengths are associated with a smaller a_0^* coefficient.

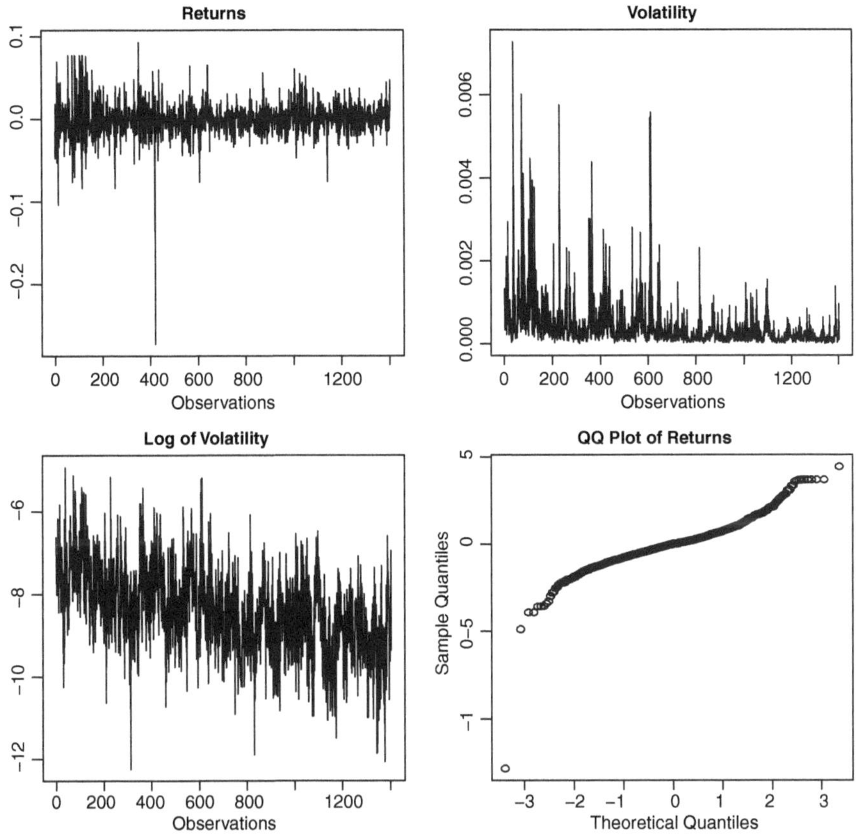

Fig. 7 Return, volatility, and QQ plots for the daily EFG series

We now turn to the out-of-sample results on the forecasting performance of NoVaS, which are summarized in Tables 6–9. The results are slightly different across the series we examine but the overall impression is that the NoVaS-based forecasts are superior to the GARCH forecasts, based on the combined performance of all evaluation measures. We discuss these in turn.

If we look at the MAD results in Table 6 the NoVaS forecasts outperform both the Naive benchmark and the GARCH-based forecasts. Note that the use of squared returns gives better results in the two series with the smallest sample kurtosis (S&P500 and USD/Yen series) while the use of absolute returns gives better results in the two series with the highest kurtosis (MSFT and EFG series). Its also worthwhile to note that the most drastic performance improvement, vis-a-vis the benchmark, can be seen for the MSFT series (smallest sample size) and the EFG series (highest

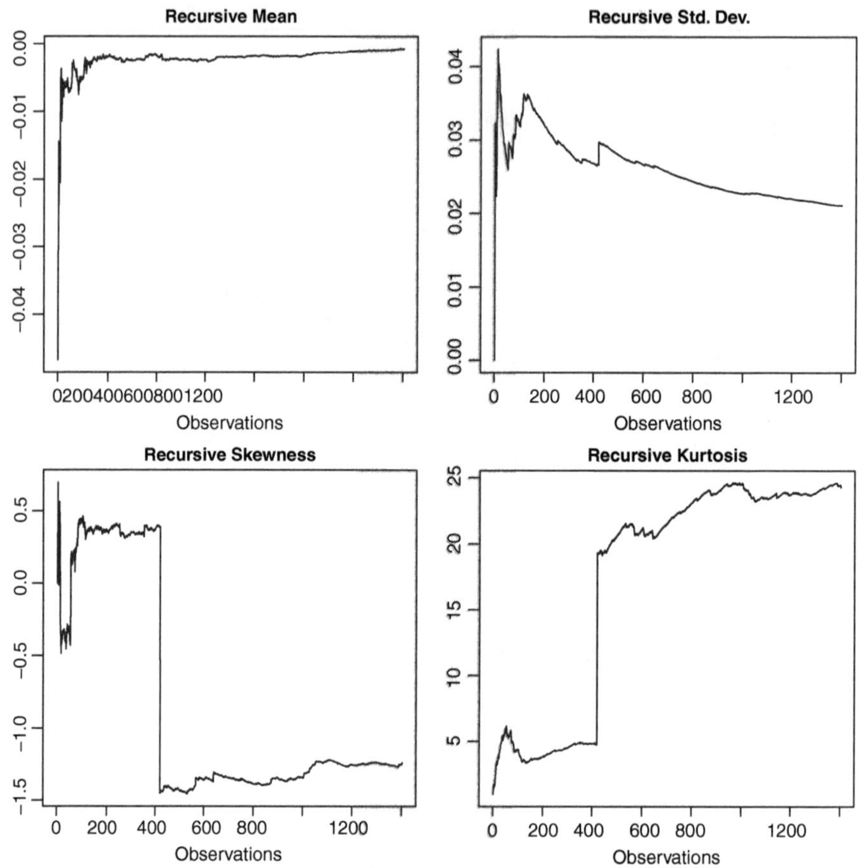

Fig. 8 Recursive moments for the daily EFG series

kurtosis).[13] This is important since we expected NoVaS to perform well in both these cases: the small sample size makes inference difficult while high kurtosis can be the result of nonstationarities in the series. Finally, the results are similar if we consider the RMSE ranking in Table 7. Based on these two descriptive evaluation measures the NoVaS forecasts outperform the benchmark and GARCH models.

To examine whether there are statistically significant differences between the NoVaS and GARCH forecasts and the benchmark, we next consider the results from the application of the Diebold and Mariano (1995) test for comparing forecasting performance. Looking at Table 7 we can see that there are statistically significant

[13] Note also the performance improvement from the use of the median GARCH versus the mean GARCH forecasts for the MSFT series. Recall that our simulation results showed that the performance of a GARCH model could be way off the mark if the training sample was small; here we use only 157 observations for training the MSFT series and the GARCH forecasts cannot outperform even the Naive benchmark.

Table 5 Full-sample NoVaS summary measures

Type	b^*	$D_n(\boldsymbol{\theta}^*)$	a_0^*	p^*	QQ_X	QQ_W
S&P500 monthly						
SQNT	0.039	0.000	0.052	34	0.989	0.996
ABNT	0.070	0.000	0.078	27	0.989	0.996
MSFT monthly						
SQNT	0.175	0.000	0.171	15	0.916	0.988
ABNT	0.251	0.000	0.231	12	0.916	0.986
USD/Yen daily						
SQNT	0.062	0.000	0.071	29	0.978	0.999
ABNT	0.121	0.000	0.124	20	0.978	0.999
EFG daily						
SQNT	0.089	0.007	0.096	24	0.943	0.999
ABNT	0.171	0.000	0.166	16	0.943	0.999

Notes (1) SQNT, ABNT denote NoVaS made forecasts based on square and absolute returns and a normal target distribution (2) b^*, a_0^* and p^* denote the optimal exponential constant, first coefficient, and implied lag length (3) $D_n(\boldsymbol{\theta}^*)$ is the value of the objective function based on kurtosis matching (4) QQ_X and QQ_W denote the QQ correlation coefficient of the original series and the transformed series respectively

Table 6 Mean absolute deviation (MAD) of forecast errors

Series	Naïve	SQNT	ABNT	Mean GARCH	Median GARCH
S&P500, monthly	0.152	0.118	0.134	0.139	0.157
MSFT, monthly	1.883	1.030	0.551	43.28	23.67
USD/Yen, daily	0.026	0.016	0.018	0.022	0.016
EFG, daily	0.251	0.143	0.120	0.225	0.141

differences between the NoVaS forecasts and the Naive benchmark for the S&P500 series and the MSFT series, with the NoVaS forecasts being significantly better.[14] For the other two series the test does not indicate a (statistically) superior performance of any of the other models compared to the benchmark.

Our empirical results so far clearly indicate that the NoVaS forecasts offer improvements in forecasting performance, both over the Naive benchmark and the GARCH models. We next discuss the results from the forecasting unbiasedness regressions of Eq. (24), where we try to see whether the forecasts are correct 'on average' and whether they make any systematic mistakes. We start by noting that the estimates from a regression like Eq. (24) suffer from bias since the regressor used, $\widehat{\sigma}_t^2$, is estimated and not measured directly. Therefore, we should be interpreting our results with some caution and connect them with our previous discussion. Looking at Table 9 we can see that in many cases the constant term a is estimated to be (numer-

[14] For the MSFT series the benchmark forecasts are also significantly better than the GARCH forecasts.

Table 7 Root mean-squared (RMSE) of forecast errors

Series	Naïve	SQNT	ABNT	Mean GARCH	Median GARCH
S&P500, monthly	0.243	0.206	0.206	0.224	0.232
MSFT, monthly	0.530	1.552	0.951	162.0	89.17
USD/Yen, daily	0.031	0.028	0.028	0.030	0.029
EFG, daily	0.227	0.208	0.194	0.211	0.212

Notes (1) All forecasts computed using a rolling evaluation sample (2) The evaluation sample used for computing the entries of the tables is as follows: 148 observations for the monthly S&P500 series, 100 observations for the monthly MSFT series, 986 observations for the daily USD/Yen series, and 503 observations for the daily EFG series (3) Table entries are the values of the evaluation measure (MAD for Table 18 and RMSE for Table 19) multiplied by 100 (S&P500 and MSFT monthly series) and by 1000 (USD/Yen and EFG daily series) respectively (4) SQNT, ABNT denote NoVaS made forecasts based on square and absolute returns and normal target distribution (5) Mean and median GARCH forecasts denote forecasts made with a GARCH model and an underlying t error distribution with degrees of freedom estimated from the data (6) The Naive forecast is based on the rolling sample variance

Table 8 Diebold-mariano test for difference in forecasting performance NoVaS and GARCH against the Naive benchmark

Series	SQNT	ABNT	Mean GARCH	Median GARCH
S&P 500, monthly				
Test value	3.369	1.762	1.282	−0.414
p-value	0.000	0.078	0.200	0.679
MSFT, monthly				
Test value	2.931	7.022	−2.671	−2.559
p-value	0.003	0.000	0.007	0.010
USD/Yen, daily				
Test value	0.101	0.083	0.037	0.096
p-value	0.919	0.933	0.971	0.924
EFG, daily				
Test value	1.077	1.301	0.259	1.095
p-value	0.281	0.190	0.795	0.274

Notes (1) See Tables 17 and 18 for column nomenclature (2) The entries of Table 19 are the test and p-values for the Diebold and Mariano (1995) test for comparing forecasting accuracy. The tests use the absolute value function for the calculation of the statistic and are expressed relative to the Naive benchmark (3) Positive values indicate that the competing model is superior, negative values that the Naive benchmark is superior

ically close to) zero, although it is statistically significant. The slope parameter b estimates show that there is still bias in the direction of the forecasts, either positive or negative, but the NoVaS estimates of b are in general much lower than those of the benchmark and the GARCH models, with the exception of the MSFT series. Furthermore, for the S&P500 and the EFG series the slope parameter is not statistically significant, at the 10 % level, indicating a possibly unbiased NoVaS forecast.

Table 9 Forecast unbiasedness regressions

Series	Naïve	SQNT	ABNT	Mean GARCH	Median GARCH
S&P500, monthly					
Estimates	(−0.003,1.824)	(0.000,0.317)	(0.000,0.879)	(−0.002,1.685)	(−0.002,3.879)
p-values	(0.597,0.540)	(0.527,0.055)	(0.344,0.000)	(0.000,0.000)	(0.000,0.000)
R^2	0.003	0.025	0.111	0.118	0.177
MSFT, monthly					
Estimates	(−0.025,0.242)	(0.004,−0.859)	(0.004,−0.729)	(0.007,−1.000)	(0.007,−1.000)
p-values	(0.000,0.276)	(0.000,0.000)	(0.000,0.000)	(0.000,0.000)	(0.000,0.000)
R^2	0.012	0.871	0.689	1.000	1.000
USD/Yen, daily					
Estimates	(0.000,−1.099)	(0.000,−0.476)	(0.000,0.355)	(0.000,−0.803)	(0.000,0.642)
p-values	(0.000,0.000)	(0.000,0.000)	(0.000,0.000)	(0.000,0.000)	(0.000,0.000)
R^2	0.188	0.055	0.017	0.136	0.029
EFG, daily					
Estimates	(0.000,−0.767)	(0.000,−0.378)	(0.000,0.058)	(0.000,0.138)	(0.000,0.567)
p-values	(0.017,0.000)	(0.000,0.000)	(0.000,0.518)	(0.038,0.318)	(0.038,0.025)
R^2	0.072	0.062	0.001	0.002	0.002

Notes (1) See Tables 17 and 18 for column nomenclature (2) The entries of Table 20 are the coefficient estimates $(\widehat{a}, \widehat{b})$ (first line), corresponding p-values (second line) and R^2 (third line) from the forecast unbiasedness regression $e_t = a + b\widehat{\sigma}_t^2 + \zeta_t$ (3) Under the hypothesis of forecast unbiasedness we must have $a = b = 0$ and $R^2 \to 0$. For any two competing models A and B for which we have that $R_A^2 < R_B^2$ we say that model A is superior to model B

The R^2 values from these regressions are also supportive of the NoVaS forecasts (remember that low values are preferred over high values): the corresponding R^2 values from the NoVaS forecasts are lower than both the benchmark and the GARCH values by at least 30 %. Note that for the S&P500 series where the value of the R^2 of the benchmark is lower than the corresponding NoVaS value, we also have a (numerically) large value for the slope parameter b for the benchmark compared to NoVaS. The only real problem with the R^2 from these regressions is for the MSFT series which we discuss below in Remark 4. All in all the results from Table 9 support the superior performance of NoVaS against its competitors and show that is a much less biased forecasting procedure.

Remark 3 Can we obtain further improvements using the NoVaS methodology? In particular, how do changes in the value of the α parameter affect the forecasting performance? This is an empirically interesting question since our results can be affected both by the small sample size and the degree of kurtosis in the data. The MSFT series exhibits both these problems and it is thus worthwhile to see whether we can improve our results by allowing the unconditional estimator of the variance to

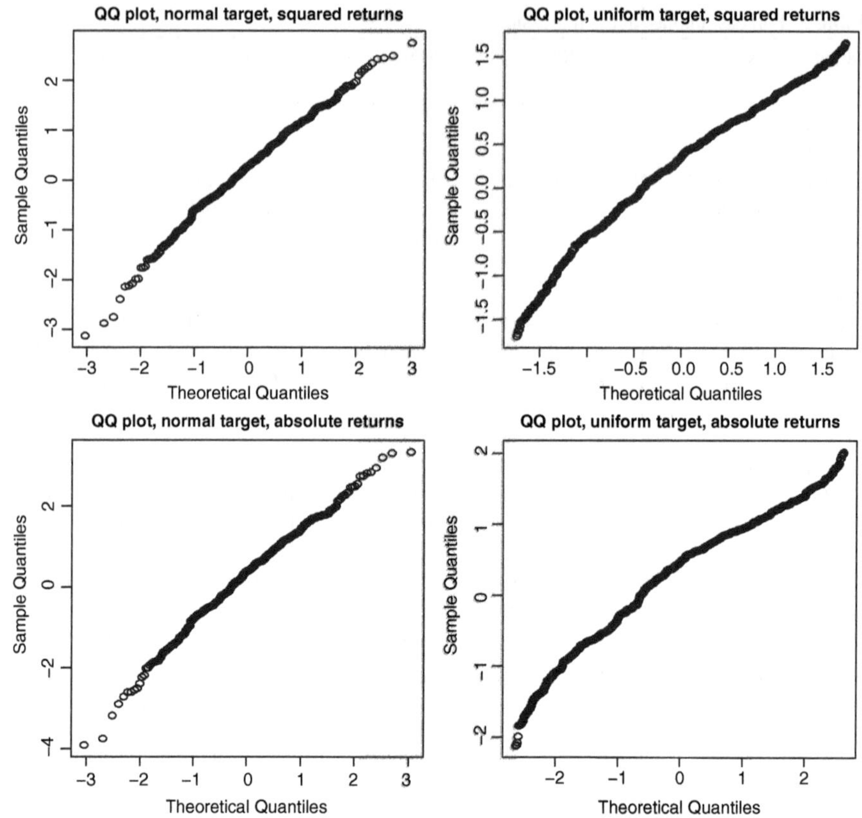

Fig. 9 QQ plots of the NoVaS -transformed W series for the monthly S&P500 series

enter the calculations.[15] We repeated our analysis for the MSFT series using $\alpha = 0.5$ and our results improved dramatically. The MAD and RMSE values from the ABNT NoVaS method dropped from 0.551 to 0.360 and from 0.951 to 0.524 respectively, with the Diebold-Mariano test still indicating a statistically significant performance over the Naive benchmark. In addition, the results from the forecasting unbiasedness regression are now better than the benchmark for the ABNT NoVaS method: the estimate of the slope parameter b is -0.145 and not statistically significant while the R^2 value is 0.010 compared to 0.012 for the benchmark.

In summary, our results are especially encouraging because they reflect on the very idea of the NoVaS transformation: a model-free approach that can account for different types of potential DGPs, that include breaks, switching regimes, and lack of higher moments. NoVaS is successful in overcoming the parameterization and estimation problems that one would encounter in models that have variability and

[15] Changing the value of α did not result in improvements in the other three series.

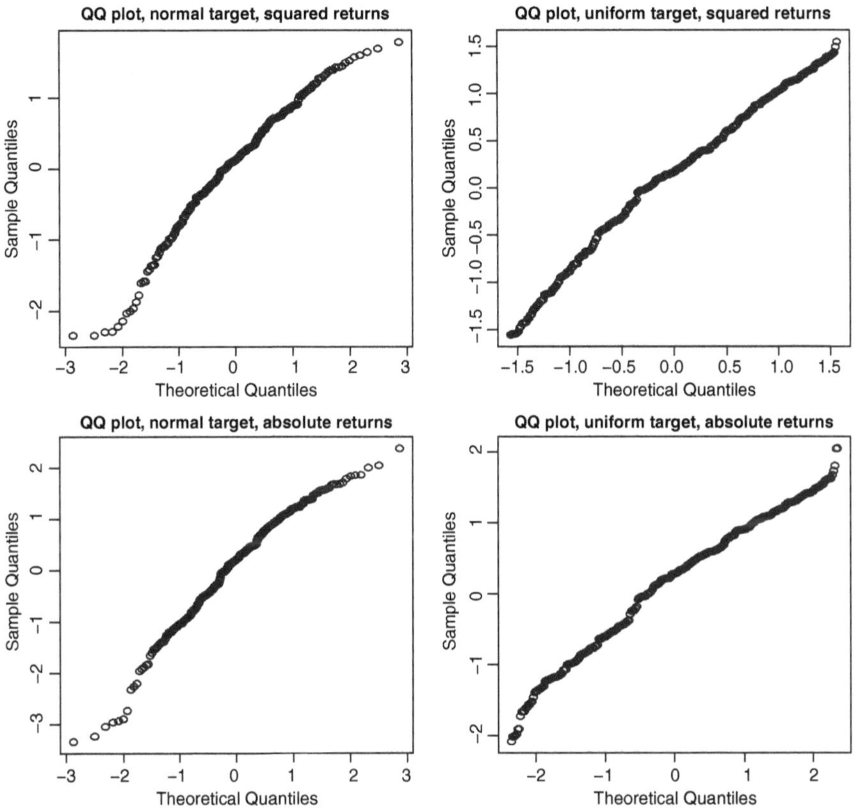

Fig. 10 QQ plots of the NoVaS -transformed W series for the monthly MSFT series

uncertainty not only in their parameters but also in their functional form. Of course our results are specific to the data sets examined and, it is true, we made no attempt to consider other types of parametric volatility models. But this is one of the problems that NoVaS attempts to solve: we have no *a priori* guidance as to which parametric volatility model to choose, be it simple GARCH, exponential GARCH, asymmetric GARCH, and so on. With NoVaS we face no such problem as the very concept of a model does not enter into consideration.

5 Concluding Remarks

In this chapter we have presented several findings on the NoVaS transformation approach for volatility forecasting introduced by Politis (2003a,b, 2007) and extended in Politis (2007). It was shown that NoVaS can be a flexible method for forecast-

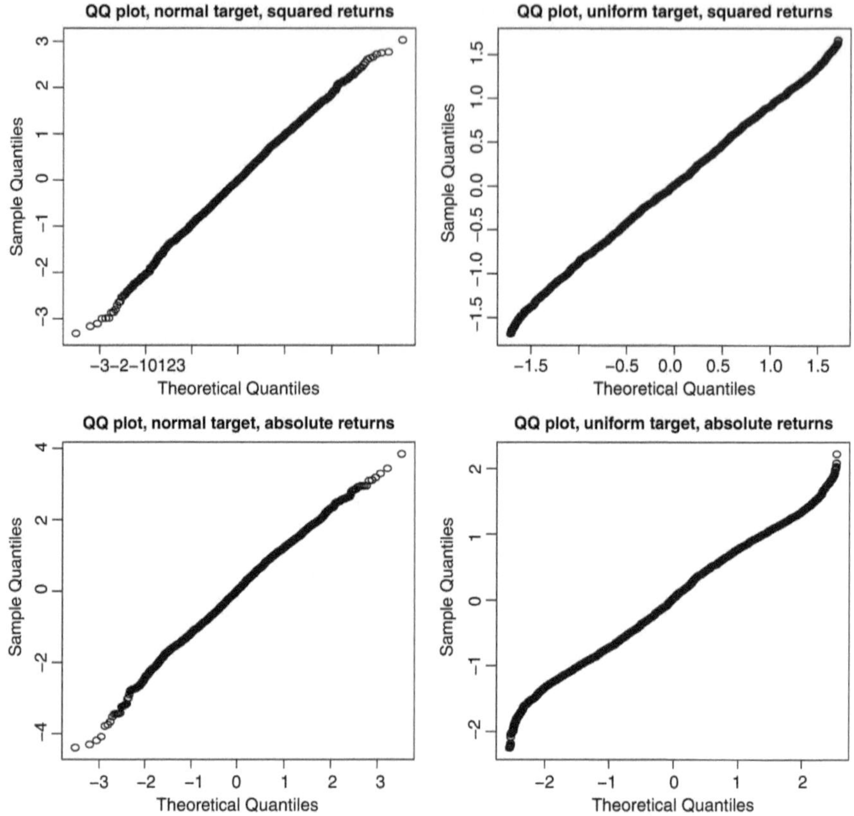

Fig. 11 QQ plots of the NoVaS -transformed W series for the daily USD/Yen series

ing volatility of financial returns that is simple to implement, and robust against nonstationarities.

In particular, we focused on a new method for volatility forecasting using NoVaS and conducted an extensive simulation to study its forecasting performance under different DGPs. It was shown that the NoVaS methodology remains successful in situations where (global) stationarity fails such as the cases of local stationarity and/or structural breaks, and invariably outperforms the GARCH benchmark for all non-GARCH DGPs. Remarkably, the NoVaS methodology was found to outperform the GARCH forecasts *even* when the underlying DGP *is* itself a (stationary) GARCH as long as the sample size is only moderately large. It was also found that NoVaS forecasts lead to a much 'tighter' distribution of the forecasting performance measure used (the MAD) for all DGPs considered. Our empirical illustrations using four real data sets are also very supportive of the excellent forecasting performance of NoVaS compared to the standard GARCH forecasts.

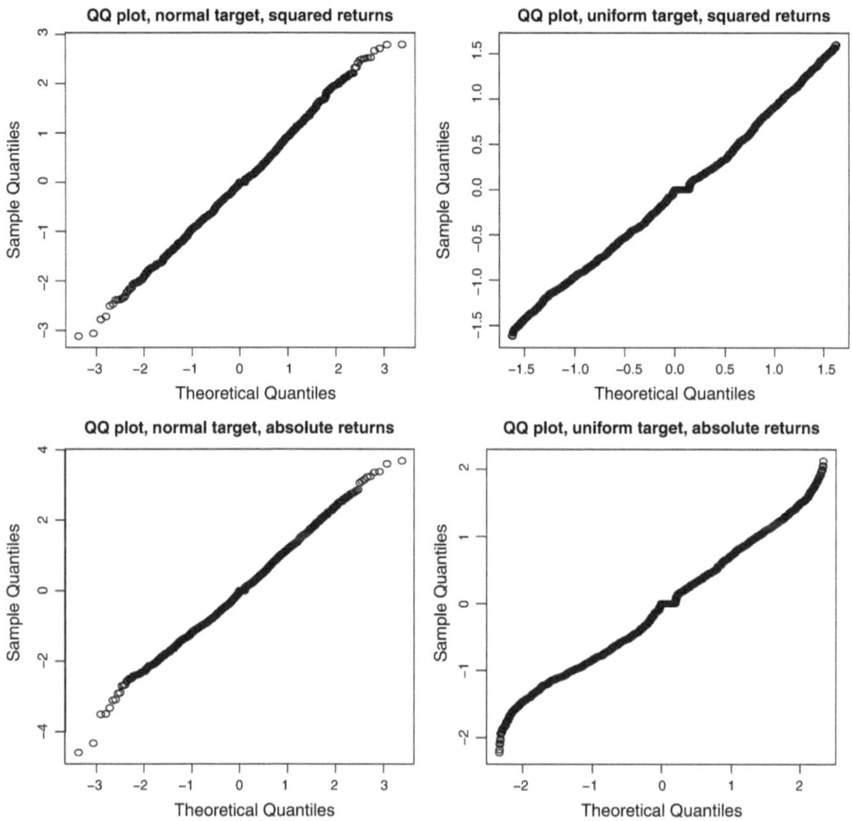

Fig. 12 QQ plots of the NoVaS -transformed *W* series for the daily EFG series

Extensions of the current work include, among others, the use of the NoVaS approach on empirical calculations of value at risk (VaR), the generalization to more than one assets and the calculation of NoVaS correlations, and further extensive testing on the out-of-sample forecasting performance of the proposed method. Some of the above are pursued by the authors.

References

Andersen, T.G., Bollerslev, T., Christoffersen, P.F., and F. X. Diebold, 2006. "Volatility and Correlation Forecasting" in G. Elliott, C.W.J. Granger, and Allan Timmermann (eds.), Handbook of Economic Forecasting, Amsterdam: North-Holland, pp. 778–878.

Andersen, T.G., Bollerslev, T. and Meddahi, N., 2004. "Analytic evaluation of volatility forecasts", International Economic Review, vol. 45, pp. 1079–1110.

Andersen, T.G., Bollerslev, T. and Meddahi, N., 2005. "Correcting the Errors: Volatility Forecast Evaluation Using High-Frequency Data and Realized Volatilities", Econometrica, vol. 73, pp. 279–296.

Bandi, F.M. and J.R. Russell, 2008. "Microstructure noise, realized variance, and optimal sampling", Review of Economic Studies, vol. 75, pp. 339–369.

Berkes, I. and L. Horvath, 2004. "The efficiency of the estimators of the parameters in GARCH processes", Annals of Statistics, 32, pp. 633–655.

Chen, K., Gerlach, R. and Lin, E.W.M., 2008. "Volatility forecasting using threshold heteroscedastic models of the intra-day range", Computational Statistics & Data Analysis, vol. 52, pp. 2990–3010.

Choi, K., Yu, W.-C. and E. Zivot, 2010. "Long memory versus structural breaks in modeling and forecasting realized volatility", Journal of International Money and Finance, vol. 29, pp. 857–875.

Dahlhaus, R. (1997), "Fitting time series models to nonstationary processes", Annals of Statistics, 25 pp. 1–37.

Dahlhaus, R. and S. Subba-Rao, 2006. "Statistical Inference for Time-Varying ARCH Processes", Annals of Statistics, vol. 34, pp. 1075–1114.

Dahlhaus, R. and S. Subba-Rao, 2007. "A Recursive Online Algorithm for the Estimation of Time Varying ARCH Parameters", Bernoulli, vol 13, pp. 389–422.

Diebold, F. X. and R. S. Mariano, 1995. "Comparing Predictive Accuracy", Journal of Business and Economic Statistics, vol. 13, pp. 253–263.

Francq, C. and J-M. Zakoian, 2005. "L2 Structures of Standard and Switching-Regime GARCH Models", Stochastic Processes and Their Applications, 115, pp. 1557–1582.

Fryzlewicz, P., Sapatinas, T. and S. Subba-Rao, 2006. "A Haar-Fisz Technique for Locally Stationary Volatility Estimation", Biometrika, vol. 93, pp. 687–704.

Fryzlewicz, P., Sapatinas, T. and S. Subba-Rao, 2008. "Normalized Least Squares Estimation in Time-Varying ARCH Models", Annals of Statistics, vol. 36, pp. 742–786.

Ghysels, E. and L. Forsberg, 2007. "Why Do Absolute Returns Predict Volatility So Well?", Journal of Financial Econometrics, vol. 5, pp. 31–67.

Ghysels, E. and B. Sohn, 2009. "Which power variation predicts volatility well?", Journal of Empirical Finance, vol. 16, pp. 686–700.

Ghysels, E., P. Santa-Clara, and R. Valkanov, 2006. "Predicting Volatility: How to Get Most Out of Returns Data Sampled at Different Frequencies", Journal of Econometrics, vol. 131, pp. 59–95.

Hall, P. and Q. Yao, 2003. "Inference in ARCH and GARCH Models with heavy-tailed errors", Econometrica, 71, pp. 285–317.

Hansen, B., 2006. "Interval Forecasts and Parameter Uncertainty", Journal of Econometrics, 127–377-398.

Hansen, P. R. and A. Lunde, 2005. "A forecast comparison of volatility models: does anything beat a $GARCH(1,1)$?", Journal of Applied Econometrics, 20(7):873–889.

Hansen, P. R. and A. Lunde, 2006. "Consistent ranking of volatility models", Journal of Econometrics, 131, pp. 97–121.

Hansen, P.R., Lunde, A. and Nason, J.M., 2003. "Choosing the best volatility models: the model confidence set approach", Oxford Bulletin of Economics and Statistics, vol. 65, pp. 839–861.

Hillebrand, E. 2005. "Neglecting Parameter Changes in GARCH Models", Journal of Econometrics, 129, pp. 121–138.

Lux, T. and L. Morales-Arias, 2010. "Forecasting volatility under fractality, regime switching, long-memory and t-innovations", Computational Statistics & Data Analysis, vol. 54, pp. 2676–2692.

Meddahi, N., 2001. "An eigenfunction approach for volatility modeling", Technical report, CIRANO Working paper 2001s–70, Univiversity of Montreal.

Mikosch, T. and C. Starica, 2004. "Change of Structure in Financial Time Series, Long Range Dependence and the GARCH model", CAF Working Paper Series, No. 58.

Parkinson, M., 1980. "The Extreme Value Method for Estimating the Variance of the Rate of Return", Journal of Business, 53, pp. 61–68.

Patton, A., 2011. "Volatility forecast evaluation and comparison using imperfect volatility proxies", Journal of Econometrics, vol. 160, pp. 246–256.

Patton, A. and K. Sheppard, 2008. "Evaluating volatility and correlation forecasts", in T. G. Andersen et al., (Eds.), Handbook of Financial Time Series, Springer Verlag.

Patton, A. and K. Sheppard, 2009. "Optimal combinations of realized volatility estimators", International Journal of Forecasting, vol. 25, pp. 218–238.

Peng, L. and Q. Yao, 2003. "Least absolute deviations estimation for ARCH and GARCH models", Biometrika, 90, pp. 967–975.

Politis, D.N., 2003a. "Model-Free Volatility Prediction", UCSD Dept. of Economics Discussion Paper 2003–16.

Politis, D.N., 2003b. "A Normalizing and Variance-Stabilizing Transformation for Financial Time Series", in Recent Advances and Trends in Nonparametric Statistics, M.G. Akritas and D.N. Politis, (Eds.), Elsevier: North Holland, pp. 335–347.

Politis, D.N., 2004. "A heavy-tailed distribution for ARCH residuals with application to volatility prediction", Annals of Economics and Finance, vol. 5, pp. 283–298.

Politis, D.N., 2007. "Model-free vs. model-based volatility prediction", J. Financial Econometrics, vol. 5, pp. 358–389.

Politis, D. and D. Thomakos, 2008. "Financial Time Series and Volatility Prediction using NoVaS-Transformations", in Forecasting in the Presence of Parameter Uncertainty and Structural Breaks, D. E. Rapach and M. E. Wohar (Eds.), Emerald Group Publishing Ltd.

Poon, S. and C. Granger, 2003. "Forecasting Volatility in Financial Markets: A Review". Journal of Economic Literature, 41, pp. 478–539.

Taylor, J., 2004. "Volatility Forecasting using Smooth Transition Exponential Smoothing", International Journal of Forecasting, vol. 20, pp. 273–286.

Wolfowitz, A., 1957. "The Minimum Distance Method", Annals of Mathematical Statistics, 28, pp. 75–88.

Regression Efficacy and the Curse of Dimensionality

Maxwell B. Stinchcombe and David M. Drukker

Abstract This chapter gives a geometric representation of a class of nonparametric regression estimators that includes series expansions (Fourier, wavelet, Tchebyshev, and others), kernels and other locally weighted regressions, splines, and artificial neural networks. For any estimator having this geometric representation, there is no curse of dimensionality—asymptotically, the error goes to 0 at the parametric rate. Regression efficacy measures the amount of variation in the conditional mean of the dependent variable, Y, that can be achieved by moving the explanatory variables across their whole range. The dismally slow, dimension-dependent rates of convergence are calculated using a class of target functions in which efficacy is infinite, and the analysis allows for the possibility that the dependent variable, Y, may be an ever-receding target.

1 Introduction

The starting point is a probability space $(\Omega, \mathcal{F}, P)$ and an independent and identically distributed (iid) sequence $(Y_i, (X_{1,i}, X_{2,i}, \ldots))_{i=1}^n$ in $L^p(\Omega, \mathcal{F}, P)$, $p \in [1, \infty)$. Interest centers on estimating the target functions,

$$f_d(x_1, \ldots, x_d) := E\left(Y \middle| (X_1, \ldots, X_d) = (x_1, \ldots, x_d)\right) \tag{1}$$

from the realization $(Y_i(\omega), (X_{1,i}(\omega), \ldots, X_{d,i}(\omega)))_{i=1}^n$. This paper provides an asymptotic analysis of the question, "How large must n be to nonparametrically

M. B. Stinchcombe (✉)
Department of Economics, U.T. Austin, 2225 Speedway BRB 1.116, C3100, Austin, TX 78712, USA
e-mail: max.stinchcombe@gmail.com

D. M. Drukker
StataCorp, 4905 Lakeway Drive, College Station, TX 77845, USA
e-mail: ddrukker@stata.com

X. Chen and N. R. Swanson (eds.), *Recent Advances and Future Directions in Causality, Prediction, and Specification Analysis*, DOI: 10.1007/978-1-4614-1653-1_20,

estimate $f_d(\cdot)$ to any given degree of precision?" Of particular interest is the relation between d and n.

1.1 Different Answers

There are, in the literature, two very different answers, the usual one, due to Stone (1982), is applicable to all nonparametric regression techniques, the second due to Barron (1993), is applicable to the nonparametric regression technique known as single-layer feedforward (slff) artificial neural networks (ann's) with sigmoidal activation functions.

1. The usual asymptotic analysis yields the following answer: if f_d belongs to a particular dense class, $\mathbb{V}_d^{\text{Lip}}$, then for a desired degree of precision, ϵ, there is a constant C, independent of ϵ, such that n must satisfy $n^{-\frac{1}{2+d}} < C\epsilon$. The C may depend on the distribution of the data and the nonparametric technique. Further, all nonparametric techniques have this property.
2. The slff ann analysis yields the following answer: if f_d belongs to a different dense class, $\mathbb{V}_d^{\text{ann}}$, then for a desired degree of precision, ϵ, there is a constant C, independent of ϵ but dependent on d, such that n must satisfy $n^{-\frac{1}{2}} < C\epsilon$. As above, C may also depend on the distribution governing the data and on the nonparametric regression technique through the specific choice of sigmoidal activation function.

If $C\epsilon = 1/100$ for both approaches, and d is a largish positive integer, say 7, the usual analysis suggests that one needs 10^{18} independent observations, not a practical data requirement, while the ann analysis suggests that one needs but 10^4 independent observations, a large but not impractical data requirement. This impracticality is known as "the curse of dimensionality."[1] It should be noted that the dependence of C on d in the ann analysis might, in principle, lead to the re-emergence of the curse. This paper shows that the ann type of analysis can be done with a constant that does not depend on d for a very wide collection of nonparametric techniques.

1.2 The Source of the Difference

The difference in the two types of analysis arises from different assumptions about the classes, $\mathbb{V}_d^{\text{Lip}}, \mathbb{V}_d^{\text{ann}} \subset L^p(\Omega, \mathcal{F}, P)$, containing the target functions $f_d(\cdot)$. In both cases, the assumed classes are dense, and being dense, they are impossible to

[1] The immense literature following on Stone's analysis has expanded the curse results far beyond his use of the sup norm to include the L^p-norms, the Sobolev norms, examined the partial role that smoothness of the target can play in overcoming the curse, and extended the analysis well beyond regression problems. Barron worked with single-layer feedforward ann's, as did Mhaskar and Michelli (1995) in a slightly different context. Yukich et al. (1995) improved Barron's result in several directions, Chen and White (1999) improved it even further, Chen (2007) is a survey.

reject on the basis of data with smooth measurement error. The **regression efficacy** of explanatory variables is the amount by which the conditional mean of Y varies as the values of $(X_1, \ldots, X_d)$ move across their range.[2] The boundedness/unboundedness of regression efficacy and the possibility/impossibility of ever-receding targets are two of the ways in which the classes differ.

1. In the dense class $\mathbb{V}_d^{\text{Lip}}$ used in the curse analysis, efficacy is unbounded in d, the number of explanatory variables. This means that there may infinitely many groups of explanatory variables, each of them having the same ability to vary the conditional mean of Y. By contrast, the dense classes used in the ann analysis have a bound on efficacy that is independent of d. This argument should not be taken as being a final statement of affairs, although unbounded regression efficacy is counter-intuitive, we give an example below of a sequence $(Y, (X_1, X_2, \ldots, X_d, X_{d+1}, \ldots))$ with efficacy that is unbounded in d.
2. The target functions in (1) above work with a fixed Y, as does the ann analysis. In particular, this means that there is a fixed joint distribution governing the data. Implicit in the curse analysis is the possibility that we are varying Y as we vary d—instead of calculating the errors in our attempts to estimate $E\,(Y|(X_1, \ldots, X_d))$, we may be calculating the errors in an attempt to estimate $E\,(Y_d|(X_1, \ldots, X_d))$ where the sequence Y_d may be divergent, i.e., ever-receding.

1.3 Outline

The next section begins with notation, two norms, and the basic implications that come from breaking up total errors into an approximation errors and estimation errors. It then explains how the main result of the paper, Theorem 1 yields the result that the total error is bounded by the estimation error in nonparametric regression. The two norms are the Lipschitz norm and the efficacy norm, which is a variant of Arzelá's multidimensional variation norm.[3] The approximation error part of the curse analysis uses sets of targets functions having uniformly bounded Lipschitz norm, the approximation error part of the ann analysis uses sets of targets having uniformly bounded efficacy norm.

The following section gives two kinds of intuition about efficacy. The first has to do with the change in the amount of 'information' contained in $(X_1, \ldots, X_d)$ and the amount contained in $(X_1, \ldots, X_{d+1})$. The second compares the implications of Lipschitz bounds and of efficacy bounds in the special case that the conditional mean functions are affine and the regressors, $(X_1, \ldots, X_d)$ are independent. In this particular case, one can directly see how bounded/unbounded efficacy works, and how ever-receding targets can arise.

[2] From the *Oxford English Dictionary*, efficacy is the "Power or capacity to produce effects." While we think of regression efficacy as causal efficacy, the referee has quite correctly pointed out that there need not be a causal or even a structural component to efficacy as discussed here.

[3] See Adams and Clarkson (1933) for an extensive comparison of the many non-equivalent definitions of bounded variation for functions of two or more variables.

The penultimate section gives the dimension independent geometric representation of nonparametric regression estimators, and demonstrates that several of the well-known estimators have this structure. The last section gives possible extensions and conclusions.

2 Norms, Density, and Rates

We begin with notation, then turn to the contrasting norms and their basic denseness property. After this, we turn to the source of the curse results and the contrast with the ann results.

2.1 Notation

$L^0 = L^0(\Omega, \mathcal{F}, P)$ denotes the set of $\mathbb{R}$-valued random variables, $L^p = L^p(\Omega, \mathcal{F}, P) \subset L^0$ the set of random variables with finite p'th norm, $p \in [1, \infty)$. For any sub-σ-field $\mathcal{G} \subset \mathcal{F}$, $L^0(\mathcal{G}) \subset L^0$ is the set of $\mathcal{G}$-measurable random variables and $L^p(\mathcal{G}) := L^p \cap L^0(\mathcal{G})$.

$\mathbb{X} = \{X_a : a \in \mathbb{N}\} \subset L^2$ denotes the set of possible explanatory variables, $\mathscr{X}_d$ denotes $\sigma(X_1, \ldots, X_d)$, the smallest σ-field making $X_1, \ldots, X_d$ measurable, and $\mathscr{X}$ denotes $\sigma(\mathbb{X})$, the smallest σ-field making every X_a in $\mathbb{X}$ measurable. We assume that $Y \in L^p$ for some $p \in [1, \infty)$ so that the set of all conceivable target functions is $L^p(\mathscr{X})$. The set of all possible targets based on some finite set of regressors is $\bigcup_d L^p(\mathscr{X}_d)$, and this set is dense in $L^p(\mathscr{X})$.

2.2 A Tale of Two Norms

By Doob's Theorem [e.g. Dellacherie and Meyer (1978, Theorem I.18, p. 12–13)], $L^p(\mathscr{X}_d)$ is the set of functions of the form $\omega \mapsto g(X_1(\omega), \ldots, X_d(\omega))$ having finite p'th moment, g a measurable function from $\mathbb{R}^d$ to $\mathbb{R}$.

For each $d \in \mathbb{N}$, $C(\mathbb{R}^d)$ denotes the set of continuous functions on $\mathbb{R}^d$, and the obvious extension/restriction identifies $C(\mathbb{R}^d)$ with $C_d \subset C(\mathbb{R}^{\mathbb{N}})$, the elements of $C(\mathbb{R}^{\mathbb{N}})$ that depend on only the first d components, $(x_1, \ldots, x_d)$ of the infinite length vectors $(x_1, x_2, \ldots, x_d, x_{d+1}, \ldots)$. For $x, y \in \mathbb{R}^d$, $e_d(x, y) := \sqrt{(x - y) \cdot (x - y)}$ denotes the Euclidean distance between the d-dimensional vectors x and y.

Definition 1 The **Lipschitz norm** of an $f_d \in C(\mathbb{R}^d)$ is

$$\|f_d\|_{\text{Lip}} = \sup_{x \in \mathbb{R}^d} |f_d(x)| + \sup_{x \neq y} \frac{|f_d(x) - f_d(y)|}{e_d(x, y)}$$

whenever this is finite. The **Lipschitz constant of** f_d is $\sup_{x \neq y} \frac{|f_d(x)-f_d(y)|}{e_d(x,y)}$. $C_d^{\text{Lip}}(B) \subset C(\mathbb{R}^d)$ denotes the set of f_d with Lipschitz norm B or less. A sequence of functions f_d in $C(\mathbb{R}^{\mathbb{N}})$ with $f_d \in C_d$ is **uniformly Lipschitz** if for some B, each f_d belongs to $C_d^{\text{Lip}}(B)$.

We will be interested in the maximal total variability in the conditional mean of Y as the explanatory variables move monotonically across their range. Recall that the **total variation** of a function $f : \mathbb{R} \to \mathbb{R}$ is $TV(f) = \sup \sum_i |f(x_{i+1}) - f(x_i)|$ where the supremum is taken over all finite subsets $x_1 < x_2 < \cdots < x_I$ of $\mathbb{R}$. A **wide-sense monotonic path in** $\mathbb{R}^d$ is a function $t \mapsto x(t)$ from $\mathbb{R}$ to $\mathbb{R}^d$ such that for each $i \in \{1, \ldots, d\}$, the function $x_i(t)$ is either non-decreasing or non-increasing.

Definition 2 The **monotonic total variation** of a function $f_d \in C(\mathbb{R}^d)$ is $\text{MTV}(f) = \sup_x TV(f_d \circ x)$ where the supremum is taken over wide-sense monotonic paths in $\mathbb{R}^d$.[4] The **monotonic total variation norm** or **efficacy norm** is

$$\|f_d\|_{\text{MTV}} = |f_d(0)| + \text{MTV}(f_d)$$

whenever this is finite. $C_d^{\text{MTV}}(B) \subset C(\mathbb{R}^d)$ denotes the set of f_d with monotonic total variation norm B or less. A sequence of functions f_d in $C(\mathbb{R}^{\mathbb{N}})$ with $f_d \in C_d$ is **uniformly efficacy bounded** if for some B, each f_d belongs to $C_d^{\text{MTV}}(B)$.

The range of functions with a Lipschitz constant B grows with d, but not so quickly as their monotonic total variation.

Example 1 If $f_d : [-1, +1]^d \to \mathbb{R}$ belongs to $C_d^{\text{Lip}}(B)$, then

$$\left[\max_{x \in [-1,+1]^d} f_d(x) - \min_{y \in [-1,+1]^d} f_d(y)\right] \leq 2B\sqrt{d} \tag{2}$$

because $\max_{x,y \in [-1,+1]^d} e(x, y) = 2\sqrt{d}$. By contrast, for f_d having Lipschitz constant B, $\text{MTV}(f_d) \leq 2Bd$ because the longest monotonic paths in $[-1, +1]^d$ are of length $2d$.[5]

An implication of the previous example is that the ratio $\|f\|_{\text{MTV}}/\|f\|_{\text{Lip}}$ is unbounded on those parts of $C(\mathbb{R}^{\mathbb{N}})$ for which both norms are finite. The next example demonstrates that $\|f\|_{\text{Lip}}/\|f\|_{\text{MTV}}$ is also unbounded.

Example 2 For $f_d(x) := \max\{0, 1 - e_d(x, 0)\}$ and $f_{d,n}(x) := \frac{1}{n} f_d(n^2 x)$, $\|f_{d,n}\|_{\text{Lip}} \uparrow \infty$ and $\|f_{d,n}\|_{\text{MTV}} \downarrow 0$.

Lusin's theorem and standard approximation results deliver the following.

Lemma 1 *If* $Y \in L^p(\Omega, \mathcal{F}, P)$, $f(x_1, x_2, \ldots) = E(Y|(X_1, X_2, \ldots) = (x_1, x_2, \ldots))$, $p \in [1, \infty)$ *and* $\epsilon > 0$, *then there exists* $g \in C(\mathbb{R}^{\mathbb{N}})$ *such that* $\|f - g\|_p < \epsilon$

[4] Taking the supremum over the subset of monotonic *increasing* paths delivers the Arzelá norm.

[5] One could reconcile these by replacing $e(x, y)$ by the distance $d_1(x, y) = \sum_{i \leq d} |x_i - y_i|$ in the definition of Lipschitz functions, but this seems to be contrary to common usage.

and the sequence $g_d := E(Y|(X_1,\ldots,X_d) = (x_1,\ldots,x_d))$ *is both uniformly Lipschitz and uniformly efficacy bounded.*

2.3 Estimation and Approximation Errors

Reiterating, interest centers on estimating $f_d(x_1,\ldots,x_d) := E(Y|(X_1,\ldots,X_d) = (x_1,\ldots,x_d))$ from iid data $(Y_i,(X_{1,i},\ldots,X_{d,i}))_{i=1}^n$ assuming that each f_d belongs to some vector subspace, $\mathbb{V}'_d$, of $\mathbb{V}_d := L^p(\mathcal{X}_d)$. Let μ be the true joint distribution of the data and $\widehat{\mu}_n(\omega)$ the empirical joint distribution of the data. A sequence of nonparametric estimators, $\widehat{f_n}$, is typically of the form

$$\widehat{f_n} = \operatorname{argmin}_{g\in\Theta_{\kappa(n)}}\left[\int (y-g(x))^2\,d\widehat{\mu}_n(y,x)\right]^{1/2} \tag{3}$$

where $(\Theta_\kappa)_{\kappa=1}^\infty$ is a sequence of subsets of $\mathbb{V}'_d$, $\kappa(n)\uparrow\infty$ and $(\Theta_\kappa)_{\kappa=1}^\infty$ are chosen so that $f\in \operatorname{climinf}\Theta_{\kappa(n)}$ with probability 1 (where $\operatorname{climinf} A_n = \{g\in\mathbb{V} : \forall\epsilon>0, \|g-A_n\|<\epsilon \text{ for all large} n\}$ is the closed liminf of a sequence of sets A_n).

A useful contrast with (3) arises if μ is perfectly known. Define $f^*_{\kappa(n)}$ as

$$f^*_{\kappa(n)} = \arg\min_{g\in\Theta_{\kappa(n)}}\left[\int (y-g(x))^2 d\mu(y,x)\right]^{1/2}. \tag{4}$$

The total error, $\|\widehat{f_n}-f\|$, can be bounded by the sum of an estimation error, ϵ_n, and an approximation error, a_n,

$$\epsilon_n + a_n := \underbrace{\|\widehat{f_n}-f^*_{\kappa(n)}\|}_{\text{estimation error}} + \underbrace{\|f^*_{\kappa(n)}-f\|}_{\text{approx. error}} \geq \|\widehat{f_n}-f\|. \tag{5}$$

The larger is $\Theta_{\kappa(n)}$, the smaller is a_n. The tradeoff is that a larger $\Theta_{\kappa(n)}$ leads to overfitting, which shows up as a larger ϵ_n. Most analyses of $\|\widehat{f_n}-f\|$ begin with a dense set, $\mathbb{V}'_d\subset\mathbb{V}_d$, of targets. The set $\mathbb{V}'_d$ is chosen so that one can calculate $\epsilon_n(\kappa)$ and $a_n(\kappa)$ as functions of κ. With this in place, one then chooses $\kappa(n)$ to minimize $\epsilon_n(\kappa)+a_n(\kappa)$.

Stone (1982) showed that the "optimal" rate of convergence is $r_n = n^{-1/(2+d)}$. By optimal, Stone meant that if the sequence f_d is uniformly Lipschitz, then for any nonparametric regression technique, any sequence of estimators, $\widehat{f_n}$, satisfies

$$\|\widehat{f_n}-f\| \geq O_P(n^{-1/(2+d)}), \tag{6}$$

and that some sequence satisfies (6) with equality.

By denseness, no data with smooth measurement error can reject the hypothesis that $f_d \in C_d^{\text{Lip}}$. It seems that this should make the Lipschitz assumption unobjectionable, but it is where dimensionality enters. An extremely clear example of how this works in $L^2(\mathcal{X})$ is Newey (1996). He shows that, if μ satisfies some easy-to-verify and quite general conditions and the target, f, satisfies the uniform approximation condition $\sup_x \inf_{g \in \Theta_\kappa} |f(x) - g(x)| = \mathcal{O}\left(\frac{1}{\kappa^\alpha}\right)$, then

$$\|f - \widehat{f}_n\|^2 = \mathcal{O}_P\left(\frac{\kappa}{n} + \frac{1}{\kappa^{2\alpha}}\right). \tag{7}$$

Ignoring some of the finer detail, the κ/n term in Newey's result corresponds to the square of the estimation error, and the $\kappa^{-2\alpha}$ to the square of the approximation error.[6] To balance the tradeoffs, one picks $\kappa = \kappa(n)$ to minimize $\frac{\kappa}{n} + \frac{1}{\kappa^{2\alpha}}$.

If $f : [-1, +1]^d \to \mathbb{R}$ has Lipschitz constant B, we must evaluate f at roughly $\left(\frac{2B}{\epsilon}\right)^d$ (carefully chosen) points to pin down f to within ϵ at all points in its domain. For many classes Θ_κ this yields, for every $f \in C_d^{\text{Lip}}$, $\sup_x \inf_{g \in \Theta_\kappa} |f(x) - g(x)| = \mathcal{O}\left(\frac{1}{\kappa^\alpha}\right)$ with $\alpha = \frac{1}{d}$. Minimizing $\frac{\kappa}{n} + \frac{1}{\kappa^{2/d}}$ yields $\kappa = n^{\frac{d}{2+d}}$, evaluating the minimand at the solution gives the cursed rate from (6),

$$\|f - \widehat{f}_n\|^2 = \mathcal{O}_P\left(\frac{\kappa}{n} + \frac{1}{\kappa^{2/d}}\right) = \mathcal{O}_P\left(n^{-\frac{2}{2+d}}\right), \quad \text{or} \quad \|f - \widehat{f}_n\| = \mathcal{O}_P\left(n^{-\frac{1}{2+d}}\right). \tag{8}$$

Artificial neural networks can accurately fit sparse high dimensional data. A theoretical basis for this empirical observations was given in Barron (1993). He showed that for every d, there is a dense set of functions, $\mathbb{V}_d^{\text{ann}}$, depending on the architecture of the networks, such that for all $f \in \mathbb{V}_d^{\text{ann}}$, the following variant of the uniform approximation condition (7), $\sup_x \inf_{g \in \Theta_\kappa} |f(x) - g(x)| \leq C(d)\left(\frac{1}{\kappa^\alpha}\right)$, is satisfied with $\alpha = \frac{1}{2}$. Ignoring the dependence on d in the constant $C(d)$, we have $\|f - \widehat{f}_n\|^2 = \mathcal{O}_P\left(\frac{\kappa}{n} + \frac{1}{\kappa^{2\alpha}}\right) = \mathcal{O}_P\left(\frac{\kappa}{n} + \frac{1}{\kappa}\right)$. Minimizing yields $\kappa(n) = \sqrt{n}$ so that $\|f - \widehat{f}_n\|^2 = \mathcal{O}\left(\frac{1}{\sqrt{n}}\right)$.

It is in principle possible that $d \mapsto C(d)$ grows explosively enough to vitiate this analysis and return us to the curse world. As we will see, this need not happen, either for ann estimators, nor for any of the other main classes of nonparametric estimators.

Theorem 1 (below) shows that for any estimator having a particular geometric representation, for any r_n converging to 0, no matter how quickly, and any $\kappa(n)$ increasing to ∞, no matter how slowly, there exists a dense $\mathbb{V}' \subset \mathbb{V}$ for which the approximation error satisfies $a_n = \mathcal{O}(r_n)$. The geometric representation covers a class of nonparametric regression estimators that includes, but is not limited to, series expansions (Fourier, wavelet, Tchebyshev and others), kernels and other locally weighted regressions, splines, wavelets, and artificial neural networks.

Through the following steps, we have dimension independent rates of convergence: First, pick $\kappa(n) \uparrow \infty$ in such a fashion that consistency is

[6] See his Eq. (A.3), p. 163, for the omitted detail.

guaranteed, typically this requires $\kappa(n)/n \downarrow 0$; Second, calculate $e_n = \|\widehat{f_n} - f^*_{\kappa(n)}\|$; Third, invoke Theorem A to guarantee the existence of a dense class of targets, $\mathbb{V}'$, such that for all $f \in \mathbb{V}'$, $a_n = \|f^*_{\kappa(n)} - f\| = \mathcal{O}(e_n)$. Fourth, observe that $\|\widehat{f_n} - f\| \le e_n + a_n = \mathcal{O}(e_n)$.

3 Intuitions About Efficacy

To gain intuition about bounded/unbounded efficacy, we will first discuss the possible decrease in the amount of 'information' gained about Y in the move from the set of regressors $(X_1, \ldots, X_d)$ to the set of $(X_1, \ldots, X_{d+1})$. After this we will specialize to the case of affine conditional expectations and bounded range, non-degenerate, independent explanatory vectors $(X_1, \ldots, X_d)$. Here, one can directly see how ever-receding targets may arise, and also count the differences in the numbers of regressors that matter.

3.1 The Information Contained in a Set of Regressors

In general, one does not expect that the X_k should be mutually independent. This might arise if the X_k are random draws from some larger set of possible explanatory variables. We first discuss the intuitions from the case that they arise from iid draws from $L^2(\Omega, \mathcal{F}, P)$, then from the case that they arise from processes that are approximately recurrent.

Let $\Delta(L^2(\Omega, \mathcal{F}, P))$ denote the set of probability distributions on $L^2(\Omega, \mathcal{F}, P)$, here viewed as the set of possible explanatory variables. Suppose first that the X_k are iid draws from some $\nu \in \Delta(L^2)$, that is, suppose that there is some probability law generating the regressors from amongst all possible regressors. By the generalized Glivenko–Cantelli theorem, the empirical distribution, ν_d, of $(X_1, \ldots, X_d)$ converges to ν. This means that the additional explanatory power to be gained by projecting Y onto the span of $(X_1, \ldots, X_d)$ must be going to 0. Another way to see how this is operating is to note that the support of any ν must be approximately flat.

Another sort of intuition would come into play if the process generating the X_k had the property that one long set of regressors, say $X_k, \ldots, X_{k+n_1}$, contained much the same information about Y as could be found in $X_{k'}, \ldots, X_{k'+n_2}$, where $k' > k + n_1$. Such a situation would arise if e.g., the X_k were drawn according to a smooth Markov process with a unique ergodic distribution ν. When the random variables X_k and $X_{k'}$ are close to each other in $L^2(\Omega, \mathcal{F}, P)$, then continuity would tend to make the distribution of the next excursion from the neighborhood containing the two of them have close to the same distribution. This would mean that we would expect that the information in $X_{k'}, \ldots, X_{k'+n_2}$ that is above and beyond what can be found in $X_k, \ldots, X_{k+n_1}$ should be small.[7]

[7] I am grateful to Graham Elliot and Jim Hamilton for these points.

3.2 Affine Conditional Expectations and Iid Regressors

In the case where the regressors are iid and all of the conditional expectations of Y given $X_1, \ldots, X_d$ are affine, it is particularly easy to see how the difference between bounded and unbounded efficacy works, and how ever-receding targets can arise. For the rest of this section, and only for the rest of this section, we assume that:

(1) the X_k, are mutually independent, take values in $[-1, +1]$, have mean 0, and are not degenerate in the limit, i.e., $\liminf_k \text{Var}(X_k) = \underline{\sigma} > 0$, and
(2) the condition expectation of Y is an affine function for all d, i.e., $f_d(x_1, \ldots, x_d) = E(Y|(X_1, \ldots, X_d) = (x_1, \ldots, x_d))$ is of the form $\beta_0 + \sum_{a \le d} \beta_a x_a$ for some sequence $(\beta_a)_{a \in \mathbb{N}}$.

In this context, we examine how efficacy interacts with properties of Y; how the uniform Lipschitz assumption allows ever-receding targets; and how bounds on the numbers of important regressors work.

Several of the arguments depend on the *three series theorem*—if R_a is a sequence of independent random variables, then the convergence of the three series, $\sum_a P(|R_a| > c)$, $\sum_a E\left(R_a \cdot 1_{|R_a| \le c}\right)$, and $\sum_a \text{Var}\left(R_a \cdot 1_{|R_a| \le c}\right)$ for some $c > 0$ implies that $\sum_a R_a$ converges a.e., and if $\sum_a R_a$ converges a.e., then the three series converge for all $c > 0$ [see e.g. Billingsley (2008, p. 290)].

We begin with an elementary result.

Lemma 2 *If $\beta_a \in \mathbb{R}$, $a \in \{0, 1, \ldots\}$ is a sequence in $\mathbb{R}$, then the sequence of affine function $f_d = \beta_0 + \sum_{a \le d} \beta_a x_a$ on $[-1, +1]^d$ has uniform Lipschitz bound B if and only if $\sup_{A \subset \mathbb{N}} \sum_{a \in A} |\beta_a| \le B\sqrt{\#A}$, and has uniform efficacy bound $2B$ if and only if $\sum_a |\beta_a| \le B$.*

Proof For any non-empty $A \subset \mathbb{N}$, if f is affine and $|\beta_a| \neq 0$ only for $a \in A$, then $\max_{x \neq y} |f(x) - f(y)|/e(x, y)$ is $\sum_{a \in A} |\beta_a|/\sqrt{\#A}$, yielding the first part of the Lemma. For the second part, note that the monotonic total variation of an affine f on $[-1, +1]^d$ is $2\sum_{a \le d} |\beta_a|$. □

The condition $\sum_a |\beta_a| \le B$ is the crucial part of Tibshirani's (1996) *least absolute shrinkage and selection operator* (lasso) models, and we will examine the connection in more detail in Sect. 3.4. Somewhat counterintuitively, one can have integrable Y, affine conditional expectations, and unbounded efficacy, i.e., $\sum_a |\beta_a| = \infty$.

Example 3 Suppose that the X_a are iid and that $\beta_a = \mathcal{O}\left(\frac{1}{a}\right)$. For any $c > 0$, for all large a, $P(|R_a| > c) = 0$. This implies that for large a, $E\left(R_a \cdot 1_{|R_a| \le c}\right) = 0$ and $\text{Var}\left(R_a \cdot 1_{|R_a| \le c}\right) = \mathcal{O}\left(\frac{1}{a^2}\right)$. The requisite three series converge, so $Y_d := \beta_0 + \sum_{a \le d} \beta_a X_a$ converges a.e. to some random variable Y. Since the variance of the Y_d is uniformly bounded, the Y_d are uniformly integrable, hence Y is integrable. Thus, conditional expectations can be affine while $\sum_a |\beta_a| = \infty$.

3.3 Receding Targets

The affine structure plus the minimal assumptions on Y necessary for the existence of a target function lead to further restrictions on the β_a's.

Lemma 3 *If* $Y \in L^1(\Omega, \mathcal{F}, P)$ *and* $E(Y|(X_1, \ldots, X_d) = (x_1, \ldots, x_d)) = \beta_0 + \sum_{a \le d} \beta_a x_a$, *then* $\sum_a |\beta_a|^2 < \infty$.

Since $\mathrm{Var}(Y) = E(\mathrm{Var}(Y|X_1, \ldots, X_d)) + \mathrm{Var}(E(Y|X_1, \ldots, X_d))$, we know that the variance of the $f_d(X_1, \ldots, X_d)$ is bounded in d when $Y \in L^2(\Omega, \mathcal{F}, P)$. A slightly more involved argument yields the same conclusion more generally.

Proof Martingale convergence implies that $Y_d := E(Y|(X_1, \ldots, X_d)) \to Y_{\mathscr{X}} := E(Y|\mathscr{X})$ a.e. If $\sum_a |\beta_a|^2$ diverges, then there exists an increasing sequence $1 = D_1 < D_2 < \cdots < D_k < \cdots$ such that $\sum_{a=D_k}^{D_{k+1}-1} |\beta_a|^2 > 2$. For every ω for which $Y_d(\omega)$ converges, the random variables $R_k(\omega) := \sum_{a=D_k}^{D_{k+1}-1} \beta_a X_a(\omega)$ must go to 0. However, for all large k, the variance of R_k is at least $3\underline{\sigma}$, contradicting the three series theorem. □

If $Y \notin L^1(\Omega, \mathcal{F}, P)$, then $E(Y|X)$ does not exist for any random vector X. The following example gives a uniformly Lipschitz class of affine $f_d(\cdot)$'s for which no $Y \in L^1(\Omega, \mathcal{F}, P)$ can satisfy $E(Y|(X_1, \ldots, X_d)) = f_d(X_1, \ldots, X_d)$.

Example 4 If $|\beta_a| = \frac{1}{\sqrt{a}}$, then $\sum_{a \in A} |\beta_a| = \mathcal{O}(\sqrt{\#A})$ so that the sequence $f_d = \beta_0 + \sum_{a \le d} \beta_a x_a$ is uniformly Lipschitz by Lemma 2. Since $\sum_a \beta_a^2$ diverges, Lemma 3 implies that there is no $Y \in L^1(\Omega, \mathcal{F}, P)$ having affine conditional expectations $f_d(x_1, \ldots, x_d) = \beta_0 + \sum_{a \le d} \beta_a x_a$.

If we define $Y_d = \beta_0 + \sum_{a \le d} \beta_a X_a$ in Example 4, then, by the three series theorem, the sequence Y_d diverges. The implication is that the Lipschitz worst case analyses may be based on ever-receding targets, so that, instead of calculating the errors in our attempts to estimate $E(Y|(X_1, \ldots, X_d))$, we may be calculating the errors in an attempt to estimate $E(Y_d|(X_1, \ldots, X_d))$ for an ever receding sequence Y_d.

3.4 Number of Regressors Intuitions

The condition $\sum_a |\beta_a| \le B$ for uniformly bounded efficacy (Lemma 2) implies that as the number of regressors grows, the amount by which any further regressors can affect the conditional mean of Y goes to 0. Another model which suggests this involves random parameters, and is also related to Tibshirani's (1996) lasso models. We will suppose that the β_a's are independent random variables with $E|\beta_a| = 1$, scale them as a function of d so that the functions $\beta_0 + \sum_{a \le d} \beta_a x_a$ satisfy Lipschitz or efficacy bounds, and ask the question, "How many of the d regressors can be ignored while still making an error of less than ϵ?"

Satisfying the Lipschitz constraint on average and being requires multiplying the β_a's by something on the order of $1/\sqrt{d}$. By contrast, if we bound the causal efficacy of the explanatory variables, we must multiply the β_a's by something on the order of $1/d$. Let $|\beta|_{(a)}$ be the a'th order statistic of the $|\beta_a|$'s. For given d and $\epsilon > 0$, let $N = N(d, \epsilon)$ be the largest integer satisfying $\frac{1}{\sqrt{d}} \sum_{a \leq N} E\,|\beta|_{(a)} < \epsilon$ and $M = M(d, \epsilon)$ the largest satisfying $\frac{1}{d} \sum_{a \leq M} E\,|\beta|_{(a)} < \epsilon$.

Example 5 If the $|\beta_a|$ are independent exponentials with mean 1, then the difference between the order statistics, $|\beta|_{(a+1)} - |\beta|_{(a)}$, are independent exponentials with means $1/(d-a)$ [e.g. Feller (1971, I.6, pp. 19–20)]. From this, $N(20, 0.05) = 4$ while $M(20, 0.05) = 13$. On average, 4 of the 20 regressors can be ignored if f has a Lipschitz constant of 1, while 13 of 20 can be ignored if the monotonic total norm of f is 1.

Since the β_a are multiplied by something going to 0 as d increases, it is their tail behavior that determines $N(d, \epsilon)$ and $M(d, \epsilon)$ when d is larger. If the tails of the $|\beta_a|$ are thinner than the exponential tails, e.g. they have Gaussian tails, then even fewer of the regressors matter, both N and M are smaller. For some tail behaviors, the ratios N/d and M/d go to 0 at different rates as $d \uparrow \infty$.

The dimension dependent growth of total efficacy is behind the slower rates of convergence in higher dimensions. Here, variation of the distributional assumptions about the regression coefficients shows that this may not be the relevant approximation. One suspects that in many empirical situations, the total efficacy is often small relative to d because relatively few regressors turn out to matter very much. This is behind the success of Tibshirani's (1996) lasso models, and, as part of an extended comparison of parametric and nonparametric methods, Breiman (2001) discusses several general classes of high-dimensional situations in which this kind of ratio result holds.

4 The Geometry of Dimension Independent Rates

The previous section strongly suggests that the rate of convergence analyses of nonparametric regression should focus on efficacy bounded classes of functions rather than the efficacy unbounded class of Lipschitz functions. The result in this section goes further, and gives a unified, dimension-independent, geometric representation of a class of nonparametric regression estimators that includes, but is not limited to, series expansions (Fourier, wavelet, Tchebyshev, and others), kernels and other locally weighted regressions, splines, wavelets, and artificial neural networks. The geometric representation allows one to identify, for each of these regression techniques, classes that function as Barron's efficacy bounded class, $\mathbb{V}_d^{\text{ann}}$.

4.1 Spaces of Targets

Let μ denote the distribution of $(Y, (X_1, \ldots, X_d))$ in $\mathbb{R}^{1+d}$ and μ_X the (marginal) distribution of the explanatory variables, $(X_1, \ldots, X_d)$. The target function is $x \mapsto f(x) := E(Y|X = x)$ from the support of μ_X to $\mathbb{R}$. Throughout, the target is assumed to belong to a space of functions $\mathbb{V} \subset L^p(\mathbb{R}^d, \mu_X)$ for some $p \in [1, \infty)$ endowed with a norm that makes it a separable, infinite dimensional Banach space such as the following.

(1) $\mathbb{V} = L^2(\mathbb{R}^d, \mu_X)$, typically used in Fourier series analysis, wavelets, and other orthogonal series expansions.
(2) $\mathbb{V} = L^p(\mathbb{R}^d, \mu_X)$ spaces, $p \in [1, \infty)$, typically used when higher (or lower) moment assumptions are appropriate.
(3) $\mathbb{V} = C(D)$, the continuous functions on a compact domain $D \subset \mathbb{R}^d$ satisfying $\mu_X(D) = 1$, with norm $\|f\|_\infty := \max_{x \in D} |f(x)|$.
(4) $\mathbb{V} = C^m(D)$, the space of m-times continuously differentiable functions, $m \in \mathbb{N}$, on a compact domain D having a smooth boundary and satisfying $\mu_X(D) = 1$, with norm $\sup_{x \in D} \sum_{|\alpha| \le m} |D^\alpha f(x)|$, typically used when smoothness of the target is an appropriate assumption.[8]
(5) $\mathbb{V} = S^{m,p}(\mathbb{R}^d, \mu_X)$, $p \in [1, \infty)$, the Sobolev spaces, defined as the completion of the set $C^{m,p}(\mathbb{R}^d, \mu_X)$, the m-times continuously differentiable functions on $\mathbb{R}^d$, with norm $\|f\| = \sum_{|\alpha| \le m} \left[\int |D^\alpha f(x)|^p \, d\mu_X(x)\right]^{\frac{1}{p}} < \infty$, are typically used when approximation of a function and its derivatives rather than uniform approximation is appropriate.

The sets C_d^{Lip}, C_d^{MTV}, and $C_d^{\mathrm{Lip}} \cap C_d^{\mathrm{MTV}}$ are dense in all of these spaces. They are also negligible in a sense to be made clear below.

4.2 Compactly Generated Two-Way Cones

An estimator of an $f \in \mathbb{V}$ is a sequence of functions $\widehat{f_n} \in \mathbb{V}$ where each $\widehat{f_n}$ depends on the data $(Y_i(\omega), (X_{1,i}(\omega), \ldots, X_{d,i}(\omega)))_{i=1}^n$. For the nonparametric techniques studied here, the $\widehat{f_n}$ are of the form $\widehat{f_n}(x) = \sum_k \beta_k c_k(x)$ where $\beta_k \in \mathbb{R}$ and $c_k \in \mathbb{V}$. What varies among the estimators are the functions c_k, the number of terms in the summation, and the dependence of both on ω. The geometry that is common to nonparametric regression estimators is that there is a sequence, $C_{\kappa(n)} = C_{\kappa(n)}(\omega) \subset \mathbb{V}$ of **compactly generated two-way cones** with the property that $\widehat{f_n} \in C_{\kappa(n)}$.

$U = \{f \in \mathbb{V} : \|f\| < 1\}$ denotes the unit ball in $\mathbb{V}$, its closure is $\overline{U}$, and $\partial U = \{f \in \mathbb{V} : \|f\| = 1\}$ is its boundary. For $E \subset \mathbb{V}$, **sp** E is the span of E, that is the set of all *finite* linear combinations of elements of E, and $\overline{\mathbf{sp}}$ E is the closure of the span of E.

[8] Here, α is a multi-index, $\alpha = (\alpha_1, \ldots, \alpha_d)$, $\alpha_i \in \{0, 1, \ldots\}$, and $|\alpha| := \sum_i \alpha_i$.

For $S \subset \mathbb{R}$, $S \cdot E := \{s \cdot f : f \in E,\ s \in S\}$ is the set of scalar multiples of elements of E with scalars belonging to S. It is worth noting that in the following definition, a cone need not be convex, e.g., the non-negative axes in $\mathbb{R}^d$ are a cone, and that a two-way cone may contain linear subspaces.

Definition 3 A set $F \subset \mathbb{V}$ is a **cone** if $F = \mathbb{R}_+ \cdot F$, that is, if F is closed under multiplication by non-negative scalars. A set $C \subset \mathbb{V}$ is a **two-way cone** if $C = \mathbb{R} \cdot C$. A two-way cone is **compactly generated** if there exists a compact $E \subset \overline{U}$, $0 \notin E$, such that $C = \mathbb{R} \cdot E$.

4.3 Examples

We turn to examples of commonly used nonparametric estimators that belong to sequences of compactly generated two-way cones. Series estimators (Fourier series, wavelets, splines, and the various polynomial schemes), as well as broad classes of artificial neural network estimators belong to *nested* sequences of compactly generated two-way cones. Kernel estimators and other locally weighted regression schemes on compact domains belong to a *non-nested* sequence of compactly generated two-way cones. Throughout, it is important to note that the sequence of cones will often depend not only on n, the number of data points, but on ω through the data, $(Y_i(\omega), (X_{1,i}(\omega), \ldots, X_{d,i}(\omega)))_{i=1}^n$.

4.3.1 Series Estimators

Fourier series, wavelets, splines, and the various polynomial schemes specify a countable set $E = \{e_k : k \in \mathbb{N}\} \subset \partial U$ with the property that $\overline{\mathbf{sp}}\, E = \mathbb{V}$. Descriptions of the specific e_k for Fourier series, for the various polynomial schemes, and for wavelets are widely available. The estimator based on n data points, $\widehat{f}_n$, is a function of the form

$$\widehat{f}_n(x) = \sum_{k \leq \kappa(n)} \widehat{\beta}_k e_k(x). \tag{9}$$

The dependence on ω arises because the function is chosen to best fit the data. The estimators $\widehat{f}_n$ belong to $C_{\kappa(n)} := \mathbf{sp}\,\{e_1, \ldots, e_{\kappa(n)}\}$. Being a finite dimension subspace of $\mathbb{V}$, each $C_{\kappa(n)}$ is a compactly generated two-way cone, e.g. generated by $\mathbf{sp}\,\{e_1, \ldots, e_{\kappa(n)}\} \cap \partial U$.

Since $\overline{\mathbf{sp}}\, E = \mathbb{V}$, having $\lim_n \kappa(n) = \infty$ guarantees that the $\widehat{f}_n$ can approximate any function. To avoid overfitting and its implied biases, not letting $\kappa(n)$ go to infinity too quickly, e.g. $\kappa(n)/n \to 0$ guarantees consistency. If $\kappa(n) \to \infty$ is regarded a sequence of parameters to be estimated e.g., by cross-validation, then $\kappa(n)$ also depends on ω, which yields the random sequence $\omega \mapsto C_{\kappa(n)}(\omega)$.

4.3.2 Kernel and Locally Weighted Regression Estimators

Kernel estimators for functions on a compact domain typically begin with a function $K : \mathbb{R} \to \mathbb{R}$, supported (i.e., non-zero) only on $[-1, +1]$, having its maximum at 0 and satisfying three integral conditions: $\int_{-1}^{+1} K(u)\, du = 1$, $\int_{-1}^{+1} uK(u)\, du = 0$, and $\int_{-1}^{+1} u^2 K(u)\, du \neq 0$. Univariate kernel regression functions are (often) of the form

$$\widehat{f}_n(x) = \sum_{i=1}^{n} \widehat{\beta}_i g(x|X_i, h_n) = \sum_{i=1}^{n} \widehat{\beta}_i K\left(\tfrac{1}{h_n}(x - X_i)\right). \tag{10}$$

Here, $\kappa(n) = n$ and $C_{\kappa(n)}(\omega) = \mathbf{sp}\,\{K(\frac{1}{h_n}(x - X_i(\omega)) : i = 1, \ldots, n\}$.

When the kernel function, $K(\cdot)$, is smooth and its derivatives satisfy $\lim_{|u|\to 1} K^{(\alpha)}(u) = 0$, and the X_i belong to a compact domain, D, the estimator $\widehat{f}_n$ belongs to $C^m(D)$ for any m, and the $C^m(D)$-norm or one of the S^p_m-norms might be used. If the kernel function, $K(\cdot)$, function is continuous but not smooth, the $\widehat{f}_n$ belong to $C_b(\mathbb{R})$, hence to $L^p(\mathbb{R}, \mu_X)$. For any compact $D \subset \mathbb{R}$, the restrictions of the $\widehat{f}_n$ to D belong to $C(D)$.

In all of these cases, the n-data points, X_i, $i = 1, \ldots, n$, and the window-size parameter h_n, define n non-zero functions, $g(\cdot|\theta_{i,n})$, $\theta_{i,n} = (X_i, h_n)$. The estimator, $\widehat{f}_n$, belongs to the span of these n functions. As established above, the span of a finite set of non-zero functions is a compactly generated two-way cone.

The considerations for choosing the window-sizes, h_n, parallel those for choosing the $\kappa(n)$ in the series expansions. They can be chosen, either deterministically or by cross-validation, so that $h_n \to 0$, to guarantee that the kernel estimators can approximate any function, but not too quickly, so as to avoid overfitting.

The considerations for multivariate kernel regression functions are almost entirely analogous. These estimators are often of the form

$$\widehat{f}_n(x) = \sum_{i=1}^{n} \widehat{\beta}_i g(x|X_i, h_n) = \sum_{i=1}^{n} \widehat{\beta}_i K\left(\frac{1}{h_n}\|x - X_i\|\right) \tag{11}$$

where $h_n \downarrow 0$ and the X_i are points in the compact domain $D \subset \mathbb{R}^d$.

Locally weighted linear/polynomial regressions have different $g_i(\cdot|\theta_{i,n})$, see e.g., Stone (1982). In all of these cases, when the domain is compact, so are the sets of possible parameters for the functions g_i, and the mapping from parameters to functions is continuous. This again implies that the $\widehat{f}_n$ belong to the span of a finite (hence compact) set not containing $\mathbf{0}$.

4.3.3 Artificial Neural Networks

Single hidden layer feedforward (slff) estimators with activation function $g : \mathbb{R} \to \mathbb{R}$ often take $E \subset \mathbb{V}$ as $E = \{x \mapsto g(\gamma'\tilde{x}) : \gamma \in \Gamma\}$. Here $x \in \mathbb{R}^d$, $\tilde{x}' := (1, x')' \in$

$\mathbb{R}^{d+1}$, and Γ is a compact subset of $\mathbb{R}^{d+1}$ with non-empty interior. The slff estimators are functions of the form

$$\widehat{f}_n(x) = \sum_{k \leq \kappa(n)} \widehat{\beta}_k g(\widehat{\gamma}_k' \tilde{x}), \tag{12}$$

where the $\widehat{\gamma}_k$ belongs to Γ. Specifically, $C_{\kappa(n)} = \{\sum_{k \leq \kappa(n)} \beta_k c_k : c_k \in E\}$ is the compactly generated two-way cone of slff estimators.

If $\kappa(n) \to \infty$, $\kappa(n)/n \to 0$, and $\overline{\mathbf{sp}}\, E = \mathbb{V}$, then the total error goes to 0. Various sufficient conditions on g that guarantee $\overline{\mathbf{sp}}\, E = \mathbb{V}$ with compact Γ in the Banach spaces listed above are given in Hornik et al. (1989, 1990), Stinchcombe and White (1990, 1998), Hornik (1993), Stinchcombe (1999). Also as above, $\kappa(n)$ may be regarded as a parameter, estimated by cross-validation.

When g is continuous and Γ is compact, then E is a compact subset of $C(D)$ for any compact $D \subset \mathbb{R}^d$. When g is bounded, as is essentially always assumed, E is a compact subset of $L^p(\mathbb{R}^d, \mu_X)$ for any $p \in [1, \infty)$. When g is bounded and measurable, as in the case of the frequently used 'hard limiter,' $g(x) = 1_{[0,\infty)}(x)$, and μ_X has a density with respect to Lebesgue measure, E is a compact subset of $L^p(\mathbb{R}^d, \mu_X)$, $p \in [1, \infty)$. When g is smooth, e.g., the ubiquitous logistic case of $g(x) = e^x/(1 + e^x)$, and Γ compact, then E is a compact subset of $C^m(D)$, and of $S^p_m(\mathbb{R}^d, \mu_X)$ for any m and any $p \in [1, \infty)$.

Aside from notational complexity, essentially the same analysis shows that multiple hidden layer feedforward networks output functions are also expressible as the elements of the span of a compact set E.[9]

Radial basis network estimators most often take E_n to be a set of the form $E_n = \{x \mapsto g(\frac{1}{\lambda_n}(x - \gamma)'\Sigma(x - \gamma)) : \gamma \in \Gamma, \lambda_n \geq \underline{\lambda}_n\}$, Γ a compact subset of $\mathbb{R}^d$ containing the domain, Σ a fixed positive definite matrix, $\underline{\lambda}_n \downarrow 0$ but not too quickly, g a continuous function. The estimators are functions of the form

$$\widehat{f}_n(x) = \sum_{k \leq \kappa(n)} \widehat{\beta}_k g(\widehat{\gamma}_k' \tilde{x}), \tag{13}$$

The continuity of g implies that the E_n have compact closure. For the common choices of g in the literature, $g(0) \neq 0$ so that $0 \notin E_n$.

4.4 Rates and Consistency

In the examples just given, the sequence of compactly generated two-way cones become dense, and may be either deterministic or random. The cones becoming dense is **consistency**.

---

[9] Consistency issues for multiple layer feedforward networks are addressed in the approximation theorems of Hornik et al. (1989, 1990), and Hornik (1993).

Definition 4 A random sequence of compactly generated two-way cones, $\omega \mapsto C_{\kappa(n)}(\omega)$, is **consistent** if for all $g \in \mathbb{V}$, $P(\cup_N \cap_{n \geq N} [d(g, C_{\kappa(n)}(\cdot)) < \epsilon]) = 1$.

4.5 Results

For any sequence of sets, B_n, $[B_n \text{ i.o.}] := \bigcap_m \bigcup_{n \geq m} B_n$ is read as "B_n infinitely often," while $[B_n \text{ a.a.}] := \bigcup_m \bigcap_{n \geq m} B_n$ is read as "B_n almost always." For a compactly generated two-way cone, C, of estimators, and $r > 0$, the set $C + r \cdot U$ is the set of all targets that are within r of set of estimators contained in C. Consistency can be rewritten as "for all $\epsilon > 0$, $P([C_{\kappa(n)} + \epsilon \cdot U \text{ a.a.}] = \mathbb{V}) = 1$." Of particular interest will be sets of the form $[C_{\kappa(n)} + r_n \cdot U \text{ a.a.}]$ where $r_n \to 0$ and $C_{\kappa(n)}$ is a sequence of compactly generated two-way cones.

This section proves Lemmas 4 and 5, which yield the following.

Theorem 1 *For any consistent nonparametric regression technique with estimators belonging to a sequence, $C_{\kappa(n)}$, of compactly generated two-way cones, and for any $r_n \to 0$, a dense, shy set of targets can be approximated at the rate $\mathcal{O}(r_n)$.*

"Shyness" is defined below, and provides useful information about the sets of targets. Within the Banach spaces of functions listed above (and many others), C_d^{Lip} and C_d^{MTV} form dense, shy sets of functions, as does their intersection.

For $M \in \mathbb{N}$, define $A_n^M := C_{\kappa(n)} + Mr_n \cdot U$. Fix a sequence of sets of estimators $C_{\kappa(n)}$. For $g \in \mathbb{V}$, there exists a subsequence, n', such that $d(g, C_{n'}) = \mathcal{O}(r_{n'})$ if and only if $g \in [A_n^M \text{ i.o.}]$ for some $M \in \mathbb{N}$. If we do not allow subsequences, we have $d(g, C_n) = \mathcal{O}(r_n)$ if and only if $g \in [A_n^M \text{ a.a.}]$ for some M.

Definition 5 The set of $\mathcal{O}(r_n)$-**accumulatable targets** is $\cup_M [A_n^M \text{ i.o.}]$, and the set of $\mathcal{O}(r_n)$-**approximable targets** is $\mathcal{T}(r_n) := \cup_M [A_n^M \text{ a.a.}]$.

Lemma 4 *$P(\mathcal{T}(r_n)$ is dense$) = 1$ if and only if the $C_{\kappa(n)}$ are consistent.*

Proof Suppose that $C_{\kappa(n)}$ is consistent. Let $\mathcal{G} = \{g_j : j \in \mathbb{N}\}$ be a dense subset of $\mathbb{V}$. Define $B_j^m = \cup_N \cap_{n \geq N} [(g_j + \frac{1}{m} \cdot U) \cap (C_{\kappa(n)}(\omega) + r_n \cdot U) \neq \emptyset]$. Since the $C_{\kappa(n)}$ are consistent, $P(B_j^m) = 1$. Therefore, $P(\cap_{m,j} B_j^m) = 1$. Finally, the event that $d(g_j, \mathcal{T}(r_n)) < 1/m$ for every m contains $\cap_{m,j} B_j^m$.

Suppose now that $C_{\kappa(n)}$ is not consistent, i.e., there exists $g \in \mathbb{V}$ and $\epsilon > 0$ such that $P([d(g, C_{\kappa(n)}) < \epsilon \text{ a.a.}]) < 1$, equivalently, $P([d(g, C_{\kappa(n)}) \geq \epsilon \text{ i.o.}]) > 0$. For all M, $Mr_n < \epsilon$ for all but finitely many n. Therefore, $P(\mathcal{T}(r_n) \cap (g + \epsilon \cdot U) = \emptyset) > 0$. That is, the probability that $\mathcal{T}(r_n)$ is dense is less than 1. □

The Lipschitz functions and the functions with bounded efficacy satisfy the following notion of a negligible subset of an infinite dimensional space.[10]

[10] There are several related notions of negligible sets in infinite dimensional spaces, detailed in Benyamini and Lindenstrauss (2000, Chap. 6). Anderson and Zame's (2001) cover some of the uses of shy (Haar null) sets in economic theory, and greatly extend the applicability of the notion.

Definition 6 A subset S of a universally measurable $S' \subset \mathbb{V}$ is **shy** or **Haar null** if there exists a compactly supported probability η such that $\eta(S' + g) = 0$ for all $g \in \mathbb{V}$.

Lemma 5 *If r_n goes to* 0 *more slowly than r'_n, then $\mathcal{T}(r_n) \setminus \mathcal{T}(r'_n)$ is shy.*

For ease of later reference, we separately record the following easy observation.

Lemma 6 *If C is a compactly generated two-way cone, then it is closed, has empty interior, and $C \cap F$ is compact for every closed, norm bounded F.*

Proof of Lemma 5 It is sufficient to show that the set of $\mathcal{O}(r_n)$-accumulatable targets is shy because $\mathcal{T}(r_n) = \cup_M [A_n^M \text{ a.a.}] \subset \cup_M [A_n^M \text{ i.o.}]$, and any subset of a shy set is shy.

A set $F \subset \mathbb{V}$ is approximately flat if for every $\epsilon > 0$, there is a finite dimensional subspace W of $\mathbb{V}$ such that $F \subset W + \epsilon \cdot U$. Every compact set is approximately flat—let F_ϵ be a finite ϵ-net and take $W = \mathbf{sp}\, F_\epsilon$. From Stinchcombe (2001, Lemma 1), for any sequence F_n of approximately flat sets, $[(F_n + r_n \cdot U) \text{ i.o.}]$ is shy. Since the countable union of shy sets is shy, $\cup_M [(F_n + M r_n \cdot U) \text{ i.o.}]$ is shy.

Fix arbitrary $R > 0$. It is sufficient to prove that $(R \cdot U) \cap [A_n^M \text{ i.o.}]$ is shy. Fix arbitrary $\eta > 0$. $R \cdot U$ is a subset of the closed, norm bounded set $R \cdot (1 + \eta)\overline{U}$. By Lemma 6, the set $F_n = C_n \cap (R \cdot (1 + \eta)\overline{U})$ is compact. Since compact sets are approximately flat, $S = [(F_n + M r_n \cdot U) \text{ i.o.}]$ is shy. Since $r_n \to 0$ and $\eta > 0$, $[(R \cdot U) \cap [A_n^M \text{ i.o.}]] \subset S$. □

Proof of Theorem 1 Lemma 4 shows that consistency of the nonparametric regression technique with estimators given by a sequence $C_{\kappa(n)}$ of compactly generated two-way cones and denseness of $\mathcal{T}(r_n)$ are equivalent. Lemma 5 shows that $\mathcal{T}(r_n)$ is shy. □

5 Conclusions and Complements

Most of the analyses of the rates of convergence for nonparametric regression arrive at dismal results with even a moderate number of regressors. The key assumption driving these results is that the target function, $f(x_1, \ldots, x_d) = E(Y|(X_1, \ldots, X_d) = (x_1, \ldots, x_d))$ is uniformly Lipschitz. This assumption can never be rejected by data. Replacing the Lipschitz functions by sets of functions sharing this unrejectability shows that the order of the rate of convergence is given by the order of the estimation error, that dimension-dependent approximation error need play no role.

Examples suggest that dimension dependence of the complexity of a regression function is more tightly tied to its monotonic total variation than to any measure of its smoothness. These examples also demonstrate that how the variation depends on the dimensionality may vary from one set of problems or distribution over problems to another. Experience suggests that the variation, both in linear and nonlinear regression, is often small.

Together, the results and examples suggest that rates of convergence calculated using Lipschitz functions are misleading, that what matters is some measure of variability. This puts correspondingly more weight on the criteria of interpretability and generalization for the judging competing nonparametric approaches.

There are a number of subsidiary points to be made.

5.1 Comparison and Estimation of Dense Sets

As well as comparing $\mathcal{T}(r_n)$ and $\mathcal{T}(r_n')$ for the same nonparametric regression technique, one can also compare these sets across regression techniques. For example, Barron (1993) fixes a pair of rates, r_n and r_n' with $r_n' = o(r_n)$, and shows that for the ann techniques that he considers, $\mathcal{T}_{\text{ann}}(r_n')$ cannot be approximated by any series expansion at a rate r_n. Reversing his example in L^2 requires a permutation of the basis elements, and gives rise to a set $\mathcal{T}_{\text{series}}(r_n')$ that cannot be approximated by any variant of his ann technique at a rate r_n.

This seems to be part of a more general pattern. Pick a pair of sequences r_n, r_n' with $r_n' = o(r_n)$. From Lemma 4, $\mathcal{T}(r_n) \setminus \mathcal{T}(r_n')$ and $\mathcal{T}(r_n')$ are disjoint, dense sets of nonparametric targets. We conjecture that for generic pairs of sequences, $C_{1,\kappa(n)}$ and $C_{2,\kappa'(n)}$, of compactly generated two-way cones, $\mathcal{T}_1(r_n') \setminus \mathcal{T}_2(r_n) \neq \emptyset$ and $\mathcal{T}_2(r_n') \setminus \mathcal{T}_1(r_n) \neq \emptyset$.

As has been noted, with smooth classical measurement error (or with errors in variables), it is not possible to reject (say) $H_{\text{Eff}} : f_d$ is uniformly efficacy bounded in favor of the larger alternative hypothesis, $H_{\text{Lip}} : f_d$ is uniformly Lipschitz bounded. If one could estimate Lipschitz or efficacy norms, then in principle one could test the alternative hypotheses against each other, but this estimation problem seems extraordinarily difficult.

5.2 Comparisons Across Rates

If r_n and r_n' both go to 0 but r_n goes more slowly, then the dense class $\mathcal{T}(r_n)$ is larger than the dense class $\mathcal{T}(r_n')$. Lemma 5 shows that the difference between the sets, $\mathcal{T}(r_n) \setminus \mathcal{T}(r_n')$, is shy. Shy subsets are an infinite dimensional extension of the finite dimensional Lebesgue null set notion non-genericity. This gives partial information about the size of the difference between the two sets. It is only partial information because the proof simply shows that the larger of the two sets is Haar null, and any subset of a null set is a null set. Two points:

(1) Much to be desired is an improvement on this partial result. Something that would, despite the impossibility of data ever distinguishing between the dense sets, allow one to distinguish, at least theoretically, more finely between sets of targets $\mathcal{T}(r_n)$ and $\mathcal{T}(r_n')$. However, Lemma 5 shows that trying to resurrect

the curse of dimensionality in rates of convergence requires one to say that one non-generic dense set of functions is clearly preferable to another non-generic dense set of functions, and that it's preferable because it yields worse results.

(2) For finite dimensional parametric estimation, superefficiency can happen on Lebesgue null sets [e.g. Lehmann and Casella (1998), Chap. 6.2)]. For infinite dimensional nonparametric estimation, Brown et al. (1997) show that it can happen "everywhere," that is, at all points in the dense sets of targets $\mathcal{T}(r_n)$ that are typically used. It seems that behind this result is the same approximately-flat-but-not-flat infinite dimensional geometry that yields the denseness of the $\mathcal{T}(r_n)$ classes.[11]

5.3 Smoothness

Another aspect of the work on the curse rates of approximation is that smoother targets lead to faster approximation. For example, if the target f is assumed to have s continuous derivatives, and these derivatives are Lipschitz, then Stone's rate of approximation is increased to $\mathcal{O}_P(n^{-1/(2+[d/s])})$. The dense classes, $\mathbb{V}_{\text{ann}}$, in the dimension independent ann rate of approximation work are defined by an integrability condition on various transforms of the gradient of the target. Niyogi and Girosi (1999) note that this suggests that $s = s(d)$ in such a fashion that $[d/s]$ stays small for the $\mathbb{V}_{\text{ann}}$ and d increases.

One might guess that something similar is at work in the classes $\mathcal{T}(r_n)$ that are analyzed here. However, this kind of smoothness argument is problematic for three separate kinds of reasons. First, for many classes of ann's, the dense set of targets are not only infinitely smooth, they are analytic. It is hard to see how smoothness could vary with dimension in this context. Second, for many other classes of ann's, the dense set of targets contain discontinuous functions, and smoothness cannot enter. Finally, the work here provides a plethora of dense classes for which the dimensionality of the regressors plays no role, and it seems unlikely that there is some special smoothness structure common to the different dense sets that work for the different techniques.

5.4 More on Negligible Sets

By definition, S is shy if and only if $\eta(S+g)$ is shy for all g and some compactly supported probability η. If $\mathbb{V} = \mathbb{R}^k$, the finite dimensional case here ruled out by assumption, one can take η to be the uniform distribution on $[0, 1]^k$ and show that S is shy if and only if it is a Lebesgue null set if and only if for every non-degenerate Gaussian distribution ν, $\nu(S) = 0$. Stinchcombe (2001) showed that there is no similar comfortable Bayesian interpretation of shy sets in the infinite dimensional

[11] I am grateful to Xiaohong Chen and Jinyong Hahn for these last two points.

contexts studied here. The complement of a shy set is a prevalent set. Other relevant properties of this class of shy sets are:

(1) shy sets have no interior so that prevalent sets are dense;
(2) the countable union of shy sets is shy, equivalently the countable intersection of prevalent sets is prevalent; and
(3) if $\mathbb{V}$ is infinite dimensional if and only if compact sets are shy.

Lemmas 5 and Theorem 1 used shy sets. These results would not hold if we replaced shy sets with the original, more restrictive, class of infinite dimensional null sets due to Aronszajn (1976). These are now called **Gauss null** sets because Aronszajn's definition is now known to be equivalent to the following: S is Gauss null if and only if for every non-degenerate Gaussian distribution, ν, on $\mathbb{V}$, $\nu(S) = 0$ (see Benyamini and Lindenstrauss 2000, Chap. 6). Every Gauss null set is shy, but the reverse is not true. It can be shown that the sets $\cup_n C_{\kappa(n)}$ of estimators are Gauss null, but not that $[C_{\kappa(n)} + r_n \cdot U \text{ a.a.}]$ is not.

5.5 Possible Extensions and Generalizations

There are several additional points to be made.

1. One can think of the analysis of affine conditional means with independent regressors of Sect. 3 as a very special class of parametrized models. Suppose, more generally, that C_κ is smoothly parametrized by a κ-dimensional vector with κ fixed. Standard results imply that $\|\widehat{f_n} - f_\kappa^*\| = \epsilon_{\kappa,n} = \mathcal{O}(n^{-1/2})$. If instead of being fixed, we let κ depend on d and on n. If $\kappa(d,n) \uparrow \infty$, as required for consistency, but $\kappa(d,n)$ grows very slowly, then the $n^{-1/2}$ rate of approximation slows as little as one desires.
2. If the data is not iid but has some time series structure, one expects that the estimation error in (5) will not be $\mathcal{O}(n^{-1/2})$ for fixed κ, but something slower. Again, since Lemmas 4 and 5 concern approximation error, total error for the nonparametric regressions covered here would also go to 0 at this ineluctably slower rate if we were outside of the iid case.
3. It is hard to imagine nonparametric techniques with estimators that do not belong to a sequence of compactly generated two-way cones. For example, in the above discussion of the locally weighted regression schemes and the artificial neural network estimators, we made use of compact domain assumptions to ease the exposition, and this led to the compactly generated conclusion. However, since the distribution of the data is tight, one can replace the compact domains with a sequence of compact domains having the property that with probability 1, the estimators belong to the associated sequence of compactly generated two-way cones.

4. The proof of Lemma 4 can be easily adapted to show that consistency is equivalent to $\mathcal{T}(r_n)$ containing a dense linear subspace of $\mathbb{V}$ with probability 1. Cohen et al. (2001) characterize some of these dense linear subspaces for wavelet expansions.
5. All of the above has been phrased as regression analysis of conditional means. Since Lemmas 4 and 5 concern the approximation error, one could also, with essentially no changes, consider, e.g., conditional quantile regression and/or loss functions other than mean squared loss. At whatever rate the estimation error goes to 0, there is a dense class of nonparametric targets with the approximation error going to 0 at the same rate.
6. The use of Banach spaces for the set of targets is not crucial. The compactly generated assumption must be slightly modified in locally convex, complete, separable, metric vector spaces, but the main result driving the shyness proofs is Stinchcombe (2001, Lemma 1), which applies in such spaces. For example, one could take $\mathbb{V} = C(\mathbb{R}^d)$ with the topology of uniform convergence on compact sets, or any other of the other Frechet spaces that appear in nonparametric regression analyses.
7. It is a reasonable conjecture that the same results hold for density estimation as hold for regression analysis. Following Davidson and McKinnon (1987), the target densities can be modeled as points in a convex subset of the positive orthant in a Hilbert space. Lemma 4 should go through fairly easily, but Lemma 5 may be more difficult. The shyness argument requires extending Stinchcombe (2001, Lemma 1) to Anderson and Zame's (2001) relatively shy sets.
8. It can be shown that if C is a compactly generated two-way cone, then the open set $C + U$ is not dense in $\mathbb{V}$. The role of the compact set E not containing 0 in the definition of compactly generated cones can be seen in the following, which should be compared to Lemma 6.

Example 6 If x_n is a countable dense subset of ∂U and E is the closure of $\{x_n/n : n \in \mathbb{N}\}$, then E is a compact subset of the closed, norm bounded set $\overline{U}$. However, the two-way cone $\mathbb{R} \cdot E$ is <u>not</u> compactly generated, not closed, and is dense, so that $\mathbb{R} \cdot E + \epsilon \cdot U = \mathbb{V}$ for any $\epsilon > 0$.

5.6 Studying the Difficulty of Nonparametric Problems

Finally, some rather preliminary simulation data suggest that it is possible to characterize the difficulty of nonparametric problems by studying when the root-n consistency "kicks in." More specifically, let d be the number of regressors and let $n(d)$ be the number of data points beyond which the root-n asymptotics provide a reasonable guide. The higher is the function $d \mapsto n(d)$, the more difficult the problem. The fact of being uniformly higher for many different nonparametric techniques constitutes a strong indication that the problem is considerably more difficult. We leave this for future research.

Acknowledgments We owe many thanks to Xiaohong Chen, Graham Elliot, Jinyong Hahn, James Hamilton, Qi Li, Dan Slesnick, Hal White, Paul Wilson, and an anonymous referee for numerous insights, questions, references, conversations and corrections.

References

Adams, C. and J. A. Clarkson (1933). On Definitions of Bounded Variation for Functions of Two Variables. Transactions of the American Mathematical Society 35(4), 824–854.

Anderson, R. and W. Zame's (2001). Genericity with Infinitely Many Parameters. Advances in Theoretical Economics: Vol. 1: No. 1, Article 1.

Aronszajn, N. (1976). Differentiability of Lipschitzian Mappings Between Banach Spaces. Studia Mathematica LVII, 147–190.

Barron, A. (1993). Universal Approximation Bounds for Superpositions of a Sigmoidal Function. IEEE Transactions on Information Theory 39(3), 930–945.

Benyamini, Y. and J. Lindenstrauss (2000). Geometric Nonlinear Functional Analysis. Providence, R.I.: American Mathematical Society, Colloquium publications (American Mathematical Society) v. 48.

Billingsley, P. (2008). Probability and Measure. John Wiley and Sons, New York.

Breiman, L. (2001). Statistical Modeling: The Two Cultures. Statistical Science 16(3), 199–231.

Brown, L. D., M. G. Low, and L. H. Zhao (1997). Superefficiency in Nonparametric Function Estimation. Annals of Statistics 25(6), 2607–2625.

Chen, X. (2007). Large Sample Sieve Estimation of Nonparametric Models. Handbook of Econometrics 6, 5549–5632.

Chen, X. and H. White (1999). Improved Rates and Asymptotic Normality for Nonparametric Neural Network Estimators. IEEE Tran. Information Theory 45, 682–691.

Cohen, A., R. DeVore, and G. Kerkyacharian (2001). Maximal Spaces with Given Rate of Convergence for Thresholding Algorithms. Applied and Computational Harmonic Analysis 11, 167–191.

Davidson, R. and J. G. McKinnon (1987). Implicit Alternatives and the Local Power of Test Statistics. Econometrica 55(6), 1305–1329.

Dellacherie, C. and P.-A. Meyer (1978). Probabilities and Potential, vol. 29 of North-Holland Mathematics Studies. North-Holland Publishing Co., Amsterdam.

Feller, W. (1971). An Introduction to Probability Theory and its Applications, v. II. John Wiley and Sons, New York.

Hornik, K. (1993). Some New Results on Neural Network Approximation. Neural Networks 6(8), 1069–1072.

Hornik, K, M. Stinchcombe and H. White (1989). Multi-layer Feedforward Networks are Universal Approximators. Neural Networks 2, 359–366.

Hornik, K, M. Stinchcombe and H. White (1990). Universal Approximation of an Unknown Mapping and its Derivatives using Multilayer Feedforward Networks. Neural Networks 3, 551–560.

Lehmann, E. L. and G. Casella (1998). Theory of Point Estimation, 2nd ed. Springer-Verlag, New York.

Mhaskar, H. N. and C. A. Michelli (1995). Degree of Approximation by Neural and Translation Networks with a Single Hidden Layer. Advances in Applied Mathematics 16, 151–183.

Newey, W. (1996). Convergence Rates and Asymptotic Normality for Series Estimators. Journal of Econometrics 79, 147–168.

Niyogi, P. and F. Girosi (1999). Generalization bounds for function approximation from scattered noisy data. Advances in Computational Mathematics 10, 51–80.

Stinchcombe, M. (1999). Neural Network Approximation of Continuous Functionals and Continuous Functions on Compactifications. Neural Networks 12, 467–477.

Stinchcombe, M. (2001). The Gap Between Probability and Prevalence: Loneliness in Vector Spaces. Proceedings of the American Mathematical Society 129, 451–457.
Stinchcombe, M. and H. White (1990). Approximating and Learning Unknown Mappings Using Multilayer Feedforward Networks with Bounded Weights. Proceedings of the International Joint Conference on Neural Networks, Washington, D. C., III, 7–16. San Diego, CA.: SOS Printing.
Stinchcombe, M. and H. White (1998). Consistent Specification Testing with Nuisance Parameters Present Only Under the Alternative. Econometric Theory 14, 295–325.
Stone, C. J. (1982). Optimal global rates of convergence for nonparametric regression. Annals of Statistics 10, 1040–1053.
Tibshirani, R. (1996). Regression Shrinkage and Selection via the Lasso. Journal of the Royal Statistical Society, Series B, 58(1), 267–288.
Yukich, J., M. Stinchcombe, and H. White (1995). Sup-Norm Approximation Bounds for Networks through Probabilistic Methods. IEEE Transactions on Information Theory 41(4), 1021–1027.

Index

X. Chen and N. R. Swanson (eds.), *Recent Advances and Future Directions in Causality, Prediction, and Specification Analysis*, DOI: 10.1007/978-1-4614-1653-1,

MIX
Papier aus verantwortungsvollen Quellen
Paper from responsible sources
FSC® C105338

If you have any concerns about our products,
you can contact us on
ProductSafety@springernature.com

In case Publisher is established outside the EU,
the EU authorized representative is:
Springer Nature Customer Service Center GmbH
Europaplatz 3, 69115 Heidelberg, Germany

Printed by Libri Plureos GmbH
in Hamburg, Germany